Frommer's®

T3-AME-091

India
3rd Edition

by Pippa de Bruyn, Dr. Keith Bain,
Niloufer Venkatraman & Shonar Joshi

Here's what the critics say about Frommer's:

"Amazingly easy to use. Very portable, very complete."

—*Booklist*

"Detailed, accurate, and easy-to-read information for all price ranges."
—*Glamour Magazine*

"Hotel information is close to encyclopedic."

—*Des Moines Sunday Register*

"Frommer's Guides have a way of giving you a real feel for a place."
—*Knight Ridder Newspapers*

WILEY
Wiley Publishing, Inc.

Published by:

Wiley Publishing, Inc.

111 River St.
Hoboken, NJ 07030-5774

ISBN: 978-0-470-16908-7

Editor: Alexis Lipsitz Flippin
Production Editor: Eric T. Schroeder
Cartographer: Guy Ruggerio
Photo Editor: Richard Fox
Production by Wiley Indianapolis Composition Services

For information on our other products and services or to obtain technical support, please contact our Customer Care Department within the U.S. at 800/762-2974, outside the U.S. at 317/572-3993 or fax 317/572-4002.

Wiley also publishes its books in a variety of electronic formats. Some content that appears in print may not be available in electronic formats.

Manufactured in the United States of America

5   4   3   2   1

Contents

List of Maps

Acknowledgments

Sincerest thanks to several individuals who assisted and contributed to updating sections of this book; they are: **Abhishek Madhukar** (Kerala, Rajasthan, and Varanasi), **Munira Rampurawala** (Mumbai, Goa, and Kumaon), **Jayati Vora** (dining and nightlife in Mumbai), **Yasmin Menon** (Chennai and Bangalore), and **André Morris** (Amritsar and Dharamsala); we'd also like to give a special mention to **Abishek Madhukar** and **John Thomas.**

An Invitation to the Reader

In researching this book, we discovered many wonderful places—hotels, restaurants, shops, and more. We're sure you'll find others. Please tell us about them, so we can share the information with your fellow travelers in upcoming editions. If you were disappointed with a recommendation, we'd love to know that, too. Please write to:

Frommer's India, 3rd Edition
Wiley Publishing, Inc. • 111 River St. • Hoboken, NJ 07030-5774

An Additional Note

Please be advised that travel information is subject to change at any time—and this is especially true of prices. We therefore suggest that you write or call ahead for confirmation when making your travel plans. The authors, editors, and publisher cannot be held responsible for the experiences of readers while traveling. Your safety is important to us, however, so we encourage you to stay alert and be aware of your surroundings. Keep a close eye on cameras, purses, and wallets, all favorite targets of thieves and pickpockets.

About the Authors

Pippa de Bruyn is an award-winning journalist, travel writer (author of *Frommer's South Africa*), and freelance editor. **Niloufer Venkatraman** has a doctoral degree in anthropology from Temple University in Philadelphia. She has traveled widely since the age of 9, and has always been as awed by other places and cultures as her own. A resident of her native Mumbai, she has worked as lecturer in sociology and anthropology, giving up the bureaucratic Indian academic scene in 2001 to turn her attention to working as a freelance writer and editor. **Shonar Joshi** is a writer by profession and explorer by heart. A strict believer in the art of drifting, she has dabbled with environmental television reporting, filmmaking, script writing, farming. and traveling—mostly in India, Nepal, and Sri Lanka. Her book *Of Past Dawns and Future Noons* is a testament to the passion with which she regards India and its rich ancient past, present, and future. **Dr. Keith Bain** has a doctoral degree in cinema. When he's not traveling the world in search of fantastic experiences, he spends his time writing and lecturing about film, media, theater, and contemporary culture.

Frommer's Star Ratings, Icons & Abbreviations

Every hotel, restaurant, and attraction listing in this guide has been ranked for quality, value, service, amenities, and special features using a **star-rating system.** In country, state, and regional guides, we also rate towns and regions to help you narrow down your choices and budget your time accordingly. Hotels and restaurants are rated on a scale of zero (recommended) to three stars (exceptional). Attractions, shopping, nightlife, towns, and regions are rated according to the following scale: zero stars (recommended), one star (highly recommended), two stars (very highly recommended), and three stars (must-see).

In addition to the star-rating system, we also use **seven feature icons** that point you to the great deals, in-the-know advice, and unique experiences that separate travelers from tourists. Throughout the book, look for:

Finds	Special finds—those places only insiders know about
Fun Fact	Fun facts—details that make travelers more informed and their trips more fun
Kids	Best bets for kids and advice for the whole family
Moments	Special moments—those experiences that memories are made of
Overrated	Places or experiences not worth your time or money
Tips	Insider tips—great ways to save time and money
Value	Great values—where to get the best deals

The following **abbreviations** are used for credit cards:

AE	American Express	DISC	Discover	V	Visa
DC	Diners Club	MC	MasterCard		

Frommers.com

Now that you have the guidebook to a great trip, visit our website at **www.frommers.com** for travel information on more than 3,600 destinations. With features updated regularly, we give you instant access to the most current trip-planning information available. At Frommers.com, you'll also find the best prices on airfares, accommodations, and car rentals—and you can even book travel online through our travel booking partners. At Frommers.com, you'll also find the following:

- Online updates to our most popular guidebooks
- Vacation sweepstakes and contest giveaways
- Newsletter highlighting the hottest travel trends
- Online travel message boards with featured travel discussions

What's New in India

It's boom time, and India is dancing to a quickened beat. In 2006 India's $1.1-trillion economy grew by a whopping 9.4%, a rate only rivaled by neighboring China, and reserves reached a staggering $212.4 billion. Nowhere is the boom more apparent than in the cities of Mumbai, New Delhi, Bangalore, and Chennai, where huge new shopping centers are being built to house the influx of international luxury goods coveted by a new, ever-expanding urban class keen to show off its newly acquired wealth and social status. Indeed, if you're planning a return trip to India, you can't help but notice the changes wrought by the country's growing affluence, from smooth new state highways and massive billboards advertising the latest designer goods to the rapidly expanding choices in upscale restaurants and chic hotels.

Once the preserve of peripatetic hippies, India is now hip, offering the sophisticated traveler a great deal more luxury. Besides exploring it with your personal chauffeur, you can now fly cross-country at the drop of a hat, book into a number of boutique-style getaways, dine at independent chef-owned restaurants, and enjoy much-improved hygiene standards throughout. Yet for all its increased sophistication, the streetscapes remain unchanged. Where else will you see the latest model Mercedes being reined in by a leisurely plodding cow or overtaking a magnificently caparisoned elephant? How many cities can blame their traffic jams on the gods, ritualistically dragged on chariots through the streets by throngs of sweating devotees? India is unlike any travel destination on earth, and you can do it in comfort and style without breaking the bank.

PLANNING YOUR TRIP The growing popularity of India in well-heeled travel circles has had a direct impact on prices, with top-end hotel tariff increases racing ahead of the official 5.06% inflation rate. It is also interesting to note how the luxury end, once utterly dependent on foreign markets, is now touting to its own countrymen—hotels that once quoted dollar-only rates are now reverting to rupee rates, subtly declaring their allegiance to the local market while simultaneously cashing in on the country's quietly strengthening currency. At press time this was Rs 44 to $1 (Rs 81 to £1); do check the exchange rates before traveling; the rates quoted in the pages of this book may have shifted by the time you read this.

For many (eco-warriors aside) the best news is that virtually every major (and a few small) airlines now offer flights into India; some have even done us the great service of arriving during the day (rather than a few hours after midnight)! You can also fly direct to India from Sydney and New York, and airlines like British Airways and Jet Airways have introduced two daily direct flights into Mumbai. Despite this, it is virtually impossible to get a seat during peak season (Dec to early Jan), so if this is the time you plan to visit, book early.

GETTING AROUND Getting around India is also much improved, thanks to the launch of a slew of low-cost airlines and the discontinuation of the iniquitous practice of charging foreigners a higher dollar fare. You'll find our recommendations for best new budget airlines in chapter 2 (it's no point purchasing a dirt-cheap fare only to have a 5-hr. delay at the airport), but do note that the domestic air travel market is still in flux. At press time several airlines' fates were up in the air as a result of takeovers, mergers, or acquisitions (among them: Kingfisher–Air Deccan, Jet Airways–Sahara, Indian–Air-India).

MUMBAI Mumbai's cab service has been given a boost with the introduction of private radio taxis, so getting anywhere should be easier, except of course when you're stuck in traffic. How could it get worse? Trust us, it has. Which is why many sensible travelers are choosing to base themselves in the **Bandra-Juhu suburbs** (closer to the airport, and good for Bollywood celeb spotting) instead of the more touristy, congested, and business-oriented downtown Colaba area. Bandra-Juhu doesn't have a tourist center, but it's studded with new restaurants, bars, endless shopping, and a vibrant nightlife, without Colaba's seedy edge.

We've added several new midrange accommodations options to suit travelers who don't want to go the five-star route.

Finally, if you're keen to take a weekend escape to the hills while you're in Mumbai, head to **Matheran,** a heavily wooded, vehicle-free town atop a hill, just a few hours from the city. It's a new addition to the chapter, but well worth it.

GOA Goa is always on the rise, given its gorgeous beaches and reputation as an essential stop on the global party circuit. Every year sees the establishment of new seasonal outfits that rise up only to get swept away by the tide, but we've found a few gorgeous additions to the lineup. Of these, the lovely **Elsewhere** is well worth highlighting, as is **Wildernest;** the latter is the ideal break for those who've had enough of sun and sand. Unfortunately,

Goa's very popularity is a threat to its long-term well-being. Outside the tourist areas are huge slums, home to migrants here to ferret for their fortune among the tourists and tat that line the beaches. In addition, unchecked development is taking its toll on the once-pristine environment. Equally worrisome is the increasing presence of Russian gangster types, here to cash in on the trance culture with drugs and prostitutes; you're unlikely to come across the hard edges of this new phenomenon, but if you encounter a couple of beefcakes touting large guns, best to back off and head for the next beach party.

KERALA With yet another additional million bodies tramping around "God's Own Country," Kerala has perhaps (hopefully?) reached saturation point. Certainly the backwaters experience—gently floating along on a *kettuvallam* **(houseboat),** passing plantations and villages while sipping a cup of *chai* made by your personal chef—is not quite what it used to be: The beautiful crafts initially propelled by pole are now usually run by motor. A mere 4 years back perhaps 15 houseboats operated out of Alappuzha; today, with that figure closer to 400, the impact is potentially disastrous. In 2007 the state government finally started taking action against those polluting engines; certainly you can place your trust in the operators recommended in our Kerala chapter.

Another area that has "enjoyed" unprecedented growth is that of **Ayurveda**—today even the smallest guesthouse offers this service. Besides the fact that a half-trained person will not provide adequate pleasure, the practice of reusing oils or using herbs indiscriminately is unhygienic and potentially dangerous. The Kerala government has reacted by providing "Green Leaf" (top) and "Olive Leaf" (good) accreditation. We have included these ratings in our reviews.

A lovely outcome of the tourism boom in Kerala has been the increase in

homestays. Olavipe, a 19th-century family home in the backwaters, is a new gem we've uncovered. And although it's not strictly a homestay, **Paradisa Plantation,** near Periyar, is so personally run by the urbane Simon that you will feel completely at home (and feast on meals unsurpassed in India).

It's worth noting that most of Kerala's place names have changed—these are all listed in the book, along with the old colonial-era name in brackets.

The last word on Kerala is that the northern regions, once thought too difficult to reach, are enjoying renewed interest—and frequented in large part by Bangalore yuppies keen to escape the city for a breath of fresh air. Increasingly, foreigners are finding their way here as well: The popular **Wyanad region,** with its lush swaths of untouched nature, saw a massive 177% increase in international arrivals in 2006.

TAMIL NADU   Tamil Nadu has experienced far less change than Kerala, and hurrah for that. That's not to say that it's in stasis: The new entry fee to the **Meenakshi Temple** in Madurai is irritating proof that tourism is having an impact. On the positive side is the growing interest in the **Chettinad region,** with its huge turn-of-the-20th-century mansions, one of which you can now stay in. And Pondicherry's new sexy beachfront hotel, nearby artsy eco-resort, and plethora of Western-influenced shops get a big thumbs-up—this is in many ways our favorite non-urban shopping destination, and together with Madurai and Chettinad an essential part of any driving tour of southern India, providing a more textured experience than just the glam beaches and plantations of Kerala.

KARNATAKA   Karnataka has two new boutique yoga retreats. Just 35km (22 miles) from Bangalore is the new ultra-luxurious **Shreyas Yoga Retreat,** where a handful of visitors follow a tailor-made wellness program in an "ashram-meets-Aman" atmosphere. On the northern tip of Karnataka, at legendary Om beach, CGH Earth has opened **Swaswara,** similarly driven to not only provide a pampered holiday, but assist you in making a long-term lifestyle change.

Bangalore continues to be one of India's hippest, happening cities with great shopping and dining (at press time the top see-and-be-seen restaurant was the newly opened branch of the fab **Olive Beach**), but other than this urban hotbed there's not much to report from Karnataka. One destination that is very beautiful and rewarding, with a barely developed infrastructure, is **Coorg.** The hills are gorgeous, the food amazing, and the people very friendly, with strikingly different customs. We've included a small section on this region should you have time to explore this area—best done before it takes off like its counterparts in Kerala (Munnar and Wayanad) and Tamil Nadu (Ooty).

DELHI & MADHYA PRADESH Over and above the mushrooming of countless high-rise chain hotels all over the capital, Delhi finally has a choice of stylish midrange accommodations. Owned, designed, and run by a French duo, **Amarya Haveli** and **Amarya Garden** offer intimate luxury in two converted mansions in residential neighborhoods south of the city center. You'll also find a host of bed-and-breakfasts opening throughout the city (the Tourism Ministry wants to develop sustainable tourism, particularly targeting the midrange travel market), and we're happy to say that you can even find a few decent, affordable accommodations right near Connaught Place. In particular, the once-awful **Hotel Place Heights** has gone from roach motel to a comfortable and aesthetically satisfying stay.

The capital has expanded at an unprecedented rate in recent years; it's all part of **Delhi Master Plan 2021,** a far-reaching government initiative to drag the rapidly growing metropolis into the future, where it is poised to be a leading world capital. The city is also gearing up to host the **2010 Commonwealth Games**—this has set off a surge in development in and around the center, not to mention throughout the burgeoning National Capital Region, which incorporates the commercial "cities" of Gurgaon and Noida. The economic shakeup has also resulted in the widespread shutting down of a number of establishments—most worrisome being a number of excellent restaurants housed in ancient buildings that have been deemed unsafe. But while some of our old favorites, like Thai Wok, have had to close their doors, there has been a marked trend toward quality dining beyond the traditional confines of the city's five-star hotels. Of these, **Véda** is certainly the most beautifully designed eatery in town and well-located in Connaught Place.

While visitors to Delhi will find fewer cows, beggars, and (apparently) pollution than just a few years ago, the sheer density of the population—and the traffic—hasn't subsided; what is changing, however, is the city ethos. Increasingly, draconian laws have been put in place to assist with modernization; in 2007, traffic violations (including all kinds of irresponsible and dangerous driving) were identified as a legal priority, while street food was officially banned. You'll have to see for yourself if these measures have any sort of real impact on the latest incarnation of Delhi. Certainly, if you visit its newest attraction, the Disneyesque **Akshardham Temple Complex** (on the eastern bank of the Yamuna River), you'll be first-party witness to the evolving aspirations—spiritual and material—of the people who now inhabit this pulsating capital, which is fast becoming a financial powerhouse.

Near Khajuraho, Madhya Pradesh, archaeologists are busy unearthing a number of previously undiscovered temples that have been buried for centuries but may well reveal secrets about India's famously erotic monuments. In Khajuraho, **The Grand Temple View** is now the most luxurious and exclusive (not to mention expensive) lodging in town.

South of Khajuraho, at **Bandhavgarh Tiger Reserve,** the sumptuous **Mahua Kothi** is the first in a range of upmarket safari lodges established by a collaboration between India's Taj hotel group and South Africa's CC Africa, world leaders in luxurious safari experiences. Thanks to Mahua Kothi, Bandhavgarh is now giving Ranthambore a run for it's money as the top tiger destination in India; certainly it's less inundated by visitors, and your chances of getting up close and personal to a tiger—on the back of an elephant, no less—are probably better here than anywhere else on the subcontinent.

RAJASTHAN Rajasthan has seen plenty of changes. Jaipur has swollen apace and is now almost always choked with traffic and crowds; the city simply cannot keep up with the commercial and industrial developments that have lured people here in droves, hoping to find their fortune. Fortunately, you can escape the city—at least between sightseeing and shopping binges—and get to stay with Jaipur socialites (their aristocratic blood palpable) at **K Country Villa,** a luxury home with a handful of smart cottages, just beyond the city limits in a countryside setting; birdlife around the nearby lake has been favorably compared with that at Bharatpur.

Like Jaipur, Udaipur is growing fast, but it remains the most charming city in Rajasthan and an essential stop on a North India itinerary. The French-designed **Verandah on the Lake** resort should be up and running by the time you read this.

If you're traveling between Jaipur and Udaipur by car (still the best way to see the state), you might consider spending a night (or two) at the lovely, peaceful **Shahpura Bagh;** it's well off the beaten track, and the aristocratic hosts have created beautiful accommodations in the vast guest rooms of two colonial bungalows. Ever-popular **Deogarh Mahal** now has a sister property, the exclusive, sexy **Fort Seengh Sagar,** with only four guest rooms; the verandas are perfect for long, lazy afternoons with cocktail in hand.

Transportation throughout Rajasthan is being steadily upgraded, and an airport is believed to be in Jaisalmer's immediate future, which means increased tourist numbers. Given Rajasthan's burgeoning infrastructure, we've included some details of what to do and where to stay if you happen to get to **Bikaner,** another intriguing desert city with a stirring medieval marketplace within the old walled center and a fascinating fort.

Finally, if you plan to visit the holy town of Pushkar, be warned that it is now more commercialized than ever; if you prefer to be away from the crowds, consider staying in a luxury cottage or tent at the new resort-style **Pushkar Bagh,** which is relatively exclusive (30 units), and not only well-designed, but brimming with amenities.

HIMACHAL PRADESH Himachal Pradesh has seen very little development—hardly surprising, since most of the hill stations in India have lost their charm to concretization and short-sighted (blind?) tourism authorities. Manali, ever popular with those in quest of marijuana, is really not worth going to for a holiday; although Indians still flock there by the hundreds for honeymoons and summer vacations, the Israelis have established entire colonies here, and a corrupt police force protects their informal drug-trade-fueled economy. We've included a few lodging options outside of town so you can enjoy what you're really here for: the scenery. But if its scenery you're after, you should be planning a trip to far-flung Ladhak. Leh has seen a huge increase in tourist traffic, and a concurrent improvement in infrastructure—we have our fingers crossed that it's not going the way of every other hill station—but make sure you have the time and resources to explore the more off-the-beaten-track spots like Tso Moreri and Pangong Tso, which are still pretty untouched.

UTTARAKHAND The tiny Himalayan foothill state formerly known as Uttaranchal is now **Uttarakhand,** having adopted the name by which it is known in the ancient Hindu sacred texts, the Puranas.

KOLKATA & EAST INDIA Moving east, the city of Kolkata remains an unexpected delight, with a plethora of dining options that will have the gourmet in you in a state of permanent bliss. It's also the perfect base to explore the northern and northeastern states—the latter are slowly emerging as new and exciting destinations in India (if you're not fazed by a lack of infrastructure), thanks to a marked decrease in the insurgency that troubled these little-known states. Of these, beautiful Assam is the most "doable," thanks to **Assam Bengal Navigation,** an enterprising Indo-British venture that offers luxury cruises on the Brahmaputra river. But if you find yourself on this side of India, there is one stop we urge you to make: the gorgeous **Glenburn Tea Estate,** with a gracious Raj-era atmosphere, gorgeous views, and the luxury of space and privacy.

Lastly, remote Sikkim has also become more popular of late, with the opening up of stunning North Sikkim (to tourists) and Nathu La (for trade with China), and a spate of lovely new homestay options. Don't expect luxury, other than the pleasure of experiencing traditional hospitality—after all, in India it is a sacred belief that the guest is king.

1

The Best of India

India will humble, awe, frustrate, amaze, and intimidate you—all on the same day. Home to some of the world's most spectacular medieval structures and largest slums; sacred rivers and filth-strewn streets; deeply religious ritual and endless traffic jams; aristocratic tigers and low-caste untouchables; jewel-encrusted tombs and pavement-bound beggars; ancient traditions and modern-day scams—there is so much to take in. Whether you're here to soak up India's spirituality, chill out on the beaches, or live like a king in the land of princes, this chapter will help you experience the very best India has to offer.

1 Experiencing Spiritual India

Visiting temples that pulsate with devotion will evoke a sense of the sacred, but in India, where religion is such an integral part of daily life, spiritual experiences occur when you least expect them.

- **See Things As They Really Are** (Vipassana Centers throughout India): Maintaining a strict code of silence with no sensory stimulation for 10 days may sound like a self-induced hell, but after attending a 10-day Vipassana meditation course, most people claim transformation and find the mental training invaluable. And it costs nothing. See chapter 2.

- **Hop on a Motorbike and Head for the Drumbeat** (Goa): Once capital of the global beach party, Goa may be past its prime, but when rumors start that an event is in the making at a to-be-announced venue, keep your ear to the ground. Why? Because only in some deserted clearing near a golden Goan beach can you trance out with the nationals of the world, and find solace in the serenity of a rural villager's smile as she hands over cups of

soothing *chai* for the duration of the party. See chapter 5.

- **Worship the Sunrise as It Touches the Southernmost Tip** (Kanyakumari, Tamil Nadu): You can't help but be moved by a sense of the miraculous when a simple daily occurrence is venerated by thousands of pilgrims who plunge themselves into the turbulent swell, believing that the tri-oceanic waters at India's southernmost tip are holy, while others delight in the glorious spectacle as if it's a Bollywood (the nickname for India's booming film industry) premiere. See chapter 6.

- **Lose All Sense of Reality in the City of Light** (Varanasi, Uttar Pradesh): Drifting at dawn on a boat on the Ganges along Varanasi's bathing *ghats* (steps leading down to the river), against a backdrop of 18th- and 19th-century temples and palaces, you will witness surreal sights—hundreds of pilgrims waist-deep in the Ganges cleansing their souls in its holy waters, while others pound laundry, meditate by staring into the sun, or limber up to wrestle. All the while, bodies burn on the sacred banks, thereby achieving *moksha*—liberation from the eternal cycle of rebirth. See chapter 9.

• **Purchase a Pushkar Passport** (Pushkar, Rajasthan): As you wander around the *ghats* of Pushkar, the beautifully serene temple town on the edge of the Thar Desert, you will almost certainly be approached by a Brahmin priest to offer *puja* (prayers) at the sacred lake. In exchange for a "donation," he will tie a red thread around your wrist—the "passport" you can brandish at the next priest who approaches. This is the commercial side of India's spirituality, and one you need to be aware of. See chapter 10.

• **Make a Wish at the Tomb of a Sufi Saint** (Ajmer, Rajasthan): The great Sufi saint Khwaja Moin-ud-Din Chisti was known as "the protector of the poor," and his tomb is said to possess the power to grant the wishes of all those who visit. His Dargah Sharif is the most sacred Islamic shrine in India, second in importance only to Mecca but frequented by Hindus and Muslims alike. The atmosphere of pure devotion is both ancient and surreal; some pray fervently, and others tie threads onto the latticework while supplicating the saint to fulfill their wish, while throughout these activities, the *qawwali* singers seated in front of the tomb repeat the same beautiful, haunting melodies that have been sung for centuries. See chapter 10.

• **Carry the Holy *Granth Sahib* to its Evening Resting Place** (Amritsar, Punjab): In Sikh temples, the *Granth Sahib*—Holy Book of the Sikhs—is an object of devotion in its own right, and nowhere is this more evocative

than at the Golden Temple, the most tangibly spiritual destination in the country. In the evenings men line up to carry the precious *Granth Sahib* from its golden sanctuary at the center of the Amrit Sarovar (Pool of Nectar), crossing **Guru's Bridge,** which symbolizes the journey of the soul after death, to **Akal Takht,** where the Holy Book rests for the night. You can take part in this ceremony by joining the line that forms behind and ahead of the heavy palanquin. Being part of this ancient tradition is a deeply moving experience and indicative of the embracing atmosphere you'll find in Sikh temples throughout India. See chapter 11.

• **Look into the Eyes of the Dalai Lama** (Dharamsala, Himachal Pradesh): There's a good chance you'll meet the Dalai Lama in person if you visit Dharamsala, home to the exiled Tibetan government, which fled its homeland in 1959. Arranging a private audience isn't easy (unless you're Richard Gere), but if you attend one of his public appearances, you will—like everyone else in the audience—receive a personal blessing. And whatever your convictions, when you look into the eyes of His Holiness, you know you are in the presence of pure energy. See chapter 11.

• **Witness a Thousand Prayers Take Flight on the Wind** (Leh, Ladakh): Take the overland journey from Manali to Leh and enter the stark world of the Trans-Himalayas—a breathtakingly beautiful yet desolate lunarlike landscape, with arid peaks and ancient Buddhist monasteries perched on rocky crags. Here prayer flags flutter against an impossibly blue sky, sending their silent prayers to the heavens. See chapter 11.

• **Clapping Along during Evening *Aarti* as the Faithful Give Thanks** to the Ganges (Rishikesh, Uttarakhand, formerly known as Uttaranchal): By day, Rishikesh is a spiritual Disneyland, where the commercial excesses of packaged meditation and two-for-one tantric yoga hang heavily about the concrete ashrams, bedecked with gaudy statues of Vishnu and Shiva. But at night, to the accompaniment of hypnotic prayers and harmonious singing, the town undergoes a magical transformation. Head for the Parmarth Niketan Ashram Ghat and feel yourself seduced by the divine rhythms during **Ganga Aarti,** when devotees gather to sing their praises at the edge of the Ganges River. See chapter 12.

2 The Best Temples, Monuments & Lost Cities

- **Cave Temples at Ajanta & Ellora** (Aurangabad, Maharashtra): Fashioned out of rock by little more than simple hand-held tools, the cave temples at Ajanta (created by Buddhist monks between the 2nd and 7th c.) and Ellora (a marriage of Buddhist, Hindu, and Jain temples, created between the 4th and 9th c.) are the finest examples of rock-cut architecture in India, and deserving of their World Heritage status. The zenith is **Kailashnath Temple,** effectively a mountain whittled down to a freestanding temple. See "Aurangabad & the Ellora and Ajanta Caves" in chapter 4.

- **Lord Gomateswara Monolith** (Sravanabelagola, Karnataka): One of the oldest (ca. A.D. 918) and most important Jain pilgrimage sites, this 18m (59-ft.) statue of the naked Lord Gomateswara—a representation of Bahubali, son of the first Jain *tirthankara,* said to have sought enlightenment by standing naked and motionless for an entire year—is the tallest monolithic statue on earth. See "Exploring the Hoysala Heartland: Belur, Halebid & Sravanabelagola" in chapter 8.

- **Hampi** (Karnataka): Scattered among the Henri Moore–like boulders in the heart of Karnataka's rural interior, Hampi was once the royal seat of the powerful Vijayanagar kingdom, its size and wealth drawing comparisons with imperial Rome. Today, the city has crumbled away to a few starkly beautiful leftovers, but the remote setting couldn't be more romantic. See "Hampi & the Ruined City of Vijayanagar" in chapter 8.

- **The Temples of Mahaballpurum** (Tamil Nadu): A visit to this once-thriving port city of the Pallava dynasty, who ruled much of South India between the 4th and 9th centuries A.D., is an essential stop on Tamil Nadu's temple tour. The earliest examples of monumental architecture in southern India (the celebrated **Arjuna's Penance** is the largest relief-carving on earth), these rock-cut shrines are best explored in the morning, leaving you time to unwind on the pleasant beach and dine on succulent seafood at village cafes for a song. See "Mahabalipuram (Mamallapuram)" in chapter 7.

- **Shri Meenakshi-Sundareshwarar Temple** (Madurai, Tamil Nadu): Alive with prayers, processions, garland-makers, and joyous devotees who celebrate the mythological romance between the beautiful three-breasted goddess and her mighty Lord Shiva, this colorful and lively complex of shrines, halls, and market stalls is almost Disneyesque, marked as it is by numerous entrance towers tangled with colorful stucco gods, demons, beasts, and mythological heroes. It truly embodies the spirit of Tamil

Nadu's deeply embedded temple culture. See "Madurai" in chapter 7.

- **Taj Mahal** (Agra, Uttar Pradesh): Nothing can prepare you for the beauty of the Taj. The perfect symmetry, the ethereal luminescence, the wonderful proportions, the sheer scale—virtually impossible to imagine from staring at its oft-reproduced image—and the exquisite detailing make this bejeweled monument to love a justifiable wonder of the world. See "Agra" in chapter 9.

- **Fatehpur Sikri** (near Agra, Uttar Pradesh): From the intricacy of the glittering white marble screens that surround the *dargah* (tomb) of Salim Chisti, to Parcheesi Court, where the emperor played a ludolike game using the ladies of his harem as live pieces, this magnificent ghost city—built almost entirely from red sandstone in 1571 and deserted only 14 years later—is a testament to the secular vision of Akbar, one of the great players in India's most dynamic dynasty. See "Agra" in chapter 9.

- **The Temples of Khajuraho** (Khajuraho, Madhya Pradesh): Built between the 10th and 12th centuries by the Chandela Rajputs, these World Heritage Site monuments are most famous for the erotic sculptures that writhe across the interiors and exteriors. But even the temple designs—their soaring *shikharas* (spires) serving as metaphoric "stairways to heaven"—are striking, and are considered the apotheosis of medieval Hindu architecture. See "Khajuraho" in chapter 9.

- **Mehrangarh Fort** (Jodhpur, Rajasthan): The impenetrable walls of this 15th-century edifice to Rajput valor rise seamlessly from the rocky outcrop on which they were built, literally dwarfing the labyrinthine city at its base; from its crenelated ramparts you enjoy postcard views of the "Blue

City" below. In the distance is the grand silhouette of Umaid Bhawan Palace, heritage hotel and residence of the current maharaja. Within the fort is one of the best palace museums in India. See "Jodhpur" in chapter 10.

- **Jain Temples of Rajasthan** (Ranakpur and Mount Abu, near Udaipur, Rajasthan): The Jains put all their devotional passion (and not inconsiderable wealth) into the creation of the most ornate marble temples; with exquisitely detailed relief carvings covering every inch, they are all jaw-droppingly beautiful. Make sure you visit at least one while you're in India, preferably either Ranakpur Temple or Dilwara Temple in Rajasthan. See chapter 10.

- **Golden Temple** (Amritsar, Punjab): Arguably the greatest spiritual monument in India. The name derives from the central gold-plated Hari Mandir—the inner sanctuary featuring gold-plated copper cupolas and white marble walls inlaid with precious stones—which sits at the center of the "Pool of Nectar." Every day thousands of disciplined devotees pay their respects, touching their heads to the glistening marble floor while singing devotional songs continuously—a wonderful, welcoming, and humbling experience. See "The Golden Temple in Amritsar" in chapter 11.

- **Tabo** (Spiti Valley, Himachal Pradesh): This 1,005-year-old Buddhist complex houses magnificent frescoes and brilliant stucco and relief figures that recount ancient myths and celebrate the deities and demons that make up the Buddhist pantheon. You'll need a flashlight to adequately explore the dark, smoldering halls and shrines lit only by thin shafts of natural light, and brought to life by the resonant chants and ringing of bells by the monks and nuns who populate this sacred center of Tibetan Buddhism. See "Exploring Kinnaur & Spiti" in chapter 11.

- **The Sun Temple at Konark** (near Bhubaneswar, Orissa): An enormous war chariot carved from a massive chunk of rock during the 13th century, this masterpiece of Indian temple art is covered with detailed sculpted scenes, from the erotic to the mythological. Guarded by stone elephants and lions, the immense structure is seen as the gigantic chariot of the sun god emerging from the ocean, not far from Orissa's 500km (310-mile) beach. See "Orissa's Golden Temple Triangle" in chapter 13.

3 Unique Places to Stay

Not surprisingly, most of these are in Rajasthan, which has almost 80 heritage properties—castles, palaces, forts, and ornate *havelis* (traditional mansions), now hotels offering varying degrees of comfort.

- **Taj Mahal Hotel** (Mumbai): George Bernard Shaw famously claimed that after staying here, he no longer had any need to visit the real Taj Mahal in Agra. Built just over a century ago by an Indian industrialist after he was treated abominably by the colonial snobs at the city's then leading hotel (since demolished), the Taj Mahal today hosts the world's rich and famous, and remains the most celebrated address in Mumbai. See p. 100.

- **Boutique Getaways in Goa:** Parisian fashion stylist Claudia Derain and her husband, Hari Ajwani, came to Goa on vacation and—like so many—never left. Together with Goan architect Dean D'Cruz, they've created an *Arabian Nights* fantasy in **Nilaya Hermitage,** with only 12 "cosmic-themed" guest suites and gorgeously informal public spaces overlooking paddy fields and coconut-palm groves. It lies 6km (3¾ miles) from the nearest beach, however; if proximity to the golden sands of bustling Goa is key, **Pousada Tauma,** another Dean D'Cruz creation, is the next contender for Goa's best boutique getaway. But if you prefer basic to boutique, **Elsewhere,** sandwiched between the river and the sea, comprises a simple beach house, a couple of double-roomed cottages, and "Otter Creek" tents—a quiet retreat, and utterly charming. See p. 147, 148, and 145.

- **Adrift aboard** *Discovery* (Kerala): The best way to experience Kerala's backwaters is floating along on a traditional *kettuvallam* (houseboat), but the stylish Malabar Group has upped the ante with *Discovery,* a funky modern interpretation of the Keralan houseboat concept. Accommodations comprise a comfortable and stylish bedroom with well-plumbed en-suite bathroom, separate lounge (can double as a second bedroom), and a rooftop deck (furnished with dining table and loungers) where you can while away the day, looked after by a dedicated staff of three, including a private chef. The packages can include a night at the aptly named **Privacy,** our favorite backwaters villa. See p. 199.

- **Gracious Keralan Homestays** (Olavipe, Backwaters/Tranquil, Wyanad): Experience life on a working plantation, then dine on exquisite home-cooked meals at the family dining table, personally hosted by urbane, charming owners—that's what the best homestays are all about. It's like finding yourself at a private house party, where you are the guest of honor. Our top picks are **Olavipe,** a stately home on an island in the backwaters, where Anthony and Rema provide the warmest welcome this side of Fort Kochi, and **Tranquil,** located at the edge of Wyanad National Park, where Victor and Ranjini ensure that you leave replenished, and heartsick to go. See p. 190 and 220.

- **Surya Samudra Beach Garden** (near Kovalam, Kerala): A small collection of traditional cottages on a terraced hillside overlooking the sea, with direct access to two picture-perfect beaches, Surya Samudra is quite simply the most Paradisiacal destination on the Malabar coast. Gazing over the Arabian Sea from your private deck (ask for a cottage near the beach), you will no doubt wish you'd spent your entire vacation here. See p. 205.

- **Mahua Kothi** (Bandhavgarh, Madhya Pradesh): The first in a highly anticipated series of ultra-luxurious safari lodges from India's Taj hotel group and South Africa's CC Africa, Mahua Kothi is not only eye-catchingly pretty and filled with whimsically stylish details, but the sumptuous guest villas are an idyllic retreat after a day of tiger-spotting with the best-trained naturalists in the country. See p. 377.

- **Amarvilãs** (Agra, Uttar Pradesh): If you've always dreamed of seeing the Taj Mahal, this is the place to celebrate that achievement. Built within the green belt that surrounds the monument, you can literally see the Taj from your bed, but you'll probably spend just as much time gazing at your immediate surroundings. With

its huge reflecting pools, colonnaded courts, terraced lawns, inlaid murals, and pillowed pavilions, this palatial hotel is worth every cent. See p. 348.

- **Rajvilãs** (near Jaipur, Rajasthan): The first of the Oberoi's flagship Vilas properties, built like a traditional fortified Rajasthani palace, Rajvilãs may not have the history of an authentic heritage hotel, but it offers a level of comfort, luxury, and service other properties cannot match, enabling even the most world-weary guest (Bill Clinton loved it) to "live in the princely style of Rajasthan." See p. 406.

- **Aman-i-Khás** (Ranthambhore, Rajasthan): Located a stone's throw from India's most famous tiger sanctuary, the superb accommodations—huge temperature-controlled Mughal-style royal tents stylishly divided by cool white drapes—and impeccable service are distinctly Aman. At night, lanterns light your way to the giant flaming *uruli* (large metal vessel) around which guests gather to enjoy the night sky and the ethereal calm, broken only by the occasional call from the wilds. See p. 427.

- **Deogarh Mahal & Fort Seengh Sagar** (Rural Rajasthan): An ornate 17th-century fort-palace with domed turrets and balconies, personally managed by the charming Thakur of Deogarh, Deogarh Mahal is one of the most authentic and best-value heritage hotels in Rajasthan, best visited on a road trip between Jaipur and Udaipur. Book the aptly named "Royal" suite, and it's not hard to feel that all you survey from your private balcony is yours. The more recently opened Seengh Sagar is an exclusive island fort that's been transformed into a sexy little villa run by the same princely family. See p. 463.

- **Rawla Narlai** (Rural Rajasthan): Rawla Narlai, the 17th-century hunting retreat of the Maharajah of Jodhpur, is another rural gem that will have you feeling like a royal guest—and it's the ideal stopover if you're traveling between Udaipur and Jodhpur. But, with activities and experiences galore (including a stiff climb to the summit of a miraculous rock), it's more than a mere stopover—you'll stay for 1 night and wish you'd planned for 3. See p. 464.
- **Lake Palace Hotel** (Udaipur, Rajasthan): Built on an island by the Maharana in 1740 as a cool summer retreat (swimming distance from his palace), this is perhaps the most romantic—certainly the most photographed—hotel in India. Whizzing across the waters to your private palace, you'll feel you've finally arrived—and if you've booked one of the heritage suites, you have. Floating like a beautiful white ship on the waters of Lake Pichola, the hotel offers good service, comfortable lodging, and picture-perfect 360-degree views. See p. 458.
- **Kankarwa** (Udaipur, Rajasthan): A short stroll from the City Palace, this ancient haveli right on the shores of Lake Pichola is the best budget heritage option in Rajasthan. Run by a family who has resided here for 200 years, double rooms cost just Rs 1,650 to Rs 2,500 ($40–$61/£20–£31). Book room no. 207—a cool, whitewashed space with a separate alcove room with a mattress where you can laze in the afternoons and gaze upon the blue waters of the lake reflected below your window. See p. 460.
- **Devi Garh** (near Udaipur, Rajasthan): If you're a modern-design enthusiast, this hotel will blow you away. The formidable exterior of this 18th-century Rajput palace-fort, towering over the tiny village at its base, remains unchanged. But step inside and you'll find a totally reinvented minimalist interior, with 14 floors transformed into 23 chic suites (with 18 more opening soon) that have clearly utilized the talents of the best young Indian designers—all of whom laid to rest the perception that design here reached its apotheosis with the Mughals. It's an unparalleled modern Indian masterpiece, and a destination in its own right. See p. 462.
- **Umaid Bhawan Palace** (Jodhpur, Rajasthan): Splurge on one of the sumptuous Deco heritage suites in this glorious, monumental palace (still partially inhabited by Jodhpur's royal family), with the city and its populace somewhere far below. It stands on the summit of a hill, with the staggering Mehrangarh Fort across the way. Guests here are treated like royalty, with access to a private cinema, fabulous lounges, a squadron of butlers, and two pools—one an indoor Deco masterpiece and another at the edge of the beautiful, lush gardens where Liz Hurley married her Indian beau. See p. 470.
- **Amanbagh** (Ajabgarh, Rajasthan): Fringed by date palms and mango and jamun trees, Aman's shimmering pink-sandstone resort is the oasis you have always wanted to stumble upon while traversing the Thar Desert. Begin your day sipping ruby-red pomegranate juice on your private porch, then hike to ancient Somsagar Lake or explore the haunted ruins at Bhangarh. Or go nowhere but your private villa pool on the edge of the palm-lined canal and listen to the joyful twittering of birds. See p. 394.
- **Killa Bhawan** (Jaisalmer, Rajasthan): Built entirely from yellow sandstone,

Sonar Qila (Golden Fort) rises like a giant sandcastle from its desert surrounds—this is the world's only living medieval fort, inhabited by families who have been here for more than 8 centuries. Within the ramparts, Killa Bhawan is a charming seven-room guesthouse with rather basic facilities (only two rooms are en-suite) but lovely furnishings and stunning views, best enjoyed from the rooftop, which is comfortably furnished with mattresses and bolsters. See p. 484.

• **Gangeshwari Suite at The Glasshouse on the Ganges** (Garhwal, Uttarakhand): It's the location—just steps away from the raging Ganges River—more than anything that gives this room its special appeal. The simply laid-out sleeping area has a four-poster canopy bed and antique furniture, while the bathroom features a tub carved into the rock, with greenery spilling down the walls. You can relax on your private balcony and watch India's holiest river gushing by,

or dive in for a refreshing dip knowing that you're far away from the pollution that enters the river much farther downstream. See p. 534.

• **Glenburn Tea Estate** (Darjeeling): Centered around the 100-year-old Burra Bungalow, which offers just four magnificent rooms, this tea plantation is by far the best place to stay in the "Land of the Celestial Thunderbolt," with great decor, delectable cuisine, and superb views of the Kanchenjunga. You can spend a night at Glenburn Lodge by the river without giving up your room at the Bungalow—the two rooms here are charming, especially at night when bathed in the orange glow of hurricane lamps (no electricity) with only the burbling of the river for music. Picnics (anywhere on the estate) will be served by liveried bearers on portable tables complete with a tablecloth, delicate crockery, and a vase of fresh flowers—all that's missing is a chandelier. See p. 581.

4 Most Memorable Moments

• **Sharing a Cup of *Chai* with a Perfect Stranger:** You will typically be asked to sit and share a cup of *chai* (tea) a dozen times a day, usually by merchants keen to keep you browsing. Although you may at first be nervous of what this may entail, don't hesitate to accept when you're feeling more comfortable, for while sipping the milky sweet brew (often flavored with ginger and cardamom), conversation will flow, and you might find yourself discussing anything from women's rights in India to the individualism that mars Western society.

• **Helping Lord Venkateshwara Repay His Debt to the God of Wealth** (Tirupati, Andhra Pradesh): Tirupati, the richest temple in India,

is the most active religious pilgrimage destination on earth, drawing more than 10 million devoted pilgrims every year (more than either Jerusalem or Rome!) who line up for hours, even days, to see the diamond-decorated black stone idol Lord Venkateshwara (aka Vishnu) for just a few seconds. Afterward, you stare in disbelief as vast piles of cash and other contributions are counted by scores of clerks behind a wall of glass. See chapter 7.

• **Watching the Moon Rise from Pushkar Palace during the Pushkar *Mela*** (Pushkar, Rajasthan): The sunset is a spectacular sight on any given evening, but on the evening of the full moon during the Pushkar *mela*, hundreds of Hindu pilgrims, accompanied by temple bells and drums, wade into a sacred lake—believed to miraculously cleanse the soul—before lighting clay lamps and setting them afloat on its holy waters, the twinkling lights a surreal reflection of the desert night sky. If you're lucky enough to have bagged a room at Pushkar Palace, you can watch this ancient ritual from a deck chair on the terrace on the banks of the lake. See chapter 10.

- **Gawking & Being Gawked At** (Dungarpur, near Udaipur, Rajasthan): As a foreigner, you may attract uncomfortably long stares (particularly on public transport), but there are a few moments that you will recall with a wry smile, like the gimlet eye of the toothless old royal retainer as he watches your reaction to the explicit *Kama Sutra* paintings he will reveal hidden in a cupboard of Dungarpur's 13th-century Juna Mahal—one of the Rajasthan's undiscovered gems. See chapter 10.

- **Playing Chicken with a Tata Truck:** The rules of the road (which is almost always single-laned, potholed, and unmarked) are hard to understand, but it would seem that (after the cow, which is of course sacred) Tata trucks, all with HORN ON PLEASE written on their bumpers, rule the road, an assumption your hired driver is likely to test—and you will, more than once, find yourself involuntarily closing your eyes as destiny appears to race toward you, blaring its horn.

- **Meeting a Maharaja** (Rajasthan): India must be the only place in the world where you can, armed with a credit card, find yourself sleeping in a king's bed, having dined with the aristocrat whose forebears built, and quite often died for, the castle or palace walls that surround it. While most heritage properties are still owned by India's oldest monarchies, many of whom live there, only some (like Mandawa Castle and Deogarh Mahal in Rajasthan, and Nilambagh Palace in Gujarat) are personally managed by these urbane aristocrats. See chapter 10.

- **Unraveling the Intricacies of Hinduism** (Master Paying Residential Guest Accommodation, Delhi): Staying here is not only the best-value deal in town, but the sophisticated, charming, and extremely knowledgeable Avnish Puri will take you on a "Hidden Delhi" tour, showing you a world not seen by many outsiders, during which he will unravel Hinduism's spiritual tenets in a profoundly logical way—no mean feat! See chapter 9.

- **Being Blessed by an Elephant:** While you may expect to see an elephant in a national park, it's always a wonderful surprise when you see one ambling down a crowded street in urban Mumbai or Delhi. Outside Thirupparankundram Temple, near Madurai, the resident temple elephant waits patiently to bestow blessings on those willing to donate a rupee.

5 Exploring Natural India

- **Watch Cows Sunbathing with Tourists on the Beach** (Goa): While there's plenty of marijuana doing the rounds in Goa, you don't have to smoke a thing to be amused by the mellow cows that wander onto the beach and chill out among the tanning tourists and hawkers. Chewing their cud while seemingly gazing out to sea, these cows really take the Goan motto, *"Sossegade"* ("Take it easy"), to heart. See chapter 5.

- **Ply the Backwaters on a *Kettuvallam*** (Alleppey & Kumarakom, Kerala): Aboard your private houseboat, you aimlessly drift past villages, temples, and churches, watching as village children, unperturbed by your drifting presence, play at the water's edge, and elephants and water buffalo wade at will. Though the facilities might strike the well-heeled as basic, you're looked after by a private team (guide, cook, and pilot) who manage to be both discreetly invisible and at your beck and call. See chapter 6.
- **Quench Your Thirst with Fresh Coconut Water on a Tropical Island** (Lakshadweep): One of India's best-kept secrets, the 36 atolls and coral reefs that make up the remote union territory of Lakshadweep are rated among the best diving destinations in Asia. Only 10 of the islands are populated, almost exclusively by Malayalam-speaking Muslims who make their living from fishing and harvesting coconuts. These relaxed islanders are supremely welcoming, happily climbing a towering coconut tree to help you quench your thirst. See chapter 6.
- **Wake to Hear a Herd of Elephants Approaching** (Periyar Wildlife Sanctuary, Kerala): The best way to experience this park—famous for its herds of wild elephants—is on a trek with the privately run Periyar Tiger Trail. Accompanied by a naturalist and a game ranger armed with a rifle, you are taken farther into the tourist zone than any other operator is allowed to penetrate. What's more, you are looked after by a team of reformed poachers, who skillfully track and spot animals, carry all the gear, strike camp, cook, clean, and—most importantly—stand sentinel throughout the night when the danger of being trampled by elephants becomes a serious risk. See chapter 6.
- **Immortalize a Wild Tiger from the Back of an Elephant** (Bandhavgarh National Park, Madhya Pradesh): With the densest population of tigers of any park in India, you are practically guaranteed a sighting at this relatively low-key, remote part of Madhya Pradesh. But it's the approach that's so exciting—elephant *mahouts* set off at dawn to track the royal cats. As soon as they've spotted one, you rendezvous with your pachyderm, who then takes you within striking distance of this most royal of cats. The tiger—unperturbed by the presence of an elephant—will then strike a pose of utter indifference for your camera. See chapter 9.
- **Pick a Picture-Perfect Beach** (Goa, Kerala): India has some of the world's best beaches, most of them on the Malabar Coast. Easily accessed, **Asvem** (northern Goa) is an idyllic haven, while just south of Goa, **Morjim** has been drawing Olive Ridley turtles to its shores for centuries. Both beaches are off the well-beaten tourist track. **Palolem** (southern Goa), a gorgeous crescent of sand backed by coconut palms and a handful of laid-back shacks where you can feast on fresh fish and bottles of cold beer, is another of India's loveliest beaches. From here, time allowing, you should head over the border to beautiful and remote **Om** Beach (Gokam, Karnataka). In Kerala, the competition is equally stiff, but we award the picture-perfect prize to the beaches at **Marari** and **Surya Samudra** resorts. The absolute stunners, if you can get that far, are at **Bangaram** and **Agatti,** in Lakshadweep. See chapters 5 and 6.

- **Find Divinity in *Devbhumi*, "Land of the Gods"** (Spiti to Kinnaur, Himachal Pradesh): The stark, rust-colored, snowcapped slopes in the Indo-Tibetan regions of Kinnaur, Spiti, and Lahaul are the stuff adventurers' dreams are made of, offering sublime mountainscapes, flower-filled valleys, terrifying roads, atmospheric Tibetan Buddhist *gompas* (monasteries), and high-altitude villages that seem to cling to the mountainsides. The region is one of the most profoundly beautiful in the world, but the drive is not for the fainthearted. See chapter 11.

- **Get a Rush While Rafting Down the Zanskar** (Ladakh): White-water rafting on the Zanskar is not only exhilarating and challenging, but you pass through the most incredibly desolate, scenic gorges and stupendous cliffs. A full river journey takes at least 12 days round-trip from Leh, so this is only for the truly committed—though there are slightly tamer options closer to Leh. See chapter 11.

6 The Best Eating & Drinking Experiences

- **Bumping into a Bollywood Idol** (Mumbai): Nowhere in India is dining more rewarding than in Mumbai, where the streets are filled with literally thousands of restaurants representing every kind of Indian cuisine. But if it's star-gazing you're after, head for places like the **Olive Bar and Kitchen** restaurant in Bandra or **Enigma** nightclub in Juhu. Alternatively, hang out at **Leopold Café**; casting agents looking for foreigners to work as extras frequently scan the clientele at this favored travelers' hangout. See chapter 4.

- **Eating Alphonso Mangoes in Mumbai:** You may have eaten mangoes in Mexico, Thailand, or even in other parts of India, but until you've had an Alphonso from Ratnagiri in rural Maharashtra, you'll be missing a sensory experience like no other. The king of mangoes has a succulent bright orange pulp, bewitching scent, and divine flavor. See chapter 4.

- **Eating with Your Hands:** Though it may initially go against the grain, there's something immensely rewarding about digging into a delicious meal with your hands. Indians generally do, and—at least once—you should follow suit. Note that ideally you only use your right hand, and in the North, where the food is "drier," you are traditionally not supposed to dirty more than the first two digits; in the South you may use the whole hand. See the appendix, "India in Depth."

- **Sipping a Sweet Lassi:** A delicious drink of liquefied sweetened yogurt, this is almost a meal in a glass and should definitely be sampled (some of the best we've tried were in Amritsar, Goa, and Jaipur). Do, however, make sure that no water has been added (including ice), and beware the *bhang* lassi—spiced with marijuana, it can make the usually surreal scenes of India a little too out of this world.

- **Sitting Around a Bonfire under a Desert Sky** (Rajasthan): There's nothing quite like eating a superb meal around a raging campfire in the peace of the desert night. Camel and horseback safaris are run out of Shekhawati, Bikaner, Pushkar, and Jaisalmer. If you opt for the latter, **Royal Desert Safaris** has a permanent tented camp with en-suite tents near Sam Dunes, run by Fort Rajwada, with food supplied by the team of chefs that cooks up a storm at Trio, Jaisalmer's best restaurant. See chapter 10.

- **Sampling *Bod-Jha*, Tibetan Butter Tea, with a Buddhist Lama** (Leh, Ladakh): Many people gag at the taste of butter tea, made with salt and— you guessed it—a good dollop of the clarified butter known as ghee. It's an acquired taste, but if you get the hang of it, sipping the buttery concoction with a friendly Buddhist monk when you visit one of the many monasteries tucked in the lunar landscapes around Leh is a truly memorable experience. See chapter 11.

7 The Best Savvy Traveler Tips

- **"You pay what you like"**: This rather annoying response from guides, drivers, and rickshaw-*wallas* to the question "How much will it cost?" will no doubt end with at least one of you feeling very disappointed. Try to find out how much something should cost *before* you enter into this dialogue (we've tried to advise this wherever possible), and always negotiate the fare or rate upfront. (Note that "I come later" is another irritating response, this time after you decline service, and you will need to remain firm or prepare to go through the entire experience again.)
- **"Just look, no buy"**: You will be urged to enter shops from all corners in both explicit and less obvious ways—your driver, guide, even the seemingly innocent bystander offering assistance, are almost all operating on the ubiquitous commission system, and whatever they make on the deal is added to the quoted price. Note that to avoid this kind of hassle, look for the fixed-rate shops or those that mark their wares with prices. But as is the case everywhere, do beware of closely named imitations of fixed-rate shops with good reputations— for example, Cottage Industries Exposition shops, often marked CIE, are seriously overpriced outlets that cash in on the fame (and closely related name) of the government-owned Central Cottage Industries Emporiums. The latter may not be the cheapest, but it offers good value, and you really can "just look, no buy."
- **"We look; we look"**: This response from a rickshaw-*walla* or driver usually means that the person either doesn't know where you've asked him to take you, or you'll end up somewhere with a similar name but nothing else to recommend it (Hotel *Chandra*, for example, rather than Hotel *Chand*). Prebook your accommodations whenever you can, so that you don't have to deal with touts and hawkers when you arrive. And be aware that a hotel or guesthouse that is successful will often have a rival opening within the year with a confusingly similar name.
- **"So where are you from, good gentleman?"** (or more commonly, "Coming from?"): You will be asked this often, so prepare yourself. One of the possible reasons Indians kick-start conversations this way is that where you come from may in the past have indicated caste or social position; whatever the reason, engage in the opener—it's far preferable to living in a five-star hotel cocoon.
- **"Hashish, taxi, guide, young girls?"**: In the well-traveled parts of India, you will be inundated with offers of assistance; again, the best response is to doggedly desist in what is essentially a game of endurance, and certainly ignore those unsolicited offers that are illicit—these can carry a hefty penalty, including a lengthy jail sentence.

- **"Cof-fay, chai; cof-fay, chai; cof-fay, chai?"**: This incessant call given by the *chai-walla* wandering the corridors of your train will put to rest any romantic notions about the relaxation of train travel. Note that you will be most comfortable aboard the overnight **Rajdhanis,** which connect all the major cities, while the best daytime trains are the **Shatabdis** (book Chair Class). Time allowing, you should definitely book a "toy train" to the hill stations of Shimla or Darjeeling—the latter approach is so spectacular it has been named a World Heritage Site.

- **"Yes, Madam"; "Yes, Sir"**: You will hear this everywhere, usually from hawkers wanting to draw your attention and con artists wanting to strike up a conversation. Unfortunately, the only way to get rid of these irritants is to completely ignore them. In places like Varanasi, even saying "no" is perceived as a willingness to interact, and your pursuer will then continue to try to draw you into conversation. Just pretend you can't be bothered, and hopefully, in a little while, you won't.

- **"You wait, no problem"**: Finally, we can't emphasize enough how important it is to simply relax and accept whatever's going on around you. Many Indians subscribe to the philosophy that life is destiny, and getting uptight or flying into a rage usually won't solve much. You'll have a far better vacation if you simply give in to the moment and enjoy the experience; after all, the only aspect you have control over is your response.

2

Planning Your Trip to India

Once the playing fields of only die-hard budget New Age travelers, India has in the past decade come into its own for top-end travelers who want to be pampered and rejuvenated as well as spiritually and culturally challenged. Given its vast size, the majority of India's top attractions are remarkably easy to get to, using a clever combination of internal flights or long-haul train journeys and chauffeur-driven cars (no sane traveler would self-drive). Hotels, particularly in the heritage category, offer excellent value-for-money in Western terms, and despite a number of potential health concerns, sensible travelers will enjoy their sojourn with little more than a brief tummy upset. It is, however, very important to plot out your itinerary and make reservations well in advance. Finally, though India has definite Third World elements—infrastructure and service levels leave much to be desired—you'll find almost everything you need here, particularly if you're armed with a credit card and *Frommer's India, 3rd Edition,* of course.

1 The Regions in Brief

India is a vast country, roughly divided—for the purposes of this book—into North, East, and South.

The South (again, for the purposes of this book), accessed most conveniently via **Mumbai** (state capital of **Maharashtra**), refers to **Goa, Karnataka** (with an excursion to **Hyderabad,** capital of Andhra Pradesh), **Kerala,** and **Tamil Nadu.**

The North refers to **Rajasthan** (and its southern neighbor **Gujarat,** which we have excluded from this edition due to recent incidents of unrest in the notoriously unsettled region); west of this area is the nation's capital, **Delhi,** and the sprawling states of **Uttar Pradesh** and **Madhya Pradesh,** which lies in the very heart of the country (only **Bodhgaya** in **Bihar** is covered in brief). Northeast of Delhi lie the largely unvisited states of **Haryana** and **Punjab** (the big exception being the Golden Temple at **Amritsar,** one of India's most wonderful attractions), and—moving even farther north—**Uttarakhand** and

Himachal Pradesh (with references to **Ladakh** in Jammu and Kashmir) in the Himalayas.

The East refers to Jharkhand (not a tourist destination), West Bengal (centered around **Kolkata,** or Calcutta), **Orissa** (with top attraction Konark), and, moving north into the Himalayas again, the mountain state of **Sikkim** and the tea-growing hill station of **Darjeeling.** Seven more states lie farther east (north and east of Bangladesh); their infrastructure is virtually nonexistent. Because travel in these areas is considered less than safe, they are not covered here.

The largest differences lie between the northern and southern regions. The former offers predominantly a plethora of medieval Mughal and Rajput architecture, ancient cities, deserts, camel safaris, heritage accommodations, tiger parks, Buddhism, and the snowcapped peaks of the Himalayas. The latter is rich with beautiful beaches, Ayurvedic spas, ancient

India

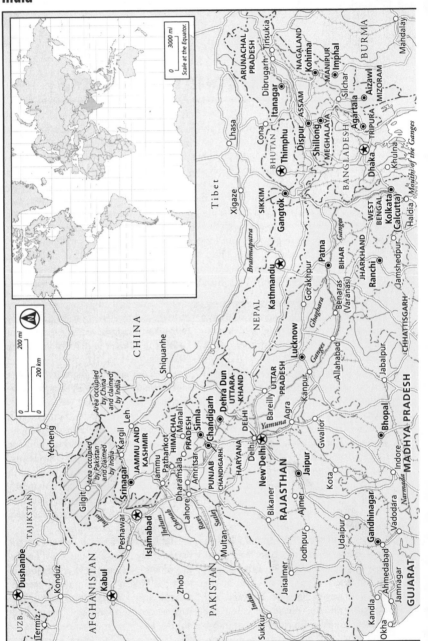

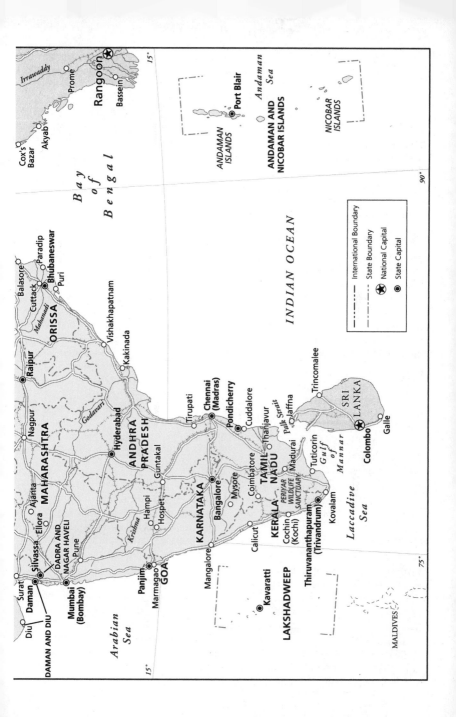

Dravidian/Hindu temples, cosmopolitan colonial coastal towns, and a generally more laid-back atmosphere. We suggest that rather than try to cover both the North and the South, concentrate your energies on one. If you do decide to combine the two, stick to two states, or you'll find yourself exhausted at the end of your vacation.

MUMBAI (BOMBAY) & MAHA-RASHTRA Teetering on the edge of the Arabian Sea, its heaving population barely contained by palm-fringed beaches, India's sexiest city is a vibrant, confident metropolis that's tangibly high on energy. The state capital of Maharashtra, this is home to many of the subcontinent's best restaurants and great hotels. It's also the ideal starting point for a tour south along the Konkan railway to **Goa** and beyond. Whichever you choose, do plan for an eastward jaunt to the ancient rock-cut caves of **Ajanta** and **Ellora,** Maharashtra's startling World Heritage Sites.

GOA Nirvana for flower children since the late 1960s, Goa still attracts a cosmopolitan mix of youngsters who cruise from beach to beach, looking for action. But Goa is more than a party in paradise. A Portuguese colonial heritage has left an indelible mark on this tiny enclave (India's smallest state), from cuisine to architecture, with plenty to see. And if the crowded beaches and vibrant markets leave you gasping for solitude, you can still find the original Goan paradise on far-flung beaches or in quiet boutique hotels, reviewed in detail in this book.

KARNATAKA & KERALA Traveling south along India's west coast, you will pass through untouched Karnataka; it's possible you'll overnight in the hip city of **Bangalore.** From there you can head to **Hyderabad,** the 400-year-old capital of Andhra Pradesh, as famous for its food and minarets as for its burgeoning software industry; or south to **Mysore,** "City of Incense." Whatever you do, set aside time to explore the lost city of **Hampi,** arguably Karnataka's most evocative attraction, or to join the Jain pilgrimage to anoint the giant feet of **Lord Gomateswara,** said to be the largest monolith in the world. There's more besides, but who can tarry long when **Kerala,** "God's own country," awaits? South India's top destination, particularly for the well-heeled traveler in search of pampering and relaxation, Kerala offers ancient backwaters plied by houseboats, herds of wild elephant, coconut-lined beaches, and, of course, the ancient healing art of Ayurveda.

TAMIL NADU Occupying a long stretch of the eastern Indian Ocean coastline, India's southernmost state seems little touched by the cocktail of foreign influences that contributed to the cultural developments in the North. This is where you'll find India's most superb Dravidian temples, from **Mamallapuram** (7th c. A.D.) to the **Madurai temple complex** (16th c. A.D.). When you're all templed out, there's always **Pondicherry,** the former French coastal town where traditional Indian snack joints feature signs proclaiming MEALS READY—BIEN VENUE and loincloth-clad locals converse in flawless French.

DELHI, MADHYA PRADESH & UTTAR PRADESH Entered through Delhi, capital of the largest democracy in the world, the central states of Madhya Pradesh and Uttar Pradesh are the real heart of India, where great rulers battled for power over vast swaths of India, and where you'll find arguably the densest concentration of top attractions on the subcontinent. From the "seven cities" of Delhi, it's a short train or road journey to **Agra,** home to the Taj Mahal and other superb examples of medieval Mughal architecture. From there you can either head west to Rajasthan, or east—via the erotic temples of **Khajuraho,** considered the pinnacle of Hindu medieval architecture—to the ancient city of **Varanasi,** India's holiest pilgrimage site, where the faithful come to die on the banks of the sacred Ganges to achieve *moksha*—liberation from earthly life. To escape the well-beaten tourist track, head south to the vast plains of Madhya Pradesh, to **Bandhavgarh National Park,** one of the best places to see tigers in Asia.

RAJASTHAN   With crenelated forts and impregnable palaces that rise like giant fairy-tale sets above dusty sun-scorched plains and shimmering lakes, Rajasthan—literally "land of princes"—epitomizes the romance of India. Whether you choose to linger in the untainted medieval atmosphere of little towns like **Bundi,** browse the bumper-to-bumper shops in **Jaipur,** track tigers in **Ranthambhore,** overnight on the lake in the beautiful city of **Udaipur,** or explore the world's oldest living fort in **Jaisalmer,** you will want to see it all.

HIMACHAL PRADESH & LADAKH Bordered by Tibet to the east, Himachal Pradesh incorporates great topographic diversity, from vast, bleak tracts of the rust-colored high-altitude Trans-Himalayan desert to dense green deodar forests, apple orchards, and cultivated terraces. Together with **Ladakh** (known as "Little Tibet"), this is also where you'll find India's largest concentration of Buddhists, their atmospheric *gompas* (monastic temples, including **Tabo,** the World

Heritage Site in **Spiti**) a total contrast to the pageantry of Hindu temples. An easy—and highly recommended—detour from the region is to Amritsar to view the **Golden Temple,** arguably the most spiritually satisfying destination in India.

UTTARAKHAND   Comprising the pre-Vedic territories of Garhwal and Kumaon, the mountains of the central Himalayan state of Uttarakhand, previously called Uttaranchal, are riven with ancient Hindu pilgrimage routes, and offer wonderful trekking routes. Non-hikers come here to practice yoga at **Rishikesh** on the banks of the holy river Ganges, or to take a road trip through the less-traveled parts of **Kumaon,** possibly ending their sojourn looking for tigers in **Corbett National Park,** which vies with Ranthambhore for accessibility from Delhi.

KOLKATA (CALCUTTA) & THE EAST   Kolkata, the much-maligned capital of West Bengal, never fails to surprise the visitor with its beautiful albeit crumbling colonial architecture, sophisticated Bengali culture, and wonderful restaurants and hotels. From here you can either head north to the cooling breezes of West Bengal's hill station, **Darjeeling,** famous for its tea, and on to the Buddhist state of **Sikkim** (in many ways even more remote than Himachal Pradesh); or you can head south to Orissa to visit the monolithic **Sun Temple** at Konark, yet another of India's awesome array of World Heritage Sites.

2 Visitor Information

India's **Tourism Information Department** is going all out to seduce international visitors, and has fairly extensive representation around the globe. Access one of its **websites** (www.incredibleindia.org or www.tourisminindia.com) for general information, but be aware that some pages may be out of date or permanently

under construction. The websites do offer links to all of India's regional tourism departments, some of which provide fantastic coverage of what's on offer.

Indian tourism offices may be found worldwide as follows. In the **U.S.:** 3550 Wilshire Blvd., Room 204, Los Angeles, CA 90010, ✆ **213/380-8855;** and Suite

1808, 1270 Avenue of the Americas, New York, NY 10020, ⓒ 212/586-4901. In the U.K.: 7 Cork St., London W1X 2LN; ⓒ 020/7437-3677. In Canada: 60 Bloor St. (W), Suite 1003, Toronto, Ontario M4W 3B8; ⓒ 416/962-3787. In Australia: Level 5, 135 King S., Glasshouse Shopping Complex, Sydney, NSW 2000; ⓒ 2/9221-9555.

WEBSITES You can access up-to-the-minute news and stories through the websites of some of the country's largest English dailies, including **www.timesof** **india.com**, **www.hindustantimes.com**, **www.expressindia.com**, and **www.the hinduonnet.com**. For up-to-date news from the two premier English-language 24/7 news channels, and updates on Bollywood movies, visit **www.ndtv.com** or **www.ibnlive.com**; for travel-related information and features, visit **www.outlook traveller.com**. Travel Spirit International (**www.tsiindia.com**) has a wide range of links as well as easy access to sites where you can book reduced-price accommodations and travel.

3 Entry Requirements

PASSPORTS

For information on how to get a passport, go to the "Fast Facts: India" section, later in this chapter. The websites listed there provide downloadable passport applications as well as the current fees for processing passport applications. For an up-to-date country-by-country listing of passport requirements around the world, go to the "Foreign Entry Requirement" Web page of the U.S. State Department at **http://travel.state.gov**.

VISAS

Travelers to India can apply for a tourist visa from their nearest Indian Consulate or High Commission. This is valid for multiple entries for a minimum of 6 months from the date of issue. Given the nature of India's bureaucracy, the rules and fees for application change regularly, so it's best to check with your travel agent or with the relevant authority for the latest visa information. Accurately completed visa application forms must be accompanied by two passport-size photographs (on a light background) and the appropriate processing fee; apply well in advance to avoid unforeseeable delays. You won't be admitted to India unless your passport is valid for at least 6 months after your entry, and it should typically also be valid for at least 3 months beyond the period of your intended stay. Check for fee structure and more details at www.indianembassy.org. In the U.S., the Indian Embassy is at 2107 Massachusetts Ave., Washington, DC 20008 (ⓒ 202/939-7000); and there are consulates in Houston, New York, San Francisco, and Chicago. In the U.K., India House is in Aldwych, London WC2B 4NA (ⓒ 020/7632-3149; www.hcilondon.net). If you're applying for a visa in a country where India does not have a representative, you are advised to make inquiries at the nearest British authority.

A special permit is required for foreigners wishing to visit the Lakshadweep Islands, as well as remote areas such as Sikkim and Ladakh. For Lakshadweep, your permit will be arranged when your accommodations are reserved. Permits for the other restricted regions can be obtained in India; specific details are given in the appropriate chapters. Carry a number of passport-size photographs and copies of the personal particulars and Indian visa pages of your passport to apply for these permits.

MEDICAL REQUIREMENTS

For information on medical requirements and recommendations, see "Health & Safety," p. 33.

CUSTOMS

For details on what you can bring in and take out of India, see "Fast Facts: India," p. 57.

4 When to Go

Your choice of where and when to go will be determined primarily by the weather. India's vastness means that the climate varies greatly from region to region, and sometimes even from day to night, as in the desert regions. The Indian year features six seasons: spring, summer, the rainy season, early and late autumn, and winter, but effectively there are but three—summer, winter, and monsoon.

You'll be better off visiting during the **high-season winter** months (Nov–Mar), when most of the country experiences pleasant, moderate temperatures (still hot enough to luxuriate in the pool), though cities in the North get chillier days as snow falls in the Himalayas. As a rule, always be prepared for warm to hot days, with the possibility of cooler weather at night. (If this has you worrying about how to pack, remember that you can pick up the most wonderful throwaway cotton garments for next to nothing and a real Pashmina scarf in every color to ward off an unexpected chill.) As with all season-driven destinations, there is a downside to traveling during peak months: From December to January, for example, Goa swells to bursting point with foreigners and city folk who arrive for the sensational beaches and parties. Lodging rates soar during these periods, so you may want to wait until the **shoulder season** (Sept, Oct, Mar, Apr), when there are fewer people and rates are very negotiable.

Summer (generally Apr–June) sees little traffic, and for good reason—the daytime heat, particularly in India's north-central regions, is debilitating, even for the locals. This is the time to plan your trip to the Himalayas instead, particularly to the Himachal Pradesh region. Ladakh, a magical region in the far north of the country, can only be visited June through September—the rest of the year it remains cut off by cold and snow.

The **monsoon** drenches much of the country between June and September, usually starting its season in Kerala. Tamil Nadu and parts of Andhra Pradesh don't get too much rain during this period; instead they get more rainfall from a second monsoon that hits just this region around mid-October and runs through December. In Rajasthan, central India, and the northern plains, the rains typically arrive by July and fall until early September. Some of the regions are at their most beautiful during the monsoon, but it can be difficult to move around, and there is a higher risk of exposure to diseases like malaria. Flooding, power failures, and natural destruction are also not uncommon.

INDIA'S WEATHER MONTH BY MONTH

The following charts indicate the average maximum and minimum temperatures for each month of the year, as well as the average rainfall, in major tourist-destination cities and towns.

THE HIMALAYA
SHIMLA

	Jan	Feb	Mar	Apr	May	June	July	Aug	Sept	Oct	Nov	Dec
Temp (°F)	48/36	50/37	57/45	66/52	73/59	75/61	70/61	68/59	68/57	64/52	59/45	52/39
Temp (°C)	9/2	10/3	14/7	19/11	23/15	24/16	21/16	20/15	20/14	18/11	15/7	11/4
Rainfall (mm)	50	50	50	25	50	150	400	375	200	50	0	25

MAHARASHTRA
MUMBAI

	Jan	Feb	Mar	Apr	May	June	July	Aug	Sept	Oct	Nov	Dec
Temp (°F)	88/61	90/63	91/68	92/75	90/79	90/79	86/79	84/79	86/79	90/75	91/64	90/55
Temp (°C)	31/16	32/17	33/20	33/24	33/26	32/26	30/26	29/26	30/26	32/24	33/18	32/13
Rainfall (mm)	0	1	0	0	20	647	945	660	309	117	7	1

SOUTH INDIA
PANJIM, GOA

	Jan	Feb	Mar	Apr	May	June	July	Aug	Sept	Oct	Nov	Dec
Temp (°F)	88/70	90/63	90/68	91/75	91/81	88/75	84/73	84/75	84/75	88/75	91/73	91/70
Temp (°C)	31/21	32/17	32/20	33/24	33/27	31/24	29/23	29/24	29/24	31/24	33/23	33/21
Rainfall (mm)	2	0	4	17	18	580	892	341	277	122	20	37

COCHIN, KERALA

	Jan	Feb	Mar	Apr	May	June	July	Aug	Sept	Oct	Nov	Dec
Temp (°F)	88/73	88/75	88/79	88/79	88/79	84/75	82/75	82/75	82/75	84/75	86/75	86/73
Temp (°C)	31/23	31/24	31/26	31/26	31/26	29/24	28/24	28/24	28/24	29/24	30/24	30/23
Rainfall (mm)	9	34	50	139	364	756	572	386	235	333	184	37

MADURAI

	Jan	Feb	Mar	Apr	May	June	July	Aug	Sept	Oct	Nov	Dec
Temp (°F)	86/70	90/72	95/73	97/77	99/79	99/79	97/79	95/77	95/77	91/75	88/73	86/72
Temp (°C)	30/21	32/22	35/23	36/25	37/26	37/26	36/26	35/25	35/25	33/24	31/23	30/22
Rainfall (mm)	26	16	21	81	59	31	48	117	123	179	161	43

HYDERABAD

	Jan	Feb	Mar	Apr	May	June	July	Aug	Sept	Oct	Nov	Dec
Temp (°F)	86/59	90/63	88/73	100/75	102/81	95/75	88/73	86/72	86/72	88/68	84/68	84/55
Temp (°C)	30/15	32/17	31/23	38/24	39/27	35/24	31/23	30/22	30/22	31/20	29/20	29/13
Rainfall (mm)	8	10	14	30	28	110	140	133	163	63	28	8

DELHI, RAJASTHAN & CENTRAL INDIA
DELHI/AGRA

	Jan	Feb	Mar	Apr	May	June	July	Aug	Sept	Oct	Nov	Dec
Temp (°F)	70/45	75/50	86/59	97/70	106/81	104/84	95/81	93/79	93/77	95/66	84/54	73/46
Temp (°C)	21/7	24/10	30/15	36/21	41/27	40/29	35/27	34/26	34/25	35/19	29/12	23/8
Rainfall (mm)	25	22	17	7	8	65	211	173	150	31	1	5

JAIPUR

	Jan	Feb	Mar	Apr	May	June	July	Aug	Sept	Oct	Nov	Dec
Temp (°F)	72/46	77/52	88/59	99/70	106/79	102/81	93/79	90/75	91/73	91/64	84/54	75/48
Temp (°C)	22/8	25/11	31/15	37/21	41/26	39/27	34/26	32/24	33/23	33/18	29/12	24/9
Rainfall (mm)	14	8	9	4	10	54	193	239	90	19	3	4

EAST INDIA
KOLKATA

	Jan	Feb	Mar	Apr	May	June	July	Aug	Sept	Oct	Nov	Dec
Temp (°F)	79/54	84/59	93/68	97/75	97/79	93/79	90/79	90/79	90/79	88/75	84/64	81/55
Temp (°C)	26/12	29/15	34/20	36/24	36/26	34/26	32/26	32/26	32/26	31/24	29/18	27/13
Rainfall (mm)	13	22	30	50	135	263	320	318	253	134	29	4

CALENDAR OF EVENTS

Indians love to celebrate, and there is no end to the list of festivals that are held in honor of the gods, gurus, and historical figures that make this such a spiritually saturated and colorful destination. Festivals usually coincide with the lunar calendar, with dates published only a year in advance, so check with the local tourism office about exact dates (some may move into another month). India has relatively few national holidays when attractions, government offices, and banks are closed: Republic Day, January 26; Independence Day, August 15; Gandhi's Birthday, October 2; and Christmas.

January/February

Basant Festival, countrywide. The onset of spring *(basant)* is marked by various celebrations. Citrus-colored clothes are worn, and there is a profusion of dancing and singing coupled with great dinner spreads and feasts to mark the season of agricultural plenty.

Carnival, Goa. It may not be on quite the same level as celebrations in Rio, but the riot of colorful costumes and processions, as well as the exuberant dancing and music, make this an especially fun time to visit the tiny state and its beautiful beaches.

Desert Festival, Rajasthan. With camel races, camel polo, a Mr. Desert competition, and even prizes for the best-looking camel, this festival is a highlight in the Jaisalmer social calendar.

Muharram. Best experienced in the city of Lucknow, the 10-day Shi'ite festival commemorates the martyrdom of the grandson of the Prophet Mohammed; during a parade of religious fervor, penitents scourge themselves with whips—often with nails or blades attached.

March

Ellora Festival of Classical Dance and Music, Maharashtran interior. This festival draws some of the country's top artists to the ancient caves at this World Heritage Site.

Holi, northern India. Celebrated predominantly in the North, this joyous Hindu festival is held during the full moon—expect to be bombarded with colored water and powder.

International Yoga Festival, Rishikesh. Spiritually inclined visitors head here to take classes with *Yogacharyas* from all over the world teaching a variety of yogic disciplines.

Khajuraho Dance Festival, Madhya Pradesh. Get a glimpse of all of India's great classical dance forms.

June/July

Rath Yatra, Puri. In Orissa's seaside temple town of Puri, this is one of the largest annual gatherings of humanity; thousands of devotees come together to help pull the Lord of the Universe and his two siblings through the streets on massive cars.

Hemis Tsechu, Ladakh. The region's most impressive monastic celebration happens on June 20 and 21, 2008, and July 8 and 9, 2009, when the birthday of the founder of Tibetan Buddhism is celebrated with lamaistic masked dances *(chaams),* chanting, and music at Hemis Monastery.

August

Nehru Cup Snake Boat Races, Alleppey. Kerala's backwaters come alive with these renowned snake boat races. Second Saturday of August.

Independence Day, countrywide. Indians unite to celebrate independence. August 15.

September/October

Ganesh Chhaturthi, countrywide. This 10-day celebration of Ganesha, the elephant-headed god, is popular across India, but Mumbai is arguably the best place to experience this vibrant event, celebrated with huge processions, fireworks, and the construction of special shrines. At the end of the festival, clay images of the god are immersed in the sea.

Kullu Dussehra. Head for the Kullu Valley in Himachal Pradesh, where you can join the crowds when idols of Hindu deities from around the region are brought together in a colorful Festival of the Gods. Similarly ecstatic revelry occurs in Mysore (Karnataka).

October/November

Diwali (Festival of Lights; also **Deepavali),** countrywide. This huge celebration among Hindu Indians is best experienced on the lawns of Umaid Bhawan Palace in Jodhpur, at a wonderful party hosted by the Maharajah (which hotel guests are invited to attend). Note, however, that just as Christmas has been exploited commercially in the West, Diwali has become a time of excessive noise, increased alcohol consumption, and all-night fireworks.

Pushkar *Mela,* Rajasthan. The annual cattle fair in the tiny temple-and-hippie town of Pushkar, is the biggest of its kind in Asia. Traders, pilgrims, and tourists from all over the world transform this budget tourist mecca into a huge tented city, with camel races, cattle auctions, huge bonfires, traditional dances, and the like.

December/January

Christmas, New Year, countrywide. Prepare for increased hotel prices as wealthy Indians celebrate both Christmas and New Year, often by taking the entire family on an extravagant vacation. New Year, in particular, may be marked by compulsory hidden extras such as special entertainment and celebratory meals. Christmas is celebrated with as much fervor, if not more, as it is in the West. City hotels take great advantage of the situation, while in certain areas, such as Goa, midnight Mass and other traditions are observed.

5 Getting There

BY PLANE

Most major airline carriers have flights to India. It's a good idea to shop around for fares on the Internet, through online travel agencies like Travelocity.com, Expedia.com, and Orbitz.com, or through airline websites. Or make use of a consolidator, which hunts for the cheapest available seats on your travel dates.

From North America Count on spending between 18 and 22 hours traveling and most flights require you to touch down at least once in Europe, the Gulf, or an Asian destination. More recently **Delta Airlines** and **Continental Airlines** have introduced 16-hour nonstop flights from New York/Newark to Mumbai/Delhi. With flights from the U.S. or Canada, the following airlines all offer service to India:

British Airways (© 800/247-9297; www.british-airways.com); **Virgin Atlantic** (© 800/821-5438; www.virgin-atlantic. com) via London; **Air India** (© 800-223-7776; www.airindia.com); **KLM/ Northwest** (© 800/447-4747; www.nwa. com); **Lufthansa** (© 800/645-3880 in the U.S., 800/563-5954 in Canada; www.lufthansa.com); and **Air France** (© 800/237-2747 in the U.S., 800/667-2747 in Canada; www.airfrance.com). Additionally, **Jet Airways** has begun flights from Newark to Mumbai via Brussels (© 877-835-9538 in the U.S.). **Etihad Airways** (© 888/8-ETIHAD) flies to Mumbai via Abu Dhabi, and **Swiss International Airlines** flies to Delhi/ Mumbai via Zurich (U.K.: © 845/601-0956; U.S.: © 877/359-7947).

Singapore Airlines, Cathay Pacific Malaysian Airlines, and other Asian carriers all fly to India via the Pacific route.

From the U.K. Many reasonably priced direct flights are available, or you can take a connecting flight in continental Europe or the Middle East; a number of European airlines (such as KLM and Alitalia) will get you there affordably if you don't mind a change of planes.

British Airways (© 0870/850-9-850; www.ba.com) has two daily direct flights to both Delhi and Mumbai, daily flights to Bangalore, and occasional direct flights to Kolkata and Chennai. **Air India** (© 800/223-7776; www.airindia.com) is the national carrier operating regular nonstop flights to Delhi and Mumbai. **Virgin Atlantic** (© 0870/574-7747) operates nonstop flights to Mumbai and Delhi. **Jet Airways** (© 0870/9101-000; www.jet

airways.com) has two daily nonstop flights between London and Mumbai and one a day to Delhi.

Emirates (© 0870/243-2222; www. emirates.com) flies to Mumbai, Delhi, and Cochin, via Dubai. **KLM UK** (© 0870/243-0541; www.klmuk.com) operates flights from all over Britain to Amsterdam, where you pick up your connection to Delhi.

Lufthansa (www.lufthansa.co.uk) has daily flights to Delhi, Mumbai, Chennai, Bangalore, and Hyderabad through Frankfurt.

From Australia & New Zealand   You can fly directly to India from Australia. From New Zealand you will more than likely be offered a flight package that incorporates more than one airline. The majority of touchdowns and changeovers are in Malaysia, Thailand, Hong Kong, and Singapore.

The following airlines offer service to India: **Singapore Airlines** (© 13-1011 in Australia; www.singaporeair.com); **Qantas** (© 13-1313 or 29/691-3636) has a direct flight from Sydney to Mumbai, (© 0800/80-8767 or 09/375-8900 in New Zealand; www.qantas.com); **Malaysia Airlines** (www.malaysiaairlines. com) via Kuala Lumpur; and **Cathay Pacific** (www.cathaypacific.com) via Hong Kong.

From South Africa   South African Airways (© 0861/359-722; www.flysaa.com) flies nonstop to Mumbai several times a week from Johannesburg. Or you can fly via Dubai to Delhi/Mumbai/Cochin on **Emirates** (© 0861/EMIRATES or 0861/ 364-728).

ARRIVING AT THE AIRPORT

India's list of international airports is constantly expanding: **Mumbai, Delhi, Hyderabad, Goa, Kolkata (Calcutta), Chennai, Trivandrum, Ahmedabad, Bangalore, Amritsar, and Cochin** all receive traffic from abroad, and a number of hitherto tiny airports—particularly in Rajasthan—are undergoing expansion to accommodate international arrivals in the very near future. Modernization at all these facilities, particularly in Delhi and Mumbai, is a priority, but there are many problems—not least of which is that the rate of expansion simply cannot keep up with the exponential increase in traffic. Consequently, the first-time traveler to India may easily be unnerved by the sheer apparent chaos and disorganization of it all. Mumbai (Bombay) receives the greatest amount of international traffic and is the best point of arrival for onward travel to Goa and South India. Be warned, however, that in spite of a recent overhaul Mumbai airport facilities are poor, and there are plans to shift terminals while new ones are under construction. Most flights arrive in India late at night, in order to leave their Western destinations during daylight hours, so booking an "immediate" onward domestic flight invariably requires some wait at the airport. Delhi's international airport—the principal starting point for journeys throughout North India, including the Himalayan regions and Rajasthan as well as east India—is substantially better. Only fly in to Kolkata (Calcutta) if you plan to explore east India exclusively. If you want to avoid spending too much time at the airport, note that Jet Airways, British Airways, Virgin, and Air-India all now have flights with daytime arrival into India.

Note: Before you leave home, know what you can carry on and what you can't. For the latest updates on items you are prohibited to bring in carry-on luggage, go to **www.tsa.gov/travelers/airtravel**.

6 Money & Costs

It's always advisable to bring money in a variety of forms on a vacation: a mix of cash, credit cards, and traveler's checks.

In many international destinations, ATMs offer the best exchange rates. Avoid exchanging money at commercial exchange bureaus and hotels, which often have the highest transaction fees.

CURRENCY

Indian currency cannot be obtained before you enter India. The Indian rupee (Rs) is available in denominations of Rs 1,000, Rs 500, Rs 100, Rs 50, Rs 20, Rs 10, and Rs 5 notes. You will occasionally come across Rs 1 or Rs 2 notes—treat them as souvenirs. Minted coins come in denominations of Rs 5, Rs 2, and Rs 1, as well as 50 and 25 paise (rarely seen now). There are 100 paise in a rupee.

Note: Badly damaged or torn rupee notes (of which there are many) may be refused, particularly in larger cities, but less fuss is made over them in small towns. Check the change you are given and avoid accepting these.

EXCHANGE RATES

Exchange rates fluctuate dramatically. At press time, US$1 bought you around Rs 44, and 1 euro equaled Rs 55, while £1 was worth around Rs 81. Bear in mind

---

Tips Small Change

When you change money, ask for some small bills (a wad of Rs 10s and Rs 20s) for tipping or *baksheesh* (see "Tipping" under "Fast Facts: India," later in this chapter). At smaller outlets and vendors, you'll also frequently be told that there is no change for your Rs 500 note. Keep your smaller bills separate from the larger ones, so that they're readily accessible.

What Things Cost in India

This is a sampling of *average* prices you're likely to pay in India. Bear in mind that big cities generally have much higher prices than smaller towns, and that any place that attracts tourists inevitably attracts rip-off artists.

	Rupees	**U.S. Dollar**	**British Pound**
Luxury hotel room	Rs 4,000–Rs 30,000	$98–$730	£49–£370
Budget–moderate hotel room	Rs 250–Rs 6,000	$6–$146	£3–£74
Cup of tea from a stall	Rs 2–Rs 7	5¢–15¢	5p–10p
Cup of tea at a hotel	Rs 10–Rs 250	25¢–$6	15p–£3
Newspaper	Rs 2–Rs 5	4¢–10¢	5p–6p
Weekly magazine	Rs 15– Rs 50	35¢–$1	20p–60p
Taxi for the day	Rs 600–Rs 3,000	$14–$73	£7–£37
1km by auto-rickshaw	Rs 9–Rs 12	20¢–30¢	10p–15p
Meal at a local diner *(dhaba)*	Rs 30–Rs 200	75¢–$5	40p–£2
Main course in a luxury restaurant	Rs 150–Rs 800	$4–$20	£2–£10

that in spite of the falling dollar/euro, a few dollars, pounds, or euros go a long way in India. For up-to-the-minute **currency conversions,** log on to www.xe.com/ucc.

You cannot obtain Indian currency anywhere outside India, and you may not carry rupees beyond India's borders. You may have to exchange at least some money at the airport upon your arrival; change just enough to cover airport incidentals and transportation to your hotel, since the rate will be quite unfavorable.

Tip: India is one destination in which it is really worthwhile to arrange an airport transfer with your hotel so that you can avoid waiting in long lines at the airport money-changer, dealing with prepaid booths, or negotiating fees with drivers and touts. After a good night's rest, head to the nearest bank or ATM for a cash infusion.

Banks offer good exchange rates, but they tend to be inefficient and the staff lethargic about tending to foreigners' needs. You run the risk of being ripped off by using unauthorized money-changers;

the most convenient option is to use ATMs while you're in the big cities. Always ask for an encashment receipt when you change cash—you will need this when you use local currency to pay for major expenses (such as lodging and transport, though you should use a credit card wherever possible). You will also be asked to produce this receipt when you re-exchange your rupees before you leave India.

ATMs (AUTOMATED TELLER MACHINES)

Getting cash from your checking account (or cash advances on your credit card) at an ATM is by far the easiest way to get money. These 24-hour machines are readily available in most Indian cities and larger towns and at large commercial banks such as Citibank, Standard Chartered, ABN Amro, and Hong Kong & Shanghai Bank. **Cirrus** (© **800/424-7747;** www.mastercard.com) and **PLUS** (© **800/843-7587;** www.visa.com) networks span the globe; call or check online for ATM locations at your destination. Be sure to find out your daily withdrawal

Tips The Battle of the Haggle

Sure, things are cheap to begin with and you may feel silly haggling over a few rupees, but keep in mind that if you're given a verbal quote for an unmarked item, it's probably (but not always) twice the realistic asking price. Use discretion though, because items that are priced ridiculously low to begin with are hardly worth reducing further—either you're being conned or you're being cruel. To haggle effectively, make a counter-offer under half price, and don't get emotional. Protests and adamant assertions ("This is less than it cost me to buy!") will follow. Stick to your guns and see what transpires; stop once you've reached a price you can live with. Remember that once the haggle is on, a challenge has been initiated, and it's fun to regard your opponent's act of salesmanship as an artistic endeavor. Let your guard slip, and he will empty your wallet. Take into account the disposition and situation of the merchant; you don't want to haggle a genuinely poor man into deeper poverty! And if you've been taken (and we all have), see it as a small contribution to a family that lives on a great deal less than you do.

---

limit before you depart. You should have no problem withdrawing Rs 10,000 (almost $250/£123) at a time from an ATM (which goes a long way in India), although some ATMs may have slightly lower limits.

Also keep in mind that many banks impose a fee every time a card is used at a different bank's ATM, and that fee can be higher for international transactions (up to $5 or more).

CREDIT CARDS

Credit cards are another safe way to carry money. They also provide a convenient record of all your expenses, and they generally offer relatively good exchange rates. You can withdraw cash advances from your credit cards at banks or ATMs, but high fees make credit-card cash advances a pricey way to get cash. Keep in mind that you'll pay interest from the moment of your withdrawal, even if you pay your monthly bills on time. Also, note that many banks now assess a 1% to 3% "transaction fee" on all charges you incur abroad (whether you're using the local currency or your native currency).

MasterCard and Visa are commonly accepted throughout India. American Express is accepted by most major hotels and restaurants; Diners Club has a much smaller following.

TRAVELER'S CHECKS

You can buy traveler's checks at most banks. They are offered in denominations of $20, $50, $100, $500, and sometimes $1,000. Generally, you'll pay a service charge ranging from 1% to 4%.

The most popular traveler's checks are offered by **American Express** (© 800/807-6233 or © 800/221-7282 for card holders—this number accepts collect calls, offers service in several foreign languages, and exempts Amex gold and platinum cardholders from the 1% fee); **Visa** (© 800/732-1322)—AAA members can obtain Visa checks for a $9.95 fee (for checks up to $1,500) at most AAA offices or by calling © 866/339-3378; and MasterCard (© 800/223-9920).

Be sure to keep a record of the traveler's checks serial numbers separate from your checks in the event that they are stolen or lost. You'll get a refund faster if you know the numbers.

Traveler's checks are useful in that, unlike cash, they can be replaced if lost or stolen, but they are far less popular now that most cities have 24-hour ATMs that allow you to withdraw small amounts of cash as needed.

7 Travel Insurance

MEDICAL INSURANCE

While the cost of quality medical care in India is nowhere near as expensive as it is in the West, you're advised to get yourself covered for any major medical emergency. A basic consultation with a specialist doctor costs between Rs 300 and Rs 1,000 ($7–$25/£4–£12), so that's not your real insurance concern. Should you need hospitalization, major medical assistance, or medical evacuation, travel medical insurance will help ease the process and cover all expenses. *Note:* Try to get "cash-free" insurance for major medical expenses, and carry a list of facilities where this is possible; otherwise you will have to pay first and get reimbursed later—which is the norm in most of India.

For travel overseas, most U.S. health plans (including Medicare and Medicaid) do not provide coverage, and the ones that do often require you to pay for services upfront and reimburse you only after you return home.

If you require additional medical insurance, try **MEDEX Assistance** (✆ **410/ 453-6300;** www.medexassist.com) or **Travel Assistance International** (✆ **800/ 821-2828;** www.travelassistance.com; for general information on services, call the company's **Worldwide Assistance Services, Inc.,** at ✆ **800/777-8710**).

Canadians should check with their provincial health plan offices or call **Health Canada** (✆ **866/225-0709;** www.hc-sc.gc.ca) to find out the extent of their coverage and what documentation and receipts they must take home in case they are treated overseas.

LOST-LUGGAGE INSURANCE

On international flights (including U.S. portions of international trips), baggage coverage is limited to approximately $9.07 per pound, up to approximately $635 per checked bag. If you plan to check items more valuable than what's covered by the standard liability, see if your homeowner's policy covers your valuables, get baggage insurance as part of your comprehensive travel-insurance package, or buy Travel Guard's "BagTrak" product.

Most airlines require that you report delayed, damaged, or lost baggage within 4 hours of arrival. Though airlines are required to deliver luggage, once found, directly to your house or destination free of charge, in India they cannot do so because Customs rules require that you clear your bags through Customs personally. Once your lost bags have arrived, you will have to make a trip to the airport to claim them.

8 Health & Safety

STAYING HEALTHY

Consult your doctor or local travel clinic concerning precautions against diseases that are prevalent in India. The following cautionary list may have you wondering whether travel is advisable at all. However, don't be alarmed: Millions of travelers leave India having suffered nothing more than an upset stomach—even this small inconvenience should settle within a few days, your system the stronger for it.

GENERAL AVAILABILITY OF HEALTH CARE

Contact the **International Association for Medical Assistance to Travelers** (IAMAT) (© **716/754-4883** or, in Canada, 416/652-0137; www.iamat.org) for tips on travel and health concerns in the countries you're visiting. The United States **Centers for Disease Control and Prevention** (© **800/311-3435;** www. cdc.gov) provides up-to-date information on health hazards by region or country and offers tips on food safety. **Travel Health Online** (www.tripprep.com), sponsored by a consortium of travel medicine practitioners, may also offer helpful advice on traveling abroad.

VACCINATIONS   You will almost certainly be advised to be vaccinated against **hepatitis A, cholera, tetanus,** and **typhoid;** also make sure your polio immunization is up to date. Longer-stay visitors should consider getting the hepatitis B and meningitis vaccinations as well. Note that travelers arriving from yellow fever–infected areas must have a yellow fever vaccination certificate.

PACKING A FIRST-AID KIT   Besides anti-diarrheal medication, of which the most important are rehydration salts (available all over India as ORS—oral rehydration salts), it may be worthwhile to carry a course of antibiotics (such as Ciprofloxacin, which is widely available in India at a fraction of what you'll pay back home) for **stomach-related illnesses.** It's also worthwhile to take an antiseptic cream, and possibly an antibacterial soap (though the type of soap used matters less than vigilance: Wash your hands regularly, particularly before eating). Pack **prescription medications** in your carry-on luggage in their original containers with pharmacy labels, so they'll make it through airport security. Also bring along copies of your prescriptions in case you lose your pills or run out (include the generic name; local pharmacists will be unfamiliar with brand names). Don't forget an extra pair of contact lenses or prescription glasses or an extra inhaler.

COMMON AILMENTS

TROPICAL   ILLNESSES   Besides malaria, India's mosquitoes are also responsible for spreading untreatable dengue fever and virulent Japanese encephalitis. Again, the best advice is to avoid getting bitten in the first place.

MALARIA   Most doctors will advise you to take a course of anti-malarial tablets, but as is the case elsewhere, the best prevention is not to get bitten. Malaria is a parasitic infection borne by the female Anopheles mosquito, and risks are greater in warm, wet areas (particularly during monsoon) and at night, when mosquitoes are at their most active. Cover all exposed skin with anti-mosquito creams (many effective creams are available in India) or sprays as evening approaches, and use repellent coils or electric plug-in mosquito repellents as a preventive measure at night, particularly in hotel rooms without air-conditioning. Note that some plug-in repellents can cause a mild throat irritation, in which case stick with creams. Wear loose, floppy clothes that cover as much skin as possible, but remember that mosquitoes sometimes do bite through thin clothing, so you may need to apply repellent on your clothes as well. Note that many travelers on anti-malarial tablets suffer side effects including nausea, vomiting, and abdominal pain; ask your doctor to suggest an alternative anti-malarial that you can take if you end up having serious side effects (but bear in mind that chloroquine is not an effective anti-malarial for India).

SEXUALLY TRANSMITTED DISEASES & BLOOD INFECTIONS Keep in mind that HIV and hepatitis B are transmitted not only through sexual contact, but by infected blood. This means that any procedure involving a used needle or a blade can be hazardous. Avoid getting tattoos or piercings, and steer clear of roadside barbers offering shaves. For haircuts and procedures such as manicures and pedicures, stick to salons in upmarket hotels. Take the usual precautions if you are about to engage in any sexual activities—AIDS numbers are not well publicized, since the disease is widely associated with taboo and "anti-Indian behaviors," but this is a huge and growing problem, and some doctors and NGO workers we have consulted suggest that India is likely to soon become the world's worst-afflicted AIDS region.

DIETARY RED FLAGS & TUMMY TROUBLES Many visitors to India fall victim to the ubiquitous "Delhi belly," an unfortunate reaction to unfamiliar rich and spicy foodstuffs that can overwhelm the system and cause symptoms ranging from slight discomfort and "the runs" to extreme cases of nausea, fever, and delirium. To avoid this, simply be sensible. Adjust slowly; move on to spicy foods in small doses. You should also be on your guard about *where* you eat; if you have any fears at all, stick to the upmarket restaurants, usually those in five-star hotels—but do venture out to those recommended in this guide. Remember that uncooked vegetables or fruit can be hazardous if washed in water that has not been boiled, so peel all your own fresh fruit and avoid salads. Unless you're in an upmarket hotel, don't eat fruit that has already been cut—any water on the knife or on the skin of the fruit is likely to seep into the flesh. Be wary of undercooked meats—they may harbor intestinal worms—and stay away from pork unless you're in a five-star hotel.

The first thing to bear in mind when diarrhea or nausea strike is that your body is trying to cleanse itself, so only use an anti-diarrhea medication (like Imodium) if you are desperate—about to embark on a long train journey, for example. Ideally, you should plan a few days of rest and cut back on all food except plain basics (a diet of boiled rice and bananas is ideal), and drink plenty of boiled water (or black tea) or bottled water with rehydration salts. If your tummy trouble doesn't clear up after 3 to 4 days, consult a physician—you may be suffering from something more serious: a protozoa (amoeba or giardia) or a viral or bacterial infection.

WATER CONCERNS More than anything else in India, it is the water that is likely to make you ill. For this reason, you should not only avoid untreated drinking water, but be on your guard against any food product that is washed with water or has had water added to it. When buying tea (or *chai*) on the streets, for example, check that the cup is washed with hot water and even ask to dry it yourself—carry a small cloth or napkins so that you can remove any and all water from anything that is going to go into your mouth; alternatively, carry your own stainless steel cup everywhere you go. Use bottled water when you brush your teeth, and do not open your mouth in the shower. Do not have ice added to your drink unless you've been assured that it's purified (as is typical of upmarket hotels and restaurants). Do be aware that in summer it is not uncommon for vendors selling *lassi* (a deliciously refreshing yogurt drink) to mix ice into their concoctions, and be exceptionally wary of enticing marketplace drinks like freshly squeezed sugarcane juice, which will be mixed with untreated water. If you purchase bottled water from roadside stalls, dodgy-looking shops, or small towns, check the seal on the cap and investigate the bottle for any signs of tampering. Also try to determine the age of the packaged water; if it looks like it's been sitting on the shelf for too long, give it a miss. The only exception to the bottled water rule may be if you are 100% sure the water has been boiled for 20 minutes. Even in very upmarket hotels and restaurants that purify their water in-house, it's advisable to stick to bottled water. Remember not to clean wounds, cuts, or sores with tap water. Instead, douse and cleanse any open wound with antiseptic solution, cover it with an adhesive bandage, and consult a doctor if it doesn't heal soon.

BUGS, BITES & OTHER WILDLIFE CONCERNS Remote areas are alive with insects and creepy-crawlies, but the greatest risk is malaria (see above). Wear shoes when trekking or in wet areas; you can be contaminated from worm-infested soil or mud, which can also be a source of microbial, bacterial, or hookworm infection. Leeches are a common problem in the rainforest regions. Do not try to pull them off your skin; dousing with salt does the trick. It's possible to prevent this nasty experience by wearing special anti-leech "socks" and dousing your shoes with lime powder. You're more likely to be bitten by a rabid dog or monkey than by a snake, spider, centipede, or sea creature, but it does occur: Wear thick trousers and boots when hiking, tread carefully, keep your eyes peeled, and in the unlikely event that you are bitten, try to get a good look at the animal so that medical staff know what antivenin to use. And yes, get to a doctor or hospital as soon as possible. Animals are seldom treated as pets in India—as a general rule, steer clear of them, and should you be bitten, use antiseptic and consult a physician immediately.

Animal lovers beware: India will horrify you if you have a real soft spot for animals. You will feel particularly sickened by the "dancing bears" in North India—sloth bears cruelly tethered and forced to perform for tourists—as well as severely malnourished dogs, feral cats, diseased pigs, and even cows, considered sacred, looking emaciated and chewing on plastic bags and cardboard for sustenance. If you can see someone to rant at, do, but for the most part you have to bear it.

SUN/ELEMENTS/EXTREME WEATHER EXPOSURE Carry high-SPF sunscreen and use it liberally. It's also advisable to wear a hat or cap during the day, and try to avoid midday sun wherever possible. In the cities, pollution often cloaks the high-level exposure, so keep that hat on. Remember that in the high-altitude Himalayan regions, you can experience cold weather and chilly winds while being burnt to a cinder. During the monsoons, certain regions can become impossible to traverse because of flooding. Orissa, Tamil Nadu, and Andhra Pradesh are prone to cyclones in November and December. Keep abreast of conditions by following weather reports.

POLLUTION Air pollution levels in many Indian cities are very high and contain high levels of suspended particulate matter. This is mostly from vehicles, but in places like Varanasi it is compounded by the use of diesel generators. The best thing to do is to always carry a cotton handkerchief with you to hold over your mouth and nose as a mask to breathe through until you are past the offending area. India is also plagued by noise pollution, and most visitors are usually shocked at how often drivers blare their horns. There's really nothing you can do other than accept that honking is usually a necessary precaution to avoid smashing into people, stray dogs, cattle, and all kinds of other obstacles (including cars).

WHAT TO DO IF YOU GET SICK IN INDIA

Don't panic. Medicines are widely and easily available in India. You can even describe your problem to your hotel concierge or receptionist and he or she will arrange for the necessary medication to be dropped off, doing away with possible translation problems. Pharmacies and chemists hand out pills and antibacterial medication upon request—even those that would require a prescription back home. (This is not always a good thing; if possible, consult a physician before resorting to over-the-counter drugs. Also beware of being given incomplete courses of antibiotics.) There are hospital listings for major cities in each chapter, but it's best to consult your hotel concierge regarding the best medical attention in town, particularly if you're in a more remote area. In fact, *do not solicit the assistance of anyone who is unknown to your hotel.* Well-documented scams operating in certain tourist destinations involve prolonging your illness in order to attract large payouts from your insurance company. If you or someone you are traveling with needs hospitalization, shell out for a well-known private one, and if you're able to travel, head for the nearest big city. Advise your consulate and your medical insurance company as soon as possible.

It's likely you'll have to pay all medical costs upfront and be reimbursed later. Medicare and Medicaid do not provide coverage for medical costs outside the U.S. Before leaving home, find out what medical services your health insurance covers. To protect yourself, consider buying medical travel insurance (see "Medical Insurance," under "Travel Insurance," above).

We list **hospitals** and **emergency numbers** under "Fast Facts" in the individual chapters.

Pack **prescription medications** in your carry-on luggage, and carry them in their original containers, with pharmacy labels—otherwise they won't make it through airport security. Carry the generic name of prescription medicines, in case a local pharmacist is unfamiliar with the brand name.

STAYING SAFE

Considering its poverty and population size, India enjoys an amazingly low incidence of violent crime, and the vast majority of visits to India tend to be trouble-free.

That said, the usual rules apply—no wandering around back alleys at night, for example, no flashing of valuables or wads of cash. Foreign visitors may be targeted by corrupt cops looking to get a handsome bribe or payoff, so you'd best steer clear of any suspicious behavior such as purchasing illegal drugs. If you're caught, even with marijuana, there is a good chance that you could be thrown in prison. If you're involved in a car accident, have your hotel manager report the incident immediately. Avoid provocative debates and arguments where alcohol may be involved. Exercise caution during festivals and religious processions, where crowds are usually overwhelming and can become unruly.

TERRORISM & CIVIL UNREST

Avoid political demonstrations—these occasionally erupt into violence. Election rallies frequently turn bitter, and you don't want to be caught in the middle of an angry mob. In recent years, there have been incidents of terrorist bombings, kidnapping, and murder in various parts of India, particularly in the northernmost state of Jammu and Kashmir, where the terrorist organization Harakat Ul Mujahideen has issued a ban on Americans, including tourists. With the exception of the eastern district of Ladakh, avoid travel in this volatile and unsafe war-torn region, no matter what tour operators and tourist offices have to say; regular terrorist attacks continue to occur in Kashmir, and civilians are often targets. Travelers should also exercise extreme caution when undertaking treks and travel to remote parts of Ladakh, where solo travelers are not permitted and can potentially be targeted by terrorist factions; in isolated cases, unaccompanied trekkers have been kidnapped or simply disappeared. Travelers to Goa and Himachal Pradesh should stay clear of any drug-related activity—the trade has begun to attract nasty criminal elements.

Surviving Scams & Con Artists

In India, scamming is an art form—and you, the tourist, a prime target. The best defense against the regular plague of touts and con men, who will try to tap into your supply of foreign currency by calling themselves "guides" or representatives of a local temple, is a combination of awareness, common sense, and fortitude. Scammers rely largely on **human psychology** to either win your confidence or tap into your irrational sense of guilt. Although it's okay to have a heart, **politeness is likely to be your enemy.** Stick to your guns when you're approached by anyone offering to get you something "cheap," "quality," or "easy" by firmly declining. In fact, get used to shaking your head and saying "no" repeatedly without losing your temper. If someone tells you upfront that they're not interested in your money, warning bells should sound; 9 times out of 10, a casual conversation or unintentional sightseeing trip will end with a suggestion that you hand over a token of your appreciation. **Don't pay for services you have not requested.** And when you do ask for help, ask if there's going to be a demand for money at the end, and decide on a price upfront. Rude as it seems, often the only way to get rid of a persistent tout, beggar, or con artist is to **pretend they don't exist** and continue along your way without pause. Often even replying "No" is seen as a window of opportunity. To some this may seem demeaning, but it is exactly the way many Indians themselves deal with the problem. If nothing works and you are being excessively harassed, try to find a policeman or other person of authority to help you. Here, then, is a guide to handling India's touts, hucksters, scam artists, and general wheeling and dealing.

- **Street touts** Touts operate under guises of friendship, wanting to practice their English or making promises of cheap accommodations or shopping. Often (but not always), the kindness turns sour when you don't comply with a suggestion to buy something or check in at a crummy hotel. When browsing a street or market, you will be accosted by men to whom shopkeepers pay a commission to bring you inside—"to look, no buy."
- **"Official" unofficial operators** Even more annoying than the con artists of the street are those who operate under the guise of perceived legitimacy by calling themselves "travel agents" or "tour operators"— and a sign saying "government-approved" often means anything but. Deal with someone who comes recommended by this book or a reputable operator recommended by your hotel.
- **Dealing with drivers** Taxi drivers are notorious for telling passengers that their hotel does not exist or has closed. Never allow yourself to be taken to a hotel or restaurant *unless it is the one you've asked to be taken to* (specified by *exact* name and address). Drivers often moonlight as restaurant and shop touts and receive a commission for getting you through the door. Taxi drivers often have meters that have been tampered with, or refuse to use fare-conversion charts issued by the city authority. If you're suspicious about a driver's conduct, ask to be let out of the vehicle immediately, or seek the assistance of your hotel

manager before paying the cab fare. When arriving at major airports and train stations, make use of **prepaid taxis** (the booths are clearly marked) whenever possible. Whenever you hire a local taxi, make sure that no one but the driver is riding with you. Do not under any circumstances agree to allow the driver's friend to ride along. If your request is not met, in the interest of your safety, get out and take another cab.

- **Bargains** *Beware of unmarked wares*—this means the goods are priced according to the salesperson's projection of your ability to pay. Any deal that seems too good to be true, is. If this all sounds too tedious, head for the government shops, where goods are sold at fixed prices. Even though the real government-owned shops have prices that are not negotiable and are sometimes slightly higher than elsewhere, they are *not* a rip-off (see "The Battle of the Haggle," under "Money & Costs," earlier in this chapter). We recommend the good-value government-owned Central Cottage Industries Emporiums for deals on high quality goods. Just be sure to double-check the name of the place before you shop, as there are stores with similar names.

- **Creating needs** Another common scam to watch for is when you are suddenly offered a service that is judiciously timed just when you need it— often because a trickster has created the very conditions that create the need. One common Delhi scam is run by shoeshine boys who suddenly appear with their polishing equipment and point to your shoes which, when you look down, suddenly have poop on them. Of course he'll offer to clean it off for you, which you should refuse, as you can be sure that the source of the poop is almost certainly the little guy himself or his accomplice.

- **Noting your notes** Swindlers will switch your Rs 500 note with a Rs 100 note and then claim that that's what you gave them. When handing out a fare or paying for a purchase, give the whole amount together and state aloud how much it is.

- **Getting the goods on precious goods** If you're shopping for **silk carpets**, ask the salesman to razor a small sample and light it with a match. Unlike wool, silk does not burn, it smolders. Tricksters will mix silk and wool—which is why you'll need to ask for a sample across the whole color range. And don't fall for anyone who tries to persuade you to purchase **precious stones** on the premise that you can resell them at a profit to a company they supposedly know back home (a Jaipur scam). Note that **gold** is imported and therefore hugely overpriced, so cheap gold jewelry is exactly that.

- **Scam doctors** Be wary when offered food or drink by a stranger. There have been isolated incidences of travelers being drugged or poisoned in order to rob them. Worse still, there are well-documented (though again isolated) accounts of these kinds of scammers in cahoots with doctors. Once you are ill, they will recommend a doctor, and after you're admitted into the care of the fraudulent physician, your medical insurance company is contacted, and you're kept ill until a substantial medical bill has been run up.

Travel to the northeastern states of Assam, Manipur, Nagaland, Tripura, and Meghalaya remains risky due to sporadic incidents of ethnic insurgent violence. These areas—and Kashmir—have not been included in this guide.

Bomb blasts believed to be connected with the unrest in Jammu and Kashmir have also occurred in public places in other parts of the country. Incidents include a series of seven bomb blasts on local commuter trains in Mumbai on July 11, 2006, that left more than 200 Indians dead. The motive for several of these bomb blasts has yet to be established. The Indian Parliament was a target in December 2001, and civil unrest between Hindus and Muslims plagued the state of Gujarat throughout 2002. There have been ongoing suggestions of political tension, highlighted by so-called "fake encounters" in which citizens, police, and leaders bamboozle one another into believing that violence and civil liberties infractions are being committed. While the media has had a field day, most level-headed people will tell you that Gujarat's problems are a result of politicians stirring an imaginary pot. Almost anywhere in India, communal violence can occur without advance warning, but such incidents rarely involve foreigners, and thus far there have been no attacks directed against Americans or other foreigners. That said, the threat here—as anywhere in the world—should not be ignored completely: Exercise vigilance and caution if you find yourself near any government installations or tourist attractions that might be regarded as potential terrorist targets; read the local papers, heeding any relevant reports and travel advisories. Access up-to-the-minute travel warnings at **www.travel.state.gov**. U.S. citizens can also contact the U.S. Embassy or the nearest U.S. Consulate for more information about the current situation in areas you plan to visit.

CRIME   Yes, India is one of the safest destinations in the world when it comes to violent assault or threat, but petty crime, like pickpocketing, can be a problem. Apply common sense at all times. Don't carry wallets prominently; and keep a firm hand on purses (women have reported having their purse straps cut or purse bottoms slit). Don't wear flashy jewelry or carry around other valuables. Most hotels have in-room electronic safes where you should stash valuables, including passports and most of your cash. Be discreet about your money, and never take out large wads of cash in public; exercise modesty at all times. Solo travelers are at greater risk of becoming victims of crime; unless you're relatively street-wise, touring India alone may be more pain than pleasure. But know that it is as a victim of a scam that you are most at risk, which at least hurts nothing but your pocket and your pride; see "Surviving Scams & Con Artists," below.

DISCRIMINATION

Africans, African-Americans, and other black travelers may sometimes face discrimination, particularly in smaller towns or nightclubs in larger cities, though this is not widespread. Some blacks and travelers from other Asian countries have also faced racist name-calling in India, usually from groups of young men in the street, completely ignorant of difference, and who are best ignored. Single female travelers do need to be careful (see section on "Women Travelers," below.)

9 Specialized Travel Resources

TRAVELERS WITH DISABILITIES

Most disabilities shouldn't stop anyone from traveling. There are more options and resources out there than ever before. However, it must be noted that India—despite the fact that it has such a high population of people with disabilities—is not well geared for travelers with disabilities. Destinations are far from wheelchair friendly, and it is hard enough for an able-bodied person to negotiate the crowded, filth-strewn, and potholed streets, where cars, animals, and rickshaws drive at will. Access to historical monuments is also difficult (though you will have the small reward of free access). Certainly you would need to be accompanied by a traveler familiar with the destination, and you must carefully sift through the accommodations options, only a handful of which have facilities specifically geared to travelers with disabilities.

Organizations that offer a range of resources and assistance to disabled travelers include **MossRehab** (© 800/CALL-MOSS; www.mossresourcenet.org); the **American Foundation for the Blind (AFB)** (© 800/232-5463; www.afb.org); and **SATH (Society for Accessible Travel & Hospitality)** (© 212/447-7284; www.sath.org).

GAY & LESBIAN TRAVELERS

Homosexuality remains frowned upon in India, and the law actively outlaws sexual acts between men (although gay women do not attract this prejudicial legislation). On the other hand, Indian men are a great deal more affectionate with one another than they are with women in public, and you'll frequently see men walking hand-in-hand, arm-in-arm, and embracing, though this is said to be an act of "brotherliness" without any sexual connotation. Recent high-profile cases have brought the issue of gay and lesbian rights into the social and political sphere, and there is increased awareness in this regard. Nevertheless, discretion is probably best observed outside your hotel room (note that no one questions same sex travelers sharing a room).

A useful website is **www.gaybombay. org**, which offers information on gay venues in Mumbai. For more information

and gay- and lesbian-friendly contacts nationwide, write to friend@gay bombay.org or **Bombay Dost** (105A Veena-Beena Shopping Centre, Bandra Station Rd., Bandra, Mumbai, 400 050); or to the **Gay Info Centre** (P.O. Box 1662 Secunderabad HPO 500 003, Andhra Pradesh).

SENIOR TRAVEL

India is not for the fainthearted, and this is definitely the one place senior travelers should utilize the services of a reliable agency and organization that targets the 50-plus market.

Members of **AARP**, 601 E St. NW, Washington, DC 20049 (© 888/687-2277; www.aarp.org), get discounts on hotels, airfares, and car rentals. AARP offers members a wide range of benefits, including *AARP: The Magazine* and a monthly newsletter. Anyone over 50 can join.

Many reliable agencies and organizations target the 50-plus market. **Elderhostel** (© 800/454-5768; www.elder hostel.org) arranges worldwide study programs for those aged 55 and over. **ElderTreks** (© 800/741-7956 or 416/558-5000 outside North America; www. eldertreks.com) offers small-group tours to off-the-beaten-path or adventure-travel locations, restricted to travelers 50 and older.

FAMILY TRAVEL

Just reading the list of inoculations and possible diseases in "Health & Safety" will probably make you think twice about taking your kids to India. But increasingly many do (to the extent that quite a few operators now customize tours to India with families in mind; see below), and if the color and pageantry of India amaze adults, they will absolutely delight smaller eyes, opening them to the rich cultural texture of the world at large. What's more, children receive the most wonderful attention, and can do no wrong in Indian eyes—for instance, restaurants are a nightmare for those who don't like children, as kids are allowed to run roughshod and make as much noise as they want while parents look on benignly. All hotels are geared toward kids (Indian parents always travel with their children), and babysitting is generally available everywhere. On the downside of taking your family with you: the extreme heat, the likelihood of tummy trouble from the water (it's very hard to avoid ingesting a single molecule), and the unavailability of suitable foodstuffs outside the big cities. To locate accommodations, restaurants, and attractions that are particularly kid-friendly, refer to the "Kids" icon throughout this guide.

Tour operators that customize holidays with families in mind include **www.kuoni. co.uk**, **www.audleytravel.com**, and **www. coxandkings.co.uk**—the latter even has a "Family Explorer" brochure that describes their custom-made trips.

WOMEN TRAVELERS

Foreign women will almost certainly experience India as sexist, but if you are confident, relaxed, and assertive, you are unlikely to experience any serious hassles. That said, traveling solo is only for the very brave and thick-skinned, unless of course you're traveling in comfort (using the accommodations selected in this book) and have hired a car and driver for the duration (using public transport is when you are at your most vulnerable). At best, you will experience being stared at intensely for an unbearable length of time, at worst you may be groped—some men are convinced that all Western women are loose and slutty. To a great extent, Western cinema and fashion trends have helped fuel the legend that women from abroad welcome these attentions, and you'd do well to take precautions, like wearing appropriate (modest) attire. On

trains, on buses, and in other public places, you are best off ignoring advances or questions from suspicious-looking men. Another strategy that often helps single women travelers ward off unwanted male attention is to wear a ring and invent a husband; if you're approached, say that you are meeting your "husband" at the next station/destination. You should have little difficulty determining when a line of questioning is likely to lead to problems. In particular, steer clear of men who have been drinking alcohol. "Eve-teasing" (the word denoting unwanted attention and public harassment by men) is an offense in certain parts of India, and you are within your rights to report inappropriate advances or remarks to the police—the easiest response, however, is to loudly tell the offender off, and even strike him—you will almost certainly be supported by those around you. You may want to ask whether or not your hotel offers a special room for solo women travelers; these are now offered in a few upmarket hotels in the larger cities, and include special privacy/security features.

Note that women are excluded from entering certain religious sites and attractions (which we have pointed out wherever relevant), but this is unlikely to impact too strongly on your plans. Menstruating women are, technically, not entitled to enter Jain temples or mosques.

AFRICAN-AMERICAN TRAVELERS

African-Americans and other travelers of African descent will face as much curiosity as someone with blond hair and blue eyes, but also some degree of discrimination, though this is neither widespread nor specific to a particular region. Mostly this takes the form of travelers being told a hotel or nightclub is full when it really isn't.

Frommers.com: The Complete Travel Resource

It should go without saying, but we highly recommend **Frommers.com**, voted Best Travel Site by *PC Magazine.* We think you'll find our expert advice and tips; independent reviews of hotels, restaurants, attractions, and preferred shopping and nightlife venues; vacation giveaways; and an online booking tool indispensable before, during, and after your travels. We publish the complete contents of over 128 travel guides in our **Destinations** section covering nearly 3,600 places worldwide to help you plan your trip. Each weekday, we publish original articles reporting on **Deals and News** via our free **Frommers.com Newsletter** to help you save time and money and travel smarter. We're betting you'll find our new **Events** listings (http://events.frommers.com) an invaluable resource; it's an up-to-the-minute roster of what's happening in cities everywhere—including concerts, festivals, lectures, and more. We've also added weekly **Podcasts, interactive maps,** and hundreds of new images across the site. Check out our **Travel Talk** area featuring **Message Boards** where you can join in conversations with thousands of fellow Frommer's travelers and post your trip report once you return.

10 Staying Connected

TELEPHONES

Phone numbers in India change at the drop of a hat, and businesses are slow in updating contact information, including websites.

To call India:

1. Dial the international access code: 011 (from the U.S. and Canada); 00 (from the U.K., Ireland, or New Zealand); or 0011 (from Australia).
2. Dial the country code: 91.
3. Dial the city code (these are provided in the relevant chapters), omitting the first zero.
4. Dial the telephone number.

Note: To call a cellphone number in India, follow up to step 2 above and then dial the 10-digit cellphone number, which should begin with "9."

Making calls within India: Hotel telephone costs are exorbitant, even when you make a domestic long-distance call. All over India, you'll see yellow ISD/STD signs indicating a privately operated "International Subscriber Dialing" and "Standard Trunk Dialing" facility; these

are very reasonably priced. Your call is monitored by a computer system, and you pay at the end of your session. Make sure you have the correct phone number with you—and check that the phone is in a quiet spot, or you run the risk of not hearing a word during your conversation. To call a mobile phone number that is not in the city in which you are based, dial "0" before the 10-digit number. Note that the Indian toll-free numbers (1/800) cannot be dialed from cellphones and land lines that don't belong to the MTNL or BSNL networks.

Making calls from cellphones: When making calls from cellphones, you'll need to punch in the full area code of the city and telephone number irrespective of where you are calling from. In other words, even if you are in Mumbai and want to call the city's Taj Mahal Hotel, you'd need to dial 022/6665-3366 from your cellphone. To call a cellphone number within a city, just dial the 10-digit cellphone number; to call a cellphone outside your city, add a "0" before the number.

To make international calls: Dial 00 and then the country code (U.S. or Canada 1, U.K. 44, Ireland 353, Australia 61, New Zealand 64). Next, dial the area code and number. For example, if you want to call the British Embassy in Washington, D.C., dial © 00-1-202-588-7800.

For directory assistance: Dial © 197 if you're looking for a local number within India, and dial © 183 for long-distance numbers within India. Don't hold your breath for accurate or up-to-date assistance, and speak slowly and clearly. There's also every chance you won't be able to get through to the number at all, or that your question will not be correctly answered. In the "Fast Facts" sections for some cities you'll find listed numbers for private, talking Yellow Pages services; these are more helpful in giving up-to-date information.

For operator assistance: If the phone you're using is not an International Subscriber Dialing (ISD) facility, you'll need operator assistance and must dial © 186. Using an ISD facility without the need for an operator will save you a great deal of time. **Toll-free numbers:** To call a 1-800 number in the U.S. from India, first contact the international operator through the Direct Access service. For a call to the U.S., call © 000-117 (AT&T Direct Access), which gives you an AT&T operator, through whom you can make your toll-free or collect call. Note, however, that these Direct Access calls cannot be made from everywhere; to ensure you won't be charged for the call, check with your hotel before dialing.

CELLPHONES

The three letters that define much of the world's wireless capabilities are **GSM** (Global System for Mobile Communications), a big, seamless network that makes for easy cross-border cellphone use worldwide. GSM phones function with a removable plastic SIM card, encoded with your phone number and account information. If your cellphone is on a GSM system, and you have a world-capable multiband phone such as many Sony Ericsson, Motorola, or Samsung models, you can make and receive calls across civilized areas around much of the globe. Just call your wireless operator and ask for "international roaming" to be activated on your account. Unfortunately, per-minute charges can be high.

If you are carrying your own phone make sure it has been "unlocked" by the provider. Then, pick up a cheap, prepaid phone **SIM card** at a mobile phone store or at tens of thousands of shops throughout the length and breadth of India, and slip it into your phone. SIM cards usually cost Rs 100 ($2/£1) or less. To get a SIM card you will need a copy of your passport, a passport-size photo, and another form of ID. You'll get a local phone number, and much, much lower calling rates and free or very cheap incoming calls. Then you can refill your talk time by purchasing a prepaid refill when you need it. Note that if you don't have a compatible phone, you can buy a decent cellphone for Rs 2,000 to Rs 4,000 ($49–$98/£25–£49) in India—buy from an authorized dealer who will give you a receipt and warranty. Later, when you leave the country, you can usually sell the phone for half what you paid for it at a local vendor dealing in second-hand phones, found everywhere in Delhi and Mumbai. Alternatively, you can buy a **CDMA (Code Division Multiple Access) prepaid phone** in India. **Reliance India Mobile** (www.relianceinfo.com) and **Tata Indicom** (www.tataindicom.com) offer countrywide network, and you can pick up a low-end phone for under Rs 3,000 ($73/£34). Note, however, that some low-end phones have difficult-to-use software; the most user-friendly ones are usually Nokia models. Once you have this phone, you can prepay a balance, and refill it when necessary. Phone calls are charged at Rs 1 to Rs 2.50 (5¢/5p) per minute within India and Rs 6 to Rs 17 (15¢–40¢/7p–20p) per minute for international calls. The disadvantage of the CDMA is that once you are ready to go home, the phone has no value and has to be discarded.

Though you can **rent** a phone in India, because of security reasons, mobile phone rental is currently not widely available; you'll need copies of your passport and go through other security checks, as well as make a hefty deposit. Most five-star hotels will rent a phone to you at a fairly high rate. In Mumbai you can also call **Colorama Centre** (© **022/2204-0362**), located in the Hilton Towers hotel. You'll pay just Rs 50 ($1/60p) per day for the handset, and you can buy and refill talk time as you require, after purchasing a new SIM card. **Matrix** offers cellular services to international customers in most of the larger cities (toll-free in India: © **800/11-1500;** www.matrix.in); you can also get your SIM card in advance overseas (U.K.: © **797/391-1620;** U.S.: © **215/359-6974**).

INTERNET/E-MAIL
WITHOUT YOUR OWN COMPUTER
To find cybercafes in your destination check **www.cybercaptive.com** and **www. cybercafe.com**. Better still, you can ask your hotel to guide you to the nearest reliable cybercafe. All big cities in India and many small towns as well have a host of cybercafes.

WITH YOUR OWN COMPUTER
More and more hotels, resorts, cafes, and retailers are going **Wi-Fi** (wireless fidelity), becoming "hot spots" that offer free high-speed Wi-Fi access or charge a small fee for usage. Most laptops sold today have built-in wireless capability. Wi-Fi facilities or dataports (and well-equipped business centers) are available in all luxury city hotels in India (as well as in many hotels outside city limits). Note that the electric current is 220–240 volts AC, and that different socket and plug standards are used in different parts of the country. Although good hotels usually have multi-socket units, you should consider bringing a universal adaptor (if you're unsure, call your hotel in advance to find out what the options are). Note that power outages are regular, as are variations in voltage, so be prepared for any eventuality.

For dial-up access, most business-class hotels throughout the world offer dataports for laptop modems.

Wherever you go, bring a **connection kit** of the right power and phone adapters, a spare phone cord, and a spare Ethernet network cable—or find out whether your hotel supplies them to guests.

11 Packages for the Independent Traveler

Package tours (not be confused with escorted tours) are simply a way to buy the airfare, accommodations, and other elements of your trip (such as car rentals, airport transfers, and sometimes even activities) at the same time and often at discounted prices.

One good source of package deals is the airlines themselves. Most major airlines offer air/land packages, including **Continental Airlines Vacations** (© **800/ 301-3800;** www.covacations.com) and **Virgin** (www.virginholidays.co.uk), Several big **online travel agencies**—Expedia, Travelocity, Orbitz, Site59, and Lastminute.com—also do a brisk business in packages.

RECOMMENDED OPERATORS FOR PACKAGE & ADVENTURE TOURS
If you're happy to pay good money for a very well-organized deluxe tailored tour, **Abercrombie & Kent** (www.abercrombie

kent.com) are the masters, not only choosing the most expensive accommodations options, but the best (there is often a difference!). The company also specializes in putting together trekking trips and packages that tap into India's great wildlife resources—in comfort, of course. The only drawback is that always traveling in style can cocoon you from the raw experiences that make India such a memorable experience. For this, consider a tour that includes houseboat and private homestays in Kerala, Tamil Nadu, and Haryana on tours organized by **Colours of India** (www.colours-of-india.co.uk); the selection is very exciting. Another Indian stalwart is **Cox & Kings** (www.coxandkings.com) who, like Abercrombie & Kent, work hard to create a really relaxing top-end holiday (rather than the hard work that India can be), tailor-made to personal preferences. Another good upmarket agency, specializing in customized travel itineraries, is **Western & Oriental** (www.westernoriental.com).

A highly recommended option if you're traveling on a budget (or even if you have money to burn) is Raj Singh, proprietor of **Exotic Journeys,** who arranges tailor-made tours throughout India—you can literally contact him and tell him your area of interest and a daily limit, and he will come up with the goods (2 weeks in Rajasthan, Agra, Delhi: upwards of $150/£75 per person per day including accommodations, entry fees, and private car and driver!). Contact him at exotic@vsnl.net or at © 011/2612-4069 through -4072.

A U.S.-based travel agency specializing in India is **United Fairfax Travel/Manaca Travel and Tours** (9864 Main St., Fairfax, VA; © 703/591-3544; vnegi@ufxtravel.com). Owned by Vinod Negi, this very professional outfit is able to plan a comprehensive itinerary and make all travel arrangements. Vinod is also extremely flexible; once you're on the road, any changes you want made are dealt with efficiently. Vinod deals directly with local agency India Travelite, located at 50H, Vandhna Building 11, Tolstoy Marg, New Delhi. **Audley Travel** (www.audleytravel.com) is a recommended U.K.–based outfit that tailors tours to suit your need.

Another reliable local operator is **Sita World Travel** for both individually tailored and escorted tours (www.sitaindia.com). Goa-based **Odyssey Tours & Travels** is also a highly dependable agent that arranges individual and customized tours all over India; they also run *The Imaginative Traveller*'s India operations (www.imaginative-traveller.com), which you can join directly through any of their offices. E-mail Odyssey's director Hans Tuinman at res@odyssey.co.in.

SPECIAL-INTEREST TOURS

COOKING   Those looking for a cooking holiday can get their aprons and bathing suits out and head to Goa where **On the Go** organizes a variety of special-interest holidays (www.onthegotours.com).

HIKING/ADVENTURE   If you're specifically looking for an agent for trekking, try **Himalayan Kingdoms** (www.himalayankingdoms.com) or **Trans Indus Travel** (www.transindus.co.uk), although the latter's itineraries are not limited to outdoor excursions. **Steppes East Ltd.** (www.steppeseast.co.uk) is another reputable option; they let you conveniently create your personal itinerary online. Other Himalayan trekking outfits are **Mountain Travel/Sobek** (www.mtsobek.com), **Geographic Expeditions** (www.geoex.com), and **Adventure Center** (www.adventurecenter.com); the latter two also have general adventure expeditions.

ON HORSE, ELEPHANT, OR CAMELBACK   **Wilderness Travel** (www.wildernesstravel.com) specializes in Rajasthan camel safaris and elephant expeditions. **Equine Adventures** organizes riding holidays in Rajasthan (www.equine adventures.co.uk).

DIVING   For diving adventures in Lakshadweep, take a look at the packages offered on www.diveworldwide.com.

WILDLIFE/BIRDING   Wildlife enthusiasts can check on the numerous options for group bird- and wildlife-watching trips from **Naturetrek** (www.naturetrek.co.uk). For small, high-end, exotic bird-watching tours of India, look no further than **Victor Emanuel Nature Tours** (www.ventbird.com), based in Austin, Texas; the tours are usually sold out as soon as they come online. Victor often includes the "Palace on Wheels," a weeklong journey through Rajasthan (including Agra) in a luxury train; for standard Palace on Wheels tours, see "Getting Around India," below.

MOTORBIKE SAFARIS   Motorbike safaris are increasingly popular; if you can handle the fabulous Enfield motorbike, get in touch with Peter Santos (info@classic-bike-india-de), and he'll put together an itinerary.

12 Escorted General-Interest Tours

Escorted tours are structured group tours, with a group leader. The price usually includes everything from airfare to hotels, meals, tours, admission costs, and local transportation.

Despite the fact that escorted tours require big deposits and predetermine hotels, restaurants, and itineraries, many people derive security and peace of mind from the structure they offer. Escorted tours—whether they're navigated by bus, motor coach, train, or boat—let travelers sit back and enjoy the trip without having to drive or worry about details. They take you to the maximum number of sights in the minimum amount of time with the least amount of hassle. They're particularly convenient for people with limited mobility and they can be a great way to make new friends.

On the downside, you'll have little opportunity for serendipitous interactions with locals. The tours can be jam-packed with activities, leaving little room for individual sightseeing, whim, or adventure—plus they often focus on the heavily touristed sites, so you miss out on many a lesser-known gem.

Dagmar von Harryegg is based in Australia but is passionate about India, particularly the desert states of Rajasthan and Gujarat, where she has developed an extensive network of contacts and friends, from elephant *mahouts* to reclusive princes. She offers personally tailored special-interest trips (anything from yoga or bird-watching to Bollywood and/or classical dance lessons) for a maximum of eight travelers—preferably friends, thereby ensuring a flexible timetable "cruising in wonderfully old-fashioned Ambassador limousines with overnight stays in off-the-beaten-track destinations." She also arranges large Hindi-style traditional weddings for couples looking for a really memorable nuptial celebration. Most trips take off in Delhi and can include a visit to the Taj Mahal. For information, contact Dagmar at dagmarvh@tpg.com.au.

For midrange and budget tours, U.K.-based **Imaginative Traveller** is popular for its mid-range-priced escorted tours (www.imaginative-traveller.com).

One of India's foremost tourism operators, **Sita World Travel** (called **SOTC** in some places) is represented throughout the length and breadth of India. Sita offers a wide range of tours to cover a range of budgets and interests. These include sightseeing trips and excursions to India's top attractions, as well as soft-adventure and special-interest tours that can really get you off the beaten track (www.e-holidaysindia.com).

Note that many of the recommended individual and adventure operators listed above offer escorted group tours.

13 Getting Around India

You can research prices and deals on travel and hotels at reliable online travel companies based in India. Try www.makemytrip.com, www.cleartrip.com, www.tcindia.com, or www.travelmart india.com. However, at press time most of these sites were not accepting foreign credit cards, at least until their online security systems were upgraded.

BY CAR

India's roads are statistically the most dangerous in the world. Self-driven rental cars are simply not available (with the exception of unauthorized operators in Goa) and if they were, renting your own car and attempting to traverse the chaos that passes for traffic is simply suicidal. That said, having your own vehicle—and a driver who knows the roads, can read road signs when they're present, and can communicate with locals—is in many ways the best way to get around. You can set your own pace, without having to worry about making public-transport connections (a major headache taken care of), and you can see the sights and experience many of the attractions without feeling anxious (your driver will be a huge help in providing advice on customs and pricing), as well as experience off-the-beaten-track towns and rural scenes that give you the only sense of real India. And by American and European standards, the luxury of being chauffeured around the country—not necessarily in a high-end luxury vehicle, keep in mind—is ridiculously cheap. Certainly this is the way to go to concentrate on certain parts of India, such as Rajasthan, but it's not advisable as a way to cover long-distance journeys—aim to spend no more than 3 to 4 hours a day in the car (there will be,

of course, exceptions). *Note:* Whatever you do, make sure your plan does not include traveling at night.

What kind of car?   Standard cars are sometimes antique-looking and very romantic Ambassadors, tough cars despite their appearance, but sometimes unpredictable; don't rely on them for long out-of-town journeys—better perhaps to opt for a modern vehicle like the compact Indica. A vehicle with off-road capabilities is essential in some of the more remote and hilly regions, including eastern Himachal Pradesh, Ladakh, Sikkim, and parts of Uttarakhand; it is also recommended for some of the awful road conditions in Madhya Pradesh and Karnataka, for example, where there may be more potholes than patches of tarmac. Air-conditioned vehicles cost more but are always recommended because you may want to keep windows closed in order to shut out the endless traffic noise and pollution.

How much will it cost?   Charges for this sort of car hire vary considerably; see our guidelines below. If you use a hotel rental service, you usually have to fork out exorbitant fees—although the vehicle and quality of service will generally be top-notch. At the other end of the scale, you can walk up to a driver in the street, negotiate an excellent deal, and spend the rest of your vacation watching the tires being changed. It's often a good idea to start by contacting the Tourist Development Corporation in whatever state you wish to hire a car (contact details are in individual chapters). Their rates are usually reasonable and fixed; you'll be spared the battle of the haggle; and you won't have to live with the misery of being overcharged. We provide price indications in individual chapters, but a good way to estimate how much a vehicle should cost for a multiday run is to calculate three things: a) the approximate distance you will travel multiplied by the per-kilometer rate (usually between Rs 8/20¢/10p and Rs 18/45¢/20p depending on the car); b) an overnight charge of Rs 150 to Rs 300 ($4–$7/£2–£4) per night, plus state taxes, tolls, and across-state permits and fees; and c) the mileage for the car to return to its place of origin, even if it returns empty.

Each chapter lists travel agencies that can assist you with car rental, many with their own fleet of vehicles and drivers; if the price doesn't seem right, shop around. Finally, when it comes to tipping your driver, a fair amount is Rs 150 to Rs 200 ($4–$5/£2–£2.50) for each day he's been with you. If you feel you got exemplary service and want to give him more, however, by all means give him what you feel he deserves. If, on the other hand, you've had to tolerate a surly, uncooperative, and inefficient chauffeur, make sure you let the agency know, and reflect it in the tip as you see fit. *Tip:* Your car driver may sometimes drive you around for an hour in a new city rather than do the sensible thing and ask for directions. Remember, in most cities the best people to ask for directions are usually auto-rickshaw or taxi drivers. If you are on foot, however, more often than not if you ask a rickshaw or cab driver for directions, he'll probably tell you your destination is "too far" and that you need to hire his services.

Bear in mind that if you are involved in an accident, it's best to get out of your vehicle and away from the scene without delay, inform your rental agency or hotel immediately, and have them inform local authorities. An accident involving the injury or death of a cow or person may result in a mob assault on all occupants of the offending vehicle as well as its incineration.

Taxis & Auto-rickshaws   These modes of transport are the ways to go within your chosen city or town. Auto-rickshaws are best for short journeys only, being slow, bumpy, and open-air—in other words, open to pollution. Always, always negotiate the rate upfront, having established the average going rate (unless the driver is using a "meter reading chart," in which case check it carefully, and make sure he is not using the night 11pm–5am chart, when charges are higher). We have tried to indicate these rates throughout, but given the potential escalation in fuel costs, it's best to ask about the going rate (your hotel or host should know) and figure out a fixed price for a given journey. To get from the station or airport to your hotel, use the prepaid taxi booths; remember to hand over your receipt only *after* reaching your destination. Be aware that in some cities it's a toss-up between forcing the driver to use his meter, only to be taken for a citywide spin, and agreeing to a slightly higher than normal price and being taken from A to B.

Remember: Carry your passport at all times—many of the borders between states have checkpoints where passports may be checked. Also always have with you at least one photocopy of your passport and visa and four to five passport-size photographs; you will need them for permits and other unforeseen bureaucratic paperwork, like getting a prepaid SIM card for a cellphone.

BY PLANE

Because train travel is time-consuming, and roads generally appalling, the best way to cover huge distances is by air. Thankfully there's been a huge spurt in domestic air traffic in India over the last 2 years, giving you great choice at bargain prices. In addition, the previous system of charging foreigners a special (higher) dollar fare has been discontinued and now all airlines advertise fares that anyone can buy. **Jet Airways** (www.jetairways. com), with its fleet of new planes, First-World service, and good connections (it's rapidly on track in its goal to link almost every significant destination in the country), is still a very good airline, but **Kingfisher Airlines** (© 1800/180-0101; www.flyingkingfisher.com) is now our favorite: Aircrafts are brand-new, cabin crew are efficient and super-friendly, and service is just exemplary—now we just await a wider network. Another contender for the domestic crown is **Paramount Airways** (© 800/180-1234; www.paramount airways.com). Predominantly based in South India but rapidly expanding, it offers full business-class cabins and service at less than economy-class fares. Basically, opt for Kingfisher or Paramount if the price is comparable, but don't hesitate to fly Jet.

If price is important, you'll be delighted to know that there has been a slew of **low-cost airlines** launched since the last edition, making travel throughout India much easier. You will certainly save money with these airlines—but don't expect top-notch service (often no meals or beverages served), and worst of all, you may (almost certainly with Deccan) have lengthy delays. Cheapest (and least reliable) is **Air Deccan** (© 98925-77008 or 080/3900-8888; www.airdeccan.net); the best (clean, reliable, relatively cheap) is **Spice Jet** (© 800/180-3333; www.spice jet.com); **Go Air** (© 800/222-111 or 09223/222-111; www.goair.in) and **Indi-Go** (© 099103/83838 or 800/180-3838; www.goindigo.in) are also worth looking into.

Note, however, that the domestic air travel market in India is in for some major changes. At press time several airlines were coming together either through takeovers, mergers, or acquisitions, forming larger, stronger conglomerates that may raise the fares of low-cost airlines. The erstwhile **Air Sahara** (© 1800/22-3020) was swallowed by Jet Airways and transformed into a low-cost airline called **Jet Lite,** and Kingfisher-Air Deccan looked set for nuptials, as did Indian-Air India (note that Indian and Air-Indian are experiences to be avoided).

India's **domestic and international check-in and preboarding procedure** may be one of the most rigorous in the world. Technically, check-in will start 180 minutes prior to international departure, and you need to produce a ticket before being allowed access to the airport building (if you plan to purchase your ticket inside the airport, speak to a security officer, who will escort you to the appropriate ticket counter). Arriving less than 60 minutes prior to domestic departure is *definitely* not recommended. Your checked baggage must be scanned and sealed before you report to the check-in counter. The list of dangerous items not permitted in your carry-on bags is fairly extensive; you will be asked to remove batteries from your camera, and these will be stowed by security until you reach your destination. Check-in closes 30 minutes prior to departure. After check-in, you should immediately head for the first security check, which will involve a body pat-down and a scan of your carry-on luggage. Boarding gates close 15 minutes prior to scheduled departure (although delays are fairly frequent), and there will be second body and carry-on checks before you are permitted to board the plane. In some instances, you will be asked to identify your checked luggage on the tarmac. While frequent travelers may be irritated by these ungainly, time-consuming methods, others find the process provides peace of mind.

Tip: Always have your concierge (or yourself to be sure) reconfirm your flight at least 72 hours before departure to save yourself the frustration of arriving at the airport only to find that your name has been deleted from the computer.

BY TRAIN

India's rail network is the second largest in the world, and you can pretty much get anywhere in the country by train. That said, train journeys between major destinations can consume massive amounts of time (often more than car travel); and the network, tiers (one of the A/C, or air-conditioned classes may, for instance, be better than non-A/C first class), and connections can be confusing. It's best to determine well in advance whether or not your destination is accessible from your point of origin and which tier is the most comfortable, and then factor in delays; some slow trains stop at every two-hut village along the way, and this can extend traveling time by hours. Generally, you should only consider long-distance train travel if you are assured of exotic scenery (like the **Konkan Railway,** which connects Mumbai with Goa, Karnataka, and Kerala, running along the Konkan coast); or if the journey is

overnight (like Delhi to Varanasi) and you have reserved a **first-class air-conditioned sleeper** or **second-class air-conditioned sleeper** berth, preferably the two-tier variety. (Never book regular **second class,** which can be torturous, claustrophobic, and distressing if you are at all intimidated by crowds.) You will be particularly comfortable aboard the overnight **Rajdhani**—the superfast train connects Delhi to Mumbai for Rs 2,210 ($54/£27) or to Kolkata (Howrah) for Rs 2,335 ($57/£29) in the two-tier A/C (air-conditioned) class; it also connects Delhi with Chennai, Bangalore, Bhubaneswar, Thiruvananthapuram, Abu Road, Ahmedabad, and Ajmer. The best daytime travel train is the **Shatabdi;** these intercity trains have several routes between important tourist destinations (Delhi to Amritsar: Rs 635/$15/£8; Mumbai to Madgaon [Goa]: Rs 675/$16/£8; Delhi to Jaipur: Rs 495/$12/£6). Book a seat in the air-conditioned **Chair Car** class;

Tips Booking Your Train Ticket at the Station: The Nitty-Gritty

Even though you will be told that there are no special lines or windows for foreigners who want to book train tickets, we assure you that this is not the case. More important, most trains have a quota of seats specifically for foreigners. This means that even if a train is completely booked up, as a foreigner you may be able to get a seat, unless other foreigners booking through the same service have already filled the seat quota. This is valuable information to keep in mind, because an agent cannot book a seat for you on this quota, nor can this be booked from the regular booking window; you must go personally to a **Foreign Tourist Rail Reservation Counter** (sometimes called Foreign Tourist Bureaus) with your passport, and pay either in foreign currency (cash or credit card) or show a currency encashment certificate or ATM receipt. The ticket costs exactly the same as the regular ticket (except for credit card surcharges). Train stations at the following Indian cities have a Foreign Tourist Rail Reservation Counter: Agra-Cantonment, Ahmedabad, Aurangabad, Bangalore, Chennai, New Delhi, Jaipur, Jodhpur, Kolkata, Mumbai, Secunderabad, Vadodara, Varanasi, and Vasco-Da-Gama (Goa). There's also a counter at the Delhi Tourism & Transport Development Corporation office at Indira Gandhi International Airport in the Arrivals lounge. In Mumbai, this office is tucked away next to the Government Tourist Office, on the first floor of the Western Railway Building, opposite Churchgate Station.

small meals, tea, coffee, and bottled water are included in the ticket price, seats are comfortable and clean, and toilets are usually usable, but not great.

For extensive railway information, log on to **www.indianrail.gov.in**, which shows routes, availability, and prices for all Indian trains, but you cannot book online from overseas. For tips on how to maneuver this rather unwieldy website to get the information you need, see the box below.

Purchasing tickets usually requires some advance planning, and it's a good idea to make all-important **ticket reservations** (particularly for overnight travel) before you leave for India, especially if you're coming during peak holiday season. You can make ticket reservations through your hotel or an agent (usually for a relatively small fee), or you can brave the possibility of long lines and silly form-filling at the train station; that said, check out "Train Booking Simplified,"

below, to see if the station you're heading to has a counter set up especially for foreigners. Not only is this an easy way to book your seat, it may be the only way to secure tickets when trains are completely full and agents can do nothing to assist.

Indian Railways Indrail Pass is a "discount" ticket for unlimited travel over a specific number of days (for example, air-conditioned chair car/first and second class: 7 days $135/£68), but these still require reservations and are only likely to benefit travelers who expect to make two or more long-distance journeys in a short time.

In every chapter we have included telephone numbers for railway stations, but don't expect too much information from these, if indeed you are even able to get through.

Tip: To avoid unnecessary stress while traveling by train (particularly on overnight journeys), use a chain and padlock to secure your luggage and fasten it to

---

Tips Booking Online: Understanding the Indian Railway Website

Using the Indian Railway website can be an exercise in frustration; here are some tips on how to master it with ease. After you log on to **indianrail.gov.in,** click on "Train/Fare Accommodation" on the top menu (third choice from the left). Next fill in where you want to depart from (source station name) and your destination, but (and here's the key), only type the first three letters of the name of the place (mum for Mumbai, ban for Bangalore, etc.). Then fill in the class of service you're interested in (safest to pick "All"). Enter your date of travel (or a fictitious date) and click "get it." This will take you to another window where you narrow your choice of source and destination from a pull-down menu (all places beginning with mum and ban). For Bangalore you may get several choices—and this is another tricky part—you have to pick one (usually the first Bangalore choice on the list). You will get a list of all the trains, with times, that run between the two cities. Now pick the train you want by clicking on the white circle to the left of the train's name to highlight it green, then choose your class of service (on the right). At this stage you can change the date if you like, and then get availability or fares. The availability is sometimes not online between 10pm to 6am Indian time, so if you don't get what you want, try again later. The availability chart basically tells you how many seats are still available in the class of service you've chosen.

The Romance of Rail: India's Special Train Journeys

India's most famous luxury train, **Palace on Wheels,** currently operates in Rajasthan, and has 14 opulently furnished en-suite saloons, a bar, and two restaurants (✆ U.S./Canada toll-free **1-888-INDIA-99,** in India call 011/2332-5939 or 011/2335-3155; www.palaceonwheels.net or www.thepalaceon wheels.com). Over 7 days, the train travels from Delhi to Jaipur, Jaisalmer, Jodhpur, Sawai Madhopur (Ranthambhore), Chittaurgarh, Udaipur, Bharat-pur, and Agra; and finishes its trip back in Delhi. The "Week in Wonder-land" trip costs $4,900 to $8,150 (£2,450–£4,075) double, including all travel, accommodations, sightseeing, and meals. Other luxury trains in India include: **Deccan Odyssey** (see chapter 4); **Fairy Queen,** the oldest operating steam locomotive in the world, dating back to 1855, which takes an overnight trip from Delhi to Alwar, Rajasthan (a visit to the Sariska wildlife sanctuary) and back (only A/C chair cars, no sleeper berths; $165/£83); and **Heritage on Wheels,** which has a 3-night trip through the Bikaner and Shekhawati regions of Rajasthan (www.heritageonwheels.net; $600/£303 per person).

For a truly exclusive train journey board the private **The Viceroy of India,** which runs just four 15-day trips a year from Mumbai to Calcutta via Jaipur, Delhi, Varanasi, and Darjeeling (two east-bound and two west-bound), and is priced at $9,995 (£5,695) (Viceroy class) or $14,995 (£8,595) (Maharaja suite) per person twin sharing (www.gwtravel.co.uk).

Getting to the hill stations of Shimla (Himachal Pradesh), Darjeeling (West Bengal), Matheran (Maharashtra), or Ooty (Tamil Nadu) can be a sce-nic novelty if you don't mind spending long hours traveling in the atmos-pheric "toy trains" that chug their ways along narrow-gauge tracks to high altitudes by way of an endless series of hairpin loops—fabulous views are guaranteed. And then, of course, there is the Konkan Railway, which runs along the Malabar coast and has truly wonderful scenery almost every click-clack of the way.

some part of your berth or cabin. Be sen-sible, and don't leave valuables lying around while you sleep.

BY BUS

Unless you are on a serious budget and traveling in India for months, we recom-mend you avoid all forms of bus travel. Often crammed full of commuters, state-operated buses are driven at blood-cur-dling speeds along dangerous and punishing roads. Numerous so-called deluxe or luxury buses, operated by private companies, often ply similarly dangerous routes overnight. You may be tempted to save time and money with this option, but be aware that safety is rarely a priority, and sleeping is almost impossible thanks to generally uncomfortable seating and/or noise. Regular stops at roadside truck stops along the way will have you arriving at your destination bleary-eyed and exhausted, wondering why you've opted for a holiday in hell. On some routes (such as Delhi–Jaipur or Cochin–Bangalore), the exception is the comfort-able "Volvo" bus with good suspension.

Another exception is the Manali-to-Leh route, where the Trans-Himalayan scenery is jaw-droppingly awesome, and an overnight stop in tents is part of the deal (see chapter 11).

Note: Buses in India do not have onboard toilets (thankfully, given the state of so many of these on trains), so stops are usually at grimy roadside *dhabas* (local diners) or just along the side of the road.

14 Tips on Accommodations

Please note that at press time most hoteliers in India had moved to a single-currency pricing policy, quoting rooms in rupees instead of both rupees and U.S. dollars. Foreigners will still be able to pay their bills in a foreign currency, however.

One of the best developments in the past decade has been the increase in **luxury boutique-type options** offering international standards of service and comfort and flavored with Indian accents—like beautiful craftsmanship and ancient traditions (we're talking Ayurvedic masseurs on tap)—which means that the subcontinent is now a very desirable destination for the visitor wanting relaxation and pampering. To find the most unusual independent hotels, guesthouses, and homestays, an excellent resource for those who don't want the classic resort or chain hotel experience is Alastair Sawday's *Special Places to Stay: India* (www.sawdays. co.uk). Though the properties listed pay to be in the book, they are all, almost without exception, special in some way; the best are included in this book (plus many more that cannot afford or choose not to pay for publicity).

Of course we all knew India had "arrived" when the ultra-luxe **Amanresorts** entered the fray with **Amanbagh,** arguably the finest resort-style property in India, but the pace was first set by the **Vilās** properties, owned by India's very own, very fabulous **Oberoi** chain. Besides the Vilās properties (the best of which is **Amarvilās** in Agra, though some rate **Udaivilās** in Udaipur as their top choice), Oberoi runs some of the very best city hotels, as well as several spa resorts in key tourist destinations and a luxury backwater cruiser in Kerala. You will pay top dollar, but you can generally count on superb service and attention to detail. Best of all, you can often get great discounts on room rates by reserving in advance over the Internet (**www.oberoi hotels.com**). Note that Oberoi also operates a tier of smaller, less opulent hotels under the **Trident Hilton** banner, aimed principally at business or family travelers.

India's other famous hotel chain is the **Taj Group (www.tajhotels.com)**, with an enormous inventory of properties, particularly in South India, where Oberoi is largely absent. Quality varies somewhat (and service does not match that of the Oberoi group), but comfort is generally guaranteed, particularly in big cities and resort destinations—the best properties are the **Taj Mahal** in Mumbai, **Rambagh Palace** in Jaipur, **Lake Palace Hotel** in Udaipur, and **Umaid Bhawan Palace** in Jodhpur.

Safari experiences are also set to change forever since the Taj group launched **Taj Safaris,** teaming up with acclaimed South African conservation group CC Africa. Their first luxury safari lodge, **Mahua Kothi,** at the Bandavgarh tiger reserve in Madhya Pradesh, is a sublime, sexy property with some of the country's best guides. They already have two more lodges in Madhya Pradech—at Kanha and Pench—and are planning dozens more in the next few years. Meanwhile, Amanresorts' tented lodge at Ranthambhore, **Aman-i-Khás,** is superlative.

HOMESTAYS   All over Kerala (and a few other places), people are converting rooms of their homes into guest rooms for tourists to rent, at incredibly reasonable prices. Guests share the public spaces with the family, which lives in the home, and often dine with them. Many of these homestays are gorgeous heritage homes and their owners extremely hospitable. It's a good way to interact with an Indian family and get a taste of local culture and cuisine (www.homestaykerala.com, for instance, has an extensive list of such properties). But don't expect room service and the kinds of amenities you get at a full-service hotel.

HERITAGE HOTELS Staying in a medieval palace or fort is a unique and wonderful option among India's accommodations (particularly in Rajasthan), especially when your host is the aristocrat whose forebears built the palace or fort in which you're overnighting; the best are discussed in detail in relevant sections throughout this guide. Many were built centuries ago, so it's not surprising that heritage hotels are seldom the most luxurious option, with the possibilities of many stairs, dodgy plumbing, low ceilings, strange room layouts, and other eccentricities. Acting principally as marketing agencies for privately owned palaces, forts, and *havelis* (Indian mansions), as well as a number of small resorts around the country (primarily North India), two websites worth checking out are **www.indianheritagehotels.com** and **www.heritagehotels.com**.

Most heritage properties are individually owned, but a group that enjoys an excellent reputation for selecting and renovating these is **Neemrana;** check out **www.neemranahotels.com** to view their select collection of really lovely boutique heritage hotels, often located in off-the-beaten-track destinations; rates generally represent excellent value for these atmospheric gems.

Tip: Be aware that any hovel will attach "palace" to its name in the hopes of attracting more customers. This is often amusing if you're walking past, but can be disastrous if you're checking in.

CITY HOTELS The biggest problem in big cities and popular tourist areas is that the good hotels are often priced way out of reach, while moderate options are thin on the ground. **Mid-range hotels** are substandard by Western standards, though considerably cheaper. Wherever possible, we've provided budget options that are scrupulously clean and moderately comfortable. A new chain of budget hotels is called **Ginger** (© **800/22-0022** or 022/66014-634; www.gingerhotels. com). Launched by Indian Hotels (owners of the Taj group) and catering specially to the middling business market, these 101-room "Smart Basics" hotels offer accommodations priced at under Rs 1,500 ($22/£19) for a double. They won't have any of the opulence of the Taj hotels; in fact, rooms are small and rather plain in design, albeit comfortable and with all the amenities, including an ATM in the hotel. Eight Ginger hotels have already opened (Bangalore, Bhubaneswar, Durgapur, Haridwar, Mysore, Nashik, Pune, and Thiruvananthapuram), and another 17 are promised by the end of 2008.

Most of the top-of-the-range city hotels are operated by major international chains, including many of the usual suspects: **Sheraton** (www.starwoodhotels. com), **Hyatt** (www.hyatt.com), **Radisson** (www.radisson.com), **Le Meridien** (www. lemeridien.com), **Shangri-La** (www. shangri-la.com), and **Marriott** (www. marriott.com).

THE RATING SYSTEM India's hotel rating system refers to size and facilities on offer, not the potential quality of your stay. Often the best hotels have no rating because they are heritage properties and—despite their overwhelming loveliness—don't conform to the norms laid down by India's tourism department.

Of Hotels & Taxes

Almost every hotel in India will quote a rate to which an additional luxury tax is added; this varies from state to state. This tax applies to all luxury hotels, or the moment the room price goes above a certain level (which depends on the state, and sometimes the city). Restaurant and hotel bills get a different tax, and alcohol and other luxuries get a different set of taxes all together. Some states such as Tamil Nadu add an astronomical 73.5% tax to imported liquor; as a rule, locally produced alcohol is taxed less than foreign imports. *Always* check whether the tax has been included in the rate you've been quoted and, if it hasn't, exactly how much it is.

Tip: One hotel chain to avoid is the so-called "five-star deluxe" government-operated **Ashok group.** Most of its properties have "five-star facilities" and an inventory of hundreds of rooms, but they are often decaying concrete blocks with disinterested staff. In fact, as a general rule of thumb, government-run properties are best avoided throughout the country.

BARGAINING In India, even hotel rates are up for a bit of hard-core bargaining. If you're thin-skinned, bargain online (many hotels offer Internet-only discounts); alternatively, show up and stay tough—when you hear the rate quoted, brazenly pretend to walk out; there's no shame in India in turning back and accepting the rate. You'll also be surprised to find that luxury hotels in cities can often be had at mid-range prices, simply because room occupancy is low. Always ask about daily specials, and call and check prices at hotels that may appear out of your reach because of high rack rates—you may actually get a room there for a song.

In remote areas, small towns and villages, and many places in Goa and the Himalayan foothills, you can find good (basic but clean) budget accommodations at unbelievable prices. The same cannot generally be said of the major cities, where a cheap, dingy hotel may expose you to bedbugs and despair; stick to the budget recommendations in this book.

Note: Prices in a number of the hotel listings throughout the book are stated in U.S. dollars or, increasingly, in euros—this is, in fact, the way hotels targeting foreign markets quote their rates.

Tip: All over India, floors are marked and understood differently from many in the U.S. First floor is the floor above the ground level, second floor is the floor above that, and so on. The ground floor or lobby level is just that.

SURFING FOR HOTELS

In addition to the online travel booking sites **Travelocity, Expedia, Orbitz, Priceline,** and **Hotwire,** you can book hotels through **Hotels.com; Quikbook** (www.quikbook.com); and **Travelaxe** (www.travelaxe.net).

Most of the budget or moderate hotel recommendations do not have websites, and many hotel websites are poorly maintained, which means you may come across tariffs and information dating as far back as the previous decade. Smaller hotels change e-mail service providers almost as often as they change sheets. For basic information on about 3,000 listed hotels in India, the website for the **Federation of Hotel and Restaurant Associations of India** (www.fhrai.com) can be a useful if undiscriminating resource.

You'll also come up against a plethora of accommodations booking services that presume to be direct representatives of the hotel you're searching for, but that actually hike up the lowest available tariff considerably, which may leave you feeling ripped off before you even bed down. Always compare the website rate with the cheapest rate offered directly by the hotel before making a reservation. On the upside, several hotel networks offer unbelievable Internet discounts that simply can't be ignored.

For Kerala and Goa, *Hip Hotels in Kerala/Goa* (www.i-escape.com) gives detailed reviews of Kerala's stylish small hotels and retreats and some interesting rooms to book in Goa.

LANDING THE BEST ROOM

Somebody has to get the best room in the house; it might as well be you. First, make sure your room has air-conditioning. Ask for a room with split air-conditioning (an air-conditioner with a separate indoor and outdoor unit); it's far less noisy—and

ugly—than a window air-conditioner. If it doesn't, ask whether there is a ceiling fan or a water-cooling system. Be sure to request your choice of twin, queen- or king-size beds. Ask for rooms with views (many hotel staff don't understand this concept in India, so it's best to look around on arrival), showers or tubs (tubs in medium or budget category are usually old and stained, so don't shy away from shower-only options), and bed size. Ask for one of the most recently renovated or redecorated rooms—bathrooms in particular seem to suffer heavy wear and tear in India.

Tip: Indians often use the term "hotel" to refer to a restaurant or eating place, so don't be surprised if someone suggests you eat at a hotel down the road, and you arrive there to find a five-table shack.

FAST FACTS: India

American Express Report lost or stolen cards by calling ℂ **0124/28-1800** from anywhere in India; or call ℂ **98109-00800** (Delhi) or ℂ **98926-00800** (Mumbai). Individual branches are listed in the "Fast Facts" sections of individual city chapters.

Area Codes The international telephone access code for India is **91**. Area codes for principal cities and towns are listed in the "Fast Facts" sections in each chapter. All numbers listed in this guide include the local area code (which you would dial from another Indian town or city); this is separated from the actual telephone number by a forward slash (/).

Business Hours Banks are usually open weekdays from 10am to 2pm and Saturday from 10am to noon, though banks in larger cities have much longer hours. Most museums are closed Monday; the Taj Mahal is closed on Friday. Hours of retail outlets vary, but many close on Sunday.

Customs **What You Can Bring into India** You can bring as much foreign currency into India as you like; if you have over $10,000 in cash or traveler's checks, however, you should complete a declaration form. You may not import Indian currency into India. In addition to your personal effects, you are allowed 2 liters of alcohol, and 200 cigarettes or 50 cigars. (Know that foreign liquors and imported cigarettes are very heavily taxed and in some areas difficult to come by.) You may carry a cellphone, camera, and pair of binoculars, but officially you may have only five rolls of film. You must complete a special Tourist Baggage

Re-Export Form if you are carrying valuables such as a laptop computer, major video equipment, special camera gear, or high-value jewelry. Although there is a strong possibility that you may encounter difficulties upon leaving if these forms are not completed, you'll discover a general malaise among Customs officials, who seldom hassle foreign visitors on international flights. Also, much of the bureaucratic heavy-handedness has eased in recent years, and there is less suspicion of foreign travelers.

What You Can Take Home from India   You may not export Indian currency. Exchange all notes at the airport before you depart. Note that airport money-changers frequently run out of certain currencies, so you might want to complete any exchange before you go to the airport. There is a restriction on the exportation of anything over 100 years old, particularly works of art and items of cultural significance. It is illegal to export animal or snake skins, ivory, *shatoosh* wool, or anything that has been produced using these materials. Generally, jewelry valued under Rs 10,000 ($244/£123) may be exported, while gold jewelry valued up to Rs 2,000 ($49/£25) is allowed.

U.S. Citizens: For specifics on what you can bring back and the corresponding fees, download the invaluable free pamphlet *Know Before You Go* online at www.cbp.gov. (Click on "Travel," and then click on "Know Before You Go.") Or contact the U.S. Customs & Border Protection (CBP), 1300 Pennsylvania Ave. NW, Washington, DC 20229 (© **877/287-8667**) and request the pamphlet.

Canadian Citizens: For a clear summary of Canadian rules, write for the booklet *I Declare,* issued by the Canada Border Services Agency (© **800/461-9999** in Canada, or 204/983-3500; www.cbsa-asfc.gc.ca).

U.K. Citizens: For information, contact HM Customs & Excise at © **0845/010-9000** (from outside the U.K., 020/8929-0152), or consult their website at www.hmce.gov.uk.

Australian Citizens: A helpful brochure available from Australian consulates or Customs offices is *Know Before You Go.* For more information, call the Australian Customs Service at © **1300/363-263,** or log on to www.customs.gov.au.

New Zealand Citizens: Most questions are answered in a free pamphlet available at New Zealand consulates and Customs offices: *New Zealand Customs Guide for Travellers, Notice no. 4.* For more information, contact New Zealand Customs, The Customhouse, 17–21 Whitmore St., Box 2218, Wellington (© **04/473-6099** or 0800/428-786; www.customs.govt.nz).

Electricity   220–240 volts AC.

Embassies & Consulates   Embassies of major English-speaking countries are listed in the "Fast Facts" section for Delhi; see chapter 9. For quick reference, here are some embassy numbers: **Australia** © **011/4139-9900; Canada** © **011/4178-2000; New Zealand** © **011/2688-3170;** and the **U.K.** © **011/2687-2161.** The U.S. State Department encourages American citizens visiting India to register at the **U.S. Embassy** in New Delhi (Shantipath, Chanakyapuri; © **011/2419-8000;** fax 011/2419-0017; http://newdelhi.usembassy.gov) or at one of the U.S. consulates in India. The U.S. Consulate General in Mumbai is located at Lincoln House, 78 Bhulabhai Desai Rd., 400 026 ((© **022/2363-3611;** fax 022/2363-0350; http://mumbai.usconsulate.gov). The U.S. Consulate General in Kolkata is at 5/1

Ho Chi Minh Sarani, 700 071 (© **033/2282-3611;** fax 033/2282-2335; http://kolkata.usconsulate.gov). The U.S. Consulate General in Chennai is at 220 Anna Salai, Gemini Circle, 600 006 (© **044/2857-4000;** fax 044/2857-4024; http://chennai.usconsulate.gov).

Emergencies Refer to "Fast Facts" sections in individual chapters for police, ambulance, and emergency contact numbers.

Internet Access Although they're not always fantastic in terms of connection speed (or cleanliness), cybercafes are a roaring trade and usually cheap, albeit frustratingly slow. Keep an eye out for **Sify iway** (www.iway.com) and **Reliance Webworld** (www.relianceinfo.com) Internet centers, both offering much faster broadband connections than average stand-alone establishments. Sify, for instance, has some 2,500 Internet browsing centers around the country, half of which also offer Internet telephone services. Log on to their website to find a list of centers in a particular city. Today even small towns have decent Internet connectivity. *Tip:* Business centers at luxury hotels often charge exorbitant rates; there's often Internet connection for 10% of the cost just around the corner.

Language You shouldn't have to battle too much if you speak English with a clear accent. Don't assume, however, that everyone in India understands or speaks English. Also don't feel affronted when you run into locals who seem to smile in acknowledgement, only to reveal much later that they haven't the foggiest notion what you're talking about; they are simply trying to make you feel more at home. Hindi is widely spoken throughout North India, while all the states are divided linguistically. For example, Tamil is spoken in Tamil Nadu, Kannada in Karnataka, Telugu in Andhra Pradesh, Malayalam in Kerala, Gujarati in Gujarat, and Konkani in Goa; and there are literally hundreds of local dialects. You'll also come across a lot of what is often called Hinglish, where local terms (in Hindi) are mixed with English phrases. This usage is becoming increasingly widespread. You'll notice it immediately in advertising billboards and on television shows, but also in general conversation.

Liquor Laws Attitudes toward alcohol vary considerably. In Gujarat, prohibition is in force and liquor can only be obtained from the permit rooms of luxury hotels, a concession made principally for foreigners and out-of-state businesspeople. In most other non-Muslim areas, alcohol is freely available and exceedingly popular. In top hotels, you'll find a full range of imported liquor, available to those who can afford the extravagance. In most cities you will encounter "country liquor" bars and insalubrious liquor "dens"; and somewhere on your travels you may be offered local bootlegged stuff—all of which you're advised to stay clear of.

Lost & Found Be sure to contact your credit card companies the minute you discover that your wallet has been lost or stolen. Also file a report at the nearest police precinct, because your credit card company or insurer may require a police report number. Most credit card companies have an emergency number to call if your card is lost or stolen. They may be able to wire you a cash advance immediately or deliver an emergency credit card in a day or two. **Visa's** U.S. emergency number is © **866/670-0955. American Express** cardholders and traveler's check holders should call © **905/474-0870. MasterCard** holders should call

☏ **636/722-7111.** If you need emergency cash over the weekend, when all banks and American Express offices are closed, you can have money wired to you via **Western Union** (in India call ☏ **1-800/44-1851** or 1-800/111-911, or go to www.moneyintime.com; in the U.S. call ☏ **800/435-2226**; www.western union.com). You can **call all these numbers collect by using the access code 000-117** (see "Telephones" under "Staying Connected" above).

Mail Buy stamps for letters and postcards from your hotel, and have your concierge post them for you. International postage is extremely affordable (letter, Rs 15/35¢/20p first 20 grams), and the Indian postal service is generally efficient. However, sending a package or parcel abroad involves a tedious process of wrapping it in cloth and sealing it with string and wax (again, ask your concierge); you'll also have to complete a Customs declaration form. All this may cost you a great deal of time at the post office (9am–5pm). Also, bear in mind that surface mail runs the risk of spending months in the system, or of never arriving at all. You can spare yourself a great deal of torment by having a local or international courier company deliver important packages or by using registered mail.

Newspapers & Magazines Major English dailies include *The Hindu* (www.the hinduonnet.com), *The Indian Express* (www.expressindia.com), *The Times of India* (www.timesofindia.com), and *Hindustan Times* (www.hindustantimes. com), as well as Kolkata's *The Statesman* (www.thestatesman.net) and *The Telegraph* (www.telegraphindia.com). These make for interesting reading and will keep you up-to-date on local and international events. You may find that much of the writing assumes a great deal on your part, however. If you haven't been following certain stories for some time, the latest update may be impossible to fathom. *The Economic Times* and *Mint* provide the most detailed business news. Each week you can pick up fresh issues of *The Week, India Today, Outlook,* and *Frontline* (which provide quite venomous analyses of the nation's social, political, and economic situations). These are available at newsstands and railway stations and not only help you pass travel time but add immensely to your understanding of India. If you're looking for general travel features, the monthly *Outlook Traveller* (www.outlooktraveller.com) features colorful articles from an Indian perspective. In Delhi, the twice-monthly *Time Out* is indispensable if you're looking for what's hot and happening.

Passports For residents of the **United States:** Whether you're applying in person or by mail, you can download passport applications from the U.S. State Department website at **http://travel.state.gov.** For general information, call the **National Passport Agency** (☏ **202/647-0518**). To find your regional passport office, either check the U.S. State Department website or call the **National Passport Information Center** (☏ **900/225-5674**); the fee is 55¢ per minute for automated information and $1.50 per minute for operator-assisted calls.

For residents of **Canada:** Passport applications are available at travel agencies throughout Canada or from the central **Passport Office,** Department of Foreign Affairs and International Trade, Ottawa, ON K1A 0G3 (☏ **800/567-6868;** www.ppt.gc.ca).

For residents of the **United Kingdom:** To pick up an application for a standard 10-year passport (5-year passport for children under 16), visit your nearest passport office, major post office, or travel agency; or contact the **United Kingdom Passport Service** at ✆ **0870/521-0410**; www.ukpa.gov.uk.

For residents of **Ireland:** You can apply for a 10-year passport at the **Passport Office**, Setanta Centre, Molesworth Street, Dublin 2 (✆ **01/671-1633**; www.irl gov.ie/iveagh). Those under age 18 and over 65 must apply for a 3-year passport. You can also apply at 1A South Mall, Cork (✆ **021/272-525**) or at most main post offices.

For residents of **Australia:** You can pick up an application at your local post office or any branch of Passports Australia, but you must schedule an interview at the passport office to present your application materials. Call the **Australian Passport Information Service** at ✆ **131-232,** or visit the government website at www.passports.gov.au.

For residents of **New Zealand:** You can pick up a passport application at any New Zealand Passports Office or download it from their website. Contact the **Passports Office** at ✆ **0800/225-050** in New Zealand or 04/474-8100; or log on to www.passports.govt.nz.

Police Emergency and police contact numbers are listed in "Fast Facts" sections for major cities.

Restrooms Avoid public restrooms in India. Always carry toilet paper or tissues with you, since they're not always provided. Walk into five-star hotels to use their facilities even if you are not staying there.

Smoking Whatever curbs the government has tried to place on cigarette usage, there are no signs of society giving in to concerns about the hazards of smoking. Nearly every male in India seems to smoke something. An exception is Trivandrum City, where, at press time, smoking in restaurants and public places was banned (and enforced). Smoking is also forbidden on all trains, so if someone is smoking on your train, you are well within your rights to ask them to stop. Most luxury hotels have introduced nonsmoking rooms; if you don't smoke, request one when you book your reservation.

Taxes The tax on hotel accommodations varies from state to state, and sometimes by city; it may be anywhere between 5% and 12.5%, and may differ within the same hotel according to the level of luxury and comfort you're experiencing. Additional taxes on restaurant food and alcohol vary from state to state. Imported liquors attract a similarly disagreeable sin tax, making local brands far more attractive than their quality might suggest. In Tamil Nadu, for example, a whopping 73.5% tax is levied on imported liquor. Restaurant bills often include additional charges (such as a service tax) that usually account for between 10% and 15% of the total cost of your meal.

Time Zone Despite India's vastness, the entire country operates according to the same time zone, 5½ hours ahead of Greenwich Mean Time. That's 9½ hours ahead of Eastern Standard Time (New York) or 10½ when daylight saving time comes into effect in the U.S. *Note:* You may find your sense of time threatened while you're in India; the rule of thumb is *don't panic.* Remember that there's no point in getting worked up about delayed trains and such. In fact, when you arrive on time or ahead of schedule, be thankful. Use "wasted time" to chat with locals.

Tipping Tipping in India is an industry unto itself, and it's a relief to find yourself in an environment like the Oberoi, where individual tipping is not encouraged, for this very reason. Money certainly speeds up most processes, and you're treated with a certain degree of dignity and respect the moment you produce a wad of cash—don't tip and you'll more than likely have to deal with a disgruntled and/or depressed porter/driver/guide. Bear in mind that many of the people who serve you are possibly living on the bread line, and your monetary contribution will be greatly appreciated; handing over an Rs 10 (25¢/10p) or Rs 20 (45¢/20p) note will hardly dent your pocket. Obviously it's not worthwhile to tip someone who hasn't eased your journey, but do reward those drivers, guides, and hotel staff who go out of their way to make your stay an enjoyable one. A driver or guide who's been with you an entire day will be most grateful for an extra Rs 150 to Rs 250 ($4–$5/£2–£3).

Tipping is but one strain of India's all-pervasive *baksheesh* system, which is apparently an accepted means of distributing wealth to the lower echelons of society. As a foreigner, you will be regarded as wealthy, and your endless charity is almost expected by those who are less fortunate. It's therefore an excellent idea to always keep a stash of Rs 10 notes in an easy-to-access pocket, so that you can hand cash to the person who has just carried your bags or given you an unsolicited tour or looked after your shoes (the list is endless), and is now hanging around hopefully. Occasionally, someone will bluntly demand *baksheesh,* which is the same term that may be used by beggars, religious mendicants, and barefoot children looking for a handout. You are not obliged to pay anything, of course, but your conscience and irritation level will probably sway you either way. *Tip:* In Hindu temples, priests will happily encourage you to hand over huge sums of cash, often insisting that the money is for the poor. Be wary of such scams, and bear in mind that many temple officials have grown wealthy on charity intended for the poor.

3

Suggested India Itineraries

India is such a vast country and has so much to see that visitors are tempted to pack in as much as possible. Begin any trip to India with the knowledge that no matter how long your vacation, it will not be long enough. Knowing this can help you make the best of your time here and prevent you from planning a punishing schedule that will not only leave you thoroughly overwhelmed, but with an uncomfortable feeling that you've rushed through most of what you did see.

Despite improved accommodations and transportation options, India is still a challenging destination, and you should always be prepared to take in stride a delayed flight, slow check-in, or upset tummy on, say, a long-distance train. Set aside time to acclimatize and simply unwind—this is, after all, a holiday.

Ideally, you should use this book's "Best of" chapter to work out a route that covers those experiences or sights that really appeal to you, as the range of possible itineraries is endless; what we've suggested below are three rather full programs covering either North or South India over a **2-week period.** If possible, extend your holiday—2 weeks is not enough time to come to grips with India—and set aside more time for those destinations that sound most appealing to you. The fourth itinerary is for those who want to experience India at a languid, easy pace while still taking in key attractions—and there is no better place to do this than in southern India.

You could, of course, combine a trip to both the North and the South, but then you really should stick to one state (even one hotel!) in each area. For instance, you can arrive in Delhi, travel through Agra and then Jaipur, Bundi, and Udaipur, covering this region in 8 days, and then head south to Kerala. In Kerala, you can cover Cochin and Kumarakom (cruising the backwaters) and finish off with a couple of days south of Kovalam, before flying out of Bangalore or Mumbai.

None of the itineraries below includes a trip into any of the fabulous Himalayan regions covered in this book. If you do in fact extend your time in India, make your way from Delhi to the Golden Temple in Amritsar, and then explore the remote valleys of Kinnaur, Lahaul, and Spiti before heading into surreal Ladakh; alternatively, you can take a road trip from Delhi through the picturesque Kumaon in Uttararkhand (formerly known as Uttaranchal), or take off from Kolkata to Darjeeling (book the famous toy train there) and Buddhist Sikkim.

Whatever you decide to do, we highly recommend that you end your holiday in one of India's natural paradises, at least to recover from the sensual assault you'll experience exploring the crowded and often polluted urban areas. These oases include the beaches on the Malabar coast and Goa, the backwaters of Kerala, the lunar landscapes and wooded hills of the Himalayas, and the wonderful hotels and resorts in Rajasthan.

Important: Should limited time force you to include only the most obvious stops in your itinerary, you will invariably only make contact with those locals who depend on you for a living, which regrettably could leave you with a frustrated sense that many of India's inhabitants are grasping, manipulative, or downright pushy. This is why it's so important to get off the beaten tourist track, and book at least one homestay in order to experience firsthand the warmth, hospitality, and generosity of the Indian people and their culture, which celebrates an ancient philosophy of the guest as god.

1 North India Highlights in 16 Days

Stunning Mughal architecture, heritage hotels, old palaces, forts, and colorful markets make North India an exciting experience that imparts a heady, sensory feeling in any visitor. No 2-week trip can exhaustively cover all the main sights, but this itinerary covers many of the most popular tourist attractions of northern India. It's a hectic schedule, so keep in mind that relaxation is required between sights, if only to catch your breath and dwell on what you've seen before leaping forward to the next equally striking sight.

Days ❶–❸: Delhi

You'll most likely arrive in Delhi in the wee hours of the morning. As a general rule, take it easy on Day 1 in India—the country takes serious acclimation. There's no better way to ease into your trip than to start your vacation at Delhi's finest hotel, **The Imperial.** Allow yourself a late morning on Day 2, and hire a car and driver for the day if you want to wander out for some slow-paced sightseeing. Take in central New Delhi's imperial architecture—beginning at **India Gate,** built to commemorate those who died in World War I. From there, set off on foot along **Rajpath** to the beautifully ornate gates of **Rashtrapati Bhavan,** official residence of the president of India. Then drive south to visit the 12th-century **Qutb Minar.** For a break, escape to **Lodi Gardens,** where lawns and golfing greens are studded with the crumbling 15th-century tombs of once-powerful dynasties. A short drive west brings you to the splendid medieval buildings of **Humayun's Tomb** and **Hazrat Nizamuddin Aulia.** Finally, stop off at **Dilli Haat** and check out the range of handicrafts and handmade goods sold by artisans from around India, before you return to The Imperial's **Spice Route** for dinner.

On Day 3, explore **Old Delhi (Shahjahanabad).** Must-sees include **Lal Qila (Red Fort)** and **Jama Masjid,** both built by Shah Jahan, the most prolific architect of the Mughal empire. You can also stop off at vibrant **Gauri Shankar Temple,** which has an 800-year-old lingam (a phallic symbol used in the worship of the Hindu god Shiva); **Sisganj Gurudwara,** an unassuming but atmospheric and welcoming Sikh temple that marks the spot where Guru Tegh Bahadur, the ninth Sikh guru, was beheaded by Aurangzeb; and **Sunehri** and **Fatehpuri masjids.** If you can handle the massive crowds, wander around **Chandni Chowk, Khari Baoli** (reputed to be Asia's biggest spice market), and jam-packed **Kinari Bazaar**—but keep a close watch on your belongings at all times.

Days ❹ & ❺: Varanasi–Khajuraho

Fly into Varanasi, a crumbling maze of a city that rises from the *ghats* (steps) on the western banks of the Ganges River. Varanasi is in many ways quintessential India—it is one of the holiest of Indian pilgrimage sites, home of Shiva, where the devout come to wash away their sins. Many come here to die with the hope that they may achieve *moksha*, salvation

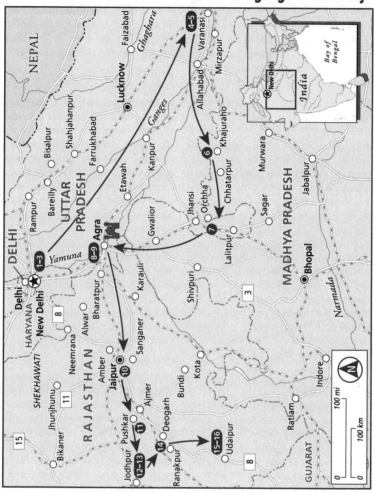

of the soul from the cycle of birth, death, and rebirth. Take a **boat cruise** past the *ghats* at dawn; you can repeat this at sunset or, better still, head for **Dasashwamedh Ghat** to watch the **Ganga Fire Arti.** For 45 minutes, young Brahmin priests perform age-old prayer rituals with conch shells and burning braziers, accompanied by drummers, while children hawk candles for you to light and set adrift. Aside from these must-sees, you should set aside some time to wander the ancient lanes of the **Old City,** particularly those around **Kashi Vishwanath Temple.** When you feel the need for peace and solitude, hire a car and visit **Sarnath,** where Buddha first revealed his Eightfold Path to Nirvana; spend a few hours exploring the archaeological ruins and the modern Buddhist temple and monasteries. Overnight at **Ganges View Guesthouse** in Varanasi, a lovely, comfortable colonial lodge at the edge of the river. On the afternoon of Day 5, take a flight to

Khajuraho. After you check in at your hotel (preferably **The Grand Temple View**), head off immediately to either the Eastern or Southern group of temples, with Samson George as your guide.

Day ❻: Khajuraho

Khajuraho is known the world over for its beautiful, taboo-breaking erotic sculptures, images that are almost as intimately associated with India as the Taj. But the temples also represent an outstanding synthesis of advanced architecture and refined sculpture. Try to enter as soon as the **Western Group** of temples opens (sunrise), not only for the light's quality, but to avoid the busloads of tourists who will arrive later. Take your time admiring the beautifully rendered friezes of gods, nymphs, animals, and energetically twisting bodies locked together in acts of hot-blooded passion. Cover the Western, Eastern, and Southern groups (unless you visited them the day before), ending your day at the 50-minute **sound-and-light show** held at 6:30pm, which provides a fascinating history of Khajuraho.

Day ❼: Orchha

From Khajuraho, drive to Orchha, the deserted royal citadel of Raja Rudra Pratap, on a rocky island on the Betwa River. This is one of India's most fabulous Mughal heritage sites and a wonderfully relaxing stop sandwiched between the intense huckster-heavy destinations of Varanasi/Khajuraho and Agra. Orchha, founded in 1531, was the capital of the Bundela kings until 1738. Today the weathered temples, palaces, and cenotaphs are the royal quarters of emerald parakeets and black-faced langurs, while traditional whitewashed, flat-roofed structures house the laid-back villagers. Besides the **palace complex,** three beautiful temples are worth seeking out, as well as 14 graceful *chhatris* (cenotaphs) commemorating the Orchha rulers, built upstream along the riverbank. Though all

these can be covered in a day, get the most out of this surreally tranquil haven by spending the night at the **Orchha Resort.**

Days ❽ & ❾: Agra

Drive to Jhansi, and take an express train to Agra, home of the **Taj Mahal.** Besides the exquisite Taj, visit the city of **Fatehpur Sikri** and the tombs of **Itmad-ud-Daulah** and **Akbar,** as well as well-preserved **Agra Fort.** If you can afford it (and this one is worth saving up for), overnight at the Oberoi's luxurious **Amarvilãs,** where your room will have a view of the Taj Mahal. Ideally, visit the Taj at dawn and spend the whole morning there. Built by Shah Jahan as an eternal symbol of his love for his favorite wife Mumtaz Mahal, the Taj has immortalized him as one of the great architectural patrons of the world. Not only does the Taj have perfect symmetry, ethereal luminescence, and wonderful proportions, but every inch of marble is covered in exquisite detail.

Day ❿: Jaipur

Drive to Jaipur, where you can explore the **City Palace** and **Amber Fort** in a day; you'll need a little more time if you want to go to **Samode Palace,** an hour's drive away. However, no amount of time is enough for shopping; Jaipur is a **bargain-hunter's** haven, where you will find gorgeous Rajasthani crafts for sale that are hard to resist. In Jaipur, overnight at **Taj Rambagh Palace** (if you prefer an authentic historical experience close to the heart of the city), or **Rajvilãs** (if you enjoy the illusion of being far away from everything combined with absolute luxury). Alternatively, stay at any of the heritage properties reviewed, which cover a range of budgets.

Day ⓫: Pushkar

Late in the afternoon, drive from Jaipur to the temple town of **Pushkar,** stopping en route to view **Dargah Sharif,** the top attraction of **Ajmer** along the way. Get your "Pushkar Passport" as early as possible, which will then free you from further harassment by priests. Spend the night on the shores of Pushkar Lake, preferably at **Pushkar Palace.**

Days ⑫ & ⑬: Pushkar–Jodhpur

Start out early to explore Pushkar, a charming (if very touristy) town surrounding a sacred lake on the eastern edge of the Thar Desert. An important pilgrimage site for Hindus, it remains a hugely atmospheric place despite its popularity with foreign hippies. Browse the **street bazaar,** where you can pick up the most gorgeous throwaway gear, great secondhand books, and CDs at bargain prices. Pushkar can be explored entirely on foot—it will take you about 45 minutes to walk around the holy lake and its 52 *ghats* (stairs). From Pushkar, move on to **Jodhpur,** where you must set aside half a day to visit fabulous **Mehrangarh Fort and Museum,** arguably Rajasthan's most impressive fort, with sheer clifflike walls that soar above the city. Situated on another raised outcrop, with sprawling grounds creating a majestic ambience, is **Umaid Bhawan Palace,** built by Maharaja Umaid Singh as a poverty-relief exercise to aid his drought-stricken subjects. Designed by Henry Lanchester, a great admirer of Lutyens (the man who designed New Delhi), it was started in 1929, took 3,000 laborers 13 years to complete, and remains one of the best examples of Indo-Saracenic Art Deco style. If you don't mind the splurge, try to spend the night at the Palace (preferably

in one of the beautiful Deco-styled historical suites), and catch the setting sun from the edge of the lovely outdoor pool. Breakfast at **The Pillars** restaurant, where you can enjoy a spellbinding view of the fort in the distance. Move on to **Rawla Narlai** or even (if you don't mind a detour) **Deogarh Mahal** (or its more exclusive sister establishment, **Fort Seengh Sagar**) to overnight.

Days ⑭ & ⑮: Udaipur

Enjoy the morning at Rawla Narlai or Deogarh Mahal, then head to Udaipur, stopping at the **Ranakpur temples** (and, if you've left early enough, Kumbhalgarh) en route. Overnight at fabulous, fabled **Lake Palace** or any of the recommended accommodations that have a lake view. Time allowing, take a sunset cruise on the lake. The following day, visit the **City Palace and Museum** in Udaipur. Prime attractions worth pursuing and doable in the time available are the temples at **Nathdwara** and **Eklingji.** Or spend the rest of the day lounging around the pool. If you wish to squeeze in an extra day, do so at **Devi Garh,** 45 minutes outside Udaipur, where you can explore the local village.

Day ⑯: Udaipur–Delhi

Enjoy a leisurely morning roaming Udaipur's lovely bazaars, or relax at the Devi Garh pool, before taking an afternoon flight back to Delhi. If you have space left in your baggage (fat chance!), stop for last-minute souvenirs and gifts before you board your flight home.

2 The Golden Triangle & Rajasthan Highlights

Though this itinerary includes Delhi, Agra, and Jaipur (the "Golden Triangle") and captures many of the essential Rajasthan sights, it does not include **Jaisalmer,** one of Rajasthan's most wonderful destinations, primarily because it's not very easy to get to. In a 2-week vacation that also takes in Delhi and Agra, it would be hard (but not impossible) to include Jaisalmer. Best to extend your stay in India by a few days if you want to cover this oldest "living" fortified city in Rajasthan. Located in the heart of the Thar Desert on India's far western border, Jaisalmer has breathtakingly beautiful sandstone mansions, though its main attraction, **Sonar Killa (Golden Fort),** is reason enough to travel this far west. Though not as impressive as Jodhpur's Mehrangarh Fort, Jaisalmer has its unique charm as an inhabited medieval fort, and the tiny guesthouses that lie within its ramparts offer fabulous views. This is a place with no heavy traffic, minimal pollution, and a wonderful sense of timelessness. So if you do come to Jaisalmer, plan to spend 2 nights here, not least because it takes so long to get to.

Days ❶–❸: Delhi

After your long flight and no doubt middle-of-the-night arrival, have a car waiting for you and check in at Delhi's finest hotel, **The Imperial,** at one of the city's superb new mid-range guesthouses, **Amarya Haveli** or **Amarya Gardens,** or at the best budget accommodations in town, the stylish **Master Paying Residential Guest Accommodation,** which will also arrange an airport transfer (book well in advance). When you feel you're ready to face the world, take in a few New Delhi sights, including **India Gate,** built to commemorate those who died in World War I. Walk from **Rajpath** to **Rashtrapati Bhavan,** where the president of India lives. After you cover the 12th-century **Qutb Minar** complex in South Delhi, grab a table at **Park Balluchi** before browsing the shops in Hauz Khas. After lunch, visit the garden tombs of **Humayun** and of **Hazrat Nizamuddin Aulia** (the saint Sheikh Nizamuddin Aulia), one of the holiest Muslim sites in India. Time allowing, stop off at **Rajghat,** the place where Gandhi was cremated in 1948. Of course if you're here to shop or want to browse, scrap these and head for **Dilli Haat,** a great place to check out the range of handicrafts you'll find on your travels through India. Pick one of Delhi's excellent restaurants for dinner (consider booking a table at the gorgeously designed **Véda,** or check if **Olive Bar and Kitchen** has reopened).

Prepare yourself for the chaos of the crowded streets of 17th-century **Shahjahanabad,** or Old Delhi—just a few kilometers from Connaught Place, it feels a hundred years away, and the pungent smells from the ancient streets are a heady reminder that you are far from home. Still surrounded by crumbling city walls and three surviving gates, the vibrant, bustling Shahjahanabad, built over a period of 10 years by Emperor Shah Jahan, is very much a separate city—predominantly a labyrinth of tiny lanes crowded with rickshaws and lined with *havelis* (Indian "mansions"), their balustrades broken and once-ornate facades defaced with rusted signs and sprouting satellite dishes. Start with imposing **Lal Qila (Red Fort)** and **Jama Masjid,** India's largest mosque. If the crowds haven't left you exhausted, visit **Gauri Shankar Temple, Sisganj Gurudwara,** and **Sunehri** and **Fatehpuri masjids.** The city's lanes and back lanes are exciting to wander through, especially **Chandni Chowk, Khari Baoli** (the spice market), and **Kinari Bazaar**—but do hold on tightly to your belongings.

Days ❹ & ❺: Shekhawati

Make an early start and drive to the Shekhawati region, the open-air art gallery of Rajasthan. Today there are some 30 "painted towns" in the region, but the most essential to include in a first-time itinerary are **Ramgarh, Nawalgarh, Fatehpur,** and **Mandawa.** Mandawa is a quaint town with a number of beautifully painted buildings; it is also centrally located and has the best accommodations in the area. Overnight at **Castle Mandawa** or, if you want to stay in a haveli, at **Mandawa Haveli.**

The Golden Triangle & Rajasthan Highlights

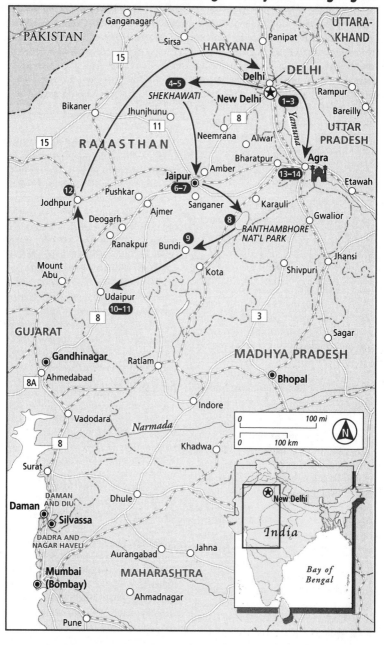

Days ⑥ & ⑦: Jaipur–Ranthambhore
Drive to the "Pink City" of Jaipur. If possible, book into the wonderful **Rajvilās** (more resort than hotel), though Jaipur is one city that has a host of pleasant heritage options to suit every budget. If you prefer the authenticity of a real heritage hotel, book a room in the opulent and well-located **Rambagh Palace** or the more low-key **Samode Haveli.** Explore the **City Palace,** including a visit to Hawa Mahal and Jantar Mantar, and then focus on sites farther afield: **Amber Fort,** first royal residence of the Maharajas of Kachchwaha, lies 11km (6¾ miles) north, while popular **Samode Palace** is an hour's drive away. Jaipur, famous for gems and jewelry, enamel and brassware, blue pottery, embroidered leather footwear, rugs, tie-and-dye cotton fabrics, hand-blocked prints, fine *Kota doria* saris, and ready-made linens and home furnishings, is a **shopper's paradise.** You could spend days bargain-hunting through the region's wonderful crafts, so be prepared to extend your stay by at least a day. If this is not possible, set off on the evening of Day 7 to **Ranthambhore National Park,** and overnight at **Aman-i-Khás,** for the finest "tenting" experience in India.

Day ⑧: Ranthambhore
Take an early-morning or afternoon game drive into the park. Set aside a few hours to visit **Ranthambhore Fort,** whose high, jagged escarpment has towered over the park's forests for nearly a thousand years. Go **tiger tracking;** the highlight of a trip here is spotting a tiger. Even if you don't see a tiger (and do be prepared for this eventuality), the physical beauty of the park is worth experiencing. Other species to watch for include *caracal* (a wildcat), crocodile, *nilgai* (large antelope resembling cattle), *chital* (spotted deer), black buck (delicate buck with spiraling horns), *chinkara* (a dainty gazelle), and sambar. The park also holds leopards, wild boars, sloth bears, and rich birdlife. At night,

unwind around a campfire and swap stories with other travelers, or discuss the fate of the highly endangered tiger.

Day ⑨: Bundi
Drive to the tiny, off-the-beaten-track town of Bundi, where life goes on pretty much as it has for centuries. Approached through a gorge, the town is embraced by the hills of the Aravalli Range, topped by Taragarh Fort. Exploring Bundi's narrow streets, with its tiny cupboardlike shops raised a meter or more above street level, is wonderful, with photo opportunities everywhere: old men beating copper pots into perfect shape; tailors working with beautiful fabrics on ancient Singers; huge mounds of orange, red, and yellow spices offset by fresh, colorful local vegetables; rickshaws carting women adorned in color-saturated saris; and temples blaring live music. Besides wandering the streets, visit **Garh Palace** and **Raniji-ki-Baori,** the state's most impressive step well. Bundi is also a great place to pick up miniature paintings. Overnight at charming **Haveli Braj Bhushanjee.**

Days ⑩ & ⑪: Udaipur
Visit Udaipur's lovely bazaars and towering **City Palace and Museum.** Take a boat ride on Lake Pichola and overnight at either **Lake Palace** or one of the other accommodations with a lake view. Or spend the night at elegant **Devi Garh** just 26km (16 miles) from Udaipur. If the lake is dry, tarry no longer than a day, moving on the next day to one of the excursions outside Udaipur. Begin with the temples at **Nathdwara, Nagda,** and **Eklingji;** then move on to the awesome Jain temples at **Ranakpur, Kumbhalgarh Wildlife Sanctuary,** and magnificent **Kumbhalgarh Fort.** Alternatively, consider another long, full-day trip to **Chittaurgarh,** site of the most legendary Mewar battles. Overnight on Day 11 at **Rawla Narlai** or **Deogarh Mahal,** from where you can head northwest for Jodhpur.

Day ⑫: Jodhpur–Delhi

Make an early start to drive to "the Blue City" of Jodhpur and explore fabulous **Mehrangarh Fort and Museum.** For many, this looming, 15th-century edifice to Rajput valor is still Rajasthan's most impressive fort, with walls that soar like sheer cliffs 122m (400 ft.) high—literally dwarfing the city at its base—and a proud history of never having fallen to its many invaders. Don't miss **Umaid Bhawan Palace,** once the largest private residence in the world—a vivid reminder of the decadence the Rajput rulers enjoyed during the British Raj (if you have an extra day, consider staying at the Palace, now a superb luxury hotel). Catch a flight to Delhi, where you can relax after a rather long day.

Days ⑬ & ⑭: Agra

From Delhi, drive to Agra to visit the jewel of India, the **Taj Mahal,** stopping en route at **Fatehpur Sikri.** Visit **Itmad-ud-Daulah's tomb** and **Agra Fort.** If you have the time, see beautiful **Jama Masjid,** built in 1648 by Jahanara Begum, Shah Jahan's favorite daughter. Overnight at the Oberoi's **Amarvilās,** a worthwhile splurge for your last night in India. Ideally, you can visit the **Taj** at dawn on Day 14 and spend as much time as you like there before you head back to Delhi for your flight out. If you get into Delhi before nightfall, you'll still have time to do last-minute shopping, as most shops are open till at least 7pm.

3 South India in 2 Weeks

South India is where the great Dravidian kingdoms were established, and anyone interested in ancient history and grand temples must visit Tamil Nadu or Karnataka. Here we've included only a few temples, but if you crave more, you'll find an exhaustive variety of exquisitely carved temples to explore. For natural beauty and rejuvenation, there are few places in India like Kerala, India's most verdant state, where we recommend you end your trip. This itinerary also takes you through its tea estates, backwaters, and wildlife parks.

Days ❶ & ❷: Bangalore or Mumbai

Fly straight into Bangalore or Mumbai. You'll probably arrive in the middle of the night, so spend the day relaxing or wandering through Karnataka's capital city. If you're in Bangalore, at some point take in **Bull Temple** on Bugle Hill. Built by the city's original architect, Kempe Gowda, this 16th-century black-granite statue of Nandi (Shiva's sacred bull "vehicle") literally dwarfs its "master," and is kept glistening by regular applications of coconut oil. Stay at either the ultra-modern **Park.hotel** or the **Taj West End** for old-world charm. If you're on a budget, book a room at lovely **Villa Pottipati.** If you arrive in Mumbai instead, you can spend the day relaxing at one of the city's

numerous luxury hotels or at a good-value option like **Gordons.** Set aside a few hours to wander around and acclimate yourself to India's most bustling metropolis.

Day ❸: Chennai–Mamallapuram

From Bangalore (or Mumbai), fly to Chennai (or take the train). You can either head straight down the coast to **Fisherman's Cove** resort (1 hr.) or take a detour to **Kanchipuram** 80km (50 miles) southwest of Chennai to visit the temples there before heading to Fisherman's Cove. If you prefer to be closer to Mamallapuram, book a room at **Temple Bay** resort instead. En route, stop along the scenic East Coast Highway at the cultural centers of **Cholamandalam** and **Dakshina Chitra** for local arts and crafts. At **Cholamandalam Artists' Village,** you can observe artists at work, while **Dakshina Chitra** is a heritage center showcasing different living styles from India's four southern states: Karnataka, Tamil Nadu, Kerala, and Andhra Pradesh.

Day ❹: Mamallapuram

Set out early and take in Mamallapuram's monolithic shrines and rock-cut cave temples, which lie scattered over a landscape heaped with boulders and rocky hillocks. Among these, the excellent **Shore Temple,** built to Lord Shiva, and the **Five Rathas,** a cluster of temples named for the five Pandava brothers of *Mahabharata* fame, are definitely worth seeking out. The celebrated **Arjuna's Penance** is the largest relief-carving on earth. When you've finished your tour, you can enjoy a great seafood meal at one of the numerous beach shacks or restaurants before continuing down the coast to the French colonial town of Pondicherry. Overnight at **Hotel de l'Orient.**

Days ❺ & ❻: Pondicherry

Besides hanging out in your antiques-filled colonial hotel or sauntering around the oceanfront **French Quarter,** you can visit **Auroville,** an interesting experiment in alternative living, also optimistically known as the City of Dawn; or you can join New Age travelers and visit the ashram of **Sri Aurobindo.** While wandering the Quarter, you may want to take a look at the **Sacred Heart of Jesus (Eglise de Sacre Coeur de Jésus),** an 18th-century neo-Gothic Catholic church on South Boulevard; and at the **Church of Immaculate Conception** on Mission Street. At twilight, stroll to **Goubert Salai** (Beach Rd.), where you'll see the colonial **Hôtel de Ville** (now the Municipal Offices building) and a statue of Gandhi standing at the pier. On the evening of Day 6, drive to Chennai, from where you

can take a flight to Madurai. Overnight at the **Taj Garden Retreat, Madurai.**

Day ❼: Madurai

Early in the morning, visit **Shri Meenakshi-Sundareshwarar Temple,** one of South India's biggest, busiest pilgrimage sites. Garish stucco gods, demons, beasts, and heroes smother the various towers in a writhing, fascinating mass of symbolism, vividly painted a riot of bright colors. Near the inner gate, a temple elephant, daubed with eye shadow and blusher, earns her keep by accepting a few rupees in exchange for a blessing—bestowed with a light tap of her dexterous trunk. From here you can wander at will, finding your way at some stage to the **Thousand Pillar Museum,** housed in the impressive 16th-century Hall of a Thousand Pillars. This hall has 985 elegantly sculpted columns, including a set of "musical pillars" that produce the seven Carnatic musical notes when tapped. All around the complex of shrines and effigies, various *pujas* (prayers) and rituals are conducted. Once you're done exploring the site and have spent an hour or so wandering the lanes adjacent to the temple, drive to Munnar, sometimes referred to as Kerala's Scottish highlands. Overnight at **The Siena Village,** a 30-minute drive from Munnar town.

Day ❽: Munnar

Munnar is a collection of vast green tea estates first established by a Scotsman in the late–19th century. Besides enjoying the rolling mists and endless greenery, you can arrange a **tea factory visit** and a stopover at the **Tea Museum.** To get up close to some of the world's last Nilgiri tahr (a variety of mountain goat or ibex), visit nearby **Eravikulam National Park.** Existing only in the mountain grasslands of the Western *ghats* at altitudes above 2,000m (6,560 ft.), the tahr is as endangered as the tiger.

South India in 2 Weeks

Day ❾: Periyar

Drive to **Periyar Wildlife Sanctuary**, originally the hunting grounds of the Maharajah of Travancore. The park covers 777 sq. km (303 sq. miles) and is divided into core, buffer, and tourist zones. Although this is a tiger reserve, tiger sightings are rare, particularly in the tourist zone, but the reserve is also home to the elephant, sloth bear, sambar, Indian bison or gaur, wild dog, leopard, spotted deer, Malabar flying squirrel, barking deer, and Nilgiri tahr, as well as some 260 species of birds. More than 2,000 species of flowering plants grow here, including at least 150 different kinds of orchids. Organize a **private boat launch** ride from where you can view animals coming to drink at the water's edge. You can also take one of the 3-hour **daily walks,** which give you the opportunity to admire the area's stunning flora. To ensure you have a close-up encounter with an elephant, go on a 30-minute **elephant ride** in the park. Overnight at **Shalimar Spice Garden Resort.**

Day ❿: Kumarakom

Drive to the heart of Kerala's backwaters region to Kumarakom, which has by far the best accommodations. Idle away the hours on a backwaters cruise, indulge in Ayurvedic therapies, and laze under the tropical sun—that's about as busy as your day is likely to get. Overnight at the **Kumarakom Lake Resort.**

Day ⑪: Houseboat

Reset your watch to a rhythm of life that has remained relatively unchanged for centuries: Board a *kettuvallam,* one of the long, beautifully crafted cargo boats that ply the waterways. The houseboat experience allows you to aimlessly drift past villages, temples, and churches and be thoroughly exposed to the rural lifestyle of the backwaters. As you drift along, you can watch women, unperturbed by your presence, wash their long ebony tresses or pound away at laundry, while children play at the water's edge, men dive for mussels, and elephants and water buffalo wade at will. Although the onboard facilities might strike some as rather basic, you'll be spoiled rotten by your private team—a guide, a cook, and a pilot—who work hard to make your experience unique and exceptional.

Days ⑫ & ⑬: Kochi (Cochin)

Travel north to Kochi and settle into a hotel in **Fort Kochi** (we suggest either The Brunton Boatyard Hotel or the Malabar Residency), then explore Fort Kochi on foot. Start your tour at the harbor near Vasco da Gama Square, where you can watch the **Chinese fishing nets,** then visit **St. Francis Church** and **Santa Cruz Cathedral.** Stop to admire the facade of **Koder House**—built in 1808 by Jewish patriarch Samuel Koder, it's a good example of the hybrid Indo-European style that developed in Cochin. Also nearby is the **Pierce Leslie Bungalow,** a charming 19th-century mansion reflecting Portuguese and Dutch influences on local architecture. Take an auto-rickshaw to Mattancherry, where you should visit the **Dutch (Mattancherry) Palace** and **Paradesi Synagogue** before discovering the fragrant scents of Kerala's **spice warehouses.** Make time to visit a few of the antiques warehouses, where some real treasures are to be found. A **sunset cruise** around the harbor is another must; it's the best way to enjoy the most-photographed of Cochin's historic sights, the Chinese fishing nets that form wonderful silhouettes against a red- and orange-hued sky.

Day ⑭: Wyanad

From Cochin, take the early Cannanore Express train to Calicut, from where you can catch a taxi for the 2-hour journey to Sulthan Bathery in Wyanad. Without a doubt the best accommodations, **Tranquil Resorts** is a wonderful homestay on a 162-hectare (400-acre) coffee and vanilla plantation at the edge of Wyanad National Park. Visit tea, pepper, cardamom, coffee, banana, and coconut plantations, or take one of the many splendid walks on this scenic estate; alternatively, take a trip into the park or to Edakkal Caves. Either way, the hospitality of Victor and Ranjini Dey at this gorgeous planter's bungalow makes for an excellent end-of-trip sojourn.

Day ⑮: Wyanad–Calicut–Home

Hearts heavy with regret, you must now make your way back to Calicut to fly to either Mumbai or Bangalore to connect to your flight home. If you arrive in Mumbai, you will need to transfer from the domestic to the international airport. En route, you can stop off for dinner at one of the superb restaurants near the airport (Dum Pukht or Dakshin at the ITC Grand Maratha Sheraton; or Stax, the Italian restaurant at the Hyatt Regency, if you'd prefer a less spice-intense meal), before you catch the late-night flight home.

4 A Leisurely Southern Sojourn

South India is perfect for a slow-paced 2-week holiday that's more unhurried escape than hectic vacation filled with must-see sights. This itinerary does explore a few tourist sites, but mostly it's about relaxing and enjoying a few beautiful and varied environments. Kerala is the ideal place to unwind and indulge; this is, after all, where succumbing to therapeutic Ayurvedic massages and treatments is as mandatory as idling away an afternoon aboard a slowly drifting *kettuvallam,* or sipping coconut water under a tropical sun.

Days ❶ & ❷: Mumbai

Though Mumbai is India's busiest city, it's also a perfect place to begin an unhurried vacation. From the airport, head either to the **Taj Mahal Palace and Tower** (only a Heritage Wing room will do) or **The Oberoi;** enjoy the warm weather on a sun-bed by the pool, or make your way to the hotel spa for the pampering you deserve after that long journey. Alternatively, a stay at **Gordon House Hotel,** Colaba's sexiest lodging option, will suit party animals who appreciate the in-house nightclub. Mumbai doesn't have a wealth of historical attractions; it's a city you *experience* rather than sightsee, and sampling the restaurants' fare should be high on your must-do list. From your hotel you can also explore on foot the **Marine Drive/Chowpatty Beach** area, and if you're at all inspired by Gothic Victorian architecture, plan a jaunt through Mumbai's older districts. Stop off at the **Gateway of India,** from where it's a 15-minute walk north to Fort, passing the **Prince of Wales Museum** as well as a host of Raj-era Gothic architectural highlights. From the museum, continue to **Flora Fountain** and beyond to **Victoria Terminus Station.** Wander back to the Fountain, taking in the impressive **High Court** building and the **Rajabai Clock Tower,** which overlooks the Bombay University complex. Some of the best restaurants in Mumbai are in this general neighborhood, so take your pick. If you want to sample the coastal seafood for which

Mumbai is famous, go no farther than **Mahesh Lunch Home** in Fort.

Days ❸ & ❹: Goa

Fly to Goa, old Portuguese colony and beach paradise. Take your pick of accommodations, from sprawling beachfront five-star hotels to small boutique hotels. If pampering is part of your plan, book into the **Pousada Tauma,** a gorgeous getaway and Ayurvedic retreat with a superb in-house restaurant. If you can drag yourself away from the beach and poolside, explore Old Goa; most sights are clustered together, so it can be covered in a few hours. These include **Arch of the Viceroys,** built in 1597 in commemoration of the arrival of Vasco da Gama in India; **Church of St. Cajetan,** modeled after St. Peter's in Rome; and **Adil Shah's Gate,** a simple lintel supported by two black basalt columns. Southwest of St. Cajetan's are the highlights of Old Goa: splendid **Sé Cathedral,** said to be larger than any church in Portugal; and the **Basilica of Bom Jesus (Cathedral of the Good Jesus).** Nearby is the **Convent and Church of St. Francis of Assisi,** while up the hill are the ruins of the **Church of St. Augustine;** below are the **Church and Convent of Santa Monica** and the **Chapel of the Weeping Cross.**

Days ❺ & ❻: Hampi

Take the biweekly train from Goa to Hampi, endure an overnight bus ride, or fly to Bangalore the previous evening, from where you can get a convenient overnight train to Hospet. Check in at **Hampi's Boulders.** Spend your time leisurely exploring the ancient city, whose isolated ruins are scattered among impossibly balanced wind-smoothed boulders and immense stretches of verdant landscape. Highlights are fabulous **Virupaksha Temple** and **Vitthala Temple,** dedicated to an incarnation of Vishnu and one of the most spectacular of Hampi's monuments; also make sure to see the **royal enclosure,** which incorporates the ruined palaces where the Vijayanagara kings would have lived and held court. Not much survives, but you can still visit **Hazara Rama Temple** (where the royals went to worship), a small **stepped tank,** and **Mahanavami Dibba** (a platform where performances and entertainment were held). On the outskirts of the royal complex, you will see the *zenana* enclosure, marked by the two-story Indo-Saracenic pavilion, **Kamala (Lotus) Mahal,** and, just outside the enclosure, the awesome **Elephant Stables.**

Days ❼ & ❽: Kochi (Cochin)

Take the train to Bangalore and from there fly to Kochi, where you should get a room in Fort Kochi (at either the **Brunton Boatyard Hotel** or the **Malabar Residency**). Fort Kochi can be explored on foot. Visit **St. Francis Church** and **Santa Cruz Cathedral;** stop to gaze at the famous **Chinese fishing nets.** Drive to **Mattancherry Palace (Dutch Palace)** and **Paradesi Synagogue** before following your nose to the **spice warehouses.** Antiques lovers will be bowled over by Kochi's antiques warehouses full of real treasures. Take a **sunset cruise** around the harbor at dusk and then dine on a seafood platter at one of Kochi's wonderful restaurants.

Days ❾ & ❿: Kumarakom

Drive to Alleppey to experience Kerala's backwaters. Spend 2 nights at one of the wonderful homestays in the region (**Philipkutty's Farm** or **Emerald Isle**) or on a **houseboat;** alternatively, book into **Coconut Lagoon** or **Kumarakom Lake Resort.** If you opt for the houseboat experience, you bed aboard a *kettuvallam,* one of the long, beautifully crafted cargo boats that ply the waterways—a wonderful way to experience the rural lifestyle of the backwaters as you aimlessly drift past villages, temples, and churches. If the facilities strike you as too basic, and if you're not keen on a homestay either, spend the night at the intimate **Kayaloram Lake Resort** and take a sunset backwaters cruise instead.

Days ⓫, ⓬ & ⓭: Kovalam & Beyond

Drive to **Trivandrum** and continue beyond it to the famous **Surya Samudra Beach Garden.** Spread over 8 hectares (20 acres) amid terraced gardens, Surya has such a glorious setting that as soon as you arrive you will wonder why you didn't come straight here in the first place. Accommodations are in the centuries-old carved wooden cottages transplanted from villages around Kerala. Much of your time here is best spent lazing by the infinity pool carved out of the rock bed or on one of the two beaches. Spend the rest of your time here enjoying Ayurvedic treatments and massages. If you can bear to tear yourself away, take an early-morning excursion to sacred **Kanyakumari,** the southernmost tip of India, where three oceans meet and crowds worship the sunrise; or to **Padmanabhapuram Palace,** for several centuries the traditional home of Kerala's Travancore royal family. Alternatively, spend a night in the hills nearby at **Duke's Forest Lodge,**

located on the edge of a river and rubber plantation near Pepara Sanctuary. Book a pool pavilion—each with a plunge pool—and enjoy a romantic getaway before heading back to Surya Samudra for your final night in India.

Day ⑭: Trivandrum–Home
Completely relaxed and rejuvenated, make your way back to Trivandrum, and from there fly to Mumbai or Bangalore for your international flight back home. If you arrive in Mumbai, where you will have many hours before your flight, enjoy dinner at one of the marvelous restaurants in Mumbai's suburbs, since the airport has no dining facilities.

4

Mumbai: City of Dreamers

Mumbai will bowl you over. Teetering on the edge of the Arabian Sea, its heaving population barely contained by palm-fringed beaches, India's commercial capital, formerly known as Bombay, is a vibrant, confident metropolis that's tangibly high in energy.

Originally home to Koli fisherfolk, the seven swampy islands that today comprise Mumbai originally commanded little significance. The largest of the islands was part of a dowry given by Portugal to England, which promptly took control of the six remaining islands and then leased the lot to the East India Company for a paltry £10. Massive land-reclamation projects followed, and by the 19th century all seven islands had been fused to form one narrow promontory and India's principal port.

Today the city continues to draw fortune-seekers from all over India. More than a hundred newcomers squeeze their way in every day, adding to the coffers of greedy slum lords and placing the city, which already has a population density four times greater than New York City's, on target for a population of 22 million by 2015. As India's economy booms, Mumbai's real estate prices are hitting an all-time high. In early 2007 1,400-square-foot apartments in what's considered a posh Mumbai neighborhood priced at over a million dollars! The effect of this of course is that prices in general have soared as businesses shell out more money for leased properties.

A city with a dual identity, Mumbai is as flamboyantly materialistic as it is

downright choked by squalor and social drudgery. The citizens of Mumbai pay almost 40% of India's taxes, yet half of its 18 million people are homeless. While the moneyed groovers and label-conscious shakers retire in luxury behind the security gates of their million-dollar Malabar Hill apartments, emaciated survivors stumble home to cardboard shacks in congested shantytowns or onto tiny patches of open pavement. At every intersection you are accosted by these destitute hopefuls, framed against a backdrop of Bollywood vanity boards and massive advertisements promoting provocative underwear and sleek mobile-phone technology. Feeding into this social schizophrenia are the one-dollar whores, half-naked fakirs, underworld gunmen, bearded *sadhus,* globe-trotting DJs, and, of course, movie moguls and wannabe starlets.

It's not just the economic disparities that are bewildering: Looking down from the Hanging Gardens on Malabar Hill, you see the assertively modern metropolis of Nariman Point—but just a little farther south, on Malabar Hill, is the Banganga Tank, one of the city's holiest sites, where apartment blocks overlook pilgrims who come to cleanse their souls by bathing in its mossy waters. Twenty-first-century Mumbai is brassy and vital, yet it can also transport you to another epoch. It is, in this sense, a quintessentially Indian city, encapsulating the raw paradoxes of the entire subcontinent.

Your plane will almost certainly touch down in Mumbai—it's the most common point of arrival for visitors, and well connected to the rest of the country (including the UNESCO World Heritage Sites of Ajanta and Ellora, also located in Maharashtra, and described at the end of the chapter). If you're looking for peace and quiet in meditative surroundings, move on as fast as jet lag and arrival times dictate. But if you want to experience modern India at its vibrant best, and dine at what are arguably some of the finest restaurants in the country, tarry for at least 2 days. You may arrive appalled by the pitiful faces of the poor, shocked by the paradox of such wealth and poverty, and overcome by the heavy, heady stench and toxic pollution. But give India's dream factory a little time, and you'll discover it has a sexy, smoldering soul, and a head-spinning groove worth getting hip to.

1 Arrival & Orientation

ARRIVING

BY PLANE   Mumbai's sprawling **Chhatrapati Shivaji International Airport** (© **022/2682-9000** or -9112) has been recently renovated, but don't expect world-class facilities. The airport is located in Sahar, 30km (19 miles) north of the center (which is why it's often called Sahar Airport). Its flights usually arrive and depart between midnight and dawn, which can make finding your feet difficult. A **Government of India Tourist Office** (© **022/2682-9248**) at the airport should be open 24 hours but—as is the case in most of India's tourist offices—it's certainly not the best place to obtain advice; you'll find the contents of this book far more useful.

Because you will no doubt have to wait in line for foreign exchange (there is only one small booth), it is advisable that you arrange an **airport transfer** to meet you—important, too, because you will be accosted by a loud, expectant mass of touts and taxi drivers the minute you exit the terminal doors, all of whom need to be treated with a degree of caution. If you are expecting a pickup, don't get sidetracked or deterred from boarding the correct hotel shuttle—ignore strangers offering help.

Should you need to hire a taxi, make use of the reliable **prepaid taxi service** (© **022/2682-9922**); a trip to a city-center hotel should cost from Rs 340 to Rs 400 ($8–$10/£4–£5) and an additional Rs 10 (25¢/10¢) per bag. (Expect to pay well over double these rates for a hotel airport transfer, but you'll also get a much better vehicle to travel in.) Because many international flights arrive late at night, traffic delays are usually not a problem, and you should be at your hotel within an hour even if you're staying downtown.

Note: **Auto-rickshaws** are banned from the city's center, so don't rely on these unless your hotel is located in the immediate vicinity of the airport.

DOMESTIC AIRPORT   If you are flying direct from Mumbai's international airport on to the next destination, note that you will have to transfer (there is a free bus; make sure you get on it) to the **Santa Cruz Domestic Airport** (© **022/2615-6500;** 4km/2½ miles from the international airport and 26km/16 miles north of the city). (Note that the domestic airport has also, bizarrely, been renamed **Chhatrapati Shivaji International Airport,** so it's best to refer to the airports by their location for example, Sahar or Santa Cruz airport). You will have to spend the rest of the night in a very uncomfortable airport seat. If you have arrived at Santa Cruz and plan to spend some time in Mumbai, you can catch a metered taxi from the airport, which should set you back about Rs 300 ($7/£4) for a trip to a hotel in the city center. Since domestic flights are likely to arrive during the day, be prepared for a long, congested,

Mumbai

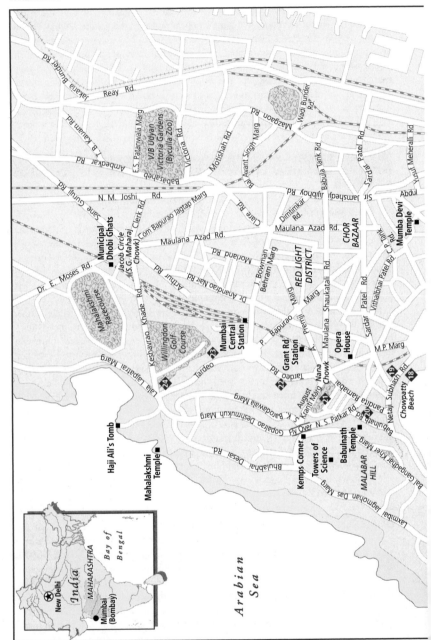

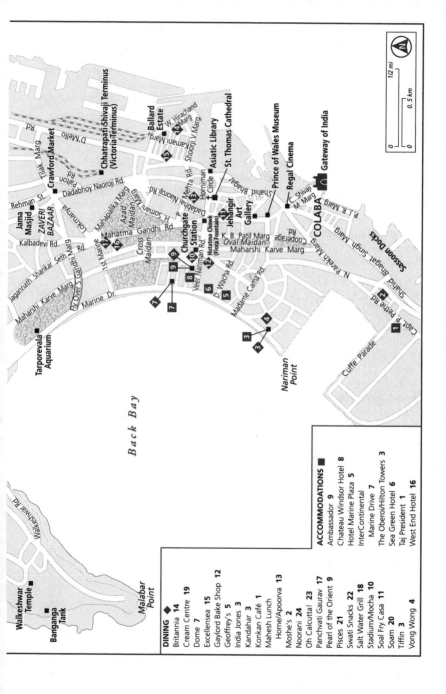

DINING ♦
Britannia **14**
Cream Centre **19**
Dome **7**
Excellensea **15**
Gaylord Bake Shop **12**
Geoffrey's **5**
India Jones **3**
Kandahar **3**
Konkan Café **1**
Mahesh Lunch
  Home/Apoorva **13**
Moshe's **2**
Noorani **24**
Oh Calcutta! **23**
Panchvati Gaurav **17**
Pearl of the Orient **9**
Pisces **21**
Swati Snacks **22**
Salt Water Grill **18**
Stadium/Mocha **10**
Soal Fry Casa **11**
Soam **20**
Tiffin **3**
Vong Wong **4**

ACCOMMODATIONS ■
Ambassador **9**
Chateau Windsor Hotel **8**
Hotel Marine Plaza **5**
InterContinental
  Marine Drive **7**
The Oberoi/Hilton Towers **3**
Sea Green Hotel **6**
Taj President **1**
West End Hotel **16**

frustrating journey into Mumbai. There's also a tourist office at the domestic airport (© 022/2615-6920; daily 7am–11pm).

BY TRAIN   If you are traveling from Central, South, or East India, you will no doubt arrive at "VT," Victoria Station (otherwise known as Chhatrapati Shivaji Terminus or CST). A taxi ride farther downtown, to Colaba, should take about 10 to 15 minutes. From the north, you'll arrive at Mumbai Central Station; from here you will have to brave the traffic and take a taxi to your destination.

WHEN TO GO

Mumbai's humidity—even in the small hours of the morning—is felt instantly, and the sun shines year-round, except in the monsoon months. You always seem drenched in warm sweat, and the heat can be terribly cruel, making sightseeing far less agreeable than a tour of the city's wonderful restaurants and drinking holes. Winter (Nov–Feb) is still hot, although not so entirely unpleasant; the sultry sea air sets the tone for an adventure in exotic dining and an intoxicating jaunt through lively, Victorian-era streets that are constantly crammed with people. The only real relief from the heat comes for brief periods in December and January, and midyear, when the annual monsoon drenches the city with heavy, nonstop tropical rains.

CITY LAYOUT

Mumbai city lies on the western coast of India, on a thin peninsula that extends southward almost parallel to the mainland. At the southern end of this peninsula are Colaba and the adjoining Fort area, on the east of which lies Mumbai's deep, natural harbor and India's busiest port. West of Fort, hugging the Arabian Sea, is the popular promenade Marine Drive, which begins at the business district of Nariman Point and terminates at Chowpatty Beach and Malabar Hill. These are the focal nodes for tourists who, unlike the locals, often refer to the area as downtown. In fact, locals say they are going "into town," by which they mean they are going toward South Mumbai, the area stretching south from Mahim Creek to Colaba. South Mumbai is where most tourists choose to base themselves (though there are those who prefer to stay in the Bandra/Juhu area). It is the historic heart of the city, with attractions like the Gateway of India and the Prince of Wales Museum, and the widest selection of restaurants and accommodations. The South Mumbai neighborhoods are described in detail below, but to see where most Mumbaikars (or Bombayites) live, including the jet-set stars, it may be worthwhile to take a trip into one of the suburbs. Of these, the most interesting (and a good alternative to South Mumbai if you're staying just 1 night—it's a great deal closer to the airport) are Bandra and Juhu. Extending northward of Churchgate is the Western Railway local train line, and moving north of Victoria Terminus (or CST; see below) is the Central Railway network. Together, these two suburban train systems transport over 6 million commuters each day.

NEIGHBORHOODS IN BRIEF

COLABA

Because of its proximity to most of Mumbai's landmarks and colonial buildings, this, the southern tip of Mumbai, is the real tourist hub. In many ways its location has contributed to Colaba's slightly seedy side, though certain areas have recently been rejuvenated. Many of the city's budget accommodations are situated along **Colaba Causeway,** punctuated by (at the northernmost end) the **Taj Mahal**

Colaba

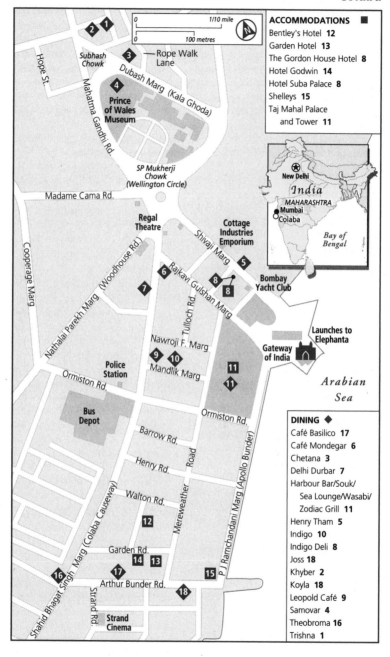

0 1/10 mile
0 100 metres

ACCOMMODATIONS ■
Bentley's Hotel **12**
Garden Hotel **13**
The Gordon House Hotel **8**
Hotel Godwin **14**
Hotel Suba Palace **8**
Shelleys **15**
Taj Mahal Palace
and Tower **11**

Hope St.
Subhash Chowk
Rope Walk Lane
Dubash Marg (Kala Ghoda)
Mahatma Gandhi Rd.
Prince of Wales Museum
SP Mukherji Chowk (Wellington Circle)
Madame Cama Rd.
Regal Theatre
Cottage Industries Emporium
Shivaji Marg
Rajkavi Gulshan Marg
Woodhouse Rd.
Nathalai Parekh Marg (Woodhouse Rd.)
Tulloch Rd.
Bombay Yacht Club
Cooperage Marg
Nawroji F. Marg
Launches to Elephanta
Police Station
Mandlik Marg
Gateway of India
Ormiston Rd.
Bus Depot
Ormiston Rd.
Barrow Rd.
Henry Rd.
Mereweather Road
Shahid Bhagat Singh Marg (Colaba Causeway)
P J Ramchandani Marg (Apollo Bunder)
Walton Rd.
Garden Rd.
Arthur Bunder Rd.
Strand Rd.
Strand Cinema

Arabian Sea

New Delhi
India
MAHARASHTRA
Mumbai
Colaba
Bay of Bengal

DINING ◆
Café Basilico **17**
Café Mondegar **6**
Chetana **3**
Delhi Durbar **7**
Harbour Bar/Souk/
    Sea Lounge/Wasabi/
    Zodiac Grill **11**
Henry Tham **5**
Indigo **10**
Indigo Deli **8**
Joss **18**
Khyber **2**
Koyla **18**
Leopold Café **9**
Samovar **4**
Theobroma **16**
Trishna **1**

Hotel, Mumbai's most famous, which is located opposite the **Gateway of India,** Mumbai's most famous marker, across from which you can see the oil rigs of Bombay High. **Apollo Bunder** refers to the area around the Gateway of India, though the easiest way to get there is to ask for directions to the Taj. Southwest of this is **Cuffe Parade,** an upmarket residential neighborhood, and farther south, the restricted navy Cantonment area.

If you travel west from Colaba to the other end of the narrow peninsula until you hit the sea, you'll arrive at **Nariman Point,** starting point of Marine Drive. Nariman Point was once Mumbai's most bustling business district but is now facing decline (though many airline offices and several foreign embassies are still situated here).

FORT

North from Colaba is the business neighborhood called Fort. By day the area comprising **Fort, Fountain, Ballard Estate,** and **VT** (or **CST**) **Station** is an extremely busy commercial district, but at night the neighborhood is rather forlorn, with many of the large parks *(maidans)* empty. A little beyond CST Station is **Crawford Market,** which leads to the heart of Mumbai's congested markets.

Just west of the Fort area is **Churchgate Station. Veer Nariman Road,** the street leading from Churchgate Station to Marine Drive, is lined with restaurants.

MARINE DRIVE/CHOWPATTY BEACH

Marine Drive stretches from Nariman Point in the south to Malabar Hill in the north. Edged by a broad promenade that follows the curve of the seafront, this is a very popular place to take a morning or evening walk. At night the streetlights along this drive accentuate the dramatic arch of the

bay, giving it the name **Queen's Necklace,** though obviously this term is less frequently used these days. Marine Drive is a long arterial road that runs along the curve of Back Bay. This road ends at **Chowpatty Beach** and then climbs uphill toward the very expensive and prestigious neighborhood of Malabar Hill.

MALABAR HILL/BREACH CANDY/PEDDAR ROAD

Malabar Hill connects to Napean Sea Road and beyond to **Breach Candy, Kemps Corner,** and **Peddar Road**— all upmarket residential areas. Several hotels in this area and particularly along Kemps Corner are good options for tourists who want to avoid the heavily touristed parts of Colaba and Churchgate.

CENTRAL MUMBAI

Central Mumbai extends beyond Crawford Market through **Mohammedali Road** and **Kalbadevi** to **Mumbai Central Station** and the fast-growing commercial areas of **Lower Parel.** The greatest developments are occurring around **Phoenix Mills,** where some of the erstwhile mill buildings have been converted into shopping complexes, restaurants, and gaming and entertainment spots. West from Mumbai Central Station are **Tardeo** and **Haji Ali,** where you drive along yet another of Mumbai's bays.

SUBURBS (BANDRA & JUHU)

North of Mahim Creek extend Mumbai's vast suburbs, from where millions commute daily. First up, just across the creek, is Bandra which, along with Juhu and Andheri (West), just north of it, is where Bollywood stars live and hang out. Although it's not really on the tourist circuit, Bandra, being home to a sizable portion of the city's elite, is packed with lively restaurants, steamy clubs, trendy bars, and countless shops. At night young people gather along Carter Road and Turner Road to drink, smoke (cigarettes or dope), and chill out before making their way to favored clubs. The area around Juhu Beach is where many of the city's middle classes escape; crowded with a host of vendors flogging popular eats, ice cream, coconuts, and fresh fruit juice, it's worth a visit to soak up Mumbai's carnivalesque atmosphere rather than contemplate sunbathing on the beach, which is filthy, or venturing into the even dirtier seawater. It does, however, have some fine hotels, restaurants, and nightclubs—Enigma at Juhu's JW Marriott Hotel is one of Mumbai's most happening spots.

Just east of Juhu lie the city's two airports and a host of upmarket hotels. The area of **Andheri (East)** around the international airport has become a crowded (and rather polluted) commercial and residential neighborhood. Yet many business visitors prefer to stay in this part of town if their business lies here, to avoid the stressful commute. Farther north in the suburbs is **Goregaon,** home to Film City, where many Bollywood films are shot; past that is **Borivali,** from where Mumbai's most popular theme park, EsselWorld, is accessible. Beyond, the city goes on (and on), with little to tempt the visitor.

VISITOR INFORMATION

Technically, there are tourist information desks at both airports, and these should be open for all flight arrivals. Don't count on it, however, and don't expect a lot of help, other than being handed a brochure or booklet and given some bland details of available hotels. That said, a good source of visitor information is the comprehensive *City Info* booklet, published monthly and available at tourist information offices as well as upmarket hotels and even certain pubs and restaurants. For the best listings of the city's current events and what's hip and happening, look no further than the twice-monthly magazine *Time Out,* available at all newsstands. The main **Government of India Tourist Office** (123 Maharishi Karve Rd., Churchgate; ℂ **022/2207-4333** or -4334; Mon–Fri 8:30am–6pm, Sat 8:30am–2pm) is where to head for general tourist-related information, but if you're staying at one of the city's better hotels, your concierge will be a good source of information on sightseeing, performances, events, and activities.

FAST FACTS: Mumbai

Airlines Domestic airlines connect Mumbai to nearly every corner of the subcontinent. For the best service, try **Kingfisher Airlines** (ℂ **022/6649-9393** or 1800/180-0101; www.flykingfisher.com) or **Jet Airways** (ℂ **022/3989-3333** or 1800/225-522; www.jetairways.com). **Indian** (ℂ **022/2202-3031** or 1800/180-1407; www.indianairlines.in) is the state-owned carrier with a wide network and somewhat indifferent service. The slew of new low-cost airlines includes **Air Deccan** (ℂ **98-9257-7008** or 080/3900-8888), **SpiceJet** (ℂ **1800/180-3333;** www.spicejet.com), **GoAir** (ℂ **1800/222-111** or 09223/222-111; www.goair.in), and **IndiGo** (ℂ **99-1038-3838** or 800/180-3838; http://book.goindigo.in). **Jet Lite** (the erstwhile Air Sahara; ℂ **1800/22-3020;** www.jetlite.com) is a low-cost airlines run by Jet Airways.

Ambulance Dial 🕿 **102** or **105** (for a cardiac ambulance). You can also contact **Bacha's Nursing Home** (La Citadelle, New Marine Lines; 🕿 **022/2203-2977** or 022/2200-0963) or **Bombay Hospital** (12 New Marine Lines; 🕿 **022/2206-7676**). Or try **Swati Ambulance** (🕿 **022/2387-1215**), which has 24-hour service.

American Express The office is near the Jehangir Art Gallery at Kala Ghoda (Trade Wings Ltd., 30 K Dubash Marg, Kala Ghoda; 🕿 **022/6634-4334**). Hours are Monday to Saturday 10:30am to 6:00pm.

Area Code The area code for **Mumbai** is **022**.

ATMs Undoubtedly the most convenient way to get local currency, ATMs are to be found throughout the city, most of them with 24-hour security guards. Your best bet for a quick transaction is to head for an ATM belonging to either HDFC, HSBC, ICICI, SBI, or Standard Chartered banking system.

Bookstores **Crossword Bookstore** (Mohammedbhai Mansion, Kemps Corner, below flyover; 🕿 **022/2384-2001** through -2004) has a Western ambience and Mumbai's largest selection of books. Alternatively, stop at **Shankar's Book Stall** (🕿 **92-2411-1790**), a tiny stall just outside Café Mondegar, Colaba Causeway; or at **Strand Book Stall** (Sir PM Rd., Fort; 🕿 **022/2266-1994** or -1719), which offers books at great discounts. Inside the Taj Mahal Hotel is **Nalanda** (🕿 **022/2287-1306**), a good spot to shop for coffee-table books and travel-related selections.

Car Hires See "Getting Around," below.

Consulates **U.S.:** Lincoln House, 78 Bhulabhai Desai Rd., Breach Candy (🕿 **022/2363-3611** through -3618); Monday to Friday 8:30am to 1pm and 1:45 to 5pm; closed second and last Fridays of the month and on Indian and American national holidays. **U.K.:** Second floor, Maker Chambers IV, J. B. Marg, 521 Nariman Point (🕿 **022/6650-2222**); Monday to Thursday 8am to 4pm and Friday 8am to 1pm. **Australia:** Maker Chamber VI, Nariman Point (🕿 **022/6669-2000**); Monday to Friday 9am to 5pm. **Canada:** Fort House, sixth floor, 221 D.N. Rd., Fort (🕿 **022/6749-4444**); Monday to Thursday 9am to 5:30pm; Friday 9am to 3pm. **South Africa:** Gandhi Mansion, Altamount Road, near Kemp's Corner (🕿 **022/2351-3725**); Monday to Friday 8:30am to 5pm.

Currency Exchange **Thomas Cook India** is located in the Thomas Cook Building, Dr. D. Naoroji Road, Fort (🕿 **022/2204-8556**), and is open Monday to Saturday 9:30am to 6pm. Or head to the American Express Office (details above).

Directory Assistance The main directory inquiry number is 🕿 **197** (if you can get through). For talking Yellow Pages service or any other useful information, call the much more helpful **Just Dial Services** at 🕿 **022/2888-8888**, **Times Infoline** at 🕿 **022/6700-5555**, or **DNA Infoline** at 🕿 **022/2666-6666**.

Drugstores In South Mumbai, **Bombay Hospital Chemist** (🕿 **022/2206-7676**) is open 24 hours. Near Juhu, call **Empire Chemists** (🕿 **022/2671-8970**).

Emergencies See "Police," below.

Hospitals **Breach Candy Hospital**, 60 Warden Rd., Breach Candy (🕿 **022/2367-1888** or -2888; casualty 022/3667-809), is open 24 hours and is one of the most advanced and reliable hospitals in Mumbai. **Bombay Hospital**, 12 New Marine Lines (🕿 **022/2206-7676**), is more centrally located and has a 24-hour ambulance service. Near Bandra/Juhu, **Lilavati Hospital** (© **022/2643-8281** or -8282) is a modern facility.

Internet Access For a cheap (about Rs 30/70¢/40p per hour), reliable connection, pop into **LSM PCO Service,** Shop no. 7B Abubakar Mansion, Mahakavi Bhushan Rd., Colaba (© **022/2202-2452**). Open daily 9am to 11pm, it's just around the corner from Café Mondegar. For better broadband speeds, try **Amrut Cyberworld Cybercafé** near Churchgate Station (8 Prem Court, behind Samrat Hotel; © **022/2284-0174**).

Newspapers & Magazines For the scoop on day-to-day city news, buy a copy of the local rag *Mid Day,* sold on street corners and at intersections from early in the morning. *The Times of India* and *Hindustan Times* are both good national dailies that provide the lowdown on current and social events. *Time Out Mumbai* is a twice-monthly magazine that has the best listings of events and happenings, as well as interesting city features.

Police Call © **1090** for a general police emergency number. Local numbers are: Colaba © 022/2285-6817; Cuffe Parade © 022/2218-8009; Juhu © 022/2618-4308; Khar © 022/2649-6030; Malabar Hill © 022/2363-7571; Andheri © 022/2683-1562.

Post Office You'll find the **General Post Office** near Victoria Terminus, off Nagar Chowk (© **022/2262-0956**). It's open Monday to Saturday 9am to 8pm.

Restrooms Make full use of your bathroom facilities *before* you head out for a day of sightseeing. Use only restrooms in hotels and upmarket restaurants.

Taxis See "Getting Around," below.

Travel Agencies Contact IATA–affiliated **NAC Travels Pvt Ltd,** 412 Raheja Centre, Nariman Point (© **022/2202-8810**; nactravels@vsnl.net), or the dependable **Travel Corporation of India (TCI)** in the Chandermukhi Building (first floor), also at Nariman Point (© **022/2202-1881** or -7120). On Colaba Causeway, near Café Mondegar, is **Uniglobe Venture Travel Services** (Metro House, Colaba; © **022/2287-6666**), which offers reliable ticketing and other travel-related services. Most travel agents will arrange to deliver tickets to your hotel.

2 Getting Around

Mumbai is a city on the go—but don't expect to get anywhere fast, because traffic is lousy at the best of times. Already, close to a million vehicles crowd the streets, and each week another 1,400 scooters and cars join the congestion caused by battered black-and-yellow taxis, Marutis, Indicas, expensive sedans and SUVs, copies of leftover red double-decker Routemaster buses, and the occasional cow. You will certainly need to take a taxi to get around (or, if you're arriving from the airport, arrange a transfer with your hotel; see "Arriving," earlier in this chapter). If you're overnighting in the Colaba–Fort area, you will, for the most part, be able to get around on foot.

PUBLIC TRANSPORTATION

BY TAXI **Metered taxis** (in which you don't bargain but pay a rate dependent on mileage predetermined by a structured fare card) are available everywhere (flag them down when you see the meter flag up), but note that you'll be riding in rather battered

Fiats from the 1960s. That said, Mumbai is one of the few places in India where using the meter is the norm—in fact, no local would go anywhere without a taxi driver using his meter. Typically, the taxi meters in Mumbai are mounted on the vehicle hoods, and taxi drivers are required to carry a conversion chart that tells passengers how much they owe, based on the original fare displayed on the ludicrously old-fashioned meters. Do not start the journey before checking to see if the driver is carrying the correct chart; these are sometimes tampered with, so vital information is missing—for example, the part of the chart informing you that the rates quoted are for nighttime travel, which are higher. If you're in any doubt, ask a policeman or your hotel doorman to decipher the fare for you (which is Rs 13/30¢/15p for the first 1.6km and Rs 8.50/20¢/10p for each subsequent kilometer), but in essence you can calculate how much you have to pay by multiplying what's on the meter by approximately Rs 13 (30¢/15p); add on 25% if you are traveling between midnight and 5am, and Rs 5 to Rs 7 (10¢–15¢/10p) per piece of sizable luggage. Nothing more.

You will also see blue-and-white Indica taxis (called Cool Cabs) with digital meters plying the streets. These can be flagged down in the same way as the yellow tops.

Mumbai now has two new taxi services. Look for green Esteem cars with large advertising banners and a white light on top (available) or red (engaged). These new taxis are called **Meru Cabs** and are equipped with GPS, digital tamper-proof meters and printers (for a receipt), radio, and A/C, and have better-trained drivers. They're a definite step up from the beaten-up black-and-yellow taxis so characteristic of Mumbai. The downside is that even though you can hail one curbside, you rarely see a vacant Meru cab, and the phone service (© 022/4422 4422; open 24/7) requires at least 4 hours' advance notice. If you want to book one several days in advance you can do so on their website (www.merucabs.com) and receive an e-mail confirmation. **Gold Cabs** (© 022/3244 3333) also runs a smaller fleet of yellow cabs in various car models; again you'll have to book a few hours ahead. Fares for both are higher than regular cabs (Rs 15/35¢/20p for first kilometer and Rs 13/30¢/15p for each subsequent kilometer), and the meter starts only after you sit in the cab (unless you call and keep it waiting more than 10 min.). *Note:* Both services are in their infancy and are not yet 100% efficient.

If you're looking for a vehicle for the day, you can strike a deal with a private taxi driver directly, but here you should negotiate the deal upfront—you should pay around Rs 700 to Rs 800 ($17–$20/£9–£10), plus a tip, for an 8-hour (or 80km/50-mile) stint. Note that it's worth shelling out extra for an air-conditioned cab—you're likely to spend long stretches waiting in traffic jams at overcrowded intersections. To rent an air-conditioned car and an English-speaking driver privately (which will cost a bit more but may remove the hassle of haggling), the following operators are recommended: **Cool Cabs** (Worli © 022/2492-7006; or at Andheri 022/2822-7006, or 022/2824-6216); **Car Hirers** (1403 Arcadia, Nariman Point; © 022/2283-4689; www.carhirers.com); **Euro Cars** (Suburban Service Station, 261 S.V. Rd., Bandra W.; © 022/2655-2424; www.eurocars-india.com); and **Ketan Travels Pvt. Ltd.** (R.T. Building, P.M. Rd., Vile Parle E.; © 022/2614-0554; www.ketancars.com). **Hertz** (© 022/6570-2126; opsmum@carzonrent.com) offers chauffeur-driven cars throughout the subcontinent.

Hiring a taxi through your hotel can get very pricey, but the fleet of cars maintained by some of the upmarket hotels is unlikely to be matched in quality by anyone in the city, and it may be convenient to have taxi charges added to your hotel bill. Do, however, remember to tip your driver directly.

Tips **Dealing with Beggars**

When long-time BBC India Bureau Chief Mark Tully was asked: "How do you cope with the poverty of India?" he responded, "I don't have to; *they* do." As a first-time visitor, you will no doubt be struck first and foremost by the seemingly endless ordeal of the impoverished masses. Families of beggars will twist and weave their way around the cars at traffic lights, hopping and even crawling to your window with displays of open wounds, diseased sores, crushed limbs, and starving babies, their hollow eyes imploring you for a few life-saving rupees. Locals will tell you that these poverty performances are Mafia-style rackets, with protection money going to gangs, and sickly babies being passed around to gain more sympathy for their "parents." In the worst of these tales of horror, children are maimed to up the ante by making them appear more pathetic. The choice is stark: Either lower the window and risk having a sea of unwelcome faces descend on you, or stare ahead and ignore them. To salve your conscience, tip generously those who have made it onto the first rung of employment.

BY TRAIN   Train travel in the city is strictly for the adventurous, but then again, a ride on a train in the afternoon (or on Sun) gives you the opportunity to see how the other half lives, as the tracks wend their ways through some of the city's most squalid slums. A first-class return ticket from Victoria Terminus to the suburb of Thane costs about Rs 210 ($5/£3). Travel only during off-peak (noon–3pm is best) times and leave luggage and valuables in your hotel room.

ORGANIZED TOURS & TRIPS

You will be offered tours of various descriptions by at least half the people you meet on the streets of Mumbai; everyone from your taxi driver to the man who asks you for the time will have a contact in the tourism industry who'll be more than happy to take you sightseeing. Use your discretion, watch your wallet, and remember that Mumbai's traffic makes it impossible to see everything in 1 day.

To arrange a legitimate tour of the city, set it up through your hotel, which should have access to the best guides (meaning those with the best English and best knowledge). Or contact **Maharashtra Tourist Development Corporation** (Madame Cama Rd., opposite L.I.C. Building; © **022/2202-6713** or -7762; Mon–Sat 9:30am–5:30pm). The department has recently converted a double-decker bus into an open-deck bus offering a 1-hour city tour (Sat–Sun evenings only) that starts from the Gateway of India and languidly makes its way past Mumbai's historic attractions. Get a seat on the top deck of the bus, called Nilambari, and experience Mumbai from a different angle (tickets at MTDC counter at Gateway; © **022/2284-1877;** Rs 90/$2/£1 top deck, Rs 40/$1/50p lower deck). For more general tourist information, contact the **Government of India Tourist Office** (123 Maharishi Karve Rd., Churchgate; © **022/2203-3144;** Mon–Fri 8:30am–6pm and Sat 8:30am–2pm). Bear in mind that there's little point in seeing Mumbai only from the back seat of a chauffeur-driven taxi; leave time to explore the city on foot. If you're keen on architecture, a group of young architects conducts **Bombay Heritage Walks** on Sunday (© **022/2369-0992;** www.bombayheritagewalks.com; mid-Sept to May 5 6:30pm, special monsoon walks June–Sept; by prior arrangement only; Rs 100/$2/£1 and up)—these tours take in various fascinating parts of the city.

Note: One of the best-organized trips in the city is the boat trip departing half-hourly from the Gateway to Elephanta Island (see "What to See & Do," below).

3 What to See & Do

Mumbai doesn't have the wealth of historical attractions of, say, Kolkata or Delhi. Rather, it is a city that revolves around its commerce, its manic pace, and the head-spinning energy exuded by the millions of diverse people who have settled here. This is a city you *experience* rather than sightsee, and sampling from the fantastic restaurants described later in the chapter should be highest on your must-do list. That said, Mumbai does have a few attractions you should make time for; and be sure to set aside time to explore at least part of the **Colaba/Fort area,** described below, on foot—do this at the beginning of the day before the heat becomes suffocating. Another good area to explore on foot is the **Marine Drive/Chowpatty Beach stretch,** possibly after a boat trip to **Elephanta Island.** Finally, you may wish to visit **Malabar Hill,** also in the South Mumbai area and home to two top attractions (see below), as well as the **Hanging Gardens** (also known as Ferozeshah Mehta Gardens). Laid out in the early 1880s, the terraced park at the top of Malabar Hill covers (or "hangs over") the city's main water reservoir, but unfortunately it fails to live up to its spectacular-sounding name. The best reason to visit here is to wander over to **Kamala Nehru Park** (across the road from the Hanging Gardens), from where you have a great view of Nariman Point's skyscrapers and the sumptuous curve of Marine Drive.

EXPLORING COLABA & FORT

If you're at all inspired by Gothic Victorian architecture, then a jaunt through Mumbai's older districts is essential. Most tours kick off at the **Gateway of India** (see below), but a more authentic place to start, given Mumbai's origins, is **Sassoon Docks** ⟨⟨ (aka the Fisherman's Market; daily 4am–noon except in the monsoon when weather dictates whether trawlers go out or not), which lies just south of the Gateway, off Shahid Bhagat Singh Marg (near Colaba Bus Station). Most of the delicious seafood dishes in the city's finest establishments start out here, where Koli women in rainbow-colored saris whip the shells off prawns while others gut and sort fish. Get here early (5am), when the boats return with their first catch, for the vibrant, communal spirit as baskets full of fish are moved around the dock through various stages of processing. It makes for absorbing viewing.

From here, catch a cab or walk to the Gateway, possibly stopping for a refresher at the Taj Mahal Hotel, situated directly opposite. From here it's a 15-minute walk north to Fort, Mumbai's cultural center, where you will find the superb **Prince of Wales Museum** (see below), nearby **Jehangir Art Gallery,** and the **National Gallery of Modern Art,** as well as a host of Raj-era Gothic architectural highlights. From the museum you can either head north along M. Gandhi Road to Flora Fountain, hub of downtown Mumbai, or travel southwest down the famous Colaba Causeway.

Surrounded by colonial buildings that testify to the solid architecture of a bygone era, **Flora Fountain** has, since 1960, had to compete for attention with a **Martyrs' Memorial** that honors those who died in the creation of the state of Maharashtra. As you head toward the fountain, take in the impressive **High Court** building (which overlooks the Oval Maidan [also called The Oval], where aspiring cricketers practice their paces), the neoclassical **Army & Navy Building,** and the 78m (256-ft.) **Rajabai Clock Tower,** which towers over the **Mumbai University** complex. East of the fountain lies

Horniman Circle, where you will find the **Town Hall,** a regal colonnaded building with original parquet wood floors, wrought-iron loggias, spiral staircases, and marble statues of leaders associated with Mumbai's history. The major drawing card here is the **Asiatic Society Library,** which has a collection of around 800,000 valuable texts. You can join the seniors and students who fill the library's popular reading room to peruse local newspapers and check out the public book collection, but you'll need special permission if you're interested in looking at some of the priceless treasures.

Also facing Horniman Circle is the late-19th-century Gothic Venetian **Elphinstone Building** and, opposite it, on Veer Nariman Road, **St. Thomas's Cathedral,** thought to be the oldest colonial structure in Mumbai. (Note that if you head west along Veer Nariman Rd., lined with restaurants, you will come to Marine Dr.) St. Thomas's Cathedral is a stark contrast to the pink and blue neoclassical **Kenneth Eliyahoo Synagogue,** Mumbai's oldest and loveliest Sephardic synagogue, located off K. Dubash Marg, on Forbes Street. North of Flora Fountain, up Dr. Dadabhai Naoroji Road, is the Art Deco–style Parsi fire temple, **Watcha Agiary.** Built in 1881, it features carvings in a distinctly Assyrian style.

If you prefer shopping (albeit of a tourist-trap nature) to architecture, opt for the famous **Causeway** (now officially renamed **Shahid Bhagat Singh Marg,** though, thankfully, no one refers to it as such). Budget travelers have long been drawn to this vibrant street, but in recent years Colaba and its side streets have begun to slip into an increasingly urbane and upmarket second skin. Hip bars, swinging clubs, and tasteful restaurants are drawing the smart crowd. Anything and everything seems to be available from the hawkers on Colaba's sidewalks and back alleys, whether it's fruit, cheap cigarettes, currency, or hashish. Shop in exclusive boutiques or rummage through heaps of cheap trinkets sold on the sidewalks, where you can bargain for everything from imitation perfume to piles of cheap, tasteless T-shirts, all the while avoiding the advances of streetwise beggars and con artists sporting half-moon smiles and incongruous American accents.

Beyond the southernmost end of the Causeway (that's if you manage to get this far south before grabbing a taxi and heading for the peace of your hotel room!), in the restricted Navy Nagar area, you will see the neo-Gothic **Afghan Memorial Church of St. John the Evangelist.** Dating back to 1858, it memorializes those who fell in the First Afghan War—proof yet again of Mumbai's mosaic past.

TOP ATTRACTIONS: DOWNTOWN

Banganga Tank ★★   Here the paradox of traditional life coexisting with unbridled modernization is all too vivid. Near the edge of the Arabian Sea at the southern tip of Malabar Hill, several small, crumbling, stone-turreted temples and flower-garlanded shrines surround a rectangular pool of holy water in an area of looming modern-day skyscrapers and encroaching urbanization. Ritual bathers who come here believe the mossy waters have healing powers and originated from a natural spring created by an arrow shot by Rama (the hero of the *Ramayana*), who rested here while on a mission to rescue his beloved Sita from the demon king's abode in Lanka. The source of the spring is said to be an underground offshoot of the Ganga, and the waters are considered just as sacred as those of the great river itself. In the shadow of one of present-day Mumbai's most prosperous neighborhoods, Banganga continues to function as an out-of-time devotional hub, its tolling bells and mantra-chanting *pujaris* drawing devotees to worship the divine. If you're here in December, scour local newspapers for news of the open-air concerts held at the Banganga Festival.

Walkeshwar Rd., Malabar Hill.

Elephanta Island Caves 🐾🐾🐾   For a taste of Mumbai's early history and an opportunity to view the city's skyline from the water (not to mention escape from the tumult of the streets), grab a ferry and head out to Elephanta Island, declared a UNESCO World Heritage Site in 1987. The hour-long trip also provides a good introduction to Hinduism; the guides on board describe the religious significance of what you're about to see, though the origins of the Shiva temple caves—thought to date from the revivalist Hindu movement between A.D. 450 and 750—remain obscure.

Entry is via the main northern entrance to a massive hall supported by large pillars, where the enormous Trimurti statue is housed. At 6.3m (21 ft.), the remarkable sculpture depicts Shiva in his three-headed aspect: as Creator (Vamadeva, facing right), Protector (Maheshmurti, the crowned face at the center), and Destroyer (Bhairadeva, facing left, with serpents for hair). Left of the Trimurti is Shiva as both male and female: Ardhanarishvara, an aspect suggesting the unity of all opposites. Other sculptures refer to specific actions of the god and events in Hindu mythology, but many were damaged or destroyed by the Portuguese, who apparently used the Hindu gods for target practice. It's practical to bring along a local guide (free) even though they rarely speak very good English. Watch listings for music and dance performances.

Tip: Plan your trip so that you can witness sunset over the Mumbai skyline on your return journey, then pop into the Taj Mahal Hotel for a post-culture cocktail. Note that music and dance festival performances are held here every year in February.

9km (5½ miles) from Mumbai. Tickets and ferries from the Gateway of India. Admission Rs 250 ($6/£3), Rs 25 (60¢/30p) camera, Rs 25 (60¢/30p) video. Ferry ticket Rs 120 ($3/£2). Boats depart from the Gateway of India every half-hour Tues–Sun 9am–2:30pm.

Gateway of India & Taj Mahal Hotel 🐾🐾🐾   Easily the most recognizable remnant of the British Raj, the Gateway was designed by George Wittet (also responsible for the Prince of Wales Museum). The Gujarati-inspired yellow basalt structure was supposed to commemorate the visit of King George V and Queen Mary, who arrived in 1911 to find a fake cardboard structure instead; the Gateway was eventually completed in 1924 and was the final departure point for the British when they left Indian soil in 1947. It is the most obvious starting point for any tour of Mumbai (and is where the boats to Elephanta are launched), and to this end it draws large numbers of visitors as well as hordes of locals keen to take money off unsuspecting foreigners. The area makes for a quick-fix introduction to Mumbai tout dynamics; expect to be offered everything from photographs of yourself posing here to hashish to young girls. Opposite the Gateway is an equestrian statue of Chhatrapati Shivaji, the Maratha hero who gives his name to several renamed Mumbai institutions.

More impressive—in beauty and size—is the hotel behind the Gateway, which in many ways symbolizes Mumbaikars' determined and enterprising attitudes. Inspired by its namesake in Agra, the **Taj Mahal Hotel** (see "Where to Stay," below) was built just over a century ago by an ambitious industrialist named Jamshedji Tata—according to legend, because he wanted to avenge the whites-only policy of Watson's, then the city's poshest hotel. Designed by a European architect who mailed the plans to India, it has been said that the hotel was mistakenly constructed back-to-front, so what was meant to be a fantastic sea-facing facade actually overlooks a side street—patently untrue, as you will see if you walk around the palatial edifice. What cannot be refuted is how much it dominates Colaba's waterfront, its six-story domed structure best viewed from an offshore boat. Alternatively, for a great view of the Gateway, head inside the Taj and make for the **Sea Lounge** or **Harbour Bar.**

Chhatrapati Shivaji Maharaj Marg. Gateway information: ☏ **022/2202-3585** or -6364. Half-hour harbor cruise Rs 50 ($1/50p) deluxe. Booking office: daily 8am–8pm.

Jain Temple ఉఉ   This is arguably the prettiest temple in Mumbai (indeed, Jain temples are generally the prettiest in India). If your itinerary does not include a visit to one elsewhere (the most famous being in Rajasthan), do make the time to visit Mumbai's. Members of the Jain community are known to be exceptionally adept in the world of business, and although they believe in self-restraint and aestheticism (orthodox Jains will not tread on an ant, and at their most extreme wear masks to avoid breathing in even tiny insects), they pour large sums into the construction and maintenance of their places of worship. Officially called **Babu Amichand Panalal Adishwarji Jain Temple,** this beautifully decorated and adorned temple has an entrance flanked by two stone elephants. The downstairs area houses an array of deities and saints, including an image of Ganesh that recalls historical links between Jainism and Hinduism.

Ridge Rd., Walkeshwar (Malabar Hill). ☏ **022/2369-2727**. Daily 5am–9pm.

Mani Bhavan Gandhi Museum ఉఉ   Mahatma Gandhi lived in this quaint Gujarati-style house from 1917 to 1934, and it was here in November 1921 that he conducted a 4-day fast in order to restore peace to the city. This quiet three-story home on a beautiful laburnum tree–lined avenue now preserves the spirit of the man who selflessly put his nation before himself. There's a library of Gandhi-related works, as well as displays of photographs, posters, slogans, and other items that document and explain Gandhi's legendary life; dioramas depicting major events and turning points in his fight for the nation's freedom draw particular attention to his devotion to the poor. You can see Gandhi's old *charkha* (spinning wheel), which in many ways symbolized the struggle for independence, as it represented a return to roots and to sustainable home industry, where anyone can weave his or her own cloth. A visit to this tranquil spot makes a welcome change from the continuous hubbub of life in Mumbai—go up to the roof to really appreciate the relative stillness of the surrounding neighborhood.

19 Laburnam Rd., near Malabar Hill. ☏ **022/2380-5864**. www.gandhi-manibhavan.org. Donations appreciated; entry Rs 10 (25¢/10p). Daily 9:30am–5:30pm.

Marine Drive & Chowpatty Beach ఉఉఉ   Marine Drive (renamed Netaji Subhash Chandra Marg) follows the sweeping curve of sea that stretches north from Nariman Point's high-rise buildings to infamous Chowpatty Beach, located at the foot of Malabar Hill. It's the ultimate seaside promenade, where Mumbaikars come to escape the claustrophobia of central Mumbai, gratefully eyeing an endless horizon while strolling or jogging along the broad windswept promenade. In the evenings, casual, single-item snack stalls are set up for brisk trade. This is the city's ultimate sunset spot, when—having watched the orange globe sink into the Arabian Sea—you can witness the street lights transform Marine Drive into the aptly named Queen's Necklace, a choker-length of twinkling jewels adorning Back Bay. The scene is perhaps best enjoyed with cocktail in hand at one of Marine Drive's classier establishments: either the rooftop restaurant at the **InterContinental Marine Drive** or The Oberoi's **Bayview Bar,** which also offers jazz music and cigars.

Once the sun has set, catch a ride (or walk) north along Marine Drive to Chowpatty, Mumbai's oldest seafront. Chowpatty is no longer the filth-ridden extravaganza its long-acquired reputation suggests (though it's still not in any state for sunbathing or swimming), and at night it assumes the demeanor of a colorful fair. Children of all ages flock to ride the ancient Ferris wheels and tacky merry-go-rounds, and fly-by-night astrologers, self-styled contortionists, snake charmers, and trained monkeys provide the flavor of the bazaar—and bizarre—especially on weekends. This is where locals love to consume the city's famous street snacks, especially *bhelpuri:* crisp puffed rice, vegetables, and fried lentil-flour noodles doused in pungent chutneys of chili, mint, and tamarind, then scooped up with a tiny, flat *puri* (puffy deep-fried bread). Chowpatty *bhelpuri* is renowned throughout India, sold here by the eponymous *bhelwallas,* who now ply their trade in Bhel Plaza, where other traditional treats like *kulfi* are on offer at dirt-cheap prices. *Tip:* It's inadvisable to eat here—unfortunately, flavor, not hygiene, enjoys top priority.

After you've watched the multitudes gorging vast quantities of assorted snack foods, cross the street and get your own *chaat* (as *bhelpuri* and similar snacks are called) at **Cream Centre** 𝕬𝕬 (25 Fulchand Niwas, Chowpatty Beach; ℭ 022/2367-9222 or -9333; all credit cards accepted; noon–midnight). For close to half a century, this vegetarian snack place has been serving up delicious food—so good, in fact, that whenever you pass Chowpatty Beach in the evening, you'll see a queue of people waiting to get in. Alternatively, make a meal of the signature *channa bhatura* (spiced chickpeas and a large *puri*), a typical Punjabi dish that is made everywhere but rarely so well as here. When you're done, step out of the restaurant, turn left, and walk down to the end of the pavement to a hole-in-the-wall (but very hygienic) juice shop called **Bachelorr's** (yes, with two r's) for deliciously refreshing seasonal fresh fruit ice creams and juices—but do make sure you ask for your juice without ice, water, or masala.

To experience Mumbai at its most exuberant, head to Chowpatty Beach for the culmination of **Ganesh Chaturthi** 𝕬𝕬𝕬, the city's biggest and most explosive celebration. Held in honor of the much-loved elephant-headed god (here called Ganpati), the 10-day festival culminates on the last day, when a jubilant procession is held and thousands of huge Ganpati idols are immersed in the sea. Ganesh Chaturthi is held in September; for exact dates contact the Government of India Tourist Office.

Prince of Wales Museum 𝕬𝕬𝕬   Renamed Chhatrapati Shivaji Maharaj Vastu Sangrahalaya, but thankfully also known just as "museum," this is Mumbai's top museum and arguably the best in India, providing an extensive and accessible introduction to Indian history and culture. The Indo-Saracenic building itself is rather lovely, but it is the collection that is outstanding, not least because it is well laid out (unlike the collections of most museums throughout the subcontinent) and aided by a useful audioguide highlighting "Curator's Choice" exhibits. The central hall features a "précis" of the collection, but don't stop there—from sculptures of Hindu deities to beautiful temple art, Buddhist *thangkas* from Nepal and Tibet to gruesome Maratha weaponry, there is much to see. Highlights are found on the first floor: Among them are the spectacular collection of more than 2,000 miniature paintings representing India's various schools of art (look for the portrait of Shah Jahan, creator of the Taj Mahal), and the exhibit relating to the Indus Valley Civilization (which is remarkably civilized considering that it dates from 3500 B.C.). Least impressive is the natural history section with its collection of stuffed animals.

Note: Art lovers may wish to include a visit to **Jehangir Art Gallery** (ℭ 022/2284-3989), located a little farther along M Gandhi Road, and open daily from 11am to 7pm, free of charge. You can probably give the main exhibition halls on the ground floor a miss—the exhibits there are fairly mediocre. Instead, head upstairs to **Gallery**

Moments Catch a Bollywood Blockbuster

You can't say you've properly done the biggest film-producing city on earth if you haven't gone to the cinema to catch a blockbuster, or tried to. Listings are found in daily newspapers, where you can also determine quality and even figure out the storyline by reading reviews written by contenders for the world's bitchiest critic; alternatively, ask your hotel concierge for recommendations. Of course, you can always get completely into the swing of things by picking up a copy of one of Bollywood's gossip magazines. *Filmfare* and *Stardust* not only fill you in on what's hot or what's not, but are crammed with glossy, airbrushed close-ups of silver-screen idols. Even though the growth of multiplexes has killed virtually all the old cinema houses, some still offer historic Art Deco appeal. Get tickets to watch a film at the once wonderful but now run-down **Eros Cinema** (opposite Churchgate Station; © 022/2282-2335) or lovely **Liberty Cinema** (© 022/2203-1196, a short walk from Eros, near Bombay Hospital), where upper-stall (at Liberty) or dress-circle (at Eros) tickets (the best in the house) still cost under Rs 100 ($2/£1). Besides the Bollywood melodrama, you get to admire the wonderful Art Deco interiors, with majestic high ceilings, white cedar and teak paneling, '60s-style soda fountain, magnificent huge etched mirrors on the stairwells, mock fountains, and old movie posters.

Chemould (© 022/2284-4356; Mon–Sat 11am–6pm), a tiny, history-filled gallery that often features some of India's best contemporary artists. For reviews of current art exhibitions, consult *Time Out Mumbai* or "The Hot List," the entertainment supplement in the local rag *Mid Day.*

159/160 Mahatma Gandhi Rd., Fort. © 022/2284-4519. www.bombaymuseum.org. powm@vsnl.com. Rs 300 ($7/£4), includes audioguide. Tues–Sun 10:15am–6pm.

Victoria Terminus (Chhatrapati Shivaji Terminus) Also rechristened in Mumbai's nationalist-inspired anti-Raj drive, but more often than not referred to as "VT," this baroque, cathedral-like building must rank as Mumbai's most marvelous Raj-era monument. India's very first steam engine left this station when it was completed in 1887; today at least a thousand trains leave every day, carrying some 2.5 million commuters in and out of the city. With its vaulted roofs, arches, Gothic spires, flying buttresses, gables crowned by neoclassical sculptures, stone carvings, and exquisite friezes, the terminus is an architectural gem, worth entering to see the massive ribbed Central Dome (topped by a statue of the torch-wielding "Progress") that caps an octagonal tower featuring beautiful stained-glass windows with colorful images of trains and floral patterns. But come, too, for the spectacle of the disparate people, from sari-clad beauties to half-naked fakirs, who make up Mumbai. Get here just before lunch to watch the famous *dabba-wallas* stream out into the city: A vast network of *dabba-wallas* transfer some 200,000 cooked lunches, prepared by housewives for their office-bound husbands, and kept warm in identical *dabbas* (metal tiffin containers), through a unique sorting and multiple-relay distribution system; later in the afternoon these empty *dabbas* are returned to their home of origin. The success of this system (no one gets the wrong lunch) is proof of how well India works, despite its reputation for obstructive bureaucracy. In fact, following a study of this network, U.S.

business magazine *Forbes* gave it a Six Sigma (99.99% accuracy) performance rating, which means that just one error occurs in six million transactions.

Dr. Dadabhai Naoroji Rd., Fort.

TOP ATTRACTION OUTSIDE DOWNTOWN MUMBAI

Dhobi Ghat 🐾🐾   It's a fascinating spectacle, looking down on row upon row of open-air concrete wash pens, each fitted with its own flogging stone, while Mumbai's *dhobis* (around 200 *dhobi* families work together here) relentlessly pound the dirt from the city's garments in a timeless tradition. Known as the world's largest outdoor laundry, Dhobi Ghat is where Mumbai's traditional washerfolk—or *dhobis*—provide a wonderful service, collecting dirty laundry, washing it, and returning it neatly pressed, all for a very small fee. Stubborn stains are removed by soaking garments in a boiling vat of caustic soda; drying takes place on long, brightly colored lines; and heavy wood-burning irons are used for pressing. At the very least, it's a great photo opportunity, though most locals think it rather amusing that their everyday work arouses such curiosity. (Note that there is another Dhobi Ghat off Capt. Prakash Petha Marg, Colaba, which may be more accessible.)

Dr. E. Moses Rd. (near Mahalakshmi Station).

MARKETS

Mumbai has more than 70 markets, and it's worthwhile to spend a couple of hours exploring at least one, not so much for the shopping (for that, see "Shopping," later in this chapter) as for the human spectacle of it all. Flowers are an intrinsic part of Indian culture, and **Bhuleshwar Wholesale Flower Market** 🐾🐾 (CP Tank Circle; dawn–noon) is the best place in the city to witness the Indian romance with color and fragrance. Note that according to Hindu beliefs, if you touch or sniff the flowers, you'll ruin them—so don't. **Chor Bazaar (Thieves' Market)** 🐾🐾 (Mutton St., off Sardar Vallabhbhai Patel Rd.; Sat–Thurs 11am–7pm) conjures up *Arabian Nights'* cloak-and-dagger intrigue and visions of precious rings sold with the finger of the former owner still attached, but in reality this is a fun place to rummage through an extravagant assortment of antiques, fakes, and junk and get into the rhythm of that favorite Indian pastime: bargaining.

If you visit only one market, make it **Crawford Market** 🐾🐾🐾 (Lokmanya Tilak Marg and Dr. Dadabhai Naoroji Rd.; Mon–Sat 11:30am–8pm), Mumbai's quintessential fresh-produce shopping experience, now officially known as **Mahatma Jyotiba Phule Market.** Dating back to the 1860s, it combines the traditional Indian bazaar experience with both Norman and Flemish architecture. (*Note:* Above the main entrance is a bas-relief frieze designed by Rudyard Kipling's father.) Admire the colorful pyramids of heavenly mangoes and ripe bananas, but steer clear of the disturbing pet stalls.

Clothing is one of Mumbai's major exports, and at **Fashion Street** 🐾 (Mahatma Gandhi Rd., across the road from Bombay Gymkhana), a motley collection of shops and stalls, you will pay a fraction of the prices asked in foreign stores. Much of what is here is surplus stock; other garments have been rejected by quality controllers. Start your haggling at under half the quoted price.

Taxi drivers get nervous when you tell them you want to visit **Zaveri Bazaar** (jewelry market) 🐾🐾 (Sheik Memon St.; Mon–Sat 11am–7pm). You'll soon discover why. Shoppers and space-fillers shuffle and push their ways endlessly through narrow gaps in this cluttered, heaving market, and it's often impossible to inch forward by car—or even on foot. Behind the street stalls and milling masses, glittering jewels are sold from family shops. If the glitzy accessories don't fascinate you, perhaps you'll be drawn to packed **Mumbadevi Temple,** where the city's namesake deity is housed. Activity around the temple is chaotic, with devotees splurging to prove their devotion to the powerful goddess.

CRICKET

Although hockey is India's official national sport, cricket is by far the best-loved game, and even watching a group of schoolboys practicing in a field is an experience unto itself. Mumbaikars play the game with an enthusiasm that's quite intoxicating—almost as if it provides some measure of relief from the hardships of daily life. In cricket-crazy India, the stars of the game are worshiped as keenly as film stars and gods, and Indian spectators at international games have the ability to transform even the blandest match into an exciting event.

During the season (Oct–Mar), several matches are held each week at **Wankhede Stadium** (Churchgate), which is where Mumbai's big national and international games are hosted. Tickets are sold by the **Mumbai Cricket Association (𝕔 022/ 2281-9910** or -2714), but it's worth asking your concierge to arrange good seats for you at a decent price (top-tier tickets can go for as much as $100 officially, and up to $300 on the black market). There's no doubt that watching a cricket match in an Indian stadium with tens of thousands of fans is one of the more fascinating experiences to be had in India, but if crowds make you nervous, watch the World Cup, Sharjah Cup, or any major cricketing event live at a local bar or lounge, with a few dozen cricket-crazy Indians to provide the spectacle.

4 Where to Stay

With greater supply than demand for rooms in Mumbai over the last few years, and the emergence of numerous five-star properties in the suburbs, rooms in downtown Mumbai can often be booked at good rates. Don't always go by a hotel's published tariff; ask about seasonal or daily discounts and cruise the Internet for bargains. It's not uncommon to find ridiculously cheap deals for rooms in hotels like the Taj President, available even during the popular winter season. That said, budget travelers should be prepared to spend more on lodging in Mumbai than in any other city on the subcontinent; standards at the low end can be difficult to stomach, so you're better off forking out a little more for a decent place to stay.

Marine Drive is a great option if you want a prime view of the Arabian Sea, but it's pricey. With a variety of options to suit every budget (top choice obviously being the Taj Mahal Hotel, reviewed below), Colaba-Fort is where most tourists end up. If you're on a really tight budget, a cheap, decent option worth noting is **Bentley's Hotel** (17 Oliver Rd., Colaba; 𝕔 **022/2284-1474** or -1733; www.bentleyshotel.com; bentleyshotel@hotmail.com), which has old, threadbare accommodations with enough character and antique furniture to make it livable. You can get a room with wooden floors, a balcony, and an attached bathroom for Rs 1,905 ($46/£23); be warned that at least several days' advance reservation might be necessary. Just a few minutes' drive from both Colaba and Marine Drive is **West End Hotel** (45 New Marine Lines, next to Bombay Hospital; 𝕔 **022/2203-9121;** Rs 3,600/$88/£44 double), a good midrange option. Most rooms have renovated bathrooms, and though the furniture and general decor is old-fashioned '70s style, there's a quaint charm about the place.

Rooms are large and spotlessly clean, and the staff very helpful. **Gourmet,** the in-house restaurant, has decent (if repetitive) breakfast and lunch buffets, and **Chez Nous,** the bar, is recommended for a quiet drink anytime between 11am and 11pm. If you are literally overnighting and have no desire to spend time in Mumbai, a number of options are located close to the international airport, but no bargains here. A good compromise is Juhu, which has cheaper choices and a great nighttime atmosphere, and is only a 30-minute drive from the airport.

Note: The prices below are sometimes given in rupees, with U.S. dollar and British pound conversions; others are stated in U.S. dollars only, which is how many hotels targeting foreign markets quote their rates.

MARINE DRIVE

Within walking distance of the city's commercial center, Marine Drive is a great place to base yourself, not least for the sea views and sense of space these provide—offering a relief from the hustling, bustling streets that lie east. Expect to pay for the privilege, however. If your budget can't stretch to pay for the suggestions below, check out **Sea Green Hotel** (🕾 022/6633-6525 or 022/2282-2294; www.seagreenhotel.com). It's the best budget option on Marine Drive, where relatively large guest rooms with French doors (and flaking paint) open onto balconies overlooking Back Bay. It has a slightly seedy air, and furnishings are quite awful, but the attached shower-toilets are large and clean, and each room comes with TV, air-conditioning, and a minibar. You can bed down on your foam mattress for Rs 3,060 ($75/£38) double.

VERY EXPENSIVE

Hotel Marine Plaza 🏵🏵   Any address along Marine Drive is highly sought after, and the blue-mirrored glass facade of this self-styled "fashionably small" upmarket establishment is no exception, though it's not in the same class as The Oberoi or Inter-Continental. Like the hotel, the marble lobby is small, its main stairway concealing a quaint lounge from which you can stare up at people swimming in the glass-bottom pool on the fifth floor. Most of the accommodations are suites, some of which are relatively well-priced but require neck-straining to get a look at the view; make sure to specify a room with a direct sea view. Besides swimming, the pool deck affords wonderful views over Back Bay and the entire Queen's Necklace strip. Like many other upscale hotels in Mumbai, Marine Plaza gets busy at weekends, especially on weekend nights and at Sunday lunch, when the popular **Bayview** and **Oriental Blossom** restaurants are filled with locals, and the bar, **Geoffrey's,** buzzes until 12:30am.

29 Marine Dr., Mumbai 400 020. 🕾 022/2285-1212. Fax 022/2282-8585. www.sarovarhotels.com. hmp@sarovar hotels.com. 68 units. $350/£176 superior double; $425/£214 executive suite; $450/£227 deluxe suite; $625/£316 special suite; plus 10% tax. AE, DC, MC, V. **Amenities:** 2 restaurants; pastry shop; bar; pool w/Jacuzzi; gym; business center; 24-hr. room service; laundry; doctor-on-call; Wi-Fi enabled. *In room:* A/C, TV, dataport, minibar, tea- and coffee-making facility, electronic safe.

InterContinental Marine Drive 🏵🏵🏵   When it comes to views, few contenders can match those of the InterContinental. Designed with business travelers in mind, yet relatively intimate (only 59 rooms), the hotel spares no expense in ensuring you a good night's sleep—there's even a "Pillow and Quilt Menu": Will it be a set of "air" pillows tonight or a mix of Korean and bamboo pillows? Satin or silk quilts? Beside the bed is your choice of oils for clarity of thought, stress relief, or peaceful sleep; in the bathroom are heavenly toiletries from Bvlgari. At a whopping 42 sq. m (450 sq. ft.), the rooms here must be the largest in the city. (While most rooms offer some view of the sea, best are the "deluxe seafront.") All rooms come with 42-inch plasma TV and DVD player. Bathrooms are large, separated from the main room only by sliding doors (in the suite) or windows, creating a feeling of spaciousness. Other personal touches include a bath menu (for prepared baths), with choices like "Skin Nourishing Bath," complete with rose petals. Although the in-house dining hasn't been exceptional, the lovely rooftop **Dome** bar (see "Hot Spots with Views," below) is perfect for a romantic evening drink, and a new Italian restaurant, **Corleogne,** promises home-style Italian cooking. Also pleasant is the lobby lounge with its leather sofas, where you can enjoy coffee, tea, and snacks; watch a humongous plasma TV; or peruse the interesting book collection.

InterContinental Marine Dr., 135 Marine Dr., Mumbai 400 020. (C) 022/3987-9999. Fax 022/3987-9600. www.mumbai. intercontinental.com. 59 units. $400/£202 deluxe double; $440/£222 deluxe bay-view double; $490/£247 deluxe seafront double; $600/£303 junior executive suite; $700/£354 deluxe corner suite; $1,900–$2,300/£960–£1161 presidential suite. AE, DC, MC, V. **Amenities:** 2 restaurants; 2 bars; health club; travel desk and car hire; tour guides, business center; 24-hr. room service; in-room massages and salon treatment; laundry and dry cleaning; DVD and CD library; currency exchange. *In room:* A/C, plasma TV, DVD player, fax, Wi-Fi, minibar, hair dryer, electronic safe, aromatherapy.

The Oberoi 🏵🏵🏵 What do Bill Gates, Richard Gere, Michael Jackson, Rupert Murdoch, and the leaders or the heads of state of the United States, Russia, Greece, China, Indonesia, and Iceland have in common? Yes, they've all stayed at the best hotel on Marine Drive, and arguably the best in Mumbai. It's particularly from a service point of view that The Oberoi wins hands-down; touches like being met at the terminal gate, your luggage dealt with for you, right through to the personal butler on each floor summoned by the touch of an "Ask Jeeves" button, and genuflecting staff members who go out of their way to make you feel revered, are typical Oberoi, and worth every dollar. If Mumbai is your first port of call, you'll find the genteel atmosphere a relief—tranquil and sophisticated, yet very relaxed, this is where you want to retreat after spending a few hours out on the crowded streets (you can walk to many of the city's best shops from here, or utilize the cheap taxis that await, like hungry fish at feeding time, the doorman's whistle). All accommodations are spacious, with tasteful decor, but the best rooms are the premium sea-view rooms, facing the bay and Marine Drive, with stunning sea views and gorgeous sunsets turning the whole room a pale pink before the Queen's Necklace starts to sparkle—a dazzling predinner spectacle. The in-house restaurants are all superb, so you won't have to go far to enjoy one of Mumbai's top-rated restaurants (see "Where to Dine," below). The top-rated **Banyan Tree spa** is equally in a league of its own. The only slight letdown is the pool area, which makes one feel stranded in a depressing wasteland, the hideous monolithic exterior a stark contrast to the classy interiors. ***Note:*** If the rates at The Oberoi are a tad stiff for your budget, overnight instead in the adjoining **Trident Towers** 🏵🏵. It may not have the same staff-to-client ratio as the more luxurious Oberoi, and the atmosphere is rather soulless, but this is still an excellent hotel, with high standards and offering relatively good value—plus you'll have access to all the facilities next door. Rates vary daily; at press time a superior room runs $330 a night, including breakfast ((C) **022/5632-4343;** www.tridenthotels.com).

Nariman Point, Mumbai 400 021. (C) 022/5632-5757; reservations 022/5632-6887. Fax 022/5632-4142. www.oberoi hotels.com. 333 units. $490/£247 deluxe room; $510/£258 premier room; $550/£277 luxury room; $600/£302 luxury sea-view room; $1,100/£554 executive suite; $1,450/£731 deluxe suite; $1,950/£983 luxury suite; $3,600/£1,814 Kohi-noor (presidential) suite. Airport transfers and breakfast included. AE, DC, MC, V. **Amenities:** 3 restaurants; bar; an additional 3 restaurants and bar in adjoining Trident Towers; pool; spa, salon, and health club; concierge; sightseeing, travel, and limousine service; business center; shopping arcade; bookshop; 24-hr. room service; laundry; dry cleaning; doctor-on-call; floor butler; currency exchange. *In room:* A/C, TV, fax, dataport, minibar, tea- and coffee-making facilities, hair dryer, electronic safe, scale. Sea-facing rooms and suites have DVD players; suites and deluxe rooms include CD players.

EXPENSIVE

Ambassador ☆   Capped by the city's only revolving restaurant, this kitsch 1940s hotel welcomes you with a baroque-inspired marble lobby adorned with cheap cherub statues, giant decorative vases, and an eclectic, extravagant mix of furniture, all under a gold-painted molded ceiling dripping with chandeliers. If you want a sea view (and that's why you're on the Drive), opt for one of the "superior" guest rooms: Clean, neat, and functional, these occupy the second, third, and fourth floors; carpeted passages are decorated with Mughlai miniatures and the theme is maroon and white. The slightly cheaper "executive" rooms on the upper floors include some units with partial sea views: Ask for room no. 8, 9, or 10. On the plus side, executive rooms are reasonably sized and have a slightly less overwhelming white, cream, and blue decor; roomy white-and-gray marble bathrooms feature large tubs. Apart from the enthusiastic turbaned doorman and the dedicated restaurant staff, service here is unexceptional.

Veer Nariman Rd., off Marine Dr., Churchgate, Mumbai 400 020. ☏ 022/2204-1131. Fax 022/2204-0004. www.ambassadorindia.com. 110 units. $220/£111 executive double; $250/£126 superior double; $290/£146 premier double; $599/£302 suite. $30/£15 extra bed; plus 10% tax. Children under 12 stay free in parent's room. AE, DC, MC, V. **Amenities:** 3 restaurants, all with bars; travel assistance and car hires; airport transfers; business center; 24-hr. room service; laundry service; dry cleaning; doctor-on-call; currency exchange; florist. *In room:* A/C, TV, minibar, hair dryer, electronic safe, bedside console.

INEXPENSIVE

Chateau Windsor Hotel *Value*   With clean, very basic rooms on the first to fifth floors of an apartment block, this "hotel" is unspectacular, but it's cheap—perhaps the best accommodations in its price bracket. Do specify that you want an air-conditioned room with attached bathroom; these units have small balconies, stone tile floors, and foam mattresses with clean white sheets and towels. The simple furnishings include an armless "sofa," a linoleum-topped table, and a small, narrow cupboard. Management is generally helpful. Although there is no restaurant, you can sit in the terrace garden and nosh, or get room service; you'll have few reasons to do this, however, given the neighborhood's large number of excellent restaurants. Morning tea is on the house, and the kitchen is available for you to do your own cooking—as long as it's vegetarian.

86 Veer Nariman Rd., Churchgate, Mumbai 400 020. ☏ 022/2204-4455. Fax 022/2202-6459. www.chateauwindsor.com. info@cwh.in. 65 units. Rs 2,390 ($58/£30) small double; Rs 3,200 ($78/£40) standard double; Rs 3,600 ($88/£44) superior; Rs 4,000 ($98/£49) deluxe. Rs 400 ($10/£5) extra person; Rs 200 ($5/£2) children ages 3–12 sharing parent's room; plus 10% tax. AE, MC, V. **Amenities:** Travel assistance; 24-hr. room service; laundry; doctor-on-call; free Internet access in lobby. *In room:* A/C, TV, fridge (in deluxe rooms), electronic safe.

COLABA

With the city's densest concentration of sights, hotels, and restaurants (of which the best are reviewed below), Colaba is an ideal location. The Taj Mahal is here, as is the excellent-value Gordon House, a personal favorite.

VERY EXPENSIVE

The Taj Mahal Palace & Tower ☆☆☆   George Bernard Shaw famously claimed that after staying here, he no longer had any need to visit the original Taj Mahal in Agra. But seriously stiff competition from the nearby Oberoi and InterContinental (and even from so-called "suburban" hotels like the JW Marriott, Hyatt Regency, Grand Hyatt, and ITC Maratha Sheraton) has The Taj in the process of reinventing itself to keep its crown as *the* most celebrated address in Mumbai. Besides launching the **Jiva** spa and a number of new restaurants and watering holes (see "Top Attractions: Downtown," earlier in this chapter), at press time all guest rooms were being refurbished in phases. Then again, the history here is tangible: Public areas are decorated with carefully chosen antiques and vintage artwork. Bombay's very first licensed drinking establishment, **Harbour Bar,** can be found here. Of its many famous and popular restaurants, **Wasabi by Morimoto** is an outstanding, world-class Japanese restaurant and highly recommended if you don't mind the price tag (meal for two Rs 8,000–Rs 20,000/$200–$488/£99–£250). **The Zodiac Grill,** now renovated, is something of a legend among the city's well-heeled for its fine European cuisine and vintage wines. If you do opt for The Taj Mahal Palace, you'll want to wallow in the luxurious old-world splendor of the Palace Wing; individually themed high-ceilinged suites transport you to another era, when the likes of Somerset Maugham and Duke Ellington bedded down in the city's best hotel. For a view of the Gateway, book a Taj Club sea-view or luxury grande sea-view room, but if money is no object, nothing less than the Rajput Suite will do. As the crowning glory of one of India's most prominent hotel chains, The Taj Mahal Palace may well double as the nerve center for moneyed mischief, but it remains a great blend of old-world charm and modern conveniences. That said, its reputation for service is less than stellar, and published rates leap by about 20% each year (ask about daily discounts). Note that the hotel's looming Tower Wing is more business-oriented, and a bit of a letdown once you've explored the original parts of the hotel.

Apollo Bunder, Mumbai 400 001. ℂ **022/6665-3366.** Fax 022/6665-0300. www.tajhotels.com. tmhbc.bom@taj hotels.com. 565 units. Tower Wing doubles: $415/£210 superior city-view, $445/£225 superior sea-view, $475/£240 deluxe city-view, $510/£258 deluxe sea-view. Palace Wing doubles: $595/£300 luxury grande city/pool view, $655/£331 luxury grande sea-view, $720/£364 Taj Club city/pool view, $770/£389 Taj Club sea-view. $1,900–$8,500/ £960–£4293 suites. (Taj Club and suites include limousine airport transfer, club floor check-in, personal valet, buffet breakfast, high tea, business services, and cocktail hour.) AE, DC, MC, V. **Amenities:** 5 restaurants; pastry shop; 2 bars; swimming pool; sports arrangements on request (golf, badminton, squash, billiards, tennis, table tennis); fitness center; concierge; travel desk; car hire; business center; shopping arcade; salon; babysitting; laundry; doctor-on-call; currency exchange; valet service; personal valet service for Grand Luxe and Presidential Suite guests; wireless newspaper service. *In room:* A/C, TV (plasma in Palace Wing only), fax, dataport, minibar, hair dryer, electronic safe, DVD player (Palace Wing rooms), MP3 stereo, 2-line speaker phones, shaving mirror. Suites have in-built personal spa.

EXPENSIVE

Taj President 𝒢𝒢   It may not be the most beautiful or luxurious hotel in Mumbai, but this classy business property offers ultra-efficient service, excellent restaurants, and a convenient location in a smart neighborhood not too far from the maelstrom of busy Colaba. At press time much-needed renovations were underway, though the old-fashioned wooden furniture and elegant bonsai trees in the lobby will remain. Standard rooms are being refurbished, so you may want to weigh that against paying double for a room on the Executive Floor (17th), which sports elegant pale tones and modern works of art. City-facing and sea-facing doubles now cost the same, so make your request known in advance.

90 Cuffe Parade, Mumbai 400 005, Maharashtra. ℂ **022/6665-0808.** Fax 022/6665-0365. www.tajhotels.com. president. mumbai@tajhotels.com. 292 units. $195/£98 standard city-facing or sea-facing double; $295/£149 deluxe double; $375/£189 executive suite. Deluxe rooms and executive suites include breakfast. Ask about daily discounts. AE, DC, MC, V. **Amenities:** 3 restaurants; pastry shop; bar; pool; fitness center (gym, steam, massage); concierge; travel desk; car hires; business center; shops; salon; 24-hr. room service; babysitting; laundry service; safe deposit lockers; doctor-on-call; currency exchange; Wi-Fi enabled. *In room:* A/C, TV (satellite), dataport, tea- and coffee-making facilities, hair

dryer, iron, scale and fax machine on request. Massage chair, massage shower (no bathtub), iPod attachments to in-room speakers, and Wi-Fi in executive suites.

MODERATE

The Gordon House Hotel ★★ *Value*   Set among a rash of rather ordinary old-fashioned hotels, Colaba's sexiest lodging option and Mumbai's only boutique-style hotel is perfect for those raring to have a good time. It's also the best choice in its price bracket. Originally owned by Arthur Gordon, an early-20th-century trader who made his fortune in Bombay, and now the pride of Sanjay Narang, one of Mumbai's most high-profile restaurateurs, this trendy pad with its toothpaste-white interiors comes as a breath of fresh air, as does the slick, attentive service that starts with the super-fast check-in. There are three themed guest room floors: The Scandinavian level offers smart, contemporary rooms with parquet floors and sleek Ikea-style furniture, timber blinds, and large Euro-themed black-and-white photographs. Mediterranean rooms are equally charming, with bright blues and yellows, tiled floors, cane chairs, John Miller posters, and cool aqua-toned bathrooms. Rooms on the feminine Country Floor are strictly floral, patchwork, and pastel fans. Accommodations are small but well proportioned, with comfortable beds and extras like a stereo system with VCD (video compact disc, a media format popular in Asia that never really caught on in the West) and CD player so you can rent a movie or request complimentary music from the hotel's library. A selection of magazines, bowls of sweets, and designer toiletries are more thoughtful touches. The bathrooms may be tiny, but they offer great walk-in showers. Opulent and over the top, the one and only suite has been themed on the Sun King's palace at Versailles, complete with crystal chandeliers and lavish gilded furniture (and available at the price you'd pay for a regular room elsewhere). **All Stir Fry,** the pleasant do-it-yourself Asian restaurant, is quite good. Breakfast is served at the rooftop restaurant (7–11am). Sadly, the place has one drawback: The nonstop thumping from the in-house nightclub **Polly Esther's,** which particularly affects rooms on the second floor.

5 Battery St., Apollo Bunder, Colaba, Mumbai 400 039. © 022/2287-1122. Fax 022/2287-2026. www.ghhotel.com. dutymanager@ghhotel.com. 29 units. $200/£101 double; $350/£177 Versailles Suite. Tariff includes continental breakfast. Ask for daily discounts. AE, MC, V. **Amenities:** 2 restaurants; bar; nightclub; health club privileges; exercise equipment; concierge; travel, transport, and sightseeing arrangements; 24-hr. room service; laundry service; dry cleaning; complimentary ironing; doctor-on-call; express check-out. *In room:* A/C, TV, minibar, tea- and coffee-making facility, hair dryer, iron and ironing board, electronic safe, CD and VCD player (CDs on request), bedside console, shaving mirror, and scale on request.

INEXPENSIVE

Hotel Godwin   The facade of this nine-story budget hotel harks back to the 1930s and suggests a faded grandeur that is sadly not realized in most of the rooms. Because the range of accommodations varies a lot here, you should specifically request a centrally air-conditioned deluxe room that has been refurbished. Also insist that it's one of the eighth-floor units blessed with a view (distant as it is) of the Taj Mahal Hotel. *Note:* Godwin's sister establishment, the **Garden Hotel** (© 022/2284-1476; gardenhotel@mail.com), immediately next door, has the same rates, but rooms are cluttered and a bit grubby. This hotel offers complimentary Internet access for those with their own laptop.

Jasmine Building, 41 Garden Rd., Colaba, Mumbai 400 039. © 022/2287-2050. Fax 022/2287-1592. hotelgodwin@mail.com. 52 units. Rs 3,000 ($73/£37) standard double; Rs 3,200 ($78/£40) deluxe double; Rs 3,400 ($83/£42) super deluxe; Rs 3,600 ($88/£44) suite. AE, MC, V. **Amenities:** Restaurant; bar; 24-hr. room service; laundry; doctor-on-call; currency exchange. *In room:* A/C, TV, minibar, tea- and coffee-making facility on request, hair dryer on request.

Hotel Suba Palace ⚅ This small, rather nondescript hotel not far from the Gateway of India is a good bet despite the side-street location and total absence of views. Rooms are clean and done up in cream hues, and service is good (such as 24-hr. room service—always useful), though the accommodations are on the small side, and there are no bedside lamps. Suba will suit the traveler looking for a reasonably smart option (as opposed to character-filled) that offers good value.

Near Gateway of India, Apollo Bunder, Mumbai 400 039. ☎ **022/2202-0636** or 022/2288-5444. Fax 022/2202-0812. www.hotelsubapalace.com. info@hotelsubapalace.com. 50 units. Rs 3,000 ($73/£37) double. Breakfast included. AE, DC, MC, V. **Amenities:** Restaurant; travel assistance; 24-hr. room service; laundry; doctor-on-call; currency exchange. *In room:* A/C, TV, tea- and coffee-making facility, hair dryer (on request), shaving mirror, scale.

JUHU & BANDRA

Mumbai's suburbs of Bandra and Juhu don't have a tourist center, but they are studded with new restaurants, bars, endless shopping, and a vibrant nightlife, sans Colaba's seedy edge. A 60- to 90-minute drive from the heavily touristed downtown area, the seaside suburb of Juhu attracts a predominantly local, moneyed crowd, and as such affords in many ways a truly genuine introduction to Mumbai. Juhu's relative proximity to the airport (it's a 30-min. drive) makes it the ideal stopover if you have no strong desire to engage with the historical side of the city, or if you need to recover from jet lag before moving on. Most of Bollywood's film stars live and hang out in this part of Mumbai, so it's definitely where you should head if you have an interest in bumping into them or simply spending time in trendy bars and restaurants. The best accommodations, the JW Marriott in Juhu and the Taj Land's End in Bandra, are reviewed below. For more midrange options, try the newly expanded **Hotel Sea Princess** (Juhu Tara Rd.; ☎ **022/2661-1111;** Rs 11,000/$268/£136 double), where you should request a sea-facing room, or the **Ramada Palm Grove** (☎ **022/2611-2323;** Rs 12,000/$293/£148 double), right on Juhu beach; the room rate includes airport transfers and breakfast. Also recommended (and on Juhu beach) is **Citizen Hotel** (☎ **022/6693-2525;** Rs 5,500/$135/£68 double; Rs 6,500/$159/£80 deluxe sea-facing double; ask for daily discounts), which has small rooms and closet-size bathrooms but great views from large windows overlooking the Arabian Sea, plasma TV in all rooms, and a very helpful staff.

VERY EXPENSIVE

JW Marriott Hotel ⚅ Designed by the renowned architect Bill Bensley, the opulent JW is Juhu's most luxurious hotel and top choice if you choose a hotel by the quality of its in-house dining. **Lotus Café,** the sprawling 24-hour coffee shop at the bottom of the split-level lobby, is a popular hangout with the local trendy crowd, who enjoy its consistently good daily buffets; authentic Italian food is found at **Mezzo Mezzo;** and **BBC (Bombay Baking Company)** is quite simply the city's best bakery. Set over five floors, the guest rooms are comfortable, with modern, albeit rather predictable, decor and amenities; each has some kind of sea view, though most are side views. The best aspect of the hotel, aside from its dining, is the expansive tropical seaside garden, with torch-lit pathways, a lotus pond, and Indian sandstone sculptures crafted by artisans from Rajasthan. It's also got two wonderful pools, as well as a well-equipped fitness center and spa—definitely required after all the extra calories you're likely to consume at BBC while staying here.

Juhu Tara Rd., Juhu Beach, Mumbai 400 099. ☎ **022/6693-3000.** Fax 022/6693-3100. 355 units. $350/£151 superior double; $425/£215 executive ocean view; $475/£240 executive premier; $550–$900/£278–£455 suite. Executive rates

Hot Spots with Views

With the waters of the Arabian Sea lapping the entire length of the city on both its eastern and western flanks, Mumbai enjoys a fabulous seaside location, yet the city has relatively few nightspots with views worth mentioning. Most can be found in five-star establishments. With the dark blue horizon just beyond the terrace's glass railing and a star-studded sky above, **Dome** ☆☆ ((☎ 022/3987-9999; reservations recommended on weekends), on the rooftop of the InterContinental Marine Drive, commands the best vista. Sink into the inviting off-white sofas and overstuffed armchairs that surround scented candles and order a Caipiroska or a Mojito, or even a Long Island Iced Tea. Give the food a pass, although you may want to sample the mango gelato with champagne. Farther along Marine Drive at the Hotel Marine Plaza, **Bayview** ☆ ((☎ 022/2285-1212) is a 24-hour restaurant. Its drinks and buffets (Rs 150–Rs 550/$4–$13/£2–£7) are great value for money; avoid weekends when the place is packed with noisy families. Alternatively, get right on the beach and grab a hammock at **Salt Water Grill** (see full review later in this chapter) on Chowpatty (H2O Water Sports Complex; ☎ 022/2368-5459). Drink in lovely views of the Arabian Sea along with heady cocktails. For an elegant evening, **Pearl of the Orient** ☆ ((☎ 022/2204-1131), the revolving restaurant atop the Ambassador Hotel, offers more lovely views of Mumbai and good service; the food is fairly satisfying and includes Korean barbecue, inauthentic Japanese, and a sprinkling of Thai and Chinese dishes.

On the opposite shore of Mumbai's southern tip, overlooking the harbor, you'll find another set of views, quite different but every bit as remarkable. For a refined setting with a splendid view of the Gateway, make your way to the **Harbour Bar** in the Taj, where martinis, champagne, and cigars are the order of the day. Also in the Taj is **Souk** ((☎ 022/6665-3366)—although

---

include access to executive lounge, breakfast, and transfers. AE, DC, MC, V. **Amenities:** 4 restaurants; bakery and cafe; bar; nightclub; pool; kids' pool; fitness center/spa; personal trainer; concierge; business center; shopping arcade; 24-hr. room service; babysitting w/advance notice; laundry service; dry cleaning; doctor-on-call. *In room:* A/C, TV, Web TV, dataport, minibar, tea- and coffee-making facility, hair dryer, iron and ironing board, electronic safe, shaving mirror, scale.

Taj Lands End ☆☆   Location, location, location! It may be away from the central tourist area of Colaba, but this hotel enjoys a lovely seaside setting in one of Mumbai's hippest suburbs. It originally opened in 1999 as the Regent, but in 2002 the Taj Group took it over and refurbished it, turning it into one of the city's finest hotels, with each and every guest room affording views of the Arabian Sea through palm trees. The lobby is done up in earth tones and has potted plants, huge metal pots, and sculptures of horses; the atrium, with its grand piano, hosts live music every evening. Plush and slightly over the top, the carpeted guest rooms feature wonderful, solid, king-size mattresses covered in soft, cool white linen. At press time, however, half the rooms were being renovated. If you don't mind shelling out the extra $115 (£58), get a Taj Club room on the 21st floor, which has wonderful wood floors, a personal butler, express check-in and -out, and a separate lounge area with complimentary French wine and

the rooftop restaurant calls its food "Eastern Mediterranean," the cuisine it serves is generally known elsewhere as Middle Eastern or West Asian. Best is the *mezze* buffet offering the usual suspects (hummus, salads, baba ghanouj, tabbouleh, falafel, and assorted olives), as well as three interesting meat- or seafood-based salads, all accompanied by delicious, hot pita bread. Souk's location is great, but the tables near the window are placed in such a way that only one person at a table for two gets the harbor view. Go figure. If you bag a window table at **Sea Lounge** ⚜ (𝄪 022/6665-3366), the Taj's renowned coffee shop, you can watch the boats float by while demanding more Earl Grey. Although you don't have to be a guest in the hotel to enjoy any of these Taj options, do note that your manner of dress (and perceived status) has a direct effect on how well you are treated.

Moving north of the city, you can take a break at **Vista,** the cafe at the Taj Land's End in Bandra; or at **Ming Yang,** the hotel's Szechuan Chinese eatery. Both afford diners fine views of the Arabian Sea and the Portuguese fort, if you can snag a table near the window (both 𝄪 022/6668-1234). Farther north near Juhu Beach is a personal favorite, the low-key, reasonably priced seaside-veranda restaurant at **Citizen Hotel** ⚜ (𝄪 022/6692-2525), which serves formulaic Indian and Continental fare in a tranquil setting that provides one of the best unobstructed views of the sea. An air-conditioned, glass-walled section also has good views. New kid on the block **Aurus** (Nichani Kutir, Juhu Tara Rd., near Reid and Taylor, Juhu; 𝄪 022/6710-6667; daily 7:30pm–1:30am; meal for two Rs 4,000/$98/£49) has a beautiful outdoor deck overlooking the sea. The Napa Valley–trained chef whips up excellent meals. Service is slow, which gives you plenty of time to study the models and air-kissing movie stars who can almost always be spotted here.

exotic dry fruits. Purge your gastronomic sins at **Pure,** the hotel's new organic food restaurant, which is well known for healthy, innovative food served in a soothing ambience.

Land's End, Bandstand, Bandra (West), Mumbai 400 050. 𝄪 022/6668-1234. Fax 022/6699-4488. www.tajhotels. com. landsend.mumbai@tajhotels.com. 368 functional units. $405/£205 deluxe double; $440/£222 luxury double; $520/£263 Taj Club; $700/£354 executive suite; $1,000/£501 luxury suite; $1,350/£682 grand luxury suite; $2,200/£1,111 presidential suite. Taj Club rooms have complimentary breakfast, cocktail hour, high tea, transfers. Daily discounts available. AE, DC, MC, V. **Amenities:** 3 restaurants; bar; pool; spa; fitness center; concierge; travel desk; car hires; business center; bookshop; salon; 24-hr. room service; laundry service; dry cleaning; doctor-on-call; currency exchange; butler on call (luxury and club lounge floors); Wi-Fi enabled. *In room:* A/C, TV, dataport, minibar, tea- and coffee-making facilities, hair dryer, electronic safe, scale, magnifying shaving mirror, electronic bedside console. Taj Club rooms have plasma TV.

MODERATE

Sun-n-Sand ⚜   This small, old-fashioned beachfront hotel was getting a much-needed overhaul at press time; however, the revamp includes an attempt to conserve water (making bathtubs now available only in the suites). Specify a sea-facing standard double room. Breakfast, cocktail hour, and airport transfers are included in the rate.

The luxury suites are done in various themes—"Suko Thai" has wooden floors, Thai rocking chair, figurines, lamps, flower-painted columns, and a pleasant circular seating area, while Galleria is apparently inspired by a contemporary art gallery, with mod lights, curved wall paneling, and a Jacuzzi bath and exercise area—but for not much more you could be at the JW Marriott, which has infinitely better service and amenities. Service borders on the adequate, but this doesn't seem to matter much to yesteryear Bollywood stars frequenting the bar.

39 Juhu Beach, Mumbai 400 049. ✆ **022/6693-8888**. Fax 022/2620-2170. www.sunnsandhotel.com. reservations@sunnsandhotel.com. 120 units. Rs 8,500 ($207/£104) superior double; Rs 9,500 ($231/£117) superior sea-facing double; Rs 10,500 ($256/£130) executive double; Rs 11,500 ($280/£142) deluxe double; Rs 13,000–20,000 ($317–$488/£160–£247) suite. Rates include buffet breakfast, airport transfers, and cocktail hours. AE, DC, MC, V. **Amenities:** 2 restaurants; bar; pool; health and fitness center; Jacuzzi; travel desk; business center; shops; salon; massage; laundry; doctor-on-call; Wi-Fi enabled lobby. *In room:* A/C, flatscreen TV, dataport, minibar, tea- and coffee-making facility, hair dryer, iron, electronic safe, shaving mirror, scale.

NEAR THE AIRPORT

The reasons for staying here are obvious, but it seems a pity to stay in these cocoons when The Taj Mahal and Oberoi beckon from Colaba.

Hyatt Regency ★★★ *Value*   As is the case with most any airport hotel, the only reason to book here is as a transit passenger, and as such the Hyatt comes up trumps. You will be picked up from the airport (the transfer costs around Rs 1,000/$23/£12—ludicrous given the distance, but book it), and swept away for the 5-minute drive to the hotel. At press time the surrounds were little more than a depressing building site, but at night (which is when you arrive) you see none of this, arriving instead to a huge space with all the dramatic design-intensive *joie de vivre* of a modern art gallery. Stacked glass walls, mood lighting, floating ebony ceiling effects, and Italian marble are offset by marigolds in tailored cube bouquets—and that's just the lobby. The sleek (and most important, silent) guest rooms deliver every comfort, with a judicious use of space, imaginative lighting, and smart fittings. One entire wall is a mirror, floors are Malaysian teakwood, desks are swivel-top slabs of glass, and the televisions are flatscreen. White-marble bathrooms offer a choice between large rain showers or separate step-down bathtubs—a welcome treat after a long plane journey. Breakfasts are superb, and the **Club Prana spa** is a popular pre- and post-flight venue. **Stax,** the in-house Italian restaurant, is the classiest dining option, good enough to attract locals who live in the vicinity of the airport for a fine dining evening. All in all the Hyatt offers a slickly professional experience for the transit passenger, and if you can get a room at a particularly low rate (these change daily, so call or check out the online rates), look no further.

Sahar Airport Rd., Mumbai 400 099. ✆ **022/5696-1234**. Fax 022/5696-1235. www.hyatt.com. 397 units. Rates on day-to-day basis but at press time Rs 11,500 ($261/£132) standard double; Rs 12,500 ($284/£143) Regency Club. Rates include breakfast. Club rate includes use of private lounge, dedicated concierge, complimentary use of meeting room, all-day tea and coffee service, and evening cocktails and canapés. AE, DC, MC, V. **Amenities:** 3 restaurants; bar; pool; lighted tennis and squash courts; spa and fitness center; 24-hr. room service; laundry; doctor-on-call. *In room:* A/C, TV, dataport, minibar, tea- and coffee-making facility, electronic safe.

ITC Hotel Grand Maratha Sheraton & Towers ★★   Since its opening in 2001, the Grand Maratha has already been recognized with at least one award as the country's best hotel. An imposing pink-sandstone neoclassical building topped by a futuristic dome, the Sheraton recalls elements of India's rich architectural legacy: thick columns, imposing contours, arches, a cobbled entrance flanked by two wooden horses and, in the porte-cochere, a Goan-inspired coffered ceiling. Rooms don't disappoint:

Beds are fabulously comfy, London-based interior designer Francesca Basu has captured the local love of bright colors, and the garden views in some rooms (ask for one) are lovely. The seven different restaurants, all of excellent quality, are reason enough to stay here: Both **Dakshin,** offering the cuisines of South India, and **Dum Pukht,** its special-ties inherited from the *Nawabs* of Awadh, are good places to go, particularly if you haven't had (or won't have) a chance to sample these cuisines elsewhere in India.

Sahar, Mumbai 400 099. © 022/2830-3030. Delhi reservations: © 011/2614-1821. Fax 022/2830-3131. www.itc welcomgroup.in. Reservations.itcmaratha@itcwelcomgroup.in. 386 units. $425/£215 Executive Club double; $475/£240 Sheraton Towers double; $525/£265 ITC One double; $500–$2,200/£253–£1,111 suites. Daily discounts available. AE, DC, MC, V. **Amenities:** 6 restaurants; bar; pool; wellness center w/gym, steam, sauna, Jacuzzi, massage, and spa treatments; concierge; travel and tour desk; car hires; business center; shops and boutiques; salon; 24-hr. room service; babysitting; laundry and valet service; doctor-on-call; currency exchange; Wi-Fi. *In room:* A/C, TV, mini-bar, tea- and coffee-making facility, hair dryer, electronic safe, scale, shaving mirror. Sheraton Towers rooms include butler service. ITC One rooms include step machine, hand-held massager, massage chair, fax machine. Sheraton Tow-ers and ITC One guests enjoy access to an exclusive lounge and library.

The Orchid ⍟   In a city this polluted, a stay at this multiple-award-winning eco-friendly hotel at least serves to relieve some tourist guilt. But that's not the only rea-son to stay here: Thankfully, the hotel's commitment to preserving the environment is combined with reasonably good taste and service. Environment-friendly considera-tions include solar-powered terrace lights, wastewater treatment technology, in-room recycle bins, and a UV-treated chlorine-free swimming pool. You'll find plants in all the rooms (which are comfortable) and understated furniture made from Nuwud medium-density-fiber "wood," the eco-conscious alternative to ripping down entire forests. Emphasizing the eco-theme, paintings and prints of orchids and flowers are found throughout the hotel, and the lobby features a six-story water curtain—recy-cled water, of course. The rooftop pool with its Mexican hacienda–style barbecue restaurant offers interesting views—particularly if you enjoy watching Mumbai's heavy air traffic come and go.

Adjacent Domestic Airport, Nehru Rd., Vile Parle (East), Mumbai 400 099. © 022/2616-4040. Toll-free 1-600-22-5432. Fax 022/2616-4141. www.orchidhotel.com. resohmu@orchidhotel.com. 245 units. $350/£177 deluxe double; $385/£193 executive suite; $430/£217 Club Privé room; $460/£232 Club Privé suite; $525/£265 Orchid suite; $800/£404 Presidential suite. $50/£25 extra bed. Children under 12 stay free in parent's room. All rates include com-plimentary breakfast and airport transfers. AE, DC, MC, V. **Amenities:** 3 restaurants; bar; pool; fitness center; travel desk; airport transfers; business center; pastry/gourmet shop; 24-hr. room service; 24-hr. tea/coffee; laundry service; dry cleaning; currency exchange; Wi-Fi enabled. *In room:* A/C, TV, minibar, tea- and coffee-making facilities, hair dryer, iron (on request), scale and magnifying shaving mirror only in club rooms and suites.

5 Where to Dine

Nowhere in India is dining more rewarding than in Mumbai. The city literally holds thousands of restaurants, and being a city of migrants, every kind of Indian cuisine is represented—though Konkan, or coastal food, is considered the local specialty. You can mingle with the city's crème de la crème at fine-dining or hip venues, or choose from a vast array of inexpensive eating places. Restaurants serving South Indian fast food (also called Udipi restaurants) can be found on every street, but if you sample only one and are willing to go the extra mile, make it either **Café Madras** (King's Cir-cle; © **022/2401-4419;** Tues–Sun) in Matunga or **A. Ramanayak Udipi Shri Krishna Boarding** ⍟⍟ (Main Market Building, first floor, near Matunga Railway Station; © **022/2414-2422;** Tues–Sun). The latter is a no-frills eatery where an authentic Madras-style meal is served on a banana leaf (Rs 60/$1/£1), and you eat with your hands. Other Indian cuisines you will come across everywhere are neighborhood kebab places (**Noorani** 𝒢; Haji Ali; ℭ 022/2353-4753 or -3054; serves good kebabs and will even deliver to your South Mumbai hotel); restaurants specializing in local favorites like *pau bhaji* (mixed vegetables and bread); Irani restaurants serving fresh inexpensive breads and *chai;* and Chinese restaurants offering "Indianized Chinese," much of it quite good, but avoid the ubiquitous and unappetizing red "Szechwan" sauce dishes.

There's an explosion of exceptional Chinese (and other Southeast Asian cuisines) and Italian eateries in Mumbai. **Royal China** 𝒢𝒢 (two branches: Fort ℭ 022/6635-5310 and Bandra ℭ 022/2642-5533) is where chef David Pang produces superb Hong Kong–style Chinese; we particularly love the dim sum. At the new, stylish, and spacious **VongWong** 𝒢 (Express Towers, Nariman Point; ℭ 022/875-633), Thai and Chinese food and Asian-style cocktails come with great service (don't get overwhelmed by the vast menu). For pan-Asian meals, the following come well recommended: **Joss** (Kalaghoda; ℭ 022/6635-6908; www.jossrestaurant.com); and in Bandra the very hip **Seijo and the Soul Dish** 𝒢 (206 Krystal, Waterfield Rd.; ℭ 022/2640-5555), which also has a great bar.

Trident Towers has two Italian restaurants. **Vetro** 𝒢𝒢, with Venetian glass interiors, serves Italian from the Mediterranean region. The kid-friendly **Frangipani** 𝒢𝒢 bakes great pizzas and other Italian dishes (among other cuisines). **Stax** 𝒢𝒢 at the Hyatt Regency (see earlier review) is one of our favorite eateries, with a wonderful open kitchen serving delicious food from the coastal provinces of Italy. If you're in Juhu, stop at **Mezzo Mezzo** (mentioned later in the Suburbs section) or across the street at **Don Giovanni** 𝒢 (ℭ 022/2612-2372), where owner Giovanni Fredrico warns diners to expect a long wait because everything is made fresh. Nearby, **Little Italy** (ℭ 022/2660-8815) is, believe it or not, an excellent vegetarian Italian restaurant. Not surprisingly, vegetarians are particularly well catered to in all Mumbai restaurants.

Tip: Bear in mind that Mumbaikars usually venture out to eat late, around 9pm, so if you're intent on eating at a popular fine-dining restaurant and don't have a reservation, ask if you can arrive at 7:30pm.

COLABA (INCLUDING MARINE DRIVE) & FORT
EXPENSIVE
Henry Tham 𝒢𝒢 CHINESE   Dining at this exclusive eatery makes you feel like royalty, beginning with the red-velvet thronelike chairs that extend several feet above your head. Take your pick from the numerous set menus in different price ranges (cheaper at lunch). Dishes on the set menu have fancy names. Some of our favorites include: Liquid Gold, a superb miso soup with seaweed and squares of tofu; Splash of Joy, delicately steamed grouper with a hint of scallion; and Drifting on the Yellow River, king prawns marinated in rice wine and yellow soybean paste and grilled. Vegetarians are also spoiled for choice. If you're going a la carte, give the soups a miss and order a bunch of the flavorful appetizers (bacon-wrapped prawns, Mongolian chicken, assorted dim sum)—it will leave you feeling quite sated. Follow this with not more than two dishes from the extensive menu (helpings are substantial), and the finale should be the "tree of life," which gets full marks for presentation—it's really only freshly cut fruit served on a bed of crushed ice with two flavors of soufflé. Overall, this is a classy affair—perfect for a celebration dinner or a special treat. Downstairs is the lounge and bar area, which is packed to the hilt (and very loud) from Thursday to Saturday night (Thurs is

Seafood Thrillers

Anyone with a penchant for seafood will love dining in Mumbai—whether it's Coastal, Konkani, Manglorean, or Malvani cuisine, you are in for a treat. Besides Mahesh Lunch Home and Trishna (see reviews below), you can try **Apoorva** *&* (Brelvi Marg, near Horniman Circle; *©* **022/2287-0335** or 022/2288-1457), which has similar Manglorean fare, as does **Excellensea** *&* (Mint Rd., near RBI; *©* **022/2261-8991**). The latter is on the first floor above **Bharat Restaurant** *&*, a non-air-conditioned economy version of Excellensea serving the same food. Note that if you are in a Konkan restaurant, you may want to try the *soul kadi,* a slightly pungent coconut milk drink and a great appetizer. Also sample fresh *appams* and *neer dosas*—both these Southern breads make excellent accompaniments to your seafood. Closer to central Mumbai is **Pisces** *&&* (*©* **022/2380-5886** or -4367), done up in the standard fish-themed decor but offering more variety in cooking styles. You haven't lived until you've tried the tamarind prawns (prawns *amtoic*)—these alone are worth the trip. Also try the *malai chingri* (a cashew nut–based coconut curry with prawns). In the suburbs in Bandra, you'll get real value for money and atmosphere at the friendly **Soul Fry** *&* (*©* **022/2604-6892**), which makes great flaky stuffed grilled *rawas* (a local fish). Monday is karaoke night, and even if you can't sing to save your life, it's a great experience to watch extremely talented locals unabashedly take the mic and have the whole place rocking well past midnight. Soul Fry is an extremely lively and friendly restaurant. Its new branch **Soul Fry Casa** (*©* **022/2267-1421**) recently opened at Fountain (near Fab India) and promises the best of the original Soul Fry, plus lots of live music to accompany the home-style Goan dishes.

live music night). Even if you're not at the bar, do try some of the excellent cocktails; we loved the cosmopolitans (the sugar cane is superb) and the Caipiroskas.

Dhanraj Mahal, Apollo Bunder. *©* 022/2284-8214. Reservations essential. Dinner set menus Rs 485–Rs 1,500 ($12–$37/£6–£19); lunch set menus Rs 490–Rs 550 ($12–$13/£6–£7); a la carte main courses Rs 215–Rs 810 ($5–$20/£3–£10). AE, MC, V. Daily 12:30–3:30pm and 7:30pm–midnight.

India Jones *&&&* SOUTHEAST ASIAN · The menu, in the form of an old traveler's map and diary, is a treasure trove of exciting Asian dishes. Start by sharing an appetizer platter—among the superb array are chicken/prawn spring roll, chicken/shrimp *siu mai,* satay chicken, and raw papaya salad with lime, mint, and basil, served with a selection of dips. Or two of you can share the platter of spring rolls from across Southeast Asia: Vietnamese rice-paper rolls, fried rice-paper rolls with crab, deep-fried mango and prawn rolls, bean-curd and chicken rolls—you name it, they roll it. But the hands-down favorite, certainly with locals who want to sample as much as possible of the extensive menu, is the "India Jones Grand Platter": an appetizer assortment; soup (*tom kha* or chicken and coriander); and a platter of green chicken curry, wok-fried prawns, stir-fried sea bass with celery, barbecued pork with honey, wok-fried mixed vegetables in black-peppercorn sauce—and the list goes on. At Rs 3,100 ($76/£43) for two, it's pricey, but it's a feast that will leave you bursting.

For the not-so-ravenous, there's plenty more: the Wok Platter (also highly recommended), live seafood (try the grouper in soy-ginger broth), and a separate *teppanyaki* counter controlled by chef Wikant. As expected of any Oberoi restaurant, the service and decor are exemplary.

Hilton Towers, Nariman Point. © 022/6632-4343. Main courses Rs 450–Rs 3,500 ($11–$85/£6–£43); platters Rs 500–Rs 1,550 ($12–$38/£6–£19) per head. AE, DC, MC, V. Daily 12:30–2:45pm and 7:30–11:45pm.

Indigo 𝕏𝕏𝕏 FUSION/INTERNATIONAL   Well-known restaurateur-chef Rahul Akerkar has created a restaurant that tops every food critic's A-list and has been listed by *Condé Nast Traveler* as one of the 60 best restaurants in the world. Angelina Jolie and Brad Pitt, Liz Hurley, the Clintons, and every other international celebrity passing through Mumbai seems to stop here. We recommend you sit upstairs in the open-air terrace section with its frangipani trees. Indigo's chic ambience is enhanced by the clientele: By 9:30pm the entire bar section is heaving with the city's Beautiful People. The international/fusion menu is not extensive, changing once a year, but specials are on offer, with something for every appetite. The celebrated lobster and shallot risotto is a constant on the changing menu, and for very good reason; it's delicious. Whether it's the tuna, *rawas,* beef tenderloin, ravioli, or tortellini mains, Indigo's dishes are simple yet utterly delightful. End the meal with the unique chocolate fondant with jalapeño peppers or the daily special soufflé (the lemon soufflé is out of this world). Indigo's Sunday brunch with accompanying jazz band and free-flowing Indian liquor is legendary; if you'd like to stuff yourself silly from noon to 3pm and rub shoulders with the city's socialites, book your table in advance.

4 Mandlik House, Colaba. © 022/6636-8984 or -8985. Reservations essential. Main courses Rs 465–Rs 1,650 ($11–$40/£6–£20); Sun brunch Rs 1,744 ($43/£22). AE, DC, MC, V. Daily noon–2:45pm and 7:30–11:45pm.

Kandahar 𝕏𝕏 NORTHWEST FRONTIER   This well-appointed restaurant, also located in The Oberoi, is a great place to sample the traditionally rich cuisine of the Northwest Frontier as well as lighter, home-style dishes. Kebabs are a specialty here, and the robust *Kabuli raan* (lamb) is soft, fragrant, and delicious, if a tad dry. Or try the rich *Patiala shahi maas,* lamb cooked in a cashew nut gravy. For a home-style dish, order the *dahiwali bhindi* (okra cooked in yogurt), a perfect complement to the heavier meat dishes. Mop up the butter-soaked, sinfully rich Kandahari or Kaali *dal* (black *dal*) with *pudina paratha* (mint bread) or *bootiwali naan* (herb-encrusted *naan*). Skip ahead to dessert: The *malpua with rabri* (pancake topped with sweet, thickened milk and nuts) is excellent. Or ask for one of the homemade *kulfis* (ice creams). Wash it all down with a refreshing *shikanjvi,* a tall glass of lemonade with spices and a slice of lime. The service here is exemplary and makes up for anything lacking in the food. (Note that Kandahar hosts regular food festivals; if you're around, don't miss one—you're sure to sample some unrivaled delights.)

The Oberoi, Nariman Point. © 022/6632-5757. Average meal Rs 1,500 ($37/£19) per person. AE, DC, MC, V. Daily 12:30–2:45pm and 7:30–11:30pm.

Khyber 𝕏𝕏 NORTH INDIAN   Khyber has been going strong for decades now, so much so that there is not even a sign outside to mark the restaurant, but its classic Mughlai cuisine and tender kebabs remain outstanding. Start with *kali mirch rawas* (fish seasoned in black pepper), firm yet meltingly good; or chicken *badami* (in rich almond sauce) and *paneer shashlik* (grilled Indian cottage cheese, spices, and vegetables). Follow these with Khyber *raan* (lamb) or mutton *chaap* Mughlai and piping-hot *naan* bread. To cleanse the palate (Mughlai cuisine is very rich), order the fresh seasonal fruit or the *ras malai*. Besides the great food, Khyber is an experience in royal dining: The opulent decor includes original paintings by some of India's most famous artists (the likes of M. F. Hussain and Anjolie Ela Menon). Seating is intimate and maximizes privacy—perfect for a romantic dinner (ask to be seated in the Anjolie Ela Menon Room). Not much changes at this Mumbai institution, and service is sometimes slow.

145 MG Rd., Kala Ghoda. ℂ 022/2267-3227 through -3229. Reservations required but are only guaranteed for seating before 8:30pm or after 10:15pm. Main courses Rs 230–Rs 650 ($6–$16/£3–£8); average meal Rs 1,000 ($24/£12) per person. AE, DC, MC, V. Daily 12:30–3:30pm and 7:30–11:30pm.

Tiffin ⓡⓡ INTERNATIONAL/FUSION The only way to do justice to Tiffin's impressive 158-item, all-day dining menu featuring food from all over the world is to come back repeatedly. Eating is a celebration here, enhanced by presentation and a lively decor. We recommend the following: salad of palm hearts, fennel, thin slices of tart apple, and water chestnut; for main courses we like the trio of Australian lamb or the pork cutlets with black truffle mash. You can also get a rigorously Japanese sushi and sashimi platter at the interactive sushi bar, where Filipino chef Francesco Balanquit takes orders. Don't miss pastry chef Ravindra Varma's ice creams, which combine unusual flavors such as wasabi and caramelized brown sugar, green tea and candied ginger (refreshing), or star anise and *rambutan* (a tropical fruit). Wash it down with a fresh juice, though some of the "healthier" ones containing *amla* (Indian gooseberry) can run a tad sour; opt instead for the more sane apple, red beet, and celery blend. For a snack, you can now also get sandwiches, burgers, and salads.

The Oberoi, Nariman Point. ℂ 022/6632-5757. Main courses Rs 525–Rs 1,300 ($13–$32/£6–£16); champagne brunch Sun Rs 1,950 ($48/£24). AE, DC, MC, V. Daily 6:30am–11:30pm.

Trishna ⓡⓡⓡ SEAFOOD Another restaurant frequented by the who's who of Mumbai, Trishna is considered one of the best in the world. Butter pepper garlic king crab is Trishna's signature dish, but you'll also find jumbo pomfrets and tiger prawns (done in any style) cooked to perfection. Despite its reputation as a somewhat snobbish restaurant, Trishna isn't about ambience (the decor in fact is somewhat tacky)— everyone is here for the food. Recommended dishes include pomfret Hyderabadi— barbecued with black pepper, it's a true masterpiece; pomfret *hariyali* enveloped in green masala and baked in a tandoor; fish *sholay* kebab; Kolhapuri prawns (spicy, so order a drink); or squid expertly prepared with butter, pepper, and garlic. Staff tends to be rather snooty, and if you ask for menu suggestions you're sure to be recommended the most expensive items on the menu. Don't expect to get in any night without a reservation, unless you're willing to arrive by 7pm and be out by 8pm.

Birla Mansion, Sai Baba Marg (next to Commerce House), Kala Ghoda, Fort. ℂ 022/2270-3213 up to -3215. Reservations essential. Main courses Rs 275–Rs 900 ($7–$22/£3–£11) depending on fish size; crab/lobster Rs 550–Rs 2,000 ($13–$49/£7–£25). AE, DC, MC, V. Daily noon–3:30pm and 6pm–midnight (from 7pm on Sun and holidays).

MODERATE/INEXPENSIVE

Now in its 34th year, **Delhi Darbar** (ℂ 022/2202-0235; daily 11:30am–midnight; average meal Rs 350/$9/£4) is a Mumbai institution serving rather standard (and oily) Mughlai food. It has several branches in Mumbai, but we recommend only the one at Colaba. No one comes here for the ambience or service—most come for the tandoori dishes or the mutton or chicken *biryani*. Ignore the Chinese menu. No alcohol is served or allowed. No alcohol at **Koyla** ⓡ either (on the roof of the Gulf Hotel, not far from the Taj; ℂ 022/6636-9999; www.koylaethniccuisine.com; Tues–Sun 7:30pm– 12:30am). It's recommended for its leisurely ambience and setting: a candlelit terrace with Arabian music playing in the background. The most popular item on the menu is not food, but the *sheesha* (hookah or pipe; Rs 200/$4/£2), with fruity flavors like green apple and strawberry. The food is mediocre, but order some kebabs just to enjoy the cool evening breeze, or come after dinner to relax, sit back, and linger over a "mocktail." The atmosphere is laid-back and no one will hustle you out—but service can be painfully slow. Reservations are recommended; even then, expect a wait. The Rs 100 ($2/£1) per-person cover charge is redeemable against your bill.

Britannia &&& *Moments* IRANI   This no-nonsense, no-frills, 90-year-old Irani (Persian) restaurant is the last of a dying breed of establishments once found on every corner of South Mumbai. The environment is simple and functional, with little room for extras like presentation and ambience. Most people come here to consume one or more of three excellent dishes: Berry *pulao* (a version of the Iranian *zereshk polow*) is the outstanding signature dish, made with succulent spiced boneless mutton (or chicken), fragrant long-grain basmati rice, and tart barberries imported from Iran. *Patra ni machchi* is pomfret fish coated in chutney made with cilantro, coconut, and assorted spices; wrapped in a banana leaf; and steamed—always moist and flaky with flavors all the way down to the bone. The mutton *dhansak* is a combination of fragrant brown rice and thick *dal* in which the meat has been cooked—a dense, hearty meal that tastes a million times better than it looks. (Vegetarians, though catered to, should give this restaurant a miss.)

Opposite New Customs House, Ballard Estate Fort. ✆ 022/2261-5264. Berry *pulao* and *dhansak* Rs 100–Rs 200 ($2–$4/£1–£2); *dhansak* or *patra ni machchi* Rs 200 ($4/£2). No credit cards. Lunch only Mon–Sat 11:30am–3:30pm.

Konkan Café && KONKAN   Chef Ananda Solomon has earned an enviable reputation for his inspired specialties, garnered from up and down the Konkan coast and served with style and an extensive collection of wines. Although the menu is constantly reinvented, look for specialties like the *meen pollichathu, rawas* cooked in a spicy tomato-onion sauce and baked in a banana leaf; and the heavenly *sukha* mutton. You can also sample specialties like *kori kachpu,* a yellow chicken curry, or fish *moilee,* pomfret rubbed with turmeric and lime and cooked in fragrant coconut milk, and of course the *feni* (the Goan liquor distilled from coconuts or cashews). Don't know what to pick? Get the consistently good seafood thali.

Taj President Hotel (see "Where to Stay," earlier in this chapter). ✆ 022/6665-0808. Thali Rs 650 ($16/£8) vegetarian, Rs 700 ($17/£9) non-vegetarian, Rs 750 ($18/£9) seafood; a la carte about Rs 750 ($18/£9) per person. AE, DC, MC, V. Daily 12:30–2:45pm and 7–11:45pm.

Leopold Café & CONTINENTAL/INDIAN/CHINESE   It's not uncommon to walk into this Colaba institution and not see a single Indian face around. Why it's such a hit with foreigners is a mystery, since the food is good but not exceptional, and the atmosphere can be noisy and rather smoky. All the same, it is consistent, and because it's one of those popular places where tourists like to share stories with other tourists over a beer, it deserves mention. It caters to Western tastes by providing items like cereals, eggs and toast, fish and chips, and club sandwiches side by side with chicken *biryani* and Indian-Chinese fare. The fresh fruit juices and *lassis* (yogurt drinks) are always a good bet if you're looking for a light pick-me-up during shopping forays on the causeway. And if you're keen to get the inside scoop on how Bollywood films are made, hang out here; casting agents looking for foreigners to work as extras on current productions frequently scan the clientele for able bodies at this favored travelers' hangout. *Tip:* Check your bill before you pay it to make sure it doesn't contain anything you didn't order.

Colaba Causeway. ℂ **022/2287-3362**. Lassis/juices/milkshakes Rs 50 ($1/£1); Mughlai main courses Rs 95 ($2/£1); Chinese main courses Rs 120 ($3/£2). AE, DC, MC, V. Daily 7am–midnight.

Mahesh Lunch Home 🎔🎔🎔 SEAFOOD   The ceiling may be too low and the tables too close together, but this Manglorean seafood restaurant should not be missed if you love fish—it's one of Mumbai's best restaurants, consistently dishing out pleasing specialties. Everything is incredibly fresh, but favorites include *surmai* fry, pomfret curry, and tandoori pomfret—all outstanding. The latter (listed as a starter, but you can order it as a main) is served flawlessly moist; eaten with butter *naan,* it provides the most heavenly gastronomic experience imaginable. Also try the scrumptious prawns Koliwada, crab tandoori, pomfret in green masala, or any of the fish curries or *gassis,* all first-rate. (Note that *gassi* refers to the thick, spicy, coconut-based Manglorean curry, while the "curries" on the menu are a thinner version of the same.) Mahesh also serves meat, chicken, and Chinese dishes, but only the misguided would come here and skip the sensational seafood.

8D Cowasji Patel St., off Pherozeshah Mehta Rd., Fort. ℂ **022/2287-0938** or 022/2202-3965. Fish fry/curry/*gassi* Rs 110–Rs 150 ($3–$4/£1–£3); jumbo pomfret/crab/lobster Rs 400–Rs 1,500 ($10–$37/£5–£19); other main courses Rs 150–Rs 300 ($4–$7/£2–£3). AE, DC, MC, V. Daily 11:30am–3:30pm and 6:30–11:30pm.

Samovar 🎔🎔 INDIAN   This long, narrow restaurant inside Jehangir Art Gallery is another South Mumbai institution that has retained its charm and low prices in spite of its popularity. With quick, efficient service and a policy of not hurrying diners even if others are waiting, this is the perfect stopover after a day roaming the Prince of Wales museum and other local landmarks. Start with a delicious seasonal fruit juice— the guava juice is the best when it's in season. *Boti* rolls (spiced meat wrapped in chapatis) rival with *parathas* (fried breads with a great assortment of stuffings) to satiate the taste buds along with the yummy bean-sprout salad. A stop here is a must: This is as close to home cooking as you are likely to get on a short visit to Mumbai.

Jehangir Art Gallery, Kala Ghoda, Fort. ℂ **022/2284-8000**. Average meal Rs 200 ($5/£2). No credit cards. Mon–Sat 11am–7:30pm. Closed Sun.

BEYOND DOWNTOWN: CHOWPATTY TO WORLI

Copper Chimney 🎔🎔🎔 KEBABS/MUGHLAI   For more than 23 years, Copper Chimney has delighted those looking for the perfect kebabs. To this end, two pages of the menu are dedicated to kebabs, from the popular *reshmi* kebab (chicken) to the *jhinga nisha* (tandoori prawn kebabs). These tender, creamy, smoky-flavored, melt-in-your-mouth kebabs can be followed by traditional Dum Pukht specialties such as chicken *makhani* (butter chicken) or the even more exquisite Peshawari lamb. No matter what you pick, you will leave satisfied. There's also a daily buffet lunch, but don't be swayed by the variety—some of the best items on the menu (such as the unfailingly wonderful butter chicken) are not offered at the buffet. Note that although Copper Chimney branches are found all over the city, the one at Worli is the only one to patronize.

Dr. Annie Besant Rd., Worli. ℂ **022/2492-0505** or -5353. Main courses Rs 199–Rs 375 ($5–$9/£2–£4); tiger prawns Rs 695 ($17/£9). AE, DC, MC, V. Daily 12:30–3:30pm and 7:30pm–12:30am.

Oh Calcutta! 🎔🎔 BENGALI   The famous hand-pulled rickshaw of Kolkata stands outside this one-of-a-kind eatery at Tardeo, not far from the Haji Ali mosque. The restaurant's specialty is its freshwater fish, flown in fresh from Kolkata. For starters, *kakra chingri bhapa,* or prawn and crabmeat cake spiced and steamed in banana leaves, is superb, but so is everything else; even the simple fish fry is outstanding. Close your eyes and order either the *daab chingri* or the *chingri malai* curry, both coconut-milk-based prawn curries, both different and gently flavorful, with steamed rice. For more robust flavors, try *illish machher patur*, hilsa fish marinated with mustard and green chili paste and steamed in banana leaf. As a Bengali restaurant, fish dominates the menu, but vegetarians are well catered to and can order a number of dishes, including the classic banana flower and potato dish *mochar ghonto*. If you don't eat fish, you can still get meat and chicken dishes from the menu. In short, after three meals here we've yet to find an item on the menu we don't like.

Hotel Rosewood, Tulsiwadi Lane, Tardeo. © 022/2353-9114 or 022/6580-6216. Reservations recommended on weekend nights. Main courses Rs 120–Rs 810 ($3–$20/£1–£10). AE, MC, V. Daily noon–2:45pm and 7–11:45pm.

Salt Water Grill *Moments* INTERNATIONAL   Alongside Chowpatty's water-sports complex H2O, this restaurant sits on the edge of the beach, a few feet from breaking waves. Well-lit terra-cotta sculptures add to the serene atmosphere of this absolutely stunning location. Pick from a variety of seating options—hammocks, lounge chairs, sofas, or traditional tables—and wiggle your toes in the sand, enjoying the sea breeze. Bar manager Naveen Kotyankar, who also designed the bar menu, makes a delicious Watermelon Caipiroska, definitely one of the best drinks on offer. Unfortunately, things go rather downhill after the cocktails, and on several occasions the food has tasted like airline food. There's a reason: We later found out the food is precooked in a kitchen 30 minutes away and reheated here. *Note:* Call ahead and check that alcohol is being served—the establishment seems to have trouble renewing their liquor license each year.

Tips The Skinny on Street Food

Street food is something you should be careful about experimenting with any-where in India. The spots we recommend are not on the street; they serve san-itized (yet authentic) versions of what is available on the street. One place where you can safely try street food while sipping chilled beer is **Vithal Bhel-wala** *, near the Excelsior Theatre, Fort (© 022/6631-7211 or -7212; daily noon–11pm). If you're into fusion street food, try their Chinese *bhel* or American *sev puri!* You get to eat real Mumbai-style street food under very sanitary (if busy and noisy) conditions at **Swati Snacks** **, in Tardeo (© 022/6580-8405 or -8406; daily 11am–11pm). Try the *sev puri, bhel, dahi batata puri* (Rs 47/$1/£1 each), or any of the numerous snack items topped with delicious sweet, sour, and spicy chutneys and sauces while you sip a hygienic sugar cane juice. Round out your meal with homemade fruit-flavored ice creams. Locals come here more for the traditional Gujarati dishes not found anywhere else. If you want to exper-iment, try the superb *peru nu shak* (spiced guava eaten with Indian bread) and *panki* (thin pancakes steamed in banana leaf). Enjoy fare similar to Swati's with-out the hour-long wait and in a quieter, more composed setting at **Soam** (Sadguru Sadan, opposite Babulnath temple, Chowpatty; © 022/2369-8080). Bandra's famous hygienic street-food stop is **Elco Pani Puri Centre & Caterers** at Elco Arcade on Hill Road (© 022/2645-7677), once a street stall and now an air-conditioned restaurant that uses bottled water to prepare its snacks.

The Thali: Gujarati & Rajasthani Cuisine at its Best

You can't leave this city without consuming at least one thali, the meal that really tests the size of your appetite! It works like this: Sit down, and in less than a minute you're expected to declare which thali you want—ordinary, special, and so on. Seconds later, a large, stainless-steel (or silver) plate *(thali)* arrives along with six to eight small bowls *(katoris)* resting on it. The waiters then fill every one of the multiple *katoris* as well as the rest of the plate with a large assortment of steaming-hot, spiced vegetables, savories, *dals,* beans, *rotis, puris,* and so on. To wash it down, you're served water and a glass of delicious, super-thin, cumin-flavored buttermilk *(chaas).* As you eat, your *katoris* will be topped up, so indicate what you want for seconds, thirds, fourths—a veritable onslaught that won't stop until you say so. Then it's a round of rice or *khichdi* (a mixture of rice and *dal*) and, in some restaurants, dessert. Not only are thalis a great value (you pay Rs 50–Rs 250/$1–$6/£1–£3), but they come pretty close to the home cooking of the country's Gujarati (or Rajasthani) population. End your visit to Crawford Market with lunch at local favorite **Rajdhani** (② 022/2342-6919; also at the Opera House ② 022/2361-3060; Rs 191/$5/£2; daily noon–3:30pm, Mon–Sat 7–10:30pm). At **Panchvati Gaurav** ⟨⟨ (opposite Bombay Hospital, Marine Lines; ② 022/2208-4877; Tues–Sun 11am–3pm and 7–10:30pm; Mon lunch only), you'll pay Rs 120 to Rs 210 ($3–$5/£2–£3) for an excellent meal (they even have a non-spicy thali). **Chetana Veg Restaurant and Bar** ⟨ (Fort; ② 022/2284-4968; daily 12:30–3:30pm, 4:30–6:30pm [snacks only], and 7:30–11:30pm) has many options and even serves a diet thali (Chetna Lite)—but doesn't that miss the point?

H2O Water Sports Complex, next to Mafatlal Swimming Club, Marine Dr. ② 022/2368-5485. Main courses Rs 310–Rs 750 ($8–$18/£4–£9); cocktails Rs 350–Rs 425 ($9–$10/£4–£5). AE, MC, V. Daily 7:30pm–12:30am; Sangria bar 4–7:30pm.

SUBURBS—BANDRA TO JUHU & NEAR THE AIRPORT

For prime people-watching, spend some time at **Prithvi Café** ⟨⟨ (② 022/2617-4118) in the Prithvi Theatre compound in Juhu. This pleasant, unpretentious cafe is where many of Mumbai's up-and-coming and/or struggling *artistes* come to nosh and discuss their art. The cafe serves great fresh *parathas* and a variety of teas and coffees over which you can linger undisturbed. If it's stargazing you're after, the restaurant that takes the prize is the **Olive Bar and Kitchen** ⟨ (near Pali Hill Tourist Hotel, 14 Union Park Khar [W]; ② 022/2605-8228), the trendiest restaurant in Bandra. This Mediterranean restaurant is expensive and the food good but inconsistent, but it's the place to see and be seen. Get there early and sit in the lovely open-air space outside, always buzzing with Beautiful People; it's a perfect spot for lingering over multiple drinks. At the other end of the spectrum is **Govinda** (② 022/2620-0337), at the Hare Krishna Temple in Juhu, where you can gorge from a 30- to 40-item all-vegetarian buffet (no onions or garlic, either). Many items are cooked in pure ghee (clarified butter), however, so expect the meal to be extremely heavy. **Papa Pancho** in Bandra's Pali Market (② 022/2651-8732) is done up like a truck stop and serves quality Punjabi food and *chaat.* **Zenzi** ⟨⟨ (② 022/6643-0670), the hip, warm-hued, lounge-bar-restaurant on Bandra's restaurant-happy Waterfield Road, has many spaces. You can sit in the quieter restaurant area or at a table near the long bar, which is filled with expats, upwardly mobile couples, and office workers. Better still, if the weather is fine, sit outside on the terrace. Fortunately, the great atmosphere comes with good food from an eclectic menu. Drinks are also good but cost as much as a main course. On varying nights, you may encounter live bands, DJs spinning modern tracks, or standup comedy acts to perk up your meal.

Some great dining options are available in the numerous five-star hotels in the vicinity of the international airport. **Dum Pukht** ✿ and **Dakshin** ✿ at the ITC Grand Maratha Sheraton are worth mentioning, as is Stax (mentioned above). **M Bar** at the Grand Hyatt hotel (✆ 022/5676-1234), closer to the domestic airport, an American-style, fine-dining grill-house, is a good place to kill a few hours before a domestic flight (the airport has no in-house dining options).

Special mention must be made of the dining options at the JW Marriott (✆ 022/ 6693-3000) in Juhu. **Saffron** is the place for unlimited kebab platters served with a heavenly buttery *dal;* **Spices** offers pan-Asian cuisine; **Mezzo Mezzo** ✿ is a fine Italian restaurant (get a table by the window); and **Lotus Café** ✿✿ has by far the best five-star buffets in the city.

6 Shopping

From internationally renowned haute couture to dirt-cheap one-season wonders, intricate jewelry and unique antiques to tawdry gifts and fabulous textiles, Mumbai is known as a shopper's paradise, and you'll find pretty much everything the country has to offer here. If you're shopping on the street or in the markets (see "Markets," earlier in this chapter), take your time, sift and sort, establish authenticity, and, if necessary, don't be afraid to bargain hard. That said, bear in mind that (as elsewhere in India) a "bargain," particularly when it comes to jewelry and antiques, is probably a cheap bauble or reproduction—fakes are a dime a dozen, as are the con men who sell them. Besides the areas described below, you will find that the suburb of Bandra has become a local shopping haven, with Linking Road, Hill Road, and several other streets overflowing with shops and street stalls selling clothes, shoes, and everything else under the sun. In addition, Western-style multistory department stores like **Shopper's Stop** and **Globus** are filled with all kinds of garments and fashions. If you're shopping in Bandra, make time to visit the very upmarket **Frazer and Haws** store (Landmark Building, Pali Naka, Bandra; ✆ 022/6675-0200), which carries eclectic and funky silver objets d'art, including sleek idols of Indian gods and goddesses like Ganesha and Laxmi. Also in Bandra are **Fab India** (see below) and dozens of trendy jewelry stores. In fact, most major stores listed below have a parallel store in Bandra/Juhu, so if you're based in the suburbs, call and check before making a trip downtown.

CLOTHING, FABRICS & HOME TEXTILES
COLABA, FORT & MARINE DRIVE
Central Cottage Industries Emporium (behind Regal Cinema; ✆ 022/2202-6564 or -7537; daily 10am–7pm) is the large, government-owned, fixed-price shop aimed at tourists, with a reputation for carrying well-crafted items that offer relatively good value (not the cheapest stuff out there but you won't get ripped off). Established during the late 1940s in an attempt to sustain traditional handicrafts, the massive showroom is crammed full of everything and anything that's likely to remind you of India. At the very least, a visit here will give you an idea of what items should more or less cost. A

better shopping experience, at least from a store and design point of view, is **The Bombay Store** (Sir P.M. Rd., Fort; ✆ 022/2288-5048, -5049, or -5052; Mon–Sat 10:30am–7:30pm, Sun 10:30am–6:30pm), where you'll find every imaginable Indian handicraft and design, from bed linens and crockery to incense and aromatherapy oils. And if you're looking for another reason to book into the **Taj Mahal Hotel,** it's worth knowing that the in-house shops are stocked with sought-after international and Indian brands and products (particularly Pashmina shawls, from simple water Pashminas at around Rs 2000/$49/£26 to high-end quality ones for around Rs 10,000/$244/£123), though obviously you pay a price for the convenience of location, and the shopping experience is relatively sterile. The same holds true for the in-house shop at the **Trident Towers.**

Having created garments for Hillary Clinton, Demi Moore, and Liza Minnelli, and earned the accolades "Crystal King" and "Czar of Embroidery," Azeem Khan is one of Mumbai's best-known designers. To find your very own slice of Indian haute couture, visit **Azeem Khan Couture** in Colaba (1 Usha Sadan; ✆ **022/2215-1028;** www. azeemkhan.com). **Ensemble** (Great Western Building, 130/132 Shahid Bhagat Singh Marg, Kala Ghoda/Fort; ✆ **022/2287-2882,** 022/2284-3227, or -5118) is an upmarket boutique, owned by designer Tarun Tahiliani, where you will find the greatest variety of East-meets-West evening wear; besides his own creations, prominent designers to look for here include Rajesh Pratap, Monisha Jaisingh, Tarana Rajpal, Abhishek Gupta, and Sunita Shankar. At the far end of Colaba (away from the Taj) is **The Courtyard** (Minoo Desai Marg, Apollo Bunder), where chic boutiques are filled with goods from a range of Indian designers; do stop at the very chic **Hot Pink** (✆ **022/6638-5482**) and **Abraham and Thakore** (✆ **022/6638-5486**). For cheap, casual, well-cut cottons, **Cotton World,** near Indigo restaurant, is the perfect stop. At **Indian Textiles** (Taj Mahal Hotel; ✆ **022/2202-8783** or 022/2204-9278), you'll find some of the best Benarasi woven silks and brocades in the country, sold by the yard, as well as authentic Pashmina shawls. Also look for hand-dyed silk stoles by **Jamnadas Khatri** (✆ **022/2242-5711** or -2277). Hand-loomed products are found in abundance at fabulous **Fab India** (Jeroo Building, 137 M.G. Rd., Kala Ghoda; ✆ **022/2262-6539;** other outlets in Bandra).

If you've loved the furnishings at many of the Taj hotels around the country, make your way to **Zeba** in Colaba or Worli (Bhaveshwar, 148–B, Dr. Annie Besant Rd., Worli Naka, ✆ **022/2495-3711;** also at Royal Terrace, 58 Wodehouse Rd., Colaba, ✆ **022/2218-8797**) for extensive collections of highly desirable home textiles, accessories, carpets, and *dhurries* in great original styles. Zeba is owned by the flamboyant Krsna Mehta, whose outfit creates in-house designs for its textiles in cotton, silk, jute, and a range of graceful fabrics, using both earthy and vibrant colors. Zeba will custom-design any living space. **Yamini** (President House, Wodehouse Rd., Colaba; ✆ **022/2218-4143** or -4145; also in Bandra, ✆ **022/2646-3645**) stocks designer linen, tablecloths, bolsters, curtains, bed covers, napkins, and even lampshades. Also at Colaba (near Indigo restaurant) is **Maspar** (Sunny building, Mandlik Rd.; ✆ **022/2287-5619**) a new store with quality home furnishings in contemporary designs and beautiful colors.

If quality is all that matters and price is not a concern, **Ravissant** (17A Cooperage Rd., New India Assurance Centre; ✆ **022/2287-3405**) has a selection of sterling-silver teapots, vases, photo frames, and assorted stylish collectibles that sport clean modern lines and hark back to the Deco period.

If you're fascinated by saris but don't know where to begin, make your way to **Kala Niketan** (☎ 022/2200-5001 or -4952) at Marine Lines, where you will be bowled over by the stunning variety, colors, and over-the-top service. Salesmen not only assist you with your purchase, but can help you get a blouse stitched and offer serious tips on how to drape that gorgeous fabric.

CHOWPATTY, PEDDER ROAD, NAPEAN SEA ROAD

Contemporary Arts and Crafts, in the residential neighborhood of Napean Sea Road (near Kemps Corner; ☎ 022/2363-1979; Mon–Sat 10am–8pm, Sun 10am–7pm), has tasteful and sometimes uncommon gifts from all over India. Famous Indian designer Ritu Kumar has several outlets specializing in silk and cotton designer-ethnic wear, much of it a blend of Western and Indian influences. **Ritu's Boutique** can be found on Warden Road (☎ 022/2367-8593 or -2947) as well as at Trident Towers and Phoenix Mills. Another boutique that is a must-see for fashionistas is **Mélange** (33 Altamount Rd., Kemps Corner; ☎ 022/2353-4492 or 022/2353-9628), known for its ultra-feminine designer dresses made from delicate chiffon. If you don't plan to visit Jaipur, stop at the Mumbai branch of **Anokhi** (Rasik Nivas, Metro Motors Lane, off Hughes Rd.; ☎ 022/2368-5761), for its East-meets-West garments, accessories, and housewares. Nearby is the turquoise-walled **Neemrana** store (Opera House; ☎ 022/2361-4436), with its gorgeous ethnic designs.

India's most famous *dhurrie* designer is **Shyam Ahuja** (78 India House, Kemps Corner; ☎ 022/2386-7372; also an outlet store in the far-out suburb of Thane), known for outstanding and expensive hand-woven products. Besides gorgeous home furnishings, table linen, bathrobes, and towels, you can purchase authentic Pashmina shawls here.

JEWELRY

Tribhovandas Bhimji Zaveri (241/43 Zaveri Bazaar; ☎ 022/2342-5001 or -5002), stretching over five separate floors, has a reputation for exceptional gold and diamond jewelry that dates back to 1865. It's very popular with Mumbai's wealthier crowd, so don't expect exceptionally good prices. **Gazdar** (Taj Mahal Hotel shopping arcade; ☎ 022/2202-3666) has been selling Indian, Western, antique, and contemporary jewelry since 1933; again, the prices go with the territory. Serious buyers looking for one-of-a-kind pieces should consider contacting **Paulomi Sanghavi** (Hughes Rd.; ☎ 022/2367-6114 or 022/6634-7475; personal meetings by appointment only) or you can browse her unique ready-made designs in the store. Alternatively, walk into any one of the numerous jewelry stores along Hughes Road, such as **U. T. Zaveri** (Dharam Palace; ☎ 022/2367-9575), where the designs are unusual and the salespeople extremely helpful.

ANTIQUES, ART & FURNITURE

For real antique finds and colonial furniture, there's no place like **Chor Bazaar's Mutton Street** (see "Markets," earlier in this chapter; closed Fri), which is a wonderful place at which to browse and discover hidden treasures. You'll spot plenty of imitation antiques and faux products here, but these are usually pretty easy to identify. Store owners will often (but not always) tell you which are genuine items and which are reproductions. If, however, walking through dirty streets and sifting through dusty shops is not your cup of tea, head straight for the more established antiques stores in the city, some of the best of which are downtown in Colaba. **Natesan's Antiqarts**

CLOSED
due to
accidental demolition

WEGEN BISSIGEN
EICHHÖRNCHEN GESCHLOSSEN

CERRADO

CABRAS

Κλειστό
Μετεωρίτες

POOL CLOSED

プール も

ELECTRIC EELS

閉鎖中

Hotel
closed for
facelifting

FERMÉ POUR
RAISON
DE GRÈVE
DES BONNES

FECHADO!
POR CAUSA DE
ATAQUES DOS CROCODILOS

— I don't speak
sign language.

A hotel can close for all kinds of reasons.

Our Guarantee ensures that if your hotel's undergoing construction, we'll
let you know in advance. In fact, we cover your entire travel experience.
See www.travelocity.com/guarantee for details.

travelocity·
You'll never roam alone.

(© 022/2285-2700), conveniently located at Jehangir Art Gallery, deals principally in stone, wood, and bronze items. Whether you pick up an ornate teak and sandal-wood carving, a bronze piece created using the 4,500-year-old lost-wax process, or a refurbished antique, Natesan's will arrange shipment. Nearby **Phillips Antiques** (opposite Prince of Wales Museum, Colaba; © 022/2202-0564 or 022/2282-0782; www.phillipsantiques.com) offers a similar service; besides four-poster beds, armchairs, writing tables, and hat stands, you'll find gorgeous porcelain and pottery, brass and sil-verware, and a range of marble items for the home, not to mention ornamental pieces, antiquarian maps, lithographs, engravings, old photographs, and lovely lamps. Filled with beautiful objects, **Heeramaneck** (below Hotel Suba Palace, Battery St., Colaba; © 022/2202-1778 or 022/2285-6340) is another essential pit stop for antiques lovers. It has an especially good collection of Victorian and Indian silverware, includ-ing tea sets, candle stands, and sometimes cutlery as well.

7 Mumbai After Dark
CAFES, BARS & LOUNGES

Join the backpackers and other Western tourists for a cold Kingfisher beer at **Leopold's Café** (© 022/2287-3362 or 022/2282-8185) on Colaba Causeway; or step into smoky, popular **Café Mondegar** or Mondy's (near Regal Cinema; © 022/2202-0591), where the atmosphere is always lively and the jukebox fires up popular Western music. **Indus,** behind the Taj Mahal Hotel, is another bar/restaurant (© 022/2202-1661) that serves relatively inexpensive alcohol and good tandoori starters, and provides a change from the overdose of Hindi remixes you hear every-where else, but not much else. Nearby is the **Sports Bar Express** (© 022/6639-6681), perfect for beer-quaffers who can get a pitcher of beer (1.5 liters) for just Rs 269 ($7/£3), and where you can also play pool or shoot hoops. If rock 'n' roll is more your taste, head for **Tavern** (Hotel Fariyas; © 022/2204-2911), farther down Colaba, where the jeans-and-T-shirt clique groove to classic rock and cheap drinks. Or grab a drink and request a song at popular but small **Ghetto** (© 022/2353-8418) at Maha-laxmi, near Haji Ali. This is where you'll find collegians and after-workers rubbing shoulders with graying hippies who still salute Bob Marley and Jim Morrison; live bands are on tap some nights (entry free). If you're in the hip suburb of Bandra, you'll find a similar scene at **Toto's Garage** (Pali Naka; © 022/2600-5494), where the main attraction, apart from the music, is the shell of a car hanging from the ceiling over patrons' heads. Call **Soul Fry Casa** (© 022/2267-1421), **Starters & More** (© 022/2281-4124) at Churchgate (which also holds Jazz Nights the first Wed of the month), or **Henry Tham Lounge** (© 022/2202-3186; see review earlier) for details of live music nights.

For über-trendy, you can't beat **Indigo** (© 022/6636-8999 or -8983; see "Where to Dine," earlier in this chapter). At Colaba's hippest joint, low tables with flickering candles light up the who's who of Mumbai as they sip fine wines and other drinks. Similarly chic but in Bandra is **Olive Bar and Kitchen** ✸✸ (Pali Hill Tourist Hotel, 14 Union Park Khar [W]; © 022/2605-8228), where celeb-spotting is the acknowl-edged pastime. Also in Bandra, **Seijo and the Soul Dish** (© 022/2640-5555) has a trendy New York look with Japanese touches and regular live music and good drinks. Farther afield, **Vie Lounge and Deck** ✸✸ (102 Juhu Tara Rd., diagonally opposite Maneckji Cooper School, Juhu; © 022/2660-3003) at the edge of Juhu Beach, is a lovely bar with an open-air lounge overlooking the Arabian Sea. Come here for the sea breeze and laid-back ambience; it's the perfect place for a wind-down martini with friends. Happy hours extend from 4 to 7pm.

The erstwhile Library Bar at the Taj President Hotel has been transformed into a classy watering hole called **Wink** (© 022/6665-0808), whose clientele consists of whiskey-swilling businesspeople and high rollers who lounge on plush sofas and boast business successes under dim lighting. If your holy grail is a chic, exclusive lounge bar, nothing beats **Opium Den** at the Trident Towers (© 022/6632-6320), which attracts well-heeled 30-something locals, expats, and hotel guests. Not far away is **Geoffrey's** (Hotel Marine Plaza; © 022/2285-1212), which is often packed with smartly dressed after-office crowds. Around the corner from Geoffrey's is **Not Just Jazz By the Bay** (© 022/2282-0957), which has live bands Wednesday to Saturday and karaoke Sunday through Tuesday.

If you're in Central Mumbai's new business districts, **Dublin** (© 022/2410-1010) in the ITC Grand Central Sheraton and Towers, with its cool green walls, leather sofas, and stained-glass panels, is a good place for a quiet drink. For more options, see "Hot Spots with Views," earlier in this chapter.

MUSIC, THEATER & CINEMA

The best way to figure out what's going on in the city is to pick up a copy of *Time Out Mumbai,* the twice-monthly magazine that has the most comprehensive Mumbai listings. "The Hot List" supplement in the daily tabloid *Mid Day* also carries extensive listings of live music events, stage productions, and film screenings. *The Times of India* features an extensive "Bombay Times" section that lists and advertises cultural activities, entertainment happenings, and movies.

Mumbai has numerous performance spaces, including its premier **National Centre for the Performing Arts** (Nariman Point; © 022/2283-3737; www.ncpamumbai.com). The NCPA houses several stages, including the city's "first opera theater," Jamshed Bhabha Theatre, which saw its first operatic production in 2003. English dramas and lavish musical concerts are held in Tata Theatre; the aptly named Little Theatre features work of a more intimate scale. For offbeat drama, student work, and small-scale music and dance, the black-box Experimental Theatre, with its audience proximity, is the place to go. The NCPA may occasionally host special film events and festivals, but these are open only to members.

Not far from Juhu Beach is one of Mumbai's best-known theaters, **Prithvi Theatre** (Janki-Kutir, Juhu-Church Rd.; © 022/2614-9546; www.prithvitheatre.org), which is owned by Bollywood's founding family, the Kapoors. Prithvi has a small, intimate, and excellent performance space with great acoustics, and the aisles and steps are often crammed with enthusiasts. The country's best plays are staged here during an annual drama festival (Nov–Dec), and the garden cafe outside is popular with the city's culturati. Over the first weekend of every month (except June–Sept), free play readings and other performances are held in the gardens at **Horniman Circle** in the Fort area; contact Prithvi for details.

NIGHTCLUBS

While you could spend your entire stay in Mumbai partying in clubs each night and recovering the following day in your hotel room—this is one Indian city that loves to party—be aware that the nightclub scene is not concentrated on a single street, and most clubs close earlier than in the West. Mumbai's partying has lately been tempered by the government's early closing rule. Although Western music is popular and has the buff and the gorgeous strutting their stuff every night of the week, Mumbaikars (thankfully) have a deep passion for contemporary Hindi songs as well, and it's not unusual to spot young studs demonstrating the choreographed rhythms of *MTV India*'s latest local video, much to the delight of their female companions. There are literally dozens of nightspots in the city, the most attractive being in the five-star hotels. The nightclub scene has largely shifted to the suburbs of Bandra and Juhu, so much so that even affluent South Mumbaikars who wouldn't normally venture to the 'burbs make a beeline for the happening clubs there. For the most up-to-date news on what's hot and what's not, get a copy of *Time Out* and talk to your concierge, because the nightclub scene changes rapidly. In particular, check whether the club recommended to you is popular with under-age kids, as some clubs are.

Here's a list of some of the most popular nightspots in mid-2007—and the ones most likely to continue to stay in top gear. Entry fees differ depending on the night, and prices are often per (heterosexual) couple; usually this entitles you to coupons that can be exchanged for overpriced drinks of a stipulated value. Note that many nightclubs charge extra for males entering alone, while most don't allow "stag" entry at all, though foreigners may sometimes sidestep this rule. Closing times vary each night; there are "official" (currently 12:30am) and unofficial hours—which essentially means that clubs may stay open later than the time stipulated by law. The popularity of a club is sustained only if it can keep the cops out and stay open into the wee hours of the morning (five-star clubs can remain open until 3am, since they are inside private hotels). *Tip:* Take a page out of a hard-partying Mumbaikar's book and tank up at one of the city's watering holes before heading to a nightclub, where drink prices are usually exorbitant. In general, party-loving locals hit more than one nightclub/bar/lounge per evening throughout this island city; if you hook up with a group, you may want to join them. *Note:* If you crave Latin and ballroom dancing, including salsa, merengue, tango, jive, and the like, several spots in the city have Latin Ballroom Nights.

Enigma 𝒢𝒢   This is one of Mumbai's hottest nightspots and a celeb-magnet. It has a circular central bar, a large dance floor, and a huge, colorful chandelier that shines almost as brightly as the Bollywood stars in attendance. Drinks are as expensive as the cover charge, but when well-known DJ Akhtar gets behind the console, most don't really care. Music is very modern—a combination of commercial Western music and Bollywood. Enigma is invariably packed to the hilt with a long queue of people waiting outside, though hotel guests can jump the line. It's open Tuesday to Saturday only, and entry costs Rs 800 to Rs 2,500 ($20–$61/£10–£31) per couple, with coupons redeemable for drinks. JW Marriott, Juhu Tara Rd., Juhu Beach. 🕐 022/6693-3000.

Poison 𝒢𝒢   One of Bandra's hippest clubs, this has a decent-size dance floor and a trendy international look. If you go on a Saturday night, you'll be one of at least a thousand guests! But don't worry: The club has 930 sq. m (10,000 sq. ft.) of space, and the air-conditioning still manages to work with that many bodies around. International DJs are often flown in to keep the swinging crowds coming, and bouncers at the door enforce a strict dress code: no shorts, sandals, saris, *salwar* suits, and (unfortunately) no stags. Entry is a dear Rs 1,500 ($30/£18) on Saturday and Rs 1,000 ($24/£12) (per couple) on other nights, giving you coupons worth Rs 1,000 ($24/£12) redeemable for drinks. Closed Monday. G 001/B Krystal, Waterfield Rd., Bandra. 🕐 022/2642-3006.

Deccan Odyssey

Western India's version of the famous Palace on Wheels train is a lavish 21-car luxury train called the **Deccan Odyssey,** which traverses Maharashtra's stunning coast. The 7-day journey begins in Mumbai and wanders down the coast to Goa via gorgeous beaches untouched by commercialization. It then stops in the historic city of Pune before moving on to Aurangabad (where you can visit the Ajanta and Ellora caves), and finally returns to Mumbai. The journey involves traveling by night and sightseeing during the day. Onboard facilities are royal and luxurious (provided by the Taj group of hotels), and you get outstanding food, the services of a personal valet, a gym, an Ayurvedic health spa, and more (**Deccan Odyssey:** in the U.S. call ℂ **888/INDIA-99;** in the U.K. call toll-free 0125/ 8580-600; in India call 011/2332-5939 or 011/2335-3155; www.thedeccan odyssey.com, www.thepalaceonwheels.com, or www.deccan-odyssey-india.com; $2,450/£1,237 for the 7-day tour, all-inclusive; discounts sometimes available).

Polly Esther's 𝕮   This Colaba nightclub (and rip-off of the American chain of nightclubs) attracts a mixed crowd, from teenyboppers to 40-somethings, with its mix of Bollywood, pop, and '80s music. The retro theme is echoed in posters of Michael Jackson and Madonna and a Polaroid man who'll take your picture for Rs 100 ($2/£1). The club's spaciousness provides a welcome break from the cramped, smoky rooms found in other clubs around the city. Drinks are relatively reasonably priced, and the entry fee is Rs 600 to Rs 1,000 ($15–$24/£7–£12) per couple. Closed Monday. Gordon House Hotel, Apollo Bunder, Colaba. ℂ **022/2287-1122.**

Ra 𝕮𝕮   In the heart of the gentrified Phoenix Mills Compound, Ra plays the latest rage in loud music, from hip-hop to Hindi remixes. It's recently redesigned its space to separate the bar (called Voyeur) and dance areas and is brimming over on weekend nights. Entry is Rs 600 to Rs 1,500 ($15–$37/£7–£19) per couple, but you get coupons for the full value to buy expensive drinks at about Rs 400 ($10/£5) each. But judging by the crowds that keep the place buzzing, nobody seems to mind. Phoenix Mills Complex, Lower Parel. ℂ **022/6661-4343.**

8 Aurangabad & the Ellora and Ajanta Caves

The ancient cave temples at Ellora and Ajanta are among the finest historical sites India has to offer, and a detour to this far-flung region of Maharashtra to view these World Heritage Sites is well worth the effort. You can cover both Ellora and Ajanta comfortably in 2 days, but for those who are truly pressed for time, it is possible to see both sets of caves in a single (long, tiring) day. To do this, you'll need a packed lunch from your hotel, and plenty of bottled water. Set out for Ajanta at about 7am, reaching the ticket office as it opens (recommended for the tranquillity of the experience, even if you're not trying to cover both in a day). Spend no more than 3 hours exploring Ajanta, before heading for Ellora; your driver should be aware of the detour along the Ajanta–Aurangabad road that will get you there much faster. The caves at Ellora are spread out, so don't drag your heels, and be sure not to miss the ultimate jaw-dropper, known as "Cave 16": the Kailashnath temple complex is more carved mountain than cave. The world's largest monolithic structure, it is twice the size of the Parthenon. Note that Ajanta is closed on Monday and Ellora on Tuesday.

ESSENTIALS

GETTING THERE   The quickest way to get here is to fly to Aurangabad's airport (in Chikalthana, Jalna Rd., just 10km/6¼ miles from the city center) with **Jet Airways** (✆ **022/3989 3333** or 1-800/225-522 in Mumbai, 0240/244-1392 in Aurangabad). The flight from Mumbai lasts 45 minutes to an hour and costs around Rs 3,500 ($85/ £43). You can also try **Indian** (✆ **022/2202-3031** or 1-800/180-1407). For a cheaper and fairly comfortable journey, book an air-conditioned chair car seat (Rs 369/$9/£5) on the **Tapovan Express** train that leaves Mumbai's VT/CST Station at 6:10am and reaches Aurangabad at 1:30pm. An alternative is the **Devagiri Express,** an overnight train that reaches Aurangabad at an inconvenient 4:10am (second-class air-conditioned sleeper berth Rs 654/$16/£8).

VISITOR INFORMATION   You'll find a tourist information booth at the airport arrivals hall, where you can pick up brochures on Aurangabad, Ajanta, and Ellora. The **India Tourism Development Corporation (ITDC) office** at Krishna Villa, on Station Road (✆ **0240/233-1217** or 0240/236-4999; Mon–Fri 8:30am–6pm, Sat 8:30am–2pm), is where you can get tourism-related information and book a **private guide** for the caves, although it's cheaper to pick one up at the caves themselves. The state tourist office in the **MTDC Holiday Resort** (Station Rd., Aurangabad 431 001; ✆ **0240/233-1143;** www.maharashtratourism.gov.in; daily 7am–1pm and 3–8pm) operates tourist buses to Ajanta (Rs 270/$6/£3) and Ellora (Rs 170/$4/£2).

GETTING AROUND   Taxis and **auto-rickshaws** are widely available in Aurangabad, and you'll be approached at the airport by the usual touts offering you a "good deal." Though the scamsters and touts here are far less aggressive or annoying than those you encounter farther north, always arrange the fare upfront; a taxi from the airport into the city should cost about Rs 250 ($61/£31). **Classic Tours and Travels** (at the MTDC Holiday Resort; see above; ✆ **0240/233-7788** or -5598; contact@ classicservices.in) lives up to its name, and will arrange just about any type of transport for travel within Aurangabad and environs (count on around Rs 2,000/$49/£25) for a full day with a car and driver; less if you're only going to Ellora), and beyond. All hotels have travel desks that will organize a car with a guide for any of the sights in the area.

AJANTA TRAVEL ADVISORY   The drive from Aurangabad to Ajanta takes between 2 and 3 hours, so you're advised to set off early in the day to avoid as much of the midday heat as possible. There are two ways of getting to the caves. Generally, visitors are dropped off in the public parking lot, several kilometers from the caves themselves; here you'll find stalls selling awful souvenirs, snacks, and tourist paraphernalia, and "guides" flogging their services. You'll also find green, eco-friendly buses that are the only vehicles allowed in the vicinity of the caves. Purchase a ticket (Rs 30/$1/£1) and hop aboard for the short drive to the Ajanta ticket office.

    A far more rigorous but rewarding alternative is to have your driver drop you at the "Viewpoint," reached via a turnoff some distance before the official parking facility. From here you can take in a panoramic view of the site across the river, then make your way down the rather difficult pathway (don't attempt this route if you're unsteady on your feet) and eventually to a footbridge that spans the Waghora River. Make for the ticket booth and proceed to the caves. Be sure to arrange to have your driver collect you from the parking lot when you're done.

ELLORA TRAVEL ADVISORY   These caves are only 30km (19 miles) from Aurangabad, but you should rent a car and driver for the day for transfers between certain caves. Starting at **Cave 1,** visit as many of the principal caves (don't miss **Cave 10**) as you have time for, until you reach **Cave 16,** where you should arrange for your driver to pick you up and then drive you to **Cave 21,** which is worth investigating. Having seen this cave, again have your driver take you to **Cave 29,** located alongside a waterfall, reachable via a rather dangerous pathway. Another short drive will take you to the **Jain Group** of temples, of which **Cave 32** is the best example.

Be warned that Ellora is enormously popular—especially during weekends and school vacations. Time your visit accordingly, or get here as soon as it opens, preferably not on a weekend. Ellora can be explored independently or with a guide (who may or may not understand English and who may sound like a recorded message); currently, the official rate is Rs 450 ($12/£6) for the first 4 hours, or—if you're really enthusiastic—Rs 600 ($15/£7) for up to 8 hours.

AURANGABAD

388km (240 miles) E of Mumbai; 30km (19 miles) SE of Ellora; 106km (66 miles) SW of Ajanta

Aurangabad takes its name from the last of the great Moghul emperors, the hard-edged Aurangzeb, who enacted an almost Shakespearean drama in the 17th century when he took control of the empire by murdering his siblings and imprisoning his father, Shah Jahan (see chapter 9), before leaving Delhi in 1693 to make this city his base. Today the sprawling city of Aurangabad is one of the fastest-growing industrial cities in India, and not a destination in its own right. However, time allowing, it has a few attractions worth noting. Best known is **Bibi-ka-Maqbara,** the "Mini-Taj," a mausoleum built for Aurangzeb's empress by his son, Azam Shah, and a supposed replica of the more famous mausoleum built by his grandfather in Agra. Set amid large landscaped gardens and surrounded by high walls, it's primarily interesting from a historical point of view, lacking as it does the fine detail and white marble of its inspiration (the builders were forced to complete the project in stone and plaster because of financial constraints). Although you can't enter the tomb itself, an amble through the grounds (admission Rs 100/$2/£1; daily sunrise–9pm; no flash photography) affords you the opportunity to compare this project with the original Agra masterpiece. If you follow the dirt road that leads past Bibi-ka-Maqbara up into the hills for some 2km (1¼ miles)—a stiff climb—you will come across the **Aurangabad Buddhist Caves** (Rs

---

Tips The Finest of Fabrics

Aurangabad is the only place in the world where Himroo art and Paithani weaving is still practiced, a millennia-old brocade-weaving craft that combines silk and cotton yarn into an almost satinlike fabric. Weavers spend around 2 to 3 months working on a single Paithani sari, even longer on more intricate and detailed designs. A custom-woven Paithani sari with gold-plated thread, featuring a design based on one of the Ajanta murals takes a year to produce and cost up to Rs 200,000 ($4,878/£2,469). A beautiful Himroo shawl can cost anywhere from Rs 1,000 to Rs 25,000 ($24–$610/£12–£309), depending on the workmanship. Pay a visit to the **Aurangabad Himroo Art & Paithani Weaving & Training Centre** (Jaffar Gate, Mondha Rd., Aurangabad) to shop or see weavers at work, or stop at **Paithani Silk Weaving Centre,** 54 P1 Town Center, behind Indian Booking Office, opposite M.G.M. College ((©) **0240/248-2811;** daily 11am–8pm).

100/$1/£1; sunrise–sunset), a series of nine man-made caves dating back to the 6th to 8th centuries. Similar to the Buddhist Caves at Ajanta (but not in the same class), they feature original painting fragments and offer spectacular views of the city and the landscape beyond.

On the way to Ellora is **Daulatabad Fort** (Rs 100/$1/£1; sunrise–sunset). Built by the Yadavas between the 10th and 11th centuries A.D., it comprises an elaborate system of mazelike tunnels that served as an ingenious defense system: Once intruders were holed up deep within the tunnels, guards would welcome them with flaming torches, hot oil, or burning coals, effectively grilling them alive.

A place largely untouched by tourism is **Lonar Crater**—created some 50,000 years ago when a meteorite careered into the basalt rock. It has a diameter of 1,800m (5,904 ft.), making it the largest crater in the world. Filling the bottom of the crater is water in which Ram and Sita are believed to have bathed while they were exiled from Ayodhya; temple ruins lie at the water's edge. Tranquil and remote, the crater is about 150km (93 miles) east of Aurangabad.

THE BUDDHIST CAVES OF AJANTA ✿✿✿

During the 2nd century B.C., a long, curving swath of rock at a sharp hairpin bend in the Waghora River was chosen as the site for one of the most significant chapters in the creative history of Buddhism. Buddhist monks spent the next 700 years carving out prayer halls for worship *(chaitya grihas)* and monasteries *(viharas)* using little more than simple hand-held tools, natural pigments, and oil lamps and natural light reflected off bits of metal or pools of water. They decorated the caves with sculptures and magnificent murals that depict the life of the Buddha as well as everyday life.

The caves were abandoned rather abruptly after almost 9 centuries of activity and were only rediscovered in 1819 (by a British cavalryman out terrorizing wild boars). Time has taken its toll on many of the murals, and modern-day restoration projects have even contributed to the near-ruin of some of the work. Despite this, the paintings continue to enthrall, and it's hard to imagine the patience and profound sense of spiritual duty and devotion that led to the creation of this, arguably the best Buddhist site in India.

It takes some time to explore all 29 caves (which are numbered from east to west), and the sensory overload can prove exhausting; try at least to see the eight described below. It's a good idea to make your way to the last cave, then view the caves in reverse numerical order—in this way you won't be running with the masses, and you won't have a long walk back to the exit when you're done.

Richly decorated with carved Buddha figures, **Cave 26** is a *chaitya* hall featuring a *stupa* (dome-shaped shrine) on which an image of the Master seated in a pavilion appears. In the left-hand wall is a huge carved figure of the reclining Buddha—a depiction of the *Mahaparinirvana,* his final salvation from the cycle of life and death. Beneath him, his disciples mourn his passing; above, celestial beings rejoice. Featuring the greatest profusion of well-preserved paintings is **Cave 17,** where maidens float overhead, accompanied by celestial musicians, and the doorway is adorned with Buddhas, female guardians, river goddesses, lotus petals, and scrollwork. One celebrated mural here depicts Prince Simhala's encounter with the man-eating ogresses of Ceylon, where he'd been shipwrecked.

Cave 16 has a rather lovely painting of Princess Sundari fainting upon hearing that her husband—the Buddha's half-brother, Nanda—has decided to become a monk.

Cave 10 is thought to be the oldest Ajanta temple, dating from around the 2nd century B.C. Dating to the 1st century B.C., **Cave 9** is one of the earliest *chaitya grihas,* and is renowned for the elegant arched windows carved into the facade that allow soft diffused light into the atmospheric prayer hall. A large stupa is found at the back of the prayer hall.

Cave 4 is incomplete, but its grandiose design makes it the largest of the Ajanta monasteries. Take a quick look, then head for **Cave 2.** The facade features images of Naga kings and their entourage. Inside the sanctum, a glorious mandala dominates the ceiling amid a profusion of beautiful floral designs, concentric circles, and abstract geometric designs with fantastic arrangements of flying figures, beasts, birds, flowers, and fruits. On the walls, well-preserved panels relate the birth of the Buddha.

Cave 1 is one of the finest and most popular of the *viharas* at Ajanta, especially renowned for the fantastic murals of two bodhisattvas (saintly beings destined to become the Buddha) that flank the doorway of the antechamber. To the right, holding a thunderbolt, is Avalokitesvara (or Vajrapani), the most significant bodhisattva in Mahayana Buddhism. To the left is bejeweled Padmapani, his eyes cast humbly downward, a water lily in his hand. Within the antechamber is a huge seated Buddha with the Wheel of Dharma (or life) beneath his throne—his hands are in the *Dharmachakra pravartana mudra,* the gesture that initiates the motion of the wheel. On the wall to the right of the Buddha is an image of the dark princess being offered lotuses by another damsel.

Last but not least, for a magnificent view of the entire Ajanta site and an idea of just why this particular spot was chosen, visit the viewing platforms on the opposite side of the river; the natural beauty of this horseshoe-shaped cliff is the perfect setting for a project so singularly inspired by spiritual fervor. It may even be the ideal starting point for your exploration.

Note: You will be required to remove your shoes before entering many of the caves, so take comfortable (and cheap) footwear that slips on and off easily.

Rs 250 ($6/£3); camera Rs 5 (10¢/5p). Tues–Sun 8am–6pm. No flash photography inside caves.

EXPLORING ELLORA ⭐⭐⭐

Ellora's 34 rock-sculpted temples, created sometime between the 4th and 9th centuries, were chiseled out of the hillside by Buddhists, Hindus, and Jains. A visit here allows for an excellent comparison of the stylistic features and narrative concerns of three distinct but compatible spiritual streams.

Of the 12 Buddhist cave-temples, carved between the 6th and 8th centuries, the largest is **Cave 5.** The "cave of the celestial carpenter, Vishwakarma" (**Cave 10),** is acknowledged to be most beautiful of the Buddhist group. A large ribbed, vaulted chamber, it houses a big figure of the Teaching Buddha, while smaller figures look down from panels above. The atmosphere here is chilling, a place for the suspension of worldly realities and for complete focus on things divine. In the three-story *vihara* (monks' domicile) of **Cave 12,** note the monks' beds and pillows carved out of rock. **Cave 13** marks the first of those carved by the Hindus which, when viewed in combination, offer a wealth of dynamic, exuberant representations of the colorful Hindu pantheon: Shiva as Natraj performs the dance of creation in **Cave 14** (where he is also seen playing dice with his wife Parvati and piercing the blind demon Andhaka with a spear); and in **Cave 15,** the manifold avatars of Vishnu tell numerous tales while Shiva rides the divine chariot and prepares to destroy the palaces of the demons.

Ellora

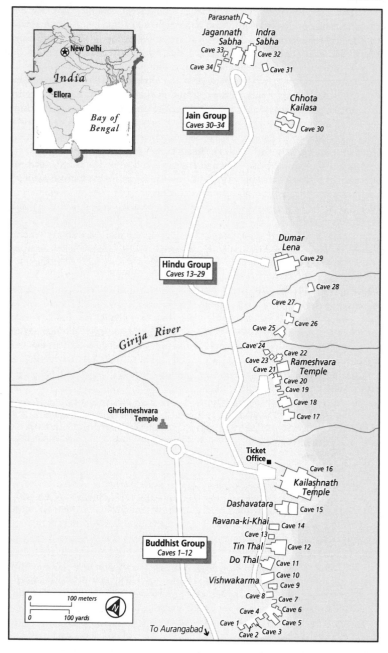

Created over 150 years by 800 artisans, **Kailashnath Temple (Cave 16)** is the zenith of rock-cut Deccan architecture, and Ellora's star attraction. A dazzling visualization of Mount Kailash, the mythical sacred abode of Shiva in the Tibetan Himalayas, it is unlike the other caves at Ellora, which were excavated into the hillside—it is effectively a mountain that has been whittled down to a free-standing temple, measuring 1,700 sq. m (18,299 sq. ft.). The intricacy of detail is remarkable; the temple basement, for example, consists of a row of mythical elephants carrying lotuses in their trunks as they appear to support the entire structure on their backs. Sculpted detail abounds in the temple and its excavated courtyard, with hardly an inch of wall space left unadorned—demons, dwarfs, deities, humans, celestial *asparas,* and animals occur in abundance. In the Nandi Pavilion facing the entrance is a beautiful carving of Lakshmi surrounded by adoring figures; seated in a pond, she is being bathed by attendant elephants carrying pots in their trunks. Also be on the lookout for *mithunas*—male and female figures in erotic situations.

Ellora Caves free. Entry to Kailashnath Temple Rs 250 ($6/£3), free for children under 15. No filming of interiors. Wed–Mon 8am–6pm.

WHERE TO STAY

A general word of caution: Don't expect too much from any category of hotel in Aurangabad; service standards even at the more expensive hotels leave much to be desired.

The Ambassador Ajanta   Set amid lovely lawns with fountains and well-maintained flower beds, The Ambassador offers good facilities and a comfortable environment—ideal for relaxing after a hectic day of cave exploration. Moghul artworks fill the white-and-beige marble lobby, creating a pleasant atmosphere (if not as stylish as at the Taj), and the public spaces are decorated with statues and objets d'art that reflect the creative spirit of Ellora and Ajanta. The best units overlook the swimming pool (ask for room nos. 201–204 or 220–225). Service here is personal but certainly not up to the standards set in larger cities.

Jalna Rd., CIDCO, Aurangabad. (✆) **0240/248-5211,** -5212, -5213, or -5214. Fax 0240/248-4367. www.ambassador india.com. 92 units. Rs 3,500 ($85/£43) executive room double; Rs 4,250 ($104/£52) superior room double; Rs 4,500 ($108/£55) deluxe suite double; Rs 750 ($18/£9) extra bed; plus 10% tax. Children under 12 stay free in parent's room. Ajanta and presidential suite tariffs on request. Tariff includes airport pickup. AE, DC, MC, V. **Amenities:** Restaurant; bar; pool; tennis court; health spa; travel assistance and car hires; business center; shopping arcade; 24-hr. room service; babysitting on request; laundry service; dry cleaning; doctor-on-call; currency exchange; Internet access; Wi-Fi (lobby); badminton court; squash court; jogging track. *In room:* A/C, TV, dataport, fridge, hair dryer, safe (except executive rooms), electronic bedside console, DVD player on request.

Quality Inn The Meadows *(Kids)*   Surrounded by 5.2 hectares (13 acres) of pleasant gardens, this small resort—built in 1996—is great if you'd rather stay out of town. Accommodations are in a variety of simple cottages, the size and level of privacy varying according to price. Deluxe cottages are quite basic, so opt for the superior category (ask for G1), with white marble flooring, stiff cane chairs, and tiled bathrooms with drench showers. There's plenty here to keep young children occupied (including rabbits) while you relax in a quiet corner after sightseeing under the Maharashtrian sun. Breakfast is served poolside, under large, umbrella-like canopies; exotic birds, wild parrots, and busy butterflies provide the entertainment. Service is inconsistent.

Gat no. 135 and 136, Village Mitmita, Mumbai-Nasik Hwy., Aurangabad 431 002. (✆) **0240/267-7412,** -7413, or -7414. Fax 0240/267-7416. www.themeadowsresort.com. Reservations (Mumbai): (✆) **022/6654-8361** or -8362. Fax 022/ 2203-3622. 48 units. $82/£41 deluxe double cottage; $89/£45 club double cottage; $152/£77 1-bedroom suite; $227/£115 2-bedroom suite; 2-night stay with sightseeing packages available. Rs 600 ($15/£7) extra bed. Rates include airport/station transfers and breakfast. AE, MC, V. **Amenities:** 2 restaurants; bar; pool; health club; business center; 24-hr. room service; laundry service; dry cleaning; currency exchange; Wi-Fi enabled; skating rink; children's playground; nature walks, paragliding, and parasailing on request. *In room:* A/C, TV, minibar in suites, tea- and cof-fee-making facilities (except deluxe), hair dryer and DVD player on request.

Taj Residency *෬෬*   Although this is the best hotel in town, catering to Aurangabad's high society crowd as well as to business and leisure travelers, the main block could do with an upgrade. The new wing with 24 deluxe rooms opened in 2005, so ask for a room there. Located away from the center, the tranquil retreat is surrounded by verdant gar-dens overlooked or accessed by guest rooms; ground-floor patios also have swings. Don't expect the type of ultra-luxurious decor you'll find in major city hotels (the mattresses are foam and the carpeting slightly tatty in places), but accommodations are reasonably spacious, with teak furniture, Mughal arch-shaped mirrors, and miniature paintings on the walls. Ask for one of the corner units (no. 201 or 221)—these have extra balcony space. Suites, which include all meals, are large and plush and have wonderful private terraces. The hotel is serviced by students of the hotel management school next door, and like elsewhere in Aurangabad, service is inconsistent.

8-N-12 CIDCO, Aurangabad 431 003. ✆ **0240/238-1106** through -1110. Fax 0240/238-1053. www.tajhotels.com. residency.aurangabad@tajhotels.com. 66 units. $90/£46 standard double; $105/£53 executive double; $145/£73 deluxe double; $250/£126 executive suite double; $325/£164 deluxe suite. All rates except standard include break-fast. AE, DC, MC, V. **Amenities:** Restaurant; bar; pool; fitness center; travel assistance and car hires; business center; 24-hr. room service; babysitting on request; laundry service; dry cleaning; doctor-on-call; currency exchange; Wi-Fi enabled; banqueting. *In room:* A/C, TV, minibar, tea- and coffee-making facilities; hair dryer and iron on request.

WHERE TO DINE

Most foreign visitors end up at **Food Lovers** (Station Rd. E., opposite MTDC Holi-day Resort), a palace of kitsch done in bamboo and fish tanks, with a separate entrance for "Families, Foreigners and Non-drinking Gents." Backpackers swear by the food (the Chinese is actually better than the Indian), and prices are very reasonable. Our money's on Tandoor, however (see review below). Another spot worth noting is **Angeethi Restaurant & Bar** (opposite Nupur Theatre, Jalna Rd.; ✆ **0240/244-1988;** Rs 65–Rs 290/$2–$7/£1–£4), one of Aurangabad's most popular restaurants, particularly with the business set. Try the Afghani chicken masala (pieces of boneless chicken cooked in a cashew-nut gravy), or the popular—and spicy—tandoori chicken masala. For something authentically Maharashtrian, order chicken *kolhapuri* (not on the menu, but ask for it anyway), a spicy-hot chicken dish with a sharp chili, onion, and garlic base; if you can handle the sting, it's delicious. But if it's real authenticity you're looking for, head to the no-frills **Thaliwala's Bhoj** (Bhau Phatak Smruti Kam-gar Bhavan, opposite Hotel Kartiki; ✆ **0240/235-9438**) and order a thali for a mere Rs 70 ($2/£1). (See "The Thali: Gujarati & Rajasthani Cuisine at its Best," earlier in this chapter.) Waiters (who generally don't speak a syllable of English) will fill your platter with wonderful concoctions—mop it all up with savory, freshly prepared chapati.

Tandoor *෬෬෬* INDIAN/MUGHLAI/CHINESE   A large square door swings open to reveal this recently refurbished eatery with walls of clay face-brick, tiled flooring, and a bold collection of Egyptian figures (King Tut's head emerges incongruously from the brickwork). Though a bit far from the main hotels, this hot favorite since 1988 is our choice for Aurangabad's best eating experience. It's greatly enhanced by wonderful service and welcoming management. You can spend ages pondering the extensive menu, or you can ask the manager, Mr. Hussain, for his choices. Okra *(bhindi)* is not on the menu but can sometimes be made to order. The house specialty is definitely the kebabs; get a mixed tandoori sizzler with a selection of chicken kebabs or the fenugreek-leaves-flavored *kasturi kebab* (chicken) and *kabuli* tandoori chicken (marinated in creamy yogurt and flavored with ginger, garlic, turmeric, and white pepper), all outstanding. If you're looking for a mild curry that's been delicately prepared to bring out the most subtle flavors, ask for chicken *korma*—the sauce is made from cashew nuts, poppy seeds, sweet-melon seeds, and white sesame seeds. Those craving a break from all things spicy can get the baked vegetables on a bed of spinach.

Shyam Chambers, Station Rd. Ⓒ **0240/232-8481**. Main courses Rs 120–Rs 405 ($3–$9/£1–£5). MC, V. Daily 11am–3pm and 6:30–11pm.

5

Goa: Party in Paradise

Nirvana for dropouts, flower children, and New Age travelers since the late 1960s, Goa peaked as a hippie haven in the '70s, when Anjuna Beach became a rocking venue for party demons and naturalists who would sell their last piece of clothing at the local flea market for just enough cash to buy more dope and extend their stay. For many, Goa still conjures up images of all-night parties and tripping hippies sauntering along sun-soaked beaches. But there is more to this tiny western state than sea and sand, hippies and hedonists. Goa's history alone has ensured that its persona, a rich amalgam of Portuguese and Indian influences, is unlike any other in India.

Arriving in 1498, the Portuguese christened it as the "Pearl of the Orient" and stayed for almost 500 years (forced to leave, finally, in 1961—the last Europeans to withdraw from the subcontinent), leaving an indelible impression on the local population and landscape. Goans still take a siesta every afternoon; many are Catholic, and you'll meet Portuguese-speaking Mirandas, D'Souzas, and Braganzas, their ancestors renamed by the colonial priests who converted them, often by force. Garden Hindu shrines stand cheek-by-jowl with holy crosses, and the local *vindaloo* (curry) is made with pork. Dotted among the palm groves and rice fields are dainty villas bearing European coats of arms and imposing mansions with wrought-iron gates—built not only for European gentry but for the Brahmins who, by converting, earned the right to own land.

Over the past 8 years Goa has become more hip than hippie, with well-heeled Indians frequenting the new crop of flashy international-style restaurants and design-conscious furniture and lifestyle stores at which they shop in order to adorn their ostentatious Goa mansions. Joining them every winter are the white-skinned package tourists, who come to indulge in the rather commercialized trance culture, and Indian youngsters who cruise from beach to beach, legs wrapped around cheap motorbikes and credit cards tucked into their Diesel jeans.

Goa is very much "India Light," a cosmopolitan tourist-oriented place of five-star resorts and boutique guesthouses. In many ways Goa is the perfect introduction to a country that, elsewhere, can be very challenging. Of course, when the crowds arrive, particularly over New Year's, Goa's beaches and markets are anything but tranquil. Sun beds and shacks line the most commercial beaches, and hawkers haggle ceaselessly with droves of Europeans here to sample paradise at bargain prices while Mumbai and Bangalore puppies crowd the shoreline bars and restaurants. If it's action you're after, there are endless opportunities for all-night partying and reckless abandon, but Goa's true pleasures are found away from the crowds, on the more remote beaches to the far north and south, on the semi-private beaches adjoining luxury resorts, or

Mayhem in Paradise: When to Groove in Goa

Every year from December 23 to January 7, tens of thousands of tourists, both domestic and foreign, descend on Goa, so if you plan to spend Christmas or New Year's here, expect to negotiate crowds everywhere, particularly along the bursting-to-the-seams Baga–Candolim stretch. You can avoid the crowds to some extent by confining yourself to your hotel or guesthouse, but all the popular bars and restaurants will be filled to capacity, with queues so long they can cause traffic jams. Besides, everything—particularly accommodations—will be extremely expensive at this time. Almost every hotel charges a separate end-of-year tariff, most with an accompanying surcharge for the in-house "festive party" (even if you don't plan to attend). If loud and raucous merriment is not your style, avoid Goa during this time; your money will go twice the distance here once the revelers have departed.

in the charming guesthouses farther inland. Come for at least 3 days, and you may end up staying for a lifetime—as a number of very content expats from around the world will attest to. However you decide to play it, live the local motto, *"Sossegade"*: "Take it easy."

1 Arrival & Orientation

ESSENTIALS

GETTING THERE   By Air   The state capital is Panjim (also called Panaji), which is pretty much centrally located; **Dabolim Airport** lies 29km (18 miles) south. Many travelers to Goa arrive on charter flights as part of ever-popular package deals direct from the U.K., Germany, Holland, Switzerland, and Scandinavia. In high season **Sri Lankan Airlines** (www.srilankan.lk) connects Goa to the U.K. via Colombo, and **Air-India** (www.airindia.com) offers one weekly flight each to Kuwait and Dubai. Or you can fly in from Mumbai (a mere 40 min.) or Delhi, as well as from Kolkata, Chennai, Kochi, Hyderabad, Bangalore, and Ahmedabad. See chapter 2 for details on airlines offering the best and/or cheapest service. A helpful government **tourist desk** (© 0832/251-2644) is in the baggage-claim hall. If you have a hotel or resort reservation, a **courtesy bus or taxi** will probably be waiting for you. If not, use a **prepaid taxi** (see chapter 2) or bargain directly with a driver; the trip to Panjim should cost Rs 500 ($12/£6.15). Given Goa's popularity with both international and domestic tourists, it's worth prebooking your accommodations here, and don't fall for a tout's offer of "discount" lodgings.

By Train   Goa's three main jumping-off points are **Thivim** in the north (20km/12 miles inland from Vagator), **Karmali** (12km/7½ miles from Panjim), and **Madgaon** in the south (also known as Margao). If you're going straight to Palolem in the far south (almost on the border with Karnataka, where the fabulous Om Beach is) on a train bound/originating farther south, jump off at **Canacona.**

Several trains travel daily from Mumbai to Goa along the **Konkan Railway;** most of these take a good 10 to 13 hours, so it's best to book the overnight **Konkan Kanya Express,** which leaves Mumbai at 11pm and gets into Madgaon at 10:45am. For a slightly quicker option, you'll need to get up early for the 5:30am **Mumbai-Madgaon Jan Shatabdi** (from Dadar Station; Thurs–Tues), which reaches Madgaon by 1.55pm.

Goa

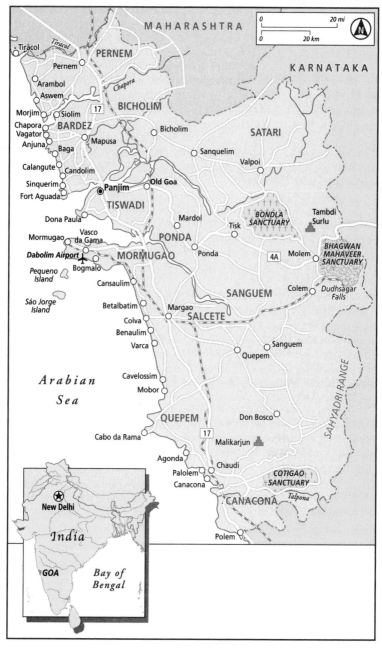

If you're traveling from the south, catch the 11am **Matsyaganda Express** from Mangalore to Madgaon (6½ hr.); the trip offers mesmerizing views along the Konkan coast. Note that it's worthwhile to book your train reservation in your home country, especially if you plan to head to Goa soon after your arrival in India or in peak season when trains between Mumbai and Goa are often fully booked. For railway inquiries, call **Madgaon** (© 0832/271-2790; reservations © 0832/271-2940).

By Bus   If you want to travel to Goa but all trains and flights are full, or if you want to save on airfare, your next-best option is a bus from Mumbai, Pune, Hyderabad, Bangalore, or Mangalore. Numerous overnight buses leave from Mumbai (near Metro Cinema–Fashion St.) every day at 7pm; try to book an air-conditioned bus. Preferably, this should be a sleeper (Rs 1,000/$24/£12). If you're traveling alone, note that you will sleep beside a stranger; if this makes you nervous, buy two tickets. Another option is to go for a semi-sleeper or "slumberette," a comfy 135-degree reclining seat for around Rs 900 ($22/£11), depending on the season and quality of the bus. Some companies provide blankets and bottled water. **Paulo Travels** (Mumbai: © 022/2643-3023 or -6764; Goa: © 0832/243-8531 through -8537) is a reliable private operator; all bookings are made at the small ticket booths near St. Xavier's College, Mumbai. If you are booking through other agents, make sure you ask for a Volvo bus (better suspension, more spacious seating) and that you get a confirmed ticket with your seat number. For the north Goa beaches, jump off at Mapusa; for the south, at Panjim. *Tip:* A single woman can request to have another woman seated beside her, though this may not always happen. Seats in the first few rows have more leg room.

VISITOR INFORMATION   For general information on the state, visit the **Government of Goa Department of Tourism office** in Panjim (Patto Tourist Home; © 0832/243-8750 through -8752; www.goatourism.org; daily 8am–6pm). Branch offices are in **Mapusa** (in the shopping complex next to Mapusa Residency; © 0832/226-2390) and **Margao** (Margao Residency; © 0832/271-5204). There's also an information counter at the **Konkan Railway Station** in Madgaon (© 0832/271-2791) and in **Vasco** (© 0832/251-2673). The GTDC also releases a twice-monthly magazine called *What's On* (© 0832/222-4132) which gives a comprehensive listing of the events and parties scheduled in all corners of Goa. Many of the upmarket hotels also keep *Travel Talk* and *See Goa* which include maps and other detailed information.

GETTING AROUND   Note that it shouldn't take much longer than 4 hours to cruise the entire coastline, so everything in this chapter is within easy reach. For quick reference, here are distances between major destinations from Panjim: Margaon 33km (21 miles); Mapusa 13km (8 miles); Old Goa 10km (6¼ miles); Calangute 16km (10 miles); Vagator 22km (14 miles); Ponda 30km (19 miles).

By Motorbike   Motorbikes are *trés* cool in Goa, and you'll encounter an endless barrage of young backpackers and old hippies zipping around Goa's roads on two-wheelers—*sans* helmets. You can rent a bike for around Rs 150 to Rs 200 ($3.40–$4.55/£1.70–£2.30) a day with a private number plate as opposed to Rs 250 to Rs 300 ($5.70–$6.80/£2.90–£3.45) a day for a government-approved bike (these are identified by their yellow number plates); note that if you are stopped by the traffic cops, you will be fined for renting a private vehicle. Have your international two-wheeler driver's license handy, and check the bike thoroughly before handing over any cash (if you don't have a license, a gearless bike is easy to use even if you've never ridden them before). Note that if you hire a two-wheeler without insurance, you must pay for the repairs. You can find motorbikes practically everywhere; in Panjim, try across the road from the post office. If you don't have a license, there are plenty of **motorcycle pilots** in Goa—which is a more cost-effective way of getting around than by taxi. When someone stops to ask if you need a lift (and they will), negotiate a price in advance. And if you don't like the pace or style of driving, say something immediately. All approved pilots will have yellow number plates. **Motorbike Safaris** are also quite popular; if you can handle the fabulous Enfield motorbike, then get in touch with Peter Santos (info@classic-bike-india-de).

By Taxi & Auto-Rickshaw   Negotiate privately with one of the many taxi drivers found around tourist areas—including those near your hotel entranceway (you can get one through your hotel, of course, but at a five-star lodging the cost will almost double). Figure on spending Rs 1,200 ($29/£15) for about 100km (62 miles), but specify which locations you hope to cover. Remember that if you need a one-way lift to a more remote region, you'll be asked to pay for the return journey. If you plan to take a day trip to a far-off beach, you're better off fixing a price for the day (Rs 1,800/$44/£22 for a trip to Palolem from north Goa). Auto-rickshaws are considerably cheaper than taxis, but a great deal more uncomfortable. **Dalesh** is a reliable taxi driver (© 98221-02964) who can be booked for the whole day or for a pickup or drop-off (Rs 750/$18/£9.25 for an airport ride from Calangute). *Note:* All rates vary according to demand and season. It's best to ask the rates from a couple of taxi drivers before settling on a ride.

By Car   Goa is also perhaps the only place in India where you can hire self-drive cars (Rs 800–Rs 1,200/$20–$29/£10–£15) for the day for a basic model; souped-up open-air jeeps cost Rs 1,000 to Rs 1,500 ($24–$37/£12–£19) but, like many of the motorbike rental services, most of these outfits aren't registered or licensed to commercially rent out vehicles. Consequently, you may not be properly insured—you hire at your own risk; if you have an accident, you pay for the repairs. For better, fully insured cars with or without a chauffeur, call Dominic of **Velankini Car Rentals** (© 0832/248-9047,** 0832/329-0584, or 98-2210-1598).

By Bus   Buses ply their way up and down the state, stopping in a rather chaotic fashion whenever someone needs to get on or off. If you're in a hurry, try to catch an express bus; otherwise you could be in for an endless series of stop-starts—it is, however, the cheapest way of getting around (Rs 30/70¢/34p from one end to the other) and a fun way of getting acquainted with local folk (and Goan music)! Buses stop after 7:30pm.

By Boat   Andy of **Marin Boat Trip** (stationed at Reggie's Café) will organize seagoing excursions anywhere in Goa. For trips to Terakol (Goa's northernmost point), he charges Rs 900 to Rs 1,000 ($22–$24/£11–£12) each, including refreshments, for a minimum of seven passengers. **Goan Bananas** (© 0832/227-6362 or -6739, at Calangute Beach) organizes dolphin-spotting trips as well as jet-skiing and parasailing. At Kenilworth Beach Resort in south Goa, **Sea Adventure** (Utorda; © 98-2216-1712) organizes bird-watching and a backwater cruise that takes in basking river crocodiles. The operation runs from late October until the end of April. For a more comfortable and luxurious cruise, book a trip on the 27-seater yacht *Solita* (immortalized in a song by India's most famous Goan rock musician, Remo). Choose between an early-morning dolphin-spotting cruise on the sea or an evening sunset cruise on the Mapusa and Mandovi rivers (Rs 1,000/$24/£12 plus taxes; inclusive of a simple lunch). Unfortunately, there are so many boats and water scooters gunning for the poor dolphins that this activity has been diminished in recent years; until tourism authorities wake up and bring some order we would urge you not to add to the harassment. If you're traveling in a small group or want a special occasion you can charter *Solita* (Rs 10,000/$243/£123 per hr. for 2-hr. minimum) for a romantic dinner cruise or party; alternatively try **Odyssey Tours** (© 0832/227-6941 or 98-2218-0826; www.traveljadoo.com).

TOURS & TRAVEL AGENTS

The **Goa Tourism Development Corporation** (Trionara Apartments, Dr. Alvares Costa Rd., Panjim; © 0832/242-7972 or -0779; www.goacom.com/goatourism; daily 9:30am–5:30pm) has full-day tours of the north and the south aimed primarily at domestic tourists. For personalized adventure expeditions to any number of Goan destinations, try **Kennedy's Adventure Tours and Travels** (© 0832/227-9381 or 98-2327-6520; www.kennedysgoaholidays.com). **MGM International Travels** has offices in both Panjim (Navelcar Trade Centre, opposite Azad Maidan; © 0832/222-5166) and Calangute (Simplex Chambers, Umtavaddo; © 0832/227-6073). Other reliable travel agents include **Trade Wings** (1st floor, Naik Building, opposite Don Bosco School, Panjim; © 0832/243-2430) and **Footprints Tours & Travels,** run by Angeline Lobo (Shelter Guest Hs, Vaddi Candolim; © 98-5047-1639; goafootprints@ yahoo.co.uk).

SCUBA DIVING   Barracuda Diving India (Goa Marriott Resort, Miramar, Panaji; © 0832/246-3333, ext. 6807, or 98-2218-2402; fax 0832/246-3300; www. barracudadiving.com; barracuda@vsnl.com) is a PADI–recognized dive center where you can rent equipment or take diving courses and get certified (from beginner to advanced levels). Venkatesh Charloo and Karen Gregory, both master diver-trainers, offer dive safaris south, in Karnataka, where visibility can reach up to 30m (100 ft.). Bookings can also be made through **Atlantis Water Sports** (see below).

WATERSPORTS   Most of the upmarket resorts offer a range of watersports facilities. Goa's best-established watersports company is **Atlantis Water Sports** (© 98-9004-7272). Jet-skiing, parasailing, windsurfing, wakeboarding, scuba diving, and other ocean-going pastimes are available from a makeshift structure roughly halfway along the beach between Baga and Aguada (at the foot of Vila Goesa Rd., Cobra Vaddo, Calangute). Just outside the Taj Holiday Village is **Thunderwave,** a higher-priced watersports outfit that provides jet skis and cruises for Taj guests, but is also open to the public.

WALKING TOURS   Goa's unique architecture has been preserved to some extent, and—away from the coastal belt, toward the interiors as well as in Panjim and Mapusa—you'll find entire lanes and villages of beautiful old houses, some crumbling, others restored but all offering great insights into the original inhabitants and their status in society. If you're interested in decoding buildings, contact Heta Pandit of the **Heritage Network** (© 98-2212-8022; www.heritagenetworkindia.com) or pick up a copy of *Walking in Goa* (Eminence Designs Pvt. Ltd.) or *Houses of Goa* (Architecture Autonomous).

FAST FACTS: Goa

Airlines Even the smallest hotels are able to make air travel arrangements for you and usually charge a small fee to process tickets, which saves you the hassle of having to travel all the way to Panjim. **Jet Airways,** the best domestic airline, is open Monday to Saturday 9am to 6pm (Patto Plaza, near the Patto Tourist Hotel and the bus stand, Panjim; © **0832/243-8790**). **Deccan Airlines** (© **0832/243-8877**) offers cheaper airfares, but is also notorious for delays and cancellations.

Ambulance Dial © **102**, or you can call the **Panjim Ambulance and Welfare Trust** (Panjim; © **0832/222-4824**). Also in Panjim, call the 24-hour **Vintage Ambulance Service** (© **98-2305-9948**). In Margao, call the local **Ambulance Trust** (© **0832/273-1759**). In Mapusa, call © **98-2298-1562.**

American Express Call **American Express** (© **1600/1801-242** or 1800/1801-245).

Area Code The area code for **Goa** is © **0832**.

ATMs Ask your hotel for the nearest ATM with credit card facilities. In Panjim. there's an ICICI ATM at the Sindur Business Centre on Swami Vivekananda Road. In Candolim there's an HDFC machine at Regal Villa (opposite SBI), and a UTI machine in the Dona Alcina Estate (also at the Brangaza Complex, opposite the Kadamba bus depot in Mapusa).

Banks & Currency Exchange For the best rates, you can exchange cash and traveler's checks at **Thomas Cook** in Panjim (8 Alcon Chambers, D. B. Marg; © **0832/222-1312;** Mon–Sat 9:30am–7pm). Another location is between Baga and Calangute, at the State Bank of India, in the Hotel Ofrill Building (© **0832/ 227-5693**).

Car Rentals Try **Sita World Travel** (101 Rizvi Chamber, Caetano Albuquerque Rd., Panjim; © **0832/222-0476**, -0477, -3134, -6477, or 0832/242-3552).

Drugstores Go to **Farmacia Universal** in Panjim (Behind People High School; © **0832/222-3740;** 24 hr.). **Walson and Walson Chemist** can be found on Calangute (© **0832/227-6366;** daily 9am–9pm).

Emergencies In Panjim, dial © **102** for an ambulance, and © **101** in case of fire. See "Police," below.

Helpline Call the aptly named "Practically Anything on Goa" (© **0832/241-2121**).

Hospitals **Dr. Bhandari Hospital** (© **0832/222-4966** or -5602) is in Panjim's Fontainhas area. For hospital emergencies in Margao, call **Margao Hospital** (© **0832/270-5664**). In Mapusa, **Vrindavan Hospital** (© **0832/225-0022** or -0033) is reputed to be the best.

Internet Access High numbers of backpackers mean plenty of Internet facilities (Rs 25–Rs 90/55¢–$1.80/30p–90p per hr.), particularly in tourist areas. Wherever you are, ask or look out for **Sify iway** cybercafes (www.iway.com).

Police Dial © **100**. **Panjim Police Headquarters** (© **0832/242-8400** or -3400) is on Malaca Road, at the western edge of Azad Maidan.

Post Office Panjim's **General Post Office** is at Patto Bridge and is open Monday to Friday 9:30am to 5:30pm.

GOA'S BEST BEACHES

Goa's reputation for having some of the world's best beaches is well-deserved, but inevitable commercialization has taken its toll, with the infamous **Baga-to-Candolim** area (north of Panjim) now part of a tourist-infested strip of sun loungers, backed by beach shacks serving beer, cocktails, and fresh seafood—the sort of packaged beach experience best avoided. A little north of Baga, **Anjuna** comes alive with parties and trance music during the winter, when full-moon festivals get the crowds howling. It also has what was once a fabulous Wednesday Market, a tad too predictable and monotonous now with almost every shack selling the same wares. Just north of Anjuna is lovely **Vagator** 🌴🌴, with Chapora Fort overlooked by stark red cliffs. **Asvem** 🌴🌴 is also a great beach, and scene of the Big Chill party in April (see sidebar "Lights! Camera! Carnival! When to Groove in Goa," below), but regulars complain that it's not quite as pristine as it was 4 years back, and of late large numbers of Russians have begun to settle on this stretch, buying land and starting private enterprises, much of it rumored to be the wrong side of legal. A little north of Asvem, **Arambol** 🌴🌴🌴, seductively far away from the package-tour masses, is one of the last refuges of hard-core hippies.

Though there are no private beaches in Goa, the southern beaches generally become the private domain of the five-star resorts fronting them because of the sheer size of property they occupy. In the far south, gorgeous **Palolem** 🌴🌴🌴 has just one large resort close by (the InterContinental Grand, a few kilometers south in Cancona), and gets our vote for the best beach in Goa: Although it's become increasingly popular in the high season and is home to a sizable hippie community, it has yet to be overwhelmed by day-trippers. Just 7km (4 miles) north of Palolem, **Agonda** 🌴🌴🌴 is even more isolated and peaceful, while to the south, **Galgibaga** 🌴🌴🌴 is another remote haven with eucalyptus trees and empty stretches of sand. And then, of course, there's **Om** 🌴🌴🌴 beach, just over the border, an hour into the neighboring state of Karnataka, considered by many to be the best beach in India. The hippies have zeroed in on it, however, and recent openings include a few relatively upmarket accommodations, including Saswari, a recommended yoga retreat (see "Om Beach: Escape to Paradise" sidebar, later in this chapter).

2 Panjim (Panaji) & Old Goa

Located at the mouth of the Mandovi River, the state capital of Panjim (moved here from Old Goa in 1759) is a breezy, laid-back town that lends itself to easy exploration. The chief attraction is the wonderful colonial Portuguese architecture, particularly in the eastern neighborhoods of Fontainhas and Sao Tome, where the atmospheric cobbled streets are lined with old mansions and churches dating as far back as the mid-1700s—look for Fontainhas's **Chapel of St. Sebastian,** where the crucifix from Old Goa's "Palace of the Inquisition" is now kept. With head upright and eyes wide open, the figure of Christ on the crucifix here is unusual, unlike the usual figures, which feature lowered head and eyes.

Dominating Panjim's town center is the imposing **Church of the Immaculate Conception,** built in the Portuguese baroque style in 1541. Nearer the water's edge is the **Secretariat;** an old palace of Adil Shah of Bijapur, this became the Portuguese viceroy's residence when the colonial administration moved here.

Wandering around Panjim on foot shouldn't take more than a few hours. If you're pushed for time, skip the walk and hop onto an auto-rickshaw or on the back of a bike

Moments Lights! Camera! Carnival!

Each year in February, during the festivities leading up to Lent, the people of Goa get down for 3 days and nights of hedonistic revelry as King Momo commands them to party hard. **Carnival,** Goa's most famous festival, is a Latin-inspired extravaganza of drinking and dancing that traces its roots to ancient Roman and Grecian ritual feasts. Cities and towns come under the spell of colorful parades, dances, floats, balls, and bands, concluding with the red-and-black dance at Panjim's Club National. Another great time to visit is in April when the **Big Chill** (www.bigchillindia.in) sets up camp. Organized for the first time in 2007 by the parent U.K.–based company, the festival took place on the delightful sands of Asvem beach and featured a weekend of classic Big Chill acts as well as newer names in the world of trance and New Age music, playing from afternoon 'till late evening. (*Note:* The Big Chill is not a camping festival, so book your accommodations early if you want a place to stay in or around Morjim and Asvem.) And then there's October, when filmmakers and stars congregate for the annual **International Film Festival of India** (http://iffi.nic.in), held in Panjim, for 10 great days of film-frenzied action.

to **Old Goa** (30 min. from Panjim), reviewed in detail below. From Old Goa, it's a short trip (and a great contrast) to view the popular Hindu temples that lie north of the dull town of Ponda, on National Highway 4. Very few Hindu temples dating back earlier than the 19th century still exist. (Affronted by the Hindus' "pagan" practices, the Portuguese tore them down.) **Sri Mangeshi Temple** was built specifically as a refuge for icons of deities smuggled from the coast during the violent years of the 16th-century Inquisition. A path lined with palm trees leads to a colorful entranceway, behind which the tiled, steep-roofed temple exemplifies a fusion of Hindu and Christian architectural styles, hardly surprising considering that it was constructed by Goan craftsmen weaned on 200 years of Portuguese church-building. Walking distance from here (15 min. south) is the slightly less commercial (no temple "guides") **Sri Mahalsa Temple.** Another half-hour from Old Goa is **Sahakari Spice Plantation** (Curti, Ponda; ℂ **0832/231-2394;** www.sahakarifarms.com; tour with lunch Rs 300/$7.30/£3.70)—if you're not heading down to Kerala you might want to take a tour here. It's quite a commercial venture, but the tours provide an interesting insight into Indian spices, along with plenty of quizzing by the well-informed guides about basic facts related to your food.

EXPLORING OLD GOA ON FOOT 👁👁

The once-bustling Goan capital is said to have been the richest and most splendid city in Asia during the late 16th and early 17th centuries, before a spate of cholera and malaria epidemics forced a move in 1759. Today, this World Heritage Site is tepid testament to the splendor it once enjoyed. The tranquillity behind this well-preserved tourist site (barring the grubby stands selling refreshments and tacky souvenirs) belies the fact that it was built on plunder and forced conversions, though you'll see little evidence (like the basalt architraves) of the mass destruction of the Hindu temples initiated by fervent colonialists.

The entire area can easily be explored on foot because the most interesting buildings are clustered together. To the northwest is the **Arch of the Viceroys,** built in 1597

Hindu Christians

In 1623 the pope agreed to tolerate converted Brahmin Catholics, who were then allowed to wear the marks of their Hindu caste. This extraordinary concession played its part in allowing Goa to ultimately adopt a practice of syncretism that embraced Hindus and Christians alike, though it drew its fair share of criticism from the more narrow-minded: The British adventurer Sir Richard Burton once noted that the "good" Hindus converted to Catholicism by the Portuguese were simply "bad" Christians.

in commemoration of the arrival of Vasco da Gama in India. Nearby, the Corinthian-styled **Church of St. Cajetan** (1651) was built by Italian friars of the Theatine order, who modeled it after St. Peter's in Rome. Under the church is a crypt in which embalmed Portuguese governors were kept before being shipped back to Lisbon—in 1992, three forgotten cadavers were removed. St. Cajetan's is a short walk down the lane from **Adil Shah's Gate,** a simple lintel supported by two black basalt columns. Southwest of St. Cajetan's are the highlights of Old Goa: splendid **Sé Cathedral** ⚔, which took nearly 80 years to build and is said to be larger than any church in Portugal; and the **Basilica of Bom Jesus** (see below). The so-called Miraculous Cross, housed in a box in a chapel behind a decorative screen, was brought here from a Goan village after a vision of Christ was seen on it—apparently a single touch (there is a hole in the glass for just this purpose) will cure the sick. The surviving tower of the Sé's whitewashed Tuscan exterior houses the Golden Bell, whose tolling indicated commencement of the *auto da fés,* brutal public spectacles in which suspected heretics were tortured and burnt at the stake. Nearby, the **Convent and Church of St. Francis of Assisi** (now an unimpressive archaeological museum) has a floor of gravestones and coats of arms; note that the images of Mary and Christ are darker-skinned than usual.

Basilica of Bom Jesus (Cathedral of the Good Jesus) ⚔   Opposite the Sé, the Basilica of Bom was built between 1594 and 1605 as a resting place for the remains of the patron saint of Goa, Francis Xavier (one of the original seven founders of the Jesuit order and responsible for most of the 16th-c. conversions). The withered body of the venerated saint lies in a silver casket to the right of the altar, his corpse surprisingly well-preserved (although one arm is on display in Rome and a missing toe is believed to have been bitten off in 1634 by an overzealous devotee looking to take home her very own relic, during the first exposition of the body—now a decennial event; the next St. Francis Festival is in 2017).

Up the hill from the Basilica are the splendid ruins of the once awe-inspiring **Church of St. Augustine;** below is the **Church and Convent of Santa Monica and Chapel of the Weeping Cross,** where a miraculous image of the crucified Christ is said to have once regularly bled, spoken, and opened its eyes.

Basilica de Bom Jesus: Mon–Sat 6am–6:30pm. Sé Cathedral: daily 7:30am–6pm. Archaeological Museum: daily 9am–12:30pm and 3–6:30pm; admission Rs 5 (10¢/5p). Convent and Church of St. Francis of Assisi: Mon–Sat 7:30am–6:30pm. Church of St. Cajetan: daily 9am–5:30pm.

WHERE TO STAY & DINE

In the unlikely event that you will stay this close to the capital, we've reviewed the best option below. The **Marriott,** an upmarket resort situated on the outskirts of the city could be another option, but **Panjim Pousada, Panjim Inn, and Panjim People's,** situated in the heart of the Fontainhas neighborhood, have more character; Pousada is also very affordable. Most of the following are open for lunch and dinner.

Panjim is filled with shabby-looking "pure veg" *udipi* eating halls. If you're in the mood for an Indian snack or a quick cheap dish, aren't afraid to get your hands dirty, and feel like hanging with the locals, try one out; **Vihar** (31 Janeiro Rd.; C **0832/222-5744**) is a good option. Opposite the Church of Our Lady of Immaculate Conception, **George Restaurant** is convenient; if a really spicy chorizo-style sausage appeals to you, order the Goan sausage. For more atmosphere, make a reservation at Luiz D'Souza's **Hospedaria Venite** (31st January Rd., Fontainhas; C **0832/242-5537**), a tiny upstairs restaurant in a 200-year-old building where you can sit on the balcony and order wonderful Goan specialties (or try the delicious shrimp salsa and stuffed crab). Close by, in a narrow alley, is another popular and consequently slightly cramped restaurant, **Viva Panjim** (Hs No.178, Rua 31 de Janeiro; C **0832/242-2405**), which has a decent menu at dirt-cheap prices. But if you're looking for a mix of Portuguese and Goan cuisine done to perfection, make a beeline for the small and cozy **Horseshoe** (Rua de Ourem; C **0832/243-1788**). The menu is extensive and striking for its complete lack of vegetarian options.

Catering to a steady stream of tourists who are told that it's the best restaurant in town for North Indian cuisine, **Delhi Darbar** (M.G. Rd.; C **0832/222-2544**) turns a heavy trade, but it's an unexciting experience. Instead, head across the Mandovi Bridge to Povorim where **O'Coquiero's** (near Water Tank; C **0832/241-7271**) has been churning out traditional Goan food for decades (try the squid masala or chicken *cafreal*). For more on Goan food, see "The Unique Flavors of Goa," below.

Down the road from the **Goa Marriott Resort** (which, incidentally, has a marvelous seafood restaurant, **Simply Fish,** an outdoor venue overlooking the bay) is **Mum's Kitchen** (Martin's Building, D. B. Marg, Miramar; C **98-2217-5559**). It has

The Unique Flavors of Goa

If you don't know your *xacuti* from your *baboti,* here's a short guide: Chicken *cafreal* is chicken marinated in green herb and garlic marinade and then fried. *Vindaloo* is a curry usually made with pork and marinated in vinegar, garlic, chilies, and assorted spices. Prawn *Balchao* is a sweetish shrimp preserve made with spices and coconut *feni.* *Ambot-tik* is a hot curry soured with *kokum* berries and usually made with baby shark. The state's favorite fish, kingfish *(isvon) recheado,* is stuffed with chilies and spices blended in vinegar. *Xacuti* is a coconut-based masala; *baboti* is a sweet and spicy ground-beef dish. *Sorpotel*—not for the fainthearted—is traditionally a spicy concoction of pork, offal, *feni,* vinegar, red chilies, and spices. *Bebinca* is the traditional layered dessert made with lots of eggs and coconut milk. *Dodol* is made with jaggery (sugar) and should always be accompanied with vanilla ice cream. Goa is famous for its cashew nuts available in many forms; get the roasted salted variety (great with any drink) from Zantye's or Kajuwala in Panjim. *Kokum* (fruit of a plant by the same name), served as a syrupy juice, is a delightful thirst quencher; when mixed with coconut milk, garlic, and salt, it becomes a digestive aid called *sol kadi.* Speaking of drinks, *feni* is the deceptively light alcoholic spirit distilled from the cashew fruit (or coconut); try it, but be wary.

a laid-back Mediterranean atmosphere and does wonderful crab *xec-xec* (cooked in thick, spicy coconut gravy) and pomfret *recheado* (fish stuffed with hot spices and pan-fried). The owner, Rony Martins, not only invites you to examine his kitchen for standards of hygiene and his fish for freshness, he is on a mission to revive authentic Goan cuisine. He sources and adopts old "grandma" recipes and has started "A Cry of Goa": an exercise to save Goan cuisine.

To sample traditional Goan sweets while wandering Fontainhas, pop into **Confeitaria 31 de Janueiro,** one of the oldest bakeries in the state (31 Janeiro Rd.; ✆ 0832/222-5791).

Panjim Inn, Panjim Pousada, and Panjim People's ✿   Situated in Panjim's historic Fontainhas district, these are the only authentically Goan guesthouses in Panjim. Retired engineer Ajit Sukhija and his son Jack provide warm Goan hospitality, regaling you with local history while proudly pointing out family photographs. The best option is **Panjim People's,** a four-room heritage hotel (formerly a prominent local school) with spacious rooms and modern bathrooms; ask for the room in which Ajit's mother's lovely rosewood four-poster bed is the centerpiece. There's nothing particularly luxurious about the restored colonial-era Hindu **Pousada,** but it offers a taste of Panjim's 19th-century upper-class lifestyle (along with hot water). The simple rooms are furnished with antiques (including four-poster beds) arranged around an empty courtyard. Windows and balconies look onto the back streets and backyards of Panjim's old "Latin Quarter." The Pousada's older Catholic sister, **Panjim Inn,** is located on an old family property dating back to 1880; as with the Pousada, rooms vary in size and price, so it's best to look around before deciding.

Panjim Inn reception, E-212, 31st January/31 Janeiro Rd., Fontainhas. ✆ **0832/222-8136** or -6523. Fax 0832/222-8136 or -6523. www.panjiminn.com. 24 units. Rs 1,350 ($33/£17) single; Rs 1,530 ($37/£19) double; Rs 1,800 ($44/£22) deluxe; Rs 2,790 ($68/£34) large suite; Rs 360–Rs 180 ($8.80–$4,40/£4.45–£2.20) extra person/child. **Panjim Pousada,** House no. 156, Circle no. 5, Cunha Gonsalves Rd., Fontainhas. 9 units. Same rates as Panjim Inn. **Panjim People's,** opposite Panjim Inn. 4 units. Rs 4,850 ($118/£60) large room; Rs 5,800 ($141/£72) superior room; Rs 900–Rs 450 ($22–$11/£11–£5.55) extra person/child. Rates are discounted or increased during off season and peak season respectively and include breakfast. MC, V. **Amenities:** Restaurant; laundry; doctor-on-call; currency exchange. *In room:* A/C, TV, minifridge, coffee- and tea-making facilities (only in People's).

3 North of Panjim

Goa's reputation as a hangout for hippies during the '60s and '70s was made on the northern beaches of **Calangute, Baga,** and **Anjuna.** Along with the relaxed lifestyle and good times came busloads of Indian men keen to observe free-spirited foreigners and, finally, a crackdown by local government. This forced fun-loving hippies to head to more remote tracts of coastline, leaving the door open for backpackers and package tourists. Thus were the north's most famous beaches transformed into tanning lots for the masses—even Anjuna has become an Ibiza-like experience—and today no card-carrying hippie would deign to set foot on the beach that stretches between Calangute and Baga (defined by resort-centered **Sinquerim** in the south to **Vagator** in the north). That said, you can't deny the beauty of the beaches (in south Vagator, **Ozran Beach** is peaceful and beautiful, with relaxed swimming in a bay at its southernmost end)—certainly this is where you'll want to be if you're here to party during the season. Baga is the smaller, slightly less-developed area of activity. Beach shacks like **Britto's** (Baga) and **Fisherman's Paradise** (Calangute) are crowded with beer-quaffing visitors recovering from the previous night's adventure at the legendary bar-cum-nightclub, **Tito's.** (Be warned that the "special lassis" served at some Goan beach

Shopping the Global Village Markets

Anjuna is the site of Goa's **Wednesday market** ✿, where a nonstop trance soundtrack sets the scene and a thousand stalls sell everything from futuristic rave gear to hammocks that you can string up between two palm trees on the nearby beach. It's a wonderful place to meet people from all over the world as well as Rajasthanis, Gujaratis, Tibetans—even drought-impoverished Karnataka farmers with "fortune-telling" cows. It's a bit like London's Camden, but everyone's tanned and the weather's almost always wonderful. Come the weekend, Goa's global residents head for either of the two **Saturday Night Bazaars—Ingoe's** ✿✿ or **Mackie's** ✿—where most of the spending seems to involve liquor and food. Ingoe's is on a larger scale, but both dole out essentially the same ingredients of live music, eclectic cuisine, and shops galore selling semi-precious stones, paintings, books, clothes, music, and handicrafts churned out by long-term international visitors.

Perhaps the most interesting market of the lot is a local affair. Once a week, folk from villages all across Goa breeze into Mapusa for the **Friday Market** ✿✿, where they set up large tables groaning under the weight of extraordinarily large-size vegetables, strings of home-made pork sausages, basketfuls of *kokum*, pickles like *chepnim* and *miscut* made out of tender mangoes, prawn *balchao* and Bombay duck pickles, a freshly baked assortment of Goan breads, all kinds of confectionary goodies like *bebinca* and *dodol*, guava cheese, and wines. If you have space to take home a souvenir, look for the red rooster water jug—you'll find one in every Goan home, ostensibly to chase away spirits! When you're pooped from shopping, drop into **Café Xaviers** (opposite the banana section), which sells refreshingly cold coffee shakes and delicious Goan sausage with *poee* (flat Goan bread). Another reason to come is the interesting **Other India Bookstore** (next to New Mapusa Clinic; ✆ **0832/226-3306**; www.otherindiabookstore.com), which stocks up on academic books related to issues like the environment, agriculture, and spirituality.

shacks will dramatically increase your amusement at the cows sunbathing alongside the tourists on Baga Beach.)

For a sense of Goa's hippie origins, head for **Arambol,** Goa's most northerly beach (36km/22 miles northwest of Mapusa). It also offers better bodysurfing—the water's a little more turbulent. It draws quite a crowd during the season (you arrive through a lane crammed with stalls selling CDs and T-shirts, and laid-back restaurants playing competing brands of music), but the setting is nevertheless lovely, with a hill looming over a small freshwater lake fed by a spring. The farther north you walk, the more solitude you enjoy. Besides looking at beautiful bodies, you can spend hours watching the surf glide. Better still, head a little farther south from Arambol for **Asvem** Beach; while the Russians may have set up camp here it's still a great beach. For a bite to eat, the best shack (at the south end of Asvem) is white-curtained **La Plage** (✆ **98-2212-1712**), run by the same French trio who own Le Restaurant Français (see review later in this chapter). Feast on great steak or fish barbecued in a banana leaf, or just sip a cool mint lassi (daily 8:30am–10:30pm; closed May to mid-Nov). Just south of Asvem is the dark sand beach of **Morjim,** popular with the Olive Ridley turtles that have been coming here for centuries and, more recently, Russian tour groups and expats keen to carve out their own place in paradise.

WHERE TO STAY

Goa offers a wide range of accommodations, but the luxury resorts tend to offer the best proximity to secluded beaches. If you're design-conscious, want to be relatively close to the beach and in the heart of the tourist zone—yet keen on a boutique "non-hotel" experience, Goa's best option is **Pousada Tauma** (reviewed below). If you're looking for something more mid-range, head for **Presa di Goa** (reviewed below). But if you're here to simply enjoy the beach, **Elsewhere** (reviewed below), is our top choice. Away from the crowds, it has an absolutely stunning beach, a lovely, simple house to stay in, and great food. And if you want to party, you can probably find something 15 to 20 minutes away.

Another good budget-oriented choice is the two suites (Rs 1,000–Rs 2,000/$24–$49/£12–£25) at **Hotel Bougainvillea** (✆ **0832/227-3270** or -3271; www.granpas inn.com; doubles from Rs 1,400/$34/£17) at Anjuna; book the one with its own garden. Inherited by Betina Faria, it was built by her grandfather and consequently is also known as Grandpa's Inn. The small accommodations are quiet and cool; there's a lovely garden, swimming pool, and old pool table. Both short and long sessions of Brahmani yoga are held on the premises. If you plan on staying anywhere near Asvem/Morjim, drop in for a very Zen experience at **Ku** (✆ **93-2612-3570**), run by Marie and Chris—it's a makeshift place that is dismantled every year when the season ends. Ku is very small, beautiful, and refreshing. At Goa's very northernmost point is the rather remote enclave of Tiracol, where the owners of Nilaya Hermitage have restored seven rooms at **Fort Tiracol Heritage Hotel** (Querim, Pernem; ✆ **02366/22-7631**; 130€ ($177/£89) standard double, 170€ ($232/£117) suite; rates inclusive of taxes, breakfast, and Goan dinner). Although the views are outstanding and the food superb, you may find life a little dull (no pool, and the beach is a 3-min. ferry away) and isolated (90 min. from Baga). However, it's hard to beat if you want to *really* get away from it all.

Casa Britona & Casa Anjuna ✿   Far away from the crowds, this 17th-century Customs warehouse, located on the riverside in the fishing village of Charmanos, has been converted by the owner of the Casa Group of Hotels, Sheela Dhody, and popular Goan architect Dean D'Cruz into a colonial-style boutique hotel. With just 10 individually furnished rooms, you are ensured privacy, though sound travels fairly easily between rooms. Ask for a room on the first floor; these share a long veranda (with planter's chairs) overlooking the pool. Almost 40 minutes from the shore, this may not be the ideal location for beach lovers (for that, book Casa Anjuna, which is a 6- to 8-min. walk from the hotel, or one of the other beach-based recommendations made here), but you are assured of peace, excellent service, and a multitude of chirping birds as backdrop while you unwind on the lounge deck by the pool or on the wooden boardwalk on the Mandovi River. On the boardwalk are tables where you can be served a lovely dinner by candlelight. There are three more Casa hotels; of these only **Casa Anjuna** offers atmosphere, style, and good cuisine, although the service is a little slow. Set in a quiet neighborhood in Anjuna, it is a lovely old bungalow with annexes, plenty of greenery, nicely turned out rooms, a lovely garden for more candlelit dinners, and a rooftop restaurant for lazy morning breakfasts.

Charmanos, Badem, Salvador-do-Mundo, Bardez. ⓒ **0832/241-0962** or 98-5055-7665. Fax 0832/241-3389. www.
casaboutiquehotelsgoa.com. 10 units. Apr 1–Sept 30, Oct & Mar, Nov & Feb, Dec 1–Dec 27 & Jan 6–Jan 31, Dec
28–Jan 5: Rs 4,500/6,000/8,000/10,000/15,000 ($110/$147/$195/$244/$366; £56/£74/£99/£124/£185) double. Rates
include breakfast. Taxes extra. No credit cards. **Casa Anjuna:** D'Mello Waddo, Anjuna, Bardez. ⓒ **0832/227-4125.**
19 units. Same rates and amenities as Casa Britona. **Amenities:** Restaurant; pool; car hire; complimentary airport
transfers; room service; laundry; doctor-on-call; TV lounge; fax and Internet; Ayurvedic treatment on request. *In room:*
A/C, hair dryer on request.

Elsewhere . . . The Beach House & Otter Creek Tents 🏝🏝🏝 If simplicity is
what works for you, then Elsewhere is where you belong. Located in the
extreme north, between Asvem and Arambol, one of the most idyllic boutique properties in
Goa is found at the end of a road and reached by crossing a bamboo footbridge
through thick green groves. You won't find chic interiors or heavy themed designs
here: The basic cottages (two- and three-bedroom villas) contain simple rooms that
are functional, tasteful, and pleasant, with planter's chairs and deck beds on sit-outs
and porches. In place of the obligatory pool you have the entire Arabian Sea to swim
in. Coming here has a definite purpose—to enjoy the salt and froth that mixes with
the air; to savor a beach that is so quiet, so pristine, so beautiful; to take lazing about
to new dimensions. Don't expect to find shacks, vendors, or shops. Come between
October and February, however, and you may spot Olive Ridley and rare loggerhead
turtles. Bargain hunters should opt for one of the three tents, which overlook the
freshwater creek; these are furnished with four-poster beds and have en-suite bathrooms with hot showers and personal sit-outs on a bamboo jetty. The food is terrific,
even though it tends to take forever to get it, and the young staff, led by manager
Vinod, is unobtrusive and ever helpful. Fashion photographer Denzil Sequeira considers his ancestral property the biggest secret in Goa, but given how long you need to
book in advance, the secret is out.

North Goa. Reservations: gaze@aseascape.com. ⓒ **93-2602-0701** (last-minute bookings or emergencies only).
www.aseascape.com. The Beach House/The Priest's House (each house goes as a whole 3-bedroom house only; sleeps
6) and the Piggery (2-bedroom villa, sleeps 4): Rs 11,076 ($270/£137). The Bakery (2-bedroom villa can be taken as
single-bedroom cottage): Rs 5,500 ($135/£68). Otter Creek Tents (3 units): Rs 3,432 ($84/£42) double. Ask for per-
week prices. Rates differ during absolute peak and off season. Closed end May to end Sept. MC, V. **Amenities:**
Restaurant; car and driver (chargeable); airport transfers (chargeable); laundry; doctor-on-call; body boards. *In room:*
The Beach House and the Priest's House: Minibar, tea/coffeemaker. The Piggery and The Bakery: A/C, minibar, tea/cof-
feemaker. Otter Creek tents: Tea/coffeemaker.

Fort Aguada Beach Resort & Hermitage 🏝🏝 (Kids) Situated on the short peninsula upon which the Portuguese built their defensive Fortress of Aguada, this Taj resort
complex (comprising the Beach Resort, Hermitage, and Holiday Village) has one of
the most spectacular locations in all of Goa, with picture-postcard views of the beach,
which stretches all the way to Baga, 8km (5 miles) away. Behind the main Beach
Resort block are 42 cottages tucked almost invisibly among groves of lantana, cashew,
and bougainvillea bush; these are the best places to stay at the Beach Resort although
you don't get a clear view of the sea from all. Alternatively, for absolute privacy (ideal
for groups or families), consider one of the 15 top-end Hermitage cottages, built as a
retreat for delegates during the 1983 meeting of the Commonwealth heads of government. The cottages are set among terraced gardens of exotic orchids, bougainvilleas,
cashew trees, jasmine, and Krishna ficus. Each villa has a separate living room; a dining area; one, two, or three bedrooms; two bathrooms; a *balcao* (balcony); and a private garden. Interiors are luxurious and include all modern amenities; request a villa
near Sunset Point, where cocktails are served while the sun descends over the Arabian

Sea. It's quite a stiff climb between the cottages and the hotel lobby (shared with the Beach Resort); courtesy vehicles are available for the short transfer. Also sharing the facilities offered by Fort Aguada Resort is the newly renovated and informal Taj Holiday Village, fronted by Sinquerim Beach, with cottages and villas in reds, pinks, blues, and yellows scattered among towering coconut trees and lush vegetation. Accommodations at this resort vary considerably, ranging from lavish sea-facing villas to less desirable suites in clustered or duplex cottages. Although its facilities make it immensely popular with families, it wouldn't be your first choice if you're looking for peace and quiet.

Sinquerim, Bardez, Goa 403 519. © **0832/664-5858.** Fax 0832/664-5868. www.tajhotels.com. 156 units. $225–$475 (£113–£239) superior garden-view with sit-out, $250–$525 (£126–£265) superior sea-view double, $275–$550 (£139–£277) superior sea-view with sit-out, $375–$675 (£189–£340) terrace suite, $325–$650 (£164–£328) cottage garden-view. Hermitage villas: $325–$650 (£164–£328) 1-bedroom garden-view, $375–$675 (£189–£340) 1-bedroom sea-view, $575–$950 (£290–£479) 2-bedroom sea-view, $1,100–$1,500 (£555–£756) 3-bedroom sea-view; $30 (£15) extra bed. Taj Holiday Village doubles: $275–$550 (£139–£277) cottage garden-view, $325–$650 (£164–£328) cottage sea-view, $425–$750 (£214–£378) villa garden-view, $475–$775 (£239–£391) villa sea-view, $675–$1,000 (£340–£504) luxury villa sunset-view; $30 (£15) extra bed. Ask about multi-day or monsoon specials that may include transfers, food, and other conveniences. AE, DC, MC, V. **Amenities:** (Taj Aguada) 3 restaurants; kids restaurant; 2 bars; pool; tennis; fitness center; spa; watersports; cycling; airport transfers; shop; salon; room service; babysitting; laundry; house doctor; currency exchange; Wi-Fi; volleyball; squash; badminton; billiards; table tennis; adventure activities (trekking, rock climbing, rappelling); activity center. *In room:* A/C, TV, minibar, tea- and coffee-making facilities, hair dryer, safe. (Similar for Taj Holiday Village as well.)

The Hobbit 🛇🛇🛇 *Finds*   This is the ultimate Goan hideaway "villa": Fashioned in and around a rock, this was once (minus windows, doors, and ceilings) the psychedelic digs of Anjuna's famed '70s hippies, and you're likely to walk right past the boundary hedge before finding it. Refurbished by the extremely chilled-out Chinmayi and her husband, rally driver Farad Bathena, the Hobbit was born in 2006, and comprises three delightful rooms on two different levels, done up simply but tastefully; a sitting and dining room, meditation alcove, and kitchenette; and plenty of sit-outs, a roof terrace, a tiny plunge pool, and semi-open bathrooms around exposed rock with sweeping views of the beach and the neighboring cliff. Even though you are right near the action (2 min. walking distance from the beach), the Hobbit remains secluded, and barring a passing hang-glider (who may be as surprised to discover you lounging on the pebbled overhang outside your room as you are seeing a man hovering above), there is little intrusion. You can choose to cook your own meals or use the services of two nearby shacks—**Curly's** (seafood) and **Shiva's** (Israeli), which are more than happy to "home" deliver via Hobbit's very own Mama and Papa (inexplicable names for two utterly sweet young Manipuri boys). The Wednesday Flea Market is a stone's throw away, and parties are fairly common in this area but (fortunately) not held on a nightly basis. Ask Chinmayi for the details if you want to make sure you're at the right place at the right time—or far away from it.

St. Michaels Vaddo, South Anjuna, Goa 403 509. © **0832/227-4629** or 98-2005-5053. www.thehobbitgoa.com. Full villa rental only; 3 units sleeping up to 6 adults. Oct/Mar–May Rs 9,000 ($220/£111); Nov–Dec 15/Jan 16–Feb 28 Rs 13,500 ($329/£167); Dec 16–Dec 24/Jan 2–Jan 15 Rs 22,500 ($549/£278); Dec 24–Jan 2 Rs 25,000 ($610/£309). Closed monsoon season (June–Sept). Rates include taxes, airport transfer, housekeeping services. MC, V. **Amenities:** Well-equipped kitchen; washing machine; iron; TV; DVD player; Internet; man servant on call. *In room:* A/C. safe. tea/coffee maker.

Laguna Anjuna 🛇   Tucked 700m (765 yards) away from the beach in a quiet area amid paddy fields, Laguna Anjuna is perfect for those who want the best of both worlds—you're close enough to Anjuna to enjoy the vibe, yet far enough away to be undisturbed by the nonstop party atmosphere. A large-size pool surrounded by lovely foliage is the first thing that greets you upon entering. With a piano and pool table inside and dining outside, the original house is extremely casual, with an eclectic mix of music playing right through the day. Behind, cottages built of laterite stone with domes and sloping roofs in red tile, each entirely unique, are set in and around the original coconut grove. With a team like Dean D'Cruz and interiors duo Sonia and Thomas of Soto Décor, there is little that can go wrong—the spacious rooms are the most astounding shapes, forming their own contours between palms, and are filled with mirrors, chests, local crafts, and wrought-iron beds covered in cool green and yellow linen. Ask for a room away from the reception, which can get a little noisy, and come prepared for the mosquitoes. Owner Farrokh Maneckshaw is a great source of information and highly amusing—he drives an absolutely fabulous '51 pink Chevy!

Soranto Vado, Anjuna 403 509. ℂ/fax **0832/274-305** or -131. www.lagunaanjuna.com. 23 units. Oct 1–Dec 19/Dec 20–Jan 15/Jan 16–Apr 30/May 1–Sept 30 1-bedroom suite, 2-bedroom suite: Rs 4,600 ($112/£57), Rs 7,000 ($171/£87)/Rs 8,500 ($207/£105), Rs 12,500 ($305/£154)/Rs 4,600 ($112/£57), Rs 7,000 ($171/£86)/Rs 3,200 ($78/£40), Rs 4,600 ($112/£57). Rs 1,200 ($29/£15) extra bed. Rates include breakfast and taxes. AE, MC, V. **Amenities:** Restaurant; bar; pool; can arrange pickups and transfers; room service; Ayurvedic massage; laundry; doctor-on-call; Internet access; pool table; backgammon. *In room:* A/C, TV, minibar, hot water.

Nilaya Hermitage 𝕣𝕣𝕣   From the moment you arrive, you know you're going to be very comfortable indeed. Ex-Parisian fashion stylist Claudia Derain and her Indian husband, Hari Ajwani, started this exclusive hillside resort when they fell in love with Goa during a vacation from Europe. Together with Goan architect Dean D'Cruz, they have created something out of *Arabian Nights,* with 12 cosmic-themed guest suites featuring vibrant colors, terrazzo flooring, and minimalist decor. Giant mosquito nets hang from high-beamed ceilings, and sweeping archways lead off to open-plan bathrooms with views of the tropical garden. Like a chic harem, the split-level, saffron-colored "Music Room" is where guests unwind on sprawling mattresses or meditate while soothing music plays beneath a high, blue-domed ceiling. Overlooking paddy fields and coconut palm groves, the setting is romantic and classy, and despite being 6km (4 miles) from the nearest beach, Nilaya is one of Goa's most celebrated getaways, as its extensive celebrity guest list (Kate Moss, Peter Lindbergh, Philippe Starck) indicates. Do also look into their **Fort Tiracol Heritage Hotel,** overlooking the sea at Goa's northernmost point.

Arpora Bhati, Goa 403 518. ℂ **0832/227-6793,** -6794, -5187, or -5188. Fax 0832/227-6792. www.nilaya.com. 12 units. Sept to end May 290€ ($395/£199) double; Dec 20–Jan 10 490€ ($667/£336) double. Rates include taxes, breakfast, dinner, and airport transfers. MC, V.Closed June–Aug. **Amenities:** Restaurant; breakfast area; bar; pool; tennis court; Ayurvedic center; spa; travel assistance; room service; laundry; doctor-on-call; meditation room; cultural performances. *In room:* A/C, TV and DVD players can be arranged.

Panchavatti 𝕣𝕣 *Finds*   If you're looking for a little peace and quiet in a soul-stirring setting and don't care too much for phones, air conditioners, bathtubs, and the like, then Isla (Loulou) Van Damme's place is the ultimate refuge from the overwhelming frenzy of India. Most people come to Goa for the beaches, but Loulou's guesthouse (also her home), with its stunning location on a hill on Corjuem Island, is where you come to put your feet up and relax, take a dip or yoga instruction, or contemplate life. With thoughtful landscaping and innate good taste, this charming Belgian woman, who provides simple, spacious rooms and Western-style set meals, has created an extraordinary getaway. Tariff includes three meals (and soft drinks)—and they are meals to die for, served on the large open colonnaded balcony that overlooks the valley. In Loulou's inimitable style, there are no latches or locks on any of the doors and bathrooms are curtained off from the bedrooms by thin cotton saris. Book one of the four rooms that open onto the large balcony (the rest overlook a central courtyard and garden). A music room is stacked with CDs and a small collection of nonfiction books. The pool is fabulously placed—on the edge of a hill. When you want to experience the beach, however, you'll have to hire a taxi for the 30-minute schlep there. Or use the bicycles to explore the island.

Collomuddi, Corjuem Island, Aldonna, Bardez, Goa 403 508. (℠ **98-2258-0632** or 0832/395-2946. http://islaingoa. com. info@islaingoa.com. 7 units. Dec–Jan Rs 9,000 ($220/£111) double; Oct–Nov/Feb–May Rs 8,000 ($195/ £99).Rates include all meals and soft drinks. No credit cards. Closed except for yoga workshops June to mid-Oct. **Amenities:** Pool; bicycles; travel assistance; limited room service; Ayurvedic massage; babysitting; laundry; music room; yoga and meditation. *In room:* Electronic safe, fan, iron and hair dryer on request.

Pousada Tauma 𝕬𝕬𝕬 This is Goa's top Ayurvedic retreat (a professional doctor presides over two excellent treatment rooms), and even though it's located in the heart of a bustling tourist center (a 10-min. walk from popular Calangute Beach), it is sheltered from the high-season madness by thick, verdant vegetation. Neville Proenca, the charming owner-manager, takes a hands-on approach—a far cry from the package-mentality tourism that's swept through the state. Working with award-winning architect Dean D'Cruz (talk about a track record!), it took Neville 3½ years to create his retreat, fashioned entirely out of distinctively Goan laterite stone and set around a pool with cascading water. Each suite has its own balcony, overlooking either the garden or pool, and is themed with eccentric pieces (a cradle-turned-table; dentist-chair-turned-recliner). The stylish bathrooms are done in shattered tile mosaics. Pousada is the perfect getaway for artists and sophisticated socialites—filmmaker Mira Nair stayed in the Mountain Suite after filming *Monsoon Wedding,* while French designer Michéle Klein enjoys the deluxe Castle Suite, a fairy-tale tower with two living rooms off a single bedroom. In addition to its Goan menu, the excellent **Copper Bowl Restaurant** offers Ayurvedic meals.

Porba Vaddo, Calangute, Bardez. (℠ **0832/227-9061.** Fax 0832/227-9064. www.pousada-tauma.com. 12 units. 155€–390€ ($211–$531/£107–£268) standard suite, 180€–440€ ($245–$599/£124–£301) superior suite, 260€–530€ ($354–$720/£178–£363) deluxe suite; 80€ ($109/£55) extra bed. Only off-season rates include taxes and breakfast. Booking for peak period (Dec 25–Jan 1) minimum 7 days. MC, V. No children. **Amenities:** Restaurant; bar; pool; gym; Ayurvedic center; travel services; airport transfers; room service (until 11pm); Internet access. *In room:* A/C, TV, mini-bar, hair dryer on request.

Presa di Goa 𝕬𝕬 *Value* Luxembourg native Edouard Spaeck and his adopted Goan son Judas (with wife, Cynthia) have turned this country house in Nagoa into a cool retreat, with friendly staff and good service. Unless you want a room close to the pool, book one of the value-for-money junior suites upstairs, which have their own balconies. Rooms, each named after a flower (we recommend Crossandra), are cozy and tastefully furnished with well-restored antiques that include four-poster beds, sofas, desks, and wardrobes or chests of drawers; the simple bathrooms contain bathtubs. Unfortunately, the closest beach is overrun Calangute, though frankly it's hard to believe this quiet place is just 10 minutes away (complimentary drop-offs 9–11am, pickups 4–7pm). If you want to head to a better beach, ask the hotel to arrange a taxi. Should you happen to be there on a Friday, hop into the car and go shopping with the cook to the Mapusa weekly market. The poolside restaurant, **La Pergola,** serves

Mediterranean, Turkish, Goan, and continental cuisine—try the grill or pan-fried kingfish, the *mezzos* platter, or the beef à la Provençale.

353/1 Arais Wado, Nagoa, Calangute, Bardez. © **0832/240-9067.** Fax 0832/240-9070. www.presadigoa.com. reservation@presadigoa.com. 7 units. Apr 1–Sep 30, Oct 1–Dec 19, Dec 20–Jan 2, Jan 3–Mar 31: $33/$50/$132/$66 (£17/£25/£67/£33) double; $55/$74/$196/$98 (£28/£37/£99/£49) junior suite double; $70/$89/$256/$118 (£35/ £45/£129/£60) junior suite triple; $70/$95/$256/$126 (£35/£48/£129/£63) Crossandra junior suite; $15/$27/ $40/$20 (£8/£14/£20/£10) extra bed. Children 2–6 get 50% discount on extra bed; taxes included except for high-season rates. Rates include breakfast and daily beach transfers. Ask about special rates for stays of 1 week or more. MC, V. **Amenities:** Restaurant; bar; pool; Ayurvedic treatment on request; airport transfers; car and motorbike hire; 24-hr. room service; laundry; doctor-on-call; Internet. *In room:* A/C, TV, hair dryer on request.

Wildernest 🏵🏵🏵 *(finds)* Miles away from the clichéd Goan image of sun and sand is an area 800m (875 yards) above sea level, sandwiched between Mahadei Wildlife Sanctuary in Goa and the proposed Bhimgarh Sanctuary in Karnataka. Lying amid this sea of green is Wildernest, the "love-child" of a group of villagers, eco-crusaders, and three forest departments that saved 450 acres from becoming a timber and mining wasteland. Having saved, resurrected, and restored the land, the team stuck fast to a self-imposed natural-material-only rule. The result is delightful; ingenuity has left its stamp everywhere: on walls, lights, even signposts, culminating in the most awesomely located swimming pool. Surrounded by forested hills, with waterfalls cascading in the distance and fed by natural spring water, the infinity pool is sheer magic. Cottages come with different views—our picks are the good-value Tulsi (Valley) and Mogra (Forest) categories. It's all managed by an efficient and ever-smiling army of young men and women. The cuisine, a delectable mix of recipes from Goa, Maharashtra, and Karnataka, is served in earthen pots. Wildernest is a haven for birders as well: You're likely to spot paradise flycatchers, Malabar grey hornbills, and long-billed vultures. Bears and leopards leave telltale signs as you go on early-morning walks on forest trails.

Swapnagandha, off Sankhali, Chorla Ghats. © **93-4111-2721** or -08838. www.wildernest-goa.com. 18 units. High season (Nov 1–Apr 14) (Forest View/Valley View/Family Cottage): Rs 6,000/7,000/10,000 ($146/$171/$244;£74/ £86/£123). Low season (Apr 15–Oct 31): Rs 3,200/4,200/6,000 ($78/$102/$146;£40/£52/£74). 1 child under 10 can stay free in Forest and Valley Cottages and 2 in Family Cottage. Rates include welcome drink, all meals, activities and hikes, folk dance/music performances, bird-watching, slide shows. No credit cards. **Amenities:** Restaurant; bar; pool; airport transfers; Ayurvedic massage; laundry.

WHERE TO DINE

Beach-shack dining is one of the essential Goa experiences—sipping *feni* while you feast on grilled tiger prawns or masala shark at unbelievable prices is a must. With at least 200 licensed seasonal shacks between Candolim and Baga, you certainly won't go hungry, but with names like Lover's Corner, Fawlty Towers, and Goan Waves, don't expect culinary magic. Best to stick to the following recommendations.

At Calangute, **Souza Lobo**'s seafood enjoys a legendary reputation, and deservedly so. Reserve a table on the beachfront patio and order the tandoor kingfish and crab-stuffed *papad,* or the expensive but excellent grilled lobster or tiger prawns (© **0832/ 228-1234** or 0832/227-6463; reservations taken before 8pm; after that, wait in line). While in Baga, check out **Casa Portuguesa** (Baga Beach; © **0832/227-7024;** closed Mon and May–Oct), set in a charming old bungalow near the beach; the chicken *caf-real* is highly recommended. Or stop at **Fiesta** (7/35 Saunta Vaddo; © **0832/227-9894**) just for the ambience (and decent pizzas but slow service) or a pick from their dessert menu. It's perched on the sand dunes near Tito's and run by Yellow and Maneck Contractor. If you have a sweet tooth, **Chocolatti** (409A Fort Aguada Rd.,

Candolim; ⓒ **93-2610-3522**) is simply irresistible when it comes to homemade chocolates and brownies.

A number of good restaurants can also be found **along the stretch of road between Arpora Hill and Baga Creek,** leading inland from Baga Beach. When Indian spices begin to take their toll, **Lila Café** (Baga River), a great breakfast and lunch cafe (and apparently where Gregory Peck, David Niven, and Roger Moore hung out when filming *Sea of Wolves*), is the perfect spot (with views of paddy fields and coconut groves) to enjoy a decent breakfast; a selection of breads and croissants is served with a variety of toppings. The fresh salads are also good, as is the catch of the day. Famous **J & A's Little Italy** 🍴🍴 (ⓒ **0832/228-2364** or 98-2313-9488; closed end of Apr to mid-Oct) is where Jamshed and Ayesha Madon serve fantastic pastas, wood-fired pizzas, and amazing organic salads in a great alfresco setting. During peak season there's always a long wait (well worth it), so do make reservations. The *regalo di mare* (prawns and squid in a tomato vinaigrette dressing served with pesto crostini) and *crespelle coi gamberi* (crepes stuffed with seafood) are personal favorites. Or try the delicious steaks or the perfect al dente pastas tossed in heavenly sauces.

Walking distance from Taj Fort Aguada are three restaurants commanding a fair amount of popularity—Burmese **Bomra's** (reviewed below), the Swiss-Italian **Santa Lucia** (ⓒ **0832/651-5213**), and the eclectic, slightly over-colorful **Sweet Chilli** (ⓒ **0832/247-9446**). But the hottest new entry this side of Panjim is undoubtedly **A Reverie** (next to Hotel Goan Heritage; ⓒ **98-2317-4927**)—you can sit in the garden or indoors beneath high ceilings and chandeliers. The food is essentially modern European with delectable exotica like smoked French duck with truffles and spiced berry sorbet or home-cured beef with mustard ice cream. With plush sofas to sink into, it also serves as a lounge and offers a great selection of drinks—all this at a price, of course, so come prepared to leave lighter in the pocket. **Sublime** (located near the Anjuna football field; ⓒ **98-2248-4051**) offers fusion food and presentational styles that are quite difficult to classify, even for American owner Christopher (for example, he uses a French recipe for fish, which is accompanied by traditional Indian green lentils and an Italian sauce!). A reasonable, well-established alternative is **Xavier's** (near the flea market; ⓒ **0832/322-6086**)—it has a lovely ambience (with additional seating in the garden), and the seafood is always fresh and the lamb chops excellent. Finally, if you're in Anjuna and seriously in need of a pizza, drop in at **Basilico** (D'mello Vaddo, near Casa Anjuna; ⓒ **0832/227-3721**). It's run by an Italian, which explains the authenticity and subtleties in flavor so often lacking in smaller restaurants. Farther north has its own share of shacks that may not be there the following season.

After-7-Seven 🍴🍴🍴 EUROPEAN   It's definitely worth tracking down this difficult-to-find (and strangely named) restaurant (located between Calangute and Candolim near the Sarkar ice factory), for it's one of the best dinner venues in Goa. Owned by the gracious Leo D'Souza and superchef Soumyen Chakraborty (both spent years at Taj hotels), this alfresco restaurant is set on the lawns of Leo's house. You can watch your meal being cooked in the glass-fronted kitchen, and discuss how you liked it afterward, when the chef visits every table. Begin with the best Camembert soufflé east of France, and move on to the delectable "Ocean's Fantasy" seafood platter, or the chargrilled filet steak with blue cheese sauce, both marvelous. Finally, whether you have room for dessert or not, we must recommend the chocolate mousse with orange Curaçao or the unbelievably light and delicious orange soufflé. Service is top-notch.

1/274B Gaura Vaddo, Calangute, Bardez. © 0832/227-9757 or 92-2618-8288. Reservations essential. Main courses Rs 300–Rs 1,000 ($7.30–$24/£3.70–£12). AE, MC, V. Daily 7pm–midnight.

Bean Me Up 🔆 *Kids* ORGANIC/VEGETARIAN   A few years ago Lisa Camps decided to open this wholesome, clean organic-food restaurant at Vagator, as an alternative to the predominantly non-vegetarian food available all over Goa. Meat-lovers won't miss anything once they sample Lisa's tofu lasagna or one of the daily house specials. But most delicious are the huge salads Lisa promises are the "safest in Goa." Expect soy in almost everything at this "Soya Station," including tofu ice cream and tofu cheesecake. If all this sounds too over-the-top healthy and New Age for you, you can sip on the unusual but tasty drinks and juices and even catch a dance performance or live Spanish band on Sundays. Children are well taken care of in the kids' corner, with its comfy floor mattresses and cushions, reading and coloring books, and—yes, 'fraid so—a TV playing Cartoon Network.

House no. 1639/2 Deul Vaddo, Anjuna-Vagator, Bardez. © 0832/227-3479. Reservations suggested for dinner during peak season. Main courses Rs 80–Rs 250 ($1.95–$6/£1–£3). MC, V. Sun–Fri 8am–4pm and 7–11pm; call about Sat hours.

Bomra's 🔆 *Value* BURMESE   With Goa bursting at its seams with every conceivable kind of restaurant, a little Burmese hangout could get entirely lost or, as is the case with Bomra's, really stand out. It's located by the side of busy Calangute road, so it's not surprising that owner-chef Bomra has chosen to open only in the evenings. With only the basic accoutrements needed to make a place pleasing to the eye—low cane chairs and paper lampshades—the main emphasis here is on the food, which is absolutely top-notch. Start with the homemade fried Shan tofu (made from gram flour) with tamarind soy sauce, or the excellent spicy rare beef salad with basil, mint, coriander, and sprouts. For a main course, try mussel curry with coconut milk and lemon grass or any of the specials—pork belly with a cashew-nut crust or the delicious steamed snapper lemon grass with chili fish sauce and jaggery (unrefined sugar) served atop a banana leaf on a wooden platter. Round off your meal with chocolate fondant and homemade vanilla ice cream. *Khow suay* (steamed rice) is served only on Wednesdays, and reservations during peak season are recommended.

Souza Vaddo, opposite Kamal Retreat, Fort Aguada Rd., Candolim. © 98221-06236. Main courses Rs 90–Rs 250 ($2.20–$6/£1–£3). No credit cards. Daily 7:30–11:30pm.

Britto's *Moments* GOAN BEACH SHACK   This is a bit of a local institution; the archetypal Goan beach shack, where owner-chef Cajie Britto has been dishing out a wicked pork *vindaloo* and prawn curry for years. If something less spicy is more your style, dig into the seafood platter or a juicy steak, and round it off with the Alpine chocolate mousse. And to quench your thirst, there are always bottles of chilled Kings available. A live one-man band plays on Monday night, karaoke is offered on Thursday and Saturday, and a barbecue is held on both nights (make a reservation in peak season).

Calangute Beach. © 0832/227-7331 or -6291. Main courses Rs 80–Rs 190 ($1.95–$4.65/£1–£2.35). MC. Daily 8:30am–midnight. Closed June 20–Aug 7.

Copper Bowl 🔆🔆 GOAN/ECLECTIC   It's not just the setting that makes dining here so pleasurable, it's the food, which is sensational. Graciously served from quaint copper pots, the typically Goan dishes are exquisite; try coconut-based chicken *xacuti* (pronounced cha-*coo*-ty) or fragrant prawn *balchao,* a mouthwatering combination of crispy prawns, aromatic spices, chili, onion, and prawn powder. If your taste leans more toward non-spicy cuisine, try the seafood in coconut-milk soup, followed by the "Seafood Treasure"—baby lobster, prawns, and two kinds of fish served in a banana leaf. Guests at the Pousada are even allowed to take over the kitchen and prepare their own specialties, but nothing will be served unless it's fresh.

Pousada Tauma, Porba Vaddo, Calangute. ✆ 0832/227-9061. Main courses Rs 300–Rs 1,400 ($7.30–$34/£3.70–£17). MC, V. Dining all day, but reservations essential if you're not a resident.

Le Restaurant Français ✦✦✦ FRENCH/FUSION   Lit by the moon, the stars, and a number of old chandeliers dangling from the branches of surrounding trees, this charming slice of Gaul shares the same magical garden venue as the daytime eatery, **Milky Way,** where Janis Joplin and The Beatles once hung out. Those erstwhile pop stars would have loved the elegant yet laid-back atmosphere that fun-loving accidental restaurateurs Morgan, Florence, and Serge brought with them from the Continent. The menu (beautifully handwritten by Florence in French, with lively English translations) features innovative dishes concocted by Morgan, who likes to "escape" (read: "experiment"), so dishes change regularly, along with the decor. Must-tries include tiger prawn carpaccio with fresh vanilla oil, and the filet of sardines on phyllo pastry with mint coulis. Be sure to leave space for the addictive chocolate cake, whose recipe Morgan once used as *baksheesh* at airport Customs.

Baga Rd., Calangute. ✆ 98-2212-1712. frenchfoodindia@hotmail.com. Main courses Rs 260–Rs 690 ($6.35–$17/£3.20–£8.50). No credit cards. Dec 10–Apr 28 Tues–Sun 7:30pm–late.

SHOPPING

Besides the vibrant markets (see "Shopping the Global Village Markets" box, earlier in this chapter), Calangute has a variety of options worth checking out. **Casa Goa** is a stylish boutique featuring designer wear by celebrated Goan designers Wendell Rodricks, Rajesh Pratap Singh, and Brigitte Singh as well as local artwork, silk drapes, restored furniture, a variety of antiques, and prints of Mario Miranda's cartoons (Cobra Vaddo, Calangute Rd.; ✆ 0832/228-1048). Then take a look at **Leela Art Palace** nearby; with any luck, proprietor Ravi will be in. You might find yourself agreeing to accompany him on an exotic journey into some of the country's remotest regions, where he regularly treks to source tribal art. Also in Calangute, **Subodh Kerkar Art Gallery,** run by Goa's well-known watercolorist, showcases contemporary Indian art including ceramics, hand-painted chests, and Rajasthani sculptures (Gauro Vaddo; ✆ 0832/227-6017). Each Tuesday (6:45–8pm; Rs 300/$7.30/£3.70), an interesting classical dance and music performance is held at the gallery.

Located in a 200-year-old Portuguese mansion, **Sangolda** is the lifestyle boutique venture by the dynamic duo behind the boutique hotel Nilaya Hermitage; here you can shop for unusual home accessories and furniture sourced from all over India—from Keralan rattan loungers to Rajasthani chests. Attached is a gallery-cum-coffee-shop (Chogm Rd., Sangolda; ✆ 0832/240-9309 or -9310). Also in Sangolda is **Monsoon Heritage,** a contemporary design studio created by internationally renowned designers Yahel Chirinian and Doris Zacheres (selected as one of the 23 most happening designers in the world by *UrbanO* magazine), who pair huge discarded tropical trees with mirrors and glass to create exclusive design pieces for the (very) rich and famous. You'll find their showrooms in Paris and Santa Monica, but their main base (and inspiration) is Goa (276/1 Livrament Vaddo, Sangolda; ✆ 0832/240-9800; www.monsoonheritage.com). Another unique duo is Sonja Weder and

Thomas Schnider, who use eco-friendly materials as much as possible and create some very striking articles ranging from furniture to lotus-leaf lazy Susans and a whole range of wall objects and gorgeous lamp shades—all of it available at **Soto Decor** (Sotohaus, 1266/f, Anna Vaddo, Candolim; ✆ **98-2298-3321;** www.sotodecor.com). Nearby is a fun boutique called **Happily Unmarried** (✆ **93-2512-2150**), where you can pick humorous knickknacks—strictly for singles.

For authentic Goan souvenirs, proceed to **Velha Goa Galleria** (✆ **0832/242-6628**) in Fountainhas, Panjim, for *azulejos,* attractive Portuguese-style hand-painted tiles and ceramics. They are happy to pack these delicate items carefully so that they survive the journey home. Also in Panjim, the government-run **Craft Complex** (✆ **0832/222-6448**) stocks basic handicrafts from all over Goa. If by the end of your stay you're sufficiently hooked on Portuguese-Goan music, head for **Rock & Raga** (June Rd., in Rizvi Tower; ✆ **0832/564-3320**), which has a good selection of local bands.

Fashionistas will be pleased with the **Wendell Rodricks Design Space** in Altinho, Panjim (✆ **0832/223-8177**). Wendell believes in affordable designer wear, and his store has everything from evening gowns to casual wear. Then there's **Sosa's,** a trendy fashion store stocking couture by Goan designer Savio Jon as well as other young and rising designers (E-245 Rua de Ourem; ✆ **0832/222-8063**). Not far from Panjim on Ribander Road, **Camelot** (✆ **0832/244-4503;** closed Apr–Sept) is an über-chic store housed in an old villa on the Mandovi River. Surrounded by walls painted gold, fuchsia, and royal blue, you can shop for designer clothing as well as exquisite silks, objets d'art, linen, and furniture.

If you don't have time to tour any heritage homes, drop in at the **Calizz museum** ௸ (Bammon Vaddo, Candolim; ✆ **93-2610-0013;** www.calizz.com). Curators here have made an extremely impressive attempt to trace the evolution of and re-create traditional Goan homes. Each house is filled with intriguing artifacts and antiques, kitchen utensils, maps, paintings, medical paraphernalia, spectacle frames, jars, bottles, and what-have-you—some of it several hundred years old, and painstakingly collected over the years by Laxmikant Kudchadkar. You can also see the differences in Goan-Portuguese and Hindu styles of architecture and enjoy a taste of traditional cuisine. The guided tour ends with a rather bizarre 3D display of Hindu gods and mythologies—perhaps the only sore point in this grand affair.

Finally, for the book hungry, **Broadway** in Panjim (18 June Rd.) has a good selection, but it's **Literatti** (E/1-282, Gaura Vaddo, Calangute; ✆ **0832/227-7740;** www.literati-goa.com) that has the atmosphere. You can sit for hours in the terrific book cafe and read or browse or buy secondhand as well as newly published works, while at the same time enjoying a delicious brownie or a tall glass of chilled *kokum* (fruit drink). Ask owner Divya Kapur about any upcoming events like poetry or book readings and writing workshops.

WHERE'S THE PARTY?

Your best bet for finding a good party is to hang out around whatever appears to be the most popular beach shack of the season, and chat up the locals (but be wary of getting lifts to unknown venues with strangers). Other excellent spots for picking up the scent of out-of-the-way parties are **Ingo's Saturday Night Bazaar,** Anjuna's **Wednesday Market,** or the ever-popular **Tito's** (✆ **0832/275028;** closed off season)—this local institution has been going for years and attracts anyone and everyone who's up for a party. The most happening clubs competing to attract the who's who

Psychedelic Journeys

Rave parties are now almost as synonymous with Goa as hippie culture. If you want to attend one of the winter rave parties, held around the full moon, you have to ask around at shacks (at little Vagator, Anjuna, or Arambol). Location is often kept secret until late in the evening to avoid harassment from cops and generally disclosed only a few hours before the party starts. These underground dance and music parties start around 11pm and go till at least 8am. Various intoxicants are freely available and consumed, and local women set up stalls outside selling *chai* and snacks. DJs play techno/psychedelic/trance music (or "psy-trance"); ravers often dress up in old-fashioned costumes and wear rave belts and colorful clothes, all part of setting the mood for their psychedelic journey. Regulars insist that these are not just massive techno freak-outs where everybody is "tripping," but a mystical, devotional experience akin to a spiritual encounter.

with great let-your-hair-down ambience, fabulous music, and terrific cuisine are **Club Cubana** (Arpora Hill; ℂ 98-2323-2910)—beautifully located atop a cliff with a swimming pool open at night and the focus on hip-hop and R&B music—and **Nine Bar,** also on top of a hill overlooking the beach, which furiously belts out deafening trance and psychedelic music—a haven for trippers and a nightmare for the rest of the world. For a less rocking atmosphere accompanied by fairly good food, check out **Kamaki** (ℂ 98-2327-6520; 6am–6pm recorded music, 6pm–6am DJ), a lounge bar up the road from Tito's that's open 24 hours; or hang out at **Mambo's,** an open-air pub where DJs Ajit and Yuri spin 1980s rock music (but no trance). If you find yourself in Anjuna on a Wednesday, ask anyone for directions to **Shorba,** which is where the revelry takes place after the flea market shuts down.

4 South of Panjim

Compared with the beach playgrounds of north Goa, the south is more about solitude and stretches of virgin sand (with the north only a short ride away). For the most part, you'll be sunning yourself on whatever beach is slap-bang in front of your resort hotel—each with its own idyllic setting, these stretches of largely untouched beaches are paradise. If you're on a tighter budget or want a bit more atmosphere, head farther south to the picturesque stretch between **Palolem-Patnem** 𝒜𝒜𝒜. Remote and tranquil (yet only 40km/25 miles from Madgaon), this is one of Goa's most beautiful stretches of coastline, a gorgeous sandy crescent cove lined with coconut palms and a few shacks and stalls. Although it's becoming increasingly popular over the high season, it remains free of sun beds, day-trippers, and large resorts, with accommodations limited to thatched tree houses or wooden houses on stilts. At sunset, Palolem becomes a natural meditation spot; the sun disappearing slowly behind the beach's northernmost promontory casts a shadow over local fishing boats, swimmers, joggers, and cavorting dogs, as the rusticated bars come to life with pleasant lounge music. Just 7km (4½ miles) north of Palolem, **Agonda** is even more isolated and peaceful, while to the south, **Galgibaga** is another remote haven with eucalyptus trees and empty stretches of sand.

GETTING THERE From Panjim you can travel directly to your beachfront resort by taxi or motorbike (the latter should take no more than 2–3 hr.), possibly stopping off for a swim at **Bogmalo.** One of the quietest of south Goa's popular beaches, it has quaint shacks (as well as a number of ugly concrete buildings), fishing boats, and a view of two small islands some distance out to sea—ask about trips to the islands at the **Watersports Goa** shack, which also has equipment for activities like windsurfing and water-skiing. The only decent accommodation is **Coconut Creek** (*✆* **0832/ 253-8090;** joets@sancharnet.in; Rs 4,000–9,500/$98–$232/£49–£117 A/C double, depending on the season), which is generally full with long-term charter groups and offers the basic requisites—pool, cottages, greenery, and beach at walking distance. Owned by the same family is **Joets** (Bogmalo Beach; *✆* **0832/253-8036**), a charming and simple guesthouse right on the beach. More important, Joets has the only "happening" restaurant with live music on Friday—make reservations and ask for a corner table by the sea. Farther south, you can stop for lunch at **Martin's Corner** *✚* (*✆* **0832/288-0061** or -0413; daily 11:30am–3:30pm and 6:30pm–midnight; follow the back road between Majorda and Colva to Betalbatim), where Martin Pereira's widow, Carafina, runs the kitchen with an iron fist. She began cooking wonderful dishes for this family restaurant back in 1994, when it opened with only two tables. Now Martin's sons operate a successful and extremely popular courtyard establishment, surrounded by mango, coconut, and jackfruit groves. Order snapper *recheado,* butter-garlic prawns, or pomfret *caldin* made with a coconut milk curry. Carafina makes a mean homemade masala, prepared according to a secret family recipe with fresh Goan spices.

Alternatively, consider a meandering trip via the Goan interior, traveling past Ponda to the Bhagwan Mahaveer Sanctuary to view Goa's oldest Hindu temple, **Mahadeva Temple** in Tambdi Surla, and the 600m-high (190-ft.) **Dudhsagar (Sea of Milk) Falls.** Constructed from slabs of black basalt, the 11th-century Mahadeva Temple is one of the few to have survived the Portuguese, thanks largely to its distance from the coast (some 75km/46 miles from Panjim). To reach the falls, you will need a jeep, so either set off with one from the outset (see "Arrival & Orientation," earlier in this chapter), or hire one in nearby Collem. Take lunch (look out for greedy monkeys) and a bathing suit for a swim in the deep, icy pool surrounded by rocks and wild greenery. There is no reason to stop in Goa's second city, **Madgaon (Margao),** which has little more to offer than a stroll through the sprawling spice-scented town market—a maze of covered stalls selling everything from garlands of flowers and peeled prawns to sacks bursting with turmeric, chilies, and tamarind—but two worthwhile house museums are nearby. In Loutolim (10km/6¼ miles north of Margao), you can tour the Araujo Alvares family home, **Casa Araujo Alvares** (arrangements through Loutolim's Ancestral Goa Museum; *✆* **0832/277-7034;** Tues–Sun 9am–1pm and 2–6pm), while 13km (8 miles) west lies the old Portuguese village of Chandor and the impressive **Casa de Braganza** *✚*, Goa's largest residence. The two-story facade of this Indo-Portuguese mansion—which practically takes up an entire street—features 28 balconies fronted by a lush, narrow garden. The land-owning Braganzas rose to prominence during the 17th century and today are divided into two clans, the Pereira-Braganzas and the Menezes-Braganzas, who occupy separate wings of the house. The large, high-ceilinged rooms (including a 250-year-old library) are filled with original antiques,

Om Beach: Escape to Paradise

Often cited as the top beach in India, **Om Beach** ☆☆☆ lies south in Gokarna, an hour across the border into Karnataka. Black rocks divide the superb white sand into three interconnected bays that more or less resemble the Sanskrit "om" symbol, the invocation that created the universe. Infrastructure here was practically nonexistent a few years back, but new shacks and small "guesthouses" have been emerging every season. The good news is that the highly respected CGH Earth group, which owns some fabulous properties in Kerala, has injected some real class here with the 2007 opening of **Swaswara** ☆ (⊘ **0838/625-7131**, -7132, or -7133; www.swaswara.com; $300/£151 double; 7-day Ayurveda package $1,685/£850 per person on twin sharing basis). Set atop a cliff above the sprawling beach and sea, this yoga retreat comprises 27 traditionally styled villas set amid 30 acres of palm trees and paddy fields. This is the place to come if you're looking for yoga, Pranayama, and meditation facilities. Alternatively, take a look at laid-back and rustic **Devbagh Beach Resort** (⊘ **0838/222-1603;** www.junglelodges.com) in Karwar, slightly north of Gokarna, where guests stay in log cabins on stilts among groves of casuarina trees. Spend your days snorkeling, visiting outlying islands, beachcombing, or lazing in your hammock. Operating under the same banner is the **Om Beach Resort** (Jungle Lodges: ⊘ **0802/559-7021** or -7024; www.junglelodges.com), located in Gokarna, which offers large, comfortable accommodation with all-modern amenities but tasteless finishes.

---

rosewood four-poster beds, mosaic floors, and Belgian glass chandeliers. Sun-lit galleries and parlors are filled with bric-a-brac, and French windows open onto an interior garden. You can arrange to have a private tour conducted by Mrs. Braganza (⊘ **0832/278-4201;** Rs 100/$2.45/£1.25 per visitor); concentrate on the west wing, which is in the best condition.

WHERE TO STAY & DINE

South Goa has more five-star resorts than north Goa, and the number is added to annually (raising the hackles of eco-watchdogs). The upmarket newcomer farthest south is the humongous **InterContinental The Grand Goa Resort,** which sprawls over 34 hectares (85 acres) and an exclusive stretch of beach; its 255 luxurious suites are currently being offered at relatively good rates (from $280/£141). At the other end, closest to Panjim, boasting the biggest pool in Goa, is the **Park Hyatt Goa Resort and Spa** (⊘ **0832/272-1234;** www.goa.park.hyatt.com; from Rs 14,500/ $354/£179)—spread over 18 hectares (45 acres) on the virgin beach of Arrossim. Midway down the south coast are the **Radisson White Sands Resort** (⊘ **0832/272-7272;** from $250/£126) at Varca Beach; and **Taj Exotica** at Benaulim (see review below). Note that all of these resorts are characterless but very child-friendly, often with separate pools and activities, and babysitters are always available.

The beach of Palolem is one of the last areas of south Goa that is free of resorts; here you'll have to venture back to nature at one of many budget options, or cozy up at the wonderful **Bhakti Kutir** eco-resort, reviewed below. Even if you've just come for the day, dine at **Aahar,** where you're served inexpensive, delicious local and organic health food under a giant cloth draped from the surrounding trees—try the *dal* and red spinach, served with organic rice, coconut chutney, and fresh, nutty hummus; or sunflower seed and *moong* (mung) bean-sprout salad with steamed spinach, toasted nuts and seeds, and tofu, served with homemade whole-wheat rice-bread. The fish curry is light and not too spicy, made with coconut gravy, and is delicious mopped up with the millet chapati. Another popular place to eat is the **Banyan Tree** (not the same as the one in Taj Holiday Village)—with Thai, Indian, Chinese, seafood, and Italian on offer and backed by a decent bar in a casual outdoor setting (**©** **98-5070-3662**).

Bhakti Kutir *Value* *Kids* This is by far Palolem's most atmospheric and comfort-able option, though don't expect any real luxury. It's the brainchild of Panta Ferrao, a Goan lawyer who (aided by his German wife, Ute) dropped out to start an ecologi-cally sensitive resort that would empower local people with skills and provide comfort-able accommodations in a fantastic location. Bhakti Kutir offers a selection of mud-plastered bamboo "cottages" made entirely from natural materials, with en-suite ablution facilities—squat toilets (organic, of course) and bucket showers. Windows are ingeniously crafted from seashells, while the cushions, fabrics, beds, and even mat-tresses (some comfortable, others hard) are all made by locals. Try to book room no. 6, which is built on different levels; no. 8, a double-story unit with an upstairs bal-cony; or the "stone house" (built with Panta's German in-laws in mind) with more tra-ditionally Western facilities (like a toilet). Come prepared for mosquitoes, dark pathways, and plenty of back-to-nature experiences. Set a short distance from the beach, the resort features a health-conscious, mostly vegetarian restaurant (fresh seafood is the exception), a bar serving beer and wine, and an assortment of esoteric activities like Ayurvedic treatments, yoga, and meditation. Workshops and cooking classes are held for those wishing to extend their knowledge of local culture. They've added an alternative school to keep the kids happy and busy. It's very popular, so reserve well in advance.

Palolem. **©** **0832/264-3469** or -3472. www.bhaktikutir.com. bhaktikutir@yahoo.com. 22 units. Oct Rs 600–Rs 2,000 ($15–$49/£7–£25), Nov & Mar Rs 1,200–Rs 2,500 ($29–$61/£15–£31), Dec–Feb Rs 1,800–Rs 4,000 ($44–$98/£22–£49). Taxes extra. Ask for off-season discounts; rates are flexible (higher Dec 15–Jan 15). No credit cards. **Amenities:** Restaurant; bar; Ayurvedic and healing center with massage, yoga, meditation, mud baths, cooling baths; air-port transfers; boutique; babysitting; laundry; kitchen; tailor; school; amphitheater; pool table. *In room:* Mosquito net.

InterContinental The Grand Goa Resort *Just* when we thought you couldn't go any farther south, the mother of all luxurious Goa resorts opens at Cana-cona Beach, south of Palolem. Its first plus, over other five-star resorts, is its long, exclusive beachfront, followed by its (*very* grand) architecture—an impressive two-level yellow baroque-Portuguese *quinta* is topped with a red-tile roof. Interiors flaunt classic mahogany furniture, patterned terrazzo flooring, and old-fashioned ceiling fans. And then, of course, there are all the trappings of a luxurious resort, including a **Champneys spa** with an exhaustive list of revitalization treatments. You will need a golf cart to take you to the beach or pool, or just about anywhere. Ask for one of the lovely, spacious, sea-facing suites that also overlook the expansive golf course. Numer-ous restaurants offer a variety of cuisines: The most interesting is **Sea BQ,** the open-air restaurant where your meal is cooked on a Japanese barbecue grill on your table. The resort also owns a three-bedroom yacht, **Blue Diamond,** which is rented out to guests. On the downside, The Grand is a 2-hour traipse to Panjim, which means you'll spend half your day traveling if you want to venture out.

Raj Baga, Canacona, Goa 403 702. **©** **0832/264-4777.** Fax 0832/264-4711. www.thegrandhotels.net. goa@interconti. com. 255 units. $275 (£139) garden-view suite; $300 (£151) sea-view suite; $500 (£252) luxury suite; $4,500 (£2,270) presidential suite. $40 (£20) extra bed. Rates include breakfast. Taxes extra. AE, MC, V. **Amenities:** 4 restaurants; 2 bars; pool; children's pool; 18-hole golf course; tennis courts; health club; spa; watersports; children's activity center; travel desk; airport transfers; business center; salon; 24-hr. room service; laundry; dry cleaning; doctor-on-call; squash courts; jogging tracks; table tennis; billiards; yoga; conference room; valet. *In room:* A/C, TV, dataport, minibar, tea- and coffee-making facilities, hair dryer, safe, Wi-Fi, weighing scale.

Taj Exotica Goa 🌴🌴   This resort features lovely surrounds (23 hectares/56 acres of landscaped gardens with 36 varieties of hibiscus trees), great accommodations, warm service, and a kick-ass beach that might as well be private. Even the cheapest "deluxe" guest rooms are spacious, with large picture windows and private patios or balconies. Ask for one on the ground floor—these are accessed via their own garden areas. The private villas are ideal if you don't want to be in the main block, which looks something like a large Portuguese hacienda—specify a sea-facing room for a sea view (the cheaper villas have garden views). The gorgeous sunset pool villas have private plunge pools—plus, the main pool is large and inviting. Another good reason to book here is the top-class restaurants. **Alegria** is where the most delicious home-cooked Goan, Portuguese, and Hindu Goan Saraswat meals are prepared. Mainstay dishes include *arroz de chorizo* (traditional Goan *pulao* of locally made spice pork sausages), *sungtache koddi* (prawns in a fragrant gravy of coconut milk and mild spices), *sungtache peri-peri* (pan-fried farm-fresh prawn marinated with red chili and toddy vinegar), and *kombdiche xacutti* (succulent chicken morsels simmered in a blend of roasted spices with coconut). Upstairs, **Miguel Arcanjo** makes some of the best pizzas in Goa. And that's not all—for starters try the shrimp glazed with honey and garlic or the Lebanese *mezze* accompanied by *horiatiki* salad, followed by delicious double lamb chops or duck roasted with dry cherry sauce. Even the oven-baked snapper is irresistible. Finally, the **Lobster Shack** (dismantled during off season) has a very informal and rather romantic setting by the sea, where you can choose your fish from the display and see it being prepared in the open kitchen.

Calwaddo, Benaulim, Salcete, Goa 403 716. © **0832/277-1234.** Fax 0832/277-1515. www.tajhotels.com. exotica.goa@ tajhotels.com. 140 units. Sept 1–Dec 21 & Jan 15–Aug 31, Dec 21–26 & Jan 4–14, Dec 27–Jan 3: $375/$475/$650 (£189/£239/£328) deluxe sea view room; $475/$575/$750 (£240/£290/£378) luxury room; $875/$975/$1,300 (£441/£491/£655) luxury suite; $350/$450/$625 (£177/£227/£315) garden villa; $450/$550/$725 (£227/£277/£365) villa garden view; $525/$625/$825 (£265/£315/£416) pool villa garden view; $575/$675/$875 (£290/£340/£441) pool villa sea view; $675/$775/$975 (£340/£390/£491) pool villa sunset view; $2,300/$3,000/$3,000 (£1,008/£1,512/ £1,512) presidential villa with private pool. $30 (£15) extra bed. Mandatory $125 (£63) per person Christmas Eve dinner and $250 (£126) New Year's Eve dinner. AE, MC, V. **Amenities:** 5 restaurants; 4 bars; pool with Jacuzzi; kids' pool; 9-hole pitch and putt golf course; 2 tennis courts; fitness center, Ayurvedic spa, yoga, aerobics; watersports; children's activity center; concierge; travel desk; car rental; complimentary airport transfers; shopping arcade; salon; 24-hr. room service; babysitting; doctor-on-call; currency exchange; beach volleyball; jogging track; table tennis; pool tables; helipad. *In room:* A/C, TV, minibar, tea- and coffee-making facilities, hair dryer, safe.

God's Own Country:
Kerala & Lakshadweep

India's most verdant state—rated by *National Geographic Traveler* as one of the world's 50 must-see destinations—is a seamless landscape of palm-lined beaches rising to meet steamy jungles and plantation-covered hills, watered by no less than 44 tropical rivers. Visitors come here primarily to unwind and indulge; this is, after all, where succumbing to a therapeutic Ayurvedic massage is as mandatory as idling away an afternoon aboard a slowly drifting *kettuvallam*, or sipping coconut water under a tropical sun before taking in a ritualized Kathakali dance. Eastward, the spice-scented Cardamom Hills and wild elephants of Periyar beckon, while a short flight west takes you to the little-known but sublime tropical reefs of the Lakshadweep islands. All of which make Kerala not just a must-see on your southern India itinerary, but a major destination in its own right.

A thin strip on the southwest coastline, sandwiched between the Lakshadweep Sea and the forested Western Ghats that define its border with Tamil Nadu to the east, Kerala covers a mere 1.3% of the country's total land area, yet its rich resources have long attracted visitors from across the oceans—it is in fact here that the first seafarers set foot on Indian soil. Legend has it that King Solomon's ships traded off the Malabar coast between 972 and 932 B.C., followed by the Phoenicians, Romans, Chinese, Portuguese, and Arabs, all of whom came to stock up on Malabar's monkeys, tigers, parrots, timber, and, of course, the abundance of spices that were literally worth their weight in gold. Seafarers not only brought trade but built synagogues and churches in the emerging port cities, while an entirely Muslim population set up shop on the islands of Lakshadweep. Despite its religious cosmopolitanism (many locals will tell you they subscribe to both Hinduism and Christianity), Kerala's Hindu tradition is deeply engrained in daily life. Most Kerala temples do not permit non-Hindus to enter, but the months of February to May bring magnificent temple processions through the streets—the most jaw-dropping being the April/May Thrissur Pooram—involving thousands of chanting devotees and squadrons of elephants adorned in flamboyant caparisons (ornamental coverings).

Contemporary Kerala was created in 1956 from the former princely states of Travancore, Kochi, and Malabar. Largely ruled by benevolent maharajas who introduced social reforms emphasizing the provision of education and basic services, Kerala remains one of the most progressive, literate, and prosperous states in post-independence India—and at the same time retains an untouched charm. In 1957, it became the first place in the world to democratically elect a Communist government, and the first Indian state to introduce a family-planning program. Despite its high population density,

Ayurveda: Kerala's Healing Balm

Drawing on some 5,000 years of Vedic culture, Ayurveda is the subconti-nent's traditional science of "life, vitality, health, and longevity" or, to tap into a more contemporary buzzphrase, "the science of well-being," and where better to experience it than Kerala, where the tradition originated. Renowned for its curative and rejuvenating powers (and a gift said to be from no other than Lord Brahma), Ayurveda works on your physical, men-tal, and emotional well-being by rectifying any imbalances in the five eter-nal elements: space (ether), air, earth, water, and fire. These elements manifest themselves in three subtle energies or humors known as the *tri-doshas—vata, pitta,* and *kapha*—when perfectly balanced, you have a healthy human constitution; if not, the imbalance translates into various ail-ments. Ayurveda is most often enjoyed by foreigners as a way to rejuvenate cells or boost the immune system, but it has a proven track record in treat-ing a wide range of specific ailments, from obesity to osteoarthritis. For these more therapeutic procedures you will need to stay a minimum of 3 days (even better: 2 to 3 weeks) and follow a dietary regimen that is pre-scribed and managed by an Ayurvedic doctor and attendant staff.

It takes 5½ years of training to qualify as an Ayurvedic doctor, who is then able to prescribe the herbal remedies and related therapies. While much of what is practiced in Ayurvedic medicine has similarities to Western medical practice (the first 3 years of training in anatomy are basically the same), the most significant difference lies in the area of pharmacology, since Ayurvedic medicines are all natural. Some may scoff, but no one can deny the sheer pleasure of the primary form of treatment: deep, thorough massage with herbal-infused oils. Which is why Ayurveda suits those skeptics who simply seek the ultimate in pampering, whether you opt for a soothing facial treat-ment, in which the face is massaged and steamed with herbal oils, or for an energizing full body massage performed with hands and feet (and often by

Keralites have the country's highest life expectancy and lowest infant mortality rates. Kerala is also considered one of the most peaceful parts of India, a claim sub-stantiated by its prosperity—the state remains a major source of India's bananas, rubber, coconuts, cashews, and ginger, and now, tourism. The downside of all this prosperity? A highly educated and com-fortable population has meant that many are unwilling to do menial jobs, and serv-ice standards are low given that tourism is for many the primary source of income. Others cash in on the tourism boom with no long-term thought for the future, and

for the first time pollution is becoming a problem in paradise. Still others head for the Gulf to seek their fortunes, returning with sufficient cash to tear down the tradi-tional carved wood dwellings that so greatly characterize the region and replace them with "modern" status symbols. Of course, many of these traditional homes have been bought and reassembled at top-notch resorts like Coconut Lagoon and Surya Samudra, a practice vilified as exploitative by Kerala native Arundhati Roy in her Booker Prize–winning *The God of Small Things.* For visitors, however, a stay in these *tharavadu* cottages is one of several masseuses simultaneously); your skin will glow and your mind will feel clear. True skeptics take note: To truly experience the strange bliss and resultant high of Ayurveda, book a *sirodhara* treatment, wherein 5 to 6 liters of warm herbal oil (selected according to the body constitution) are poured steadily onto your "third eye" (the forehead) for the better part of an hour while (or after which) you are massaged—said to retard the aging process (by arresting the degeneration of cells), it certainly relieves the body of stress (some compare it to taking a tranquilizer), and is likely to turn you into a complete convert.

No matter which balm you choose, you'll find that the well-practiced masseuses of Kerala will treat your body like a temple; for them, the massage or treatment is almost a spiritual exercise. Of course, it helps to know that your body is being worshiped when you're lying there in your birthday suit (note that in strict accordance with Indian piety, you will be assigned a same-sex therapist). Whatever its purported virtues and pleasures, Ayurveda lures thousands of Westerners to Kerala, which in turn sustains a thriving industry that puts food on the table for many people. The downside of this has been an unprecedented mushrooming of quick-fix Ayurvedic "centers" throughout the state. Almost every hotel in the country now offers Ayurvedic "treatments," many staffed with therapists back from a short training stint in Kerala and having insufficient knowledge of technique (reusing oils that should be discarded, for example). To ensure that you get the real deal, look for the top-of-the-range "Green Leaf" certification issued by the Department of Tourism, or the equally trustworthy (for non-therapeutic programs) "Olive Leaf" centers. These certifications are based on strict criteria covering the quality of the physicians, programs, medicines, and facilities offered. We review the best resorts with this accreditation in this chapter.

the most charming aspects of a trip to Kerala, along with its tropical beaches and backwater cruises; and lounging in a hammock at one of the region's top resorts can make you forget you're in India.

If you're interested in experiencing a more authentic experience of the subcontinent, combine your trip with a few days in neighboring Tamil Nadu, the spiritual heartland of southern India (see chapter 7). But if all you're looking for is rejuvenation, head straight to the backwaters, then wash up on some of the world's most beautiful beaches. "God's Own Country" is one tourist slogan that really does deliver.

1 Kochi (Cochin)

1,080km (670 miles) S of Mumbai

Kochi is not the capital of Kerala, but it is a great deal more charming than Trivandrum, and, blessed with a good airport and infrastructure, is for many the ideal gateway to the state. In fact, this has been the case since 1341, the year nature carved out

Kochi's harbor with a massive flood, and the city became the first port of call for Arabs, Chinese, and, finally, European sea merchants, who sailed for barter into what came to be known as the "Queen of the Arabian Sea."

Lured by the promise of pepper, the Portuguese under Vasco da Gama arrived in 1500, and the Franciscan friars who accompanied the explorer Pedro Alvarez Cabral established a church and set about converting the locals. By 1553, the Maharaja of Kochi had granted permission for the construction of the first European fort in India, and what had been an obscure fishing hamlet became India's first European settlement. In 1663, Kochi fell to the Dutch, and 132 years later, to the British. Each of these foreign influences left their mark, resulting in a distinctly Indo-European culture, most evident in the architecture.

Today, Kochi (or Cochin, as it was formerly known) comprises three distinct areas. The down-at-heel but wonderfully atmospheric Mattancherry and its more pristine neighbor, Fort Kochi, lie on one of two peninsular arms that shield the Kochi harbor. Opposite it, on the mainland that creates the eastern peninsula, lies modern Ernakulam. Between the two are islands, now well connected by bridges.

Fort Kochi, the oldest European settlement in India, retains an old-world charm. Although it has now largely been given over to tourism, the town's heritage buildings and broad, peaceful streets make this the preferred place to overnight. Its battlements no longer stand, but the combination of Portuguese, Dutch, Jewish, British, and local influences is evident in the tiled, steep-roofed bungalows that line its quaint streets, and it's home to the oldest synagogue in the Commonwealth. From here Mattancherry, with its wonderful warehouses filled with antiques and trinkets, is a short rickshaw drive away. Plan to spend 2 nights in Kochi, enjoying its charming atmosphere and low-key sights at a lazy, relaxed pace. Take in a Kathakali performance, dig into the delectable seafood, enjoy a romantic sunset cruise around the harbor, and, if you're at all interested in bargains in antiques, get ready to wade through stores packed with unexpected curiosities.

ESSENTIALS

VISITOR INFORMATION   Kerala (www.keralatourism.org) has the best tourism organization in India, and Kochi is no exception. In Ernakulam you will find the helpful **Kerala Tourism Development Corporation** (**KTDC,** Shanmugham Rd., Ernakulam; © **0484/235-3234;** ktdccok@sancharnet.in; Mon–Fri 10am–5pm), but because of the sort of bureaucratic nonsense you might expect to find in the India of a decade ago, you then have to pick up brochures and maps from the nearby **Department of Tourism** (a 2-min. walk). If you can find one, pick up *Hello Cochin,* a bimonthly free booklet filled with useful listings. If you're traveling farther afield and need general information (excellent brochures on anything from arts and crafts to top museums in the country) but don't mind sullen service, visit the **Government of India Tourist Office** (near the Taj Malabar, Willingdon Island; © **0484/266-8352;** Mon–Fri 9am–5:30pm, Sat 9am–1pm). A **tourism information counter** (© **0484/ 261-0115**) at the airport is usually open for all arrivals.

GETTING THERE & AWAY   By Air   Kochi International Airport (© **0484/ 261-0115**) is one of India's best. It's located alongside National Highway 47, in Nedumbassery, which is 42km (26 miles) from the historic heart of Fort Kochi. There are flights to and from most major centers in India; international flights are mostly from the Middle East, including Dubai, Singapore, and Sri Lanka

Kerala

Kochi (Cochin)

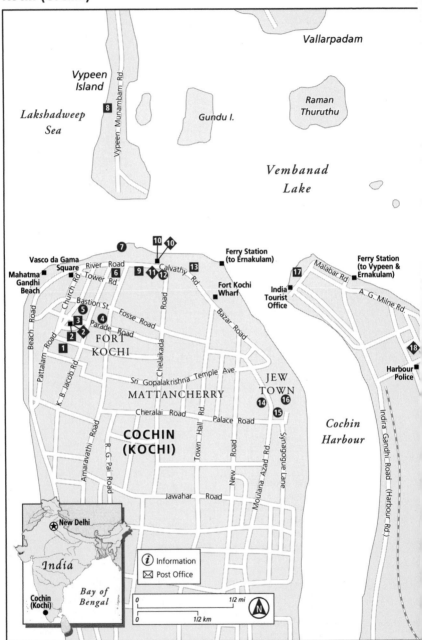

Vallarpadam

Vypeen Island

Lakshadweep Sea

Gundu I.

Raman Thuruthu

Vembanad Lake

Vypeen Munambam Rd.

8

7

10

10

Ferry Station (to Ernakulam)

Vasco da Gama Square

River Road

6

9 **11** **12** Calvathy Rd. **13**

Fort Kochi Wharf

Ferry Station (to Vypeen & Ernakulam)

17

Malabar Rd.

A. G. Milne Rd.

India Tourist Office

Mahatma Gandhi Beach

Church Rd.

Tower Rd.

Bastion St.

5

Fosse Road

4

Parade Road

Road

Chelakada

Bazar Road

Beach Road

Pattalam Road

K. B. Jacob Rd.

3

2

1

FORT KOCHI

Sri Gopalakrishna Temple Ave.

MATTANCHERRY

18

Harbour Police

JEW TOWN

14 **16**

15

Cheralai Road

Palace Road

Cochin Harbour

COCHIN (KOCHI)

Amaravathi Road

R. G. Pai Road

Town Hall Rd.

New Road

Moulana Azad Rd.

Synagogue Lane

Indira Gandhi Road (Harbour Rd.)

Jawahar Road

New Delhi

India

Bay of Bengal

Cochin (Kochi)

(i) Information

✉ Post Office

0   1/2 mi

0   1/2 km

N

164

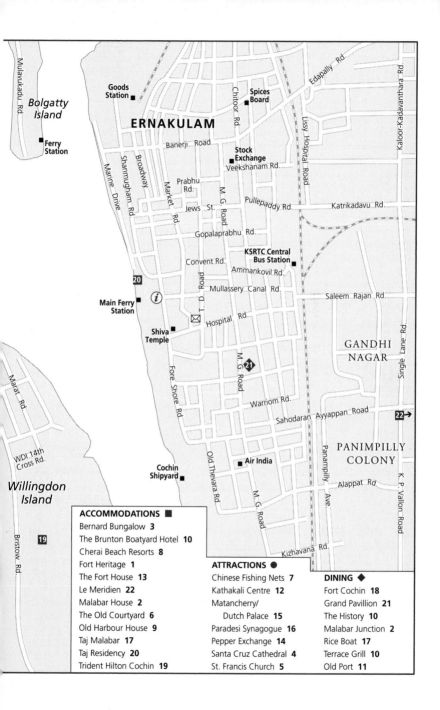

Bolgatty
Island

Mulavukadu Rd.

Ferry
Station

Goods
Station

Spices
Board

ERNAKULAM

Chitoor Rd.

Edapally Rd.

Lissy Hospital Road

Kaloor-Kadavanthara Rd.

Banerji Road

Stock
Exchange
Veekshanam Rd.

Marine Drive

Shanmugham Rd.

Broadway

Market Rd.

Prabhu
Rd.

M. G. Road

Jews St.

Pullepaddy Rd.

Katrikadavu Rd.

Gopalaprabhu Rd.

KSRTC Central
Bus Station

Convent Rd.

Ammankovil Rd.

Main Ferry
Station

Shiva
Temple

T. D. Road

Mullassery Canal Rd.

Saleem Rajan Rd.

Hospital Rd.

Fore Shore Rd.

M. G. Road

21

GANDHI
NAGAR

Single Lane Rd.

Warriom Rd.

Sahodaran Ayyappan Road

22→

Cochin
Shipyard

Old Thevara Rd.

Air India

M. G. Road

Panampilly

Panampilly Ave.

PANIMPILLY
COLONY

Alappat Rd.

K. P. Vallon Road

Marat. Rd.

WDI 14th
Cross Rd.

Willingdon
Island

Bristow Rd.

19

Kizhavana Rd.

ACCOMMODATIONS ■
Bernard Bungalow **3**
The Brunton Boatyard Hotel **10**
Cherai Beach Resorts **8**
Fort Heritage **1**
The Fort House **13**
Le Meridien **22**
Malabar House **2**
The Old Courtyard **6**
Old Harbour House **9**
Taj Malabar **17**
Taj Residency **20**
Trident Hilton Cochin **19**

ATTRACTIONS ●
Chinese Fishing Nets **7**
Kathakali Centre **12**
Matancherry/
    Dutch Palace **15**
Paradesi Synagogue **16**
Pepper Exchange **14**
Santa Cruz Cathedral **4**
St. Francis Church **5**

DINING ◆
Fort Cochin **18**
Grand Pavillion **21**
The History **10**
Malabar Junction **2**
Rice Boat **17**
Terrace Grill **10**
Old Port **11**

A prepaid taxi service into the city is available at the airport; transfers to Fort Kochi cost around Rs 650 ($16/£8); Rs 550 ($13/£7) if you're lucky. A better plan is to e-mail or call **Kerala Adventures** (② **94-4703-5627** or 0484/231-3744; touch@ keralaadventure.com) with your flight details a few days in advance, and have a driver waiting for you on arrival; price for a non-A/C car costs Rs 650 ($16/£8); with A/C Rs 840 ($20/£10).

By Train   Kochi is well connected by rail to almost every part of India. Some of the journeys can be long and grueling, however, so check on times, or opt for train travel only within Kerala. Departing from Delhi, the biweekly (Tues and Sat) **Trivandrum Rajdhani** makes its way to Kozhikode, Kochi, and Trivandrum; this is one of the best connections in Kerala—some of the journey is very scenic but it's a punishing 48 hours if you start from Delhi. For schedules, see www.indianrail.gov.in.

Kochi has two principal commuter railway stations: **Ernakulam Town Station** (② **0484/239-0920** or -5198) and **Ernakulam Junction** (② **1364**). The **computerized reservations office** is at the Junction Railway Station (Mon–Sat 8am–2pm and 2:15–8pm; Sun 8am–2pm). For reservations, call ② **132;** for status of current reservations, call ② **1316.**

By Road   Traveling around Kerala with a rented car and driver can be wonderful and exhilarating; there's plenty of natural beauty worth taking in, and Kerala's main roads are in relatively good shape; see "Guided Tours & Travel Agents," below, for our top recommendation here. North of Kochi, coast-hugging National Highway 17 passes through Kozhikode and runs all the way to Mangalore and Mysore in Karnataka, and on to Mumbai. Traveling south between Kochi and the capital Trivandrum (6 hr.), National Highway 47 has been resurfaced in recent years, and the highway really spreads out for the popular segment between Kochi and the backwater towns of Alleppey and Kottayam. For journeys between Kochi and Madurai, you can expect long but beautiful stretches along National Highway 49, which traverses hairpin mountain passes, or you can detour via Periyar for equally scenic views. Private and state buses connect Kochi with many cities and towns throughout South India; these provide something bordering on a theme-park experience, however, and have a reputation for thrill-ride speeds. For long-distance private bus schedules (much more comfortable and punctual) to (and from) Ernakulam, contact **Kerala SRTC Office** (② **0484/237-2033**); alternatively the **Karnataka SRTC** (② **0484/236-0229**) and **Tamil Nadu** (② **0484/237-2616**).

GETTING AROUND   **By Taxi & Auto-Rickshaw**   Speak to your hotel management about the most up-to-date rates. For the most part, it's best to negotiate a mutually agreeable fare before starting off; in 2007 auto-rickshaws charged a minimum of Rs 10 (25¢/12p) for a trip, with Rs 7 (15¢/10p) per kilometer thereafter; alternatively Rs 30 (70¢/35p) per hour for sightseeing within Fort Kochi and Mattancherry. After 10pm the rate is one and a half or double. Taxicabs are reasonable (1 hr. around Rs 40/90¢/45p) but really only useful if traveling farther afield: A one-way trip between Fort Kochi and Ernakulam shouldn't cost more than Rs 350 ($9/£4).

Note that the bridges connecting the mainland and Fort Kochi with the islands usually charge a toll, which you will be expected to pay.

By Ferry   The ferry is a cheap way to get to and from any of Kochi's main areas; the journey between Fort Kochi/Mattancherry and the mainland takes around 30 minutes and departs every half-hour; Willingdon lies around 15 minutes away. Ernakulam's

Homestays in Kerala

A homestay, in which you board with a local household, is a great way to immerse yourself in real Indian culture and hospitality. It is highly recommended as an alternative or addition to the one-size-fits-all hotel or resort experience. The concept has proven hugely popular throughout the country, but particularly in touristic Kerala, which now has homestay options on every corner. Note that the lines are currently a little blurred, however, regarding the definition of "homestay"—a household that employs a manager trained in the hospitality industry should not, to my mind, be described as a homestay, nor should a house entirely given over to guests, with no presence of a host to provide a personal introduction to the area or family presence at mealtimes. These distinctions have not been drawn in certification procedures (which simply specify a "homely environment"). That said, our top Kerala homestays are **Olavipe,** located on the backwaters just south of Kochi, and **Tranquil** in Wyanad, both reviewed in this chapter. For full listings, take a look at **www. homestayskerala.com,** or call the agency **Homestay Kerala** at ℂ **0484/231-0324.** *Tip:* Though it's not expected of foreigners, it's courteous to remove your shoes before entering a home and greet the owners by pressing your palms together and saying *"namaskaram."*

most important jetty is the **Main Boat Jetty** (off Fore Press Club Rd.) for services to Willingdon Island, Fort Kochi, and Cherrai Beach; at Fort Kochi the main jetty is next to Brunton Boat Yard. **High Court Jetty** off Shanmugham Road, from where you can get to Bolgatty Island, is less regular since the construction of the bridge between Bolgatty and the mainland. Ferry services begin at 6am and continue until 9:30pm; fares are nominal.

GUIDED TOURS & TRAVEL AGENTS Babu John of **Kerala Adventures** (ℂ **94-4703-5627** or 0484/231-3744; 24-hr. number ℂ **94-4703-5627;** www.kerala adventure.com; journey@asianetindia.com or comvoyge@vsnl.net) is an excellent local agent with a fleet of reliable vehicles and drivers, and extremely knowledgeable about the best places to stay in Kerala and Tamil Nadu. He specializes in customizing itineraries according to budget, time, and preferences and is well-versed in the needs of foreign clients, with all services provided at excellent rates. For example, a 7-day package covering Kerala and Tamil Nadu will cost you around Rs 12,000 ($273/£138) for a non–A/C car, including driver and taxes, and around Rs 17,000 ($386/£195) for an air-conditioned vehicle—hard to beat. If you're the kind who doesn't plan ahead, you can even arrange for Babu to pick you up at the airport, and ask to be shown a few hotels in your preferred price range before deciding where to stay. Other reputable agents, but offering a less personal service, are **Sita Travels** (Tharakan Building, M.G. Rd., Ravipuram, Ernakulam; ℂ **0484/236-3801** or 0484/237-4122; www.sitaindia. com) and the upmarket U.K.–based **Cox & Kings** (www.coxandkings.co.uk). **Kerala Tourism Development Corporation** (**KTDC,** Shanmugham Rd., Ernakulam; ℂ **0484/235-3234**) and the privately run **Tourist Desk** (Main Boat Jetty, Ernakulam; ℂ **0484/237-1761**) offer half-day boat cruises of Kochi as well as daily tours and longer *kettuvallam* houseboat cruises of the backwaters near Kochi. **KTDC** offers car rentals, and a wide range of tours and packages to suit different budgets, but be aware that most of these will include accommodations at state-run hotels, which are of varying standards, usually on the poor side. For details and bookings, contact KTDC central reservations in Trivandrum, the capital (Mascot Sq.; ✆ **0471/231-6736;** fax 0471/233-4780; www.ktdc.com; ktdc@vsnl.com; Mon–Sat 8am–6pm, Sun and public holidays 10am–4pm).

WHEN TO GO   Climate-wise, the best time to visit Kerala is between October and March. December and January are peak-season months, and many resorts charge accordingly, some even tripling their rates; if you plan to visit during this time, book well in advance. Note, however, that August is when boat races are held, and September can be really pleasant—not too muggy, with the lakes filled with monsoon water and prices low. Rates are also favorable in April, which is temple festival time (though the heat is a little more intense, you're catching the tail end of the season, when most resorts start routine maintenance). In fact, from February to May, caparisoned elephants often take to the streets to participate in spectacular temple festivals; by far the biggest and most colorful is the **Thrissur Pooram Temple Festival,** which takes place at the end of April/early May, 74km (46 miles) north of Kochi. With two rival temple groups, each armed with 15 elephants and gorgeously heisted parasols, vying with each other to make their procession and fireworks display grander than preceding years, this is a photographer's dream and well worth planning a trip around. Bear in mind, however, that most hotels in Thrissur will be booked for many months in advance, so plan well ahead, and ask Babu John (see "Guided Tours & Travel Agents," above) for assistance—given enough warning, he can even arrange for you to witness the festival (which sees thousands of ecstatic devotees crushed into the streets around the temples—potentially as frightening as it is thrilling) from a hotel rooftop. Thrissur is (58km/36 miles) from Kochi airport.

FAST FACTS: Kochi

Airlines For the **Jet Airways city office,** call ✆ 0484/235-8879; for the **airport counter,** call ✆ 0484/261-0037. For **Deccan,** call ✆ 0484/261-0288; **Kingfisher** (✆ 0484/261-0055); **Indian Airlines** (✆ 0484/261-0041); **Air-India** (✆ 0484/261-0040); **Emirates** (✆ 0484/261-1194); **Qatar** (✆ 0484/261-1305).

Ambulance Dial ✆ 102.

Area Code The area code for **Kochi** is ✆ 0484.

ATMs Kochi has hundreds of ATMs; ask your driver or host for the nearest.

Banks There are more than 50 banks in Kochi. Hours are Monday to Friday 10am to 3pm (some 9am–1pm); Saturday 10am to 1pm (some 12:30pm). Some have evening counters and a few open Sunday; ATMs offer 24-hour banking. See "Currency Exchange," below.

Bookstores Both branches of **Idiom Books** are wonderful for a wide variety of books on India, its culture, and its literature. In Fort Kochi, the store is at the corner of Bastion and Quirose streets (✆ 0484/221-7075; Mon–Sat 9am–9pm, Sun 10am–6pm). In Mattancherry, it's opposite the Boat Jetty on Jew Street (✆ 0484/222-5604).

Car Hires & Taxis On average, you can expect to pay Rs 150 ($4/£2) per hour or Rs 8 (19¢/9p) per kilometer for a taxi. The **Government of India Tourist Office** (near Taj Malabar Hotel, Willingdon Island; ✆ **0484/266-8352**; Mon–Fri 9am–5:30pm, Sat 9am–1pm) has a fleet of Ambassadors. Also try **Sita Travels** (Tharakan Building, M.G. Rd., Ernakulam; ✆ **0484/237-4122**) or **Kerala Adventures** (see "Guided Tours & Travel Agents," above).

Currency Exchange You can exchange currency and traveler's checks at any of the many banks in Kochi, like **Canara Bank** in Fort Kochi (Kunnumpuram Junction, Amaravathy Rd.; ✆ **0484/221-5467**; Mon–Fri 10am–2pm and 2:30–3:30pm, Sat 10am–noon) or **Standard Chartered** (M.G. Rd., Ernakulam; ✆ **0484/235-9462**; Mon–Fri 9:30am–4:30pm, Sat till 1pm). **Thomas Cook** is also on M.G. Rd. (✆ **0484/236-9729**; Mon–Sat 9:30am–6pm) and has a branch at the airport (✆ **0484/261-0052** or -0032). Note that credit cards outside of big hotels are not the norm (and some of these accept only MasterCard and Visa), so always carry some cash.

Drugstores **Medilab** (Doraiswamy Iyer Rd., Ernakulam; ✆ **0484/236-8963**) is open around the clock, as is **Ernakulam Medical Centre** on the NH Bypass (✆ **0484/280-7101**).

Emergencies For police emergencies, dial ✆ **100**; to report a crime, call ✆ **1090**. For fires and other emergencies, including medical services, call ✆ **101**.

Hospitals There are more than 500 hospitals and clinics in Kochi, some specializing in particular ailments, and a number of them highly respected. If you have a medical emergency, your hotel should be able to organize the best medical match.

Internet Access Fort Kochi has plenty of Internet "cafes" (back rooms behind shops). These generally charge more than any of the options in Ernakulam. **Call'n'Fax/Shop'n'Save** (Princess St.; ✆ **0484/221-5438**; Mon–Sat 8am–10pm, Sun 9am–10pm) charges Rs 40 (90¢/45p) per hour.

Post Office Use the **General Post Office** in Mattancherry (✆ **0484/236-0668**) or the **Kochi Head Post Office** in Fort Kochi (behind St. Francis Church).

WHAT TO SEE & DO

Lazy and laid-back, Fort Kochi offers a tranquillity that is in complete contrast to the heaving city experience of Ernakulam. Comprising **Mattancherry** and **Jew Town,** Fort Kochi is the historic heart of the city—it is, after all, a town where 14 different languages are spoken, and tumbled-down mansions line narrow ancient lanes. Near the water's edge, old warehouses (or *godowns*) are filled with the state's treasured cash crops—pepper, tea, Ayurvedic herbs, whole ginger, and betel nuts—being dried, sorted, and prepared for direct sale or auction. The area is wonderful for historic walks, particularly into Jew Town, which hosts the remains of a community that dates back to the 1st century A.D., augmented during the 16th century when the Inquisition brought a fresh wave of Jewish immigrants here. Today only a small handful of aging "white Jewish" families remain in Kochi, but their residential quarter retains a charming ambience, with cobbled streets and fascinating antiques shops and spice markets.

Man-made **Willingdon Island,** a short ferry ride or bridge journey away, was created in the 20th century by large-scale dredging. There is a good hotel here, but the island is primarily concerned with naval and commercial port activity and is not worth visiting unless you're based here. **Bolgatty Island,** reached by ferry, is of no interest other than the rather lovely heritage "palace" on its shores, which has been converted into a poorly managed state-government hotel.

EXPLORING FORT KOCHI ON FOOT

Start your 2-hour walking tour at the harbor near Vasco da Gama Square, where you can watch fishermen hoisting their catch from the cantilevered **Chinese fishing nets** that line the shore, then head along Church Road to **St. Francis Church** (see below). Keep going toward Parade Road (where you'll see the Malabar House Residency; see "Where to Stay," below). Turn right into Parade Road then left along Dutch Cemetery Road, passing **Thakur House** and the **cemetery** on your right, as well as the remains of the 16th-century **Fort Immanuel.** Just after this you will turn north up Elephinstone Road, making a left onto Ridsdale Road. After popping into Cinnamon (see "Shopping," below) and the adjacent Cottage Expo Crafts, drift down Bastion Street, in the direction of **Santa Cruz Basilica** (see below). If you're ready to take a break, turn right before this into **Peter Celli Street,** where you can't miss the lovely **Tea Pot** (see "Where to Dine," below); service is excruciatingly slow but the ambience is lovely. Or take the next street left into Burgher and stop at **Kashi Art Café** (see below), where the contemporary art and vibrant atmosphere provide a contrast to the historic surroundings.

When you're ready, head toward Tower Road, where you will find the lovely redbrick **Koder House.** Built in 1808 by Jewish patriarch Samuel Koder, Koder House is a good example of the hybrid Indo-European style that developed in Cochin. It's also an example of an overpriced guesthouse, so if you want to appreciate the interiors, ask to see a room—until they drop their rates they'll more than likely have one to show. On the same road, Old Harbour Hotel has made a more successful transition (see "Where to Stay," below); beyond is the **Pierce Leslie Bungalow,** a charming 19th-century mansion reflecting both Portuguese and Dutch influences.

Afterward, catch an auto-rickshaw to Mattancherry, where you should visit the **Mattancherry (Dutch) Palace** and **Paradesi Synagogue** (see below) before discovering the fragrant scents of Kerala's **spice warehouses.** Make time to visit a few of the antiques warehouses, and don't be put off by the layers of dust—there are some real treasures to be found. End your day full circle with a **sunset cruise** around the harbor; this is the best way to enjoy the most-photographed of Kochi's historic sights: the Chinese fishing nets that form wonderful silhouettes against a red- and orange-hued sky.

Chinese Fishing Nets Said to have been introduced by traders from the court of Kublai Khan, these cantilevered nets, set up on teak and bamboo poles, are physical remnants of Fort Kochi's ancient trade with the Far East. Fishermen work the nets all day long, lowering them into the water and then hauling them up using a remarkably efficient pulley system. The best place to watch them at work is from **Vasco da Gama Square** or from a boat at sunset. Nearby, the Indo-European **Bastion Bungalow** (now the official residence of the Sub Collector) dates back to 1667; built on the site of the old Dutch Fort's Stromberg Bastion, it is believed to stand above a network of secret tunnels.

Vasco da Gama Sq. is on the water's edge along River Rd.

Mattancherry Palace 🎔🎔   Also known as the Dutch Palace, this large two-story 16th-century building was actually built by the Portuguese, who gave it to the Raja of Kochi as thanks for trading rights and favors granted to them. When the Dutch claimed Kochi in 1663, they took control of the palace and gave it a makeover. The large two-story building with its sloping roofs and pale walls is now a shadow of what it must have once been. Part of it is open to visitors, and displays include a collection of coronation robes, palanquins, and royal family portraits, but the real reason to visit is to view the bedroom chamber, where vibrant murals, executed in vivid red, green, and yellow ocher, are truly exquisite. Particularly notable are erotic scenes of the divine lover, Krishna, surrounded by enraptured female figures. Vishnu, Shiva, and various Hindu deities fill the large walls, their eyes wide and bodies full. These are among the first examples of a school of painting specific to Kerala.

Palace Rd., Mattancherry. Admission Rs 5 (10¢/5p). No photography. Sat–Thurs 10am–5:30pm.

Paradesi Synagogue 🎔🎔🎔   Kochi's first Jewish settlers arrived from Yemen and Babylon as early as A.D. 52; this—the oldest synagogue in the Commonwealth—was originally built 1,500 years later. Set in a corner of Jew Town and rather hemmed in by other buildings, with only the 18th-century clock tower visible from the outside, it must be entered before you can view its most interesting feature: the beautiful blue-and-white Cantonese ceramic floor tiles—each individual tile hand-painted, so no two are alike. Above, glorious Belgian chandeliers dangle from the ceiling. At one end of the hall, old Torah scrolls are kept behind the gilded doors of the holy tabernacle.

At press time, only a handful of Jews remain in Kochi, though they uphold the traditions of their ancestors, and the synagogue is moving testament to the effects of the Diaspora. The number remaining are not enough to form a *minyan* (the number of men needed to sustain a synagogue), so Jews from outlying areas travel to Kochi to worship in this historic Judaic monument. The synagogue elders are understandably concerned about tourist numbers, and numerous signs warn that NO ONE IS ALLOWED UPSTAIRS, NO ONE IS ALLOWED INSIDE THE PULPIT, and NO ONE IS ALLOWED TO TOUCH ANYTHING. You are also expected to be demurely attired.

Jew Town Rd., Mattancherry. Admission Rs 2 (5¢/5p). No video. Sun–Thurs 10am–noon and 3–5pm; closed for Jewish holidays.

St. Francis Church 🎔   India's earliest European church was originally constructed in wood, but this was replaced by a stone structure in 1546. It was also originally Roman Catholic, but under the British it became Anglican. Vasco da Gama was originally buried here when he died in Kochi on Christmas Eve, 1524; although his body was later moved to Lisbon, he is still memorialized here with a tombstone. Having passed through the hands of Franciscan friars, Dutch Protestants, and Anglicans, the presiding Church of South India continues to hold its services here every morning at 8am. Note that, as at Hindu temples and Muslim mosques, you are required to remove your shoes before entering.

Church St., Fort Kochi. Mon–Sat 9:30am–1pm and 2:30–5:30pm.

Santa Cruz Basilica 🎔   Pope Paul IV elevated this Portuguese church to a cathedral in 1558, but the original building was destroyed by the British in 1795. A new building was commissioned on the same site in 1887; it was declared a basilica in 1984 by Pope John Paul II. The basilica's interiors are worth a look, especially the caryatids and exquisite stained glass.

Black Gold

In Kerala, pepper is still sometimes referred to as *karuthu ponnu,* or "black gold," and represents the backbone of the state's international spice trade. Although the furious trade around spices has subsided considerably these days, the sorting houses, warehouses, and auction houses from which these valuable products find their way to the rest of the world still operate in much the same way they have for centuries (though given the current crises surrounding many of the traditional cash crops, there is a possibility that these side-street sights will not be around forever). Ask your guide or auto-rickshaw driver to take you to the ginger, black pepper, betel nut, and Ayurvedic medicine warehouses, reminiscent of Salman Rushdie's *The Moor's Last Sigh;* or head for the **Kochi International Pepper Exchange** on Jew Town Rd., Mattancherry (© **0484/222-4263),** where until recently you could see Kerala's black gold being furiously sold off to the highest bidder; sadly, this is now done electronically.

Parade Rd. and K. B. Jacob Rd., near Bastion St., Fort Kochi. www.santacruzbasilica.org. Mon–Sat 9:30am–5pm; Sun morning Mass only.

WHERE TO STAY

The area with the most charm and relaxing atmosphere is Fort Kochi; best here are Brunton (waterfront location), Malabar (chichi decor), and Old Harbour (best value). Alternatively, opt for Willingdon Island, just across the bay, and useful if you want to shop at both historic Fort Kochi and busy, bustling Ernakulam.

If you don't mind being far from the ambience of Fort Kochi and the harbor, two out-of-town options are worth considering: the truly upscale "5 Star Diamond" **Le Meridien Cochin** (NH 47 Bypass, Kundannur Junction, Kochi 682 304; © **0484/270-5777** or -5451; from $240/£121 double excluding taxes), which gives a foretaste of life on the backwaters (albeit in a huge, 223-room hotel). Guests have access to an excellent range of resort facilities and services, including one of only a handful of Green Leaf–accredited Ayurvedic spas in Ernakulam (the other being at the Taj Malabar)—check it all out on www.cochin.lemeridien.com. If, on the other hand, you want Kochi backwaters with a bit of beach, laid-back **Cherai Beach Resorts** is 30km (19 miles, or 40 min.) north of Kochi by road, or 15km (9⅓ miles) from the Vypeen jetty. Ask for a heritage cottage with an open-air bathroom and patio on stilts overlooking the backwaters; although the newer rooms are sleeker, they lack the charm of these. The resort is pretty basic in terms of service and amenities, but the Ayurvedic rejuvenation massages are good, and you get decent Kerala food. Best of all, the rate offers very good value at Rs 2,000 to Rs 5,500 ($48–$134/£25–£68) (© **0484/248-1818** or 0484/241-6949; www.cheraibeachresorts.com).

Note: The prices below are sometimes given in euros with U.S. dollar and U.K. pound conversions (in other words, no rupee rate)—this is how hotels targeting foreign markets quote their rates.

FORT KOCHI

If you're on a tight budget, make an advance booking (do make sure that it's one of three that has a balcony) at the five-room **Raintree Lodge** (1/618 Petercelli St; www.nivalink.com/raintreelodge; raintree@fortcochin.com; Rs 2,000/$49/£25 double). It's located in the heart of the old town; guest rooms are basic but clean, and the beds are comfortable; tubs look worse for wear but overhead showers mean you don't have to lie in them. Because it's so small with no public amenities (bar a rooftop with a relatively nice view), it feels rather like renting a tiny flat. If you're looking for a homestay experience, the best in town is **Bernard Bungalow** (1/297 Parade Rd.; *©* **0984/ 742-7999;** www.bernardbungalow.com; Rs 1,000–Rs 3000/$24–$73/£12–£37 double, depending on room and season), run with an iron hand by Coral Bernard. She's a bit of a battleaxe but her rooms are so clean you could practically eat off the floor. Pick a room upstairs and you'll feel very much a part of the home she's lived in for the past 30 years, without actually encroaching on her space (don't bother with the rooms on the ground floor). Pick room 105 and you get to overlook pretty Malabar House; room 103 has the possibility of an additional bedroom for families. Another recommended option is **Napier House** (Napier Lane; *©* **0484/221-5715;** www.napier house.com). Designated a heritage homestay by the tourism department, the spick-and-span eight-room house is more guesthouse than homestay, with a very friendly manager rather than owner Sajeev on hand, and no sense of it being anyone's home any longer. That said, prices are pretty good (Rs 1,400–Rs 2,000/$34–$49/£17–£25), the place is exceptionally clean, and the large airy "suite," with its own balcony, is a rather good option at Rs 1,750 to Rs 3,000 ($40–$68/£20–£34), depending on the season, though it doesn't have the waterfront location and atmosphere of Fort House (see below).

The Brunton Boatyard Hotel *ᏪᏪᏪ*   Situated at the water's edge on the site of a bustling boatyard, this is the best located hotel in Fort Kochi, and the space (wide corridors run around a large central grassed courtyard, leading to a generous-size pool on the waterfront) gives it the edge on Malabar House, particularly for those traveling with kids. A smart, whitewashed colonial warehouse-style building with sloping tiled roofs, deep verandas, and spacious high-ceilinged rooms, the designers have successfully captured the gracious ambience of a bygone era, but with all the comforts of modern living. An open-plan lobby—the only disappointment, with no comfortable seating—spills into spacious passages that lead to the guest rooms, all of which overlook the busy harbor. Each room has its own balcony from which to enjoy views of the fishing boats and ferries that cruise between the islands; those on the second floor are better for views, which you also enjoy from the bathroom, so make sure you book one of these. Original and reproduction antiques include typical Kerala four-poster beds, high enough off the ground to make the footstools a necessity. The complimentary sunset cruise from the hotel's own jetty is a great way to kick off the evening, and the cooking demonstrations on the rooftop terrace make you feel part of a BBC food program. The only possible drawback to staying here is the hotel's proximity to the active and noisy waterways, but on the other hand, the low-level soundtrack lends an air of authenticity.

Near Aspinwall, Calvathy, Fort Kochi. Inquiries: CGH Earth, Casino Building, Willingdon Island, Cochin, Kerala, India 682 003 *©* **0484/221-5461** through -5465. Fax 0484/221-5562. Reservations: *©* **0484/266-8211** or 0484/301-1568. www.cghearth.com. bruntonboatyard@cghearth.com. 26 units. Doubles: low season $150–$210 (£76–£106); high season $270–$385 (£136–£194). $40 (£20) extra person. Rates include breakfast; exclude 15% tax. AE, DC, MC, V. **Amenities:** 2 restaurants; bar; tea lounge; pool; boat rental; car hire; business facilities; shop; room service; laundry; doctor-on-call; Ayurvedic center; complimentary sunset cruise; cooking demonstrations; yoga and guided walking tour. *In room:* A/C, TV, minibar, hair dryer, electronic safe, scale. Suites include personal butler, kitchenette.

The Fort House *Ꮺ*   The best feature of this budget "hotel" is undoubtedly its location right on the waterfront—it even has a private jetty and a boat (though no rooms overlook the water as such). The owners have also sadly ditched their eco-friendly origins and built a characterless new concrete wing on the property, increasing the room count from 9 to 25. While new rooms are in some senses more "comfortable" than the original rooms—the latter comprising two single-level wings strung along two shared verandas, a stark contrast to the new three-story building opposite—they are cheaply done and already look a little tired, with none of the character of the original (and cheaper) bamboo rooms. Of these, rooms 8 and 9 (nearest the water, with views through the arches) are still the ones to book (though keen readers should note that they are dimly lit). The restaurant has a very good reputation, thanks to owner Nova Thomas's Portuguese-influenced Keralan dishes (her great-grandmother being of Portuguese descent) like pork *vindaloo*—though personally I'd stick to the seafood and vegetarian dishes on offer. Local guides and sightseeing can be arranged, and an in-house tailor can whip up casual clothing in a matter of hours at incredibly low prices. There is also a brand new Ayurvedic center planned, but still no pool.

2/6 A, Calvathy Rd., Kochi 682 001. (℃) **0484/221-7103** or 989/519-6236. www.forthousecochin.com. fort_hs@ yahoo.com. 25 units. High season Rs 1,800–Rs 2,800 ($44–$68/£22–£35) A/C double new block, Rs 1,200–Rs 2,200 ($29–$54/£15–£27) non-A/C double; low season Rs 950–Rs 1,400 ($23–$34/£12–£17) double. Rates include breakfast. MC, V. **Amenities:** Restaurant; boat rental; travel desk; laundry service; dry-cleaning; doctor-on-call; Internet access; tailor. *In room:* A/C (2 rooms only).

Hotel Arches ⊛ *(Value)*   "The guest is running the show here," says the smiling manager, before pointing out that Hotel Arches made it to the number-three spot on Trip Advisor a mere year after opening in December 2005. And it's true: This is a sweet hotel, albeit one with rather bland rooms (reproduction furniture, with nothing decorating the bare walls). The rooms to request are the four with balconies on the street, or number 10, a deluxe room with plenty of natural light. Guest rooms are almost all twin bedded, but these can be made up into king-size beds (request when you book). Bathrooms are new, which is nice, but afflicted with the horrid cheap plastic tubs typical of most South Indian hotels. Still, if you're looking for hotel-like amenities (including 24-hr. room service), but don't want to shell out for the Brunton, Old Harbour, or Malabar, this is the best bargain in town. It also has a lovely rooftop restaurant, but no pool.

1/341 Rose St. (℃) **0484/221-5050.** Fax 0484/221-5704. www.hotelarches.com. 11 units. High season 60€–70€ ($82–$95/£41–£47) deluxe; low season (May–Sept) 40€ ($54/£27) deluxe. Nidra Suite 60€–100€ ($82–$136/£41– £68) depending on season. 10€ ($14/£7) extra bed. All rates include breakfast; exclude taxes. MC, V. **Amenities:** Restaurant; coffee shop; travel assistance; business center; 24-hr. room service; laundry; doctor-on-call; currency exchange; Internet access; cultural activities. *In room:* A/C, TV, fridge.

Malabar House Residency/Trinity ⊛⊛⊛   Step inside this chunky white 18th-century colonial British bungalow at the edge of the Parade Maidan, a grassy expanse for schoolboy cricketers and frolicking goats, and you're immediately cooled by rooms in vibrant colors, a lush courtyard, and the sound of trickling water. Infused by architect Joerg Drechsel with a contemporary edge, this is a tiny boutique hotel with a tropical inner courtyard (trees, potted shrubs, and stone pathways) with a lovely plunge pool, wooden foldaway chairs, a small open-air theater area, and a covered restaurant, the main focus. Rooms feature waxed black Kadapa stone floors offset by bright red, turquoise, or yellow walls; each features a selection of paintings, sculptures, and period furniture reflecting the cultural heritage of Kerala, while the beds, solid in every sense, are made from carved teak and rosewood. All the entry-level deluxe rooms are on the ground floor—of these, 14 and 15 are the best, with private minicourtyards at the back. The five suites all have private roof gardens—of these, the best are 9, 11, and 17. The **Trinity** annex is just across the maidan, but bar the Red Suite (which is huge and has the best bathroom in Kochi), Malabar House has more atmosphere, and offers better value as a result (though it pains me to see how much the rates have risen in just 2 years). The first operation in India to be certified by Green Globe, the global environmental certification program for travel and tourism, Malabar also has one of the best backwater properties in Kerala, **Privacy,** and a super houseboat (see "The Backwaters," below); while we don't generally promote package holidays, this is one worth considering.

1/268, 1/269 Parade Rd., Fort Cochin 682 001. ✆ 0484/221-6666. Fax 0484/221-7777. www.malabarhouse.com. Malabar: 17 units. Trinity: 3. There are 3 seasonal rates. Malabar: 120€–245€ ($163–$333/£81–£166) deluxe double; 160€–325€ ($217–$442/£108–£220) roof garden suites; 200€–380€ ($272–$517/£135–£257) Malabar suite. Trinity: 120€–330€ ($163–$449/£81–£23). Rates include breakfast. AE, MC, V. **Amenities:** Restaurant; pool; Ayurvedic spa; boat rental; bicycles; airline bookings; travel desk; car hire; boutique; 24-hr. room service; babysitting (with prior notice); laundry; doctor-on-call; currency exchange; tailor. *In room:* A/C, TV, mosquito net.

The Old Courtyard ✦ *Value*

This pleasant, intimate heritage hotel, located in a 200-year-old Portuguese mansion in the heart of Fort Kochi's quiet back streets, has a charming, authentic atmosphere and is relatively well maintained; best of all, accommodations are well priced. Each of the eight guest rooms—located on two floors in wings that lead off a central cobblestone courtyard—is different, but all have wooden floors and high-beamed ceilings, and most are furnished largely with antique furniture. Adjacent to the courtyard is a semi-enclosed restaurant serving a wide range of cuisines; traditional dances are performed here during the season. Premium rooms and suites have lovely original Portuguese four-poster beds and large, clean bathrooms (the cheapest room is strictly for bargain-hunters). A good option if you're looking for a real heritage atmosphere, but service and lack of pool are drawbacks.

1/371–372 Princess St., Fort Kochi 682 001. ✆ 0484/221-6302. www.oldcourtyard.com. 8 units. Rs 2,250–Rs 3,500 ($55–$82/£28–£43) regular non-A/C double; Rs 2,700–Rs 3,700 ($66–$90/£33–£46) regular A/C double; Rs 3,450–Rs 5,100 ($84–$124/£43–£63) suite. Rs 750 ($18/£9) extra bed. MC, V. **Amenities:** Restaurant; travel assistance; airport transfers; laundry; doctor-on-call; currency exchange; cultural performances; small book collection.

Old Harbour Hotel ✦✦ *Value*

A possible case of two dogs (Malabar House and Brunton) fighting over a bone, and a third getting away with it, this new heritage hotel (opened in Dec 2006) has aimed low in terms of rates, and high in terms of decor and atmosphere, and as a result it's almost always full. It's not positioned right on the waterfront like Brunton (but pretty darn close), nor does it offer the boutique design ethos of Malabar, but it's got class and offers excellent value. Until such time as it decides to change the tariff, this is going to remain fully booked, so best to make inquiries now. The 1808 bungalow was until recently the residence of an old tea-broking family, and renovation has been rather sensitive; even the entry-level superior rooms retain a sense of history and space. Garden-view rooms are a little more generous, but the garden "cottages" are the best options, with lovely outdoor bathrooms. Usually suites are not worth the money (unless you're on an expense account or traveling with kids), but the huge Princess Suite, with a harbor view, is a bargain and worth every one of its 200 dollars (not so the Bastion Suite with its weirdly angled bed). The pool is good-sized, but the garden needs time (and effort) to become established—early days yet.

Tower Rd., Fort Kochi. ✆ 0984/702-9000. www.oldharbourhotel.com. 13 units. $100–$130 (£51–£66) superior garden view; $150 (£76) garden cottage; $175–$200 (£88–£101) suite. Rates include breakfast; exclude taxes. AE, DC, MC, V. **Amenities:** Restaurant; pool; travel assistance; Ayurvedic massage on request; laundry; Wi-Fi. *In room:* A/C, TV.

WILLINGDON ISLAND

Taj Malabar *★★* A hostel built for those traveling by steamship from England is today the Heritage Wing of Willingdon's only waterfront hotel, an elegant property and the most chichi hotel option in town. Prices, as a result, have seen a rather steep increase in tandem with Kochi's popularity as the gateway to Kerala. The generously proportioned Heritage Wing rooms feature wood floors, period-style furniture, and assorted knickknacks, but for truly spectacular views book one of the Superior Sea Views or Deluxe Sunset Views in the Tower Wing; make sure you're on the fifth or sixth floor and that your room ends in 01, 09, or 10 (the latter the aptly named Sunset View category). The chic Ayurvedic center in the Tamara Spa is Green Leaf–accredited and occupies its own traditional-style building overlooking the gorgeous rim-flow pool. Enjoy sunset drinks on the pool deck or on one of the hotel's daily harbor cruises. Or—for those who prefer privacy—book *Cinnamon Coast,* the private yacht available for hire. The Taj Malabar has two highly rated restaurants and the biggest and best-located infinity pool, right on the harbor edge.

Willingdon Island, Kochi 682 009. *©* **0484/266-6811** or -8010. Fax 0484/266-8297. www.tajhotels.com. malabar. cochin@tajhotels.com. 96 units. Tower Wing: $245 (£128) superior double; $270 (£136) superior sea-view double; $295 (£149) deluxe sunset-view double; $395 (£199) executive suite. Heritage Wing: $245 (£124) superior double; $320 (£162) superior sea-view double; $425 (£215) deluxe suite. AE, MC, V. **Amenities:** 4 restaurants; bar; pool; gym; Jacuzzi; boat rental; travel desk; sightseeing; car hire; business center; salon; 24-hr. room service; babysitting; laundry; doctor-on-call; currency exchange; Wi-Fi enabled; valet service; Ayurvedic center. *In room:* A/C, TV, minibar, tea- and coffee-making facility, hair dryer, electronic safe, Wi-Fi.

Trident Cochin *★* This upmarket business hotel is quiet, tasteful, and replete with modern conveniences plus arguably the best service standards in town. Accommodations surround a pleasant courtyard where you can swim in the pool and dine alfresco. An effort has been made to personalize the public spaces with traditional artifacts and ornaments, and the entrance is dominated by a giant *uruli* cooking pot mounted on old black-and-gold snake-boat prows. The modestly sized guest rooms are cool, with blond timber and marble floors and blue-and-white themed decor, and bathrooms are in good nick. All in all, it's a very slick, professional place, and were it not for its location (neither in the heritage area nor on the waterfront), it would be a top pick. But then the rates—which offer very good value when compared with those of the nearby Taj—would not be so enticing.

Bristow Rd., Willingdon Island, Kochi 682 003, Kerala. *©* **0484/266-9595** or -6816. Fax 0484/266-9393. www.trident hotels.com. 85 units. $180 (£91) superior double; $200 (£101) deluxe double; $265 (£134) deluxe suite double. Ask about specials. AE, DC, MC, V. **Amenities:** 2 restaurants; bar; pool; gym; travel desk; sightseeing; car hire; business center; gift shop; book shop; salon; 24-hr. room service; babysitting; laundry valet service; currency exchange; Wi-Fi enabled. *In room:* A/C, TV, minibar, tea- and coffee-making facility, hair dryer, electronic safe, Wi-Fi.

ERNAKULAM

If you can't get a room at Fort Kochi or Willingdon Island, or are here for business reasons (or just want to shop in earnest in the heart of the city), **Taj Residency** (Marine Dr.; *©* **0484/237-1471;** www.tajhotels.com; $150–$250/£74–£123 double), which sits right on the harbor's edge and has its own jetty, is by far the best option in Ernakulam proper; make sure to book a harbor-view room. Alternatively, **The Woods Manor** is located slap-bang on busy M.G. Road, with no views to speak of but a rooftop pool (*©* **0484/238-2055** through -2059; www.thewoodsmanor.com; from Rs 2,530/$62/£31 double, includes breakfast). Also on M.G. Road is **The Grand** (*©* **0484/238-2061** or 0484/236-6833; www.grandhotelkerala.com; Rs

1,750–Rs 2,800/$43–$68/£22–£35 double), Ernakulam's oldest hotel. The restaurant is a local institution—it's worth staying just so you can dine here every night, then wedge yourself into the lift and just roll down the corridor into bed!

WHERE TO DINE

Seafood, always fresh, should be at least one course. Seerfish, a large, meaty white-fleshed fish, is by far the most reliable, as are prawns. Kochi's best eating establishments are for the most part still located in hotels, but two exceptions worth trying are Old Port and Dal Roti, both very unpretentious venues and the only stand-alone restaurants to offer any serious competition to the hotels in Fort Kochi. **Old Port** is conveniently located next to one of the better Kathakali centers (opposite the entrance to Brunton), and specializes in tandoor seafood. Here kingfish *tikka* is the dish to order (assuming it's available); alternatively, try the snapper or prawns Kerala style. Prices are usually determined by weight, but it's not expensive. If you're bored with seafood and South Indian spicing, **Dal Roti** (1/293 Lilly St.; © **0984/619-0052;** dhal.roti@gmail.com) serves up delicious North Indian fare in a lovely, casual atmosphere: whitewashed walls and simple pine benches and tables arranged around a terra-cotta Nandi (a sacred Hindu bull). It's new, so hopefully standards won't decline, but at press time you could expect to find deliciously rich yet simple "village"-style cooking, very good, and wonderful value. The most expensive item is the *murg mussalam* (spicy chicken with yogurt) at Rs 175 ($4/£2), and it serves four! Best bet is to order the non-veg thali, and devour with *alu paratas* (stuffed whole-wheat bread).

For pit stops during the day while wandering around Fort Kochi, there are two good options: **Kashi Art Café** (Burgher St.; © **0484-221-5769;** www.kashiartcafe.com), located in a restored Dutch heritage house, is a novel cafe-cum-art-gallery with tables and benches made out of coconut trunks. It serves up hot and cold beverages with cakes or sandwiches. Another charming venue is **Tea Pot** (Peter Celli St.; © **0484/221-8035;** tpleaz@hotmail.com), run by Sanjai, a laid-back hippie type. Order the *appam* with vegetable stew (chopped vegetables in a very mild coconut base; Rs 100/$2/£1) and a ginger lime soda (or one of more than 30 teas), then settle down with a good book or a garrulous partner—the food takes a while to get there, but it's almost always worth the wait.

Fort Cochin 𝕲𝕲𝕲 SEAFOOD   Considered one of the state's best seafood restaurants, this casual catch-of-the-day semi-alfresco pad—located in the otherwise unprepossessing Casino Hotel—is something of a Kerala institution. The atmosphere is rustic: Tables are set around a huge banyan tree and the menu is scrawled on a blackboard. Choose from a range of freshly caught seafood displayed on a cart that makes its way from table to table, and decide how you would like it prepared—grilled whole with heaps of spices, or delicately sliced with subtle herbs; the obliging maitre d' will help you make up your mind. Seafood is prepared at an open grill adjacent to a large waist-level fish tank filled with Chinese carp.

Note: If you'd prefer a more fine-dining atmosphere, the **Rice Boat** (© **0484/266-6811**) is the gorgeous seafood restaurant at the Taj Malabar, a small specialty restaurant with floor-to-ceiling glass walls and a curved cane ceiling, located right on the water's edge. It's an excellent place to indulge in some fusion dishes, like rice hoppers (traditional rice "pasta cakes") served with smoked salmon, tropical fruit, and coconut chutney, or cubes of seerfish cooked with ground coconut and raw mango, and served with *idlyappams*. It's not cheap by Kerala standards, and seafood is not as good as the more simple fare served up at Fort Cochin, but it's still darn good!

Traditional Keralite Feasts

If you're invited, don't pass up the opportunity to enjoy a traditional *sadhya* feast while in Kerala. In truth, even the simplest breakfast meal is a feast in Kerala, so forgo the eggs and toast and order whatever's going. The most well-known feast food is of course the *dosa,* a crispy thin pancake, or the *idly* (also spelled *iddly* or *idli*), a small compressed rice and lentil wedge—both are served with *sambar* (a vegetable and lentil gravy) and various chutneys (coconut, mint, peanut, tomato, and chili). The famous *"masala dosa"* is when the pancake is stuffed with a spicy potato dish. Also delicious is *puttu,* a fine rice powder and grated coconut "cylinder," which is often served with baked banana and mildly spicy chickpea stew. Or there's the steamed rice pancake known as *appam,* served with vegetable "stew" (chopped vegetables and cashews in coconut milk). At traditional feasts, expect rice and ghee (clarified butter), served with various stews and curries like *sambar, rasam, kootu, pacchadi, appalam,* and *payasam,* all of which will be heaped endlessly upon your *ela* (leaf). Seafood in Kerala is exquisite and plentiful. A popular dish is *meen moilee,* a delicate fish curry tempered with fresh coconut milk (*chemeen,* incidentally, means "prawns"). Coconut is a staple used in many dishes: *Avial* is a mixed-vegetable "dry" curry prepared with coconut, cumin, and turmeric; and *aadu olathiyathu* is a coconut-based curry made with cubes of fried mutton.

Casino Hotel, K.P.K. Menon Rd., Willingdon Island. ℂ **0484/266-8221** or **-8421**. Prices determined on the day and by weight. Mixed-seafood platter Rs 875 ($21/£11). AE, DC, MC, V. Daily 7–11:45pm.

The Grand Pavilion 🌟🌟🌟 INDIAN   Okay, this may not be grand in the decor sense, but the Keralan and Indian food is delicious. And cheap. Which is why the place is always jam-packed with locals, and apparently has been since the '60s when The Grand really was. Seafood is superb, with the signature *karimeen pollichathu* a definite must-have. If you're not feeling that hungry, start with a plate of *chemeen ularthiyathu* (tiny prawns; ask that they not be too spicy), then follow with vegetable stew to be mopped up with the most delectable crisp-edged, soft-centered *appams,* and a plate of tender *malai* chicken, prepared in the tandoor, and served with mint sauce. All that food, and still the bill won't top Rs 700 ($17/£9) for two. A huge dining hall, filled to the brim with a loyal Indian clientele, and faultless food makes this 20-minute trip from Fort Kochi most definitely worth it. Make sure you book ahead.

M.G. Rd., Ernakulam. ℂ **0484/238-2061.** www.grandhotelkerala.com. Main courses Rs 60–Rs 130 ($1–$3/£1–£2). MC, V. Daily 12:30–4pm and 7–11:30pm.

The History & Terrace Grill 🌟🌟🌟 KERALITE   The Terrace Grill has a great location overlooking the busy Vypin boat jetty and waterfront section, and you can spend hours watching the passing parade while you dine on the superb signature seafood platters (Rs 1,200/$29/£15), filled with lobster, tiger prawns, scampi, squid (a little tough), and the catch of the day. Order a combination of Mattencherry Spiced and lemon garlic butter, then move inside if you wish (some nights the mosquitoes can be bothersome). *Note:* In a somewhat cumbersome arrangement, guests of the Terrace may move inside to what is named The History, where the chef will then serve you the same seafood platter, but if you've booked at The History, you cannot order a seafood platter from the Terrace Grill. Go figure. The History has a much more varied menu, with most of the recipes borrowed from the kitchens of Kochi families.

The Brunton Boatyard Hotel, 1/498 Fort Cochin, Kochi. © 0484/221-5461 through -0465. Main courses Rs 250–Rs 400 ($6–$10/£3–£5); seafood platter Rs 1,200–1,400 ($29–$34/£15–£17). AE, DC, MC, V. Daily 7:30–10:30pm.

Malabar Junction ✫✫ MEDITERRANEAN FUSION   Along with **Rice Boat** (Taj Malabar's pretty restaurant), this is Kochi's answer to fine dining, though here it is alfresco, with guests seated in the small, lush courtyard area, watching (at night) a performance on the adjacent stage, the hotel and plants lit up to great effect. The atmosphere is very romantic, and if Indian food is not your thing, this is the place to be. Though the food is very good (and said to be homemade), it's a little weird to be ordering pasta in India. Opt instead for dishes (none of which are very hot) like fragrant lemon grass skewered tiger prawns, marinated with spring onion, coriander, ginger, and garlic; or the combination of seerfish, rice fish, and tiger prawn cooked in a coconut milk, onion, tomato, turmeric, chili, and ground coriander sauce. Malabar also does a seafood platter for Rs 980 ($24/£12). A good lunch option is the thali. Malabar has a great atmosphere, but service can be a tad snooty.

Malabar House Residency, 1/268–1/269 Parade Rd., Fort Kochi. © 0484/221-6666. Menu changes regularly, but expect to pay Rs 250–Rs 550 ($6–$13/£3–£7) for a main course, Rs 980 ($24/£12) for a seafood platter. AE, DC, MC, V. Daily 7–10:30am, noon–3pm, and 7–10:30pm.

SHOPPING

With the exception of Cinnamon (see below), where Bangalore-based buyers show off their exceptional eye for modern Indian design, and a small branch of the ever-popular **FabIndia** (1/279 Napier St., near Parade Ground; © **0484/304-3517;** www.fabindia.com), Fort Kochi itself caters to mass tourist tastes. The goods on offer are neither cheap nor exceptional. You'll have far more fun exploring the antiques dealerships in neighboring Mattancherry, most of which are jam-packed with weird, wonderful, and genuine pieces from Kerala's multifangled past; catch a rickshaw to Crafters (see below), then wander around this area. The biggest outfit in the area, Crafters is less likely to offer discounts, but dig around the dark corners of the little shops in the area around this legendary antiques shop, and bargain hard: Try offering half of the quoted price, and settle halfway between the two. Also in Jew Town and worth popping into is **Galleria Synagogue Art Gallery** (© **0484/222-2544;** www. galleriasynagogue.com), where local artists are well represented; art and antiques lovers should also check out **Lawrence Art Gallery** in Synagogue Lane (© **0484/222 3657**).

If you're looking for fabrics or clothing, or just want to experience a totally vibrant and more authentic Indian city shopping experience, get a cab to Ernakulam, where the locals shop. You'll find almost everything on **M.G. Road,** a great street to just wander at will, but be on the lookout for **Music World** for music, **Seematti** and **Jayalakshmi** for textiles (particularly silks and saris), and **Bhima and Brothers** (www.bhima jewellery.com) for jewelry. **Marine Drive** is another good shopping street—it's worth setting aside half an hour just to explore the huge selection of brass- and silverware at **AKP Metalodrome** (next to the cinema) alone. Both these streets have scores of shops trading in a variety of goods and offering excellent value (note that shops in Ernakulam, catering as they do to locals, are usually "fixed price"—in other words, don't expect to gain anything but disdain by haggling here). A larger **FabIndia** (© **0484/ 301-8682**) is on Old Thevara Road, near the Kochi Shipyard Ravipuram; unlike most Kochi shops, both FabIndias are open daily 10am to 8pm.

Cinnamon ★★★   A branch of Bangalore's trendy store, and managed by the Malabar House, this is Kochi's most fashionable outlet. With a cool gallery-like ambience, Cinamon sells modern *objets,* shoes, and fashions that are entirely homegrown and produced by some of the best designers in India. Find fishing nets made into pillowcases, coconuts fashioned into purses, vintage prints of Hindu deities, silk caftans, and cotton dresses and tunics ideal for the Indian heat. (If you don't like the modern interpretation of Indian skills, head next door to **Kala Nilayam Cottage Expo Crafts,** which showcases a huge array of traditional arts and crafts from across the country.) Open Monday to Saturday 10am to 7pm. 1/658 Ridsdale Rd. © 0484/221-7124.

Crafters   In the heart of historic Mattanchery's Jew Town, Crafters is an antiques fetishist's dream come true. A huge selection of unique antiques and handicrafts, ranging from religious curiosities to that perfect doorway, are displayed in five different stores, and piled up high in a massive warehouse style, with so much to take home you'll find it hard to leave empty-handed; staff members are dab hands at arranging for purchases to be shipped abroad. Before you purchase anything, though, do look around the other antiques shops in Jew Town; Crafters has the best selection, and prices are fair, but you won't find real bargains here. VI/141, Jew Town. © 0484/222-3346, -7652, or 0484/221-2210. www.craftersantique.com.

KOCHI AFTER DARK

When the sun starts to sink, you should be watching it turn the harbor waters pale pink, either on a harbor cruise or, a cocktail in hand, from the **Harbour View** bar at the **Taj Residency** in Ernakulam (see above). Once the sun has set, head down M.G. Road to the Avenue Regent hotel and grab a sofa at **Loungevity,** a cool white minimalist lounge bar, and watch the city of Kochi network at what is currently the trendiest nightspot in town (© 0484/237 7977; www.avenueregent.com). Alternatively, if you want to stay in Fort Kochi, a Kathakali or Kalaripayattu demonstration (see below) can easily fill the gap before a fine seafood dinner.

KATHAKALI PERFORMANCES

In Fort Kochi, the **Kerala Kathakali Centre** ★★★ (River Rd., opposite entrance to Brunton Boatyard; © 0484/221-5827; www.kathakalicentre.com) hosts the best Kathakali demonstration in the city (see "Kathakali & Kalaripayattu: Kerala's Colorful Art Forms," above). This rustic, atmospheric "theater" also hosts Indian Classical Music nights. Kathakali performances (Rs 150/$3.40/£1.70) are held daily from 6:30 or 7pm to 8pm, with make-up demonstrations from around 5pm; the hour-long music performances are from 8:45pm. Alongside the theater is **Old Port Restaurant** (© 0484/221-5341), a good venue for pre- or post-show meals (a good idea to bring mosquito repellent for both the show and the restaurant). If you're interested in attending a proper all-night Kathakali performance at a temple, speak to one of the organizers at Kerala Kathakali; some of their top performers are often involved in authentic rituals.

The other, more famous Kathakali venue, featured on a number of television programs, is in Ernakulam, near the Junction Railway station. **India Foundation Traditional Theatre** (Kalathi Parambil Cross Rd; © 0484/237-6471; kathakalidevan@ hotmail.com) is presented by P. K. Devan, who reveals the religious roots and philosophy behind the *katha* (story) and *kali* (play). Performances are held daily between 6:45 and 8pm; makeup starts at 6pm.

Kathakali & Kalaripayattu: Kerala's Colorful Art Forms

A stay in Kochi affords you the opportunity to sample Kerala's best-known classical art form—Kathakali, a performance style that delves into the world of demons, deities, soldiers, sages, and satyrs, taken from Indian epics such as the *Mahabharata*. Combining various theatrical and performance elements, it is said to have developed during the 16th century under the auspices of the Raja of Kottaraka, and today the best Kathakali school is in Kalamandalam, founded by a poet named Vallathol Narayan Menon in 1930. Here, students undergo a rigorous training program that lasts 6 years and includes massage techniques, extensive make-up training, and knowledge of the precise and subtle finger, body, and eye movements that constitute the language and grand emotions of Kathakali. There is also a host of instruments that may be mastered, as no performance is without musical accompaniment. So striking are the costumes, make-up, and jewelry associated with this form of dance-theater, that the image of the elaborately adorned, heavily made-up, and almost mask-like face of the Kathakali performer has become the state's most recognizable icon. Performers employ exaggerated facial expressions (only enhanced by the make-up—bright paint applied thickly to the face) and a highly technical set of symbolic hand gestures (known as *mudras*). Vocalists and musicians help set the mood, utilizing the *chengila* (gong), *elathalam* (small cymbals), and *chenda* and *maddalam* (drums). Traditionally, Kathakali performances are held for entire nights, often as part of festival events. In Kochi, however, a number of Kathakali groups stage short extracts of the longer pieces specifically for tourist consumption. Kerala is also renowned for its unique martial arts form: the supremely acrobatic Kalaripayattu, believed to be the oldest defense-combat system in the world. Apparently discovered in ancient times by traveling Buddhist monks who needed to protect themselves against marauding bandits, Kalaripayattu is believed to predate more recognizable forms, like kung-fu, that emerged farther east. For demonstrations of Kathakali and Kalaripayattu, see recommendations below.

KALARIPAYATTU PERFORMANCES

While there are a number of dedicated training schools *(kalaris)* where Kerala's traditional martial arts form, Kalaripayattu, is taught for its intended purpose, it is usually performed in a staged environment for tourists. **Shiva Shakti Kalari Kshetram** (Kaloor, Ernakulam; ✆ **98-9529-0635**) holds daily demonstrations of Kalaripayattu from 5 to 6pm; the institute also provides training and Ayurvedic massage based on principles derived from the art of Kalari.

2 The Backwaters ★★★

Alappuzha is 85km (53 miles) from Kochi; Kumarokum is 95km (59 miles) from Kochi; Periyar is 190km (118 miles) from Kochi and 145km (90 miles) from Madurai

Kerala's backwaters comprise a web of waterways that forms a natural inland transport network stretching from **Kochi,** the northern gateway, to **Kollam** (or **Quilon,** as it's been renamed), the backwaters' southernmost town. At its heart is Vembanad Lake, on the east of which lie the top-notch resorts of **Kumarakom** and its Bird Sanctuary, and on its southern shores, the little town of **Alappuzha,** the unofficial capital of the backwaters. Inland, just 12km (7½ miles) east of Kumarakom, is **Kottayam,** the bustling town described by Arundhati Roy in her Booker Prize–winning *The God of Small Things*. Located at the foot of the Western Ghats, it has two historically significant (but ultimately missable) early Syrian Christian churches.

Kumarakom has the most luxury accommodations, all strung along the shores of Vembanad Lake, but unless you're a keen birder, there's not a great deal to do here. Indulge in Ayurvedic therapies, and laze under the tropical sun—that's about as busy as your day is likely to get; then board a houseboat cruise, where the passing scenery and slow pace (and discreet service on tap) is enough to lull you into a comfortable coma. Between November and March, the local **Bird Sanctuary** becomes home to numerous migratory flocks, many of which fly in from Siberia. Regularly seen here are little cormorants, darters (or snake birds), night herons, golden-backed woodpeckers, tree pies, and crow pheasants. Given its exclusivity and sublime setting, Kumarakom does not offer accommodations for budget-oriented travelers; for that you'll need to look farther south to **Alappuzha** (pronounced Ala-*purd*-ha, or Alleppey if you can't be bothered), also the focal point of backwater cruise operators, and the only backwater town worth spending a few hours indulging in a bit of retail therapy.

Home to the coir (fibers made from coconut husks) industry, Alleppey once bore the nickname "Venice of the East" because of its famed palm-fringed canal network, the intricate byways and narrow streams that allow boats to transport huge bales of coconut fibers. Of the many **snake boat races** (see "Snake Boat Races," below) that take place in the backwaters during August and September, Alleppey's Nehru Trophy event is the most significant. If you're keen to witness the event, book a houseboat with an elevated platform—preferably the *Discovery* (see "Hiring the Best Houseboat," below).

The entire backwaters region is a tranquil paradise and sustains a delightfully laid-back way of life that has endured for centuries—perfect for sultry, languid, do-nothing houseboat adventures that take you into the heart of Kerala country life. Despite the huge increase in traffic from the tourist boom, floating along these waters will be the highlight of your sojourn in south India (see "Hiring the Best Houseboat," below).

Snake Boat Races

Every year Kerala's backwater canals host the world's largest team sport, when scores of streamlined *chundan vallams,* the ram-snouted boats commonly known as snake boats, are propelled across the waters at impressive speeds, cheered on by an exuberant audience. Typically, snake boats are manned by four helmsmen, 25 singers, and up to 100 oarsmen rowing in unison to the terrific rhythm of the *vanchipattu,* or "song of the boatman." The oldest and most popular event is the **Champakulam Moolam Boat Race,** held in monsoon-soaked July, but the most famous water battle is undoubtedly the **Nehru Trophy Boat Race,** held on the second Saturday of August on the Punnamada backwaters of Alleppey in conjunction with Kerala's important *Onam* harvest festival. Tickets for the event, which features at least 16 competing *chundan vallams* and attracts thousands of excited supporters, are available from the **District Tourism Promotion Council office** (see "Visitor Information," below), but best to ask your hotel or houseboat operator to arrange these.

ESSENTIALS

VISITOR INFORMATION The official authority responsible for dishing out information to visitors is the **District Tourism Promotion Council,** which has various offices in the different backwaters towns. The main office is in **Alappuzha,** on Boat Jetty Road (© **0477/225-3308;** daily 9am–5:30pm). If your main interest is getting information on houseboats, see "Hiring the Best Houseboat," below.

GETTING THERE   By Road   Taxis are easily available in all major towns and cities. From Kochi a taxi should cost at most Rs 950 ($23/£12) and get you to Kottayam in about 1½ hours; farther south, Alappuzha is better connected (better road) and should take around 1 hour. It is a 5-hour journey from Idukki/Periyar, the same from Munnar. Trivandrum lies 4 hours away.

By Air   For the northern backwater towns, the nearest airport is at Kochi; around 76km (47 miles) by road by car to Kottayam/Kumarakom, or 85km (53 miles) to Alappuzha.

By Train   Though there are railheads in Kottayam (15 min. from the Kumarakom resorts), Alappuzha, and Kollam, your best bet is to get to Trivandrum or Kochi and then head out by road; all resorts offer transfers.

GETTING AROUND   By Water-Taxi & Ferry   Kottayam, Alappuzha, and Kollam are all connected by ferries that ply the route, with six departures to Kottayam daily. State Water Transport Department ferries between Alappuzha and Kottayam (a 3-hr. round-trip) depart from the tourist boat jetty near the bus station. Ferries between Alappuzha and Kollam take 8 hours, departing from both the Alleppey and Kollam boat jetties at 10:30am and arriving in Kollam/Alappuzha around 6:30pm (cost is Rs 300/$7/£4); after this you can catch a road taxi back. If you're in a hurry you can ask about speedboats, which more than halve the journey time.

GUIDED TOURS & CRUISES   Alappuzha's well-meaning **District Tourism Promotion Council** (Boat Jetty, Alappuzha; © **0477/225-3308**) organizes tickets for the daily backwater ferry between Kollam, Kottayam, and Alappuzha (see above). DTPC also offers private cruises that work out to about Rs 250 ($5.70/£2.90) per hour on a motorboat, and around Rs 150 ($3.40/£1.70) per hour on a "country boat"; an overnight trip (22 hr.) on a *kettuvallam* houseboat will run you Rs 3,500 ($85/£43). See "Hiring the Best Houseboat," below, for recommended guided overnight trips. Alternatively, any of the accommodations listed below can organize backwaters cruises—for many it's part of the package, though this is definitely not the same as having a houseboat to call your own.

CRUISING THE BACKWATERS

Reset your watch to a rhythm of life that has gone unchanged for centuries by boarding a *kettuvallam,* the long, beautifully crafted cargo boats that ply the waterways with cargo (if you don't mind being referred to as such). An engineering feat, a *kettuvallam* is made from lengths of ironwood, *anjili,* or jackwood, and not a single nail is used in the construction—it's joined together with thick coir ropes, and sealed with fish oil and a black caustic resin produced by boiling cashew kernels.

The houseboat experience allows you to aimlessly drift past villages, temples, and churches and be thoroughly exposed to the rural lifestyle of the backwaters. As if you're on the very large set of a reality TV show, you can watch as women, unperturbed by your drifting presence, wash their long ebony tresses or pound away at laundry; children play at the water's edge and men dive for mussels; and elephants and water buffalo wade at will. Fishermen suavely holding umbrellas above their heads suddenly drift by, while floating vendors using single-log canoes and other modest craft deliver commodities such as rice and coir fiber. On the shore, toddy tappers whisk up palm trees (note that you can ask to stop at a village to buy unforeseen necessities like beer or coconut toddy); see "Toddy Tappers," below. And when the sun sets, the sky lights up in magnificent shades of orange and red. Gliding past the rural communities that cling to the banks is without a doubt one of the most relaxing and romantic ways to witness a timeless lifestyle, where people rely on impossibly tiny tracts of land to cultivate subsistence crops and keep a few animals, using slender jackfruit wood canoes to get around, deliver goods, and do a spot of fishing. And of course it is always rather marvelous to be waited on hand and foot by three servants.

The original concept of turning cargo boats into tourist cruise vessels was the brain-child of Babu Varghese of TourIndia (an outfit that has incidentally fallen into disarray since Varghese employed a hit man to punish his partner—high business drama, India-style). Varghese transformed the *kettuvallam* into a livable houseboat by expanding the original size to include two or three rooms, a flush toilet, a shower, and a small viewing or sunbathing platform. With designs that owe some allegiance to the Chinese junk but that more closely resemble a small Sydney Opera House, these beautiful crafts were initially propelled by pole but now more usually by a small (and

Cruising Kerala on the World's Smallest Luxury Liner

Leave it to Oberoi to take the traditional backwater cruise to new heights with the **MV** *Vrinda*—not exactly a liner, but the ultimate in luxury on Kerala's backwaters, and very Agatha Christie. After all, only on board the MV *Vrinda* can you find yourself watching life along the river from a comfy rattan chair on the breezy upper-deck lounge, or from your plush settee in the air-conditioned dining room while staff keeps a watchful eye out for a raised finger. On the first night, after a scenic 4-hour cruise on Vembanad Lake, you dock at a jetty for dinner (a thoroughly elegant affair accompanied by Kathakali dancers), then bed down in one of only eight smart cabins, each decked out with luxuries like TV and DVD, en-suite showers, and lovely king-size beds. The following day, the boat makes its way to Lake Pamba, where you can climb aboard a small rice boat to explore the narrower backwaters; the following day another rice boat excursion takes you to see an 18th-century church and century-old Hindu temple at Nedumudy, with a qualified guide. Three nights later you wend your way back by road to Kochi. Typical of the Oberoi, food is outstanding (there's an a la carte menu but you can pretty much get what you want) and you are treated like royalty—perfect if you prefer to travel in a somewhat sanitized manner, ensconced in a luxurious cocoon. The 3-night package runs from October to April and costs Rs 88,000 ($2,146/£1,086), including all meals, excursions, and Kochi airport transfer. For reservations, call the Oberoi at © **1600/11-2030** (www.oberoihotels.com).

Toddy Tappers

For generations, agile young village men have been clambering up coconut palms to tap into the sweet sap known as toddy, or *kallu*. Like their fathers and their fathers' fathers, these "toddy tappers" have made a good living over the years harvesting the sap to drink right away (sweet and refreshing, but definitely an acquired taste) or to ferment into an alcoholic drink. The morning's toddy is already a heady tipple by evening—by the next day, it's prodigiously potent.

hopefully quiet) motor. In 2007 the state government finally started taking action against those engines that pollute, and not a minute too soon: A mere 4 years back there were perhaps 15 houseboats operating out of Alappuzha; today the figure is closer to 400—all the more reason to be careful with whom you book.

While the general idea is to wind your way aimlessly through the waterways, one of the most popular stop-off points for visitors is **Champakulam,** where 500-year-old **St. Mary's Church** shows definite traces of Hindu influence, from a small statue of Christ assuming a pose typical of Krishna to the custom of leaving one's footwear outside. Another stop worth scheduling is at the **Amma's Ashram** (✆ **0476/289-6179** or -6278; 2 hr. away by speedboat), home of a female guru endearingly known as the "Hugging Mother." The Mother is said to believe in physically manifesting her love and compassion for humanity, and has embraced thousands of devotees; if she's not on tour, this is exactly what she will do to you! If this sounds a little too touchy-feely, visit just to wander the ashram grounds and have lunch with those residing there; the Raheem Residency (see "Where to Stay," below) organizes visits here.

Note: Two more stops worth considering (reached this time by vehicle) are the **Elephant Orphanage,** where you can get up close and personal with the elephants (usually including at least one baby) that are cared for here, as well as **Mannar** and **Aranmula,** towns famous for their metal icons and mirrors respectively.

WHERE TO STAY

Ideally you will combine a night or two at one of the resorts or guesthouses recommended below with at least two more on a houseboat. Most of the top luxury resorts are strung along the eastern shores of Lake Vembanad; the exceptions are the top-rated Privacy and Olavipe (reviewed below) and Green Lagoon (see "Green Lagoon: The Best Villa Stay in Kerala," below), all of which lie on backwaters on the northern end of the lake. You can reach virtually all of them by car, but many prefer to pick you up from a prearranged jetty, which heightens the sense of escape. Some, like Coconut Lagoon and Green Lagoon, can in fact only be reached by water. In short, this is one area you should plan and book in advance regardless of season, so that the necessary transfer arrangements can be made. Alleppey is the only town worth exploring at any length, and perhaps a better contrast to a lakeside resort; thanks to Raheem Residency (reviewed below), there is also a good guesthouse here. *Note:* Taxes usually run 10% to 15%; do check whether it's included when asking for rate quotes. From May to September, rates are generally half those of the peak season, which is December and January; September is a particularly good month to visit for houseboat excursions.

HIRING THE BEST HOUSEBOAT

This will possibly be the highlight of your holiday, so make sure you hire a good boat. *Kettuvallam* houseboats are available at various levels of luxury, and may be rented for day trips or for sleep-in journeys of several days; we recommend that you spend 2 nights on board, since it takes one to realize how relaxing the process is, and the major attractions are watching the setting sun turn the lake orange before settling down in the middle of the lake for the night (all boats must be moored or anchored by 6pm for the fishermen to cast their night nets), and witnessing the activities of households on the smaller backwaters at dawn and dusk (usually the second day). Most houseboats feature solar-panel power and heating, bio-toilets, and an average cruising speed of 8 to 10km (5–6 miles) per hour. Although the facilities might strike some as rather basic, you'll be spoiled rotten by your private team—usually a cook and two pilots—who work hard to make your experience unique and exceptional (and discreetly manage to leave you to experience the backwaters in peace). Meals are authentic Kerala fare—if you're curious about Kerala cuisine, you're welcome to observe proceedings in the tiny kitchen at the rear end of the boat. With the huge increase of traffic on the backwaters, don't expect exclusivity—try to avoid booking over the peak season, and opt instead for shoulder times. September is to our mind the best month, when the water is high, harvest is due, races are scheduled, and tourist numbers are relatively low.

One of the simplest and most sensitive conversions of the *kettuvallam* has been done by **Spice Coast Cruises** ★★ (House Boats, Puthenangadi, Alleppey; © 0484/266-8221 or 0478/258-2615; spicecoastcruise@cghearth.com), who have cleverly increased the number of "awnings" (for views as well as breeze) and created a comfortable sun deck "bed" with white bolster cushions on the elevated section of the boat up front—perfect for lounging around with a book (though the "captain" steers from the front, you soon forget his presence); just behind is your coir-carpeted dining room, furnished with unpretentious antiques. The tiny bedroom comes with A/C (running at night only), and in our experience staff struck just the right balance between attentiveness and discretion. Rates are $135 to $460 (£68–£232) double, depending on season, all meals included; while a two-bedroom (sleeping four) costs $205 to $650 (£103–£328) depending on season. Two other reputable companies are **Lakes & Lagoons** (© 098-4705-1566; lakes_lagoon@satyam.net.in) and **Rainbow Cruises** (© 0477/224-1375; www.backwaterkerala.com; reservations@rainbowcruises.in). The former has a huge reliable fleet; the latter has 16 craft in three categories but specialize in the luxury end, offering boats with TVs and relatively large air-conditioned bedrooms. Part of the Somatheeram Group, **Soma Houseboats** is another outfit worth looking into, particularly for boats with a separate elevated viewing platform; for this luxury make sure you book one of its "Upper Deck" houseboats (© 0471/226-8101; www.somahouseboats.com); from Rs 4,750 to Rs 8,500 ($116–$207/£59–£105) (one bedroom) and Rs 8,250 to Rs 12,500 ($201–$305/£102–£154) (two bedrooms) for 1-night cruise; 2- and 3-night cruises are also available. Both Rainbow and Soma have earned Gold Star classification from the state government and are considered the top of their class.

But if you don't mind forgoing the traditional *kettavallam* design, the best houseboat experience is on the Malabar House's *Discovery* ★★★ (© 0484/221-6666; www.malabarhouse.com; 400€/$544/£271 per night, including all meals). Launched in 2006/07, this is a gorgeous modern interpretation of the houseboat concept, with a totally private upper deck (furnished with dining table and loungers), a comfortable

Finds Green Lagoon: The Best Villa Stay in Kerala

Opened at the end of 2007, this is the new venture from Klaus Schleusener, the Chennai professor who put the Keralan coast on the tourism map when he created Surya Samudra way back in the 1980s. He sold the resort to retire on his Green Lagoon islands near Kochi but, never one to sit still (or stint on the one real luxury he cannot forego: privacy), he built another beautiful dwelling, this one on one of the separate islands, all now linked with small bridges—for friends. Then he built another two dwellings, this time with a lovely infinity pool, on another island. The result is three totally separate and totally private units, each with their own large pool and own butler. At 1,000€ ($1,375/£680) (that includes all meals, butler, speedboat tours, airport transfers, day excursions), it's not exactly cheap, but trust me, if you can afford it, the **Green Lagoon** (www.green-lagoon.com) is the best-value deal on the backwaters, with Privacy's Waterfront Suite (see below) the second.

and stylish bedroom with well-plumbed en-suite bathroom (most of the *kettuvallam* bathrooms are pretty substandard, with low water pressure for showering and flushing), and a separate lounge that can double as a second bedroom since your "living" is done almost entirely on the top deck. The team works hard to create routes where you won't come across other houseboats, and the packages come with a night at the wonderful Privacy (see below), where you start your journey and one of our favorite backwaters villas. It has an edge of modernity and style typical of the Malabar group, making it our personal pick. But for 100% luxury and genuflecting service from India's best-trained hoteliers, the top-of-the-range choice is of course the *Vrinda;* see "Cruising Kerala on the World's Smallest Luxury Liner," above.

LAKE VEMBANAD & SURROUNDS

A stay on the backwaters has become an essential stop on any Kerala itinerary; small wonder then that there has been a surge in development on the eastern shores of Vembanad Lake, with its spectacular sunset views to the west. The very latest of these is the **Radisson Plaza Resort & Spa,** which opened in September 2006 with much fanfare on a 7.2-hectare (18-acre) lake-facing property (© **0481/252-7272;** www. radisson.com/kumarakomin). However: Unless you book one of the rather pricey lake-view pool villas ($1,265–$1,725/£639–£871 double, depending on season)—which are indeed lovely, positioned as they are right on the shore of the lake, each with its own generously sized plunge pool—you are paying a lot of money (from $402/£203) for a nice new room with a view of another nice new room. For some reason the architects saw fit to design the entire resort around a man-made "lagoon," so rooms circle what is really just a rather large pond, and are built in double-story wings, so there's no hope of the garden one day creating pools of privacy. In the Radisson's defense, it offers everything you'd expect from a five-star resort, though it's hard to see why you wouldn't rather settle for Kumarakom Lake Resort. Far less luxurious than either of these, but offering lake-facing rooms at a fraction of the price, is nearby **Whispering Palms,** where a lake-facing cottage (make sure you specify "lake," not "lagoon") costs only $145 (£73) double (© **0484/238-1122;** www.abadhotels. com; including all meals, excluding 15% tax). **Backwater Ripples,** another relative newcomer that opened in 2005, also has 12 "lakeview rooms" that go for $165 to $275 (£83–£139) double (includes breakfast but not taxes; rate changes with season). Note that this is really the only category you want; the upstairs Executive Rooms aren't bad, but make sure it's an upstairs unit with a partial lake view. The small so-called "garden cottages" are just too bland and boring to spend your holiday in. Better-looking than these two, but situated near Alappuzha (on Vembanad Lake but without the sunset views), **Punnamada Backwater Resort** offers four lake-view villas that are charmingly decorated with four-poster beds, and a real bargain at $155 (£78) double (including breakfast, excluding 15% tax). But neither of these have the charm of the two top heritage resorts, Coconut Lagoon and Kumarakom Lake Resort (see below).

Coconut Lagoon ⭑⭑ *Kids*   If private alfresco showers and hammocks rather than room service and television are your idea of bliss, then this is your kind of lakeside idyll. Comprising reassembled wooden *tharavads* (traditional Kerala houses), all the cottages are set among coconut trees, hibiscus flowers, and specially grafted orchids, and the resort has splendid views of Lake Vembanad and the Kavanar River (though very few of the actual cottages do). Most accommodations are in the traditional *tharavads*. The best values are the "standard" heritage bungalows numbered 219 to 221, 223, and 225 to 228—these face the Kavanar River yet cost no more than those clustered around pathways. If you're traveling with kids (and this is a great place to come with a family, with three naturalists on staff to take you on walks in the adjoining bird sanctuary; there is also a butterfly garden and turtles to feed in the fish sanctuary), the best duplex-style "mansions" (an unfortunate choice of room description) are lake-facing units nos. 201 to 204. Some of the homes here date back to the early 1700s, and each historic teak, *anjili*, or jackfruit building has been reassembled according to ancient carpentry rules known as *thachu shashtra*. The emphasis here is on providing an authentic Kerala feel and having as little impact as possible on the natural environment—indeed, much of the resort's rustic charm lies in its simplicity. Pool cottages are set on the shores of the lake, but a lack of foresight has the pools (small) situated behind the rooms; for a private pool with a lake-facing view you will need to book at the new Radisson (see above), and pay dearly for the privilege. Coconut Lagoon is not as fancy as Kumarakom, but it has a wonderfully warm and laid-back atmosphere; it also does a great sunset cruise with live Indian musicians to serenade the setting sun. *Note:* Coconut Lagoon has a Green Leaf–certified Ayurvedic center, with a host of reasonably priced treatments, from Rs 575 ($14/£7) for a head massage to a general body massage for Rs 1,006 ($25/£12).

Kumarakom, Kottayam, Kerala. Contact c/o Casino Hotel, Willingdon Island, Kochi 682 003, Kerala. ✆ **0481/252-5834** through -5836. Fax 0481/252-4495. www.cghearth.com. coconutlagoon@cghearth.com. 50 units. High season $235–$270 (£119–£136) bungalow, $295–$330 (£149–£167) mansion, $470–$550 (£237–£278) pool villa; summer (low) season $110–$210 (£56–£106) all categories. $35–$50 (£18–£25) extra person. Rates include breakfast. AE, DC, MC, V. **Amenities:** 2 restaurants; bar; pool (cottages also have private pools); shop; 48-hr. laundry service; traditional performances; Ayurvedic center; houseboats; boat shuttle service; sunset cruise; hamper service; butterfly garden; village expeditions; yoga; bird-sanctuary visits; cooking demonstrations. *In room:* A/C, minibar, tea- and coffee-making facility.

Emerald Isle ⭑⭑   Yet another backwater treasure, and far from the resort crowd, this 150-year-old heritage villa, located between the Pamba River and Vembanad Lake, will suit travelers looking for an authentic Kerala backwater homestay experience. The magic begins when a boatman picks you up in a dugout canoe from "Landing Point" (next to Nazareth church) and rows you to the Job family home. There you are welcomed with filter coffee, tea, coconut water, or toddy. The home is sparklingly clean and has a glorious old-world charm—history-lovers will enjoy the 250-year-old property deed etched in palm leaves, newspaper cuttings from 1909, and even the ancient cooking pot–turned–coffee table in the living room; others might opt to do nothing but sink into the inviting wicker chairs. The en-suite guest rooms have ancestral carved teakwood furniture; ask for one of the two with great open-air bathrooms. (Only one room is air-conditioned, but the attached bathroom for this is small.) Freshly prepared meals are eaten with the family, but you can pick what's on the menu: Choose among chicken curry and *appams* (lace pancakes), *karimeen pollichathu* (pearl spot fish), *avoli* fry, *neimeen* curry, egg roasts, or catch of the day. The place is filled with history, which the Jobs are happy to share; they can also provide information on local culture, cuisine (you're invited into the kitchen), or anything that piques your curiosity. In addition, the Jobs will organize boat cruises, backwater trips, fishing, walks through paddy and coconut plantations, and village tours. Beautifully maintained, this retreat has 3 hectares (7 acres) of plantations and gardens and is a wonderful way to experience a Kerala that's a world away from the posher but sometimes sterile five-star accommodations.

Kanjooparambil-Manimalathara, Chathurthiakary P.O, Alleppey 688 511. ☏ **0477/270-3899**, 0477/309-0577, or 94-4707-7555. www.emeraldislekerala.com. info@emeraldislekerala.com. 4 units. Rs 4,000 ($98/£49) double; Rs 4,800 ($117/£59) A/C double. Children 5–12 Rs 350 ($9/£4). Rates include boat transfers and all meals. Rs 500 ($12/£6) extra Dec 15–Jan 15. AE, MC, V. **Amenities:** Ayurvedic massage; boat sightseeing cruises; free cooking classes; fishing; toddy tapping.

Kayaloram Lake Resort ★ *(Value)*

Kayaloram is a relatively intimate and very private lakeside resort, with watery views that seem to stretch forever (or at the very least to distant Kumarakom and Kollam). The 12 guest rooms are in four transplanted and remodeled 75-year-old *tharavads* with wraparound teak verandas and intricately patterned gables. Rooms are uncluttered and feature the de rigueur high-beamed ceilings, bamboo blinds, coir carpets, terra-cotta tiled floors, and paneled walls of dark jackfruit wood. Outdoor bathrooms come with open-air showers. The best views are from room nos. 2, 3, and 5, which face the lake, less than 10m (33 ft.) away, and allow you to watch the prawn fishermen's lights twinkling on the lake at night. During the day, the continuously changing spectacle of passing boats, canoes, and *chundan vallams* (snake boats) is equally magical. In keeping with the personalized service, individual lunch and dinner orders are taken a few hours in advance (Ayurvedic cuisine is available) to ensure that tastes, needs, and moods are adequately met. Complimentary sunset backwater cruises are also on offer; alternatively, the resort will organize longer backwater trips for you, for which you'll be picked up from the lawn outside your room. The manager is fond of taking guests on walking tours through some of the backwater villages located near the resort. The Ayurvedic treatments, while not extensive, are considered some of the best in India.

Punnamada, Alleppey 688 006. ☏ **0477/226-2931**, 0477/223-2040, or -1573. Fax 0477/225-2918. www.kayaloram. com. kayaloram@vsnl.com or kayaloram@satyam.net.in. 12 units. $95–$118 (£48–£59) pool-facing double; $118–$147 (£59–£74) lake-facing double. Rates include 2 transfers and breakfast. Meals are $7 each. AE, MC, V. **Amenities:** Restaurant; beer available; pool; doctor-on-call; Ayurvedic treatments. *In room:* A/C.

Kumarakom Lake Resort ★★★ *(Kids)*

This large award-winning resort is still the swankiest of the backwater resorts. Like so many of its predecessors, it comprises exquisite *tharavadu*-style carved teak and rosewood houses with curved terra-cotta tiled roofs, many of them reassembled originals salvaged from Kerala villages. The interiors are decidedly more luxurious than those of their neighbors, however, with rooms furnished to a very high standard; some feature expensive antiques and lovely examples of temple mural art but all have a sense of luxury. Each room has a tiny garden into which open granite-floored drench showers and basins have been installed. The main pool is at the water's edge with a bar adjacent—perfect for sundowners— while in the resort's newest section a second meandering pool snakes its way past the "pool villa" cottages, which means you can swim around the property directly from your back door. The best of these is number 144, which is right on the edge of the lake, with fabulous views. Most of the pool villas are surrounded by lush greenery and feel quite private, but some, like 138, face directly onto a public concourse. Should you fancy a night or two on the lake, the resort has a small fleet of well-equipped houseboats, among the most luxurious on the lake, and highly recommended if money is no object. The resort also has an excellent seafood restaurant (pity about the singer doing cover versions of "Hello" and other mainstream dirges) and an extensive Ayurvedic spa—one of Kerala's best (Green Leaf–accredited, of course), offering a wide range of treatments. It's not as well priced as Coconut Lagoon, but still incredibly affordable given the standards. And complimentary additions like the Indian "high tea" and sunset cruises offer a good sense of generosity.

Kumarakom N., Kottayam 686 566. ⓒ **0481/252-4900,** -4501, -5020, or -5021. Fax 0481/252-4987 or toll-free 600/ 425-5030. www.klresort.com. klresort@vsnl.com. 50 units plus 3 houseboats. There are 4 seasons, with May–Sept being lowest season and peak season from Dec 23–Jan 5. Rs 12,000–Rs 24,000 ($293–$585/£148–£296) luxury pavilion rooms (garden view); Rs 13,000–26,000 ($317–$634/£160–£321) meandering pool villa; Rs 14,000–Rs 28,500 ($341–$695/£173–£352) heritage lake-view; Rs 15,000–Rs 35,000 ($366–$854/£185–£432) meandering pool duplex villa; Rs 16,000–Rs 72,000 ($390–$1,756/£198–£889) heritage villa with private pool. Rates include breakfast. Houseboats are full board: Rs 15,000–Rs 22,500 ($365–$549/£185–£278) 1-bedroom; Rs 25,000–Rs 35,000 ($610–$854/£309–£432) 2-bedroom. AE, DC, MC, V. **Amenities:** 3 restaurants; 2 pools; gymnasium; Jacuzzi; cycling; children's play area; travel desk; business center; curio shop; salon; 24-hr. room service; babysitting; laundry; currency exchange; Green Leaf Ayurvedic center; yoga; billiards; table tennis; activity room; sightseeing/boat rides; fishing; cultural program; computer rentals. *In room:* A/C, TV, minibar, tea- and coffee-making facilities, hair dryer, electronic safe.

Olavipe ⊛⊛ ⓥalue   This is currently our favorite homestay in India, complete with a stately and authentic family home dating back to 1851, a sophisticated family with an illustrious and long history, a working farm (entertaining guests is just a sideline, pursued because the family is gregarious), a superb family cook, and very comfortable accommodations. With luck you may be there when a group of yuppies from Bangalore install themselves for a weekend break, in which case you've stumbled into your very own Indian house party. The fourth-generation Tharakans are clearly very proud of their ancestral home and roots, and the house feels rather like a private museum, with old farm records and implements and photographs and paintings charting events from their great-grandfather's time. Even more touching is the fact that almost every guest who has every stayed here is photographed, framed, and placed on the wall—a small but significant insight into how this family sees the people they share their home with; as clichéd as it sounds, here you truly do arrive as a stranger and leave a friend. There isn't much to do, nor is there a pool, so if you're the type that has to rush around and tick off a sightseeing list, you're likely to get bored, but if all you want to do is experience the rhythm of farm life (you'll be the only foreigners in the nearby village) and sit down to meals with an intellectually stimulating and charming family, prepared by the talented and crotchety 71-year-old chef, then you will feel blessed at

Olavipe indeed. Besides, Kochi is less than an hour away, and Antony and his sophisticated wife, Rema, will arm you with the best shopping tips in town!

Olavipe, 25km (16 miles) from Kochi. ☏ **0484/240-2410** or 0478/252-2255. www.olavipe.com. homestay@olavipe.com. 8 units. Rs 7,000 ($171/£86) double. Includes all meals. **Amenities:** Cycling; assistance with sightseeing; Internet access; canoes; windsurfing; table tennis; badminton; basketball; volleyball; trails.

Philipkutty's Farm ★★ *Value*   This is a real gem, ideal for those who find the whole resort experience a little pretentious but want more privacy than the average homestay offers. Here you get to experience first-hand the hospitality of a local farming family, albeit in the privacy of your very own waterfront cottage, surrounded by 18 hectares (45 acres) that include banana, mango, nutmeg, coconut, and pepper plantations. The first villa (Chempakam) was designed by Karl Damschen, a Swiss architect who combined traditional Keralite design—open-plan living, carved wooden doors, and a veranda—with personal touches; the rest, designed by a Kochi architect, have separate living areas. The breezy cottages (up to 18 windows/doors to create a wonderful flow of air), named after flowers growing in the courtyard, feature antiques, while the en-suite bathrooms are modern; one of the villas has two en-suite bedrooms and separate living area, ideal for a family. Hosts Vinod and Anu Mathew treat guests as part of the family yet provide privacy (they stay in a separate house) and time to soak up the tranquillity. Vinod's mother and Anu are the kitchen genies, preparing three marvelous feasts a day, and you're welcome to watch them cooking in the kitchen. Ask for your breakfast to be served in the pleasant open-air pavilion. The only real drawback is that there's no pool, but some guests cool off as locals do, by venturing into the waters of Vembanad Lake. As it is, you're taken on informative excursions of the plantations and get to enjoy a free backwater cruise on a canoe. Children are very warmly welcomed.

Pallivathukal, Ambika Market P.O., Vechoor, Kottayam. ☏ **04829/27-6529**, -6530, or 98950-75130. www.philipkuttysfarm.com. 5 units. Rates vary across 3 seasons. Rs 5,000–Rs 11,000 ($125–$275/£62–£136) double; Rs 6,000–Rs 12,000 ($150–$300/£74–£148) 2-bed Villa. Children 6–12 Rs 1,500–Rs 2,000 ($37–$49/£19–£25). Children over 12 Rs 2,500–Rs 3,000 ($61–$73/£31–£37). Rates include all meals, tea and coffee, sunset cruise on country boat, and farm excursions. Credit cards for overseas bank deposits only. **Amenities:** Dining facilities. *In room:* Minibar, tea- and coffee-making facilities.

Privacy ★★★   If you're more of a "villa stay" person and hate the impersonal resort vibe, this is one of the top options on the backwaters: two secluded traditional bungalows situated at the edge of Vembanad Lake. The waterfront suite is exactly that, with superb unobstructed views from your bed, while the cottage is set slightly farther back, behind the pool and deck, with its own, more traditional charm. The location and atmosphere certainly live up to its name, with a maximum of only two parties present and even then set quite far apart from each other, meeting only for meals (if you choose) and at the pool. Besides the fabulous location, interiors are in a class of their own, designed by talented owner Joerg Drechsel (of super-stylish Malabar House), who incorporated local skills and elements with his personal take on Kerala style. Polished black-oxide flooring contrasts with blue and mustard-yellow fabrics in the bedrooms, latticed walls, large mirrors framed in teakwood, antiques, and traditional masks. On the porch, wooden rocking chairs with extendable leg-rests invite hours of relaxation. The front door is just steps from the lake, where *kettuvallams* idle and birds swoop down to catch fish. Completing the idyll, guests enjoy the personal attention of a dedicated chef and housekeeper. Privacy may make you feel a million miles from anywhere, but it's only 45km (28 miles) from Kochi and 15km (9⅓ miles) from the backwater-access town of Alleppey.

Reservations through Malabar House Residency, 1/268–1/269 Parade Rd., Fort Kochi 682 001. © **0484/221-6666.** Fax 0484/221-7777. www.malabarhouse.com. 2 units. 200€–330€ ($272–$449/£135–£223) waterfront suite; 120€–195€ ($163–$265/£81–£132) 2-bedroom cottage. 30€ ($41/£20) extra bed. Rates include breakfast. Cottage rented to 1 party at a time. MC, V. Amenities: Pool; mountain bikes; electric country boat. *In room:* TV, fax machine, kitchenette w/tea- and coffee-making facility.

BEACHFRONT: MARARIKULAM TO ALAPPUZHA

The beachfront options stretch from an area known as Mararikulam south to the backwaters town of Alapphuzha. Of the many lodgings, two options are leagues ahead: Marari Beach and Raheem Residency, both reviewed below. Bar these, two more are well worth considering, among them the beach homes, particularly if you like a holiday that moves at your own pace.

Pollathai is a contender to nearby Marari Beach resort, offering a more exclusive feel with only 10 units (five more planned by late 2008), most in single-unit cottages scattered throughout the property (www.oldcourtyard.com; Rs 5,250–Rs 13,000/ $128–$317/£65–£160 double, depending on season and including breakfast). It only opened in September 2006, so everything is still in good nick, with attractive furnishings (book cottage number 4, and you have the most private unit); the beach is an 8-minute walk away though. That said, the exclusive atmosphere comes at the expense of important facilities like Green Leaf–accredited Ayurvedic treatments and the generally high standards of service you get at Marari.

If the whole resort experience leaves you cold, your best bet is to rent your very own beach bungalow: **Marari Beach Homes** is a collection of renovated fishermen's cottages located right on the beach (© **0477/224-3535;** www.mararibeachhomes.com; $90–$260/£45–£131, self-catering rate dependent on season/house; breakfast $5/£3, other meals $10/£5). Make sure you book Papaya House, not only because it's closest to the beach, large (two bedrooms, outside bathroom), and with lovely sea views from the dining table and recliners on the deep balcony, but it's freestanding, so you can imagine you're in your own beach villa far from civilization. Second best is Wood House, slightly set back but with sea views from the small terrace, furnished with tables and chairs, and, round the back, outside bathrooms; the only drawback is the small size and shared wall. The other houses currently look a bit too dirty and disheveled to bother with. Amenities throughout are very basic (some would say rundown), but you really do feel as if you've been washed ashore on some primitive beach idyll, and if you don't mind forgoing resort luxuries, this is a close contender to Karikkathi Beach House in the south (see "Chandra, Surya & Vizhinjam," p. 204).

Marari Beach 👫👫 *(Kids)* This is a truly great beach resort, with every amenity and facility laid on, and a good choice if you have neither the time nor the inclination to travel farther south to the better-known Kovalam beach resorts. It has a big-resort vibe, with 58 comfortable and very spacious (but relatively basic) stand-alone thatched cottages spread over 15 hectares (36 acres) of lawns and pathways enveloped by coconut groves. Everything is very far set back from the beach (you can hardly see the sea, even from the best rooms, which happen to be nos. 18–20, located along the beach-facing front, and conveniently located near the bar, restaurants, and pool). But the sea is just one of Marari's many laid-back charms, from great tours to Kochi, Alleppey, and farther afield to slick cooking demonstrations. The extensive Ayurvedic center (Green Leaf) is also considered one of Kerala's best, serviced by excellent doctors and therapists who offer wonderful pampering at really reasonable rates. And while the size of the resort is a little off-putting, it is comforting to know how committed management is to eco-friendly undertakings (like all CGH Earth properties), including an effective water-recycling plant, an organic vegetable garden, rainwater harvesting, and a solar-heated hot-water project. But the best aspect is the resort's *au naturelle* setting, with a 25km (16-mile) beach shared only with fellow guests, local fishermen, and a Laurel-and-Hardy duo who serve as the resort's lifeguards.

Mararikulam, Alleppey 688 549, Kerala. ⓒ **0478/286-3801** through -3809. Fax 0478/286-3810. www.cghearth. com. 62 units. $200–$220 (£101–£111) garden villa; $350–$410 (£177–£207) pool villa; $410–$465 (£207–£235) deluxe pool villa. $40 extra bed. Rates include breakfast. AE, DC, MC, V. **Amenities:** 2 restaurants; 2 bars; pool; 2 tennis courts; bicycles; car hire; business center; shop; laundry; doctor-on-call; currency exchange; volleyball; badminton; Ayurvedic center; yoga; numerous excursions including houseboat trips and elephant visits; cooking demonstrations; sari and dhoti demonstration; library. *In room:* A/C, minibar, tea- and coffee-making facility, safe.

Raheem Residency 🌟🌟   An absolutely charming guesthouse, located opposite the main Alappuzha beach, with a very organized travel desk to arrange all your sightseeing, be it shopping for temple umbrellas in town, arranging a four-stop temple walking tour, riding an elephant, or booking a short- or long-term houseboat cruise. The bungalow, built in 1868 by Gujurati traders, was skillfully renovated in 2003 by Bibi, an Irish expat, and her Indian business partner, Flemin, to create seven gracious guest rooms catering to guests looking for a low-key boutique-style destination. The highlight of your stay is likely to be dinner, taken early on the covered but otherwise open-to-the-elements rooftop and the perfect theater seat from which to watch the locals thronging to the beach at sunset (particularly on a Sun) or, on the other end, spy on young adults receiving their first driving lessons, carefully avoiding the boys playing cricket in the dusty park. It's by no means a five-star hotel, but staff is attentive and charming, and the whole experience is very nurturing. Note that water is solar powered, so it takes a while for the shower to heat up and can be a little erratic. ***Tip:*** If you are a keen shopper, Bibi is full of great advice. Don't miss a trip to the famous **Bhima Jewellers** (established here in 1925, with only certified gold on sale, and branches now throughout India) located on Mullackal, the main shopping street in Alleppey, as well as the **Maheshwari Fabric Showroom** and the wooden handicrafts near the KSRTC bus stand—all within walking distance from the Residency; ask for a map.

Beach Rd., Alleppey. ⓒ **0477/223-9767** or -0767. www.raheemresidency.com. 7 units. Doubles: low season 90€– 160€ ($122–$218/£61–£108); high season (Oct–Mar) 130€–250€ ($177–$340/£88–£169). Extra bed 30€ ($41/ £20). Rates include breakfast; exclude 15% tax. Meals 8€–15€ ($10–$20/£5–£10). MC, V. **Amenities:** Restaurant; bar; pool; bicycle hire; travel and tour assistance (www.keralatours.com); car hire; room service; laundry; doctor-on-call; currency exchange; Internet access; Ayurvedic center; in-room beauty treatment on request. *In room:* A/C.

3 Thiruvananthapuram (Trivandrum) & Varkala

1,200km (744 miles) S of Mumbai

Thiruvananthapuram ("City of the Sacred Serpent") is the mouthful of a name given to Kerala's seaside state capital, but thankfully almost everyone calls it Trivandrum (if you want to impress locals, though, try saying it slowly: "Tiru-vanan-tha-poo-ram"). Although the city has some interesting museums and a temple that's of great significance to Hindus (and off-limits to non-Hindus), the main reason you'll find yourself here is to utilize the city's excellent transportation connections and head for the beautiful beaches that surround it. North lies Varkala, which has been a popular seaside vacation spot for more than 70 years—no doubt because of its proximity to Trivandrum (a mere 10- to 20-min. drive south)—and as a result has become overcommercialized and saturated with tourist-hungry businesses. If you're looking for Kerala's most stunning, upmarket seaside options, many with more-or-less private beaches, you'll have to travel farther south of Kovalam (see "From Kovalam to the Tip of India," later in this chapter).

ESSENTIALS

VISITOR INFORMATION As the state capital, Trivandrum has plenty of outlets for tourist information. There are two **Tourist Information Counters** at the airport; one is run by the Government of India (© **0471/250-2298**) and the other by the Government of Kerala (© **0471/250-1085;** daily 10am–5pm, closed a flexible hr. for lunch); the latter also has counters at the Central Bus Station in Thampanoor (© **0471/232-7224**) and at the Railway Station (© **0471/233-4470**), both of which are open daily from 8am to 8pm. Kerala's **Department of Tourism** operates a 24-hour toll-free information line (© **1600/425-4747**). Also providing tourist information is **Kerala Tourism** (Park View, Museum Rd., opposite the museum complex; © **0471/ 232-1132;** daily 10am–5pm). For local tour information, go to the **Kerala Tourism Development Corporation** or KTDC (at Hotel Chaithram, adjacent to Central Bus Station in Thampanoor; © **0471/233-0031;** daily 6:30am–9:30pm).

In Kovalam, visit the **Tourist Facilitation Centre** (© **0471/248-0085;** Mon–Sat 10am–1pm and 1:30–5pm) at the ITDC Compound. Besides giving information, the center assists with tour bookings, car hires, boat rides, and lodging. *Tip:* Consider any government-owned accommodations carefully.

GETTING THERE & AWAY By Road As mentioned earlier, Kerala is ideal for exploration with a hired car and driver; roads are relatively good, the countryside is spectacular, and Trivandrum is connected by principal roads and highways with all parts of the country. For car/driver hire recommendations, see "Guided Tours," below. Super Deluxe bus services are operated by the **Kerala State Road Transport Corporation** (© **0471/232-3886** or 0471/246-3497 for the Central Bus Station in Thampanoor; © **0471/246-3029** for the City Bus Stand in Fort; www.keralartc.com; mdkeralartc@yahoo.com). Private operators run so-called deluxe coaches to more distant towns and cities in South India, but note that most overnight buses stop regularly, making sleep impossible. Make sure you've booked a nonstop overnight (Volvo) bus between the major cities. Though the journey is long, it's relatively comfortable and cheap (an overnight bus from Bangalore to Kochi for instance, takes 10 to 11 hours and costs less than Rs 1,000 ($24/£12); buses are air-conditioned, have reclining seats, usually provide blankets, and stop only two or three times for toilet/food breaks.

By Air Trivandrum is connected by air to Delhi, Mumbai, Kochi, Chennai, Bangalore, Hyderabad, and Tiruchirapali. The **international airport** (© **0471/250-1424** for international flight information) is served by all the Indian airlines including **Jet Airways, Kingfisher, Paramount,** and **Spice Jet** (airlines rated the most reliable, with the best service standards). There are also international flights from various Asian cities, including Dubai, Abu Dhabi, and nearby Malé in the Maldives. The airport is 6km (3¾ miles) from the city center, and you can pick up a set-fee prepaid taxi for the journey into town inside the terminal, or shell out a little more and arrange with John Thomas for one of his drivers to pick you up (Kerala Adventures; touch@kerala adventures.com; Rs 450–Rs 660/$11–$16/£6–£8 depending on where you need to go; Rs 630–Rs 920/$15–$22/£8–£11 for A/C vehicle).

By Train There are regular trains between Trivandrum and other important destinations in Kerala, including Kochi (under 4 hr.), Alleppey (3½ hr.), Kollam (1½ hr.), and Varkala (1 hr.). If you're coming from Chennai in Tamil Nadu, the overnight **Trivandrum Mail** is convenient. Trains also reach India's southernmost point, Kanyakumari; the journey takes around 2½ hours.

Thiruvananthapuram **Central Railway Station** is just east of M.G. Road, on Station Road; for general railway inquiries, call 🕐 **131.** For reservations, call 🕐 **132** or 0471/232-3066, or you can access the **Interactive Voice Response** service by calling 🕐 **1361.**

GETTING AROUND **By Taxi & Auto-Rickshaw** In this region you will probably need a taxi from the airport (or your hired car and driver if you've been traveling around the state) to take you to your Kovalam resort; after this you're unlikely to need transport, with the exception of a possible brief foray to a nearby market. For this you're best off using a rickshaw; these usually charge upward of Rs 12 (30¢/15p) for the first kilometer; Rs 4 (10¢/5p) for each kilometer thereafter. A one-way trip from Kovalam into Trivandrum (or vice versa) will cost around Rs 150 ($3.40/£1.70). To hire a car and driver, see "Guided Tours," below.

By Motorcycle & Scooter You can rent an Enfield or Honda on a daily basis from **Kerala Adventures** (🕐 **0471/231-0796**) in Trivandrum.

GUIDED TOURS **KTDC** (Hotel Chaithram, adjacent Central Bus Station, Thampanoor; 🕐 **0471/233-0031;** Mon–Sat 6:30am–9:30pm) organizes sightseeing tours in and around the city. Because they are aimed primarily at domestic tourists, they are not recommended. A far better option is to hire a private car and driver and plan a personalized trip from Trivandrum. We recommend you arrange this through local outfit **Kerala Adventures** (House No 101 Geeth, Golflinks Rd.; 🕐 **0471/243-3398** or 0471/231-9548; 24-hr. emergency contact no. 0999/507-6829; www.kerala adventure.com; touch@keralaadventure.com or comvoyge@vsnl.net). You could also get a quote from **Sita World Travel** (🕐 **0471/247-0921** or 0471/257-3180; trv@ sitaindia.com).

FAST FACTS: Trivandrum

Airlines The airline with the most frequent flights is **Jet Airways** (🕐 **0471/272-1018** or **-8864**); you can also contact Jet at the airport (🕐 **0471/250-0710** or 0471/250-0860).

Area Code The area code for **Trivandrum** is **0471.**

ATMs Numerous ATMs in Trivandrum accept Visa and MasterCard; note that there are far fewer facilities south of the capital, so best to draw cash for incidentals in the city.

Banks You can exchange currency and traveler's checks at any bank; a conveniently located bank is **Canara Bank** at Spencer Junction, M.G. Road (🕐 **0471/233-1536;** Mon–Fri 10am–2pm and 2:30–3:30pm, Sat 10am–noon). Alternatively use one of the many ATMs throughout the city.

Car Hire See "Guided Tours," above.

Currency Exchange See "Banks," above. The Thomas Cook is also located on M.G. Road (🕐 **0471/233-8140** or **-8141**).

Drugstores **City Medical Service** (Statue; ✆ **0471/246-1770**) or **Central Medical Stores** (Statuel; ✆ **0471/246-0923**).

Emergencies For fires and other emergencies, including medical services, call ✆ **101.**

Hospitals Medical tourism is becoming quite a trend in Kerala; here are a few reputable options in Trivandrum: **Kerala Institute of Medical Sciences,** P.B. No.1, Anayara; ✆ 0471/244-7575 or 0471/244-7676; www.kimskerala.com. **SUT Hospital,** Pattom; ✆ 0471/244-7566; www.suthospital.com. **Sree Chitirathirunal Medical Centre,** Medical College; ✆ 0471/244-3152. **Cosmopolitan Hospital,** Pahaya Rd., Kumarapuram; ✆ 0471/244-81182. **Regional Cancer Centre,** Medical College; ✆ 0471/244-2541; www.rcctvm.org.

Internet Access Look for the signs for **Sify iway** or **Reliance Webworld**—these Internet centers usually provide faster connections than most.

Police Dial ✆ **100.** Thampanoor Police Station (✆ **0471/233-1843**) is on Station Road. For road accidents, call the police **help line** at ✆ **98-4610-0100.**

Post Office The **General Post Office** (✆ **0471/247-3071**; Mon–Sat 8am–7pm, Sun 10am–4pm) is along M.G. Road.

WHAT TO SEE & DO IN TRIVANDRUM

With palm-lined beaches beckoning, Trivandrum is unlikely to detain you longer than it takes to arrange your transfer out of there, but it has a number of interesting buildings, including the stately **Secretariat and Legislative Assembly,** situated along Mahatma Gandhi Road, which is the main boulevard and center of activity through town. M.G. Road runs more or less north to south and links the two most significant areas of tourist interest: the **Museum Complex,** to the north of the city; and the Fort area, which houses **Sree Padmanabhaswamy Temple** and **Puthen Malika Palace Museum,** to the south. It is possible to walk from one area to the other (about 45 min.), and there are numerous shops en route. Alternatively, auto-rickshaws continuously buzz along the road's length, and you will have no trouble catching a ride from one area to the other. It's worth wandering M.G. just to shop; if this is all you feel like doing, don't bother with the sights and make a beeline for **Natesan's** (✆ **0471/233-1594;** www.natesansantiqarts.com), the city's largest and most reputable antiques and art dealer, with original bronze, silver, teak, sandalwood, stone, and wood carvings as well as manufacturer's replicas. **Hastakala** (Gandhariamman Kovil Rd.; ✆ **0484/233-1627**) specializes in Kashmiri goods including hand-woven carpets, quality Pashminas, and Tibetan and tribal jewelry. For a uniquely Keralan souvenir, go to the **SMSM Institute** (behind the Secretarial Statue; ✆ **0471/233-0298**) and pick up an Aranmula mirror, or browse the **Gram Sree Craft Centre.** Book lovers could spend a day in **DC Books,** the biggest in Kerala (www.dcbooks.com); there are four branches in the city, but your best bet is to head to the one in Karimpanal Statue Avenue. And if you're looking for clothing for all ages, **Aiyappas,** opposite the SL Theatre Complex (✆ **0484/233-1627**), is a good place to start, while **Karalkada** (www.karalkada.com; ✆ **0471/2474520**) has the most superb hand-woven cotton fabrics, saris, *kavanis, kurthas,* and dhotis, and is *the* place locals come to shop when looking to buy something special for an imminent wedding or religious ceremony.

Museum Complex ⊛ Many of Trivandrum's cultural sites are clustered in a huge formal public garden at the northern end of the city. **Napier Museum** occupies an early Indo-Saracenic building, created in 1880 in honor of the then-governor of Madras, Lord Napier. This priceless collection includes excellent 12th-century Chola bronzes, wood carvings, stone idols, and fascinating musical instruments, while more unique pieces include a temple chariot, a 400-year-old clock, and a royal cot made from herbal wood. Fine-art enthusiasts should visit **Sri Chitra Art Gallery,** which holds an assortment of miniature paintings from the Rajput, Moghul, and Tanjore schools, as well as more exotic works from Japan, China, Bali, and Tibet. One of the country's foremost artists, Raja Ravi Varma (1848–1905), whose well-known oil paintings explore Hindu mythological themes, is represented here. **K.C.S. Paniker Gallery** is a wholly unnecessary diversion, as is the **Natural History Museum** (unless you want to see stuffed animals and dolls in traditional costumes)—the anthropological exhibit at Kolkata's Indian Museum is far superior. And stay away from the **zoo,** particularly if you're an animal lover—like most zoos in India, it lacks the funding to build bigger, more humane habitats for its animals.

Museum Rd. Purchase tickets for all museums at the ticket booth. Admission Rs 6 (15¢/10p). Thurs–Sun and Tues 10am–4:45pm; Wed 1:30–4:45pm.

Puthenmalika (Kuthiramalika) Palace Museum ⊛⊛ A secret, private passage is believed to connect Padmanabhaswamy Temple with this Travancore-style palace, built in the early–18th century by the social reformer Maharajah Swathi Thirunal Balarama Varma, a poet and distinguished musician. Known as the Horse Palace because of the 122 carved horse brackets that buttress the exterior walls, the buildings include elaborate carvings, among them two extravagant thrones—one made from 25 elephant tusks, another made entirely from Bohemian crystal. Visitors are also allowed into the maharaja's music room, from where you get the same view of the temple that was apparently a source of inspiration to the erstwhile ruler. Despite the value of much of the collection, the buildings are in need of renovation; the beauty of the carved teakwood ceilings and collected objets d'art are sometimes masked by insufficient lighting and neglectful curatorship. You'll be taken around by an "official" guide— obviously he'll require a small tip.

100m (328 ft.) from the temple, Fort. ℂ 0471/247-3952. Entrance Rs 20 (45¢/25p) adult, Rs 10 (25¢/15p) children. Tues–Sun 8:30am–1pm and 3–5:30pm.

Shri Padmanabhaswamy Temple ⊛ This Dravidian-style Vishnu temple, said to be the largest in Kerala, may be off-limits to non-Hindus, but the "temple guides" manage to target foreigners with great ease, leading them to the obligatory spots from which to photograph the seven-story-high entrance tower, or *goparum,* which is pretty much all that can be viewed from the outside. The temple is believed to have come into existence on the first day of the Kaliyuga era (3102 B.C.)—legend has it that the temple "materialized" after a sage prayed to Vishnu asking him to appear in a form that he could comprehend with his limited human vision—but the greater part of the complex was built during the 18th century. The temple is fronted by a massive tank, where devotees take ritual dips. Alongside a promenade are stalls selling ritual items, religious souvenirs, and flowers for use inside the temple.

Fort, Trivandrum. ℂ 0471/245-0233. Closed to non-Hindus. 4am–noon and 5–7:30pm.

ARTS & ENTERTAINMENT

Shree Karthika Thirunal Theatre (alongside Lucia Continental Hotel; ℭ 0471/
247-1335), in Trivandrum's Fort district, holds regular classical dance-theater performances (mostly Karnatic, but also Hindustani) throughout the year. The theater
has its own company but hosts outside groups showcasing various genres, including
Kathakali, Mohiniattam, and Bharatanatyam.

You can observe **Kalaripayattu** martial arts classes, and even arrange special performances or lecture demonstrations, through **C.V.N. Kalari Sangham** (Fort, Trivandrum;
ℭ 0471/247-4182; fax 0471/245-8996; www.cvnkalarikerala.com). Established in
1956, this institution has represented India at numerous international festivals.

WHERE TO STAY & DINE

Walk up the spiraling incline of **Maveli Coffee House** (between the Tourist Reception Centre and KSRTC bus stand; daily 7:30am–10pm), if only to be able to say
afterward that you've dined in one of the world's oddest restaurants, which somewhat
resembles a squat, ocher-colored version of Pisa's leaning tower. Located diagonally
opposite the railway station, this unique coffeehouse was designed by Laurie Baker,
the renowned English architect who pioneered environmentally sustainable architecture and worked on hundreds of projects in southern India before passing away in
Trivandrum, his adopted home, in 2007. It's a favorite hangout for the locals and an
interesting spot in which to spend some time rubbing shoulders with the groundlings
and businesspeople who come here for their *idlis, dosas,* and *chai* or coffee.

If you're exploring the Secretariat, head across the road to **Arul Jyothi** (Mahatma
Gandhi Rd.; daily 6:30am–10pm). The capital's civil servants pile in here at lunchtime,
when there's much ordering of *thalis* (the ubiquitous platter featuring Indian breads and
various curries and chutneys) and wonderful *masala dosas.* If you're keen to browse newspapers from back home, stop at the British Library nearby; it has a good collection of
magazines and international dailies (just show your passport to enter). Alternatively,
Kadaleevanam (Prakrithi Bhojanasala Hotel Mas Annexe, near the SL Theatre, Chet-
tikulangara; ℭ 0471/247-2780; daily 8am–9:30pm; no credit cards), where the owners pride themselves on the fact that they have no fridges or freezers (all food, cooked on
wood fires, is served within 3 hr. or not offered to customers) and use only organically
grown vegetables and whole grains. The set meal will run you a mere Rs 100 ($2/£1).

Warning: Banana Chips Are Addictive

Although tourists are normally advised to avoid street food, there's one kind of
street snack you can sample without a problem in Trivandrum. Banana chips are
a Keralite's favorite snack, and you'll see *thattu kadas,* temporary food trolleys
(particularly at night), with men slicing and frying bananas in coconut oil right
on the street, almost all over Kerala. Buy them piping-hot and lightly salted—
they're even more scrumptious than potato chips. Good spots to buy these
fresh are near the British Library, or at a small shop in Kaithamukku (about
3km/2 miles west of the central train station), where A. Kannan has been frying some of the best banana chips in Kerala for close to 15 years. Note that
banana chips come in myriad flavors depending on the variety of banana used.
Those made with ripe bananas are slightly sweet, but we suggest you go for
the thinly sliced variety. Be warned, however: They are seriously addictive.

For more salubrious surrounds, the smart **Tiffany's** at the Muthoot Plaza is rated by locals as the best restaurant in town (Punnen Rd.; © **0471/233-7733;** daily 12:30–3pm and 7:30–10:30pm).

There is little reason not to head south before nightfall, but if you really must stay in the city, **Muthoot Plaza** is (until the proposed Taj opens) Trivandrum's best hotel (© **0471/233-7733;** www.themuthootplaza.com; from Rs 4200/$102/£52 double, including breakfast). A seven-story steel-and-glass hangout for foreign visitors and businesspeople who come to the state capital to pay *baksheesh* to various government representatives, Muthoot is functional, with good service and a convenient location, but it has no pool. A more interesting option, and within walking distance of the Muthoot is **Varikatt Heritage,** a green oasis off bustling Puynnen Road. This is the best homestay in town, filled with beautiful furniture and presided over by the welcoming Colonel Roy Kuncheria, who enjoys playing the gracious host to a handful of guests. Make sure you book one of the three rooms off of the front veranda; these are by far the best (© **0471-233-6057;** www.varikattheritage.com; roy@varikatt.com; Rs 3,500–Rs 4,500/$85–$110/£43–£55). Budget travelers just looking for a decent en-suite room for the night should head for **Ariya Nivaas Hotel** (© **0471/233-0789;** www.ariyanivaas.com), an office-block-style hotel that offers good, clean lodging conveniently located near the Central Railway Station for Rs 1,000 ($24/£12). Staff is friendly and can help with travel arrangements. The hotel has a decent restaurant and a useful 24-hour checkout policy. It's often full, so book in advance.

NORTH OF TRIVANDRUM: THE RED CLIFFS OF VARKALA

A 55km (34-mile) drive north of Trivandrum (1 hr. by train), the seaside resort of Varkala draws numerous Hindu pilgrims who come to worship in the 2,000-year-old **Sri Janardhana Swami Temple** and ritualistically cleanse themselves in the mineral spring waters that gush from Varkala's ruby-red laterite cliffs. The cliffs overlook the aptly named "Beach of Redemption." Varkala attracts scores of backpackers searching for an untouched beach paradise—and a decade ago, they might have found just that. Over the years, hawkers and shack-dwellers have drifted in and set up shop along the tops of the cliffs; the coconut palms have been replaced by cheap guesthouses and open-air cafes; and children flog cheap jewelry, yards of cloth, and back-to-nature hippie gear.

Nonetheless, being a holy beach, the sand at the base of the cliffs stays relatively free of human pollution—it's neither a convenient public ablution facility nor a waste-dumping ground. Instead, devotees of Vishnu attend to earnest *puja* sessions, offering banana leaves piled with boiled rice and brightly colored marigolds to be carried away by the ocean. Usually, the sand is soft and lovely, and you can find a quiet cove for sunbathing without the crowds that are inescapable in Kovalam. In fact, you can find relative peace and calm if you restrict your beach activities to the morning; by lunchtime the gawkers (female bathers are advised to be discreet), hawkers, and dreadlocked Europeans start to file in, and it's time to venture back to the hotel or guesthouse.

Other activities for visitors here include Kathakali demonstrations, elephant rides, village tours, and backwater trips. You can also take a pleasant evening walk (or auto-rickshaw ride) to the cliffs to visit Sunset Point. If you don't want to walk back, keep the rickshaw for your return trip (round-trip Rs 30–Rs 40/70¢–90¢/35p–45p; more if you want to go farther up the cliff).

WHERE TO STAY & DINE

Varkala has plenty of accommodation choices, virtually all below par, with the predominant market clearly more the backpacker or budget end of the spectrum. Bucking this trend is the classy **Villa Jacaranda** ★★. By far the best option in Varkala, this is a genteel four-room guesthouse on South Cliff, with gorgeous rooms and a lovely garden (© **0470/261-0296;** www.villa-jacaranda.biz; Rs 3,600–Rs 4,400/$88–$107/ £44–£54 double). In the evenings you'll return to your candle-lit veranda and hosts who make you feel well and truly pampered; book room 2 or 4 and you'll have the additional pleasure of sea views. The only drawback? No pool. And, for families, no kids.

If you prefer hotels, your best bet is the newly opened **Hindustan Beach Retreat** (© **0470/260 4254/55;** www.hindustanbeachretreat.com; standard double Rs 4,000–Rs 5,500/$98–$134/£49–£68 depending on season; executive Rs 500/$12/£6 more). Hindustan is an unattractive five-story hotel, but it's right on the beach and has a pool. Rooms, all with views of the Arabian Sea, are comfortable and bathrooms spick-and-span, but it's all a bit sterile; on the other hand this is the closest you get to the beach, lined with casual resto-shacks (one the best of which in 2007 was the Somatheeram Beach Restaurant), so you could spend the day with your toes in the sand pretending to be a beach bum and then retreat to your middle-class box.

Neatly set on the slopes of Varkala's red North Cliffs and overlooking a beautiful length of coastline, the **Taj Garden Retreat** (© **0470/260-3000;** www.tajhotels.com; from $110/£55 double) has long considered itself Varkala's premier hotel; certainly it wins first prize for the most fantastic gardens and longest list of facilities, but it is ugly, with the pastel rooms substandard chain hotel fare. Worst of all, you have to drive to reach the beach; it's one thing getting there, but a real pain trying to get back. Staff members have the usual touch of Taj arrogance; with nothing to back it up, it's very irritating here. A better bet is the less flashy but more professionally and warmly run **Krishnatheeram** (© **0470/215-6444;** www.krishnatheeram.com), with an excellent Ayurvedic center and lovely lawned alfresco dining area with sea views; a "black beach" is a 15-minute stroll away. There are only 18 rooms, all very simply constructed with palms and bamboo and furnished with the basics (all en-suite); the best located are called "A Thanal" and "B Thanal" and go for Rs 3,500 ($85/£43); rates are reduced in the summer.

The two best places to eat in Varkala, with clean kitchens, good food, nice atmosphere, and great views, are **Clafoutis** (Papasham Beach, North Cliff) and **Cafe Del Mar.** Clafoutis has a large menu with Indian, Thai, Italian, and Chinese options; Cafe Del Mar has a much smaller menu, offering Indian, Italian, and Mexican options. Both serve good fresh fish and seafood.

4 From Kovalam to the Tip of India

1,216km (754 miles) S of Mumbai

A mere 16km (10 miles) south of Trivandrum, Kovalam has been a haunt for beach tourism since the 1930s, but its fame as a coastal idyll has wrought the inevitable. Discovered by hippies and then by charter tour groups, it is now home to a virtually unbroken string of holiday resorts, its once-virgin charm plundered by low-rise concrete hotels. Even so, Kovalam's three crescent-shaped sandy beaches, flanked by rocky promontories and coconut palm groves, remain quite impressive. You can watch fishermen ply the waters in so-called catamarans (derived from the local word *kattu-maram*, these are simply a few timbers lashed together) as they have for centuries, at night assisted by the red-and-white lighthouse that beams from Kovalam's southern-most beach.

Lighthouse Beach is, in fact, a guiding light to the charter types, and where you'll find the bulk of cheap hotels, restaurants, and bars, with fishing-net-strewn Hawa Beach and less-crowded Samudra Beach lying to the north. After the rigors of India's crowded cities and comfort-free public transport, budget travelers are lured by the easy, comfortable (and high) life offered here, often staying until money (or good weather) runs out. You can rent umbrellas and watersports equipment along the beach, or hop aboard a fishing boat for a cruise out to sea. Stalls sell colorful fabrics, pseudo-ethnic hippie trinkets, and fresh fruit, fish, and coconut water; music wafts from shack-style cafes, and unofficial bars survive strict liquor laws by serving beer in ceramic mugs and teapots. (***Party animals note:*** The vibe at Kovalam is far, far tamer than Goa's.)

Immediately south of Kovalam is **Vizhinjam Beach,** the site of the erstwhile capi-tal of southern Kerala's first dynastic rulers and, between the 8th and 13th centuries, a major natural port for local kingdoms. Now a poor fishing hamlet of thatched huts overlooked by a pink mosque, Vizhinjam is an interesting contrast to the tourist hub-bub of Kovalam; swimming here, however, is dangerous, no doubt the reason for its relatively untouched atmosphere. A number of shrines are found in Vizhinjam, including a rock-cut cave enclosing a shrine with a sculpture of Dakshinamurthy; the outer wall of the cave includes a half-complete relief depicting Lord Shiva and his con-sort, Parvati.

Farther south, the Ayurvedic resorts that can still lay claim to the beach idyll that put Kovalam on the map dot the coast (see "Where to Stay & Dine," below). Visitors staying at any of these should seriously consider a day trip that takes in **Padmanab-hapuram Palace** (see review below), on the way to **Kanyakumari,** India's southern-most tip, where you can enjoy one of the most interesting cultural experiences on the subcontinent (see box below).

From a terraced viewing area, you will see two rock islands, one of which is the site of the **Swami Vivekananda Rock Memorial** (Rs 15/35¢/20p daily *darshan* or view-ing of a deity; 8am–4pm), reached by the half-hourly ferry. The memorial commem-orates a Hindu guru and social reformer's meditative sojourn on the island in 1892. Several bookstores selling spiritual tomes are found on the island, but the best experi-ence is to be had in the **Dhyana Mandapam,** a room where absolute silence is main-tained so that pilgrims can meditate before a golden *om* symbol. A set of **Parvati's footprints** is enshrined in a temple built for it on the island. On the adjacent rocky island, a massive sculpture of the celebrated ancient Tamil poet-savant **Thiruvalluvar** stands 40m (131 ft.) high, punctuating the horizon like some bizarre homage to New York's Statue of Liberty.

The only attraction in the town itself is famous **Kumari Amman Temple** ⚐ (daily 4:30am–noon and 4:30–8:30pm), dedicated to Kanyakumari, a virgin goddess. Devotees enter the temple through the north gate, making their way around various corridors and bridges before viewing the deity, here depicted as a young girl doing penance with a rosary in her right hand. It's said that her sparkling nose jewel—seen glowing from some distance away—was installed by Parasurama (Lord Rama, an avatar of Vishnu) himself. Non-Hindus wishing to enter the temple must remove shoes, and men must remove shirts and wear a dhoti (although a *lungi* passes; purchase one before you leave Kovalam). A willing temple priest will lead you on a very brisk

Moments Watching the Sun Rise from the Subcontinent's Southernmost Tip

Just 87km (54 miles) southeast of Trivandrum, across the border with Tamil Nadu, **Kanyakumari** (also known as Cape Comorin) is not only India's southernmost tip but the much-venerated confluence of the Arabian Sea, the Bay of Bengal, and the Indian Ocean. **Watching the sun rise from the subcontinent's southernmost point** ✮✮ is an age-old ritual that attracts thousands of Indian pilgrims each morning. They plunge themselves into the turbulent swell, believing that the tri-oceanic waters are holy. Others revel in the glorious spectacle as though it were a major Bollywood premiere. Nature's daily show here becomes something akin to a miniature festival, with excited pilgrims besieged by *chai-*, coffee-, and souvenir-*wallas* selling everything from kitschy crafts (how else to describe conch shells with plastic flower bouquets glued to the top?) to ancient postcards and outdated booklets. But it's all part of the experience, which is quite wonderful; you can't help but be moved by the mass of people who gaze on a natural daily occurrence with such childlike wonder, effectively bestowing upon the event the spiritual significance that draws the crowds in the first place.

To get here, you need to arrange for an early-morning wake-up call and have your hotel organize a taxi. You should reach Kanyakumari at least half an hour before sunrise in order to take in the mounting excitement as the crowds prepare to greet the new day. (*Note:* **Kanyakumari sunsets,** which are obviously more convenient to reach, also draw a crowd but are only visible mid-Oct to mid-Mar and are not quite as atmospheric, except perhaps for *chaitra purnima,* the full-moon evening in April when the sunset and moonrise can be viewed simultaneously along the horizon.)

(queue-jumping) tour of the temple, ending with the obligatory suggestion that a donation would be quite acceptable.

If, for some reason, you get trapped in this ramshackle, pilgrim-choked town, head for **Hotel Maadhini** (East Car St.; ✆ **0465/224-6857** or -6787; www.hotelmaadhini. com), where you will be woken pre-dawn with tea and an urgent suggestion to watch the rising sun from your balcony.

En route back towards Kerala, you can buy cheap, delicious palm fruits from children on the roadside and visit the fantastic palace in the town of **Padmanabhapuram,** capital of Travancore until 1790 (see below).

Padmanabhapuram Palace ✮✮✮   Although technically in Tamil Nadu (but a mere 55km/34 miles south of Trivandrum), this gorgeous palace—one of the finest examples of secular architecture in India—was for several centuries the traditional home of Kerala's Travancore royal family. It's still well-maintained, and a meditation room features two lamps that have burned since its construction, tended by two dutiful women. Built over a number of generations during the 17th and 18th centuries, the palace exemplifies the aesthetic and functional appeal of Kerala's distinctive architectural style: sloping tiled roofs; elaborate slatted balconies; cool, polished floors; and slanting walls and wooden shutters—all effectively designed to counter the intense sunlight and heat. The private living quarters of the royal family are a maze of open corridors and pillared verandas; outside, small garden areas feature open courtyards where the sunlight can be enjoyed. Note that the king's chamber is furnished with a bed made from 64 different types of medicated wood and has its own beautifully decorated prayer room.

Padmanabhapuram is located 55km (34 miles) south of Trivandrum. Admission Rs 10 (25¢/15p). Rs 25 (55¢/30p) camera, Rs 100 ($2.30/£1.15) video. Tues–Sun 9am–4pm. Ticket office closed 1–2pm. Visitors must be accompanied by a guide and must remove footwear at the entrance.

WHERE TO STAY & DINE

Backpackers head for the budget hotels on the fringes of Kovalam's beaches, which, during peak season (Dec and Jan), are completely overrun by tourists and relentless hawkers. With the notable exception of The Leela, most lodging in Kovalam is less pleasant than cheap, and you're likely to be at the constant mercy of blaring music from the beach and its sprawl of cafes. Note that these cafes are fine for a snack, but each should be judged according to the number of customers. The rule of thumb is: If it's empty, the food has been standing around too long.

The resorts reviewed below have been chosen because they are situated away from mainstream Kovalam and offer peace, tranquillity, and charm, as well as some of the world's most pristine stretches of coastline. The prize for top location still goes to Surya Samudra; if you haven't opted to stay here (see below), it's definitely worthwhile taking a drive out to dine at **Octopus.** The restaurant's open-to-the-elements semi-circular terrace is perched high above the ocean and palm-fringed beach and cooled by the fresh sea breezes. Seafood is the order of the day: Don't miss the superb grilled tiger prawns or the fish curry (succulent pieces of white fish in a spicy red sauce; order with chappatis). Vegetarians can opt for the vegetable *theeyal* (spicy gravy), this time with Kerala *paratha* (flatbread). And for the truly unadventurous, there is a selection of Western dishes.

KOVALAM

Not as great on location as the Leela, but worth a mention is the Taj's **Green Cove Resort & Spa,** offering 59 rooms spread over 4 hectares (10 acres) of tropically landscaped gardens on the Kovalam cliffside, with a private beach below. Cottages have traditional Kerala-style thatched roofs and are hidden among palm trees—maintaining privacy from the outside, but still offering good views. Make sure to ask for a seaview room—at $240 (£121) a mere $20 (£10) more than a standard garden view unit. Both of the Taj's restaurants, **Chemmeen,** an alfresco space specializing in Kerala cuisine, and **Curries,** serve good Indian food. The resort also has a great-looking **Jiva** spa, but reports of the services haven't been good (✆ **0471/248-7733;** fax 0471/248-7744; www.tajhotels.com).

Lagoona Davina 🌟🌟   Described as "barefoot chic" (though Indian travel agents refer to it slightly more disparagingly as "ethnic"), this small, lagoon-facing property (just outside Trivandrum, on the way to Kovalam) was converted into a laid-back boutique sanctuary by adventuress Davina Taylor Phillips over a decade ago. While the tourism boom has spawned encroaching development (the charmless Lake & Lagoon hotel is now also here, and the beach is increasingly littered with debris), the views of the lagoon and beach—where fishermen pull in nets every morning in a kind of synchronized dance—are still splendid. Rooms are small and bathrooms very basic, but there are lovely touches throughout, like hand-loomed linens, a personally selected assortment of toiletries, and the caftans and camisoles Davina has made for you to live in while you're here. If Davina is in residence, you're sure to hear some wonderful stories (a true eccentric, she opened with two rooms at the tender age of 55), but be warned: She is starting to get itchy feet—Morocco and Libya beckon—so get here soon. Guests in the main "guest house" (a low-slung, single-story rectangular building facing the lagoon) and more spacious Maharaja rooms also enjoy the services of a personal room attendant; also available are "light" Ayurvedic treatments, the services of a tailor, and special floating dinners for two. *Note:* Although the beach is close by, it's not good for swimming.

Pachalloor 695 527. (*C*) **0471/238-0049** or -4857. Fax 0471/246-2935. www.lagoonadavina.com. 6 units, 1 cottage. Main guesthouse sea-view double and Maharaja Room (without sea view) double $133 (£67) high season; $80 (£40) low season. Other rooms $30–$86 (£17–£28) depending on size and season. 20% supplement and conditions for Christmas and New Year's. MC, V. Credit card payments made in India incur 5% service charge. **Amenities:** Restaurant; pool; travel assistance; car hire; Ayurvedic massage; cultural programs in season; boating; backwater excursions to be arranged; small library with indoor games; yoga, meditation, and Reiki; tailor.

Leela Kempinsky Kovalam Beach 𝒜𝒜𝒜   If you're looking for five-star resort-style amenities and snappy service (a boon in sometimes irritatingly laid-back Kerala), along with stunning views over the Lakshadweep Sea, this is the place to be. Following a Rs 700-million makeover, the ITDC's run-down Kovalam Ashok Beach Resort (briefly taken over by Le Meridien) emerged as the self-styled "capital" of Kovalam tourism in 2006. With the opening of the new Sea View Club wing, it's now the largest resort in Kerala. Like most Kovalam beach resorts, it is built into a cliff-face, but to Leela's advantage, the resort is well connected with the beach, thanks to elevators and golf carts that traverse the hill between reception and sea (well-suited to the infirm and lazy). The original hotel rooms—the "Beach View" category—are a little too like living in a large hotel, with low-ceilinged rooms ranged along corridors; equally so the much more luxuriously appointed (and very pricey) rooms and suites in the Sea View Club wing. Our money is on the Sea View Pavilions, 22 freestanding bungalows (each comprising two split-level units with semi-private verandas) right next to the beach (which, incidentally, has serviced deck chairs and a comfortably furnished restaurant—surreal given the activities of the traditional fishermen nearby). The Garden View Pavilions are just behind these and on a slight incline so not entirely viewless—and at $240 to $280 (£121–£141) double depending on season, the best-value category in the resort. But if you like your luxury with a great deal more nature and exclusivity, and you don't mind lax service, Surya Samudra still pips it at the post.

Kovalam Beach, Thiruvananthapuram 695 521. (*C*) **0471/248-0101.** Fax 0471/248-1522. www.theleela.com. 182 units. Low season (Apr–Sept) $240 (£121) Beach View Superior & Garden View Pavilion, $265 (£134) Beach View Deluxe, $290 (£146) Sea View Pavilion, $360–$550 (£181–£278)Sea View Club Wing, depending on room/suite; high season $280 (£141) Beach View Superior & Garden View Pavilion, $310 (£157) Beach View Deluxe, $360 (£182) Sea View Pavilion, $645–$1,500 (£326–£758) Sea View Club Wing. All rates exclude 15% tax. AE, MC, V. Surcharge and conditions for Christmas and New Year's period. **Amenities:** 3 restaurants; 2 bars; 3 pools; tennis; gym; Ayurvedic & wellness spa; cycling; travel desk; airport transfers; business center; 24-hr. room service; laundry; 2 exclusive beaches; yoga; snooker; beach volleyball; jogging track; table tennis; badminton; library. *In room:* A/C, TV, minibar, tea- and coffee-making facilities; hair dryer, Internet access; butler service in Sea View Club Wing.

CHANDRA, SURYA & VIZHINJAM

When Klaus Schleusener, a German professor who was based in Chennai in the '70s and '80s, first laid eyes on these aptly named beaches (Chandra means "moon," for the moonrise; Surya means "sun," above where it sets), he knew he had to own the cliff promontory that divided them. Naming the property Surya Samudra, Klaus built the original octagonal "Sea Front Deluxe" unit as his personal getaway. Alarmed at how centuries-old carved wooden cottages from villages around Kerala were being torn down to make way for modern homes—he came up with the inspired idea to transplant them, and so created a trend that helped set Kerala's huge tourism industry in motion. Today he's moved on (see "The Best Villa Stay in Kerala," under the Backwaters section above), but the resort is in many ways still a winner (see review below).

Sharing Surya's unbeatable location (though it's not nearly as elevated, and you'll miss the pool) is **Karikkathi Beach House** ✿✿ (✆ 098-4706-9654 or 0471/240-0956; www.karikkathibeachhouse.com), which vies with Green Lagoon as the best villa stay in Kerala. This totally charming two-bedroom bungalow is located right on Surya Beach; both en-suite bedrooms feature sea views and come with a personal chef and servants. A room costs 200€ ($272/£135) (including breakfast and lunch/dinner; excluding taxes) daily from May to October; 400€ ($544/£271) December to February, and 500€ ($680/£339) December 23 to January 7. If you book just the one en-suite room, the rate varies between 100€ and 250€ ($136–$340/£68–£169).

Located on the other side of Surya Samudra, on Chandra beach, is the very basic **Bethsaida Hermitage** resort (✆ **0471/248-1554;** fax 0471/248-1554; www.bethsaida-c. org). This collection of thatched bamboo and stone beach cottages was begun by a local priest who wanted to start an eco-friendly endeavor that could be used to aid a local orphanage. It's looking a little run-down at present and not worth booking unless you can reserve one of the most recently built "standard sea-facing" rooms (60€–80€/$82–$109/£41–£54) behind the pool. These rooms are spotless, spacious, and close to the beach. Hot water is at the mercy of an occasionally moody electrical system, and you need to bring your own toiletries. Don't arrive expecting luxury and you'll feel good knowing that your room's rate (slightly overpriced, considering) contributes to the welfare of some 2,500 children.

Out of sight, but not far from here, is **Coconut Bay** (✆ **0471/248-0566;** www. coconutbay.com), one of the most efficiently run resorts on the coast, with an unpretentious and low-key atmosphere and a very serious focus on Ayurveda, for which it has earned a deserved Green Leaf accreditation. It's small (only 25 units), but accommodations are in a variety of categories. If you're a single traveler, the best units are one of only five non-air-conditioned beach rooms (✆ **098-4706-9654;** 44€–66€/$60–$90/£30–£45, depending on season), which are off to one side and right above the beach; book room 301 and you have a semi-private veranda area with the best view at the resort. Other units with great views are deluxe beach villas 205 and 206 (77€–121€/$105–$165/£52–£82, depending on season) and super deluxe villas 201 and 203 (99€–143€/$135–$194/£67–£97, depending on season). Like that of the Somatheeram group, the specialty here is on Ayurvedic package deals, so check the website for specials and treatment details.

Surya Samudra Beach Garden ✿✿✿   This is Kerala's most famous resort (at least for those who subscribe to *Condé Nast Traveler* or who have flipped through the picture-perfect *Hip Hotels*), and deservedly so. Having resisted the greed to go big, the current owners have kept numbers relatively small: It accommodates a maximum of 44 guests, who stay in traditional-style cottages sitting high on a terraced hillside overlooking the sea, amid gardens of hibiscus trees, banyans, and coconut palms interspersed with rustic pathways and statues. Surya is not as slick (or coolly detached) as a five-star hotel, but the atmosphere is romantic and the setting totally glorious. Start the day with a yogic salutation to the sun, then laze by the infinity pool carved out of the rock bed or head to one of the two beaches. End the day by being lulled into dreamland by the sound of the ocean. You have a variety of accommodations to choose from, most with antique beds, beamed ceilings, heavy rosewood shutters, planter's chairs, peaceful verandas, and fans whirring lazily overhead; they are all charming and the pool is one of the most gorgeous in India; food too is excellent. You can be picky and find faults such as loose toilet seats, the presence of an insect or lizard, and other housekeeping oversights, and you may be irritated by an exceptionally lazy attitude to service, but the luxury of unfettered tranquillity and the gorgeous setting makes up for these inconveniences. Totally cut off from civilization yet a mere 40 minutes from Trivandrum airport, this is still one of the best destinations in India and a great place to end a frenetic-paced itinerary.

Pulinkudi, Mullar P.O. Thiruvananthapuram 695 521. ✆ 0471/226-7333. Fax 0471/226-7124. www.suryasamudra. com. 21 units. Low season–high season $100–$160 (£51–£81) small beach cottage; $160–$170 (£81–£86) garden cottages; $210–$350 (£106–£177) bungalows and sea-view rooms; $240–$460 (£121–£232) sea-front deluxe double. Dec 20–Jan 10 around 30% surcharge and special conditions apply. Children under 6 stay free if no extra bed required; extra bed 20% more. All rates include breakfast. MC, V. **Amenities:** Restaurant; pool; Ayurvedic spa; tour arrangements; room service; babysitting (by prior booking); doctor-on-call; currency exchange; beach lifeguard (in season); boating; small library. In room: Minibar, tea- and coffee-making facility. A/C only in garden rooms.

CHOWARA BEACH

Located below the small village of Chowara, within verdant cliffs towering along it, this long stretch of powdery white sand is located 12km (7½ miles) south of Trivandrum and 30 to 40 minutes from the airport. Chowara Beach is not only very pretty, but the sea here is usually rather tame—hardly surprising then that it has several resorts strung along it, the best of which are rated below.

Nikki's Nest 🌟🌟   Despite nearly doubling in size, this resort has retained a warm and intimate atmosphere, with either the Baileys on hand to ensure personalized assistance or a small staff complement that is well versed in making guests feel very welcome. Accommodations are in roomy thatch-roofed cottages/deluxe doubles (rooms 203 and 204 are closest to the beach) or in restored traditional wooden Kerala houses (202 is the one to book here; alternatively, 201). Keen to include travelers that are not necessarily well-heeled, the Baileys developed a palm grove plot opposite their entrance, with an additional 17 non–A/C cottages offering good value at $70 to $100 (£35–£56), depending on the season. Like the Somatheeram properties, this Green Leaf–accredited resort is the place to come for first-rate Ayurvedic treatments, after which you can trundle down to the beach or spend hours daydreaming at the restaurant, which has equally spectacular views and heavenly fresh fruit juices. Note that the Baileys also run **Duke's Forest Lodge,** situated at the edge of a river and rubber plantation near the Pepara Sanctuary some 50km (31 miles) away. This is a wonderfully untouched area, perfect for a romantic, secluded getaway ($75–$150/£38–76, depending on season, including breakfast).

Azhimala Shiva Temple Rd., Pulinkudi, Chowara, S. Kovalam, Thiruvananthapuram 695 501. ✆ 0471/226-8821, -8822, or 0471/226-7822. Fax 0471/226-7182. www.nikkisnest.com. nest@sancharnet.in. 20 units. $100–$170 (£51–£86) nest double; $70–$135 (£35–£68) big Kerala house double; $65–$125 (£33–£63) deluxe double; $50–$85 (£25–£43) non-A/C double. Add 20% per extra person. Rates include breakfast. AE, DC, MC, V. **Amenities:** Restaurant; pool; Green Leaf Ayurvedic spa; travel desk; airport and railway transfers; shop; room service; laundry; doctor-on-call; currency exchange; Internet access; cultural programs; library.

Somatheeram Ayurvedic Health Resort ✫✫   As much beachfront hospital as holiday destination, this resort has been inundated with awards for "Best Ayurvedic Centre" for the past 6 years. That is still the primary reason to book a Somatheeram package: Massages and treatments are provided in a hygienic environment by a team of experienced, professional staff (12 doctors and more than 50 therapists) who offer serious Ayurvedic rejuvenation and therapeutic packages (average stay here is 2 weeks) rather than just luxurious pampering. Some accommodations are in traditional wooden Kerala houses, which have the standard shaded verandas and hand-carved pillars and are usually the most comfortable rooms. Opt for an ordinary *nalukettu* room in one of these four-bedroom houses—the best by far (for the fabulous sea views) are nos. 102 and 101. Substantially cheaper, the four beachfront "mini-cottages," located within a stone's throw from the beach, are very basic round thatched structures with two shared bathrooms; of these, no. 301 has the best view from its sit-out area. *Note:* To confuse matters, the owners, brothers Polly and Baby Matthew, split the company in 2006, but in a typically Indian way—the split is designed to obfuscate the original brand, so neither can gain the upper hand. In short, on either side of Somatheeram Ayruvedic Health Resort (now owned by Mr. Polly and a partner, and still with the greatest variety of accommodation categories), you will now also come across **Somatheeram Ayurvedic Beach Resort** (✆ **0471/226-8101;** www.somatheeram.in) and **Manaltheeram Ayurvedic Beach Resort** (✆ **0471/248-1610;** www.manaltheeram. com), both owned by Baby Matthew. Of the latter two, Manaltheeram, which incidentally also enjoys Green Leaf accreditation for its Ayurvedic treatment center, created before the split, is our pick—not only because it has a great sea-view pool (Somatheeram currently shares this), but it is relatively flat, so there's less toiling up and down stairs. Most of Manaltheeram's accommodations are in "Ordinary" and "Special" (read: sea-view) cottages: These are standard thatched round villas. Book Special cottages 525 to 530 for the most privacy—at $51 to $101 (£26–£51), these are better value than the so-called "Kerala houses." If you're on a budget, Manaltheeram Ordinary cottages, located behind the Special cottages, go for $31 to $80 (£16–£40). Do check all three websites for specials on Ayurvedic packages.

Chowara P.O. 695 501. ✆ **0471/226-6501.** Fax 0471/226-6505. www.somatheeram.org. info@somatheeram.org. 59 units. $104–$226 (£53–£114) Sidharta deluxe suite; $74–$182 (£37–£92) Kerala deluxe house; $62–$136 (£31–£69) ordinary Kerala house; $50–$100 (£25–£50) special cottage; $30–$80 (£15–£40) ordinary cottage; $19–$59 (£10–£30) mini-cottages. 20% extra per person sharing. AE, DC, MC, V. **Amenities:** Restaurant; Internet cafe; travel and tour assistance; car hire; gift shop; 24-hr. room service; laundry; currency exchange; tailor; Ayurvedic hospital/center; cultural performances; beach guards; boating; yoga and meditation; indoor games. *In room:* Fridge in deluxe units.

Travancore Heritage ✫✫   Generally considered to be at the top end of the Kovalam lodging spectrum (and self-proclaimed "best heritage resort on Kerala"), this relatively luxurious resort, set on 6 hectares (15 acres) of land amid tamarind and jackfruit trees and coconut palms, is the place to come if you prefer your heritage faux. With sloping red-tile roofs, wooden walls and floors, high-pitched ceilings, and covered pillared verandas, structures recall the traditional style of the region. The main building is modeled on the royal palace at Edapally and features some wonderful reproductions and charming views from its upstairs balcony. The best rooms are the heritage premiums (which have sea views, as opposed to the non-sea-view heritage homes); these are for the most part furnished with high, wood-frame beds, old wicker-backed planter's chairs, and blinds made from gilded white *lungi* material. The best-value bungalow is number 43, a dinky freestanding heritage home with a sea view but categorized as a mere home (rather than a premium) because of its size. If you want to be near the beach, book a room in the bland Beach Grove wing, reached thankfully with an elevator, and with its own pool. Avoid the so-called Premium "Mansion," which is a similarly bland wing, with no freestanding units; it's more expensive than the heritage homes and hard to tell why. Beach chairs and lifeguards are shared with Somatheeram. There's a fine Ayurvedic center, though it is currently only Olive Leaf accredited, and the food is good.

Chowara P.O., Trivandrum 695 501. ⓒ **0471/226-7828** or -7832. Fax 0471/226-7201. www.thetravancoreheritage.com. travancoreheritage@vsnl.net. 65 units. $65–$135 (£33–£68) Beach Grove; $95–$185 (£48–£93) Premium Mansion; $80–$175 (£40–£88) heritage home double; $115–$200 (£58–£101) heritage premium double; $200–$350 (£101–£177) pool mansion. $25–$40 (£13–£20) extra bed. AE, MC, V. **Amenities:** Restaurant; 2 pools; Jacuzzi; travel, car hire, and tour assistance; room service; doctor-on-call; currency exchange; library; Ayurveda center; cultural performances; beach volleyball; indoor games. In room: A/C, TV, coffee-making facility.

POOVAR ISLAND

Kerala's southernmost resort destination (40 min. from Trivandrum), at the border between Kerala and Tamil Nadu on a remote stretch of river lagoon, provides a taste of the backwaters, with palm-fringed rivers and the ocean views of a beach resort. That said, the sea here is rough, so it's not a great place for ocean swimming, and with the proliferation of resorts in a relatively small area in the past 4 years, its tranquillity has been compromised. Don't be fooled by the glossy brochures and designs of Poovar Island Resort, whose romantic "floating cottages" have ongoing sewage problems; best of the five options is **Isola Di Cocco** (ⓒ **0471/221-0008;** www.isoladicocco.com; standard from Rs 3,000–Rs 5,500/$73–$134/£37–£68 depending on season), mostly due to the fact that it takes its Ayurvedic treatments and packages very seriously at very good value—this is the only Green Leaf–accredited center that offered a general body massage for a mere Rs 660 ($16/£8) in 2007. Accommodation is perfectly comfortable if a little unimaginative, with no personal touches or design forethought (or, more tellingly, sea views), but everything is spotless and spacious. The best of the lot are the 10 lake-view rooms (16, 17, and 53–60), which fall in the Heritage Category (Rs 3,500–Rs 6,000/$85–$146/£43–£74 double depending on season). Service is friendly, and the Indian food is good.

If you're a back-to-basics nature lover, the tiny eco-lodge **Friday's Place** (ⓒ **0471/ 213-3292;** www.fridaysplace.biz) is where you can reconnect with your eco-warrior. It comprises only four wooden cottages (two high on stilts) in the wilderness extending straight out into the Neyyar backwaters, so the impact on the environment is negligible. Designed by owners Mark and Sujeewa Reynolds (who personally run the retreat), the cottages are outfitted with palm-leaf roofs to ensure that they are cool even on warm days, and each has a veranda with hammock—just the place to admire the glorious birdlife at your door. The cottages are solar-powered and sport an eco-friendly sewage system—two rooms lack an attached toilet, but the common bathroom is spacious, with a central copper-floor shower area. It's all pretty basic, and there are no real facilities (most important, no pool), so the rates (full board around $50–$75/£100–£150) may seem a little steep. Note that the retreat has no road access, is only open mid-October through April, serves vegetarian meals only, has no credit card facilities, and has an inflexible minimum-3-night-stay policy.

5 Lakshadweep

Between 200km (124 miles) and 450km (279 miles) W of Kerala's coast

Ask any globe-trotting island-hopper if the world still holds any undiscovered gems, and Lakshadweep will be among the first names to crop up. One of India's best-kept secrets, the 36 atolls and coral reefs making up the remote Union Territory of Lakshadweep are an extension of the better-known Maldives island group. Only three Lakshadweep islands—Agatti, Kadmat, and Bangaram—are open to foreign tourists, and the Indian government employs a strictly enforced entry-permit system. All the islands are "owned" by the indigenous people, and land is unavailable for purchase by non-natives—even a man marrying a local woman may not buy land here.

Ten islands in the archipelago are populated, almost exclusively by Malayalam-speaking Sunni Muslims who make their living from fishing and harvesting coconuts. Only Minicoy Island, which is closest to the nearby Maldives, shares aspects of its neighbor's culture, including a Maldivian dialect known as Mahl.

Being Muslim, the islands are officially dry, and alcohol is only available on Bangaram, which is technically uninhabited by locals; avoid carrying any liquor with you. You are strongly advised to bring insect repellent since the mosquitoes become alarmingly active once the sun descends.

ESSENTIALS

PERMITS   No foreigner may visit the islands without prebooked accommodations. Visitors intending to stay at the Bangaram Island Resort can have all permit arrangements made through the **CGH Earth central reservations** (Casino Hotel, Willingdon Island, Kochi 682 003; ✆ **0484/266-8221;** fax 0484/266-8001; www.cghearth. com). Foreigners must supply the hotel with name, address, place and date of birth, passport number, place of issue, date of issue, and expiration date. Permits usually take 2 full working days to be processed. The CGH Group will also book your flight to and from Kochi (or Bangalore, direct flights introduced in 2007) for you.

To make your own permit arrangements (a laborious process; best avoided), contact the **Society for Nature, Tourism and Sports (SPORTS)** run by Lakshadweep Tourism (✆ **0484/266-8387**) in Kochi. Or contact their Delhi office (✆ **011/2338-6807**).

VISITOR INFORMATION   See "Permits," above. For details about Lakshadweep, contact the Assistant Manager, SPORTS, Lakshadweep Administrative Office, Willingdon Island, Kochi (✆ **0484/266-8387;** 10am–1pm and 2–5pm; closed Sun and second Sat of the month).

GETTING THERE   Unless you fancy a time-munching trip from Kochi by ship (14–20 hr.), you'll have to get to Bangaram by air: The flight will cost around $440 (£222) and arrives at the tiny airfield on Agatti (Agathi) Island. Here you'll be met by a resort representative who'll usher you to a waiting boat anchored near the shore not far from the airport for a memorable 90-minute journey to nearby Bangaram Island ($30/£15). Alternatively, transfer via helicopter for around $185 (£93).

DIVING THE REEFS

Experienced divers rank the reefs of Lakshadweep among the best diving destinations in Asia, particularly the coral islands of Bangaram, Tinakara, Pirelli 1, and Pirelli 2. Bangaram Island Resort hosts **Lacadives,** a small dive center that was the first CMAS (an international underwater-sports federation) dive organization in India, with its headquarters on the island of Kadmat. Lacadives offers diving courses, rents out equipment, and conducts two dives a day (9:30am and 2:30pm). If you're not a qualified diver, you can rent a mask and go on one of the resort's snorkeling trips to a nearby wreck where an assortment of marine fauna will have you begging for more. The resort can organize big-game fishing with local boats, but anglers should bring their own equipment. For details, contact the **Lacadives Diving Centre,** Bangaram Island Resort, Bangaram (℃ **93-8861-9494;** fax 0484/220-6766; in Mumbai: E-20, Everest Building, Tardeo Rd.; ℃ **022/6662-7381** or -7382; fax 022/6666-9241; www.lacadives.com; lacadives@gmail.com).

WHERE TO STAY

Bangaram Island Resort ★★★   Up against the biggest hoteliers of the day, CGH (now CGH Earth) won the rights to host visitors here based on their commitment to ecological principals more than a decade ago, long before these were fashionable. Borrowed from the pages of an old-style holiday brochure, this peaceful 50-hectare (123-acre) island is all untouched beaches and towering coconut palms—no newspapers, television, minibars, or even air-conditioning get in the way of experiencing the island's beauty. Eco-consciously designed so as to all but disappear into the surroundings, the modest 17-year-old resort remains quite basic, with emphasis on the captivating setting rather than fussy luxuries. Guest cottages, arranged in a row a short distance back from the beach, are spartan and clean: palm-frond thatch-covered huts with simple cane furniture, mesh screen windows, and private porches from which to admire the ocean. It won't suit the Aman types: For example, shower water is heated, but because it's taken straight from the ground it has a detectably high salinity level and a slight sulfuric smell. But the atmosphere here is so removed from workaday worries that you'll find no excuses not to recline in your hammock and stare into the magnificent cobalt waters, or discover a new addiction to diving, which is a major draw. On foot (take shoes for coral-covered stretches), you can skirt the entire island in about an hour; en route you will discover a host of stunning milky-white beaches to call your own. There's an Ayurvedic massage center for those days when sunbathing gets too stressful, and early risers can salute the rising sun with yoga on the helipad at 6:30am. The buffet meals are served outdoors so long as weather permits, but the best spot to be in the evenings is at the circular bar near the water's edge where, among other things, the barman mixes a mean Bangaram Binge—a feisty blend of dark Indian rum and coconut milk, complete with one of his signature palm frond swizzle sticks.

Bangaram Island, Lakshadweep. Reservations: Casino Hotel, Willingdon Island, Kochi 682 003. ℃ **0484/266-8221.** Fax 0484/266-8001. www.cghearth.com. casino@vsnl.com. 29 cottages. $320–$390 ($162–£197) standard hut double, $135 (£68) off season; $580–$640 (£293–£323) 2-bedroom deluxe double hut, $245 (£124) off season. (May 1–Sept 30 off season). Rates include all meals. Boat transfers $30 (£15) per person. AE, DC, MC, V. **Amenities:** Restaurant; bar; Ayurvedic center; yoga; boat transfers; dive center; deep-sea fishing; island trips; kayaks; catamarans.

6 The Cardamom Hills & Periyar Wildlife Sanctuary

190km (118 miles) E of Kochi

Each year, around half a million travelers make their way up into the Cardamom Hills, where the crisp, cool air is redolent with the scents of spices, and soaring mountains give way to tea plantations and dense jungle. Most people intent on seeing the best of Kerala head from the backwaters to the village of Thekaddy, gateway to Periyar Wildlife Sanctuary, the stomping grounds for large herds of wild elephants. Although it's true that Periyar is one of India's largest and most popular elephant reserves, this is not a wilderness experience in the true sense. Unless you opt for an overnight trek or one of the full-day hikes, the popular boat trip on the lake feels much like being processed like sheep by regimented nature rangers, and the intense tourist activity around the roads leading to the gates is quite disheartening.

However, with a couple of lovely places to stay, it is well worth overnighting here if you are traveling by car from Kerala to Tamil Nadu (or vice versa), though the most direct (if your route is Madurai-Kochi) is **Munnar,** which lies 4 hours due north. At a much greater altitude than Periyar (and site of Aneimudi, highest peak south of the Himalayas), Munnar is a collection of vast green-tea estates first established by a Scotsman in the late 19th century—it's hardly surprising, then, that the area is sometimes referred to as Kerala's Scottish highlands. In the days of the Raj, it became a popular "hill station"—a place to escape from the summer heat in the plains. Today the landscape—for the most part—retains a classic hill station atmosphere. Watched over by Mount Anamudi, South India's highest peak, Munnar's primary attractions are its gorgeous views of rolling hills covered with tea and cardamom plantations, and the cool climate—great, if you intend to stay more than 1 night, for leisurely walks and cycletours (not to mention a close encounter with the endangered Nilgiri tahr, a variety of mountain goat).

ESSENTIALS

VISITOR INFORMATION   All Periyar Wildlife Sanctuary inquiries should be made through the **Divisional Forest Office,** Thekkady (© 04869/22-2027; Mon–Sat 10am–5pm, closed second Sat of the month). Note that entry to the park costs Rs 300 ($7/£4) and is only open between 6am and 6pm. Easiest by far is to ask your hotel to make arrangements; all the resorts will book and transfer you to the KTDC-arranged excursions (see "The Periyar Wildlife Sanctuary," below).

In Munnar, the **Tourist Information Centre** (© 04865/23-1516; www.munnar.com; Mon–Sat 9am–7pm) in Old Munnar is relatively helpful.

GETTING THERE   From Kochi   Periyar/Thekaddy is a 4-hour drive east of Kochi, a long but enjoyable drive that traverses mountain roads ascending 900m (2,952 ft.) above sea level. Munnar is about 3-hours from Kochi (and a 2- to 3-hour drive north of Periyar), and another beautiful drive; you'll pass tea plantations and spice-growing embankments and drive through lovely sections of forest.

From Madurai, Tamil Nadu   Both Munnar and Thekkady lie around 4 hours away from Madurai; if you're really in a hurry, Munnar will shave a few minutes off. *Note:* Traveling by bus is arduous and time-consuming, at worst hair-raising, but if you want to save money, this is the way to go.

GETTING AROUND   You can pick up a ride on a auto-rickshaw or taxi almost anywhere in the Periyar area, with hordes of vehicles waiting at the bus stand. Overcharging foreigners is common; try to ascertain from your hotel what the going rate for a particular route is, and bargain upfront. Taxicabs and auto-rickshaws are readily available in and around **Munnar,** or you can arrange a car and driver through your hotel.

THE PERIYAR WILDLIFE SANCTUARY

Originally the hunting grounds of the Maharajah of Travancore, Periyar Wildlife Sanctuary was declared a wildlife reserve in 1933. In 1979 it became a Project Tiger

---

Kids Another Lovely Villa: Finding Serenity on the Way to Periyar

If you're traveling as a family or a group, another great Kerala villa stay is **Serenity** ⭐⭐, which makes a good stop between Kochi or Kottayam and Periyar (or, like nearby Paradisa Plantation Retreat, a destination in its own right). A converted 1920s bungalow in the heart of a rubber plantation, Kanam Estate, it offers six guest rooms, high wood-beam ceilings, polished floors, cane chairs, four-poster beds, traditional masks mounted on display stands, and a gorgeously located pool. You can arrange for an elephant to come in and play for the day, a great hit with kids, but make sure it's not ceremony or harvest season, when elephants throughout the state are in huge demand, leaving the Malabar team with red faces. Reservations are made through the **Malabar House Residency** (© **0484/221-6666**; www.malabarhouse.com; rates 120€–195€/$163–$265/£81–£132).

Reserve—India's homegrown initiative to protect the big cats' dwindling numbers. Today Periyar covers 777 sq. km (2,012 sq. miles), and is divided into core, buffer, and tourist zones. Although tiger sightings are very rare, particularly in the tourist zone, the reserve is home to elephants, sloth bears, sambar, Indian bison or gaur, wild dogs, leopards, spotted deer, Malabar flying squirrels, barking deer, Nilgiri tahr, and some 260 species of birds. It contains over 2,000 species of flowering plants, including at least 150 different kinds of orchid.

The best way to experience Periyar is with a Periyar Tiger Trail (see below); other than this, all access to the park is cheap, making excursions popular with exuberant domestic tourists who tend to be noisy, which somewhat inhibits one's enjoyment of natural scenery. Most opt for the 2-hour **boat cruise** on Periyar Lake, from where—if you're lucky—you can view animals coming to drink at the water's edge. Unfortunately, you're more likely to experience nonstop din from children (and their parents) who refuse to obey pleas for silence, preferring to rove around the boat and camcord each other. Boats depart at 7 or 7:30am, 9:30am, 11:30am, 2pm, and 4pm; there is some confusion about tickets at press time but you're certainly not looking at more than Rs 200 ($4.50/£2.25) for an Upper Deck seat. Less subscribed are the **daily walks;** these 3-hour treks depart at 7am, 11am, and 2pm and cost Rs 100 ($2/£1 per person; maximum five in a group), and provide you with the opportunity to admire some of the stunning flora of the region; better still are the **bamboo rafting trips** in which a maximum of 10 tourists are taken on a full day out (Rs 1,000/$24/£12 per person; 8am–5pm), combining walking with rafting. Check **www.periyartiger reserve.org** for details on these and other adventures such as jungle patrol, a night hike, and the park's Periyar Tiger Trail. However you choose to explore the park, do bear in mind that temperatures can be freezing from November through February, so pack warm layers.

Note: Whatever activities you have in mind, you're better off making all your arrangements through your hotel. Avoid any unsolicited offers from "guides" promising to take you on walks or tours into the reserve; this will only waste your time and test your patience.

PERIYAR TIGER TRAIL ✸✸

By far the most exciting and tranquil way to experience the park is a 2- or 3-day "Periyar Tiger Trail." Armed with anti-leech footwear and a sleeping bag (supplied), and accompanied by two forest officials and five guides, you are taken farther into the tourist zone than any other operator is allowed to penetrate. What's more, you are being led and looked after by a team of reformed poachers (sandalwood, cinnamon bark, and bison being their loot of choice) who know the terrain and the wildlife better than anyone. They skillfully track and spot animals, carry all the gear, strike camp, cook, clean, and—most important—stand sentinel throughout the night when the danger of being trampled by elephants becomes a serious risk. They also now play an essential role in catching poachers who remain active in the reserve.

You'll almost certainly come across elephants, wild pigs, sambar, black monkeys, wild dogs, and bison, and when you're not trekking to your next campsite, you'll be relaxing under forest cover or alongside a lake tributary. Meals are wholesome, authentic Kerala vegetarian fare: sweet *chai* and pleasant snack lunches served on silver trays with the grass for a tablecloth and a beetle symphony as background. Ablutions are performed in the great outdoors. ***Note:*** These exceptional hiking expeditions are limited to five visitors at a time, and only 20 participants are accepted per week (maximum six persons per trail), so book well in advance, particularly in peak (winter) season, when it is often booked a year in advance. The trek starts between 8 and 9am, so you'll have to stay in the area the previous night. At press time the 1-night trail was Rs 3,000 ($73/£37) per person; Rs 5,000 ($122/£62) if you happen to be the only person on the trail; the 2-night trail is Rs 5,000 ($122/£62), Rs 7,500 ($183/£93) minimum. For bookings or information, contact tourism@periyartigerreserve.org or call ✆ **04869/224571.**

Note that all trails are run by the park, so while there are tour operators offering Periyar Trails excursions, all you essentially get by booking through them is an additional middleman fee (though you might think the $30/£15-odd additional charge per person worth it if you're struggling to contact the park or get confirmation on your booking). If you prefer to go this way, contact the Trivandrum-based **TourIndia** (✆ **0471/233-0437** or -1507; www.tourindiakerala.com; tourindia@vsnl.com), which charges $150 (£76) per person; $600 (£303) for two persons only. If you have any special interests, such as ornithology, TourIndia will make arrangements to have a specialist guide you.

WHERE TO STAY & DINE IN & AROUND PERIYAR

With the exception of the atmospheric KTDC Lake Palace, which is inside the park, visitors to Periyar are limited to accommodations that lie within a few minutes of each other along Thekkady Road (which links nearby Kumily with the park gate). Of these, Shalimar Spice Garden Resort (see below), located just off Thekkady Road, is by far the most atmospheric. If you're just passing through and looking for a cheap, excellent Indian meal, the restaurant at Hotel Ambadi (www.hotelambadi.com) is the place. Packed to capacity with domestic tourists, it offers superb value (the most expensive items are half a chicken for Rs 90/$2/£1 and prawns for Rs 110/$3/£1), delicious (very spicy) food, and surly service.

KTDC Lake Palace ✸✸   Located on its own promontory in the Periyar Lake, this is a truly charming option, and one of the most romantic in India. It is however by no means a palace but a lovely low-slung stone, wood, and tile-roofed bungalow—the former game lodge of the Maharajah of Travancore. The best reason to book here is for the sense of exclusivity (it takes a maximum of 12 guests and is very popular, so book well in advance) and the remote setting, best enjoyed from the wraparound veranda from which you're likely to spot a variety of game and plenty of birds. In fact, the sense of getting away from the hustling around Periyar kicks in as soon as you take the 15-minute boat ride across Periyar Lake, watching the tourists streaming into the KTDC boat turn to a column of ants as you glide, alone, across the waters to reach a forested peninsula, inhabited only by a handful of staff and fellow guests and the wild animals of Periyar. The six "deluxe" guest suites are also the best in the KTDC stable, spotlessly clean and charmingly old-fashioned, with a few pieces of antique teak furniture, including four-poster twin or double beds. Don't expect luxury or high levels of service (the manager is efficient and kind, but the team is tiny), but do look forward to plenty of peace and tranquillity; bring a few books and arrange for a predawn wakeup call and guide to take you into the forest on foot.

Inside Periyar Wildlife Sanctuary. Reservations: Aranya Nivas and Lake Palace, Thekkady 685 536. © **04869/22-2024.** Fax 04869/22-2282. www.ktdc.com. aranyanivas@vsnl.com. 6 units. Rs 7,850–Rs 9,800 ($191–$244/£97–£121) double. Rs 1,900 ($46/£23) extra person. Rates include all meals and boating. AE, DC, MC, V. **Amenities:** Restaurant; travel assistance; room service; boat cruises. *In room:* TV.

Paradisa Plantation Retreat *★★★*

Located an hour's drive from Periyar's entrance, but with stupendous views of the reserve hills from a wonderful elevated position, this is our favorite inland lodge in Kerala. The central dining and entertainment area—a circular space where the charmingly decadent and almost aristocratic owner, Simon Paulose, holds court—is where the easy socializing is done, accompanied by the most unbelievably delicious meals. It's more than you can possibly eat, but eat you will, if only because you will never taste this exact combination of flavors again, more's the pity. Like so many top-notch Keralan lodges, accommodation is in traditional teak houses, but Simon has done a superb job of reconstructing them to provide a decent amount of space and located them in such a way that makes the most of the views. Each has gorgeous, unobstructed views of the rolling green hills, covered in dense jungle in which wild spices grow as casually as grass in a middle-class suburb. Simon has also situated these houses so that you enjoy total privacy once you're retreated to your '"home"; he's also kept the numbers down (only 12 units) to ensure that he can continue to manage his retreat in a very hands-on way. Simon is a superb host, his staff the most on-the-ball and loyal we've come across in Kerala. The spartan elegance and layout of the bungalows makes them by far the most livable of this genre. Pity about the threadbare towels, but really, we'd opt for a night in Paradisa over the most luxurious resorts in Kumarakom any day.

Murinjapuzha P.O. Idukki District, Kerala 685 532. Central Office © **0469/270-1311.** Retreat © 04869/288-119 or 0944/7088-119. Fax 0469/260-2828. www.paradisaretreat.com. info@paradisaretreat.com. 12 units. 150€–180€ ($204–$245/£102–£122) double. Rates include breakfast; meals 15€ ($20/£10). MC, V. **Amenities:** Superb dining; room service; laundry; doctor-on-call; excursions to Periyar; authentic Ayurvedic treatments arranged at nearby medical center; walks. *In room:* TV.

Shalimar Spice Garden Resort *★★★*

In the off-the-map "village" of Murikkady, just 4km (2½ miles) from Thekkady, this laid-back resort, situated on a 2.4-hectare (6-acre) plantation of palms, hardwood, fruit, coffee, and fragrant spices, offers the most enchanting accommodations in the Periyar area. Scattered over a landscaped terraced hillock behind the lobby (a 300-year-old traditional *pathayam,* or granary), granite and pebble pathways lead you to the thatch-roofed guest rooms and cottages. Enter through the teak and rosewood doorways to cool interiors—very basically furnished, but with a lovely polished terrace from where you can watch the light dim and listen to the rustling forest sounds as night falls, and "houseboys" bring a citronella candle (and, if requested, a G&T) at sundown. Cottage interiors feature whitewashed walls and terra-cotta tile floors; a few have stained glass and breezy loggias. The en-suite bathrooms all have windows letting in natural light; the best options from a jungle view and privacy point of view are 212 and 214. The rooms are smaller and less private than the cottages; instead of bathtubs, they feature drench showers. Up the terraced hill, along garden pathways decorated with stone bowls once used for grinding spices, the granite-bordered pool sits in a sun-drenched clearing. Outside and in, the scents of cinnamon, tea, pepper, cardamom, jasmine, guava, orange, gooseberry, mulberry, tapioca, passionfruit, and tamarind fill the air. Service is atrociously slow, but it's all very well-meaning, and the location is so lovely that you simply have to adapt to the pace and enjoy it.

Murikkady P.O. 685 535. ⓒ **04869/22-2132** or -3232. Fax 04869/22-3022. www.shalimarkerala.com. shalimar_resort@vsnl.com. 15 units. 120€–180€ ($163–$245/£81–£122) double; 150€–225€ ($204–$306/£102–£152) cottage. Extra bed is 20% of room rate. New Year surcharge. Children under 6 free without extra bed. Rates include breakfast. MC, V. **Amenities:** Restaurant; pool; taxi rental; laundry; doctor-on-call; currency exchange; Ayurvedic treatments; yoga; boat rides; sightseeing; trekking excursions.

Spice Village *Finds* *Kids*   Alive with the fragrant smell of lemon grass (used on all the patios), this huge "rustic village" resort is the most professionally run in the area, with groomed grounds, well-maintained bungalows, and the best staff-to-guest ratio in Thekaddy. Spread over a huge area around a network of pathways and intersections (if you're averse to walking, choose a low-numbered room—these are closer to the public areas), the whitewashed bungalow cottages are very pretty, each one topped with thatch—a swell of thick elephant grass propped up by slim timber poles. Interiors are spacious but simply furnished (no need to shell out for the "deluxe" units; standard villas provide ample space). From the moment you arrive, when you're welcomed with a mint-lime soda and the delicate smell of incense, staff is eager to please: They are happy to arrange guided plantation tours, Periyar excursions, excellent Ayurvedic spa treatments (two doctors and six therapists), and various cultural and wildlife activities, including the dedicated services of a qualified naturalist and an in-house Wildlife Resource Center. We like the more casual, unkempt, and jungly atmosphere of Shalimar, but Spice Village is a great option if you prefer things super-neat and tidy, efficient service, and an array of facilities laid on.

Thekkady-Kumily Rd., Thekkady 685 536. ⓒ **04869/22-2314** through -2316. www.cghearth.com. 52 units. $110–$270 (£56–£136) standard villa; $210–$395 (£106–£199) deluxe villa. Rates include breakfast. Extra person $35–$50 (£18–£25). AE, DC, MC, V. **Amenities:** Restaurant; bar; pool; tennis; Ayurvedic spa; recreation room; shop; limited room service; doctor-on-call; cultural performances; badminton; nature center; wildlife excursions; cooking demonstrations; plantation visits.

MUNNAR: HOME OF TEA & TAHRS

Munnar town itself is rather unpleasant and increasingly clogged by impulsive development; thankfully, the region's real attractions lie on its outskirts and have so far withstood the onslaught of tourist exploitation.

With tea plantations spread out as far as the eye can see, watching the mists creep over the valleys and come to rest like a blanket on the jade-colored hills is almost as refreshing as luxuriating in the cool climate—a welcome relief before you descend to the tropical Kerala coast or to sultry Madurai in neighboring Tamil Nadu.

Almost all the plantations are owned by the powerful Tata company, the same mighty conglomerate that produces India's buses, Sumo four-by-fours, and the Taj hotel chain. **Tea factory visits** can be arranged either through your hotel or by contacting Tata's regional office (© **04865/23-0561** through -0565), through which you can also visit the **Tea Museum** and the tea factory's processing unit (Tues–Sun 10am–4pm). To get up close to some of the world's last Nilgiri tahr (a variety of mountain goat or ibex), arrange a visit to nearby **Eravikulam National Park.** Existing only in the mountain grasslands of the Western Ghats at altitudes above 2,000m (6,560 ft.), the tahr is as endangered as the tiger, with fewer than 2,000 left. That said, the park has been a great success, with dedicated tea planters, once the primary hunters of the tahr, now doubling as voluntary wildlife wardens. The 2007 census shows a healthy population of 800, almost double what it was 30 years ago. Note that you can participate in the annual census, which will ensure up-close encounters with both the tahr and the planters and rangers who protect it. It is held for a week in April; for more information call the park office (see contact information below). Of course, sighting what is basically a goat, no matter how rare, may not be as exhilarating as spotting a tiger, but your chances are far higher—in fact the tahrs have grown so used to visitors that you can get within a few yards of them. Enter the park at the Rajamala entrance, 15km (9⅓ miles) from Munnar, where you can buy tickets at the park office (© **04865/23-1587;** entry Rs 50/$1/60p, light vehicles Rs 10/24¢/12p; daily 8am–5pm). Avoid the usual noisy crowds by arriving early.

WHERE TO STAY

If Windermere and Tall Trees are full, you might want to look at the **Siena Village.** With 28 units and a long list of facilities, it's very much a resort, but the location, a striking half-hour drive from Munnar in what feels like genuine hill country, is really lovely. Accommodations are comfortable enough without any flair (a single framed print, hung too high, is the only wall decoration) and are spread around a wide expanse of neatly trimmed lawns and a central open-air pavilion. Ask for one with an upstairs bedroom (© **04868/24-9261;** www.thesienavillage.com; from Rs 2,750/$67/£34 standard double, rates include breakfast). Before booking with a resort that isn't recommended here, it's worth knowing that the Keralan authorities are taking a very hard line against resorts erected illegally on reserve land. In June 2007 some 30 resorts were razed to the ground, including the popular 24-unit Cloud Nine resort, built in 2003. Two of the partners are allegedly related to former revenue minister and Kerala Congress chief KM Mani.

The Tall Trees ✿ Located 8km (5 miles) outside of scruffy Munnar town, this aptly named miniresort has 19 attractive cottages, many of them stilted and all designed and placed in such a way that not one of the 531 trees in the 26-hectare (66-acre) woodlands had to be felled. Of the three cottage categories, the standard—very spacious, with a balcony—should suffice; if you need more space, the deluxe cottages offer a separate dining-cum-living-room, with two balconies, while the two-bedroom luxury cottages will suit families. Interiors, with bland furnishings, lack the character the exteriors promise, but nothing is jarring, and the environment is peaceful, with great bird-watching from your veranda. It can be a long walk uphill to the restaurant, so request a cottage close by if you're not that fit. The standard of meals (and service) is inconsistent. With the emphasis firmly on nature, the resort has no TVs in rooms, but if you really must indulge, a few are for rent.

Baison Valley Rd., Munnar 685 618. © 04865/23-0641 or -0593. www.ttr.in. holiday@thetalltreesresorts.com. 19 units. Rs 5,000 ($122/£62) standard cottage; Rs 6,000 ($146/£74) deluxe cottage; Rs 10,000 ($244/£123) suite. Rs 500 ($12/£6) extra bed. In peak season 2-night minimum stay required. Rates include breakfast and dinner or lunch. MC, V. **Amenities:** Restaurant; cycling; laundry; indoor games; trekking, bird-watching; mountaineering; golf and aquatic pursuits by prior arrangement.

Windermere Estate ⟨★⟨★   Also located just outside Munnar, on a 24-hectare (60-acre) cardamom estate, this is by far the best place to stay in the region (and as a result often booked months in advance). The best-value accommodation options, almost all with views of the surrounding tea-clad hills and forests, comprise five rooms in the original stone split-level farmhouse and four Valley View Rooms; if you're staying more than 1 night and like your space, there are six very spacious rooms (big enough to take another person) called "cottages," and four Planter's Villas currently under construction. Warm service makes visitors feel like the personal guests of owner Dr. Simon, an ophthalmic surgeon, and the discreet level of service is designed to make you feel as if you're lord of your very own plantation estate. Accommodations are bright and clean, with wooden ceilings and floors and dark cane furniture; opt for one of the cottages, which are spacious with large bathrooms. The surrounding landscape is exceptionally good for scenic early-morning walks, organized daily, and you can try your luck fishing in one of several nearby streams. Food is fresh family cuisine, with everything sourced from local farms; like so many homestay-type experiences, it far surpasses the buffets you get at five-star resorts.

P.O. Box 21, Pothamedu, Munnar 685 612. © 04865/23-0512. Fax 04865/23-0978. Reservations: c/o Molly Simon, Trikkakara, Kochi 682 021. © 0484/242-5237. Fax 0484/242-7575. www.windermeremunnar.com. info@windermere munnar.com. 15 units (soon to be 19). $125 (£63) farmhouse double; $155 (£78) Valley View double; $225 (£113) cottage; $315 (£159) Planter's Villa. May–July off-season 25% discount. Rates include breakfast and lunch or dinner. Payment in advance by direct transfer or at Kochi banks. No credit cards. **Amenities:** Dining room; doctor-on-call; fishing; trekking; TV in lounge.

7 Malabar: Northern Kerala

Even though northern Kerala's history as a major spice-trade destination is well documented, it remains relatively untouched by tourism. This is largely because of the 8-hour drive it takes to get here from Kerala's better-favored beaches and backwaters. Nevertheless, this can be a wonderful region to explore if you are looking to get away from the tourist crowds, and have time to spare. Certainly if you're traveling overland from Mysore, Karnataka, to Kerala, it makes excellent sense to spend a day or two exploring this relatively untouched part of subcontinent, particularly the **Wyanad Hills,** which remains one of India's last true wilderness areas. As a result, the area has begun to see a big increase in visitors keen to escape the predictable tourist hot spots.

ESSENTIALS

VISITOR INFORMATION   In Kozhikode (until recently known as Calicut), a **Kerala Tourism information booth** (© 0495/270-2606; daily 10am–1pm and 2–5pm) is located at the railway station. In Kannur, inquire at the **Kannur District Tourism Promotion Council** (Taluka Office Campus; © 0497/270-6336; Mon–Sat 10am–5pm, closed Sun and second Sat of the month).

GETTING THERE   By Road   Kannur and Kozhikode are both on National Highway 17, which gets tricky in places as you head farther north. To get from Kozhikode to Vythiri in the Wyanad mountain ranges, you'll need to take the

Kozhikode–Bangalore highway; best to hire a car and driver (see "Getting Around," under Kochi). If you have more time (and less money), look into bus connections; call the local KSRTC Office in Kozhhikode on 📞 **0495/2723-796.**

By Air There are regular flight connections to **Karipur Airport** (📞 **0495/271-2630** or -1314)—located 25km (16 miles) south of Kozhikode—with Mumbai, Chennai, and Coimbatore, and less frequent connections with Goa.

By Train Kozhikode is an important jumping-off point for trains running up and down the coast of Kerala; there are daily trains from Mumbai and Delhi. Daytime journeys are wonderful if you're keen on enjoying fantastic views. Dial 📞 **133** or 0495/270-1234 for inquiries at the **Kozhikode Railway Station,** or 📞 **0495/270-3822** for reservations.

GETTING AROUND **By Taxi & Auto-Rickshaw** Auto-rickshaws are fine for short trips in Kozhikode and Kannur, but for longer journeys you will have to hire a car and driver.

KOZHIKODE & THE WYANAD RAINFOREST
Kozhikode is 146km (91 miles) NW of Kochi

Archaeological evidence suggests that civilizations inhabited the fertile forests of the Wyanad around 3 millennia ago. Today pockets of tribal populations still practice time-old rituals and eke out a simple existence in harmony with nature, but the wonderfully temperate climate and almost permanently sodden soil has also meant that the region supports a sprawling network of coffee, cardamom, pepper, and rubber plantations, stretching over the undulating hills in every direction.

Malabar trade, which is still largely focused on spices and textiles, once centered on the teeming coastal town of **Kozhikode,** the unofficial capital of the North. Until recently known as Calicut—incidentally where the term *calico* (or white, unbleached cotton) originated—this is one of India's cleanest cities. Vasco da Gama was first welcomed here in 1498; at the nearby village of Kappad, a commemorative plaque memorializes the spot where the Portuguese explorer is said to have landed. Now also known as Kozhikode, the city is of marginal interest to travelers, being more of a go-between point for journeys farther south or north, or inland to Kerala's highest rainfall region, the **Wyanad Hills** 𝒦𝒦𝒦. One of India's last true wildernesses, the hills are home to **Tranquil Resort,** a wonderful, sophisticated homestay surrounded by a 160-hectare (400-acre) working coffee plantation (see below).

KANNUR
92km (57 miles) NW of Kozhide; 266km (165 miles) N of Kochi

Kannur is a pretty coastal town predominantly inhabited by what is locally known as the "Malabar Muslim." Unlike North India, where Islam was more often than not established through violent conquest, here it arrived initially through trade, and grew through love; Arab sailors coming to Malabar in search of precious spices married local women, establishing the Mappila (or Malabar Muslim) community, which in turn developed its own Arabi-Malayalam songs and poems and the "Mappila Pattu." This oral record of the unique history of the broad-minded Calicut rulers stands in stark contrast, for instance, with that of the intolerant Portuguese tyrants.

Tourism in this northerly region of Kerala is only recently coming into its own, which has distinct advantages if you're looking to get away from the crowds. It also means that infrastructure remains undeveloped—although rising tourist numbers

Placating the Gods with *Theyyams*

Peculiar to the tribal region of northern Malabar, this ritual dance form evolved as a means of placating ancient village gods and ancestors. Combining temple ritual, rustic ballads, and folk art, *theyyams* are essentially representations of the collective consciousness of the village. Heavily made-up men with masks, elaborate costumes, spectacular jewelry, and often 2m-high (6 $^1/_2$ -ft.) headgear essentially become oracle-like incarnations or manifestations of the godhead or of a valorous ancestor. The ceremony begins with a song of praise, performed in honor of the presiding deity; this is followed by a dance strongly influenced by Kalaripayattu, the traditional Kerala martial art thought to predate the better-known Far Eastern forms like kung fu. *Theyyams* traditionally last an entire day and include a great deal of music, singing, and lighting of torches—oil lamps are ceremoniously brandished as shields and swords. *Theyyams* are usually held between December and April. To ensure your chances of seeing a performance, visit **Sri Muthappan Temple** at Parassini Kadavu, 18km (11 miles) from Kannur, which has early-morning and evening performances throughout the year.

warrant future increased investment in basics like roads. Don't be put off, particularly for those traveling by road between Karnataka and Kerala.

If you're looking for a safe, practically untouched sunbathing and swimming spot, head for **Muzhapilangad Beach,** 15km (9⅓ miles) south of Kannur, where you'll probably have much of the 4km (2½-mile) sandy stretch all to yourself. Closer to the city, which the Europeans called Cannanore, the Portuguese built imposing **Fort St. Angelo** (free admission; daily 8am–6pm), a monumental laterite edifice from which visitors can view the fishing harbor below. Seventy kilometers (43 miles) north of Kannur lies **Bekal,** Kerala's largest fort, thought to date back to the mid–17th century, though there is no accurate account of its construction. **Bekal Fort** (✆ **0467/227-2900** or -2007) is open to visitors daily between 9am and 5pm; admission is $2 (£1).

WHERE TO STAY
KOZHIKODE

Kozhikode has a dearth of good places to stay. Your best bet is the Taj Residency, the only five-star hotel in town (but don't expect five-star quality). Unless you're sold on the anonymity of hotels—in which case the **Fortune Park Hotel** (✆ **0495/276-8888;** www.fortunehotels.in) is a cheaper alternative to Taj Residency—a far more interesting option is the **Harivihar Ayurvedic Heritage Home** (✆ **0495/276-5865;** www.nivalink.com/harivihar; 90€/$122/£61 including all meals). In the heart of Kozhikode, but a million miles from the hustle and bustle of the city, this is the gracious family home of Neethi Srikumar and her husband, the good doctor, but now host to visitors from across the globe who come to learn about (and experience) the healing art of Ayurveda as well as immerse themselves in Indian culture and philosophy. It has only eight rooms, so you're assured of individual attention. You'll leave this haven rejuvenated, restored, and ready to tackle anything.

Taj Residency, Calicut (Kozhikode) ✫✫   This luxury business-oriented hotel, the best in town, is steadily drawing more leisure and health travelers as the hinterland region grows in popularity. The lobby is bright and welcoming, with wood-paneled pillars, cast-iron chandeliers, and wood-beam pitched ceilings; guest rooms are clean and neat if totally forgettable. Staff are well-meaning and definitely the best in town. If you do go for an Ayurvedic rejuvenation program (and you should), you can be assured of professional service, and all treatments are made in consultation with the resident doctor. It's also minutes from the spice market. This is a good hotel for an overnight stop, but in no way a place you should choose to tarry; for that you'd be better off at Harivihar, the guesthouse reviewed above.

P.T. Usha Rd., Kozhikode 673 032. © 0495/276-5354. Fax 0495/276-6448. www.tajhotels.com. residency.calicut@ tajhotels.com. 74 units. Rs 4,100 ($93/£47) standard double; Rs 4,700 ($107/£54) residency double; Rs 6,900 ($157/£79) executive suite. AE, DC, MC, V. **Amenities:** 2 restaurants; bar; pool; kids' pool; health club; travel assistance; car hire; business center; shopping arcade; 24-hr. room service; laundry; dry cleaning; doctor-on-call; currency exchange; Ayurvedic center. *In room:* A/C, TV, safe.

IN & AROUND WYANAD

It takes about 2 hours to drive the 90km (56 miles) from the coastal city of Kozhikode to Vythiri, the nearest village to many of Wyanad's resorts, the best of which is **Tranquil Resorts** (reviewed below). Note that Green Magic Nature Resort, once considered "the best tree-house experience in Asia," has had some bad press; unless you hear otherwise think twice before you book here. Besides Tranquil, which is a classic classy homestay, you may want to check out the 36-unit **Vythiri Resort** ✦ (© 04936/ 25-5366; fax 04936/25-5368; www.vythiriresort.com), not least for its excellent Serena spa with Ayurvedic facilities. Doubles cost around $75 (£38) for a tribal hut (avoid) and $90 to $110 (£45–£55) for a cottage (recommended); all meals are included. This resort is extremely popular with large family and tour groups, however, especially in the summer, so if you're looking for a little more peace and quiet, head instead to **Rain Country Resorts** ✦✦ with only five remotely situated traditional Keralan cottages in 8 hectares (20 acres) of untouched jungle (© 0493/620-5306 or 09447/245288; www.raincountryresort.com; Rs 2,500–Rs 3,500/$61–$85/£31–£43). Alternatively, **Edakkal Hermitage** ✦ (© 04936/22-1860; www.edakkal.com) is located near the Edakkal Caves (which feature wall carvings dating from the Neolithic Age), where cottages have good views. The resort organizes unusual and rather romantic candlelit dinners in one of the caves. Book a cottage rather than the unconvincing tree house.

Tranquil Resorts ✦✦✦   This is one of the best ways to experience life on a 160-hectare (400-acre) working coffee and vanilla plantation, located at the edge of the Wyanad National Park, thanks to the warm hospitality of Victor and Ranjini Dey. Situated in a 70-year-old planter's bungalow with rosewood floors, accommodations are aptly named Coffee, Cloves, and Cardamom, and are individually and tastefully designed, some with a glass-ceiling bath area that allows natural light to stream in. If you've always dreamed of sleeping in a tree house with the sights and sounds of a rainforest canopy, then request a stay in the gorgeous tree villa 40m (131 ft.) above ground and spread across three bright Flame of the Forest trees. You get a personal balcony and deck with cane chairs and table, TV, and telephone. The elegantly designed bathroom comes with flush toilet and shower. Do bear in mind, however, that this is a forest, so insects may be the accompaniment to your sundowner on the deck in the evenings, though the villa itself has been secured with window nets. The Deys, both fine raconteurs, are very good about arranging tours of tea, pepper, cardamom, coffee, banana, and coconut plantations as well as a variety of walks on the estate, all clearly signposted, taking you through fabulous scenery. You can also see the workings of the estate, explore local sights, or take a trip into the park or to Edakkal caves. The staff cooks wonderful meals with guest preferences in mind. The resort has a pool and an Ayurvedic Wing.

Kuppamudi Coffee Estate, Kolagapara P.O., Sultan Bathery, Wyanad 673 591. ℂ **04936/22-0244.** Fax 04936/22-2358. www.tranquilresorts.com. homestay@vsnl.com. Reservations: TravelsKerala, Karimpatta Rd., opposite Medical Trust Hospital, Pallimukku, Kochi 682 016. ℂ **0484/238-1038.** Fax 0484/236-4485. info@travelkerala.com. 6 units. $275 (£139) deluxe double; $330 (£167) Tree Villa. Rates include all meals, some sightseeing, and taxes. AE, MC, V (credit cards taken for room only; all other charges require cash payment). **Amenities:** Restaurant; pool; laundry; Ayurvedic treatments; plantation tours; sightseeing. *In room:* TV.

NEAR KANNUR

The best place to overnight in this northernmost part of Kerala is a family-run guesthouse called **Ayisha Manzil** ✿✿ in Thalassery, which enjoys a majestic position atop a cliff with a terrace overlooking the sea. Built by an East India Company tradesman in 1862, this lovely two-story mansion was bought by a family of Muslim spice traders in 1900. Today, it is still run by the Moosas, and combines modern facilities (like a beautiful pool overlooking the ocean) with sumptuous wooden antiques and unique family heirlooms. The guesthouse has a pool and a dining room where traditional Keralite and Malabari dishes are served, and you can take a 5-day cookery course, "Tellichery Pepper," a great introduction to traditional Malabar cuisine. The six en-suite guest rooms differ in size and layout; upstairs accommodations are more private. Each room has either one or two double beds. Doubles, including all meals and beach transfers, cost around $175 (£88). If you want to drink anything more than beer, you must bring your own alcohol. If it's a thoroughly unusual dining experience you're after, ask if you can be served breakfast on "the island"; if not, settle for breakfast on the beach instead. Nearby excursions include outings to Thalassery's fruit markets, a temple tour, a visit to the local martial arts school, and a tour through the property's original cinnamon plantation, apparently once the largest in Asia. Ayisha Manzil (Court Rd., Thalassery 670 101; ℂ **0490/234-1590;** cpmoosa@rediffmail.com; from $200/£101, including all meals) is 80km (50 miles) from Kozhikode airport, and Thalassery (or Tellicherry) is served by trains from Kozhikode as well as Bangalore and Chennai. Transfers are easily organized.

7

Tamil Nadu: The Temple Tour

If your idea of India is one of ancient temples thick with incense and chanting masses worshiping dimly lit deities covered with vermilion paste and crushed marigolds, then Tamil Nadu is where your mental images will be replaced by vivid memories. Occupying a long stretch of the Bay of Bengal coastline known as the Coromandel Coast, India's southernmost state is dominated by a rich cultural and religious heritage that touches every aspect of life. For many, this is the Hindu heartland—home to one of India's oldest civilizations, the Dravidians, who pretty much escaped the Mughal influence that permeated so much of the cultural development in the North. Ruled predominantly by the powerful Chola, Pallava, and Pandyan dynasties, Dravidian culture flourished for more than a thousand years, developing a unique political and social hierarchy, and an architectural temple style that has come to typify the South. In spite of globalization and the political dominance of the North, Tamil Nadu has retained its fervent nationalist sensibility—an almost zealous pride in Tamil language and literature, and in its delicious and varied cuisines. Outside of Chennai and the coastal stretch south to Pondicherry, it is also a state that remains virtually unchanged despite the tourism boom of the past decade, and exploring it provides a far more textured experience than provided by its popular neighbor, Kerala.

Thanks to heavy summer downpours, Tamil Nadu is green and lush—particularly in the Cauvery Delta toward the west, where the great Dravidian kingdoms were established and some of the finest temples built, like the 11th-century **Brihadeshvara Temple,** situated in Thanjavur, the Chola capital for 400 years, and the nearby temples of Kumbakonam. By contrast, **Chennai** (or Madras, as some still refer to it), the capital established by the British in the 17th century, exudes no such appeal. It's primarily of interest as a gateway to some of the region's best attractions, like nearby **Kanchipuram,** one of the seven sacred cities of India, and **Sri Venkateshvara Temple** (in Tirupati, just over the border in Andhra Pradesh), said to be the wealthiest temple in the world. There, devotees line up for hours—even days—to hand over an annual 1.5 billion rupees to help Vishnu settle his debt with the God of Wealth. Just 2 hours south of Chennai lies the seaside village of **Mamallapuram,** where, right near the water's edge, the Pallavas built the earliest examples of monumental architecture in southern India during the 5th and 9th centuries. From here it's a relaxing drive farther south to the former French coastal colony of **Pondicherry,** which—with its charming mansions, eclectic community, and bohemian atmosphere—is perhaps the best shopping destination in southern India. Although the French officially left years ago, Pondicherry's Gallic spirit is still very much alive—traditional Indian snack joints feature signs proclaiming MEALS READY; BIEN VENUE; locals clad in *lungis* (traditional Indian clothing) converse in French; and gorgeous antiques-filled

Tsunami Aftermath

On December 26, 2004, an earthquake measuring 9.0 on the Richter scale struck Indonesia's coast, triggering the infamous tsunami that sped across the Indian Ocean, destroying everything in its path. The Andaman Islands and Tamil Nadu were the worst-affected Indian states, with an estimated loss of 8,000 lives. In Tamil Nadu, the districts of Nagapattinam and Cuddalore suffered most, but the Coromandel Coast's tourist sites emerged more or less undamaged; in fact, a new discovery was made at Mamallapuram when the wall of water receded (see below). The destruction also produced some good initiatives. Besides plans to install an internationally coordinated high-tech tsunami early-warning system, a program called the Loyola Empowerment and Awareness Programme has offered alternative, more secure career paths for hundreds of children on the north coast. Linked to Chennai's respected educational institutions, the program has offered a new generation of kids—once slaves to their destiny as fisherfolk—opportunities to pursue careers in diverse new sectors such as catering and publishing.

Indo-French colonial mansions have been restored as hotels—the kind of "temple" that will appeal to the lazy hedonist in you. Having caught your breath in the wide boulevards and air-conditioned shops of Pondicherry, you can travel to Tiruchirappalli, exploring the holy temple town of **Srirangam** and the "Big Temple" at nearby **Thanjavur,** then overnight in the **Chettinad** region, where the wealthy Chettiars built palaces and painted mansions to rival the havelis constructed by the merchants and aristocrats of Rajasthan. Either way, your final Tamil Nadu stop will be the temple town of Madurai, to visit the magnificent **Sri Meenakshi-Sundareshwar Temple.** A place of intense spiritual activity, this temple is where up to 15,000 pilgrims gather daily to celebrate the divine union of the goddess Meenakshi (Parvati) and her eternal lover, Sundareshwar (Shiva)— one of the most evocative experiences in all of India.

Note: **Kanyakumari,** the venerated southernmost tip of Tamil Nadu, and another worthwhile addition but best reached from Kerala, is discussed in chapter 6.

1 Chennai

Chennai, India's fourth largest city, is neither ancient nor lovely but it is—like Bangalore and Hyderabad—booming. Established on the site of a fishing village in 1639 as the first British settlement in India, the capital of Tamil Nadu (formerly Madras) is a teeming, sprawling, bustling industrial metropolis, a manufacturing hub known as the "Detroit of the South," where 9 of the top 10 Indian IT companies are located. Unless you're here on business, or keen to shop, the city itself is only marginally fascinating— a strange mix of British Raj–era monuments, Portuguese churches, Hindu temples, and ugly 21st-century buildings, massive billboards, and concrete flyovers; even one of the longest urban beaches on earth is not enough to hold the attention for long. Most travelers arrive here simply because it's a transport hub and soon leave, distracted by the attractions that start only a few hours away—among them, **Kanchipuram,** city

Fun Fact   **Rule of the Screen Gods. And Money.**

It's not just temple gods who are worshiped here—screen gods are adored by the local population, enough to elect them to the highest political office: In fact, the majority of Tamil Nadu's leaders have kick-started their careers on the big screen, and nowhere else is politics quite as colorful (Arnie, move over). Across the state, you'll still see massive billboards featuring the swollen face of **Jayalalitha,** the controversial actress-turned-politician who has been in and out of political power for almost 2 decades. Kicked out of office on corruption charges in 2001, she jumped back in to reclaim her position a few years later, tossing her successor in jail in a drama worthy of a high-voltage Bollywood spectacle; Jayalalitha is currently the incorrigible leader of Tamil Nadu's opposition party. Despite the Tamils invariably voting out the incumbent, hampering delivery, the state registered a 6.3% annual growth rate during the '90s, ahead of 15 major states; it's one of the few states to have a surplus power supply and attracts a large chunk of direct foreign investment flowing into India. With a boom in automobile and technology industries, global players like Nokia, Ford, Hyundai, Dell, BMW, and Samsung are flocking to find their place under Tamil Nadu's sun; equally so the world's banks, who are choosing to open their headquarters in this state. All of which will, it is projected, translate into 800,000 jobs by 2011.

of "a thousand temples," is a day excursion away, while the beach resorts near **Mamallapuram,** a World Heritage Site, are only 2 hours south. Even charming **Pondicherry** is only 2½ hours away, making Chennai a destination of choice only with businessmen here to catch onto the coattails of one of India's fastest-growing cities.

ESSENTIALS
GETTING THERE & AWAY   By Air   There are daily flights to Chennai's **International Anna Airport** (Airport Information Centre; © **044/2256-1818**) and the **Kamaraj Domestic Airport** from all major destinations in India; both Madurai and Tiruchirappalli can be reached by flights from here. Anna International Terminal and Kamaraj Domestic Terminal are situated just over 12km (7½ miles) from the center. The 30-minute taxi ride from the airport to downtown (Mount Rd.) Chennai should cost around Rs 175 to Rs 350 ($4–$8/£2–£4) for a prepaid taxi.

By Train   Chennai has two major railway stations. **Chennai Central** (Georgetown) connects Chennai with most major destinations around India, while **Egmore** (© **131**) is the point of arrival and departure for trains within Tamil Nadu or Kerala. Some trains from within the state now also pull in at **Tambaram** Station, an hour from Chennai. You can get recorded train information by dialing the computerized © **1361** (remember to have your train number); alternatively call general inquiries on © **133** for arrivals and departures. To plan train travel, we suggest you go online to **www.indianrail.gov.in** or **www.southernrailway.org**. Or book your train at your hotel, at a travel agency (see below), or at the Rajaji Bhavan Complex (ground floor) in Besant Nagar.

Tamil Nadu

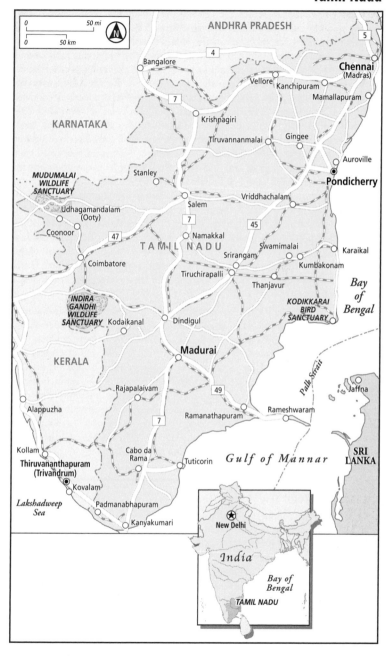

By Road   You may not realize it by glancing at a map, but Tamil Nadu is a fairly massive chunk of India, and it will take more than 15 hours to drive from Chennai to Kanyakumari in the far southwest of the state. Nevertheless, getting around is best done from the relative comfort of a rented car, with the wonderful rural landscape unfurling mile after mile (keep the window open to smell the freshness of turned earth and roasting cashews) and a driver who knows the way. **Kerala Adventures** ✦✦✦ (✆ **0484/231-3744;** www.keralaadventure.com; touch@keralaadventure.com) has a well-run office in Chennai, headed by the charming Mr. Prem (✆ **094-4261-2988**). Proprietor John Babu is knowledgeable and will help plan an itinerary that takes in the best of Tamil Nadu, before moving across the mountains into Kerala's Cardomom Hills, west to the coast, and—time allowing—north to Karnataka. Best of all his tariff structure is not only transparent, but offers excellent value. For tours within Tamil Nadu, you can use **GRT Tours & Travels** (✆ **044/6550-0000**), but they will try to push you to stay in their hotels and resorts, all of which are comfortable but not necessarily the best in each class; however, it's worth getting a comparative quote from them. Also reliable, and worth getting quotes from, are: **Balakrishna Tourist Taxis** (✆ **044/2641-6340**), **Sita World Travel** (www.sitaindia.com), **Travel House** (www.travelhouseindia.com), or **Madura Travel Service** (www.maduratravel.com). Regular buses are available for travel to almost any point in the state, Bangalore, and Tirupati; contact the **State Express Transport Corporation Bus Stand** (✆ **044/2479-4707;** daily 7am–9pm).

VISITOR INFORMATION   For general tourist information, contact **Indiatourism** (✆ **1913**). Staff at the Indiatourism offices (154 Anna Salai; ✆ **044/2846-0285** or -1459; fax 044/2846-0193; indtour@vsnl.com; Mon–Fri 9am–6pm, Sat 9am–1pm), across the road from Spencer's, is busy but attentive. CityInfo's useful *Chennai This Fortnight: The City in Your Hands* is a useful bimonthly booklet; it highlights hotels, restaurants, and shopping options and has listings for just about everything, from suggested walks to entertainment events. But the most useful pre-trip planner may be the following websites: **www.chennaibest.com** covers everything from art and shopping and restaurants (by cuisine style, with short reviews) to e-shopping; and **www.chennaihub.com** is similarly useful, only with even more detail (dance academies in Chennai? pool parlors?) and the option to book.

⎛ Tips **Heritage Walks**

Mylapore Times conducts two interesting heritage walks on Sundays from July to March (other months by special request); the walks start early (between 6:30 and 7:30am) to make the most of the coolest, most pleasant part of day. The **Mylapore–Santhome Walk** (some of which is by vehicle; Rs 150/$4/£2) covers the ancient temples and churches and heritage houses of Chennai's old neighborhoods, the predominantly Hindu Mylapore, and the adjoining Christian Santhome. The **Fort St. George Walk** (Rs 100/$2/£1) covers the 370-year-old fort, continues through old British offices and residences, St. Mary's Church, and army barracks, and ends at the Fort Museum. Each walk takes 3 hours; call Vasantha (✆ **044/2498-2244**).

ORIENTATION & NEIGHBORHOODS   Extending westward from the Bay of Bengal, Chennai is quite unwieldy. Linking the north and south of the city is Anna Salai, which starts out as G.S.T. Road (or Mount Rd.) near the airport in the southwest, and terminates at Fort St. George in George Town in the northeast. Two major rivers snake their way through the city—the Cooum River in the north, and the Adyar River several kilometers south. Between these, the most popular section of Marina Beach stretches between the sea and the city's busiest districts, where you'll find most of its hotels and a number of attractions. George Town lies just north of the Cooum's confluence with the Bay of Bengal. Southwest of George Town (around the Cooum River), Egmore and Triplicane form the heart of the commercial city. Farther south, the neighborhoods of San Thome and Mylapore are where you'll find the most significant religious monuments—**San Thome Cathedral** and **Kapaleshvara Temple.**

GETTING AROUND CHENNAI   By Taxi & Auto-Rickshaw   Chennai is a large, sprawling city, and its many sights are spread out and quite impossible to cover on foot. Auto-rickshaw drivers in this city are particularly adept at squeezing impossible fares out of foreign visitors—you would be well-warned to always fix a price upfront. Unlike other large cities, Chennai does not have taxis cruising the streets or idling at taxi stands. If you want a taxi, you will have to phone for one—for short distances, this is hardly worth the long wait or cost. For longer rides, **call taxis** are a good option and run by fairly reliable meters that start at a minimum base fare of Rs 50 ($1/60p) for 3km (2 miles), with Rs 10 (25¢/15p) for every additional kilometer. You can also negotiate flat rates. After 9pm, fares are surcharged anything from 25% more to double. Try **Bharat Call Taxi** (✆ **044/2814-2233**) or **Chennai Call Taxi** (✆ **044/2598-4435**). In "Fast Facts: Chennai" below, see "Taxis" for more call-taxi options, and "Car Rentals" for longer (1 or more days) excursions.

FAST FACTS: Chennai

Airlines Phone numbers you may need are: **Jet Airways** (✆ **044/2841-4141**, or airport 044/2256-1818); **Spice Jet** (✆ **098-7180-333** or 098-7180-3333); **Kingfisher** (✆ **1800/233-1131**).

Ambulance Dial ✆ **044/2815-0311** or -0700 or **Apollo** ✆ **1066.**

American Express 501 Spencer Plaza, Anna Salai; ✆ **044/2849-2582.** Open Monday to Friday 9:30am to 6:30pm; Saturday 9:30am to 2:30pm.

Area Code The area code for **Chennai** is **044.** For directory inquiries dial 197; time in English 174; change of telephone number in English 1952; 24-hour tele-information service 4444-4444.

ATMs There are numerous ATMs around the city; ask your hotel concierge or driver about a machine near you, or head for Spencer mall.

Banks & Currency Exchange There are a large number of foreign exchange dealers. **Thomas Cook:** Eldorado Building, 112 Nungambakkam High Rd. (✆ **044/2827-2610**); Ceebros Centre, 45 Monteith Rd. (✆ **044/2855-3276** or -4600); 20 Rajaji Rd., George Town (✆ **044/2534-2374** or 044/2533-0105). Open Monday to Saturday 9am to 6pm.

Bookstores **Landmark** (3 Nungambakkam High Rd./M.G. Rd.; ✆ **044/2827-9637** or 044/2823-7438; daily 9am–9pm) is said to be Chennai's largest and most popular bookstore, and also has a selection of music, stationery, and other items. **Higginbothams** (116 Anna Salai; ✆ **044/2256-0586**; daily 9am–7:30pm) is another recommendation with a great selection of books as well as Indian music.

Car Rentals See "Getting Around Chennai" above. **Welcome Tours and Travels** (✆ **044/2846-0614** or -0908; www.allindiatours.com; agnesh@vsnl.com) has a wide range of vehicles for rent at reasonable rates: you're looking at around Rs 630 ($15/£8) a day. Compare rates with **Bala Service** (✆ **044/2822-4444**) or **International Travel House** (✆ **044/2811-1206**).

Drugstore Located on the second floor of Spencer Plaza (769 Anna Salai) is **Health & Glow** (✆ **044/ 5205-6013**; Mon–Sat 9am–8pm, Sun 11am–7pm).

Embassies & Consulates **U.K.:** 20 Anderson Rd.; ✆ **044/5219-2151**; Monday to Friday 8:30am to 4pm. **U.S.:** 220 Anna Salai; ✆ **044/2811-2000**; Monday to Friday 8:15am to 5pm. **New Zealand:** "Maithri," 132 Cathedral Rd.; ✆ **044/2811-2473**; Monday to Friday 8am to 12:30pm, Saturday 8 to 11:45am.

Emergencies Police ✆ **100**. Fire ✆ **101**. Ambulance ✆ **102** (also see "Ambulance," above).

Hospital Internationally acclaimed **Apollo Hospital** (21 Greams Lane, off Greams Rd.; ✆ **044/2829-3333** or -0200) offers the city's top medical services; it also has a good round-the-clock pharmacy.

Internet As is the case in other cities, your most reliable bet is to find a **Sify iway** (when in Mylapore, head for the outlet on 59 Dr. Radhakrishnan Rd.) or **Reliance Web World** (there's one in Spencer Plaza).

Police For emergencies, dial ✆ **100**. For traffic police, dial ✆ **103**.

Post Office Although the **General Post Office** (Rajaji Salai; ✆ **044**) is in George Town, you're best off making use of the **Head Post Office** on Anna Salai (✆ **044/2852-1892** or 044/2851-8668). Its hours are daily 10am to 8:30pm.

Taxis For call-taxi services worth recommending, see "Getting Around in Chennai," above. Additional call-taxi services include **Fast Track** (✆ **044/2473-2020**) and **Dial-a-Car** (✆ **044/2811-1098**).

WHAT TO SEE & DO

Unfortunately, the city's attractions are very spread out, and getting around can be nightmarish; select a few choice attractions and get an air-conditioned taxi for the day. Presuming you've already spent the night in Chennai, get a predawn start by taking in the early-morning activities along the 12km (7½-mile) **Marina Beach** including fishing boats being launched (around 6am). If you'd rather sleep in, save the beach for dusk, when it becomes a colorful pageant of boys playing cricket, families strolling, vendors flogging souvenirs, and food carts offering fast-food snacks. Given that it's the world's second-longest city beach you might want to concentrate your energies on the best area: the vicinity of Triplicane, along Kamaraj Road.

The 8th-century **Parthasarathy Temple** (off Triplicane High Rd., west of South Beach Rd.; daily 7am–noon and 4–8pm) is near the main drag of Marina Beach;

dedicated to Krishna, it is believed to be Chennai's oldest temple, though extensively renovated by the Vijaynagar kings in the 16th century. South, near the lighthouse, lies Mylapore's **Basilica of San Thome** (San Thome High Rd., Mylapore; daily 6am–6pm), where the so-called final resting place of Thomas the Apostle has become a neon-lit attraction. Legend has it that St. Thomas, one of Christ's disciples, was martyred at St. Thomas Mount (see below) after spending the final years of his life preaching on a nearby beach. Stained-glass windows recount the saint's tale, and wooden panels depict Christ's final days on earth. The interior is also decked with bits of tinsel and neon-pink polystyrene hearts dangling from the ceiling; other modern kitsch additions include a halo of fairy lights.

Near the basilica is another 8th century temple, **Kapaleshvara** (also spelled Kapaleeshwar; off Kutchery Rd. and Chitrukullan N. St., Mylapore; daily 6am–12:30pm and 4–8:30pm), still a classic example of Dravidian architecture, where thronging devotees will give you an idea of what Tamil Nadu's devout worship is all about. The temple is marked by a 36m (118-ft.) *goparum* (gateway) tower adorned with detailed figures and inscriptions dating back to A.D. 1250. The place really comes alive during the Arupathumoovar Festival, 10 days in March.

Built by the Portuguese, **Luz Church** (Luz Church Rd.), also in Mylapore, is the oldest church in Chennai but if it's peace and quiet that appeal to you, visit the 16th-century **Church of our Lady of Expectations (Senhora da Expectação),** atop **St. Thomas Mount.** Built in 1523 by the Portuguese, the little church provides fine views over the city and is serenely removed from the city's nonstop commotion. Alternatively, spend some time roaming the gardens of the **Theosophical Society,** a sprawling 108 hectares (270-acre) campus of rambling pathways and shaded by trees including the Adayar Banyan tree, said to be 400 years old. The society's headquarters are the Huddlestone mansion, built in 1776, where relief imagery and quotations representing various faiths are on display (E. Adyar; ☎ **044/2491-3528,** -7198, or -2904; daily 9am–4:30pm).

Chennai's **Government Museum and National Gallery** (Pantheon Rd.; ☎ **044/2819-3238;** admission to Pantheon Complex Rs 250/$6/£3; Sat–Thurs 9:30am–5pm) is considered one of the finest receptacles of 10th- and 13th-century bronze sculpture in the country; visit if you're interested in Indian art (also 11th- and 12th-century handicrafts and Rajasthani, Mughal, and Deccan paintings) or simply need to escape from the sun. One of the buildings in this complex is the beautifully renovated **Museum Theatre,** where you can perhaps catch a dance or a music performance. While in Egmore, pop into **St. Andrew's Kirk** (off Periyar E.V.R. High Rd., northeast of Egmore Station, Egmore; ☎ **044/2561-2608;** daily 9am–5pm)—inspired by London's St. Martin-in-the-Fields, St. Andrew's steeple rises 50m (164 ft.) into the air; you can climb this to reach a small balcony for a good city view. To experience grand architectural heritage, set aside a few hours to visit **Fort St. George** (Kamaraj Rd.)—the first bastion of British power in India, constructed in 1640. The cluster of gray and white colonial buildings with pillared neoclassical facades now houses the Tamil Nadu State Legislature and the Secretariat. Visit its **Fort Museum** (☎ **044/2567-1127;** admission Rs 100/$2/£1; Sat–Thurs 10am–5pm; still camera without flash allowed with permission from tourist office) to see the collection of portraiture, oil paintings, sketches, and etchings that reveal the nature of colonial life in early Madras. In the compound is Asia's oldest existing Anglican church, **St. Mary's** (daily 9:30am–5pm), incidentally where Yale University's founder, Gov. Elihu Yale, was married. The church has numerous 17th- and 18th-century gravestones—look for the Latin memorial to Mrs. Elizabeth Baker (1652), believed to be the oldest British inscription in India.

Just north of the fort is the red-sandstone **High Court** (Mon–Sat 10am–5pm), built in the mid–19th century in the Indo-Saracenic style, and still in use today. Guided tours of the building take in the various courtrooms, many of which are remarkably decorated. Busy **George Town,** bounded by Rajaji Salai and N.S.C. Bose Road, was once known as "Black Town," a racist appellation for a settlement occupied by East India Company textile workers who came from Andhra Pradesh in the mid-1600s (the name "Chennai," incidentally, is derived from the name given to the area by the dyers and weavers who lived here: Chennapatnam). Today, George Town is a bustling collection of streets that should be explored on foot—not a good idea in the middle of the day.

DAY TRIP TO THE SACRED CITY OF KANCHIPURAM ★★★

All of Kanchipuram's roads lead to *goparums,* the unmistakable temple gateways that tower over you as you prepare to enter the sacred shrines. This 2,000-year-old city of "a thousand temples"—also called Kanchi—features on many travel itineraries, and is best seen as a day trip out of Chennai. With a rich heritage, it's famous as a seat of both Shaivaite and Vaishnavite devotion and for exquisite silk saris. It was here that the Dravidian style really had its roots, and the sheer profusion of temples makes this an ideal place to get a feel for how South Indian temple architecture has developed over the centuries. The oldest structure in town is **Kailasnath Temple** (Putleri St.; 1.5km/¾ mile out of the town center; daily 6am–12:30pm and 4–8pm), entered via a small gateway. Built by the same Pallava king responsible for Mamallapuram's Shore Temple, Kailasnath shows signs of evolution from its seaside forebear; it's also less overwhelming than many of the more grandiose Tamil temples.

The 57m (187-ft.) white *goparum* marking the entrance to the 9th-century Shaivite **Ekambareswara Temple** (Puthupalayam St.; 6am–12:30pm and 4–8pm; non-Hindus not allowed in sanctum) was added as late as the 16th century. Through a passageway, visitors enter a courtyard and the "thousand-pillared" hall (though the number of pillars has dwindled significantly over the years). Within the temple, a mango tree believed to be 2,500 years old apparently yields four different varieties of the fruit. Legend has it that it was here Shiva and Parvati were married, and that Parvati fashioned a lingam (phallic symbol) of earth, one of the five sacred Hindu elements. As a test of her devotion, Shiva sent a flood through the town that destroyed everything in its path except the lingam, which she protected from the deluge with her body. Be on the lookout for touts who will aggressively try to get a donation out of you at this temple.

Dedicated to the *Shakti* cult, which celebrates creation's female aspect, the 14th-century **Kamakshi Amman Temple** (Mangadu; daily 6am–12:30pm and 4–8:30pm) was built by the Cholas. Apparently, the tank there is so sacred that demons sent to bathe were cleansed of their malevolent ways. Other worthwhile temples include **Vaikunta Perumal Temple** and **Varadaraja Temple,** both of which are dedicated to Vishnu.

Note that, like elsewhere, Kanchi's temples close from 12:30 until 4pm, which means that you'll need to head out rather early or—better still—arrive in time for evening *puja* (prayer). However, traffic into and out of Chennai can get hellish during peak hours. If you're hot and hungry, head for the air-conditioned room at the vegetarian restaurant in **Hotel Saravana Bhavan** (504 Gandhi Rd.; ✆ **04112/22-2505;**

Silk Route

In general, visitors are drawn to **Kanchipuram** for two main reasons: its famed Kamakshi Amman temple, where the goddess Shakthi is worshiped, and—with 75% of the population employed in the hand-loom industry—its silk. The city is famous for producing the most exquisite hand-loomed silk saris in the world—called *Kanjeevarams*, the bridalwear of choice that become coveted heirlooms. A single *Kanjeevaram* sari costs anything from Rs 2,500 to Rs 100,000 ($61–$2,439/£31–£1,235), and can—depending on the intricacy of the pattern (often taken from temple carvings) and vividness of the colors (*zari*, or gold thread, is often interwoven with the silk)—take from 10 days to a month to weave. Of course, you don't have to wear a sari to covet the silk; plenty of haute couture designers have discovered its beauty, and any fashionista worth her salt will include Kanchipuram silk on her wish list.

6am–10:30pm), where you can feast on reasonably priced South Indian *dosas* (savory pancakes) or order a thali (multicourse platter).

Kanchipuram is 80km (50 miles) southwest of Chennai. Ask about guided tours of the temple town at the tourist office. Otherwise, guides can be picked up around Kailasnath Temple for around Rs 250 to Rs 350 ($6–$8/£3–£4); ask to see certification.

WHERE TO STAY

Given the generally insalubrious conditions of much of Chennai city, you're best off forking over some cash for a decent hotel, of which Chennai has a large inventory of business-orientated options, providing reliable comfort and standardized service. Better still, skip the city and head down the coast to **Fisherman's Cove** resort, which is right on the beach, a mere 50 minutes' drive (28km/17 miles) from Chennai airport and about 20km (12 miles) from Mahabalipurum (see lodging reviews for Mahabalipurum, later in this chapter).

Should you decide to spend the night in town, **The Park** (reviewed below; don't confuse it with the **ITC Park Sheraton and Towers** on TTK Rd.), which blew the lid off Tamil Nadu's hospitality industry when it opened in 2002, is *the* place to be mainline straight into Chennai's nightlife, with a sexy rooftop pool deck for daytime people-watching. If, on the other hand, you prefer old-world charm and a place with some history, the lovely, laid-back **Taj Connemara** is your best bet (again, reviewed below). Note that if you're just in transit, a few good hotels are located near the airport, the best of which is the low-rise **Trident Hilton** (© **044/2234-4747;** www.trident-hilton.com). It's 3 minutes away from the airport, and staffers have all benefited from the Oberoi school of training, so service levels are among the best in the city; the CBD is about 20 minutes away. With 167 elegantly outfitted rooms (bar slightly tarnished tub fittings) aimed at the business traveler, it has all the mod-cons you need to keep in touch. Mindful of their core market, rooms are also soundproofed, with blackout blinds to further cocoon the jet-lagged traveler. The pool area is also delightful; you'd never know you were in a semi-industrial area (until aircrafts take off, of course). If the rates strike you as steep (from $200/£101 double), you should see what neighbor **Radisson GRT** (www.radisson.com) is offering; at press time it was identical, and the Trident Hilton definitely has the edge.

Note: Many of the city's upmarket hotels offer significant discounts on published rates depending on the season and occupancy; ask about options. Also ask hotels about courtesy airport shuttle/transfers.

The Park 🏵🏵   The Park hotels see themselves as India's premier boutique chain, not realizing perhaps that being a chain means you more or less have to forgo the "boutique" moniker. Besides, while attempting to be super-trendy, some effects are looking a little dated, with fittings and finishes due for a refurb. But there's no doubting its place in the hearts of Chennai movers and groovers, who flock here to dine at the 24-hour eatery off the lobby, **Six-O-One (601),** recommended for its unusual, varied menu (and one of the best *masala dosas* in the city), as well as to the **Leather Bar** and **Pasha,** the city's most popular nightclub (see below). The Park's other celebrated dining options include **Lotus,** a popular Thai restaurant, and **Aqua,** a cool cafe where the outdoor seating, on *diwans* (Indian recliner sofas) near the pool, is terrific. Having covered Chennai's social scene (which being a guest here gives you automatic access to), you can retreat to your extremely comfortable "pod," and sleep off events on one very comfortable mattress. Next day, stroll down to the Ispahani Centre for some retail therapy.

601 Anna Salai, Chennai 600 006. ✆ 044/4214-4000. Fax 044/4214-4100. www.theparkhotels.com. fo.che@the parkhotels.com. 214 units. $275 (£139) deluxe double; $300 (£151) luxury double; $350–$900 (£177–£455) suite. Extra bed $25 (£13). AE, DC, MC, V. **Amenities:** 3 restaurants; bar; nightclub; health club; gym; spa; travel assistance; car hire; secretarial services; 24-hr. room service; laundry; doctor-on-call; currency exchange. *In room:* A/C, TV, mini-bar, tea- and coffee-making facilities, hair dryer, electronic safe.

The Residency Towers 🏵 *Value*   This is a modern, comfortable, well-run hotel, in no way a luxury property but nothing that will depress you (though I take personal offense at the fabric cover on the toilet seat). The most cheer-inducing aspect is that it's the best-value deal in town. It's also conveniently located in downtown Chennai but only 12km (7½ miles) from the airport. Book a room on the 11th floor (the only nonsmoking floor, with standard rooms); book a Residency Club room and they'll throw in a complimentary airport transfer (though you can get a taxi for less than the additional Rs 1,800/$44/£22 this will run you). Room decor changes from floor to floor but you're basically looking at gold touches paired with a green-blue theme or rich maroon. Dining options are nothing to write home about; just cross the road to dine at the **Copper Point,** the in-house restaurant at neighboring hotel **GRT Grand** (very similar, by the way, but with rates running at around Rs 2,500/$61/£31 higher; www.grtgrand.com) offering very, very good Indian fare. The pool area is a little drab, but at least it's there for when the Chennai heat really has you beat.

Sir Thyagaraya Rd., Chennai 600 018. ✆ 044/2815-6363. Fax 044/2815-6969. www.theresidency.com. restowers@ vsnl.net. 174 units. Rs 4,200 ($102/£52) double standard; Rs 5,000 ($122/£62) Residency Club double; Rs 6,300–Rs 20,000 ($154–$488/£78–£247) suite. Rates include breakfast. MC, V. **Amenities:** 3 restaurants; resto-pub; pool; health club; car hire; business center; room service; laundry; doctor-on-call; salon/parlor. *In room:* A/C, TV, minibar, Wi-Fi (fee charged per hr.).

Taj Connemara 🏵🏵🏵   Book a heritage room at Chennai's oldest five-star hotel (it's been around since 1891) for a sense of colonial splendor and old-world charm right in the heart of modern Chennai (Spencer Plaza, the city's biggest shopping complex, is directly opposite). Although the exterior is very unprepossessing, enter and you are transported into another era, with gracious public spaces, wide corridors, and high-ceilinged rooms, all tastefully decorated with wooden engravings, temple sculptures, and luxury fabrics. Add an attentive staff and the best restaurant in town, and you have a recipe for total comfort. All categories of rooms are super spacious and elegant, with top amenities (but no views to speak of). However if you're here to celebrate something special, your choice without a doubt should be one of the striking heritage rooms: largest in the city, with antique furniture, rich drapes, and soft furnishings; the luxurious setting is fit for a king—even the room's ceiling fan rotates both ways, letting you decide which way the breeze should blow.

Binny Rd., Chennai 600 002. ℂ **044/5500-0555**. Fax 044/5500-0000. www.tajhotels.com. Connemara.chennai@ tajhotels.com. 150 units. $240(£121) superior double; $275(£139) deluxe double; $300 (£151) heritage double; $350–$625 (£176–£316) suite. Extra bed $40 (£20). AE, DC, MC, V. **Amenities:** 2 restaurants; bar; 24-hr. coffee shop; pool; health club; travel desk; business center; room service; laundry; doctor-on-call; currency exchange; salon. *In room:* A/C, TV, minibar, tea- and coffee-making facilities, hair dryer, ironing equipment, Wi-Fi.

WHERE TO DINE

With most Chennaites preferring to dine at home, the city has a dearth of fine-dining options, with most remaining cloistered in the city's five-star hotels. But with the greater economic prosperity, that pattern is slowly changing. We'd like to encourage you to experience the delicious and varied flavors of South India, particularly the cuisine of the Chettinad, surrounded by Chennaites. Two of the best places to do this are the superb **Karaikudi** ⭐⭐ (84 Radhakrishna Salai; ℂ **044/2491-0900**) and **Saravana Bhavan** (see "Eating with Your Hands," below). Karaikudi is more "upmarket" than Saravana Bhavan, with carpeted floors and waiters wearing the traditional Panchakacham style; at the entrance two large brass pots are supposed to emulate that of a Chettinad home. But it's in no way fine dining (for that you'd best stick to the five-star hotels), with indifferent service. But the food is truly superb; try the special Chettiar chicken pepper roast with *appams,* the (fried) pigeon *Varuval,* or best of all, order the thali (multicourse platter). An average meal here will run you Rs 60 to Rs 150 ($1–$4/50p–£2) per person.

If you're bored with South Indian food, you'll also find many of the world's tastes represented in the city. If you're mood is for Thai, don't miss the highly rated **Benjarong,** reviewed below; if it's Italian, head for **Bella Ciao** (4 Shree Krishna Enclave, off Water Land Dr., Kottivakkam Beach; ℂ **044/2451-1130**), where Ciro Cattaneo serves authentic pizzas and pastas at a pleasant outdoor venue near the beach. **Hip Asia** ⭐ (ℂ **044/5500-0000**), the Taj Connemara's stylish restaurant, is where imported chefs twirl knives and jars at the Japanese *teppanyaki* counter. Delicate Vietnamese and Thai (avoid the Malay) dishes are superbly crafted, and served in a trendy setting that transforms itself from a lunch to dinner space.

Chennai also has several shop-and-unwind stops worth considering. **Moca Café,** better known by the store's name, **Amethyst** (Jeypore Colony, Gopalapuram; ℂ **044/ 2835-1627**), is set in a delightful old colonial bungalow where you can choose to sit indoors or outdoors under the shade of huge, century-old trees. Kiran Rao, the cafe/ shop owner, serves organic gourmet coffee and great cakes. Upstairs you'll find designer clothing in Western designs and Indian fabrics. Some evenings, performances or book or poetry readings are on offer. **Chamiers** (Chamiers Rd., across from ITC Park Sheraton; ℂ **044/2431-1495**), situated in a charming bungalow, offers food similar to that at the Moca Café, juices, and fresh salads served in the shade of an almond tree. It's attached to Anokhi, the leading Jaipur design store (see chapter 10), where you can buy Western-style clothes designed in traditional India hand-block-print fabric. Both Moca Café and Chamiers (and the stores) are open every day of the week.

Benjarong ⭐⭐⭐ THAI   Popular with Chennai's international diplomats and bankers, as well as visiting Bollywood stars, Benjarong (the name refers to the hand-painted gold porcelain used in Royal Thai households) is perhaps the city's only non-hotel

---

(Moments Eating with Your Hands

A superb and authentic introduction to South Indian cuisine is a lunch at an outlet of **Saravana Bhavan** (the one near the station may be most convenient). We recommend that you sit in the large hall where the locals eat with their hands (there is usually a small, drab air-conditioned room where "refined" Indians and foreigners eat the same food with cutlery—not nearly as much fun, and pricier to boot). It can be a bit intimidating to eat with your hands, given that many of the dishes are quite liquid, and none of the servers who wander around with huge pots dishing out spoonfuls speak English. If you find this daunting, or you're simply not sure how to proceed with the many courses that are piled onto your banana leaf (which you rinse with the water on the table), ask your driver (assuming you have one) to join you for lunch and follow his lead. Ask what each spoonful is, and by the end of your meal you'll have taken a crash course in South Indian food. Come hungry: The special Tamil Nadu thali is an assortment of 23 items for just Rs 95 ($2/£1). If that much food seems overwhelming, order a minitiffin (an assortment of tasty breakfast items, including the "definitive taste" of Sambar, a gravy that is mopped up with a variety of pancakes) and a traditional South Indian coffee.

---

fine-dining option; certainly it's Chennai's best Thai restaurant. You're welcomed with a ginger-flavored drink—a delicately refreshing concoction to whet the appetite—and with a selection of taste-size treats called *mein kam,* wrapped in pandanas leaves. The spicy *tom yam* soup is possibly the best you'll get outside Bangkok, made using *goong* (prawn brains) and tempered with ginger. Signature dishes include chargrilled duck *(ped yang)* done to perfection; also wonderful is spicy *gai pahd bai graprou,* ground chicken tossed with chilies and hot basil. If you're up for something simpler, green curry prawn is a standout favorite, as is the chicken wrapped in banana leaf; or go for fish delicately flavored with tamarind. Top off the evening with *tub tim siam* (water chestnut in chilled coconut milk), jackfruit custard (in summer), or *sankaya fathong* (coconut-pumpkin custard) and ice cream.

146 T.T.K. Rd., Alwarpet. © 044/2432-2640. Reservations essential on weekends. Main courses Rs 148–Rs 428 ($4–$10/£2–£5). AE, DC, MC, V. Daily 12:15–3pm and 7:15–11:30pm.

Raintree ✹✹✹ CHETTINAD   It was in this atmospheric outdoor restaurant— one of the best in the state—that Chettinad cuisine first emerged from the Chettiar family kitchen and into the commercial arena. The rain trees were sadly swept over by a massive storm some years back, but a number of palms still bravely screen off Spencer mall, and the ambience, lit with fairy lights and candles, is very pleasant indeed. Try to book a table in front of the stage, featuring a slick classical dance and music program. After sipping a welcome drink—a wide-brimmed copper goblet of *vasantha neer,* honey-sweetened tender coconut water, delicately flavored with mint leaves—you can't go wrong with crunchy *Karuveppilai year,* prawns marinated in a curry leaf paste and deep fried, as a starter, along with *Urugai idli vathakkal* (pickle-filled cocktail *idlies*) and *Kuzhi paniaram* (rice and lentil batter tempered with spices and shallow fried on a special griddle). Leave space for mains, of which the *kozhi Chettinad,* deliciously tender boneless chicken in an authentic Chettinad gravy, best had with *appams* (rice flour pancakes) and *Meen kozhumbu* (spicy fish curry with shallots, garlic, onion, tamarind pulp, and fresh mango—have this with lemon rice, or mop up with a *dosa*), will blow you away. Even if you don't have a sweet tooth, do not leave without trying the *elaneer paayasam*—tender coconut kernels, coconut milk, and condensed milk—it's unlike anything you've ever tasted, and you'll wish this was home.

Taj Connemara, Binny Rd. © 044/5500-0000. Reservations essential in winter season. Main courses Rs 265–Rs 525 ($6–$12/£3–£6). AE, DC, MC, V. Daily 7:30pm–midnight.

CHENNAI AFTER DARK

Chennai doesn't have much of a nightlife, with the police keeping a strict eye on closing time: midnight. If all you want is a drink, the best place to do so is the **Leather Bar** ★★★ (© 044/5214-4000), at The Park hotel. Go not just for the beautiful leather floor and suede-covered walls or the gorgeous clientele, but for the super-hip tunes belting from the orbital DJ booth, transporting you far away from Chennai's heat and hectic crowds. Afterwards, saunter over to The Park's nightclub, **Pasha** (© 044/5214-4000), a crowded, happening place to see and be seen—it warrants a visit even just for a few minutes to see the cool crowd (easy if you're residing at The Park, which automatically gives you free access). Alternatively, head for **Platinum Dance Bar** at the Quality Inn Aruna, formerly known as HFO (an amusing acronym for Hell Freezes Over), the 557 sq. m (6,000-sq.-ft.) steaming pit that was once the most popular nightclub in town; check around to find out if the place is still pumping.

For a more subdued evening (well, that depends on the night, actually), head over to **Distil** (© 044/5500-0000) at the Taj Connemara: With large-screen TVs, it has a bit of a sports-bar feel, but when it's full it has an energetic buzz. The fresh fruit cocktails are great; try the lychee vodka or the watermelon martini.

SHOPPING

Chennai isn't charming, but it does offer good shopping—if you want a one-stop shopping destination, head to **Spencer Plaza** (opposite Taj Connemara), or **City Centre,** the latest addition to Chennai's mall lineup. With around 400 shops, Spencer Plaza is said to be the largest shopping complex in South India: Two outlets worth looking for here are the famous **FabIndia,** where you can pick up cotton garments, *kurtas* (tunics), and ethnic furnishings and linens (if you hate huge malls, you can try the outlet at Ilford House, 3 Woods Rd.; © 044/2851-0395 or 044/5202-7015); and **Hidesign,** the latter a Pondicherry-based outfit renowned for top-quality leather goods, created by Indian craftsmen as well as internationally renowned Italian designers. (Hidesign is also in the **Ispahani Center** on Nungambakkam High Rd.; © 044/2833-2111 or 044/5214-149; here you can also pop into Casablanca for men and women's wear, don't miss the Gecko linenwear). While you're on Nungambakkam, head over to **Khader Nawaz Khan Road** for the most dense concentration of designer wear in the city (as well as, bizarrely, a Marks & Spencer). If you're not going to Pondicherry, this is where you can browse the goods produced by the community in the City of Dawn at **Naturally Auroville Boutique** (© 044/2833-0517). For housewares, handicrafts, and antique furniture, visit **Kalpa Druma** (71 Cathedral Rd.; © 044/2811-7652 or -1695). Go to the Taj Coromandel's **Khazana Shop** (37 M.G. Rd.; © 044/5500-2012 or -2827), for silks, saris, and various objets d'art in an upmarket, luxurious environment. Across the road from the Coromandel, **Central Cottage Industries Emporium** (672 Anna Salai; © 044/2433-0809 or -0898) is the fixed-price government emporium with a virtual monopoly on package tourist shoppers. Farther up the road is **Poompuhar,** the government emporium of Tamil Nadu

(818 Anna Salai/Mount Rd., near Higginbothams), which has a better selection of art pieces unique to the state—pick up a Tanjore painting or woodcarving or bronze figurine. The **Victoria Technical Institute,** also on Anna Salai, showcases embroidered and crocheted linens and smocked children's wear made by nuns for charity.

   The Design Store on C. P. Ramaswamy Rd. (✆ **044/2499-7157**) is a fine option for trendy, quality home decor with an ethnic touch. Eco-warriors should head for **Prana: Live Natural** (D6 6th St., near Chintamani, Anna Nagar East; ✆ **044/4217-0077**) for organic clothing for men and women, all natural or naturally dyed (or "safe-chemical" dyed). **Cane & Bamboo** (21 Marshalls Rd., Egmore; ✆ **044/2852-8672**) is a good shop for curios and gifts—trays, bowls, spoons, lamps, and other handicrafts made of different species of wood sourced from all over India—and managed by the knowledgeable Mrs. Thangam Philip, who can tell you about the different artifacts she stocks. **Amethyst** (see "Where to Dine," above) is excellent for lovely Western-style clothing and other souvenir handicrafts made with Indian fabrics and design elements. Even if you have absolutely no intention of buying a silk sari, you must visit **Nalli Chinnasami Chetty** ✵✵ (9 Nageswaran Rd., T. Nagar, near Panagal Park; ✆ **044/2434-4115;** www.nallisilk.com), a Chennai institution, where you can't help but fall in love with the exquisite silks, including the famous Kanchipuram silks. T. Nagar also has an outlet of **Kazaana Jewellery** (the other is on Cathedral Rd., the first shop in India to introduce a "guarantee card" to buy back any item at market rate); this street is incidentally also the best place to look for clothing bargains, while Pantheon Road is the place for cheap but attractive linen.

THE WORLD'S WEALTHIEST TEMPLE: A SIDE TRIP TO TIRUPATI IN ANDHRA PRADESH ✵✵

Situated on a peak of the Tirumalai Hills, overlooking Tirupati (just across the Tamil Nadu border into Andhra Pradesh), is the second busiest and richest religious center on earth (after the Vatican), drawing more than 10 million devoted pilgrims every year. Certainly the richest temple in the world, the Dravidian-style **Sri Venkateswara Temple** is said to be the heart of Hindu piety, but in many ways it appears to exist expressly for the collection of wealth connected to a legendary loan: Lord Venkateswara, the living form of Vishnu, apparently borrowed an enormous amount of money from the God of Wealth in order to secure a dowry for his bride. Devotees donate generously in order to help their god settle his debt—the loan must be repaid in full, with interest, before the end of this epoch. Annual donations of jewelry, cash, and gold (along with sales of *laddus* or sweets and donated human hair) total around 1.5 billion rupees. Much of this goes to the temple kitchens that prepare meals, free accommodations for pilgrims, and various charitable hospitals and schools.

   The inner shrine is presided over by a diamond-ornamented 2m (6½-ft.) black idol that stands at the end of a narrow passage. Pilgrims queue for hours, sometimes days, excitedly preparing for *darshan*—the extraordinarily brief moment when you're all but pushed past the god by guards to ensure that the sanctum doesn't become clogged with devotees, many of whom succumb to the moment by falling to the ground. Waiting amid the mass of anxious, highly charged pilgrims, you'll get a good sense of the religious fervor of the Hindu faith. By the time you reach the moment of *darshan,* thousands of excited, expectant worshipers will be behind you, chanting Vishnu's name. Once out of the inner shrine (one of the few in South India that non-Hindus can enter), you'll make your way past a massive fish-tank-like enclosure, where temple clerks count the day's takings—possibly the most cash you're ever likely to see in one place.

Tips Jumping the Queue

Wealthier pilgrims can now make use of a computerized virtual queue system that streamlines the *darshan* experience. Pilgrims buy an armband imprinted with their *darshan* time, shaving hours—even days—off their wait in line. Foreign visitors should bring their passports and appeal to the Assistant Executive Officer or A.E.O. (ask one of the temple police for directions) for a special *darshan* ticket, which costs anywhere from Rs 200 to Rs 4,000 ($5–$98/£2–£49) depending on the kind of speedy access you request (you will also be fingerprinted and photographed at this stage; ask your hotel if you need to book this a day in advance). Paid for at a special counter, it cuts waiting time to around 2 hours. Note that men must wear long pants or *lungis;* women must be conservatively dressed with long skirts and shoulders covered. Prior to entering the queue, you'll be asked to sign allegiance to the god. Avoid taking part if you suffer from claustrophobia, since you'll still have to spend an hour or two within cagelike passages designed to prevent line-jumping. Temple activities commence at 3am with a wake-up call to the idol *(suprabhatham)* and continue until 12:45am the following morning. On Sundays the temple closes.

Note: As you're waiting in line, you'll see many shaven heads—it's common practice for believers to have their heads tonsured before going before the deity as a devotional sacrifice. As a result, a lucrative human hair business contributes significantly to the temple coffers—Far East and Italian wig manufacturers are major consumers of world-renowned Tirumalai hair, shorn by a fleet of barbers permanently in the service of the temple.

ESSENTIALS   For information you can log onto **www.ttdsevaonline.com** for tickets, but you'll more than likely find everything sold out—in which case you can try calling the call center (© **0877/223-3333** or 0877/227-7777, ext. 3679). The easiest ways to get here are by plane (the nearest airport, Renigunta, has regular flights from Chennai, Hyderabad, and Bangalore); alternatively travel by train from Chennai (or Hyderabad, Bangalore, or Mumbai). To overnight, prebook a room at the dependable (and popular) **Fortune Kences** (© **0877/225-5855;** www.fortunehotels.in; kences@fortuneparkhotels.com; doubles $55–$65/£28–£33), which is located in the heart of the town and draws the well-heeled devotees. Service is very good, and the hotel is comfortable (but not luxurious).

2 Mahabalipurum (Mamallapuram) ★★★

51km (31 miles) S of Chennai

A visit to this once-thriving port city of the Pallavas, a dynasty that ruled much of South India between the 4th and 9th centuries A.D., is an excellent introduction to South Indian temple architecture, and a much more pleasant base to kick off your Tamil Nadu itinerary than Chennai. Established by Mamalla, "the Great Wrestler," the tourist town of Mahabalipurum attracts thousands to view the earliest examples of monumental architecture in southern India—incredible rock-cut shrines that celebrate Hinduism's sacred pantheon and legends. Even today, the descendents of these early sculptors continue to create carvings for temples, hotel foyers, and tourists; the sounds of sculptors chipping away at blocks of stone echo through the narrow lanes, an aural reminder of the sort of devoted craftsmanship that must have possessed the original masons who created the World Heritage monuments. It's possible to survey the best monuments in a morning, provided you get an early start (ideally, long before domestic tourists arrive en masse around mid-morning). This leaves you time to unwind on the pleasant beach and dine on a plate of simply prepared fresh seafood. You could even overnight, enjoying its charming villagelike atmosphere, a million miles from the 21st century hustle that is Chennai. Alternatively, you can move on to Pondicherry after lunch and be sipping Gallic cocktails before sundown.

ESSENTIALS

GETTING THERE & AWAY   Mahabalipuram is 2 hours south of Chennai, on the East Coast Highway. Buses from Chennai arrive and depart every half-hour from the suburban Koyambedu bus stand (state-owned buses at Mofussil and private buses at Omni stand). Pondicherry is around 40 minutes away by road.

VISITOR INFORMATION   The **Government of Tamil Nadu Tourist Office** (Kovalam Rd.; ✆ **04114/242-232;** Mon–Fri 10am–5:45pm) can supply you with limited information (like a map of Tamil Nadu) and a few booklets on the town. Peak season is December to February; July and August, when the French are on holiday, is also busy.

GETTING AROUND   All of the town's attractions can be reached on foot, or you can catch an auto-rickshaw.

EXPLORING THE SHRINES & TEMPLES

Mahabalipuram's monolithic shrines and rock-cut cave temples lie scattered over a landscape heaped with boulders and rocky hillocks. Among these, the excellent **Shore Temple,** built to Lord Shiva, and the **Five Rathas,** a cluster of temples named for the five Pandava brothers of *Mahabharata* fame, are definitely worth seeking out. The celebrated **Arjuna's Penance** is the largest relief-carving on earth—try to see these as early in the day as possible, before busloads of noisy holiday-makers descend. Also try to view **Mahishamardini Mandapa** (and give the nearby government-run Sculpture Museum a miss). If you feel the need to visit an active temple, head for **Talasayana Perumal Temple,** dedicated to Vishnu. It stands on the site of an original 9th-century Pallava temple but was rebuilt during the 14th century by the Vijayanagar King Parang Kusan, who feared that the sea would eventually erode Shore Temple. Half-hour *puja* (prayer) sessions are conducted daily at 9am, 11:30am, and 7:30pm. About 4km (2½ miles) north of Mahabalipuram, **Tiger Cave** (★ (Covelong Rd.) is the site of an 8th-century shrine to the tiger-loving goddess Durga. It's thought that the shallow cave, with its sculpted *yalis* (mythical beasts) framing the entrance, might have been used for open-air performances. Seventeen kilometers (11 miles) west of Mahabalipurum, in the Kanchipuram district, **Tirukkazhukundram,** named for the holy kites (eagle-type birds) that make their home here, are popular with pilgrims who come to witness the Brahmin priests feeding the two birds of prey at midday. *Note:* Herpetologists and beleaguered parents may wish to make a pilgrimage of a very different kind: Set up by the famous herpetologist Romulus Whitaker, **Crocodile Bank** (15km/9 miles north of Mahabalipuram; Rs 20/45¢/25p; Tues–Sun 9am–5:30pm) is an extremely successful breeding and research center that currently sustains around 2,500 crocodiles, including 14 of the world's 26 species.

Arjuna's Penance ✫✫✫   Opposite Talasayana Perumal Temple, the world's largest bas-relief is commonly referred to as "The Descent of the Ganges," depicting the sacred penance performed by one of the Pandava brothers. Standing on one leg, the meditative Arjuna contemplates Shiva—a painful reparation performed while lively representations of the gods, celestial nymphs, elephants, monkeys, and other creatures look on. A naturally occurring cleft down the rock is said to represent the Ganges, a symbol that comes to life during the rainy season when water flows into a tank below. Just a few meters away, to the left of Arjuna's Penance, is **Krishna Mandapam** ✫, another bas-relief, carved in the mid–7th century; this one depicts Krishna using his divine strength to lift a mountain to protect people from imminent floods. The duality of the god's nature is expressed in carvings of him going about more mundane activities, including flirting with his milkmaids. Near Arjuna's Penance, to the north, is the huge spherical boulder known as **Krishna's Butter Ball,** balancing on a hillside.
W. Raja St.

Mahishasuramardini Cave ✫✫   A lighthouse tops the hill where you'll find a number of superb rock-cut shrines—seek out **Mahishasuramardini Mandapa,** remarkable for the two impressive friezes at each end of its long veranda. In the panel to the right, Durga, the terrifying mother of the universe, is seated astride her lion *vahana* wielding an assortment of weapons. She is in the process of destroying the buffalo-headed demon, Mahisha, who disturbs the delicate balance of life. At the opposite end of the veranda, Vishnu is depicted sleeping peacefully on his serpent bed, the sea of eternity; gathered around him, the gods appeal to him to continue the creation. Also atop the hill, **Adivaraha Mandap** features various sculpted figures and mythical scenes, including one large panel of Vishnu as a gigantic boar.
W. Raja St.

Panch Pandava Rathas ✫✫✫   The initial sight of these five *(panch)* monolithic stone shrines, set in a sandy fenced-off clearing, is dramatic, even though the structures themselves—named for the five brother-heroes of the *Mahabharata* and resembling temple chariots *(rathas)*—are incomplete. The ancient sculpting techniques are astonishing: Carved out of single pieces of rock from the top down, these shrines reveal perfect, precise planning. The dome-shaped *shikhara* (tower finial) found on some of the temples became the template for later South Indian temples, successful experiments that were further refined and enlarged.
E. Raja St., 1km (a half-mile) south of Arjuna's Penance. Tickets available from ASI booth at the entrance. Single ticket for both Five Rathas and Shore Temple costs Rs 250 ($6/£3). Daily 6:30am–5pm. Approved guides can be hired at the entrance.

Shore Temple ✫✫✫   Perched at the edge of a sandy beach on the Bay of Bengal, where it has been subjected to centuries of battering by salt water and oceanic winds, this early-8th-century stone temple is considered one of the oldest temples in South India, and a forerunner of the Dravidian style. Its two carved towers inspired a style that spread throughout the region and to more distant Asian shores. Vishnu is found reclining inside one shrine, while two others are dedicated to Shiva. A low boundary wall topped by rock-cut Nandi bulls surrounds the temple, and a veritable pride of lions rear their heads from the base of the pillars.
Northeast of the Panch Pandava Rathas, at the beach. Tickets available from ASI booth at the entrance. A single ticket for entrance to both the Five Rathas and the Shore Temple costs Rs 250 ($6/£3). Daily 6:30am–5pm. Approved guides can be hired at the entrance.

Lost City: The Temple Uncovered by the Big Tsunami

When the powerful wall of water began to recede from the shores of Maha-balipurum, it uncovered ancient rock sculptures of lions, elephants, and pea-cocks—all fairly common motifs used to decorate walls and temples during the Pallava period in the 7th and 8th centuries. Could this be the remains of a once thriving city, submerged below the sea when the shoreline changed? Archaeol-ogists working off the coast after the December 2004 tsunami have already uncovered the remains of a massive collapsed temple, built entirely of granite blocks, renewing speculation that Mahabalipurum was a part of the legendary Seven Pagodas, written of in the diaries of European travelers, and that six temples remain submerged in the ocean.

WHERE TO STAY & DINE

The best place to stay (and eat) in Mahabalipurum itself is a very small, very basic out-fit, located right on the beach, and a real find if you don't mind giving up on hotel comforts for a night or two. **Santana** (© **094/4429-0832** or 098/4078-9576; babu-santana@rediffmail.com), owned by the affable Babu Santana, comprises six rooms on the rooftop of his tidy beachfront restaurant, and they're the best deal in town. Rooms share a patio that runs the length of the building; rooms 101 (the top choice corner room; Rs 800/$20/£10) and 102 (Rs 700/$17/£9) have views of the Shore Temple from their patio chairs. The others (Rs 600/$15/£7 each) are set further back and have no views, but they are neat as a pin, and besides, you can spend the better part of the day reading your book on the restaurant deck, snacking on plates of fresh grilled cala-mari and chips (Rs 150/$4/£2), masala-fried prawns and salad (Rs 100/$2/£1), or vegetable *kuruma* with chapati (Rs 50/$1/50p), or just enjoy the view of the Shore Temple with the cooling sea breeze. Note that July through August is lobster season; Babu can also arrange outings on the traditional fishing boats that line the beach in front of the restaurant.

The best resort option (other than Fisherman's Cove, about an hr. north of the Mahabalipurum temples) is **GRT Temple Bay.** The GRT is located right on the beach, with hotel and chalet-style units, most with sea views; best of all it's close enough to Mahabalipurum to enjoy a view of the Shore Temple from the restaurant. It has typical resort-type amenities (including a beautiful rim-flow pool) and plenty of children's activities. The best accommodations are in the chalet sea-view category (ask for a "front sea-facing upstairs unit"), with private ocean-facing patios; these have air-conditioning, TV, and semistocked minibars (© **044/2744-3636;** www.grttemple bay.com; mail@grttemplebay.com; from Rs 7,000/$159/£80 double, with additional supplement charged over the festive season). The so-called **Ideal Beach Resort,** located just a little farther away (3km/2 miles from Mahabalipurum), is your next bet; it's very old-fashioned and indifferently managed, but offers a range of standard amenities. Again, ask for an upstairs front unit with an ocean view; no. 38 is a good choice (© **044/2744-2240;** www.idealresort.com; doubles Rs 1,850–Rs 6,000/$42–$136/£21–£69). Whatever you do, give the newly opened (Feb '07) **Fortune Char-iot Beach Resort** a miss—ill-conceived and badly designed, with few sea views, and depressingly ugly. Not even the pool has a view (it faces the back-end of the presiden-tial suite) and, given these mistakes, the rates are prohibitive.

Taj Fisherman's Cove ✰✰✰   Built on the site of a 17th-century Dutch fort, this bright, breezy, beachfront resort is set on 8.8 manicured hectares (25 acres) with a labyrinth of tidy, shrub-lined pathways. It's a great refuge, within easy striking distance of both Chennai and Mahabalipurum, but this means it is also very busy, with plenty of businessmen choosing to base themselves here, while weekends see it packed with family trippers. Most guest rooms are in the main hotel block, which can be incredibly noisy; better by far to book one of the shell-shaped cottages scattered about the cropped lawns—these are delightful, with bamboo-enclosed alfresco showers, private hammocks, bright interiors in shades of orange, yellow, and green, and breezy patios with Chettinad swings. Those cottages facing the sea directly (nos. C4–C14) are the best spots from which to admire the surf. Larger luxury sea-facing villas are also available; each one has a semi-private garden with palm trees supporting your own hammock and cane-strung rockers on a covered porch. Interiors are a little more formal and old-fashioned, but also more spacious, with high-pitched ceilings and an indoor bathroom that has a separate tub and shower. When you're not out exploring ancient temples, you can try out the huge number of activities on offer, laze around a pool with a sunken swim-up bar, stroll along the beach to the nearby village of Kovalam (also known as Covelong; not to be mistaken for its more famous namesake in Kerala), peruse the menu at the thatched beachside **Bay View Point,** or dine on Mediterranean fare at the new **Upper Deck.** Both are lovely dinner locations, particularly when the moon rises ahead, creating a glittering crease in the swirling velvet black of the ocean.

Covelong Beach, Kanchipuram District, Chennai 603 112. (C) **04114/27-2304** through -2306. Fax 04114/27-2303. www.tajhotels.com. fishcove.Chennai@tajhotels.com. 88 units of which 38 are cottages. $210 (£106) standard double room; $235 (£119) standard sea-view double; $270 (£136) cottage garden-view double; $320 (£162) sea-view cottage; $370 (£187) sea-view villa with private garden. Supplements charged Dec 22–Jan 8. AE, MC, V. **Amenities:** 3 restaurants; 2 bars; pool; kids' pool; tennis; health club; bicycles; children's activity center; indoor games; concierge; travel desk; car hire; shopping arcade; 24-hr. room service; Ayurvedic massage center; babysitting; doctor-on-call; currency exchange; library; beach volleyball; badminton; catamaran trips; fishing excursions; ecology tours. *In room:* A/C, TV, minibar, tea- and coffee-making facilities, hair dryer.

3 Pondicherry (Puducherry) ✰✰✰

189km (117 miles) S of Chennai

Pondicherry's ancient history dates back to the Vedic era; the Romans traded here 2 millennia ago, and the Portuguese arrived in 1521. Dutch and Danish traders followed, but it was the French—who purchased the town in the late 17th century, only relinquishing their hold in 1954—who left the most enduring legacy. Now a Union Territory, with its own local government, this seaside colony retains its French élan, tempered by South Indian warmth, making it one of India's most relaxing destinations. After hanging out in your antiques-filled colonial hotel and sauntering around the broad boulevards of the tranquil **French Quarter** (where you'll see old men in thick-rimmed spectacles under the apparent illusion that they're in a Parisian *arrondissement*), it comes as a pleasant shock to step over the "Grand Canal" into a typical Tamil town, where cracked pavements are jam-packed with people and shops, and wares on offer, blend Indian craftsmanship with Western-influenced designs. Even if you're not a keen shopper or particularly interested in French colonial architecture, you can immerse yourself in the spirituality of Puducherry (as it is increasingly referred to) by joining the New Age travelers and Indian pilgrims here to pay their respects at the ashram of **Sri Aurobindo,** their blissful commitment making this a bizarrely authentic spiritual experience. Or you can visit nearby **Auroville,** an interesting experiment in alternative living, also optimistically known as the City of Dawn. Ashramic allure and Aurovillian aura aside, Pondi (as it is affectionately called) is the type of charming seaside town where you arrive for a quick overnighter and end up staying; like Goa, it has a number of expats whizzing around on scooters to prove it. And, yes, it's far friendlier than Bordeaux.

ESSENTIALS

GETTING THERE & AWAY   Pondicherry is best reached by road from Chennai, a 3½-hour drive (140km/87 miles from the airport), mostly along a two-lane highway; a taxi will run you around Rs 1,800 ($41/£21) (Rs 1,500/$34/£17 if you're coming from Pondi). There are also regular buses (Rs 50–Rs 60/$1.15–$1.35/60p–70p) connecting Pondi with Chennai. To get here by train from Chennai (or Madurai/Trichy), you must first travel to Villuparam station (30 min. away; buses every 10–15 min. in peak time) to catch the train; it takes 5 hours from Chennai. See chapter 2 for online rail reservations or inquire at the **railway station** (South Blvd.; ℂ **0413/233-6684**).

VISITOR INFORMATION   Pondicherry's helpful **Tourism Information Centre** (40 Goubert Ave.; ℂ **0413/233-9497** or -4575; fax 0413/235-8389; www.tourism. pon.nic.in; daily 9am–5pm) can help you with maps, brochures, and tour bookings. *Repos The Images of Pondicherry* (www.thetravelmate.com) carries extensive local listings. A good locally based travel agent is **Travelmate** (ℂ **0413/420-0525;** www. thetravelmate.com).

GETTING AROUND   By Taxi & Auto-Rickshaw   Auto-rickshaws prowl the streets in some areas, actively soliciting fares. Overcharging is rife, but if you've got several kilometers to cover, it may be worthwhile to hire one; the minimum charge is Rs 30 (70¢/35p) for 6km (3¾ miles). Pondi to Auroville costs around Rs 200 ($4.55/£2.30) by auto-rickshaw and Rs 350 ($7.95/£4) by taxi.

By Bicycle   Parts of Pondicherry are immaculate and ideal for exploration by bike. You can rent a bike (Rs 35–Rs 40/80¢–90¢/40p–45p per day) from the Pondicherry Tourism Information Centre (see above). Ask about hiring the services of a guide who can cycle along with you.

By Boat   Offshore cruises are available through the **Tourism Information Counter** (40 Goubert Ave.; ℂ **0413/233-8643**), where you can arrange a sea cruise for Rs 1,250 ($28/£14) an hour.

GUIDED TOURS   Guided tours and sightseeing trips can be arranged through Pondicherry Tourism (see above); Rs 90 ($2.05/£1.05) for a half-day or Rs 110 ($2.50/£1.25) for a full day. Alternatively, heritage tours are offered by the **Indian National Trust for Art & Cultural Heritage** (INTACH, 14 Labourdonnais S.; ℂ **0413/222-5991** or -7324; www.intach.org; ashokpan@yahoo.com).

WHAT TO SEE & DO

The joy of Pondicherry is the fact that you need no car to have it all. Simply wander through its tree-lined French Quarter, one of India's most prepossessing neighborhoods, with wide boulevards, uncluttered roads, bilingual signs, stately government buildings, and gorgeous residential villas. Then step into another world by crossing the "Grand Canal" aqueduct, into the area the French used to call "black town"—typically Tamil, with tiny shops lining crowded streets, beeping rickshaws, and—at night—an almost carnival atmosphere. Besides strolling the streets, browsing shops, and taking the seaside promenade, the only other attractions—and really, this is one place you will feel entirely guilt-free—are **Aurobindo Ashram,** and a trip to **Auroville** (the "City of Dawn"), a must for anyone who remains a hippie at heart.

It's lovely just wandering through the Quarter, but you may want to make sure your walk takes you past the **Sacred Heart of Jesus (Eglise de Sacre Coeur de Jésus),** an 18th-century neo-Gothic Catholic church on South Boulevard, as well as the facade of the **Church of Immaculate Conception** (Mission St.) which has an air of pageantry enhanced by colorful banners (it's interesting to note that many Christian devotees remove their shoes before entering). Dedicated to Ganesha, the elephant-headed god, **Sri Manakula Vinayagar Temple** is off a side street so popular that it's cordoned off during the early-evening hours; a temple elephant marks the entrance. For a quick glimpse of local historic memorabilia and collectibles, visit the **Pondicherry Museum** (49 Rue St. Louis; ✆ **0413/233-6203;** Tues–Sun 10am–5pm), housed in a 17th-century colonial mansion once occupied by the French administrator. The museum features a collection of carriages and carts, stone sculptures, and a formidable bronze gallery. Along the same road, which runs along the northern end of a square known as **Government Place,** is **Raj Nivas,** the late-18th-century mansion occupied by Pondicherry's lieutenant governor.

At twilight, head for **Goubert Salai** (Beach Rd.). The most interesting sights along the promenade (aside from the locals enjoying themselves) include the colonial **Hôtel de Ville** (now the Municipal Offices building) and the 4m (13-ft.) statue of Gandhi standing at the pier. If you're here for a few nights, it's also worth looking into the cultural events, art exhibitions, and film screenings conducted regularly by Pondicherry's **Alliance Française** (✆ **0413/233-8146;** fax 0413/233-4351; afpondy@satyam.net.in; Mon–Fri 8:30am–12:30pm and 2:30–6pm.

Aurobindo Ashram 🐦🐦   Located in the French heart of Pondicherry, Aurobindo Ashram draws a global mix of ardent devotees and ordinary people searching for peace or looking to improve their meditation skills. Sri Aurobindo, a politically active British-educated Bengali who sought asylum from the British in this small French enclave, took to meditation and yoga while developing theories of enlightenment that integrated his personal spirituality with the tenets of modern science. He met Mirra Alfassa, a Paris-born artist on a similar spiritual quest, in 1914; she became his soul mate, and her ministrations earned her the appellation "The Mother." Founded as a place to foster evolution to a higher level of spiritual consciousness, the ashram opened in 1926. With a significant following and numerous published titles to his credit, Aurobindo left the running of the ashram to Mirra, retreating into solitary confinement for 24 years before finally passing away in 1950; The Mother followed in 1973. Today, those who share their vision of a better world come to pray and meditate aside the memorial chambers *(samadhis)* of Sri Aurobindo and The Mother, which lie in the center of the peaceful main courtyard. It's a very humble place, not like the huge or ancient temples typical of Tamil. Within the house (where the couple once lived) you will find the wise elders of the ashram, who are available for questions—if you have any burning spiritual issues, this is the place to air them; the answers you will receive will inspire. Note that unlike Auroville, outsiders cannot join the Ashram.

Rue de la Marine. ✆ 0413/223-3649. Free admission; no children under 3. Daily 6am–noon and 2–6:30pm.

WHERE TO STAY
IN PONDICHERRY

For spotlessly clean budget accommodations right on the sea, look no further than **Sea Side Guest House** (14 Goubert Ave.; ✆ **0413/233-6494;** seaside@sriaurobindo

The City of Dawn: Sixties Sci-Fi in the 21st Century

Conceived in 1964 by Sri Aurobindo's French-born disciple, Mirra Alfassa (aka "The Mother"; see "What to See & Do: Aurobindo Ashram"), the **Auroville Project** was founded on a tract of land some 8km (5 miles) north of Pondi. It was based on Mirra's vision of a place that could not be claimed or owned by any nation, one where all humanity could live freely and in peace—a city that would ultimately become a living embodiment of human unity. Largely designed by French architect Roger Anger, **Auroville** drew a group of citizens from all corners of the globe and was inaugurated in 1968, when soils from around the world were symbolically placed in an urn along with the Auroville Charter. Today it is still home to a diverse population, a number of whom were here from its inception, but many more continue to arrive over the years, making this the most interesting, globally representative community in India, and effectively its only privately owned "suburb," built almost entirely on the hippie principles typical of the '60s.

At its spiritual and physical heart is the huge futuristic spherical structure known as **Matrimandir**, a symbolic space devoted to the "divine creatrix." An ongoing project, the structure is a flattened dome spanning 36m (118 ft.) in diameter. Covered in glistening gold discs fixed to the outer surface of the dome, it looks like a faux UFO from a 1960s sci-fi film set. The inner marble chamber houses 12 meditation "petals" (each concerning attitudes towards the Divine and humanity worth striving for, such as sincerity, humility, gratitude, courage, generosity, and peace). At the center is a huge man-made crystal (said to be the largest in the world) that reflects the sun's rays and produces a concentrated light to enhance meditation. Visitors who obtain passes can have a brief peek at this chamber between 4 and 5pm each day, and it's possible to stay for meditation until 6pm (note that the interior was closed at press time for renovations).

sociaety.org.in). It's basically a small hostel-like hotel, run by the Aurobindo Society, so service is either benign or indifferent, and there are no real amenities. But the combination of location and price is unbeatable: a double A/C room with sea view costs a mere Rs 775 ($18/£9)! Sea-facing suites cost Rs 975 ($22/£11) a day; extra mattress Rs 150 ($3.40/£1.70). The only possible irritant is the fact that the gates are locked at 11:15pm, and no alcohol is allowed on the premises. It's understandably popular, so book well in advance. If you'd like to stay in Auroville, contact Pierre Elouard, owner-chef of Satsanga; he also has a guesthouse with room located next to the ashram for Rs 1,500 ($34/£17) (© 093-4542-3637; pierree@auroville.org.in).

Hotel de l'Orient   Tamil and Cajun spices scent the air of this award-winning heritage hotel—more guesthouse than hotel, this is a slightly run-down but charming 1760s manor house located in the heart of the French Quarter. Sensitively restored and furnished with French colonial antiques, it captures the period grandeur of a colonial nobleman's mansion. With none of the modern touches or stylish flair displayed at Le Dupleix (see below), some may find this more authentic, but be warned that

Radiating from the Matrimandir and its gardens, which also have an amphitheater built with red Agra stone where the occasional performance is held, the city is architecturally conceived along the lines of a galaxy, evolving organically within certain preset parameters. The original design planned accommodations for 50,000 residents; currently there are about 1,500 from 35 countries, all apparently committed to being "willing servitors of the Divine Consciousness." Every year new citizens are accepted into the City of Dawn, based on the needs of the existing population (schoolteachers are always welcome!) and following a stringent evaluation. Far more than a place for devotional meditation, Auroville is an experiment in self-sufficient living that supposedly takes both nature and culture into account, with all members providing some service to the community. Certainly its architectural innovation and utopian idealism make this a place of interest for anyone with a penchant for the unusual, the ethereal, or the novel, but living here is no doubt a great deal more challenging since the mediating presence of The Mother is no longer there to smooth over the flaws of life among mere mortals. But it is the global residents of Auroville who give Pondicherry its unique flavor, with many running restaurants and retail outlets in the coastal town and beyond.

As a day visitor you will need to stop at the **Tourist Information Centre** (𝒞 **0413/262-2239**; www.auroville.org), where you can pick up brochures, shop, snack, and watch a video presentation before moving on to visit the Matrimandir (Mon–Sat 9:45am–12:30pm and 1:45–4pm; Sun 9:45am–12:30pm) and surrounding gardens.

service is very laid-back. Each of the guest rooms—set around an inner courtyard shaded by citrus and neem trees—is themed and named for a former French colony (a renovation of the adjacent bungalow has produced a new wing with four new rooms that are not as charming as the original manor house rooms). Comfortable and airy, with shuttered windows, high ceilings (some original wood ceiling beams), and tall French doors, the rooms are elegantly attired in whites, pinks, yellows, or cool emerald. Top favorites are Karikal (a truly "Grand Room" with terrace and veranda) and Yanaon (a bargain, given its size, at Rs 3,750/$85/£43). Arcot, which has a patio, is also recommended (Rs 3,250/$74/£37), while Masulipatam is a good choice in the Rs 2,500 ($57/£29) category. Most accommodations overlook or are linked to the romantically candle-lit courtyard restaurant, **Carte Blanche,** where local "Creole" cuisine, a blend of South Indian and French, is served. Don't miss the gift shop; it has some wonderful and fair-priced souvenirs sourced from all over India.

17 Rue Romain Rolland, Pondicherry 605 001. 𝒞 **0413/234-3067.** Fax 0413/222-7829. www.neemranahotels.com. orient1804@satyam.net.in. Delhi reservations: Neemrana Hotels Private Ltd., A–58 Nizamuddin E., New Delhi 110 013. 𝒞 **011/2435-6145** or -8962. Fax 011/2435-1112. sales@neemranahotels.com. 14 units. Rs 2,500–Rs 3,750

($57–$85/£29–£43) double room; Rs 5,000 ($114/£57) luxury suite. AE, MC, V. **Amenities:** Restaurant; gift shop; laundry. *In room:* A/C, tea- and coffee-making facilities, hair dryer on request.

Le Dupleix ✺✺✺   Owner Dilip Kapur (creator of the internationally renowned leather brand Hidesign) and his glamorous wife restored and modernized this 18th-century French colonial villa (originally built for the French governor of Pondicherry), blending old-world and au courant styling with ease. Every room in this urbane, compact hotel is unique, with super-modern bathrooms, comfortable beds, French reproduction writing desks, and louvered shutters. The best rooms are the two luxury penthouses (modern glass and teak boxes of which no. 15 is best; no. 14 is bigger); of the deluxe rooms, no. 9 is best. If your budget can't stretch that far, opt for no. 6 or 7 (superior rooms); note that nos. 3 and 4 are really tiny. The public spaces have lovely touches—on the entrance terrace, an old-fashioned gas lamp hangs from trees, a traditional swing hangs in the hallway, and everywhere you'll find plenty of ornate woodwork (salvaged by Kapur when the house belonging to French governor of yore Marquis Joseph Francois Dupleix was demolished). A granite waterfall by French sculptor Francois Weil is reflected in the glass staircase landings, and walls are covered in a special Chettinad plaster—a mixture of egg white, powdered sea shells, and yogurt. Open-air dining is at the **Courtyard Restaurant,** where Pondicherry-French and Indian-fusion cuisine are served, and presentation is as important as freshness of ingredients. The first boutique hotel in Pondicherry, Le Dupleix is in many ways the best option in town; in fact it would be if the staff wasn't so snooty.

5 Rue De La Caserne, Pondicherry 605 00. ✆ **0413/222-6999.** Fax 0413/233-5278. ledupleix@sarovarhotels.com. www.sarovarhotels.com. 14 units. $65 (£33) superior double; $100 (£50) deluxe suite; $120 (£60) luxury penthouse; $130 (£66) luxury suite. MC, V. **Amenities:** Restaurant; bar; travel desk; Chennai airport transfers; 24-hr. room service; in-room spa massages; laundry. *In room:* A/C, TV, minibar, tea- and coffee-making facilities, hair dryer, safe, DVD player on demand, Wi-Fi.

The Promenade ✺✺✺   The latest addition to Pondicherry's fashionable boutique scene, The Promenade is a small, newly built seaside hotel from the same team that brought us Le Dupleix. It doesn't have the charm of its heritage sister, but if you bag a sea-facing room you'll have the glistening waters of the Bay of Bengal to make up for it. Rooms are well designed and classy, with huge leather headboards, raw-silk bed throws, teak-framed doorways and floors (not a cheap laminate strip in sight), and Zenlike low-level beds and floating cupboards; bathrooms are compact and ultramodern. The public spaces are more spacious than that at Le Dupleix, and there's a plunge pool to cool off in; best of all is the rooftop terrace, **The Lighthouse,** which opens at night. It's an atmospheric restaurant, with the sounds and smells of the sea, a view of the nearby lighthouse, and dining that is as good as the views; get here before sunset and watch the passing parade strut the Promenade.

23 Goubert Ave., Pondicherry 605 001. ✆ **0413/222-7750.** Fax 0413/222-7141. www.sarovarhotels.com. promenade@ sarovarhotels.com. 35 units. $75 (£38) deluxe double; $95 (£48) sea-facing double; $120–$180 (£60–£91) suite. Rates include breakfast. MC, V. **Amenities:** 2 restaurants; lounge bar; plunge pool; travel desk; airport transfers; 24-hr. room service; laundry; doctor-on-call; Wi-Fi access throughout; rooftop aerobics; board games. *In room:* A/C, TV, minibar, tea- and coffee-making facilities, hair dryer, safe, DVD player on demand, Wi-Fi.

Villa Helena ✺   Owned by Roselyne Guitry, a perfumer from Burgundy who has lived in Bangkok, Delhi, and now Pondicherry, this guesthouse started out as an annex in which Roselyne could keep her collection of antiques and traditional furniture. A natural decorator, she claims the place was "thrown together," and operates her villa as a nonprofit hobby and an opportunity to meet people from around the world. A communal porch with gracious arches and pillars, where you can relax in planters' chairs, is a plus, while the guest rooms are in a heritage building with lovely high ceilings on the ground floor. It's all rather quirky and charming, if not in any way luxurious, and a good value as such, but don't expect a staff complement or any real service—for that you're better off at Hotel de l'Orient.

13 Lal Bahadur Shastri (Bussy St.), Pondicherry 605 001. (C) 0413/222-6789, or 0413/420-0377. Fax 0413/222-7087. villahelena@satyam.net.in. 5 units. Rs 2,000 ($45/£23) standard double; Rs 2,500 ($57/£29) deluxe. Coffee and soft drinks on demand. No credit cards. **Amenities:** Limited room service; laundry. *In room:* A/C, TV (in deluxe).

OUTSKIRTS OF PONDICHERRY

Pondicherry is a charming town and made for pedestrians, so you'll probably want to base yourself in the center and wander at will. That said, there are two good beach resorts within easy striking distance, so if you prefer to do nothing but relax around a pool, with the option of popping into Pondi, these are well worth looking in to. The Dune Village (below) is a one of the most interesting resorts in India, but **Kailash Beach Resort** ((C) **04132/619-700;** www.kailashbeachhotel.com; from Rs 3,000/$68/£34 double), a 37-unit retreat situated about 20 minutes south of Pondi, and run by the well-traveled Raj, an ex-publisher, and his French wife, Elisabete, is another good bet. It's billed as a "beach" resort, but there are no sea views (the beach is a short stroll away), and you're more likely to find yourself by the massive pool than braving the pounding surf. The sprawling pink buildings are apparently inspired by Sikkim architecture, with plenty of carved doorways and deep terraces with comfortable seating; rooms are cool and comfortable though positively bland when compared to the Dune Village.

The Dune Village 🌟🌟 *Kids* This is one of the quirkiest destinations in India, and will appeal to those with an artistic and/or ecological bent. It features "thematic guesthouses" and installations peppered throughout the 12-hectare (30-acre) coastal stretch (many of them created during artist-in-residence programs), so that each unit is totally unique (which, it must be said, makes for an architecturally messy look). Set aside expectations of a single harmonious design ethos, and a one-on-one inspection evokes sheer delight at the highly creative expressions of the people and artists who have fashioned this ever-evolving village. The Tower Suite soars above Grecian-style block units painted in peacock blue, while farther along a playful interior showcases high kitsch in glossy plastics and wall-to-wall Bollywood posters. The array of options runs from eco-designed traditional thatched single-room units on stilts right on the beach to double-story and walled L-shaped villas, ideal for families. Even the pool, a deep, seemingly cantilevered bowl, is interesting. Like elsewhere on the Coromandel coast, the sea is usually too rough to swim in, but staff are on hand to keep an eye out should you wish to challenge the surf (don't do this alone). It's a very laid-back place (no reception as such, and you're handed a mobile phone to summon staff in what is a huge sprawling area), but manager Sunil is an absolute charmer and will bend over backwards to ensure a pleasant stay. There is nothing he can do about the lack of pressure in some of the toilets, however, the temperature in some of the showers, the ugly spotlights at the adjoining fishing village (built post-tsunami), or the heavy maintenance a unique property like this requires: Eco-friendly practices (solar, water treatment plant, natural ventilation, organic vegetable farm) exact a small price, so don't book here if you're all for 21st-century comfort. *Tip:* The Village, a great party venue, is host to live music concerts from December to February; make sure you book in advance for one of these.

Pudhukuppam Keelputhupet, 605 014 Tamil Nadu. ℂ 0413/265-5751. Fax 0413/265-6351. www.thedune.in. booking@thedune.in or booking@epok.in. (www.artistsinresidence.org.) 35 units. Rs 3,300–Rs 11,000 ($75–$250/ £38–£126) non-A/C double; Rs 6,500–Rs 14,500 ($148–$330/£75–£166) A/C double. All rates include breakfast. Additional person Rs 1,000 ($23/£12); child Rs 400 ($9/£4.55). Children under 5 stay free in parent's room. 20% off Apr–June. AE, MC, V. **Amenities:** 2 restaurants; bar; pool; tennis; bicycles; children's playground & activities; travel desk; 24-hr. room service; laundry; Ayurvedic treatments; beach volleyball; table games; library; day trips to Pondi/Auroville; open-air auditorium. *In room:* A/C (some), minibar (some), DVD player, guest cellphone.

WHERE TO DINE

Given the Indian and French influences, it's hardly surprising that you're spoiled for choice in Pondicherry, and space constraints are the only reason the following restaurants are not reviewed in full. All of them, incidentally, are walking distance from one another. For daytime dining, it's a toss-up between **The Bistro** (38 Rue Dumas St.; ℂ 0413/222-7409), located in the gardens of a rather run-down heritage hotel, and the nearby **La Terrasse** (5 Subbiah Salai; ℂ 0413/222-0809). Set beneath a thatched roof, with roll-down blinds, cane furniture (green plastic seats for the spillover), and potted plants, The Bistro (aka Indochine) has a lovely, laid-back courtyard-garden atmosphere. However, the more basic La Terrasse has the edge when it comes to food, which is simple but good (the fruit lassis are out of this world). Both are semi-alfresco; if you're looking to escape the heat by stepping into an A/C icebox, **Ayar Bakery** (12 Jawaharlal Nehru St.; ℂ 0413/420-5210) is a spotlessly clean vegetarian multi-cuisine canteen-style restaurant near the ashram; order the delicious *navrattan korma.*

When night falls and temperatures are balmy, you'll definitely want to dine alfresco: Aristo's rooftop (reviewed below) is the place to go for delicious, authentic and inexpensive Indian food, but if you're looking for a special-occasion venue, the following three options are tops. **The Lighthouse Grill** ⭐⭐, the rooftop restaurant at The Promenade (see above), is a sexy, atmospherically lit evening space, with a slick bar/club-type atmosphere—bizarre given that you're in a sleepy coastal town. Book a table up against the wall (so you can watch the passing parade as it strolls the Promenade), order the tandoori seafood assortment (Rs 600/$14/£7.05 for 2), and splash out on a chilled bottle of white wine. Alternatively, the *skiandari raan* (tender marinated leg of lamb cooked in a clay oven), washed down with Kingfisher beer, should have you smiling from ear to ear. For a more cosseted old-fashioned atmosphere, head over to the leafy, candle-lit courtyard at Hotel de l'Orient (see above for address): At press time the menu at **Carte Blanche** ⭐⭐ had undergone an extensive revamp by the French executive chef, fusing French recipes with Indian ingredients (predominantly coconut and curry leaves). Start with the carrot mousse and cumin, and follow up with one of the super fresh fish dishes on offer. Steamed seerfish filets are spiced with a green, pink, and black pepper sauce; red tuna is served with an olive sauce. Or sample the quartet of fish matched with a delicate saffron sauce. **Satsanga** ⭐ (30 Labourdonnais St.; ℂ 0413/222-5867), another alfresco restaurant specializing in French cuisine, is where you'll find many of Pondi's French inhabitants, as well as a large contingency of tourists. Owner-run by Pierre Elouard, an expat from the south of France who has been living in Auroville for 33 years, Satsanga is a Pondi institution, and more laid-back than the Lighthouse Grill or Carte Blanche. If you're a carnivore, opt for the legendary green-pepper filet *(filet au poivre vert)* or the fish Provençal. If Satsanga is full, you could also try **Rendez-vous Café** (30 Rue Suffren; ℂ 0413/233-9132), where owner Vincent (another expat) claims to serve the best pork (bred by Jesuit priests in Kodaikanal); try it Indian style (pork *vindaloo*) or the more conventional roast pork.

Finally, if you find the French-influenced cuisine a little pretentious here on the subcontinent and prefer the deadly spices of the local Chettinad cuisine, an alternative to Aristo's A/C room (see below) is nearby **Appachi** (8 Rangapillai St.; ℂ **0413/222-0613**). It's very popular with locals, so get here early or be prepared to wait for a table.

Aristo ⭐⭐ *Value* CONTINENTAL/INDIAN   If you aren't in the mood to spend excessively, find Indian cuisine tasty, and want quick service (a rarity in Pondi), then head for Aristo, a rooftop restaurant overlooking chaotic Nehru Street. Expect little from the decor—plastic seating and plain crockery—but the place is breezy, clean, and cool. Enthusiastically twittering birds in a cage compete with a background soundtrack of pop songs and below, the honks and beeps of busy traffic. Evenings, with the rooftop lit with fairy lights, are more peaceful. The food is very reasonable and for the most part pretty good. Make a beeline for the *biryanis* (prepared for 4 hr.) or the steaks; if you find it's too hot to eat something meaty (often the case) try the *poisson du chef:* Chef Anwar's special fish in mushroom sauce. If you feel like having spicy local cuisine, then head for the first floor, where a totally different menu awaits you in an air-conditioned room that fits about eight tables. An absolute must is the Ceylon egg *paratha* (pancakelike bread, stuffed with meat and onions, wrapped in egg, and fried lightly); accompany that with just about anything that strikes your fancy— it's all extremely tasty and excellent value for money.

114 Nehru St. ℂ **0413/233-4524** or 0413/430-8202. Main courses: Rooftop Rs 90–Rs 180 ($2.20–$4.40/£1–£2.20); Chettinad restaurant everything under Rs 100 ($2.45/£1.25). MC, V. Daily 11:30am–4:30pm and 6:30–10pm.

SHOPPING

Pondicherry is paradise for shoppers: Just about everything is within walking distance (and there are plenty of eager rickshaws if not), and, thanks to the Auroville and ashram communities, the goods on offer are of a far superior quality to that in any other Tamil town. First stop has to be Mission Street to spend at least an hour at Auroville's best outlet, **Kalki** ⭐⭐⭐ (132 Mission St.; ℂ **0413/233-9166**), where you browse for superb leather footwear (for men and women), hand-painted silk clothing, perfumed candles, incense, oils, ceramics, jewelry, and handmade paper items to the accompaniment of artsy, esoteric music. It's not cheap, but the atmosphere and selection is fantastic. If there's anything you want that's not in your size, you can arrange to have it made and couriered to your next destination. Across the road is **Casablanca** (165 Mission St.; ℂ **0413/222-6495** or 0413/233-6495), one of South India's funkiest department stores (owned by the glam couple who created Le Dupleix and The Promenade), with top international brands spread over three floors. If you love linen, head straight upstairs and peruse the gorgeous Gecko stock (gecko@auroville.org.in). Casablanca is also a great place to pick out a new handbag from the **Hidesign** selection on offer. Around the corner is the **Titanic Factory Outlet** (33 Aambalathadayar Madam St.; ℂ **0413/234-2075**), for international brands (Guess, Ralph Lauren, Gap, Tommy Hilfiger, Timberland, and the like) at Indian prices—a great place to dig for clothing bargains. Also on Mission Street, next to the Church of Immaculate Conception, **Focus** bookstore (ℂ **0413/234-5513**) has hundreds of books on Indian culture and religion, owned and run by the ashram.

The tiny **Boutique Auroshree** (18 Jawaharlal Nehru St.; ℂ **0413/222-2117**) sells clothes and handicrafts from all over India; it has a small selection of silver jewelry, paintings, and handcrafted bronze, brass, and sandalwood items. **La Boutique d'Auroville** ⭐ (J.N. St.; ℂ **0413/262-2150**) sells more goods from Auroville, from lovely pottery and handmade paper to original garments. **Curio Centre** (40 Roman

> ## *Tips* Carting the Shopping Back Home
>
> For many people, India is the number-one place to shop, and Pondicherry is quite possibly our favorite village-style town to do so; problem is, you'll soon run out of luggage space, and the last thing you want is to be weighed down. Here's the plan: Head down to the nearest domestic counter (there are dozens, virtually on every street; try Best Cargo on 71 Aurobindo St.) and courier your shopping to your final destination. It costs no more than around Rs 40 to Rs 50 (90¢–$1.15/45p–60p) per kilo and takes around 3 days—worth it given the inflated prices you pay for goods in Mumbai and Delhi.

Rolland St.; ✆ **0413/222-5676**) has a selection of objets d'art as well as indigenous and colonial antique furniture. Next door is **Art Colony** (32 Romain Rolland St.; ✆ **0413/233-2395**), with mostly antiques (as well as some reproduction furniture), wood carvings, and handicrafts. If you're interested in art, specifically paintings, don't miss **Cottonwood** 𝕲𝕲𝕲 (Rue Nidarajapayer, next door to Touchwood, a great cafe with Internet service), which showcases the work of five top local artists—you'll be hard-pressed to leave here without a canvas signed by Dhanasegar or Stridher.

For funky gifts (lights, bags, tops, sandals), don't miss **Nirvana Boutique** 𝕲 (53B Rue Suffren, opposite Alliance Française), which is also near the Pondi outlet of **FabIndia** (59 Rue Suffren); while you're on that side, pop into **Kasha-Ki-Aasha** (23 Rue Surcouf; www.kasha-ki-aasha.com); upstairs is a good place to snack and stop for tea (though service is atrocious).

Back on the promenade, it's worth popping into **Splendour** (16 Goubert Ave.; ✆ **0413/233-6398**), with more goods exclusively produced by the Aurobindo Society. Besides toys, belts, bags, and incense, you can pick up a wide range of books on the Society and Sri Aurobindo.

Finally, if you're looking for a shopping experience to fill your camera (rather than just suitcases), head down **M.G. Road** on Sunday to peruse the market. Packed with people and stalls, this is exuberant local life at its best and pure Tamil Pondi. Equally so the fish market, held daily (5am–2pm) on M.G. Road: It's pure mayhem (and rather smelly; take a hanky if you have a sensitive nose), but it's the real deal, and a far cry from the land of chichi boutiques.

4 Tiruchirappalli (Trichy), Thanjavur & Chettinad Region

Trichy: 325km (202 miles) from Chennai; 55km (34 miles) from Thanjavur; 90km (56 miles) from Chettinad

Tiruchirappalli, "City of the Three-Headed Demon," sprawls at the foot of colossal **Rock Fort,** where the Vijayanagar empire built its once-impregnable citadel when they wrested power from the Cholas in the 10th century. During the bitter Carnatic wars, French and British forces battled for control of the city, both keen to establish control of the looming hilltop fortress. Today a number of neo-Gothic Christian monuments remain as evidence of the British influence during the 18th and 19th centuries, when a cantonment was established here and when the present-day city was built. But it is the nearby temple town, lying just beyond Tiruchirappalli, that draws visitors here. Another legacy of the mighty Vijayanagars, the holy town of **Srirangam** occupies an island in the Cauvery and is considered one of the most impressive temple towns in South India.

Almost directly east of Tiruchirappalli (or Trichy, as you may refer to it if you can't master the tongue-twister), is **Thanjavur,** once the capital of the Chola empire—which included present-day Kerala, Sri Lanka, and parts of Indonesia. Here its 11th-century **Brihadeshvara Temple,** a World Heritage monument, is (together with Mahabalipurum and Madurai) the most important stop on Tamil Nadu's temple route. Having visited the Brihadeshvara Temple, plan to overnight in the **Chettinad** region, which lies around 1½ hours south. Known predominantly for its pungent, spicy cuisine, this little-known area, comprising some 75 villages centered around the town of Karaikudi, is enjoying a slow revival. Visitors, keen to explore the palatial mansions built by the wealthy Nattukottai Chettiars, wander dusty lanes to admire the peeling facades and enjoy the peace of semi-deserted streetscapes. The place to stay is Kanadukathan, a tiny heritage village sprawled around the Chettinad Palace, with tranquil village scenes that form a wonderful contrast to the bohemian sophistication of Pondi and the chaotic temple town of Madurai.

ESSENTIALS

GETTING THERE & AWAY   You can fly to Trichy from major southern cities (including Chennai or Trivandrum, in Kerala). Trichy airport is 8km (5 miles) from the city. Chennai is 7 hours away by road; slightly quicker by train—several daily trains then also connect Trichy with Madurai. To get to Thanjavur, 50km (31 miles) east of Trichy, either hire a car or travel by separate train for the 1-hour journey. From Pondicherry, the fastest way to get to Trichy is by hired car; alternatively, via train from Villapuram. The Chettinad region is connected by road and train. It lies about 2 hours by car from Trichy, 1½ hours from Thanjavore, and 2 hours from Madurai, making it the ideal overnight stop.

VISITOR INFORMATION   **Government of Tamil Nadu Tourism Department** (1 Williams Rd., Cantonment (Trichy); ℂ **0431/246-0136;** Mon–Fri 10am–5:45pm) can supply you with information, maps, and brochures. **Thanjavur's tourist office** (Hotel Tamil Nadu Complex Jawan Bhavan; ℂ **04362/230-984;** Mon–Fri 10am–5:45pm) provides good information on local sights and can help you with transport. Your best source of local information in Chettinad region is your host.

GETTING AROUND   This is definitely one area where it is worthwhile to hire a car and driver. If you've arrived in Trichy by train, do this through your hotel or the tourist information center, and you can manage to see Srirangam and Brihadeshvara Temple in a single, exhausting day, leaving for Madurai the following day.

WHAT TO SEE & DO
TIRUCHIRAPPALLI

Spend anywhere from a half- to a full day here, devoting the majority of your time to the atmospheric temple town of **Srirangam.** In the evening, climb the steps to the summit of **Rock Fort** in time to witness the sun setting over the city (entrance at China Bazaar; small admission fee and camera fees; daily 6am–8pm). This is also the time you're likely to encounter the greatest number of devotees coming to worship at the Shiva temple (off-limits to non-Hindus) and paying tribute to the elephant-headed god, Ganesh, at his summit shrine. Little of the old fortification has survived (though some inscriptions date back to the 3rd c. B.C.), but you may be interested to know that at 3,800 million years old, the rock itself is said to be one of the oldest on earth, predating the Himalayan range by around a million years. Alongside Rock Fort is the huge **Teppakulam Tank,** and across from this, **Our Lady of Lourdes Church,** built in 1840.

Srirangam ✩✩✩ Just 7km (4⅓ miles) beyond Trichy, the vibrant, ancient holy town of Srirangam—one of India's biggest temple complexes—is the site of sprawling **Sri Ranganathaswamy Temple,** whose seven concentric boundary walls *(prakarams)* enclose 240 hectares (600 acres) devoted to the Hindu faith. Within the temple walls, a web of lanes lined with houses, shops, and businesses is also enclosed, making for fascinating exploration of what feels like a heaving medieval village. Dedicated to Vishnu (worshipped here as Ranganatha), the town sees almost nonstop feverish and colorful activity, with communal gatherings and festivals held throughout the year. The original 10th-century temple was destroyed by a Delhi sultan, but reconstruction began in the late 14th century. Ongoing expansion by Trichy's successive rulers culminated in the late 20th century, with the elaborately carved and brightly painted **Rajagopuram,** not only the largest of the 21 *goparums* (tower gateways) that surround the immense complex, but said to be the largest in Asia, soaring to a height of 72m (236 ft.). The most important shrines are within the inner four boundary walls, entered via a high gateway where smaller shrines mark the point beyond which lower-caste Hindus could not venture. Within this enclosure, you'll find a temple to the goddess Ranganayaki, as well as the **thousand-pillared hall,** which dates back to the Chola period. Arguably the most impressive of all is nearby **Seshagirirayar Mandapa,** where the pillars are decorated with stone carvings of rearing horses mounted by warriors. For a memorable view of the entire complex, make sure to purchase a ticket to climb to the rooftop.

7km (4⅓ miles) north of Trichy on an island on the River Cauvery. Free admission. Rs 50 ($1.15/60p) still camera, Rs 100 ($2.30/£1.15) video camera. Daily 6am–noon and 2 or 4pm–8 or 10pm. No photography allowed inside the sanctum.

THANJAVUR

Brihadeshvara Temple ✩✩✩ This granite temple, a World Heritage Site built by the Chola kings a thousand years ago, is still very much alive, with devotees lining up in the hundreds to pay their respects. Standing in a vast courtyard, surrounded by a number of subsidiary shrines, the temple was built—at great expense—by the Chola Rajaraja I for the worship of Shiva. Pyramidal in shape, the monumental tower or *vimana* over the inner sanctum rises almost 70m (230 ft.) and is visible for miles around. It's capped by an octagonal cupola carved from a single block of granite that was hauled into place along a ramp that is said to have been 6km (3¾ miles) long. Within the sanctum is a 4m (13-ft.) lingam; facing the sanctum, a colossal 25-ton Nandi monolith, carved from solid granite, dominates the courtyard. Numerous extant inscriptions on the molded plinth describe the enormous wealth of the temple (much of it booty from Rajaraja's successful campaigns), as well as the copious acts of ritual and celebration that took place here. In its heyday, an enormous staff was maintained to attend to the temple's varied activities; these included everything from administration to procuring dancing girls.

West of Thanjavur bus stand. Visitors may be able to make prior arrangements for entry to the sanctum and the upper floors of the temple by contacting the local tourist office. Daily 6am–noon and 3:30–8:30pm.

Thanjavur Palace Complex & Art Gallery ✩✩ Built as the home of the Nayak rulers, the 16th-century **Royal Palace** has fallen into a state of minor ruin but is home to the impressive **Rajaraja Museum and Art Gallery** (daily 10am–1pm and 2–5pm; admission Rs 15/35¢/20p), which houses an eclectic collection of stone and bronze idols, mostly from the Chola period. Within the palace, you should also climb the narrow and tricky steps of the **arsenal tower** for fantastic views of the complex and the entire city, including Brihadeshvara Temple. Inside 17th-century **Durbar Hall,** built by the Marathas, who ruled after the Nayaks, are 11th-century statues of Vishnu and Parvati, exhibited in Washington, D.C., in 1865. Near the museum is **Saraswati Mahal Library,** which houses a collection of rare books—including Sanskrit works and 18,623 palm-leaf manuscripts—assembled by the Maratha ruler Serfoji II, who ruled until 1832 and was a great patron of the arts. The attached **Museum** has highlights from the collection, including detailed drawings of Chinese torture and punishment techniques. Give both the **Sadar Mahal Palace** and its **Royal Museum** a miss.

E. Main Rd. For information about Thanjavur Art Gallery, contact the Art Gallery Society (✆ 04362/239-823). Free admission. Daily 9am–1pm and 3–6pm.

CHETTINAD REGION

Known as the Marwadis of the South, the Nattukottai Chettiars were a powerful trading community that rose to prominence during the 19th and 20th centuries, specializing in money lending and wholesale trading with the East. While not particularly ostentatious, the Nattukottai Chettiars gave expression to their immense wealth by building massive fortified mansions and temples in the rural villages that spawned them. Their fortunes waned somewhat after World War II, with the new generation of ambitious Chettiars seeking their own pots of gold in the cities of India and beyond, and the majority of these mansions are now padlocked and empty for much of the year, opened only for the occasional marriage ceremony or Bollywood film shoot. Some of the larger homes are opened for visitors keen to view the teak and stone-pillared courtyards, ornate doorways and ceilings, crystal chandeliers, and dusty portraits of the powerful patriarchs who once ruled these now-empty corridors. If you see only one, make it the **Chettinad Palace,** the family home of Raja Sir Annamalai Chettiar, noted educator and business magnate, who built this most ornate of the mansions at the turn of the 20th century in Kanadukathan. The best way to arrange access is through the proprietors of the guesthouses who have opened their homes to paying guests (the best of which is the neighboring Chettinadu Mansion; see below). Equally pleasurable is to simply wander alone through the tiny village of Kanadukathan, watching wizened tailors behind ancient Singer machines and browsing the smattering of stalls; keen shoppers should also set aside a few hours to plunder the antiques shops in nearby Karaikudi, unofficial "capital" of the region.

WHERE TO STAY & DINE

If you're not traveling on your own steam (with car and driver), you'll probably have to make do with a hotel in either Trichy or Thanjavur—a pity, because neither has exciting accommodations. Of the two, Thanjavur has the better option in **Hotel Parisutham** (✆ 0436/223-1801; www.hotelparisutham.com; Rs 5,500/$125/£63 double). This is not because of its particularly superior accommodations—though adequate, it's an old-fashioned hotel (built in the 1980s but refurbed in 2005) with no real defining attributes. But the delightful manager, Mr. Sridharan, and his wife (the couple have been running the hotel for 20 years, and appear inseparable) are charm personified. Rooms are spotless, there is a sparkling pool, and it's a 5-minute walk to the temple and another 5 minutes to the station. The best luncheon stop in the area is the **Ideal River View Resort** (✆ 0436/225-0533; www.idealresort.com; 3km/2 miles from Thanjavore); the service is awful, but it has a large alfresco terrace with distant views of the Cauvery river. If you find yourself stuck in Trichy with no transport, your best bet is **Hotel Sangam Tiruchirappalli** (© 0431/241-4700 or -4480; www.hotelsangam.com); it's a short distance from the city center, clean and comfortable, with good facilities—but ultimately a rather depressing place to find yourself on a hard-earned holiday.

In the Chettiar region there are two alternatives to the Chettinadu Mansion: **The Bangala** is an extremely friendly and efficiently run guesthouse (owner Mrs. Meenaksh Meyyapan has an excellent eye for staff), with a legendary reputation for its Chettiar cuisine, served, as is traditional, on banana leaves. The bungalow is in charmless Karaikudi, however, and accommodations are nowhere near as delightful as that at the Mansion, reviewed below. But do try and arrange a lunch or dinner here (prebook by at least a day; © 04565/220-221; www.thebangala.com). A new option, scheduled to open by the time you read this, is **Visalam:** Another restored and renovated Chettiar home, also in the heritage village of Kanadukathan, this is the first Tamil venture from the excellent Kerala-based CGH Earth (www.cghearth.com). It will no doubt bring some slick hotel standards to this otherwise rough tourism gem.

Chettinadu Mansion 🏵🏵 (Value   This is the closest you get in southern India to experiencing a night in a Rajasthani heritage hotel, with a semi-aristocratic (in nature if not title) host at the helm and a palace as neighbor. In the heart of the Chettinad region, in the tiny heritage village of Kanadukathan, this immaculately kept 126-room mansion, built around four pillared courtyards, is the family home of larger-than-life Mr. Chandramouli (cousin of Raja Sir Annamalai Chettiar, owner of the neighboring Palace) and his diminutive wife, Aachi. Step past the deep *thinnai* (veranda, where you will find Mr. Chandramouli and retinue at sunset) through the arched entrance ("HEARTY WELCOME TO YOUR EXCELLENCIES" painted above) into a vast reception hall, with black-and-white marble tiles from Italy and massive granite pillars. Through here is the first of the mansion's four courtyards, lined with brilliant blue cast-iron pillars imported from Birmingham. Upstairs you'll find the most delightful rooms (insist on one of these seven rooms), each painted with *trompe l'oeil* Art Nouveau–style tile patterns ("glazed" with egg white to give them a sheen) and furnished with antique beds and reproduction fittings and furnishings thematically in keeping with the turn-of-the-20th-century origins of the house. Bathrooms are immaculate and, best of all, there's an outdoor terrace from which to enjoy the rooftops of the heritage village as the sun starts to dip, as you sip the best *chai* in Tamil Nadu.

11 AR St. (SARM House, behind Raja's Palace), Kanadukathan, Sivaganga Dist, Tamil Nadu 630 103. © 04565/273-080. www.chettinadumansion.com. chandramoulia@yahoo.com. 11 units. Rs 3,800 ($86/£43) double. Meals Rs 500 ($11/£5.55). MC, V. **Amenities:** Dining hall; station transfers; room service; laundry.

Sterling Swamimalai 🏵🏵   Even though it's not exactly conveniently located (Thanjavur lies an hr. away; Trichy 2 hr.), this award-winning eco-resort, centered around an 1896 villa and surrounded by coconut palm and mangrove plantations, is generally considered to be the best base from which to explore the region. Designed to mimic a typical Indian village, the resort sprawls over 2.4 hectares (6 acres) of land adjoining the Cauvery River. The sense of being in a non-hotel atmosphere, with free-ranging deer, unexpected shrines, and fresh *kolams* (floor "paintings") done daily, is both refreshing and restorative. Service is attentive, and the facilities are by far the best in the area (a great Ayurvedic Center; big pool; yoga; theater performances; delicious—albeit somewhat pricey—veg-only menu; interesting museum). As a result it is hugely popular, with a guest list that includes the likes of Deepak Chopra and William

Dalrymple (though in reality you are more likely to share the dining room with a busload of package tourists). Rooms are comfortable but pretty spartan in design, furnished with reproduction or authentic Chettinad antiques. The old block has the more atmospheric rooms, while the new block rooms are bigger (if you can, book no. 125, off a delightful courtyard). This is a great place to base yourself if the focus is on day trips to Thanjavur and Trichy, with Ayurvedic treatments in between—but to our mind Chettinadu Mansion (above) is a great deal more interesting.

6/30B Timmakudi Agiraharam, Baburajapuram PO, Swamimalai (4km/2½ miles from Kumbakonam) 612 302. ⓒ 04352/480-044. Cellphone 094-4441-0396. www.sterlingswamimalai.net. Sterling_kmb@sancharnet.in. 27 units. $110 (£55) standard double; $128 (£65) suite. MC, V. **Amenities:** Restaurant; pool; travel assistance; laundry; yoga; Ayurvedic center; pottery. In room: A/C, TV, minibar (soft drinks only).

5 Madurai ⓐⓐⓐ

498km (309 miles) SW of Chennai; 160km (99 miles) W of Trichy

Located on the banks of the Vaigai River, the temple town Madurai—apparently named for the nectar that flowed from Shiva's hair as a blessing for the new city (*madhuram* is the Tamil word for sweetness)—was built by the Pandyan king Kulasekara. The oldest living city in the Indian peninsula, it was the capital of a kingdom that ruled much of South India during the 4th century B.C., and that conducted trade as far afield as Greece and Rome.

Madurai also became a center for the great festivals of poetry and writing—the **Tamil Sangams**—that were being held more than 2 millennia ago. Through the millennia, various dynasties have battled over the city. The Vijayanagars built much of the temple during their reign, which lasted until the 16th century, when the Nayaks came to power, who in turn ruled until the arrival of the British in 1736. Today Madurai is also Tamil Nadu's second-largest city, a hodge-podge of chaotic streets and rutted lanes leading into industrial sectors plagued by pollution and traffic jams and other ills characteristic of unchecked development. It is a fascinating city, a place of pilgrimage and joy, and in many ways the embodiment of Tamil Nadu's temple culture. Certainly the labyrinthine **Meenakshi Temple**—celebrating the love of the Meenakshi goddess and her groom, Sundareswarar (the "Handsome God"), an avatar of Lord Shiva—is easily our first choice among Tamil Nadu's temple destinations.

ESSENTIALS

GETTING THERE & AWAY   There are flights connecting Madurai to Chennai, Tiruchirapalli, Bangalore, and Mumbai. The **airport** is 12km (7½ miles) south of the city center. For information about **Jet Airways'** daily flights, call ⓒ **0452/269-0771** through -0774; **Air Deccan** (www.flyairdeccan.net) also offers low-cost flights, but be prepared for delays. Trains from all over southern India pull in at **Madurai Junction Railway Station** (W. Veli St.; ⓒ **0452/274-3131**). The train journey from Chennai is 8 hours (via Trichy); from Bangalore, 11 hours. From Pondicherry you'll need to catch a cab to Villipuram (30-min. drive) then travel for 6 hours by train. If you're traveling by car, it's best to overnight along the way, preferably in the Chettinad/Kodaikanal area. The drive between Madurai and Kochi in Kerala takes 8 hours; best to overnight in Munnar or the Periyar area.

VISITOR INFORMATION   Staff at the **Government of Tamil Nadu Tourist Office** (W. Veli St., next to the Tamil Nadu Hotel; ⓒ **0452/233-4757;** www.maduraicity.com; Mon–Sat 10am–5:45pm) provides maps, advice on government-sponsored hotels and shops, and recommendations on guides. As elsewhere, beware of fake "official guides" you meet on the streets.

GETTING AROUND   Auto-rickshaw drivers tend to have a field day with foreign visitors; establish a flat rate before heading off.

FESTIVALS   Try to time your visit to coincide with the **Chittrai Festival,** held at the end of April/early May, when Shree Meenakshi's marriage to Lord Sundareswara is celebrated by dragging the divine couple from temple to temple on magnificent chariots, accompanied by elephants and drummers, with revelers reaching fever-pitch radiance. The couple is again heralded during the **Teppam Festival** (Float Festival), held sometime in January and February, when they are set afloat in the tank near the Thirupparankundram Temple. Another good time is during the **Avanimoola Festival,** held in late August through early September, when temple cars are heaved through the streets by hundreds of devotees.

WHAT TO SEE & DO

The principal reason to visit Madurai—for you as well as for tens of thousands of Hindu pilgrims—is to experience the ecstatic spiritual life of **Meenakshi Temple;** though the numbers of international tourists traipsing about (and the introduction of an entrance fee for foreigners) has unfortunately made the experience a little more commercial, it is still a magnificent temple, particularly at 8:30pm when the evening *"aarti"* takes place (see below).

Legend recalls that Meenakshi began life as a glorious princess, born of fire with three breasts and eyes like a fish. As she grew older, she overpowered all the gods with her impossible beauty until she encountered Shiva, who transformed her heart to ghee (butter) and married her. While sitting inside the temple itself can provide hours of entertainment and a palpable sense of Tamil Nadu's deep spirituality (as well as a sense of its religious commerce), the streets immediately near the great temple are full of character, and are best experienced by wandering around. Head down Nethaji Road (exit from the West Gate) and keep your camera handy for the great view back down the narrow stall-lined lane, over which the magnificent *goparum* towers.

Fans of the Mahatma may be interested to know that it was in Madurai in 1921 that Gandhi historically exchanged his *kurta* and *dhoti* wardrobe for the loincloth, typically worn by the poor. Today the bloodstained *khadi* loincloth he wore when he was assassinated is encased in a glass shrine at **Gandhi Memorial Museum,** which chronicles India's history leading up to independence (Tamukkam, 5km/3 miles east of the city center; ✆ **0452/253-1060;** www.madurai.com/gandhi.htm; free admission; daily 10am–1pm and 2–5:45pm). Avoid the adjacent **Government Museum,** where visitors experience 2 million years of history in 30 seconds as they whiz past a 9th-century Vishnu statue, 12th-century Pandyan works, undated Chola statues, and a stuffed polar bear.

If Meenakshi doesn't blow you away, and you'd like to experience a truly authentic temple experience as yet untainted by tourism, take a rickshaw to **Thirupparankundram Temple** ⍟, supposedly 8km (5 miles) from Madurai center, but very much part of the continuous sprawl of the temple town. While it's by no means as decorative as the Meenakshi Temple, this evocative cave temple is older and has a more sacred atmosphere than the Meenakshi Temple, particularly on Friday, when women with marriage or family troubles place candles or sit on the temple floor and create *rangoli* patterns on the ground, using colored powders, ash, and flowers as offerings to Durga.

Take a few rupees along to offer to the resident temple elephant, **Owayat,** who shuf-
fles and waits to bestow blessings after gracefully accepting your offering in his cupped
trunk. If you make it into the inner sanctum (strictly speaking not allowed, but the
friendly priests may turn a blind eye) you will see the ghee-blackened carvings of the
gods, carved into the holy mountainside on which the temple has been built.

Lastly, if you're up for one more temple experience, set aside a day or two to visit
Rameshwaram. Situated on an island on the southern tip of India, it has a legendary
role in the epic of Lord Rama and is today considered by many to be the second holiest place in India for Hindus (after Varanasi). It's a little far for a day trip (350km/217
miles round-trip), and bear in mind that the Temple is not open to non-Hindus, but
the drive is scenic and the carnival-like atmosphere—created by domestic rather than
foreign tourists—is what a trip to the temple destinations of India is all about, so if
you have time this is definitely a detour worth considering.

Shri Meenakshi-Sundareshwarar Temple 𝒜𝒜𝒜 One of South India's biggest,
busiest pilgrimage sites, attracting up to 15,000 devotees a day, this sprawling temple,
always undergoing renovation and repairs, is a place of intense spiritual activity. A
high wall surrounds the complex, and 12 looming *goparums* (pyramidal gateways)
mark the various entrances. Garish stucco gods, demons, beasts, and heroes smother
these towers in a writhing, fascinating mass of symbolism, vividly painted in a riot of
bright Disneyesque colors. Traditionally, entrance to the complex is through the eastern **Ashta Shakti Mandapa,** a hall of pillars graced by sculptural representations of
the goddess Shakti in her many aspects. Adjacent to this, **Meenakshi Nayaka Mandapa** is where pilgrims purchase all manner of devotional paraphernalia and holy souvenirs. Near the inner gate, a temple elephant, daubed with eye shadow and blusher,
earns her keep by accepting a few rupees' donation in exchange for a blessing—
bestowed with a light tap of her dexterous trunk. From here you can wander at will,
finding your way at some stage to the impressive 16th-century Hall of a Thousand Pillars. This hall (or museum, as it is also called) has 985 elegantly sculpted columns,
including a set of "musical pillars" that produce the seven Carnatic musical notes
when tapped (a ticket officer will gladly demonstrate in exchange for a tip).

All around the complex of shrines and effigies, various *pujas* (prayers) and rituals
are conducted, some under the guiding hand of a bare-chested Brahmin priest, others
as spontaneous expressions of personal, elated devotion. Layer upon layer of ghee and
oil have turned surfaces of many of the statues smooth and black, with daubs of
turmeric and vermilion powder sprinkled on by believers seeking blessings and hope.

At the heart of the complex are the **sanctums** of the goddess Meenakshi (Parvati)
and of Sundareshvara (Shiva). What often eludes visitors to the heaving temple at
Madurai is the city's deeply imbedded cult of fertility; behind the reverence and sever-
ity of worship, the Meenakshi Temple is a celebration of the divine union of the eternal lovers, represented symbolically at around 8:30pm when they are ceremoniously
carried (a ritual you can observe until they enter the inner sanctum, which is off-limits to non-Hindus) before Shiva is deposited in the Meenakshi's chamber, no doubt
for an evening of celestial fornication. This is the time to head for the stairs around
the great tank, where devotees gather to chat and relax at the end of the day. Many of
the groups of people you see sitting around are in fact arranging their own unions; the
temple is a place where men and women of marriageable age are presented to families.
Note: Visitors must be discreetly dressed to gain access—no exposed shoulders or bare
midriffs or legs. It's great just to wander around and enjoy the atmospheric scenes, but

if you'd prefer to have a guide, contact **Maheswari** (✆ **0934/413-1160**), who will do a half-day tour for Rs 300 ($6.80/£3.40).

Bounded by N., E., S., and W. Chitrai sts. ✆ **0452/234-4360.** www.maduraimeenakshi.org. Admission Rs 50 ($1.15/ 60p). Daily 5am–1pm and 4–10:30pm. Evening *aarti* 8:30pm. Thousand Pillar Museum: Rs 5 (10¢/5p). Daily 7am– 8pm. No entrance to main sanctum for non-Hindus. Deposit shoes outside entrance.

WHERE TO STAY & DINE

Though Royal Court (reviewed below) currently has the edge in terms of location, bathroom fittings, and amenities, **GRT Regency** (✆ **0452/237-1155;** www.grthotels. com; mail@grtregency.com) is a fair alternative, charging similar rates (Rs 2,750/ $62/£31 double). It's big and bland, but it may be useful to look into a package deal (there's a GRT in Chennai and a pleasant beach resort near Mahabalipurum), particularly if you decide to also include Rameshwaram in your itinerary, as the GRT-affiliated hotel is probably the best in Rameshwaram. **Hotel Royal Park** is just 2km (1¼ miles) from the Rameshwaram Temple, with good amenities and average room facilities (✆ **04573/221-680;** www.hotelroyalpark.in).

The most atmospheric place to dine at night, weather permitting, is **On Board,** the terrace at the Taj (not to be confused with The View), with the city sparkling below. Cuisine is predominantly tandoor-style kebabs (Rs 600–Rs 800/$14–$18/£7–£9). Food is not consistent, but the views are superb. If you're watching your budget, you'll enjoy better value at the pleasant **Mogul Rooftop Barbeque Grill House** 🦶 at Royal Court (see below), where a good meal won't break the bank (note no alcohol served). For a truly authentic experience, pop into one of the numerous scruffy dining halls (just make sure that it's well attended by locals)—thali (multicourse) meals served in these dime-a-dozen joints are delicious and extremely economical, but you will be expected to eat with your fingers.

Royal Court 🔺*Value*   This is a great option if you want to be right in the heart of this bustling temple town. It's literally a stone's throw from the station and a 10-minute walk from the Meenakshi Temple and the fascinating lanes that surround it (20 min. from the airport). The Royal Court is not in any way as luxurious as the Taj Garden Retreat, but it's very comfortable, with basic hotel rooms aimed at business travelers who require certain standards: double-glazed windows ensure that you're cocooned from the chaos below, there's Wi-Fi connectivity in every room, and the bathrooms are in remarkable shape given that the hotel opened in 2003. Another good reason to stay here is the food; the **Mogul Rooftop Barbeque Grill House** is arguably the best restaurant in town. (Do note however that in strict accordance to the beliefs of the owners, no alcohol is served in the hotel.) All in all, this is an unpretentious, professionally run hotel that offers very good value—certainly the standard rooms are the best in this price category. The only drawback: There's no pool to cool off in.

4 West Veli St., Madurai 625 004. ✆ **0452/435-6666.** Fax 0452/437-3333. www.royalcourtindia.com. 69 units. $85 (£43) standard double; $125 (£63) executive double; $165 (£83) suite. $15 (£7.55) extra bed. Taxes extra. AE, DC, MC, V. **Amenities:** 2 restaurants; gymnasium; travel desk; 24-hr. room service; laundry; doctor-on-call; Internet. *In room:* A/C, TV, Wi-Fi.

Taj Garden Retreat, Madurai 🦶🦶   Situated on a hillock known as Pasumalai and blessed with 25 hectares (62 acres) of tree-filled grounds, this colonial-style hotel—without a doubt your best option in Madurai—offers panoramic views of the sprawling town, the tall *goparums* of its temples the only high-rise outlines on the horizon. Arrived at by a long driveway (a sign en route warns of PEACOCKS CROSSING), this was the original residence of Sir William Harvey. The main building, built in 1891, is decorated with hunting trophies and includes a well-stocked colonial-style bar with deep verandas, wicker chairs, and whirring overhead fans. Accommodations are spread over five different blocks; the best are the very spacious deluxe rooms, offering fantastic views of the city and temple from wide bay windows (book room no. 21 or 22) and balconies. Superior rooms are also comfortable, offering either pool or garden views; no. 12 is a corner standard worth booking for the additional space; nos. 15 to 17 have sit-outs. Dining at **The View** is disappointing (the food, not the view); better by far are the tandoori-style offerings at **On Board,** the alfresco terrace, with even more spectacular views and a romantic setting. *Caveats:* Service can be extremely slow for a so-called five-star hotel, the Ayurvedic treatments at press time were very much below par, and unless you have a car and driver at your beck and call, you may find it a little cut off from the city.

40 T.P.K. Rd., Pasumalai, Madurai 625 004. © **0452/237-1601.** Fax 0452/237-1636. www.tajhotels.com. 63 units. $135 (£68) standard double; $165 (£83) superior double; $190 (£96) deluxe double. $15 (£7.55) extra bed. Taxes extra. AE, DC, MC, V. **Amenities:** 2 restaurants; bar; pool; tennis court; travel desk; car hire; 24-hr. room service; babysitting; laundry; dry cleaning; doctor-on-call; Internet access; badminton court; jogging track; Ayurvedic center; nursery; pharmacy service; palmist. *In room:* A/C, TV, minibar, hair dryer. Deluxe rooms have tea- and coffee-making facilities.

8

Karnataka & Hyderabad: Kingdoms of the South

Sixteenth-century visitors to the royal courts of present-day Karnataka returned to Europe with stupendous tales of wealth—cities overflowing with jewels, and streets littered with diamonds. Over the centuries, the lush green state that occupies a vast chunk of India's southwestern seaboard and much of the Deccan plateau saw numerous kingdoms rise and fall, powerful dynasties that left legacies of impressive palaces and monumental cities that lie scattered throughout the interior, some of them well off the beaten track, but worth the effort and time it takes to seek them out.

The post-independence state of Karnataka, unified in 1950 on the basis of common language, is predominantly made up of the once-princely state of Mysore and the Berar territories of the Nizam of Hyderabad's kingdom. Once one of the richest cities in India, Hyderabad is now the vibrant capital of neighboring Andhra Pradesh, and a possible excursion from Bangalore, state capital of Karnataka. **Bangalore** may have been renamed Bengalooru in yet another attempt to strip away the Raj legacy, but it remains in many ways the country's most "Western" city, famous for its energetic nightlife and highly evolved computer and technology industries. Although it offers little by way of

sightseeing attractions, it's a great place to relax; you can shop by day and explore the bars and clubs at night before taking an overnight train to explore the ancient city of **Hampi.** The great medieval Hindu capital of the south is said to have once rivaled Rome in wealth and, with the ruins of the 14th-century Vijayanagar kingdom set in a boulder-strewn landscape that proves fascinating in its own right, this is deservedly Karnataka's most famous attraction.

Karnataka's other primary destination is Mysore, the famous "City of Incense," where vibrant markets are perfumed with the scents of jasmine, musk, sandalwood, and frangipani. Ruled by India's most enlightened maharajas, Mysore is home to some 17 palaces, of which Amba Vilas is arguably India's most opulent. Just a few hours south of Mysore is Rajiv Gandhi National Park, home to herds of wild elephant and the more elusive Bengal tiger. Northward lie the "Jewel Box" temples built by the mighty Hoysala warriors in the cities of Belur and Halebid, best reached via Sravanabelgola, home to one of the oldest and most important Jain pilgrimage sites in India: an 18m (60-ft.) statue of the naked Lord Gomateswara, said to be the tallest monolithic statue on earth and one of the most spiritually satisfying destinations in India.

1 Bangalore

If you've been in India a while, the capital of Karnataka will probably feel like a long, soothing break from endless commotion. The first city in India to get electricity, Bangalore continues to blaze the trail in terms of the country's quest for a modern identity. Once known as the Garden City (and less encouragingly as Pensioner's Paradise), the country's most pristine city evolved significantly when the high-tech revolution arrived and Bangalore suddenly found itself at the center of the nation's massive computer hardware and software industries. Its cosmopolitan spirit, fueled as much by its lively bar and cafe culture as by the influx of international businesspeople, gives India's high-tech hub a high-energy buzz, yet it's tangibly calmer and cleaner than most other places in the country, with far and away the best climate of any Indian city—no doubt one of the reasons the majority of upwardly mobile Indians rank it the number-one city in which to live.

Unless you go in for cafe society or are keen to see India's new moneyed elite flash their bling and wads of cash, you won't find very many attractions in Bangalore—perhaps a relief in a country that is so saturated with historic must-sees. The city's real appeal is its zesty contemporary Indian lifestyle and its usefulness as a base for getting to the extraordinary temples and ruins of the Deccan interior and the cities of Hyderabad and Mysore.

ESSENTIALS

GETTING THERE & MOVING ON   By Air   Bangalore's airport (8km/5 miles from M.G. Rd.) is the busiest in South India, connected to most of the major cities in India (including Hyderabad). Several international flights to the Far East, Europe, London, and the U.S. fly out of the airport as well. To get to your hotel from the airport, it's best to use a taxi (about Rs 150–Rs 300/$3.65–$7.30/£1.85–£3.70) from the prepaid counter.

By Train   As a major transport hub, Bangalore is reached by a significant number of rail connections. Journeys from North Indian cities, however, are extremely time-consuming; the fastest connection with Delhi takes 35 hours, while Mumbai is 24 hours away. From Chennai (capital of Tamil Nadu), take either the evening or the morning 5-hour Shatabdi Express or the overnight Bangalore Mail which leaves late and gets in early. To get to Mysore from Bangalore, catch the 2-hour Shatabdi Express (departs Wed–Mon at 11am) or else take an ordinary passenger train (which departs several times a day and takes only 1 hr. more than the Shatabdi) and enjoy the sights and sounds of local commuters, many of whom begin impromptu song competitions in order to pass time. For Hyderabad, catch the comfortable overnight Rajdhani Express (departs four times a week at 8:20pm). At press time, there was talk of a passenger train linking Bangalore with Mangalore, a journey done by road so far. Bangalore City and Bangalore Cantonment are the two railway stations; the latter is a bit closer to the main downtown area.

By Road   For the greatest amount of freedom, you should hire a car and driver, particularly if you plan to get off the beaten track.

VISITOR INFORMATION   Karnataka State Tourism Development Corporation (KSTDC) information counters are found at the railway station (✆ **080/2287-0068;** daily 6:30am–9:30pm) and at the airport (✆ **080/526-8012;** 24 hr.). **Karnataka Tourism** (Khanija Bhavan, Race Course Rd.; ✆ **080/2235-2901** through

-2903 or 080/2227-5869 or -5883; www.kstdc.nic.in; Mon–Sat 10:30am–5:30pm, closed Sun and second Sat of the month) is reliable for sightseeing information rather than info on accommodations and dining; ask for a copy of *Bangalore This Fortnight.* The **Government of India Tourist Office** is at the KSFC Building, 48 Church St. (© **080/2558-5417;** Mon–Fri 9:30am–6pm, Sat 9am–1pm), where you can pick up a copy of the free quarterly guide *City Info.*

GETTING AROUND   By Auto-Rickshaw & Taxi   Insist that auto-rickshaw drivers use their meters. Generally, the first kilometer will cost Rs 12 (30¢/15p); each kilometer after that costs Rs 7 (15¢/10p). After 10pm, drivers will try to make you pay double; pay no more than 50% above the recorded fare. You won't find taxis that you can just hail off the street, but metered **"call taxis"** are available almost all over the city; see our recommendation in "Fast Facts: Bangalore," below; or ask your hotel for a reputable number. Expect to pay minimum fare of Rs 45 ($1.10/55p) for 4km (2½ miles), Rs 10 (25¢/15p) each additional kilometer, plus extra for waiting and luggage.

With Car & Driver   Plan on spending in the region of Rs 150 ($3.65/£1.85) per hour, or Rs 480 ($12/£6) for a 4-hour tour, which will include 40km (25 miles) of free mileage (Rs 12/30¢/15p for every extra kilometer). To hire a car and driver, try **Hertz** (© **080/5537-5404** or -4901), which operates around-the-clock as does **Cel Cabs** (© **080/2346-6666**).

GUIDED TOURS & TRAVEL AGENTS   KSTDC (address above; © **080/2235-2901**) conducts sightseeing tours around the state. **Sita Travels** (1 St. Mark's Rd.; © **080/2558-8892**) and **Marco Polo Tours** (2 Janardhan Towers, Residency Rd.; © **080/4122-1222**) are reliable all-rounders. **Cosmopole Travels** (© **080/2228-1591** or 080/2220-2410) is useful for event-related destinations such as the Nrityagram Dance Village.

FAST FACTS: **Bangalore**

Airlines **Jet Airways:** © **080/2522-9873** or airport 080/2522-6576 and 080/4151-1111. See chapter 2 for details on more airlines, almost all of which service this busy hub.

Area Code The area code for **Bangalore** is **080.**

ATMs Visit the shop-intensive vicinity of M.G. Road.

Bookstores **Strand Book Stall** is at S113-114 Manipal Centre, Dickenson Road (© **080/2558-0000**). **Higginbothams** is at 68 M.G. Rd. (© **080/2558-6574**). **Sankar's Book Stall** is at 15/2 Museum Rd. (© **080/2558-6867**). The huge **Landmark** bookstore can be found at Forum Mall in Koramangala, far from downtown Bangalore.

Car Rentals **Gullivers Tours & Travels** is at B2-SPL Habitat, no. 138, Gangadhara Chetty Rd. (© **080/2558-0108** or -3213). Another reliable name is **Srushti Travels** (© **98-4503-2213**).

Currency Exchange Exchange cash or get credit card advances from **Wall Street Finances** (3 House of Lords, St. Mark's Rd.; © **080/2221-4300** or 080/2227-8052; Mon–Fri 9:30am–6pm, Sat 9:30am–5pm) or from **Standard Chartered** (Raheja Towers, 26 M.G. Rd.; Mon–Fri 10:30am–5pm, Sat 10:30am–1:30pm). Alternatively,

Karnataka

you can go to **Thomas Cook** (55 M.G. Rd.; ℂ **080/2558-1337** or 080/2559-4168; Mon–Sat 9:30am–6pm) or **American Express** (180 Imperial Court, Cunningham Rd.; ℂ **080/2220-0251**).

Directory Assistance The number ℂ **080/2222-2222** operates much like a talking Yellow Pages service, where you get free updated telephone numbers and addresses for various city establishments.

Drugstores Twenty-four-hour chemists include **Cash Pharmacy** (ℂ **080/2212-6033**), **Manipal Hospital** (ℂ **080/2526-8901**), and **Mallya Hospital** (Vittal Mallya Rd., south of Cubbon Park; ℂ **080/2227-7979**).

Emergencies Dial ℂ **100** for police emergencies.

Hospital Both **Manipal Hospital** (98 Rustum Bagh, Airport Rd.; ℂ **080/2526-8901** or -6447) and **St. John's Medical College and Hospital** (Sarjapur Rd.; ℂ **080/2553-0724** or -2411) are decent options.

Internet Access Cybercafes abound in this IT-savvy city. You'll find a **Sify i way** on Residency Road (ℂ **080/4121-3971** or 080/4112-4226; www.iway.com) and a **Reliance Webworld** on M.G. Road (ℂ **080/3033-6666**; www.relianceinfo.com); outlets of both are found all over the city.

Police Contact **Cubbon Park Station** at ℂ **080/2294-2591**, -2087, or 100.

Post Office As always, your best bet for sending mail is through your hotel. The **GPO** (ℂ **080/2286-6772** or 080/2289-2036; Mon–Sat 10am–6pm, Sun 10:30am–1pm) is, however, architecturally interesting. It's located at the intersection of Raj Bhavan and Ambedkar Road.

Railway For inquiries, dial ℂ **131** or 132.

Taxis Call **Gopinath Radio Call Taxi** (ℂ **080/2360-5555** or 080/2332-0152; 24 hr.); alternatively **Spot City Taxi** (ℂ **080/4110-0000**).

WHAT TO SEE & DO

Although it was ruled by various dynasties, Bangalore's chief historical sights date back to the 18th-century reign of Hyder Ali and his son Tipu Sultan, "the Lion of Mysore," who put up the most spirited resistance to British imperialism. But more than anything, Bangalore is about experiencing an Indian city that brims with bars, restaurants, clubs, and positive energy—a great place for walking, window-shopping and, at night, letting your hair down. The Garden City also has lovely parks, some of which date back over 2 centuries, of which the botanical gardens at **Lal Bagh** are the most impressive.

Set off early for Bugle Hill, site of the **Bull Temple** (sanctum timings daily 7:30am–11:30am and 4:30–8:30pm). Built by the city's original architect, Kempe Gowda, this 16th-century black-granite statue of Nandi (Shiva's sacred bull) literally dwarfs his "master," and is kept glistening by regular applications of coconut oil. Nearby is a Ganesha temple (Sri Dodda Ganapathi), which houses an enormous statue of the elephant-headed deity made of 100 kilos of rank-smelling butter. Apparently this idol is remade every 4 years, and the butter distributed to devotees as *prasad* (blessed food).

Picnicking with the family, cricketing with the boys, and holding hands in secret (with all possible gender combinations) are popular pastimes in **Cubbon Park** (Cantonment), laid out in 1864 by the Mysore engineer, Richard Sankey and named after the longest serving Commissioner of Bangalore. Today many visitors come to view the lovely buildings that surround the park as well as to visit the **Government Museum and Venkatappa Art Gallery** (© 080/2286-4483; Rs 4/10¢/5p; Tues–Sun 10am–5pm), which focuses on sculpture. It contains works from Khajuraho, Bihar, and Madhya Pradesh dating back to the 10th century, Buddhist figures from the 4th- and 5th-century Gandhara school, and Hoysala carvings from Belur, Halebid, and Hampi—not that these are really a match for the real thing, seen on location. While in the vicinity, take a walk or drive past **Vidhana Vidhi** to admire its Greco colonial–style buildings, including India's largest state headquarters, **Vidhana Soudha,** Karnataka's State Legislature and Secretariat building (no entry allowed), to marvel at what is termed "neo-Dravidian" architecture. Its blend of styles from across India is capped by one of India's most recognizable symbols—the four-headed gold lion of Ashoka, India's celebrated early Buddhist king. Over the entrance, a gleaming gold-lettered sign bears the somewhat optimistic slogan GOVERNMENT WORK IS GOD'S WORK. Across the road from the Vidhana Soudha, fringing Cubbon Park, is Karnataka's two-story High Court building, or **Attara Kacheri,** an attractive design with red bricks and monumental Corinthian columns.

Learn the "Art of Living" with India's Hot New Age Guru

Sri Sri Ravi Shankar, once a disciple of Maharishi Mahesh Yogi (renowned spiritual guide of The Beatles), is the subcontinent's hottest New Age guru—many consider "The Art of Living," his nonsectarian philosophy of enjoying life for the moment, the perfect spiritual currency for our material times. His main ashram lies on 24 hectares (60 acres) of lush green hillside in south Bangalore, where every evening thousands of the city's well-heeled gather for the evening lecture and *satsang* (devotional singing). The articulate Sri Sri's appeal lies in the fact that he does not emphasize incarnations or abstinences, but encourages his disciples to enjoy the present without guilt while also encouraging them to contribute towards humanitarian and environmental concerns. His adherents—predominantly from India's growing urban elite (including Kingfisher's Vijay Mallya, the "Branson of Bangalore"), but also hugely popular on foreign shores (apparently San Franciscans have a real penchant for his teachings)—can go about their hectic lives and remain relatively apolitical yet feel good about not discarding all sense of religion and tradition.

A philosophy of convenience, some say, but even his fiercest detractors admit the value of *sudarshan kriya,* an ancient breathing technique taught when you attend the "Art of Living" course. The 30-minute-a-day practice is said to encourage the flow of oxygen to the whole body, ostensibly discouraging the storage of toxins and thus helping release anxiety, frustration, depression, and anger, leaving you with a genuine sense of calm and well-being.

To attend an evening session or a 14-hour Art of Living course spread over several days, call ahead (21st Km, Kanakapura Main Rd., Udayapura, Bangalore 560 082; © 080/2843-2273, -2274; www.artofliving.org).

If it's a real garden you're after, head straight for the botanical gardens at **Lal Bagh** (Rs 2/5¢/5p; daily 7am–6pm), conceived and laid out by Sultan Hyder Ali in 1760. His son, Tipu, expanded the gardens further, planting exotic plants from Persia, Kabul, Turkey, and Mauritius over 96 hectares (240 acres). Highlights include the Lawn Clock and the British-built glasshouse, structurally based on London's Crystal Palace. After visiting the gardens, be sure to pop in for a meal at *the* Bangalore lunch institution, **Mavalli Tiffin Rooms** (see "Where to Dine," below), a short distance from the entrance.

Tipu Sultan's Summer Palace (Rs 2/5¢/5p; daily 9am–5pm), built toward the end of the 18th century entirely from timber, is a relic in a city committed more to progress than to preservation. It has a somewhat sophomoric exhibition with extensive text about Tipu's life and military conquests as well as those of his father, Hyder Ali Khan. Next door is an enormously active 17th-century temple, built by the Wodeyar kings; and just north are the ruins of **Bangalore Fort,** largely destroyed during the Anglo-Mysore War.

WHERE TO STAY

Bangalore has a huge range of excellent top-quality hotels, of which our personal favorites are **The Park.hotel** for its contemporary über-slick styling and in-house nightlife, and the **Taj West End Hotel** for its heritage atmosphere (both reviewed below). However, you may want to compare online rates with the following round-up of the city's best hotels, which offer the same or similar top-end luxury and amenities. As you'll find elsewhere in Indian destinations frequented by foreigners, many of the lodgings in Bangalore quote their rates in dollars or euros. Not so however at charming **Villa Pottipati** (also reviewed below), the best-value deal in town.

ITC Hotel Windsor Sheraton & Towers (25 Windsor Square, Golf Course Rd.; ℂ 080/2226-9898; fax 080/2226-4941; www.welcomgroup.com), popular with Bollywood's elite and high-profile businesspeople and politicians, retains the look and character of a neoclassical English country house; ask for a room in the Manor Block. The **Oberoi** (37/39 M.G. Rd.; ℂ 080/2558-5858; www.oberoihotels.com; doubles from $550/£278) is another excellent hotel, with the usual high standards we have come to rely on from India's best hotel group. It's extremely picturesque, with balconies draped with blue blossoming creepers and set amid gardens with lovely views over the lawns and the swimming pool. Standard units are not quite as large or as elegant as those at the ITC Windsor Sheraton, but they're spacious enough and luxuriously decorated with floral fabrics and antique finishes; ask for a room on an upper floor for better views. But for over-the-top opulence, **Leela Palace Kempinski**—judged by *Forbes Magazine* as one of the world's best new business hotels when it opened in 2001 and garnering CNN's Ultimate Service Award for 2 years in a row—is the hands-down winner. A baroque rendition of contemporary Indo-Saracenic architecture, looming large in pale pink, it offers enormous "conservatory" rooms with private balconies and, along with all the modern conveniences, elegant four-poster beds, rococo gold-gilt lamps, and silk duvet covers. Deluxe rooms are also very spacious and styled in the same manner (23 Airport Rd.; ℂ 080/2521-1234; www.theleela.com; doubles $470/£238 deluxe, $500/£253 conservatory [including breakfast]; suites range from $725/£367 to a whopping $3,500/£1,774 for the Maharaja suite). In the (comparatively) moderate price range, opt for the Taj-run **Gateway Hotel on Residency Road;** its best accommodations are the cheapest and recently refurbished "executive" guest rooms priced at $265 (£134). Ask for an even-numbered, pool-facing room on the fourth floor (ℂ 080/6660-4545; fax 080/66614542, www.tajhotels.com).

Much cheaper and less luxe but perfectly serviceable, **St. Mark's** is a small, neat business hotel (℘ **080/2227-9090;** www.stmarkshotel.com) with doubles from Rs 4,800 ($117/£59); alternatively, **Ivory Towers** (℘ **080/2558-9333;** Rs 3,600/$88/ £44) has 12 spotless suites with great views (ask for one with a balcony) and all amenities (including Wi-Fi). Its restaurant, Ebony, is reviewed below. Perched on the 12th and 13th floors of Barton Centre, gob-smack on busy M.G. Road, Ivory Towers is conveniently located if you want to be downtown.

The Park.hotel ✻✻✻   Themed around Bangalore's reputation as India's information-technology city and its historic connection with silk production, this compact boutique hotel features top-class interiors by Tina Ellis (of London-based Conran) and has been rated as one of the 101 best hotels worldwide by *Tatler.* In the lobby—dominated by a gigantic silk curtain—rough, smooth, and suede textures are offset with brushed metal and a row of large white orbs of light, while staff are smartly turned out in pale gray jackets over white T-shirts, an efficient look that is matched by service levels. The four floors are styled around a palette of strong chromatic elements that apparently refer to the Indian landscape; pale lime and iris purple suggest the mountains, while a desert oasis is alluded to with ultramarine and saffron. Guest rooms are on the small side and don't have great views (ask for a pool-facing room), but they are beautifully finished—oak flooring, designer rugs, black-and-white photographs of Bangalore, oak-and-leather director's chairs, and minimalist metal-framed four-poster beds with the softest goose feather pillows and duvets. Bathrooms are great, with large rain showers that adjust to give you a water massage. On the downside, the temperature of the water isn't quite right for a luxurious soak in the tub. Rooms on the desert-themed Residence Floor come with a host of additional services, including airport transfers, late checkout, sparkling wine on arrival, head and shoulder massage, in-room fax and laptop on request, DVD player, and access to the elegant private lounge, where breakfast and all-day tea and coffee are served.

14/7 M.G. Rd., Bangalore 560 001. ℘ **080/2559-4666.** Fax 080/2559-4667. www.theparkhotels.com. resv.blr@the parkhotels.com. 109 units. $350 (£177) deluxe double; $375 (£190) deluxe balcony double; $385 (£195) deluxe terrace double; $400 (£203) luxury double; $450 (£228) Residence Floor; $600 (£304) suite. All rates include breakfast and one-way transfer. AE, DC, MC, V. **Amenities:** 3 restaurants; lounge bar; pool; health spa; indoor games; travel services; business center; gift shop; 24-hr. room service; babysitting; laundry; doctor-on-call; currency exchange; valet; sightseeing; theater; library. *In room:* A/C, TV, minibar, Wi-Fi enabled.

Taj West End Hotel ✻✻✻   A member of The Leading Hotels of the World, West End dates back to 1887, when it was a 10-room Victorian boardinghouse. Today the luxury hotel has expanded hugely but retains its old-world charm while providing guests with 21st-century conveniences. The stately lobby features a central atrium with skylight, dark walnut paneling, teakwood fluting on the walls, lots of plants, plush sofas, and a grand piano. It opens onto **Mynt,** the hotel's 24-hour coffee shop serving Mediterranean, Italian, and Indian food at separate counters, each with a chef who interacts with guests. Accommodations are spread over more than 9 hectares (22 acres) of gardens with wonderful old banyan trees—thankfully, there is a buggy to whisk you to your room after check-in. Rooms comprise various pitched-roof-veranda blocks and more recent structures modeled on similar colonial architecture; each has a private balcony overlooking the extensive gardens. Try to book in the Heritage Wing, which has four-poster beds and old-Bangalore-theme lithographs. "Superior" rooms are by comparison rather ordinary, but the private balcony with lovely views is a consolation. If you value your space, fork out the extra cash for an executive suite; these are massive, warm-toned, carpeted spaces with long balconies and high, arched ceilings. Bathrooms are large, with separate tub and shower and a walk-in dressing room.

Race Course Rd., Bangalore 560 001. ℂ 080/6660-5660. Fax 080/6660-5700. www.tajhotels.com. 122 units. $425 (£216) superior double; $450 (£228) luxury double (includes one-way airport transfer); $500 (£254) Grand Luxury; $575 (£292) Taj Club; $650–$1,250 (£330–£634) suite. $23 (£12) extra bed. Taj Club rooms and suites include breakfast and airport transfers. AE, DC, MC, V. **Amenities:** 3 restaurants; 2 bars; golf and riding on request; 2 tennis courts; fitness center; travel assistance; car hire; shopping arcade; salon; 24-hr. room service; babysitting; laundry service; dry cleaning; doctor-on-call; currency exchange; Internet access, Wi-Fi, laptop computers for hire. *In room:* A/C, TV (some wall-mounted plasma), minibar, hair dryer. Taj Club units: fax machines on request, DVD players, personal butlers.

Villa Pottipati 🌟🌟🌟 *Value*   Surrounded by mango, jackfruit, avocado, jacaranda, and gulmohar trees, and heady *shivalinga* blossoms at the entrance, this is the most authentic and reasonably priced heritage experience you can have in the heart of this city of steel, glass, and concrete. Pottipati, a stately villa of red cement floors, teakwood beams, and high ceilings, gets its name from a village in Andhra Pradesh, where the Reddy family (who own the property, now managed by the Neemrana group) originally resided over a century ago. Service is personal and exceptional, with the kind of attention guests probably enjoyed a century ago, and furnishings in keeping with the heritage character: teak and rosewood antiques and beautiful artifacts. Dining is indoors, surrounded by teak and bronze, or outdoors under a canopy of mango trees; everything we tried was delicious. As at all Neemrana properties, each guest room is different. No matter which room you stay in, do ask for a tour of unoccupied others, named after traditional South Indian saris. The Venkatagiri Suite, with a turquoise-blue Venkatagiri sari covering the bed, offers incredible value, with a living room, a private dressing area, an area for kids, two large wardrobes, a bathroom with a large bathtub, and a veranda. The Rajadurga Suite rewards early birds with spectacular sunrise views. The fabulous Kanchipuram Suite has a private pillared balcony, an anteroom for kids, an old-fashioned, lime-green bathroom, and an antique gramophone.

142, 8th Cross, 4th Main Rd., Malleswaram, Bangalore 560 003. ℂ 080/2336-0777 or 080/4128-0832 through -0834. Fax 080/5128-0835. www.neemranahotels.com. 8 units. Rs 4,000–Rs 5,000 ($98–$122/£49–£62) double; extra bed ($11/£5.60). Rates include bed tea, evening tea, and breakfast. Taxes extra. AE, DC, MC, V. **Amenities:** Dining room; restaurant; bar; pool; concierge; travel desk; car hire; laundry service; dry cleaning; doctor-on-call; currency exchange. *In room:* A/C, TV, hair dryer, safe, Wi-Fi enabled.

WHERE TO DINE

With Bangalore's IT boom, the number of professionals with disposable cash keeps rising exponentially—leading in turn to an explosion of options on the dining scene. We've reviewed a combination of upmarket eateries with excellent and very atmospheric budget alternatives.

As in Tamil Nadu, you can get a good, clean, wholesome vegetarian tiffin ("light meal") all over Bangalore. Most famous of all is **MTR** (reviewed below); but equally good for its Tamil Iyengar food, especially the must-have *puliyogere* (a kind of tamarind rice), is **Kadambam** (112 C South Block, Manipal Centre, Dickenson Rd.; other branches as well). Gold-framed pictures of deities line the wall, the simple open kitchen is spotless, the food is cheap and delicious, and the filter coffee—if, that is, you've developed a taste for sweetened South Indian filter coffee—extraordinary. For authentic Karnataka cuisine, **Halli Mane** (no. 14, 3rd Cross Rd., off Sampige Rd., Malleswaram; ℂ **080/2346-9797**) is Bangalore's busiest restaurant, serving pure vegetarian, dirt-cheap thalis, or buffet meals (Rs 69/$1.70/85p). Its tiled roof, basic furnishings, and stainless-steel crockery evoke the ambience of a typical rural home; chat with the friendly manager, Mr. Baburao, who will assist you in selecting just the right dishes for your palate. For affordable, nonvegetarian coastal Karnataka cuisine, **Unicorn** (94/3 Infantry Rd.; ℂ **080/2559-1670**) is great. The menu changes every week, but expect fish, coconut milk, and lots of flavor. And if you aren't hopping across to Hyderabad, have a taste of excellent Andhra cuisine at **Bheemas** (No. 31 Asha Building, Church St.; ℂ **080/2558-7389**)—be sure to order the chilly chicken, Andhra style. The most delicious ice creams and sundaes are available at **Corner House** (44/1 Residency Rd.; ℂ **080/2521-6312**), which, owing to its popularity, is arguably the narrowest space with the biggest vibe in Bangalore. The Death By Chocolate (Rs 90/$2.20/£1.10) is just that—no trip to Bangalore is complete without at least one shot at surviving it.

In the big hotels, besides **Karavalli,** reviewed below, the following are worth a mention: For North and South Indian cuisine, **Jamavar** at Leela Palace Kempinski (ℂ **080/2521-1234**) is one of Bangalore's class acts, with arguably the best tandoor dishes in town. For specialty South Indian cuisine, there's no better place than **Dakshin** (ℂ **080/2226-9898**), the upmarket restaurant at the Hotel Windsor Sheraton, with a menu that represents the best of all four southern states. It's hard to know what to order from their extensive menu ($25–$50/£13–£25), so go with the maitre d's recommendation or get a thali (the seafood thali, Rs 1,000/$24/£12, is fab). If your system needs a break from spicy cuisine, **i-t.ALIA** (reviewed below) is Bangalore's most stylish Italian restaurant; it's situated in The Park.hotel.

If you want to get out of the hotel atmosphere, head for **Sunny's** (Embassy Diamante, Vittal Mallaya Rd.; ℂ **080/2224-3642**), which has a spacious outdoor and indoor seating area and lounge bar. The eclectic menu is a reflection of Bangalore's growing sophistication. Favorites here include baked brie with toasted almonds; stir-fried calamari with basil and garlic; angel-hair pasta with fresh chunky tomatoes and extra-virgin olive oil; and the flavorful, slightly spiced lamb lasagna, served piping hot. Even better is **Shiok,** which means "yummy" in Malay (Indiranagar; ℂ **080/4116-1800;** www.shiokfood.com), a fine-dining restaurant-cum-cocktail-lounge run by owner-chef Madhu Menon, who has traveled extensively in the Far East to study different styles of cooking. Thai, Malay, Indonesian, and Singaporean dishes are on offer, with—apparently—more than 60% of the ingredients flown in from overseas, making it rather pricey in terms of "food miles"; that said, lemon grass chili prawns (Rs 300/$7.30/£3.70), spiced fish grilled in banana leaves (Rs 210/$5.10/£2.60), and vegetables in chili, garlic, and basil (Rs 125/$3/£1.55) are all recommended. If you happen to visit on the weekend, be sure to try the Singapore black-pepper crab ($23/£12).

Part of a chain, **Olive Beach** 🍴 (16 Wood St., Ashok Nagar; ℂ **080/4112-8400**) lives up to its high culinary style and pulls in the city's who's who, just as it does in Mumbai and Delhi. Try just about any of the exoticas on the menu but definitely end with the Affogato—a combination of coffee bean and Kahlua ice cream with *amaretti* bitter almond cookies.

Blue Ginger 🍴🍴🍴 VIETNAMESE Lush tropical foliage, a lotus pond, and the scent of frangipani in bloom set the mood for Taj West End's Vietnamese restaurant. The decor is Vietnamese-chic: water-hyacinth fiber and dark silks; leather ottomans and natural stone tables; silk lanterns and flaming torches. You can watch the chefs at work in their open kitchen. The hands-down favorite starter is the crunchy raw mango salad, followed by the coconut-based Vietnamese *caris* (curry) served in a clay pot, and accompanied not by rice but a baguette. You could also try shrimp and chicken rice paper rolls served with peanut sauce and salad leaves. For a light meal, we recommend the braised fish with pepper and garlic, the succulent grilled prawns, or the stir-fried chicken with lemon grass and chili (vegetarians should try the crisp stir-fried greens with garlic). End with coconut crème brûlée, sweet sticky rice and mung bean in banana leaves, the mung bean ice cream, or the fresh fruit ice creams in seasonal flavors.

Taj West End. 𝄢 080/6660-5660. Main courses Rs 450–Rs 1,000 ($11–$24/£5.55–£12). AE, DC, MC, V. Daily 12:30–3pm and 7:30–11:45pm.

Ebony 𝜌 ECLECTIC INDIAN   Here's an unexpected treat on the rooftop of a lurid city-center building. After the unpromising elevator ride up, you can dine alfresco and enjoy the best city views in Bangalore. Try the Parsi dish mutton *dhansak* made out of a combination of different lentils and served with brown rice. Another fantastic meat dish is Manan's pepper mutton; this comes from the temple town of Kumbakonam (Tamil Nadu), where Manan is the owner of a small eatery. The mutton is cooked in a paste made from roasted pepper, coriander seeds, and Indian spices. If you'd prefer to avoid meat, try *paneer kairi dopiaza,* made from *paneer,* green mangoes, onions, and fresh coriander; have it with garlic *naan* (bread). Thai food is served daily.

13th Floor, Ivory Tower Hotel, Barton Centre, 84 M.G. Rd. 𝄢 080/2558-9333 or -5164. Main courses Rs 175–Rs 350 ($4.30–$8.55/£2.15–£4.30). AE, DC, MC, V. Daily noon–3pm and 7:30–11:15pm.

i-t.ALIA 𝜌𝜌𝜌 ITALIAN/INTERNATIONAL   Rated the best Italian restaurant in Bangalore by the *Times Food Guide,* i-t.ALIA is led by the globetrotting team of Abhijit Saha and Mandaar Sukhtankar. The menu may have items that are a mouthful to pronounce, but once you taste them, you will be left speechless. Flavor enjoys top priority here, but for the maestros in the kitchen, creative presentation is equally important. Begin with the light and gentle-on-the-palate lettuce and asparagus soup or the *insalata di mela verde, noci arrostite sedano e gorgonzola,* a green apple and rocket lettuce salad with walnuts and Gorgonzola dressing. Whether you pick a simple tapenade-stuffed potato gnocchi or the *gamberoni grigliati conpatate arrosto, carciofi e pomodoro* (king prawns with artichokes, roasted potatoes, and tomato), you will be served a platter as beautiful as it is delicious.

The Park.hotel, 14/7 M.G. Rd. 𝄢 080/2559-4666. An average 3- to 4-course meal is Rs 1,000–Rs 2,000 ($24–$49/£12–£25) with wine and dessert. AE, DC, MC, V. Daily noon–2:45pm and 7–11:45pm.

Karavalli 𝜌𝜌𝜌 SOUTH INDIAN   For more than a decade, this indoor-outdoor restaurant has been wowing guests and winning awards. Sit in the open-air courtyard under the huge canopy of a rain tree on wrought-iron garden chairs, or inside, in what resembles a Mangalorean home, with high ceilings, antique furniture, and walls adorned with old seafarer maps and a grandfather clock. For seafood lovers, Karavalli is a godsend, with Goan baby lobster, Mangalorean black pomfret, and pearlspot caught off the shores of Cochin in Kerala. The west coast also provides fresh *bekti,* shrimp, tiger prawns, scampi, squid, sear, sole, and ladyfish, while the varying cuisines of India's southern coastal regions provide inspiration for dishes originally found in home kitchens. Chef Jose Thomas drums up sensational starters like the Coorg fried chicken, which you can follow with dry Malabar-style tiger prawns or Kane fry (ladyfish). If you've any room left for the main course, try the Alleppey fish curry or the Karavalli mutton curry with *appams* (savory rice-batter pancakes).

Taj Gateway Hotel, 66 Residency Rd. 𝄢 080/6660-4545. Main courses Rs 1,000–Rs 1,500 ($24–$37/£12–£19); lunch thali Rs 575–Rs 675 ($14–$16/£7–£8.35). AE, DC, MC, V. Daily 12:30–3:00pm and 7:30–11:30pm.

Swinging in the Hip City of Bangalore

Spend at least an hour schmoozing on beanbags at The Park.hotel's **i-BAR** ✹✹✹—one of Bangalore's most happening spots—or dancing to house and trance on the small dance floor, where DJ Deepak mixes up a swinging party (Rs 500/$12/£6.15 entry). Alternatively, head for **13th Floor** ✹✹ (Ivory Tower Hotel; M.G. Rd.), a sexy 120-seater rooftop cocktail lounge where you get a large dose of the Bangalore skyline while you sip cocktails named after weapons. **Liquor Café** ✹✹ is a groovy lounge bar on the covered rooftop of a building that houses several smart restaurants; it attracts a hip young crowd who come for the funky, laid-back acid lounge music (Cosmo Village, Magrath Rd.; ✆ 080/4112-7373).

Named for the Greek god of sleep, **Hypnos** ✹ is a cocktail lounge that does anything but, even in the Moroccan Square, where you can smoke *sheeshas* (hookahs) filled with apple, strawberry, or grape tobacco while tucking into Lebanese and Mediterranean fusion cuisine (Gem Plaza, Infantry Rd.; ✆ 080/4111-3361 through -3364; Rs 500/$12/£6.15 entry fee). Single men are technically unwelcome at **1912—The Living Room** ✹✹ (previously **180 proof**), where the Mafioso-style management ensures that the industrial-chic atmosphere is enhanced by the highest-profile Bangalorean crowd. Housed in a lovely stone building that looks like a historic monument, this is probably *the* place in Bangalore to strut your stuff on the dance floor: Three locally based DJs run the show with a blend of rock, hip-hop, and from 8:30pm on, trance music, occasionally joined by record-spinners from Mumbai, San Francisco, and the U.K. (40 St. Marks Rd.; ✆ 080/2299-7290). **Fuga** ✹✹ (No. 1 Castle St., Ashok Nagar; ✆ 080/4147-8625 or 98-4524-7914) is the city's latest lounge bar; elegantly wasted would be the way to be if one had to blend in—it's got plush interiors, a mix of hip-hop, house, and club seeing the night through, great food, and a trendy crowd. **Noir** (Le Meridien; ✆ 080/2226-2233) has taken the place of the club previously known as Insomnia, and competes quite comfortably with the top rung as it belts out retro and house music till 11:30pm. Also in Le Meridien is **F-Bar and Lounge**, a franchise of the Fashion TV bar chain, with screens beaming Fashion TV while fashionistas nibble Japanese and Korean starters or dance to the music of DJ Ganesh; the bar occasionally hosts live fashion shows. Another see-and-be-seen nightclub is **Spinn**, located in a 1940s Art Deco bungalow (80 3rd Cross, Residency Rd.; ✆ 080/2559-0902 or -0901) where hip-hop, funk, and house music rule. **NASA** (1/A Church St.; ✆ 080/2558-6512) is worth a giggle: Staff is decked out in pilot outfits, and the interior is like the inside of a sci-fi space module; the bar is called the "Fuel Tank" and the loo is known as the "Humanoid Disposal" area. It's good for an afternoon pint, but happy hours draw massive crowds. For loud rock music and a crowd that likes to sing along, **Purple Haze** (M.G. Rd., near Richmond Circle; ✆ 080/2221-3758) is one of Bangalore's more popular nightclubs. The Oberoi Hotel's smart **Polo Club** combines deep leather sofas with the ubiquitous TV sports entertainment. Cigar aficionados should head for the **Jockey Club** (✆ 080/6660-4444) at the Taj Residency, popular with expats; while **Dublin,** the watering hole at the ITC Windsor Sheraton (✆ 080/2226-9898), serves up—yep, you guessed right—an Irish pub vibe.

Koshy's Restaurant and the Jewel Box *(Value* INDIAN/CONTINENTAL   Easily the most popular eating and meeting place on M.G. Road, this 50-year-old restaurant has changed little over the years. Food is varied, but it's more or less beside the point; you come here for the energetic buzz—it's a favorite gathering spot and has a distinct local flavor, attracting the coffeehouse intellectual and budding artist alike. You won't be bothered at all if you prefer to linger endlessly over a beer (Rs 100/$2.45/ £1.25) and your book. Those who would rather steer clear of the action can sit in the quieter, but rather bland, air-conditioned section, the Jewel Box.

39 St. Mark's Rd. ✆ 080/2221-3793 or -5030. Average meal Rs 350 ($8.55/£4.30). AE, DC, MC, V. Daily noon–3pm and 7–11pm.

Mavalli Tiffin Rooms (MTR) ✦✦ *(Moments* SOUTH INDIAN VEGETARIAN   Possibly *the* essential Bangalore eating experience, this is an excellent spot to sample the chaos of a traditional "tiffin" room, where scores of locals rush in for the Indian version of fast food, served since 1924 with attitude and gusto from shiny silver buckets by notoriously surly waiters in white. If you're here during lunch, order a thali and eat with your fingers from a silver tray onto which various authentic South Indian concoctions are heaped and continuously replenished. You can also try the lighter fare, especially the *Bisi Bele Bath,* made out of rice, lentils, tamarind, chilies, ground spices, coconut, and vegetables and, last but not least, topped with calorie-intensive ghee. You sit in rather indecorous surroundings (the current venue was built in 1949 and hasn't changed at all in over 40 years) on brown plastic chairs at marble-top tables with orange steel legs; grab a table upstairs. Adjacent, the **MTR Store** sells a wide range of South Indian treats and delicacies, including popular sweets (like *badam halwa* and *ladu*) and ready-to-eat savories.

14 Lal Bagh Rd. ✆ 080/2222-1706. Typical meal Rs 75 ($1.85/95p); individual items Rs 5–Rs 20 (10¢–50¢/5p–25p). No credit cards. Tues–Sun 6:30am–noon, 12:30–2:30pm, and 7:30–9pm.

SHOPPING

You'll find the city's major shopping centers along and around **M.G. Road, Commercial Street,** and **Brigade Road.** M.G. Road is where you'll find the fixed-price touristorientated (no bargains or bargaining) **Cauvery Arts and Crafts Emporium, Central Cottage Industries Emporium,** and **Karnataka State Silk Industries Emporium.** Fabulous silks and home textiles, as well as contemporary silverware from Neemrana and traditional silver jewelry from Amrapali and Jaipur, are some of the highlights available in **Shop Ananya,** located next to the Hotel Sarovar at 9/1 Dhondusa Annexe, Richmond Circle (✆ 080/2299-8922). For antiques and other collectibles in bronze, stone, teak, and silver, call on **Natesan's Antiqarts** (76 M.G. Rd.; ✆ 080/ 2558-8344 or -7427). Pick up beautiful ethnic home accessories, rugs, and other gifts at **The Bombay Store** (99 EGK Prestige, M.G. Rd.; ✆ 080/2532-0014 or -0015). With four levels of saris and *salwar kameez* (for women) and *sherwanis* (for men), and a nonstop clientele, you can understand why staff at **Deepam Silk International** insists that there is "nowhere else in the whole world" better to shop for silk garments (67 Bluemoon Complex, M.G. Rd.; ✆ 080/2558-8760). It's not exactly in the most characterful surroundings, but the **Leela Galleria** (The Leela Palace Hotel, 23 Airport Rd.; ✆ 033/2521-1234) boasts some of the hottest and biggest brands both from India and overseas. Haute couture from Mogra, ffolio, and Sanchita Ajampur, a delicious range of rich linen fabrics at Svisti, and perfumes from Baccarose's Parcos are just some of the reasons to take the trip to this end of town.

Rejuvenation City: Tip-Top Spas

Prompted by the emergence of an overstressed, well-heeled workforce, Bangalore has a number of well-known luxury and medical spas. Besides **The Spa** at Leela Palace Kempinski (✆ **080/2521-1234**) in the city, three luxury spas lie about an hour outside Bangalore. **The Golden Palms Spa** (✆ **080/2371-2222**), owned by Bollywood director Sanjay Khan, is part of an upmarket resort that not only provides routine spa treatments, but is the spot for discreet cosmetic surgery and anti-aging treatments. The attitude toward pampering is more laid-back at the internationally-affiliated **Angsana Oasis Spa and Resort** (✆ **080/2846-8893**; www.angsana.com), offering spa packages from $825 (£418.35) for 2 nights (including taxes, meals, airport transfers, and a few treatments). Neither of these spas will restrict your diet or ban smoking or alcohol, and on weekends you can wholeheartedly tuck into their barbeque and grilled cuisine. In contrast, **Soukya International Holistic Health Centre** (in Whitefield, 30 min. from Bangalore; ✆ **080/2794-5001** through -5004; www.soukya.com) is a medical spa that focuses on therapeutic and complementary therapies. Run by Dr Isaac Mathai, his nutritionist wife Suja, and a battery of experts, this is a nonsmoking, alcohol- and meat-free spa where everything is low fat, low salt, low spice, and organic. The focus is on individually created "holistic wellness programs" (from Hawaiian hot stone to specialized Ayurvedic treatments) that strengthen the body's immune system, including those belonging to some rather famous people, like healthy-living guru Andrew Weil, Fergie, Princess of York, and Archbishop Desmond Tutu. If this all sounds a little militaristic, then look no further than the latest luxury entrant: **Shreyas Yoga Retreat** ★★★ (near Gollahalli Gate, 35km from the city; ✆ **080/2773-7183**; www.shreyas retreat.com; from $350 double including all meals, yoga classes, and wellness consulations), voted one of the best yoga retreats by Harper's & Queen and Business Week. The brainchild of Wall Street banker Pawan Malik, the boutique retreat is set in gorgeously landscaped gardens, with Bali-inspired accommodations. It's a great blend of the simple ashram style (someone describes it as ashram meets Aman!), no-nonsense (but challenging) yoga lessons, very relaxing "rejuvenation" massages, stress management and wellness programmes, all aimed at assisting you long-term in maintaining a more balanced life. Also adhering to the no alcohol/meat lifestyle, it prides itself on its massive vegetable garden where you are welcome to get your hands dirty. Emphasis is on practicing a bit of *ashthanga* and *hatha* yoga (mornings and evenings, but not compulsory), which is taught outdoors under swaying palms. Limited to 4 cottages and 8 tented cottages set in 25 acres, the atmosphere is discreet and personal, amenities are luxurious and service excellent. *(Note:* If you are planning to carry on to Goa from Karnataka, also take a look at **Swaswara**—a yoga retreat on the northern tip of Karnataka's coast, bordering Goa: see chapter 5, under "Om Beach: Escape to Paradise".)

Cinnamon ★★★ Some of India's best designers (Sonam, Vivek Narang, Sujit Mukherjee) are represented in this cool, stylish boutique, which often hosts small exhibitions, and has interesting objects, some at really good prices. Apparently Bangalorean designer Jason Cheriyan refuses to sell his work anywhere else; certainly the store buyer's eye is well honed. Hours are Monday to Saturday 10:30am to 8pm and Sunday noon to 8pm. 11 Walton Rd., off Lavelle Rd. © 080/2222-9794.

CULTURAL ACTIVITIES

Check the local dailies for information about cultural events. Besides art exhibitions and traditional dance and music performances, Bangalore draws major international artists, including pop and rock stars.

The violin-shaped auditorium known as **Chowdaiah Memorial Hall** (Gayathri Devi Park Extension, Vyalikaval; © 080/2344-5810) hosts regular classical music performances, as well as film, dance, and drama. Plays are regularly staged at **Rabindra Kalakshetra** (Jayachamarachendra Rd.; © 080/2224-1325), where you can also catch occasional art exhibitions. Numerous art galleries around the city host contemporary Indian art and other exhibitions. **Venkatappa Art Gallery,** attached to the Government Museum (Kasturba Rd.; © 080/2286-4483; Rs 10/25¢/15p; Tues–Sun 10am–5pm), displays more than 600 paintings year-round. **Chitrakala Parishat** (Art Complex, Kumara Krupa Rd.; © 080/2226-1816) has a varied collection of traditional paintings, leather puppets, and artifacts from all over Karnataka. Visit its various art studios and gallery spaces, the open-air theater, and (in particular) the Roerich and Kejriwal galleries. For high-end art, check out **Gallerie Zen** (121 Dickenson Rd.; © 080/2671-0412; by appointment only).

Nrityagram Dance Village (along the Bangalore-Pune Hwy., 35km/22 miles from Bangalore) is a renowned center for Indian dance training. Performances feature students as well as established artists. Organized tours of the facility include lecture-demonstrations designed to introduce you to Indian culture, life philosophy, and both *kathak* and *odissi* dance forms (© 080/2846-6313; tours Rs 20/50¢/25p per person; Tues–Sun 10am–5:30pm, dance classes 10:30am–1pm). A through-the-night dance and music festival is held in February; it attracts almost 30,000 spectators, so decent seating is at a premium.

2 Mysore ★★★

140km (87 miles) SW of Bangalore; 473km (293 miles) N of Chennai; 1,177km (730 miles) SE of Mumbai

A city of palatial buildings and tree-lined boulevards, laid-back Mysore is possessed of a quaint charm, a dignified hangover from the days when it was the capital of a rich princely state. It remains a popular destination for travelers, particularly for its **Maharajah's Palace.** Built over a period of 15 years at the turn of the 20th century at a cost of over Rs 4 million, this astonishing Indo-Saracenic palace is testament to the affluence of one of India's greatest ruling dynasties. During the 10-day **Dussehra Festival,** held here during the first half of October, the entire city is dressed up in show-off style; each night **Mysore Palace** is lit up by 80,000 bulbs, and on the final evening of festivities, the maharajah, dressed in royal finery, leads one of the country's most spectacular processions on elephants through the city streets. But Mysore is also an ideal base from which to explore the temples known as the **"Jewel Boxes"** of Hoysala architecture, which lie some 3 hours north, as well as the nearby Jain pilgrimage site at **Sravanabelgola.**

ESSENTIALS

GETTING THERE & AWAY Trains from Bangalore (3 hr.) and Hassan (for Hoysala heartland; 2–3 hr.) pull in regularly at the **railway station** (© **131** or 0821/ 242-2103), situated at the intersection of Jhansi Laxmi Bai Road and Irwin Road. For Rajiv Gandhi National Park, your best option is to hire a car.

VISITOR INFORMATION For information, visit the **Karnataka Tourist Office** (Mayura Yatri Niwas, JLB Rd., near railway station; © **0821/242-3652;** daily 7am–9pm).

GETTING AROUND Negotiate **taxi** prices in advance, or hire a vehicle for the day. **Auto-rickshaws** are cheap and plentiful; you can either insist that the driver use his meter (Rs 12/30¢/15p at the start) or fix a price upfront; the latter is likely to get you to your destination quicker (see chapter 2). Don't pay for any taxi or vehicle without first checking its condition. You can organize a car through your hotel travel desk, but it's likely to be more expensive.

GUIDED TOURS & TRAVEL AGENTS Operating since 1976, **Seagull Travels** (8 Best Western Ramanashree Hotel Complex, Bangalore–Niligiri Rd.; © **0821/ 252-9732,** or 0821/426-0054 and -3653; fax 0821/252-0549; www.seagulltravels. net; daily 9:45am–8:45pm) handles a wide range of travel needs, including ticketing, taxi arrangements, and individually packaged tours (although prices can fluctuate arbitrarily). Seagull is Mysore's only agent for the popular government-owned Jungle Lodges and Resorts, including the popular Kabini River Lodge (see below). Another local travel agent is **Skyway International Travels** (3704/4, Jansi Laxmibai Rd.; © **0821/244-4444** or 0821/242-3767; fax 0821/242-6000; www.skywaytour.com; skyway@vsnl.com).

WHAT TO SEE & DO

Besides Mysore's most famous palace, the Maharajah's Palace, and Keshava Temple, you might want to visit **Jagan Mohan Palace** (west of Mysore Palace, Dewan's Rd. ; Rs 10/25¢/15p; daily 8:30am–5pm), which once served as the royal auditorium. The building now exhibits South India's oddest assortment of kitsch memorabilia from the massive private collection of the Wodeyars. Southeast of downtown (3km/2 miles away), **Chamundi Hill** is where you can join throngs of huffing-puffing pilgrims, some of who recite or read Hindu verses along the way. Stop first at the **Shiva Temple,** where devotees circumambulate the statue in a clockwise direction while a friendly priest dishes out sacred water and dollops of vermilion paste. The summit of the hill is very active with pilgrims come to pay their respects to Durga. You can buy a *darshan* ticket from the computerized ticketing booth and join the queue for a peek at the deity inside **Sri Chamundeswari Temple** (3:30–6:30pm); or you can wander around the hilltop exploring smaller temples, many of which serve as bases for bright-robed grinning *sadhus* (holy persons) wanting to sell you a private photo opportunity. Near the Race Course is the **Karinji Lake,** a particularly beautiful spot during the early hours of the morning when you get to see a large number of birds.

Finally, no trip to Mysore is complete without getting lost in the dizzying scents of jasmine, musk, sandalwood, frangipani, and incense as you wander through the city's vibrant **market.** Mysore is also famous for its silk and sandalwood oil, and you can witness the production of both by taking a side trip to Vidyaranyapuram, 15 minutes away. For an escorted tour of the **Government Silk Weaving Factory,** call © **0821/ 248-1803** (visiting hours daily 7am–2:30pm; shop hours 9:30am–6:30pm); the

Government Sandal Oil Factory is right next door (daily 11:30am–4pm). If time is short, you can also hop into **Cauvery Arts and Crafts Emporium** (Sayaji Rao Rd.; 10am–6pm) which is like a one-stop shop for all that Mysore has to offer.

Keshava Temple ✦✦✦ Situated 38km (24 miles) from Mysore in the small village of Somnathpur, this is perhaps the best-preserved and most complete Hoysala monument in existence. Also referred to as Chennakeshava Temple, this beautiful religious monument is presided over by Vijayanarayana, one of the 24 incarnations of Vishnu. Built as early as 1268, it is constructed entirely of soapstone and rests on a raised plinth; typical of Hoysala temples, it has a star-shaped ground plan and exquisitely sculpted interiors. It's really worth exploring in detail; you may have to urge or bribe the caretaker to crank up the generator so that you have enough light to properly observe the three shrines in the temple. Somnathpur is serene and remote, and the lawns around the monument are ideal for picnicking—ask your hotel for a packed lunch. The best time to photograph the temple is around 4:30pm, when the sun creates a fantastic play of shadow and light, especially along the row of pillars.

Somnathpur is 38km (24 miles) east of Mysore. Admission Rs 100 ($2.45/£1.25). Daily 8am–5:30pm.

Maharajah's Palace (Amba Vilas) ✦✦✦ Generally considered *the* palace in South India, this was designed by Henry Irving at the turn of the 20th century; 15 years of nonstop construction produced a fabulous domed, arched, colonnaded, and turreted structure with lavish interiors—teak ceilings, carved marble handrails, gilded pillared halls, ivory deities, rococo lamp stands, Italian crystal chandeliers, stained-glass windows, miles of white marble floors, and ceilings made from stained glass brought all the way from Glasgow. You'll be hard-pressed to find an undecorated section of wall or ceiling; frescoes, paintings, statues, and delicate relief carvings recall religious as well as secular scenes, including glorious state processions. Within the inner courtyards, growling stone felines guard stairways, while elsewhere, elaborately carved rosewood doors mark the entrances of yet more splendid halls and chambers. Paintings by Raja Ravi Varma, golden chariots, gilt-framed mirrors, stately family portraits (including a wax sculpture of the maharajah), and all manner of ornate fantasy objects add to the spectacle of abundant wealth. Overlooking the parade grounds, brought to life during the **Dussehra Festival** (Sept or Oct), a terraced grandstand pavilion is covered by a heavily decorated and frescoed ceiling, while huge, decaying chandeliers dangle precariously over the seating.

Don't bother to purchase an additional ticket for the disappointing **Maharajah's Residential Palace,** where, sadly, a display of items gathers dust.

Ramvilas Rd., Mizra Rd., and Purandara Rd. ✆ 0821/242-2620. Admission: Amber Vilas Rs 20 (50¢/25p); Residential Palace Rs 20 (50¢/25p). Daily 10am–5:30pm.

WHERE TO STAY

Although small, Mysore offers a good variety of hotels, ranging from business hotels, heritage properties, and resorts to dirt-cheap establishments. If you're interested in the latter category, walk around Gandhi Square and take your pick, or head straight into **Hotel Dasaprakash,** a local institution. It has clean, modest rooms with running hot water 5 to 10am (✆ 0821/244-2444 or -4455; from Rs 420/$10/£5.20 double). Another extremely low-end place with no frills whatsoever is **Hotel Siddhartha** (Guest House Rd., Nazarbad; ✆ 0821/428-0999 or -0888; siddhartahotel@hotmail.com), situated at a convenient distance from the palace, station, and bus stand. The rooms are small but were recently renovated and have a fresh feel. The range starts from Rs 860 to Rs 1,460 ($21–$36/£11–£18)—some rooms have Indian-style bathrooms (the wc is sunk into the ground), so make sure you ask beforehand. The in-house restaurant **Om Shanthi** has a great local atmosphere and is extremely popular with regulars, who have been coming for 25 years—*rawa dosai* (a flat kind of pancake made out of rice powder), *mallige idli* (in Kannada "mallige" means jasmine, and these slightly flattened balls of rice flour are reputedly as soft as the flower itself), and the filter coffee are all top class. Adjacent, **Hotel Sandesh the Prince** is loud and gaudy in appearance but has decent rooms and offers all the basic facilities including a pool and gym (Guest House Rd., Nazarbad; ✆ **0821/243-6777;** doubles from $80/£41). **Regaalis** (known in a previous incarnation as Southern Star) is a pretty good business hotel and combines a fair amount of luxury (wood paneling, marble flooring, and lovely photographs of flowers by Tom Baril) with value for the money. The poolside barbecue is popular, while **Gardenia,** its multi-cuisine restaurant, serves the best buffet in town and is a steal at Rs 380 ($9.25/£4.70) (13-14 Vinoba Rd., Mysore 570005; ✆ **0821/242-6426;** www.ushashriramhotels.com; doubles from Rs 5,500–Rs 11,000/$134–$268/£68–£136).

In the heritage category, it's a bit of a toss-up between The Green Hotel (reviewed below, and better a value) and the 120-year-old **Royal Orchid Metropole,** built by the Maharaja of Mysore to entertain his foreign guests (5 Jhansi Lakshmibai Rd., Mysore 570005; ✆ **0821/425-5566;** www.royalorchidhotels.com; doubles from $125/£63). The stately colonial structure is a striking contrast to neighboring Hotel Regaalis (mentioned above) and extremely popular with foreign tourists for its laid-back ambience and good cuisine. The standard rooms are small and very bland but located away from the road, while the bigger royal rooms hear a fair amount of traffic noise—still, these are preferable given the greater charm of antique furniture and sit-outs, or balconies. The bathroom of the only suite in the hotel incidentally features the first bathtub to be brought to India from England, still functioning today without leaks! Real silver swings and chairs from Rajasthan adorn the tiny lobby, while a 100-year-old portrait of Tipu Sultan looms large in the restaurant.

The Green Hotel 🐟🐟 This award-winning hotel began as Chittaranjan Palace, built in the 1920s by Wodeyar IV as a retreat for his three sisters. Today it looks and feels pretty much how you would imagine the home of a royal family in decline would look—all faded glamour and lots of character. The hotel is owned by a charity that employs disadvantaged people on good wages and, true to its name, tries to be environmentally conscious (only 25 hotels in the world are listed as "Eco Hotels," and the Green Hotel ranks 15th). The palace proper has a motley assortment of antique furniture and colorful memorabilia that rivals other tourist distractions in town. Light filters through stained-glass windows, and the large, open public spaces are swathed in teak and brimming with old-world charm, despite the incessant noise from the main road alongside. This erstwhile princesses' retreat also offers interesting lodging options. Choose one of the seven guest rooms in the original palace: The Princess's Room is enormous, with antique furniture, blue Indian throws, and sheer curtains over narrow slit windows. For added color, try the Deluxe Bollywood Room, where the antique wooden headboards are decorated with brightly colored renditions of old Bollywood starlets on painted glass. The Rose and Marigold rooms, however, are quite tiny and only worth booking if you're traveling alone. Though all rooms are garden-facing, guest rooms in the New Wing (built when the palace became a film studio), while offering value, lack the historical flavor of the palace.

Chittaranjan Palace, 2270 Vinoba Rd., Jayalamipuram, Mysore 570 012. ℂ **0821/251-2536** or 0821/525-5000, -5001, and -5002. Fax 0821/251-6139. www.greenhotelindia.com. 31 units. New Wing: Rs 1,950—Rs 3,250 ($48–$79/ £24–£40) double. Palace Rooms: Rs 4,750 ($116/£59) Marigold, Rs 3,250 ($79/£40) Writer and Small Bollywood. Palace suites: Rs 6,000 ($146/£74) Maharni Suite, Rs 5,500 ($134/£68) Princess's Room, Rose, and Large Bollywood. Rs 575 ($14/£7) extra bed. Rates include breakfast. MC, V. **Amenities:** Restaurant; bar; indoor games; travel services; room service on request; laundry; doctor-on-call; Internet facilities in lounge; library; TV room; volleyball; croquet; boule; green auto-rickshaw service. As part of the eco-friendly image, none of the rooms have carpets or individual TVs; no newspapers are delivered either.

The Windflower Spa and Resort 🌟🌟

Situated in the quiet environs of the Mysore race course and flanked in the distance by the Chamundi Hill, the 4-hectare (10-acre) Windflower property, midway between a high-end hotel and boutique resort, exudes a sense of space from the moment you walk into its delightful reception area. With nothing save a couple of chairs and a sofa or two, the high-ceilinged hall is open on two sides, giving a glimpse of shimmering water beyond, while the exterior looks exquisite with rows of areca-nut wood cladding. (*Warning:* You will probably be greeted by a snow-white Australian cockatoo called Rosy who has a fondness for punching holes in footwear.) The 39 white cottages with Mangalore-tiled roofs are lined along a shallow canal-like pond with gorgeous giant brass *urlis* (cauldrons) placed at intervals, and plenty of swaying palms. Almost the entire resort has been designed using furniture from Indonesia—massive low beds with a wooden step, chunky teak wood coffee tables, sofas with silk covers, and lots of cane and bamboo everywhere; your best bet is one of the Deluxe rooms, which are big. The spa (known technically as **Emerge**) is also very artfully designed, with Sri Lankan artifacts peeping from niches and plenty of treatments (Ayurvedic, Balinese, hydrotherapy, and beauty) to suit your fancy and— wonder of wonders—will not leave your pockets empty. The biggest drawback (or blessing!) is that you are a little far (3km/2 miles) from central Mysore.

Maharanapratap Rd., Nazarbad, Mysore 570 010. ℂ **0821/252-2500.** Fax 0821/252-2400. www.thewindflower. com. 39 units. Rs 4,200 ($90/£45) Executive; Rs 5,100 ($120/£61) Deluxe; Rs 6,300 ($150/£76) Club Class Suite, Rs 9,000 ($200/£101) Royal Presidential Suite. Rs 800 ($19/£10) extra bed. Rates include breakfast. AE, MC, V. **Amenities:** Restaurant; bar; pool; fitness center in the making; spa; indoor games; business center; room service; laundry; doctor-on-call; currency exchange; Wi-Fi enabled. *In room:* TV, DVD player, hot and cold water, fresh fruit basket.

WHERE TO DINE

Visitors with a sweet tooth will get a kick out of the local specialty, Mysore *pak (mysurpa)*, made from gram flour and liters of ghee (clarified butter). You'll find a number of outlets at Devaraja Market. Try the famous and long-established **Guru Sweet Mart** (Sayaji Rao Rd.) or any of the Nandini milk stalls for your sugar rush. Hotel Dasaprakash's canteenlike restaurant **Akshaya** (Gandhi Sq.; ℂ **0821/244- 2444**) serves simple, hygienic vegetarian fare, typical of the region, and a sumptuous thali that costs just Rs 45 ($1.10/55p).

Le Olive Garden 🌟 (Finds) NORTH INDIAN/ECLECTIC

The in-house restaurant at the new Windflower Spa and Resort (reviewed above) offers alfresco dining in a leafy garden with geese and wind chimes for company. Arranged on landscaped terracing, the dining area is surrounded by water and reached by tiny bridges. Most of the dishes are Indian, with a good range of kebabs on offer, but you can also order Chinese or choose from a small selection of Continental dishes. We recommend the *murgh malai kebab* (chicken cubes grilled with fresh yogurt cream) or the *Peshawari kebab* (pistachio- and almond-flavored grilled chicken cubes); consult the enthusiastic Vicky if you want more clarity on what to order. The owner of the resort is also the proprietor of Joy ice cream, famous in this part of the country, so it makes perfect sense to end with a bowl of delicious butterscotch ice cream or the Olive orange-flavored caramel custard. Incidentally, you won't find better iced coffee (don't ask for ice cream in it) anywhere else in Karnataka.

Maharanapratap Rd., Nazarbad. © 0821/252-2500. Main courses Rs 150–Rs 250 ($3.65–$6/£1.85–£3). MC, V. Daily 11:30am–3:30pm and 7–11:30pm.

VISITING RAJIV GANDHI NATIONAL PARK

Originally the private property of the Maharajah of Mysore, Karnataka's most popular elephant hangout became a national park in 1955, 3 years after the princely state of Mysore was absorbed into post-colonial India. Situated 95km (59 miles) southwest of Mysore, and spread over 511 sq. km (199 sq. miles) filled with teak, rosewood, sandal, and silver oak trees, Rajiv Gandhi National Park is also generously populated by *dhole* (wild dogs), *gaur* (Indian bison), antelope, sloth bears, panthers, otters, crocodiles, cobras, pythons, falcons, eagles, and great Indian horned owls. Keep an eye peeled for tiny *muntjac* deer; they stand only .6m (2 ft.) tall and are crowned by finger-length antlers. The big draw, of course, are the tigers (between 60 and 65 reside here), but sightings are subject to a great deal of luck—although when Goldie Hawn came here to shoot a documentary, she apparently spotted several. Ms. Hawn stayed at the popular **Kabini River Lodge,** the most practical place to be if you want to have access to the park without any organizational fuss. A charmingly rustic retreat some 6 hours by car from Bangalore (3 hr. from Mysore), Kabini is spread over 22 hectares (55 acres), incorporating lush forest and largely untamed vegetation, just the way a "jungle resort" should, with the maharajah's original 18th-century hunting lodge as centerpiece. Accommodations with the best positions are the river-facing cottages. Expect small bathrooms, dated green sofas, and lumpy mattresses covered with charming Indian throws. Eyeball the skies for birds like hoopoes and drongos, try a brief coracle (boat) trip, go for an elephant ride or tiger spotting, and—of course—partake of the meals and tea laid out for you according to a precise schedule. The lodge was set up by Col. John Felix Wakefield, who at 90 still takes his meals on the terrace overlooking the river. A tiger hunter in his youth, now a celebrated sanctuary-tourism reformer, Wakefield can be a lively source of information about the region. Book a room at Kabini well in advance, and plan to arrive there at least an hour before the afternoon safari, which begins at 4:30pm (© 08228/26-4402 through -4405; head office in Bangalore © 080/2559-7021, -7024, or -7025; www.junglelodges.com; standard package 2 days, 1 night per person, $62–$79/£31–£40; includes all meals, safaris, park entrance, and elephant and boat rides). For companies that offer the services of a car and driver for the 3-hour drive, see "Guided Tours & Travel Agents" under Mysore "Essentials," above.

Another resort worth looking into is **Orange County Kabini.** Built along the lines of a tribal village, replete with palm-thatched mud huts lit with bottle-gourd lamps and other ethnic bric-a-brac, the new luxury lodge opened in mid-2007 and offers two kinds of lodging—private pool huts and Jacuzzi huts, ranging between $400 and $500 (£203–£253). Contact the marketing agents Trails for details (St. Patricks Business Complex, 1st floor, 21, Museum Rd., Bangalore; © 080/2558-2425).

OF COORG & COFFEE

Legend has it that in 1670, Baba Budan, a Muslim pilgrim, carried seven coffee beans from Arabia (where the export of only processed beans was allowed) and planted them in the Chikmagalur region of Karnataka, thus introducing coffee to India. Today the state is the largest producer of coffee in the country, and a large chunk of it comes from a gorgeous area known as Kodagu, or, as the British called it, Coorg, an elevated region that lies 3 hours southwest of Mysore. With undulating hills, this is a superb trekking destination, and as yet still somewhat of a secret.

The capital of Coorg is **Madikeri,** an unexceptional town but a convenient base for treks in the area. If you don't intend to hike, however, you could opt for a quieter, more luxurious getaway in the midst of a coffee plantation at Orange County (reviewed below). As is the case elsewhere, a number of homestay options have opened in the last few years, but most don't meet our standards of hygiene and ambience. Having said that, the best way of getting acquainted with the Coorgi way of life is to attend a wedding—nonstop fun, and full of interesting rites and ceremonies. Essentially agriculturists, the Coorgis, also known as the Kodavas, are a distinct community, with strict adherence to the code of merry-making, and occasions to celebrate are never wanting. Interestingly, they are said to be descendents of Alexander's army, something that could well be true given that they always carry some form of weapon—thankfully, rarely ever used.

Orange County Coorg ⍟ From the moment you arrive at this lovely 16th-century Tudor-style resort, surrounded by a 120-hectare (300-acre) coffee and pepper plantation, and are welcomed with a delicious glass of fresh sugar-cane juice, you know you're in for a treat. Connected by cobbled pathways, the thatched and tiled cottages are divided into clusters and spread out over almost 20 hectares (50 acres). The Private Pool Villas are worth the money, with huge bedrooms and spacious dining and sitting areas that lead out to a decent-size private pool set in the middle of a garden with your very own pepper tree. Fringing the picturesque lake is the Camp, where eight luxury tents have been set up for couples only—a hit with Indian honeymooners. (It's worth noting that Orange County is extremely popular with Indian tourists, especially entire families on vacation, so don't come if you prefer intimate retreats, and particularly avoid the months of May–June and Dec, when the resort is unbearably full and noisy.) There are three restaurants to choose from—the multi-cuisine **Granary,** which doles out extensive buffets three times a day, the purely vegetarian **Plantain Leaf,** and **Peppercorn,** the specialty restaurant located by the lake—don't miss Chef Shivaprasad's *Pandhi* curry (pork flavored with *kachempulli,* a strong kind of tamarind) and *bamballoos* (fresh bamboo shoot with a coconut base) with *akki roti* (thin flatbread made out of rice). Caffeine addicts can get their fix in the lounge, where coffee is free of charge. *Tip:* If too much coffee produces an energy rush, head for **Bylekuppe,** 30km (19 miles) away. The second largest Tibetan settlement outside Tibet, its Golden Monastery is spectacular, featuring three gigantic gold-plated statues and huge wall frescoes. There are plenty of smaller monasteries in town, along with slightly drab carpet-, incense-, and noodle-making units.

Karadigodu Post, Siddapur, Coorg 571253. ⍟ **08274/258-481** or -482. Fax 08274/258-485. www.orangecounty.in. 66 units. $240 (£122) County Cottages; $270 (£137) Presidential Villa; $300 (£152) tent at the Camp; $400 (£203) Pool Villa; $490 (£249) King's Court (4-person suite); $53 (£27) extra bed. Rates include all meals and taxes. MC, V. **Amenities:** Coffee lounge; bar; 2 pools; gymnasium; health spa; cycling; indoor games; travel desk; shop; room service; laundry; doctor-on-call; library; boating; fishing; trekking; spice tour; badminton. *In room:* A/C, TV, coffee- and tea-making facility.

3 Exploring the Hoysala Heartland: Belur, Halebid & Sravanabelagola

Halebid is 220km (136 miles) W of Bangalore; Belur is 14km (9 miles) SW of Halebid; Sravanabelagola is 85 km (53 miles) SE of Belur.

The Hoysalas were ferocious warriors who, despite regular military campaigns, found time to allow their love for the arts to flourish. What remains of this once-powerful dynasty are their beautiful temples, usually commissioned to commemorate their victories or successful covenants made with their gods. Situated at the edge of the Western Ghats, the temples of the once-powerful cities of **Belur** and **Halebid** are often referred to as the "Jewel Boxes" of Hoysala architecture, and are comparable with the religious monuments of Khajuraho (in Madhya Pradesh) and Konark (in Orissa). The artists who created these compact, assiduously sculpted temples demonstrated enormous regard for the rules of proportion, and went to extreme lengths to ensure absolute spatial precision. Exterior temple walls are invariably covered in detailed sculpted decoration, while inside you will discover hand-lathe-turned filigreed pillars and figures with moveable jewelry, also carved from stone. The gods paraded at these temples are over 8 centuries old, yet continue to impress with the vigor with which they carry out their superhuman duties, slaying demons and moving mountains, while celestial maidens admire their reflections in eternally reflecting mirrors.

In quite a different vein, the living pilgrimage center at **Sravanabelagola** is where you will find the world's tallest monolithic sculpture. The statue of Gomateswara, a naked ascetic saint, is the object of one of the biggest Jain pilgrimages in the country—lacking any decoration whatsoever, yet awesome in its sheer grandeur.

To see these highlights of Karnataka's religious heritage, you have to veer off the main drag a little. Fortunately, if you're pressed for time, it is possible to cover all three destinations with ease in a single day. Most visitors base their exploration of this region out of the dull and dusty town of Hassan, but the coffee-growing town of Chikmagalur, 25km (16 miles) from Belur, offers far more glowing surroundings, and the pleasant accommodations of the **Taj Garden Retreat.**

ESSENTIALS

GETTING THERE & AROUND   The most convenient way to see the Hoysala sights is to hire a car and driver in Mysore or even Bangalore. A more affordable option is to catch a train from Mysore to Hassan (3 hr. away), from where you can pick up a taxi for a full day of sightseeing (approximately Rs 1,300/$32/£16). Hassan can also be reached overland from Mangalore (see "Traveling Via Mangalore," below). If you need to hire a vehicle in Hassan, we recommend **Mr. Altaf** (© **94-4825-6479;** or ask the manager at Hotel Southern Star to give him a call), who offers excellent rates.

VISITOR INFORMATION   Visit the friendly **Regional Tourist Office** (Vartha Bhavan, B.M. Rd.; © **08172/26-8862;** 10am–5:30pm, closed Sun and second Sat of the month) if you need to stock up on brochures. You can also deepen your knowledge at Hotel Mayura Velapuri's **Belur Tourist Information Centre** (Temple Rd.; © **08177/22-2209;** daily 9:30am–6:30pm). In Halebid, there's a **Tourist Help Desk** (Mon–Sat 10am–5:30pm) at Hoysalesvara Temple. You can pick up ASI-certified **guides** outside each of the two main temples in Belur and Halebid.

BELUR

Now a sleepy hamlet, Belur was the capital of the Hoysala kings at the height of their reign. The magnificent soapstone **Temple of Lord Channakeshava** ✦✦✦ (free admission; daily sunrise–sunset), built over a period of 103 years, was commissioned to commemorate the victory of Vishnuvardhana over the Cholas from Tamil Nadu; apparently, it was so admired by Belur's iconoclastic Muslim invaders that they decided to leave it intact.

Built on a star-shaped plan, the temple stands on a raised platform within a courtyard surrounded by an outer wall. After you survey the courtyard, approach the temple by climbing the short flight of steps. Despite its compact scale, the profusion of carved decoration is spectacular, the multicornered shape of the temple allowing maximum space for sculptures of Vishnu and a vast retinue of Hindu images. Covering the flat-roofed building are detailed representations of myriad themes—ranging from erotica to religious mythology, everyday events to episodes from the *Ramayana*—arranged in bands that wrap the entire exterior in delightful compositions. The temple itself is borne by almost 650 stone elephants. Don't miss the various bracket figures, which are considered the highlight of Hoysala workmanship. Use a torch to study the temple interior, at the center of which is a pillar adorned with smaller versions of the temple's 10,000 sculpted images. Belur is a living temple, and a silver-plated image of Vishnu within the inner sanctum is still worshiped; *puja* (prayer) is performed at 9am and 7pm each day, and the inner sanctums are closed between 1 and 3pm and 5 and 6pm.

HALEBID

Once known as Dwara Samudra, "the gateway to the sea," Halebid usurped Belur's position as the Hoysalan capital in the 12th century. Unfortunately, when the Muslim invaders arrived, Halebid failed to escape their wrath. Appropriately, its current name means "old city," as it consists of only a dusty road and some well-crafted temples amid a lush landscape with the Western Ghats as a distant backdrop. Exquisitely sculpted **Hoysalesvara Temple** ✦✦✦ (free admission; shoe-check Rs 1/5¢; sunrise–sunset) is the largest of the Hoysala temples. Hoysalesvara actually consists of two distinct temples resting upon a star-shaped platform, both dedicated to Shiva. It has more complex and detailed carvings than those at Belur. You can discover the 20,000-odd sculptures in and around the temple on your own, or enlist the services of a **guide** (who will approach you as you arrive at the monument; expect to pay around Rs 150/$3.65/£1.85, but do include a tip). You can visit the on-site **Archaeological Museum** (Rs 2/5¢/5p; Sat–Thurs 10am–5pm) to see more stone statues of Hindu gods, gathered from Halebid and its immediate environs. If you want more of the same, without the touristy vibe, head for **Kedareshvara Temple,** 300m (984 ft.) away and marked by its serene location.

Also in Halebid are several **Jain Bastis** that allude to the religious tolerance of the Hoysala kings, who extended patronage to other faiths. Although lacking the immense carved decoration of the Hindu monuments, **Parswanathasamy Temple** (free admission; daily sunrise–sunset) enjoys a lovely lakeside location.

SRAVANABELAGOLA ✦✦✦

For members of the peace-loving, nonviolent Jain faith, this is one of the oldest and most important pilgrimage centers, famous for its colossal 18m (59-ft.) statue of Lord Gomateswara, said to be the tallest monolithic statue on earth, and reached by climbing

> ## Tips Traveling Via Mangalore
>
> Once a seaport of some significance, Mangalore is an important center for the processing and export of Karnataka's spices, coffee, and cashews, and known as the *bidi* cigarette capital of the world. (The *bidi*, effectively a roll of dried tobacco leaf, is also known as the "pauper's puff." Apparently 90 people die every hr. in India from tobacco-related cancer.) Its greatest significance for travelers is that it makes a convenient pit stop on the section of the Konkan Railway that runs between Goa and Kerala, and provides road access to Belur, Halebid, and Sravanabelgola, as well as Mysore. **Taj Manjarun** (© 0824/566-0420; www.tajhotels.com; doubles from $80/£41) is the best hotel in Mangalore. Accommodations are comfortable, if not particularly luxurious. Suite no. 401 ($120/£61) has the best views, taking in the river and the ocean. Staff will arrange trips to the beach and local temples, as well as tours of a cashew-nut factory or tours to see how Mangalore's famous red-clay roof tiles are made.

the 635 steps that lead to the hill's summit. Naked and imposing, the statue is a symbolic representation of worldly renunciation.

Commissioned in A.D. 981, the **Statue of Gomateswara** ★★★ is a representation of Bahubali. Son of the first Jain Tirthankara Adinatha, Bahubali renounced his kingdom and sought enlightenment by standing naked and motionless for an entire year while contemplating the meaning of life. Seen in detail on the legs of the statue, the creepers and plants twisting their way up his body are symbolic of his motionless mission of spiritual discovery. A special celebration (*Mahamastakabhisheka,* or the Great Annointing) is held here every 12 years, when the giant monolith is bathed with bucketfuls of milk and honey. The next ceremony takes place in 2018.

WHERE TO STAY & DINE

Accommodations close to the temples are limited and hardly the stuff of kings. You'll find a number of government-run hotels in both Belur and Halebid; these have restaurants of questionable quality and extremely basic rooms. In Halebid, the tourism department's **Hotel Mayura Shanthala** (Temple Rd.; © 08177/27-3224; doubles Rs 260/$6.35/£3.20) is within striking distance of a number of temples, but you pay for what you get. Equally so at Belur's **Hotel Mayura Velapuri** (© 08177/222-209; doubles Rs 300/$7.30/£3.70), located just outside the temple entrance. Better to opt for **Hotel Southern Star Hassan** (© 08172/22-51816 or -51817; www.ushashriramhotels.com; doubles from Rs 1,600/$39/£20), which offers pleasant service (including sightseeing advice) and safe dining. It's certainly not luxury level, but guest rooms are comfortable and clean. Views from odd-numbered rooms are of a less built-up part of the town.

Taj Garden Retreat, Chikmagalur ★★   Located just outside the small coffee-growing town of Chikmagalur, this hillside retreat—originally built as a government rest house—is comfortable and idyllically remote, with sloping red-tile roofs echoing the style of the local colonial Malnad plantation homes. Reserve one of the cottages (only $10–$15/£5–£7.50 more); these have high-pitched ceilings, polished floors, two double beds, and large balconies with scenic views. (Reserve no. 119 for an especially large balcony.) The attached bathrooms are spacious but have showers only. Visits to nearby coffee plantations set off Monday to Saturday at 3:30pm. Taj has also opened a Ayurvedic massage center, so you can kick back and allow yourself to be stroked into good health.

K.M. Rd., opposite Pavitravana Jyothinagar Post, Chikmagalur 577 102. (C) 08262/22-0202 or -0404. Fax 08262/22-0222. www.tajhotels.com. 29 units. $85 (£43) standard garden view double; $90 (£46) superior pool-view double; $100 (£51) cottage mountain view. $20 (£10) extra bed. AE, DC, MC, V. **Amenities:** Restaurant; bar; pool; cycling; travel assistance; car hire; room service 7:30am–10:30pm; laundry; doctor-on-call; currency exchange; pool table; table tennis; fax service. *In room:* A/C, TV, minibar, tea- and coffee-making facilities.

4 Hampi & the Ruined City of Vijayanagar ★★★

Hampi is 460km (285 miles) NW of Bangalore and 13km (8 miles) E of Hospet

The surreal, boulder-strewn landscape of Karnataka's hinterland is the backdrop to the largest complex of ruins in India. Hampi, capital of one of India's most formidable empires, the powerful Vijayanagara—whose rule stretched from the Arabian Sea to the Indian Ocean—was home to a population of half a million, and protected by more than a million soldiers. Set in a vast valley sprawling from the banks of the Tungabhadra River, the splendid "City of Victory"—where even the king's horses were adorned in jewels—is now a ghost city with numerous temples, fortification ramparts, stables, royal apartments, and palaces, popular with determined sightseers and trance and rave party disciples. Long popular with Bollywood as a shooting location, Hampi is also where scenes from the 2005 Jackie Chan thriller *The Myth* were shot. Hampi may be a little difficult to get to, but this remoteness is to a large extent its charm. You can easily enjoy 2 or 3 days in this serene atmosphere, particularly if you've booked at **Hampi's Boulders** (see "Where to Stay," below), a comfortable resort within striking distance of the ruins.

ESSENTIALS
GETTING THERE   The overnight **Hampi Express** leaves Bangalore daily at 10:20pm, arriving in unremarkable Hospet, the nearest town, at 7:40am. From Hyderabad, the Rayalseema Express departs at 5:25pm and arrives early the following morning, at 5:10am. Hampi is 15km (9⅓ miles) away. Taxis charge around Rs 300 ($7.30/£3.70) for the one-way trip; be sure to negotiate. Hampi is also connected to Goa by an overnight bus service. **Air Deccan,** India's cheap flight service, operates flights from Goa and Bangalore to Vidyanagar airport at Toranagallu (38km/24 miles from Hospet)—check the website (www.airdeccan.net) for details.

VISITOR INFORMATION   If you reserve lodging at **Hampi's Boulders** (see "Where to Stay," below), you'll have no better source of information than your host, Bobby. In Hampi Bazaar, the unusually helpful staff at the government-run **tourist office** (C) 08394/241-339; Apr–May daily 8am–1:30pm, June–Mar daily 10am–1:30pm and 2:15–5:30pm) can provide information and organize coach bookings (not recommended) and English-speaking guides. At Hotel Malligi (see "Where to Stay," below), you can hire an **audioguide** for around Rs 50 ($1.20/60p). In Hampi, you can pick up information and guides (Rs 500/$12/£6.15) from the **information office** (C) 08394/241-339) on Bazaar Street. If you're a stickler for detail and thorough research, pick up *New Light on Hampi* (Marg Publications) by John M. Fritz and George Michell.

GETTING AROUND   By Taxi & Auto-Rickshaw   Hampi's ruins cover 39 sq. km (15 sq. miles), and should be explored on wheels. Bicycles (for rent in Hampi Bazaar) are fine for the energetic, but only in winter. Taxis (Indicas around Rs 800/$20/£10 for a full day, without air-conditioning or Qualis at Rs 1,500/$37/£19) or even auto-rickshaws (count on Rs 350–Rs 400/$8.55–$9.75/£4.30–£5) are better if you'd rather not deal with maps, heat, and dirt tracks. Do, however, get out on foot whenever you can.

EXPLORING THE RUINED CITY OF VIJAYANAGARA

For anyone with dreams of Indiana Jones–style adventuring, the Hampi ruins provide the perfect setting—an ancient city with isolated ruins scattered among impossibly balanced wind-smoothed boulders and immense stretches of verdant landscape. Listed as a World Cultural Heritage Site, various excavations have uncovered evidence to suggest that Vijayanagara was occupied as long ago as the 3rd-century-B.C. Mauryan era. During early medieval times, armies were regularly dispatched to the Deccan by the Delhi Sultanate as part of its campaign to establish an empire that would encompass the whole of India. During one such campaign in the early 14th century, the invading forces captured Harihara and Bukka, two princes of Warangal, and took them to Delhi, where they fell in with the Sultanate. This allegiance eventually saw Harihara being crowned king of the region that is today known as Hampi. In celebration, Harihara lay the foundations of Vijayanagara, his new capital, on the southern banks of the Tungabhadra. His brother, Bukka, succeeded him 20 years later and ensured widespread support by issuing an edict that granted all religions equal protection. The monarchs who followed extended patronage to all manner of artists, poets, philosophers, and academics, effectively making Vijayanagara a center of learning that, in its grandeur, captivated visitors from as far away as Arabia, Portugal, and Italy.

The kingdom reached its zenith during the reign of Krishna Deva Raya (1509–29), when international trade flourished under progressive commercial practices and foreign trade agreements. Early accounts of the city tell of its massive fortifications, broad boulevards, grand gateways, efficient irrigation systems, and splendid civic amenities. The kingdom of Vijayanagara fell in 1565 when five allied Deccan sultans laid siege to the city, which they then apparently ransacked—their soldiers looting, killing, and destroying at will.

While some of the individual ruins can only be visited upon purchase of a ticket, most of Hampi is a veritable free-for-all, with tame security in the form of a handful of guards at the major monuments. This means that you can mix and match your itinerary as you see fit, moving between the different locations in a taxi or—if you're up for it—on a bicycle. Before you set off, pick up information or engage the services of an official guide from the government tourist office in Hampi. You can see Hampi's highlights in a morning if you set out early enough. However, it's spread over a vast area, and exploring can be quite exhausting, particularly in the midday heat—don't overdo it, or even the most impressive monuments begin to look like more of the same. In fact, with Vitthala Temple now illuminated at night and plans afoot to light up more of Hampi's main monuments, it may be worth returning at twilight.

Hampi Bazaar is a broad, dusty boulevard lined with stalls and restaurants. It leads to the entrance of **Virupaksha Temple** ✸✸✸, which predates the Vijayanagara kingdom yet remains a center of living Hindu faith (even though Hindu idols have been removed from the surrounding temples). Virupaksha's towering *goparum* is lavishly sculpted and rises several stories; within its courtyards, monkeys and children career around ancient pillars, while a sad-faced temple elephant takes tips for much-rehearsed blessings granted with her trunk. In the far right corner of the complex, tucked within a chamber, look for the shadow of the main *goparum,* which falls—miraculously, it would seem—as an inverted image on the temple wall, created by light passing through a small window. South of Virupaksha Temple is a temple housing a massive **Shiva lingam** (phallic symbol) standing in a pool of water. Carved from a single rock, the lingam is adjacent to a fantastic **monolithic statue of Narasimha** ✸✸, the man-lion avatar of Vishnu. Although partially damaged, the one-piece carving dating to the early 16th century is one of the finest sculptures at Hampi.

Some distance from the bazaar, on a high elevation, is the spectacular **Vitthala Temple** ✸✸✸, dedicated to an incarnation of Vishnu, and one of the most fabulous and famous of Hampi's monuments. One of Hinduism's most enduring images, an ornate **stone chariot** ✸✸✸, is found here. With solid stone wheels that can turn on their axles, the chariot faces a shaded dance hall where ancient musical dramas were once played out and from where you can now enjoy panoramic views of Vijayanagara. The pillars of the temple are commonly referred to as "musical pillars," each one producing a different note when tapped.

Nearby, the **King's Balance** was once a scalelike instrument used to measure out grain or even gold against the weight of the king. The weighed item was then given to the priests (or to the poor, depending on your guide's story).

The **royal enclosure** ✸ incorporates the ruined palaces where the Vijayanagara kings would have lived and held court. Not much survives, but you can still visit **Hazara Rama Temple,** where the royals went to worship, a small stepped tank, and **Mahanavami Dibba,** a platform where performances and entertainments were held. On the outskirts of the royal complex, you need to buy a ticket to see the *zenana* enclosure, where the two-story Indo-Saracenic pavilion known as **Kamala (Lotus) Mahal** ✸✸ features massive pillars, delicately punctuated arches, and fine stucco ornamentation; its unusual design blends elements of Muslim and Hindu architecture. Within the same enclosure are quarters believed to have been used by Hampi's Amazonian female guards, described by several Portuguese travelers. Just outside the enclosure are the superb domed **Elephant Stables** ✸✸✸.

13km (8 miles) east of Hospet, Belary District. Guides can be hired through the government tourist office in Hampi Bazaar for Rs 300 ($7.30/£3.70) half-day and Rs 500 ($12/£6.15) full day. Entrance to Virupaksha Temple Rs 2 (5¢/5p); 6am–12:30pm and 2–8pm. Entrance to both Lotus Mahal and Elephant Stables $5 (£2.50); 8am–6pm. The Hampi Festival takes place between Nov 3 and 5.

WHERE TO STAY

You may come across signposts sporting the name Kishkinda Heritage Resort—it is anything but "heritage" and extremely full in high season with children, thanks to the amusement and water park attached to it. KSTDC's **Hotel Mayura Bhuvaneshwari** at Kamalapuram (✆ **08394/241-574;** http://kstdc.nic.in; A/C doubles Rs 1,600/ $39/£20) is a cheaper option to Hampi's Boulders in case it's full. They can also arrange a Hampi tour (Rs 110/$2.70/£1.35).

Hampi's Boulders ✸✸   This resort, established and run by the enterprising proprietor Bobby Vallabhchandra and his cousin Vikram, is set in and among the enormous natural boulders that define Karnataka's splendid landscape, and is your best bet here. Private, remote, and immersed in nature, Boulders resides alongside the Tungabhadra River on a 16-hectare (40-acre) spread, amid bamboo trees, coconut groves, mango trees, and the namesake rocks. It's a mere 6km (3¾ miles) from Hampi, reached by crossing the river in a coracle (small boat) after a pleasant half-hour walk or a 10 minute drive. Nearby, in the 4,800-hectare (12,000-acre) animal sanctuary, you can spot wolves, panthers, hyenas, foxes, jackals, sloth bears, and crocodiles. A 15-minute walk through scrub and over rickety bridges will reveal some fantastic natural rock formations. Another option is to drive 5 minutes away from the resort to see hundreds of roosting birds—egrets, cormorants, ibis, open-billed storks, grey herons. Accommodations in the Executive Cottage are top-notch; living rock boulders bulge through the walls, and the entire structure feels like a miniature castle (where, in the huge bathroom, the "throne" allows the occupant to gaze onto the river). There's also a great veranda and a rooftop viewing platform. Guest cottages are pleasant, with attached bathrooms and private patios; the floors are marble and the ambience and furniture simple, but they're still far better than anything else near Hampi, and the setting is unmatched. Meals are served in a semi-exposed circular granite-walled thatched-roof dining area; there's no menu, but a buffet with a predominantly South-Indian selection is served.

Narayanpet, Bandi Harlapur–P.O., Via Munirabad-R-S, Koppal District and TQ. ©/fax **08539/265-939**, or catch Vikram on 94-4803-4202 or 92-4264-2552 and Bobby on 94-4818-9939. 13 units. Rs 3,000 per person or Rs 4,000 per couple ($73–$98/£37–£49) standard non-A/C double; Rs 4,000 per person or Rs 5,000 per couple ($98–$122/£49–£62) standard A/C double; Rs 10,000 ($244/£123) executive double. No credit cards. **Amenities:** Restaurant; pool; hand-washed laundry; doctor-on-call; play area; guided tours and safaris; fishing; beach volleyball; birding.

Hotel Malligi (Value   Long-standing base for visitors to Hampi, this huge campus of guest rooms, restaurants, and modest tourist facilities began as a small retiring house for medical reps supplying Hospet's first pharmacy, and today offers a wide range of accommodations, with the only disadvantage of being almost 45 min away from the ruins. Guest rooms are generally comfortable—those in the "super luxury" category are clean, with tiled floors, wood-paneled walls, and very '80s fittings and furniture in shades of brown. At just $5 (£2.50) more, executive suites are slightly more attractive, in shades of gray and blue, with large bathrooms with tubs (not in best nick) and private balconies. Bollywood stars shooting films in the area, however, book only the Honeymoon Suite, where a ceiling mirror hovers over the circular bed. Budget rooms are ridiculously cheap, considering the hotel's amenities (including a pool, essential after a grueling day of sightseeing under the pounding sun), though they offer little in the way of comfort or taste. Ask for the informative CD-ROM on Hampi.

10/90 J.N. Rd., P. B. no. 1, Hospet 583 201. © **08394/228-101.** Fax 08394/227-038. www.malligihotels.com. 200 units. Rs 300–Rs 500 ($7.30–$12/£3.70–£6.15) non-A/C budget double; Rs 2,000 ($49/£25) super luxury double; Rs 2,250 ($55/£28) executive suite, Rs 2,500 ($61/£31) honeymoon suite. AE, MC, V. **Amenities:** 2 restaurants; bar; pool; children's play area; travel desk; car hire; limited business facilities; salon; gift shop; bookshop; room service 6am–10pm; massage; laundry; currency exchange; pool table; banqueting; conferencing. *In room:* A/C, TV, minibar (in most rooms).

WHERE TO DINE

Mango Tree (Moments VEGETARIAN   Although the food here is unremarkable, the rustic setting is undeniably welcoming. A lovely walk through a banana plantation takes you to an unassuming gateway; enter and you sit under an enormous mango tree with a swing, in the backyard of a local family home, surrounded by boulders, acres of greenery, and kingfishers darting through the air. In front of you, the Tungabhadra River glides by. There's no electricity; you dine sitting on the ground on straw mats at low, portable tables set at terraced levels, while the proprietor, Krishna, and his family wait on you. Start with a special *samosa* with a touch of cream cheese on top,

stuffed with tangy tomatoes and chopped potato. Follow it up with a Mango Tree special thali or Mango special curry served on a banana leaf; finish with a cup of *chai* or
quench your thirst with a banana coconut lassi. If you want to know more about how
this quaint place evolved, speak to the lively Seena, who will be happy to fill you in.

400m (1,312 ft.) downriver from the main Virupaksha temple tank, Hampi. (✆) **94-4876-5213** or 08394/241-944.
Meals under Rs 150 ($3.65/£1.85). No credit cards. Daily 7am–9:30pm.

5 Side Trip to Northern Karnataka ★★★

If you'd like to get off the principal tourist beat and discover the Deccan's architectural
treasures in less-chartered territory, set aside a few more days to explore the splendid
remains of the erstwhile **Chalukyan Empire** and—tucked within one of the state's
northernmost corners—the Muslim city of **Bijapur,** filled with mosques, minarets,
mausoleums, and palace ruins.

The easiest way to get to these sites is to rent a car and driver in Hospet (you can
arrange one through Hotel Malligi; Rs 2,100/$51/£26 for a return trip), and drive to
Badami, stopping at Aihole and Pattadakal either on your way in or out. It is quite possible to spend a long day traveling from Hospet or Hampi to all three Chalukya sites,
including a stop at **Mahakuteshwara** and **Mallikajuna temples** en route. After that you
can either proceed to Bijapur, or return to Hampi before nightfall. If you prefer something a little less hectic, however, overnight in Badami, and then continue your journey
the following day. The best accommodations choice is **Hotel Badami Court** (✆ **08357/
220-230** through -233). It's located 2km (1¼ miles) from the town center and has a pool
and decent air-conditioned rooms with TVs and bathtubs (ask for one of the garden-facing rooms, which are quieter) for around $62 (£31) including breakfast.

BADAMI, AIHOLE & PATTADAKAL

Around 4 hours by car from Hospet, the remote, modest town of **Badami** was established around A.D. 543 when it became the capital of the Chalukyas, one of the most
powerful of the Deccan dynasties. Today its most significant attraction is the complex
of **cave temples** ★★★ ($5/£2.55; daily sunrise–sunset) carved into the imposing
horseshoe-shaped red-sandstone cliff that once formed a natural fortification at the
southern end of the town. Enter the pillared interiors and you'll discover elaborate
symbolic and mystical carvings of the highest quality (not to mention a few scampering monkeys). It's worth hiring the services of a guide (around Rs 150/$3.65/£1.85
for up to 3 hr.) to gain some understanding of the symbolism. Also worth exploring
are the **Bhutanatha temples,** built over 4 centuries at a picturesque location at the
edge of the Agastyatirtha water tank; and atop the hill, 7th-century **Malegitti Shiv-
alya Temple,** unusually decorated with dwarfs, geese, and various geometric patterns.
Time allowing, stop at the **Archaeological Museum** (✆ **08357/22-0157;** Rs 2/5¢/5p;
Sat–Thurs 10am–5pm) to see well-preserved sculpted panels depicting the life of
Krishna, and the **Lajja Gauri** sculpture, an extraordinary fertility cult symbol. Less
than 30km (19 miles) from Badami, en route to Aihole, is the small settlement of **Pattadakal** and its UNESCO World Heritage–listed **temple complex** ★★★ ($10/£5;
daily sunrise–sunset), where Chalukyan temple architecture reached its zenith in the
7th and 8th centuries. Some, like Papanatha Temple built around A.D. 680, are in the
northern Indo-Aryan style, while others, like the main Virupaksha Temple built 80 years
later, are in the South Indian Dravidian architectural style, with tiered pyramidal

rather than conical roofs. A dance festival is held at Pattadakal each January. (Note that if you're pressed for time, the Pattadakal stop can be skipped.)

About 17km (11 miles) away, the riverbank village of **Aihole** ✸✸✸ is strewn with some 70 abandoned temples, built between A.D. 450 and 650 as architectural experiments by the early Chalukyan kings. Historians theorize that these obsessive rulers had a guild of architects, artists, and artisans working for them, and the variety of styles, including the Gupta (northern), incipient Dravidian, and elements of Buddhist architecture, reflect the various stages in the development of Chalukyan architecture. The chief attraction among these, fashioned along the lines of a Buddhist *chaitya* (prayer hall), is **Durga Temple** ✸✸✸, with its magnificent circular colonnaded veranda studded with stunning sculptures and intricate carving. Contrast this with the Jain **Meguti Temple** ✸✸ situated atop a nearby hill—with an inscription putting its construction at A.D. 634, this was perhaps the last temple to be built in Aihole.

The interiors aren't lighted, so you should carry a flashlight—the detailing is well worth studying. In some temples, you'll discover images of fierce Chalukyan warriors in action, while elsewhere, amorous couples engage in a different sort of action. Admission to the main complex of temples is free; entrance to Durga Temple is $2 (£1). Hours are daily sunrise to sunset.

BIJAPUR

The walled city of **Bijapur,** in the far north of Karnataka, is often referred to as the "Agra of the South" because of its profusion of Muslim architecture. First founded during the reign of the Chalukyan dynasty, between the 10th and 11th centuries, Bijapur passed into Muslim rule and later into the hands of the Bahamani kings. When these rulers fell into decline, the city was taken over by its governor, Yusuf Adil Khan, the founder of the Adil Shahi dynasty, who established rule over the Deccan during the 16th and 17th centuries, with Bijapur as their capital. Muslim mausoleums, mosques, palaces, pavilions, and *burkha*-clad women will remind you that this is a city unlike any other in Karnataka. Head to the very helpful local **tourism office** (Station Rd.; ✆ **08352/250-359;** daily 10am–5:30pm) to hire a guide and get assistance with sightseeing. Monuments are open from sunrise to sunset and entry is free except where listed. Within the fortified **Citadel** in the city center lie the remains of royal structures, including **Anand Mahal** (Pleasure Palace), and **Saat Manzil.** Outside Saat Manzil is beautiful **Jal Mandir,** or water pavilion, now dry, so you can admire its carvings and porticos. Not far away (near the tourist office) is incomplete **Bara Kaman** ("12 Arches"), the roofless tomb of Ali Adil Shah II—a wonderful piece of architecture comprising 12 arches—surrounded by a garden.

Outside the Citadel's walls, near the edge of the city, is **Ibrahim Rouza** ✸✸✸, the gorgeously proportioned and heavily decorated mausoleum of Ibrahim Adil Shah II and his wife, Taj Sultana (admission $2/£1; daily 6am–6pm; leave shoes outside). Ignore the garbage dump near the entrance and admire what is considered the most beautiful Muslim structure in the Deccan, featuring richly engraved walls and inscribed ornamental stone windows. Move on to **Gol Gumbaz** ✸✸✸, the world's second-largest dome (after St. Peter's in Rome), atop the mausoleum of 17th-century sultan Muhammad Adil Shah (Mahatma Gandhi Rd.; admission $5/£2.55, video cameras 50¢/25p; leave shoes outside; daily 6am–6pm). Renowned for its remarkable engineering and stereophonic acoustics, the Gol Gumbaz can get noisy as visitors test the echo effect created by the massive dome—multiple distinct echoes are said to be produced for each sound uttered in the whispering gallery upstairs. Most visitors don't

bother to whisper, however, which may leave you with an experience akin to an audi-
tory hallucination. As is the case with the Taj, try to arrive as soon as the gates open
for the most atmospheric visit. It's worth scaling the 115 steps to reach the dome's terrace for the excellent views of the formal gardens and tombs.

Jami Masjid (free admission; daily 6am–6pm), close to Gol Gumbaz, is the city's
other major attraction. Also incomplete, this is the largest mosque in the region, dating back to A.D. 1576, when Ali Adil Shah I reigned. Consisting of a large dome and
gorgeous white arcaded bays, this impressive mosque is spread over some 10,000 sq.
m (107,639 sq. ft.).

WHERE TO STAY & DINE IN BIJAPUR

Hotel Madhuvan International   Bijapur's top business hotel doesn't offer the luxuries you might expect in cities catering to substantial numbers of Western visitors.
Accommodations are comfortable enough, however, and some rooms have views of
Gol Gumbaz. All bathrooms have tubs. You can organize your sightseeing through the
hotel, and take meals in the relaxing garden restaurant (which serves only vegetarian
food, by the way).

Station Rd., Bijapur 586 104. ℂ **08352/25-5571** through -5573. Fax 08352/25-6201. www.hotelmadhuvan.com. 36
units. Rs 950 ($23/£12) non-A/C double; Rs 1,200 ($29/£15) A/C double. Taxes extra. MC, V. **Amenities:** Restaurant;
limited room service; laundry; doctor-on-call; sightseeing. *In room:* TV.

6 Hyderabad

490km (304 miles) N of Bangalore

Named after Hyder Mahal, wife of Muhammad Quli, a 16th-century ruler of the
Qutb Shahi dynasty, Hyderabad was one of the largest and wealthiest of India's former princely states. The city built its fortune on the trade of pearls, gold, steel, fabric,
and, above all, diamonds, which some believe remain hidden beneath the foundations
of **Golconda Fort,** precursor to the city some 10km (6¼ miles) away. Once the most
famous diamond mining area in the world, Golconda was where the 108-carat Kohi-Noor diamond (not to mention the Orloff, Regent, and Hope diamonds) was excavated. It was in fact Golconda's legendary wealth that attracted the attention of the
voracious Mughal emperor Aurangzeb, and with the aid of an inside agent he captured
the fortress in 1687. Aurangzeb's invasion marked the temporary decline of the city,
but when the Mughal empire began to fade, the enterprising local viceroy, Asaf Jah I,
promptly proclaimed himself *Nizam,* and established independent rule over the Deccan state. Under the notoriously opulent Nizams of the Asaf Jahi dynasty, their power
cemented by an alliance forged in 1798 with the British East India Company, Hyderabad again became a major influence, and even contributed to the British military
campaigns against the recalcitrant Tipu Sultan of Mysore.

Hyderabad is more than 400 years old, but today the state capital of Andhra
Pradesh is as famous for its burgeoning information technology and biotech research
industries as it is for its minarets. Like Bangalore, this is one of India's fastest-growing
cities (with a projected population of 7.5 million by 2015) with what could be considered as the worst driving etiquette in the country, but unlike most Indian cities,
Hyderabad is actually getting greener and cleaner. A substantial part of the city is the
suburb of **Cyberabad,** where Microsoft and Oracle are but two major players in the
development known as Hi-Tech City, responsible for the city's economic upswing.

Despite its newfound attractiveness as a business destination, the city remains steeped in history, and you're just as likely to share the road with camels and bullock carts, and haggle alongside Muslim women covered from head to toe in black *burkhas,* as you are to converse with cellphone-wielding yuppies. There may not be much by way of specific sights to see in Hyderabad, but it's a pleasantly manageable city with a vibrant culture, excellent-value luxury hotels, and a heavenly cuisine—perhaps the most enduring legacy of the decadent tastes and patronage of the cultured *Nizams* who first put the city on the map.

ESSENTIALS

GETTING THERE & AWAY   Hyderabad is pretty much slap-bang in the middle of very little else, so you're best off flying in, not least because you're unlikely to spend much time in Hyderabad proper (unless you plan to shop endlessly for pearls and eat yourself stupid). International flights (British Airways, Air-India, Lufthansa, North-west Airlines, Thai Airways, Singapore Airlines, Malaysia Airlines) connect Hyderabad to the rest of the world. There are daily 2-hour flights from Delhi and 1-hour flights from Bangalore, Mumbai, Chennai, Kolkata, and Tirupati. **Begumpet Airport** (off Sardar Patel Rd.; ✆ **1407** for Indian Airlines inquiries, 142 for recorded flight information) is 8km (5 miles) north of the city; a taxi into town should cost between Rs 150 ($3.65/£1.85) and Rs 300 ($7.30/£3.70). **Trains** to and from Bangalore, Tirupati, Chennai, and Mumbai take at least 14 hours; book an overnight journey several days in advance. There are two main stations: Nampally (also known as Hyderabad Station) and Secunderabad, with most longer-distance trains arriving at the latter. Call ✆ **1345** for specific information about outbound services.

VISITOR INFORMATION   For the lowdown on sights, tours, and events, visit **Andhra Pradesh Travel & Tourism Development Corporation** (✆ **040/2345-3036** or -0444; open 24 hr.), on the corner where Secretariat Road becomes Tank Bund. Avoid **Andhra Pradesh Tourism** right next door; the stench that hangs in the air from the fish market nearby competes with the staff's incompetence. The railway stations also have information counters. *Channel 6* (Rs 15/35¢/20p) is a monthly booklet listing a wealth of information about the twin cities of Hyderabad and Secunderabad. *Hyderabad CityInfo* (Rs 30/75¢/35p) appears every 2 weeks and provides extensive information about hotels, restaurants, and current events. *Primetime Prism* (monthly; Rs 10/25¢/15p) is filled with useful information about destinations all over the state.

If you want to do some serious reading up on Hyderabad other than the brochures supplied by the Tourism Department, then try two of the bigger and better bookstores in the city—**Walden** (6-3-871 Greenlands Rd., Begumpet; ✆ **040/2341-3434** with a branch at Trendset Towers, Road No. 2, Banjara Hills; ✆ **040/2335-1613;** open daily) and **A.A.Husain & Co.** (5-8-551 Abid Rd.; ✆ **040/2320-3724;** closed Sun).

Useful numbers: For **24-hour pharmacies** call **Apollo** (✆ **040/2360-7777**) or **New-citi** (✆ **040/2780-5960**). The local **telephone search engine** (✆ **040/2444-4444**) can be quite helpful.

GETTING AROUND   Actually comprising the twin cities of Hyderabad and Secunderabad, Hyderabad is spread over a vast area, and its few sights are scattered, so you're best off renting a car and driver for a half- or full day. See **SOTC** (details below) for 24-hour car-hire service; or call **Cosy Cabs** (Karan Apartments, Begumpet; ✆ **040/2776-7146** and -0409). Note that the Old City is best explored on foot.

GUIDED TOURS & TRAVEL AGENTS   The **Andhra Pradesh Travel & Tourism Development Corporation** (see "Visitor information," above) runs full-day guided tours of the city (Rs 230/$5.60/£2.85) and 3-day trips to Tirupati (Rs 1,600/$39/£20 including a night's accommodations). There are also daily tours to Nagarjuna Sagar (150km/93 miles away; Rs 350/$8.55/£4.30), where excavations during the construction of a dam revealed an ancient Buddhist site. All the salvaged structures and antiques are now housed in a museum on an island. **SOTC** (3-5-874 Hyderguda Rd.; ☏ **040/6699-9922;** Mon–Sat 10am–6pm) can make all your travel, sightseeing, and car-hire arrangements. For alternate quotes, call **Mercury Travels** (☏ **040/5520-2200** or 040/2781-4399). You can also try **Sai Bon Voyage** (☏ **98-8562-8111** or 040/6684-3333). For short-distance commuting, contact **City Cabs** (☏ **040/6631-6001**) or **Cab Services** (☏ **040/6631-6000**)

WHAT TO SEE & DO

To see Hyderabad in a day, first drive to **Qutb Shahi Tombs** (9:30am-4:30pm; closed Fri), where Hyderabad's dynastic rulers are buried. The tombs, built in grey granite with stucco ornamentation, are an interesting mix of Persian, Pathan, and Hindu styles. Standing at the center of its own garden, Sultan Muhammed Quli Qutb Shah's tomb is considered the most impressive. Built around the same time as his tomb, the mortuary bath **(Hamaam)**—where the dead were washed before being laid to rest—lies at the center of the enclosure. From here, consider walking to **Golconda Fort;** have your driver show you the route, which is about 2km (1¼ miles) and takes you through lively villages where you may even be invited in for a cup of *chai* and a chat. Allow at least an hour to explore the ruins of the historic citadel, arranging for your driver to pick you up at the entrance.

Next, head to **Charminar,** a four-sided archway with soaring minarets. It was laid out by Muhammad Quli Qutb Shah as the centerpiece of a great new city when Golconda's disease epidemics forced him to move his seat to the banks of the Musi River. Explore the Old City quarter on foot, heading westward into **Laad Bazaar** ✦✦✦, where double-story houses with tiny wooden shutters line narrow lanes. Wandering through these perpetually congested narrow lanes, you'll encounter numerous *burkha*-wearing women scanning the stalls for bargains, and you're likely to score a deal on anything from old saris, pearls, *bidri* (surface ornamentation) work, and silver and gold jewelry to paper kites, henna, turmeric, and cheap china. *Lac* bangles, made from shellac encrusted with shiny, colorful stones, are a Hyderabadi specialty that you'll find in huge quantities here. It's also where the people of Hyderabad go to buy traditional bridal wear, or *Khopdia Joda,* consisting of a *kurta* pajama, *choli,* and *ghunghat.*

When you've had your fill of the Old City, the interiors of **Salar Jung Museum** are a cool diversion, filled with an unprecedented assortment of kitschy collectibles and works of art (see below). Also interesting for antiques-lovers is **Purani Haveli,** near the Salar Jung Museum, where several *Nizams* were born and lived. When Nawab Mir Mehboob Ali Khan, the sixth *Nizam,* lived here, he had a 73m-long (240-ft.) wooden chamber built with 150 huge cupboards (probably the world's largest walk-in closet), to stock his extensive collection of fine clothing and shoes (also called Nizam Jubilee Pavilion; Rs 40/$1/50p; daily 10am–6pm). Alternatively visit the recently opened **Chowmohalla Palace,** located near Charminar: After 5 years of restoration work, the complex has lovely courtyards and fountains and is now used increasingly for traditional music soirees in Urdu and Persian. Or visit India's second-largest mosque (purportedly the seventh largest in the world): **Mecca Masjid** (Kishan Prasad Rd., near

Charminar) is said to have been built with a few bricks brought from Mecca, and attracts thousands of worshipers during *Namaaz,* Friday prayers. It's off-limits to non-Muslims during prayers, but visitors are welcome at other times. Leave your shoes with an attendant before making your way through a long room that houses the tombs of the Nizams of the Asaf Jahi dynasty. Non-Muslims cannot enter the prayer hall but can view proceedings through a screen. In Gulzar Hauz is **Jami Masjid,** Hyderabad's oldest functioning mosque, dating back to 1597.

Round off the day by watching the sun set over Cyberabad from white-marble **Birla Mandir** ⚑ (Kalabahad Hill; free admission; daily 6am–noon and 3–9pm). Commissioned by the Birlas, India's foremost industrial magnates, the main temple is dedicated to Lord Venkateshwara, and is pleasantly free of greedy "guides" and the like. Perched on a hilltop, it looks beautiful when lit at night.

If you're here for another day, consider a half-day excursion to the **Ramoji Film City** (Rs 200/$4.85/£2.45) for an amusing and interesting exposure to the South Indian film industry. It's packed with local star-struck tourists, and you have a good chance of coming face to face with the top actors of the day—one of their song-and-dance sequence may just be the highlight of the trip. (Check to see what's on by calling ✆ **040/2323-5678.**) If all you want is to find yourself in a green lung, the best option lies in the middle of the city: The semi-forested **KBR Park** allows for a pleasant stroll.

Golconda Fort ⚑⚑   Sitting at an elevated height on the outskirts of Hyderabad, Golconda—seat of the Qutb Shahis—was once a magnificent citadel and center of the world diamond trade. The fort took 62 years to build, and when it fell to Aurangzeb in 1687, he tore the place apart looking for diamonds and gold. Left to the birds of prey that circle high above the once-daunting battlements, Golconda would have become a tranquil retreat were it not for its popularity with visitors, who noisily explore the ramparts of Hyderabad's most illustrious attraction. That's why it's best if you visit it as soon as it opens, or around twilight (when it's far cooler and the dimming evening sky sheds a mysterious aura over the stone ruins).

Enclosing the graffiti-smeared remains of bazaars, homes, fields, barracks, armories, mosques, camel stables, Turkish baths, and water reservoirs, the battlements incorporate 87 bastions and extend some 5km (3 miles) in circumference. Four of the original eight gates are still in use; present-day visitors enter via the **Bala Hissar gate**—large teakwood doors with metal spikes designed to withstand charging elephants. Guides can assist by demonstrating the tremendous acoustics of the structure—a clap here is heard clearly when you are at the fort's highest point, 1km (½ mile) away; this was once an invaluable security-cum-intercom system. The Royal Palace complex comprises buildings constructed by the Qutb Shahi kings during different periods. Most

---

ⓘ *Tips* **Getting a Good Guide**

You'll be confronted by many would-be guides at the entrance to the Golconda Fort—ask around for **M. D. Rathmath** or **Shaikh Rajiv,** who both have a good grasp of English. The going rate is Rs 300 ($7.30/£3.70) for 2 to 3 hours (you could up this to Rs 400/$9.10/£4.60 if the service is really good). At the end of the day, the guides gather on the lawn outside the fort entrance, near the ticket booth; join them if you're interested in learning more about Hyderabad culture.

Asthmatics Say "A-aah!"

One of the world's largest alternative medicinal gatherings takes place annually at **Nampally Exhibition Grounds** in Hyderabad, usually on June 7 or 8. Just as the monsoon sets in and brings with it all sorts of seasonal respiratory illnesses, hundreds of thousands of asthmatics from all over India flock to the city to receive an unusual cure administered orally by the Bathini Goud brothers. A special herbal medicine, prepared by using water from the family well only, is stuffed into the mouth of a 2- or 3-inch *murrel* (sardine). The fish is then slipped into the patient's mouth, who swallows the slithering creature alive (the Gouds claim that the wriggling fish increases the efficacy of the medicine because it clears the patient's throat; for those who are strict vegetarians or particularly squeamish, a banana acts as a substitute, albeit a poor one). The result: For more than 162 years, countless people have reported relief from a variety of respiratory-type disorders. Said to have been given to an ancestor of the present-day Gouds by a Hindu holy man back in 1845, the secret formula has been passed down through the generations and administered free of charge in accordance with the saint's wishes. Visit **www.fish-medicine.org** for details.

are decorated with floral designs, glazed tilework on the walls, and cut-plaster decorations indicative of the Qutb Shahi style. Sadly, where royalty once went about their daily lives, rats, bats, garbage, grime, and tourists have taken over. At the top of the fort is the **Baradari,** reached by three stone stairways. As you make your way up, look along the walls for the remains of limestone pipes once part of a sophisticated plumbing system that used Persian wheels to carry water up the hill, so that it could be piped in for bathing, flushing cistern systems, and keeping the palace cool. The climb to the top is worth it for the excellent views alone.

The fort hosts an extremely popular **sound-and-light show** that recounts the history of Golconda using the illuminated ruins as a backdrop. There are performances in English each night; but be warned that power failures can disrupt the performance—and be sure to take insect repellent.

Situated 6km (3¾ miles) west of the city. ℂ **040/2351-3984.** Admission Rs 100 ($2.45/£1.25). Daily 9am–6pm. English sound-and-light show: Admission Rs 40 ($1/50p). Mar–Oct daily 7–8pm; Nov–Feb daily 6:30–7:30pm. Tickets available 30 min. before the show; line up early.

Salar Jung Museum ⟨⟨⟨   Marketed as the world's largest private collection of art, artifacts, and antiques, this eclectic assortment of more than 30,000 different exhibits was assembled by Salar Jung III, who served as prime minister *(wazir)* to the Nizam of Hyderabad. It's a truly fascinating collection—particularly the textiles and fine art section, which includes a fine collection of Indian miniature paintings demonstrating the evolution of styles and the differences between Rajput, Deccan, Pahari, and Mughal paintings, though the displays are somewhat disorganized. One of the most valuable pieces must be a 9th-century edition of the *Koran,* written in beautiful Kufic script. The weaponry collection includes a diamond-encrusted sword used ceremonially by the Salar Jungs, as well as pieces used by Mughal emperors. There's something to be said for the sheer profusion of design objects, ranging from boxes studded with precious gems and vessels blown from Indo-Persian glass to a chair made of solid ivory, a gift from Louis XV to Tipu Sultan. In one room, large crowds are drawn to a famous musical clock with a toy watchman who emerges from behind a door every hour in time to beat a melodious gong. Give yourself at least 90 minutes to explore.

C. L. Badari, Malakpet. ℂ **040/2452-3211.** Admission Rs 150 ($3.65/£1.85). Sat–Thurs 10am–5pm, 4:15pm last entry. There is also a separate entrance to view the famed jewels of the *Nizams* for which the admission is Rs 500 ($12/£6.20), Sat–Thurs 11 am–6pm. Cameras not allowed.

WHERE TO STAY

At press time, exquisite **Falaknuma Palace** (Tank Bund Rd.), a work of astonishing architectural opulence that has hosted the likes of King George V, was in the process of being converted into a heritage hotel by the Taj hotel group. This is likely to be the best place to stay in Hyderabad when it opens in late 2008; visit www.tajhotels.com for ongoing developments.

A good budget option is **Green Park;** it may not rank high in terms of luxury and sophistication, but it's clean, comfortable, and convenient to the nearby airport. Ask for a garden-facing room (ℂ **040/2375-7575** or 040/6651-5151; www.hotelgreen park.com; doubles from Rs 4,995/$122/£62, breakfast included).

Aalankrita ⓡ *Value*   Resorts are mushrooming in Hyderabad just as they are elsewhere in the country, but only the award-winning Aalankrita stands proud. A doctor couple infatuated with antique furniture went on a buying spree almost a decade ago until they found they had no more space to keep their treasured finds, so they bought some land, built one room styled as a typical village house, with antique stairs, frames, and doors—all this multiplied, and today they own a full-blown resort. Lovely antiques, mostly from the Chettinad region in Tamil Nadu, Kerala, and Rajasthan, are in all the rooms (sadly a dearth of art), and there's also an Ayurvedic massage center, beautiful gardens, friendly staff, and good cuisine. Accommodation is available as independent cottages (Gruha) as well as rooms in a main block (Devkrupa). Designed to resemble a village, it's replete with a traditional *mandapam,* where Indian marriages can take place—if you'd rather not become an inadvertent wedding guest, check before confirming your booking.

20 min. from Secunderabad Club, Shameerpet Rd., Thumkunta Village, Shameerpet Mandal, R.R. District 500 078. ℂ 08418-247464/161/162. Fax 08418-247013/014. www.aalankrita.com. 46 units. $51 (£26) standard room; $59 (£30) studio cottage; $71 (£36) deluxe cottage; $147 (£75) crystal suite; $226 (£115) presidential suite; $13 (£6.60) extra bed. Rates include bed tea, breakfast, and taxes. AE, MC, V. **Amenities:** 3 restaurants (multicuisine/barbecue/vegetarian); lounge bar; pool; business center; meditation center; banquet halls; arts and crafts gallery; playground. *In room:* A/C, TV, 24-hr. hot and cold water.

Hyderabad Marriott ⓡ *Value*   Previously known as the Viceroy, this new addition to the Marriot stable has retained its appeal to the business sector but also welcomes leisure travelers with the confidence and ease that comes naturally to those who have been in the hotel business for years. Much of the Viceroy staff has been absorbed into the new setup, but the decor has had a thorough revamping. A richer, more plush and sophisticated ambience greets guests on entering, whether it is from the sober coffee-colored interiors or the smart and attentive approach of the staff. Rooms have also been remodeled, and despite their compactness look fresh and livable, with the best offering prime views of the Hussain Sagar Lake.

Opposite Hussain Sagar Lake, Tank Bund Rd., Hyderabad 500 080. ℂ **040/2752-2999.** Fax 040/2752-8888. http://marriott.com. 297 units. $199 (£101) Superior Double; $224 (£114) Deluxe Double; $450 (£228) Deluxe Suite. Rates include breakfast. AE, MC, V. **Amenities:** 2 restaurants of which only 1 is operational at the moment; bar; pool; fitness center; 24-hr. concierge; travel desk; car rental; business center; same-day laundry and dry-cleaning facility;

doctor; currency exchange; nonsmoking floors; executive floor and lounge; parcel and post service; city tours; meeting and conference rooms. *In room:* A/C, TV, dataport, hair dryer.

ITC Hotel Kakatiya Sheraton & Towers ✹✹✹   Not as opulently over-the-top as Taj Krishna, this fully Wi-Fi–enabled hotel is billed as the best business hotel in town. Public spaces are smartly dressed in a vibrant and culturally evocative assortment of objets d'art typical of the region—decorative silver *bidri* pieces, detailed frescoes, and elegant furniture in rich fabrics. Guest rooms are wonderfully spacious; even the cheapest corporate rooms are large and nicely finished (twins only). The best views are of Hussain Sagar Lake, the city, and the pool (book a room with a number ending in 01, 03, or 05 for the least obstructed view). The atmosphere here is one of down-to-earth sophistication. Staff is friendly and helpful, if not always on the ball.

Begumpet, Hyderabad 500 016. ☎ 040/2340-0132. Fax 040/2340-1045. www.welcomgroup.com. 189 units. $375 (£190) executive club double (includes breakfast and happy hour); $475 (£241) Sheraton Tower; $900–$1,400 (£456–£710) suite. Tower rooms and suites include breakfast, airport transfer, and happy hour. AE, MC, V. **Amenities:** 3 restaurants; 2 bars; tea pavilion; patisserie; tie-up with army golf course; pool with Jacuzzi; health club; concierge; travel desk; shopping arcade; florist; salon; room service; laundry; dry cleaning; doctor; currency exchange; Wi-Fi enabled. *In room:* A/C, TV, minibar, tea- and coffee-making facilities, weighing scales in some rooms.

Taj Krishna ✹✹✹   Situated in the upmarket suburb of Banjara Hills, Hyderabad's most luxurious hotel is fashioned to emulate the opulence and (sometimes high-kitsch) style of an Indian palace; guests have included the late Lady Di, the Dalai Lama, Aga Khan, and Kofi Anan. Between its sumptuous arches, *zardozi* (embroidered) panels, and mother-of-pearl inlaid marble pillars, its lobby is packed full of Belgian chandeliers, ornately engraved mirrors, rococo marble statues, Asian vases, an original French gold-encrusted ornamental grandfather clock, and a fountain spouting water into a dark marble koi pond. The best guest rooms are those on the two Taj Club floors, which have beautiful wooden floors, embroidered sheer curtains, and large bathrooms; club benefits include breakfast, cocktails, and airport pickup. Book an even-numbered room facing the lake and the acre-long pool area. Note that if you opt for a cheaper room, you'll be more comfortable at the Sheraton. Krishna has some of the city's most exclusive restaurants (see "Where to Dine," below), its best nightlife option, and proximity to shopping outlets. The Krishna is very popular, which can tax the general efficiency of staff and elevators when occupancy is up. (Note that the Taj group has a less opulent brother in town.)

Rd. no. 1, Banjara Hills, Hyderabad 500 034. ☎ 040/6666-2323 or 040/2339-2323. Fax 040/6666-1313. www.taj hotels.com. 261 units. $375 (£190) deluxe double; $480 (£243) Taj Club (includes breakfast and airport transfers); $475 (£241) executive suite; $625 (£317) deluxe suite; $800 (£406) luxury suite; $1,200 (£609) presidential suite. $30 (£15) extra bed. AE, MC, V. **Amenities:** 4 restaurants; bar; tea lounge; nightclub; pool; clay tennis court; health club; concierge; travel desk; car hire; limousine service; florist service; bookshop; pearl shop; salon; 24-hr. room service; laundry; dry cleaning; doctor-on-call; currency exchange; Wi-Fi; library; squash, badminton, golf, and sightseeing by arrangement. *In room:* A/C, TV, dataport; minibar, tea- and coffee-making facilities, iron on request.

WHERE TO DINE

In Hyderabad, food is as important as life itself, a world-view no doubt inherited from the *Nizams*, who reveled in culinary intemperance. Hyderabad is known for its *dum*-style cooking (with its origins in Lucknow): the practice of sealing the pot or dish and gently simmering its ingredients over a slow fire, thereby increasing the absorption of aromatic spices. Lavishly decorated in vibrant blues and distinctively Hyderabadi objets d'art, **Dum Pukht** ✹✹✹ (ITC Kakatiya Sheraton & Towers; ☎ **040/2340-1032;** Rs 400–Rs 1,250/$9.75–$31/£5–£15) is the city's most celebrated upmarket restaurant, and known for its *dum*-style dishes. (*Dum Pukht* literally means cooking by locking in steam.) Try the chef's *kareli ki nahari,* mutton shanks cooked in their own juices and marrow, tinged with cardamom and saffron. Melt-in-the-mouth *kakori* kebabs prepared from finely minced mutton, green papaya, cloves, and cinnamon are skewered, chargrilled, and eaten with *sheermal,* saffron-and-milk-infused flaky bread.

One of the best examples of *dum*-style cooking is *biryani,* Hyderabad's most time-honored dish, best made with marinated mutton which, together with basmati rice and spices, is prepared in a sealed pot for an aromatic result. Available practically anywhere, it's best enjoyed with a spicy *mirch ka salan* (chili curry) and yogurt salad; lately, however, most of the restaurants are taking a shortcut and cooking *biryani* in open cauldrons—although tasty, it's not quite the same thing. Try **Azizia,** adjacent the Nampally railway station: It is said to be the home of *biryani,* and its chefs claim to be descended from the *Nizams'* master chefs; alternatively try **Paradise** (Paradise Circle, M.G. Rd.), **Café Bahar** in Himayatnagar, or **Medina,** in the Old City. Finish your meal with Hyderabad's famous desserts: *khubani ka meetha* (apricots and cream) or *double ka meetha* (bread pudding with cashews and almonds). Another place that serves authentic *biryani,* this time in an elegant atmosphere, is **Firdaus** ⓕⓕⓕ (Taj Krishna, Rd. no. 1, Banjara Hills; ⓒ **040/6666-2323;** Rs 305–Rs 1,275/$7.45–$31/£3.75–£16). Another good meal here is the *raan-e-firdaus:* tender lamb steak marinated in assorted spices and tandoor grilled. But really, all the meals are fit for a *Nizam,* especially enjoyed against a backdrop of live *ghazal* music. Also in Banjara Hills, on Road no. 1, is a three-in-one restaurant: At **Fusion 9** you can select food from nine different parts of the world. **Deli 9** is famous for its deliciously rich pastries—after polishing off a few Norwegian pork chops or tenderloin steak, order the must-have Black Magic pastry (ⓒ **040/6550-6662**).

If you're keen to sample more regional Andhra cuisine without forever losing your sense of taste (it is intensely fiery), take a table at **Chutney's** (ⓒ **040/2335-8484;** Shilpa Arcade Rd. no. 3, Banjara Hills) to sample their *pesarattu* (spiced mung bean flour pancake) eaten with *allam pachadi* (ginger pickle). Better still, make your way to the first floor and take your pick of a huge variety of vegetarian dishes from North and South India at their reasonably priced all-you-can-eat daily buffet spread (Rs 140/$3.40/£1.70). Another value-for-money restaurant is **Abhiruchi** on S.D. Road (**040/2789-6565** or -2227). It has superfast service and excellent food for dirt-cheap prices—along with the thali, order the *mutton gongura* as a side dish (a spinachlike leaf that grows in Andhra mixed with goat meat).

One of the best buffets in town is at **Okra** ⓕ, the 24-hour dining at the new Hyderabad Marriott. Priced at Rs 525 ($13/£6.50), it offers a large variety of Indian, Continental, and traditional fare, but its current claim to fame is the highly unusual *Teppannayaki* method of making ice cream. Open kitchens, a relaxed atmosphere, and location overlooking the pool make Okra a good choice; with the candles lit in the evening, it's charming.

An absolute find is **Finjaan** (opposite Mughal Residency Apts., Main Rd. Toli Chowki; ⓒ **040/2356-1738;** www.finjaan.com), the first teahouse to open in Hyderabad in 2006. Brothers Salman and Mohammed Taiyebi are only too happy to educate on all 37 kinds of tea and the health benefits of your particular cuppa. India, China, Thailand, and Africa all meet in a steaming pot at Finjaan (meaning "small cup without handle in which decoction is served").

SHOPPING

Pearls are a major draw in Hyderabad—it is said that 9 out of 10 pearls in the world travel through Hyderabad for piercing and stringing—the craftsmanship is unsurpassed here. But do be careful: There are a lot of fakes out there. **Kedarnathji Motiwale** (near Bata, Pathergatti; © 040/2456-6667; www.kedarnathji.com) has been supplying authentic pearls and jewelry since 1908; hardly surprising then that a number of impersonators sporting the same name have cropped up—make sure you're in the shop with the photograph of the President of India giving an award to the owners. **Meena Jewellers** (Babukhan Estate; © 040/2329-9509) is also recommended, particularly if you're after exotic-looking pieces typical of Indian bridalwear. Catering to the wealthy is **Krishna Pearls & Jewellers** (www.krishnapearls.com), with branches in several of the upmarket hotels, including Taj Krishna (© 040/2339-5015), Taj Residency (© 040/5556-4822), and the ITC Kakatiya Sheraton & Towers (© 040/2340-0811 or 040/5556-4844); the main city showroom is at 22-6-209 Pathergatti Rd. (© 040/2441-7881). Another well-known and reliable name is **Jagdamba Jewellers** (Gupta Estate, Basheerbagh Circle; 040/2323-6486; www.jagdamba.com). Besides high-quality Hyderabadi pearls, these jewelers also design and manufacture gold jewelry and various traditional handicrafts.

For high-quality traditional Indian garments, visit **Kalanjali,** a Hyderabadi institution, with four floors of air-conditioned shopping under one roof (opposite Public Gardens, 5-10-194 Hill Fort Rd., Saifabad; © 040/2323-1147 or 040/2342-3440). And to absorb the scents and colors of one of India's most evocative bazaars, spend some time in **Laad Bazaar** ☆☆ near Charminar (see "What to See & Do," above).

As in any of India's growing and constantly changing cities, Hyderabad too has its share of new malls—**Hyderabad Central** (Panjagutta Cross Roads; © 040/6684-8000 or -9000) draws the maximum crowd and is a hangout for the young; **Lifestyle** (© 040/2341-0013) and **Shopper's Stop** (© 040/2776-1084), both at Begumpet, are other popular malls with a variety of branded stores. Hyderabad's version of the Dilli Haat in Delhi is called **Shilparamam** ☆☆ (© 040/2310-0455)—artisans and craftsmen from all parts of India gather and demonstrate, create, and sell their craftwork and handlooms here. The annual crafts fair is held here in December.

9

The Heart of India: Delhi, the Taj, Uttar Pradesh & Madhya Pradesh

The capital of India, Delhi, and its neighboring state, Uttar Pradesh, compose the geographical and historical heart of India, with ancient cities and awesome monuments that make for definite inclusion in the itineraries of most first-time visitors to the subcontinent.

With comfortable accommodations and a host of interesting sights, Delhi is a good place to acclimatize. But the main reason most visitors touch down here is its proximity to some of North India's most impressive sights, like the **Golden Temple** at Amritsar, one of the most spiritual destinations in India (see chapter 11); **Jaipur,** capital of Rajasthan, "land of princes" (see chapter 10); and **Agra.** The Mughal capital of Agra is famed for the timeless beauty of its monuments, of which the **Taj Mahal** is the most famous, but it is in the city of **Varanasi** that time has indeed stood still. Believed to be the oldest living city in the world, Varanasi is the holiest destination in Hindu India, where true believers come to die in order to achieve *moksha*—the final liberation of the soul from the continuous rebirth cycle of Hindu life. Rising like a densely populated crust from the banks of the Ganges, the city is saturated with a sense of the sacred, but while the experience is almost mind-altering, the crowds and filth you may encounter in the city's tiny medieval lanes are not for the fainthearted. (For those who prefer to keep the chaos of India at arm's length, you might want to take a side trip to **Lucknow,** the state capital, where space and serenity prevail, and where the decadence and good taste of the ruling *Nawabs*—Shiite Muslim rulers or landowners—live on in the rich cuisine and majestic *imambaras,* or tombs. Lucknow is not included in this guide.)

South of Uttar Pradesh sprawls **Madhya Pradesh,** a vast landlocked state that contains some of the loveliest untouched vistas on the subcontinent. The most famous sights here are the deserted palaces of **Orchha** and the erotic shrines of **Khajuraho**—both easily included as side trips between Delhi or Agra and Varanasi. Deeper south, which sees a great deal less tourist traffic, lie **Sanchi,** one of the finest Buddhist *stupa* (commemorative cairn) complexes in Asia, and **Mandu,** an exotic Mughal stronghold. To the east lies **Bandhavgarh National Park,** with the densest concentration of tigers in India. These excursions will suit those keen to escape the hassle of more tourist-orientated destinations, but they take careful planning to reach; details are provided throughout the chapter.

1 Delhi

200km (124 miles) NW of Agra; 261km (162 miles) NE of Jaipur; 604km (375 miles) NE of Jodhpur

The capital of the world's largest democracy has a fascinating history, but with a population of 14 million sprawling over some 1,500 sq. km (585 sq. miles), and plagued by the subcontinent's highest levels of pollution, growth, and poverty, Delhi's delights are not immediately apparent. Even Delhiites, most of whom were born elsewhere, seldom show pride in the city they now call home, bemoaning its drab mix of civil servants, aspiring politicians, and avaricious businessfolk; the ever-expanding slums and "unauthorized" colonies; the relatively high levels of crime; and the general demise of traditional ways. Yet Delhi is in many ways the essence of modern India, with its vivid paradox of old and new, rich and poor, foreign and familiar.

Today, to the return visitor, what is startlingly noticeable is the unprecedented growth; to some extent, this is a natural, organic expansion, but it's also part of a mapped-out initiative to prepare the city for its highly anticipated role as host of the 2010 Commonwealth Games and as a leading Asian capital. Beyond the "Games City" moniker, there's the somewhat draconian-sounding "Master Plan for Delhi 2021," which aims to thrust the capital—kicking and screaming if need be—into a better, brighter (and, perhaps sadly, thoroughly Westernized) future. It's clearly a role that local government is taking seriously, because the change is palpable. As the city spreads, giving rise to entire new cities (like Gurgaon and Noida)—devoted almost entirely to economic growth—high rises and malls and residential colonies are mushrooming everywhere. Some residents are left with their jaws hanging in disbelief, while others worship furiously at the altar of capitalist expansion. The expanding megalopolis of Delhi really is more "National Capital Region" than mere city.

Delhi is on the move, and some believe the mobilization of capital and resources is responsible for quite positive transformation. Pollution levels are supposedly dropping, and government officials seem to introduce new modernization schemes every

---

The Plight of the Delhi Beggars

Some 50,000 people live on Delhi's pavements or squalid open lots. These squatters are predominantly from rural areas, many of them forced to move off their ancestral lands to make way for a network of dams that are being constructed across North India despite fierce opposition. Oblivious to the blatant injustice these people have suffered, Delhi's municipal authorities passed a law in September 2002 that makes it an offense to give money to beggars at traffic lights, in part because "it portrays an adverse picture of our country." Begging has in fact been illegal since the 1959 Beggars Act, and those arrested have to bribe the police to avoid spending up to 3 years in jail, but this was the first time the *actual act of giving* has been penalized. Whether or not this inhuman law has any bearing on the situation, you'll notice relatively little by way of begging, and when you do, it's heart-breakingly evident that only the poorest of the poor and the most desperate (often with a malnourished infant curled into the crook of a mother's arms) spend their days pounding the tarmac, usually at traffic intersections. In this city, even homeless pre-teenagers have taken to selling newspapers or flogging fragrant strings of flowers. And their inexpensive merchandise is always accompanied by a smile.

The Heart of India: Delhi, Uttar Pradesh & Madhya Pradesh

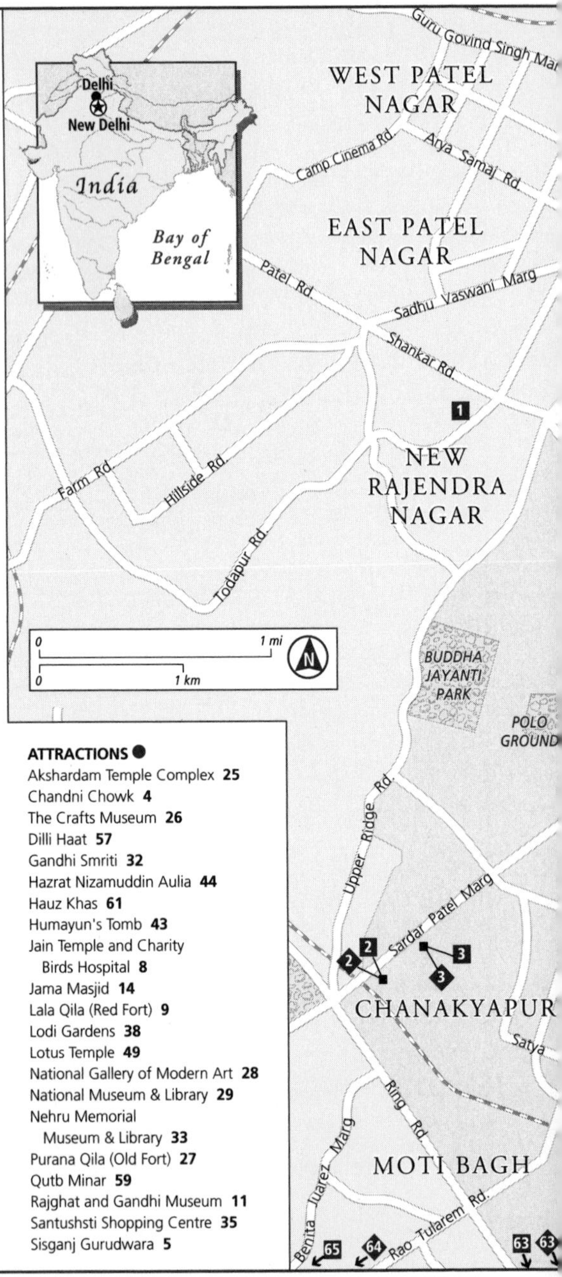

Delhi

WEST PATEL NAGAR

Guru Govind Singh Marg

Delhi
New Delhi

India

Bay of Bengal

Camp Cinema Rd.

Arya Samaj Rd.

EAST PATEL NAGAR

Patel Rd.

Sadhu Vaswani Marg

Shankar Rd.

Farm Rd.

Hillside Rd.

Todapur Rd.

NEW RAJENDRA NAGAR

1

BUDDHA JAYANTI PARK

POLO GROUND

Upper Ridge Rd.

Sardar Patel Marg

2

3

CHANAKYAPUR

Satya

Ring Rd.

MOTI BAGH

Benito Juarez Marg

Rao Tularam Rd.

65 **64** **63 63**

0 _____ 1 mi
0 _____ 1 km

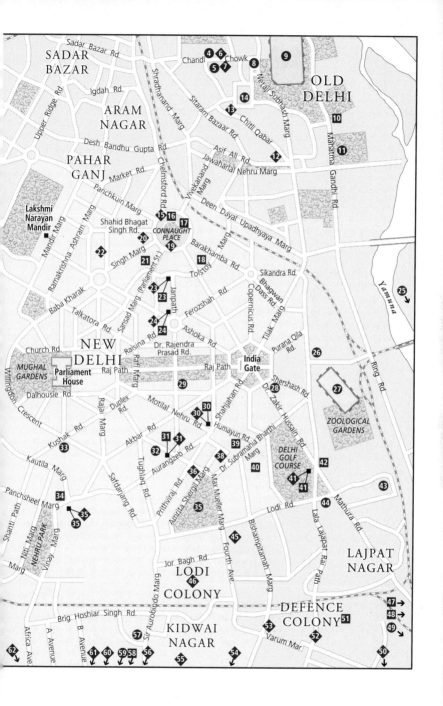

A Tale of Seven Cities

Chosen by the strategically astute invaders who attacked from the north, east, and west, Delhi was not only the gateway to the fertile Gangetic plains and watered by its own Yamuna River, but it enjoyed some protection from the west by the Aravalli Mountains that cross latter-day Rajasthan, and by the Himalayas to the north. Despite this, waves of invaders resulted in the creation—and more often than not destruction—of at least seven distinct cities. The earliest accounts and archaeological finds date back to 1000 B.C., when—according to the *Mahabharata* epic, most revered of Hindu religious texts—the Pandavas and their cousins the Kauravas battled for the city of **Indraprastha,** thought to be located under the present ruins of Purana Qila, citadel of the sixth capital. But the earliest existing ruins date back to A.D. 736, when the Tomara Rajputs, one of the self-anointed warrior clans to which Rajasthan gave birth, built the fortress **Lal Kot,** around which grew **Qila Rai Pithora,** today known as the first city of Delhi. In 1180 the Tomaras were ousted by the Chauhan Rajputs, who were in turn forced back to Rajasthan by the Slave King Qutb-ud-din Aibak, a Turkish general. He built the **Qutb Complex,** which remains one of the most interesting sights in the city (see "The Top Attractions," later in this section). Aibak served under the Afghani Muhammad Ghori until Ghori's assassination in 1206. Aibak took over the Indian spoils of war, founding the Delhi Sultanate, which was to rule Delhi and the surrounding region for almost 2 centuries. In 1303, the Delhi Sultan Ala-ud-din Khilji built the second city, **Siri,** near present-day Hauz Khas. Then the Tughluqs built **Tughlaqabad,** 8km (5 miles) east of the Qutb Complex, but this was deserted in 1321 and little remains of the third city. After a brief sojourn in latter-day Maharashtra, the Tughluqs moved the city again in 1327, this time between Lal Kot and Siri, and named this fourth city **Jahanpanah.** A mere 27 years later it was moved again, this time some distance north to an eminently sensible position on the Yamuna River. Named **Ferozabad,** this sprawling fifth city was, according to legend, one of the richest in the world. But how the mighty do fall or, according to the Persian prophecy, "Whoever builds a new city in Delhi will lose it." Timur drove the Tughluqs out of Delhi, and while his successors, the Sayyids and Lodis, did not build brand-new cities, their tombs are found scattered in the appropriately named **Lodi Gardens.** Their defeat by the Mughal Babur signaled the end of Sultanate rule and the start of the Mughal empire, one of the world's greatest medieval dynasties, which ruled the region for over 200 years.

It was Babur who first moved the capital to nearby Agra, but his son **Humayun** chose to return to Delhi in 1534, only to be forced into exile by the advancing army of the Afghan Sher Shah, who took possession of **Purana Qila** (literally "old fort") in 1540, rebuilt this sixth city, and renamed the citadel **Shergarh.** Fifteen years later, Humayun finally ousted the Afghan, only to die an ignominious death a year later, falling down his library steps—his tomb, which can be seen from the southern gate of Purana Qila, remains one of Delhi's top attractions.

Humayun's son, Akbar—generally revered for his religious tolerance and diplomacy—again chose to move the capital back to Agra. Only after Akbar's grandson, Shah Jahan, built the Taj Mahal for his wife, did Delhi again become the capital in 1638. Shah Jahan, the greatest architect of the Mughal dynasty, rebuilt an entirely new city, using materials from the ruins of Ferozabad (and, it is said, leaving the corpses of criminals to settle in the foundations). Not known for his humility, he named it **Shahjahanabad.** Shahjahanabad is still very much inhabited, and is today usually referred to as "Old Delhi," home to many of the city's top attractions. After Shah Jahan was viciously deposed by his son, Aurangzeb (see "The Life & Times of the Mughal Emperors," later in this chapter), Mughal power began to wane, and with it the importance of Delhi. It was only with the advent of British power that Delhi again played a pivotal role in the affairs of India. After the "Indian Mutiny" (or "The First War of Independence," depending on who's talking), a direct result of the racist and exploitative policies of the British East India Company, India was annexed by Britain as its colony in 1858, and Delhi was declared the capital of the Raj in 1911. The last (at least for the time being) of Delhi's cities to be built, **New Delhi** took shape between 1911 and 1933. Designed by the British imperialist architects Lutyens and Baker, the New Delhi's major buildings have a simple, almost brutal classicism and are considered the finest artifacts of the British Empire, their sheer scale symbolizing its fascist ideals. But again Delhi was lost to her rulers, and in 1947 India's first democratically elected prime minister was sworn into power. The bungalows of New Delhi became home to Indian masters. Ever a city of paradoxes, Delhi's jubilation was tinged with tragedy, for this was also for many the demise of ancient Delhi: With the division ("Partition") of the subcontinent into India and Pakistan, bloody street battles between Hindu and Muslim broke out, leading to the wide-scale immigration of Delhi's urbane Muslim population to Pakistan, and to an even bigger, reverse influx of Punjabis from what is now Pakistan. Primarily farmers, but with a reputation for hard work and business acumen, the Punjabi immigrants effectively doubled the population of Delhi and forever changed its image of itself as a birthplace of civilization. As William Dalrymple describes it in *City of Djinns,* Delhi—"grandest of grand old aristocratic dowagers"—had become "a nouveau-riche heiress: all show and vulgarity and conspicuous consumption." But if one thing is constant, it is Delhi's ability to reconstitute herself. Indeed, with fierce development in the adjunct metropolitan areas of Gurgaon and Noida, a rapidly expanding Metro system, and a stringent plan in place to drastically develop the city's infrastructure ahead of the 2010 Commonwealth Games, there are signs that Delhi's desire is to become a city of the future, molded along capitalist ideals and increasingly in line with Western expectations for a high-yield international hub. And, with pressure from the Supreme Court, local government has been consistently installing an ever-tightening schedule of laws designed to gentrify and unclog the city of cows, beggars, illegal businesses, and pollution-spewing vehicles, it's certain that the desire for rapid evolution exists. One only hopes that Delhi's historic heartbeat will not be lost in the process.

week. You're unlikely to see cows roaming the streets of the capital any more; those that dare are rounded up and taken to stray cow facilities, and in May 2007, the traffic department vowed to crack down on all forms of dangerous driving. But there are ill-considered political choices, too. In 2007, street food was officially banned in the capital, and there was fervent talk of outlawing cycle-rickshaws in Old Delhi. Sadly, such decisions often come from wealthy politicos who have never even been into the heart of the old city and have little idea how much a part of daily Delhi life the roadside food stalls really are. So, not only is Delhi hurtling into the future, but it remains a symbol of many of the challenges faced by India in its bid to catch up with the West.

Delhi is also an excellent starting point for exploring North India, not only because of ample transport connections and relatively sophisticated infrastructure, but because the history of Delhi, one of the oldest cities in the world, is essentially the history of India (see "A Tale of Seven Cities," above).

The city is littered with crumbling tombs and ruins, most of which are not even on the tourist map. They—like the elephant trundling alongside a traffic-logged road, where handwritten posters for CUSTOM CONFISCATED GOODS SOLD HERE vie with glossy fashion billboards—are just part of the strange fabric of Delhi. It doesn't have the vibrancy of Mumbai or the atmosphere of Kolkata, but in 1 day you can go from marveling at the sheer grace of the soaring **Qutb Minar Tower,** built in 1199 by the Turkish Slave King Qutb-ud-din Aibak to celebrate his victory over the Hindu Rajputs, to gawking at that 1920s British imperialist masterpiece, palatial **Rashtrapati Bhavan.** You can wander through the sculptural **Jantar Mantar,** a huge, open-air astronomy observatory built in 1725 by Jai Singh, creator and ruler of Jaipur, experience the tangibly sacred atmosphere surrounding the **tomb of the 14th-century Sufi saint,** Sheikh Nizamuddin Aulia, or admire the **16th-century garden tomb of Mughal Emperor Humayun,** precursor to the Taj. Or, after the chaos of exploring the crowded streets of 17th-century **Shahjahanabad,** Delhi's oldest living city, you can escape to **Rajghat,** the park where Mahatma Gandhi was cremated in 1948; or to **Lodi Gardens,** where lawns and golfing greens are studded with the crumbling 15th-century tombs of once-powerful dynasties. And still you haven't covered the half of it . . .

But despite its host of attractions, unless you're staying in one of its top hotels (of which The Imperial is almost a destination in its own right), Delhi is not a very relaxing destination, and it is as famous for its pollution (it was rated the fourth-most-polluted city in the world through the 1990s) as it is for its sights. Unless you're a history buff or here on business or like to get caught up in the hustle and bustle of a big city, spend as much time as you need to recover from jet lag, choosing to view only a few of its many attractions (the best of which are listed below), and then move on. The rest of India, with its awesome array of experiences and beauty, awaits you.

ESSENTIALS

VISITOR INFORMATION To pick up a free map of Delhi or to get up-to-date information on sights, city tours, and taxi/rickshaw prices, head for the **India Tourism Office** at 88 Janpath (near Connaught Place; ✆ **011/2332-0005** or -0008; www. incredibleindia.org; Mon–Fri 9am–6pm, Sat 9am–2pm). You will also find Government of India Tourist offices at both airports (open 24 hr.). Do not confuse these with so-called "government authorized" tourist offices, which are not authorized by anyone and are very adept at fleecing the unsuspecting. You will find these fakes particularly along Janpath and at the New Delhi railway station; make sure you seek assistance only at 88 Janpath or from one of the recommended tour operators (see below). If you intend to travel anywhere during your sojourn in India by train, you may choose to make all your reservations in Delhi (though these are just as easily available in other big cities). You can make bookings at the helpful Indian Railways Counter at the airport. Alternatively, for information, visit the **Delhi Tourism and Transport Development Corporation** (DTTDC; Bombay Life Building, N-Block, Connaught Place; ℂ **011/2331-5322;** www.delhitourism.nic.in; Mon–Sat 9:30am–6pm), or see "Getting There: By Train," below.

GETTING THERE   By Air   Most major international airlines operate in what is one of the best-connected cities in south Asia. Delhi has separate domestic and international airports that lie 8km (5 miles) apart; a free hourly shuttle bus runs between them. Note that the domestic airport has two terminals, 1A and 1B, also connected by free shuttle bus (1A is for Indian Airlines; check which one you need to be at when leaving). **Indira Gandhi International Airport** (ℂ **011/2569-6021** or 011/2565-2011; www.delhiairport.com) lies 20km (12 miles) southwest of Connaught Place (the city center), 25 to 50 minutes away. The cheapest way (but one to be avoided) to get into town is to catch a State Transport bus (Rs 50/$1.25/65p plus luggage fee), but if you've just crossed time zones you'll want to opt for a taxi; **Easycabs** (ℂ **011/4343-4343**) is the best option, with rates ranging from Rs 200 to Rs 450 ($4.90–$11/£2.50–£5.60) for rides from the airport to the main hotels in town. If you've just arrived in India, it's also not worthwhile to hire a rickshaw; they may be cheaper than taxis, but they're very slow and bound to be uncomfortable if you're burdened with luggage—plus, you will almost certainly be pressured into handing over more money even if the price has been discussed upfront. Choosing, let alone negotiating with, a taxi driver is likely to make your head spin, so it's best to book a taxi at the official **prepaid taxi kiosk** (just outside the arrivals hall; ask for directions, and don't be sidelined). It offers fixed rates, with a small fee for each piece of large luggage, but expect to pay between Rs 195 and Rs 300 ($4.75–$7.35/£2.40–£3.70) into the center of town (25% more after 11pm). Better still, ask your hotel to arrange the transfer, though this will more than likely double the price, unless you have booked a "Club Room" at one of the upmarket chains—these usually include chauffered transfers in the rate. Note that you can change money at the international airport at the State Bank of India or Thomas Cook counters (both 24 hr.), but you can't draw money on your credit card.

By Train   Of the five stations, most trains arrive at either **New Delhi Station,** a 10-minute walk from Connaught Place, or at **Old Delhi Station** in Shahjahanabad. (Note that if you're traveling on to Agra, you may need to catch the passenger train that leaves from **Nizamuddin Station,** south of Connaught Place.) For rail inquiries and reservations, call ℂ **131** from 8am to 8pm. All stations are well-serviced by taxis and auto-rickshaws. Again, negotiate the fare upfront—expect to pay Rs 50 ($1.25/65p) to Connaught Place, slightly more to Shahjahanabad/Old Delhi—or insist on using the meter (see rates under "Getting Around," below). Note that if you plan to travel elsewhere in India by train, you don't necessarily need to prebook all your train trips in Delhi (see chapter 2 for details on train travel). It's easiest to do this with a recommended travel agent like **Sadhana Travel** (ℂ **011/2646-5312,** 011/4161-8278, or 98-1005-2471), which also does air travel and tour itineraries; or work with a travel agent attached to your hotel. Keep in mind that on some trains a small quota of seats is set aside for foreign travelers. A travel agent cannot book these seats; you will need to go to the station to a special counter to book them (again, see chapter 2).

GETTING AROUND The **Delhi Metro** can be useful for covering longer distance (like getting to Oberoi Maidens in the north), but as is the case elsewhere, subways also provide no sense of the city layout or passing sights. During peak hours, the tube can also get overcrowded and claustrophobic, and women traveling alone may get unwelcome attention. Ticketing agents are still not very clued in or helpful, either. If you want to try out the Metro, consider buying a 1-day card.

The best way to get around is still in Delhi's **black-and-yellow taxis** or, for short distances, **auto-rickshaws** (run on eco-friendly CNG—compressed natural gas), but be sure to agree on the price upfront. For instance, traveling from Connaught Place to Red Fort shouldn't cost more than Rs 100 ($2.45/£1.25) by auto-rickshaw, Rs 150 ($3.65/£1.85) by taxi. Delhi has the most complacent lot of auto-rickshaw drivers in the country; if they don't feel like going where you're asking, they'll simply refuse you service. Often, this is a ploy to press you for more money (official rates are Rs 8/20¢/10p for the first kilometer, and Rs 3.50/9¢/4p for every kilometer thereafter). If you feel you're being overcharged, accuse the driver of cheating and threaten to report him (often simply pretending to dial the police on your mobile phone does the trick); to really complain, dial ℂ 011/**2337-8888** (24 hr.). If the idea of having to haggle like this turns your stomach, **Mega Cab** (ℂ **011/4141-4141**) is a radio taxi outfit that offers a convenient, marginally more expensive, alternative, with a fleet of air-conditioned cars outfitted with working meters (Rs 15/37¢/19p per kilometer at press time) available around-the-clock; their drivers usually keep you abreast of their arrival via cellphone.

If you'd prefer to hire a car and driver for a half- or full day, arrange this through your hotel or, for the best possible rate and reliable drivers, through **The One** (ℂ **011/2687-7434**), which has given us nothing but joy in Delhi. Better still, contact **Shahabuddin Khan** (ℂ **99-1087-1230** or 93-1203-2182) directly; he's the best driver we've had in the city, speaks wonderful English (and several other languages), has had experience abroad, and at press time was planning to start his own company.

If you plan to tour North India by car, setting off from Delhi, contact **Greaves Travels India** (ℂ **011/2437-3523** or -2426; www.greavesindia.com), a reputable operator with good drivers. At press time there was talk of a new **Heritage Bus,** which will certainly make visits to the city's top sights easier and more affordable.

Note: It is inadvisable to travel anywhere during rush hour—you will almost certainly find yourself in a traffic jam in one of the most polluted cities in the world.

GUIDED TOURS You can book an air-conditioned bus tour of New Delhi (daily 9am–1:30pm) and/or Old Delhi (daily 2:15–5:45pm) through **Delhi Tourism** (see "Visitor Information," above). Tours cost Rs 158 ($3.85/£1.95) each, or Rs 263 ($6.45/£3.25) for both; monument admission fees are extra. Both also offer long-distance tours that include trips to Agra, Jaipur, and Rishikesh, but we definitely recommend you opt for a private operator like **Go Delhi Luxury Tours** (ℂ **98-9988-8207;** www.godelhi.net), or **TCI** (ℂ **011/2341-5367** or 011/2341-6167). Their tours are more personal, and the higher tariff (upward of Rs 1,000/$24/£12 per person, excluding monument entry) ensures that you get a decent English-speaking guide and an air-conditioned vehicle.

For an excellent introduction to Hinduism, as well as visits to some of the lesser-known sights in Old and New Delhi, book into **Master Paying Residential Guest Accommodation** (see "Where to Stay," later in this section)—the erudite proprietor gives one of the best tours we've had in India, and runs the best-value guesthouse in Delhi, too.

If you'd care to learn more about life on the streets of Delhi, and fancy a walking tour, contact **Salaam Baalak Trust City Walk** (© 98-7313-0383; sbttour@yahoo.com), although you'd better be prepared to have your heart broken. The daily walks through the city's hodge-podge streets and back alleys are led by street children who will share views on life that will possibly change your reality forever. **INTACH** (The Indian National Trust for Art and Cultural Heritage; 71 Lodhi Estate; © 011/2464-1304) conducts 2-hour morning walks through Chandni Chowk on Saturdays. For very comfortable customized tours of the city and farther afield, contact **Navigator Holidays** or **Banyan Tours and Travel** (see "Fast Facts: Delhi," below), or that U.K.-based stalwart in Indian travel, **Cox & Kings** (see chapter 2). Another company worth highlighting is **Exotic Journeys**—all you need to do is supply proprietor Raj Singh with your budget (as low as $100/£50 per day, including car, driver, and accommodations—or higher, of course), number of days, and area of interest, and he will customize an excellent trip, kicking off with 2 days of sightseeing in Delhi. Contact him at exotic@del2.vsnl.net.in or exoticjourney@vsnl.com, or call © **011/2612-4069.**

FAST FACTS: Delhi

Airlines Most international airline offices are located on Janpath, Connaught Place, and Barakhamba Road. The best domestic airline, **Jet Airways,** is located at Jetair House, 13 Community Centre, Yusuf Sarai; there's a walk-in office at N-40 Outer Circle, Connaught Place (Reservations © **011/4164-1414,** or 011/4164-3636). **Indian Airlines** is located at Safdarjung Airport (© **011/2462-2220**) and is open 24 hours; for general inquiries call © **1600/180-1407,** or 011/1407 from your mobile. Other airlines: **Air Sahara** (© **011/2332-6851** or 011/2335-2771); **Kingfisher Airlines** (© **1600/180-0101**); **Spice Jet** (© **1600/180-3333** or 98-7180-3333).

Ambulance For an ambulance call either © **102,** or **East West Rescue** at © **011/2469-9229,** -0429, or -3738.

American Express The office is located at A-Block Connaught Place (© **011/2332-6129** or 011/2330-8035).

Area Code The area code for **Delhi** is **011.**

ATMs There are hundreds of ATMs in the city; ask your hotel which is the closest. Alternatively, head for Connaught Place, where (among others) HSBC, Standard Chartered, and Citibank ATMs offer 24-hour cash machines that take Visa and MasterCard.

Banks Hours are normally Monday to Friday 10am to 2pm, Saturday 10am to noon, though many banks are also open 9am to 5pm. It's quickest to use 24-hour ATMs. See "ATMs," above.

Bookstores The best are in Khan Market—try **Bahri & Sons** (© **011/2469-4610**), or **Full Circle** (© **011/2465-5641**). If you're looking for something downtown, **Bookworm** (29 B-Block Connaught Place; © **011/2332-2260**) is excellent, and will often obtain a book you want within 24 hours even if it's not in stock. In Jor Bagh, **The Bookshop** (© **011/2469-7102**) is another good option.

Car Hires See "Getting Around," above. For upmarket cars and other travel arrangements, a recommended operator is **Banyan Tours and Travels** (© 011/4173-4810; www.banyantours.com). Another operator to try is **Navigator Holidays** (L-5 2nd floor, Radiant Limo, Lajpat Nagar II; © 011/5172-5020).

Currency Exchange The international airport has 24-hour currency exchange but no facilities to let you draw money on your credit cards, so bring foreign notes or traveler's checks if you intend to catch a taxi from here. Thomas Cook is located at the airport (open 24/7) and at The Imperial hotel (Mon–Sat; see "Where to Stay," later in this section). See above for American Express. For cash withdrawals or exchange, see "ATMs" and "Banks," above.

Directory Assistance To get numbers texted to your mobile phone (or e-mailed to you), call **Just Dial** (© 011/3999-9999).

Doctors & Dentists All hotels listed here have doctors on call. The hotels are also your best bet for finding a reputable dentist.

Drugstores There are numerous 24-hour drugstores throughout the city. Best to ask your hotel to arrange a delivery or pickup.

Embassies & Consulates U.S.: Shanti Path, Chanakyapuri (© 011/2419-8000; Mon–Fri 8:30am–1pm and 2–5:30pm). U.K.: Shanti Path, Chanakyapuri (© 011/2419-2100; Mon–Fri 9am–1pm and 2–4pm). Australia: 1/50-G Shanti Path, Chanakyapuri (© 011/4139-9900; Mon–Fri 8:30am–1pm and 2–5pm). Canada: 7/8 Shanti Path Chanakyapuri (© 011/4178-2000). New Zealand: 50-N Nyaya Marg (© 011/2688-3170).

Emergencies For police call © **100**; for local stations ask your hotel or call the Government of India Tourist Office. See "Ambulance," above. For complaints about taxi or auto-rickshaw drivers, dial © **96-0440-0400**. For any tourism-related emergencies, call the **Tourism Hotline** (© 011/2336-5358).

Hospitals **All India Institute of Medicinal Sciences** (© 011/2658-8500), on Ansari Nagar, has a 24-hour trauma unit. Alternatively, head for **Ram Manohar Lohia Hospital** (Baba Khadak Singh Marg; © 011/2336-5933 or -5525) or, farther afield, is **Apollo Hospital** on the Delhi–Mathura Road (© 011/2692-5858 or -5801); both have 24-hour emergency service.

Internet Access Numerous outlets are located all over the city and charge Rs 25 to Rs 75 (60¢–$1.85/30p–95p) per hour.

Mobile Phones You can buy prepaid cellphone cards almost anywhere in Delhi (see chapter 2); however, the procedure has been severely complicated by various anti-terrorism laws that will require you to supply ID photos and copies of your passport and visa, and possibly proof of residence. Call pricing options also vary considerably according to network and package purchased. Best to ask your hotel about the best (and simplest) rental scheme, or call **Matrix** at © 011/2680-0000; they promise to deliver a phone to you within 2 hours.

Newspapers & Magazines **Indian Express, Hindustan Times,** and **The Times of India** are good national dailies that provide the lowdown on (largely) the political scene. *Outlook* and *India Today* are weekly news magazines that cover a range of issues; of the two, *Outlook* is more populist and interesting to read. *Time Out New Delhi* (Rs 50/$1.25/65p) hit the streets in April 2007 and is a superb source of (sometimes sycophantic) information about every conceivable activity in town, with good accounts of new establishments and entertainment events. It's considerably better than *First City,* a reasonable monthly magazine recommended for its comprehensive reviews and listings. *Delhi Diary* is a city guide published weekly, and *The Delhi City Complete Guide and Magazine* (Rs 20/50¢/25p) is published every 2 weeks; both are available at hotels and tourism offices and include events listings. You can also check out the latter's website at www.thedelhicity.com. *Outlook Traveller* (www.outlooktraveller.com) is a top-quality locally produced travel magazine.

Police See "Emergencies," above.

Post Office Try the P.O. at Parliament Street (© **011/2336-4111**) or the **GPO** at Gol Khana, 5 minutes from Connaught Place. But best to ask your hotel to post items.

Restrooms Avoid public restrooms. Period.

Safety Delhi, like the rest of India, is relatively safe, though the city has seen an increase in crime. It's unwise for women to travel alone at night.

Taxis See "Getting Around," above.

Weather Delhi's summers are notoriously unbearable; October/November to February are the best times to go.

THE TOP ATTRACTIONS

India's capital has more sights than any other city in India, but they are concentrated in three distinct areas—Old Delhi, New Delhi, and South Delhi (known as the **Qutb Minar Complex**)—which can be tackled as separate tours or grouped together. Most organized tours spend a half-day covering the top attractions in New Delhi, and another half-day exploring the 17th-century capital, Shahjahanabad. Commonly referred to as "Old Delhi," Shahjahanabad lies a mere 5km (3 miles) north of centrally located Connaught Place, the commercial heart of New Delhi, but it feels a few hundred years away (400 to be exact). If you do only one sightseeing excursion, make it here, for this is most authentically India, where imposing **Lal Qila (Red Fort)** and **Jama Masjid,** India's largest mosque, pay testament to the vision and power of Shah Jahan, and the chaos and pungent smells from the overcrowded and ancient streets are a heady reminder that you are far from home. Surrounding and immediately south of Connaught Place is New Delhi, built by British imperialist architects Baker and Lutyens. Its primary attractions are the architectural gems centered around **Rajpath** and **Rashtrapati Bhavan,** official residence of the president of India. Of Delhi's remaining cities, all of which are today deserted and in ruins, only the 12th-century **Qutb Minar,** a World Heritage Site monument built in Delhi's first city and surprisingly intact, is definitely worth inclusion in your itinerary.

SHAHJAHANABAD (OLD DELHI) ✦✦✦

Still surrounded by crumbling city walls and three surviving gates, the vibrant, bustling Shahjahanabad, built over a period of 10 years by Emperor Shah Jahan, is very much a separate city—predominantly a labyrinth of tiny lanes crowded with rickshaws, and lined with 17th-century *havelis* (Indian mansions), their balustrades

Museum Monday

Most of the important museums in Delhi close on Mondays; if you're at loose ends, there are a handful of hangouts for the culturally inclined. First up is the totally unique and utterly original **Sulabh International Museum of Toilets** (Sulabh Gram, Mahavir Enclave, Palam-Dabri Marg; © **011/2503-1518**; Mon–Sat 10am–5pm), which takes visitors on a journey through everything "loo"-related, from Thomas Crapper's first flushable commode to present-day innovations in Indian sanitation technology. If you have an interest in Tibetan art (particularly Buddhist *thangka* paintings and religious objects), visit the **Tibetan House Museum** (Tibet House, 1 Institutional Area, Lodhi Rd.; © **011/2461-1515**; Mon–Fri 9:30am–5:30pm).

broken and once-ornate facades defaced with rusted signs and sprouting satellite dishes. Old Delhi is inhabited by a predominantly Muslim population whose lives revolve around work and the local mosque, much as it was a century ago.

The best way to explore the area is to catch a taxi or auto-rickshaw to Red Fort (see below), then set off in a cycle-rickshaw (agree on Rs 100/$2.45/£1.25 per hr.), or on foot if it's too congested. Head down the principal street, **Chandni Chowk,** which leads from the main entrance to Red Fort. Along this busy commercial street are mosques, a church, and a number of temples. First up, opposite the fort, is **Digambar Jain Temple,** the oldest of its kind in Delhi and surprisingly simple compared with other Jain temples, which are renowned for the intricacy of their carvings. Attached is a **bird hospital,** which smells less charming than it sounds. If you're pressed for time, skip these and proceed to vibrant **Gauri Shankar Temple** (look for the mounds of marigolds, sold to worshipers as they enter), which has an 800-year-old lingam. Or stop at **Sisganj Gurudwara,** an unassuming but superbly atmospheric and welcoming Sikh temple, which marks the spot where Guru Tegh Bahadur, the ninth Sikh guru, was beheaded by the fundamentalist Aurangzeb (Shah Jahan's intolerant son). You will be expected to hand over your shoes at a super-efficient kiosk and wash your hands and feet at the cheap taps plumbed right at the temple entrance; on the way out you may be offered food—politely decline (it's rich with ghee, clarified butter). Then, either turn left into Kinari Bazaar (see below) or head the length of Chandni Chowk to **Fatehpuri Masjid,** designed by one of Shah Jahan's wives. Take a detour to the right into Church Mission Marg and then left into **Khari Baoli**— reputed to be Asia's biggest spice market—the colors, textures, and aromas that literally spill out into the street are worth the side trip, but be careful with your belongings in these packed streets. Then double back down Chandni Chowk, turn right into jam-packed **Kinari Bazaar,** and stop to admire the cheap gold (we're talking mostly tinsel) and silver trinkets and accessories. Or keep going until the right turn into **Dariba Kalan,** "the jewelers' lane," where you can bargain hard for gorgeous baubles. Go south down Dariba Kalan to reach **Jama Masjid,** India's largest mosque, keeping an eye out on the right for the tall spire of **Shiv Temple.** Having explored Jama Masjid (see below), you can head west down **Chawri Bazaar** for brass and copper icons and other souvenirs, then up **Nai Sarak** (which specializes in the most magnificent stationery, some bound into diaries). Or head south to **Churiwali Galli,** the "lane of bangle-sellers," and make a final stop at **Karim's** to sample the authentic Mughlai cooking that has kept patrons coming back for over 100 years. A little farther along is

Sunehri Masjid, recognizable by its three gilt domes from where the Persian invader Nadir Shah enjoyed a bird's-eye view as his men massacred some 3,000 of Shahjahan-abad's citizens in 1739.

This done, you've pretty much covered Shahjahanabad's top attractions by rick-shaw. A few more sights of interest within the old city walls may attract the die-hard tourist. Pretty **Zinat-ul Masjid (Daryaganj),** or "Cloud Mosque," built in 1710 by one of Aurangzeb's daughters, lies south, but doesn't see as much traffic as nearby **Rajghat** (Mahatma Gandhi Rd.; daily sunrise–sunset; leave shoes outside with atten-dant for a small tip), where Mahatma Gandhi, "Father of the Nation," was cremated. There's not much to see besides the black granite plinth inscribed with his last words, "Hé Ram!" ("Oh God!"), but it's worth getting here at 5pm on Friday (the day of the week he was assassinated), when devotees gather to sing melancholic *bhajans.* Nearby, **Gandhi Memorial Museum** (*©* **011/2331-1793;** Tues–Sun 9:30am–5:30pm) doc-uments his life and last rites, which must have been immensely moving. Also within the old city walls is **Feroze Shah Kotla (Bahadur Shah Zafar Marg),** the ruins of the palace of the fifth city, Ferozabad. The principal attraction here is the pristine polished sandstone pillar from the 3rd century B.C. that rises from the palace's crumbling remains. One of many pillars left by the Mauryan emperor Ashoka throughout North India, it was moved from the Punjab and erected here in 1356. North of Red Fort is **St. James Church** (Lothian Rd. near Kashmiri Gate; daily 8am–noon and 2–5pm). Consecrated in 1836, Delhi's oldest church was built by Col. James Skinner—the son of a Scotsman and his Rajput wife, who became one of Delhi's most flamboyant 19th-century characters—to repay a promise made during battle.

Jama Masjid ☆☆   Commissioned by Shah Jahan in 1656, this mosque took 5,000 laborers 6 years to complete and is still the largest in Asia, accommodating up to 25,000 worshipers during holy festivals such as Id. Sadly, non-Muslims are not allowed in during prayers, but photographs (sold elsewhere) of the thousands of sup-plicant worshipers provide some idea of the atmosphere as you wander the huge expanse within. The central pool is for washing hands, face, and feet; to the west (fac-ing Mecca) is the main prayer hall with the traditional *mihrab* for the prayer leader. You can ascend to the top of the southern minaret to enjoy fantastic views from Old Delhi to the distinctly different rooftops and high-rises of New Delhi—the climb is pretty stiff, but worth it. *Note:* If your knees or shoulders are bare, you'll have to rent a scarf or *lungi* (sarong or cloth) at the entrance to cover up.

Off Netaji Subhash Marg. Free admission; Rs 20 (50¢/25p) for minaret rooftop viewing; Rs 150 ($3.65/£1.85) camera or video. Daily 8:30am–12:15pm and 1:45pm to half-hour before sunset; opens at 7am in summer. Closed during prayers 12:15–1:45pm. Shoes to be removed outside.

Lal Qila (Red Fort) ☆☆   Built by Shah Jahan, the most prolific architect and builder of the Mughal empire, Lal Qila must have been a very modern departure from labyrinthine Agra Fort (which is older but a great deal better preserved and atmos-pheric). It was the seat of Mughal power from 1639 to 1857. Named after the red sandstone used in its construction, Red Fort covers an area of almost 2km (1¼ miles). Visitors enter via three-story **Lahore Gate,** one of six impressive gateways. You'll pass through **Chatta Chowk,** which has quaint shops selling cheap souvenirs (some rather nice handbags). You'll arrive at **Naqqar Khana,** where the emperor's musicians used to play. From here you look up into **Diwan-I-Am,** the 60-pillared "hall of public audi-ence," from where Emperor Shah Jahan used to listen to his subjects' queries and com-plaints as he sat cross-legged upon the beautifully carved throne (an age-old custom that his nasty son, Aurangzeb, discontinued). Behind this lie **Rang Mahal,** the royal quarters of the wives and mistresses, and **Mumtaz Mahal,** probably used by a favored wife or by Princess Jahanara, who evoked such envy in her sister's heart (see "Agra" introduction, later in this chapter). Next up are **Khas Mahal,** which housed the emperor's personal quarters (he would greet his subjects across the Yamuna River from the balcony); gilded **Diwan-I-Khas,** where the emperor would hold court with his inner circle from the famous jewel-encrusted Peacock Throne (taken by Persian invader Nadir Shah in 1739 and still in Iran); and finally the **Hamams,** or royal baths, whose fountains of rose-scented water would give modern-day spas a run for their money. In front of the *hamams* is **Moti Masjid,** built by Aurangzeb exclusively for his own use—a far cry from the huge Jama Masjid his father built to celebrate the faith together with thousands of his subjects.

A few examples of beautiful carving, inlay, and gilding remain, particularly in Diwan-I-Khas, but after so many years of successive plunder it takes some contemplation (and a guide) to imagine just how plush and glorious the palaces and gardens must have been in their heyday; they were ruined when the British ripped up the gardens and built their ugly barracks (the fort is incidentally still a military stronghold, with much of it off-limits). Consider hiring a guide at the entrance, but negotiate the fee upfront and don't expect much by way of dialogue (guides often speak English by rote and don't understand queries); do expect to be hassled for more money. If you're staying in an upmarket hotel, arrange a guide through the concierge.

Chandni Chowk. ✆ 011/2327-7705. Rs 100 ($2.45/£1.25) entry; Rs 25 (60¢/30p) video; Rs 100–Rs 150 ($2.45–$3.65/£1.25–£1.85) guide. Tues–Sun sunrise–sunset. Evening light show 7:30pm Nov–Jan, 8:30pm Feb–Apr, 9pm May–Aug; Rs 50 ($1.25/65p); inquiries ✆ 011/2327-4580.

NEW DELHI

Almost all of New Delhi's attractions lie south of **Connaught Place,** which you will no doubt visit to make onward bookings, get cash, eat, or shop. Built on concentric circles surrounding a central park, the retail heart of New Delhi was designed by Robert Tor Russell in the late 1920s. With its deep colonnaded verandas, gleaming banks, and host of burger joints and pizzerias, it's a far cry from Chandni Chowk but is still quite chaotic, crawling with touts and hucksters whose aim is to part you from your money as quickly and seductively as possible. From here, the closest attraction well worth visiting (unless you're moving on to Jaipur) is **Jantar Mantar** ⊀ (daily sunrise–sunset), which lies on Sansad Marg, on the way to Rashtrapati Bhavan. It's one of five open-air observatories built in the 18th century by Maharaja Jai Singh II, the eccentric genius who built Jaipur. The sculptural qualities of the huge instruments he designed are worth a visit alone, but note that Jantar Mantar in Jaipur, built by the same king, is both bigger and better preserved (see chapter 10).

The easiest way to take in central New Delhi's imperial architecture—for many the chief attraction—is to drive to **India Gate,** built to commemorate those who died in World War I. There an eternal flame burns in memory of those who gave their lives in the 1971 Indo-Pakistan war, their names inscribed on the memorial. Set off on foot west along **Rajpath** (the 3.2km/2-mile boulevard once known as King's Way) to the beautifully ornate gates of **Rashtrapati Bhavan,** flanked by the two almost identical **Secretariat buildings.** Having covered the architectural attractions of New Delhi, you can double back to **The National Museum** (see below) or catch a ride to the **National Gallery of Modern Art,** which lies near India Gate (Jaipur House; ✆ 011/2338-2835; Rs 150/$3.65/£1.85; Tues–Sun 10am–5pm). Farther west lies **The Crafts**

Museum (see below). Although the National Gallery is one of India's largest museums of modern art, it's pretty staid fare and unlikely to thrill those used to such Western shrines as London's Tate Modern or New York's Museum of Modern Art.

Other museums you may consider in the area include the **Eternal Gandhi Multimedia Museum** at **Gandhi Smriti and Darshan Samiti** ☆ (5 Tees January Marg; ℭ **011/3095-7269** or 011/2301-2843; www.eternalgandhi.org; Tues–Sun 10am–5pm, closed second Sat of the month). The colonial bungalow where Gandhi stayed when he was in Delhi, and where he was assassinated, it's more atmospheric than the museum near Raj Ghat in Old Delhi. **Nehru Memorial Museum and Library** (Teen Murti Marg; ℭ **011/2301-6734;** free admission; Tues–Sun 9:30am–5pm) was the grand home of India's own "Kennedy clan": Nehru was India's first prime minister, a role his daughter and grandson, Indira and Rajiv respectively, were also to play before both were assassinated. Those interested in contemporary Indian history may wish to visit **Indira Gandhi Memorial Museum** (1 Safdarjung Rd.; ℭ **011/2301-0094;** free admission; Tues–Sun 9:30am–4:45pm). A huge force in post-independence India (see "India Past to Present," in the appendix), Indira Gandhi was murdered here by her Sikh bodyguards. Among the displays (which provide a real sense of the woman) is her blood-soaked sari, as well as the clothes worn by her son Rajiv when he was killed in 1991.

The best temples to visit in central New Delhi are **Lakshmi Narayan Mandir** ☆ (west of Connaught Place, on Mandir Marg; leave cameras and cellphones at counter outside), an ornate yet contemporary Hindu temple built by the wealthy industrialist B. D. Birla in 1938; and **Bangla Sahib Gurudwara** ☆☆ (off Ashoka Rd.), Delhi's principal Sikh temple. If you aren't heading north to the Golden Temple at Amritsar (see chapter 11 for more on Sikhism), a visit to the *gurudwara* is highly recommended, if only to experience the warm and welcoming atmosphere that seems to pervade all Sikh places of worship—evident in details like the efficient shoe deposit, a scarf to cover your head (both free), genuinely devoted guides who expect no recompense (available at the entrance), devotional hymns (sung constantly sunrise–9pm), free food (served three times daily), and *prasad* (communion) offered as you leave—be warned that it's very oily and you won't give offense if you decline. The *gurudwara* is certainly an interesting contrast to Lakshmi Narayan Mandir; a visit to one of the first Hindu temples to open its doors to all castes (including "outcasts" like the foreign Britishers) makes you feel very much like a tourist, whereas the more embracing atmosphere of the *gurudwaras* has you feeling rather humbled.

If all this sightseeing has you beat, you can retreat to **Lodi Gardens** (5km/3 miles south of Connaught Place), where green lawns surround the crumbling tombs of the 15th-century Sayyid and Lodi dynasties—the tombs are not well-preserved, but the green, shaded oasis may suffice as a break from the hectic traffic or shopping at nearby Khan Market (though I'd opt for a hotel pool). The 18th-century **Safdarjang's Tomb** lies just south of Lodi Gardens, but more impressive by far is **Humayun's Tomb** (a short rickshaw ride west) and, across the street, **Hazrat Nizamuddin Aulia** (both discussed below).

Finally, for the special-interest traveler, you can view India's largest collection of rare stamps free of charge at the **National Philatelic Museum,** located at the post office at Dak Bhavan (Sansad Marg; enter at back of post office; Mon–Fri 9:30am–4:30pm, closed 12:30–2:30pm).

Humayun's Tomb ☆☆☆   This tomb, built for the second Mughal emperor, launched a great Mughal architectural legacy—even the Taj, which was built by Humayun's great-grandson, was inspired by it. Though the Taj's beauty (and the money spent) eclipsed this magnificent example of a garden tomb, it's well worth a visit, even if your intention is to visit its progeny. Paid for by Humayun's "senior" wife, Haji Begum, and designed by the Persian (Iranian) architect Mirak Mirza Ghiyas, it's another grand testimony to love. Set in peaceful surrounds, the tomb features an artful combination of red sandstone and white marble, which plays with the wonderful symmetry and scale used by the makers of the Mughal empire. Though it doesn't have the fine detailing of the Taj, aspects such as the intricately carved stone trellis windows are lovely. If you're traveling on to Agra, it is interesting to see how the Mughals' prolonged stay in India started to influence design elements (the Persian finial that mounts the central marble dome was, for instance, later supplanted by the lotus). There are a number of outlying tombs, and if you want to do more than simply wander through the beautifully restored gardens and walkways and marvel at the sheer generosity of scale, this is again one place where the services of a guide are worthwhile. Hire one through your hotel or the central tourism office.

Lodi and Mathura Rd. ✆ 011/2435-5275. Rs 250 ($6.10/£3.10); Rs 25 (60¢/30p) video. Daily sunrise–sunset.

The National Museum ✿✿　Okay, so this museum boasts 150,000 pieces covering some 5 millennia, but it is frustratingly hard for the layperson to traverse these hallowed corridors, some of which lie boarded up and empty, and all of which have displays with little or no information. That said, you can still find gems, like the **12th-century statue** of the cosmic dance of Lord Shiva (South Indian bronzes), which is almost an Indian archetype; and the truly wonderful collection of **miniature paintings**—this is one area (second floor) where you could easily spend a few hours. And if you have any interest in history, the sheer antiquity of many of the pieces will amaze you—here lies the country's finest collection of Indus Valley relics (ca. 2700 B.C.), as well as those garnered from central Asia's "Silk Route," but again very little is displayed in an accessible manner. It takes time and effort (and preferably a guide) to appreciate the wealth of history that lies throughout the 30-odd galleries spread over three floors. If your visit coincides with one of the free tours offered, join in for a bit.

Corner of Janpath and Rajpath. ✆ 011/2301-9272. Rs 150 ($3.65/£1.85). Tues–Sun 10am–5pm.

New Delhi's Imperial Architecture ✿✿✿　Nehru wrote that "New Delhi is the visible symbol of British power, with all its ostentation and wasteful extravagance," but no one with any design interest fails to be impressed by the sheer scale and beauty of these buildings and the subtle blending of Indian influence on an otherwise stripped-down Western classicism—a far cry from the ornate Indo-Saracenic style so deplored by chief architect Sir Edwin Lutyens. Lutyens, known for his racist views, in fact despised all Indian architecture (he conveniently convinced himself that the Taj was actually the work of an Italian designer), but he was forced to include some "native" elements in his designs. Clearly, at first glance the Lutyens buildings of Central Delhi are symbols of imperial power intended to utterly dwarf and humble the individual, yet the Indian influences, such as the neo-Buddhist dome, tiny helmetlike *chattris* (cenotaphs), and filigree stonework, add a great deal to their stately beauty. Once the home of the viceroy of India, **Rashtrapati Bhavan** is today the official residence of the president of India and is closed to the public (though the Mughal Gardens, spread over 5.2 magnificent hectares [13 acres] and among the best in India, are open to the public Feb 14–Mar 14). It's worth noting that this is the largest residence of any president on earth, with over 350 rooms (the White House has a mere 132). Do take note of the slender 145 foot Jaipur Column near the entrance gates; donated by the Maharaja of Jaipur, it is topped by a bronze lotus and six-pointed glass star. The two Secretariat buildings, designed by Sir Herbert Baker, show a similar subtle blend of colonial and Mughal influences and today house the Ministry of Home Affairs and the Home and Finance ministries. Northeast, at the end of Sansad Marg, is Sansad Bhavan (Parliament House), also designed by Baker, from where the country is managed (or not, as Booker Prize–winner Arundhati Roy argues so succinctly in *The Algebra of Injustice*—a recommended but somewhat depressing read). Take a drive around the roads that lie just south of here (Krishna Menon Marg, for instance) to view the lovely bungalows, also designed by Lutyens, that line the tree-lined avenues.

The Crafts Museum ⊛

If you plan to shop for crafts in India, this serves as an excellent introduction to what's out there, though when it comes to the antiques, like the 200-year-old life-size Bhuta figures from Karnataka or the Charrake bowls from Kerala, picking up anything nearly as beautiful is akin to winning a lottery. Some 20,000 artifacts—some more art than craft—are housed in five separate galleries, showcasing the creativity that has thrived here for centuries, not to mention the numerous ways in which it's expressed, depending on where you travel. The **Crafts Museum Shop** is also worth your time, at the very least to again familiarize yourself with the best crafts and textiles, and there are live demonstrations by artisans.

Bhairon Rd., Pragati Maidan. © 011/2337-1641. Free admission. Tues–Sun 10am–5pm. Closed July–Sept.

Hazrat Nizamuddin Aulia ⊛

Originally built in 1325, but added to during the following 2 centuries, the tomb of the saint Sheikh Nizamuddin Aulia (along with a few prominent others, including the favorite daughter of Shah Jahan) is one of the holiest Muslim pilgrimages in India. It is certainly one of Delhi's most fascinating attractions, not least because the only way to get here is to traverse the tiny, narrow medieval lanes of old Nizamuddin on foot. The entire experience will transport you back even further than a foray into Shahjahanabad. This is not for the fainthearted (or perhaps the recently arrived), however—the lanes are claustrophobic, you will be hassled by hawkers (perhaps best to purchase some flowers as a sign of your good intentions upfront), and the smells are almost as assaulting as the hawkers who bar your way. Once there, you may be pressured into making a heftier donation than is necessary (Rs 50/$1.25/65p is fair). This would in fact be a three-star attraction if it weren't for the sense that outsiders are not really welcome (though many report otherwise)—note that the main structure is a mosque, Jam-at Khana Masjid, off limits to women. Best to dress decorously (women should consider covering their heads), pick up some flowers along the way, get here on a Thursday evening when *qawwals* gather to sing the most spiritually evocative devotional songs, take a seat, and soak up the medieval atmosphere.

Nizamuddin. 6km (3¾ miles) south of Connaught Place. Donation expected.

SOUTH DELHI

Delhi's sprawling suburbs keep expanding southward, impervious of the remnants of the ancient cities they surround. Die-hard historians may feel impelled to visit the ruins of **Siri** (the second city), **Tughlaqabad** (the third), and **Jahanpanah** (the fourth), but the principal attraction here is the **Qutb Complex** (see below), built in the area that comprised the first city of Delhi. Located in Mehrauli Archaeological Park, it has a number of historic sites centered around the Dargah of Qutb Sahib, as well as a number of cafes and boutiques frequented by Delhi's well-heeled.

Nearby is **Hauz Khas** on the Delhi–Mehrauli road. Once a village, Haus Khas is now a gentrified upmarket suburb known more for its glossy boutiques and restaurants

Delhi's Spiritual Disneyland

Already a landmark, Delhi's youngest attraction is the modern-era pilgrimage center **Akshardam**. This temple and cultural complex rises from the banks of the Yamuna River in east Delhi, surrounded by landscaped lawns and an air of civility. Supposedly, visitors come here to worship—largely in the main temple, expectedly splendid in white marble and pink sandstone, and borne on the shoulders of 149 life-size stone elephants; ornate pillars and domes, thousands of sculpted idols, and a 3.3m (11-ft.) gold-plated version of Swaminarayan give the place an air of spiritual decadence. At a cost of $50 million, the modern architectural landmark took 5 years to complete, involving the efforts of some 11,000 artisans and craftsmen who toiled for an estimated 300 million man hours. And in a tribute to Disney-style theme parks, visitors can take a boat ride through key moments of Indian cultural and religious history. But one can only speculate at the significance of the attached shopping complex and IMAX theater. Akshardam is open Tuesday to Sunday 9am to 6pm; temple entry is free, but there's a fee (Rs 125/$3.05/£1.55) for exhibitions and to see the ecclesiastical feature film on the life of Lord Satyanarayan.

than for its 14th-century reservoir and ruins, including the **tomb of Feroze Shah Tughlaq** (Rs 100/$2.45/£1.25). If you happen to have a train fetish (although just traveling by train on India will probably sort that out), you shouldn't miss **The National Railway Museum** (✆ 011/2688-1816; Rs 10/25¢/15p; Tues–Sun 9:30am–7:30pm, closes 5pm in winter), said to be one of the world's most impressive—hardly surprising given India's huge network. You can ogle all kinds of saloon cars and locomotives, and even swoon at models trains and railway maps of yore. It is situated southwest of Lodi Gardens, on Chanakyapuri.

If you've traveled this far south, why not head a little east to the **Bahá'i House of Worship**, or "Lotus Temple," where 27 huge and beautiful marble "petals" create the lotus-shaped dome. Often likened to a miniversion of the Sydney Opera House, this contemporary temple invites people of all faiths for worship. It's sometimes described as a modern counterpoint to the Taj, but unlike the Taj, it's more photogenic than it appears in real life, with a lack of detailing and a drab interior (Kalkaji; ✆ 011/2644-4029; Apr–Oct Tues–Sun 9am–7pm, Nov–Mar Tues–Sun 9:30am–5:30pm).

Qutb Complex ⋆⋆⋆ Originally built by Qutbuddin Aibak, first of the Delhi Sultanates who were to rule for some 4 centuries, the complex surrounds Qutb Minar, the sandstone Victory Tower that he started in 1193. The Minar was added to by his successor, Iltutmish (whose tomb lies in one corner); and the topmost stories, reaching 70m (230 ft.), were built in 1368 by Feroze Shah Tughlag. It is remarkably well preserved, and photographs don't really do the tower justice—not in scale, nor in the detail of its carving. The surrounding buildings show some of the earliest Islamic construction techniques used in India, as well as the first mingling of Islamic and Hindu decorative styles—Koranic texts are inscribed in the Minar and Alai Darwaza (old gateway), while Hindu motifs embellish the pillars of Quwwat-ul-Islam ("Might of Islam") mosque. The iron pillar in the courtyard dates back to the 4th century.

Aurobindo Marg, near Mehrauli. 15km (9⅓ miles) south of Connaught Place. Rs 250 ($6.10/£3.10); Rs 25 (60¢/30p) video. Daily sunrise–sunset.

WHERE TO STAY

The capital draws countless diplomats and businesspeople, which in turn has led to a thriving (and ridiculously pricey) five-star accommodations sector, meaning that you'll probably need to dig a little deeper in your pockets if you want a certain level of luxury—not a bad idea if this is your first stop in India. Although a five-star hotel may serve as a gentle introduction to India, most are bland reproductions of what you can expect anywhere in the world, and some are downright hideous despite the hefty price tags. While big luxury hotels are more numerous than we need to mention, there are a few very special options for travelers looking for affordability, style, and something out of the ordinary. We've long acknowledged the innovations offered by **Master Paying Residential Guest Accommodation** (reviewed below), the best place by far to stay if you're watching your rupees and would like to live among charming Delhiites. A small chain of slightly more formal guesthouses, **Amarya Haveli** and **Amarya Gardens,** is owned and operated by a pair of Frenchmen; these stylish digs are truly in a league of their own, and reviewed below. Two more to consider seriously are **Oberoi Maidens,** Delhi's oldest hotel, and **The Manor,** the city's first boutique-style option; both offer an alternative to the anonymous atmosphere of larger hotels, not to mention great value.

With so much parity in the top-end market, our hands-down recommendation is **The Imperial,** a classy hotel with an authentic colonial old-world atmosphere, friendly staff, superb restaurants, and the most central location (it's walking distance to Connaught Place); the only drawback is the temperamental approach to honoring reservations. More of a brand, but still the ultimate in luxury, **The Oberoi** has the most lavishly cozy rooms of all the top-end hotels in Delhi, but you'll shell out for the privilege. It's worth checking the going rate at **Hyatt Regency,** which is not as conveniently located as either of these but operates a daily rate, so you never know what special deal you might strike. Another unadventurous big hotel option, which is a resounding favorite with foreigners (including Bill Clinton), is the **ITC Maurya Sheraton Hotel and Towers** ☆☆ (☏ **011/2611-2233;** www.welcomgroup.com; from $500/£250 double). Its location in the diplomatic sector and the expensive rooms are major drawbacks, but foodies will enjoy easy access to Bukhara, widely considered the best restaurant in the country (see "Where to Dine," below). Note, too, that there is now a second Sheraton property in south Delhi (Sheraton New Delhi Hotel, District Centre, Saket; ☏ **011/4266-1122**), with typically sumptuous rooms starting at a far more affordable $300 (£150).

Note that if you're literally in transit, the **Radisson** ☆ (National Highway 8, New Delhi 110 037; ☏ **011/2677-9191;** fax 011/2677-9090; www.radisson.com) is your best bet near the airport. It's perched on the edge of a major highway, but guest rooms (from $265/£133) are large and sumptuous, with contemporary furnishings and king-size beds. Ask for a pool- or garden-facing unit.

Note: The prices below are sometimes given in rupees, with U.S. dollar conversions; others are stated in U.S. dollars only, which is how many hotels targeting foreign markets quote their rates.

NEW DELHI
Very Expensive
Claridges ☆   With over half a century behind it, this elegant hotel—in an upmarket residential neighborhood, convenient to many Central Delhi sights—retains some of its authentic old-fashioned charm and period sophistication. Renovations in recent

years have been met with several steep jumps in price, which is pretty much in keeping with the trend in all the five-star options, but it's nowhere nearly as expensive—or as impressive—as The Imperial (reviewed below). Accommodations are a very mixed bag, and you'll pay according to the relative level of comfort and aesthetic appeal you enjoy. The cheapest accommodations are in the Premium Wing, while Deluxe Wing rooms are more elegant and considered. Claridges rooms in both wings have private balconies and a more sumptuous look. More expensive still, are the Club suites; these are chic and contemporary, with wooden floors and muted tones, and they're designed with business travelers in mind (bedside control panels, interactive computer technology via plasma TVs); nos. 128 and 228 face the central pool. When you book, indicate whether you want a slightly antique or swish, modern look to your room. Claridges may not offer the same posh luxury as the city's overrepresented Western chains, but in many ways you'll find better comfort in the smart, down-to-earth restaurants and watering holes that feature highly on the local social barometer. **Dhaba** is the Punjabi restaurant, done up like a roadside truck stop; it serves a refined, hygienic version of the simple, tasty food found along North India's busy highways, and **Sevilla** is a new semi-alfresco Mediterranean restaurant under a canopy of trees and thatch; the attached vodka bar is sublime.

12 Aurangzeb Rd., New Delhi 110 011. ☎ **011/4133-5133**. Fax 011/2301-0625. www.claridges.com. info@claridges.com. 129 units. Premium Wing: $350 (£175) deluxe double, $380 (£190) Claridges Room double, $450 (£225) Club double; Deluxe Wing: $380 (£190) deluxe double, $410 (£205) Claridges Room double, $500 (£250) Club double; $800–$1,500 (£400–£750) suite; $60 (£30) extra bed. Taxes extra. AE, DC, MC, V. **Amenities:** 4 restaurants; 2 bars; tea lounge; patisserie; pool; kiddies' pool; health club; gym; spa; sauna; steam; travel agency; car hire; business center; shopping arcade; salon; 24-hr. room service; babysitting; laundry; dry cleaning; doctor-on-call; currency exchange; Wi-Fi enabled. *In room:* A/C, TV, minibar, hair dryer, iron on request, electronic safe, Internet, scale, DVD on request.

The Imperial 🏵🏵🏵   This gracious establishment (built in 1931) is the best hotel in Delhi—certainly for anyone wanting something a little more atmospheric than any chain, no matter how luxurious, can hope to offer. Only at The Imperial can you recover from your jet lag in luxury while experiencing something of the elegance of colonial-era Delhi—without even setting foot out of the lobby. It's also incredibly convenient (only a short stroll to Connaught Place) yet tranquil (it has one of the deepest, largest pools in Delhi). It's comfortable as well, having undergone a major renovation that left the Raj-era atmosphere untouched but loaded with every amenity you'd expect from a five-star hotel. Spacious guest rooms (no need for a suite; opt for an Imperial or Heritage Room) with wonderfully high ceilings are furnished in colonial-era elegance. However, it is the public areas, like the double-volume colonnaded veranda and grand 1911 bar, that are a sheer delight—huge, elegant (it's a word that tends to crop up whenever you try to describe The Imperial), and everywhere a showcase of Delhi's imperial past. A huge collection of original art adorns every corridor (a veritable museum of 18th- and 19th-century art, which you can explore with the resident curator). Silver-service breakfasts are among the best in the world. Despite all this praise for what we've ranked as one of the most dignified and perfect places in Delhi, and even the world, we're sad to report that this award-winning hotel may have taken to resting on its laurels; not only have we heard horror stories of fudged reservations (legitimately booked guests being turned onto the streets midstay—with staff arriving at the rooms to "help pack"), but we've had little joy in our own attempts to book without the aid of an agent.

1 Janpath, New Delhi 110 001. ☎ **011/2334-1234** or 011/4150-1234 Fax 011/2334-2255. www.theimperialindia.com. luxury@theimperialhotel.com. 231 units. $550 (£275) Imperial double; $600 (£300) Heritage double;

$750–$4,200 (£378–£2,117) suite; $75–$150 (£38–£75) extra bed. AE, DC, MC, V. **Amenities:** 5 restaurants; 2 bars; pastry shop; pool; fitness center; concierge; travel desk; car hire; boutique; gift store; bookshop; salon; 24-hr. room service; babysitting; laundry; doctor-on-call; Thomas Cook currency exchange; Wi-Fi enabled; valet; art gallery. *In room:* A/C, TV, dataport, fax machine (on request), minibar, tea- and coffee-making facilities or butler service, hair dryer, electronic safe, scale, DVD player (all except Imperial Rooms).

The Oberoi ✸✸✸   If you like being treated with the reverence of a celebrity, this is the place to stay—just ask Harrison Ford, Mick Jagger, Nelson Mandela, and Salman Rushdie. Even if you're not a star, staff is trained to genuflect—a typical characteristic of all the Oberoi hotels. Service aside, the hotel's location—east of the Lodi Gardens (near Humayun's Tomb) and surrounded by the green oasis of Delhi's golf course—makes for tranquillity, although, considering the heady buzz in the lobby and even in the popular coffee shop, **Threesixtydegrees,** you need to be in your room, sheltered downstairs in the spa, or at the pool to really escape it all. The carpeted guest rooms are richly textured, with upholstered carved wood furniture and bright pink scatter cushions offset with pale floral and paisley fabrics; walls feature artworks illustrating the rich variety of Indian culture. Bathrooms are unexpectedly small, but are impeccably decked out with top-notch fittings. The higher up your room, the better the view; odd-numbered rooms look towards Humayun's Tomb. The massive deluxe suites have private balconies, timber floors with rugs, large bathrooms with Jacuzzi tubs and bidets, cabinets with decorative inlay, and two-poster beds; executive suites are similarly lovely but more compact and not quite as lavish. Guest rooms on the top four floors not only have the benefit of excellent views, but also DVD players, complimentary breakfast, and free airport transfers.

Dr. Zakir Hussain Marg, New Delhi 110 003. (**✆** 011/2436-3030. Fax 011/2436-0484. www.oberoihotels.com. reservations@oberoidel.com. 300 units. $425 (£213) deluxe double; $525 (£263) premiere double; $600 (£300) luxury double; $700 (£350) executive suite; $900 (£450) special executive suite; $1,200 (£600) deluxe suite; $1,700–$4,500 (£850–£2,250) luxury suite. Rates include breakfast. Deluxe rooms and suites include airport transfers. Taxes extra. AE, DC, MC, V. **Amenities:** 4 restaurants; bar; *enoteca* (wine bar); patisserie; pool; health club; spa; concierge; travel desk; car hire; limousine service; shopping arcade; bookshop; salon; 24-hr. room service; babysitting; laundry; dry cleaning; doctor-on-call; Wi-Fi enabled; valet. *In room:* A/C, TV, fax machine (except 1st floor), minibar, tea- and coffee-making facilities or butler service, hair dryer, electronic safe, wireless Internet, scale. Deluxe rooms and suites have DVD player.

Shangri-La Hotel ✸✸   This late-2005 addition to Delhi's five-star high-rise hotel scene still gleams with polished marble and sparkling chandeliers, giving it the advantage of freshness, evident not only in the pleasant, contemporary design (which makes good use of space and light) but also in the demeanor of the staff. There's a lively buzz almost everywhere in the hotel, making it seem less pretentious than some of the city's more established luxury hotels. Most guest rooms enjoy great views of the city; the higher up you go, the more intriguing the city scene through the window—ask for a "Parliament View" if you'd like to see a greener Delhi. Deluxe rooms start on the 12th floor; they're carpeted and dressed in earthy tones, and feel spacious compared to that of many other large city hotels. Horizon rooms are on higher (17th and 18th) floors and are priciest, but come with a host of amenities, including access to the 19th-floor lounge, airport pickup, breakfast, and cocktail hour. What we like best here is probably the gorgeous pan-Asian restaurant, **19 Oriental Avenue,** which is not only beautiful to look at, but features two live kitchens and hard-working kimono-clad waitresses. Outdoor areas, although small, include a fabulous pool surrounded by trees.

19 Ashoka Rd., Connaught Place, New Delhi 110 001. (**✆** 011/4119-1919. Fax 011/4119-1988. www.shangri-la.com. slnd@shangri-la.com. 320 units. $425 (£213) superior double; $465 (£233) deluxe double; $495 (£248) premiere double; $525 (£263) Horizon superior double; $565 (£283) Horizon premiere double; $900–$2,000 (£450–£1,000) suite;

$40 (£20) extra bed. Taxes extra. AE, DC, MC, V. **Amenities:** 2 restaurants; bar; lobby lounge-bar; pastry shop; pool; health club; spa; indoor and outdoor Jacuzzis; steam; sauna; travel services; limousine service; business center; shopping arcade; salon; 24-hr. room service; Ayurvedic massage; babysitting; laundry; doctor-on-call. *In room:* A/C, TV, minibar, tea- and coffee-making facilities, hair dryer, iron and ironing board, safe, Internet.

Taj Mahal Hotel 🦋🦋   Listed among *Travel & Leisure's* World's Best in 2006, this opulent, slightly brash hotel is not quite so massively over the top or as overwhelming as its older sister, the Taj Palace Hotel, but it does have an exciting atmosphere and a range of super-efficient amenities. Its major drawing card, however, is the high esteem in which it is held locally—this is one of the best places to watch the Delhi glitterati at play and work. Capped by *zardozi* domes, the carefully decorated lobby sees a variety of beautiful models and high-powered execs swishing in and out the front door. Not only that, but it's hosted the world's elite: Bill Gates, Tony Blair, Kofi Annan, the Aga Khan, and the Prince of Wales have all ended up here. Despite wonderful service and every amenity you could wish for, guest rooms are unexceptional, designed more for efficiency and all-round comfort than to keep you staring at the walls (or boxed in the little bathrooms). No matter: After a day's sightseeing, head for the pool, where you can watch as raptors cut their way through a darkening sky, or chill out in the spa before dressing up for a night of martinis at **Rick's,** Delhi's best bar. You can splurge on a luxurious room on the Taj Club floor, where you'll enjoy a dedicated check-in (the alternative in hotels this size can be tiresome) after being fetched from the airport in a limousine, but at this price you may as well consider The Oberoi. Slightly cheaper, the **Taj Palace Hotel** 🦋 (ⓒ 011/ 2611-0202; www.tajhotels.com; doubles from $425/£214) pulsates with the energy of Delhi's bourgeoisie; at night it becomes a haven for see-and-be-seen weddings and gigantic corporate functions. The Western-style deluxe guest rooms are large and overlook the pool. Unfortunately, all the high-end social functions seem to have had a negative impact on service (this hotel has the longest checkout line in Delhi), and the location in the Diplomatic Enclave is a drawback.

Number One Mansingh Rd., New Delhi 110 011. ⓒ **011/2302-6162.** Fax 011/2302-6070. www.tajhotels.com. mahal.delhi@tajhotels.com. 296 units. $440 (£220) superior double; $510 (£255) deluxe double; $625 (£313) Taj Club double (includes breakfast, limousine airport transfers, valet, and cocktail hour); $1,400–$6,000 (£700–£3,000) suite. Taxes extra. AE, DC, MC, V. **Amenities:** 5 restaurants; bar; pool; health club; spa and gym; yoga; concierge; travel desk; car hire; shopping arcade; bookshop; florist; salon; 24-hr. room service; babysitting; doctor-on-call; DVD and CD library; wireless Internet; currency exchange. *In room:* A/C, TV, fax machine (all except superior), Wi-Fi, minibar, tea- and coffee-making facilities, electronic safe.

Expensive
The Ambassador Hotel 🦋   Not far from Lodi Gardens and Humayun's Tomb, and practically next door to Khan Market, this hotel—operating since 1945—has an old-fashioned edge, with plenty of wood paneling and understated luxury. The bright lobby is usually incense-scented, providing a fragrant welcome when you return from sightseeing. It's not particularly elegant, and you might find standard guest rooms small and cluttered, but you'll be pleased with the old-world ambience and good value. Our recommendation is to book a superior guest room (only $25/£13 extra), where French doors open onto private balconies (not that there's all that much to see). The bathrooms are large and enjoy natural light. Also a pretty good value are the suite-size executive rooms, where a sliding door divides the bedroom from the comfortably furnished sitting room; sadly, the original Victorian fireplaces are now used for potted plants. Buffet breakfasts are taken in the bright, laid-back **Yellow Brick Road** coffee shop, which has an outdoor section that can be lovely in the morning (get there ahead of the crowds); nearby is the newly added pool. Less opulent and grandiose than some

of the other upmarket hotels in town, this is a comfortable alternative with less formal but pleasant service.

Sujan Singh Park, Cornwallis Rd., New Delhi 110 003. © **011/2463-2600.** Fax 011/2463-8219. www.tajhotels.com. ambassador.delhi@tajhotels.com. 88 units. $240 (£120) standard double; $265 (£133) superior double; $290 (£145) executive double; $325 (£163) deluxe suite; $15 (£8) extra bed. Taxes extra. AE, DC, MC, V. **Amenities:** 2 restaurants; bar; pool; spa (at Taj Mahal hotel); travel desk; bookshop; shopping arcade; salon; 24-hr. room service; babysitting; doctor-on-call; currency exchange; Wi-Fi enabled. *In room:* A/C, TV, minibar, tea- and coffee-making facilities, iron and hair dryer on request, scale (except standard).

The Manor ⟨☆☆⟩   If you favor the trend toward intimate, boutique-style hotels, this is a preeminently classy option situated in Friends Colony, a smart residential quarter in the southwestern part of New Delhi. The Manor has been featured in a number of design books and magazines like *Tatler* and *Condé Nast Traveler.* It may not be within walking distance of any attractions, but the neighborhood provides a wonderful respite from the madness and traffic of the city; it's also where you'll most likely meet a refined social elite, either in one of the many restaurant spots nearby (ask for recommendations) or at the local Friends Club (entry to which your host should be able to organize). Guest rooms have a smart, contemporary look; units on the ground floor have private terraces. This is really one of the most elegant (all muted colors) and contemporary (a great mix of materials like silk, terrazzo, onyx, and granite) options in Delhi, with pleasing designer furnishings, yet without any over-the-top opulence; it's simply a lovely, relaxing, and friendly place to experience Delhi at it's most hassle-free (management will attend to any and all travel and transport needs, leaving you to get on with the business of enjoying your vacation). The Manor also has a fabulous chef, and the little restaurant, **"77",** has quite a reputation about town. Service is gracious, with an intimate atmosphere unmatched by the larger city hotels. Besides the soothing terrace and lawn (lit up with lanterns at night), there are promises of the imminent relaunch of the in-house swimming pool, and a spa is on the cards for 2008.

77 Friends Colony (West), New Delhi 110 065. © **011/2692-5151** or -7510. Fax 011/2692-2299. www.themanor delhi.com. info@themanordelhi.com. 12 units. $225 (£113) standard double; $350 (£175) suite; $450 (£227) Manor suite; $50 (£25) extra bed. Rates include breakfast and transfers. Taxes and service charge extra. AE, DC, MC, V. **Amenities:** Restaurant; bar; pool (expected soon); concierge; travel and car hire service; 24-hr. room service; laundry; doctor-on-call. *In room:* A/C, TV, minibar, high-speed Internet, DVD (selection of movies available).

The Park ⟨☆☆⟩   Fabulous and fun, the colorful Park has set its aspirations high and gone against the grain of smart and serious luxury so idolized by Delhi's other five-star properties. With its recent chichi designer makeover that extends from the cool drama of the prettily festooned lobby, to the ultra-trendy restaurants and bar, and right into the elegant, lovely guest rooms, it's certainly a hotel that keeps people talking. Accommodations really are gorgeous; even the standard "luxury" rooms have wooden floors, designer light fittings, plush 10-inch mattresses, and delectable white linens accented with flashes of color (which varies according to the floor you're on); a frosted glass sliding door leads to an intelligently designed little bathroom (shower only), and all rooms have bathrobes *and* kimonos to help you feel that much more pampered. If you require a tub, book a "luxury premium" room, which is enormous. Because of the curved shape of the hotel, guest rooms vary in size somewhat: The largest are at the corners of each floor—request these specifically. The "Residence" on the 9th and 10th floors are club rooms with access to a library and special lounge overlooking the Jantar Mantar; these rooms are even more aesthetically pleasing, with a host of extra amenities (a docking station for your complimentary iPod, remote-controlled curtains, bedside electronic console) to make you feel special; there are also Jacuzzis and TVs in the sumptuous bathrooms. For indulgences, there's a full spa; and there's often a party in and around the funky pool, which not only has a bar but a net—so guests can play water volleyball—and a giant mirror ball to remind them that they're on holiday! This is probably our favorite chain hotel in its price range, with enough hard-working visual fabulousness to make up for disconcertingly poor service.

15 Parliament St., New Delhi 110 001. ℭ **011/2374-3000.** Fax 011/2373-4400. www.theparkhotels.com. resv.del@ theparkhotels.com. 220 units. $350 (£175) luxury double; $385 (£193) premium double; $450 (£225) Residence double; $600 (£300) deluxe suite; $1,200 (£600) presidential suite. Rates include breakfast. Premium and Residence units, and suites, include airport transfers. Taxes extra. AE, DC, MC, V. **Amenities:** 3 restaurants; 2 bars; pool; health club; gym; spa; sauna; steam; travel desk; confectionery shop; gift shop; salon; 24-hr. room service; massage; babysitting; laundry; doctor-on-call; wireless Internet; library of DVDs and CDs. *In room:* A/C, TV, dataport, minibar, hair dryer, electronic safe, DVD. Residence rooms and suites include iPod, laptop on request.

Moderate

Ahuja Residency ❀ Situated adjacent to a park in Golf Links, the most expensive residential area in Delhi, this family-run hotel offers reasonable comfort, a peaceful retreat from the city, and well-meaning service. The owners also spend good money to maintain standards and upgrade facilities regularly; the most recent face-lift was in 2007, so if you prefer a more intimate lodging experience and can't quite afford to stay at Amarya (or, more likely, can't get a reservation there), Ahuja is certainly worth considering, not least because of the relative comfort of the rooms (particularly when compared with similarly priced options like La Sagrita Tourist Home and the awful 27 Jor Bagh). Guest rooms are done out in pale tones with earthy accents; floors are tiled with rugs, and there are armchairs and a small desk; try to reserve no. 12, a slightly larger-than-average corner unit, or fork out on no. 13, recently converted to a suite. You may find mattresses a trifle soft, but cool white linens make up for this. There is only one room with a tub (instead of the standard drench shower). Guests tend to make a beeline for the lovely terrace overlooking the park and the neat little lawn out front. There's a quaint country-style dining room for homey Indian meals. The Ahuja family also offers serviced apartments and has an alternative guesthouse in Defence Colony.

193 Golf Links, New Delhi 110 003. ℭ **011/2461-1027.** Fax 011/2464-9008. www.ahujaresidency.com. info@ahuja residency.com. 12 units. Rs 2,800 ($68/£35) double. AE, DC, MC, V. **Amenities:** Dining room; travel and transport assistance; transfers; limited room service; laundry; doctor-on-call; Internet. *In room:* A/C, TV, minibar, tea- and coffee-making facility.

Amarya Haveli & Amarya Gardens ❀❀ Alexandre Lieury and Mathieu Chanard are the visionary young Frenchmen behind two delightful Delhi guesthouses, resetting the bar for affordable comfort in a city that has long been the preserve of five-star anonymity and backpacker drudgery. Here are exclusive lodgings that combine eye-catching style with useful amenities. Besides offering boutique-style luxury and a great sense of intimacy, these low-key glamour pads are spaces where guests can really ease into a gentler, more refined take on this chaotic, bustling city. **Amarya Haveli** is in Hauz Khas and has six beautifully decorated en-suite bedrooms, each inspired by a different region of India; these spaces are refreshing and original, with fabulous textures, striking colors, smart finishes, and luxurious fabrics, all tied together in a timeless integration of traditional and contemporary. Come evening, guests gather on the rooftop terrace under a pink and orange canopy or hang out in the beautiful lounge with its rugs, antique furniture, objets d'art, fresh flowers, and bright silken cushions. At **Amarya Gardens,** a little farther south in a wonderfully transformed Defence

Colony mansion, there are even fewer rooms (including two suites), each big and airy, and a cheerful, tree-shaded garden. The signature here is the magnificent use of white, outside and in, offset by Alex and Mathieu's obvious love of dashing colors. Here, you can enjoy meals in the garden or sip cocktails in the gorgeous chandeliered lounge. The Amarya properties are a real find in a city that is often quite standoffish: Sublime, sexy, and characterful, they're artful enough to be destinations in themselves. The only potential drawback is that your hosts are not native Delhiites, but that may just mean that they're the perfect eyes through which to encounter the city for the first time.

Haveli: P-5 Hauz Khas Enclave, near Safdarjung Dev. Area, New Delhi 110 016. ✆ 011/4175-9268. Fax 011/4265-1106. 6 Units. Rs 6,200 ($151/£77) double; Rs 1,000 ($24/£12) extra bed. **Gardens:** C 179 Defence Colony, New Delhi 110 024. ✆ 011/4656-2735. Fax 011/4656-2734. www.amaryagroup.com. amaryahaveli@hotmail.com. 4 units. Rs 7,800 ($190/£96) deluxe double; Rs 8,800 ($215/£109) master suite. Rates include breakfast. AE, MC, V. **Amenities:** Lounge; bar; spa treatments; travel and transport assistance; transfers; business center; 24-hr. room service; massage; laundry; doctor-on-call; currency exchange; Internet; rooftop terrace (Haveli); garden terrace (Gardens). *In room:* A/C, TV, wireless Internet.

Delhi Bed and Breakfast   Although it really can't compare with the more afford-able Master Paying Residential Guest Accommodation (reviewed below) in terms of style (and is also a lot farther from Connaught Place), this is an excellent homestay-style option if you prefer to have your own bathroom (shower only), and don't mind being a little way out of the center. Besides a comfortable, homey bedroom (with fresh flow-ers, back-supporting foam mattresses, framed artworks, and plenty of cupboard space) and the option of regular home-cooked meals (served in a tiny family dining room, microwave lurking in the background), you'll have access to the advice, assistance, and lively repartee of your enthusiastic host, Sheikh Pervez Hameed, who can hook you up with quality guides, the best taxis in town, and all sorts of tours and experiences; his wife, Lubna, will even take you shopping. Your hosts have Bollywood DVDs for you to watch, and they'll probably join you in the living room as you experience the Sur-round Sound through their supersize speakers. It's essential to know that you're not just coming here to stay, but to receive fairly hands-on attention from a vibrant family as eager to learn from you as you are from them. Bear in mind that you'll be in a fairly busy neighborhood: The sounds of the traffic are never far away (no fear of oversleep-ing here), and a nearby commercial center has dozens of restaurants and bars. But you get to live like a pampered local: You could have the family barber summoned to give you a trim or escape to a plant-dappled terrace and meditate on suburbia. At press time, Pervez was planning to convert a rooftop space into a guest room with a private "gar-den" sit-out area; ask for this if you crave a little extra privacy.

A-6, Friends Colony East, Delhi 110 065. ✆ 98-1105-7103. Fax 011/2691-3201. www.delhibedandbreakfast.com. delhibedandbreakfast@gmail.com. 4 units. Rs 3,550 ($87/£44) double; Rs 1,250 ($31/£15) extra bed. Rate includes breakfast. No credit cards. **Amenities:** Dining room; travel and transport assistance; transfers; massage and certain beauty treatments on request; laundry; doctor-on-call; wireless Internet; TV lounge; cooking lessons; mobile phone hire. *In room:* A/C.

The Hans Hotel   Staff at this small hotel, conveniently located near Connaught Place, are wonderfully friendly and enthusiastic, which is a major draw, particularly after expe-riencing the horror of the building's revolting facade (the hotel occupies only the ground and upper floors of some sort of office block). Inside, things have recently been spruced up quite dramatically, with a modern makeover in shades of brown against white mar-ble floors working to create a vaguely contemporary look, underscored by lounge music filling the lobby. Guest rooms vary quite a bit: Ask for a deluxe unit on the 16th or 19th floor and you'll enjoy a king-size bed with a firm, comfortable mattress and old-fashioned sofas set on marble floors—all very neat, clean, and unexceptional; ask for an executive room on the 17th or 18th floor, and you'll have a decent wood-floor room with larger windows, but not the same good bed or furniture. Like practically every hotel in Delhi, The Hans was, at press time, introducing "Club Rooms," here located on the top floor, with great views. The rooftop restaurant and bar afford grand views of the city.

15 Barakhamba Rd., Connaught Place, New Delhi. ℭ 011/2331-6861 through -6870. Fax 011/2331-4830. www. hanshotels.com. 80 units. $170 (£85) executive double; $200 (£100) deluxe double; $250 (£125) Club room; $250 (£125) suite. Rates include breakfast. Some rates include transfers. Taxes extra. AE, DC, MC, V. **Amenities:** 2 restaurants; bar; travel assistance; 24-hr. room service; babysitting; laundry; dry cleaning; doctor-on-call; currency exchange. *In room:* A/C, TV, dataport, minibar, tea- and coffee-making facility, hair dryer, iron on request, electronic safe, magnifying mirror, scale.

Hotel Palace Heights *(Value*   Considering its location in the very heart of Connaught Place and just a 2-minute walk to the Rajiv Chowk Metro station, this contemporary upgrade of a former hovel (under the same name but different ownership for 50 years) is a real find. Two things: It is not a palace, and the only sense of height you'll get is the view from either the restaurant or the rooftop terrace, from where you can watch the mayhem on the street below or the fairly ugly urban scene created by the surrounding Connaught Place buildings. Accommodations, which occupy a single floor, have been entirely refurbished in a modern, clean aesthetic: wall-mounted plasma TVs, small marble bathrooms with glass-walled showers, and fairly comfortable mattresses, all packaged in a neutral, pleasing palette. Windows, thankfully, have both blinds and curtains to keep out the unsightly "view" of adjacent premises (and double glazing to keep out the noise). While it's not a place to be if you need dozens of amenities and space to roam, you can rest assured that the manager, Mr. Mahipal Singh Rawat, goes beyond the call of duty to assist guests and make them feel comfortable and safe. If you're in town with an urgent need to be in a very central location, and don't demand too much from your lodgings, this is a great value.

D 26/28, Connaught Place, New Delhi 110 001. ℭ 011/4358-2610, -2620, or -2630. Fax 011/4358-2640. www. hotelpalaceheights.com. admin@hotelpalaceheights.com. 14 units. Rs 5,000 ($122/£62) double. Rate includes breakfast. Taxes extra. DC, MC, V. **Amenities:** Restaurant; bar; 24-hr. room service; laundry; doctor-on-call. *In room:* A/C, TV, safe, wireless Internet.

Inexpensive

Master Paying Residential Guest Accommodation * (Value*   Staying here is quite simply your best opportunity to discover what "real" Delhiites are all about: sophisticated, charming, and extremely knowledgeable. Filled with warmth and good taste, the guesthouse is owned and run by Avnish and Urvashi Puri. It's their energy and creative panache that make this a satisfying experience, as amenities are pretty basic. The four modest, beautiful guest rooms occupy the two floors above their home; two rooms are located on the rooftop terrace. All rooms share two sets of immaculately clean bathroom facilities (showers only). You'll find comfortable beds, writing tables, and a carefully sourced objet d'art in each room, while the entire house is decorated with sculpted gods, handicrafts, and artworks. There's an aqua purification system, so you'll shower in cleaner water than the bottled stuff you drink, and an emergency inverter deals with Delhi's unpredictable electricity supply. Hot-water bottles and heaters are provided in winter, and there's air-conditioning when it gets warm. Home-cooked meals are prepared from fresh market ingredients and served in a small dining room—simply order by ringing a bell and jotting down your request. Meals are also served on the rooftop terrace; you'll find a scented garden nook as well as a meditation room cluttered with images of gurus and gods. We highly recommend at least one Reiki session with Urvashi, a master. The guesthouse is a mere 4km (2½ miles) from Connaught Place, but Avnish offers a wonderful "Hidden Delhi" experiential tour through the city, showing you a world never seen by most visitors to Delhi, and he'll unravel Hinduism's spiritual origins in a profoundly logical way. Reserve in advance, and arrange for a pickup if you want to avoid haggling with taxi drivers at the airport; Avnish will also assist with onward transfers. The drawback is that you'll have to book several months in advance, for word of India's gentlest introduction is out.

R-500 New Rajinder Nagar, New Delhi 110 060. (C) **011/2874-1089** or 011/6547-9947 or 011/2874-1914. www.master-guesthouse.com. urvashi@del2.vsnl.net.in. 4 units. Rs 1,995 ($49/£25) double. No credit cards. **Amenities:** Dining room; transport assistance; airport transfers; laundry; Internet access; yoga; meditation; Reiki; sightseeing; excursions; hospital nearby. *In room:* A/C, electronic safe, heater.

SOUTH DELHI

Hyatt Regency *★★*   A persistent buzz around the many public spaces and the city's most contemporary-looking guest rooms mark this as one of the city's most popular hotels, not least because you can at times score a bargain: Room tariffs fluctuate like the stock exchange, so it's always worth checking for daily deals. The hotel is not all that spectacular at first glance: like all the city's big, modern hotels, the exterior is forgettable, and the lobby, with its faint resemblance to a Hindu temple (mirrored panels and vaulted ceilings over rug-covered marble floors), feels dated. Although accommodations have been styled with business travelers in mind, they're constantly updated to keep with the times. They're not huge, but the parquet-wood floors, sleek furnishings, and queen-size beds with lovely white duvets and thick mattresses will certainly make you feel comfortable. The modern bathrooms have glass basins, large walk-in showers, and tubs. When booking, ask for a renovated room, for the most up-to-date room styling, and also consider a slightly more expensive room facing the pool—the so-called "bay rooms" are also a fraction more spacious. Hyatt Regency features the city's most authentic Italian restaurant (don't miss the pizzas here), and the **Polo Bar** is rated one of the city's best after-dark hangouts.

Bhikaji Cama Place, Ring Rd., New Delhi 110 066. (C) **011/2679-1234.** Fax 011/2679-1122. www.delhi.hyatt.com. 508 units. Rates change daily. From Rs 18,000 ($439/£222) double; Rs 22,000 ($537/£272) Regency Club double; suite rates on request. Taxes extra. AE, DC, MC, V. **Amenities:** 4 restaurants; bar; patisserie; pool; 2 tennis courts; fitness club; travel desk; shopping arcade; 24-hr. room service; babysitting; laundry; dry cleaning; doctor-on-call; currency exchange. *In room:* A/C, TV, dataport, minibar, tea- and coffee-making facilities, iron.

NORTH DELHI

Oberoi Maidens *★★* *Value*   This Georgian gem is a little out of the center of Delhi, but it has more character and charm than competitors charging twice its tariff. Operating since 1903, it retains much of its grand architectural ambience, hinting at what it might have been like when Lutyens stayed here while supervising the development of the Raj Bhavan. It's also a great deal quieter than the bigger city hotels, with a smaller staff contingent. Stained-glass windows, thick columns, stately arches, and deep corridors open to huge rooms on one side and small sunlit balconies on the other, all recalling a bygone style. Accommodations have been adequately renovated but are nevertheless still carpeted, have high ceilings, and done out in elegant old-fashioned textiles (paisley bedcovers and striped upholstery). Of the standard ("superior") rooms, no. 105 is a particularly good option, with a second, smaller bedroom, and a large bathroom. It receives plenty of natural light, whereas most rooms have small windows, many of which have been strategically frosted to block unsightly rooftop views. Lovely grounds, with plenty of established trees and shrubs, and a period kidney-shaped pool add further serenity, only disrupted when parties and weddings are hosted here (it's an understandably popular venue for wealthy families). Good news is that the Maidens is just a short stroll from the nearest Metro station, so getting into the city center is a breeze.

7 Sham Nath Marg, Delhi 110 054. ⓒ 011/2397-5464. Toll-free ⓒ 800/11-7070. Fax 011/2389-0595. www.maidens hotel.com. 56 units. $225 (£113) superior double; $275 (£138) executive suite; $325 (£163) deluxe suite. Taxes extra. Check online for good off-season discounts. AE, DC, MC, V. **Amenities:** 2 restaurants; bar; pool; 2 tennis courts; travel assistance; car hire; 24-hr. room service; babysitting; laundry; doctor-on-call; currency exchange. *In room:* A/C, TV, minibar, tea- and coffee-making facility, hair dryer, iron on request, safe, deluxe suites have DVD player.

WHERE TO DINE

Delhi's dining scene is booming, and when you ask locals to name their favorite restaurant, you're sure to get more than a simple response. You'll hear fierce criticism of Bukhara (Delhi's long-reigning restaurant champion) and high praise for some modest hole-in-the-wall. The point is that the culinary revolution is finally in full swing, and it's no longer necessary to hide out in the overpriced hotel eateries for fear of contracting a bellyache or being swindled by fly-by-night "restaurateurs." More likely, you'll experience a dent in your budget if you choose to eat in the hotels, and you'll miss out on a highly recommended opportunity to see where the city's innumerable foodies are feasting these days. To help you make the leap of faith, we're discussing five-star hotel restaurants in a separate box, and hope you'll find your way to at least one of the stand-alone choices we've reviewed below. For many more options (thousands, in fact), you'd do worse than to consult the annual *Times Food Guide,* written by opinionated *Times of India* food critic Sabina Sehgal Saikia; it's available at booksellers and magazine vendors (Rs 100/$2.45/£1.25).

EXPENSIVE

An irritating trend (at least for voyeurs) among the moneyed crowd is to eat at "members only" restaurants. The most popular of these very hip joints is **Oriental Octopus** (Habitat World, India Habitat Centre, Lodhi Rd.; ⓒ **011/2468-2222** or 011/5122-0000, ext. 2512), where you dine at curved, meandering tables shared by gorgeous designer-clad Delhiites—a million miles from the streets of Shahjahanabad. See if your concierge can arrange a reservation, or find a member and tag along. The food isn't bad either—start with Singaporean steamed spring rolls, and move on to Malaysian black-pepper prawns tossed in garlic and crushed pepper. It also has an interesting bargain-priced buffet spread.

Even more irritating (especially for restaurateurs) has been the city's recent clampdown on health and safety regulations, which saw the closure of numerous venues in 2006, usually because of unsound architecture (a problem in some of the city's more ancient structures). In mid-2007, for example, the sublime and wonderful **Olive Bar and Kitchen** ✸✸ (Haveli No. 6-8, One Style Mile, Kalka Das Marg, Mehrauli; ⓒ **011/2664-2552**) had been closed for several months and was awaiting an imminent comeback.

For superb Italian by one of Delhi's most celebrated restaurateurs, Ritu Dalmia (who's also responsible for Vama, in London), try to get a table at **Diva** ✸✸ (M-8, M Block Market, Greater Kailash I; ⓒ **011/2921-5673**), which has drawn countless accolades despite fever-pitch prices. You simply can't go wrong here; any of the seafood starters are recommended, and the lamb chops in red wine are superb.

Ploof ☆ SEAFOOD/ECLECTIC   This is not only an underpublicized Gandhi-clan hangout, but it's also where our dearest Delhiite friends choose to take us when we're in town. It may not be the swishest eatery in town, but it's bright, comfortable, and reliable, and the seafood is always fresh. The biggest drawback here has to be deciding what to have; the menu is notoriously long-winded and draws such diverse inspiration that you'll be hard-pressed to order. Here's a suggestion: Start with the Fisherman's Basket (grilled baby octopus, prawns, and fish) and use the wine list to find out what Indian vintners are getting up to. Then choose from garlic-flavored grilled jumbo prawns, Singaporean chili crab, pepper-crusted Japanese bluefin tuna, Kerala-style fish curry, or even braised abalone. Besides a rather extensive (slightly befuddling) list of a la carte options (including some chicken dishes and vegetarian items), you can also choose from the seafood marketplace menu and then select how you'd like your crab, lobster, prawns, or fish prepared; the choices range from simply chargrilled with lemon butter to stir-fried with basil leaves and lemon grass.

13 Main Market, Lodhi Colony. ✆ 011/2464-9026. Reservations recommended. Main courses Rs 275–Rs 950 ($6.70–$23/£3.40–£12); marketplace seafood priced by weight. 10% service charge. MC, V. Daily 11am–3:30pm and 7–11pm.

Shalom ☆☆ LEBANESE/MEDITERRANEAN   If you're on the hunt for a hipper, potentially younger upmarket dining crowd, you could do worse than to reserve a table in this smart, sexy spot in the south. You'll sense from the smartly attired waitstaff, upbeat lounge music soundtrack, and soothing decor (hand-plastered walls, burnt-wood furniture) that you're in for a night of fun, starting perhaps with one of the legendary *mojitos,* and then moving swiftly on to a meze platter of hummus, baba ghanouj, tabbouleh, cacik, and various other dips and morsels. Or tuck into a decadent tapas selection that includes skewered fish in a lemon, paprika, and garlic sauce, or dates stuffed with spicy chorizo (absolutely scrumptious). For mains, the Moroccan lamb stew is highly recommended (it's served with wild rice), as are the prawns with *romesco* paste (made from walnuts, saffron, and pine nuts), and the *gallina en pepitoria* (grilled chicken breast in a rich wine sauce with toasted almonds). Vegetarians will love the Spanish corn crepes, as well as the goat's cheese and ricotta galette. The decent wine list is dominated by Chilean and Argentinian vintages. Do not pass up the chocolate lasagna when you're offered dessert.

N-18, N Block Market, Greater Kailash I. ✆ 98-1004-8084. Reservations highly recommended. www.shalomdelhi. com. Main courses Rs 425–Rs 1,395 ($9.65–$32/£4.85–£16). 10% service charge. AE, MC, V. Daily 12:30–3:30pm and 7:30pm–midnight.

Véda ☆☆ NORTH INDIAN   An offshoot of the now-defunct Michelin-rated New York restaurant, Dévi, this is certainly the most atmospheric and downright beautiful restaurant in Delhi; designed by iconic fashion guru Rohit Bal, the interior space has a dreamlike elegance—a careful balance of baroque fantasy and contemporary appeal—that feels light-years away from the chaos of Connaught Place just outside. Large decorative mirrors, a candle-lit ceiling, table votifs, walls studded with inlay mirror work, and a gigantic red centerpiece chandelier are standout elements in an intimate space that's ultimately a lot friendlier once you get past the unsmiling viper who works the door. Although Véda has quickly garnered an armful of accolades (it hit *Conde Naste Traveler*'s Hot List in 2006), the food here doesn't necessarily match the ambience. Nevertheless, you could do worse than to order one of the seven-course tasting menus. You get to sample such imaginative items as chicken stuffed with lamb and goat's cheese and tomato. Alternatively, order a plate of curry leaf and lotus leaf

Five-Star Culinary Flagships Where You Can't Go Wrong

Delhiites love to discover that a world-renowned establishment is not up to scratch and then report their findings to anyone who will listen. Whatever you're told, it's unlikely that you'll be disappointed if you reserve a table at one of our top hotel choices. The advantages of settling on a meal at one of the city's five-star hotels include relative consistency and refined service; you'll find addresses under "Where to Stay," above. Needless to say, reservations are essential. Expect to fork out substantially for the opportunity to dine with the elite.

Staff at **Bukhara** ✿✿✿ (✆ 011/2611-2233), the Maurya Sheraton's Indian restaurant, are immensely proud that Bill Clinton apparently chose to stay at the hotel "because of our restaurant." In a busy display kitchen, where meat and vegetables hang from swordlike kebab spears, chefs slave to produce delicacies from a menu that hasn't changed in 30 years and continues to earn accolades as one of the world's finest Asian restaurants. Start by ordering an assorted kebab platter (there's even one named in Clinton's honor), and follow that up with any of the classic lamb *(raan)* dishes, best savored with thin butter *naans.* Finish off with a traditional rice-based *phirni* pudding or one of their amazing *kulfis* (ice cream). Next door to the Sheraton is the glitzy Taj Palace Hotel, where the city's elite line up (sometimes literally) to get a table at **Masala Art** ✿✿✿ (✆ 011/2611-0202), which makes a very conscious (usually successful) attempt to dazzle. The chefs turn cooking into performance art, putting on engaging food demonstrations at mealtimes; spectators eat whatever delicacies are produced. Of the daily a la carte specials, look for *achari jhinga* (prawns flavored with raw mango), and *galouti* kebabs prepared with finely minced lamb and 126 different herbs. If you're up for sharing a small feast, order *khushk raan,* a whole leg of lamb pot-roasted in a secret, heavenly marinade. Be sure to have a glass of fresh sugar-cane juice or *bhune jeere ki chaas,* buttermilk seasoned with roasted cumin. Taj Palace also does old-school dining pretty well, so if you prefer a stiff, formal (and potentially very romantic) evening in the company of exquisite French cuisine, dress smart for **Orient Express** ✿✿ (✆ 011/2611-0202), where you dine in a posh replica of a Pullman train carriage. Enjoy pre-boarding drinks on the "platform," as the bar area is called, and scan the humidor for an expensive cigar. Your four-course journey is inspired by the countries through which the Orient Express passes on its Paris-to-Istanbul run, and is likely to include items such as Camembert soufflé with paprika sauce, pan-seared reef cod with raw papaya salad, and the extremely popular oven-roasted New Zealand rack of lamb, encrusted with herbs and almonds and served with lamb jus. Fish is flown in fresh daily—from France. Although the menu changes three or four times a year, one item will never be replaced: the sinful but wonderful warm chocolate pudding with a liquid chocolate center.

If you need a good excuse to swan through the lobby of The Imperial, why not reserve at **The Spice Route** ✿✿✿ (✆ 011/2334-1234)? Voted one of the top 10 restaurants in the world by *Condé Nast Traveler,* it's still living up to its promise with a vast menu that makes the mouth water at the variety of flavors and ingredients. The decor alone is worth a visit—every nook and cranny is hand-painted by temple artists flown in from Kerala. If the evening is balmy, sit in the tranquil courtyard and be prepared to be blown away by the food, which, as the name suggests, takes you on a complex culinary journey, from the Malabar Coast to Sri Lanka, Malaysia to Indonesia, Thailand to Vietnam. Certainly, it has the best ever *tom kha kai* (classic Thai soup, made with spicy chicken and coconut milk, flavored with lemon grass and kafir leaves) and mouthwatering *chemeen thoren* (Kerala-style prawns, stir-fried with coconut, curry leaves, and black tamarind, and flavored with mustard seeds). *Kung nang phad khing* is stir-fried lobster with ginger and Thai black mushrooms, and *malu miris* contains vegetables, coral mushrooms, and water chestnuts cooked in a Sri Lankan curry.

There's a veritable war going on among supporters of Delhi's top Chinese restaurants. Many lean toward **Taipan** ★★★ at The Oberoi (© **011/2436-3030**), where you can fill up on amazing *dim sum* (tiny dumplings filled with an assortment of tasty morsels, steamed, and served in bamboo baskets), best enjoyed at lunchtime with fantastic views over Delhi Golf Course. But these days our Delhi connections say they're far more satisfied with the range of Oriental dishes served at the Shangri-La's beautiful **19 Oriental Avenue** ★★★ (© **011/4119-1919**), where you can savor close-to-perfect Thai, Japanese, and Chinese cuisine. Thai chicken soup (flavored with galangal and lemon grass), Cantonese-style steamed red snapper (green spring onions and top-notch soy sauce bring out the flavor), Peking duck, and silky-smooth *teppanyaki* tofu steak are just a handful of recommendations from a diverse menu. There's also an exquisite sushi bar (arguably the finest in town). The Taj Mahal Hotel boasts the excellent **House of Ming** ★★★, which is gorgeously decorated and, thanks to a recent revolution in the kitchen, has emerged as a formidable culinary force focusing on Cantonese and Szechuan cooking; it now also offers delectable dim sum and seafood selections and has an enviable tea menu.

If you want to focus on Japanese, you could head straight to **Sakura** at The Metropolitan Hotel Nikko (Bangla Sahib Rd.; © **011/2334-2000**), where the sushi is fresh, authentic, and award-winning, but we prefer **TK's Oriental Grill** ★★ (Hyatt Regency) for great *teppanyaki* grills and remarkable sashimi. If you're too nervous to dive headlong into the region's heavily spiced cuisine, the Hyatt is also where you'll find the best pizzas in town, at **La Piazza** ★★ (© **011/2679-1234**). Chef Mitele Sbardellini from Milan dishes out authentic Italian cuisine; an extensive wine list includes superb vintages from around the world, though the prices may have you gagging into your glass.

Finally, if you simply want to sit back and relax with a good bottle of wine and a choice of pretty much anything from anywhere around the world, the flavor of the moment has got to be The Oberoi's smart, contemporary **Threesixtydegrees** ★★ (© **011/2436-3030**), open all day and somehow almost always buzzing. Sure, it's a smart place to impress business associates, but the buffet spread is legendary, and the attached *enoteca* is stellar.

chips to start and then try the lamb Véda special, an unusual combination of lamb on the bone and minced lamb, or have the highly recommended Parsi sea bass *(paatra ni machi)*. The tandoori-grilled lamb chops are simple and delicious. Dishes are generally spiced to suit an international palate, so you'll need to ask if you want the heat turned up. Oh, and plan on serious contemplation of the wine offerings.

H 27, Outer Circle, Connaught Circus. ℂ 011/4151-3535 or 011/4151-3940/1. Reservations essential. Main courses Rs 291–Rs 651 ($7.10–$16/£3.60–£8.05); tasting menus Rs 975–Rs 1,175 ($24–$29/£12–£15). AE, MC, V. Daily noon–3:30pm and 8–11:30pm.

MODERATE

One Connaught Place institution you certainly shouldn't pass up is **United Coffee House** 𝒜, which began 5 decades ago as a coffeehouse and is now also a multi-cuisine restaurant where we can sit for hours ogling the fantastic array of people who come here to feast, drink, strike deals, play cards, and pass the time. Interesting Art Deco interiors, lit by chandeliers, make this more about nostalgia than particularly inspiring cuisine, but the reasonable Indian food, and prolonged two-for-one happy hours make this a favorite with locals and travelers alike. And, yes, the coffee is freshly brewed and brought to your table in a French press. Reserve for dinner, just in case (E-15, Inner Circle; ℂ 011/2341-1697 or -6075). A popular lunchtime venue is **Basil and Thyme** 𝒜 (Santushti Shopping Complex, New Wellington Camp; ℂ 011/ 2467-3322), where you can sample playful experiments with healthy Eurocentric fare from the kitchen of octogenarian gourmand Bhicoo Manekshaw. The day's special and other healthy selections rarely fail to please, and the fabulous homemade cheesecakes and ice creams should be declared illegal. Reserve ahead.

If you fancy a theme restaurant that goes quite over the top in its attempts to be more Indian than is perhaps necessary, head for the Garden of Five Senses and grab a table at **Baujee ka Dhaba** (Saed Ul Ajab; ℂ 011/3261-6707). Folk art decorates the mud-effect walls, and even the waitstaff is in traditional getup. The food is distinctively Mughlai and Punjabi fare, rich and heavy, but unquestionably well-made and delicious. Get the ever-popular *shammi* kebab or *dum pukht* chicken. Or just nibble on assorted kebabs while you enjoy a reasonably priced chilled beer. A fairly recent addition to a Delhi dining scene is **Oh! Calcutta** 𝒜𝒜 (E Block, International Trade Towers, Nehru Place; ℂ 011/2646-4180), which is obsessed with just one thing: authentic, excellent Bengali cuisine. A visit here should be prefaced with a warning, though: Don't come for the decor, service, or even the slightest hint of romantic atmosphere. The only thing you get by way of entertainment is the opportunity to watch dozens of local middle-class families making a right royal night of it. They, like you, are here for reliable, reasonably priced meals. And the food really is scrumptious, no doubt necessary to take the bite out of the surly demeanor of the waiters, who make very competent recommendations, so go with them.

Chor Bizarre 𝒜𝒜 NORTH INDIAN/KASHMIRI   A fantasy of kitsch twisted into a unique space that is more irreverent museum than diner, this is one restaurant that lives up to its name. A pun on *chor bazaar,* which literally means "thieves' market," Chor Bizarre is packed with fascinating odds and ends, mismatched settings, out-of-place furnishings, and reassembled bits and pieces (matchboxes, coins, chessboards, antique combs, ivory sandals, jewelry, chandeliers, a jukebox . . .), innovatively displayed to create one of India's most visually dynamic restaurants (a branch of which is now also open in London). One table was previously a maharaja's bed, while a 1927 vintage Fiat has become the buffet-carrying "*Chaat* mobile." Start with deep-fried lotus roots, prepared Kashmiri-style, and move on to *kakori kebab,* lamb marinated in 36 different spices and grilled in a tandoor. Cardamom-flavored lamb meatballs (*goshtaba*) are another delicious Kashmiri specialty, slow-cooked over an open flame. Alternatively, if you're up for a feast, try the Kashmiri *taramis* (thali), filled with treats and served from a traditional royal platter. Ask about walking tours that combine lunch with sights in Old Delhi.

Hotel Broadway, 4/15 A Asaf Ali Rd. (central New Delhi). ℂ 011/2327-3821. Main courses Rs 155–Rs 365 ($3.80–$8.90/£1.90–£4.50). AE, DC, MC, V. Daily noon–3:30pm and 7:30–11:30pm.

Park Balluchi ✿✿✿ MUGHLAI/AFGHANI   A regular winner of India's Tourism Award for the country's best restaurant, Park Balluchi enjoys a prized location on the grounds of Delhi's leafy Deer Park, in Hauz Khas. Turbaned waiters in waistcoats serve an extensive range of kebabs and spicy tandoor items. For some light drama, order Afghani-style *murgh-potli* (tandoori chicken): chicken breast stuffed with minced mutton and served over a flaming sword. The specialty at Balluchi is the *lazeez dohra kebabs,* tantalizing combinations of two meats (chicken and prawn marinated in herbs, or minced lamb with minced chicken). Newer favorites include *raan sikandari,* roast leg of lamb marinated in herbs, spices, and rum and then grilled in the tandoor. Vegetarians should order *mewa paneer tukra,* chunky Indian cottage cheese stuffed with raisins, sultanas, walnuts, and other nuts; preparation of this dish takes at least 12 hours. Be sure to get a side order of *peshawri naan,* bread cooked in the tandoor oven with poppy seeds and coriander leaves. If you book for lunch, you may even catch a glimpse of scampering rabbits, strutting peacocks, or one of 300 spotted deer that roam the park. And we haven't even started on the cocktails . . .

Deer Park, Hauz Khas Village. ℂ 011/2685-9369 or 011/2696-9829. Reservations for dinner and weekends essential. Main courses Rs 140–Rs 650 ($3.45–$16/£1.75–£8.05). 5% service charge extra. AE, MC, V. Daily noon–11:45pm.

Punjabi By Nature ✿ PUNJABI   You'll know from the many Sikh families that eat here that this is one of Delhi's best-regarded Punjabi restaurants (and now a reliable chain); at this venue there are two floors for diners and a pub upstairs, all a mere 10 minutes' drive west of Haus Khas Village (or 15 min. from Safdarjung's tomb, the Hyatt Regency, or the Santushti Shopping Complex). On the first floor is a display kitchen where you can watch tandoori items and desserts being made; ask for a table here, where it's more atmospheric. Try masala quail (*bataear masaledar*) or fresh *tandoori* pomfret, and take heed of the wine suggestions. The staff is particularly proud of the *raan-e-Punjab,* marinated whole leg of lamb cooked in the tandoor—you're served the tender meat as it literally falls off the bone. Vegetarians can look forward to tandoori broccoli, prepared in a mustard marinade, or *sarson ka saag,* fresh mustard greens served with homemade cornmeal bread. If you're adventurous, arrive for happy hour (4–8pm) and try the house specialty, a "golguppa" shot: a tiny *puri* (fried puffed bread) filled with spicy vodka, which you pop into your mouth whole.

11 Basant Lok, Vasant Vihar. ℂ 011/5151-6665 through -6669. Main courses Rs 245–Rs 695 ($6–$17/£3–£8.60). 10% service charge. AE, DC, MC, V. Daily 12:30pm–midnight.

Swagath ✿✿ INDIAN COASTAL/ECLECTIC   This might just be the best seafood restaurant in Delhi. Frequented by a seasoned crowd and always busy, the place has a no-nonsense ambience over several floors in Defence Colony Market, a popular shopping area in a relaxed residential area. The menu brings together many classic South Indian dishes—Mangalorean, Maharashtran, Keralan, Malabari, and Chettinad cuisines are represented, each with their peculiar spices and gravies and varieties of fish—a great testament to the diversity of Indian culinary influences. This is also the only place in town where you can sample "Bombay Duck" (or *Bombil*), dried, crispy fish that makes a finger-licking starter. We also love the garlicky prawns, done in butter and pepper and absolutely potent with fresh garlic. For a main course, we usually go straight for the "special fish," but be sure to specify *"surmai,"* which is the less bony kingfish (*bangda*—mackerel—is the bonier alternative). If you're fond of Thai curries, you might like the taste of fish *gassi,* a Mangalorean-style dish with coconut gravy, which comes highly recommended. And, we've heard nothing but good reports about the scrumptious garlic-butter crabs, prawns *gassi,* and green masala pomfret. *Tip:* If you're feeling adventurous, the little mobile vendor stationed near Swagath's entrance prepares excellent *paan.* Considered a digestive and a stimulant, these parcels of tobacco, betel nut, and other assorted ingredients (some even include low traces of opiate) may not be something you want to do regularly, but they're certainly a vital part of Indian street culture. Ask for one of the sweeter blends and remember to chew, not swallow!

14 Defence Colony Market. ℂ 011/2433-0930 or -7538. Reservations highly recommended. Main courses Rs 125–Rs 625 ($3.05–$15/£1.55–£7.75). AE, MC, V. Daily 11am–11:30pm.

INEXPENSIVE

Sagar is one of Delhi's favorite restaurant chains, serving reliable vegetarian South Indian food at reasonable prices till 11pm. Have one of the South Indian thali platters, and eat with your hands. End your meal with Madrasi filter coffee, or you can start your day the same way—the restaurant opens at 8am, which is the best time for traditional *idli* (South India's favorite breakfast dumplings) and chutney. You'll battle to spend more than Rs 90 ($2.20/£1.10) on food here. There's a good outlet at 18 Defence Colony Market (ℂ **011/2433-3110** or 011/5565-0961), just 10 minutes from India Gate. When in Old Delhi, one must-see eatery is **Haldiram's** 𝕽𝕽, always bustling with frenetic activity as locals flock to pick up the city's most legendary range of Indian sweets. Another legendary stop, even if only to bask in the historic glow of a place that served both Nehru and Indira Gandhi (not to mention other Indian prime ministers), is a *paratha* shop recognizable by the sign reading THE POWER OF PRANTHAS—PT. GAYA PRASAD SHIV CHARAN (ℂ **98-1126-3137**), which you'll probably need your guide to help you seek out (it's at 34 Gali Pranthe Wail, Chandni Chowk). This shouldn't be too difficult, as the little eatery has been satisfying locals since 1872 and any guide worth his salt should know it. There are 20 different varieties of *paratha* available, and each comes with a thali-like plate filled with *sambals,* vegetables, lentils, and sauces to make a more substantial meal out of the popular street food. Grab a seat and join the Old Delhi locals.

Karim Hotel 𝕽𝕽 MUGHLAI   In the heart of Old Delhi, not far from the Jama Masjid, this legendary eatery dates back to 1913, when it was opened by a chef who claimed to have hailed from a family of royal cooks who served, among other guests, the great Mughal emperor Akbar. Come here for the food, and don't be put off by the informal setting; this is the genuine thing. It's primarily a meat-eaters' hangout, and the real princely treats are mutton *burra* kebabs. The butter-cooked chicken *(makhani murgh)* is also wonderful, as is the *badshahi badam pasanda,* mutton cooked with blended almonds and yogurt and fragrant spices. If you're really adventurous, you can also sample exotic fare such as spiced goat trotters, or the advance-order *bakra* feast—lamb stuffed with chicken, rice, eggs, and dried fruit, a meal made for a dozen people (about $100/£50). No doubt about it: This is the real deal.

Moments **Saucy Fingers**

One of our absolute favorite eating experiences in Delhi has got to be **Khan Chacha Kabab Corner** ★★ (© **98-1067-1103;** Mon–Sat noon–10pm, Sun 4–10pm), a hole-in-the-wall kebab counter in Khan Market serving legendary mutton *seekh kababs,* wrapped in light *roomali rotis* (Rs 55/$1.35/70p), from a tiny kitchen manned by a squadron of brothers who've continued what their father started back in 1972. These delicious, juicy meat-filled rolls are prepared while you wait and served as a take-away snack; you can hang around and munch them on the spot, or smuggle a batch into your hotel room and sit down to a feast. But be warned: They're utterly addictive. Ask for onions and green chutney if you'd like to add a spicy edge, and be prepared for a deliciously decadent sauce to dribble down your chin. To get there, seek out the crowd of devotees that inevitably forms (at 75 Middle Lane); it's right next to The Kitchen, a pretentious and anonymous neon-lit cafe.

16 Gali Kababian, Jama Masjid. © **011/2326-4981** or -9880. www.karimhoteldelhi.com. Main courses Rs 51–Rs 200 ($1.25–$4.90/65p–£2.50). No credit cards. Daily 7am–midnight.

Naivedyam ★★ SOUTH INDIAN VEGETARIAN   Delhi has five branches of this fantastic, cramped, and always busy little South Indian restaurant; the one in Hauz Khas is the original, atmospherically decorated with mirror-framed Tanjore paintings and pillars that have been beautifully carved and embossed. Not that you'll notice this; you'll be too busy checking out the crowd (if it's full, just wait until a table opens up). You start your meal with a spicy peppery lentil soup, called *rasam,* which is drunk as a curative and is something of an acquired taste. Thalis, or multicourse platters, are served at meal times, and are a good way to sample a variety of tastes from the South. Alternatively, you can choose from a whole range of *dosas* (rice and lentil flour pancake); the variety can be quite intimidating, so ask the waiter for some advice—be warned that *dosas* easily become addictive. On the side you'll be served chutney made from ground coconut and green chilies, and *sambar,* a souplike concoction of lentils, tamarind, and vegetables. Tea and coffee are served in the style typical of the South, but there's no alcohol. You'll recognize the restaurant by the stone Nandi bull statue that faces the front entrance.

1 Hauz Khas Village. © **011/2696-0426.** Main courses Rs 45–Rs 75 ($1.10–$1.85/55p–95p); thali Rs 90 ($2.20/£1.10). AE, DC, MC, V. Daily 11am–11pm.

SHOPPING

The Delhi shopping experience is every bit as exciting as that found in Mumbai and Jaipur, but the sprawling size of the city makes it difficult to cover all in one day— best to concentrate on one area at a time. And if this is your first port of call, try not to load your luggage too early with stuff to take home. It is a good idea, however, to pop into Dilli Haat (reviewed below) to get a perspective of the range of regional arts and crafts and approximate prices. If something here really captures your heart, by all means get it and have it shipped home, for it may not be available when you return. Note that most shops (and markets) are open from 10am to 7pm and are closed on Sunday, unless mentioned otherwise. Besides the areas described below, you can spend an entire day covering the old city of Shahjahanabad (see "The Top Attractions," earlier in this section). Finally, keep in mind that the recommended shops that follow are only a fraction of what's out there; if you know what you're looking for, it's best to inquire at both your hotel and the Janpath tourist office for alternatives.

Connaught Place   If you want to get an idea of what lies ahead on your travels, visit a few of the 22 **State Government Emporiums** that line Baba Kharak Singh Marg; some recommended options are Himachal for blankets and shawls in particular (© 011/2336-3087); Tamil Nadu ("Poompuhar") for sandalwood objects (© 011/2336-3913); Uttar Pradesh ("Gangotri") for the stone-inlay work made famous by the Taj, as well as copper/brasswork and leather goods (© 011/2336-4723); **Kashmir Emporium** for superb carpets; and Orissa (Utkalika) for fabrics and traditional paintings (the latter off the beaten tourist track). If you're not moving on to Rajasthan, don't miss visiting both this and **Gurjari Emporium.** These State Government Emporiums (like the poorly managed **Central Cottage Industries Emporium** on nearby Janpath) have fixed prices, so you are spared the incessant haggling you'll have to master elsewhere. One place where it's worth bargaining is **Tibetan Market** (on Janpath), where it is said you will pick up a better selection of items (from antique locks to silver jewelry) at better prices than you will anywhere in Tibet. Having walked its length, you will find yourself in Connaught Place, the retail heart of imperial Delhi, where hundreds of outlets vie for your rupees. Visit **Banaras House** for saris and the most beautiful fabrics on earth (N-13 Connaught Place, opposite Scindia House; © 011/2331-4751). Head to **Jain Super Store** (172 Palika Bazaar, Gate 6; © 011/2332-1031; www.jainperfumers.com) for perfumes, incense, and teas; it also has a store on Janpath called **Arihant Fragrances** (17 Main Market; © 011/2335-3959), which sells lovely silver jewelry alongside fabulous scented products. Stop at **Shaw Brothers** (Shop 8, Palika Bazaar; © 011/2332-9080) for pure, high-quality Kashmiri shawls and elegant Pashminas—even if you don't buy, this is pretty much a must-see (note that the main showroom is in Defence Colony; call © 011/4155-0858 for free transport if you're very serious about buying). For beautiful (and expensive) gemstones, gold jewelry, and bridalwear, try **Bholanath Brothers** (L-23 Connaught Circus; © 011/2341-8630) or nearby **Kapur di Hatti** (L-16; © 011/2341-7183), which also has Kundan jewelry. The most famous shop in Connaught Place is **Fabindia** (see review below), specializing in stylish ethnic Indian homewear and clothing for all ages.

Khan Market & Sunder Nagar Market   Sunder Nagar is considered the best market to trawl for authentic antiques, interesting secondhand goods, and unique artworks; it has a few good permanent stalls such as **Natesans** (13 Sunder Nagar Market; © 011/2435-9320), renowned for the quality of its artifacts and antiques (though these can be pricey). Khan Market is good for books, music, and DVDs and increasingly for designer stores. Browse **Anokhi** (32 Khan Market; © 011/2460-3423), patronized by expats and locals alike for its highly fashionable blend of Western- and Eastern-style clothing (see "Jaipur: Shopping" in chapter 10 for full review of the Anokhi headquarters). **The Neemrana Shop** (12-B, Middle Lane, Khan Market; © 011/2462-0262) has a range of homewares, trinkets, and souvenirs that make ideal gifts and usable memorabilia; you can buy Kama Ayurvedic toiletries, gorgeous pewter teapots, and simple and stylish light cotton garments, perfect for you to wear during your travels in India. Whatever you do, don't miss **Good Earth** (🏵🏵 (9 Khan Market; © 011/2464-7175), which opened in 2007. It's filled with fabulous homewares, furniture, and accessories and the perfect place to pick up beautiful linens, silk cushions, fragranced candles, glass votives, or colorful tea sets. There's also a branch at **Santushti** (see below).

South Delhi   Seek out **Ravissant** (© 011/2683-7278; www.cest-ravissant.com) in New Friends Colony for beautiful contemporary pewter and silver houseware items (or visit the outlet conveniently located in The Oberoi hotel lobby). **Santushti Shopping Complex** 𝒜𝒜 is an upscale collection of shops (predominantly boutiques) housed in landscaped gardens 15 minutes from the center. Shopping here is wonderfully hassle-free (and there's parking); pick up cigars at **Kastro's,** visit **Tulsi** for beautiful garments, and step into **Anokhi** for off-the-shelf cottonwear.

Even farther south (convenient to visit after viewing Qutb Minar) is trendy **Hauz Khas Village,** set against a 12th-century backdrop; and, slightly southeast (40 min. from the center), **Greater Kailash**—the latter shopping area (divided into M and N blocks) is the least atmospheric but has a large variety of shops in an upmarket atmosphere. Hauz Khas is the place to seek out designer boutique outlets, like **Ritu Kumar** (E-4; © **011/2656-8986** or 011/4165-5340). Or head straight for **Ogaan** (H–2; © **011/2696-7595**)—the formalwear version of Anokhi, it's perfect for unusual Indo-West and contemporary Indian designer clothing, and stocks a number of well-known labels; be sure to seek out the cute '60s-inspired minidresses by Puja Arya. **Natural Selection** (1 Hauz Khas; © **011/2686-4574**) is an excellent space to browse for larger items like antique furniture; the proprietors can make all shipping arrangements. Hauz Khas also has a number of fine restaurants (see "Where to Dine," above), although some have been shut down because of unsound ancient architecture. For wonderful tailor-made garments, make your way to **Kavita & Vanita Sawhney** (B-78 Greater Kailash I; © **011/2646-4633**).

Dilli Haat 𝒜𝒜   This open area imitates a *haat* (rural marketplace), where 200 little stalls form a permanent open-air arts-and-crafts market. It's a unique shopping experience, and the most authentic and affordable in Delhi. Dilli Haat offers you the opportunity to buy directly from rural artisans and craftspeople who are allotted space rotationally for 2 weeks, making this a great place to browse the variety of crafts from all over India, whether you are traveling farther afield or not. From Bihar's *Madhubani* art to silver jewelry and furniture, as well as unusual gifts and souvenirs or colorful linens and other furnishings, the range is exhausting, the prices excellent. If you are in Delhi in early December, be sure to check out the **Master Crafts Fair** (normally held Dec 1–15), where award-winning artists and craftspeople display and sell their work. Numerous food stalls serve food from all over India, but the hygiene is questionable, and there's more flogging of Coke and mineral water than anything else. It's open daily from 10am to 10:30pm Aurobindo Marg, opposite INA Market. © 011/2611-9055. Entry Rs 10/25¢/15p.

Fabindia 𝒜𝒜   If you've coveted Indian ethnic-chic at stores like the Conran Shop in London or New York, here's your chance to buy the fabrics and crafts at one-tenth the price. Fabindia sources its products from more than 7,500 craftspeople and artisans around India. Their distinctive use of handloom weaving techniques, natural dyes, and both vivid and earthy colors have made their products both fashionable and desirable. Do bear in mind that these fabrics usually require gentle hand washing and drip-drying. Also, sizing and quality are inconsistent, so it's best to try on any item of clothing before you buy. There are branch stores all over India as well as in Rome and Dubai. The Connaught Place store is open daily from 10am to 7pm; the Khan Market store is open Monday to Saturday from 10am to 7pm. N-Block Market, Connaught Place: © 011/4151-3371 or -3372. Greater Kailash Part I: © 011/2923-2183 or -2184. Fabindia Craft Store: Central Hall, Khan Market. © 011/4175-7142 or -7143. www.fabindia.com.

DELHI AFTER DARK

"The dawn breaks orange . . . The peacock sings . . . And Delhi still swings . . ." go the words to an uplifting dance track by Delhi's top ethno-electronic-music outfit, the MIDIval PunditZ. While we're still not convinced that this isn't slightly tongue-in-cheek, and despite the capital's reputation for early nights and boring diplomatic gatherings, you certainly won't want for a buzz these days. The trick is to sniff out the latest fad or craze before it's died out; your best bet—and where you'll find the most extensive news about current events and entertainment—is the twice-monthly *Time Out New Delhi*. And, if contemporary music is your thing, do try to catch the PunditZ live.

MUSIC, DANCE & FILM   **Dances of India** is an organization that regularly stages classical and folk dance performances, showcasing styles from around the subcontinent; call ℂ **011/2358-5357** to find out what events are lined up. Call the **India Habitat Centre** (Lodhi Rd.; ℂ **011/2468-2222**) for information on theater, film festivals, and other cultural events held almost nightly. Nearby is **India International Centre** ((ℂ **011/2461-9431**), which also hosts a variety of cultural performances and film screenings (mostly in the cooler months of the year), as does **Poorva Sanskritik Kendra** (14 District Centre, Laxmi Nagar; ℂ **011/4244-8840**). Entry to most events is free.

BARS & PUBS   Cultural attractions aside, Delhi is in many ways most interesting at nighttime, when the "conspicuous consumers" to whom William Dalrymple refers in his *City of Djinns* head out and schmooze. Of course, unless they're in hotels, most restaurants and bars (many of which double as both) close around midnight.

Fancying itself Delhi's most exclusive pub is **Dublin** (ℂ **011/2611-2233**), although with its Irish theme, we can't imagine why. It does have a dance floor, however, as well as the largest selection of single malts in Delhi; on Friday and Saturday regular DJs spin popular commercial tracks—a mix of fast-paced rhythms from hip-hop to '90s rock and even London bhangra. For a more genteel and upmarket atmosphere, head to **Rick's** 𝕘𝕘 at the Taj Mahal Hotel (1 Mansingh Rd.; ℂ **011/2302-6162**), where you can sip some of the best cocktails in Delhi while watching the city's fashionable set unwind. A DJ (Wed–Sat) plays retro music from 10:30pm onwards. Far more formal, and perhaps a tad demure, is **Club Bar** (The Oberoi, Dr. Zakir Hussain Marg; ℂ **011/2436-3030**); relaxed and spacious, and good for cigar smokers, it's the sort of place where you find yourself discussing business deals. **1911 Bar** in The Imperial ((ℂ **011/2334-1234**), with its horseshoe-shaped bar, quilted leather Montana chairs, vintage portraits, and stained-glass roof, is an elegant place to enjoy an evening drink; despite the TV stuck on sports channels, it attracts a discriminating clientele that includes expats, celebs, and political bigwigs. All the rage among the jet-set crowd is **Aura** 𝕘𝕘, the sublime vodka bar at the Claridges (ℂ **011/2301-0211**); schmoozing on the black leather armchairs here is greatly enhanced by the 68 varieties of vodka on offer.

Beyond the hotels, another popular watering hole and lounge is **Q'Ba** (E 42-43, Inner Circle, Connaught Place; ℂ **011/5151-2888;** www.qba.co.in). It features a funky island bar on the lower level and dining upstairs—a good place to hang out with travel companions and swap stories; there are two terraces from which to admire the mayhem down below. After 8:30pm the DJ plays commercial music. The downstairs bar at **Turquoise Cottage** (81/3 Adhchini, Sri Aurobindo Marg; ℂ **011/2685-396**), is *the* place for rock music, and fills up with a vibrant mix of westerners and locals Wednesdays through Saturdays. The Western-obsessed decor (one nook is dedicated to vintage cars, another is filled with Rolling Stones album covers, another celebrates saddles) may feel out of place this far east, but the young crowd of habitual smokers doesn't seem to mind. If you prefer a venue that looks and feels a bit more local (we're talking Khajuraho-inspired erotic sculptures and wall-mounted Harappan seals), head to **Urban Pind** (N-4, N Block Market, Greater Kailash I; ℂ **011/3251-4646;** www.urbanpind.com); you can sip Masala Martinis or cocktails infused with Indian spices while tapping your feet to commercial tracks spun by resident DJ Praveen. The crowd is as eclectic as the decor; although it's a rather sedate eatery by day, there's dance floor action at night, with danceable tunes from the likes of Costa Del House. Another decent option for a night of unwinding is **Baci Bar** (23 Sundar Nagar Market; ℂ **011/4150-7445**), which is also an authentic Italian restaurant.

NIGHTCLUBS   Delhi has its fair share of nightclubs, though most play standard commercial music. Unfortunately, stand-alone restaurants, bars and clubs within Delhi proper must close at midnight; this is why you'll notice so much late night carousing at hotels, and why there's such a major after-hours exodus to Noida and Gurgaon (suburbs which are actually in different states), especially on weekends.

There's also no getting around the megalithic popularity of The Park's ultra-chic and trendy **Agni** ⭐⭐⭐ (ℂ **011/2374-3000**) the popular (and undeniably sexy) bar—with a small dance floor for bhangra swingers—designed by London's Conran & Partners; it's worth popping into, not least for its funky decor, beanbags, and leather sofas, and nifty bar staff in designer gear by Rohit Bal. On weekends there's sure to be a crowd you won't be able to take your eyes off, although things shut down around 1am. If you want to party into the wee hours (5am), make your way to **Elevate** ⭐⭐ (Fifth Floor, Centre Stage Mall, Noida; ℂ **0120/436-4611** or 99-6795-9789), a spacious three-story club that plays a variety of sounds including commercial, R&B, and electronic music, with some trance/psychedelic stuff thrown in for good measure. Strictly for those who need to feel the music pulsate through their bodies, the club regularly has an international DJ playing the latest world trends; Paul Oakenfold stirred the crowd into a frenzy here in May 2007, hinting at Delhi's evolving love of a good time. With its black walls and pink lights, **Decibel** (Hotel Samrat, Kautilya Marg; ℂ **011/2611-0606**) in Chanakyapuri is a trendy nightclub with a large dance floor that draws a jet-setting crowd. The in-house DJ spins commercial music while night owls sip fine cocktails and dance away the calories. And then, of course, there's Delhi's very own pumping house club, **Ministry of Sound** ⭐⭐ (ℂ **98-7380-0060**) at The Pyramid in Vasant Kunj, although city authorities might have closed it down—again—by the time you're in town.

Note: Bars and nightclubs in Delhi can be extremely popular for months, or even years, and then suddenly and inexplicably the crowds stop coming. All the establishments listed above have been popular for a significant period of time and are unlikely to turn into has-beens by the time you get there, but fads and trends guide people's movements, so it's best to ask around once you're there, consult *Time Out,* and also check out the score at www.delhievents.com.

2 Agra

200km (124 miles) SE of Delhi; 60km (37 miles) E of Bharatpur; 120km (75 miles) N of Gwalior

Agra is invariably included on every first-time visitor's itinerary, for who visits India without visiting the Taj? Home to three generations of one of the most dynamic dynasties in the medieval world, their talent and wealth immortalized in stone and marble, Agra is home to the finest examples of Mughal architecture in India, of which the Taj is simply the most famous. The beauty of these buildings will bowl you over, but knowing something of the history that played itself out on these stages (akin to reading a Shakespearean drama) makes the entire Agra experience come alive.

To soak up this fascinating history in the walls and rooms that resonated to Mughal voices, you should ideally set aside 2 full days here and hire the services of a good guide. And, if your budget can stretch that far, there's only one place to stay: the palatial Amarvilās, where every room has a view of the Taj.

ESSENTIALS

VISITOR INFORMATION   The **Government of India Tourist Office** is at 191 The Mall (© **0562/222-6378;** goitoagr@sancharnet.in; Mon–Fri 9am–5:30pm, Sat 9am–2pm). A 24-hour **Tourism Reception Centre** is at Cantonment Railway Station (© **0562/242-1204**). Not as much on the ball, the **U.P. Tourism Bureau** is at 64 Taj Rd. (© **0562/222-6431;** Mon–Sat 10am–5pm; closed second Sat of the month).

GETTING THERE & AWAY   By Road   Agra lies less than 4 hours away, on a good double-carriage highway from Delhi. Many Delhi operators offer bus tours to Agra; see "Essentials" in the Delhi section, above. If you don't mind being part of a bus tour, a good option is to take a day trip from Delhi with **TCI** (see "Guided Tours" below); alternatively, hire a car and driver. Should you need to stop for refreshments, the **Country Inn** at Kosi, 99km (61 miles) from Delhi, is a good bet.

By Air   At press time, the only flights into Agra are charters; it is unknown whether commercials flights (suspended several years back) will ever resume.

By Train   The **Bhopal Shatabdi** leaves New Delhi at 6am daily, arriving at **Agra Cantonment Railway Station** (inquiries © **131** or 133, reservations 0562/242-0998) at 8am; it returns to Delhi at 11:05pm. Alternatively, you can catch the **Taj Express,** which leaves Delhi's Nizamuddin Station at 7:15am, returning to Delhi at 10:05pm. The station has a prepaid taxi/auto-rickshaw service (Rs 50–Rs 120/$1.25–$2.95/65p–£1.50), and is 2km (1¼ miles) from downtown; this is also where you can book a city sightseeing tour. *Note:* Trains from Rajasthan pull in at the Agra Fort Station. (If arriving from elsewhere, avoid inconveniently located Agra City Station.)

GETTING AROUND   By Taxi & Auto-Rickshaw   As is the case everywhere in India, make sure you negotiate your taxi or auto-rickshaw rate upfront (or use the prepaid facility). Hiring an air-conditioned car for 4 hours should run you around Rs 800 ($20/£10), while a full day will cost upwards of Rs 1,450 ($35/£18), depending on how far you want to go. Unless you're traveling to Sikandra or Fatehpur Sikri, an auto-rickshaw should suffice. In an attempt to cut down on the air pollution that threatens the Taj, motorized transport is not allowed in the Taj Sanctuary area (2km/1¼-miles radius); walk or hire a cycle-rickshaw.

GUIDED TOURS   Uttar Pradesh Tourism operates city tours that cover all the major sights. The tour usually starts at 10:15am, costs Rs 1,650 ($40/£20), and covers the Taj, Agra Fort, and Fatehpur Sikri and includes all entrance fees, a guide, and transport by air-conditioned bus; book with the manager of Hotel Taj Khema (© **0562/233-0140;** tajkhema@up-tourism.com). A recommended private tour operator from Delhi is **TCI** (C-35, Connaught Place; © **011/2341-6081** through -6085; www.tcindia.com). The TCI bus departs Delhi at 7am and returns by 10pm, covering Agra Fort and the Taj; it costs Rs 2,000 ($49/£25), including breakfast, sightseeing,

Agra

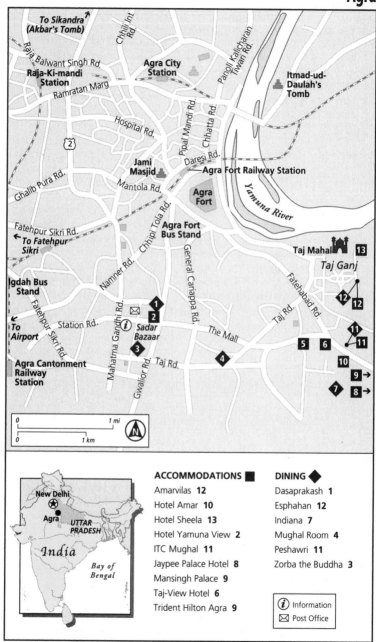

ACCOMMODATIONS ■

Amarvilas **12**
Hotel Amar **10**
Hotel Sheela **13**
Hotel Yamuna View **2**
ITC Mughal **11**
Jaypee Palace Hotel **8**
Mansingh Palace **9**
Taj-View Hotel **6**
Trident Hilton Agra **9**

DINING ◆

Dasaprakash **1**
Esphahan **12**
Indiana **7**
Mughal Room **4**
Peshawri **11**
Zorba the Buddha **3**

ⓘ Information
✉ Post Office

The Life & Times of the Mughal Emperors

Babur, the first Mughal emperor—inspired by the Persians' belief that a cultured leader should re-create the Islamic ideal of a "garden of paradise" here on earth—built three gardens on the banks of the Yamuna. But Agra only took shape as a city under his grandson, Akbar, the third Mughal emperor. Son of the poet-astronomer-philosopher Humayun (whose tomb is in Delhi, described earlier in this chapter), Akbar moved the capital here in 1566. While Akbar was as versatile as his father, he was also a better statesman, revered for his religious tolerance and relatively understated lifestyle. He took the throne at age 13 and ruled for almost 50 years, during which time he consolidated the Mughal empire and wooed the Hindu "underlings" by abolishing taxes, banning the slaughter of cows, promoting Hindu warriors within his army, and taking a Rajput princess as his bride, who bore him a son, Jahangir. In gratitude for the appearance of an heir, Akbar built a brand-new city, **Fatehpur Sikri,** which lies 40km (25 miles) southwest and is today one of Agra's top attractions.

   The grandeur of this statement of gratitude indicates that Akbar must have, at least at first, been a very indulgent father, though his joy must later have been tinged with disappointment, for at an age when he himself was ruling India, Jahangir (who was to be his only surviving son) was relishing his reputation as a womanizer and acquiring a deep affection for alcohol, opium, painting, and poetry. When Jahangir fell in love with **Nur Jahan,** his "light of the world," who was at the time married, Akbar opposed the alliance. But after her husband died (under mysterious circumstances, it must be said), Jahangir promised to give up "the pleasures of the world," so Akbar gave his consent. Jahangir had a coin minted in her honor, and when he was crowned emperor in Agra Fort in 1628, it was in fact the strong-willed and ambitious Nur Jahan who ruled the empire from behind the *jalis*

lunch at the Taj View Hotel, snacks, and an English-speaking guide; you pay your own entry fees at monuments). Traveling around with a tour group is, however, far from the ideal way to experience the mystery and magical allure of the Taj or Fatehpur Sikri. To book one of the best guides in Agra (one of the best, in fact, in India), contact the intelligent and knowledgeable **Rajiv Rajawat** (© 98-3702-3601; rajivrajawat@ yahoo.com) before you even get to India, to ensure he is available on the days you'd like to use his services (Rs 1,000–Rs 1,500/$24–$37/£12–£19 per day). Pitching himself more affordably is **Sudhir Agarwal** (© 98-3714-2946 or 0562/260-2441; sudhir_ agra@rediffmail.com), who charges as little as Rs 600 ($15/£7.40) for the day, from 8am through 5pm.

WHAT TO SEE & DO

Agra is today a large industrial city with a woeful infrastructure, but sightseeing is quite manageable given that there are five major attractions and very little else to keep you here. Ideally, you will see the **Taj** at dawn, then visit **Itmad-ud-Daulah's Tomb** and **Agra Fort,** and move on to **Fatehpur Sikri** the following dawn. Besides those (screens) for 16 years. She also built a magnificent garden tomb, another of Agra's top attractions and affectionately referred to as the "mini-Taj", for her father. By the time Jahangir died in 1644, reputedly a drunkard, Akbar must have been turning in his tomb (yet another of Agra's top attractions).

It was Jahangir's third son, **Shah Jahan** (not incidentally born of Nur Jahan), who came to power—apparently after murdering his two elder brothers, their two children, and two male cousins. Known as the "architect" of the dynasty, the fifth Mughal emperor began renovating the Agra Fort at age 16, but achieved the apotheosis of Mughal design when he built the Taj Mahal for his beloved **Mumtaz** (the niece of Nur Jahan). Bored, he moved the capital to Delhi when he was 47, building an entirely new city from scratch, designing modern geometric palaces (including a separate royal apartment for his favored daughter, Jahanara Begum) and beautiful gardens within the new Red Fort. But he was to pay a bitter price for the favoritism he showed Jahanara and his son, **Dara Shikoh**. His pious third son, **Aurangzeb**, aided by **Roshanara Begum** (Jahanara's embittered younger sister), seized the throne by betraying and/or murdering most of their siblings. Aurangzeb, the last of the great Mughal emperors, became the most repressive ruler North India had yet seen, destroying Hindu temples and images throughout the region and banning the playing of music or any other form of indulgent pleasure. Known as much for his cruelty as his ambition, Aurangzeb allegedly poisoned his ally Roshanara when he caught her in an illicit liaison in her quarters at the Red Fort. Having imprisoned his father in Agra Fort, Aurangzeb sent him a platter upon which he garnished the head of his favorite son, Dara. According to legend he instructed his servant to present it with the words, "Your son sends you this to let you see that he does not forget you."

sights listed below, you may also want to make time to visit beautiful **Jama Masjid,** built in 1648 by Jahanara Begum, Shah Jahan's favorite daughter, who clearly inherited some of his aesthetic sensibilities. It is in the heart of the medieval part of Agra, best approached by cycle- or auto-rickshaw; you can stop along the way to bargain for jewelry, fabrics, or carpets. The other sight worth swinging by is **Dayal Bagh Temple**—begun 95 years ago, it is still under construction and is being built by the progeny of the laborers who built the Taj. The families guard their traditional craft techniques like gold, passing them on only to the sons in the family. Other minor attractions are ill-kept and a disappointment after viewing those reviewed below. Note that Bharatpur, where Keoladeo Ghana National Park lies (see chapter 10), is only 54km (34 miles) from Agra, with a stop at Fatehpur Sikri along the way.

Taj Mahal _ᏩᏩᏩ_   You expect to be disappointed when coming face to face with an icon that is almost an archetype, but nothing can really prepare you for the beauty of the Taj Mahal. Built by Shah Jahan as an eternal symbol of his love for his favorite wife, whom he called Mumtaz Mahal ("Jewel of the Palace"), it has immortalized him

---

Tips **Be the First to Arrive**

Get to the Taj entrance at dawn, before it opens, then rush—run if you must—straight to the cenotaph chamber (remember to remove your shoes before ascending the marble steps). If you manage to get there first, you will hear what might aptly be described as "the sound of infinity"—the vibration created by air moving through the huge ventilated dome. As soon as the first visitor walks in, jabbering away, it reverberates throughout the room, and the sacred moment is lost until closing time again.

---

forever as one of the great architectural patrons of the world. It's not just the perfect symmetry, the ethereal luminescence, the wonderful proportions, or the sheer scale (which is virtually impossible to imagine from staring at its oft-reproduced image), but the exquisite detailing covering every inch of marble that justifies it as a wonder of the world. What appears from afar to be perfectly proportioned white marble magnificence is in fact a massive bejeweled box, with *pietra dura* adorning the interior and exterior—said by some to be an Italian technique imported to Agra by Jahangir, but more likely to be a craft originating in Persia. These intricately carved floral bouquets are inlaid with precious stones: agate, jasper, malachite, turquoise, tiger's eye, lapis lazuli, coral, carnelian—every stone known to man, as well as different shades of marble, slate, and sandstone. Beautiful calligraphy, inlaid with black marble, is carefully increased in size as the eye moves higher, creating an optical illusion of perfectly balanced typography, with the letters the same size from whichever angle you look. Carved relief work, again usually of flowers, which symbolized paradise on earth for the Mughals, decorates much of the interior, while the delicacy of the filigree screens that surround the cenotaph, carved out of a single piece of marble, is simply astounding. The tomb is flanked by two mosques—one is a prerequisite, but the other is a "dummy" built only in the interests of symmetry; both buildings are worthy of examination in their own right. At the center of it all lies Mumtaz Mahal's cenotaph with the words HELP US OH LORD TO BEAR WHAT WE CANNOT BEAR; Shah Jahan's cenotaph was added later.

Work started in 1641, and the structure took 20,000 laborers 22 years to complete—legend has it that Shah Jahan cut off the hands of the architect (Persian-born Ustad Ahmad Lahori) and his laborers to ensure that they would never build another, but there is little to substantiate this sensational story.

The Taj changes color depending on the time of day, and many recommend that you witness this by visiting in the morning and evening; however, your ticket is valid for one entry only. Eat a hearty breakfast before you head out (no food is allowed past security), and stay the day, or come in the early morning.

Finally, to understand the symbolism of the Taj, as well as what has been lost since Shah Jahan's day (such as the plunder of the pearl-encrusted silks that covered Mumtaz's cenotaph), it's definitely worth hiring the services of a good (read: official), well-spoken guide. Besides **Rajiv Rajawat** and **Sudhir Agarwal** (for contact details, see above), you can consider arranging a reputable guide through your hotel.

If you're an absolute romantic, you might like to check with your hotel whether or not one of the **full moon Taj-viewing experiences** is likely to fall on one of the nights during your stay. Since early 2005, the Taj has been open for night viewing for 5 days each lunar cycle: the full moon night and the 2 nights before and after. These after-hours sessions happen between 8pm and midnight and are highly regulated (and certainly no substitute for day-time visits); try to time such a visit for around 10pm.

Note: The Taj is closed on Friday. Your Taj ticket also entitles you to a small discount at the other four major attractions (Agra Fort, Itmad-ud-Daulah, Sikandra, and Fatehpur Sikri), so keep it on hand and show it when paying to enter the others.

Taj Ganj. (✆ **0562/233-0498**. Admission Rs 500 ($12/£6.20), children under 15 free; Rs 50 ($1.25/65p) limited video use. Sat–Thurs sunrise–sunset. Only water, camera, film, batteries, medicines, and other similar essentials are allowed. No food, sharp objects, tripods, or electronics—if you have any of these items, you can leave them at reception. Mobile phone use is a criminal offense.

Agra Fort ⟨⟨⟨ Built by Akbar (or rather, by his 4,000 workmen) on the west bank of the Yamuna, Agra Fort first took shape between 1565 and 1573, but each successive emperor was to add his imprint, and today the towering red-sandstone ramparts house a variety of palace apartments, representing the different building styles of Akbar and his grandson Shah Jahan. Akbar's son, Jahangir, installed a **"chain of justice"** (1605) by which any of his subjects could call on him, which provides some insight into the ruling qualities of the man many dismiss as a drunkard. Entrance is through impressive **Amar Singh Gate.** On your right-hand side you pass **Jahangiri Mahal,** the palace that housed the women of the court, dating to Akbar's reign (ca. 1570). In front is a stone pool with steps both inside and outside—legend says it was filled with rose petals during Nur Jahan's time, so that she could bathe in their scent. Much of the exterior (the jutting *jarokhas,* for example, and the domed *chattris*) and almost the entire interior were clearly built by Hindu workmen, who used Hindu building styles and decorative motifs—indicative of Akbar's all-embracing religious tolerance. Adjacent, facing **Anguri Bagh (Grape Garden,** where flowing water, flower beds, hidden lamps, and hanging jewels would have transformed it into a fantasy garden), is **Khas Mahal** (1636), built overlooking the cooling breezes of the Yamuna. You are now entering Shah Jahan's palaces, immediately recognizable by the extensive use of white marble. Historians also point out that here—unlike in Akbar's buildings, which feature straightforward Hindu elements next to Islamic—a subtle blend of Hindu and Persian elements resulted in a totally new style, referred to as the "Mughal style," with its classical purity. The Khas Mahal is flanked by two **Golden Pavilions** (a reference to the fact that they were once gilded): the bedrooms of the princesses Jahanara and Roshanara, before the latter plotted the downfall of her father and sister. On the left is **Mussaman Burj,** an octagonal tower open to the cooling breezes, which may have been the emperor's bedroom. Romantic accounts would have us believe that Shah Jahan, imprisoned by his son in this room, would gaze at the Taj Mahal until his death of a broken heart in 1666. However, evidence points to death by a massive dose of opium, complicated by the prolonged use of aphrodisiacs. Near the tower are the mirrored **Sheesh Mahal** and **Mina Masjid (Gem Mosque);** adjacent is **Diwan-i-Khas (Hall of Private Audience;** 1637), its marble columns inlaid with semi-precious stones in *pietra dura* floral patterns. In front of Diwan-i-Khas are two **thrones** (from where the emperor watched elephant fights below); facing these is **Machchhi Bhavan (Fish House),** once filled with the sounds of trickling water. Beyond lies **Diwan-i-Am (Hall of Public Audience),** the arcaded hall where the emperor would listen to the complaints of his subjects, seated on the Peacock Throne (see Lal Qila [Red Fort], in Delhi, earlier in this chapter). Note the insensitive placement of the tomb of John Russell Colvin, who died here during the Mutiny and was laid to rest in front of

Diwan-I-Am. The ugly barracks to the north are also 19th-century British additions. From here on, most of the buildings (except for **Nagina Masjid,** the private mosque of the ladies of the court) are closed to the public, undergoing extensive excavation at press time. (*Note:* A sound-and-light-show is held each evening at 7pm—when the machinery is working, that is.)

Yamuna Kinara Rd. Admission Rs 300 ($7.35/£3.70). Rs 50 ($1.25/65p) discount with Taj ticket. Keep ticket until visit is over. Daily sunrise–sunset. *Son-et-lumiere* (sound-and-light show) Rs 75 ($1.85/95p). **Note:** Avoid Fri, when the Taj is closed and entry is half-price for Indian visitors, making the place crowded.

Fatehpur Sikri ✸✸✸   Built from scratch in 1571 by Akbar in honor of the Sufi saint Salim Chisti, who had predicted the birth of a son (see "The Dargah Sharif & Other Ajmer Gems" in chapter 10), this grand ghost city is carved entirely from red sandstone. It was only inhabited for 14 years, after which—some say because of water shortages—it was totally abandoned. It's a bizarre experience to wander through these magnificent, architecturally fascinating sandstone arches, courtyards, and buildings. (Try to get here right when it opens, the only time it's peaceful.) The buildings combine a fine sense of proportion—indicative of Akbar's Persian ancestry—with strong Hindu and Jain design elements, indicative again of his embracing attitude to the conquered and their faiths. Upon entering, you will see **Diwan-i-Khas,** thought to be a debating chamber, on the right. Facing it is **Ankh Michali,** thought to be the treasury, which has mythical Hindu creatures carved on its stone struts. To the left is large **Parcheesi Court,** where Parcheesi (from which games such as backgammon and ludo were subsequently derived) was played with live pieces: the ladies of the harem. It is said that Akbar learned much about the personalities of his court and enemies by watching how they played, won, and lost. Surrounding the court are, from the left, **Diwan-i-Am,** a large pavilion where public hearings were held; the **Turkish Sultana's House,** an ornate sandstone pavilion; and **Abdar Khana,** where drinking water and fruit were apparently stored. Walk between the two latter buildings to enter **Akbar's private quarters.** Facing **Anoop Talao**—the four-quartered pool—are the rooms in which he slept (note the ventilating shaft near his built-in bed) and his personal library with shelves carved into the walls. Also overlooking Parcheesi Court is **Panch Mahal,** the tallest pavilion, where Akbar's wives could watch the games and enjoy the breeze without being seen. Behind Panch Mahal are the female quarters, including **Maryam's House** and the **Haram Sara Complex.** The harem leads to **Jodha Bai's Palace,** a large courtyard surrounded by pavilions—note the green glazed roof tiles. To the east is **Birbal's House,** a two-story pavilion noted for its carvings; beyond lie the **servants' cells.** From here you exit to visit **Jama Masjid,** a mosque even more spectacular than the larger one Akbar's grandson built in Delhi. Set like a glittering pearl amid the towering red-sandstone bastions, punctuated by a grand gateway, is the white marble *dargah* (tomb) of Salim Chisti, which has some of the most beautiful carved screens in India. It attracts pilgrims from all over India, particularly (given the good fortune he brought Akbar) the childless, who make wishes while tying cotton threads onto the screens that surround the tomb.

Again, the services of a good guide are indispensable to a visit here (don't bother hiring one of the "official" guides at the entrance, however). Also note that if you are moving on to Rajasthan and plan to visit Bharatpur (for its bird sanctuary), Fatehpur Sikri can be visited en route.

37km (23 miles) west of Agra on the road to Bharatpur. No phone. Admission $5 (£2.50) Daily sunrise–sunset.

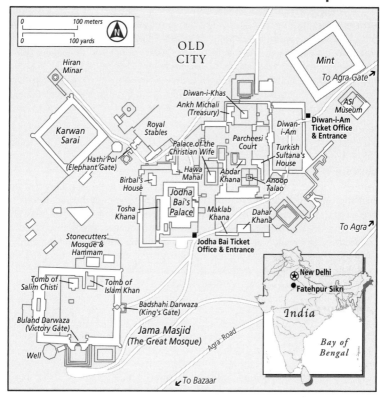

Itmad-ud-Daulah's Tomb ✮✮✮ Described as a mini-Taj, this is the tomb of Mirza Ghiyath Beg, who served under Akbar and fathered Nur Jahan, the powerful wife of Jahangir who helped promote her father to his position as Lord of the Treasury and enshrined him here in this "bejeweled marble box"—proof of her powerful hold on the purse strings. Also built of translucent white marble, it was the most innovative building of 17th-century India, and marked the transition from the heavy red sandstone so favored by previous Mughal emperors. It no doubt inspired Shah Jahan with its beautiful symmetry and detailing; the *pietra duras* are as delicate as embroidery, and the dense gilding and paintwork feature typical Persian motifs, such as the wine-vase and the dish and cup, much favored by Jahangir at the time. The scale may be far less grand than that of the Taj, but the polychrome geometric ornamentation is more obviously decorative, and given the beauty of the proportions and the intricacy of its inlays and mosaics, it's amazing how little traffic this tomb sees relative to the Taj. It definitely warrants a short visit, if only to get a sense of how almost generic opulence was to the Mughal court.

Eastern Bank of Yamuna (30 min. from Taj). Admission Rs 110 ($2.70/£1.35). Rs 10 (25¢/15p) discount with Taj ticket. Daily sunrise–sunset.

Sikandra (Akbar's Tomb) ✮✮ Someone once described the rise and fall of the Mughal empire as rulers who started "as titans and finished as jewelers." To this end,

Akbar's tomb is a less-elegant version of the bejeweled tombs of his great-granddaughter (or his daughter-in-law's father), yet more ornate than that of his father Humayun (see "Delhi: The Top Attractions"). That said, the perfect symmetry is typical of Persian architecture, and the scale is huge; the gateway alone, featuring more than 20 panels inlaid with intricate geometric patterning, will stop you in your tracks. Geometric patterning in fact dominates, with relatively few floral designs, as befits the last "titan" ruler. It's not surprising to hear that the tomb is believed to have been designed by Akbar; the detailing reflects the altogether more restrained lifestyle and masculine personality of this great ruler.

8km (5 miles) from Agra on NH 2. (℃) **0562/264-1230**. Admission Rs 110 ($2.70/£1.35). Rs 10 (25¢/15p) discount with Taj ticket. Rs 25 (60¢/30p) video. Daily sunrise–sunset.

WHERE TO STAY

Given that it is one of the most-visited tourist destinations in the world, Agra's accommodations can be disappointing, no doubt a case of resting on the Taj's laurels. The big exception is **Amarvilās,** which—even if it means scrimping elsewhere—is worth every cent, not least for its proximity to the Taj and the matchless views. Within the moderate price category, all located south and southwest (known as the Cantonment) of the Taj, there is incredible price parity; of these only the **Trident** offers good value. The best budget option, conveniently located within Tajganj (where the Taj is located), is the **Hotel Sheela,** reviewed below.

VERY EXPENSIVE

Amarvilās 𝒢𝒢𝒢   It's one of the most talked-about hotels in India—or rather, the world—and your experience visiting the Taj Mahal and Agra will simply be enhanced by a thoroughly worthwhile splurge at this extraordinary property. It's been enjoyed by a global "who's who": from Salman Rushdie to William Dalrymple, Will Smith to Meg Ryan, not to mention a host of world leaders. This is a sublime choice and our favorite of the Oberoi's celebrated Vilās properties (thanks in no small part to the hands-on management). No matter what anyone tells you, there's little to beat the satisfaction of enjoying all-day views of the Taj from your bedroom—just 600m (1,968 ft.) away. Every room has a beautiful view. You can literally sip a cappuccino in your king-size bed at dawn, watching the subtle color variations the monument undergoes as the sun rises; or you can order a cocktail on your private balcony at sunset, admiring the ethereal marble silhouette as staff light the burners that line the hotel's grand stepped terraces leading down to the central pool. The lobby, bar, and lounge all offer the same surreal views of the Taj, but even those public spaces that don't offer a monument view are lovely, with large reflecting pools, colonnaded courts, terraced lawns, and pillowed pavilions. By day some of the exteriors look a little bland and in need of the detailing featured in the interior, but at night it's a pure *Arabian Nights* fantasy, when burning braziers provide a wonderful contrast to the fountains and trickling streams. The rooms are compact but extremely luxurious, showcasing the best-quality Indian craftsmanship available but with every modern amenity, including a walk-in cupboard and marble bathroom with separate tub and shower. The only significant choice you need make is whether or not to pay extra for a balcony (recommended!). The in-house spa also has views of the Taj—lying there, gazing at the dreamlike monument, you might just have to ask the masseuse to pinch you. While the hotel scores high points for its understated opulence, it's the silky smooth service that accompanies your encounter with the Taj that really makes a difference; be sure to make use of the courtesy golf cart rides to just within striking distance of the monument's East Gate. And make every effort to spend more than a single night!

Taj East Gate Rd., Taj Nagari Scheme, Agra 282 001. © **0562/223-1515.** Fax 0562/223-1516. www.oberoihotels.com. 102 units. $665–$765 (£333–£383) premiere double; $725–$825 (£363–£413) premiere double with balcony; $1,200–$3,800 (£600–£1,900) suite. Taxes extra. AE, DC, MC, V. **Amenities:** 2 restaurants; lounge; bar; pool; fitness center; Banyan Tree spa; travel services; business center; boutiques; salon; 24-hr. room service; laundry; doctor-on-call; golf cart drop-off at Taj; cultural performances (Oct–Mar). *In room:* A/C, TV, minibar, hair dryer, DVD, personal butler.

EXPENSIVE

Jaypee Palace Hotel ⚜ This huge hotel and convention center at the edge of town tends to feel very busy, which can prove a real nuisance. Nevertheless, the red-sandstone buildings (more reminiscent of a modern library than a palace) are wonderfully set on 10-hectare (25-acre) grounds with well-tended gardens, lovely walkways, fountains, and pergolas—you can even take a camel ride through the grounds. Unfortunately, the hotel's size and the rather brusque staff can make your stay here memorable for the wrong reasons: Here you pass through a security scanner on your way in (a silly homage to terrorist paranoia), but you're more likely to feel threatened by the large numbers of tourist and conference groups that regularly flood the newly enlarged lobby area. One revamped wing has given rise to so-called Palace Rooms: Escape here to avoid the crowds. Approached via a red carpet, these spacious guest rooms have wood-paneled floors and little semi-private terraces that look onto the garden. Along with various in-room freebies (snacks and wine), Palace Rooms also come with a free massage, which you can enjoy in Agra's largest health club. This is also a good option for parents of kids disinterested in Agra's architectural pleasures; youngsters can lose themselves at Leisure Mall, which offers a bowling alley, virtual reality games, and other kinds of entertainment you never came to India for.

Fatehabad Rd., Agra 282 003. © **0562/233-0800.** Fax 0562/233-0850. www.jaypeehotels.com. 350 units. $220–$290 (£105–£140) double; $370–$2,000 (£178–£960) suite. $25 (£12) extra bed. Taxes extra. Ask about discounts. AE, DC, MC, V. **Amenities:** 4 restaurants; tea lounge; bar; disco; pool; putting greens; tennis; health club; spa; travel and transport counter; airport transfers; florist; beauty parlor; barber shop; 24-hr. room service; babysitting; laundry; doctor-on-call; currency exchange; Wi-Fi enabled; squash; jogging track; bowling alley; billiards; aerobics; children's play areas; virtual reality games; helipad. *In room:* A/C, TV, minibar, tea- and coffee-making facilities, hair dryer. Executive & Palace rooms have electronic safe.

MODERATE

If for some reason our reviewed recommendations below are full, note that you can get an even better deal at the **Mansingh Palace** (Fatehabad Rd.; © **0562/233-1771;** www.mansinghhotels.com; doubles from $155/£78), where you'll have the option of getting a room from which you can (just) see the Taj. Styled as a faux fortress-palace, Mansingh Palace has similar amenities to the Taj and Trident, but the ambience is just a touch more cluttered; on the upside, however, this tends to mean that staff goes that little bit extra to try make you feel more comfortable. The previously government-run **Hotel Yamuna View** (6B, The Mall Rd.; © **0562/246-2990** or 0562-329-3777; www.hotelyamunaviewagra.com; doubles from $108/£54) has neat and fairly spacious guest rooms and a number of amenities such as an in-house restaurant, 24-hour room service, a pool, a travel desk, and laundry. But don't come expecting luxury, lavish trimmings, or above-average service.

Taj-View Hotel ⚜ Don't be put off by the unattractive exterior of this stalwart Agra hotel. What from the outside looks a bit like an unfortunate 1970s apartment block, actually offers a wide range of amenities and, thanks to a massive refurbishment, provides bright, comfortable guest rooms, the best of which offer views of the monument you're in town to see. Whatever you do, reserve a Taj-facing room, and do your best to secure room 518, which has the best view. Generally, the deluxe rooms have more appeal, with marble floors and colorful throws and cushions, but they aren't that much different from the slightly smaller, cheaper superior rooms. You'll be pleased to know that, while you'll never beat the close-up views offered at Amarvilãs, here your picture of the Taj (albeit from 1km/½ mile away) is more complete, despite overlooking the fairly ugly city; a pair of binoculars might come in handy. What can't be helped, however, is the constant intrusion of the dull drone of noise from the streets. With extensive landscaped lawns and a marble pool with its own swim-up bar, this is a fair place to come home to after the rush of sightseeing. It's more competitively priced than the brash Sheraton, but not as good value as the Trident.

Fatehabad Rd., Taj Ganj, Agra 282 001. ℂ **0562/223-2400** through -2418. Fax 0562/223-2420. www.tajhotels.com. 100 units. $195 (£98) superior city- or pool-facing double; $215 (£108) superior Taj-view double; $240 (£120) deluxe Taj-facing double; $375 (£188) luxury Taj-facing suite. Taxes extra. AE, DC, MC, V. **Amenities:** 2 restaurants; bar; seasonal poolside barbecue; pool; putting green; tennis court; health club and spa; travel services; car rental; airport transfers; shops; 24-hr. room service; babysitting; laundry; doctor-on-call; currency exchange; cultural performances by arrangement; sightseeing; astrologer. *In room:* A/C, TV, minibar, tea- and coffee-making facility, hair dryer, Wi-Fi.

Trident Agra 🌟🌟 *(Value* In a low-key attempt to emulate Agra's architectural heritage, this hotel uses the same red sandstone favored by the Mughal kings, but that's where the similarity ends. In fact, the moment you step into the lobby, you'll feel thoroughly located in the 21st century. Public spaces were given a shape-shifting contemporary makeover, bringing in modish sofas and light fittings set off by gorgeous yellow cushions and vases filled with matching yellow roses. This may be something of a shock for those after Agra's historical ambience, but the result is an atmosphere of soothing tranquillity, carried through to the bar and restaurant. What's more, service is generally a great deal slicker here than elsewhere in Agra—not surprising given that it's partially managed by the distinguished Oberoi hotel group. Guest rooms continue the theme of using bright yellows to inject energy into the otherwise ordinary spaces; the effect is refreshing, although hardly a stand-in for a bedside view of the Taj. Accommodations are arranged around a central garden, with manicured lawns, trimmed hedges, and a swimming pool; try to reserve a room facing this. Check online for daily price variations: You can sometimes get an ultra-low bargain rate.

Taj Nagri Scheme, Fatehabad Rd., Agra 282 001. ℂ **0562/233-1818** through -1826. Fax 0562/233-1827. www. tridenthotels.com. 138 units. $180 (£90) deluxe garden view double; $195 (£98) deluxe pool-view double; $300 (£150) suite; $20 (£10) extra bed. Actual rate varies daily. Taxes extra. Children under 12 stay free in parent's room. Rates include breakfast. AE, DC, MC, V. **Amenities:** Restaurant; bar; pool; travel agent; airport transfers; bookstore; jewelry store; salon; 24-hr. room service; babysitting; laundry; doctor-on-call; table tennis. *In room:* A/C, TV, dataport, minibar, tea- and coffee-making facilities, electronic safe.

INEXPENSIVE

If you're watching your rupees but want to be near the Taj, the Hotel Sheela (reviewed below) is less than a minute's walk from the entrance; it's ideal for travelers who can put up with absolute basics. Away from the main hype, the **Hotel Amar** (Tourist Complex Area, Fatehabad Rd.; ℂ **0562/233-1884** through -1889; www.hotelamar. com) offers clean rooms with en-suite baths; renovations have given the lobby a modern feel, but the rooms are fairly tawdry, with standard amenities. All the rooms may be noisy given the proximity of traffic: Be sure to insist on an upstairs room looking toward the pool, which is well-maintained and sets the Amar apart from the other faceless options along busy Fatehabad Road. Doubles start at Rs 2,600 ($63/£32).

Hotel Sheela *(Value)* As far as budget lodging goes in the immediate vicinity of the Taj Mahal, you won't do better than this peaceful ochre-colored complex of simple and very basic accommodations in a pleasant garden courtyard surrounded by trees. Aimed squarely at the budget traveler, guest rooms are very spartan, with patterned vinyl flooring and wallpaper designed like faux miniature brickwork. Beds are firm with thin mattresses, but you're provided with bedding. Reserve well ahead for one of the two units that have both air-conditioning and en-suite bathrooms (which are clean and are provided with towels; hot water is available in winter). Cheaper guest rooms have fans and mosquito screens over the windows, and a few more rooms have aging air coolers for summer. The managers, Manish and Rohit, can help with sightseeing endeavors, guides, and organizing a taxi; however, service standards are generally in keeping with the ultra-low tariffs. *Note:* During the busy winter season, you're advised to reserve in advance or risk ending up in one of the nearby hovels. Alternatively, if you prefer something more substantial, yet still want to save rupees, ask about **Sheela Inn**, the sister property, which is pricier but has better in-room facilities (TV, telephone) and is half a kilometer away from the Taj.

East Gate, Taj Ganj, Agra 282 001. ✆ 0562/233-1194. www.hotelsheelaagra.com. 22 units. Rs 200–Rs 400 ($5–$10/£2.50–£5) double; Rs 500–Rs 700 ($12–$17/£6–£9) A/C double. No credit cards. **Amenities:** Restaurant; taxi hire; sightseeing assistance. *In room:* A/C (2 rooms), air cooler (some).

WHERE TO DINE

Dining (and nightlife) options are limited in Agra, and you may as well dine in your hotel, particularly if you're staying at Amarvilās. But if you're "slumming" elsewhere and have cash to burn, **Esphahan** (reviewed below) is definitely worth a splurge. Among the dining options in the big hotels, one of the finest remains **Peshawri** in the Mughal Sheraton, still a firm favorite among locals in the know, or **Mughal Room** in the Clarks Shiraz, where live *ghazals* (poetry readings) add to the experience.

If you want to get away from the hotels, you could do far worse than the delicious and satisfying dishes served at **Indiana** (✆ 0562/400-1192; daily 7:30am–10:30pm), which is hardly an inspiring venue (behind Hotel Ratan Deep on Fatehabad Rd.), but will satisfy any hunger. Portions are rather large (you may even consider sharing some of the dishes between two people). The best dishes are North Indian specialties, although the habit of adding Western and Chinese items persists. If you don't mind something spicy, order *murg boti masal,* chicken in a wonderfully tasty gravy, or go for the spiced fish curry *(rasili machhli).* If you really can't decide, opt for a thali, a platter covering all the courses and including dessert or lassi.

You can get a satisfying, reasonably priced meal at **Zorba the Buddha** (E13 Shopping Arcade, Gopi Chand Shivare Rd., Sadar Bazaar; ✆ 0562/236-3757), which serves excellent, nongreasy vegetarian food. This tiny eatery is extremely hygienic, reason enough to go. Go early to get a good table and order the light spinach *parathas,* any of the Indian fare, or even a salad—all quite passable, if a trifle bland. Vegetarians (or others avoiding meat) have another option: **Dasaprakash** (✆ 0562/236-3535), located in the Meher Theatre Complex at 1 Gwalior Rd., is the city's best-known South Indian restaurant. Regular fare includes *sada dosa* (plain rice and lentil pancakes), *masala dosa* (pancake with potato stuffing), *uttappams* (thicker pancakes), and *idlis* (steamed dumplings), all served with coconut chutney and *sambar* (spiced *dal*). No alcohol is served. At some point, you will hear of **Only** restaurant on Taj Road, mentioned in every guidebook on the planet, but we find it avoidable.

Note: Agra is renowned for moneymaking restaurant scams. Besides the fact that guides, taxi drivers, and auto-rickshaw *wallas* earn commissions for taking you to certain eateries, you need to be wary of getting caught up in more dangerous pursuits. Some unsuspecting diners have been taken for a ride by unscrupulous restaurateurs working in tandem with rickshaw-*wallas* and so-called doctors. Everyone involved might feign major concern over your health, but you'll pay dearly for the experience. *Bottom line:* Be careful where you eat, and if you feel sudden illness coming on, don't rely on the restaurateur to call a "doctor"—insist on being taken back to your hotel.

Esphahan ✹✹✹ INDIAN   Even if you aren't staying at Amarvilās, you should dine at this exceptional restaurant—not only are the cuisine, service, and live Indian music superb, but arriving at the flame-lit latter-day palace is one of Agra's most memorable moments. (When you reserve, ask to have your predinner cocktail on the veranda so you can watch the sunset hues color the Taj and the magnificent pool area below.) Start with *tandoori phool,* stuffed cauliflower in a yogurt and star anise marinade; *Balai ka jheenga,* tiger prawns marinated in black pepper and homemade cream; or the succulent chicken *tikka,* prepared in saffron and garlic. Highly recommended is *Bharwaan gucchi malai* (Kashmiri morel mushrooms stuffed with cottage cheese and raisins) and the *aab gosht,* a Persian lamb dish in which the meat is braised in milk and flavored with dry ginger and fennel—extraordinary. There's also delicious Persian-style quail. All dishes are served with *dal,* seasonal vegetables, and a choice of Indian bread. Alternatively, you could loosen your belt and make room for a filling thali (platter), which affords the opportunity to sample a range of tastes. All in all, a most memorable evening out, and the perfect place to celebrate seeing the Taj.

Amarvilās, Taj East Gate End. ✆ 0562/223-1515. Reservations essential. Main courses Rs 550–Rs 1,250 ($13–$31/£6.80–£15). AE, DC, MC, V. Daily 7–10:30pm.

SHOPPING

Agra is famous for its marble and soft-stone inlay, as well as *zardori*-embroidered fabrics, leather goods, brassware, carpets, and jewelry. However, it's hard work dealing with what is probably the worst concentration of touts and scamsters in all India, so if you can, avoid shopping here. Don't be fooled by Cottage Industries Exposition, which is not a branch of the similarly named government-owned (Emporium) shops in other parts of the country. This one is overpriced, and whatever is sold here can quite easily be obtained in Delhi at half the price. If you absolutely must buy something to remind you of your visit here, **Subhash Emporium** (18/1 Gwalior Rd.; ✆ **0562/222-5828**) sells good-quality inlay work, souvenirs, and other gifts. Or make your way to one of the *official* government emporiums for reasonably priced sources of local handicrafts.

3 Varanasi (Benaras)

320km (198 miles) SE of Lucknow; 765km (474 miles) SE of Delhi

A crumbling maze of a city that rises from the *ghats* (steps) on the western banks of the Ganges, Varanasi is in many senses the quintessential India. With an ancient history—Mark Twain famously described it as "older than history, older than tradition, older even than legend, and looks twice as old as all of them put together"—it is also one of the most sacred cities in the world today. Kashi, or "City of Light, where the eternal light of Shiva intersects the earth," as Varanasi is seen by devotees, is the holiest of Indian pilgrimages, home of Shiva, where the devout come to wash away their

Varanasi

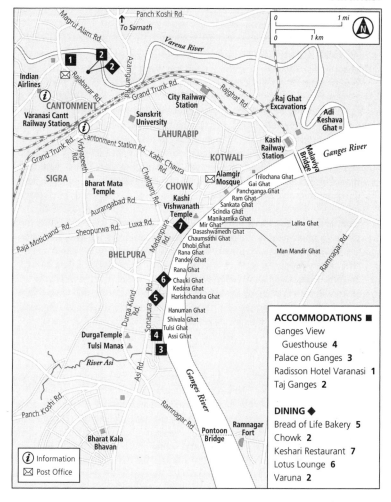

↑
To Sarnath

Panch Koshi Rd.

Varena River

Magrul Alam Rd.

Azamgarh Rd.

Rajabazar Rd.

Indian Airlines

CANTONMENT

Varanasi Cantt Railway Station

Grand Trunk Rd.

Grand Trunk Rd.

Cantonment Station Rd.

City Railway Station

Sanskrit University

LAHURABIP

Rajghat Rd.

Raj Ghat Excavations

Adi Keshava Ghat

Kashi Railway Station

Malaviya Bridge

Ganges River

Vidyapeeth Rd.

Kabir Chaura Rd.

Chaitganj Rd.

KOTWALI

Alamgir Mosque

Trilochana Ghat
Gai Ghat
Panchganga Ghat
Ram Ghat
Sankata Ghat
Scindia Ghat
Manikarnika Ghat
Mir Ghat
Dasashwamedh Ghat
Chaumsathi Ghat
Dhobi Ghat
Rana Ghat
Pandey Ghat

Lalita Ghat

SIGRA

Bharat Mata Temple

Aurangabad Rd.

CHOWK

Kashi Vishwanath Temple

Madanpura Rd.

Raja Motichand Rd.

Sheopurwa Rd.

Luxa Rd.

BHELPURA

Durga Kund Rd.

Sonapura Rd.

Rana Ghat
Chauki Ghat
Kedara Ghat
Harishchandra Ghat

Hanuman Ghat
Shivala Ghat
Tulsi Ghat
Assi Ghat

Man Mandir Ghat

Ramnagar Rd.

DurgaTemple
Tulsi Manas

River Asi

Asi Rd.

Ganges River

Panch Koshi Rd.

Ramnagar Rd.

Pontoon Bridge

Ramnagar Fort

Bharat Kala Bhavan

(i) Information
✉ Post Office

ACCOMMODATIONS ■

Ganges View Guesthouse **4**
Palace on Ganges **3**
Radisson Hotel Varanasi **1**
Taj Ganges **2**

DINING ◆

Bread of Life Bakery **5**
Chowk **2**
Keshari Restaurant **7**
Lotus Lounge **6**
Varuna **2**

0 ___ 1 mi
0 ___ 1 km

sins. It is also one of the holiest *tirthas* (literally a "crossing" or sacred place where mortals can cross over to the divine, or the gods and goddesses come to bathe on earth), where many return to die in the hope that they may achieve *moksha,* the salvation of the soul from the cycle of birth, death, and rebirth.

Named after the confluence of two rivers, Varuna and Asi, the city is centered on the *ghats* that line the waterfront, each honoring Shiva in the form of a *linga*—the rounded phalliclike shaft of stone found on every *ghat.* Cruise the waterfront at dawn and you will witness the most surreal scenes, when devotees come to bathe, meditate, and perform ancient rituals to greet the sun. Or even come at sunset, when *pundits* (priests) at Dasashwamedh Ghat perform *aarti* (prayer ritual) with complicated fire rituals, and pilgrims light candles to float along the sacred waters.

Moments **Up in Flames**

You need a pretty strong constitution to hang around Varanasi's burning *ghats* (**Harish Chandra** or **Manikarnika**) and watch a human corpse, wrapped in little more than a sheet, being cremated in public view. Bodies are burned around the clock at these famous open-air cremation sites, which draw a constant crowd of grievers, curious pilgrims, bug-eyed travelers, and confused cows. Only Varanasi's "Untouchables" are allowed to touch the bodies or perform the cremation. After bathing the body one last time in the holy Ganges, they place it on wood piles, and cover it with more logs (ask your guide about the kinds of wood—teak, sandalwood, and so on—used and their significance) before being doused in a flammable paste, or ghee, and lightly coated with incense powder (the latter used to hide the smell of burning flesh). Then a male relative, usually the son (female relatives of the deceased, even wives, rarely if ever visit the cremation grounds), lights the pyre. No photography is allowed, and you should treat the mourners with the respect their grief deserves. Avoid touts offering to show you a cremation up close and personal; not only do many drug addicts trying to part tourists from their cash hang around these areas, but gawking at an unknown person's funeral pyre from close quarters is considered fairly offensive. To get a quiet glimpse of a cremation ritual from a respectable distance, without causing any offense, take a boat ride down to Manikarnika Ghat.

Earliest accounts of the city go back 8,000 years, and "the city of learning and burning," as it is affectionately referred to, has attracted pilgrims from time immemorial, not all of them Hindu—even Buddha visited here in 500 B.C. after he achieved enlightenment, sharing his wisdom at nearby Sarnath. Successive raids by Muslim invaders (the last of whom was the Mughal emperor Aurangzeb) led to the destruction of many of the original Hindu temples, which means that most of the buildings here date back no further than the 18th century. Yet the sense of ancient history is almost palpable. Getting lost in the impossibly cramped labyrinth, you are crowded by pilgrims purchasing flowers for *puja* (offering or prayer), grieving relatives bearing corpses, chanting priests sounding gongs, and sacred cows rooting in the rubbish—an experience you will never forget.

ESSENTIALS

VISITOR INFORMATION   The **India Tourism Office** is located at 15B The Mall, Cantonment (✆ **0542/250-1784;** indiatourvns@sify.com; Mon–Fri 9am–5pm, Sat 9am–2pm). A satellite information counter is open during flight arrivals. The **U. P. Tourist Office** is on Parade Kothi (✆ **0542/220-6638;** Mon–Sat 10am–5pm); a satellite counter is at the railway station (✆ **0542/234-6370;** daily 9am–7pm).

GETTING THERE   **By Road**   Unless you have a lot of time on your hands, driving to Varanasi means spending too much time on a bumpy road with no interesting stops.

By Air   The airport is 23km (14 miles) from the Cantonment (Cantt.) area, where the large chain hotels are located, and 30km (19 miles) from the riverfront. The flight from Delhi lasts 75 minutes. Best to fly in with **Jet Airways** (reservations ✆ **0542/ 250-6444** or -6555, airport 0542/262-2795 through -2797), or—for the best deal— with **SpiceJet** (www.spicejet.com), which offers flights from Delhi for just over Rs 2,000 ($49/£25). **Indian Airlines** (reservations ✆ **0542/250-2527** or -2529, airport 0542/262-2090) flies in from Delhi, Mumbai, Katmandu, and Khajuraho. **Air Sahara** (central ✆ **0542/250-7871** through -7873, airport 0542/262-2547) connects the city with Delhi, Kolkata, and Bangalore. A taxi should run you Rs 380 ($9.30/ £4.70) to the Cantonment, and Rs 500 ($12/£6.20) to Assi Ghat; use the prepaid service and try to inspect the vehicle before jumping in. Ignore all attempts by drivers to get you to stay at hotels they recommend (or "own").

By Train   Varanasi is conveniently reached by overnight train from Delhi; the Swatantrata Express and Shiv Ganga Express take 12 to 13 hours. It is also connected with a host of other cities and towns. For inquiries, call ✆ **1331;** for Varanasi Cantonment reservations, call ✆ **0542/250-4131** or -4031. Prepaid taxis are available from the station. Be sure to disembark at Varanasi Cantonment station.

GETTING AROUND   By Auto-Rickshaw & Cycle-Rickshaw   The narrow lanes and extremely crowded streets of the Old City and the lanes in and around Godaulia (also Gowdalia) are penetrable only by two-wheelers and extremely determined cycle-rickshaws. These are also useful—if sometimes bone-jarring—ways of getting from your hotel to the area near the *ghats* and other attractions. Once at (or near) the *ghats,* set off on foot. Note that most cycle-rickshaws don't have functioning brakes; their technique of stopping is to merely roll into the cycle-rickshaw in front; hold on and try not to be alarmed, although you must know that they're very uncomfortable, and tend to have you constantly sliding forward.

Bear in mind that Varanasi is a city of transport tricksters, and you have little chance of escaping at least one rickshaw-related con job. Ask your hotel what the current going rate is for any trip in either an auto- or cycle-rickshaw, and bargain for the correct fare. Be further warned that rickshaw-*wallas* will readily agree to take you somewhere without having the faintest idea where it is. Once you've been onboard for several minutes, you will suddenly be asked where you want to go and, more likely than not, you will end up at a shop where the driver expects to make a commission off your purchase. To avoid falling into this annoying and time-wasting trap, ensure that the driver can repeat the name of your destination (or the nearest prominent landmark), in recognizable English. In addition, avoid the shopping scam by using a bit of trickery yourself. To begin with, never use the word "shopping" with a rickshaw-*walla.* If you're heading to the shopping area in Godaulia, ask to be taken to Dasashwamedh Ghat, as if you plan to go there for a stroll. When you're almost there, you'll pass the Old City shopping area and Godaulia; stop your rickshaw and get off before you reach the *ghats,* or get to the *ghats* and take the 5-minute walk back into the market. To hire a car and driver to tour the surrounds, expect to pay at least Rs 650 ($16/£8) for a half-day or Rs 1,200 ($29/£15) for a full day.

GUIDED TOURS   We recommend that you explore the area with a personal guide, if only to know which temples you can enter or which street food to sample, and to avoid getting lost or conned. One of Varanasi's best guides is **Ajit Kumar Yadav** (✆ **0542/258-1052** or 94-1522-5994; ajitashay@yahoo.com; book him in advance), an official, government-approved guide; he's often engaged for group tours during peak season. Ajit is perfect for those looking for an understanding of the city that goes beyond its history, covering religious rituals and mythological stories as well. His knowledge of Hinduism and Buddhism (for Sarnath) is unmatched; most important, he never asks if you want to shop, unless you express a keen interest. **Dhananjay (Deejay) Singh** is another government-approved guide who has a wealth of knowledge and is an absolutely charming host; contact him at © **983905-8228.** Alternatively, you can arrange both guide and car through your hotel, or contact the **India Tourism Office** (see "Visitor Information," above) to arrange for an approved guide and vehicle (© **0542/250-1784**). To hire a boat (with oarsman), head for Dasashwamedh; the price should be around Rs 100 ($2.45/£1.25) per hour.

FESTIVALS   Varanasi is in many ways like a huge trippy trance party that started centuries ago and has kept on going, its revelers refusing to discard their costumes and come down to earth. So there's no real reason to time your visit with a festival—on the contrary, any increase in numbers is worth avoiding. That said, the huge **Dev Deepavali (Diwali)** festival is by all accounts a spectacle, held during the full moon in October/November. Almost every *ghat* and building is covered by glowing earthen lamps, and the river is aglitter with floating candles (but with about 100,000 pilgrims about, you may never even get to the river). Other auspicious occasions are **Mahashivratri** (Jan/Feb), **Holi** (Mar/Apr), **Ganga Dashehra** (May/June), and **Sri Krishna Janmashtami** (Sept/Nov).

WHAT TO SEE & DO

If you do only one thing in Varanasi, take a **boat cruise** past the *ghats* at dawn (see below); you can repeat this at sunset or, better still, head for **Dasashwamedh Ghat** to watch the **Ganga Fire Arti.** For 45 minutes, young Brahmin priests perform age-old prayer rituals with conch shells and burning braziers accompanied by drummers, while children hawk candles for you to light and set adrift. Aside from these two mustsees, you should set aside some time to wander the ancient lanes of the **Old City,** particularly those centered around **Kashi Vishwanath Temple** (see below)—but a few hours of picking your way past cow pats amid the incessant din of clanging temple gongs, not to mention striking out to view the 24-hour cremations at **Manikarnika Ghat,** are likely to have you craving peace and solitude. Hire a car and visit **Sarnath,** where Buddha first revealed his Eightfold Path to Nirvana, and where you can spend a few hours exploring the archaeological ruins, visit a modern Buddhist temple, and admire the beautiful Indo-Greek and Mathura styles of Buddhist art and sculpture at the museum. Alternatively, stay in Varanasi to explore the fascinating collection in the **Bharat Kala Bhavan Museum** at Benaras Hindu University. Both experiences are enriched by having a good guide with you.

   Ramnagar Fort (Rs 12/30¢/15p; Oct–Mar daily 8am–noon and 2–6 pm, Apr–Sept daily 10am–5pm), the palace of the former Maharaja of Varanasi, is billed as another worthwhile attraction. Although the actual palace is beautiful in a run-down sort of way, and the location (the only Varanasi site on the east bank of the river) is lovely, the museum is filled with dusty, moth-eaten, decaying exhibits, such as the once-ornate *howdas* (elephant seats) that transported the royal family—fascinating in a way to see such beauty so discarded. Do stop for a glance at the palace's grand Durbar Hall, though it's hard to see through the filthy windows. The lack of care says much about the dedication of the current young maharaja. Although he is said to involve himself in local tourism, his name does not enjoy the reverence that the Maharajas of Rajasthan still evoke. That said, attempts at renovation continue, so do check for improvements. Last but not least of Varanasi's fascinating sights, **Bharat Mata,** or **Mother India Temple**

(located just north of the Old City) is worth highlighting, if only because it is the incarnation of the spoken Hindu belief that the very land of India is sacred (ironic, given the pollution). Pilgrims walk around a large relief map of the subcontinent before Partition, featuring all its holy *tirthas,* mountains, and rivers.

Varanasi has produced some of India's most talented musicians (the great Ravi Shankar was born here; if you're unfamiliar with his genius, purchase without delay the CD *Chants of India,* produced by George Harrison—highly recommended). Ask your hotel what performances are being hosted while you are in town, or head for the **International Music Centre** in Ganesh Mahal on Wednesday and Saturday (check with your hotel for exact dates and times) for live Indian classical music performances by up-and-coming artists. **Naach Ghar** (Bungalow no. 25, Cantonment, near SSP Residence; ✆ 93-3549-3084) is another place that puts on a dance performance almost every evening around 7:15 for Rs 500 ($12/£6.20) per head.

If you'd like to learn to play the **tabla** (set of two small drums) in Varanasi, which is renowned for its tabla merchants, head for **Triveni Music Centre** (D24/38 Pandey Ghat) and ask for Nandlal. Nandlal and his father also stage regular concerts at Triveni.

Yoga schools and teachers are a dime a dozen in Varanasi; even your hotel will likely have a morning yoga session. If you're more serious, however, contact **Dr. Vagish Shastri** at his residence behind the Bread of Life Bakery (Vagyoga Chetanapitham, B3/131A, Shivala; ✆ 0542/31-1706; vagyoga@hotmail.com) between 7 and 9am. He operates a range of courses in yoga as well as Kundalini meditation and Sanskrit; it's worth contacting him well before you intend traveling.

Note: If you take a cycle-rickshaw for the evening *aarti* ceremony, you will encounter terrible pollution. Additionally, because the supply of electricity to Varanasi is erratic, most hotels and restaurants use diesel generators. Unfortunately, their exhaust pipes are often at face level, spewing diesel fumes into Varanasi's narrow streets as you walk or cycle by. Carry a cotton handkerchief/scarf with you, cover your nose and mouth with it, and breathe through the cotton to make your way through an otherwise suffocating environment.

⟨Fun Fact⟩ The Polluted Elixir of Life

According to religious belief, the Ganges is *amrita,* elixir of life, "cleanser of sin," "eternal womb," and "purifier of souls." Even from a scientific point of view, the river once had an almost miraculous ability to purify itself—up to 100 years ago, microbes such as cholera could not survive in these sacred waters. Sadly, the Ganges is today one of the most polluted rivers in the world. This is mostly due to the chemical toxins dumped by industrial factories that line the river, but Varanasi's ancient sewers and a population with equally ancient attitudes toward waste disposal (including the dumping of an estimated 45,000 uncremated corpses annually) are problems the Uttar Pradesh Water Board struggles to overcome. Several eco-groups like the Sankat Mochan Foundation at Tulsi Ghat are working to alleviate the environmental degradation of the Ganges, but as you will find abundantly clear within an hour of being in Varanasi, much more needs to be done. Still, it may be something of a miracle that so many people perform their daily ablutions—with full-body immersions—in the waters and apparently suffer no harm; it's even a popular stunt with braver tourists.

CRUISING THE GHATS ✩✩✩

Drifting along the Ganges, admiring the densely textured backdrop of 18th- and 19th-century temples and palaces that line the 84-odd bathing *ghats,* you will be confronted with one of the most spiritually uplifting or downright weird tableaus on the entire crazy subcontinent: Down below, waist-deep pilgrims raise their arms in supplication, priests meditate by staring directly into the rising sun or are frozen in complicated yoga positions, wrestlers limber up, and disinterested onlookers toss live rats from the towering walls of the Old City, among other assorted goings-on. Note that you'll need to get here between 4:30am and 6am (check sunrise times with your hotel, as well as the time it takes to get to the *ghats),* so plan an early wake-up call. You should be able to hire a boat anywhere along the *ghats,* but most people either catch one from **Assi Ghat,** the southernmost *ghat,* or—particularly if you're staying in the Cantonment area—from **Dasashwamedh** (literally "10-horse-sacrifice," referring to an ancient sacrificial rite performed by Brahma). Situated roughly halfway, this is the most accessible and popular *ghat* and is always crawling with pilgrims, hawkers, and priests surveying the scene from under bamboo umbrellas. Boats operate at a fixed rate (at press time) of Rs 100 ($2.45/£1.25) per hour—this hasn't changed in years. The following descriptions of the 100-odd *ghats* assume that you will leave from here; note that it's worth traveling both north and south. You can do another trip in the evening as the sun is setting, but don't travel too far—boating is limited after sunset (except at the time of *aarti,* when you can sail up to watch the ceremony from the water).

Heading North from Dasashwamedh Ghat   From here, you pass **Man Mandir Ghat** which, along with the beautiful palace that overlooks it, was built by the Maharaja Man Singh of Amber in 1600. Jai Singh, who built the Jantar Mantars, converted the palace into an observatory in 1710. Hours are 7am to 5:30pm; entrance costs Rs 100 ($2.45/£1.25). Next is **Mir Ghat,** where the New Vishwanath Temple, Vishalakshi shrine, and Dharma Kupa (where the Lord of Death relinquished his hold over those who die in Varanasi), are found. North lies **Lalita Ghat,** with its distinctive Nepalese Temple, and beyond it is the "burning" **Manikarnika Ghat,** the principal and favored *smashan ghat* (cremation ground) of Varanasi, where you can see funeral-pyre flames burning 24 hours, tended by the *doms,* or "Untouchables"—touching the dead is considered polluting to all but these low castes. Boats are requested to keep their distance as a sign of respect. On this *ghat* is the venerated **Manikarnika Kund,** the world's first *tirtha,* said to have been dug out by Vishnu, whose sweat filled it as he created the world as ordered by Shiva. Some say that Shiva shivered in delight when he saw what Vishnu had created, dropping an earring into the pool; others say that it was the earring of Sati, Shiva's dead wife, hence the name Manikarnika: "jeweled earring." Between the Kund and the *ghat* is what is supposed to be Vishnu's footprint. Adjacent is **Scindia Ghat,** with its distinctive, half-submerged Shiva temple, toppled by weight; then **Ram Ghat** and **Panchganga Ghat** (said to be empowered by the five mythical streams that flow here into the Ganges), and one of the five *tirthas* at which pilgrims perform rituals. Behind the *ghat* glowers **Alamgir Mosque,** built by Aurangzeb on a Hindu temple he destroyed; note also the almost submerged cells where the Kashi pundits (priests) are freeze-framed in meditation poses. Proceed from here to **Gai, Trilochana,** and **Raj** *ghats,* but it's best (if you still want to proceed south) to turn back at Panchganga (or explore the north banks further on foot).

Heading South   Passing **Chaumsathi Ghat,** where the temple houses images of Kali and Durga; and **Dhobi Ghat,** alive with the sound of laundry workers rhythmically beating clothing that have been "cleansed" by the Ganges, you come to **Kedara Ghat,** notable for its red-and-white-striped South Indian–style temple. Farther south lie **Harishchandra Ghat,** Varanasi's second cremation *ghat* (though less popular because it also houses an electric crematorium); and **Tulsi Ghat,** named in honor of Goswami Tulsidas, a revered Hindu poet. Nearby is **Lolark Kund,** where childless women come to bathe and pray for progeny. The final stop (or the first, if your accommodations make a south-north journey more convenient) is **Assi Ghat,** a simple clay bank situated at the confluence of the Ganga and Assi rivers. From here you can walk to **Durga Temple,** which lies farther west from the *ghat. Note:* If you want to walk from Assi Ghat to Dasashwamedh, the trip will take a leisurely 60 to 90 minutes. Although the best time to walk or cruise the river is at sunrise or before sunset, you may wish to see the river in a completely different and relatively quiet "avatar," in which case take a late-afternoon stroll down the *ghats* in winter.

Bharat Kala Bhavan Museum *ꝑꝑ* As is so often the case in India, this museum suffers from poor curatorship, with exhibits—which are marvelous—haphazardly displayed and poorly labeled. You may even have trouble persuading the guards to turn on all the lights and show you the rooms behind the screen—hence the need for a good guide. The miniature-painting collection is superb, as are many of the Hindu and Buddhist sculptures and Mughal artifacts, though again, without a guide there is no way to know, for instance, that the otherwise nondescript coin behind the glass was minted by the Mughal emperor Akbar—and in keeping with his legendary religious tolerance, it has a Hindu symbol printed on one side and an Islamic on the other. Set aside 2 hours to explore.

Benaras Hindu University. Admission Rs 100 ($2.45/£1.25); still camera free, video not allowed. July–Apr Mon–Sat 11am–4pm; May–June closes at 12:30pm.

Kashi Vishwanath Temple *ꝑꝑ* Of the more than 2,000 temples in Varanasi, the most important is Kashi Vishwanath Temple, or "Golden Temple," dedicated to Lord Shiva, the presiding deity of the city. Because of repeated destruction by the invading sultans and later by Aurangzeb, the current Vishwanath is a relatively modern building: It was built in 1777 by the Maharani of Indore, and the *shikhara* (spire) and ceilings were plated with 820 kilograms (1,808 lb.) of gold, a gift from Maharaja Ranjit Singh, in 1839. Five major *aartis* are held daily, but the temple is always abuzz with worshipers. Sadly, non-Hindus may not enter, but by taking a stroll through the Vishwanath Galli (pronounced *Gul*-ley, meaning lane) that runs the length of it, you can get a glimpse of the interior, which exudes pungent smells and constant noise. For a small donation, you can climb to one of the second floors or rooftops of the shops that line the lane and get a good view. Note that adjacent is **Gyanvapi Mosque,** built by Aurangzeb on a Hindu temple site and heavily guarded to ensure that no trouble erupts. Ironically, this is also the starting point for many pilgrims on their quest to visit all the *tirthas* in a ritual journey, accompanied by a priest who recites the *sankalpa,* or "declaration of intent." Nearby is **Annapurna Temple,** dedicated to Shakti.

Vishwanath Galli. Temple is closed to non-Hindus; compound is accessible. No cameras or cellphones allowed within the Galli and temple compound.

A SIDE TRIP TO SARNATH

After gaining enlightenment, **Sarnath** *ꝑ* is where Buddha gave his first sermon some 2,500 years ago, and continued to return with followers. For many centuries after this, it was renowned as a Buddhist center of learning, housing some 3,000 monks, but successive Muslim invasions and later lootings destroyed the monasteries and much of the art. Today it still attracts many pilgrims, but—unless you're very familiar with Buddha's personal history or are an archaeologist—the site itself is nowhere near as inspiring as his teachings, and you're likely to experience it all as nothing more than a boring pile of bricks. The most impressive sight is **Dhamekh Stupa,** if only for its sheer age. Built around A.D. 500, with a massive girth, it still towers 31m (102 ft.) into the air and is said to mark the very spot where Buddha revealed his Eightfold Path leading to nirvana. The ruins of **Dharmarajika Stupa** lie immediately north of the entrance. Beyond is the **Ashokan Pillar**—the stupa is said to have been one of 28 built by Ashoka, the 3rd-century-B.C. Mauryan king and bloodthirsty warrior who was to become one of the most passionate converts to Buddhism. Beyond these are the ruins of monasteries. Across the road from the entrance to the main site is **Sarnath Archaeological Museum,** where you can view the four-headed lion that once topped the Ashoka Pillar; created in the 3rd century B.C., it's made from sandstone, polished to look like marble. The lion capital, with the wheel beneath representing Buddha's "wheel of dharma," is today a national emblem for India, found on all currency notes and official government documents. East of the Dhamek Stupa is **Mulagandha Kuti** (main temple), which houses an image of Buddha (ironically enough, against his wishes, images of Buddha abounded after his death). The walls contain frescoes pertaining to his life history—a good crash course for the novice if accompanied by a guide. You can also visit the peaceful **Tibetan Buddhist Monastery,** a lovely, bright space with display cases filled with hundreds of miniature Buddhas.

Sarnath is 10km (6¼ miles) north of Varanasi. Admission Rs 100 ($2.45/£1.25). Daily 7am–6:30pm. Museum Rs 2 (5¢/3p); Sat–Thurs 10am–5pm; cameras not allowed (lockers provided). Mulagandha Kuti 4–11:30am and 1:30–8pm. Daily chanting Rs 5 (12¢/6p) for use of still camera, Rs 25 (60¢/30p) video; Nov–Feb 6pm, Mar–May 6:30pm, June–Oct 7pm. Tibetan Buddhist Monastery free admission; 5am–noon and 2–6:30pm.

WHERE TO STAY

In a general sense, you have two options: You can stay in one of the waterfront lodgings, most of which (with the exception of the two reviewed below) are very basic; or you can spend the night in the relative peace and comfort of the Cantonment area, where the most "luxurious" options are. Still, with a few exceptions (including our two choice picks, below), the Cantonment hotels tend to look very frayed, if not downright decaying. And the downside of staying in the Cantonment is that you feel very cut off from the real Varanasi, and require an earlier morning wake-up call to get to the *ghats;* for the sunset *aarti,* when the streets are often jammed, it may take 30 minutes (and a blood-curdling taxi or rickshaw ride) to get there, and you'll walk the last part. These issues can be solved by staying in a hotel on the Ganges, but this also means you have no chance of unwinding at a pool, eating meat, or drinking alcohol— still, if you manage to bag a river-facing room, you will have the delight of a waterfront view, with the surreal experience of Varanasi on your doorstep. *Note:* Staying in one of the budget hotels away from the *ghats* is inadvisable unless you're used to budget traveling; many have no windows, and the noise is incessant.

CANTONMENT

Radisson Hotel Varanasi ★★ *Value*   One of only two of Varanasi's so-called top-end hotels, the Radisson offers a host of modern conveniences and ultra-contemporary accommodations, but is quite a distance from the riverside action. Guest rooms are large and comfortable (the thick, plush mattresses are the best in town), with thick drapes and chocolate-brown furniture offset by pale walls. The marble bathrooms—also the best in town—are moderately proportioned, with green marble floors and gleaming fittings. The most recently upgraded rooms are the very smart Club Floor units; these have snazzy wooden floors with rugs (superior rooms are carpeted), plasma screen TVs, and wonderful rainfall showers. There's also a full spa and a small-ish pool with wooden deck chairs and its own bar; breakfasts are served in the bright sunflower-themed coffee shop. The free railway station transfer is very convenient if you're arriving by overnight train from Delhi. The drawback of this otherwise good chain hotel? None of the rooms have views worth mentioning.

The Mall, Cantonment, Varanasi 221 002. ℂ 0542/250-1515. Fax 0542/250-1516. www.radisson.com. radvar@sify.com. 116 units. $160 (£80) superior double; $280 (£140) suite; $20 (£10) extra bed. Rates include breakfast and railway transfers; taxes extra. Check online for special deals. AE, DC, MC, V. Amenities: 2 restaurants; bar; lounge and pastry bar; pool; health club; spa; travel desk; business center; 24-hr. room service; babysitting; doctor-on-call; currency exchange; palmist; resident artist. In room: A/C, TV, minibar, tea- and coffee-making facilities, hair dryer, iron and ironing board, safe, wireless Internet.

Taj Ganges ⭐⭐   Before the Radisson opened, the Taj Ganges was undisputedly the best hotel away from the *ghats,* but this had more to do with the pathetic competition than any superior features. Within an ugly 1970s monolith, rooms have been reno-vated over the past few years to create a more contemporary ambience; even the cheap-est (superior) rooms have wooden floors and white cotton linens, but you'll be far more comfortable in one of the stylish deluxe rooms, which not only have comfy divans and plasma TVs to increase the illusion of glamour, but also rugs, throws, cush-ions, and colorful paintings set against the pale cream walls. Best of all, the small bath-rooms have been completely upgraded. You'd do well, however, to consider one of the lovely, cozy suites (book no. 527, which occupies a top corner and is very spacious and gracious, with a huge bathroom). What distinguishes this old five-star stalwart are service and the vast array of amenities, as well as a real passion for the region; the hotel hires the best guides in the city, shopping tips are excellent, and the travel desk will arrange tours as far afield as Bodhgaya. It also has huge, sprawling grounds, a great pool, and two of the best restaurants in town (this does not mean that the meal will be the best you have in India, however). If you don't mind attracting a lot of atten-tion, there's also an unusual boat tour: A beautiful old horse-drawn carriage, once belonging to the maharajas, clip-clops through the old city to the *ghats,* after which you board a luxury boat and experience the Ganges in style. You can also take a car-riage ride around the 16-hectare (40-acre) hotel property, which includes a genuine little palace; long-term plans to turn **Nadesar Palace** into luxurious suites began in April 2007, so ask about the current status of this heritage property.

Nadesar Palace, Varanasi 221 002. ℂ 0542/250-3001 through -3019. Fax 0542/220-4898. www.tajhotels.com. 130 units. $190 (£95) superior double; $225 (£113) deluxe double; $235 (£118) executive suite; $290 (£145) deluxe suite. $25 (£13) extra bed. AE, MC, V. Amenities: 2 restaurants; bar; pool; golf; tennis; health club; spa; indoor games; travel desk; business center; shop; 24-hr. room service; massage; laundry; doctor-on-call; badminton; table tennis; yoga; astrologer. In room: A/C, TV, minibar, tea- and coffee-making facilities, electronic safe, Wi-Fi enabled.

WATERFRONT

Ganges View Guesthouse ⭐⭐ *(Value)*   You're required to remove your shoes upon entering this lovely colonial lodge at the edge of the Ganges, and it's an appropriate gesture of respect given the effort that has turned this budget guesthouse—the best on the Ganges—into such a comfortable haven. In fact, it's so popular with certain repeat guests (many of them artists and musicians) that you'd do well to book your room up

Mindless Necrophagy or Road to Salvation?

Of all the *sadhus* (ascetics) and holy men you will see in Varanasi, perhaps the hardest to understand without brutal judgment are the Aghori sect and their bizarre rituals. You may spot the occasional Aghori at a *smashan ghat* (cremation ground) in Varanasi, usually with matted hair and no clothing, or just covered in white ash, or at most wearing a funeral shroud. The skull he carries is his cranial eating and drinking bowl. Aghoris roam the cremation grounds, where they may smear themselves with the ash from the pyres and/or meditate sitting atop a corpse. It is alleged that as a once-in-a-lifetime act they sometimes also eat a piece of a corpse's flesh. While their rituals are extremely radical and even abhorrent to most, it's interesting to understand what underlies this bizarre behavior. Aghoris believe that acting contrary to the accepted norms and taboos of Brahmin ritual and belief is the necessary path to enlightenment. As a result, they eat meat, drink alcohol, and smoke intoxicants. By seeking to reverse all values entrenched within mainstream Hinduism, they choose to embrace all that a Brahmin considers impure. Close contact with the dead, they believe, is a way of focusing on their single-minded quest to live with reality. The funeral pyre is thus for the Aghoris a continual reminder that everyone has to die, and their obsession with death an attempt to live in intimate awareness of it.

---

to a year in advance. The gorgeous, simple guest rooms feature marble floors and French doors that open onto enclosed corridors filled with ornamental columns, charming bric-a-brac, antique furniture, and animal trophies. Straw mats and colorful Indian throws add character to the tiny bedrooms. Book an upstairs room if you want air-conditioning (and specify clearly if you also want a waterfront view). Evening meals (which should be booked in advance) are traditional affairs taken in the pretty dining room, but the large, open-air upstairs terrace (packed with potted plants and stylish cane furniture) is a delightful spot for breakfast, accompanied by excellent views of activity at the *ghats* down below. Cheerful and homey, with books to peruse and covetous objets d'art to admire, this guesthouse somehow feels just right.

B1/163 Assi Ghat, Varanasi 221 006. © **0542/231-3218.** Fax 0542/236-9695. hotelgangesview@yahoo.com. 14 units. Rs 1,500 ($37/£19) non-A/C double; Rs 3,000 ($73/£37) A/C double. Rates are discounted Apr–Sept. No credit cards. **Amenities:** Dining room; taxi and sightseeing arrangements; room service; laundry; musical performances. *In room:* A/C (most).

Palace on Ganges ⊕   It's no palace, but for the waterfront this is a reasonably smart option. Guest rooms are small but attractive, with marble or parquet floors and rugs, king-size beds with hard foam mattresses, and the best amenities on the Ganges. Walls are decorated with artworks reflecting aspects of Indian heritage sites, and each room is a tribute to a different regional style. Bathrooms (showers only) are tiny, modern, and done in colorful tiles. The heritage theme is carried throughout, with polished brown marble stairways, dark wood paneling, and intricately carved period furniture featuring inlaid decorative tiles. Although its location overlooking the Ganges is one of the selling points, you aren't guaranteed a river-view room (do request one, though longer stays enjoy first dibs), and views from the rooftop terrace restaurant (Jain food only) include an unpleasant garbage dump at the water's edge.

B-1/158 Assighat, Varanasi 221 001. © **0542/231-5050,** -4304, or -4305. Fax 0542/220-4898 or 0542/231-4306. www.palaceonganges.com. info@palaceonganges.com. 24 units. Rs 3,500 ($85/£43) double; off season (May–July)

Rs 2,000 ($49/£25) double. Taxes extra. AE, MC, V. **Amenities:** 2 restaurants; travel desk; car hire; 24-hr. room service; laundry; doctor-on-call. *In room:* A/C, TV, minibar.

WHERE TO DINE

Be warned that Varanasi is not known for its culinary finesse. Varanasi's best and smartest restaurant is **Varuna** (© 0542/250-3001), in the Taj Ganges hotel, which features a vast menu of Indian specialties (illustrated with chilies to indicate those that are super-strength), a comfortable air-conditioned interior, and helpful service. For the works, served on a traditional Varanasi silver platter, order the Satvik Thali (Rs 505/$12/£6.25). That said, this is very much a hotel restaurant, and you may not be in the Cantonment area at lunchtime. The Taj's **Chowk** restaurant does dinner buffet spreads that are popular with foreign tour groups, and at Rs 600 ($15/£7.40), the buffets offer very good value.

For a hygienic meal while exploring the Old City, your options are remarkably limited. Varanasi caters rather haphazardly to the budget Western traveler, with a split focus on affordability and cleanliness, presumably implied by the involvement of foreign management. If you want authentic Indian food, we recommend calling ahead to find out about the possibility of a meal at **Ganges View Guesthouse** (see above) or that old stalwart Keshari (reviewed below). There's the rather iconic **Bread of Life Bakery & Restaurant** (B3/322 Shivala; © 0542/227-5012; www.bolbar.com), a basic cafe established by James and Monika Hetherington, an American interior designer and a German flight attendant. The decor is very sterile (white-vinyl-top tables), and staff borders on comatose, but you can enjoy wholesome Western dishes and freshly baked breads and muffins knowing that you are making a positive contribution—all profits from the bakery and the silk shop above (which, incidentally, has a good selection of scarves and linen made by local weavers) go to local charities, including the Mother Teresa Hospice. Daily specials include steaming-hot vegetable moussaka, chickpea goulash, ratatouille, and warm Portuguese salad. Hot dishes take a while to arrive, so you can be certain that everything is freshly prepared and, in a city known for food-related mishaps, that hygiene is a priority. We've noticed standards lagging in recent times, so you might instead consider laid-back **Lotus Lounge** (D14/27, Mansarowar Ghat; © 98-3856-7717), an open-air eatery on the *ghats,* benefiting from a bird's-eye view of the Ganges. Perfect for all-day chilling (lounge on floor cushions or sit at tables set with candles at night), the space is lorded over by a serene-looking Buddha mural and operated by an Indo-German couple, Martina and Atul, who vary the menu seasonally and plan to introduce a bakery in 2008. Count on fresh ingredients and wide-ranging international choices: gazpacho (made with ginger), red Thai curry, impressive ravioli, and wonderful Tibetan-style *momos* (dumplings). While meat is generally an absolute no-no anywhere near the river, here you can even order fresh chicken. It's open September through mid-May.

The Keshari Restaurant *(Value* INDIAN   A stern-looking, bespectacled clerk sits counting cash at the entrance of this busy, cramped restaurant (ideal if you're exploring the Old City) hidden away down a near-impossible-to-find back street (to get here, head down the lane opposite the La-Ra Hotel). Inside, wall-mounted fans and ancient cooling systems blast away while waiters dash between tables packed with locals, pilgrims, and bewildered foreigners. There's a huge selection of Indian, Chinese, and other dishes, all vegetarian, but we recommend you stick to the Indian fare, which includes an admirable assortment of curries, *biryanis, pulao,* and traditional breads. It also contains a list of commandments for diners that includes "AVOIDING

COMBING OF HAIR" and "NOT WASHING HANDS IN UTENSILS"! If you're particularly ravenous, order the huge Keshari Thali, with a selection of finger-licking curries served on a platter that includes *dal,* curd, rice, *naan,* and *roti.* The Keshari special *dosa* (pancake) is filled with creamy *paneer* and cashew nuts. Lassis are all fantastic. It may not be particularly relaxing, but this is certainly a place to mingle with real Indians.

D14/8 Teri Neem, Godaulia (Off Dasashwamedh Rd., near Godaulia crossing). (C) **0542/240-1472.** Main courses Rs 35–Rs 80 (85¢–$1.95/45p–£1); thalis Rs 55–Rs 100 ($1.35–$2.45/70p–£1.25). No credit cards. Daily 9am–10:30pm.

SHOPPING

Varanasi is famous above all for its silk—every Indian bride wants a Benarasi silk sari in her trousseau, and around 3,000 kilograms (6,614 lb.) of silk are consumed by the weaving units daily. Wander through the Old City, or ask at your hotel or the tourist office for recommended wholesalers. **Silk Ways** ((C) **0542/221-0791**), near Chhave Mahal Cinema, has the most gossamer-like scarves, among other things. Or head for one of these two recommended sari shops in Chowk: **Narayan Das Jagdish Das** ((C) **0542/240-0561** or -0593) or **Ushnak Mal Mool Chand** ((C) **0542/227-6253**).

For an excellent selection of Indian fiction and books on philosophy and religion, not to mention good CDs, visit **Kashi Annapurna Book House** (B1/185B, Main Assi Ghat; (C) **0542/231-5992**), a small enterprise near Ganges View Guesthouse.

4 Khajuraho ⭒⭒⭒

600km (372 miles) SE of Delhi; 415km (257 miles) SW of Varanasi; 395km (245 miles) SE of Agra

Legend has it that when the Moon God saw the young maiden Hemavati bathing in a river, her beauty was such that he descended to earth to engage in a passionate affair. Before his return to the celestial realm, he swore she would bear a son who would one day erect a great temple to celebrate the beauty of their divine love. Thus the founder of the mighty Chandela dynasty, a robust clan of the warrior Rajputs, was born, and between A.D. 900 and 1100, the Chandela kings—who settled in remote Khajuraho, where they were clearly unhindered by the usual distractions of fighting off invading forces—built not 1 but 85 temples, almost all of them featuring exquisite sculptures of men and women joyfully engaging in the most intimate and erotic acts. The Chandelas held sway here until the start of the 13th century, when the Sultans of Delhi strengthened their hold over vast swaths of central North India. By the end of the 15th century, the temples were abandoned, hidden deep within thick jungle, until their accidental discovery by a British military adventurer in 1838. By this time, 7 centuries after the political decline of their Chandela creators, only around 24 of the original 85 temples were found. Today these UNESCO World Heritage Site monuments are famous for their erotic sculptures, images that—despite being transgressive by India's conservative contemporary standards—are almost as intimately associated with India as the Taj. But the temples also represent an outstanding synthesis of advanced architecture and refined sculpture, and their beauty means that a trip here should definitely be included in your North India itinerary, particularly if you plan to fly from Agra or Delhi to Varanasi.

ESSENTIALS

GETTING THERE & AWAY   By Air   It's most convenient to fly in from Varanasi (a mere 35-min. hop), on Jet Airways' connecting flight from Delhi (about the same price as Indian Airlines, but with better service). You can then continue on to Delhi or Varanasi the following day. Note that you should stay 2 nights if you really want to

Khajuraho

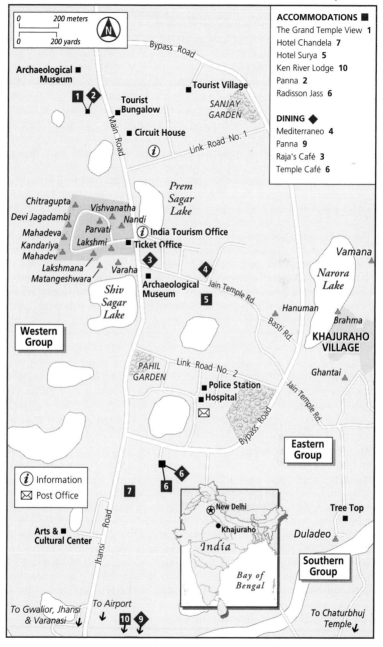

Scale: 0 — 200 meters / 0 — 200 yards

ACCOMMODATIONS ■
The Grand Temple View **1**
Hotel Chandela **7**
Hotel Surya **5**
Ken River Lodge **10**
Panna **2**
Radisson Jass **6**

DINING ◆
Mediterraneo **4**
Panna **9**
Raja's Café **3**
Temple Café **6**

Bypass Road

Archaeological ■ Museum

1 **2**

Tourist ■ Bungalow

Tourist Village ■

SANJAY GARDEN

Main Road

■ Circuit House

(i)

Link Road No. 1

Prem Sagar Lake

Chitragupta ▲
Devi Jagadambi ▲ Vishvanatha ▲
Mahadeva ▲ Parvati ▲ Nandi ▲
Kandariya ▲ Lakshmi ▲
Mahadev
Lakshmana ▲ Varaha ▲
Matangeshwara ▲

Shiv Sagar Lake

(i) **India Tourism Office**
■ **Ticket Office**

3

4

■ **Archaeological Museum**

5

Jain Temple Rd

Hanuman ▲

Basti Rd

Vamana ▲

Narora Lake

Brahma ▲

KHAJURAHO VILLAGE

Western Group

Eastern Group

PAHIL GARDEN

Link Road No. 2

■ **Police Station**
■ **Hospital**
⊠

Ghantai ▲

Jain Temple Rd

Bypass Road

(i) Information
⊠ Post Office

■ **6**

6

7

India

New Delhi ✪
Khajuraho ●

Tree Top ■

Duladeo ▲

Southern Group

Bay of Bengal

Arts & ■ Cultural Center

Jhansi Road

To Gwalior, Jhansi & Varanasi ↓

To Airport ↓

10 **9**

To Chaturbhuj Temple ↓

Fun Fact India's Ancient Sex Manual

Khajuraho's shops are filled with an endless variety of versions of the *Kama Sutra,* an ancient avatar of modern-day do-it-yourself sex manuals. With information about everything from "increasing the size of the male organ" to the benefits of "slaps and screams" and "bites and scratches," the ancient treatise on sensory pleasures—recorded by the scribe Vatsyayana from oral accounts sometime between the 1st and 6th century A.D.—remains the most famous Indian text in the world. The first English translation was published in 1883 by the Victorian adventurer Richard Burton, who adapted the text in order to dodge charges of obscenity; among other confusing details, he used the Sanskrit words *lingam* and *yoni* to denote the sexual organs. Meanwhile, the debate around the purpose of the erotic temple carvings continues: Some have suggested that they allude to the fact that worshipers were meant to leave all sexual desires at the door. Another interpretation is that the images are "manifestations of tantric practices," which is why these temples were known as Yogini temples, where images of exotic sexual positions possessed the power to ward off the evil eye. Another theory suggests that the erotica served to educate young men who as boys lived in hermitages, obeying the Hindu law of being *"brahmacharis"* until they attained manhood. Studying the sculptures— and the earthly passions they depicted—were the only way they could prepare themselves for the worldly role of husband. In other words, they were a form of sex education!

explore the temples thoroughly or visit the nearby Panna National Park. Daily Jet Airways flights leave Delhi at 10:40am and take off from Varanasi at 12:20pm, arriving in Khajuraho by 1pm. During the high season (winter), these are usually pretty full of package tour groups, so you'll need to book well in advance; by April, however, the planes are quite empty. Khajuraho's airport is 3km (2 miles) from the town center; taxis operate according to very strict fixed rates.

By Train & Road Khajuraho is expected to have its very own railway station by mid-2008; we're not holding our breath, but it's part of the state government's plan to stimulate domestic tourism in Madhya Pradesh. Until then, if you're traveling by train from Delhi or Chennai, you will disembark at Jhansi (175km/109 miles from Khajuraho). From New Delhi, catch the Bhopal Shatabdi, which leaves the capital's Nizamuddin Station at 6am and pulls in at Jhansi at 10:40am. From here, MPSRTC runs a bus service from Jhansi to Khajuraho, scheduled to meet the train from Delhi (around Rs 90/$2.20/£1.10—not recommended), or you can catch a taxi (Rs 2,500/ $61/£31) to Khajuraho (4 hr.). You can also rent a car and driver for a few days if you have plans to see more of the region—note that Orchha (20km/12 miles from Jhansi) is definitely worth a stop en route to Khajuraho (Orchha is discussed later in the chapter); try to spend the night if you have time. If you're traveling by train from Mumbai, Kolkata, or Varanasi, you will arrive at Satna, which is 117km (73 miles) or 3 hours from town. Note that it is possible to rent a vehicle and driver for the arduous overland journey onwards from Khajuraho to Bandhavgarh (discussed below); this should set you back a maximum of Rs 4,800 ($117/£59) for a non-A/C vehicle, or Rs. 6,000 ($146/£74) for a car with A/C, during peak season.

Note: We cannot overemphasize the appalling state of the roads in Madhya Pradesh. Avoid lengthy road trips, ensure sufficient stops, and don't travel at night. If you must, rent the services of a sturdy 4WD and driver, and check that your vehicle has at least one spare wheel.

VISITOR INFORMATION   M. P. Tourism (① **07686/27-4051;** mptkhaj@ sancharnet.in; Mon–Sat 10am–5pm, closed Sun and second and third Sat of the month) is in the Chandela Cultural Centre, Khajuraho. The more helpful **India Tourism office** (① **07686/27-2347;** Mon–Fri 9:30am–6pm) is located opposite the Western Group of Temples. Note that the state tourism website, **www.mptourism.com**, as well as the unrelated **www.khajuraho-temples.com**, are both decent sources of information.

GETTING AROUND   By Taxi, Auto-Rickshaw & Cycle-Rickshaw   You will be flooded with offers to take you from Khajuraho's airport to your accommodations; in return, touts and drivers expect you to use their services for the duration of your stay, and will even continue to lurk outside your hotel. Make it clear that yours is a one-time fare, and stick to cycle-rickshaws and walking for the duration of your stay (average rickshaw costs are Rs 150/$3.70/£1.85 for a half-day trip including a stop at the Southern Group). To visit the Panna National Park, expect to pay Rs 1,200 ($29/£15) for a taxi.

GUIDES   Guides charge Rs 350 ($8.55/£4.35) for a group of one to five people for 6 hours. You can hire the services of a guide at **Raja Café** (opposite the Western Group of temples; see below). Alternatively, the MPSTDC offers a "Walkman Tour"—an audioguide tour purchased at the M. P. Tourism counter at the entrance to the Western Group; this costs Rs 50 ($1.25/65p), but do check that everything is in working order before you set out. Be warned that most guides in Khajuraho are just plain dreadful. They may be fine for pointing out details you might otherwise miss, but they regularly spout fundamentalist nonsense and provide the most unbelievable explanations for why erotica was carved on these temples (one classic explanation is that the scenes were created to tell people what "*not* to do"). An exception to the normal drivel is **Samson George** (① **98-9317-3280**), a light-hearted guy who provides savvy historical information, with explanations that separate fact from legend.

FESTIVALS   The **Khajuraho Dance Festival** ✹✹ is held between February 25 and March 2, when the temples are transformed into a magical backdrop for India's top classical dancers, who perform traditional Odissi, Kuchipudi, and Bharatnatyam dance forms, as well as contemporary Indian dance styles. For up-to-date information, visit **www.khajuraho-temples.com**. *Tip:* Hotels get packed during this time, so you may need to book months ahead.

Tips Services Unlimited

As you wend your way around town, all sorts of men and boys will try to "adopt" you by starting up polite conversations—a pattern you will quickly recognize—before getting down to the business of offering their services for a range of possible needs: tour guides, transport, bicycle hire, shopping assistance, advice, or a tour of the local village school. All are moneymaking enterprises of which you should be wary; best to make it very clear that you have no intention of parting with your money, and leave it to your new friend to decide whether or not to stick around.

EXPLORING KHAJURAHO'S TEMPLES

Known for the profusion of sculptural embellishments on both exterior and interior walls, Khajuraho's temples are also recognizable for the exaggerated vertical sweep in the majority of the temples, with a series of *shikharas* (spires) that grow successively higher. Serving as both metaphoric and literal "stairways to heaven," these *shikharas* are believed to be a visual echo of the soaring Himalayan mountains, abode of Lord Shiva. Most of the sculpted temples are elevated on large plinths (often also shared by four smaller corner shrines), and follow the same five-part design. After admiring the raised entrance area, you will enter a colonnaded hall that leads to a smaller vestibule and then an inner courtyard, around which is an enclosed sanctum. You can circumnavigate the sanctum (move around the temple in a clockwise direction, in the manner of the ritual *pradakshina,* with your right shoulder nearest the temple building) to view the beautifully rendered friezes of gods, nymphs, animals, and energetically twisting bodies locked together in acts of hot-blooded passion.

Originally spread across a large open area, unprotected by walls, the temples—most of them built from sandstone lugged on bullock carts from the banks of the River Ken 30km (19 miles) away—are today roughly divided into three sections according to geographic location: the Western, Eastern, and Southern groups. The most spectacular—and those most obviously dripping with erotic sculpture—are within the Western Group. The Eastern Group is located near the old village, and the Southern Group, which is the most missable, lies south of this. As none of the temples outside the Western Group are likely to evoke quite the same delighted reaction, see these first if you're pushed for time or tired; they're also conveniently located near the majority of hotels. Try to enter as soon as they open (sunrise), not only for the quality of light but to avoid the busloads of tourists who will almost certainly detract from the experience.

You can cover the Western Group in 2 hours. The baritone voice of Amitabh Bachchan, arguably India's most popular screen icon, narrates the fascinating history of Khajuraho for the 50-minute **sound-and-light show** held here each night at 6:30pm (an hr. later in summer). Try to time your visit to the Eastern Group for about 3 or 4pm, so you can enjoy the sunset while you return either to the Western Group or to the imminently more peaceful Chaturbhuj Temple in the Southern Group. To save time and get the most out of the experience, an official guide—hired through the Raja Café, tourist office, or your hotel—is highly recommended; avoid all unofficial touts and guides. Note that you can rent an audioguide, which is useful if you don't want to be accompanied by a guide.

Tip: When setting out to explore the temples, be sure to wear shoes that you can easily slip on and off. Each time you enter a temple building—even if it is no longer in use—you are required to "please put down your shoes."

WESTERN GROUP 👁👁👁

As you make your way around the complex in a clockwise direction, the first important structure you'll encounter is **Lakshmana Temple** 👁👁👁, one of the three largest in Khajuraho. Built in commemoration of military victory and temporal power, it is thought to be one of the earliest Chandela temples, completed around A.D. 954, yet relatively intact. The structure is as high as it is long, and its raised platform is, like the entire temple, heavily decorated with a variety of sculptures that allude to the pleasures, pastimes, lifestyle, desires, and conquests of the Chandela dynasty. Here you will witness an astonishing diversity of scenes: horse-mounted hunters pursuing their prey, musicians providing lively entertainment for the court, couples drunk on love and liquor, female attendants fanning their king, elephants engaged in playful battle, soldiers on the march, and, of course, amorous couples keeping themselves occupied in the most literal of pleasures. Higher up, above bands of images of Shiva and Vishnu, are the voluptuous depictions of women engaged in worldly activity while draped in little more than jewelry and gossamer-like garments. Inside the temple, covered with more depictions of gorgeous women and deities in their various avatars and incarnations, light pours in through high balconies on each side of the structure, and shadows are cast seductively over the imaginatively carved walls. The main shrine was built to house the three-headed image of Vishnu-Vaikuntha, which features one human head and the head of two of Vishnu's avatars (incarnations), a lion and a boar.

Opposite the temple are two smaller structures, **Devi Mandap** and **Varaha Mandap** ⊀. The latter is an open sandstone pavilion on a high platform with 14 pillars supporting a high pyramidal roof with a flat ceiling carved with lovely lotus designs. A large stone sculpture of Varaha, the incarnation of Vishnu as the boar, dominates the space. Varaha's polished monolithic body is carved with hundreds of tiny Brahmanical gods and goddesses.

At the northeastern end of the Western Group complex, a number of magnificent temples are found in proximity to one another. Thought to have been built between A.D. 1017 and 1029, elegantly proportioned **Kandariya Mahadev Temple** ⊀⊀⊀ is considered the finest temple in Khajuraho, with 872 statues adorning the interior and exterior. Within niches around the temple are images of Ganesh and the seven mother goddesses or *Sapta Matrikas.* Again, among the sculptures of Shiva and the other deities is a profusion of female figures engaged in daily activities made lovely by the sheer exuberance of the sculptural technique: A woman stretches, another plays with a ball, another admires her reflection in a mirror. You won't have to search too hard to find fascinating erotic panels; kissing, caressing couples are depicted with their bodies entwined in blissful union, while others, sometimes in groups of three or four, engage in more lascivious activities. To enter the temple building, you pass through the beautiful entrance *toran;* sculpted from a single piece of stone, this is a floral garland that stems from the mouths of *makaras,* ever-watchful mythical crocodiles, and is carried across the doorway by flying nymphs. Within the temple, walls are covered with exquisite carvings: Don't forget to look upward to appreciate the sculpted flower and leaf motifs of the ceilings. There's a Shiva lingam deep within the *garbha griha,* or "womb chamber"; devotees today place flowers on and around the lingam.

Next to Kandariya Mahadev Temple is small **Mahadev Shrine,** which features a sculpted figure of what is thought to be the emblem of the Chandela dynasty, a raging lion fighting with a kneeling figure. Alongside it is **Devi Jagadambi Temple** ⊀⊀ — note the graceful woman who stands half-naked as she interrupts her bath, possibly to catch a glimpse of Shiva's wedding procession. The southern wall includes a panel with a woman climbing up her lover's stout, standing body so that she can kiss him passionately. Although originally dedicated to Vishnu, the temple now houses a large image of Devi Jagadambi, the goddess of the universe, also known as Kali, one of the avatars of Shiva's divine consort. In both this and nearby **Chitragupta Temple** ⊀, images of Parvati and Shiva in the throes of amorous passion are symbolic of the "cosmic union that makes the world go round." Chitragupta, which was poorly renovated by the Maharaja of Chattarpur, is dedicated to Surya, the sun god; the relief carving around the entrance is the temple's highlight. Within the temple is the figure of Surya riding his sun chariot across the eternal sky.

Back near the entrance of the complex stands the **Temple of Vishvanatha** ⚐, built in A.D. 1002 by King Dhanga, and notable for three female figures that decorate the building. One maiden plays the flute, her back sensuously exposed to the viewer, another cradles a baby, and the third has a parrot seated on her wrist. Opposite the main entrance is **Nandi Pavilion** (or *mandap*), in which one of the largest figures of Shiva's companion, Nandi the bull, can be found, sculpted from a single piece of stone.

Outside the walls of the Western Group complex, but right alongside the Lakshman Temple, is the still-functioning **Matangeshvar Temple.** It is here that the annual Maha-Shivratri Festival culminates when the Shiva-Parvati marriage ceremony is accompanied by latter-day wedding rituals, lasting through the entire night in a fantastic collaboration of myth and reality.

Planning a major upgrade and a move is the **Archaeological Museum,** at press time still situated across the road from the entrance to the Western Group. By the time you visit, the museum will have relocated to fancy new quarters just outside the town, adjacent to the Grand Temple View hotel. Hopefully, the modest collection of sculptures sampling various Khajuraho sites will be expanded and improved upon. The advantage of spending a few minutes here is that you get to see close-up details of carved figures that usually occur high up on the temple *shikharas.*

Main Rd., opposite the State Bank of India. Admission Rs 250 ($6.10/£3.10) or pay $5 in foreign currency. Daily sunrise–sunset. English-language sound-and-light show Rs 250 ($6.10/£3.10); Mar–June 7:30pm, Sept–Oct 7pm, Nov–Feb 6:30pm. Archaeological Museum Rs 5 (12¢/6p); Sat–Thurs 10am–5pm. No photography in the museum.

EASTERN GROUP

The Eastern Group comprises both Hindu and Jain temples. The entrance to the Jain **Shantinath Temple** is guarded by a pair of mythical lions; inside, you are confronted by esoteric charts detailing some of the finer points of Jain philosophy. Photographs of important sculptures and Jain architecture line some of the walls, while the individual shrine entrances are carved with amorous, non-erotic couples and other figures. The main shrine contains a large sculpted image of a naked saint. Throughout the temple, devotees place grains of rice and nuts as tributes at the feet of the various saints.

Parsvanatha Temple ⚐ dates to the middle of the 10th century A.D. and is the finest and best preserved of Khajuraho's old Jain temples. Since Jainism promotes an ascetic doctrine, there are no erotic images here, but the sculptural decoration is rich nonetheless. In a large panel at the right side of the entrance are images of meditating and naked Jain saints *(tirthankaras),* while the temple exterior is covered in decorative sculptures of voluptuous maidens, embracing couples, and solo male figures representing various Hindu deities. This is a strong indication that the temple—which recalls the temples of the Western Group—was perhaps originally Hindu. In the same complex, **Adinath Temple** has been modified and reconstructed with plastered masonry and even concrete.

Moving north to the Hindu temples, you will pass **Ghantai Temple;** built in A.D. 1148, it is named for the pretty sculpted bells that adorn its pillars. Passing between Javari Temple and the granite and sandstone "Brahma" Temple (more likely to be dedicated to Shiva given the presence of a lingam), you come to the northernmost of the Eastern Group temples, the Hindu **Vamana Temple,** built between A.D. 1050 and 1075. Vamana is the short, plump, dwarf incarnation of Vishnu. The entrance to the inner sanctum of this temple is decorated with small erotic relief panels; within the sanctum you will see Vishnu in many forms, including the Buddha, believed to be one of his incarnations.

SOUTHERN GROUP

One of the last temples to be built, **Duladeo Temple** dates back to the 12th century A.D. but has been subjected to later restoration. Standing on the banks of Khuddar Stream, facing east, the temple is dedicated to Shiva. Elaborately crowned and ornamented *apsaras,* flying *vidyadharas,* crocodile-mounted *ashtavasu* figures, and sculptures of over-ornamented and stereotypically endowed characters in relatively shallow relief decorate the interior. As at Parshwanath Temple, the walls of Duladeo feature a narrow band of sculptures that depict the celestial garland carriers and musicians in attendance at the wedding of Shiva and Parvati.

The unexceptional **Chaturbhuj Temple,** 3km (2 miles) south of Duladeo, sees very little traffic but has a remarkable sculpture of Vishnu and is a peaceful place at the best of times, not least at sunset. Nearby excavations continue to unearth new temple complexes, as Khajuraho keeps revealing more hidden gems.

WHERE TO STAY

If you're simply overnighting, it's best to stay in the village, from where you can walk to the majority of temples—the Grand Temple View is your best bet here. For those who want a more adventurous, earthy experience and a visit to Panna National Park, Ken River Lodge is currently the place to be. Also in the pipeline is a fabulous new safari lodge being established at Panna by the Taj-CC Africa team responsible for the exquisite Mahua Kothi (see Bandhavgarh accommodations later in this chapter). Also *still* under discussion is the proposed creation of Khajuraho's first heritage accommodations, at the hitherto deserted 19th-century **Rajgarh Palace.** Situated some 25km (16 miles) from the village, at the foot of the Manijagarh Hills, this beautiful palace has exceptional views, and the end result is likely to be spectacular. You can get updated information about developments from the local tourism bureau.

IN KHAJURAHO

During winter, groups of tourists pass fast and furious through this dusty little town, and hotels (some with almost 100 rooms) fill up quickly, so it's a good idea to plan ahead. A few self-billed "luxury" options are situated along Khajuraho's main road; if they're not included below, it's because they really aren't worth it. A large strip of hotels and guesthouses is dedicated to backpackers; rooms vary considerably. Budget travelers should head for **Hotel Surya** (Jain Temple Rd.; ✆ **07686/27-4145;** www.hotel suryakhajuraho.com), where Rs 750 to Rs 950 ($18–$23/£9–£12) buys you a clean, spartan deluxe room with an air-conditioner, attached drench shower, and a balcony, from where you can watch early risers practice yoga in the garden. A bit more expensive are the "executive" rooms, distinguished by their relative newness and their considerable size; non-A/C rooms (with fans) are much cheaper. Surya has a decent dining facility and bikes for hire, and guests can take cooking classes.

The Grand Temple View ★★   Signaling a minor revolution in sleepy Khajuraho, this 2007 newcomer is the result of brilliant renovations and is positively palatial compared with everything else in town. Benefiting from a great location (just beyond the town and 200m/656 ft. from the Western Group of temples), The Grand has meticulously landscaped gardens, fashioned from the previously insipid grounds of the former government-run hotel. A tall, red-turbaned gent stands sentry at the wide glass doors leading into a big, bright, square lobby, where the design concept might be called "contemporary Indian chic"—a reasonably pleasing integration of modern furnishings and passable replicas of artful artifacts that tie the hotel in with the heritage town you've come to visit. The effect is a rather soothing atmosphere (and although we visited when there weren't too many other guests around, it has relatively few rooms, so is unlikely to become crowded), underscored at night by piped temple chanting and flickering candles. Accommodations are comfortable and contemporary (wall-mounted flatscreen TVs) and easy on the eye (marble tile floors and pale sandstone walls offset by colorful throws). Drapes and blinds hang over massive picture windows, the best of which enjoy views of little lotus ponds outside (ask for a slightly more expensive executive suite facing the clover-shaped pool; the "garden-facing" units look toward the new archaeological museum, away from the Western temple group). The stylish bathrooms, with walk-in showers, are a bit cramped. Of all the distractions here, the beautiful spa is where you'll want to spend the most time between temple-spotting, and even the gym's treadmill has a view of the main temples. We found **Panna,** the multicuisine restaurant, a little soulless (with a large plasma TV blasting away), despite its carefully selected items on the decently priced menu.

Opposite Circuit House, Khajuraho 471 606. (C) **07686/27-2111** or -2333. Fax 07686/27-2123. www.thegrandhotels. net. 47 units. Rs 13,500 ($330/£167) superior/deluxe double; Rs 15,500 ($378/£191) executive suite; Rs 22,000 ($537/£272) luxury suite; Rs 30,000 ($732/£370) presidential suite. Special rates on request. Taxes extra. AE, DC, MC, V. **Amenities:** Restaurant; bar; pool; fitness center; spa; bicycles; business center; gift shop; 24-hr. room service; laundry; doctor-on-call; yoga; jogging track; children's playground; sightseeing excursions; cultural performances; billiards; table tennis; board games. *In room:* A/C, TV, minibar, dataport, tea- and coffee-making facility, hair dryer, safe.

Hotel Chandela ★

Located a kilometer from Khajuraho's main temple complex, on the main road into town, this reliable low-rise Taj chain hotel has peaceful gardens, comfortable accommodations, and staff who (considering the small-town atmosphere) are fairly willing to oblige. It won't win any awards for design or innovation, but guest rooms have been refurbished with marble tile floors, a lick of white paint, shiny drapes, and bright scatter cushions, making them smart if not particularly luxurious (particularly since we found mountains of dust behind the furniture and some ancient wiring in need of an electrician). Ask for a ground-floor room that opens directly onto the pool mezzanine with its lawns and palms; those nearest the lobby are best (some of the passages appear endless) and 117, 121, and 125 have double beds.

Airport Rd., Khajuraho 471 606. (C) **07686/27-2355** through -2364. Fax 07686/27-2365 or -2366. www.tajhotels. com. chandela.khajuraho@tajhotels.com. 94 units. $120 (£60) superior garden-facing double; $130 (£65) superior pool-facing double; $150 (£75) junior suite; $200 (£100) deluxe suite. Taxes extra. AE, DC, MC, V. **Amenities:** 2 restaurants; bar; pool; minigolf; tennis court; fitness center; travel desk; book shop; salon; 24-hr. room service; laundry; doctor-on-call; pool table; badminton; table tennis; archery. *In room:* A/C, TV, minibar, tea- and coffee-making facility, hair dryer, safe.

Radisson Jass ★

Guest rooms at the Jass—which has a bizarrely futuristic appearance from the outside—are no longer the best in town, but remain elegant and luxurious. Bright white marble-floored public spaces are decorated with attractive Indian artworks including a fine collection of large Mughal paintings. After Radisson took over management, extensive renovations were undertaken throughout 2005, with new "super deluxe" rooms now available and a few new amenities added. Guest rooms have a plush contemporary look (off-white hues offset by framed Indian textiles and art prints) and are fairly spacious with private balconies and either garden, pool, or mountain views; those on the first floor (reached via a twisting marble staircase with an impressive chandelier hanging from a domed ceiling) overlooking the lawn-fringed pool are best. Half the rooms have wooden floors; the rest are marble. Sadly, since the Radisson took over management, service standards have dropped considerably (we dare you to get a "hello" out of the doorman).

By-Pass Rd., Khajuraho 471 606. © **07686/27-2344** or -2777. Fax 07686/27-2345. reservations@radissonkhajuraho. com. 90 units. $110 (£55) super deluxe double; $225 (£113) suite. Taxes extra. AE, DC, MC, V. **Amenities:** Restaurant; bar; pool; tennis court; health club; travel assistance; sightseeing; guides; car hire; airport transfers; shopping arcade; 24-hr. room service; babysitting with prior notice; laundry; doctor-on-call; currency exchange; billiards room. *In room:* A/C, TV, minibar, tea- and coffee-making facilities, hair dryer, iron and ironing board on request, safe.

OUTSIDE KHAJURAHO

Ken River Lodge *Finds* *Value*   A short distance from the entrance to Panna National Park (about 30 min. from Khajuraho), this 18-hectare (45-acre) "resort," located right on the river, was extensively destroyed during the monsoon of 2005; it's been rebuilt with much of its former rustic charm (although no longer with any tents), and it's a far better option for nature lovers than any of its pricier counterparts in town. Three kilometers (2 miles) off the main road, it's an ideal hideaway in a gorgeous forest setting, where fishing enthusiasts can cast a line and hope for one of India's famous fighting *mahseer,* and there are experienced naturists to make your safaris all the more thrilling. Accommodations are in 10 cottages or in 10 mud-walled huts; unless you're with children and want to be in a larger structure, choose the latter. They have straw roofs, fireplaces, separate dressing areas, and big, simple attached bathrooms (round-the-clock hot water; shower only); there's an overhead fan, wooden beds, and a rather loud cooling system. The massive two-roomed cottages feel old and colonial, not to mention a bit run-down. Great, fairly flexible eating arrangements and a popular bar on a raised wooden platform contribute to the resort's appeal. If this isn't good enough, romantic dinners can be arranged on a tiny private island in the middle of the river.

Village Madla, District Panna 488 001. © **07732/27-5235.** In Delhi contact Manav Khanduja (© 981002-4711). www.kenriverlodge.com. wildlifer@vsnl.net. 20 units. Rs 4,000 ($98/£50) double, including all meals, tea and coffee, and taxes; Rs 10,000 ($244/£124) jungle plan double (includes 2 all-inclusive safaris with naturalist). No credit cards. **Amenities:** Restaurant; bar; laundry; doctor-on-call; boating; fishing; tours and jeep safaris with naturalist; elephant rides; room service only in exceptional circumstances. *In room:* Water coolers (some units).

WHERE TO DINE

If you're down with a case of culinary homesickness, you may find some comfort in the fact that Khajuraho is awash with eateries offering "multi-cuisine" menus; in fact, the term seems to be a favorite among staff in most of the top hotels. Unfortunately, the hotels are where you'll find the best dining options, headed up by the **Temple Café** at the Radisson, and **Panna,** the multi-cuisine eatery at The Grand Temple View (an altogether easier, and cheaper, option for lunch). If you don't mind something a little more down-home, sample the Italian fare offered at **Mediterraneo** (Jain Temple Rd., opposite Surya Hotel; © **07686/27-2246;** no credit cards; daily 7:30am– 10:30pm), an alfresco rooftop restaurant with friendly staff and little pretense beyond the gigantic letters along the side of the building exclaiming MEDITERRANEO CHEF TRAINED IN ROME. While this bit of ambitious advertising is something of an exaggeration, Rama, the owner, *is* from Rome, and he has personally trained all his staff. The menu offers a range of Italian favorites, including wood-fired pizza (when available; Rs 150–Rs 240/$3.65–$5.85/£1.85–£3), pasta, and tasty Roman-style chicken. Don't expect to be blown away, but you can be sure your meal will be made with fresh ingredients, and there's real espresso. Another local hangout—conveniently situated across the road from the Western Group entrance—is **Raja Café Swiss Restaurant** (© **07686/27-2307;** no credit cards), which has a rooftop terrace and a ground level courtyard under a shady peepul tree. The only real advantage here is that you get to enjoy excellent views of the Western Group (it's an ideal place for a beer after you've visited the site); we're afraid that since the longstanding Swiss proprietor passed away several years ago, the food has gone from unremarkable to just passable.

SHOPPING

Khajuraho can be a nightmare. In contrast with the tranquil village atmosphere, hawkers and touts ooze from every corner and have record-setting persistence. You'll no doubt develop a gut-wrenching dislike for the overstretched shopping areas in and around the main square, where everyone seems to demand that you step into yet another handicrafts shop to "just look, no buy." Do not enter any shop in Khajuraho with anyone other than fellow travelers. If you make a purchase on your own, you'll save yourself around 20%, which is the standard commission, borne by you, demanded by "agents" (taxi drivers, guides, or someone who has "befriended" you) for their "service" of bringing foreign business to local stores.

If you're looking to buy miniature artworks—perhaps an erotic interpretation inspired by the temple carvings—consider stopping in at **Artist** (Surya Hotel Complex, Jain Temple Rd.; ✆ **07686/27-4496**), an appropriately named outlet for Pichhwai and Mughal paintings rendered by Dilip Singh and his two brothers, whose late father was a recipient of a National Award for Art many years back. Their paintings vary in subject, size, and quality, but the selection includes something to suit everyone's pocket. Miniatures on silk, fabric, or paper start at a mere Rs 10 (25¢/12p), and go up to Rs 13,000 ($317/£161); you can also commission a work if there's something in particular that you want to take home with you.

5 Bandhavgarh National Park ★★★

237km (147 miles) S of Khajuraho

Known as "Kipling Country," despite the fact that the writer never set foot here, the nature reserves of Madhya Pradesh are archetypal India, with vast tracts of jungle, open grassy plains, and, of course, tigers. Bandhavgarh National Park occupies 437 sq. km (168 sq. miles), making it a great deal smaller than its more famous cousin, Kahna National Park. But despite its relatively diminutive size, the park is home to some 50 to 70 tigers; around 25 of these are in the tourist zone, and at press time there are several new litters on their way contributing to what is probably the highest density of tigers in any park on earth. Once the personal hunting grounds of local maharajas who almost wiped out the tiger population, Bandhavgarh continues to experience problems with wayward poachers, usually suppliers for China's lucrative traditional medicine industry. But, as locals will assure you, your chances of seeing a wild tiger (those at Ranthambhore are almost tame) are still unmatched anywhere else in India. Best of all, you will approach your predator on elephant-back, giving the entire experience a totally unreal air. Besides the sought-after tiger, the sanctuary is home to spotted deer, *sambar*, *nilgai* antelope, barking deer, shy *chinkara* (Indian gazelle), and wild boar; leopards and sloth bears are far more elusive. The varied topography includes dramatic cliffs that proved a natural location for the 14th-century **Bandhavgarh Fort.** If you give enough notice, you can arrange to visit the reserve's rock-cut caves, with inscriptions dating as far back as the 2nd century B.C. And now, with the arrival of the Taj/CC Africa luxury lodge, **Mahua Kothi,** Bandhavgarh has become *the* place to blow your savings and settle back into exquisite pampering.

> ⌒ *Fun Fact* **The White Tiger of Rewa**
>
> The last elusive white tiger ever to roam free was a Bandhavgarh cub that was
> snared by Martand Singh, who bred the animal in captivity in order to exploit
> his deviant genes and so produce a new "genus"—the "White Tiger of Rewa."
> Today, the only places you'll see white tigers are zoos.

ESSENTIALS

VISITOR INFORMATION   Entry to Bandhavgarh is via the tiny village of Tala,
where a number of lodges and resorts, a handful of *dhabas* (snack shacks), and several
souvenir stalls are the only distractions from park activities. Try to get any information you require in advance, but you can pretty much rely on your chosen lodge to
make all local arrangements for you. Contact **M. P. Tourism** at the White Tiger Forest Lodge at Bandhavgarh (✆ **07627/26-5308;** www.mptourism.com) or the **Project
Tiger Field Director** in Umaria (✆ **07653/22-2214;** fdbtr@rediffmail.com).

GETTING THERE   By Road   Set aside an entire day for road journeys from destinations within Madhya Pradesh; surfaces are terrible at best, consisting of little more
than endless potholes linked by clusters of asphalt and islands of sand. The nearest
town of tourist interest is Khajuraho—a rather bumpy 5-hour drive away.

By Air   If you can afford it, take advantage of the helicopter trips from Delhi offered
by several of the upmarket resorts in Bandhavgarh. If you decide to catch a commercial flight, Jabalpur is the nearest airport. It is situated 165km (102 miles) away; the
4-hour onward taxi trip will cost upward of Rs 3,200 ($78/£40).

By Train   Umaria, 45 minutes from Tala, is the nearest railhead. The best train from
Delhi is the **Kalinga Utkal Express,** which leaves Nizamuddin Station at 12:50pm
and arrives in Umaria the following day at 6:15am, a little too late for early entry to
the park. Taxi rides to Tala cost around Rs 900 ($22/£11); **Anil Gupta** has a reliable
service (✆ **94-2518-1604**). Other nearby railheads are Katni and Jabalpur.

WHEN TO GO   The park opens as early as October (depending on the monsoon situation), but sightings are best February through June, when the heat forces more animals to search for water. Although the park attracts smaller crowds than Corbett and
Ranthambhore, avoid Bandhavgarh the week before and after Diwali, Holi, and New
Year's holidays, when the park is filled with queue-jumping VIPs and noisy families.

ORGANIZING YOUR BANDHAVGARH SAFARI

Regarding entry fees and permits, the best plan is to book accommodations that include
everything; the resorts and lodges we've reviewed below will take care of all your safari
arrangements. Get to the park first thing in the morning, when you will join the line of
open-top jeeps and other 4WDs waiting at the entrance for the daily rush, which starts
promptly at dawn. If you've hired a vehicle and driver privately, you will have to pay a
small fee for the services of a park guide who will accompany you; this and other charges
for entry permits, cameras, and such are all paid at the park entrance. Jeep safaris can
cover a relatively large area within the park, but most sightings occur as a result of information shared among the various drivers and guides. Drivers must take a lottery-decided
route to a central point where a token is collected; this token then allows access to the
rest of the park. In particular, the token enables your jeep to join the queue for the

much-anticipated elephant-back tiger-viewing experience. Elephant-mounted *mahouts* head out early to search for tigers; once they locate them, they wait at the nearest road until the jeeps begin to congregate and word spreads, ensuring the arrival of other vehicle-driven visitors. Rs 600 ($15/£8) buys you an elephant-back ride for an unnervingly close-up view of the tigers, usually encountered minding their own business deep within the sal forest. You then have around 5 minutes to capture the elusive cat on film before your elephant returns to the road to pick up new passengers.

Tip: Being at the rear of the queue of jeeps may involve some waiting, but *mahouts* usually allow the last elephants-trippers a few extra moments with the tigers. During the afternoon, the park offers more-substantial elephant safaris that are as much relaxing as they are a good opportunity to see more tigers in the wild, this time without feeling like you're part of a tourist conveyor belt.

With any luck, your guide will be as interested in showing you the terrain, which is rugged and beautiful, as he is in finding your tiger. He may point out other species such as the *chital,* blue bull antelope, and *sambar;* and the many bird species such as spotted black kites, crested serpent eagles, storks, ibises, hornbills, white-eyed buzzards, black vultures, golden-backed woodpeckers, kingfishers, and dove parakeets. If all else fails, there are plenty of black-faced langur monkeys and rhesus macaques ("red bummed monkeys") to keep you amused.

Park entrance is at Tala. Park fees: Rs 500 ($12/£6.20) admission; Rs 150 ($3.65/£1.85) vehicle entry; Rs 105 ($2.60/£1.30) guide; Rs 200 ($4.90/£2.50) video; Rs 600 ($15/£7.40) elephant ride per person; Rs 10,000 ($244/£124) 6-hr. elephant ride. Daily 6:15–10am and 3–6pm.

WHERE TO STAY

Note that rates quoted here are "Jungle Plan" packages, which include all meals and two safaris into the park as well as all entrance, guide, and vehicle fees, and that all are situated within striking distance of the entrance. Besides the thoroughly swish and sexy Mahua Kothi (reviewed below), there are two more options worth considering, and they won't break the bank in quite the same way. Located on the park's southern edge, 15 minutes from Tala gate, **Camp Mewar on Ketkiya** ✪ (☎ **07627/26-5395** or 94-1415-9797; www.campmewar.com; Oct 15–Apr 15) is a reasonably luxurious option which is both tasteful and wonderfully integrated with nature. This 4-hectare (10-acre) property is not only quite enchanting, but represents good value; $350 (£175) gets you the jungle plan option for two in either a "tent" (really a stone house with a canvas canopy providing a tented feel) or thatch hut. If you don't mind forking out a bit extra, opt for an *aodhi* (cottage in the design of hunting towers of old), which are also quite lovely ($400/£200 double). All rooms have attached marble bathrooms with bathtubs, bidets, and other resort trimmings. Mewar benefits from being some distance from the entrance to the park, but note that you should book well in advance because with only 12 rooms, it packs out quickly.

One of the newer ventures near the park entrance is **King's Lodge** ✪ (☎ **98-1002-4711;** reservations **011/2588-5709;** www.kingslodge.in), operated by the same team responsible for Ken River Lodge near Khajuraho. Accommodations (most of which are raised off the ground on stilts) have large covered porches, mud-effect walls, and sliding doors that open to bedrooms with high A-frame ceilings; floors are stone tiled and there's plenty of wood, including entire branches and tree trunks used as part of the decor. They're smart and have working iron fireplaces, air-conditioning, and good, firm mattresses covered with white cotton linens; bathrooms have tubs and showers. The lodge also offers a good range of amenities, including a pool, and there's a mellow atmosphere enhanced by the breezy layout of the public spaces. Rates start at Rs 13,500 ($330/£167) for two people on the Jungle Plan.

Mahua Kothi ⭐⭐⭐ This is the most stylish safari lodge in the state, if not in all of India. The groundbreaking collaboration between India's Taj luxury hotel chain and South Africa's renowned high-end safari operator CC Africa, Mahua Kothi brings glamour, even sexiness, to the jungle and a level of intelligent guiding that tiger tracking in this region has not previously known. With interiors by smart-eyed designer Chris Browne, the original homestead has been lavishly furnished and decorated to become a homey public space with an open-plan interior filled with memorabilia that suggests the collected history of several generations; mixed in are colorful, whimsical pieces that add a dash of fun. Lunches are taken at the tremendous dining tables with fat tree-stump legs, and a deep, comfortable veranda is just the spot for post-safari gin and tonics. Then slink off to one of 12 gorgeous village-style *kutiyas,* or mud-walled suites: Each is a clever synthesis of modern luxury and design that works harmoniously with the forested setting. An entrance porch leads to a large room with wood-tiled floors, lime-washed walls, magnificent built-in bed, and big picture windows. Behind the bed a spacious dressing area leads to a bath (filled by your personal butler by the time you return from your evening game drive) and massive rainfall shower. Dinners are quite festive, often taken on the rooftop under the stars, preceded by cocktails (staff are steadily acquiring the knack of mixing a proper martini) and warm snacks. Mahua Kothi's naturalists, who are passionate about the outdoors and have been impeccably trained by CC Africa, have set a whole new standard in game tracking on the subcontinent. Gone are the days of racing through the forest charging after tigers; you'll learn about the fragile ebb and flow of life in the jungle. Although luxury like this comes at a stiff price, a stay here is enchanting enough to make this easily the best all-round tiger-spotting experience in the world.

Bandhavgarh National Park, Village Tala, District Umaria 484 661. Reservations: Worldwide toll-free ☎ 008-004-588-1825. In India ☎ 92-1230-5607. www.tajsafaris.com. tajsafaris@tajhotels.com. 12 units. $1,200 (£600) double. AE, MC, V. **Amenities:** Dining room and various dining areas; bar; pool; bicycles; travel arrangements; gift shop; massage; laundry; doctor-on-call; library; jeep safaris; camel safaris; butler. *In room:* A/C, hair dryer, safe, flashlight (torch).

6 Orchha ⭐⭐⭐

440km (273 miles) SE of Delhi; 238km (148 miles) S of Agra; 120km (74 miles) SE of Gwalior

Located on a rocky island on the Betwa River, the deserted royal citadel of Raja Rudra Pratap is one of India's most fabulous Mughal heritage sites, yet Orchha (literally "hidden place") is mercifully free of development, making this a wonderfully relaxing stop. Founded in 1531, it was the capital of the Bundela kings until 1738. Today the weathered temples, palaces, and cenotaphs are the royal quarters of emerald parakeets and black-faced langurs, while traditional whitewashed, flat-roofed structures house the laid-back villagers. Besides the palace complex, three beautiful temples are worth seeking out, as well as 14 graceful *chhatris* (cenotaphs) commemorating the Orchha rulers, built upstream along the riverbank. Most of these sights can be covered in a day excursion on the way to Khajuraho, but to get the most out of this surreally tranquil haven, spend at least 1 night here.

ESSENTIALS

VISITOR INFORMATION The **MPSTDC Sheesh Mahal** (☎ 07680/25-2624) acts as an informal tourism office (see "Where to Stay," below). They will arrange day trips and transfers.

The Gems of Gwalior

If you've chosen to travel by rail or road from Agra, 118km (73 miles) north, to Khajuraho via Orchha, 120km (74 miles) south, set aside a day to explore Gwalior's fine sights. To see them all necessitates an overnight stay in the palace that is part of the attraction and one of central India's best heritage properties.

Looming over the three cities of modern Gwalior—Lashkar, Morar, and Gwalior—its 3km-long (2-mile) thick walls built atop steep cliff surfaces, **Gwalior Fort** ⓡ ($2/£1 entrance allows you into most sites, Rs 25/60¢/30p video; daily sunrise–sunset) is believed to date back to the 3rd century A.D. The oldest surviving Hindu fort in the Bundelkund, it changed hands repeatedly and was admired by all who invaded it—even the first Mughal emperor, Babur, who admired very little else of India, famously described it as "the pearl among the fortresses of Hind" (though he still allowed his army to desecrate the Jain rock-cut sculptures, viewed as you approach the Urwahi Gate). Within the ancient walls are a number of palaces, temples, step wells, and underground pools (best to hire a taxi, available at the entrance), but its most significant structure is the monumental **Man Mandir Palace,** built by Raja Man Singh of the Tomara dynasty in the 15th century. Ornamented with a variety of glazed tile patterns, this is considered one of the finest examples of pre-Mughal Hindu palace architecture in India. Now housing a rather good **Archaeological Museum** (Tues–Sun 10am–5pm), **Gujari Mahal** was also built by Man Singh, this time for his favorite wife, a queen of the Gujjar tribe; he famously fell in love with her after he witnessed her courageously separate two warring buffaloes.

The oldest temple in the fort is **Teli-ka Mandir,** or **Temple of the Caste of Oil Sellers,** dating back to the 9th century. Built in the South Indian, or Dravidian, style, it was originally dedicated to Vishnu before apparently being used as a soda factory by the British when they occupied the fort in the 1800s. Just north of here is a large pool of water known as **Suraj Kund.** It was here that a divine hermit named Gwalipa, for whom the fort is named, is believed to have cured the fort's founder, King Suraj Sen, of leprosy. Other notable temples are late-11th-century **Sas Mandir (Temple of the Mother-in-law)** and **Bahu Mandir (Temple of the Daughter-in-law),** which form an elegant pair. Guides hired at the fort should cost Rs 250 ($6.10/£3.10) for 2 hours; **Samar Singh** (ⓒ 98-2623-0564) is a reliable choice—his grandfather was the very first guide to work here.

The last rulers of Gwalior were the Scindia clan, and during the British era the Scindia Maharaja, Jiyaji Rao, was known to be one of the most decadent of the Rajput rulers. In 1875 he built the over-the-top 19th-century **Jai Vilas Palace** ⓡ for the express purpose of impressing the Prince of Wales. He filled it with treasures imported from Europe; in the Durbar Hall are the world's heaviest chandeliers, each weighing 3½ tons, which hang over the largest handmade carpet in Asia. In the dining room you can see the electric silver-and-crystal toy train the maharaja used to dispense drinks and cigars around the massive dinner table—apparently refusing to stop the train in front of those he disliked. Jai Vilas Palace (© **0751/232-1101;** Rs 200/$4.90/£2.50, Rs 30/75¢/40p camera; Thurs–Tues 10am–5pm) is still occupied by his descendants (if the flag is flying, royalty is in residence); there's also a torturous series of museum galleries filled with a mix of banal and unusual trifles. You might be shocked to see the collection of stuffed tigers and cheetahs labeled "Natural History Gallery."

Gwalior's has a long-standing tradition of musical excellence and innovation, and to this end **Sarod Ghar** 𝒜 traces and showcases this legacy in the beautiful sandstone home of the Bagnash family. You might inquire about the **musical recitals** occasionally held in the museum's marble courtyard (© **0751/ 242-5607;** www.sarod.com; entry free; Tues–Sun 10:30am–4pm); don't pass up the chance of hearing Amjad Ali Khan, an internationally recognized master. Or find out whether musicians are performing at the simple white memorial **Tomb of Miyan Tansen.** One of India's greatest musicians, Miyan Tansen was considered one of the *navratna* (nine gems) of Mughal Emperor Akbar's court. For recital information, contact **M. P. State Tourism Development Corporation** (© **0751/234-0370;** mptrogwalior@sancharnet.in; open 24 hr.).

The best place to overnight is the Taj's luxurious **Usha Kiran Palace Hotel** 𝒜𝒜 (© **0751/244-4000;** www.tajhotels.com), located right next door to the Jai Vilas Palace. Scindia royalty once resided here, and this handsome heritage hotel, extensively renovated in 2005, retains an evocative old-world atmosphere. Most accommodations (with A/C, TV, and minibar) are arranged around a courtyard and are tastefully furnished, with high ceilings, pleasant sitting areas, and furniture that once belonged to the maharaja. Of the massive deluxe rooms, 201 and 202 offer the best value ($235/£118 double). A stay here is definitely a taste of luxury, particularly if you stay in one of the fabulous **new villas** 𝒜𝒜𝒜 added in 2006, which have private pools and smart designer interiors (from $550/£225). The hotel offers guests several royal experiences, notably at the gorgeous poolside spa; among the decadent offerings is a bathing ritual *(Mangal snana)* where you soak in a tub infused with rich traditional ingredients while live musicians play from behind a curtain. Around the hotel building, you'll discover broad passages, 51 differently designed sandstone trellises, ornate chandeliers, and an upstairs terrace affording views of Jai Vilas Palace and Gwalior Fort, ideal as a sundowner venue. If you do spend the night, you might want to watch the 45-minute sound-and-light show (Rs 150/$3.65/£1.85; tickets available at the fort; closed July–Sept 15) held at the fortress each night at 7:30pm November through February and 8:30pm March through October.

GETTING THERE   The best way to get to Orchha is to catch a train to Jhansi, where trains from Delhi, Mumbai, or Chennai pull in, carrying visitors on their way to Khajuraho (see "Khajuraho: Getting There & Away," earlier in this chapter). You can catch an auto-rickshaw from Jhansi to Orchha (20km/12 miles) for about Rs 200 ($4.90/£2.50). Alternatively, with time on your hands, you can hire a car and driver and travel by road from Agra, overnighting at Gwalior (see "The Gems of Gwalior," below).

EXPLORING ORCHHA'S FORGOTTEN MONUMENTS

The monuments of Orchha are fairly spread out, but close enough to be explored entirely on foot. You can spend a quick-paced morning poking through the ruins in which you're most interested, or take your time and spread your explorations over an entire day. A few of the sights require a ticket, which you can purchase from a booth at the front of the Raj Mahal (daily 9am–5pm); the Rs 30 (75¢/37p) ticket provides access to all the main monuments.

Visible as you enter the village, Orchha's fortified palace complex is approached by a multi-arched medieval bridge. Once over the bridge, you'll first encounter the earliest of the palaces, **Raj Mahal** ⭐, built during the 16th century by the deeply religious Raja Madhukar Shah, who befriended the Mughal Emperor Akbar, an alliance that was to serve the rulers of Orchha well. Look for the bold, colorful murals on walls and ceilings, and climb to the uppermost levels of the palace for a more complete view of the entire complex. A pathway leads to the two-story **Rai Praveen Mahal;** according to legend, it was built in the mid–17th century for a concubine who the then-ruling Raja loved to watch dance. Surrounded by lovely lawns, the palace includes a ground-level hall where performances were once held, and naturally cooled subterranean apartments. Deemed Orchha's finest palace, with delicate *chhatris* (dome-shaped cenotaphs) and ornate stone *jalis* (screens) along its outer walls, **Jahangir Mahal** ⭐⭐ is distinguished by its domed pavilions, fortified bastions, and ornamental gateway flanked by stone elephants holding bells in their trunk, perhaps to announce the entry of the man in whose honor the palace was built: Emperor Jahangir, Akbar's son (see "The Life & Times of the Mughal Emperors," earlier in the chapter). He is said to have promised to visit, but accounts vary as to whether he actually arrived. The sandstone exterior bears the remains of beautiful turquoise- and lapis lazuli–tiled embellishments, while interior walls are decorated with lovely carvings. **Sheesh Mahal,** now a hotel, is a section of the palace complex built by a local king as a country getaway some time after Orchha's decline. If you wander along the paths away from the palace complex (to your left after you cross the bridge), you'll find the ruins of a number of small, atmospheric temples amid fields belonging to local farmers.

With both Persian and Rajput architectural influences, seven-story **Chaturbhuj Mandir** ⭐ looms hauntingly over Orchha village. Reached by a steep flight of steps, the 16th-century temple consists of an expansive vaulted assembly hall with impressive spires; make your way up the narrow spiral staircases for lovely views from the temple roof. Never used, the temple was supposed to have housed an image of Lord Rama brought from Ayodhya by the wife of Orchha's king. Upon arriving, she found the temple incomplete, so she temporarily installed the deity in her palace. When Chaturbhuj was finally completed, the god refused to be moved, so the queen's palace became **Ram Raja Mandir** (daily 8am–noon and 8–10pm), today one of Orchha's main attractions for Hindus, despite its secular architecture.

Behind Ram Raja Mandir is a paved path that leads to **Lakshminarayan Mandir** ⭐⭐, atop a low hill less than 1km (a half-mile) from the village. The walk takes you past lovely flat-roofed houses that line part of the pathway. The 17th-century temple features interesting murals depicting military battles and religious myths. Although it's usually open to ticket-holders between 9am and 5pm, the temple is sometimes locked up, with no trace of the attendant.

After exploring the village and its trinket-filled stores, don't miss the 14 sandstone *chhatris,* or cenotaphs, along the Betwa River. Built as memorials to expired rulers of the Bundelkhand, they celebrate old alliances, mixing elements of Mughal architecture, such as the arches, and Hindu temple design, such as the *shikharas* (spires).

WHERE TO STAY

Orchha is small but popular, with few decent lodging options, so be sure to book well in advance, particularly in winter when tour groups can arrive en masse. The best room in Orchha is the **Maharaja Suite** ★★ in the **Sheesh Mahal Hotel,** which was renovated in 2004 (✆ **07680/25-2624** or 011/2336-6528; www.mptourism.com; Rs 4,990/$122/£62). An enormous room, with a domed ceiling over an assortment of paintings, cabinets, and fascinating Raj-era relics, the suite has its own dining area and a wonderful terrace with magical views. Even the bathroom is huge, with a marble tub and polished stone flooring. Despite the recent refurbishment, the rest of the hotel's guest rooms are quite ordinary. And, like most government-run establishments, the place is poorly managed, and the second-rate food is only to be consumed if you have no other option. Despite these shortcomings, the Sheesh Mahal—no doubt because of its heritage status—is usually booked up days in advance.

The Orchha Resort ★ Orchha's smartest hotel enjoys a good location on the banks of the Betwa River near the cenotaphs. Popular with European tour groups, the resort is built in attractive pink sandstone and includes 11 deluxe tents (pitched Oct–Apr 15) arranged around the tennis court; these really are the best value. They're comfortably furnished and include all the regular amenities as well as en-suite toilets and showers and a small porch from where you have an incredible, close-up view of several impressive cenotaphs. Guest rooms in the main building are more expensive; they have marble floors, smallish bathrooms with tubs, and good-quality fabrics in shades of green and cream. Do beware of the slippery area around the pool when you go for a post-sightseeing dip. Owned by Jains, the restaurant is strictly vegetarian, but the food is fresh and appetizing.

Kanchanaghat, Orchha, Tikamgarh District 472 246. ✆ **07680/25-2222** through -2224. Fax 07680/25-2677. www.orchharesort.com. Reservations: Oswal Motels and Resorts, 30 Munro Rd., Agra 282 001. ✆ **0562/222-5712**. Fax 0562/222-6520. 45 units. Rs 2,950 ($72/£36) tent double; Rs 5,050 ($123/£62) double; Rs 5,900 ($144/£73) deluxe double; Rs 800 ($20/£10) extra bed. Taxes extra. AE, MC, V. **Amenities:** Restaurant; pool; tennis court; health club; sauna; gift shop; 24-hr. room service; massage room; babysitting; laundry; doctor-on-call; table tennis. *In room:* A/C, TV, minibar.

7 Bhopal & Sanchi

Bhopal is 744km (461 miles) S of Delhi; Sanchi is 46km (29 miles) NE of Bhopal

Despite its exciting marketplaces, grand old mosques, and lovely palaces, the capital of Madhya Pradesh is perhaps best known as site of the world's worst urban industrial disaster (see box below). But most foreign visitors find themselves in Bhopal in order to visit nearby Sanchi, a UNESCO World Heritage Site, and one of the most impressive Buddhist monuments in Asia. Architecturally unique and far from the beaten tourist track, the monuments and surrounding ruins are tranquil, free of hawkers and touts, and a worthwhile diversion from the more frequented destinations of Varanasi, Agra, Khajuraho, and Delhi.

The Bhopal Gas Tragedy

On the night of December 2, 1984, a tank at the Union Carbide pesticide manufacturing plant near Bhopal ruptured, leaking highly poisonous methyl isocyanate gas into the atmosphere. By the time it had dissipated, 1,600 people were dead—but final estimates are as high as 20,000. A claim of $6 billion in compensation was initially demanded by the government, but it settled out of court for $470 million. Adding insult to injury, the money, paid to the government, took 7 years and many more deaths before even a fraction of it reached the victims. Almost 2 decades later, survivors continue to protest the haphazard and inadequate manner in which the families of the victims were compensated. Evidence suggests that the continuing effects of the gas disaster may have affected as many as 300,000 people afflicted with various cancers and birth defects. Effigies of the Union Carbide bosses are regularly burned at memorial protests (failing to reach more than the evening news), and many victims continue to go without aid or recourse from the law. Meanwhile, Union Carbide, having abandoned the factory, has started up elsewhere as Eveready Industries India Ltd.

If Bhopal's few monuments, its market, and the glorious Buddhist monuments at Sanchi leave you with time on your hands, head for the caves of **Bhimbetka,** where red-and-black prehistoric drawings recall the antics of ancient dancers and hunters, sticklike in the company of tigers and charging bulls.

ESSENTIALS

VISITOR INFORMATION   For extensive information about any destination in Madhya Pradesh, as well as transport options, contact the **Madhya Pradesh State Tourism Development Corporation (MPSTDC)** at its Bhopal hotel, Palash Residency (45 Bungalows, New Market, T.T. Nagar; © **0755/255-3006;** www.mptourism. com). Sanchi is 46km (29 miles) from Bhopal, less than 2 hours by road. Regular train services from Bhopal pass through Sanchi.

GETTING THERE & AWAY   As the state capital, Bhopal is well connected by air with numerous cities (including Delhi, Mumbai, Gwalior, and Indore). Bhopal is also on a main railway line, and frequent **trains** connect the city with Delhi, Agra, Gwalior, Jhansi (for Orchha), Mumbai, and Hyderabad.

GETTING AROUND   Taxis and auto-rickshaws are easy to flag down.

GUIDED TOURS   Mrs. Rekha Chopra, of **Radiant Travels** (243/B, First Floor, Krishna Palace, M. P. Nagar, Zone I; © **0755/273-8540** or 0755/254-0560), is not only an experienced tour guide, but introduces visitors to basic Indian cuisine with vegetarian meals at her home.

WHAT TO SEE & DO IN BHOPAL

No one spends much time in Bhopal itself, but the "City of Lakes" is not without its charms, and a handful of sights are worth setting time aside for. Note that most places are closed on Monday, and on Friday mosques are off-limits, unless you're Muslim.

A visit to the **Chowk (Bazaar),** in the heart of the Old City, can be a wonderful way to gain insight into the daily lives of Bhopal's warm, friendly citizens. Its ramshackle streets are lined with old havelis and atmospheric stalls; it's impossible not to get involved in the village vibe, where shopping, hard-core haggling, and gossiping occupy one's time. Shop around for embroidered velvet cushions, *tussar* silk, silver jewelry, and intricate beadwork. While you're in the Chowk, visit lovely **Jama Masjid;** built in 1837, it features gold-spiked minarets, distinguishing it from the "Pearl Mosque," or **Moti Masjid** (1860), farther south. Sporting three large white Mughal domes and two soaring minarets, **Taj-ul-Masjid** ℛ, one of India's largest mosques, was started at the end of the 19th century by Bhopal's eighth ruler, the great queen Shah Jahan Begum, but was only completed in the 1970s.

Designed by the preeminent Indian architect, Charles Correa, the breezy, modern **Bharat Bhavan** ℛℛ (Shamla Hills; ℂ **0755/266-0353;** Rs 10/25¢/15p, Fri free; Feb–Oct Tues–Sun 2–8pm, Nov–Jan Tues–Sun 1–7pm), overlooking Upper Lake, is one of the best cultural centers in the country, showcasing some wonderful contemporary and tribal art exhibitions.

If you're set on seeing a white tiger, **Van Vihar National Park** is the place to do it. Zoo conditions at this "safari-park" are better than elsewhere in India, but it's still a depressing place to see a wild animal (Zoo Rd.; Rs 100/$2.45/£1.25, vehicle entry Rs 30/75¢/35p; Wed–Mon 7–11am and 3–5:30pm; carnivores are fed around 4pm).

EXPLORING THE BUDDHIST COMPLEX AT SANCHI ℛℛℛ

Now a deserted site resembling an *X-Files* set, the monuments of Sanchi have not only survived despite nearly 2,000 years of neglect, but the stupa at Sanchi is considered India's finest and most evocative example of ancient Buddhist architecture. The Mauryan emperor Ashoka—famous for converting to Buddhism during a personal spiritual crisis after massacring thousands during his military campaigns in Orissa—was responsible for laying the foundations in the 3rd century B.C. Set upon a squat hill affording lovely views of the surrounding countryside, the complex of *stupas* (fat, domelike monuments housing Buddhist relics), monasteries, and temples probably owes its location as much to the serenity of the site as it does to its proximity to the once-prosperous city of Vidisha, where Ashoka's devoted Buddhist wife, Mahadevi, lived. Located at the confluence of the Bes and the Betwa rivers and two important trade routes, the Buddhist complex elicited the patronage of Vidisha's wealthy merchant communities. Even during the invasions of the Hun, life at Sanchi appears to have gone undisturbed, and is believed to have continued until the 13th century A.D., when a resurgence of Hinduism and an increasingly militant Islamic movement led to a decline of Buddhism in India. The site was deserted for more than 500 years before its rediscovery—again by a British military adventurer-type—in 1818. Today, aside from the attractive complex of ruins, Sanchi is little more than a railway station, a few guesthouses, snack stands, a museum, a restaurant, and a shop.

During the excavation that has taken place over the last century, the ruins of around 55 temples, pillars, monasteries, stupas, and other structures have been unearthed. It appears that Sanchi is unique in that its monuments cover the gamut of Buddhist architectural structures—dating from the 3rd century B.C. to the 12th century A.D.

The star attraction is Ashoka's large hemispherical **stupa,** which rises from the ground like a massive stone-carved alien craft. Around the middle of the 2nd century B.C., a balustrade was erected around the stupa, and the mound was covered in stone by the rulers of the Sunga dynasty. Facing the cardinal directions and contributing to the mystical appearance of the main stupa are the four intricately carved gateways, erected around 25 B.C. under the later Satvahana rulers. These striking entranceways feature finely detailed panels depicting incidents from the life of the Buddha and tales from the *Jatakas.* Note that, at that time, the depiction of the Buddha in human form had not yet emerged, so instead he is depicted symbolically, as a Bodhi tree, lotus, wheel, pair of feet, or stupa.

The Sanchi monasteries consist of a central courtyard surrounded by cells that served as the sleeping quarters for the nuns or monks. Of these, the best is **Monastery 51,** which was first excavated in the 19th century.

WHERE TO STAY & DINE

Jehan Numa Palace ★★ (Value) Built in 1890 as a royal guesthouse, this handsome low-rise white colonial-era building is fronted by attractive lawns with fountains, hedges, and colorful bougainvilleas. The two original heritage suites (ask specifically for either "Bourbon" or "Goddard") are very swish, with huge bedrooms, poster-beds, Regency furniture, spacious bathrooms with separate tubs and showers, and private patios. "Regal" guest rooms are off verandas around a fountain courtyard; these are large, with French doors and high ceilings. Standard rooms are best avoided, as are the "cottage rooms." Colored with natural vegetable dyes, the eco-friendly linens are handmade by a local cottage industry, and walls are decorated with local handicrafts. Service is excellent. Facilities include the state's largest pool and a fitness center offering Ayurvedic massage.

157 Shamla Hill, Bhopal 462 013. (©) **0755/266-1100** through -1105. Fax 0755/266-1720. www.hoteljehanuma palace.com. 98 units. Rs 3,200 ($78/£40) cottage double; Rs 4,250 ($104/£53) standard double; Rs 4,750 ($116/£59) Regal double; Rs 5,950 ($145/£74) Imperial double; Rs 8,000 ($195/£99) suite; Rs 10,000 ($244/£124) Heritage Suite; Rs 800 ($20/£10) extra bed. Rates include airport pick-up and breakfast. Taxes and 5% service charge extra. AE, DC, MC, V. **Amenities:** 3 restaurants; bar; club-cum-pub; garden barbecue; patisserie; pool; minigolf; tennis court; health club; concierge; business center; boutique; barber shop; 24-hr. room service; massage; laundry; doctor-on-call; currency exchange; jogging track; horse riding; table tennis; pool table; children's playground. *In room:* A/C, TV, minibar, Wi-Fi. Suites and Imperial rooms have tea- and coffee-making facilities, hair dryer.

8 The Fortress City of Mandu ★★★

90km (56 miles) from Indore

Built at a cool height of over 600m (1,968 ft.) on the southwestern edge of the Malwa Plateau, with sweeping views of the Nimar Plains below, Mandu was once the largest fortified city on earth, and playpen to some of central India's most powerful rulers. Initially christened by the Malwa sultans as the "City of Joy," the medieval capital inspired its rulers to celebrate the most pleasurable of pastimes—one of Mandu's most famous palaces was built solely to house some 15,000 concubines, and it is said that the Mughal emperor Humayun was so mesmerized by Mandu's sanguine beauty that he developed an opium habit during his stay here. Today the exotic ghost city—still one of the most atmospheric destinations in India—draws but a handful of tourists, which makes the excursion here all the more rewarding. It's just 2 hours away from the industrial hub of Indore, yet Mandu, even more so than Orchha, is rural India at its best: a place of enduring beauty, both natural and man-made, with panoramic views. It's the perfect antidote to the well-traveled North India circuits. You can visit Mandu as a rather long day trip out of Indore, but for those willing to sacrifice luxury for serenity, it's worth spending a night or two here to revel in silence, fresh air, and wide-open space. Then again, you could stay in the lovely Ahilya fort-palace at nearby Maheshwar and combine serenity with luxury.

ESSENTIALS

GETTING THERE & AWAY To visit Mandu, most people travel via Indore, which is connected to important regional centers by daily flights and regular train services. The airport ((©) **0731/262-1782** or -0758) is 8km (5 miles) out of the center. The train trip from Bhopal lasts 6 hours; the **Intercity Express** from Delhi takes 13 hours; and the **Avantika Express** from Mumbai takes 15 hours. A far more convenient option is to base yourself in the small town of Maheshwar, 35 miles from Mandu, and about 2 hours by road from Indore. To get to Mandu (or Maheshwar) from Indore, hire a taxi through **President Travels** (Hotel President, 163 R.N.T. Rd.; ✆ **0731/252-8866**); you can arrange a pick-up at the airport/station, and drive straight to Mandu (around Rs 2,000/$49/£25 for an A/C car); M. P. Tourism (see below) also arranges cars. If you're traveling on the cheap, there's a long, tiring bus trip to Mandu.

VISITOR INFORMATION   **Madhya Pradesh Tourism** has an office on the ground floor of Jhabua Tower, R.N.T. Road, in Indore (✆ **0731/252-8653** or -1717; mptourismind@airtelbroadband.in; Mon–Sat 10am–5pm, closed Sun and second and third Sat of the month). In Mandu, ask the manager at MPSTDC-run **Malwa Resort** (✆ **07292/26-3235**) for assistance.

GETTING AROUND   Indore has plenty of **taxis** and **auto-rickshaws;** ask the driver to use his meter. In Mandu, you can hire a **bicycle,** or ride on the back of a **motorcycle** with a local guide as your driver.

EXPLORING MANDU

After passing through the narrow gates of the fortress and continuing for some distance, you'll arrive in "downtown" Mandu (a collection of shops and stalls in the vicinity of the **Central Group** of monuments). As soon as you emerge from your car or bus, you'll no doubt be approached by a local guide who will offer his services. Even if your guide—and there are only a couple in Mandu—is not a certified expert, this is one place where it can be fun to have someone show you around and enrich your experience with a version of history that overdoes the myth, romance, and fantasy. Establish that he speaks passable English, and agree on a price upfront; expect to pay up to Rs 500 ($12/£6) for the day. Monuments are open from 8am to 6pm.

If you don't plan to spend the night in Mandu, start your tour immediately with 15th-century **Jama Masjid** 𝒜. Said to have been inspired by the mosque in Damascus, this colossal colonnaded structure bears some Hindu influences, such as the carvings of lotus flowers and decorative bells. Adjacent to the mosque is the **mausoleum of Hoshang Shah,** the first white marble tomb in India, said to have inspired those in Agra; it's ultimately missable. The **Royal Enclave** 𝒜𝒜 (Rs 100/$2.45/£1.25; daily 8am–6pm) is dominated by enormous **Jahaz Mahal,** commonly known as the "ship palace." Built between two artificial lakes, it certainly was intended to be the ultimate stone pleasure cruiser, where the sultan Ghiyas Shah kept his 15,000 courtesans and an additional 1,000 Amazonians from Turkey and Abyssinia to guard them. Behind the ship palace is **Hindola Mahal;** its oddly sloping buttress walls have given it the nickname "Swing Palace."

Mandu's main road stretches southward, through open fields dotted with ruins and a few village houses, and continues into the **Rewa Kund** group of monuments, where the passionate romance between Maharaja Baz Bahadur, the last independent sultan of Malwa, and the beautiful Hindu shepherdess, Rupmati, is preserved in striking stone constructions. Apparently smitten by Rupmati's glorious singing voice, Baz built the **Rupmati Pavilion** 𝒜𝒜 (Rs 100/$2.45/£1.25) so that she could see her village in the Narmada Valley below, but things went awry when the Mughal emperor Akbar came to hear of her legendary beauty and voice and wanted to take her home as a souvenir. After a fierce battle in which Baz was defeated, his beloved committed suicide. The view from the pavilion, which stands on the edge of a sheer precipice rising 365m (1,197 ft.) from the valley floor, is still sublime. On the way back from the pavilion, stop at **Baz Bahadur's Palace** (Rs 100/$2.45/£1.25), where the acoustics enjoyed by the musically inclined king remain quite astonishing, even if some of the restoration work is a bit ham-fisted.

WHERE TO STAY & DINE

While there are basic lodgings in Mandu, we highly recommend a stay at Ahilya Fort (reviewed below), a fantastic destination in itself, situated on the Narmada River in the town of Maheshwar, some 91km (56 miles) from Indore. From either city, the journey to Mandu should take 2½ hours. If you arrive in Indore too late to move on to Mandu or Maheshwar, you'll easily find a room in one of the city's standard business hotels; the best of these is **Fortune Landmark** (✆ 0731/25-5770; www.fortune hotels.com; doubles from $95/£48). The amenities and comforts here match those of any smart city hotel, and the surrounding lawns and gardens are lovely. If, however, you'd prefer a more personal experience, see if you can manage to stay at **Rashid Kothi** (22 Yeshwant Niwas Rd., Indore 452 003; ✆ 0731/243-4377; ashanu@hot mail.com), a family home run by Anuradha Dubey and Arshad Rashid. Of the two rooms, one is a garden cottage; furnishings are comfortable and contain thoughtful touches that enhance the homey atmosphere. All meals (strictly vegetarian) are included in the room rate (100€/$134/£67 double without air-conditioning).

If you decide to stay in Mandu itself, be prepared to rough it somewhat. Our first choice among the small selection of spartan lodgings is **Hotel Rupmati** (Mandu 454 010; ✆ 07292/26-3270 or -3279; reservations in Indore: ✆ 0731/270-2055), a budget charmer with 12 simple rooms (from Rs 550/$13/£7 double). Close to the village bazaar on the edge of a cliff, the hotel enjoys sublime views. Guest rooms are in a long stone building; all are large with whitewashed walls and a thin, rock-hard mattress with white linens and a blanket (most also have A/C and a TV for double the price). The view can be enjoyed from a small private balcony. Attention has been paid to the grounds, which feature a children's play area, and the cleanliness and tranquillity of the place make up for the budget facilities.

Ahilya Fort 🐾🐾   A haven of tranquillity, the hassle-free sacred town of Maheshwar is home to one of the loveliest heritage properties in the state—a place of good taste and serenity. The summer palace of Indore's Prince Richard Holkar (a whiz in the kitchen with a number of cookbooks to his name), the fort is a labyrinthine 18th-century palace, complete with English flower gardens and evocative battlements of rough-hewn stone. Each guest room is a unique combination of colonial period furniture and personal touches, with smart attention to detail. Choose between a river-facing unit (the "royal" rooms have balconies overlooking the river) or one with a private courtyard, or ask to stay in one of two luxurious tents. Then spend some time discovering all manner of delightful spaces; ease onto the silken comfort of the *jharokha* overlooking the holy Narmada River below. Besides visiting Mandu (just 56km/35 miles away), you can explore the Maheshwar temple just next door or visit the local Holkar-resuscitated handloom center. Have dinner on the river under moonlight, or select a terrace, courtyard, or battlement to be your preferred dining spot; the refined meals are a real highlight.

Maheshwar 451 224. ✆ 0728/327-3329. www.ahilyafort.com. info@ahilyafort.com. Reservations in Delhi: ✆ 011/ 4155-1575. Fax 011/4155-1055. 14 units. 145€ ($194/£99) standard and tent double; 185€ ($248/£126) superior double; 210€ ($281/£143) royal double. Rates include all meals, soft drinks, Indian alcoholic beverages, massages, laundry, boating, local sightseeing, and taxes. 2-night minimum stay. 50% discount mid-Apr through mid-Oct. MC, V. **Amenities:** Various dining areas; pool; TV and game room; gift shop; massage; babysitting; laundry; doctor-on-call; guided excursions; picnics; boat trips; e-mail facility. *In room:* A/C (suite and superior rooms), tea- and coffee-making facility, hair dryer on request, air-cooler (standard rooms and tents).

10

Rajasthan: Land of Princes

For many, Rajasthan is the very essence of India, with crenelated forts and impregnable palaces that rise like giant fairy-tale sets above dusty sun-scorched plains and shimmering lakes. India's second-largest state—similar in size to France—is largely covered by the ever-encroaching Thar Desert, but despite its aridity, Rajasthan was once remarkably prosperous: Traders from as far afield as Persia and China had to cross its dry plains to reach the southern ports of Gujarat, something the warrior princes of Rajasthan were quick to capitalize on. Today the principal attraction of Rajasthan—the post-independence name for Rajputana, literally "land of princes"—is the large variety of forts and palaces its aristocrats built throughout the centuries, making it one of the most popular destinations in India. But Rajasthan offers so much more than desert castles and culture—from tracking down tigers in the Ranthambhore jungle (arguably the best place to spot wild tigers in Asia) to gaping at the world's most intricately carved marble temples on historic Mount Abu. Peopled by proud turbaned men and delicately boned women in saris of dazzling colors, the "land of princes" is rich with possibilities. It's also high on contrasts: You could bed down amid some of the most sumptuous luxury on earth and then spend the day roaming ancient villages, exploring medieval marketplaces.

You could plan to spend your entire trip to India in Rajasthan, which is within easy striking distance of Delhi (and the Taj Mahal) by train, plane, or road. Certainly you'll need at least a week to take in the major destinations, of which the lake city of Udaipur and the desert fort of Jaisalmer—the only fort in the world still inhabited by villagers—are top highlights. Also vying for your time is the "blue city" of Jodhpur, which has the state's most impressive and best-preserved fort as well as the largest palace in India; the tiny town of Pushkar, built around a sacred lake and host to the biggest camel *mela* (fair) in Asia; the painted *havelis* (historic homes or mansions) of the Shekhawati region, referred to as India's open-air gallery; the tiny Keoladeo "Ghana" National Park, which boasts the largest concentration and variety of bird life in Asia; the untainted, almost medieval atmosphere of little towns like Bundi; and the bumper-to-bumper shops and bazaars in Jaipur (the state and retail capitals of Rajasthan). Shopping, in fact, is another of the state's chief attractions: Because of the liberal patronage of the wealthy Rajput princes, skilled artisans from all over the East settled here to adorn the aristocrats and their palaces. Today these same skills are on sale to the world's designers and travelers, and no one—from die-hard bargain-hunters to chichi fashionistas—leaves Rajasthan empty-handed. The question is how to choose from an unbelievable array of textiles, jewelry, paintings, rugs, pottery, diaries—even kitchen utensils—and then how to fit them into your bulging suitcase.

Land of Thirst: Rajasthan Today

Although the revenue you bring to Rajasthan is a welcome boon, don't be fooled by the sumptuous luxury, deep bathtubs, and infinity swimming pools you'll encounter and no doubt be seduced by. Still very much a traditional, feudal society, the country's second-largest state is also one of its poorest. Although official estimates indicate that poverty is on the decrease, sheer numbers rather than percentages paint a more depressing picture—more than a million city-dwellers live in slums. Some 400,000 have no regular access to pure drinking water, and 330,000 have no access to proper toilet facilities. The plight of Rajasthan's people has in recent years been exacerbated by the worst drought in living memory—years of little rain have resulted in the widespread deaths of livestock and the decimation of crops. Many blame the government for undermining traditional ways of coping with drought: Widespread irrigation schemes have made farmers rely on taps and tanks rather than take a frugal approach to water. As you drive through the state, you'll see massive concrete pipes being installed, ready to bring water to even the driest regions. Regardless, the fact remains that—even with the prayed-for return of rain—it will be difficult for the rural sector to fully recover, particularly since there is every reason to suspect that the global warming phenomenon has forever altered local seasons; monsoon rains in 2006 were accompanied by unexpected floods that wreaked havoc in unprepared desert regions, while hail during the 2007 harvest in Jaisalmer, for example, undid the good work of the previous year's rainfall.

But perhaps the best reason to visit Rajasthan is to experience its unusual hotels: The state has at least 100 heritage properties—castles, palaces, forts, and ornate havelis—many of which are still home to India's oldest monarchies. This must be the only place in the world where, armed with a credit card, you can find yourself sleeping in a king's bed, having earlier dined with the aristocrat whose forebears built and quite often died for the castle walls that surround it. Known for their valor and honor, and later for their decadence (see "Once Were Warriors: The History of the Rajput," below), the Rajputs are superb hosts, and it is almost possible to believe that you, too, are of aristocratic blood, as a turbaned aide awaits your every wish while you marvel at the starry night from the bastion of your castle. Long live the king (and queen), for you are it.

1 Planning Your Trip to Rajasthan

Rajasthan has so much to see, with long travel distances between top sites, that a trip here requires careful planning (particularly if you hire a car and driver, which is the best way to tour the state). The following overview can help you plan your itinerary.

The three biggest cities in Rajasthan, all with airports, are **Jaipur,** the "Pink City"; **Jodhpur,** the "Blue City"; and **Udaipur,** the "White City." All are worthwhile destinations, not least because they offer easy access to great excursions. The tiny **Jaisalmer,**

0
100 mi
0
100 km

Lahore

Amritsar

HIMACHAL PRADESH

Ravi

PUNJAB

Simla

Chandigarh

CHANDIGARH

Sutlej

Multan

Dehra Dun

PAKISTAN

HARYANA

15

DELHI

Delhi

SHEKHAWATI

New Delhi

Bikaner

Jhunjhunu

Mandawa

11

Neemrana

Amanbagh (Ajabgarh)

Yamuna

Jaisalmer

15

SARISKA WLS

Alwar

Bharatpur

RAJASTHAN

Amber

KEOLADEO NP

Agra

Jaipur

Jodhpur

Pushkar

Ajmer

Sanganer

Karauli

Deogarh

RANTHAMBHORE NP

Ranakpur

Sawai Madhopur

Gwalior

Bundi

Mount Abu

Chittaurgarh

Kota

15

Udaipur

8

3

LITTLE RANN OF KACHCHH

Gandhinagar

8A

Ahmedabad

New Delhi

RAJASTHAN

NALSAROVAR NP

Vadodara

Narmada

India

Palitana

8

Bay of Bengal

Surat

or "Golden City," is the most awkward to reach, and while some find it the highlight of their Rajasthan trip, others feel it isn't worth the schlep it takes to get there.

For most, the entry point is the state capital of Jaipur, near the eastern border, which is the third point (the others being nearby Delhi and Agra) of the much-traveled **Golden Triangle.** Should you choose to start your trip here, you are in fact well positioned to visit some of Rajasthan's top sites: Only a few hours from the city is **Ranthambhore National Park**—where you have good chances of spotting a wild tiger—and Bharatpur's **Keoladeo National Park,** a must-see for birders, and literally on the way from Agra. Jaipur is also within driving distance of **Bundi,** an untouched, off-the-beaten-track rural town that lies some hours away by train or car, as well as nearby **Ajmer,** gateway to the sacred lake of **Pushkar,** site of the world's most famous camel fair.

Other than its proximity to these sites, however, as well as the excellent rail and flight connections to the rest of India, the only good reason to dally in Jaipur itself is to indulge in some retail therapy. Most visitors planning to travel farther by car circle Rajasthan in a counterclockwise direction, starting off in Jaipur and traveling the rather circuitous route west to Jodhpur (with a sojourn in Pushkar—a highly recommended option, particularly for younger travelers); then, from Jodhpur, you make the 5½- to 6-hour drive west to Jaisalmer for a few nights before you return to Jodhpur. An alternative route to Jaisalmer, which means you don't have to travel both to and from Jodhpur, is to travel from Delhi through the Shekhawati region to **Bikaner,** known for the nearby **Temple of the Rats,** and from there on to Jaisalmer, before you travel east again to Jodhpur. (The other alternative is to skip Jaisalmer altogether, and if you're short on time this is what you may have to do, but we think it's a must-see city.) From Jodhpur you then travel south to Udaipur and, finally, head back north to Jaipur, stopping en route at one of many lovely palace hotels (or at Amanbagh) for a most relaxing end to your journey.

For someone with limited time (say, only enough to visit one of Rajasthan's cities), it's far better to fly direct to Udaipur—with great lodging options in all price brackets, this is arguably Rajasthan's most attractive city (though you should check the status of the lakes, which have gone dry for an entire season in recent years, before planning your entire trip around it). From Udaipur you can take a wonderful (but long) day trip to **Kumbhalgarh Reserve** to take in Ranakpur's exquisitely carved **Jain temples** and impressive **Kumbhalgarh Fort** before overnighting at **Devi Garh,** one of India's top hotels. Alternatively, you can head east from Udaipur to Bundi, via the historic fort of **Chittaurgarh,** and then move on to **Ranthambhore National Park.** Or take the short trip directly south to the relatively undiscovered **palaces of Dungarpur,** or head much further out west to **Mount Abu,** the state's only hill station and sacred pilgrimage of the Jains, who come to visit the famous **Dilwara Temples.** Jodhpur and its majestic **Mehrangarh Fort** lie only 5 hours north of Udaipur by road, and you can break up the trip by overnighting at one of the recommended heritage properties along the way.

As mentioned, the state's other must-see city is Jaisalmer, which is rather inconveniently situated on the far-flung western outreaches of Rajasthan's Thar Desert; of course, its remote setting is greatly responsible for its desirability as a destination. To get there, you have to either set off from Jodhpur, or travel via the desert town of Bikaner—both routes involve a lot of driving (Jodhpur is a 5½- to 6-hr. drive away; Bikaner a 6- to 7-hr. drive). You can opt to travel from Jodhpur to Jaisalmer by overnight train, but make sure to get a berth in the air-conditioned compartment of the Delhi–Jaisalmer Express (even though the desert nights can be bitterly cold, this is your best option until Jaisalmer's airport arrives) and carry a warm blanket.

Your Carriage Awaits . . .

The most hassle-free way to experience Rajasthan is by train, and by this we're in no way suggesting that you slum it with the rest of the country's commuters. Instead, consider spending your nights aboard the famous **Palace on Wheels** (www.palaceonwheels.net; see chapter 2 for details). The drawback of train packages (or any package tour, for that matter) is a relative lack of autonomy and independence; virtually everything is prearranged and you do feel like you're part of a group, or herd, jostling from one significant attraction to the next. But if you want to save time and energy and forgo daily haggling and making key choices—like where to stay, eat, and shop—training through the state is ideal.

You can fly between Rajasthan's major cities and hire a vehicle and driver from one of the recommended operators for the duration of your stay in each region, but the long-term hire of a car and driver is highly recommended—this is really the best way to tour Rajasthan because it means you can travel at your own pace, avoid public transport (or the daily grind of haggling with taxis), and get right off the beaten track. That said, Rajasthan's potholed roads make for slow going, drivers have unknown rules (but clearly the big trucks and cows rule, no matter what the circumstances), and traveling by night is only for the suicidal—even day trips will have you closing your eyes in supplication to some higher being.

Many operators are not keen to provide a breakdown of pricing, leaving you with the distinct feeling that you are being ripped off. To avoid this, get a per-kilometer rate for the specific kind of car you wish to hire, and the overnight supplement for the driver. Establish a ballpark per-kilometer rate from the **RTDC Transport Unit**—their rates are usually slightly higher than those offered by private operators, so it's worth going there first for a quote. The RTDC in Jaipur owns a number of vehicles or will contract out specific requests for vehicles; call them at (✆ **0141/220-0778** (or write to cro@rajasthantourism.gov.in or rtdcpr@sancharnet.in). At press time, an air-conditioned car and driver in Jaipur cost about Rs 1,200 ($29/£15) for a full day (8 hr.), up to 80km (50 miles), plus a negotiated fee for every hour after that. For out-of-town trips, expect to pay Rs 7.50 to Rs 10 (20¢–25¢/10p–15p) per kilometer plus Rs 200 ($4.90/£2.50) per night out. A romantic way to go is in an air-conditioned Ambassador, India's quaint homegrown brand of sedans, which provides you with a real sense of being in another world, not to mention another era. They're also pretty hardy. The best organized travel company in Rajasthan is **Rajasthan Tours** (www.rajasthan touronline.com), which has branches in each of the main cities; rates are somewhat pricier than you'll find elsewhere, but they're fixed, so there's no bargaining, and service is of an excellent standard. If you'd prefer to support an entrepreneurial independent driver, contact **Hari Ram Choudhary** (✆ **94-1444-2618;** around Rs 2,000/ $49/£25 per day in Rajasthan), who owns a Toyota Qualis, speaks good English, and knows his way around the state (he's been driving travelers since 1984); you might want to book him well in advance of your trip by e-mailing his friend at anilsharma. jaipur@gmail.com.

Note: At press time, tax on Rajasthan hotel accommodation varied between 8% and 10% (depending on the city), although this does not apply to economy rooms; sales tax of 12.5% is charged on dining bills.

Once Were Warriors: The History of the Rajput

Rajasthan's history is inextricably entwined with that of its self-proclaimed aristocracy: a warrior clan, calling themselves *Rajputs,* that emerged sometime during the 6th and 7th centuries. Given that no one too low in the social hierarchy could take the profession (like bearing arms) of a higher caste, this new clan, comprising both indigenous people and foreign invaders such as the Huns, held a special "rebirth" ceremony—purifying themselves with fire—at Mount Abu, where they assigned themselves a mythical descent from the sun and the moon. In calling themselves Rajputs (a corruption of the word *Raj Putra,* "sons of princes"), they officially segregated themselves from the rest of society. Proud and bloodthirsty, yet with a strict code of honor, they were to dominate the history of the region right up until independence, and are still treated with deference by their mostly loyal subjects.

The Rajputs offered their subjects protection in return for revenue, and together formed a kind of loose kinship in which each leader was entitled to unequal shares within the territory of his clan. The term they used for this collective sharing of power was "brotherhood," but predictably the clan did not remain a homogenous unit, and bitter internecine wars were fought. Besides these ongoing internal battles, the Hindu Rajputs had to defend their territory from repeated invasions by the Mughals and Marathas, but given the Rajputs' ferocity and unconquerable spirit, the most skillful invasion came in the form of diplomacy, when the great Mughal emperor Akbar married Jodhabai, daughter of Raja Bihar Mal, ruler of the Kachchwaha Rajputs (Jaipur region), who then bore him his first son, Jahangir.

Jahangir was to become the next Mughal emperor, and the bond between Mughal and Rajput was cemented when he in turn married another Kachchwaha princess (his mother's niece). A period of tremendous prosperity for the Kachchwaha clan followed, as their military prowess helped the Mughals conquer large swaths of India in return for booty. But many of the Rajput clans—particularly those of Mewar (in the Udaipur region)—were dismayed by what they saw as a capitulation to Mughal imperialism. In the end it was English diplomacy that truly tamed the maharajas. Rather than waste money and men going to war with the Rajput kings, the English offered them a treaty. This gave "the Britishers" control of Rajputana, but in return the empire recognized the royal status of the Rajputs and allowed them to keep most of the taxes extorted from their subjects and the many travelers who still plied the trade routes in the Thar Desert.

WHERE TO STAY & DINE EN ROUTE FROM DELHI

Instead of hightailing it from the capital, consider breaking up your journey and enjoying some of the marvelous luxury and architectural heritage on offer between Delhi and Jaipur. We highly recommend overnighting at Neemrana Fort-Palace on your way into Rajasthan (it's not far from Delhi, and many Indian families head there

This resulted in a period of unprecedented decadence for the Rajputs, who now spent their days hunting for tigers, playing polo, and flying to Europe to stock up on the latest Cartier jewels and Belgian crystal. Legends abound of their spectacular hedonism, but perhaps the most famous surround the Maharaja Jai Singh of Alwar (north of Jaipur), who wore black silk gloves when he shook hands with the English king and reputedly used elderly women and children as tiger bait. When Jai Singh visited the showrooms of Rolls-Royce in London, he was affronted when the salesman implied that he couldn't afford to purchase one of the sleek new models—he promptly purchased 10, shipped them home, tore their roofs off, and used them to collect garbage. The English tolerated his bizarre behavior until, after being thrown from his horse during a polo match, he doused the animal with fuel and set it alight. Having ignored previous reports of child molestation, the horse-loving British finally acted with outrage and exiled him from the state.

Above all, the Rajput maharajas expressed their newfound wealth and decadence by embarking on a frenzied building spree, spending vast fortunes on gilding and furnishing new palaces and forts. The building period reached its peak in Jodhpur, with the completion of the Umaid Bhawan Palace in the 1930s, at the time the largest private residence in the world.

When the imperialists were finally forced to withdraw, the "special relationship" that existed between the Rajputs and the British was honored for another 3 decades—they were allowed to keep their titles and enjoyed a large government-funded "pension," but their loyalty to the British, even during the bloody 1857 uprisings, was to cost them in the long run.

In 1972 Prime Minister Indira Gandhi—sensibly, but no doubt in a bid to win popular votes—stripped the Rajputs of both stipends and titles. This left the former aristocracy almost destitute, unable to maintain either their lifestyles or their sprawling properties. While many sold their properties and retired to middle-class comfort in Delhi or Mumbai, others started opening their doors to paying guests like Jackie Kennedy and members of the English aristocracy, who came to recapture the romance of Raj-era India. By the dawn of a new millennium, these once-proud warriors had become first-rate hoteliers, offering people from all walks of life the opportunity to experience the princely lifestyle of Rajasthan.

for Sun lunch); from here you can move on either to Jaipur or directly into the Shekhawati region. Stay at Amanbagh after your tour of Rajasthan, and set aside at least 2 nights for the unadulterated pampering you'll receive; the state can be hard work, filled with tourist crowds in winter, and a stay at Amanbagh will ensure you return home rested and restored.

Amanbagh ★★★   For its inspired location alone, this fabulous Amanresort property deserves three stars. Date palms and mango and jamun trees dominate this truly exotic natural oasis in the Thar Desert, adjacent to Sariska National Park, near Alwar (142km/88 miles northeast of Jaipur). Made almost entirely of pink sandstone by local stonemasons, Amanbagh was designed by architect Ed Tuttle, who took inspiration from local structures, particularly in evidence when you visit the nearby ghost city, Bhangarh (truly, an undiscovered gem). The best and most expensive suites are the palatial pool pavilions: A light-filled entrance foyer leads to a gorgeous, massive bedroom on one side and a humongous bath chamber on the other. All three "rooms" have glass doors that open out onto the private pool area, complete with sun beds and a sunken marble dining table atop a sandstone pedestal. Interiors are spacious and exceedingly tasteful: Marble floors and ultra-smooth pink sandstone walls are complemented by neutral tones, wood, black, and silver, while in the bathroom green marble predominates—an impressive bathtub has been carved out of a single piece of Kesariya green marble. The same marble lines your private pool, which is cooled in summer and heated in winter; begin your day listening to twittering birds and watching for cheeky monkeys while sipping ruby-red pomegranate juice on the porch facing the canal, thick with vegetation, that flows along the resort's periphery. For significantly fewer dollars, you can forgo the pool while still being thoroughly ensconced in luxury in one of the three categories of haveli suite (terrace units are best; ask for one facing the canal rather than the pool). If you can bear to leave the premises, you can take picnics into the countryside, hike to ancient Somsagar Lake, explore the haunted ruins at Bhangarh, or visit the archaeological sites in the Paranagar area. Amanbagh's staff is enchanting: warm, discreet, and remarkably helpful (many are locals, and rather than graduating from hotel schools, understand the culture, wildlife, and history of the region, which makes for a wonderfully intimate and personable experience). Guests are assigned a personal manager who takes care of your every need, and—a boon, this—suggests itineraries for the duration of your stay, so you can comfortably combine excursions with spa appointments and more mundane leisure time at the pool.

Ajabgarh, Rajasthan. ⓒ **01465/22-3333.** Fax: 01465/22-3335. amanbagh@amanresorts.com. www.amanresorts.com. Reservations: Amanresorts Corporate Office ⓒ **65/6887-3337** in Singapore 24/7. Fax 65/6887-3338. reservations@ amanresorts.com. 40 Units. $1,050 (£525) pool pavilion; $750 (£375) terrace haveli; $650 (£325) garden haveli; $600 (£300) courtyard haveli. Rates exclude 10% tax and 10% service charge. AE, DC, MC, V. **Amenities:** 2 restaurants; bar; 2 heated pools; gym; spa; boutique; 24-hr. room service; laundry; doctor-on-call; Internet; library; guided excursions; trekking; horse safaris; camel safaris; jeep safaris; shopping excursions. *In room:* A/C, minibar, hair dryer, safe, Internet connectivity, CD player, pool pavilions have private heated pool.

Neemrana Fort-Palace ★★   Since it first opened in the early 1990s, Neemrana Fort has become the flagship of the highly regarded Neemrana Group (check out the website for many more atmospheric heritage properties). Purchased by historians Aman Nath and Francis Wacziarg, who spotted the ruined fort while researching a book on Rajasthan, it has been sensitively and painstakingly rebuilt into what is billed a "non-hotel." Almost every room has an arresting view, though no two are alike and not all will please you, so do ask for a description before paying. For instance, Lehsuniya Mahal is windowless, Geru Mahal has just a short wall separating living and bathing space, only a few rooms have double beds, and others have tiny bathing spaces; getting to the most far-off rooms (usually with private terraces) may require some fitness. Among the standard rooms, Jalaj Mahal (Lotus Palace) is quiet and located near a pretty lotus pond, while the Chandra Mahal suite, formerly a court room, is spacious and cool and once roomed Kate Winslet; Deva Mahal is a huge apartment conveniently located near the pool. Service is well-intended, but lacks rigor. Buffet meals are served in the courtyard and adjoining hall; stick to the Indian food and avoid the French restaurant, which doesn't cut the mustard. An evening spent sipping a drink while watching the sunset or under the stars at any of the lovely outdoor spaces will no doubt be one of the highlights of your Rajasthan trip. An enchanting destination, Neemrana will inspire contemplation and creativity. It's highly recommended.

Village Neemrana, District Alwar, Rajasthan 301 705. *C* **01494/24-6006** through -6008. Reservations: 13 Main Market, New Delhi 110 013. *C* **011/2435-6145** or 011/4182-5001. Fax 011/2435-1112. www.neemranahotels.com. 50 units. Rs 3,000–Rs 6,600 ($73–$161/£37–£82) standard double; Rs 5,400–Rs 10,200 ($132–$249/£67–£126) grand room; Rs 7,800–Rs 9,000 ($190–$220/£96–£111) suite; Rs 10,200–Rs 19,200 ($249–$468/£126–£237) luxury suite; Rs 600 ($15/£8) extra bed. Rates include bed tea and evening tea. Taxes extra. 20% off-season discount May–Aug. AE, DC, MC, V. **Amenities:** Restaurants and multiple dining areas; bar; pool; Jacuzzi; spa; indoor game room; concierge; travel desk; Ayurvedic massage; library; cultural programs; yoga and meditation facility; TV lounge; camel cart rides. *In room:* A/C (most rooms), tea- and coffee-making facilities (some suites).

2 Jaipur

262km (162 miles) SW of Delhi; 232km (144 miles) W of Agra

After independence, Jaipur became the administrative and commercial capital of what was known as Rajputana, a suitable conclusion to the dreams of its founder Maharaja Sawai Jai Singh II, a man famed for his talents as a politician, mathematician, and astronomer. At age 13 he ascended the throne of the Kachchwaha Rajputs, a clan that had enjoyed tremendous prosperity and power as a result of their canny alliance, dating back to Humayun's reign, with the Mughal emperors. It was in fact the emperor Aurangzeb, a fanatically pious Muslim, who—despite the fact that Jai Singh was a Hindu prince—named him Sawai, meaning "one and a quarter," for his larger-than-life intellect and wit. Having proved his prowess as a military tactician for Aurangzeb, increasing the emperor's coffers substantially, Jai Singh felt it safe to move his capital from the claustrophobic hills surrounding Amber to a dry lake in the valley below.

Begun in 1727 and completed in just 8 years, Jaipur was the first city in India to enjoy rigorous town planning according to the principles laid down in "Shilpa Shastra," an ancient Indian treatise on architecture. The city is protected by high walls, with wide, straight avenues that divide it into nine sectors, or *chokris* (apparently reflecting the nine divisions of the universe, resembling the Indian horoscope), each named after the commodity and caste who lived and practiced their specific skills here—the order and space was at the time a total revolution in Indian cities. Although these market names still provide some clue as to what was once found in the otherwise rather uniform rows of shops that line the streets, the overall significance of these historic divisions is today lost to the traveler on foot trying to negotiate the chaos of the filth-strewn streets and pushy traders.

Despite the romantic nickname the "Pink City," Jaipur is not one of Rajasthan's most attractive cities, which is why, after taking in the centrally located City Palace (where the principal sights are located), it's probably wise to concentrate on sites farther afield: **Amber Fort,** first royal residence of the Maharajas of Kachchwaha, lies 11km (7 miles) north; and popular **Samode Palace** is an hour's drive away. But if the heat has you beat and the very thought of traipsing through another fort or durbar hall leaves you feeling exhausted, check out the shopping recommendations. A central repository for the region's wonderful crafts, Jaipur is famous for its gems and jewelry, enamel- and brassware, blue pottery, embroidered leather footwear, rugs, tie-and-dye

Jaipur

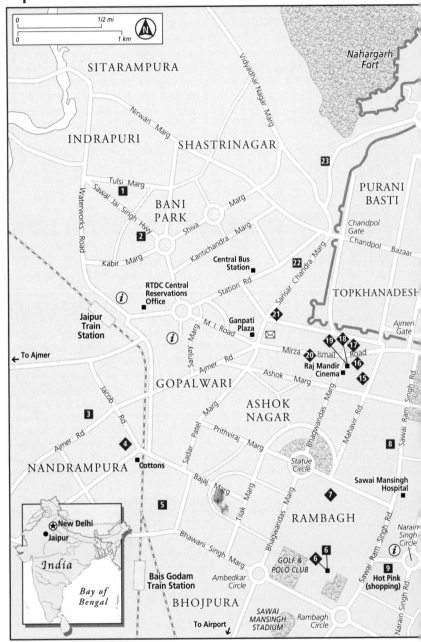

SITARAMPURA

Nahargarh
Fort

INDRAPURI

SHASTRINAGAR

Ninwan Marg

Vidyadhar Nagar Marg

23

PURANI
BASTI

Tulsi Marg

1

Waterworks Road

Sawai Jai Singh Hwy

BANI
PARK

Shiva

Marg

Chandpol
Gate

2

Chandpol Bazaar

Kabir Marg

Kantichandra Marg

Sansar Chandra Marg

TOPKHANADESH

Central Bus
Station

Station Rd.

22

Ajmeri
Gate

RTDC Central
Reservations
Office

M. I. Road

Ganpati
Plaza

21

19 18 17

Jaipur
Train
Station

Sanjay Marg

Mirza

Ismail

Road

16

← To Ajmer

Ajmer Rd.

20

Raj Mandir
Cinema

15

Ashok

Marg

GOPALWARI

Jacob Rd.

ASHOK
NAGAR

Sadar Patel Marg

Prithviraj

Marg

Bhagwandas Marg

Mahavir Rd.

Sawai Ram Singh Rd.

3

Ajmer Rd.

8

4

Cottons

Statue
Circle

Sawai Mansingh
Hospital

NANDRAMPURA

Bajaj Marg

Tilak Marg

7

Bhagwandas Marg

RAMBAGH

Narain
Singh
Circle

5

New Delhi

Jaipur

India

Bhawani Singh Marg

GOLF &
POLO CLUB

6

6

Sawai Ram Singh Rd.

9

Hot Pink
(shopping)

Narain Singh Rd.

Bay of
Bengal

Bais Godam
Train Station

Ambedkar
Circle

BHOJPURA

SAWAI
MANSINGH
STADIUM

Rambagh
Circle

To Airport

0   1/2 mi
0   1 km

N

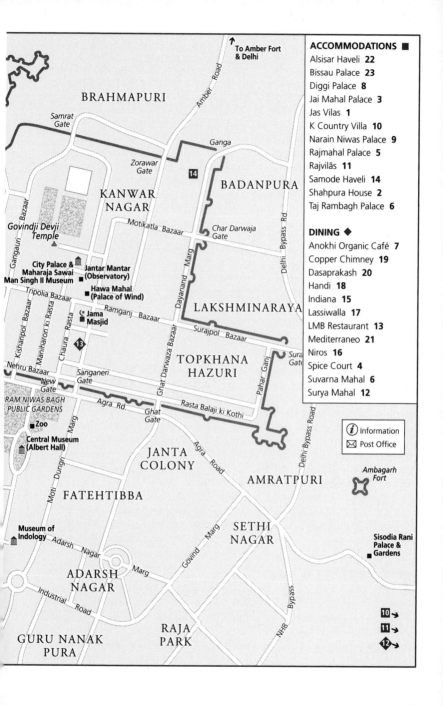

ACCOMMODATIONS ■
Alsisar Haveli 22
Bissau Palace 23
Diggi Palace 8
Jai Mahal Palace 3
Jas Vilas 1
K Country Villa 10
Narain Niwas Palace 9
Rajmahal Palace 5
Rajvilās 11
Samode Haveli 14
Shahpura House 2
Taj Rambagh Palace 6

DINING ◆
Anokhi Organic Café 7
Copper Chimney 19
Dasaprakash 20
Handi 18
Indiana 15
Lassiwalla 17
LMB Restaurant 13
Mediterraneo 21
Niros 16
Spice Court 4
Suvarna Mahal 6
Surya Mahal 12

ⓘ Information
✉ Post Office

(Fun Fact Why Pink?

Jaipur is known as the Pink City, a highly idealized description of the terra-cotta-colored lime plaster that coats the old part of the city's walls, buildings, and temples. The reasons for painting the town pink are unknown, but various theories have been tossed about, from using pink to cut down glare, to Jai Singh II's apparent devotion to Lord Shiva (whose favorite color is reputedly terra cotta). Others believe Singh wanted to imitate the color of the sandstone used in the forts and palaces of his Mughal emperor-friends. The most popular reason (spread no doubt by "Britishers" during the Raj era) is that pink is the traditional color of hospitality, and the city was freshly painted and paved with pink gravel to warmly welcome Edward VII for his visit here in 1876. The city is painted pink once every 10 years by the Municipal Corporation, and in 2000 the painting was timed for a state visit, this time by former U.S. president Bill Clinton. A few streets became off-limits to cars, but this is not the case anymore, and cars and rickshaws crowd areas such as Bapu Bazaar, which otherwise is one of the better places to browse. If you are being driven around, especially at peak hour, it will take a very long time to get to your destination.

---

cotton fabrics, hand-blocked prints, fine *Kota doria* saris, and ready-made linens and home furnishings.

ESSENTIALS

VISITOR INFO   The **Rajasthan Tourism Development Corporation (RTDC)** information bureau is located on Platform 1 at the Jaipur Railway Station (© 0141/220-3531; open 24 hr.). There's an RTDC **tourist help desk** at Hotel Swagatam (behind Sadar Thana; © 0141/220-2586 or 0141/220-3531; Mon–Sat 10am–5pm; closed second Sat of every month). The **Tourist Reception Centre** is located at the Government Hostel, Paryatan Bhawan (© 0141/511-0595 through -0598; same hours as station office; mainly for emergencies or problems) on M.I. Road, the main thoroughfare in Jaipur. You'll find the less helpful **Government of India Tourist Office** at the Khasa Kothi hotel (© 0141/237-2200; Mon–Fri 9am–6pm, Sat 9am–2pm), or call their **24-hour help line,** © 1363, for information or assistance in an emergency, or to organize a guide. For predeparture planning, check out the RTDC's website (www.rajasthantourism.gov.in), or contact secretary@rajasthantourism.gov.in.

To find out about any events or festivals or current arts and entertainment listings, pick up a copy of the daily *Hindustan Times* or the *Jaipur Vision.*

GETTING THERE & AWAY

BY AIR   Both **Jet Airways** (© 0141/511-2222 through -2225) and **Indian Airlines** (© 0141/274-3500 or -3324) have daily flights between Jaipur and Delhi (40–60 min.), Jodhpur (45 min.), Udaipur (50 min.), and Mumbai (directly 1 hr., 30 min.). Indian also flies to Kolkata (2 hr., 25 min. to 3 hr., 45 min.) four times a week. **Sanganer Airport** lies 15 minutes south of the center of town; most hotels are 30 minutes away. Use the prepaid taxi service for the most convenient trip into the city (unless your hotel provides a complimentary transfer); a taxi ride to the Old City should cost under Rs 300 ($7.35/£3.70). It's a terribly grueling auto-rickshaw ride (but slightly cheaper at around Rs 200/$4.90/£2.50).

BY TRAIN   The Jaipur Railway Station is located west of the Old City (reservations Mon–Sat 8am–2pm and 2:15–8pm, Sun 8am–2pm). You can reach Jaipur by train from just about anywhere. The Ajmer Shatabdi connects Jaipur with Delhi in 4½ hours (daily except Wed); from Agra the Marudhar Express (early morning, alternate days) takes about 5 hours, while the late night Howrah Express (arriving midnight) takes 4 hours. You will be inundated with offers from rickshaw-*wallas* upon your arrival at Jaipur Station—to avoid this, go to the prepaid auto-rickshaw counter. Dial *©* **131** for railway inquiries, *©* **0141/220-4531** for recorded arrival and departure information, and *©* **135** for reservations. Reservations for foreign tourists are made at counter 8. To book a ticket, your easiest option is to get your hotel or a travel agent to do it for you. Either will charge a service fee of Rs 50 to Rs 100 ($1.25–$2.45/65p–£1.25) per passenger.

BY BUS   Buses arrive at the Inter-State Bus Terminal (called Sindhi Camp bus stand) on Station Road. For information, call *©* **0141/511-6043** for regular buses; or *©* **0141/511-6031** or 0141/220-5790 for deluxe buses. Deluxe Volvo coaches from Delhi will drop you off at Bikaner House, near India Gate. Departing from the same depot, you'll pay Rs 460 ($11/£5.70) for a seat on an A/C deluxe bus to Delhi; these leave half-hourly between 6am and 12:30am. It's a 5½-hour trip.

BY CAR   As is the case everywhere, you will need to hire a driver with your car. The Jaipur–Delhi National Highway no. 8 is a dual carriage road that should get you between the two cities in 4 hours. The single-road highway between Agra and Jaipur through Fatehpur Sikri and Bharatpur is in reasonable condition, too. There's not much you can do about the driving habits of other drivers, but you can certainly say something if you feel yours is driving rashly.

GETTING AROUND

Unprecedented commercial development in the state capital in recent years has not been accompanied by infrastructural change; rush-hour traffic is probably worse here than anywhere else in the country, although there are plans afoot to address the crisis. The best way to get around the crowded city center is on foot or by rickshaw. A rickshaw should set you back Rs 50 ($1.25/65p) per hour—always discuss the fare upfront before you get into the rickshaw. If you're in a bind and simply need a taxi right away, call **Pink City Taxi** (*©* **0141/220-5000**). More viable, however, is to hire an air-conditioned car and driver for use within the city for approximately 4 hours (40km/25 miles) at Rs 700 ($17/£8.65); 8 hours (80km/50 miles) at Rs 1,200 ($30/£15). If your intention is to hire a car and driver to tour Rajasthan at your own pace, contact **RTDC Transport Unit** (*©* **0141/220-0778**). For more information on hiring a car and driver from elsewhere, see chapter 2. **K. K. Holidays and Vacations**

Moments **Sunset over Jaipur**

See the pink city at its rosiest from Nahargarh Fort (or "Tiger Fort") when the sun sinks behind the Aravalli Hills. Then—as night falls—watch the city skyline turn into the twinkling jewels for which it is famed. The view is always a winner, but during the festival of Diwali in November, when firecrackers explode above the city, it's one you will never forget. The fort (Rs 5/10¢/5p) itself is largely in ruins, but the great vantage point alone is worth the trip. An RTDC-run cafe serves drinks and snacks.

(105 Neelkanth, 1 Bhawani Singh Rd., opposite Nehru Sehkar Bhawan; ✆ **0141/ 510-6820**, -2241, or -2245) is a reliable travel agency that charges the standard going rate for hiring a car (local or outstation) and has a fleet of vehicles to suit all budgets and needs. Mahender Singh, the director, and his GM, I. V. Singh, are not only helpful but Internet-savvy and can prebook all of your car and hotel arrangements if you e-mail them in advance (kkholidays@tantramail.com). If you like to support small local businesses, we suggest you contact Shankar Meena (✆ **98-2939-6947**) of **Rama Tours & Travels** (Srinath Colony, Near Airport, Sanganer) to arrange a car of really excellent quality at standard rates. Chances are Shankar or his brother Ramavtar will be your driver, and although their English may not be all that great, service is good-natured, and you'll be doing your bit for local entrepreneurship. You can also contact **Hari Ram Choudhary** (✆ **94-1444-2618**) for trips in the city or farther afield; he's been in the business for nearly 25 years and knows his way around.

GUIDED TOURS   Official guides, who hang around outside attractions (and charge Rs 100/$2.45/£1.25 per monument) tend to have their commentary down pat, but their enthusiasm wanes as soon as they've been hired and a price has been settled upon; while they often can't engage in dialogue, they will convince you that the tour is going to last a lot longer than it needs to be. Don't take chances with these professional amateurs: Hire **Jaimini Shastri** (✆ **93-1450-9684;** shastri_guide@yahoo.co.in; Rs 600/$15/£7.40 for the day), one of the most respected guides in Jaipur and well-versed in the city's history, culture, and arts and crafts. He can give you the best guided tour of Jantar Mantar, speaking at length on astronomy, astrology, and the observatory. Book him well in advance, and—if you are planning to tour the whole state—consider booking him for the entire trip. Alternatively, organize a guide through your hotel, or contact **Rajasthan Travel** (✆ **0141/236-5408**) or **Sita World Travel** (✆ **0141/237-3996** or 0141/510-2020); you will inevitably pay a higher rate if you use a middleman, but the official rate is Rs 600 ($15/£7.40) per day. If you don't mind groups (and a guide that may, once again, have limited knowledge of English), **RTDC** (✆ **0141/231-5714**) offers several tours. A packed half-day (5-hr.) tour, departing 8am, 11:30am, and 1:30pm, covers Hawa Mahal, Amer Palace and Fort, Jal Mahal, the Gaitor Maharaja Cenotaphs, the City Palace and Museum, Jantar Mantar, Albert Hall (Central Museum), and Jawahar Kala Kendra. The 8am tour (Rs 110/$2.70/ £1.30) is advisable. The full-day tour (9am–6:30pm) includes all of the above as well as Nahargarh and Jaigarh forts, and Birla Planetarium; it costs Rs 160 ($3.90/£2). The **Pink City by Night Tour** is essentially a bus tour to view various city monuments (including the Secretariate) as they are lit up in the evening; a vegetarian dinner at Nahargarh Fort is included (6:30–10:30pm; Rs 100/$2.45/£1.25). Night tours depart from the Government Hostel on M.I. Rd.

Tip: Consider picking up a copy of Dharmendar Kanwar's *Jaipur—10 Easy Walks* (Rupa; Rs 295/$7.20/£3.65) from the excellent new **Crossword** bookstore (First Floor, K.K. Square, C 11, Prithvi Raj Marg; ✆ **0141/237-9400**), which will also deliver books to you.

CITY LAYOUT

The major attractions and best bazaars lie within the walls of the Old City. Just south of the wall lies **Mirza Ismail (M.I.) Road**—running west to east, this major thoroughfare is where most of the primary retail outlets and a few good restaurants are located, and divides the city between the old (north) and new (south). The Old City is clearly distinguishable by its terra-cotta-colored walls and ramparts, and the new by its modern shops. Station Road, Sansar Chandra Marg, and Bhagwan Das Marg all intersect M.I. Road. Along these you will find all the services you need, from travel agents and money-changers to ATMs, restaurants, and Internet cafes. Farther south (but still within walking distance), diagonally opposite both Ajmeri Gate and New Gate of the Old City, lie Albert Hall and the Museum of Indology.

FESTIVALS

As is the case everywhere in India, Jaipur seems to celebrate something new every month, but the following are worth noting: In February during the **Harvest Festival (Basant Panchami)** the city celebrates a Kite Festival, when hundreds of colorful kites sail the blue Jaipur sky, especially around the City Palace area; there's also a competition and display. In March, when Holi celebrants throughout the country splash color on anything that moves, Jaipur celebrates an **Elephant Festival.** The massive pachyderms—dressed to the nines and decorated with paint—march through the city's streets to the City Palace, accompanied by loud drumbeats and chanting. The event sees a tug-of-war between the elephants and their *mahouts* (elephant trainers/caretakers), as well as men playing polo—on elephant-back, of course. Make sure you book accommodations in advance during this period.

The following month (Apr) is **Gangaur,** when the women of Rajasthan pray to the goddess Parvati (also known as Gangaur) for the longevity of their husbands or for husbands fair and kind. This culminates in a procession to Gangaur Temple by the symbolic Siva, accompanied by elephants, to take his bride home. **Teej** (July–Aug) sees Rajasthan's always colorfully clad women dressed in full regalia to celebrate the onset of the monsoon, while **Diwali (Festival of Lights),** the Hindu New Year, is celebrated throughout India in November.

Tip: Although all festivals are meant to be fun celebrations, a few unruly young men may try to ruin it with their aggressive behavior, especially during Holi and Diwali. Ask your hotel where it is advisable to go, and make sure you have your own transport if you are going to watch the festivities; single women travelers are advised to go with a male companion.

FAST FACTS: Jaipur

American Express Located on M.I. Road ((C) 0141/237-0117 or -0119) near Ganpati Plaza, the office is open daily 9am to 6pm.

Area Code For Jaipur, the area code is **0141**.

Banks You'll find several banks and ATMS on M.I. Road. The **Thomas Cook** office for foreign exchange is at Jaipur Tower ((C) 0141/236-0940; Mon–Sat 9:30am–6pm). There's a Citibank ATM next to the General Post Office, HDFC Bank ATM on Ashok Marg, ICICI Bank ATM in Ganpati Plaza, and others within the Old City.

Climate Summers have a mean maximum temperature of 104°F (40°C) and a minimum of 75°F (24°C), while winters range between a mean maximum of 70°F (21°C) and minimum of 48°F (9°C). The best weather occurs October through February.

Directory Assistance For telephone numbers call ℂ **197**. The number ℂ **0141/
274-4447** is a privately operated general information number (talking Yellow
Pages) that you can call for directory inquiries or information on shopping,
restaurants, and the like.

Emergencies Ambulance ℂ **102**; fire ℂ **101**; police ℂ **100**.

Hospitals **Santokba Durlabji Memorial Hospital** (ℂ **0141/256-6251** to **-6257**) is
located on Bhawani Singh Marg. **SMS Hospital** (ℂ **0414/256-0291**) is on Sawai
Ram Singh Road.

Newspapers & Books You can pick up an amazing selection of newspapers,
magazines, and books from tiny, inconspicuous **Books Corner** on M.I. Road;
Jaipur Vision is a local newspaper.

Police **Sindhi Camp Police Station** can be reached at ℂ **0141/220-6201**.

Post Office The GPO (ℂ **0141/236-8740**) is on M.I. Road (Mon–Sat 10am–6pm).

Tourist Help Desk Calll the **24-hour tourist help desk** (ℂ **1364**) if you want to
report a theft or register a tourism-related complaint. If you can't get through,
you can call the help desk's Delhi office at ℂ **98-1157-3315**.

WHAT TO SEE & DO

The principal attraction of the Old City of Jaipur is its **City Palace** (see below),
nearby **Jantar Mantar** (also described below), and much-photographed **Hawa Mahal
(Palace of Wind).** Built by Sawai Pratap Singh in 1799, Hawa Mahal (ℂ **0141/261-
8862;** Rs 5/10¢/5p entry, Rs 30/75¢/40p camera, Rs 70/$1.70/90p video; daily
9am–4:30pm) is principally a five-story facade of 593 latticed-stone screened windows, behind which the ladies of the palace could view the city without being seen.
You can walk along the corridors that line the windows, which are mostly one room
thick, but the building's principal attraction is the facade, which was undergoing renovation in 2007, and can be viewed from street level (entrance from Tripolia Bazaar,
Police HQ lane). Also within the city complex, opposite Chandra Mahal, is **Govindji
Temple** (daily 5–11am and 6–8pm), the most famous in the city and dedicated to
Lord Krishna, installed here so that Jai Singh II could see his favorite deity from the
Chandra Mahal. The Krishna image was brought here from Brindavan in the late 17th
century; devotees are allowed only a glimpse of it seven times a day.

In the new part of the city lies **Ram Niwas Bagh,** the city garden, which houses a
depressing zoo and aviary. At the heart of the garden lies Albert Hall, which houses
the **Central Museum** (ℂ **0141/257-0099;** Rs 35/85¢/45p; daily 10am–4:30pm;
cameras not allowed). Designed by the prolific architect and past master of the hybrid
Indo-Saracenic style of architecture, Swinton Jacob, this is of principal interest from
an architectural point of view, and a slow turn around the building in a car will suffice for many. That's not to say that the exhibits are devoid of interest—the eclectic
collection covers a wide range from musical instruments to bottled organs, and the
tiny terra-cotta figures demonstrating myriad yoga positions are worth a look. A short
drive due south lies the even stranger **Museum of Indology** (ℂ **0141/260-7455;** Rs
40/$1/50p, Rs 100/$2.45/£1.25 camera, Rs 500/$12/£6.20 video; Sat–Thurs
9:30am–4:30pm), where an incredible selection of objects—all collected in one lifetime by the writer Acharya Ram Charan Sharma "Vyakul"—has been crammed into

countless dusty display cases in every nook and cranny of his house. The collection is as eclectic as they come, including a map of India painted on a grain of rice, mis-printed rupees, a 180-million-year-old fossil, a letter written by Jai Singh, and the Gayatri Mantra written on a single strand of hair. It's a great shame more money is not available to edit and present this collection professionally.

On M.I. Road, near the Panch Batti intersection (where you'll see a **statue of Sawai Jai Singh II**) is **Raj Mandir** (© **0141/237-9372** or 0141/236-4438)—one of the most over-the-top cinemas in the country. This is the place to watch a Bollywood blockbuster, though you will need to book tickets in advance to avoid waiting in line for hours. If the film is a new release, book a day in advance (daily 10am–2pm and 3–6pm). If you don't fancy sitting through 3 hours of Hindi melodrama, request that the doorman let you in for a sneak peak; he may oblige for a small tip if the hall isn't packed. Or arrive a few hours before the film, purchase your ticket, and kill time over a coffee and a pastry across the street at Barista, while you browse books on Rajasthani art and architecture, magazines, and bestsellers.

The most disappointing attraction in the city is **Jawahar Kala Kendra.** Designed by the Indian architect Charles Correa in 1993, it has enjoyed exposure as a great example of contemporary Indian design and is celebrated as a center for the arts, with large exhibition spaces and studios for artists. Although the architecture may impress some, it is now all but empty of artists, and the exhibition spaces contain little more than a few broken chairs and the mattress of a homeless student—which may pass for art in the minds of the Turner Prize judges, but looks very much like a failed project.

CITY ESCAPES If the populous nature and heavy traffic of Jaipur gets to be too much, take a trip to **Amber Fort** (see below), which can be covered in a few hours. Do bear in mind, however, that even here the crush of people can be exhausting, par-ticularly over weekends; try to get here as soon as it opens. Time allowing, you may want to include a visit to **Jaigarh Fort** (Rs 50/$1.25/65p; City Palace entry ticket includes Jaigarh; daily 9am–4:30pm), whose walls snake high above Amber, creating a crenelated horizon. Built for defense purposes by Sawai Jai Singh II, it has a num-ber of buildings, gardens, and reservoirs as well as the world's largest cannon on wheels and the only surviving medieval cannon foundry, but its principal attraction is the panoramic view across Amber.

On the way to Amber you'll see the turnoff for the imposing hilltop fort of **Nahar-garh** (see "Sunset over Jaipur," above). Just below it is **Gaitor** (free admission, Rs 10/25¢/15p camera), a walled garden that houses the marble *chhatris*—erected over cre-mation platforms—of the Kachchwaha rulers. Needless to say, the most impressive one belongs to Jai Singh II. Farther along Amber Road you will see **Jal Mahal,** a lake palace originally built by Sawai Pratap Singh in 1799, who spent much of his childhood at Udaipur's Lake Palace. Sadly, Man Sagar Lake is dry from the protracted drought, strip-ping it of much of its romance. If it's romance you're after, take a leisurely drive to **Samode Palace** (see "Where to Stay," below; lunch Rs 500/$12/£6.20) where, after touring Diwan-i-Khas and Diwan-i-Am, you can enjoy tea in the lovely courtyard, where bold sparrows will attempt to nibble your biscuits. Or—even better—book a table at **Rajvilās** for dinner (see "Where to Dine," later in this chapter).

TOP ATTRACTIONS

Amer (or Amber) Fort 🐾🐾   Amber was the capital of the Kachchwahas from 1037 to 1727, when Sawai Jai Singh II moved the capital to Jaipur. The approach is through a narrow pass, and the fort, an imposing edifice that grew over a period of 2 centuries, is naturally fortified by the Aravalli Hills, making it an ideal stronghold. It's a stiff 20-minute climb to **Suraj Pol (Sun Gate),** beyond which lies a beautiful complex of palaces, halls, pavilions, gardens, and temples. Either travel by car or pretend you are of royal blood and ascend on elephant-back (Rs 450/$11/£5.55) for one to four riders; if you want to take pictures of the elephants, they pose for you for around Rs 50 ($1.25/65p). After entering Jaleb Chowk through Suraj Pol (more elephants take riders for a turn around the courtyard), dismount and take the flight of stairs up through **Singh Pol (Lion Gate)** to **Diwan-i-Am (Hall of Public Audience),** a raised platform with 27 colonnades. Opposite you'll see the ornately carved silver doors leading to **Shila Devi Temple,** which contains an image of the goddess Kali, the appropriate family deity for the warring Rajput Kachchwaha. Massive, three-story, intricately decorated **Ganesh Pol (Elephant Gate)** leads to the private apartments of the royal family, built around a Mughal-style garden courtyard. **Sheesh Mahal (Mirror Palace)**—covered in mirror mosaics and colored glass—would have been the private quarters of the maharaja and his maharani, literally transformed into a glittering jewel box in flickering candlelight; guides will point out the "magic flower" carved in marble at the base of one of the pillars around the mirror palace—recognizable by the two butterflies hovering around it, the flower can be seen to contain seven unique designs (a fish tail, a lotus, a hooded cobra, an elephant trunk, a lion's tail, a cob of corn, and a scorpion). Above is **Jas Mandir,** a hall of private audience, with floral glass inlays and alabaster relief work. Opposite, across the garden, is **Sukh Mahal (Pleasure Palace)**—note the perforations in the marble walls and channels where water was piped to cool the rooms. South lies the oldest part, the **Palace of Man Singh I.** If you want to explore the old town and its many temples, exit through Chand Pol, opposite Suraj Pol. *Note:* As is the case elsewhere, the press of bodies and noise levels can seriously detract from the experience—try to get here as soon as it opens to avoid the heat and crowds, and, if possible, avoid visiting on weekends. Also detracting from the historic splendor is the major renovation being carried out (finally) to bring the fort up to a more magnificent standard.

Amber, 11km (7 miles) north of Jaipur. ℂ 0141/253-0293. Rs 50 ($1.25/65p), Rs 75 ($1.85/95p) with camera, Rs 150 ($3.65/£1.85) video. Free lockers to store cameras. Daily 8am–5:30pm.

Anokhi Museum of Hand Printing 𝒢𝒢

While you are in the Amber Fort area, take time to stop at this little gem, a largely undiscovered (and undermarketed) venture by the highly successful boutique chain of the same name. You may be told the museum doesn't exist, but persist by asking for Biharji Temple and looking for a (fabulously restored) pink haveli nearby. Anokhi began as an arts-and-crafts movement 30 years ago, and in this beautifully designed museum you can admire the textile traditions the movement has helped preserve. Each room is dedicated to a different style of fabric printing, displayed in glass cases along with artisans' implements. Curator Emma Ronald is very hands-on (an approach that is drastically lacking throughout much of India) and goes to great lengths to bring innovative and interesting exhibitions to the museum; in winter, the top-floor gallery usually hosts loan exhibitions from around the world. Best of all, for those interested in a more hands-on understanding of block-printing, there's a full-time artisan who demonstrates the craft, as well as a woodcarver who makes printing blocks (Thurs–Sat only). End your visit at the pleasant cafe (great for organic coffee and biscuits), and then arm yourself with a credit card at the exquisite museum shop, which has a great range of goods, from books to homewares (see "Shopping" section, later in this chapter).

Anokhi Haveli, Kheri Gate, Amber. ℂ 0141/253-0226 or 0141/253-1267. www.anokhimuseum.com. Rs 30 (75¢/ 40p) adults, Rs 20 (50¢/25p) students, Rs 15 (40¢/20p) children, Rs 50 ($1.25/65p) still camera, R 150 ($3.65/£1.85) video camera. Tues–Sat 10:30am–5pm; Sun 11am–4:30pm. Closed May 1–July 15.

City Palace 🏵🏵 Although the former ruling family still lives in the seven-story Chandra Mahal (Moon Palace) built by Sawai Jai Singh II, most of what you'll experience here is the poorly managed **Maharaja Sawai Man Singh II Museum** and an overwhelming number of overpriced shops (even here you won't be free of India's omnipresent hustling; most guides are keen observers of the commission system—you have been warned!). Depending on which entrance you use, the first courtyard is where you'll find **Mubarak Mahal (Welcome Palace),** a "reception center" constructed by Maharaja Sawai Madho Singh II, grandfather of the present maharaja. Mubarak houses the textiles and costume section, where regal costumes provide insight into the tremendous wealth and status that the family enjoyed, as well as the extraordinarily high level of craftsmanship available to them over the centuries. These include embroidery so fine it looks like printwork, some of the best *bandhani odhnis* (tie-dye scarves/veils) to come out of Sanganer, Kashmiri shawls, gossamer muslin from Bangladesh, and silk saris from Varanasi. There's also insight into the lifestyles of Jaipur's royals in the form of a specialized billiards outfit worn by the king. The **Armoury,** with a selection of exquisitely crafted yet truly vicious-looking daggers and swords, is housed in the adjacent palace—if Mughal history, with all its valor and intrigue, has caught your imagination, ask one of the red turbaned attendants to point out the items belonging to the emperors Akbar, Jahangir, and Shah Jahan. The next courtyard reveals the raised **Diwan-i-Khas (Hall of Private Audience),** built in sandstone and marble. Look for the sun emblems decorating the walls—like most Rajput princes, the Kachchwaha clan belonged to the warrior caste, who traced their origins back to the sun (see "Once Were Warriors: The History of the Rajput," earlier in this chapter). To the west is **Pritam Niwas Chowk (Peacock Courtyard),** with its four beautifully painted doorways—from here you can search for signs of life from the royal residence that towers above. Move on to **Diwan-i-Am (Hall of Public Audience),** which houses a simply fantastic collection of miniature paintings, carpets, manuscripts, and photographs. Unfortunately, the entire exhibition is poorly lit, and display cases make browsing very awkward, but do try to look for the self-portraits of eccentric Ram Singh II, who found expression for his vanity in a passion for photography. The **Friends of the Museum** section is a bazaar selling art and crafts by respected artisans; it's a good place to pick up a quality miniature painting or Kundan jewelry, although prices are blatantly inflated. During our last visit we were also horrified to notice that not a single woman artist was represented.

Chokri Shahad, Old City. Entrance through Atish Gate or Nakkar Gate. ℂ 0141/260-8055. www.royalfamilyjaipur. com. Admission Rs 180 ($4.40/£2.25) includes still camera; Rs 75 ($1.85/95p) children aged 5–12; Rs 200 ($4.90/ £2.50) video. Daily 9am–5pm. Get here as soon as it opens.

Jantar Mantar 🏵🏵 Living proof of the genius of Sawai Jai Singh, this medieval observatory is the largest of its kind in the world, and the best preserved of Jai Singh's five observatories. There are 18 instruments in all, erected between 1728 and 1734— many of Jai Singh's own invention. The observatory looks more like a modern art exhibition or sci-fi set—hard to believe these instruments were constructed in the 18th century and remain functional. Some are still used to forecast how hot the summer will be, when the monsoon will arrive, and how long it will last. Whether or not you understand how the instruments are read (and for this, you should try to avoid

---

Tips Elephant Etiquette

A word to the wise about taking elephants seriously: It wasn't too long ago that a tourist was killed by an Amber Fort elephant after her belligerent tour leader ignored the elephant's *mahout* (handler), who insisted that the pachyderm was in a bad mood and that a ride was a bad idea. When it comes to elephants—even ones that *seem* completely tame—always take the word of the *mahout* above all else; if they tell you there's a problem, you probably don't want to be anywhere near the animal.

---

coming on an overcast day—almost all the instruments require sunlight to function), the sheer sculptural shapes of the stone and marble objects and the monumental sizes of many (like the 23m-high/75-ft. Samrat Yantra, which forecasts crop prospects based on "the declination and hour of the heavenly bodies") are worth the trip and make for great photographs (evidenced by the Indian visitors who like to pose atop many of them as if they were starring in some Bollywood blockbuster). In 2007, a major upgrade of the observatory was under way; hopefully improvements will include more visitor-friendly explanations of how everything works. Failing this wishful thinking, you can hire a guide at the gate for Rs 100 ($2.45/£1.25), but you'll do far better booking **Jaimini Shastri** (see "Guided Tours," earlier in this chapter); be sure to book him well in advance. *Tip:* If you'd prefer a forecast of future events that are more focused on yourself, you could always call upon the renowned (and very important) **Dr. Vinod Shastri,** who practices palmistry, predictive dice-throwing *(ramal),* and computer-aided astrological predictions in an office just around the corner (Chandni Chowk, behind Tripolia Gate; © **0141/261-3338**). A professor of astrology and palmistry at Rajasthan University, Dr. Shastri is available between noon and 7pm, but you should know that his asking fee ranges from Rs 600 to Rs 3,000 ($15–$73/£8–£37) for a session lasting just 10 minutes.

Follow signs from city palace. © **0141/261-0494.** Rs 10 (25¢/15p), Rs 50 ($1.25/65p) still camera, Rs 100 ($2.45/£1.25) video. Daily 9:30am–5pm.

WHERE TO STAY

Jaipur has a plethora of places to stay, from standard Holiday Inns to the usual backpacker hostels. But no one in their right mind comes to Rajasthan to overnight in a bland room in some nondescript hotel chain when you could be sleeping in the very room where a maharaja seduced his maharani, or in the royal apartments of the family guests—hence our focus on heritage hotels. The following reviews represent the best heritage accommodations in the city, in a variety of price categories. The exceptions to this are the good-value Shahpura House, K Country Villa—where you get to mingle with aristocratically connected locals—and the decadent Rajvilās, which not only imitates the heritage property concept, but in many ways improves upon it. *Note:* The prices below are sometimes given in rupees, with U.S. dollar and pound sterling conversions; others are in U.S. dollars with sterling conversions only (or in euros with both), which is how hotels targeting foreign markets quote their rates.

VERY EXPENSIVE

Rajvilās 🏨🏨🏨   Rajvilās is one of those luxury hotels that is a destination in its own right, albeit along a rather industrial-looking road some distance from Jaipur's center.

Nevertheless, it has won numerous awards since it opened a decade ago and is certainly a trendsetter in terms of Indian hospitality. With a budget of $20 million, no expense was spared in showcasing the fine craftsmanship typical of the region to create and decorate what is ostensibly a traditional fortified Rajasthani palace. Although it may not have the history of an original heritage hotel, it more than makes up for this with a level of comfort and luxury that is only matched by the better-located Rambagh Palace. Set amid 13 hectares (32 acres) of orchards, formal gardens, and decorative pools, accommodations are separate from the main fort (which houses the public spaces) in clusters of rooms—between four and six around each central courtyard—and a few luxury tents. Given the enormity of the property, you might expect the rooms to be larger—they're dominated by massive four-poster canopied beds, and the armchairs, writing desk, and tables do seem a little cluttered—but they're luxuriously decorated in a colonial style offset by Rajasthani elements (fabrics, textiles, and miniatures). Tents have a more opulent atmosphere, and are more spacious. There are rough areas (like long, dimly lit pathways between the rooms and restaurants), and service is not quite in the same magnificent league it was just a few years back. In fact, pool service is downright patchy, and you aren't even brought complimentary mineral water to slake your thirst while sunbathing (as you are at Rambagh, for example). **Surya Mahal,** the long-standing international restaurant, has a well-deserved reputation, and by late 2007, a dedicated Indian eatery should be up and running. Don't pass up on at least one session at the award-winning Banyan Tree spa, offering every conceivable treatment and featuring a beautiful Ayurvedic therapy room; insist on a bath of milk and rose petals when you're done. Come here to relax and get away from it all; for these top-scale prices, you'll totally disconnected from Jaipur and often quite happy to simply stay within the blissful confines of the resort.

Goner Rd., Jaipur 303 012. ✆ 0141/268-0101. Fax 0141/268-0202. www.oberoihotels.com. ✆ 800/5-OBEROI toll-free in the U.S. and Canada. 71 units. $665–$765 (£333–£383) premiere double; $775–$875 (£388–£438) luxury tent; $1,600–$1,800 (£800–£900) royal tent; $2,200–$2,400 (£1,100–£1,200) luxury villa; $3,600–$3,800 (£1,800–£1,900) Kohinoor villa. Taxes extra. AE, DC, MC, V. **Amenities:** 2 restaurants; library/bar; pool; 5-hole putting green; 2 tennis courts; health club; spa; concierge; travel and sightseeing arrangements; airport transfers; gift boutique; 24-hr. room service; babysitting; laundry; doctor-on-call; yoga; croquet; elephant safari; horse riding; helipad; horse and cart rides. *In room:* A/C, TV, minibar, tea- and coffee-making facility, hair dryer, electronic safe, scale, DVD player (complimentary access to CD and DVD library); villas have private pools, butler, sound system.

Taj Rambagh Palace ★★★ If you're hell-bent on experiencing the blue blood of heritage properties, Rambagh Palace is both the largest (19 hectares/47 acres) and most elegant option in Jaipur. Its origins date back to 1835. What started as a garden developed by the maharani's handmaid, Rambagh has been a hunting lodge and a private boarding school (for a prince, of course). Converted into a hotel in 1957, it was the first heritage hotel in India, and remains a favorite of Bollywood stars and socialites: It's where Jaipur royalty celebrate birthdays, and where the elite gather to strike deals and friendships. It's worth visiting for a drink or dinner even if you're not staying here. Guests are treated to an early evening tour culminating with a glass of bubbly in the **Polo Bar** (one of Rajasthan's classiest watering holes). In recent years, a fortune has been spent upgrading all the guest rooms, so that a sense of grandeur accompanies every stay (even in the simpler, more affordable "luxury" rooms, which were enlarged and emptied of clutter in 2006—ask for one with a private terrace). If you want to feel as if you're actually living in a royal apartment, however, opt for a "palace" room (no. 317 is just fabulous)—old-fashioned in a colonial rather than Rajasthani sense, with electric fireplaces and canopied beds, and most with comfortable, cushioned window seats. Bathrooms are relatively small, but feature delightfully concealed walk-in cupboards. Historic suites, while expensive, are disarmingly luxurious, with thoughtful in-room luxuries that make a big difference: a bedtime drinks menu, a selection of pillows and quilts, honey for your tea, and real filtered coffee. Then again, you probably won't spend a great deal of time in your room; you'll be too busy luxuriating in the beautiful palace buildings or lolling around the fabulous new outdoor swimming pool, tucked away some distance from the main palace buildings, alongside the spa and indoor pool. Dining at the swish **Suvarna Mahal** is a grand affair (see review below). The more recently opened drinking and dining venue, **Steam,** which inhabits an old train carriage, has quickly become popular on the local social scene. Certainly the hotel has every amenity you could wish for, and modern conveniences are wonderfully supported by the authentic atmosphere and welcoming staff.

Sawani Sing Rd., Jaipur 302 005. ⓒ **0141/221-1919.** Fax 0141/238-5098. www.tajhotels.com. rambagh.jaipur@taj hotels.com. 85 units. $650 (£325) luxury double; $750 (£375) palace double; $1,600 (£800) historical suite; $2,600 (£1,300) royal suite; $4,000 (£2,000) grand royal suite. Taxes extra. AE, DC, MC, V. **Amenities:** 3 restaurants; bar; indoor and outdoor pools; golf on request; tennis; health club; outdoor Jacuzzi; spa; concierge; travel desk; car hire; business center; gift shops, boutiques, jewelry store; 24-hr. room service; laundry; doctor-on-call; camel rides; astrologer; buggy rides; polo viewing in season; cultural performances; butler service; badminton; squash court; croquet; table tennis. *In room:* A/C, TV, minibar, tea- and coffee-making facility, hair dryer, safe, Internet; some suites have Jacuzzi, electric fireplace.

EXPENSIVE

A couple of heritage properties deserve a mention, such as the **Jai Mahal Palace** *ℛℛ* (Jacob Rd., Civil Lines; ⓒ **0141/222-3636;** www.tajhotels.com; $330/£165 double). The hotel is architecturally splendid, with buildings dating back to 1745, and it's recently undergone a life-altering renovation that has made it quite the talk of the town. Guest rooms are bright, and dining venues funky (particularly **Cinnamon,** known as much for its cocktails as it is for its Indian cuisine), but it's neither as grand as Taj Rambagh nor as romantic or authentic as Samode or Alsisar havelis (both of which offer better value for money). Also vying to compete with the Rambagh is **Raj Palace** *ℛ* (ⓒ **0141/263-4077;** fax 0141/263-0489; www.rajpalace.com; from $350–$450/£175–£225 double), which has very posh rooms (each of which has its own display cabinet of museum-worthy artifacts) in elegant buildings that look as though they were converted from palace to hotel by an Indian Gianni Versace. Think Swarovski crystal chandeliers, real gold decorative effects on the pillars, an in-house cinema, and a full-on shopping arcade. Yet, while there's gold, glitz, and glamour aplenty, we can't understand where the plastic sun loungers and piped trite classical music fit in with a look that's trying so hard to be bling.

Samode Haveli *ℛℛ*   Ever since Samode Haveli made it into that glossy tome to style, *Hip Hotels: Budget,* and was selected by the author, Herbert Ypma, as one of his top 10 hotels in the world, it has enjoyed unprecedented popularity (and was one of *Tatler's* 101 Best Hotels in 2006). One of the few accommodations within the old walled city (and a better value than the nearby ritzy Raj Palace), this 200-year-old city mansion enjoys an unbeatable location and oozes authenticity, with higgledy-piggledy rooms of various sizes furnished in typical Rajasthani antiques and featuring pillars and cusped arches painted with traditional motifs, tiny colored-glass windows, marble floors, and deep alcoves for lounging. Accommodations are generally beautiful, bright and spacious; some face the pool, some look on to the garden, while others are off courtyards or passageways that help enhance privacy. The best rooms are those housed in the *zenana* (traditionally the part of the house where women were secluded), particularly the Sheesh Mahal Suite, in which every inch of wall and ceiling is covered in tiny glass mirrors or delicately executed miniature paintings—the effect in candlelight is not dissimilar to the celebrated Sheesh Mahal at Amber Fort (though it's worth mentioning that some find the extra-low ceilings and numerous pillars claustrophobic). The main drawbacks here are the dining hall that, despite being beautifully decorated, feels gloomy and oppressive (particularly during the day), serves mediocre food, and has friendly, but unpredictable service. That said, there's nothing to stop you from insisting that you take breakfast on the cozy terrace right outside the dining hall. Finally, Samode scores with Jaipur's most handsome pool, a great place to unwind with a drink or snack after a day of hectic shopping. *Note:* At press time, there were plans to introduce 10 more guest rooms, which may impact somewhat on the degree of exclusivity experienced by guests who prefer to avoid the crowds.

Samode Haveli, Ganga Pol, Jaipur 302 992. (℃ **0141/263-2407,** -2370, or -1942. Fax 0141/263-1397. www.samode. com. reservations@samode.com. 40 units. Low season (May 1–Sept 30) to high season (Oct 1–Apr 31): 90€–170€ ($121–$228/£61–£116) deluxe double; 110€–198€ ($147–$265/£75–£135) deluxe suite; 170€–248€ ($228–$332/£116–£169) Sheesh Mahal or haveli suite; 40€–60€ ($54–$80/£27–£54) extra bed. Rates include breakfast; taxes extra. AE, MC, V. **Amenities:** Dining hall; bar; pool; fitness center; steam room; airport transfers; massage; laundry; Internet facility; children's playground; doctor-on-call. *In room:* A/C, TV, minibar, hair dryer, safe.

MODERATE

Travelers looking for a comfortable stay at modest rates should check out **Jas Vilas** (C-9 Sawai Jai Singh Hwy.; (℃ **0141/220-4638** or -4902; www.jasvilas.com), the large 1950s family home of the gracious Singh family (proud members of a Shekhawat clan) that has been converted into a 11-room hotel staffed by affable hosts Mahendra and Rajyashree. It's an excellent option if you're looking for warmth, quiet, and a homey feel (and tub baths) but still want to be close to the heart of Jaipur; the Singhs have gone to great trouble to add personal touches, like embroidered patterned quilts featuring elephants or camels. The hotel has verandas on every floor, and here you can lounge on cozy cane chairs watching the action around the pool (definitely ask for a poolside room; units at the front of the hotel get noise off the busy street). Standard doubles cost Rs 2,800 ($69/£35), while the newly added "heritage room" goes for Rs 4,000 ($98/£50); breakfast and taxes are extra.

The shabby-chic **Rajmahal Palace Hotel** (℃ **0141/510-5665** through -5667; www.royalfamilyjaipur.com) is a 14-room mansion with an additional 16, very boxy, standard rooms (from Rs 3,500/$86/£44 double) in the newer "Neem Tree Wing." In its heyday (when Man Singh II and his beautiful wife, Gayatri Devi, moved here from Rambagh), it hosted the likes of Jackie Kennedy and Princess Diana. It still has a gracious feel (not to mention the biggest hotel rooms in India), but is badly in need of refurbishment. If you're into nostalgia, consider booking room no. 107, where the maharaja hosted Mrs. Kennedy. This is also the best place to bring kids, with its huge royal suites (you could host a tennis match in the maharaja suite, although it's looking terribly run-down; Rs 10,000/$244/£124), large grounds, and a pool. Service, starting with lazy guards who stagger to their feet at the front entrance, is complacent—to the extent that no one has bothered identifying the source of the various moldy smells in the heritage guest rooms.

A similar air of decay has long hung over **Bissau Palace** (℃ **0141/230-4371** or -4391; www.bissaupalace.com; from Rs 2,400/$59/£30 A/C double), at press time undergoing much-needed renovations, unfortunately with the insensitive addition of potentially inappropriate modern facilities (like a coffee shop serving "authentic" European food prepared by a chef brought in from New York); we only hope that the frightening electrical system will be fixed and bathrooms substantially upgraded. Built by the Rawal (Duke) of Bissau, with original buildings dating back to 1787, it offers much the same facilities as the cheaper Diggi Palace, with the advantage of a recently refurbished pool, now enlarged to look like a large footprint. Oddly, the hotel received a President's Award for heritage restoration before the job had even been carried out, but management insists that accommodations will be further enhanced by the importation of artifacts from the family castle.

Alsisar Haveli 🞵🞵 (𝘝alue)   This is the most elegant heritage property in its price category in Jaipur, offering excellent value for money, and in slightly better condition than Narain Niwas. Built in 1892 and still owned by the Kachchwaha clan of Rajputs, it has all the traditional elements of Rajput architecture—scalloped arches and pretty cupolas, painted ceilings and colored glass windows, and a maze of corridors and stairs around and through inner courtyards. Rooms vary in size, but all are furnished with antiques and the block-printed fabrics typical of the region, and most have a padded alcove area for lounging. The only drawback is that some of the mattresses are a tad soft. You can take tea around the pool, or retreat to the tables on the lawn for total peace. The lounge is beautifully furnished, but it is the dining hall that sets the place apart: Unlike the oppressive rooms so typical of heritage properties (like the much-vaunted Samode Haveli), Alsisar's is filled with light, thanks to the floor-to-ceiling glass walls and spotless white tablecloths. The food is quite satisfactory, albeit not particularly memorable; breakfast will run you Rs 275 ($6.70/£3.40), while lunch and dinner (both buffets) costs Rs 400 ($9.75/£4.95) plus taxes.

Sansar Chandra Rd., Jaipur 302 001. ☏ **0141/236-8290** or -4685. Fax 0141/236-4652. www.alsisar.com. 37 units. Rs 3,500 ($85/£43) double; Rs 4,100 ($100/£51) suite; Rs 750 ($18/£9) extra bed. Rates exclude taxes. AE, MC, V. **Amenities:** Restaurant; bar; pool; travel desk; limited room service; Ayurvedic massage; laundry; doctor-on-call. *In room:* A/C, TV, hair dryer.

Narain Niwas Palace 🞵   Like Alsisar, Narain Niwas provides you with an opportunity to live in a heritage property for relatively little money (though Alsisar currently has the edge in terms of atmosphere and service). Built in 1928 by Gen. Amar Singh, Thakur of Kanota and then commander of the Jaipur State forces, this was originally a country residence to which the *Thakur* would retreat from the walled city. The 3-hectare (7-acre) property remains an oasis, but the city now surrounds it. Since opening as a heritage hotel in 1978, it has been featured in glossy design publications like Taschen's *Indian Interiors*. Not surprisingly, staying in a room like the much-photographed suite no. 36, with its high ceilings, four-poster antique bed, fresco-painted walls and ceilings, and Raj-era chandelier, is like overnighting in a museum, albeit one with serious drawbacks, including ugly and dangerous-looking electrical fittings, a very disappointing bathroom (with no tub and in serious need of a face-lift), and a constant din emanating from the adjacent dining hall and kitchen. Standard room nos. 51 to 57 are worth booking; individually furnished with antique beds and chairs, these feature pretty frescoes and block-print fabrics (on rather thin mattresses) and are close to the pool, opening onto a particularly lush part of the garden—an essential balm after tackling Jaipur's streets. Avoid the monstrously overpriced new "garden suites," which have been tackily renovated and packed with such silly luxuries as oversize wall-mounted TVs and massage shower fittings, but have gloomy bed chambers and no sofa. Buffet-style meals are taken on the lawns or in the dining hall, which, like the antiques-filled lounge, features scalloped arches decorated with frescoes, and colored-glass windows and baubles.

Kanota Bagh, Narain Sing Rd., Jaipur 302 004. © **0141/256-1291** or -3448. Fax 0141/256-1045. www.hotelnarain niwas.com. 31 units. Rs 3,800 ($93/£47) double; Rs 4,600–Rs 5,500 ($112–$134/£57–£68) suite; Rs 8,000 ($195/£99) garden suite; Rs 1,400 ($34/£17) extra bed. Breakfast included; taxes extra. AE, MC, V. **Amenities:** Dining hall; bar; pool; travel desk; car hires; limited room service; Ayurvedic massage; laundry; doctor-on-call; Internet; yoga and meditation facility; table tennis; crafts shop. *In room:* A/C, TV in some, minibar, hair dryer.

Shahpura House ⭐ *Value*   Located in the heart of a relaxed residential neighborhood, one of Jaipur's best-value hotels was built just half a century ago by a noble member of the Shekhawat's Shahpura clan (Shahpura is 65km/40 miles from Jaipur). It's still a family-run affair, managed with a great deal more flair and charm than many of its more historically positioned competitors. The aristocratic owner has dressed the place in what might be termed "haveli style," with decor that runs from framed black-and-white family photographs to elaborate chandeliers to detailed frescoes. To emphasize the family's military heritage, there are antique shields, spears, arrowheads, and daggers throughout. Accommodations are very comfortable, with marble floors, antique furniture, block-print curtains, and beds covered with smart white linen. The cheaper deluxe rooms are more boxy, but if you can book no. 206, you'll have a spacious bathroom, large bed, and a window overlooking the pool. Of the decently priced suites, no. 306 has a balcony overlooking the pool. Rooms are tastefully, colorfully decorated and, remarkably, are spruced up (with new throws and fabrics) every 3 months or so. Soak up the sun on one of the loungers around the pool, or find comfort (and order drinks) in pretty lounges around the hotel; besides choices from the well-stocked bar, there's excellent fresh watermelon juice.

Devi Marg, Bani Park, Jaipur 302 016. © **0141/220-2292** or -2293. Fax 0141/220-1494. shahpurahous@usa.net. www.shahpurahouse.com. 35 units. Rs 3,000 ($73/£37) deluxe double; Rs 4,000 ($98/£49) suite; Rs 4,500 ($110/£56) Royal suite; Rs 600 ($15/£7.40) extra bed. Taxes extra. AE, DC, MC, V. **Amenities:** Restaurant; bar; limited room service; laundry; transport assistance; airport transfers; complimentary station and bus stand pickup; Internet; currency exchange; doctor-on-call. *In room:* A/C, TV, minibar, hair dryer.

INEXPENSIVE

Diggi Palace ⭐ *Value*   This to our mind is the best budget option in Jaipur, where you get the opportunity to overnight in a 200-year-old haveli for a fraction of the rate charged by Alsisar Haveli and Narain Niwas (though service and facilities are correspondingly not in the same class). Architecturally, the pale, cool blue buildings reflect traditional Rajput style. The "palace"—which it is not—lies at the edge of a big open lawn and is within walking distance of Ram Niwas Gardens and the Central Museum. The drawbacks of this backpacker haven are that it's invariably full, it's a long walk from the Old City, and it has no pool, but the leafy, well-established gardens are a wonderful respite, filled with bird song. Rooms vary in size, but all feature cool, clean white tiles and whitewashed walls; some have antique furniture offset with bright block-printed fabrics. The cheapest accommodations are basic rooms without A/C, TV, or minibar. Book an air-conditioned room to beat the heat—they're substantially larger and still great value; unit 108 is a gorgeous first-floor room with a large four-poster metal frame bed and big bathroom; framed Hindu paintings and an antique wall clock suggest attention to detail (the drawback may be the noise of chatting staff coming off the inner courtyard just below). We suggest one of the newly added cottage rooms (Rs 1,850/$44/£23), which have marble floors and bright block-print fabrics—these all have tubs *and* showers, and some have antique furniture; most significantly, they're away from the potentially noisy main building and overlook the garden. If you want access to a semi-private veranda, ask for no. 209, a spacious "suite" with a large bathroom and shared balcony overlooking the courtyard. Meals are served on the open-air, first-floor veranda; dinner costs about Rs 150 ($3.70/£1.85). Call ahead for a complimentary pick-up from the train station.

Shivaji Marg, C-scheme, Sawai Ram Singh Hwy., Jaipur 302 004. ✆ **0141/237-3091**, 0141/236-6120, or 0141/236-6196. Fax 0141/230-359. www.hoteldiggipalace.com. 48 units. Rs 700 ($17/£9) air-cooled double; Rs 1,800–Rs 2,300 ($44–$56/£22–£29) A/C double. Taxes extra. AE, V. **Amenities:** Dining hall; bar; station and airport transfers; shop selling basic items; limited room service; laundry; Internet facilities; phone booth; doctor-on-call. *In room:* A/C in most, TV in most, minibar in most.

AROUND JAIPUR

K Country Villa 🐫🐫   Here's an opportunity to be swathed in luxury and mingle with your impeccably debonair hosts, Ridhiraj ("Tony") Singh and his wife, Rithu, both of whom love to pamper and indulge their guests. A top choice for anyone grown weary of hotel anonymity, this dressed-to-kill luxury home just outside Jaipur provides a fine introduction to aspirational Indian life. The plush accommodations, beautifully decorated by Rithu personally with a gracious attention to detail and considerable concern for personal comfort, are outfitted with top-quality fabrics, furnishings, and fittings (with some borderline kitsch thrown in for good measure) and artworks collected from across the country. You can stay in one of the large guest rooms in the main house or in one of the huge cottages a short distance away. The cottages each have a private outdoor area (with a Jacuzzi) designed for romance, separate dressing rooms, and gleaming bathrooms. Meals are taken in the company of your hosts, with pre-dinner drinks in any of the different lounge spaces (the best being the sunken lounge, where you can listen to music while browsing coffee-table tomes); conversations can be a real eye-opener (ask about astrology and you'll eventually get to politics and the joys of Jaipur). Various sightseeing trips can be arranged (Rithu is the ideal source of lowdown shopping information), and you can go horseback riding or fishing if you'd like to take a break from polluted city life. K Country Villa is just 9km (5½ miles) from central Jaipur and 7km (4⅓ miles) from Sisodia Rani ka Bagh, but you really do get a sense of being in the country. Plus, there's great bird-watching down by the nearby lake (it's been favorably compared with that at Bharatpur).

Near Malpura Hill, Kanota Irrigation Dam, Vill. Post—Sumel, Jaipur 303 012. ✆ **98-2906-3897** or 98-2921-3897. Fax 0141/237-7531. www.kcountryvilla.com. kcountryvilla@mail.com. 7 units. Rs 9,500 ($232/£117) luxury double; Rs 12,000 ($293/£148) luxury deluxe double; Rs 17,000 ($415/£210) premium cottage; Rs 1,200 ($29/£15) extra bed. Rates include breakfast, dinner, and soft minibar; taxes extra. MC, V. **Amenities:** Dining room; bar; lounge with hi-fi; pool; travel assistance; transfers; room service; Ayurvedic massage and yoga on request; laundry; doctor-on-call; currency exchange; cultural performances; library; horse riding; jeep safari; camel safari; bird-watching; billiards table. *In room:* A/C, TV, minibar, tea- and coffee-making facility, hair dryer, DVD; luxury deluxe room and cottages have Jacuzzi; cottages have massage chairs.

Samode Palace 🐫🐫   An hour's drive (45km/28 miles) from Jaipur, 400-year-old Samode Palace is popular, pretty, and very commercialized. Once an exclusive retreat for those in the know, it was put on the map by its starring role in the 1984 miniseries *The Far Pavilions*, resulting in some touristy additions like the new wing with its charmless low-ceilinged rooms; simply avoid these. The original palace suites are beautiful, however: huge, with loads of natural light and furnished with a mix of antiques and contemporary pieces. Best value-for-money option is one of the rooms overlooking the lovely pool area (nos. 207, 216, 308, and 405 are a few)—ask for one with a balcony and a renovated bathroom (206, 207, 208, or 216). Many visitors use this as a relaxing retreat from Jaipur, whose major attractions can be covered in a day trip, and it's also a good stepping-stone into the Shekhawati. However, the palace is far more commercial than, say, Deogarh Mahal (a 280km/174-mile drive from Jaipur), and there's not much to see or do here besides wander around the cobblestone streets of town to meet the tourist-savvy locals or shop for block-print fabrics and bangles (though Dukaan, the crafts shop located inside the palace, stocks a pretty good selection of jewelry and trinkets). It must be said, however, that the palace itself is worth exploring (especially for the gorgeous 250-year-old frescoes in Durbar Hall, or the even lovelier Sultan Mahal, with its blue and silver terrace). At press time, a heated rooftop pool was planned for the palace. An interesting and good-value alternative to the palace lies 10 minutes away, at **Samode Bagh,** a large garden established by the royal family, where the current owners have pitched 44 delightful air-conditioned tents with stone floors and permanent attached bathrooms (showers only). The tent walls feature beautiful Mughal-inspired patterns and are attractively furnished with carpets, standing lamps, and pretty wooden beds and chairs. The Bagh has its own pool and tennis courts, and all in all is an extremely peaceful getaway. Though the tents are situated a little too close to each other, the tent area is seldom full; the real problem is the claustrophobic dining tent—definitely ask about meals served on the spacious lawns. You will, of course, need your own car and driver, and be warned (as at all Samode properties) that service is at best unpredictable.

Samode, Jaipur 303 806. © **01423/24-0023.** Reservations through Samode Haveli, Ganga Pol, Jaipur 302 992. © 0141/263-2407, -2370, or -1068. Fax 0141/263-1397. www.samode.com. 35 units (Palace); 44 units (Bagh). Low season (May 1–Sept 30)–high season (Oct 1–Apr 30): **Samode Palace** 125€–215€ ($168–$288/£85–£146) deluxe double; 165€–253€ ($221–$339/£112–£172) deluxe suite; 355€–420€ ($476–$563/£241–£286) Royal Suite (includes dinner); 55€–65€ ($74–$87/£37–£44) extra bed. **Samode Bagh** 88€–110€ ($118–$147/£60–£75) double; 40€–50€ ($54–$67/£27–£34) extra bed. Rates include breakfast; taxes extra during high season. AE, MC, V. **Amenities:** Restaurant; bar; pool; gym; travel desk; business center; 24-hr. room service; massage; laundry; doctor-on-call; Internet; camel safari; jeep safari; Bagh includes tennis, badminton, volleyball, table tennis, and bicycles. *In room:* A/C, TV, minibar, tea- and coffee-making facility, hair dryer, safe.

TRAVELING BETWEEN JAIPUR & UDAIPUR

Shahpura Bagh ☆☆ *Value*   Located precisely midway between Jaipur and Udaipur, this peaceful 40-hectare (100-acre) wooded estate is on land that was gifted to the present owners' forebears by Shah Jehan himself for success in battle against the Afghans; ask to see the title deed bearing the emperor's handprint. Against a backdrop of mango and guava orchards, the buildings now used to lodge guests are colonial-era, a sense of which you'll get, thanks to the sense of spaciousness. In a building that's part bungalow and part flat-roofed cathedral, with a veranda lined by fat, squat pillars, most guest rooms are vast, double-volume affairs with tall, arched windows that make for plenty of light. The effect is heightened by the bright double-volume interiors, where splendid pure white lime floors are offset by block-printed curtains, rugs, paisley sofas, and cushions in soothing, natural tones. This is a place for calm contemplation and serious relaxation, coupled with two primary distractions: boating (and canoeing) and bird-watching. The large manmade dam at one end of the property is particularly lovely, and the lush surrounds attract jungle cats, jackals, and peacocks. Outside the immaculate accommodations, Shahpura Bagh has an incredibly homey atmosphere. It's run with hands-on enthusiasm and genuine concern for guest comfort and personal needs; even the Dalmatian, sausage dog, and collection of cats make you feel welcome. Meals are of the home-cooked variety (ask about authentic Rajasthani cooking lessons), and arrangements can be made to decamp to various romantic spots around the property if you tire of meals around the family table (just ask). Packed lunches for picnic walks and cycle tours make it easy to spend the day exploring the lush surrounds (or the off-the-beaten-track village, where you should investigate *phad* painting, which originated here and is still practiced by the renowned Vijay Joshi). Planning for a pool is under way, and there is also talk of getting some horses. It won't be too long, either, before the family's 480-year-old Dhikola Fort (12km/7½ miles away) is restored and open to guests; until then, you can visit on a day trip.

Shahpura, District Bhilwara 311 404. (C) **98-2812-2012** or -2013. Fax 01484/22-2077. www.shahpurabagh.com. res@shahpurabagh.com. 9 units. $144 (£72) double; $187 (£94) royal suite; $40 (£20) extra bed. Rates include breakfast; taxes extra. 20% discount May–Sept. AE, DC, MC, V. **Amenities:** Dining room; lounge; bar; bicycles; transfers; room service; laundry; doctor-on-call; library; TV lounge; boating and canoeing; yoga and meditation. *In room:* A/C, tea- and coffee-making facility, hair dryer, WorldSpace radio.

WHERE TO DINE

All the hotels reviewed above have dining halls or restaurants that usually serve buffets featuring mediocre to good North Indian food and mediocre to inedible international ("Continental") options. If you're spending more than 1 night or looking for somewhere local to lunch, check out the following. Note that you'll find the largest concentration of restaurants along M.I. Road, which is also the main shopping drag outside the Old City. Two popular choices here, both close to the very famous Niro's, are **Copper Chimney** and **Handi.** Also on M.I. Road is the famous **Dasaprakash** ((C) **0141/237-1313**), which serves fresh pomegranate juice with which to wash down excellent *dosas* (filled South Indian pancakes). When the heat gets to you, and you still have dozens more shops to visit, you may want to forgo a large lunch and opt for something healthy and light; for this, your prayers have been answered in the form of **Anokhi's organic deli** (see "Shopping," below). With daily specials and great, healthful salads, this is the eatery with far and away the freshest fare in town.

Widely considered one of Jaipur's best, **Indiana** ⭐ (J2-34, Mahaveer Marg, behind Jai Club; (C) **0141/236-2061** or -2062) is a bit of a tourist trap, owned by a local graduate of Purdue University who harbors considerable fondness for his alma mater and has a keen eye for kitsch (watch how a tacky fountain issues an upward spray from the head of a stone god). Although locals are hardly ever seen here, the Indian fare is reasonable, and prices are only marginally inflated to cover the nightly "complimentary" open-air folk dance show (which can be a lot of fun, although it's very inauthentic—more like a floor show—and tellingly pitched at a dumbed-down foreign audience). Although service is abysmal, you can watch some of the kitchen action and appreciate the spectacle of *naan* and *roti* being prepared before making its way to your table. Although there's not much serious focus on Rajasthani cuisine, you can feast on thali (multicourse platter), or ask for regional specialties like *ker sangri* (spicy capers and desert beans) and *laal maas* (spicy meat curry), which aren't on the menu; main courses start at Rs 130 ($3.20/£1.60), and a non-veg thali is Rs 400 ($9.75/£4.95). Another tourist-oriented place, with a firmer focus on food and a more stylish ambience, is **Spice Court** (Hari Bhawan, Achrol House, Jacob Rd., Civil Lines; (C) **0141/222-0202;** www.spicecourtindia.com), which has a pretty all-encompassing menu but also offers regional Rajasthani specialities, served at tables designed like large display cabinets for spices and other dry food ingredients. It's also well located for shoppers, being right near **Cottons,** a great little place to pick up cool, summery garments.

If it's atmosphere you're after, not to mention a highly memorable visual experience, reserve dinner at the Rambagh Palace's **Suvarna Mahal** ((C) **0141/221-1919**), a grand

(*Moments* Lassi Heaven

Across the road from Niros is **Lassiwalla,** favored by locals as *the* place to experience a *lassi* (cold yogurt drink). Not only is the lassi (salty or sweet; sadly, no banana) exquisitely creamy, but the price (just Rs 20/50¢/25p for a large) includes the handmade terra-cotta mug it's served in—to be kept as a memento or (as the locals do) thrown away after use. You need to buy a token at the front and then join a second thronging mass at the side to exchange it for your rewarding drink. Imitators have sprung up next door, so make sure you go to the right one; the original *lassi-walla* is *always* busy, and a sign above the stall reads "OLDEST SHOP IN JAIPUR" and features an image of baby Krishna. The current owner is Ashok Agarwal (© **0141/237-6892**), grandson of Govind Narain, who started the stall decades ago. He serves nothing but *lassis* and is usually sold out by 4pm.

double-volume colonial dining room behind enormous doors that signal a night of opulence. Start your evening with a drink at the elegant Polo Bar, or grab a seat on the deep veranda that overlooks the Rambagh's lawns (a puppet show or Rajasthani dancers may serve as predinner entertainment). While the menu changes regularly, you can ask your waiter for suggestions, taking time to enjoy the old-world ambience, proudly set off by the glow of four alabaster lamps and enhanced by huge gilded mirrors, walls covered in rich gold fabric, and an Italian Renaissance ceiling. Indulge in the magic and try to forget the cost of dining amid such extravagance (main courses range from Rs 500 to Rs 1,700 ($12–$42/£6.20–£21).

LMB (Laxmi Misthan Bhandar) ★★ INDIAN/VEGETARIAN/SWEET SHOP
If you're headed for Johari Bazaar to shop, make sure you stop at this renowned local hangout, first and foremost known for its selection of Indian sweets. Anyone with even half a sweet tooth shouldn't miss stepping out of the madness of the bazaar into this cool oasis—even if it's just to salivate over the huge selection of sweets beautifully (and hygienically) displayed behind glass counters in the sweet *(mithai)* shop section. Sample the *paneer ghewar* (honeycomb-like dessert soaked in sugary syrup)—supposedly the best in India. Beyond the takeout area lies the large air-conditioned restaurant. Perhaps renovated by a set designer with a love for the flamboyant 1980s, it remains strictly vegetarian, and no onion or garlic (believed to inflame the senses) is used in food preparation. No meat or alcohol is allowed on the premises, and only snacks are served between 4 and 7pm. Try the freshly prepared *samosas* or potato and cashew-nut *tikkis,* and wash them down with delicious *lassis* (yogurt drinks) or exotic pomegranate juice. For an authentic, filling meal, order the Rajasthani thali, which begins with tangy *papad mangori* soup and includes traditional *ker sangri,* Rajasthani *kadhi* (dumplings in a yogurt sauce), five different vegetables, and three kinds of bread.
Johari Bazaar. © **0141/256-5844**. Rs 50–Rs 225 ($1.25–$5.50/65p–£2.80). AE, MC, V. Daily 8am–11pm.

Niros ★★ NORTH INDIAN/CHINESE   Although the name sounds terribly inauthentic, and the appalling covers of '80s pop songs are almost unbearable, this remains the favored haunt of extended bourgeois Indian families, visiting Bollywood celebs, and foreign travelers, all drawn by its reputation for excellent food. Well-situated on the shopping route, Niros does good Chinese as well as typical Rajasthani meat and vegetarian dishes, and you can order ice cold beer, as well as wine from

India's very own Sula vineyards. Plus, if your stomach is starting to curdle from the traditional (and liberal) use of ghee as a cooking medium, you'll be happy to know that Niros's chefs use only refined soybean oil. House specialties include *laal maas* (mutton cooked in spicy red gravy) and *reshmi* kebab (mutton marinated in traditional spices and chargrilled). The *korma* dishes are all prepared in a deliciously creamy cashew-nut-based sauce, while the ever-popular chicken *tikka masala* is spicier than usual. You certainly won't want for choice: The numbered menu runs right up to 286! Forgo dessert and head across the street to Lassiwalla (see box below).

M.I. Rd. ✆ **0141/237-4493** or 0141/221-8520. www.nirosindia.com. Rs 65–Rs 380 ($1.60–$9.30/80p–£4. 70). AE, DC, MC, V. Daily 10am–11pm.

Surya Mahal ✸✸✸ INDIAN/INTERNATIONAL   Although only used for evening meals during the winter season, the courtyard adjoining this all-day fine dining restaurant at Rajvilās is arguably the most romantic place to have dinner in Jaipur. Lit by huge burning braziers, the courtyard features a raised platform where beautiful Rajasthani women give a short performance of their traditional dance (Sept 15–Mar only). Apart from the live entertainment—and there's always melodic musical accompaniment—Surya Mahal is all about rather formal dining, offset by a wonderful serving staff who do their best to bring zest to a menu that certainly doesn't take too many chances. Although the head chef, Marc Hegenberg, is Australian, his team is capable of dishing up some mean Indian dishes. You can sample the tastes of the region with a Rajasthani thali (multicourse platter), or, if you're up for something spicy, have the *laal maas* (lamb braised with Mathania chilies and yogurt, and smoked with cloves and garlic), which goes wonderfully with rice or *naan* bread. Specialty Indian dishes include the kebab platter (any of the tandoor dishes are highly recommended) and traditional thali. Tantalize your taste buds with the *shammi kebab,* minced lamb flavored with mace and cardamom and then filled with hung yogurt. If you fancy a simple, tasty chicken dish, try *rarha murgh,* tender morsels of meat cooked off the bone with tomato and roasted cumin. Or you can give the Indian dishes a break, and choose from roasted Chilean sea bass, Australian milk-fed pork loin in a sour cherry glaze, or perfectly roasted Australian rack of lamb.

Rajvilās, Goner Rd., Jaipur. ✆ **0141/268-0101.** Reservations essential. Rs 500–Rs 1,650 ($12–$40/£6.20–£20). AE, DC, MC, V. Daily noon–3pm and 7–10:30pm.

SHOPPING
Only Mumbai or Delhi comes close to offering the array of goods found here, and foreign buyers for wholesale and retail outlets descend in droves to stock up on textiles, rugs, pottery, jewelry, shoes, miniature paintings, and ready-made clothing and housewares. It's a cornucopia here, and the pressure to buy is immense—not least because everyone seems to be a tout for someone (see "Understanding the Commission System," below). Finding your way around the Old City is relatively easy—the divisions based on what is produced still hold true, though you'll find much more besides. Following are a few rough guidelines.

For jewelry and gems, head for **Johari Bazaar** in the Old City—the gem center of Jaipur (look for Bhuramal Rajmal Surana). While you're there, pick up a cool pair of *jootis* (traditional camel-hide sandals) at **Shivam Nagara Palace** (Shop 11, Johari Bazaar; ✆ **0141/257-1468**). Alternatively, wander through **Chameliwala Market,** beyond Zarawar Singh Gate, on Amber Road, particularly if you're in search of silver, tribal, or ornamental jewelry. **Silver Mountain** (✆ **0141/237-7399**) and **Maneeka** (✆ **0141/237-5913**), both located at Chameliwala Market, are recommended.

Tips **Understanding the Commission System**

Like everywhere in India, your rickshaw-*walla,* guide, or driver—even the well-spoken gentleman who strikes up a conversation, then offers to show you around (or wants "to practice his English")—is without fail out to earn commission from the shops they suggest you stop at, and this gets added to the price you're quoted. Even on foot you will be accosted by who appears to be the owner of the shop but is in fact one of a host of men paid by shop-keepers if they bring you inside—"to look, no buy, madam." It's an irritation you simply have to get used to, but establish upfront how much the commission is. Also, be aware of credit card fraud—unscrupulous traders will run off extra dockets, then forge your signature: Best not to let your credit card out of sight. And don't fall for anyone who tries to persuade you to purchase precious stones on the premise that you can sell them at a profit to a company they supposedly know of back home.

Numerous factories and showrooms run the length of Amber Road, including those specializing in hand-blocked prints and antiques. And if you're looking to take home some of Jaipur's famous blue pottery, Amber Road is also where you'll find the largest concentration of outlets: **Jaipur Blue Pottery Art Centre** (near Jain Mandir, Amber Rd.; ✆ **0141/263-5375**) is a reliable place to pick up items like blue pottery vases, trays, coasters, and wall plates. If you're considering redecorating your home with a classy, upscale Indian look, definitely venture into **AKFD** (B-6/A-1 Prithviraj Rd., C-Scheme; ✆ **0141/236-4863**), a fantastic one-stop interior design store with beautiful creations by the hard-working owners and covetable items from across the country.

The cutting, polishing, and selling of gems and the making of silver jewelry take place in the predominantly Muslim area of Pahar Ganj in the **Surajpol Bazaar.** Jewelry designers from all over the world continue to nurture the superlative gem-cutting and -setting skills of these craftspeople, but here, as in Johari Bazaar, be aware that bargains are hard to come by—more often than not, you really do get what you pay for. If you're knowledgeable enough, shop for gems and jewelry in the bazaars, but for most, a trip to the shops listed below is recommended.

Fabric is another must-buy, as the finest quality silk, chiffon, and cotton are transformed through traditional block printing and tie-and-dye techniques into intricately patterned fabrics with vibrant contrasts and colors. The finest tie-dye process is known as *bandhani* (literally "to tie"): Tiny circles are made by tying the cloth with thread in a detailed design; the cloth is often sold with the thread still tied on (to be removed before first use) and is traditionally worn unironed, showing off the crinkly circles. **Bapu Bazaar** (around the corner from Johari Bazaar; closed Sun) is where you can bargain for a wide range of textiles and ready-made garments, as well as traditional camel-leather shoes *(jootis)* and bangles of glass and lacquer; it's also by far the most pleasant shopping street because it's pedestrianized. If you're looking for great inexpensive gifts, take a look at the tiny workshops producing beautiful bangles in **Maniharon Ka Rasta,** an alley off Tripolia Bazaar (closed Sun).

For block-print fabrics, a trip to Sanganer, a village 16km (10 miles) south of Jaipur, is a must—here printing takes place in the courtyard of almost every house. Famous as the birthplace of block-work (and home to the largest handmade-paper industry in India), this is where you'll find the most refined block-print work in the world. Visit **Shilpi Handicrafts** (© 0141/273-1106) or **Sakshi** (© 0141/273-1862) for fabrics, and **Salim Paper** (© 0141/273-0222) for a range of handmade paper you'll be loathe to write on! If you are really serious about picking up block-printed fabrics, make an appointment to visit the colorful workshop of **Surabhi Exports** (© 0141/237-2202), where creative powerhouse, Gitto, works with renowned interior designers to come up with looks that are unique and totally fabulous. Also visit **Anokhi** (reviewed below) for lovely block-print garments.

One of the most reliable shops for knickknacks is **Neelam Handicrafts** at the Arya Niwas (© 0141/237-2456 or 0141/510-6010). This little shop stocks maps, post-cards, and books on India as well as some music CDs. It also has a small collection of silver jewelry, Indian teas, handmade paper, and souvenirs—all good quality and sold at a fixed marked price (a rarity in Jaipur); incidentally, they are half the price quoted at most other city shops.

Finally, if you'd like to find all the finest jewelry, designerwear, Pashminas, books, and selected homewares under one roof and aren't against traveling some distance out of town, consider undertaking the 90-minute drive to **Amanbagh,** in the Ajabgarh valley. This remote, beautifully situated resort has one of the finest boutiques we've encountered. Christina Patnaik (a Mexican who married locally) sources exceptional items from all over India, and some of the clothing and jewelry displayed here costs marginally less than what you'd find in Jaipur (only here you won't have to contend with heavy traffic, the commission system, or trying to figure out high quality from average items; everything at Amangagh is top-notch). There's some extraordinary jewelry (including chunky tribal ankle bracelets), and funky Indian twists on Western garments by sought-after Delhi-based designer Malini Ramani; check out her colorful miniskirts with mirror-work and detailed *sitara* (sequin) designs—gorgeous, if pricey, at around Rs 9,000 ($220/£111). Pashmina shawls of the highest quality start at $500 (£250).

BLUE POTTERY
Kripal Singh Shekhawat 🏵🏵🏵   If you want to make sure you're purchasing top-quality blue glazed pottery, make an appointment to view the work of Jaipur's most famous ceramist, Kripal Singh, often credited with reviving this dying art. Made from ground blue quartz stone, glass, borax, and clay, and utilizing traditional designs, his work is nothing short of exquisite. B-18A Shiv Marg, Bani Park. © 0141/220-1127.

BOOKS
Books Corner 🏵   You could easily miss this corner shop, but even though it's tiny, it's chockablock with magazines and books. If you're looking for more information on India, coffee-table books on Rajasthan, or just a good paperback read, this has the best selection around, at the fairest prices. M.I. Rd. © 0141/236-6323.

CLOTHING & HOUSEWARES
Anokhi 🏵🏵🏵   This company was created in the 1960s by a British designer who had items made here for export to the U.K. and elsewhere. The combination of Eastern and Western influences has resulted in elegant and flattering designs that have become hugely popular around the world. Anokhi is part of a growing design movement that taps into the skills of local craftspeople and gives those crafts a modern twist. Hand-blocked prints, hand-woven fabrics, and natural dyes are the hallmark of Anokhi's products, which include gorgeous garments for men, women, and children,

(Moments Bargaining Is Part of the Deal

If you'd like to take home a couple of pairs of inexpensive leather sandals or sequined slippers, head for the string of shops beneath the Hawa Mahal on Tripolia Bazaar; you'll find mountains of shoes, as well as the opportunity to try your hand at bargaining. To the local tradesman, this activity—so often frowned upon by Westerners—is almost inbred, and is actually not as trying or tiring as perceptions might lead you to believe. The trick is to go at it with gusto, enthusiasm, and, most important, good humor and a smile. To the shop-keeper, there is almost nothing worse than failing to make a sale, and it would be unprecedented for him to start with a reasonable opening price: He expects you to challenge his offer (usually about five times any acceptable amount), so sets off by suggesting an outrageous amount (based on what you look like you can afford) at which you must shake your head despondently. Then (and you may well remember the famous bazaar bargaining scene from Monty Python's *Life of Brian*) make an equally impossible counter-offer and you'll find yourself locked in a battle of psychological warfare that's more exciting than chess. After all, even when you've shaved several hundred rupees off the price, you'll have no idea what your prize is really worth. But you'll have something to wear to remind you of your very Indian interaction.

and a wide range of feminine home furnishings—anything from duvet and cushion covers to napkins. Prices are significantly higher than those in the bazaars, but the quality of design is in another league. After stuffing your shopping basket, eat a healthy lunch at the **Organic Cafe,** which serves daily specials, salads, desserts, and fresh juices. 2nd Floor, C-11, K.K. Sq., Prithviraj Marg, C-Scheme. © **0141/400-7244.** www.anokhi.com.

Hot Pink 🅖🅖🅖   We love the small, cool, stylish space of this designer boutique in the garden of Narain Niwas Palace. Browse for beautiful garments, fashion accessories, and textiles from 25 hot Indian designers; look for gorgeously stylish clothing by Rajesh Pratap Singh or the almost avant-garde designs of Manish Arora (who's branded as "Fish Fry" internationally). The menswear is highly desirable too, and there are some fantastic, bright, daring cushion covers that you'll want to cram into your luggage. If you're particularly interested in Indian fashion, this is a great place to strike up conversation with western designers who base themselves here because of great local innovations (Thierry Journo is the French in-house designer). Narain Niwas Palace, Marain Singh Rd. © **0141/510-8932.** www.hotpinkindia.com.

JEWELRY

Amrapali 🅖🅖   In 1980, two young entrepreneurs, Rajesh Ajmera and Rajiv Arora, saw a gap in the market and started adapting traditional jewelry styles to appeal to a broader international market. Conveniently situated near Panch Batti and the city gate that leads into Jauhri Bazaar, Amrapali is famous for its tribal silver jewelry, but the gold showroom also contains some rare examples of *kundan* jewelry, a technique in which each gem is set by pressing fine strips of highly purified gold around it. Depending on how much you spend, you may be able to negotiate a discount. M.I. Rd. © **0141/237-7940** or 0141/236-2768.

Gem Palace ✦✦✦   When the maharajas of Rajasthan were suddenly deprived of their privy purses in 1972, many were forced to sell off the family jewels. Gem Palace, whose owners had been serving their needs for four generations, was a discreet place to do so. Today you can admire these priceless items, now owned by the Kasliwals and displayed in this beautiful store, along with antiques from the Mughal period. You can also view the craftspeople here creating new pieces, destined for the necks, wrists, and fingers of the privileged all over the world; its celebrity customers have included Princess Diana, Bill Clinton, and Paul McCartney. This is arguably the best and most exclusive jewelry shop in Jaipur, but it's not the place to pick up a bargain. M.I. Rd. ✆ 0141/236-3061 or 0141/237-4175. www.gempalacejaipur.com.

K. S. Durlabhji, Emerald House ✦   When a new emerald mine was discovered in Rhodesia (now Zimbabwe) in the 1920s, Mr. M. S. Durlabhji got on the very next boat and traveled south. Once there, he took one look at the deep-green quality of the emeralds and purchased the entire consignment, then continued to purchase every stone until the mine ran dry. Today his son Yogendra has a collection of emerald jewelry that makes jewelers across the world green with envy, and their buyers include a who's who of the world's top jewelers: Van Cleef, Harry Winston, Tiffany, Cartier, and Boucheron, to name a few. Subhash Marg, C-Scheme. ✆ 0141/237-2318 or -6044.

PASHMINAS

New Gandhi Handloom Coop ✦✦ *Value*   This tiny store is stuffed with a selection of Pashminas of varying quality—the cheapest cost Rs 100 ($2.45/£1.25) and are available in just about every color under the sun, though at that price you're hardly getting much of the real Pashmina wool in it. The extremely helpful Kashmiri gentleman will of course tempt you to spend a great deal more on one of his pure Pashminas—prices aren't going to be any lower, even in Kashmir. Johari Bazaar, Old City.

3 The National Parks

The two most famous parks in Rajasthan, both within easy striking distance of Jaipur, are **Bharatpur-Keoladeo Ghana National Park,** a 2,600-hectare (6,400-acre) tract of land that attracts the largest concentration and variety of birdlife in Asia; and **Ranthambhore National Park,** which enjoys an enviable reputation as the one area where you are virtually guaranteed to see a tiger. Also relatively close to Jaipur (110km/68 miles; 2 hr.) is **Sariska National Park** where, sadly, tigers no longer roam (see "Wanted: Tigers," below), though there are currently plans underway to repopulate the park with tigers from Ranthambhore. The Sariska Palace Hotel, an aspiring luxury hotel built by the Machiavellian Maharaja Jay Singh of Alwar (see "Once Were Warriors: The History of the Rajput," earlier in this chapter), is a rather lovely French-Indo concoction (if you like your buildings to resemble over-the-top confections) furnished with many original pieces (rotting trophies included). Reports of service have been less than satisfactory, and it's really only worthwhile to pop in for tea if you're in the area. By contrast, Ranthambhore is far more beautiful and has two excellent accommodations as well as a fascinating conservation history.

BHARATPUR & THE KEOLADEO GHANA NATIONAL PARK

Referred to as the Eastern Gateway to Rajasthan, Bharatpur lies almost exactly halfway between Delhi (152km/94 miles) and Jaipur (176km/109 miles), and is a mere 55km (34 miles) from the Taj Mahal. The town itself holds no fascination, but a few kilometers south on National Highway 11 is Keoladeo "Ghana" National Park. Recognized by UNESCO as a World Heritage Site, the park is definitely worth visiting if you're a keen birder, but it's not a must-see for people who don't know the difference between a lark and a peacock.

A natural depression of land that was initially flooded by Maharaja Suraj Mal in 1726, the park abounds in large tracts of wetlands (covering more than a third of the terrain) as well as wood, scrub, and grasslands, a combination that attracts a large number of migratory birds that fly thousands of miles to find sanctuary here. It was not always so— for centuries, the area was the Maharaja of Bharatpur's private hunting reserve, and in 1902 it was inaugurated by Lord Curzon as an official duck-shoot reserve (some 20 species of duck are found here). In the most shameful incident in the park's history, Lord Linlithgow, then Viceroy of India, shot 4,273 birds in one day—the inscription of his record can still be read on a pillar near Keoladeo Temple. Thankfully, the park became a sanctuary in 1956 and was ultimately upgraded to national park status in 1982.

Today the park supports more than 375 bird species, including a large variety of herons, kingfishers, pelicans, storks, and ducks. It is the only known wintering region of the rare and endangered Siberian crane, which flies 8,050km (5,000 miles) to get here. The numbers are indeed staggering, and birds will fill your vision throughout your visit—particularly during the winter months (Oct–Feb), when the resident bird population swells to over half a million. The park is also home to 13 snake species (including the oft-spotted python); six species of large herbivores; and mongoose, civet, and otter. Although a dead tiger was discovered here in June 2005, Bharatpur is not regarded as a tiger sanctuary, and you sense that the signs urging caution are there to inject a sense of romance and wildness into what is otherwise a very tame experience. In fact, it is hard to understand how a World Heritage Site that attracts more than a million visitors a year can be so undervalued by those administering it—at

Wanted: Tigers

On October 10, 2003, Chinese Customs officials apprehended a truck on the road to Lhasa. Wrapped in Delhi newspapers were the skins of 581 leopards, 778 otters, and 31 tigers—the latter representing 1% of the entire estimated tiger population of India. While wildlife non-governmental organizations (NGOs) like the Wildlife Protection Society of India have persistently highlighted the high level of organized wildlife crime and its inevitable effect on the tiger population, these facts were always denied by local authorities, who invariably reported increased tiger populations. But poaching remains rampant, with tigers in particular danger because of the Chinese belief that ingesting their crushed bones imbues potency. This was proven in February 2005, when a journalist blew the whistle on the complete disappearance of all tigers from the Sariska Sanctuary during the monsoon of 2004. The ensuing public outcry led to the formation of several high-level committees that attempted to get to the truth about tiger numbers. After a nationwide manhunt, kingpin wildlife butcher Sansar Chand—allegedly responsible for the poaching of at least 100 tigers—was arrested in Delhi on July 1, 2005. But unless sterner measures are instituted, conservationists and environmentalists remain skeptical of the continued survival of India's endangered tigers.

dawn scores of people (as well as a few illegal vehicles) take the main road through the park as a shortcut into Bharatpur, feral cattle blithely grazing the grasslands transform the scene into one of ordinary farmland, the loud *khudu-khudu* of generators pumping water disturb the peace in many areas, and a general lack of facilities and tawdry appearance leave a lot to be desired, though the drought has no doubt exacerbated the situation over the past few years.

Tip: If you are staying in the area for a couple of days, an excursion well worth considering is to the architecturally beautiful **Deeg Palaces** (free admission; daily 8am–sunset), 30km (19 miles) northwest of Bharatpur, particularly in August during the 3-day Monsoon Festival, when the 500-odd fountains are turned on.

ESSENTIALS

VISITOR INFORMATION   The **wildlife office** is located at the main gate on National Highway 11 (© **05644/22-2777**). Entry is Rs 200 ($4.90/£2.50) per person, Rs 200 ($4.90/£2.50) per video camera. To really get into the excitement of birding, you should borrow a copy of Sálim Ali's *The Book of Indian Birds* (OUP India), or Rajpul Singh's *Birds of Bharatpur,* and start ticking off those sightings! If you're staying at The Bagh (reviewed below), you'll find an excellent range of guides, including several copies of Krys Kazmierczak's *A Field Guide to the Birds of India.*

GETTING THERE   Bharatpur is a 4½-hour drive from Delhi; it's 55km (34 miles) west of Agra and 175km (108 miles) east of Jaipur. If you travel by train from Delhi, it will take 2½ hours by the convenient Kota Janshatabdi; it takes a little over 2 hours for this train to link you with Sawai Madhopur (Ranthambhore National Park). From Agra, the Marudhar Express gets you here in just 55 minutes.

GETTING AROUND   Park hours are 6:30am to 5pm in winter, and 6am to 6pm in summer. You can set off **on foot** or rent your own **bicycle** near the entrance to the park (Rs 25/60¢/30p per hr.; some rental shops ask that you leave your passport or a deposit of no more than Rs 500/$12/£6.20), but roads aren't great and you will often find yourself on foot, actually burdened by the bike, especially if you try to traverse the dirt tracks. You can explore certain areas by **boat** (Rs 100/$2.45/£1.25), though if the drought persists, these will continue to be out of operation. The best way to get around the park is with a **cycle-rickshaw** or **horse-drawn tonga** (Rs 100/$2.45/£1.25 per hr.); many of the rickshaw-*wallas* have spent years trundling visitors around and now have a good knowledge of the birdlife as well as keen eyesight (though a less than satisfactory command of English). If you want them to double as guides, they will expect a tip (Rs 100/$2.45/£1.25 is fair, depending on how long you use them). Official guides (Rs 70/$1.70/90p per hr.) carrying binoculars are also available at the entrance to the park; in a rather unwieldy arrangement, they travel alongside on their bicycles. The park now offers battery-operated **minibus tours** and **electric auto-rickshaw** rides through the park; these are considerably quieter than you might imagine; a 90-minute ride costs Rs 250 ($6.10/£3.10).

WHERE TO STAY & DINE

The government-run **Hotel Bharatpur Ashok** or Forest Lodge (© **05644/22-2722** or -2760; www.theashokgroup.com; itdchba@sancaharnet.in; Rs 2,700/$66/£33 double) is the only option inside the park. The 17 rooms are clean but charmless, there is no pool, and you have to pay an entry fee every time you enter the park. On the plus side, it does have a lovely bougainvillea-lined terrace—though you'll have to contend with monkeys should you choose to eat here (and you don't have to travel far to find the very reason you've come in the first place!). It's overpriced, however, which is why our money is on **The Bagh** (see below), a far more lavish option just a 15- to 20-minute drive away. If you're on a tighter budget, consider **Hotel Sunbird** (*C* **05644/ 22-5701** or -1533; www.hotelsunbird.com; from $20/£12 double, or $28–$33/£16–£19 with breakfast and dinner) or **Birder's Inn** (*C* **05644/22-7346** or in Delhi 011/ 2683-1792; www.thebirdersinn.com; Rs 1,570/$39/£20 double, including breakfast). Located on National Highway 11 (which can be noisy) and within walking distance of the gates, both offer pretty basic but scrupulously clean en-suite accommodations, with Birder's Inn set farther back from the road and run by avid birders Tirath Singh and Laxmi Mudgal (the resident naturalist).

The Bagh *🏠🏠🏠*   Leave tatty Bharatpur behind and wander into this relaxed oasis set in an enchanting garden filled with fruit trees and abuzz with birdlife and an ambience of tranquillity. The Bagh is a truly classy, good-value retreat, and a perfect base—not only from which to explore the bird sanctuary, but also as an alternative to busy, overrun Agra. The resort layout emphasizes space, peace, and privacy, and once you step through the gate, you'll feel far away from everything. There are three separate residential complexes, each set a considerable distance from the other and each comprising various large suites set along wide verandas with crenellated archways, classic cane armchairs, and the odd fountain or two. Guest rooms have marble floors with a few rugs, huge beds, and tasteful antique furniture; double blinds fold down over the windows that look into the garden. Bathrooms are a joy: big spaces with glass-encased showers and separate tubs (although we hope your conscience will keep you from using the latter). Here, the absence of televisions and minibars only adds to the thrill of the setting; when you're not out spotting birds, entertain yourself by lounging at the pool, getting rubbed down with Ayurvedic oils at the spa, or simply wandering through the property. The excellent **Gulmohar** restaurant (breakfast $10/£5; dinner $20/£10) is presided over by chef Gambhir Singh, who prepares something for everyone; do try the local Brij dishes, like *dum aloo brijwasi* (potatoes stuffed with *mawa* and spices and then cooked in a sealed pot and dusted with coriander and green chilies). Or, if you want to dine like royalty, try the "chicken from Bharatpur *ki degchi*," a lively dish that originated in the local royal kitchen.

Old Agra-Achnera Rd., Pakka Bagh Village, Bharatpur 321 001 (3.5km/2¼ miles from town; 55km/34 miles from Agra). *C* **05644/22-8333** or 05644/22-5191. Fax 05644/22-58051. www.thebagh.com. thebagh@hotmail.com. 23 units. $150 (£75) deluxe double; $170 (£85) junior suite; $30 (£15) extra bed. Taxes extra. AE, MC, V. **Amenities:** Restaurant; coffee shop; bar; pool; gym; spa with Ayurvedic massage, Jacuzzi, sauna, and steam room; travel assistance; gift shop; laundry; yoga; library; guided tours and bird sanctuary guides; art gallery. *In room:* A/C.

Laxmi Vilas Palace *🏠*   This is not a palace in any sense of the word, but a rather pretty double-story heritage hotel, decorated with frescoes around the windows, doorways, and alcoves. Known for its legendary duck shoots (look for the official photographs that catalog the slaughter), Laxmi Vilas was originally built in 1899 for the Maharaja of Bharatpur's younger brother; members of the royal family live in a separate wing and still manage the property. It's not luxurious, or particularly stylish, but the rooms—ringing a central courtyard—have historical ambience, the layout differing from room to room. Some are decorated in original Rajasthani antiques, with the best featuring small double doors leading onto the narrow balcony that circumambulates the exterior. Suites are, as always, more spacious. A personal favorite is room no. 301, the "penthouse suite," which is hardly ever rented out because it has no air-conditioning (something you won't need in winter). It's the only room on the rooftop, affording you wonderful privacy, with five double doors, three of which open onto a small private balcony overlooking the fields behind the house. During our most recent visit, in early 2007, hasty construction of a new luxury property next door was under way. The planned 20-room hotel will share some facilities (like the pool) with the original palace and will feature reproduction furniture and an "upmarket" ambience (or so it is envisioned); rates start at $100 (£50) double. Areas of the original hotel look a tad run-down, but it is hoped that when the new wing opens, the heritage wing will receive a much-needed upgrade. Service is mostly friendly, although when we asked for some of the offered amenities, like train reservations, the response made it clear that we'd have to sort it out ourselves. Food is of the tasty home-cooked variety, although during peak season you'll need to put up with buffets. Grab a table in the inner courtyard rather than the more claustrophobic dining hall, where stuffed tiger heads may suppress your appetite; the dinnertime music and puppet show is short but sweet. The hotel jeep can take you to the park or on any other excursions.

Kakaji Ki Kothi, Bharatpur 321 001 (2.5km/1½ miles from town; 55km/34 miles from Agra). *C* **05644/22-3523** or 05644/23-1199. Fax 05644/22-5259. www.laxmivilas.com. reservations@laxmivilas.com. 30 units. Rs 3,500 ($86/£44) double; Rs 4,000 ($98/£50) suite. AE, MC, V. **Amenities:** Dining hall; pool; kids' pool; Jacuzzi; travel desk; car rental/transfers; bookstore; massage; laundry; doctor-on-call; currency exchange; Internet; cultural performances; jeep safari. *In room:* A/C, TV, hair dryer.

RANTHAMBHORE NATIONAL PARK

Ranthambhore—for many decades the hunting preserve of the princes of Jaipur—covers a mere 40,000 hectares (98,800 acres) but offers a fascinating combination of crumbling monuments, living temples, wild beauty, and your best chance to spot a wild tiger. Set within a high, jagged escarpment, **Ranthambhore Fort** (save a few hr. for a visit) has towered over the park's forests for nearly a thousand years and has witnessed many a bloody combat—even the Mughal emperor Akbar fought a battle for supremacy here in the 16th century. Inside the fort (open dawn–dusk at no cost) lie a number of ruined palaces, step wells, and a celebrated Ganesha temple visited every year in September by two million pilgrims who come to worship during the Lord Ganesha's birthday. But it is the forests, that lie shimmering in the gorges below, scattered with more ancient crumbling monuments, that attract the foreign pilgrims, who come during the winter months to catch a glimpse of the mighty Bengal tiger. Sightings are recorded fairly regularly—it is said that between 75% and 95% of all the photographs ever taken of a tiger in the wild have been taken in Ranthambhore. This has meant that the 26-odd tigers living here have become totally habituated to human observation and are almost entirely indifferent to the sight and sound of vehicles and flashing light bulbs.

The success of the park is due in no small measure to the efforts of Fateh Singh Rathore. A member of the princely family of Jodhpur, Rathore was made field director of Ranthambhore in 1972, the year tiger hunting was banned in India. Almost single-handedly, Rathore mapped and built the park's roads and persuaded 12 entire villages to move voluntarily, having arranged financial compensation and constructed new villages with modern facilities that included schools, wells, and electricity. He also used a powerful spiritual argument: It is the tiger that always accompanies the goddess and demon-slayer Durga (who embodies the power of good over evil), so it therefore deserves protection; however, its survival remains forever compromised in a habitat shared with humans (see "Wanted: Tigers" above).

Under Rathore's protection, the Ranthambhore tiger population increased from 13 to 40, and his dedicated study and photography of the subjects brought much of the tiger's beauty and plight into the international spotlight. But at no small cost—Rathore was awarded the WWF International Valour Award after a mob of villagers, angry at no longer having access to their ancestral lands for grazing and hunting, attacked him, shattering his kneecaps and fracturing his skull. On his release from the hospital, Rathore simply returned to the village and challenged them to do it again.

After a brief scare in the early 1990s, when poaching (apparently by the park's own wardens) almost halved the resident tiger population, numbers stabilized by the year 2000. Today, people like Rathore and Valmik Thapar, one of India's foremost campaigners for the protection of the tiger, are once again fighting a crucial battle against widespread poaching; they argue that the authorities set up for the protection of the reserve are doing little. In fact, unofficial stories tell that Rathore was summarily banned form the park at one stage, having been too vocal against corrupt officials and their hopeless policies. But Rathore and Thapar were proven right; in mid-2005 an independent committee appointed to carry out a tiger census discovered that numbers in Ranthambhore had dwindled from 40 to 26, in spite of the presence of several new cubs. Some local tiger afficionados are more positive, however, and will remind you that by mid-2007 there had been a 2-year period without any poaching incidents; apparently there are now six cubs in the tourist zone and 12 in the entire reserve.

If you're keen on understanding the tiger politics of the region, you will no doubt find yourself engaged in intense discussion at Sher Bagh and Ranthambhore Bagh, both good accommodations. Fateh Singh's daughter-in-law manages Sher Bagh, while his son Goverdhan, a doctor, runs the nearby charitable hospital for the welfare of local people; it's one of the best-run rural hospitals in India. They also run an excellent rural school (visitors are welcome to visit both the school and hospital)—all this based on the philosophy that unless one develops solutions in concert with local people, it won't be possible to save the tiger for posterity. With an estimated 90,000 humans and almost a million livestock living within a 5km (3-mile) radius of the park, the pressure on this island of wilderness remains immense, but its popularity and the efforts of many wildlife supporters will hopefully stand it in good stead. You can also go to the website of **Travel Operators For Tigers** (www.TOFTiger.org), a U.K.–based organization promoting responsible tiger tourism and tiger research.

While tiger sightings are relatively common, don't expect the experience to be necessarily a romantic one. It can be ruined by the presence of other vehicles, particularly the open-topped 20-seater Canters buses with whooping kids on board. Only a limited number of vehicles are allowed at any sighting, but this regulation is not always respected, hence the designation of different routes (see "Game Drive Formalities," below) to keep number densities spread throughout the park. Even if you don't spot a tiger (and do be prepared for this eventuality), the sheer physical beauty of the park is worth experiencing—from lotus-filled lakes and dense jungle to craggy, boulder-strewn cliffs and golden grasslands. Other species worth looking for include caracal (a wildcat), crocodile, *nilgai* (large antelope resembling cattle), *chital* (spotted deer), black buck (delicate buck with spiraling horns), *chinkara* (a dainty gazelle), and sambar (their distinctive barking call often warns of the presence of a tiger nearby). The park also has leopards (notoriously shy), wild boars, and sloth bears, and is rich in birdlife—over 400 resident and migrant species.

Note, too, that park authorities are planning to introduce a small safari park that should provide impatient visitors who are hell-bent on spotting tiger with an almost zoolike experience. If you're desperate, ask your host about this development.

ESSENTIALS

VISITOR INFORMATION   Ranthambhore National Park is closed July through September due to the monsoon. Unlike at Bharatpur, traffic and numbers are closely regulated. For general information, call the **Sawai Madhopur Tourist Centre** (Sawai Madhopur Railway Station; © **07462/22-0808;** Mon–Sat 10am–1pm and 2–5pm).

GETTING THERE   The nearest airport is Jaipur's, which lies 180km (112 miles) away; it is just under a 4-hour drive. Alternatively, the sprawling village of Sawai Madhopur (10km/6¼ miles from the park gates) is well connected by rail to Jaipur (just over 2 hr.) and to Jodhpur (8 hr.), and is on the main line between Delhi (5½ hr.) and Mumbai. All accommodations listed will arrange pick-ups from the station.

GAME DRIVE FORMALITIES   Only official vehicles with sanctioned drivers and guides are permitted to take visitors into the park. There are two types of vehicle: jeeps and Canter buses. The latter—ferrying up to 25 passengers—should be avoided, even though they're slightly cheaper. To ensure your place in a game-drive jeep, it's best to arrange well in advance through your hotel. Places on the 40 vehicles that are allowed into the park for each drive session are often booked up to 2 months in advance. For bookings in a jeep, call the **Project Tiger office** (© **07462/22-0223;** Mon–Sat 5–7am and noon–2pm for advance booking). If you have no alternative, Canters buses can be booked a day in advance at the tourist reception center at RTDC's Hotel Vinayak. If you book with any of the accommodations recommended below, they will arrange all this for you (they also enjoy unofficial priority access to the park, and seem to be able to arrange entrance at short notice, although you shouldn't count on it). Please note, however, that you must let your host know when and how often you would like to go on a game drive as soon as possible—these officially need to be booked 60 days in advance. The price of a seat in a jeep varies depending on where you stay; the official rate charged by the park is Rs 800 ($20/£10) for a seat on a jeep (which includes park entry, but excludes a Rs 200/$4.90/£2.50 video fee), but you can also book through your lodge, essentially sparing you the bother of exchanging cash at the park entrance. For a wonderful introduction to the park, ask your host to find a copy of *The Ultimate Ranthambhore Guide* (Rs 175/$4.30/£2.20) by Sheena Sippy and Sanjna Kapoor, also sold at the park's gate.

Tip: Although the park's seven routes are assigned randomly, and you are normally not allowed to choose which route you would like to go on, you *can* request that your host either try to have at least one game drive near a body of water in the park or in an area where a tiger was spotted the day before. The best time to visit the park is between November and April (Jan–Apr is best for tiger sightings). The park closes during the monsoon season (July–Sept).

There are two game drives: The early-morning drive (winter 7:30–10:30am; summer 6:30–9:30am) is often preferable to the afternoon drive (winter 3–5:30pm; summer 4–6:30pm), given that temperatures can make for muggy afternoons. However, you should pack something warm—it can get cold both early in the morning and once darkness approaches.

Routes (which drivers are pretty much forced to stick to) and guides are randomly allotted, which means you may be on a tight budget yet find yourself in a jeep with an excellent guide, watching a tiger bathe in the lotus lake that fronts the beautiful 250-year-old Jogi Mahal, while a hapless guest paying top dollar for the same trip trundles around with a monosyllabic guide with halitosis. Note that the overhaul of tourist entry procedures and rules are a constant topic for bureaucratic debate, and procedures may change on a whim at any time, so do check ahead.

WHERE TO STAY & DINE

Almost all the best options are on Ranthambhore Road, which flanks the park. If you're watching your dollar, a good-value option is the tastefully rustic **Ranthambhore Bagh** (② **07462/22-1728,** reservations in Delhi ② 011/2691-4417 or 94-1403-0221; www.ranthambhorebagh.com), where you can book twin-bedded luxury tents for Rs 4,280 ($105/£53) with all meals included; $20 (£10) per person for a game drive by jeep. Located 5km (3 miles) from the park gate, accommodations here are simple but comfortable (it has slightly cheaper traditional walled rooms—with A/C—if the tents sound too rough), and the fixed-menu buffet meals are often served outdoors. Frequented by photographers and conservationists, this is a good place to meet and talk with wildlife enthusiasts.

Aman-i-Khás 🕷🕷🕷   This is surely the most stylish tented wilderness accommodations in all India. Unlike Vanyavilās, it lacks peripheral constructed walls, which gives it the ambience of the true outdoors, with its own small watering hole where you can watch for visiting animals. Each of the spacious air-conditioned (or heated) white tents, located a sensible distance away from one another, features typical Aman touches of discreet luxury, with spaces stylishly divided by cool white drapes. Sip a cocktail as you relax on the cowhide and teak chairs (with footstools, of course) or on the *charpais* (traditional woven bed) on your patio; browse glossy coffee-table books on India, wildlife, or Rajasthan in the library-cum-lounge; or get pampered silly with an Aman Raj massage in the spa tent. Designed to echo the look of a traditional step-well, the pool here is blissful—another perfectly idyllic spot to unwind between game drives. Each room is assigned a batman who is superbly efficient yet completely invisible unless you need him—screen windows open and close, beds are turned in, bathrobes replaced, all quite magically. Food is simply superb—fresh organic produce from the garden enhances refreshingly delicate flavors. At night, lanterns light the path from your room to the outdoor lounge, where a giant *uruli* (traditional bronze bowl) forms the central fireplace, and guests gather to enjoy the night sky, the ethereal calm, and the occasional call from the wild. A stay here is truly magical, utterly romantic, and certainly the most perfect integration of luxury and nature in Rajasthan.

Ranthambhore Rd. (just beyond Sher Bagh), Sawai Madhopur. ② **07462/25-2052** or -2224. Fax 07462/25-2178. Reservations, in Singapore: ② **65/6887-3337.** Fax 65/6887-3338. www.amanresorts.com. reservations@aman resorts.com. 10 units. Oct–Apr only. $1,000 (£500) double. Minimum 2 (preferably 3) nights' stay required, arriving Mon or Thurs. Rate includes all meals and drinks; 10% tax and 10% service charge extra. Game drives $60 (£30) minimum per person. AE, MC, DC, V. **Amenities:** Dining tent; library/lounge; spa tent; room service; laundry; outdoor lounge with fireplace; safety deposit box; CD Walkman on request. *In room:* A/C, cooler box.

Dev Vilas 🕷 *Value*   Upon approach, this modern pale peach-colored hotel (which is the closest lodge to the park entrance) may not look like much, but it has been designed to echo the simple, unfettered layout of an old hunting lodge, only on a somewhat grander, more spacious scale. In fact, it's space that is emphasized here, especially in the large, uncluttered accommodations, where you're meant to focus on your safari experience rather than unnecessary luxuries (rooms are very comfortable, but not particularly smart). From the rooms and rooftops you can enjoy interesting and often lovely views of the surrounding landscape and catch the daily routines of neighboring villagers. Guest rooms are arranged along two wings on either side of a wide lawn, and seven new tent-covered cottages (no. 7 is the most private, with the largest bed) lie just beyond the large pool. Here, as you soak up the sun on wooden sunbeds, veteran waitstaff administer midday drinks and inquire after your morning game drive. The affable hotel owner, Balendu Singh, is passionate about the park, and with whiskey in hand he'll happily wax lyrical about Ranthambhore eco-politics. And, pachyderm-lovers will be excited to know that this is the only lodge in Ranthambhore with its own pet elephant, "Pawan Kali," available for rides (Rs 500/$13/£7 for 45 min.) or camera opportunities. The drawback, for some, is that meals are strictly buffet, although the variety is wide. Should you be bold enough to ask, you can always get away from the crowd and dine beneath the stars. *Note:* Dev Vilas is the most wheelchair-friendly lodging option in the region.

Village Khilchipur, Ranthambhore Rd., Sawai Madhopur 322 001. ℂ 07462/25-2168. Fax 07462/25-2195. www. devvilas.com. devvilas@datainfosys.net. 28 units. $225 (£113) double; $240 (£120) tented bungalow; $250 (£125) superior suite; $35 (£18) extra bed. Rates include all meals and morning and afternoon tea; taxes extra. MC, V. **Amenities:** Dining hall; bar; pool; travel assistance; station transfers; gift shop; Ayurvedic massage; laundry; doctor-on-call; Internet; elephant rides; game drives; birding excursions; nature drives. *In room:* A/C, TV.

Sher Bagh 🐾🐾   If you're looking for a safari experience in India, this intimate camp is a great choice (though unlike its African counterpart, it's not situated in a reserve, but is as close to the park as you are likely to get). The irrepressible and charming owner, Jaisal Singh, is a superb host when he is around, and a member of what could be described as Ranthambhore royalty. (He is Fateh Singh Rathore's godchild and practically grew up in the park between bouts of polo playing and hobnobbing with the rich and famous.) Accommodations comprise a semicircle of comfortable tents (originally designed for the Maharaja of Jodhpur's hunting expeditions), each with an en-suite bathroom (no bathtubs; satisfying showers, but the hot water sometimes runs out). Tents are a little too close together and hot during the day (there are fans, but no air-conditioning), but there are a number of places to relax; the coolest is the first-floor bar/lounge area (it enjoys a breeze and has a great selection of books) in the main building, which looks and feels a bit like a Spanish hacienda. Sadly, Sher Bagh has no pool. Meals are a welcome relief from standard North Indian fare; a full breakfast is served after the morning game drive ($30/£15 per person per drive) followed by a light lunch (pesto pasta and salad, perhaps; almost all ingredients are grown on the farm). Cucumber sandwiches and delicious *chai* (tea) are served immediately after the afternoon game drive, followed by a lavish buffet dinner. At night, when the lanterns and torches are lit, the camp really comes into its own. Engaging in idle chatter while imbibing G&Ts, your feet in the sand and stars above, makes this one of the most relaxing experiences in North India. And just when you thought a good thing couldn't get any better, Sher Bagh's owners decided to improve the size of the tents in 2007.

Sherpur-Khiljipur, Sawai Madhopur 322 001. ℂ 07462/25-2120 or -2119. Reservations: ℂ 011/2374-3194 or -3195. Fax 011/2334-5429. www.sherbagh.com. delhioffice@sherbagh.com. 12 units. $325/£163 double. Rate includes all meals, morning and evening tea, and transfers. Taxes extra. MC, V. Closed Apr 15–Oct 1. **Amenities:** Dining tent; bar and jungle bar; complimentary station transfer; limited room service; massage; laundry; hospital-on-call; excursions.

Vanyavilās 🐾🐾🐾   Set on 8 hectares (20 acres) of landscaped gardens, this superb resort retreat exemplifies the type of cosseted luxury found in many Oberoi properties. Surrounded by a mud wall enclosing a wraparound garden (private except for the odd strutting peacock), the tent rooms are not as safari-like as those at Aman-i-Khás, and the overall outdoor setting not quite as back-to-nature, but they are nevertheless gorgeous, featuring huge canvas roofs shot through with gold sparkles, teak floors, solid walls hung with artwork, opulent Indo-colonial furnishings, and all the modern conveniences you could possibly need. Bathrooms are the sizes of most hotel rooms and have freestanding claw-foot tubs, fabulous showers, and doors leading out to private terraces with comfortable day beds on which to rest after plundering the well-stocked minibars. The property does sprawl somewhat amid lotus ponds and lush bird-filled vegetation, forcing a rather long walk to the pool or restaurant (you can, of course, call for a golf cart), and, unlike Sher Bagh and Aman-i-Khas, the well-manicured surroundings give you little sense of being on the edge of a wilderness. But the superb service, great dining (either in the restaurant or adjacent courtyard), excellent spa, and sheer opulence of the public spaces more than make up for this. Best of all is the opportunity to sit in on one of the regular lectures given by Fateh Singh Rathore, the man who put Ranthambhore on the map—not to mention the bliss of a sparkling pool, where many snow-white guests seem to spend their days.

Ranthambhore Rd., Sawai Madhopur 322 001. ✆ 07462/22-3999. Reservations: ✆ 800/6-OBEROI in the U.S., or toll-free 1600/11-2030. www.oberoihotels.com. 25 units. $775–$875 (£388–£438) double. Taxes extra. AE, DC, MC, V. **Amenities:** Restaurant; library bar; pool; fitness tent; spa; chauffeur-driven cars; complimentary station transfer; business center; salon; laundry; doctor-on-call; currency exchange; Internet; yoga; billiards room; observation tower; game drives; elephant safaris. *In room:* A/C, TV, minibar, tea- and coffee-making facilities, hair dryer, safe, wireless Internet, DVD, CD music system (including selection of CDs and DVDs).

4 Bundi

210km (130 miles) S of Jaipur; 279km (173 miles) SE of Udaipur; 438km (272 miles) SW of Agra

If you see only one off-the-beaten-track town in Rajasthan, the small town of Bundi, established in 1241, should be your first choice. It's worth a visit not just for the architectural magnificence of the palace that clings to the cliff above; the town's lack of modernization and abundance of temples, cenotaphs, and step wells; or even its renowned school of miniature paintings (arguably the best-value paintings in Rajasthan); it's the lack of hustling, which comes as a truly welcome relief. Approached through a gorge, the town is protected by the embracing hills of the Aravalli Hills, topped by Taragarh Fort, and life here goes on pretty much as it has for centuries. Because the population is in no way dependent on tourism, you are either greeted with real affection or total indifference. There's absolutely no sales pressure—a refreshing change after the constant barrage of "Please come see," and "Special price for you" that follows you everywhere in the cities and more popular towns.

Exploring Bundi's narrow streets, with tiny cupboardlike shops raised a meter or more above street level to avoid the monsoon floods, feels like seeing the real India. Followed by giggling children trying to touch your hand or clothes, you will pass old men beating copper pots into perfect shape; tailors working with beautiful fabrics on ancient Singers; huge mounds of orange, red, and yellow spices offset by purple aubergines, red tomatoes, and green peppers; rickshaws carting women adorned in saris of saturated colors; and temples blaring live music—fresh and natural images that will have you grabbing your camera every 2 minutes. Besides wandering the streets, you can walk to a number of attractions, of which **Garh Palace** 🐾🐾🐾 (described by Rudyard Kipling as "the work of goblins" and one of the few examples of pure Rajput style) is not to be missed. Garh Palace's exterior is astounding, but sadly, much of the interior is falling apart; nevertheless, entry to some areas (with spectacular views of the blue-tinged town below) is now allowed (entry Rs 50/$1.25/65p, Rs 50/$1.25/65p camera, Rs 100/$2.45/£1.25 video; dawn–dusk) and makes for fascinating, hassle-free

For the Pleasures of the Raj

Traveling to and from Kota and Bundi, you will see fields of wheat, castor beans (from which castor oil is made)—and opium poppy. An ancient crop grown for the pleasures of Rajput kings and queens and Mughal emperors, the poppy is today ostensibly grown for the pharmaceutical industry. However, much of it makes its way into the hands of the Mumbai Mafia, and addiction in the area is reported to be rife; you may even come across locals getting high as you wander more remote parts of town.

exploration. The labyrinthine network of rooms, chambers, balconies, and nooks and crannies turns up a good number of surprises, including murals in various states of faded elegance. Above the main part of the palace, you can also visit the arcaded **Chitra Shala,** which is decorated with many of the fine murals in the miniature style the town is famous for (free entry; dawn–dusk). Chitra Shala alone is worth the steep walk up to the imposing gates, as are the views of the town—much of it painted the same blue seen in the more famous "blue city" of Jodhpur. For an even better vantage point, keep ascending the rough path that leads up to Taragarh (not necessarily to the top), for a great sense of peace (you're unlikely to encounter anyone, bar the Hanuman langur monkeys and a lone goat herder) and superb photo ops of the town. Back down in town, take a few minuts to visit **Raniji-ki-Baori** ★★ (the state's most impressive step well), which lies in a small park in the center of town; it dates back to the 17th century and features ornately carved gates, pillars, and friezes.

Sights farther afield, like **Sukh Mahal,** a summer palace where Kipling wrote *Kim,* are best explored with Haveli Braj Bhushanjee's picnic and sightseeing tour.

ESSENTIALS

VISITOR INFORMATION   The **Tourist Information Bureau** (© 0747/244-3697; Mon–Sat 10am–5pm, closed second Sat of the month and Sun) is located at Circuit House, but the owners of the Haveli Braj Bhushanjee heritage hotel (see below) are a mine of information, supplying you with maps, arranging transport, and ready with advice on anything from how much to pay for a rickshaw to opening hours.

GETTING THERE   Kota is 130km (81 miles) by road from Sawai Madhopur and 155km (96 miles) from Chittaurgarh, so you can either visit it after you see Ranthambhore and/or Jaipur or combine it with a trip from Udaipur via Chittaurgarh. To get to Bundi, you have to travel through the industrialized town of Kota. If you have arrived by train (Kota is well connected to the rest of the state, including the main Delhi-to-Mumbai line, Jaipur, Sawai Madhopur, and Chittaurgarh), you will then have to catch a bus, jeep, or taxi to Bundi. A taxi to Bundi will run you Rs 650 ($16/£8); a jeep costs Rs 550 ($14/£7). Kota, which dates back to the 12th century, has a number of impressive monuments (particularly the Palace Fort), but it is only worth stopping at if you have arrived too late to catch a taxi to Bundi. If this is the case, recommended overnight options are **Brijraj Bhawan Palace** (© 0744/245-0529; Rs 2,950/$72/£36 double); and Welcomgroup's **Umed Bhawan Palace** (© 0744/232-5262; www.welcomheritagehotels.com), where doubles start at $70 (£35).

GETTING AROUND   You can get around the town on foot with ease. Should you tire, auto-rickshaws traverse the narrow lanes. If you book into Haveli Braj Bhushanjee, the proprietor will arrange all your transport at very reasonable prices—yet another reason the hotel is so highly recommended. Expect to pay around Rs 1,200 ($29/£15) for an air-conditioned taxi for the day.

WHERE TO STAY & DINE

Haveli Braj Bhushanjee ⭐⭐   This is without a doubt the best place to stay in Bundi, and—despite the small size of the rooms and basic facilities—one of the most authentic heritage properties in India. Situated on a narrow lane inside the walled city, just below the palace, it also happens to be one of the most professionally run guesthouses in India, managed by the discreetly proud Braj Bhushanjee brothers (four of whose ancestors were prime ministers of Bundi State in the 19th c.). Many of the walls are covered with exceptional-quality murals, again typical of the Bundi school of miniature painting, and though each room (like those in so many other guesthouses) is traditionally decorated, the choice of objects, fabrics, and carpets (all sourced from Bundi and surroundings) shows a great deal of thought and innate flair. All the rooms are beautiful (though those overlooking the lane are a tad noisy at times) and feature en-suite "shower rooms"—mostly small, but freshly whitewashed and gleaming. An adjacent building was commandeered and restored in 2002, and in late 2006 two fairly lavish super-deluxe rooms were introduced. Still, our favorite choice is big, lovely white-marble-floored deluxe room no. 22; it has large windows and a massive shower and is decorated with gorgeous silver statues and an antique gramophone player. No alcohol is served—you can bring your own, however—and meat is definitely not permitted on the premises. Though garlic and onion are rarely used in the cooking, dining is of exceptional quality. Rather than choosing from a menu, you are served a selection of simple, flavorful, home-cooked dishes, either in the Darikhana—akin to a carpeted temple, where images of ancestors glower and large colored glass baubles hang from the ceiling—or on the terrace, from where you have a picture-perfect view of the illuminated palace at night. The brothers are a wealth of information about the area and can arrange wonderful sightseeing tours on request (they will, for instance, pack a picnic and carry it up to the fort for you). They also have an excellent (and extensive) collection of miniature paintings and other tribal and traditional crafts for sale—you may pay a little more than you would if you purchased directly from the artist (see "Shopping," below), but be assured that the brothers know the difference between a pretty souvenir and a real investment. At press time, a swimming pool, Jacuzzi, and sauna were being added.

Below Fort, opposite Ayurvedic Hospital, Bundi 323 001. ✆ **0747/244-2322** or -2509. Fax 0747/244-2142. www.kiplingsbundi.com. 25 units. Rs 750 ($18/£9.25) economy double; Rs 1,500 ($37/£19) standard double; Rs 1,850 ($45/£23) deluxe double; Rs 2,500 ($61/£31) super deluxe double. Taxes extra. MC, V. **Amenities:** Dining hall; pool; travel and transport assistance; artwork shop; 24-hr. room service; laundry; doctor-on-call. *In room:* A/C, TV, hair dryer (except economy); super-deluxe rooms have iron, tea- and coffee-making facility.

SHOPPING

If you want to take home a few miniature paintings (and you do—the style is exquisite and the prices laughably cheap), Bundi is one of the best places to do so. If the vast selection at Haveli Braj Bhushanjee doesn't suffice, the charming **Gopal Soni** has a little shop, **Mayur Art** (Nahar Ka Chohatta; ✆ **0747/244-7297** or 0747/244-7710; Aug–Apr daily 8am–noon and 1–8pm, May–July daily 9am–noon and 4–7pm) near the haveli where he paints beautiful miniatures (mostly copies of those in Chitra Shala) on anything from marble and silk to antique Raj-era paper documents. They make a delightful souvenir or gift (prices start from Rs 50/$1.25/65p); plus, for a small fee, you can have each of your fingernails adorned with a miniature elephant, peacock, or tiger.

5 Shekhawati

200km (124 miles) SW of Delhi; 160km (99 miles) NW of Jaipur

Shekhawati, known as the open-air art gallery of Rajasthan, lies in the roughly triangular area between Delhi, Jaipur, and Bikaner, and encompasses the districts of Jhunjhunu, Sikar, and Churu. Its largely semi-desert, wide-open (uninhabited) spaces offer a peaceful respite from the cities. But the primary drawing card is its remarkable art collection—unusual for the unique painting styles and for the fact that the exhibition space consists of the exterior and interior walls of literally hundreds of havelis, temples, cenotaphs, wells, and forts in the region. The trend for decorating walls in this way was imported from the courts of Amber and Jaipur, where the Rajput princes in turn were inspired by the Mughal emperors' patronage of the miniature-mural art form. The Shekhawati's patronage was funded by duties imposed on merchandise carried across that section of the Spice Route that traversed their region (cleverly, the local barons here ensured that their duties were lower than those of the house of Jaipur, thereby diverting trade), or by raids across the borders, but patronage truly flourished during the British Raj, a period when the Shekhawati merchants, renowned for their business acumen, moved to the ports of Calcutta, Madras, and Bombay to capitalize on the growing trade in these new centers. There they made small fortunes and celebrated their wealth by adorning their mansions—an age-old urge, but the result here is a great deal more interesting than anything Martha Stewart might have suggested.

The demand was such that skilled artists could not paint fast enough. Even local masons tried their hand, injecting a wonderful naiveté into many of the paintings. Subject matters vary tremendously, from mythological stories and epics such as the *Ramayana* and *Mahabharata* to local legends of battles and hunts; but perhaps the most amusing are copies of British photographs featuring hot-air balloons, trains, and cars—objects most of the painters had never set their eyes on but faithfully rendered according to the descriptions and prints supplied by their employers.

Today there are some 30 "painted towns" in the region, but the most essential to include in a first-time itinerary are **Ramgarh** (the town with the most painted buildings), **Nawalgarh** (second in number, but with a superior selection, some better preserved than Ramgarh's, particularly the restored Anandi Lal Poddar Haveli), **Fatehpur** (together with Jhunjhunu, this is Shekhawati's oldest town, featuring murals that predate any others in the region as well as the **Haveli Française;** see box below), and **Mandawa** (a quaint town with a number of beautiful painted buildings, and centrally located with the best accommodations in the area).

Armed with a good map (see "Visitor Information," below) and a car, it is relatively easy to explore the surrounds on your own—not least because of the usual army of small kids eager to accompany you and point out the relevant sights. But to know more about the history of the buildings, the artisans, and the area, you may wish to hire the services of a guide through the hotels listed below. Most of the buildings are still inhabited and are accessible for a small fee (Rs 10–Rs 20/25¢–45¢/15p–25p per haveli to the caretaker or watchman); negotiating payment (and whether you should offer to pay at all) is where a guide comes in handy. (Remember that, as is the case in all temples, you may need to *remove your shoes* to enter the inhabited havelis; ask before you enter.) Although the region evokes real passion in some and has resulted in a number of excellent books, it must be said that many of the murals are mere shadows of their former selves, either defaced by human indifference—posters and graffiti mar many of the walls—or faded by the increased water supply to the region, the rise in the water table creating damper conditions. Including this area in your itinerary can be tricky as well, unless you are intent on traveling the long haul through Bikaner to Jaisalmer, or journeying directly from Delhi and then moving on to Jaipur or vice versa, both of which mean many hours spent on the road.

Note: If you've missed out on a camel safari elsewhere in Rajasthan, Shekhawati is a good place to try it out; camel rides lasting 1 to 2 hours cost Rs 300 ($6.85/£3.45) per person; overnight safaris cost Rs 3,000 ($68/£34) for two. For a reliable operator, contact **Dinesh Dhabhai,** the owner of Mandawa Haveli (© **94-1336-6546;** see below), who is also an extremely useful and helpful source for local travel information and advice.

ESSENTIALS

VISITOR INFORMATION Jhunjhunu has a tourist office (© **015945/23-2909;** Mon–Sat 10am–5pm; closed Sun and second Sat of the month), but you'll have more success finding information and arranging a guide through your hotel. Ilay Cooper's illustrated *The Painted Towns of Shekhawati* (Mapin Guides) is still the original bible, with a concise history of the region as well as a breakdown of towns, easy-to-follow maps, and listings of all the sites worth visiting. You can purchase a copy at Books Corner in Jaipur, at Mandawa Castle, or at Desert Resort. Another book worth considering is *Shekhawati: Rajasthan's Painted Homes* by Pankaj Rakesh and Karoki Lewis (Lustre Press Roli Books).

Tip: Traditionally dressed local women often approach tourists to have their picture taken and then demand tips of up to Rs 50 ($1.25/65p) a head. If you don't want to encourage this, ignore them as they follow you around town. Another popular local scam is children asking for a donation for their school—a ploy that will most likely fall apart if you ask to be taken to the school to receive an official receipt.

GETTING THERE Public transport is relatively limited, so the easiest way to explore the area is to hire a car and driver in Jaipur, stop at a few towns along the way, and overnight at Mandawa or Nawalgarh. Or you could take a 2-day detour to Mandawa en route from Delhi to Jaipur (driving time Delhi–Mandawa 7 hr.; Mandawa–Jaipur 4 hr.) or vice versa.

GETTING AROUND Again, you will need a car and driver to go from town to town with ease. Once there, it is relatively easy to explore each area on foot with a guide or by following Ilay Cooper's maps in *The Painted Towns of Shekhawati.*

DRIVING TOUR Travel from Jaipur (or Samode Palace) to Sikar, stopping to look at the *havelis* (historic homes or mansions of wealthy merchants) in Nawalgarh. Have lunch at Roop Niwas, then set off for Mandawa and overnight there. The following day, visit Fatehpur (see "Haveli Française," below) and Lachhmangarh before heading south to Sikar and back down to Jaipur or onward to Delhi.

WHERE TO STAY & DINE

If you're traveling here directly from Delhi, a highly recommended overnight stop is **Neemrana Fort-Palace** (see "Where to Stay & Dine En Route from Delhi," earlier in this chapter). Situated a few hours from Delhi on the eastern outskirts of Shekhawati, it is considered one of the best fort conversions in the country.

Once you're in the Shekhawati region, the two properties reviewed below are your best bets, providing you with both central location and comfort. Worth mentioning if you're looking to save money and live in one of the original Shekhawati havelis is

Haveli Française

In 1999 French artist Nadine Le Prince bought a 19th-century haveli in Fatehpur and, with the help of Dinesh Dhabhai of Mandawa Haveli, spent the next year locating the right artisans, paints, and methods of restoring it. Now called **Haveli Nadine** (though locals call it *angrez ki haveli*—Englishwoman's haveli), it's been converted into a cultural center that's aimed at bringing together the art of Rajasthani with that of foreign artists, and preserving the art forms of Shekhawati. When rain and humidity damaged her newly restored haveli in 2003, Nadine waited for the walls to dry up, and began restoration work in earnest again. Serious art lovers should make an effort to stop here, particularly when an exhibition is on; you can discover Rajasthan through paintings or sculptures not available in any of the regular tourist centers. Either way, touring this gorgeous, painstakingly restored haveli is one way you can visualize what this region's art might have looked like in its heyday. It's generally open between 8am and 7pm each day, but call to check (✆ **01571/23-3024**; nadine.leprince@free.fr; Rs 100/$2.45/£1.25 admission).

Hotel Mandawa Haveli (Mandawa, Jhunjhunu District; ✆ **01592/22-3088,** 01592/31-4463 or 94-1336-6546; http://hotelmandawa.free.fr), not to be confused with Mandawa Haveli in Jaipur. Carefully restored, with its frescoes in excellent condition, the 115-year-old haveli has some good rooms, several with renovated bathrooms; ask for the Nilesh Room on the first floor (Rs 1,950/$48/£24; meals and taxes extra). Alternatively, splurge on one of the suites, which are a really good bargain at Rs 2,950 ($72/£37). Staff can organize superb candlelit dinners on the rooftop for Rs 375 ($9/£5) per head. Alternatively, **Hotel Heritage Mandawa** (✆ **0159/22-3742** or -3743; Rs 1,300–Rs 2,000/$30–$46/£15–£23) offers similar facilities and has hospitable owners.

Another good-value option is **Roop Niwas Kothi** ✪ (Nawalgarh, District Jhunjhunu; ✆ **01594/22-2008** or -4152; www.roopniwaskothi.com), a rather unlikely choice if you're looking for a bit of action. Situated on the outskirts of Nawalgarh, the town that boasts the largest number of painted havelis in Shekhawati (yet nary a place to shop), the hotel doesn't see half as much traffic as the Mandawa properties, and as a result has a slightly desolate air. The rural atmosphere and gracious Indo-colonial architecture make up for some run-down areas (and potentially hazardous plumbing). Rooms are clean and furnished with colonial and Rajput pieces, all with en-suite bathrooms (none with tubs), and air-conditioning. Horse lovers will find the stables offer a great way to explore the countryside (there's an in-house guide), and camel safaris are available. This is a good choice if you're after real tranquillity, but if your budget can stretch that far, Desert Resort (reviewed below) is a better bet. Doubles are Rs 2,100 ($51/£26) deluxe, or Rs 3,000 ($73/£37) for a suite.

If you're interested in unusual architecture, you might consider a night at **The Piramal Haveli** (Village Bagar, Jhunjhunu District; ✆ **01592/22-1220;** from $40/£20 double), particularly if you've grown fond of the Neemrana way of doing things (see review of Neemrana Fort-Palace in "Where to Stay & Dine En Route from Delhi," earlier in this chapter). This Rajasthani-Italianate-style villa certainly does look out of place in the desert—a squat lime-green confection with slender columns, pretty gardens, and some baroque ceiling frescoes that seem to have turned up for the wrong party. That said, the hotel conversion is aimed more at history buffs than visitors who want luxury or great comfort (or double beds), so you'll find plenty of antique styling amid a restoration job that's been rather kind.

Unfortunately, the Shekhawati region is under serious threat of environmental and cultural devastation, a potentially disastrous situation that many blame entirely on poorly managed tourism. Of course, the problem runs a lot deeper than thoughtless visitors filling their bathtubs and flaunting their foreign ways, but eco-conscious travelers will be pleased to know that there is a sensible, "low-impact," extremely good-value accommodation option that is doing its bit for future generations. Along the road from Sikar to Jhunjhuna is **Apani Dhani Eco Lodge** (Jhunjhunu Rd., Nawalgarh; © **01594/22-2239;** www.apanidhani.com; Rs 895–Rs 995/$22–$24/£11–£12), eight en-suite huts with ocher mud-effect walls and thatched roofs created by hands-on owner Ramesh Jangid. Interiors are designed to emphasize harmony with nature and local heritage; they're simple, with a sort of rustic-chic look—earth tones with wooden furniture and regional handicrafts displayed in little wall nooks. A paved courtyard with cane chairs, potted plants, and a canopy of bougainvillea is where traditional meals are served and guests get to pester Ramesh with requests for guided haveli tours or yoga sessions. Best of all, your stay will be practically guilt-free, not least because of the savings you'll be enjoying by forgoing unnecessary luxuries.

Castle Mandawa ✦✦   The castle, well situated to explore the region, is one of the most authentic heritage properties in Rajasthan, not least because of the presence of urbane host Kesri Singh, who was one of the first to start converting the rooms of his 16th-century castle into a hotel in the late 1970s. A thoroughly gregarious and charming host, he usually (assuming he's in residence) invites guests to share a drink with him on one of the turreted battlements that tower above the town roofs before he ushers you to a table on a large roof terrace under the stars. If the hotel is hosting a group, a special fire dance is given by one of the castle's oldest retainers, during which guests help themselves to a tasty buffet. Given the age of the property, its conversion to modern hotel has been remarkably sensitive, maintaining much of the original feel of the castle (no doubt to the approval of the Mandawa ancestors, whose portraits decorate many of the walls) without sacrificing comfort. (Bear in mind that this cannot be said of the most recently added wing, which features boring, uniformly sized rooms with none of the authentic charm of the original castle.) If you have a poor sense of direction, the journey from the veranda bar to your room can be challenging, but really, getting lost and clambering up and down the narrow staircases is half the fun. Rooms vary hugely in size, and some have special features like built-in swings and alcoves furnished with bolster cushions. Nos. 304 and 313 are particularly lovely rooms; no. 215 is smaller (standard) but also a good choice. For more luxury, pick the Peacock Suite (no. 401), which has a marble water fountain; or no. 303, the Tower Suite. Both are located in the castle turrets. The hotel has a few small drawbacks: Situated in the middle of town, it makes for a strangely urban experience—the town's blaring temple music ceases to charm when it's turned on at the crack of dawn.

Mandawa, Jhunjhunu District, Shekhawati 333 704. Reservations: © **0141/237-4112** or -4130. Fax 0141/237-2084 or 0141/510-6082. www.castlemandawa.com. reservation@castlemandawa.com. 70 units. Rs 3,500 ($85/£43) standard double; Rs 6,000 ($146/£74) deluxe cottage; Rs 9,000–Rs 15,000 ($220–$366/£111–£185) suite. Taxes extra. AE, MC, V. **Amenities:** Various dining areas; bar; pool; spa; Ayurvedic massage; laundry; doctor-on-call; billiard room; pool table; badminton; table tennis; camel, horse, and jeep safaris; vintage car rides; cultural performances; heritage walk. *In room:* A/C, minibar (suites only), hair dryer (on request).

Desert Resort Mandawa 🏵🏵 Situated in the semi-arid Shekhawati Desert and built in the style of a Rajasthani village, this is arguably Shekhawati's most peaceful option, which is no doubt why—together with its unusual architecture—it's featured in the glossy coffee-table tome *Hip Hotels: Escape.* Ethnic accommodations consist primarily of circular mud-thatch huts, their organic shapes charmingly decorated with tribal motifs—stark white on dark brown—making features of even the air-conditioning units. Beds are covered in pretty embroidered linen traditional in the area—in fact, almost everything in each hut has been sourced from the Shekhawati. The rustic charm is endearing, though some may find the hard mud beds and thin mattresses a bit uncomfortable; if you do, ask the hotel for an extra mattress and they'll gladly provide one. Our recommendation is to book the suite right next to the pool—it makes no overtures to the tribal theme, being squared off and comfortably furnished with a mix of colonial-era antiques, and it's huge, with some great desert views, even from the bathroom. And you'll be hard-pressed to leave the pool, which is filled with fresh spring water, wonderfully soft, and a fabulous temperature (lounge chairs and fresh towels provided). As at Castle Mandawa, dinners are tasty buffets accompanied by entertainment and served under the stars, but this time on the manicured lawns; you can also request seating at the pool.

Mandawa, Jhunjhunu District, Shekhawati 333 704. Reservations: 📞 **0141/237-1194** or -4112. Fax 0141/237-2084 or 0141/510-6082. www.castlemandawa.com. desertresortmandawa@gmail.com. 60 units. Rs 3,500 ($85/£43) standard double; Rs 6,000 ($146/£74) deluxe cottage; Rs 9,000–Rs 15,000 ($220–$366/£111–£185) suite. Taxes extra. AE, MC, V. **Amenities:** Restaurant; bar; pool; Ayurvedic massage; laundry; billiard room; badminton; table tennis; croquet; card room; cultural performances; camel, horse, and jeep safaris; crafts shop; helipad; in-house dairy. *In room:* A/C, minibar (suites only), hair dryer (on request).

SHOPPING

Outside some havelis, caretakers sell Rajasthani puppets and postcards. You can see artisans and craftspeople at work in their shops in Mandawa, along Sonthaliya Gate and the bazaar. *Lac* bangles in bright natural colors make pretty gifts (from as little as Rs 15/40¢/20p each); if you find the sizes too small, have a pair custom-made while you wait. Another good buy is the camel-leather Rajasthani shoes *(jootis),* once a symbol of royalty. The shop at Mandawa's Desert Resort sells handicrafts in vivid colors, all produced by rural women of the region.

6 Pushkar

288km (179 miles) W of Jaipur

On the eastern edge of the vast Thar Desert, with a beautiful backdrop in the embracing arms of the Aravalli Hills, Pushkar is one of the most sacred—and atmospheric— towns in India. Legend has it that the holy lake at its center was created when Brahma dropped the petals of a lotus flower *(pushpa)* from his hand *(kar).* The tiny temple town that sprung up on the lake shores remains an important pilgrimage site for Hindus, its population swollen dramatically in recent years by the hippies who came for a few days and never left—a sore point for visitors who remember its untouched charm, and a real nuisance for first-time travelers who now discover a town steeped in commercial prospectors who thrive on making a quick buck, often at the expense of Pushkar's spiritual roots. Their presence has transformed the sleepy desert town into a semi-permanent trance party, however, with *bhang* (marijuana) lassis imbibed at the myriad tiny eateries, falafels on every menu, long-bearded rabbis on bicycles, boys perfectly dressed up like Shiva posing for photographs, and world music pumping from

ACCOMMODATIONS ■
Bharatpur Palace **1**
Jagat Palace **4**
Pushkar Bagh **7**
Pushkar Palace **2**

DINING ◆
Baba **5**
Sai Baba Restaurant **6**
Sun-Set Café **3**

ⓘ Information
✉ Post Office

speakers that line the street bazaar that runs along the lake's northern edge. This street bazaar is the center of all activity in Pushkar and incidentally one of the best shopping experiences in Rajasthan, where you can pick up the most gorgeous throwaway gear, great secondhand books, and mountains of CDs at bargain prices.

Pushkar is something akin to Varanasi, only without the awful road traffic—it really is possible to explore the town entirely on foot, and outside the annual camel *mela* (fair) it doesn't have the same claustrophobic crowds you find in Varanasi. What you will find exasperating, however, is the tremendous commercialization of just about everything—particularly "spirituality"—except without service standards to match. It takes about 45 minutes to walk around the holy lake and its 52 *ghats*. Built to represent each of the Rajput Maharajas who constructed their "holiday homes" on its banks, *ghats* are broad sets of stairs from where Hindu pilgrims take ritual baths to cleanse their souls. Note that you will need a "Pushkar Passport" to perambulate without harassment (see "Passport to Pushkar: Saying Your Prayers," below), that shoes need to be removed 9m (30 ft.) from the holy lake (bring cheap flip-flops if you're worried about losing them), and that photography of bathers is prohibited.

Surrounding the lake and encroaching on the hills that enhance the town's wonderful sense of remoteness are some 500 temples, of which the one dedicated to Brahma, said to be 2,000 years old, is the most famous, not least because it's one of only a handful in

Finds The Dargah Sharif & Other Ajmer Gems

Ajmer is not an attractive town, and most foreigners experience it only as a jumping-off point to the pilgrim town of Pushkar. However, it is worthwhile to plan your journey so that you can spend a few hours exploring Ajmer's fascinating sights (particularly the Dargah, one of the most spiritually resonant destinations in India) before you head the short 11km (7 miles) over a mountain pass to the laid-back atmosphere of Pushkar and its superior selection of accommodations.

Founded in the 7th century and strategically located within striking distance of the Mewar (Udaipur) and Marwar (Jodhpur) dynasties, as well as encompassing most of the major trade routes, Ajmer has played a pivotal role in the affairs of Rajasthan over the years. The Mughal emperors realized that only by holding this city could they increase their power base in Rajasthan. This is principally why the great Mughal emperor Akbar courted the loyalty of the nearby Amber/Jaipur court, marrying one of its daughters. But Ajmer was important on an emotional and spiritual level too, for only by gaining a foothold in Ajmer could Akbar ensure a safe passage for Muslim pilgrims to **Dargah Sharif (Khwaja Moin-ud-Din Chisti's Dargah).** The great Sufi saint Khwaja Moin-ud-Din Chisti, "protector of the poor," was buried here in 1235.

Said to possess the ability to grant the wishes and desires of all those who visit it, the **Dargah Sharif** ★★ is the most sacred Islamic shrine in India, and a pilgrimage here is considered second in importance only to a visit to Mecca. After a living member of the Sufi sect, Sheikh Salim Chisti, blessed Akbar with the prophecy of a much-longed-for son (Emperor Jahangir, father of Shah Jahan, builder of the Taj), Emperor Akbar himself made the pilgrimage many times, traveling on foot from distant Fatehpur Sikri and presenting the shrine with cauldrons (near the entrance) large enough to cook food for 5,000 people. It was not only Akbar and his offspring who made the pilgrimage—even the Hindu Rajputs came to pay homage to "the divine soul" that lies within.

Today the shrine still attracts hundreds of pilgrims every day, swelling to thousands during special occasions such as Urs Mela (Oct/Nov), the anniversary of Akbar's death. Leaving your shoes at the entrance (Rs 10/25¢/15p at exit), you pass through imposing **Nizam Gate** and smaller **Shahjahani Gate;** to the right is **Akbar's mosque,** and opposite is the equally imposing **Buland Darwaza.** Climb the steps to take a peek into the **two huge cauldrons** (3m/ 10 ft. round) that flank the gates—they come into their own at Urs when they are filled to the brim with a rice dish that is then distributed to the poor. To the right is **Mehfil Khana,** built in 1888 by the Nizam of Hyderabad. From here you enter another gateway into the courtyard, where you will find another mosque on the right, this one built by Shah Jahan in his characteristic white marble. You'll also see the great **Chisti's Tomb**—the small building topped by a marble dome and enclosed by marble lattice screens. In front of the tomb, the *qawwali* singers are seated, every day repeating the same beautiful haunting melodies (praising the saint) that have been sung for centuries. Everywhere, people abase themselves and sing, their eyes closed, hands spread wide on the floor or clutching their chests, while others feverishly pray and knot bits of fabrics to the latticework of the tomb or shower it with flowers. The scene is moving, the sense of faith palpable and, unlike the Dargah in Delhi, the atmosphere welcoming (though it's best to be discreet: no insensitive clicking of cameras or loud talking). Entry is free, but donations, paid to the office in the main courtyard, are welcome and are directly distributed to the poor. Entered off Dargah Bazaar, the Dargah is open daily, from 4 or 5am to 9 or 10pm (except during prayer times) depending on the season.

Having laid claim to Ajmer through a diplomatic marriage, Akbar built a red-sandstone fort he called **Daulat Khana (Abode of Riches)** in 1572. This was later renamed the Magazine by the British, who maintained a large garrison here, having also realized Ajmer's strategic importance. In 1908 it was again transformed, this time into the largely missable **Rajputana Museum** (small fee; Sat–Thurs 10am–4:30pm). The fort is significant mostly from a historical perspective, for it is here in 1660 that the British got a toehold in India when Sir Thomas Roe, representative of the British East India Company, met Emperor Jahangir and gained his permission to establish the first British factory at Surat.

The British also established a number of first-rate educational institutions, particularly **Mayo College** ⟨ℛ⟩, known as the Eton of the East. Originally designed to educate only the sons of the aristocracy, it opened its doors in 1875 to princes arriving on elephant-back, followed by retinues of 1,000 servants. The school is worth visiting, even just to view the building from the road; it's a superb example of Indo-Saracenic architecture, with much symbolic detailing. The sun and the moon, for instance (featured on the college hall roof and on the school coat of arms), signify the mythical descent of the maharajas (see "Once Were Warriors: The History of the Rajput," earlier in this chapter). To enter the school, you will need to get the principal's permission (with a bit of patience, this can be arranged through the gate attendant).

Another Ajmer attraction definitely worth seeing is **Svarna Nagari Hall** ⟨ℛℛ⟩ behind the Jain Nasiyan Temple in Anok Chowk. It's a totally unassuming building from the outside, but ascend the stairs to the second floor and you gaze down upon a fantasy world; a breathtaking display that fills the double-volume hall with tiny gilded figures celebrating scenes from Jain mythology. Sadly, no guide is available to explain what it all means, but the workmanship and sheer scale of the display are spellbinding.

Tips **Passport to Pushkar: Saying Your Prayers**

Proof of Pushkar's charm lies in the passport control as you enter the town—many foreigners (mostly Israeli hippies, hence the inclusion of falafels and pitas on the menu of even the most traditional Brahmin eatery) have come to experience its idyllic location and quaint, laid-back vibe and have never left, marrying locals and starting small businesses. As a result, there is now a moratorium on the length of time you can stay—a maximum of 3 months. So even though this measure is not always enforced, have your passport on hand as you enter. For those who wish to walk onto the *ghats* lining the lake, you'll need an entirely different kind of passport: Brahmin priests will bully you into performing *puja*—prayers that involve a scattering of flowers into the lake—after which you will be expected to make a hefty donation (inquire at your hotel for the going rate or you will almost certainly be ripped off). The priest will then tie a thin red thread around your wrist, which you can brandish at the next Brahmin priest who will almost certainly approach you, but who will quickly retreat upon seeing your "passport." To experience Pushkar from a pilgrim's perspective, gain a closer insight into what makes this an important place for Hindu pilgrims, and gain your wrist thread without being ripped off, call on **Giriraj** (© **94-1430-0053**; *puja* fee Rs 150/$3.65/£1.85), a local priest who is also a licensed guide. His English isn't perfect, but he can throw some light on the history and background of the area, and help out with practical information; he charges Rs 350 ($8.55/£4.35) a-half day, and Rs 500 ($12/£6.20) a full day.

India dedicated to the Hindu Lord of Creation. The doors to the enshrined deity are shut between 1:30 and 3pm, but you can wander around the temple courtyard during these hours. The other two worth noting (but a stiff 50-min. climb to reach) are dedicated to his consorts: It is said that Brahma was cursed by his first wife, Savitri, when he briefly took up with another woman, Gayatri—to this day, the temple of Savitri sits sulking on a hill overlooking the temple town, while across the lake, on another hill, no doubt nervous of retribution, the Gayatri Temple keeps a lookout. Ideally, Savitri should be visited at sunset, while a visit to Gayatri should coincide with the beautiful sunrise. ***Note:*** The Vishnu temple, encountered as you enter town, is the only temple off-limits to non-Hindus, but photography is permitted from outside the temple gates.

Unless you're expecting authentic untouched India, Pushkar is a delight to visit any time of the year, with its laid-back, almost European atmosphere offset by the unique aromas of India and tons of tiny shops, temples, Brahmin eateries, and operators offering camel- and horseback safaris into the surrounding desert (camels are about Rs 100/$2.45/£1.25 per hr., Rs 400/$9.75/£4.95 full day; horses are Rs 250/$6.10/£3.10 per hr.). But the town is most famous for its annual *mela*—the largest camel fair in Asia. Attracting an estimated 200,000 rural traders, red-turbaned Rabari and Bhil tribal folk, pilgrims, and tourists, the *mela* stretches tiny Pushkar into sprawling villages of temporary campsites—interspersed with food stalls and open-air theaters—created solely to house, feed, and entertain the swollen population that flocks to the specially built amphitheater on the outskirts of the town to watch the races and attend the auctions. Like most desert destinations, however, it is at night that the atmosphere takes on an unreal intimacy, as pilgrims and tourists get to know each other around the many campfires, and Rajasthani dancers and traditional folk singers create a time-less backdrop. The Pushkar *mela* takes place in the Hindu month of Kartik, over the waxing and waning of the full moon that occurs in late October or in November.

On the evening of the full *mela* moon, as the desert sun sets behind the low-slung hills (a spectacular sight at the best of times), temple bells and drums call the devout to *puja,* and hundreds of pilgrims wade into the lake—believed to miraculously cleanse the soul—before lighting clay lamps and setting them afloat on its holy waters, the twinkling lights a surreal reflection of the desert night sky. If you're lucky enough to have booked a room at Pushkar Palace, you can watch this ancient ritual from a deck chair on the terrace (it can be quite a scramble to get a view from the *ghats* them-selves)—a wonderful sight and one of those mystic moments that make a trip to India among the most memorable of your life.

ESSENTIALS

VISITOR INFORMATION   Pushkar doesn't have its own tourist office. The rather useless **RTDC office** is located at the very mediocre RTDC Hotel Sarovar (*C* **0145/277-2040**), and is open daily from 9am to 5pm.

GETTING THERE   Pushkar lies about 3 hours west of Jaipur; a deluxe bus here costs about Rs 80 ($1.95/£1).

GETTING AROUND   Pushkar is easily explored on foot. There is no public trans-port system (cycle- or auto-rickshaws) in town. If you prefer not to walk, the only option is to hire a private taxi, motorbike, or scooter (the latter costs around Rs 300/$7.35/£3.70 per day).

WHERE TO STAY

You really want to get a room overlooking the sacred lake—despite the early-morning and evening chanting calls to *puja* and blaring temple music, it's by far the most atmospheric location in Pushkar. Of the surprisingly limited options that offer direct lake views, Pushkar Palace (reviewed below) is the only luxurious option; for the rest you'll have to rough it (we're talking basic furnishings—a plastic chair and bed and the possibility of sharing a bathroom and toilet).

Far and away the best budget option in town is **Inn Seventh Heaven** *(R) (Value* (next to Mali ka Mandir; *C* **0145/510-5455;** www.inn-seventh-heaven.com; Rs 450–Rs 2,000/$11–$49/£6–£25), located in a 100-year-old haveli with rooms (with names like "Hilly Billy" and "Rapunzel") around a fountain and garden courtyard. Anoop, the enterprising young owner, has ensured that rooms are clean and dressed with some sense of style; despite its location (away from the lake), it has a pleasant, informal, homey feel, and the great second-floor restaurant does satisfying Indian food. If you plan well in advance, you can bag the most recently added room, "Asana," also the most expensive, but it's bright and situated on the roof, where there's a good view. It has antique furniture and four-poster beds (as do some of the other rooms).

If you want a truly peaceful option, far from the madding crowd (and ideal if you're traveling with children), the brand-new **Pushkar Bagh** *(R) (C* **0145/277-3929;** 24-hr. reservations: 94-1403-0669; www.thepushkarbagh.com), with 15 luxury cottages and 15 very smart en-suite "tents" (with stone walls and canopy roofs), is a great option. Overlooking the camel *mela* grounds, bordered by open fields, with views of the surrounding hills, this is probably the most upmarket option anywhere near Pushkar, with an emphasis on relaxation and an atmosphere that's akin to an intimate resort. Buildings are constructed from pink sandstone, and there are lovely courtyards to relax with a drink (which you won't find anywhere around the sacred lake). Since you're pretty cut off from the town and its spiritual-cum-hippie energy, activities like jeep and camel safaris are thrown into the mix to keep you occupied; tribal village tours and traditional evening meals (called *mehfils*) are a highlight. There's also a spa, and the lawns are a fine place for yoga. Cottages cost $100 (£50) double, and tents cost $155 (£128); rates soar to around $300 (£150) during the *mela*.

Note that if you haven't prebooked well in advance for the Pushkar *mela,* which takes place when the full moon appears in late October or early November, finding a decent bed anywhere in town can be hell. During the fair, the RTDC sets up additional accommodations in the **"Tourist Village Camp,"** with huts, Swiss tents, and standard tents. Rates vary considerably depending on dates, but these options are infinitely preferable to the "caravan dormitories" also on offer.

Note: All accommodations have different tariffs for the period of the Pushkar Fair, anything from double to 10 times the normal rate.

Pushkar Palace ★★ (Value   This pretty 400-year-old palace—its thick white walls reflected in the holy waters of the lake—is by far the best place to stay in Pushkar, not least because of the extensive renovations undertaken in 2002. The best rooms are the suites below the terrace (nos. 101–105)—these are the closest to the lake, with windows that provide serene (or surreal, depending on the time of day) views directly onto it; do bear in mind, however, that such proximity to the lake also means picking up most sounds that occur on or near it. Room no. 102 is a particularly good option—it's a corner suite with additional windows. Alternatively, ask for a suite with a balcony. In the deluxe category, the corner rooms (nos. 209, 309, and 409), despite being significantly smaller but comfortably furnished, have the best views—you can literally lie in bed and watch the sunsets, which are stupendous. This is, in fact, one of the best reasons to stay here: the views of the lake, temples, and hills, behind which the sun sets, are both thrilling and exclusive to guests. Even if you don't have a room with the best of views (most are set behind the open-air corridors that link the rooms), you can enjoy it all from the terrace, where waiters are on hand to provide the necessary liquid refreshments (be aware that, as elsewhere, no alcohol is allowed). Pushkar Palace also arranges a **Royal Desert Camp** during the *mela* ($150/£75 double, with meals), which is the most luxurious temporary accommodations in town.

The Palace has a sister establishment, **Jagat Palace,** a relatively luxurious property built on the outskirts of town. The same rates apply for an experience that's somewhat isolated and disconnected from Pushkar, but with the added incentive of a fabulous pool. The design pays homage to Hindu elements, with really lovely rooms furnished with antiques and modern amenities, but many of the public interior spaces are gloomy, the soulless atmosphere clearly designed to deal with large groups of package tourists. That said, it's probably the most luxurious hotel option if Pushkar Palace is full, though you'll need a car or taxi to get to town; if you want to walk, it's a 15-minute trek along a dusty main road.

Pushkar 305 022, Rajasthan. © **0145/277-2001** or -2402. Fax 0145/277-2226 or -2952. www.hotelpushkarpalace.com. hppalace@datainfosys.net. Pushkar Palace: 53 units. Jagat Palace: 72 units. Rs 3,400 ($83/£42) deluxe double; Rs 6,600 ($161/£82) suite; Rs 600 ($15/£8) extra bed. Taxes extra. AE, DC, MC, V. **Amenities:** Restaurant; travel desk; room service; laundry; doctor-on-call; camel/horse safaris; Jagat has 2 restaurants, pool, Ayurvedic massage. *In room:* A/C, TV, minibar.

WHERE TO DINE

Dining options are plentiful but far from spectacular, catering largely to budget travelers more concerned with imbibing marijuana than partaking of quality cuisine; if you're staying at Seventh Heaven or Pushkar Palace, you'd be well advised to make full use of their dining facilities. However, if you're up for a culinary adventure of the backpacking kind, you'll find numerous strange and unusual places around the lake, many of them proud of their multifarious global cuisines, all fairly Indianized. Do be aware that you won't find meat, eggs, or alcohol served anywhere near the sacred lake of Pushkar.

Sai Baba Haveli Restaurant is a favorite with young foreign tourists and aging hippies—it serves gratifying baked goods and decent (egg-less) croissants (although their idea of espresso is simply stronger-than-usual coffee). We're sure most people come here because of the liberal attitude toward smoking intoxicants, which tends to happen in the garden, lorded over by a statue of Sai Baba ("the living god") himself; on Saturday nights, festivities include a desert gypsy (Kalbeliya) dance program and party. There's also a rooftop restaurant. Nearby, closer to the post office, is **Baba,** which feels like a hippie grotto in which you're surrounded by psychedelic murals of green pixies and luminous aliens. Claiming that all their food is "cooked with love," the laid-back staff (an old man hands you a grime-laden menu and a pad to jot down your own order) serve everything from Lebanese to Indonesian dishes, and they're now purporting to make wood-fired pizzas, which are cheap (around $2/£1) but difficult to chew. **Prems Venkatesh,** a basic eatery overseen by a Brahmin who cooks his delicious chapatis with vegetables of the day and *dal* over a wood-burning fire, is widely considered the best in town for cheap Indian food; ask anyone to direct you there, but don't expect it to be sparkling clean. *Beware: Bhang* (or "special") *lassi* is served at numerous outlets around Pushkar; these seem innocent, and invariably taste sweet, but the narcotic after-effects take a while to set in and will have you losing all sense of reality (and direction). Be sure you know your way back to your hotel.

Moments Sunset over Pushkar

The aptly named **Sun-Set Café** (on the same road as Pushkar Palace, just a little farther along; ℂ **0145/277-2382**) has just a few tables on the popular terrace overlooking the lake (there is much more space indoors); get here early if you want to enjoy the spectacle of the sun over the lake with something cold to drink (there's alcohol-free Beck's beer). Although the food is middling (the vegetable curry isn't too bad) and service can be unbearably slow, the late-afternoon/early-evening vibe here represents one of those real tourist moments, complete with glaring cows, pigeons strung along the power cables, a nest of parked motorcycles, and an array of street musicians (which may include some wonderfully practiced drumming; tip appreciated) who show up to help make fantastically kitsch magic of the daily setting of the sun. As the sun fades, an assortment of neon lights and fires around the *ghats,* temples, and havelis on the far side of the lake add a shimmering backlight to the scene.

SHOPPING

The main thoroughfare, **Sadar Bazaar,** is just over 1km (a half-mile) long, and is lined with tiny shops selling ridiculously cheap (though usually low-quality) clothing, jewelry, leather sandals, excellent music (anything from Hindu temple to Hindi pop to global trance), and the best selection of books in Rajasthan. This is definitely the place to come with empty bags—its almost cheaper to stock up on a new wardrobe here than pay hotel laundry fees, and you can pick up a huge selection of Indian music to listen to back home and make you long to return.

7 Udaipur

405km (251 miles) SW of Jaipur; 260km (161 miles) S of Jodhpur

The "City of Sunrise," often described as the most romantic city in India, was built around four lakes, the placid blue waters reflecting ethereal white palaces and temples, beyond which shimmer the distant Aravalli Hills. Udaipur has a real sense of space and peace, and the city is mercifully free of the kind of intense capitalist hucksterism that so marks the Indian street experience. This may have something to do with its proud Hindu history, for the city is not only known for its gracious palaces, temperate climate, and beautiful views, but for maintaining a fierce independence from even the most powerful outside influences. It fought bloody wars to repel Turkish, Afghan, Tartar, and Mongol invaders and rejected allegiances with the Mughals, only to acquiesce in 1818, when the state grudgingly came under British political control.

Capital of the legendary Sisodias of Mewar, believed to be direct descendants of the Sun (an insignia you'll see everywhere), Udaipur was built on the shores of Lake Pichola by Udai Singh II in 1559, who returned here after the third and final sacking of the previous Mewar stronghold, Chittaurgarh (see "Top Excursions," later in this chapter). Udai Singh's son, Pratap, kept the Mughal invaders at bay for a further 25 years and is said to have been so disgusted by Man Singh and the Jaipur raja's obsequious relations with the Mughals that, after one historic meeting, he had the ground where Man Singh had walked washed with Ganges water in order to purify it. Maharana Fateh Singh was also the only Rajput prince who refused to attend the Delhi Durbar held for King George V in 1911, despite the fact that the British had acknowledged him as the head of the princely states of Rajputana.

Much of Udaipur, particularly the old part located on the shores of Lake Pichola, is where you'll find the city's most striking landmarks—the towering **City Palace** and **Lake Palace**—and it still feels remarkably like a 16th-century Rajput stronghold, with the benevolent maharana still treated like a reigning king by his devoted and loyal subjects. You can witness this firsthand by attending the temple at nearby Eklingji on a Monday evening, when the maharana—the 76th ruler of one of the world's oldest surviving dynasties—often joins his subjects to pay his respects to Shiva.

Try to spend at least 3 to 4 days in Udaipur, whether you spend them aimlessly wandering its mazelike lanes, taking a slow cruise on Pichola Lake, exploring the giant medieval fortress and palaces that rise from its shores, or setting off to see the intricately carved Jain temples of Ranakpur and the ancient fort of Kumbhalgarh—or whether you do nothing but loll on a comfortable divan overlooking the lake. You'll find the City of Sunrise the most relaxing part of your sojourn in Rajasthan.

Udaipur

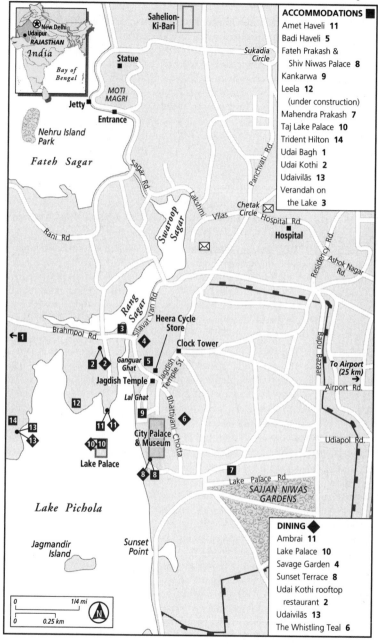

ESSENTIALS

VISITOR INFORMATION   Rajasthan Tourism Development Corporation (RTDC), though inconveniently located in the Tourist Office at Fateh Memorial in Suraj Pol (© 0294/241-1535; Mon–Sat 10am–5pm), can arrange accommodations, licensed guides, maps, and brochures. Ask for the helpful young Yogesh Joshi in room no. 1, who can caution you about the latest scams to avoid. You can also call the RTDC Hotel Kajri at © 0294/241-0501 through -0503 for tourist information and assistance. Satellite tourist offices can be found at the airport (© 0294/265-5433; open at flight times) and at the railway station, which was scheduled to reopen once new train services begin (see "Getting There: By Train/Bus," below).

The most convenient place to draw money against your credit card/ATM card is near the Jagdish Temple (City Palace Rd.). There is also an ICICI Bank next to the Jet Airways office (Madhuban), an SBI ATM next to Indian Airlines (Delhi Gate), and several others near Town Hall, Bapu Bazaar. There are two convenient LKP foreign exchange offices on Lake Palace Road (next to Rang Niwas Palace Hotel) and near Jagdish Temple. A useful private hospital is **American International Hospital** on Kothi Baugh, Bhatt Ji Ki (© 0294/242-8701 through -8704).

GETTING THERE   By Air   Dabok Airport is 25km (16 miles) from Udaipur. As always, **Jet Airways** is the preferable option (© 0294/256-1105-60), connecting the city with Delhi, Mumbai (both 1 hr., 15 min.), and Jaipur (45 min.). **Indian Airlines** (© 0294/265-5453 airport, 0294/241-0999 Delhi Gate) covers the same routes, as well as Jodhpur. A regular non-air-conditioned taxi into town should cost about Rs 375 ($9.15/£6.65). **Parul Tours and Travel** (details below) offers air-conditioned taxis from the airport to the city for Rs 475 ($12/£5.90).

By Train/Bus   The **Mewar Express** departs Delhi's Nizamuddin station at 7pm and arrives at Udaipur City station at 7am the following morning; significant stops en route are Bharatpur, Sawai Madhopur (for Ranthambhore), and Chittaurgaur. There's an evening train from Jaipur, departing 9:40pm, which arrives at 7am the following morning. There are deluxe bus connections from Jaipur, Jodhpur, and Ahmedabad (roads are in fairly good condition). In the unlikely event that you've opted for a bus, you will most likely be dropped off just north of the City Railway Station.

GETTING AROUND   The best way to get around the main tourist sights (the area surrounding the City Palace) is on foot, but if you want to spend a rather satisfying day taking in all the sights in the city, consider renting a **moped** or **bicycle** from **Heera Cycle Store & Tours & Travels** (inside Hotel Badi Haveli, 86 Gangaur Ghat Rd., easy walking distance from Jagdish Temple; © 0294/513-0625; copy of passport and driver's license required; daily 7:30am–9pm).

For journeys farther afield, hiring a car with driver is probably the only way to go; you will certainly need one for the recommended trips described below. To hire one for the day, or for a self-planned tour in Rajasthan, head for the RTDC at Suraj Pol (see "Visitor Information," above). This is also where to check out the range of half- or full-day government tours on offer, though note that organized tours can be too rushed or too slow, and can place you in close contact with odious fellow travelers; the quality of guides often leaves a lot to be desired as well. Should you wish to hire a car and driver from one of the many travel and tour agents that are more conveniently located in the Old City (see recommendations below), you might want to call the RTDC just to discern their going rate, but we'd urge you to waste no time in contacting the very efficient Ramesh

Dashora, proprietor of **Parul Tours and Travel,** opposite Jagat Niwas Hotel, at 32 Lal Ghat (© 0294/242-1697; info@rajasthantravelbycab.com); he offers English-speaking guides (Rs 1,000/$24/£12 per day), plus A/C Ambassadors (or Indicas) for Rs 1,500 ($37/£19) for a full day; this includes 250km (155 miles) with each additional kilometer costing Rs 6 (15¢/10p), and there's an overnight fee of Rs 150 ($3.65/£1.85). More substantial vehicles will push prices up considerably. You can even reserve a car online (www.rajasthantravelbycab.com). Alternatively, call **Mohan Singh** (© 98-2938-1935), who drives an air-conditioned Ambassador. He understands enough English to take you sightseeing and is very well versed in routes and attractions. You can probably arrange a good deal with him for the duration of your stay.

FESTIVALS   Udaipur's biggest festivals are the **Mewar Festival,** held every March or April, and the **Holi Festival,** held every March. October's Ashwa Poojan is another celebration worth inquiring about (your hotel should be able to advise you on exact dates and where best to experience the festivities). The **Gangaur Festival** is celebrated with special zeal by the women of Udaipur (end of Mar to Apr). During this festival, unmarried women pray to the goddess Gauri (manifestation of Parvati, Shiva's wife) for a good husband, while the married pray for the well-being of their husbands and a happy married life. Women decorate their hands and feet with *mehendi* (tattoos of henna paste) and carry colorful images of Gauri and terra-cotta lamps on their heads as they dance and sing songs in street processions. At the end of the festival they break these lamp-pots and celebrate with a feast. Festivities last 18 days and include many colorful processions and a fireworks display.

WHAT TO SEE & DO

To make Udaipur's intriguing and valorous history really come alive, consider taking on the services of **Arun Achariya** (© 0294/252-5967), easily one of the best guides in the city, and highly recommended.

If your idea of a holiday is lying by a pool with a good book, only visits to the City and Lake palaces (see "Top Attractions," below) need top your list of things to do in Udaipur proper. The city is the ideal base for a number of day trips, however. The most highly recommended is a round-trip through Kumbhalgarh Wildlife Sanctuary and Fort, taking in the temples of Ranakpur along the way, and possibly stopping at Eklingji on the way back (see "Top Excursions," below). The lovely, scenic drive passes picture-postcard rural hamlets and fields of mustard, scattered with boys tending cattle and women clad in bright saris tilling the soil.

For those interested in seeing more of the city, the following day tour—to be tailored to your needs—provides an overview of the top sights in and around Udaipur. Start your day by exploring the City Palace, which usually towers over the city's raison d'etre, Lake Pichola. Two more palaces can be seen on what would be the islands of Jag Niwas and Jag Mandir (see "Top Attractions," below). Exit through Tripolia Gate to explore the Old City of Udaipur, which sprawls north of the palace. **Jagdish Temple** ⊕, the largest in Udaipur, is its chief attraction. Despite some lovely exterior carvings (including hidden erotic pieces your guide will point out), the temple itself is rather ordinary (if you've seen a number of them elsewhere, that is), but its attraction lies in its massive popularity. The temple has seen a constant stream of people who come to worship Lord Jagannath, an aspect of Vishnu (the black stone image enshrined within), since it first opened its doors in 1652. *Aarti* takes place at around 10am, 7:30pm, and 10pm—try to time your visit for when the *bhajans* (prayer-songs) make for a most atmospheric experience. (Remove your shoes before entering, and an attendant will look after them for a small tip; no photography inside.) The bronze half-man, half-bird statue of Garuda outside is the vehicle of Vishnu. From Jagdish Temple you can wander the mazelike streets of old Udaipur, admiring the whitewashed havelis and popping into tiny shops before reaching the clock tower that marks the northern edge. Near the lake edge, at Gangaur Ghat, you can visit the **Bagore-ki-Haveli Museum** (© 0294/242-2567), a restored royal haveli with plenty of idiosyncratic design detail that's now part of a museum and cultural center; it's best visited on evenings for the nightly music and dance performances. If you haven't picked up a bicycle from **Heera Cycle Store** (86 Gangaur Ghat Rd., near Jagdish Temple), catch a taxi from here (or have your driver waiting) to **Bharatiya Lok Kala Museum** (Panch Vati Rd.; entry Rs 35/85¢/45p, Rs 20/50¢/25p camera; daily 9am–6pm), Udaipur's unofficial "Puppet Museum" (Rajasthan being the birthplace of this favored Indian storytelling medium), where you can watch a good show, staged almost hourly throughout the day. The best is held each evening at 6pm (Rs 30/75¢/40p) with traditional folk dances added on (though note that most hotels have a puppet show as part of their evening's entertainment). The folk museum also contains models, instruments, and photographs documenting other local traditions and crafts, but for this you're better off visiting **Shilpgram** (© 0294/241-9023; www.shilpgram.org). This rather faux rural arts-and-crafts "village" is located 3km (2 miles) out of town; follow the road that runs along the north of Fateh Sagar Lake; daily 11am to 7pm, folk dances 11am and 7pm; admission is just Rs 25 (60¢/30p), but you'll pay for extras such as camel rides and the use of cameras. Created to "promote and preserve the traditional architecture, music, and crafts of the tribal village of western India," Shilpgram has a distinctly artificial feel but interesting cultural performances; you can also ride a camel and browse for tribal knickknacks that the "traditionally" attired craftspeople will be only too delighted to finally off-load. If you're in a particularly touristy mood, you can dress up in a traditional Rajasthani outfit and have your picture taken. Along the way, stop for a brief wander through **Saheliyon-ki-Bari (Garden of the Maids of Honour)** north of Bharatiya Lok Kala Museum—turn left at Sukadia Circle. It's open daily 8am to 7:30pm (small admission fee). Created by Sangram Singh in the 18th century for the ladies of his household (some say to re-create the monsoon climate for his sickly daughter), this is billed as Udaipur's finest garden, but it suffers from neglect, with none of the fountains operating. Still, it's a peaceful place, and the array of established indigenous trees may interest keen botanists. If the monsoon has been good and lake levels in Udaipur have risen, from Saheliyon-ki-Bari make your way to nearby **Fateh Sagar Lake,** passing **Moti Magri** on your left, atop which is the statue of Maharana Pratap and his beloved horse, Chetak (largely missable, but the views from here are lovely). Fateh Sagar, the large lake that lies north of Lake Pichola, has a small island garden of its own, the rather neglected **Nehru Park.**

An excellent place to view the sunset is **Sajjan Garh (Monsoon Palace),** built by the Maharana Sajjan Singh as an observatory in the late 19th century. You can enter the palace building by tipping the guard (though it's a restricted security area). Head to one of the alcoves from where views of the surrounding mountains are breathtaking. If this sounds like one stop too many after a rather exhausting day, head straight for one of the rooftop or garden restaurants in the city; get a table on the **Sunset Terrace** (near the Dovecoat lobby of the Fateh Prakash hotel); or sit on the "deck" at the Lake Palace, where you can relax with a drink as the sun sinks behind the distant jagged outline of the Aravalli Hills.

TOP ATTRACTIONS

City Palace and Museum ✫✫✫   For full effect, the staggering, monumental City Palace complex is best viewed from either of the islands on Lake Pichola; the palace's cream-colored stone walls tower some 30m (98 ft.) above its mirrorlike reflection in the lake and stretch almost 250m (820 ft.) across its eastern shore. The 300-year-old complex actually comprises 11 palaces (or *mahals*) built by its successive maharanas, making it by far the largest palace complex in Rajasthan. Purchase the useful guidebook at the entrance (or hire the services of a guide through your hotel; those who hang around the ticket office charge Rs 300/$7.35/£3.70 for a 2-hr. tour) to help you maneuver the sprawling museum, much of it connected by a maze of rather claustrophobic tunnel-like stairways designed to confuse and slow down potential invaders. (This is why it's essential to get here as soon as the palace doors open—finding yourself trapped between busloads of jeering families who mysteriously come to regular standstills in these airless passages is sheer purgatory.) The entire palace is a delight, but highlights include the large peacock mosaics in the 17th-century **Mor (Peacock) Chowk;** mirror-encrusted **Moti Mahal;** the glass and porcelain figures of **Manak (Ruby) Mahal,** which has a central garden; the collection of miniatures featuring Krishna legends in **Krishna Vilas** (dedicated to a 16-year-old princess who committed suicide here); exquisite Zenana Mahal (Palace of the Queens); and the Chinese and Dutch ceramics of **Chini Mahal.** When the lake levels are normal, the cusped windows provide superb views of the serene waters of Pichola Lake, on which white-marble Lake Palace appears to float. The last two palaces built, both now open to visitors wishing to overnight or dine, are the grand but rather staid **Shiv Niwas** and gorgeous **Fateh Prakash.** The latter can be visited for high tea (a rather dull affair) to view the Durbar Hall's royal portrait gallery, with its massive chandeliers and Venetian mirrors, and to see the Crystal Gallery, which has a huge collection of rare cut-crystal furniture and ornaments imported by Maharana Sajjan Singh from England in 1877. (For more on these palaces, see "Where to Stay" and "Where to Dine," later in this section.) Vintage-car lovers should ask about the tour of the Mewar family's Classic Car Collection. Set aside 3 hours to do the palace justice.

City Palace. ℂ 0294/241-9021. Rs 50 ($1.25/65p) Jagdish Temple end, Rs 75 ($1.85/95p) via Hotel Fateh Prakash; Rs 200 ($4.90/£2.50) any camera. Daily 9:30am–4:30pm. **Crystal Gallery** Rs 350 ($8.55/£4.35); daily 10am–1pm and 3–8pm; no photography.

Lake Pichola & Lake Palace ✫✫✫   Most beautiful at sunrise and sunset, Lake Pichola reflects what seems to be a picture-perfect inversion of the many whitewashed and cream buildings that rise majestically from its shores and islands, known locally as Jag Niwas and Jag Mandir. Jag Niwas island is entirely covered by the Lake Palace, built by the maharana in 1740 as a summer idyll and today perhaps the most romantic—certainly the most photographed—hotel in India. What you will see if the lake remains parched is a magnificent palace that should be floating on water but instead sits on a vast, dry lake bed. A little farther south is the slightly larger Jag Mandir, upon which domed Gul Mahal stands. Famous as the star location in the movie *Octopussy,* it has also been a place of refuge: first for the young prince Shah Jahan who—in a typical Mughal ascension—was plotting to overthrow his father, Jahangir (incidentally, Udaipuris believe that Gul Mahal is what later inspired Jahan to build Taj Mahal); and later for European women and children, whom Maharana Swaroop Singh protected during the Mutiny. You can catch a boat to Jag Mandir from the City Palace (Bansi Ghat) jetty, but once you have alighted, there's not much to do but purchase overpriced refreshments;

> ## *Fun Fact* Indian Solutions to a Global Problem
>
> The current Maharana Shri Arvind Singhji, 76th custodian of the house of
> Mewar, combines philanthropic interests with a keen capitalist eye—he owns
> some 12 heritage hotels throughout Rajasthan, from which a sizable part of
> the profits are funneled back into his **Maharana of Mewar Charitable Foun-
> dation**. Long concerned about the effects of global warming, particularly in
> Udaipur, which has seen a significant rise in average temperatures, this par-
> ticular descendant of the sun has perhaps fulfilled his destiny by helping to
> pioneer the world's first solar-powered water taxi and the world's first solar
> rickshaw, which were successfully tested in Udaipur, with the ultimate aim of
> making Udaipur a solar-powered city. Because 86% of all the vehicles in India
> are two-stroke two-wheelers (motorcycles, mopeds, gas-powered scooters),
> which are responsible for a major percentage of the country's carbon dioxide
> emissions, this could go a long way toward solving India's pollution problems.
> In 2005, the foundation won the prestigious Eurostar prize for its work on
> solar-powered vehicles. Now we only hope to actually see some of them on
> the roads.

the trip around the lake includes a visit to Sunset Terrace (near Dovecoat Wing) or the
Lake Palace Hotel. If you haven't booked a room at the hotel, make sure you come for
dinner—the views alone are worth it, and the opulent and elegant setting is sublime (see
"Where to Stay" and "Where to Dine," later in this section).

To make a table reservation at Lake Palace, call ✆ **0294/252-7961**. To charter a boat, or book a seat on one, call
✆ **92-1473-2149**; Launches are from Lal Ghat and there are prices to suit all budgets.

TOP EXCURSIONS
A number of recommended excursions from Udaipur can either be tackled as round-
trips or as stopovers on your way elsewhere in the state. The first option is the easiest,
a half-day excursion (at most) that takes in some of the most important temples in
Udaipur. The second option—which you can combine with the first for a rather grueling but very satisfying round-trip—takes you to the awesome Jain temples at
Ranakpur through Kumbhalgarh Wildlife Sanctuary, past wonderful pastoral scenes
that haven't changed since medieval times, to view magnificent Kumbhalgarh Fort.
From here you can either head northwest for Jodhpur or double back to Udaipur, possibly taking in the temples at Nathdwara, Nagda, and Eklingji. (If you're pressed for
time, leave out Nathdwara—beyond the superb examples of *pichhwai* paintings,
there's not much to see, as non-Hindus may not enter the temple.) To plan this as a
round-trip, you will need to hire a driver familiar with the distances and terrain, and
overnight along the way (see the listing for Kumbhalgarh Fort, below).

The third option is another long full-day trip, this time with the sole purpose of
viewing Chittaurgarh, site of the most legendary Mewar battles. From here you can
return to Udaipur or push on east to the little town of Bundi (see earlier in this chapter), and from there proceed to Jaipur or Ranthambhore National Park. For those
interested in an off-the-beaten-track experience to the south, the fourth option, relatively undiscovered Dungarpur Palace, is well worth the time, not least for Deco fans

who will relish overnighting in the family manse—Udai Bilas Palace, a living Deco museum—before returning to Udaipur. If Ranakpur's temples have whet your appetite for more, a fifth option, an excursion to the west ascending the Aravalli Hills to Mount Abu, the only hill station in Rajasthan and home to Dilwara—the most famous Jain temples in India—can also be tackled from Udaipur, though the distances will necessitate an overnight stay. Details of distances for all excursions are given below.

An excursion to an attraction that is not described in detail below, but which may interest birders or those in search of more peace, is **Jaisamand Lake,** the second-largest man-made lake in Asia, created in 1691 by Maharana Jai Singh and, thankfully, still containing water. Located a little over an hour away from Udaipur, it has a number of marble pavilions but is more famous for the many aquatic birds that have found a home in what is now **Jaisamand Wildlife Sanctuary.**

DAY TRIP 1: A HALF-DAY TEMPLE EXCURSION

Eklingji & Nagda Temples ⟨★★⟩ Housing a manifestation of Shiva, the god who guards the fortunes of the rulers of Mewar, Eklingji is a lovely marble complex made up of 108 temples, the first of which was built in A.D. 734 by Bappa Rawal, legendary founder of the Sisodia clan, who ruled the Mewar kingdom for hundreds of years. The entire complex, most of it rebuilt in the 15th century, has a wonderfully uplifting atmosphere, particularly during prayer times (see below), and never more so than on the Monday evenings when the Maharana of Udaipur is in town and comes to pay his respects here, walking among his subjects as a mere mortal despite the attendant bowing and scraping. The four-faced black lingam (phallic symbol) apparently marks the spot where Bappa Rawal (that's him riding the peacock) was given the title Darwan ("servant") of Eklingji by his guru; outside, facing Shiva, is Nandi, Shiva's vehicle. Wander around the temple complex and you'll find a number of carvings from the *Kama Sutra;* your explorations won't exceed 30 minutes. Deserted **Nagda,** which lies 2km (1¼ miles) north, is a far cry from this vibrant place of worship. All that survives of the site of the ancient capital of Mewar, which dates back to A.D. 626, are the ruins of the **Saas Bahu,** a 10th-century Vaishnavite twin temple (*Saas* meaning "mother-in-law" and *Bahu* "daughter-in-law") and the remains of Adbhutji Temple. Regrettably, the temples have been vandalized over the years and look much the worse for wear—unless you're of the archaeological bent, skip them if you're pushed for time.

22km (14 miles) north of Udaipur (30–40-min. drive one-way). Eklingji daily 4:15–6:45am, 10:30am–1:30pm, and 5:15–7:45pm. Prayer times: 15-min. *aartis* are performed at 5:30am, 8:15am, 9:15am, 3:30pm, 4:30pm, 5pm, and 6:30pm; a 45-min. *aarti* is performed at 11:30am.

Nathdwara ⟨★⟩ Said to be the second-richest temple in India, Nathdwara's **Shri Nathji Temple,** home to a 600-year-old black marble statue of Lord Krishna, is one of the most important pilgrimage sites in India, attracting thousands, particularly during the festivals of Diwali, Holi, and Janmashthami. According to legend, in 1669 as the statue was being carried from Mathura to protect it from the destructive blows of the pious Mughal emperor Aurangzeb, it fell off the wagon at this site; the carriers (no doubt pretty exhausted) took this as a sign and built the temple around the statue. That said, the interior is closed to non-Hindus, so many of you won't even get a glimpse of the statue. The main reason to visit is to view what many believe are the finest examples of *pichhwai* paintings that adorn the interior and exterior of the temple. Hand-spun cloth painted with vibrant scenes depicting Krishna's life, these were originally created to teach illiterate low castes (who in the past were also barred from entering the sacred inner sanctum). You can purchase your own *pichhwai* paintings in the local bazaar, or look for more examples in Udaipur. Note that this is also a center for traditional *meenakari* (enamel) work.

48km (30 miles) from Udaipur (1-hr. drive one-way).

DAY TRIP 2: A TEMPLE, A FORT & A WONDERFUL DRIVE

Ranakpur Temples ★★★   If you visit only one temple complex in Rajasthan, it should be Jain. Those at Ranakpur offer the finest examples of the complex and sustained levels of craftsmanship the Jains are renowned for, comparable in every way to the more famous Dilwara Temples at Mount Abu. If anything, a visit here is preferable—despite being a great deal more accessible, the area is infinitely more peaceful, with less traffic. Known for their aestheticism and religious fervor (Jains are not only strict vegetarians, but the most orthodox among them walk with care to ensure no hapless insect should die underfoot due to their carelessness, and wear permanent masks to protect even the tiniest bug from the possibility of being ingested), the Jains put all their passion (and not inconsiderable wealth) into the creation of ornately carved temples. The Ranakpur Temples are jaw-droppingly beautiful, with exquisitely detailed relief carvings (and strangely, a few pieces of tinfoil) covering every inch of pillar, wall, and ceiling. The main triple-volume Chaumukha Temple, built from 1446 and dedicated to Adinatha Rishabdeva, the first Jain *tirthankara*, or "Enlightened One," is surrounded by 66 subsidiary shrines; inside are 1,444 intricately carved pillars—not one of them the same. (Incidentally, the land was donated to the Jains by Rana Kumbha, the warrior who built 32 forts, of which Kumbhalgarh is the most famous.) Note that no leather items (including belts and handbags) are allowed on the premises, no photography of the statues or enshrined deities is allowed (general temple pictures are permitted), and you are requested to dress conservatively (legs and shoulders must be covered; you can hire garments at the ticket desk should you require). Jain customs also strictly forbid menstruating women from entering. *Note:* There are no good accommodations in the immediate vicinity; best to push on to the **Aodhi Hotel,** near Kumbhalgarh Fort (see below) or, if you're on your way to Jodhpur, **Rawla Narlai** or **Deogarh Mahal** (see "Traveling between Udaipur & Jaipur/Jodhpur," later in this section). If you want to grab an early lunch of authentic Jain food, make your way to the canteen-style eatery near the main temple, which operates between 11:30am and 1pm; if you're visiting late, perhaps stay for an early dinner, served from 5pm until sunset (5:45pm in winter, and around 7pm in summer).

Tip: Two kilometers (1¼ miles) north of Ranakpur, you will pass **Tribal Dhurrie Udyog,** a traditional *dhurrie* (carpet) "shop" (© **0294/241-7833**), where you can pick up a beautifully crafted 4×6m (13×20-ft.) carpet for around $75 (£38)—a great deal cheaper than what you'll pay in the cities.

65km (40 miles) from Udaipur (2½-hr. drive one-way). Rs 50 ($1.25/65p) camera. Summer 11:30am–5pm; winter noon–5pm. Any queries, contact office manager, Prema Ramji © 02934/28-5019.

Kumbhalgarh Fort ★★★   Built in the 15th century by Rana Kumbha, this mountain fortress is, together with Jodhpur's Mehrangarh Fort, one of the most impressive sights Rajasthan has to offer. Take one look at the impenetrable walls that snake for 36km (22 miles) along 13 mountain peaks, and you know that this is one of the most inaccessible fortifications ever built by humans. It was in fact only captured once, when the Mughal emperor Akbar had its water supply poisoned. This is also where the infant Udai Singh, who was spirited here by his nanny while Chittaurgarh (see below)

Battling for a Glimpse of Beauty

It is said that the rapacious sultan Allauddin Khilji laid siege to the fort because he had become obsessed with tales of the legendary beauty of the Maharana (or Rana) Ratan Singh's queen, Rani Padmini. He promised to withdraw, provided Singh allow him an opportunity to lay eyes on her—an outrageous demand considering that a strange man's gaze was tantamount to the defilement of a Rajput royal woman. But in the spirit of compromise, Singh reluctantly agreed to present him with her reflection in the lotus pond that lay below the palace's women's quarters. The sultan used this opportunity to betray the king, ambushing and capturing him on his departure. The next day a bereft Padmini sent word to the sultan that she would give herself to him in return for her husband and the withdrawal of his troops. She then descended through the seven *pols* (gates), surrounded by what appeared to be her maids-of-honor—Singh's troops, disguised as women. Singh was rescued from the sultan's camp, but the ensuing battle cost the lives of some 7,000 of Singh's men—a crippling loss. When it was clear that the Rajputs would be defeated, the funeral pyres were lit, and Padmini and 13,000 women and children committed *jauhar,* flinging themselves onto the flames, after which the last of Singh's men went to meet certain death below the ramparts.

was being sacked, spent his formative years. The wall, the second longest in the world, culminates in a fairy-tale fort within which lie the **Palace of Rana Kumbha** and **Badal Mahal** (or **Palace of Clouds,** so named because it literally is in the clouds during the monsoon months). The fort is situated deep within Kumbhalgarh Wildlife Sanctuary, and the drive there—through tiny villages and pastoral countryside—is one of the great highlights of a trip to Rajasthan and a great contrast to the crowded cities. Kumbhalgarh is considered the most important fort after Chittaurgarh, but its relative accessibility and the charm of the drive make this the preferable option. That said, while the sheer size and initial spectacle of the fort stays with you, be warned that the climb to the palaces is steep and stiff, and the buildings themselves are pretty lifeless (there's hardly anything left to suggest anything of the life and times of the people who once occupied these lofty chambers). The real reward for your physical exertions will be the unforgettable views of the surrounding valleys—let your imagination soar and you may just be able to hear the sounds of war.

To have adequate time to explore the fort, or to take in Eklingji on the return journey, it's worth overnighting near the fort. The closest and best choice is the **Aodhi Hotel,** a former royal hunting lodge now owned by the Udaipur king's hotel chain (© **02954/24-2341** through -2346; www.hrhindia.com; Rs 6,000/$146/£74 double, Rs 7,000/$171/£86 suite). Built of packed stone and rock, it mimics a hillside fortress, complete with cannons and crenellated walls. Accommodations are spacious and reasonably neat (each with A/C, TV, and tea- and coffee-making facilities and big, thick, comfortable new beds) and overlook a large pool and a pretty alfresco dining area. Room nos. 4, 5, 10, 11, and 23 enjoy good views, but you'll no doubt find yourself sharing the hotel with groups during the winter season. Even if you don't stay here, consider stopping for a special drink at the bar—ask for a tot of *kesar kastari,* a unique heritage liqueur made with saffron and 20 other herbal ingredients. ***Note:*** There is now an evening **sound-and-light show** at the fort; it starts at 7pm, which means you almost *have* to be a guest at Aodhi if you want to see it.

90km (56 miles) from Udaipur (2-hr. drive one-way; 1 hr. from Ranakpur Temples). Admission $2.45 (£1.25). Sunrise to sunset.

DAY TRIP 3: A HISTORY OF VALOR

Chittaurgarh (Chittor)   Chittaurgarh is 3 hours (115km/71 miles) from Udaipur and covers 280 hectares (700 acres), making it a rather long day trip (it takes around 2 hr. to explore), but it's well worth it if you're armed with information and a good imagination (both of which can be supplied by a good guide; ask your hotel for recommendations). Thrusting 180m (590 ft.) into the sky, the fort houses a number of monuments and memorials, but with much of it in ruins, its primary importance lies in its evocative history. The fort has witnessed some of the bloodiest battles in history, and songs recording the valor and sacrifice of its inhabitants are still sung today.

Built in the 7th century, it remained the capital of Mewar until 1568, when the capital shifted to Udaipur. During this time Chittaurgarh was ravaged three times, but the story of the first sacking that took place in 1303 during the reign of Rana Ratan Singh is perhaps the most romantic (see "Battling for a Glimpse of Beauty," below).

Chittaurgarh returned to Rajput rule in 1326 and the Mewar enjoyed 2 centuries of prosperity before it was again laid siege to, this time by Sultan Bahadur Shah of Gujarat. To save the life of the Rajput heir Udai Singh, his nursemaid Panna Dai sacrificed her own infant son, leaving him as a decoy for the murderous sultan and spiriting the tiny heir away to Kumbhalgarh Fort. The women and children of Chittaurgarh committed *jauhar* (mass ritual suicide) while their men died in battle.

When, at the age of 13, Udai was reinstated at Chittaurgarh, he searched in earnest for a new site for the capital, building Udaipur on the shores of Lake Pichola. Eight years later, the Mughal emperor Akbar, trying to contain the arrogance of Udai Singh—who poured such contempt on Jai (of Jaipur) Singh's collaboration with the emperor—attacked Chittaurgarh. This time 30,000 Rajput lives were lost, and the women and children again flung themselves on the flames rather than be captured by the Muslims. Chittaurgarh was given back to the Rajputs in 1616, much of it in ruins, but by this time the royal family was comfortably ensconced in Udaipur, and the fort was never lived in again.

The fort is approached through seven massive ***pols,*** or gates—look for the *chhatri* (cenotaph) of the chivalrous Jaimal and his cousin Kala near Bhairon Pol. Jaimal was seriously wounded defending Chittaur against Emperor Akbar but he refused to give up and was carried back into battle on the shoulders of Kala, where both were slain. At Ram Pol is a **memorial to Phatta** who, at 16, having lost his father in battle and witnessed the deaths of his sword-wielding mother and young wife on the battlefield, led his saffron-robed men to certain death while the women of the fort yet again ended their lives by committing *jauhar.*

As you enter the final *pol,* you will see **Shingara Chauri Mandir,** a typically adorned Jain temple, and the crumbling **15th-century palace** built by Rana Kumbha up ahead. Under the palace lies a series of cellars where Padmini reputedly committed *jauhar* (see box). Rana Kumbha was one of the Mewar's most powerful rulers: In addition to the palace, he built nearby **Khumba Shyam Temple,** dedicated to Varah (an incarnation of Vishnu), as well as **Meera Temple,** dedicated to the poet and princess

Meera, whose devotion to Krishna reputedly saved her from being poisoned. (Incidentally, Krishna is usually depicted as blue as a result of the poison he consumed, thereby saving the world.) Within the cenotaph in front of the temple is a **carved figure** of five human bodies with one head—in a rare overture to tolerance, this supposedly demonstrates caste equality. Farther south lies Kumbha's **Vijay Stambh (Tower of Victory)**—a lavishly ornamented tower built by Maharana Kumbha to commemorate his victory over the combined forces of Malwa and Gujarat.

Other sites of interest are **Padmini's Palace,** where the sultan Allauddin Khilji gazed upon Padmini's reflection in the lotus pond; **Kirti Stambh,** a 12th-century tower ornamented with figures, dedicated to the first Jain *tirthankara;* **Fateh Prakash Palace,** built for the maharana during the 1920s and housing a dry archaeological museum (small fee; Sat–Thurs 10am–4:30pm); and **Kalika Mata Temple,** originally built as a Sun Temple by Bappa Rawal in the 8th century but rebuilt during the 14th century and dedicated to Kali, goddess of power and valor. Some of the best views are from **Gaumukh (Cow's Mouth) Reservoir,** so-called because the spring water trickles through a stone carving of a cow's mouth.

Note: You can get here by train from Udaipur, but it's a late-night trip, departing at 9:40pm and arriving 2 hours later, so you would have to overnight, and perhaps consider moving on to Jaipur the following evening (on the same connecting train). Accommodations in Chittor are limited, with no luxury options. If you *have* to overnight, the best option is **Pratap Palace** (© 01472/24-0099; Rs 1,200–Rs 2,500/ $30–$61/£15–£31 double); the priciest rooms are recently added A/C units with tubs in the attached bathrooms.

115km/71 miles) from Udaipur (3-hr. drive one-way). No admission charge.

DAY TRIP 4: UNDISCOVERED PALACES & DECO DELIGHT
Dungarpur's Palaces ✦✦✦ *(Finds*   It's hard for anyone flipping through Angelika Taschen's book *Indian Style* to refrain from gasping when they come to the pages recording the magnificent apartments of 13th-century **Juna Mahal.** A seven-story fortresslike structure that appears to spring forth from its rocky surrounds, the palace doesn't look like much from the outside, but inside, it houses one of the world's most interesting "art galleries": Every wall and column is covered with beautiful, intricate frescoes—tiny paintings; mosaics with glass, mirror, and tiles; or artfully used porcelain plates embedded into the walls. And don't forget to look above you: On one ceiling panel, gorgeous images of Krishna depict the playful god getting up to all kinds of shenanigans. In one of the massive downstairs reception rooms, the entire floor is covered with huge decaying Persian carpets. Yet even though it houses a treasure trove of art and design, the palace is far from being a tourist attraction: There are very few visitors and not a single hawker in sight, only the toothless old retainer whose trembling hands hold the keys while he waits for you to drink it all in before he opens another, even more stunning room. Perhaps it is precisely this—viewing such beauty in absolute solitude—that makes the experience so special, but the artworks are considered to be of the very best in Rajasthan. Don't miss (you're unlikely to, as long as the old man is around to leer at your reaction) the collection of miniature paintings depicting scenes from the *Kama Sutra;* modestly hidden behind cupboard doors in the Maharaja's Suite on the top floor, it's a veritable A to Z of erotic possibilities, including some near-impossible feats (definitely bring a flashlight).

Although Dungarpur is a mere 2 hours' drive from Udaipur, you might want to consider combining the tour with a stay at nearby **Udai Bilas Palace** ✦ (Dungarpur,

Rajasthan 314 001; © **02964/23-0808** or 93-1465-3967; www.udaibilaspalace.com), which has a rather magical lakeside setting and offers no hardship, as this, too, is a wonderful experience, particularly if you have any interest in the Deco period or relish a sense of nostalgia. Built on the shores of Gaibsagar Lake (great for birders, with 122 species recorded), it is both scenic and secluded and combines Rajput architecture and murals with original Art Deco furnishings and fittings—the work of Maharawal Laxman Singhji, who had three new wings built around lovely Ek Thambia Mahal ("One-Pillared Palace") in 1940. Still the royal residence of the Maharawal and his family, the palace offers 20 old-fashioned rooms (old plumbing, beautiful Deco furniture in need of new springs, no in-room amenities aside from air-conditioning—but wonderfully authentic) as well as a great pool on the water's edge. If you can afford it, book a suite (from Rs 5,300/$130/£66); our personal preference is no. 20, but really, it all depends on whether you fall in love with a particular lounge suite, carpet pattern, or view. Ask whether you can wander around and take your pick; no. 7 is the best standard room (Rs 4,450/$109/£55 double). *Note:* The Juna Mahal is roughly 15 minutes beyond Udai Bilas Palace, which is where you must purchase a ticket

Dungarpur is 120km (75 miles) south of Udaipur (a 2-hr. drive one-way), and 175km (109 miles) from Ahmedabad, Gujarat. Admission: Rs 150 ($3.65/£1.85).

DAY TRIP 5: ASCENDING MOUNT ABU

The Rajputs are said to have held the fire ceremony in which they were "reborn" as warriors on these lofty heights, but Mount Abu, so-called "Abode of the Gods," only became a destination for mere mortals a millennium later, when the British persuaded the Sirohi State to allow them to use it as a retreat from the searing heat of the plateaus that shimmer below. They were later joined by the Rajput princes, who built mini-palaces to show off and entertain the Britishers. At a cool 1,220m (4,002 ft.) above sea level, this is the only hill station in Rajasthan, and it's within easy striking distance of many of Gujarat's big cities, providing welcome relief for thousands of domestic visitors who come to partake of freely available alcohol (Gujrat is a dry state), paddle central **Nakki Lake** in giant swan boats, and view the exquisite sunsets, all accompanied by the inevitable high-spirited carousing of friends and families.

Indeed, unless you put on your walking shoes and head for the hills, this is not the most peaceful of places; it's filled with a year-round festive spirit as families and honeymooners throng the streets, clutching ice creams or the manes of the ponies that clatter along, shaking their bells and feathered heads at passersby. Every evening at sunset, literally hundreds of people set off for **Sunset Point,** riding in large pramlike vehicles pushed by stringy men or mounting the ponies that congregate here in the hope of making their masters a few more rupees before the onset of night. The sun sinking into the plains thousands of miles below is a truly wonderful sight, not least because you are sharing it with so many people, the smell of roasting peanuts permeating the air. There is a rare sense of camaraderie as the crowd gives a roar of approval when the sun finally slips behind the horizon.

If you have no anthropological bent, however, the real reason to venture so far off the beaten track (and unless you approach it from Gujarat, Mount Abu is a long and not altogether satisfactory detour, some 190km/118 miles from Udaipur and a 5-hr. drive one-way) is to view the **Dilwara Temples** ★★★, widely considered the best examples of Jain architecture in India. Not to be confused with Delwara (just north of Udaipur), these "hymns in marble" were built between the 11th and 13th centuries.

Every interior wall and pillar is covered with the most intricate carvings, none of which are repeated, and all of which inspire great devotion. Of the five temples, **Vimala Vasahi** (1031), which took 1,500 artists and 1,200 laborers 14 years to complete, and **Luna Vasahi** (1231) are the most impressive. The full-color guidebook at the entrance is worth purchasing (not least because photography is not allowed here); it gives a breakdown of what you are looking at in each temple. Alternatively, hire the services of a guide through your hotel. The Dilwara Temples are said to be unparalleled anywhere else in India, but we thought the temples at Ranakpur equally beautiful. Dilwara is open from noon to 6pm; see the rules for visiting Jain temples under Ranakpur Temples, above.

There's a plethora of hotels in town, most awful, but two are recommended. **The Jaipur House** (© **02974/235-176;** delhi@palacesofindia.com), which the Maharaja of Jaipur transformed into an intimate hotel in 2002, is by far the best situated. Because of close family ties, the Jaipur Maharaja was given first choice of land by the then-ruler of Sirohi State, and in 1897 he built his Rajput-style mansion on the highest hilltop overlooking Nakki Lake. Guests have a choice of nine rooms in the heritage wing (avoid the 14 on offer in the new wing). All suites have views of the lake (for truly stupendous views, no. 201, "the Royal Suite," is fantastic); room no. 107 has no lake view but with two small balconies is a good option. Avoid no. 106, a horrid "junior suite." Rates are Rs 3,500 to Rs 6,000 ($85–$146/£43–£74) per suite.

If you prefer a more old-fashioned, laid-back atmosphere and more personable service, **Palace Hotel (Bikaner House),** once the summer residence of the royal Bikaner family, was designed by that master of Indo-Saracenic style, Sir Swinton Jacob, in 1893. Enjoying a tranquil location near the Dilwara Temples, it is surrounded by sprawling grounds and forests. A million miles from the jovial madness that reigns in town, it will suit those who enjoy the timeless elegance of good design. Rooms in both wings have been given a new lease on life with extensive renovations carried out in 2005, adding updated plumbing and bathroom fixtures and other modern comforts to the old-world charm; further renovations are planned. Make sure you have a room in the main house; the service (under the kind, professional Rajvirsinh) is faultless, and the genteel atmosphere very much captures the graciousness of a bygone era. For bookings, contact © **02974/23-5121** or 02974/23-8673 (bikhouse@sancharnet.in; www.palacehotel bikanerhouse.com). Rates start at Rs 3,500 ($85/£43) for a double room, and from Rs 5,000 ($122/£62) for a suite. The hotels will happily arrange guides or transfers.

WHERE TO STAY

Note: The prices for the accommodations below are sometimes given in rupees, with U.S. dollar conversions; others are stated in U.S. dollars only, which is how many hotels targeting foreign markets quote their rates.

Sadly, there is always the remote possibility that the fabulous Lake Pichola will again succumb to climactic pressure and dry up; we strongly urge you to call ahead and check on the status of the lake waters to make an informed lodging choice; we'd hate for you to fork out a load of cash for a special lake-facing room, only to end up staring at a parched lake bed. For instance, without a view you can rule out the Fateh Prakash and Lake Palace and consider instead a room at the Kankarwa or one of the other more reasonably priced options, then head off to spend a night at Devi Garh, or stay at Deogarh Mahal, Shahpura Bagh, or Rawla Narlai en route elsewhere.

Udaipur on the Rise

While we last visited Udaipur, a number of new hotels were undergoing furious construction. Most prominent is the rather large (and potentially very intrusive) **Leela** property; rumors abound that the scheduled 2008 opening might be postponed until the following year. A **Radisson** is also believed to be opening in the near future. We had a walk through the building site of **Verandah on the Lake** (www.verandahonthelake.com; from Rs 2,500/$61/£31 double), a 16-room boutique-style hotel with French-designed interiors, teak decks, and a small infinity pool at the lake edge; the lake-facing rooms (each with a little balcony) overlook the less popular northern portion of Pichola, as the hotel has its "back" to the palaces. Nonetheless, when Chandpole is lit up at night, it's rather pretty, and owners plan to adopt and beautify one of the islets on the lake. You're likely to have a real sense of lodging among the people of Udaipur here (as opposed to being in the center of an entire bank of hotels and guesthouses), which could also imply a lot of noise. It opened in October 2007.

Assuming that the lake is full of water, we urge you to book into a hotel or haveli with a view of the lake; accommodations on the eastern shore are best for sunsets, but this is also the best time to be at the Lake Palace itself, or on Jag Mandir. The best accommodations are reviewed below, but if you're literally counting your rupees, **Badi Haveli** (© **0294/241-2588;** hotelbadihaveli@yahoo.com; Rs 300–Rs 550/$7.30–$13/£3.70–£6.80) is the well-run, well-located (near City Palace) 350-year-old home of Mr. Samant Bhatt, with monastic but scrupulously clean rooms. Some top-floor rooms have lovely views of the lake. Several notches higher but still in the budget category, **Mahendra Prakash** on Lake Palace Road is without lake views, but it does have a swimming pool and a cool garden and attractive decorative touches like colored window panes, wooden doors with ormolu mountings, and solid brass door knockers. Service is prompt and friendly. Make sure you get an air-conditioned room on the first floor; these have pretty carved balconies with cushioned seats (© **0294/24-19811;** udai99@hotmail.com; first-floor A/C double Rs 1,800/$44/£22). Also see the review of Kankarwa, below.

At the other end of the scale is the **Trident** (© **1600/11-2122** or 0294/243-2200; www.tridenthotels.com). A large, mellow, purpose-built hotel set behind Udaivilas, it has plenty of amenities and facilities but is set some way from the lake among the tranquil Aravalli Hills, about a 25-minute drive from town. At $240 to $290 (£120–£145) per double (check online for daily rates and deals), this comfortable option offers relatively good value (pool-facing rooms, which also have views towards the hills, are best) and will suit the less-adventurous traveler, but it's a bit soulless for our taste.

LAKE PICHOLA

Lake Palace Hotel 🏆🏆🏆   Just looking at a photograph of this 18th-century island palace is enough to make you want to start planning a trip to India. On our recent stays here, it's certainly lived up to its promise, from the experience of being ferried to the "lobby" by boat to exploring the various courtyards, with their flowerbeds and fountains, to ascending the roof, getting lost down a passage, or being treated like royalty in the beautiful bar. Both standard and deluxe rooms feature wood paneling and murals, lovely marble bathrooms, well-crafted furniture, opulent fabrics, and blissful

Egyptian cotton linens; recent renovations have also improved many of the public spaces. Best of all, everywhere you look—be it from the mango-shaded pool, your room, or the restaurant—you have picture-perfect views: the statuesque City Palace walls and crenelated rooftops to the east, the whitewashed havelis and temples of the Old City lining the shores of the lake to the north, the Aravalli Hills to the west, or Jag Mandir to the south. Our favorite spot is on a poolside lounger; here, you face the City Palace directly and are brought selections of refreshing drinks and tasty nibbles, and there are glossy magazines to peruse. The best rooms (besides the fabulous suites) are the deluxe rooms facing east—the City Palace is lit up at night, giving you a 24-hour view. The huge and opulent suites (of which no. 116 and 117 housed the queen and the king, respectively) were thankfully left more or less as inherited from the royal family and have a timeless grandeur that the City Palace hotels could only wish for: stained-glass windows, marble floors, crystal chandeliers, antique Rajasthani furniture, and old-fashioned pieces that wouldn't be out of place at Balmoral (Queen Elizabeth's favorite residence)—making them the epitome of 20th-century royal splendor. Note that the luxury rooms with City Palace views tend to be smaller than those facing the hills, which are like miniature suites (albeit with cramped bathrooms), and be very careful to insist on a room with a view over the lake—a few deluxe units overlook the lily pond in the internal courtyard

P.O. Box 5, Udaipur 313 001. ✆ **0294/252-8800.** Fax 0294/252-7975. www.tajhotels.com. 85 units. $700 (£350) luxury double; $800 (£400) palace double; $2,600 (£1,300) royal suite; $4,000 (£2,000) grand royal suite. Taxes extra. AE, DC, MC, V. **Amenities:** 2 restaurants; bar; pool; minigym; spa; 2 outdoor Jacuzzis; travel desk; car hire; shops; 24-hr. room service; babysitting; doctor-on-call; currency exchange; boat trips; 24-hr. water taxi; reading room; astrologer. *In room:* A/C, TV, minibar, hair dryer, safe, DVD/CD player, personal butler.

EASTERN SHORES OF LAKE PICHOLA

Fateh Prakash & Shiv Niwas Palaces   The last two palaces built within the City Palace walls are now both hotels, but unless you want to overnight in what feels like a wealthy old aunt's large but stuffy apartment, there's only one section worth considering: the relatively new **Dovecoat Wing** ⟨𝕗 in Fateh Prakash. After the Lake Palace, this is the next-best location in Udaipur: Almost all the rooms in this wing, which stretches along the shoreline, have the most wonderful views of the lake and its palace, as well as views beyond the distant Aravalli Hills (perfect at both sunset and dawn); room nos. 511 and 617 even have little sitting rooms that jut over the water. Furnishings are elegant (predominantly salmon and white), bathrooms adequate (obviously done before bathrooms became a real focus in hotel design), and rates offer by far the best value in the palaces. By contrast, Fateh Prakash's much pricier "Regal Suites," while a great deal larger, are overdressed, overcarpeted, and old-fashioned—these definitely need sprucing up; certainly those that don't even face the lake are a definite no-no. Management may try to persuade you to "upgrade" to these older apartments, but if you don't like the musty, almost claustrophobic atmosphere, insist that they honor your booked room in the lighter, breezier Dovecoat Wing. Crescent-shaped Shiv Niwas Palace, built around the pool courtyard, is positioned farther south, and without the lovely Lake Palace floating before you, its views are a great deal less magical (although staff is trained to encourage excitement about seeing Jag Mandir from your room). And that's *if* you get a lake view—again, don't bother staying here if you don't have one since it's hardly worth the price (rooms with lake views are listed with rates below). Service in both hotels is well-meaning but will almost certainly try your patience. The aptly named **Sunset Terrace** (see later in this section) is the best place to dine—the views are great, but don't expect much from the cuisine.

City Palace Complex, Udaipur 313 001. ℂ **0294/252-8016** or -8019. Fax 0294/252-8006. www.hrhindia.com. Fateh Prakash 28 units. Shiv Niwas 31 units. **Fateh Prakash:** $350 (£175) Dovecote doubles and Regal suites. **Shiv Niwas:** $300 (£150) palace double (no views); $600 (£300) Terrace Suite (nos. 15 and 16 lake-facing); $800 Royal Suite (nos. 5, 6, 7, and 18 lake-facing); $1,000 (£500) Imperial Suite (no. 17 lake-facing). AE, MC, V. **Amenities** (shared by hotels): 3 restaurants; pool; spa; travel desk; massage; doctor-on-call; squash; billiards. *In room:* A/C, TV, minibar, hair dryer.

Jagat Niwas 🖈 Like its neighbor the Kankarwa, this 17th-century haveli literally rises from the waters of Lake Pichola. The difference is that Jag Niwas is more hotel than guesthouse, with a laid-back staff, a good travel agent, and in-room amenities like air-conditioning, TVs, and telephones. Approached through a narrow street that runs into the entrance, it is essentially a cluster of buildings around a central courtyard. Rooms vary considerably, with only suites and deluxe rooms providing lake views—of these, no. 102 (super deluxe) and nos. 101, 110, and 116 (suites), are particularly pleasing options, and the latter is the most romantic. Note that deluxe rooms with lake views are generally much smaller than those without. Ceilings often feature colored glass baubles typical of Rajasthani havelis; walls have painted murals; fabrics are traditional Rajasthani block prints; and many rooms have alcoves with mattresses. In an irritating oversight, not a single room has a bedside reading lamp. Not all rooms have split air-conditioning—units with this are a great deal quieter than window units, so you might want to request it. The best part of the hotel is the wonderful covered terrace that overlooks the lake and hosts evening shows; the in-house boutique has a fine silver collection. Unless you prefer hotel-like amenities, choose the more stylish Kankarwa (see below), and come and relax on the terrace here as a visitor. If you want a pool, Udai Kothi (see below) is a better option.

23–25 Lal Ghat, Udaipur 313 001. ℂ **0294/242-0133** or -2860. Fax 0294/241-8512. www.jagatniwaspalace.com. mail@jagatniwaspalace.com. 29 units. Rs 1,350 ($33/£17) standard double; Rs 1,895 ($46/£23) regular deluxe double; Rs 2,300 ($56/£28) lake-facing deluxe double; Rs 3,300 ($81/£41) super deluxe double; Rs 4,999 ($124/£62) suite; Rs 500 ($12/£6) extra bed. Taxes extra. AE, MC, V. **Amenities:** Restaurant; bar; travel desk; car hire; boutique; 24-hr. room service; laundry; doctor-on-call; currency exchange; Internet; horseback riding and safaris. *In room:* A/C, TV, hair dryer (on request).

Kankarwa 🖈🖈 *Value* A short stroll from the City Palace, this is by far the best budget option in town, if not the whole of Rajasthan. It's an elegant and professional family-run guesthouse in an ancient haveli right on the shores of Lake Pichola. We loved room no. 204; the simple whitewashed space has white bedding and traditional Rajasthani antiques; a single blood-red lamp perfectly offsets the cool white—this family has innate style. The compact bathrooms (most with shower only) are also whitewashed or tiled, only adding to the refreshing, clean atmosphere. Room no. 206 is a good twin-bed option with white-pillowed alcove (colored by stained-glass windows and hanging red baubles) and a great big bathroom with a window and tub. Other good options are nos. 217 (pastel green), 216, and 203 (pale pink)—all with the same sense of cool offset with touches of intense color. But our favorite has got to be no. 207, with a large bathroom and a separate alcove room where you can lounge on a mattress or poke your head out over the lake. Meals are taken at wrought-iron tables on the rooftop terrace (with the lake spread out before you), and there's a strict policy of introducing guests to authentic local cuisine; expect home-cooked dishes straight from the family kitchen. The only possible drawback is the lack of amenities, but the family works hard at providing assistance, and the affable proprietor, Janardan, regularly entertains guests for hours with his mordant observations on travel, Indian culture, and the great spiritual benefits of visiting his fine country. Budget travelers can get an excellent deal on two very small but comfortable single rooms (no views) for just Rs 1,000 ($24/£12).

26 Lal Ghat, Udaipur 313 001. ⓒ 0294/241-1457. Fax 0294/252-1403. www.indianheritagehotels.com. khaveli@ yahoo.com. 15 units. Rs 1,000–Rs 2,500 ($24–$61/£12–£31) double. Taxes included. MC, V. **Amenities:** Rooftop dining terrace; travel and sightseeing assistance; laundry; Internet; library. *In room:* A/C (some).

WESTERN SHORES OF LAKE PICHOLA

Amet Haveli ⓐ Located on the shores of Lake Pichola, with views of Kankarwa and Jag Niwas directly opposite, this pretty 350-year-old haveli has enough charm to have found its way into glossy books on Indian style, but it's rather basic for anyone wanting lots of amenities. Nevertheless, all accommodations face the lake, and if you book suite no. 7, a corner unit with a large mattressed *jarokha* that juts over the water, you'll have lovely views of the City and Lake palaces, which you can even see from your king-size bed. Freshly whitewashed, with simple furnishings, the room is airy and light, and very good value. Suite no. 8 is almost twice as large—a bright, marble-floored space with antique furnishings—but the views are not nearly as spectacular. The five new upstairs guest rooms are completely modern additions. Despite the bitterly standard menu, the **Ambrai** restaurant has a good reputation for its tandoori dishes, and its lakeside setting makes it an ideal sunset spot. Service is the real letdown here, so don't come with any expectations in that department.

Outside Chandpole, Udaipur 313 001. ⓒ 0294/243-1085 or 0294/243-4009. Fax 0294/252-2447. regiudr@datainfo sys.net. 11 units. Rs 2,500 ($61/£31) double; Rs 3,000 ($73/£37) suite; Rs 500 ($12/£6) extra bed. Taxes extra. AE, MC, V. **Amenities:** Restaurant; bar; transport assistance; laundry; doctor-on-call; Internet. *In room:* A/C, TV, hair dryer on request.

Udai Kothi ⓐ ⓥ*alue* The fragrant scent of marigold fills the air at this laid-back hotel built by entrepreneurial Vishwa Vijay Singh and decorated by his keen-eyed shopaholic wife. Together, they've created a relatively authentic replica of a traditional haveli. It may not be as well located (with regards to top attractions) as Jagat Niwas or Kankarwa, but it's an easy stroll to the Old City and a great value, with Udaipur's only rooftop pool, situated on a trellised terrace where meals are served—the views at night are breathtaking. Accommodations are comfortable, with canopied beds, block-print fabrics, frescoes, and individually sourced pieces—all with comfortable *jarokhas* (window seats) from which to enjoy the lake or garden view (the latter are sold as standard rooms). Ask for a room on the third floor for the best views. Underscoring the immense popularity of this unassuming place, eight new suites will be available by 2008, and there are plans to double the size of the property over the next 2 years; depending on when you check in, expect to see two new pools, an additional restaurant, and a launch for budget-conscious jet-setters who fancy arriving by boat.

Udai Kothi, Udaipur 313 001. ⓒ 0294/243-2810 or -2812. Fax 0294/243-0412. www.udaikothi.com. 23 units. Rs 4,600 ($112/£57) standard double; Rs 5,200 ($127/£64) deluxe double; Rs 6,000 ($146/£74) suite; Rs 1,000 ($24/£12) extra bed. Taxes extra. MC, V. **Amenities:** 2 restaurants; bar; pool; health club; Jacuzzi; travel desk; bookshop; room service; laundry; doctor-on-call; cultural performances; roof terrace; garden; boating. *In room:* A/C, TV, hair dryer.

Udaivilās ⓐⓐⓐ You'd be forgiven for relinquishing all sightseeing responsibilities and simply giving in to your inner indolence at this highly relaxing resort, which, with its numerous domes, has become a significant part of Udaipur's western skyline; shimmering in the distance across Lake Pichola, it could well be mistaken for another of the city's most majestic palaces but is actually a completely contemporary 2002 addition. The palatial property features magnificent grounds (beautifully landscaped gardens as well as a wildlife conservatory where deer and peacock roam) and stunning interiors, including a massive central dome, lit up at night, that wouldn't look out of place on St. Peter's. Intricately crafted pieces and fabrics are artfully combined with Western decor to create the most elegantly dressed rooms and luxurious bathrooms in Udaipur; accommodations include comforting touches—piles of colorful cushions, linens in the most perfect cotton, and highly original artworks. If you're interested in landscaping, it'd be well worth your while to explore the resort extensively, seeking out the many beautiful touches—like water easing its way down sky-blue channels or spouting from the trunks of stone elephants—that make this property so special. That said, if you're a first-time visitor to Udaipur, you'll want to reserve a lake-view room (which automatically has access—from your own personal porch—to a semi-private infinity pool that forms a veritable moat along the length of the accommodations wing); this is the best way of ensuring round-the-clock visual access to the city's favorite sights. (Then again, some guests find that the shared pool spoils their sense of exclusivity.) Otherwise, book a cheaper room and plan on spending your days at the spa pool (the main resort pool, designed like a monumental step-well, is lovely but lacks views). Service is generally world-class but can be a little matter-of-fact at times. Dining experiences, too, can be quite wonderful, particularly if you reserve an outdoor table for dinner. Even if the food isn't 100% and tables get cleared before the last guest has left, lights from the historic palaces glitter across the surface of the lake, stars twinkle above, and regular fireworks displays underscore the utter romance of the place.

Haridasji Ki Magri, Udaipur 313 001. Ⓒ **0294/243-3300.** Oberoi hotels: Ⓒ 800/562-3764. Fax 0294/243-3200. www.oberoihotels.com. 87 units. $665–$765 (£333–£383) premiere double; $775–$875 (£388–£438) premiere lake-view double; $3,000–$3,800 (£1,500–£1,900) suite. Taxes extra. AE, DC, MC, V. **Amenities:** 2 restaurants; lounge/bar; 2 pools; Banyan Spa (with Ayurvedic treatments); travel desk; limousine transfer from airport on request; boutique; salon; 24-hr. room service; babysitting; laundry; doctor-on-call; Wi-Fi; butler service; boating; adjacent wildlife conservatory; CD/DVD library. *In room:* A/C, TV, minibar, tea- and coffee-making facilities, hair dryer, iron on request, electronic safe, flashlight (torch), Internet, DVD/CD, semi-private pools (some); suites have private pools.

AROUND UDAIPUR

Reviewed below is Devi Garh, one of our favorite places to stay in all India; it's quite a distance from Udaipur (26km/16 miles or 45 min.), however, and definitely aimed at the well-heeled. If it doesn't suit your budget, or if you'd prefer to be within easy striking distance of the city, you'll be pleased to learn that the owners of popular Udai Kothi have come up with a marvelous little property just 6km (3¾ miles) from Lake Pichola. Surrounded by dramatic hilly landscape, **Udai Bagh** ⃰ (see Udai Kothi, above; www.udaibagh.com) is a serene country retreat with a big pool and just seven luxury tents; there are plans in the not-too-distant future for an upmarket destination spa with additional rooms ($200/£100 double), to be designed by Nimesh Patel, who had his hand in Udaivilās. The air-conditioned en-suite tents—outfitted with clay tile floors, block-print-fabric ceilings, and metal frame beds (reserve no. 1 if you want a double bed)—have lovely wooden furniture and piles of magazines and books to keep you entertained (there's also a TV, minibar, Wi-Fi, and room service if reading doesn't suffice). Bathrooms have big, smart showers, and there's a little porch with seats out front (it's not very private, but you won't be sharing the property with too many people). Udai Bagh is great value too: just Rs 4,000 ($98/£49) double, with breakfast. There's no restaurant, but a butler brings you whatever you want, and there's a free shuttle service to and from Udaipur.

Devi Garh ⃰⃰⃰ "Went to see the City Palace this morning and couldn't wait to return to our very own," one guest remarked, and really, it *is* hard to tear yourself away from what is arguably the best hotel on the subcontinent. Devi Garh is more than beautiful, it is *inspiring*, particularly if you're a modern-design enthusiast. Little wonder it's become a popular Bollywood location. Staff are exceptional, all looking as if they've stepped out of an Armani ad for India. The service levels are unbeatable: extensive, personal, discreet, and intelligent. But what makes this an unparalleled masterpiece is the marriage of the towering exterior of an original 18th-century Rajput palace (which remains totally unchanged) with a reinvented minimalist interior. Utilizing the best young designers in India (which put a lie to the perception that design here reached its apotheosis with the Mughals) and financed by the latter-day patron Lekha Poddar, it took 15 years to transform the higgledy-piggledy rooms spread over 14 floors into 23 huge suites, with more "garden" suites (much cheaper, but without the same ambience) added in 2005. Within the almost stark, soothing space of each suite, there's none of the familiar Rajasthani accents, yet it remains uniquely Indian: Almost everything, from the bed and sofa bases to ashtrays and vases, is carved out of white marble, offset with flashes of color—flower motifs in semi-precious stones, bold swaths of gold inlay, or asymmetrical relief sculpture—designs that reinterpret India's centuries-old craftsmanship in dazzlingly modern ways. If that's not enough, the views of the majestic Aravalli Hills and tiny Delwara village, where life continues as it has for centuries, are perfectly framed by large sheets of squared-off glass—a modern element that is successfully hidden when viewing the pretty *jarokha* windows from the exterior. Below lies a heated green marble pool, tennis court, and spa (with great Ayurvedic treatments on offer), as well as the dining areas where more superb views (and wonderful cuisine) await. The hotel will arrange camel or horse safaris, jeep treks, or chauffeured tours: Udaipur, Eklingji, Nagda, Nathdwara, Kumbhalgarh Fort, and Ranakpur are all easily explored from here. Make every effort to include a night at this acclaimed (by, among others, *Condé Nast Traveler, Vogue, Wallpaper*) hotel, though it will no doubt have you wishing you'd planned nothing other than to stay here for the duration of your trip.

Devi Garh, Delwara Village 313 001. ⓒ **02953/28-9211.** In Delhi: 011/2335-4554 or 011/2375-5540. www.devi resorts.com. devigarh@deviresorts.com. 49 units. Low season (Apr–Sept)/High season (Oct–Mar): $400/$450 (£200/£225) garden suite; $700/$750 (£350/£375) palace suite; $900/$1,100 (£450/£550) Aravalli suite; $1,300/ $1,500 (£650/£750) Devi Garh suite; $35 (£18) extra bed. Taxes extra; certain ultra-peak season supplements apply. Oct 1–Mar 31: $150 (£76) tent. AE, DC, MC, V. **Amenities:** Restaurant; bar; pool; tennis court; health club/gym; spa; cycling; travel desk; salon; 24-hr. room service; babysitting; doctor-on-call; horse/camel riding; kite flying; pool table; table tennis; croquet; astrologer; library. *In room:* A/C, TV, dataport, minibar, DVD/CD.

TRAVELING BETWEEN UDAIPUR & JAIPUR/JODHPUR

Note that if you are traveling by road from Udaipur to Jaipur, another excellent option is **Shahpura Bagh** (reviewed earlier in this chapter).

Deogarh Mahal & Fort Seengh Sagar 🕉🕉 Deogarh Mahal is one of the best and most authentic heritage hotels in Rajasthan, though it's not as good a value as the lovely Rawla Narlai, with its magical setting. Comprising an ornate 17th-century fort-palace with domed turrets and balconies, it towers over the little village below. Immaculately restored suites and deluxe rooms feature original frescoes and antiques. Rooms vary considerably (you are welcome to look around when you arrive, and choose one), but all are beautifully furnished, with little done to change the authenticity of the architecture (right down to the slightly erratic plumbing). Book one of the six gorgeous suites (no. 235 is a particularly beautiful deluxe suite) and pretend that all you survey from your private balcony is yours. There's also a gorgeous pool, and the village is worth exploring. Deogarh's international repute has now been greatly bolstered with the opening of a nearby sister establishment, **Fort Seengh Sagar,** which promises grand exclusivity: an island fortress converted into a sexy little luxury villa with just four suites (you can rent the whole thing for yourself), each a rich amalgam of traditional Rajasthani furniture and modern elements blended with a designer's eye, and shot through with eye-catching colors and lovely fabrics. Each room has a private balcony, but there is a sublime public terrace where you can catch views of the forest around the lake, and on winter nights a roaring fire vies with the stars for attention. The palace and fort are personally managed by Col. Randhir Singhji, the Thakur of Deogarh, who makes you feel like a long-lost aristocrat. He is supported by a small, discreet, professional staff. The traditional Rajasthani cuisine is delicious (dinner costs Rs 650/$16/£8). Note that Deogarh is a good place to stop after you've visited the Ranakpur Temples and Kumbhalgarh Fort. From here you can proceed to Jodhpur (170km/105 miles away) or to Jaipur (280km/174 miles away), but while you're here, there's everything from horseback riding to bird-watching to exotic train rides to keep you amused.

Deogarh Madaria, District Rajsamand, Rajasthan 313 331. ℭ **02904/25-2777.** Fax 02904/25-2555. www.deogarh mahal.com. info@deogarhmahal.com. Deogarh: 50 units. Rs 7,000 ($171/£86) deluxe double; Rs 9,000 ($220/£111) deluxe suite; Rs 12,000 ($293/£148) royal suite. Seeghh Sagar: 4 units. Rs 15,000 ($366/£185) per suite, with discounts on each additional suite; Rs 48,000 ($1,171/£593) for all 4 suites. Taxes extra. AE, DC, MC, V. **Amenities:** Restaurant; bar; coffee shop; lounge; pool; kids' pool; gym; Jacuzzi; bicycles; travel desk; car hire; souvenir shop; Ayurvedic massage; babysitting; doctor-on-call; Internet services; library; in-house movies; snooker; table tennis; horse riding; jeep safaris. *In room:* A/C, TV (not Seeghh Sagar), minibar, hair dryer, safe; tea- and coffee-making facilities in suites (and at Seeghh Sagar).

Rawla Narlai ★★ ⓥalue   A 17th-century hunting retreat of the Maharaja of Jodhpur, located in the heart of the arid Aravalli Hills halfway between Udaipur and Jodhpur, the lovely Rawla Narlai was only opened to paying guests in 1995 (and soon after was featured in numerous glossy magazines charmed by its pretty decor and low prices). Over a decade later, it remains an excellent-value destination, but the addition of a pool, and the ongoing luster of good taste and attention to the individual needs of guests (not to mention the myriad activities on offer), make it one of our favorite places in all Rajasthan. The hotel was sensitively renovated to ensure that authenticity wasn't lost in the process of attaching bathrooms and enlarging the spaces. Each guest room is unique, but all are characterized by a sense of simple elegance (we particularly love nos. 18 and 19), with touches like sepia photographs of the maharaja's ancestors, cusped window frames, frescoed walls, stained-glass windows, pretty alcoves, colored ceiling baubles, and *jarokhas;* many rooms have views of the Shiva temple that rises from the Ganesh Rock "mountain" that can be seen for miles from the surrounding countryside. In fact, it's the proximity to this rock that seems to give Rawla Narlai that extra something special; it was at the summit that a saint once meditated and performed miracles, before founding the village of Narlai. You can—and should—enjoy the stiff sunrise walk up the rock (views are intoxicating) before breakfast. Service is attentive, with plenty of warm touches (not least the hot-water bottle slipped between the sheets in winter). If you're on your way to Jodhpur, this makes an ideal and well-priced overnight stop after you visit the Jain temples of Ranakpur (less than an hr. away) and/or Kumbhalgarh Fort. It's also a destination in its own right, one completely free of touts, shops, and pushers; your dapper host, "Tikka," will gladly provide a guide to take you on a relaxed walk through the village, and on visits to local temples or the *baoli* (step well). Or you could go riding on beautiful Marwari horses. Follow these activities with cocktails in the idyllic garden and a delectable, romantic rooftop dinner.

140km (87 miles) from Udaipur (via Ranakpur 125km/78 miles); 160km (99 miles) from Jodhpur. Reservations through Ajit Bhawan, Near Circuit House, Jodhpur 342 006. ℂ 0291/251-0410, -1410, or -0610. Fax 0291/251-0674. www.narlai.com. reservations@ajitbhawan.com. 25 units. $130 (£65) standard double; $190 (£95) deluxe double; $238 (£119) luxury tent; $355 (£178) luxury room double; $25 (£13) extra bed. Taxes extra. AE, MC, V. **Amenities:** Restaurant; pool; laundry; doctor-on-call; horse riding; camel safaris; rock climbing; excursions. *In room:* A/C.

WHERE TO DINE

When it comes to Udaipur's fine-dining experiences, an almost unmissable evening can be spent at the **Lake Palace Hotel,** where you can watch beautiful young Rajasthani women twirl to a hypnotic drumbeat (while behind them are sublime views of the City Palace turning pink). This waterside dance routine is usually followed by a more elaborate performance in an open-air courtyard alongside the fabulous bar where you can order a cocktail and enjoy canapés served by the splendid waitstaff. After the show, head to one of the hotel's very smart restaurants; be prepared to shell out considerably for the privilege of dining in one of the most special spots in India, and make sure to book in advance (ℂ **0294/252-8800**)—you'll need a reservation in order to get ferried to the hotel in the first place.

If you're gathering memorable (and pricey) dining experiences and don't mind journeying to the far western shore of Lake Pichola, you could check out the alfresco dining at **Udaivilas** (ℂ **0294/243-3300**); be warned that although most dishes are excellent, the food is not the best we've had in the state (the signature *laal maas,* for example, tasted watered down, and even the *naan* bread was unexpectedly doughy). Nevertheless, a meal here might give you the chance to explore the hotel's spectacular architecture, and service is on a par with that at the Lake Palace, which you can see here from your table.

If you really feel deserving of excellent cuisine and don't mind traveling out of town to a gorgeous country scene, set aside time for a midday tour to fabulous **Devi Garh** 🟎🟎🟎 (see details above), one of the classiest little hotels in India. The food is exquisite (and expectedly pricey), and if you are here for a midday sojourn, you can admire the brilliant restoration of the castle and perhaps explore the little village after you've dined. The menu is limited, but if you want to know where Udaipur's informed movers and shakers take their out-of-town guests for a special treat, this is an ideal venue. Reservations are essential.

A more casual dining experience is the **Sunset Terrace** at the Fateh Prakash Palace (see earlier in this section). This is indeed the perfect place to watch the sunset, and when the sun finally disappears behind the Aravalli Hills, the ambience just gets more romantic as candles are lit and the Lake Palace, which floats in the foreground, glows like an ocean liner on the lake. That said, the food—which ranges from toasted sandwiches (adequate) to tandoori (overcooked)—is a bit of a letdown. Better fare and more comfortable seating are to be had at nearby **Jagat Niwas** (see details above). Unlike almost everywhere else in town, this restaurant terrace is open to the cooling breezes but covered by a roof, which provides some escape from the midday heat. It has comfortable mattressed alcoves with bolsters where you can curl up with a book or appreciate the sublime views of the lake. This is the kind of place where you could spend an entire afternoon relaxing; in fact, one guest, who wasn't even staying in the hotel, did exactly that every day for the duration of his stay in Udaipur. Service is slow but friendly (some of the waiters have been here 18 years), and food is average to good. Stick to the Indian dishes, either the vegetarian (*paneer matar masala,* Indian ricotta-like cheese simmered in a thick gravy with peas and tomatoes; or *paneer do pyaja,* cheese cooked with onion, tomato, and chilies) or local dishes like fish *a la* Jagat (slices of the local freshwater fish from Jaisamand Lake, caught daily, cooked in a lemon sauce, and served with chips) or Afghani *murgh malai tikka* (creamy chicken kebabs). Main courses cost between Rs 65 and Rs 275 ($1.60–$6.70/80p–£3.40).

Two other dining options are worth considering, both with lake views. **Ambrai,** at the Amet Haveli (details above), serves decent enough tandoori dishes (and some Indo-Chinese and "Continental" as well). The place has a mellow ambience created by the warm light from candlelit tables, and wrought-iron chairs in the pleasant sprawling garden right on the edge of Lake Pichola. **Udai Kothi's** rooftop restaurant is a lovely spot at night (especially with the terrace pool lit up), with good service. Choose a small alcove by the pool—with mirrored dome, cushions, candlelight, and a good butter chicken, this could be one of the most memorable meals you have in India.

Set in the garden courtyard of Jhadol Haveli, **The Whistling Teal** (103 Bhatiyani Chohatta; ✆ **0294/242-2067** or 094-1416-3727) is one of the most romantic dining spots in Udaipur. Despite its lack of lake views, it's a relative oasis in the city. You can saddle up (literally) to the bar (where seats are made of horse saddles), or chill out with a hookah (sheesha) pipe, sampling different flavored tobaccos. There are various seating areas, either on the lawn or under canopies, and you can sample an array of traditional Rajasthani dishes. The royal Jhadol family also organizes some of the most intriguing visits to rural areas, where you get to come to grips with the customs of the tribal Bhil people. For more information, visit **www.jhadol.com**.

Finally, if you're after something light, healthy, and affordable, particularly for lunch, consider the ironically named **Savage Garden** (22 Inside Chandpole; ✆ **0294/ 242-5440**), set over several floors of a pleasant building with cascading bougainvilleas and a towering banana tree in its blue-walled courtyard. Besides some standard Indian fare, you can order toned-down, simplified versions of traditional cuisine, such as "spinach mutton," served with boiled potatoes (*boiled,* not fried!), or grilled fish with mash, and even an unusual vegetarian "Kela curry": slices of banana in an onion-curd sauce, seasoned with fragrant spices from the south. There are basic, healthy salads and a few pasta dishes, not to mention a delicious mulligatawny soup. You'll pay Rs 70 to Rs 110 ($1.70–$2.70/85p–£1.35) for a main course.

SHOPPING

Udaipur has a number of attractive handicrafts. You're probably best off purchasing them directly from small factories whose touts will beg you to visit, but do beware that the commission system can add significantly to the price, so don't buy the first beautiful thing you see. The main shopping streets run from the City Palace along Jagdish Temple Street to the clock tower and beyond to Hathi Pol. Good areas are Suraj Pol, Bapu Bazaar, Chetak, and Ashwini markets. **Rajasthali** (Chetak Circle; beware similarly named stores elsewhere), the government-run handicraft shop, is a good place to both pick up basic handicrafts and gauge fair prices. **Mangalam** (Sukhadia Circle; ✆ **0294/ 256-0259**) is best for textiles, handicrafts, *dhurries,* and a variety of products.

If you'd like to contribute to local communities, visit the city showroom of **Sadhna** (Jagdish Temple Rd.; ✆ **0294/241-7454;** www.sadhna.org) where you can browse hand-stitched garments, homewares, and linens. A purchase here means contributing to the income of 500 rural and tribal women who are involved in this enterprise. If you're looking for silver, a great place to start is **Boutique Jagat Nikhar** at the Jagat Niwas hotel (see details above); here, Mr. Harish Arora offers advice on silver items, and his excellent collection comes with fixed prices. Udaipur is considered a good place to purchase miniature paintings (it has its unique style, but if you're looking for a bargain, you're better off purchasing in off-the-beaten-track towns, like Bundi) and *pichhwai* paintings—wall hangings painted on cloth or silk, often featuring scenes from Krishna's life, that originated in Nathdwara; see "Top Excursions," earlier in this chapter. Alternatively, you could pick up some of these at the **City Palace Museum shop;** the prices are higher but well worth the quality.

Other goods worth keeping an eye out for are puppets and wooden folk toys, enamel or Meenakari work, *dhurries* (rugs), tie-dye and block-printed fabrics, embroidered bags and clothing, and silver jewelry. As is always the case, consider carefully before you buy (cheaper is not always better and often means the object is a poor imitation), and try to bargain. Plenty of places will try to sell you paintings, but if you're looking for top quality (or at least want to understand the difference), you'll need to visit the artist **Kamal Sharma** (15A, New Colony, Kalaji-Goraji; ② **0294/242-3451** or 98-2904-0851). A four-time national award winner, Sharma works on paper, marble, and silk. Nearer the City Palace, you can visit **Shreenath** (City Palace Rd.), where a father-and-son team has been in business for years and conducts considerable export trade; ask to view the more elaborate (and expensive) paintings in the back room, bearing in mind that quality is determined by the intricacy of the brush strokes, which (at first) really need to be viewed under a magnifying glass. You'll soon develop a knack for spotting finer paintings at a glance. For a really kitschy souvenir, you can even commission a traditional miniature with your own face in the scene; just bring a photograph!

To view traditional Udaipur (and Gujarati) embroidery, visit **Jagdish Emporium** on City Palace Road; but note that a far superior and more affordable outlet, **Rama Art Gallery** (Haridas ji ki Magri; ② **0294/512-0771**), is located near Udaivilās and the Trident. For beautiful beaded bags, head for **Chandpole Road,** where you will also find a number of jewelry stores.

8 Jodhpur

336km (208 miles) E of Jaipur; 260km (161 miles) NW of Udaipur; 295km (183 miles) SE of Jaisalmer

Founded in 1459 by Rao Jodhaji, chief of the Rathore Rajputs who ruled over Marwar, "land of death," Jodhpur was to become one of Rajputana's wealthiest cities, capitalizing on its central position on the Delhi–Gujarat trade route and protected by one of the most impenetrable forts in history. Today it is the state's second-largest city, much of it a sprawling, polluted metropolis, but within the old walls—where every building is painted the same light blue hue, earning Jodhpur the nickname "Blue City"—you'll find a teeming maze of narrow medieval streets and bazaars, where life appears much as it has for centuries. Towering above is **Mehrangarh (Majestic) Fort,** its impenetrable walls rising like sheer cliffs from the rocky outcrop on which it is built. From its crenelated ramparts you enjoy postcard views of the ancient blue city below and, in the distance, the grand silhouette of **Umaid Bhawan Palace,** residence of the current Maharaja and heritage hotel. Within the fort is a typical Rajput palace that today houses one of the state's best-presented museums, artfully displaying the accumulated accouterments of the royal house of Rathore in the beautifully preserved royal apartments.

The labyrinthine Old City is a more visually exciting experience than Jaipur, but besides exploring these medieval streets and visiting Mehrangarh Fort and Umaid Bhawan Palace, there's not much to hold you here for more than a day or two—most people use Jodhpur as a jumping-off point to Jaisalmer or as an overnight stop before traveling on to Jaipur or Udaipur.

ESSENTIALS

VISITOR INFORMATION The tourist reception center is located in the **RTDC Ghoomar Tourist Bungalow,** on High Court Road ((C) **0291/254-5083** or 0291/254-4010; Mon–Sat 10am–5pm; closed second Sat of the month). Your own hotel's reception will assist with reservations for sightseeing and day tours. The tourist **help line** number is (C) **1364** (Mon–Sat 9am–5pm). Convenient places to withdraw cash against your credit card are the HDFC or ICICI ATM at Ratanada Chauraha, **UTI Bank** (near Kwality Inn, Chandra Hotel), or **Bank of Baroda** (Sojati Gate).

GETTING THERE Traveling by car from Udaipur takes approximately 5½ hours with no stops; the journey from Jaipur takes about 6½ to 7 hours. However, Jodhpur is very well connected by rail and air. As always, try to book flights with the more professional **Jet Airways** ((C) **0291/510-3333** or -2222 city office, 0291/251-5551 or -5552 airport), though you'll have to use **Indian Airlines** ((C) **0291/251-0757** or -0758 city office, 0291/251-2617 airport) if you want to fly to Udaipur. Jodhpur's **airport** ((C) **0291/251-2934**) lies 4km (2½ miles) south of the city. Expect to pay about Rs 200 ($4.90/£2.50) for a taxi into town; this will be less if you use the pre-paid taxi service. Jodhpur's main **train station** ((C) **131** or 132) is on Station Road, just south of the Old City walls. The overnight Mandor Express links the city to Delhi in 12½ hours; the Jaipur Intercity Express gets you here from Jaipur in 5 hours. There are two daily trains from Jaisalmer (6 hr.), early morning and late at night. At press time, train services to/from Udaipur were still suspended until the completion of the new railway line.

GETTING AROUND Rickshaws are the most useful way to get around the Old City (a 15-min. ride should cost around Rs 50/$1.25/65p), but you'll need to hire a taxi if you plan to visit the outlying attractions. To hire a car and driver for the day (or longer—for instance, for a round-trip to Jaisalmer or to Udaipur), contact **Rajasthan Tours** ((C) **0291/251-2428** or -2932; www.rajasthantouronline.com). **K. K. Holidays and Vacations** (33-B/34-A, opposite Custom House, Airport Rd.; (C) **0291/264-5767;** karnikripajodhpur@tantramail.com) is reliable, and arranges excursions, hotels, and transport at prevailing rates (at press time Rs 1,800/$44/£22 for 8 hr./80km/50 miles within Jodhpur).

FESTIVALS **Diwali,** the Hindu New Year celebration that takes place in October/November, is celebrated all over India, but the "Festival of Lights" is particularly exciting when viewed from the lawns of Umaid Bhawan Palace. At the grand bash held by Maharaja Gaj Singh II, you can experience firsthand the deep reverence with which the former ruler of Jodhpur and Marwar is still treated—everyone wants to kiss the hem and touch the hand of their beloved father figure. The 2-day **Marwar Festival,** held during the full moon in October, is also worth attending, particularly to see the fire dance held on the Osian dunes. Celebrations include classical folk music concerts, puppet shows, camel polo, and even turban-tying contests. The end of the festivities is heralded with the **fire dance,** when men jump over burning wood to the rhythm of drums and chants. Sometimes dancers perform on top of red-hot coals, moving in an almost trancelike state to percussion beats.

WHAT TO SEE & DO

Having visited the fort and Umaid Bhawan Palace, there's no reason to overextend yourself, but you may opt to include a trip to **Mandore,** which lies 9km (5½ miles) north of the Old City. The previous capital of Marwar (not to be confused with Mewar, the princely state of Udaipur), Mandore has as its principal attractions today

Moments The Future in the Palm of Your Hand

Even if you don't believe in predestiny (which forms part of the Hindu belief system), one of Jodhpur's most delightful citizens, the astrologer and palmist **Mr. Sharma,** will make a believer out of you. Honing his craft, or rather his science, for nearly 50 years, Mr. Sharma will (with often startling accuracy) provide insights about your personality, habits, genetic health, work, and romantic life; on top of it all, he'll share heartfelt advice that you dare not ignore. You can put your palms in his hands at the Mehrangarh Fort; he works in a small consulting office on Moti Mahal Chowk (toward the end of your tour) from 9am to 5pm daily. If requested, he'll come to certain hotels after hours. To make an appointment, call the fort (ⓒ **0291/254-8790,** ext. 39), his mobile (ⓒ **94-1413-0200**), or his residence (ⓒ **0291/251-4614** or -1751). Remember to remove your nail polish, and be prepared for one of the more intimate moments of your trip to Rajasthan.

gardens (in dire need of attention) in which lie the templelike cenotaphs built to honor the Rathore rulers before final rites were moved to Jaswant Thada (see Mehrangarh Fort & Museum, below). The largest and grandest of the red-sandstone structures was also the last to be built here; it commemorates the life of Maharaja Dhiraj Ajit Singh, who died in 1763. Beyond, in a totally separate section (pious to the end), is a group of smaller cenotaphs, built to commemorate the female counterparts. Opposite the weird but ultimately missable museum is the **Hall of Heroes,** a collection of 18th-century deities and Rajput heroes carved out of a rock wall. If you haven't tired of temples by now, you can move on to visit the Hindu and Jain temples at **Osian,** 65km (40 miles) north of Jodhpur. You first come across the **Vishnu** and **Harihara temples,** which were built between the 8th and 9th centuries, but more impressive (or at least still alive with worship) are **Sacchiya Mata** (12th c.) and **Mahavira Jain temples** (8th and 10th c.). See Ranakpur Temples, earlier in this chapter, for rules on entering a Jain temple. Virtually every hotel and agent in town arranges **village safaris,** in which you are taken into the arid surrounds to make contact with the rural Bishnoi people, sample their food, and learn about their traditional remedies and crafts; expect to pay around Rs 1,200 ($30/£15) for 2 people for a 5-hour trip that should include some wildlife sightings. If you're curious, ask your operator or hotel if you can also see a traditional opium ceremony, which forms part of the daily rituals of village life. You can arrange these safaris through the RTDC at the tourist office (see "Visitor Information," above), but you'll save yourself much effort by asking your hotel to make all arrangements.

Mehrangarh Fort & Museum ⭐⭐⭐   "The work of angels, fairies and giants . . . he who walks through it loses sense of being among buildings; it as though he walked through mountain gorges . . ." wrote Rudyard Kipling in 1899. Little has changed since then, and for many this looming 15th-century edifice to Rajput valor is still Rajasthan's most impressive fort, with walls that soar like sheer cliffs 120m (400 ft.) high, literally dwarfing the city at its base, and a proud history of never having fallen to its many invaders. Before you start exploring the fort, get an audioguide (free with entry fee; passport or driver's license required as deposit). This is one of the best audioguides you will get at a tourist site in India, with sound effects and commentaries from former rulers of Jodhpur recorded on an MP3 player in seven languages. It contains additional information on subjects like the caste system, the maharajas, miniature paintings, and more. If you prefer a more interactive tour, hire a local guide (Rs 100/$2.45/£1.25) from your hotel or at the fort entrance, most of whom consider the audioguide useless but will ultimately steer you toward some ill-considered shopping in order to reap a commission (you have been warned). There is an elevator, but choose to walk past cannon-pockmarked and *sati*-daubed **Loha Gate** (the maharajas' wives would traditionally immortalize their lives by leaving handprints on the fort walls before tossing themselves on the flames to join their deceased husbands). Once at the top, you enjoy not only the most spectacular view, but you enter one of India's finest museums, with a rich collection of palanquins, royal cradles, miniature paintings, musical instruments, costumes, furniture, and armor. Every room is worth exploring (allow at least 2 hr.), but among the highlights are the gorgeous **royal chamber** where the Maharaja entertained his 30-plus wives (we're not even counting concubines); **Moti Mahal,** featuring the throne on which every Marwar Maharaja has been crowned; and **Phool Mahal,** the "dancing hall" with its pure gold ceiling. A massive **silk and velvet tent,** taken from Emperor Shah Jahan in Delhi, is a vivid illustration of the superlative wealth and decadent pomp with which the Rathore rulers lived. After visiting the courtyard of **Chamunda (Sun Goddess) Temple** (remember to remove your shoes), take the lane that leads to the left to view what is apparently among the rarest collections of cannons in India—again, the view alone is worth it. There is a very good museum shop (look for the exquisite silk and chiffon fabrics made by award-winning Tyeb Khan) and a restaurant where you can catch your breath.

On the road that leads to and from the fort, you will notice **Jaswant Thada,** a white marble cenotaph built to commemorate the life of Maharaja Jaswant Singh II, who died in 1899, and where the last rites of the Jodhpur rulers have been held since then. It's pretty enough, but after the magnificence of the fort's museum and forts, it can be a bit of a letdown. If you finish with the fort before sunset, descend to the cobbled streets of **Sadar Market,** where the sights and aromas of India's ancient and narrow streets—packed with cows, people, goats, carts, and chickens, and remarkably untouristed—may leave you wondering whether you've wandered onto the set of a movie about medieval times. If it all gets too claustrophobic, hire a rickshaw in which to sit in relative comfort and watch the passing parade. All in all, this will be one of your most satisfying outings in Rajasthan.

The Fort, Jodhpur. (📞 0291/254-8790. **Mehrangarh Fort:** Rs 250 ($6.10/£3.10), includes camera fee and audioguide; Rs 200 ($4.90/£2.50) video; Rs 15 (35¢/20p) elevator. Apr–Sept 8:30am–5:30pm; Oct–Mar 9am–5pm. **Jaswant Thada:** Rs 20 (50¢/25p); Rs 25 (60¢/30p) camera; Rs 50 ($1.25/65p) video. Daily 8:30am–5:30pm.

Umaid Bhawan Palace 🏛🏛🏛   Situated on another raised outcrop, with sprawling grounds creating an almost rural ambience, this splendid palace was built by Maharaja Umaid Singh (the current maharaja's father) as a poverty-relief exercise to aid his drought-stricken subjects. With 347 rooms, including a cinema, it was at the time the largest private residence in the world—a vivid reminder of the decadence the Rajput rulers enjoyed during the British Raj. Designed by Henry Lanchester, a great admirer of Lutyens (the man who designed New Delhi), it was commenced in 1929, took 3,000 laborers 13 years to complete, and remains one of the best examples of the Indo-Saracenic Art Deco style, topped with a massive dome which rises 56m (184 ft.) high, beyond which the buildings are perfectly symmetrical. If you don't choose to overnight here, you should still visit—if only to sip coffee at The Pillars, from where you enjoy a spellbinding view of the fort in the distance (note that non-staying guests are technically required to pay a cover charge even when dining at The Pillars; to avoid disappointment, try acting the part and say your keys are at reception, or else cough up the dough). There is also a museum that features photographs of the construction and a model of the building, as well as items collected by the maharaja's ancestors; it's not quite what you want out of a palace visit.

Umaid Bhawan Palace, Jodhpur. ✆ 0291/251-0101. Admission to hotel restaurants Rs 1,500 ($37/£19), payable at reception, and deductible from your dining bill. Museum: Rs 50 ($1.25/65p). Daily 9am–5pm.

WHERE TO STAY & DINE
If you want to experience the medieval spirit of daily life within the Old City, your best bet is Pal Haveli (reviewed below). There are also a number of good budget options, including many family-run affairs that are listed with the tourist office. If you don't want to take your chances, the following are worth noting. **Haveli Guest House** (✆ **0291/261-4615;** www.haveliguesthouse.com) is a very hospitable and well-run establishment (more of an inn than a haveli) with simple en-suite rooms—make sure you book one that has a view of the fort. The best of these are 15 new rooms added in 2007; they're the most expensive, but are relatively attractive, with murals and window seats where you can enjoy the view (and spy on the street life down below). If you're not staying here, pop in for lunch at the **rooftop restaurant;** views are unbeatable. Doubles range from Rs 350 to Rs 1,500 ($8.55–$37/£4.35–£19).

If living in the Old City sounds a little rough, head for the outskirts of town (20 min. from the fort) to **Taj Hari Mahal** ⌘ (5 Residency Rd.; ✆ **0291/243-9700;** www.tajhotels.com; from $300/£150), a very smart hotel built in the style of a Marwari palace. Aimed predominantly at the wealthy business market, this will suit those who have simply had enough of the chaos of India and want to be cocooned from it all in a modern hotel with professional service. Guest rooms are huge and elegantly dressed, with state-of-the-art conveniences and tip-top bathrooms. Public spaces are also luxurious and cool. The hotel's very modernity and mass-produced furnishings make it somewhat dull, with none of the charm of the haveli hotels; if you can afford it, you'll be far better off at the Taj-managed Umaid Bhawan Palace (reviewed below).

Jodhpur is not renowned for its restaurants; you're pretty much limited to dining in hotels. Even if you're not overnighting at Umaid Bhawan, consider whiling away a few hours at **The Pillars,** the hotel's informal cafe-restaurant where you sit at the base of a cavernous colonnaded veranda that steps down to the palace lawns—get there before the sun goes down to watch the almost surreal changing hues of the sky over the fort, but don't expect miracles from the kitchen. Widely regarded as the best restaurant in town, with a great nighttime atmosphere (do make sure they're serving in the garden), **On the Rocks** (next to Ajit Bhawan; ✆ **0291/510-2701** or -7880) is famous for its barbecue dishes—skewers of spicy vegetables, *paneer,* or meat tenderized in a yogurt-based marinade and cooked over an open fire. For a more leisurely dinner, with decent Indian food and enchanting views of the Fort, head to **Indique,** the rooftop restaurant at Pal Haveli (reviewed below).

Ajit Bhawan ⌘ (Kids)   Built at the turn of the 20th century for Maharaj Ajit Singh (younger brother of the Maharaja Umaid Singh), this hotel incorporates crenelated castlelike walls and traditional Hindustani elements, resulting in a weird, rather kitschy mishmash with the atmosphere of a small resort. But it's a hugely popular place, and some prefer its more laid-back, down-home atmosphere to Umaid's plush palace. It's also significantly cheaper and has a wonderful outdoor pool and a good restaurant. The kitsch continues inside as you wander through what appears to be a faux Rajasthani "village," with stone cottages and low-slung mud walls leading off the central dining area and pool. Decor ranges from quite whimsical (which some may find amusing), to tremendously smart; the rooms are the work of Raghavendra Rathore, the owner's son and one of the country's top 15 designers. His smartest, most contemporary work is notable in the 12 new executive rooms, which are relatively luxurious, with wooden floors, unique, elegant furniture, and great bathrooms with tubs. That said, a few rooms have taken the kitsch theme a step too far (like no. 26, which has an indoor waterfall cascading over a rock, buck horns sprouting from its light fixtures, and a tiger skin behind the bed). Still, rooms are in mint condition, and a selection of gorgeous luxury tents features built-in bathrooms and wrought-iron furniture. If you can bag deluxe-room nos. 101 to 104 (also with wooden floors), each with a little balcony overlooking the pool (the best reason to book here), you'll have a better reason for smiling. Car enthusiasts may dig the fleet of 10 vintage cars on offer—the oldest Buicks and Fords date back to 1928.

Near Circuit House, Jodhpur 342 006. ⓒ **0291/251-1410.** Fax 0291/251-0674. www.ajitbhawan.com. 54 units. $95 (£48) Shikar tent double; $130 (£65) standard double; $190 (£95) deluxe double; $215 (£108) executive double; $238 (£119) luxury tent double; $355 (£178) luxury double room. $25 (£13) extra bed. Taxes extra. AE, DC, MC, V. **Amenities:** Restaurant; pool; health club; spa; travel desk; fleet of vintage cars for hire; airport transfers; business center; gift shop; salon; 24-hr. room service; laundry; doctor-on-call; currency exchange; wireless Internet; horse, camel, and village safaris; evening folk dancing. *In room:* A/C, TV, minibar, hair dryer.

Devi Bhawan 🏵🏵 *(Value)*   This low-slung sandstone residence is a great surprise—a bungalow with free-standing cottages set within a lush, tranquil garden and personally overseen by a wonderful husband-and-wife team. You won't find such value—a fabulous pool, good restaurant, and friendly service—anywhere else in town. Ask for an air-conditioned semi-deluxe (bungalow) room (particularly no. 10), or spend a little extra on deluxe unit no. 11, a large and lovely room that has a big bathroom with tub. All the rooms are wonderfully clean and neat with simple, casually stylish furnishings—there's not a hint of plastic anywhere. Completely overhauled in 2007, with the added advantage of air-conditioning, the restaurant spills out onto a neat little lawn surrounded by greenery; you can (and should) dine here under the stars (bring insect repellent) at tables prettily laid out with fabric tablecloths. Service is very personal, and the hard-working manager, Rakesh, will not only arrange practically anything you need, but can probably list train times and transport tariffs in his sleep; these people go well out of their way to be of assistance. All in all, this is a very comfortable, relaxing, good-value option, and once seduced by the pool, you may just find yourself extending your stay in Jodhpur.

1 Defence Lab. Rd., Ratanada Circle, Jodhpur 342 011. ⓒ **0291/251-1067** or 98-2803-5359. Fax 0291/251-2215. www.devibhawan.com. devibhawan@sify.com. 13 units. Rs 850 ($21/£11) standard/garden double; Rs 1,200 ($29/£15) semi-deluxe/bungalow double; Rs 1,500 ($37/£19) deluxe double. 10% luxury tax on rooms over Rs 1,200. MC, V. **Amenities:** Restaurant; bar/lounge; pool; travel desk; laundry; doctor-on-call; Internet access; jeep/horse safaris. *In room:* A/C (most rooms), TV.

Pal Haveli 🏵   A relatively recent addition to Jodhpur's heritage scene, this is the only original haveli in the Old City and *the* place to stay if you want to be in the real heart of the bustling (and admittedly noisy) town; at press time it was undergoing a thorough renovation, transforming it into a truly worthwhile heritage experience. Once you enter—via a steeply sloped ramp and through massive painted, traditional doors—you can shut out the world and imagine you're living in a bygone era. Rooms are a mixed bag: All are spacious (some are now massive) and decorated to enhance the ambience of an earlier era; expect to find murals or framed miniatures and plenty of antique furniture. Beds are comfortable, and bathrooms (with either tub or drench shower) are exquisitely clean. At press time, rooms had not yet been assigned names or numbers, but you have a choice of either lake-facing, fort-facing, or heritage room; those arranged around the fountain courtyard tend to be quieter, with a more sophisticated look. Meals at the alfresco rooftop restaurant, **Indique,** are accompanied by superb views of the fort, the palace, and the lake.

Gulab Sagar, Jodhpur 342 001. ℂ 0291/329-3328 or 0291/263-8344. www.palhaveli.com. info@palhaveli.com. 20 units. Rs 2,100 ($51/£26) standard double; Rs 2,500 ($61/£31) heritage double; Rs 3,500 ($85/£43) suite; Rs 500 ($12/£6) extra bed. Taxes extra. MC, V. **Amenities:** 2 restaurants; bar; travel and tour assistance; complimentary station pick-up; transfers; room service; laundry; doctor-on-call; village safaris; billiards room. *In room:* A/C, TV, minibar, tea- and coffee-making facility.

Ratan Vilas ⟨R⟩ ⟨*Value*⟩   Built in 1920 by current owner Brij Raj Singh's grandfather, this haveli has been painstakingly restored, preserving its traditional character while adding modern comforts—which makes it an excellent option in this price category (a great deal better than places like Karni Bhawan, which charges twice the rates here). Until the planned pool is installed (presumably in 2008), however, it's not quite as good a value—or as good an experience—as a stay in Devi Bhawan, which also benefits from a lush, beautiful garden. It offers better value than anything you'll find inside the Old City, though. Air-conditioned rooms are immaculate and simple, tastefully styled with antique furniture (which Brij Raj collects) and traditional handblock-printed curtains and bed sheets (book deluxe room no. 101, 102, or 104, or bag one of the slightly larger units in the new wing). The breezy, plant-filled central courtyard has a lovely swing where you can spend hours with a book. It's a homey place with old family photographs and souvenirs adorning the walls—no five-star amenities, of course, but the food has home-cooked freshness, service is prompt and personalized, and you can even ask to step into the kitchen for a demonstration of traditional Rajasthani cooking. Until the pool arrives, sun-worshipers can take advantage of the sun-deck chairs on the terrace and veranda, and Brij Raj (a keen polo player) maintains a stable of well-bred Marwari horses for residents to ride.

Loco Shed Rd., Ratanada, Jodhpur 342 001. ℂ/fax 0291/261-4418. www.ratanvilas.com. info@ratanvilas.com. 20 units. Rs 800 ($20/£10) non-A/C double; Rs 995 ($24/£12) A/C double; Rs 1,650 ($40/£20) deluxe double; Rs 1,950 ($48/£24) superior double; Rs 350 ($9/£4) extra bed. Taxes extra. MC, V. **Amenities:** Dining hall; bar; travel desk; complimentary pick-up; laundry; doctor-on-call; currency exchange; Internet; horse riding; village jeep safari. *In room:* A/C, TV.

Umaid Bhawan Palace ⟨R⟩⟨R⟩⟨R⟩   Far and away the grandest lodging in Jodhpur, this is also one of the proudest pieces of architecture in the state. Its formidable sense of grandeur is made all the more dramatic by the unique hilltop position, seemingly miles away from humdrum city life below. Although the palace was built in the last century, its splendor has been restored to bring alive an authentic opulence and luxury, making guests feel as though they really are royalty, a point underscored by the galley of turbaned staff who greet you at every turn, even thanking you for visiting their part of the hotel. Monumental in scale, with lavish attention to detail, this palace is not just breathtaking to behold (and every visitor to Jodhpur *must* gaze upon it), but interior spaces have a certain magic that makes a stay here utterly memorable. After the spectacle of the 32m (105-ft.) central dome in the Palm Court (where you really need to pause and let your eyes drink it all in), you'll want to spend some time exploring the various public spaces (decorated in Art Deco furniture and fittings), swanning up and down the sweeping marble staircases, and heading down to the indoor pool—which will transport you to back to the 1940s with its bold blue zodiac-sign mosaics. Guests are taken on a personal tour of the entire palace (excluding the private residence of the royal family); do ask if you can see the Maharaja and Maharani suites, which have not been renovated but represent another opportunity to peek back in time. There's even an in-house cinema, which you can reserve (ask the concierge to recommend a big-budget Bollywood DVD). The quality of rooms varies according to what you're able to spend. That said, this is a good place to indulge if you can afford one of the historical suites; these grand spaces are packed with gorgeous period furniture, lovely artworks, and every possible amenity. Bathrooms are sumptuous Deco affairs with original, unusual tubs and massive showers. Ask for a room with a private terrace. A wonderful new pool sits beyond a superb garden of shaped bougainvilleas and the vast lawn where Liz Hurley staged her much-publicized wedding to her Indian beau, Arun Nayar. The outdoor pool is also a tranquil spot to unwind at the end of the day and, with cocktail in hand, watch the fort light up as the sun descends and sets the sky ashimmer.

Umaid Bhawan Palace, Jodhpur 342 006. ✆ **0291/251-0101.** Fax 0291/251-0100. 75 units. $600 (£300) luxury double; $750 (£375) palace double; $1,600 (£800) historical suite; $2,600 (£1,300) royal suite; $4,000 (£2,000) grand royal suite. Taxes extra. AE, DC, MC, V. **Amenities:** 3 restaurants; bar; smoking lounge/reading room; outdoor pool; indoor pool; tennis; gym; health club; spa; concierge; travel desk; gift boutique; 24-hr. room service; laundry; doctor-on-call; squash; billiards room; cinema; DVD library. *In room:* A/C, TV, minibar, hair dryer, safe, personal butler; DVD player.

OUTSKIRTS OF JODHPUR

Bal Samand Lake Palace & Garden Retreat 👁★★   Built in 1594, Bal Samand is a relatively tiny palace that was carved out of red sandstone and appears to grow out of the dam-wall terrace that overlooks its namesake lake, some 7km (4⅓ miles) from Jodhpur. Surrounded by water, scrubland, and what once must have been beautifully landscaped gardens, it's a grand rural oasis second to none, not least because you share it with a maximum of only 16 other guests. Keep in mind that what is being reviewed here are the palace or "Regal Suites" in the actual Bal Samand palace, *not* the standard "garden" rooms in the relatively new wing in the 120-hectare (300-acre) gardens near the property entrance—the latter are terribly ordinary. If the Regal Suites aren't available, you may as well book into the Ajit Bhawan. Book room no. 1 for wonderful garden views, or the more private room no. 6, which is simply beautiful—a massive double-volume space with fabulous sandstone detailing, lots of lamps for atmospheric lighting, a gorgeous mix of Rajasthani and colonial furniture, a Jacuzzi-size bath, and an atmosphere fit for a king. Room no. 2 is a great choice as well, with fantastic, detailed stonework, two sets of bathrooms (one with tub, one with glassed-in shower), yards of huge picture windows showing off the pretty gardens, and a delightful swingbed. Some of the rooms on the ground floor have the benefit of doors that open directly on to the lovely, fairy-tale garden, lorded over by a stunning, ancient banyan tree; they're also a little closer to the large, remotely situated outdoor pool, which takes considerable effort to get to. Traditionally, the biggest drawback has been the thin service, which is well-meaning and steadily improving but certainly not up to scratch. Fortunately, residents in the palace have their own, exclusive dining facility, together with a plush royal bar. Check in here for a truly romantic retreat.

Mandore Rd., Jodhpur 342 026. ✆ **0291/257-2321** through -2326, or -1991. Fax 0291/257-1240. www.jodhpur heritage.com. reservations@jodhpurheritage.com. 35 units. $130 (£65) garden double; $325 (£163) regal suite. 10% tax extra; off-season discount may apply. AE, MC, V. **Amenities:** 3 restaurants; 2 bars; pool; 9-hole golf course;

24-hr. room service; massage; laundry; doctor-on-call; horse and buggy rides; croquet. *In room:* A/C, TV, minibar, tea- and coffee-making facilities, hair dryer and iron on request.

Fort Chanwa ⊛   This red-sandstone fortress is an oasis of relative luxury at the end of a potholed road to Luni, a tiny village just 35km (22 miles) from Jodhpur. Some- how this makes it feel a great deal more remote than Rohet Garh, but logistically it's actually a great deal closer to Jodhpur. Belonging to the present Jodhpur Maharaja's uncle, the 200-year-old property was renovated in 1998, and not always that sensi- tively. However, interiors (designed by the maharani) are very tasteful, and there's a pool, an Ayurvedic massage center, and a very sharp staff to oversee all your needs. The Maharaja Suite (no. 9)—a deluxe twin room, with a deep double bed–size alcove, is particularly lovely; a family or group should book nos. 12 and 14, which share a large terrace. Rooms in the newer wing are very standard, with limited atmosphere (and fewer windows) to inflame your imagination. Just a 40-minute drive from Jodhpur, this rural retreat will suit travelers who want to see Jodhpur's top attractions but who prefer to spend the night away from the city's chaos and pollution. Transfers from Jodhpur are easily arranged.

Luni village. On the NH68, 9km (5½ miles) off the main road. ⓒ **02931/28-4216.** Reservations: 1 PWD Rd., Jodh- pur 342 001. ⓒ **0291/243-2460.** www.fortchanwa.com. 67 units. Rs 4,000 ($98/£49) standard double; Rs 4,500 ($110/£56) deluxe double. AE, DC, MC, V. **Amenities:** Restaurant; pool; Jacuzzi, steam, and sauna; travel desk; gift shop; limited room service; massage; babysitting; laundry; doctor-on-call; currency exchange; evening entertainment; croquet; horse rides; village safaris; camel safaris; excursions to Jodhpur. *In room:* A/C, minibar in some, hair dryer on request.

Rohet Garh ⊛ *(Value)*   Professionally run and lorded over by its aristocratic owner, Sidharth Singh, Rohet Garh may be farther away from Jodhpur, but is far more ele- gant than Fort Chanwa. The rural peace is intoxicating—peacocks lazily strut on the lawns and pose on the rooftops, while the adjacent village makes for heady exploration without the hassle of wandering the streets of the city. More important (for hydrohe- donists at least), it has a lovely pool in the central courtyard, from which you can access the dining room, smartly attired with white linen tablecloths and napkins (and a wonderful absence of hunting trophies) and serving good-quality Rajasthani food. Rooms, as is always the case with heritage properties, vary dramatically (ask to see what's on offer when you arrive), but all are relatively spacious, featuring frescoes and Rajasthani antiques in rather bright, minimalist arrangements tied together with dif- ferent color palettes. Book the most recently renovated rooms (nos. 6 and 7) for the best bathrooms (most are small, but neat), though you are warned that these are around the pool, so they are not that private (for more privacy, ask for no. 15 or 30). Room 14 is especially large, with a big shower and a huge carved bed, while the lake- view suites (particularly no. 27) have lovely window seats for lazing about with a good book. A couple of the rooms have direct views into the stables, where there are 12 Marwar steeds—great for kids who haven't outgrown the *Black Beauty* phase—and where you might even glimpse a mare with newborn foal. As with practically every hotel in Jodhpur, outings include visits to traditional Bishnoi villages, with the possi- bility of witnessing traditional opium ceremonies. If you have the time, ask about the miniature paintings workshops or sign up for a cooking class. ***Note:*** This is a practi- cal option if you are looking to overnight en route to Udaipur but haven't managed to get that far away from Jodhpur. Also available for travelers with a greater sense of adventure are six luxury tents (Rs 7,500/$183/£93 double, including all meals, evening tea, and village safari), pitched in the desert, 17km (11 miles) away.

Rohet Garh, Vill P.O. Rohet, District Pali, Rajasthan 306 401. © 02936/268-231 or reservations in Jodhpur 0291/
243-1161. Fax 0291/264-9368. www.rohetgarh.com. 34 units. Rs 4,500 ($110/£56) deluxe double; Rs 6,000
($146/£74) suite. Taxes extra. AE, MC, V. **Amenities:** Restaurant; bar; pool; health club; travel desk; gift shop; limited
room service; laundry; doctor-on-call; currency exchange; jeep; horse and camel safaris; bird-watching by bicycle; picnic lunch; cooking demonstrations. *In room:* A/C, hair dryer in some; suites have minibar and tea- and coffee-making
facilities.

SHOPPING

Jodhpur is famous for its antiques dealers, most lining the road that runs between Ajit
Bhawan and Umaid Bhawan. These can be prohibitively pricey, however, particularly
when you factor in freight prices. Jodhpur is also good for tie-dye fabrics. The best
bazaars are around Sojati Gate, Tripolia, Khanda Falsa, and Lakhara—the latter specializes in colorful *lac* bangles, which make great gifts. If you're looking for more serious jewelry, head for Station Road. Traditional Jodhpur coats and riding breeches are
now only made to order; ask your hotel to recommend a tailor. *Tip:* Beware of making any purchases in or around the fort, particularly if you are encouraged to do so by
the local guides; not only will you be paying inflated prices for anything you buy, but
guides are paid a hefty commission to get you to part with your cash.

9 Jaisalmer

285km (177 miles) W of Jodhpur; 333km (206 miles) SW of Bikaner

Jaisalmer was founded by Rao Jaisal in 1156, making it the oldest "living" fortified
city in Rajasthan. For many, a visit here is the start of an enduring romance. Located
in the heart of the Thar Desert on the far western border of India (55km/34 miles
from Pakistan), it was strategically positioned on one of the central Asian trade routes,
and fortunes were made by the Rajputs and Jain merchants who levied enormous taxes
on caravans laden with silks and spices, particularly during the 14th and 16th centuries. In the 18th century, some merchants, wanting to expand their homes, moved
out of the fort to settle on the plateau below. Much as in the Shekhawati region, the
wealth generated by their taxes was used to decorate the havelis of these wealthy Jain
businessmen. Where frescoes satisfied the Shekhawats, here power was expressed by
the construction of mansions whose soft sandstone facades were embellished with
intricate, almost lacelike carvings. These oft-photographed sandstone mansions are
indeed breathtakingly beautiful, but it is Sonar Killa, literally "Golden Fort," that
makes it worth traveling this far west. It may not be as impressive as Jodhpur's
Mehrangarh Fort, but its charm lies in the fact that this is the world's only inhabited
medieval fort, its families living in homes they have colonized for more than 800
years. Built entirely from yellow sandstone, the fort rises like a giant sandcastle from
its desert surrounds, with great views from the tiny guesthouses that lie within its ramparts; stare down on the city and desert vista, and you get a sense of how forts such as
these once served the most basic of needs: protection against invaders from the plateau
below. Within you will find a place with almost no traffic, minimal pollution (watch
out for the cow dung), and an awesome sense of timelessness (bar the motorcycles and
persistent salesmanship). It takes no more than a few hours to tour the fort, including
stops to visit the Jain and Hindu temples. And if you want to ride a camel into the
sunset, Jaisalmer is probably the place to do it. So plan to spend 2 or more nights here,
not least because it takes so long to get here (until the new airport is finished, that is).

ESSENTIALS

VISITOR INFORMATION You'll find the **RTDC tourist office** near Gadi Sagar Pol (℃ **02922/25-2406;** Mon–Sat 10am–6pm; closed second Sat of every month and Sun).

GETTING THERE At press time, Jaisalmer's new airport was expected to open anywhere between late 2007 and 2009, finally making it possible to fly to India's easternmost city directly from Delhi. Until flights commence, the nearest airport is at Jodhpur (a 5½-hr. drive; about 2 hr. longer in a bus—not recommended). *Tip:* The best place to stop for lunch or a snack on this route is **Manvar Desert Resort** (near Shergarh; ℃ **02928/266-137;** www.manvar.com), which serves a mean chicken *pakora.* It takes 6 to 7 hours to get from Bikaner to Jaisalmer by road. The train journey from Jodhpur takes 5½ hours (on the overnight Jodhpur–Jaisalmer Express), arriving at the station 2km (1¼ miles) east of town. Avoid the touts soliciting riders by asking your hotel to arrange a transfer. From Delhi, take the Delhi–Jaisalmer Express from Delhi's Sarai Rohilla Station; it departs at 5:25pm, arriving in Jaisalmer at 1:30pm the next day.

GETTING AROUND Both inside and outside the fort, the town is small enough to explore on foot; for journeys farther afield you will need to hire an auto-rickshaw (at the station or Gadsisar Tank) or taxi (Sam Dunes). For the latter, you'll probably take an all-inclusive trip with your hotel, almost all of which offer safaris of various duration; or contact Harish Bhai at **K.K. Travels** (℃ **02992/253-087;** kktravels_2000@yahoo.com). You'll also find taxis around Suraj Pol or through one of several travel agencies at the entrance to the fort.

FESTIVALS The **Desert Festival** held at the end of January or in February (incidentally, the best time of the year to visit Jaisalmer) is the highlight of the year, when dance shows, turban-tying competitions, and camel races are held below the fort, cheered on by colorful crowds who are as much a part of the spectacle as the entertainment. While its relative inaccessibility keeps tourist numbers down, during the festival the town is packed.

WHAT TO SEE & DO

Jaisalmer's main attraction is its yellow sandstone **fort,** whose 9m (30-ft.) walls grow in a roughly triangular shape, springing from Trikuta (Triangular) Hill, on which it is built, and buttressed by 99 bastions. Within you will find a number of elaborately carved havelis overlooking the narrow streets, but the best examples of Jaisalmer's unique **havelis** are situated in the town below. Hordes of tourists end the afternoon by taking a trip out to Sam Dunes or Khuhri to watch the **setting desert sun** from the back of a camel; with a little planning, however, you can enjoy a totally unique **dune-and-camel experience** that will have you falling in love with the desert (see "Camel Safari," below, for our recommendation). If you're more sedentary, head for **Saffron,** the rooftop terrace at the Nachana Haveli, for a view of the fort, which starts to glow as the sky darkens; you'll also witness all manner of daily life on the town's rooftops.

Other attractions are **Gadsisar Tank,** excavated by the Maharaja Gadsi Singh in 1367, which has a few temples and a *chhattri* (cenotaph) overlooking it, but is principally worth visiting to access the nearby **Folklore Museum.** The private museum contains some interesting exhibits, particularly the handcrafted items (look for the mobile temple, and the depiction of the tragic love story of Princess Moomal and King Mahendra, which, incidentally, is told in detail on the Palace Museum audio tour).

Exhibits are not well labeled, however; if the proprietor, Mr. Sharma, is not on hand, a guide could prove useful here. The small entrance fee is not always charged, but do leave a donation; hours are 8am to noon and 3 to 6pm, daily. A shop at the end of the museum sells reasonably priced postcards (and overpriced books).

The best way to experience Jaisalmer's desert surrounds is on a **camel safari** (see below), many of which include the following places of interest. **Amar Sagar** is a small settlement with a palace and a restored Jain temple built around the shores of a lake that lies 5km (3 miles) northwest of Jaisalmer. **Barra Bagh,** which lies 6km (3¾ miles) north of town, is a minioasis where you can view a collection of cenotaphs to Jaisalmer's Rajput rulers. Another 10km (6¼ miles) north lies **Lodurva,** once the capital of the Bhatti Rajputs before Jaisalmer was built. The main attractions here are more restored Jain temples, with the usual fine carvings. The entrance to **Thar Desert National Park** lies about an hour (45km/28 miles) from Jaisalmer, near Khuhri. Wildlife you are likely to encounter include deer, desert fox, black buck, and the rare long-necked bird known as the Great Indian Bustard.

EXPLORING THE GOLDEN FORT

Some 1,000 people still live in the tiny village inside **Sonar Killa,** or Golden Fort, which has twisting lanes so narrow they can be blocked by a single cow (be warned that these animals *know* that they have the right of way, so step aside). Exploring the fort is easily done in a morning—you access the fort through Gopa Chowk, ascending the battle-scarred ramparts to enter the main courtyard, overlooked by seven-story Raja Mahal, or Maharaja's Palace, which now operates as the **Fort Palace Museum & Heritage Centre** ★★★ (© **02992/25-2981**). Thanks to a brilliant audioguide tour, the palace has become one of the most alluring tourist attractions in the state, packed with information that not only brings to life the history of this unique place, but waxes vividly about the aristocrats who built and frequently defended it. It also does an excellent job of shedding light on intriguing aspects of regional culture. Set aside around 2 hours for the tour; admission is Rs 250 ($6.10/£3.10) and includes the audioguide (passport, credit card, driver's license, or $40/£20 as deposit) as well as still camera use (video is Rs 150/$3.65/£1.85).

After the palace, the other great reason to visit the fort is to check out the panoramas of the city below and the distant desert vistas (although a number of exquisite bird's-eye views are afforded throughout the palace tour) from various perspectives. There are a number of interesting vantage points (a few are specifically marked), but do be aware that buskers may try to take advantage of you by starting up a tune and then insisting on a donation. Stop for a cup of *chai* on the rooftop of Hotel Paradise for sublime views, or head straight for the beautiful **Jain temples,** which lie west (just ask for directions). The best among these (Rishabnath and Sambhavnath) are open only to non-Jains after 11am. Entry is Rs 20 (50¢/25p) and you'll pay Rs 50 ($1.25/65p) to take a camera in, double that for video. No leather is allowed within the temple, and menstruating women are restricted from entering. Constructed between the 14th and 16th centuries, these temples are typical of Jain craftsmanship, with every wall and pillar as well as the ceiling covered with the most intricate relief carvings, and large statues representing the Jain *tirthankaras,* or "Enlightened Ones"—note that you cannot enter the caged sanctuaries in which these sculptures sit, or touch or photograph them. A small library has a collection of rare manuscripts, books, and miniature paintings. Take a breather at **Toap Khana (Place of Cannon)** for the views, then head north, turning right at some stage to find **Laxminath Temple** (again, just ask). Although the

Jain temples are worth a visit to see the intricacy of the carvings, it is the Hindu temple that pulsates with energy, particularly if you get here when worshipers chant their *bhajans,* devotional songs (about 10:30am and at several other times during the day; check with your hotel). From here it's a short walk back to the main courtyard.

THE JAISALMER HAVELIS

Haveli refers to a traditional, ornate Rajasthani "mansion," with one or more internal courtyards. Steps lead up to an ornate door through which you enter a central courtyard, around which the family apartments are arranged. The facades of the Jaisalmer havelis, built as elsewhere by the town's wealthy merchants, are unsurpassed for the delicacy of their relief carvings, filigreed windows, and lacelike screens and *jarokhas* (small projecting balconies). A testament to the softness of the sandstone but even more to the skill of the *silavats,* Jaisalmer's community of stonemasons, these beautiful facades, some of which date back more than 300 years, have been perfectly preserved, thanks largely to the hot, dry climate. You will find them dotted all over town, but the most impressive are Patwon ki Haveli, Salim Singh ki Haveli, and Nathmalji ki Haveli. **Patwon ki Haveli** actually comprises five ornate houses built by the wealthy Patwon for his five sons between 1800 and 1860. The houses are connected from within (though some are privately owned and not open to the public) and have flat-topped roofs. Inside one of the houses is the **Basant Art Emporium,** where you can pick up truly exquisite handicrafts—but certainly not at bargain prices—collected by the owner from the desert tribes. Patwon ki Haveli is open daily between 10am and 5pm (8:30am–7pm in summer); admission is Rs 20 (50¢/25p; cameras extra). South of this, near the fort entrance, is **Salim Singh ki Haveli,** built by a particularly mean-spirited and greedy prime minister who extorted the hell out of the Rajput's kings' subjects, and even squeezed the royal family by providing huge loans and then charging exorbitant interest rates. It was apparently once two stories higher, but legend has it that the Rajput king blew away the top floors in a fit of pique, and Salim Singh was later stabbed to death. It's not necessary that you enter, and it's not always open (though times advertised are 8am–6pm, up to 7pm in summer). You can't enter **Nathmalji ki Haveli,** but it's still worth swinging by to play "spot the difference" with the beautiful facade. The right and left wings look identical at first glance, but they were separately carved by two brothers—the numerous tiny differences can take hours to discover (this is where a guide comes in handy!). It's on the road to Malka Pol (just ask for directions). Note that many of the havelis now house overpriced handicraft shops; you will have to bargain hard to get the prices down.

CAMEL SAFARI

Spending some time in the desert on camelback is touted as one of Jaisalmer's must-do activities, and although you can spend a night or even two "camping" out in the desert (some outfitters have semi-permanent camps, with en-suite tents), trekking to sites of interest during the day, most people choose to spend only a few hours in the desert, usually watching the sun set from **Sam Dunes.** Keep in mind that the popularity of these short trips means you will more than likely be surrounded by noisy travelers in areas that are looking increasingly degraded—with discarded bottles and cigarette packets, and kids cajoling you to buy warm colas and make "donations." The whole experience can be unbearable if you value solitude and want a unique experience that doesn't feel like an overhyped tourist trap. If the idea of a communally enjoyed sunset doesn't ruin the romance for you, you can either take a camel ride at sunset from Sam Dunes, about an hour from town by car, or from Khuhri, which lies almost 2 hours away by car. The latter is obviously less popular, so it's not as busy, but it is no longer the unspoiled experience it was 15 years ago. Almost every hotel and innumerable agents offer camel trips in various locations (you can opt for one just outside of town, where there are no dunes, but lovely fort views), or you can drive out yourself and negotiate directly with one of the camel drivers who line the road with camels—the state of the saddle is a good indication of which one to choose. In any case, your backside is likely to start aching after a while—the best part of the ride might be getting out of the saddle and strolling over a dune or two; or, if you're feeling adventurous, ask your camel-*wallah* to climb up behind you and take you for a canter.

If you'd rather escape the tedium of done-to-death camel safaris, contact without hesitation **Shakti Singh** of Nachana Haveli (see "Where to Stay" below); he'll arrange a unique, tailor-made, and totally private **desert experience** ✦✦✦ that will combine a camel safari with visits to remote villages, perhaps a meal on the dunes, and a delightfully intimate knowledge of the environment. Shakti, the unassuming son of a maharaja, lived in the desert for 2 years getting to grips with a way of life most sophisticated urbanites could hardly conceive. He's knowledgeable about the flora and fauna that you come across as you traverse the dunes; although young and modest, he knows the region better than the multitude of "professionals" offering camel safaris.

If you can cope with staying "on board" a camel train for 2 to 3 hours every morning and afternoon, you can go on a trek that stops at various desert villages and temples and lets you enjoy meals around bonfires under the stars and sleep in a temporary but comfortable camp—you will need to pack warm sleepwear for this, and you're pretty much at the mercy of fate when it comes to the group you land up with.

Should you wish to saddle up with the masses, the most reliable camel safari agent is **Royal Desert Safaris** (Nachana Haveli; ✆ **02992/252-538;** rsafari@sancharnet.in). Expect an all-inclusive late-afternoon camel ride, with dinner and jeep transfers, to cost Rs 1,050 ($26/£13) per head. The camel ride without food and transfers is Rs 250 ($6/£3). Also offered are overnight packages for camping out in the desert in Swiss cottages (Rs 4,500/$110/£56 double, including rides, entertainment, and meals).

WHERE TO STAY

Jaisalmer offers three general choices: Stay inside the fort, stay in the town that sprawls at its base, or head out into the desert and stay at one of the "resorts" targeting travelers who want to feel like they're in the middle of nowhere. The ecologically sensitive make a strong argument for not staying in the fort: The increase in water usage (mostly due to tourist traffic), which relies on medieval drainage systems, has started to literally pulp the ancient sandstone fort, and clearly the best way to preserve it is to avoid staying in the fort itself. The most luxurious accommodations are a few minutes' drive from the town itself, built where there is space for such luxuries as swimming pools and gardens. The best of these is Fort Rajwada (reviewed below); from here, you can see the fort, but you'll miss out on the daily rituals of the people who live inside the fort's ramparts. Even if tourism is for most now the major source of income, waking up in the fort affords visitors an authentic experience of a totally unique way of life. Note, however, that if you choose to stay inside the fort, cars are not allowed, so you'll need to use an auto-rickshaw or a porter get your luggage up the steep approach to the fort. Also be aware that, for some, the medieval lodgings can be claustrophobic, while the cramped living conditions make for a noisy environment (certainly contributing to the unique atmosphere), and in the midday heat you'll probably long for a pool. A surprising number of options are found inside the fort, but none comes near the standard of **Killa Bhawan** (reviewed below). If Killa Bhawan is full, try the new **Hotel Garh Jaisal** (*(C)* **02992/25-3836**), which has a less stylish ambience but a full complement of en-suite air-conditioned accommodations; guest rooms are a mixed bag, each accented according to a different color theme, but they're also quite atmospheric, catching a refreshing breeze and plenty of light ("Blue Sky" is a decent choice with a balcony). Views are fantastic, and doubles start at around $100 (£50).

If you're watching your rupees, but don't fancy slumming it, consider **Hotel Monsoon Palace** (*(C)* **02992/25-2656** or 94-1414-9631; Rs 2,500/$61/£31 double with breakfast), which has just two small, bright, clean en-suite air-conditioned guest rooms in a skinny building hidden in the fort's back-alley maze. Rooms have large metal-frame beds with silk bedcovers; bathrooms are outrageously tiny, however. You can watch the street below from your window seat, but the loveliest spot to relax and enjoy the sumptuous views is the windswept rooftop terrace (where breakfasts are served); complimentary tea and coffee are served here all day. Your Brahmin hosts will arrange and accompany you on camel safaris, during which you can visit desert villages, overnight in a tent, and learn traditional cooking. If you're looking for a really inexpensive experience in the fort, don't be put off by the crudely ambitious name of the popular **Hotel Paradise** (*(C)* **02992/252-674;** www.paradiseonfort.com; Rs 350–Rs 1,500/$9–$37/£4–£19). Aimed at budget travelers, Paradise offers very basic, cell-like rooms ranging from units with shared baths to spruced-up rooms with tiny, precarious balconies. Because it's situated right on the fort ramparts, however, it has awesome desert views (make sure you book a room with one); it also has a great rooftop terrace.

Choices in town are a mixed bag, but if you're looking for historic ambience and a friendly atmosphere, nothing beats **Nachana Haveli** (Govardhan Chowk; *(C)* **02992/25-2110;** nachana_haveli@yahoo.com; winter rates from Rs 2,300/$56/£28 double), the best heritage option outside the fort, particularly good if you're young at heart and want to hang with Jaisalmer's groovy elite. At almost 3 centuries, this atmospheric mansion (next door to the royal palace) has seen better days, but it has character, with cavernous, individually styled rooms designed for the extremes of the desert climate. Most have four-poster beds and stone floors with rugs (decent choices are room nos. 111 and 107). The family-run hotel is the brainchild of Vikram, the globe-trotting playboyish son of the Maharaja of Nachana (an area spanning the desert and across into Pakistan) and cousin of Jaisalmer's own king. He's a bit of a collector, so all spaces are decorated with eclectic paraphernalia; the vaulted ground-floor lounge, in particular, feels like a motley family museum, stuffed full of antique furniture, portraits, statues, hobby toys, and relics of a bygone era. Of the two suites built on the roof, no. 112 is quite lovely, with white marble flooring and a view of the fort from the bathroom. Note that Vikram's younger brother, Shakti, will gladly arrange unique desert experiences for you, provided you give him sufficient warning (see "Camel Safari," above). At press time, Vikram was planning an underground lounge bar and rooftop pool, both welcome prospects. *Note:* As with most hotels, rates double during the Desert Festival.

Finally, if you want to feel the desert sand between your toes (perhaps quite literally), consider **Royal Desert Resort** (operated by Royal Desert Safaris; see above), a simple, lovely new place that's unfortunately situated right next to the main road used by everyone to get to the Sam Dunes. The "resort" comprises a number of mud huts and tents (each with attached bathrooms and a fan), and there's a pleasant dining hall. Camels pick guests up for safaris right outside the entrance. It's quite good value at Rs 2,500 ($61/£31) double.

Bikaner & the Temple of the Rats

With a bustling city sprawling around a higgledy-piggledy historic center, **Bikaner** is another desert oasis worth visiting if you have a few extra days or a penchant for the unusual. Bikaner is a popular stop-off between Jaipur (or Pushkar) and Jaisalmer and is also easily accessible from the Shekhawati region. Some like to compare Bikaner with Beirut. The city's historic center has a lovely medieval market atmosphere, offset by grandiose havelis (many owned by trade-merchants who made their fortunes in Calcutta and built their houses here), and the city also boasts an impressive fort, India's only **camel-breeding farm,** some pretty heritage accommodations, and a wide range of temples, many of them Jain. Founded in 1498 by Rao Bika, a Rajput descendant who established his own kingdom on the lucrative spice trade route, Bikaner really is a desert oasis, and it's quite surprising to find a city here—seemingly in the middle of nowhere. At its heart is a fascinating walled Old City packed with spice markets, havelis, Jain temples, and a wonderfully medieval way of life. This is also a good place to be based for desert safaris that are less commercialized than those in Jaisalmer. Bikaner will certainly strike you as somewhat unusual, remote, and tangibly cut off from the rest of the world. Two of its biggest claims to fame are that it has remained, throughout its history, a battle-free state, and it is host to an awesome kite-flying festival (usually in Apr).

Most visitors scramble to visit the bizarre **Temple of the Rats** or rather, **Karni Mata** (entry free; Rs 20/50¢/25p camera), no doubt expecting to witness some arcane rodent ritual. Instead, they experience a rather pleasant 600-year-old temple with the unusual addition of thousands of harmless little rats dashing about and feasting on sweets left by worshipers and competing with cheeky pigeons. The temple is dedicated to an incarnation of the goddess Durga (whose mythology of miracles is remarkably similar to that of Christ); her father apparently found a husband for her near the place where the temple now stands, in the remote village of Deshnoke (less than an hr. by bus from Bikaner). The rats have apparently been living here for 6 centuries, and scientific tests have shown them to be quite healthy (we think they look a bit malnourished, no doubt suffering the effects of too much ghee); they are given water and milk, and there has never been an incident of plague. While you may tremble at the thought of a rat scrambling over your foot (which must be bare in the temple, of course), this is actually considered a good omen—and if a white rat runs over you, it's very lucky indeed.

Locals consider **Junagarh Fort** (*($ (© 0151/254-2297; daily 10am–4:30pm) the finest in Rajasthan, and while this is highly debatable, the monumental construction (built from 1589 and only completed in 1937) is fiercely impressive and filled with interesting collections, architectural details, and hints of royal excess run amuck; at times it seems as if each successive maharaja insisted on establishing his personal authority by building yet another bejeweled private audience chamber. You can only visit as part of a guided tour (and you will be pushed for a tip at the end), but it's really worth it, not least for the great views from the ramparts and roofs.

Myriad heritage properties in Bikaner have been converted to accommodations for those wanting a taste of a bygone era. While some of the most important royal properties (like Lalgarh Palace) are now hotels, these are often poorly managed and in a rather unfortunate state of disarray, not to mention overpriced. In a different league altogether is **Bhanwar Niwas** ✹✹ (Rampuria St.; ✆ **0151/20-1043;** www.bhanwarniwas.com; Rs 4,000/$98/£49 double), a smart haveli built in the 1920s by a Jain textile merchant whose descendents still live here. Rooms range over two floors around a central courtyard; it's not opulent or pretentious like the royal properties, but it's comfortable and well-maintained (the frescoed walls are touched up regularly). Each guest room is unique, from the patterned floors and framed paintings to the stained-glass doors, canopied beds, and antique furnishings. Much of it is more Versailles than desert haveli: European baroque hangs heavily, all swirling floral arrangements and heavy pastels. In the drawing rooms and corridors, black rococo figures, flamboyantly dressed in gold, hold electric flames, while gold-plated wooden thrones stand on either side of a fireplace beneath an underlit bejeweled peacock.

The haveli is right near the heart of the old city, so you can set out on foot to explore medieval Bikaner, passing unique architectural facades along the way. Many are crumbling, and many are still home to families that have lived here for centuries. While exploring (or getting lost), ask for directions to the gorgeous **Bhanda Shaha Jain Temple,** which (unusually for Jain temples) is richly decorated with wildly colorful frescoes (rather than carvings). The local priest will tell you that the temple (apparently 540 years old) predates the city and that the mortar used in its construction was mixed with butter instead of water; the stone used in its construction was brought all the way from Jaisalmer. If it's quiet, the priest will probably even let you into the inner sanctuary, strictly off-limits to all except Jain priests. Climb to the top of the temple for views of the surrounds.

Staff at Bhanwar Niwas will gladly assist with your transport needs (a car and driver for the day will cost around Rs 800/$20/£10). Incidentally, should you want a guide (highly recommended in this bustling city where attractions are spread out), try to recruit **Jayant Singh** (✆ **98-2919-0488**), a veteran and arguably the best guide in Bikaner. Situated several miles from the city, the **camel breeding farm** (entry Rs 10/25¢/15p, Rs 20/50¢/25p camera; daily 2–6pm) is where you can get up close and quite personal to the most intensely studied camels in India; the farm is actually a research facility where you can ask questions about why these animals look so content traipsing through hostile desert environments. More likely you'll want to hop aboard for a short ride or even ask to sample some camel milk, which is definitely an acquired taste. But if you really want to enjoy a proper desert dune **camel safari,** you'll be better off heading for **Kakoo,** a tiny village near Bikaner that serves as a starting point for camel-back adventures that include a night or two in simple desert tents and dining under the stars. The experience hasn't yet been discovered by the tourist hordes that flock to Jaisalmer's Sam Dunes; you can book by contacting Bhagwan Singh, the manager at Bhanwar Niwas.

Fort Rajwada ★★ (Value The dapper and stylish entrepreneur Jitendra Rathore, who built Gorbandh, is the energy behind the most luxurious option in Jaisalmer, and he's a mine of information about the town that he loves. Set on the outskirts, on 2 hectares (5½ acres) of land, the hotel has been built in the style of a palace but has all the comforts of the 21st century (barring the constant power failures that, thanks to generators, affect only the TV). Interiors were fashioned by the opera stage designer Stephanie Engeln, and the public spaces, particularly the dazzling double-volume bar, which could have been designed by Philippe Starck, feel like a grand set. Guest rooms are more standard but very comfortable and have great modern bathrooms; ask for one with a fort view. Cuisine at the Sonal and Roopal restaurants is superb (the *laal maans* here is infinitely better than we had at Udaivilās), and service is exceptionally friendly. The hotel is the best choice in town if you value amenities such as a pool and a sense of uncluttered space. Fort Rajwada also runs Royal Desert Safaris, where you can either dine or overnight after a camel ride at Sam Dune (see above).

1 Hotel Complex, Jodhpur–Barmer Link Rd., Jaisalmer. ℂ 02992/25-3233, -3533, -4608, or -4609. Fax 02992/ 25-3733. www.fortrajwada.com. sales@fortrajwada.com. 96 units. $170 (£85) double; $265–$340 (£133–£170) suite; $55 (£28) extra bed. Children under 10 stay free in parent's room. Taxes extra. AE, DC, MC, V. **Amenities:** 2 restaurants; bar; sunset bar; pool; health club; travel desk; boutiques; bookstore; salon; 24-hr. room service; Ayurvedic massage; laundry; doctor-on-call; billiards room. *In room:* A/C, TV, tea- and coffee-making facilities, hair dryer, safe.

Killa Bhawan ★ This intimate and well-run little guesthouse is the most luxurious and stylish option in the fort. It really is a delightful choice given that it's been hewn out of a dwelling that's been around for 700-odd years. Only the lack of amenities, and the fact that most rooms share a communal shower and toilet, stop this lovely guesthouse, created by Swiss-Italian Luca Borella, from getting two stars. And bear in mind that the shared shower room is large and luxurious (and cleaned between showers), unlike the usual communal cupboard standard elsewhere. All rooms are beautifully furnished with lovely fabrics (and such thoughtful touches as gowns for guests to don before showering). Two suites (one expected to open by 2008) are available for families traveling with children. The rooftop, which has stunning views, is comfortably furnished with mattresses and colorful cushions. Manager Manu and his brother Bharat are always on hand to arrange complimentary tea or coffee or to assist with anything from travel arrangements to dining choices.

Inside the fort. No. 445. ℂ 02992/25-1204 or -0232. Fax 02992/25-4518. www.killabhawan.com. kbhawan@yahoo. com. 9 units. $68 (£34) non-A/C double with shared shower; $112 (£56) A/C deluxe double; $125 (£63) A/C super-deluxe double; $161 (£81) suite. Rates include breakfast; taxes extra. MC, V. **Amenities:** Breakfast terrace; tours arranged; travel assistance; laundry; doctor-on-call; currency exchange. *In room:* En-suite units have A/C and hair dryer.

WHERE TO DINE

Eateries within the fort (like **8 July Restaurant,** opposite the palace entrance) serve marginally acceptable basics; you'd do better to head into town for more substantial meals. Besides The Trio and Desert Boy's Dhani (both reviewed below), you can also get tasty dishes at **Saffron** at Nachana Haveli (see above).

Desert Boy's Dhani ★★ ECLECTIC/VEGETARIAN Just below the fort, this atmospheric restaurant has a lovely outdoor section; you can sit in the garden courtyard or get closer to the ground on thin mattresses at one of the low tables, where lazy reclining is definitely encouraged. The nostalgic strains of old Hindi film music sets the mood, and at night the garden is lit up with candles, creating a romantic atmosphere; from November through January, traditional dance performances are held from 9 to

11pm. The specialty here is tasty vegetarian dishes (including veggie burgers and thin-crust pizzas smothered with cheese from the Punjab), and you really should consider Desert Boy's specialty, *kair sanagari,* a delicious yogurt-based concoction made with capers and a local desert-dwelling string bean that's purported to have antibiotic proper-ties. If that doesn't appeal, another Jaisalmer speciality is *govind gatta,* chickpea-flavored balls stuffed with dried fruit and served with yogurt spiced with turmeric, coriander, and chili. Finish off with a *kaju dakh* milkshake, made with cashews and raisins.

Near Nagar Palika. ✆ **02992/25-4336.** Rs 50–Rs 120 ($1.25–$2.95/65p–£1.50). No credit cards. Daily 9am–11pm.

The Trio 𝒦𝒦𝒦 RAJASTHANI/ECLECTIC   This unassuming eatery, with its open walls and thin cotton flaps providing a welcome through-breeze (not to mention views of the town and the Maharaja's palace), is Jaisalmer's top restaurant and one of the best in Rajasthan. It's not just that the food is delicious, but the chef brings a few interest-ing variations to signature Rajasthani dishes—a welcome relief to one who has exhausted the almost standardized North Indian menu. The *murgh-e-subz*—succu-lent, boneless strips of chicken stir-fried with shredded vegetables—is one not to miss. If you want to reward your taste buds, order the very tasty mutton *nabori,* a somewhat creamy Thar Desert specialty; be warned, however, there's enough garlic in it to scare camels away. If you have a hearty appetite, the tandoor thali is tops: two chicken preparations (including the ubiquitous but delicious *tikka*), vegetable kebab, mint sauce, and *naan.* Sensitive stomachs can opt for the *kadhi pakora,* fried graham-flour dumplings dunked in yogurt sauce, or *bharwan aloo* (potatoes stuffed with mint paste and simmered in gravy). Their masala *chai* is not quite as spicy as you'd expect, how-ever. Wash all of it down with the coldest beers and Cokes in the state.

Gandhi Chowk, Mandir Palace (Near the Amar Sagar Gate). ✆ **02992/25-2733.** Rs 60–Rs 180 ($1.45–$4.30/ 75p–£2.25). MC, V. Daily 11am–10:30pm.

SHOPPING

Whatever you do, don't miss **Barmer Embroidery House** (near Patwon ki Haveli); it's owned by Abhimanyu Rathi, legendary for his fine eye for antique textiles. Design-ers have been known to cross the Thar just to plunder his exquisite selection. Jaisalmer is also famous for its wool products, particularly *dhurries* (rugs), as well as its fine hand embroidery, which turns average skirts and tops into real conversation pieces. Because the town is so easily explored, the best shopping experience is to set aside a morning and wander around, comparing prices before making your selection. Start by explor-ing the main **Bhatia Market** (begins at the entrance to the fort) and follow your nose. Note that **Rangoli** has a large collection of embroidered garments, particularly for children, and is a fixed-rate shop (you don't have to bargain), which can be quite a relief. You'll find it opposite the Bank of Baroda, in Gandhi Chowk.

Kanu Swami (✆ **98-2909-7319**) is a skillful miniaturist who produces original and beautiful paintings, typically of birds and trees; you'll see evidence of his affinity for nature in the near-microscopic detail that figures into his work. Not satisfied with portraits of trees featuring well over 4,000 individual leaves, he continues to attempt record-breaking images that have the quality of computer-generated graphic artworks but are executed with an artist's touch. If you'd like to take home a painting that com-bines traditional skills with a contemporary look, spend some time surveying Kanu's work; you'll spend a mere Rs 800 ($20/£9.90) for a beautifully crafted artwork that's taken 2 full days to complete. Kanu's workshop-cum-outlet is adjacent to the entrance of 8 July Restaurant (opposite the palace entrance).

11

Himachal Pradesh: On Top of the World

Proclaimed by ancient Indian texts as *Devbhumi*—"Land of the Gods"—and believed to be the earthly home of the mighty Lord Shiva, this beautiful, far-flung region has an almost palpable presence of divinity. Bordered by Tibet to the east, Jammu and Kashmir to the north, and the Punjab to the west, the land-locked state is one of great topographic diversity, from vast bleak tracts of rust-colored high-altitude Trans-Himalayan desert to dense green deodar forests, apple orchards, cultivated terraces, and, everywhere you look, sublime snow-capped mountains. This is also where you'll find the largest concentration of Buddhists, their atmospheric *gompas* (monasteries) a total contrast to the pageantry of Hindu temples.

Shimla, the state capital, is easily accessed from Delhi by train, preferably via the Punjabi town of Amritsar, where the shimmering **Golden Temple** of the Sikhs takes the honors as India's best cultural attraction. Shimla shouldn't hold you longer than it takes to get ready to tackle one of the greatest road adventures in Asia—negotiating the ledges, land-slides, and hairpin bends of the **Hindustan-Tibet Road** through the remote valleys of Kinnaur, Lahaul, and Spiti. Hidden from the world for most of the year by a cloak of thick, impenetrable snow, these easternmost districts emerge from their wintry slumber to reveal white-capped Himalayan mountains,

lush green meadow-valleys dappled with flowers, and Tibetan Buddhist *gompas,* of which **Tabo,** a World Heritage Site, is one of the most spiritual destinations in India. Due to limited accessibility (the region only opened to visitors in recent years and requires a special permit) and the impassability of the roads, the region—despite an upturn in tourist numbers in the last few years—remains the least visited and most exhilarating part of Himachal Pradesh. You should set aside at least 3 to 4 days to explore the area after arriving in Manali, a town somewhat enlivened (some say ruined) by its designated role as Himachal Pradesh's "hippie hot spot" and local honeymoon destination. You can either set off on a trek from this popular adventure center, or head west (via Mandi) to the tea-carpeted hills of the westernmost Kangra Valley and the hill station of **Dharam-sala**—seat of the Tibetan government-in-exile and home to the Dalai Lama. Another option is to head north to the lunar landscapes of **Ladakh.**

Although Jammu and Kashmir, India's northernmost state, is a no-go area for many travelers, Ladakh, the western J&K province on the border of Tibet, is the exception. It sits astride the Ladakh and Zanskar mountains, surrounded by two of the world's highest ranges—the Greater Himalayas and the mighty Karakoram—and nothing will prepare you for the breathtaking, stark beauty of

Himachal Pradesh

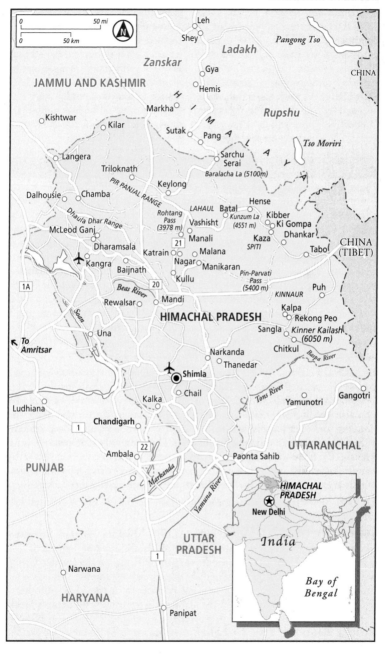

the landscape. Jagged peaks, rocky uplands, and vast barren plateaus are the dominant features of this harsh, dry land swept by dust devils and dotted with Buddhist *gompas,* large whitewashed *chortens* (commemorative cairns), and chest-high *mani* walls made from stacks of engraved stones. Aptly nicknamed "Little Tibet," this is India at her remote best. Only visited for the few months of summer when the roads are passable, the communities outside of Leh (capital of Ladhak) and Padum (capital of Zanskar) remain literally frozen in time, with small Buddhist communities living as they have for centuries, miraculously untouched by outside influences. Spend at least 4 days here (adjusting to the high altitude takes time), then fly out to Delhi and rejoin the 21st century.

1 Staying Active

Himachal Pradesh and Ladakh are exceptional destinations for adventurous travelers. The area has a phenomenal array of trekking routes, and numerous tour operators offer anything from gentle strolls to walks lasting several days—including trips to serious rock faces for seasoned climbers. Besides the scenery, a visit here is an ideal opportunity to meet people more or less untouched by the modern world—outside of a handful of towns, much of the population in this region is rural and dependent on agriculture. It is also home to some of the world's last nomadic people. **Manali** is a popular starting point for treks into the lush Kullu and Parvati valleys, while **Dharamsala** is a good base from which to explore the Dhauladhar mountain range. In Ladakh, expeditions out of **Leh** visit the many fascinating Buddhist monasteries, and the **Indus** and **Zanskar rivers** are excellent for white-water rafting. Note that most of the companies listed below are happy to arrange a variety of adventure activities almost anywhere in the Himalayas, including Sikkim (discussed in chapter 13).

IN MANALI If you arrive in Manali with no prearranged outdoor activities, you can contact two places. **Himalayan Outdoor Centre** (en route to Rohtang Rd., 1.5km/1 mile from Manali; ✆ 01902/25-2581 or 98-1600-3035) offers a wide range of adventure activities, including rafting on the Beas River, skiing (Apr to mid-May), snowboarding, treks, jeep safaris, and tandem paragliding. Besides organizing trekking in Himachal and Ladakh, **Himalayan Journeys The Adventure Company** (The Mall, Manali; ✆ 01902/25-4397; www.himalayanjourneysindia.com; info@himalayan journeysindia.com) arranges ski courses, jeep safaris, river-rafting expeditions, mountain-biking tours, and, for well-heeled adventurers, luxury heli-skiing packages.

IN LEH For details on active vacations in Leh, see "Leh & Environs," later in this chapter.

JEEP & MOTORCYCLE SAFARI SPECIALISTS **Banjara Camps & Retreats** ☆☆ (www.banjaracamps.com) operates a number of Trans-Himalayan jeep safaris, which generally start in Delhi and explore different parts of Himachal and Ladakh. Comfortable accommodations (some in beautifully situated deluxe campsites) and good meals accompany you along the way, and you can even customize your safari. Another outfitter that allows you to traverse the top of the world in comfort, **Wilderness Trekkers** (www.wilderness-trekkers.org) runs a weeklong adventure that takes in Himachal's Rohtang Pass, as well as some of Ladakh's most mesmerizing Buddhist *gompas*. **Shepherds Realms, Camps & Adventures** ☆ (C-8/8115, Shepherd's House, Vasant Kunj, New Delhi; ✆ 98-1871-2970; www.asiasafari.com; shepherdsrealms@gmail.com), run by an ex-army captain, specializes in custom-made motorcycle and jeep safaris through Ladakh, as well as Tibet, Nepal, and Bhutan, along with other adventure activities in these regions.

2 The Golden Temple in Amritsar

410km (254 miles) NW of Delhi

Amritsar (pronounced Um-*rit*-sir) has been the capital of the Sikh religion since the 16th century. Located in the northwestern state of Punjab, a wealthy and prosperous region and home to the majority of India's Sikhs, Amritsar is also home to India's most dazzling temple. A shimmering monument in marble, bronze, and gold leaf, and a vivid architectural celebration of Sikhism's devotion (a faith that actively preaches unity and equality among all religions), **The Golden Temple** is both fascinating and spiritually invigorating, combining sheer physical beauty with a truly sacred atmosphere. The way in which its devotees worship is enough to hold your attention—and your heart—completely captive.

ESSENTIALS

VISITOR INFORMATION   The best place to get information about the Golden Temple and the Sikh faith is at the temple's own **Information Office** (✆ **0183/255-3954;** Apr–June daily 7:30am–7:30pm, July–Mar daily 8am–7pm). The **Punjab Government Tourist Office** (✆ **0183/240-2452;** http://punjabgovt.nic.in; Mon–Sat 9am–5pm) is at the Palace Hotel, opposite the railway station.

GETTING THERE & AWAY   You can fly from Delhi (or Chandigarh) with **Indian Airlines** (39A Court Rd.; ✆ **0183/221-3392,** -3393, or -3141; Mon–Sat 10am–5pm) or **Jet Airways** (Main Market, Ranjit's Ave. Shopping Complex; ✆ **0183/ 250-8003**), but the best way to get here is on the Shatabdi Express or the overnight Golden Temple Mail from Delhi—it is far more economical and quite a comfortable option. Taxis, auto-rickshaws, and bicycle-rickshaws are always available at the station to take you to your hotel. You'll want to avoid spending time tracking down tickets, so either book your return or onward journey in advance, or have your hotel handle your reservation. If you're stuck, there is a computerized train reservation facility located at the Golden Temple complex.

GETTING AROUND   Note that both Mrs. Bhandari's Guesthouse as well as Ranjit's Svaasa (see below) will make all your transport and sightseeing arrangements for you. You can hire the services of a guide for Rs 650 ($16/£8) half-day, or Rs 1,100 ($27/£14) full day; car hire will be in addition to this. Cycle-rickshaws are popular, but if you're in a hurry, don't want to deal with the glaring sun, or need to cover more than a few kilometers, opt for a car or auto-rickshaw instead.

FAST FACTS: Amritsar

Ambulance   Dial ✆ **0183/250-6053** for Kakkar Hospital's 24-hour ambulance service.

ATMs, Banks & Currency Exchange   Several banks around The Golden Temple area provide necessary services. Twenty-four-hour ATMs can be found at HDFC Bank, Mall Road; Bank of Punjab, Court Road; ICICI Bank, Katcheri Chowk, and Grindlays Bank on Mall Road for Foreign Exchange.

Hospital **Apollo Hospital** (© 0183/254-5599) at Bhushapura near Sultanwind Gate is one of the city's best. Excellent care is also available at **Kakkar Hospital** on Green Avenue (© 0183/250-6053 or -6015).

Post Office The **General Post Office** (© 0183/256-6032; Mon–Sat 9am–5pm) is located on Court Road. There's also a post office with the same hours at The Golden Temple.

THE TOP ATTRACTIONS

The Golden Temple ✦✦✦ *(Moments* Prepare to be humbled by the most tangibly spiritual place in the country, one that, in its status as a living monument, even has the edge on the Taj Mahal. Arrive with a few good hours set aside and get lost in its magical beauty. Leave your shoes at the free facility near the entrance, cover your head (bandanas are provided, or you can purchase a "Golden Temple" souvenir bandana from a vendor), and wash your feet by wading through the shallow pool before entering. The most sacred part of the complex is **Hari Mandir Sahib (Divine Temple)** or **Darbar Sahib (Court of the Lord),** which you'll instantly recognize as the marble-and-gold sanctuary at the center of a large body of water within the temple complex. The name "Golden Temple" comes from this gold-plated building, which features copper cupolas and white marble walls encrusted with precious stones arranged in decorative floral patterns that show strong Islamic influence. Four *chattris* flank the structure, which is decorated inside and out with verses from the *Granth Sahib* (the Sikh Holy Book). Construction of the temple began in 1574, with ongoing restoration and embellishment over the years, including the addition in the 19th century of 100 kilograms (220 lb.) of gold to cover the inverted lotus-shaped dome.

To reach the temple, follow the *parikrama* (walkway), which circumscribes the sacred water tank—known as **Amrit Sarovar,** or the Pool of Nectar—in a clockwise direction. You'll need to cross a marble causeway, **Guru's Bridge,** which symbolizes the journey of the soul after death, in order to reach the *bangaldar* pavilion on which the temple stands. Access to the bridge is through marvelous **Darshani Deorhi,** a gateway marked by magnificent silver doors. Here, you will join the many devotees who, especially early and late in the day, pass through the temple to pay their respects (and give a donation) to their Holy Book. Within Hari Mandir, the scene—which is almost constantly being televised for Sikh viewers around India—is fascinating. Beneath a canopy studded with jewels, scriptures from the Holy Book are sung, while a crowd of fervent yet solemn devotees immerse themselves in the moment. A *chauri,* or whisk, is repeatedly waved dramatically in the air above the Book, while new musicians and singers continually join the ensemble after another participant has paid his respects. Like an organic human machine, lines of Sikhs pay their respects by touching their foreheads to the temple floor and walls, continuing in a clockwise direction at a moderate pace. Being among such gracious devotion will fill you with a sense of inner calm. Once you've passed through Hari Mandir, either climb the narrow stairwells and take your time to drink in the atmosphere or head back along Guru's Bridge. It is along this bridge that the *Granth Sahib* is carried between Hari Mandir and **Akal Takht** (see "Spiritual Weightlifting," below), the seat of the Sikh parliament, built in 1609 and located directly across from Hari Mandir.

Don't miss **Guru-ka-Langar,** a community kitchen where each day around 35,000 people are fed by temple volunteers. In an act that symbolizes the Sikh belief in equality of all people, irrespective of caste or creed, anyone and everyone is welcomed and invited to join the communal breaking of bread—a simple and unlimited meal of chapatis (wheat bread), *dal* (lentils), and sweet porridge is served. (***Note:*** You must raise your hands palm-up in order to receive the chapatis.) Guest quarters are also available for international Sikh visitors (for a nominal fee), and at least 400 simple rooms are provided free of charge to pilgrims. In the **Central Sikh Museum** at the main entrance, galleries display images and remembrances of Sikh gurus, warriors, and saints; note that it includes some graphic portraits of gurus being tortured and executed in terrifying ways.

Unlike in many other temples in India, here you feel genuinely welcome and not at all pressured to take out your wallet. In fact, so proud of their religion, culture, history, and temple are the local Sikhs that you will almost certainly be offered enthusiastic conversation and valuable information by one of the regular devotees—in return for nothing more than your attention. The welcoming information office to the left of the main gate gives helpful advice and information, as well as free guides and booklets on Sikhism (see the appendix for a brief précis).

For further information, contact the **Temple Manager** (© 0183/255-3953, -3957, or -3958; fax 0183/255-3919), or call the **Information Office** (© 0183/255-3954). Daily 7:30am–7:30pm in summer and 8am–7pm in winter. Activity at the temple goes on till late, and even when the last ceremonies of the evening have been concluded, volunteers get to work by cleaning or preparing for the next day. The main gate never closes, and Hari Mandir is open according to hours determined by the lunar cycle—some 20 hr. in summer and 18 hr. in winter. In summer, the closing ceremony takes place at 11pm and the sanctum is reopened at 2am. Winter times are usually 9:30pm and 3am; however, best to call and check.

Jallianwala Bagh   It was here, just a short walk from The Golden Temple, that one of the most dastardly events of British rule in India took place. On April 13, 1919, Brig.-Gen. Reginald Dwyer ordered the brutal massacre of hundreds of citizens who had gathered to protest the "imprisonment without trial" of two of their leaders under the newly passed Rowlatt Act. Now a leafy garden memorial, the park is surrounded by buildings on all sides; the British officers blocked the only access in and indiscriminately opened fire, gunning down many women and children. You can visit the martyr's gallery, and take a look at the bullet-pocked wall and the well where many, escaping bullets, jumped to their death. Unfortunately, the atmosphere inside is more

Bloody History of the Holy Temple

In 1984, the Sikh fundamentalist Sant Bhindranwale and his followers armed themselves and occupied The Golden Temple as part of a campaign for a separate Sikh state, which they wanted to call Khalistan. Acting on Prime Minister Indira Gandhi's orders, the Indian Army attacked, killing Bhindranwale and others and causing serious damage to the temple. Sikh honor was avenged when Indira Gandhi was later assassinated by two of her Sikh bodyguards, which in turn led to a massacre in which thousands of Sikhs lost their lives. The Sikh community refused to allow the central government to repair the damage to the temple, instead undertaking the work themselves. Although most of the cracks and crevices have been repaired, the incident has not been forgotten, and you will find many people in Amritsar keen to explain the Sikh side of the story.

Moments **Spiritual Weightlifting**

The best time to visit The Golden Temple is during *Palki Sahib,* or the **night ceremony,** during which the *Granth Sahib* is carried from the main shrine in Hari
Mandir to the sanctum, where it rests for a few hours until the opening ceremony the following morning. Any man can take part in this ceremony by joining one of the vibrant lines that form behind and ahead of the heavy palanquin
on which the Holy Book is moved. Several devotees simultaneously help support
each arm of the palanquin, giving each person a few seconds to take part in the
auspicious event. As though it were being transported along a human conveyor
belt, one person from each side moves away from the palanquin and is replaced
by a new shoulder from each of the lines; in this way, everyone gets at least one
chance to participate, and you can join the end of the line again and again until
your shoulder refuses to cooperate.

---

akin to a picnicking revelry, with India's post-independence generation displaying
only cursory curiosity, more intent on shooting photographs to show back home.

Jallianwala Bagh. Daily 5am–7pm.

AN UNUSUAL OUTING

Flag Ceremony at Wagah Border *Moments*   One of the world's oddest spectator
activities, this pompous display of military bravado is a major drawing card for Indian
tourists who travel long distances to watch the "Beating the Retreat," a high-kicking,
toe-stepping, quick-marching ceremony wherein the Indian and Pakistani flags are
lowered on either side of the only border that remains open between the two more-
often-than-not hostile countries. A number of officers from each team put on a raised-
eyebrow performance to the satisfaction of the cheering, chanting crowds, seated on
concrete grandstands on either side. The pointless exercise ends with the furious slam-
ming of the border gates, at which time each side's flag is urgently carried to a room
for overnight safekeeping. For anyone interested in unbridled nationalist pride, the
Flag Ceremony is a memorable outing (only half an hour from Amritsar). Arrive well
ahead of the crowds in order to get a close-up seat—the grimaces of the mighty military men in their rooster caps add to the fun, and you'll get a better look at the Pakistani delegation. Alternatively, find a way of organizing a VIP spot across the road
from the crowd; a friendly call to a local politician might do the trick.

Wagah is at the border between India and Pakistan, 32km (20 miles) from Amritsar. Round-trip taxi around Rs 550
($13/£6.80) basic model car, Rs 1,000 ($24/£12) four-wheel-drive.

WHERE TO STAY & DINE

That the people of Amritsar live to eat is obvious from the scores of *dhabas,* Punjabi-
style "fast-food" joints serving tasty and filling thalis (multicourse platters), that showcase various traditional dishes everywhere. This is the land of *desi-ghee* (clarified
butter) and butter, added to almost every dish: Those watching their weight or unable
to consume rich, heavy food should take it easy on the Indian fare here. But if you're
up for the adventure, this is a culinary exploration like few others in India, where for
as little as Rs 50 ($1.20/60p) you'll be served a sizable spread that you eat with your
fingers, dipping piping-hot *parathas* (fried flatbread) into *maa ki dal, channa,* and
other concoctions arranged in little heaps on your platter.

For close to a hundred years, simple **Kesar da Dhaba** 🍴🍴 in Bazaar Passian has been serving superb vegetarian dishes. For Amritsari fish—here, fabulous batter-fried sole from the Beas River, flavored with lovage (a thymelike spice)—you must go to **Makhan Dhaba** (Lawrence Rd.). For a simple budget meal, **Bharawan Da Dhaba** 🍴 (*©* **0183/2532575**), conveniently located near town hall and the railway station, dishes out the most delicious *paratha* and *dal* in town, to be washed down with an utterly decadent lassi. In fact, as far as these thick yogurt drinks go, Amritsar sets the standard; try the tiny but brilliant **Gian Sweets** (Chowk Regent, Katra Sher Singh) or just about anywhere else you see a crowd. **Surjit Chicken** (Lawrence Rd.) is the spot if you're looking for a sit-down meal of delicious butter chicken and *kulchas* or *lachedar parathas*. **Kulcha Land** (opposite M.K. Hotel, Ranjit Ave.) also comes highly recommended. If you're looking for a clean, glitzy restaurant that serves a wide range of dishes, head for **Crystal** (Crystal Chowk, Queens Rd.; *©* **0183/222-5555** or -9999; Rs 90–Rs 250/$2.20–$6/£1–£3). It may not win any awards for atmosphere, and service is atrocious (especially on weekends and after 8:30pm when the place is often packed), but it's the most popular "upmarket" restaurant in town, and the food is an eclectic array of dishes (including Chinese and Continental, but with the emphasis on North Indian specialties—don't miss the *malai tikka*). A new contender you may want to consider is **Astoria:** Tucked into a posh colony and run by young Navneet Singh, Astoria also offers an extensive menu and great value for money (SCO 38 DSC Ranjit Ave.; *©* **0183/250-5722**).

Amritsar has several fairly decent hotels, including the **Ritz Plaza Hotel** (45 Mall Rd.; *©*/fax **0183/256-2836** through -2839; www.ritzhotel.in), which has comfortable rooms, a pool, and all the basic facilities for Rs 4,000 ($97/£49) double (including breakfast). But if you're only here for a night or two and prefer a more personal environment, the two homestay-oriented options below offer not only value for money, but a more intense experience.

Mrs. Bhandari's Guesthouse 🍴 *Value*   Situated along a wide avenue in the peaceful, leafy Cantonment neighborhood, this is a very pleasant, comfortable, and, above all, homey place in which to enjoy genuine Punjabi hospitality. The well-preserved late-Raj family estate packs in beautiful gardens, a welcoming pool, and its own team of curious water buffalo; these provide the essential ingredient (fresh dung) for homemade fire "briquettes." Accommodations vary in size and location, arranged in and around Mrs. Bhandari's home. Most rooms resemble "chummeries," the bachelor quarters assigned to Raj officials of junior rank with an attached room for their Indian servant. Interiors are modest but atmospheric, featuring high ceilings, Art Deco tiles, fine Indian throws over firm mattresses, and bathrooms with drench showers or old-fashioned tubs and original piping. Mrs. Bhandari has been living here since 1930, but the guesthouse is now run by her daughter, who will help you plan an enjoyable itinerary and organize all transport and temple visits. A one-way transfer from the railway station to the guesthouse is included in the room rate. It's not faultless, but service and management are hands-on and well meaning, and really, given the price, it's relatively good value (though the additional charge for using the fireplace, for instance, irks).

No. 10, Cantonment, Amritsar 143 001. *©* **0183/222-8509**. Fax 0183/222-2390. http://bhandari_guesthouse. tripod.com. bgha10@gmail.com. 15 units. Rs 1,400 ($34/£17) double; Rs 1,700 ($41/£21) double with A/C and heater; Rs 1,100 ($27/£14) single; Rs 1,400 ($34/£17) single with A/C and heater. Rs 300 ($7.30/£3.70) extra bed. Camping Rs 170 ($4.15/£2) per person with own equipment. MC, V (3% surcharge). **Amenities:** Restaurant; pool open Mar–Nov; kids' play area; transport and taxi arrangements; limited room service 8am–10pm; laundry; Internet; TV in lounge; tour guide; camping facilities. *In room:* A/C, heater, fireplace (extra charge).

Visiting Le Corbusier's Chandigarh

Fans of the father of modernism, Le Corbusier, will appreciate the form and functionality of **Chandigarh**. When Punjab was divided after Partition, Lahore went to Pakistan, leaving the state without a capital; Chandigarh was envisioned as the new headquarters. When Punjab was once again divided into smaller states, the city became a Union Territory serving as the administrative capital for both Punjab and Haryana. Le Corbusier is largely responsible for designing the mesh of rectangular units, or "sectors," into which the city is divided. Characterized by exposed brickwork, boulder stone masonry, broad boulevards, large landscaped parks with abundant trees, and quadrants of tidy, self-sufficient neighborhoods made up of buildings with louvered screens *(brise-soleil)* and unfinished concrete surfaces, Le Corbusier's city doesn't quite function as the living organism it's intended to be. Urban decay and waste have crept in, but architecture buffs will find Le Corbusier's structural contributions intriguing. Architectural attractions in Chandigarh include the **Capitol Complex** ⋒⋒ (Sector 1), where the geometrical concrete buildings of the **Legislative Assembly, High Court,** and **Secretariat** represent structural innovation. At the southern end of the complex piazza, the **Vidhan Sabha (Legislative Assembly)** building is capped by a startling cupola, a pyramidal tower, and a cuboid tower, while within the portico is a bright **Cubist mural** by Le Corbusier himself. Also within the complex is the **Open Hand Monument,** a giant metal hand standing 26m (85 ft.) high that is able to rotate in the wind. Symbolizing the give-and-take of ideas, the hand has become the city's official emblem. Technically, tours of the complex start from the reception area, but these half-hourly episodes don't always materialize; check with someone from the **Chandigarh Industrial & Tourism Development Corporation (CITCO)** (✆ **0172/270-4761** or **-4356**) in advance. Locals go to walk, jog, and relax in the 8km-long (5-mile) linear park known as **Leisure Valley.** In Sector 16, the **Rose Garden** is the largest of its kind in Asia. In Sector 10, the **Sculpture Park** adjoining the Cultural Complex is worth exploring. Within the Complex, the **Art and Picture Gallery** (Tues–Sun 9:30am–5pm) includes Modernist works. If you'd like to

Ranjit's Svaasa ⋒⋒   Set in a 250-year-old colonial redbrick mansion on Amritsar's Mall Road, Rama Mehra's retreat is not only an environmentally- and health-conscious one, it's also atmospheric: Rooms are furnished with colonial-era furniture (including four-poster beds) and open onto a cool balcony overlooking a landscaped garden. Pleasant rooms aside, the focus here is on serving delicious, healthy, organic-style food and providing healing therapies at the Spa Pavilion, where you can choose from an assortment of therapies ranging from Lime and Ginger aromatherapy (to detox) and an Abhyangam Ayurvedic massage (for pure relaxation). A yoga hall and gymnasium round out the healthy living facilities of this friendly spa-hotel, managed by the very efficient Abhimanyu Mehra. Hot water is heated by solar energy and rainwater saved during the monsoon. Ask for East Court, which overlooks the courtyard deepen your knowledge of Chandigarh's planning and construction, visit the **City Museum** (Sector 10), where exhibits document the realization of the city.

Chandigarh's highlight is the **Rock Garden of Nek Chand** ★★★, a surreal fantasyland created by "outsider artist" Nek Chand—a road inspector—from rocks, concrete, and urban rubbish. Set on 8 hectares (20 acres) of wooded landscape, the "garden" comprises a series of mazelike archways, tunnels, pavilions, waterfalls, and bridges, with passages leading from one open-air gallery to another. Each gallery is occupied by unusual characters, figures, and creatures fashioned from an unbelievable array of materials Chand started collecting in 1958; almost half a century later, the garden continues to grow. If the artist is in residence, he'll be happy to chat with you about his project.

Chandigarh can be visited en route between Amritsar and Shimla, or directly from Delhi by train. The best connections between Delhi and Chandigarh are several daily Shatabdi Express trains or the Himalayan Queen. From Amritsar, choose the Paschim Express, a section of which also links Chandigarh with Kalka, starting point for the "toy train" to Shimla. The **railway station** (✆ **0172/265-3131**, 0172/264-1651, -1131, or -1132) is in Sector 17, around 8km (5 miles) from the city center. For railway inquiries, call the **city reservation center** (✆ **0172/270-8573**; Mon–Sat 8am–8pm, Sun 8am–2pm). **Chandigarh Tourism** (✆ **0172/270-3839** or 0172/505-5462) has offices at the airport and at the railway station. If you decide to spend the night, book into the newly opened **Taj** (Block No. 9, Sector 17-A; ✆ **0172/651-3000**), by far the best accommodation in the city. If you're able to make your visit to Chandigarh a day trip, **Fort Nalagarh** (www.caravantraveltalk.com/nalagarh-fort.htm) lies 60km (37 miles) away and offers doubles from Rs 2,700 ($66/£33) onward. Built in 1421, this heritage property, surrounded by sprawling lawns, is eccentric but a great improvement on anything in Chandigarh itself.

and has lovely large windows, a wooden swing, and seating, or the Regal, which opens out into the terrace and has a lounge as well.

47 A The Mall, Amritsar 143 001. ✆ **0183/256-6618** or 0183/329-8840. Fax 0183/500-3728. www.svaasa.com. spa@svaasa.com. 17 units. Rs 5,000 ($122/£62) Rai Bahadur Luxury Suite; Rs 6,500 ($159/£80) Svaasa Suite; Rs 10,000 ($244/£123) Presidential Suite; Rs 15,500 ($378/£191) Svaasa Penthouse. Rs 800 ($195/£10) extra bed. Rates include breakfast and taxes; ask about half- or full-moon spa packages. AE, MC, V. **Amenities:** Dining hall; pool; gym; limited room service; laundry; doctor-on-call; Wi-Fi in lounge; naturopath on-call; health shop; small library; TV in lounge. *In room:* Tea- and coffee-making facilities, hair dryer; minifridge in superior suites.

SHOPPING

Although it's unlikely you would spend more than a day visiting Amritsar, there are a few things you can carry home. Everywhere in the city you'll see signs for "PAPAD AND WARIAN"; if you want to learn more about these edible "snacks" made out of dried lentil mixed with an assortment of spices, pop into **Dry Fruit Corner** (Chowk Goal Hatti, Hall Bazaar; ℂ **0183/254-1174**) and speak to the proprietor. If you're looking for more durable purchases, Amritsar is known for its woolen shawls and stoles in rich colors and weaves. For quality at a reasonable price, drop into either or both **Essma** (ℂ **0183/222-6252**) and **OCM** (ℂ **0183/225-9171**) factory outlets, known to every driver in the city, on the road leading to the Wagah Border (G.T. Rd., Putlighar). Finally, the traditional Amritsari-styled *juttis* (slipperlike shoes made out of leather with embroidery or cutwork) can be found in a row of shops just opposite the Gandhi Gate near Hall Bazaar.

3 Shimla

107km (66 miles) NE of Chandigarh

In the days when Shimla inspired scenes from Rudyard Kipling's *Kim,* it was a popular pick-up center for lusty British officers and flirtatious maidens keen to create a stir among the scandalmongers who gathered along The Mall during the summers. Shimla enjoys a proud history as the preferred mountain escape retreat from the unbearable summer heat of the plains (or "downstairs," as many Himachalis refer to their low-altitude neighbors)—a cool spot in which to sink into a life of idle gossip, romantic conquests, and military brown-nosing. Today, this romantic image has been somewhat ruined by unchecked urbanization and reckless construction. Development has now been curbed, but the clogged roads and ugly concrete tenements that cling to the mountainsides beneath Shimla detract significantly from the town's former glory.

Sprawling over seven hills fringed by dense forest and magnificent mountains, Shimla is a useful starting point from which to explore more untouched parts of Himachal, and the town's timbered cottages and wood-gabled buildings retain a degree of charm, but if you're expecting a quiet hill station, you may be disappointed. The Mall, a promenade on the southern slopes of the ridge, remains a pedestrian preserve, thronged by tourists and local Anglophiles who tend to echo the social mannerisms of the Raj at its most British. Below the ridge, however, an overwhelmingly Indian conglomeration of buildings constitutes the bazaar, and a sweep of modern dwellings has the distinctly untidy appearance of unplanned urban sprawl. Shimla is, however, in close proximity to a number of lesser-known hill resort getaways: Naldehra, Narkanda, Kufri, and Chadwick Falls are all destinations offering relative peace and quiet as well as scenic splendor guaranteed to capture your imagination. And for those seeking adventure and remote beauty, Shimla is a useful confluence of roads leading west to the Kangra Valley; north to Kullu, Lahaul, and Ladakh; and east into the valleys of Kinnaur and Spiti.

ESSENTIALS

GETTING THERE & AWAY By Road All of the more reputable hotels (see "Where to Stay & Dine," below) will arrange transfers from practically any starting point in India, should you wish to arrive in chauffeured style. From Delhi, you'll take National Highway 1 (Grand Trunk Rd.) north to Ambala (in Haryana) and then continue on a fierce and beautiful journey along a hillside road that snakes all the way up to Shimla. You can also drive directly from Chandigarh, following National Highway 21 south until you join the main Delhi–Shimla road.

By Air Weather can interfere with flights in and out of Shimla's **Jubbarhatti Airport,** 23km (14 miles) from the city (taxi into town around Rs 550/$14/£7). Daily

 **Tips** **You Can't Eat Plastic**

Obtaining cash against credit cards can be problematic in Himachal Pradesh and Ladakh. Make sure you draw cash (easiest at ATMs) in the tourist hubs of Shimla, Dharamsala, and Manali before heading into the mountains.

flights connect Shimla with Delhi (1 hr.). These also stop at Kullu's **Bhuntar Airport,** which serves northern Himachal Pradesh.

By Train   The most romantic way to get to Shimla, the **Himalayan Queen** runs from New Delhi to Kalka (640m/2,099 ft. above sea level), where the train switches to a narrow-gauge track and continues on to Shimla (2,060m/6,757 ft.). Traveling at an average speed of 25 to 30kmph (15–19 mph), the "toy train" journey will consume nearly a full day of your itinerary. Its 96km (60 miles) travels through some 100 tunnels, numerous bridges, and sharp curves, taking in picturesque views of green forests and meadows, capsicum fields, and red-roofed chalets. The train back to Kalka departs Shimla at 10:35am, arriving in time for you to make the onward connection to Delhi, where you'll arrive before midnight. Check out **www.indianrail.gov.in** (see chapter 2 for more information). *Note:* During the high season (May–June; Dec/Jan), it's difficult to secure tickets without at least several days' advance booking, so do so through the Internet or an agency.

VISITOR INFORMATION   For friendly, helpful, and enthusiastic assistance on the entire Himachal region, pop into the **Himachal Pradesh Tourism Development Corporation (HPTDC) information centre;** © **0177/265-4589;** www.himachal tourism.nic.in), where Geeta Ram Ranote will provide you with everything from trekking tips to details of his favorite itineraries; beware, however, of taking his advice on accommodations—he, like many other government officials, is committed to sending you to HPTDC-run establishments, of which 99.9% are undesirable.

GETTING AROUND   On Foot   Central Shimla is free of traffic, which means that you'll spend much of your time exploring on foot. You'll need some degree of stamina to deal with the numerous steep inclines. A two-stage elevator, **The Lift,** operating between 8am and 10pm, connects The Mall with Cart Road; ticket prices are nominal.

By Car   Shimla has a number of restricted and sealed roads, and farther routes are no-go zones for heavier vehicles. Should you arrive in town by train, you can find a taxi (or even the odd auto-rickshaw), which will drop you at your hotel—although you may be surprised at the route necessary to get around "no traffic" zones. Day trips (see "Shimla Excursions," below) will generally require a taxi or jeep—but the prices can fluctuate wildly. Get advice from your hotel on hiring a car and driver at reasonable rates. For prepaid taxi trips, contact the government-run service at © **0177/ 265-8892,** or **Vishal Himachal Taxi Operator Union** at © **0177/265-7645.**

GUIDED TOURS & TRAVEL AGENTS   For intelligent, entertaining, and exclusive **tours of Shimla** itself, your best bet is to make contact with noted local writer Raaja Bhasin, author of *Simla—The Summer Capital of British India.* Raaja conducts interesting and tailor-made walks around Shimla and will provide you with fond memories of the town and an acute understanding of its juicy history. E-mail or call Raaja in advance to make sure he's available (© **0177/265-3194;** www.raajabhasin.

com; mail@raajabhasin.com). Tours normally start from your hotel and run from 10am to 5pm for a charge of $150/£76 (for up to eight people; meals and transport, if required, cost extra). Additionally, he does shorter tours (2–3 hr.; cost varies) and all-day excursions outside Shimla.

Government-operated tours are annoying, claustrophobic excursions, best avoided unless you're on a tight budget. The office of the **Himachal Pradesh Tourism Development Corporation** (**HPTDC;** ✆ **0177/265-2561** or -8302; www.hptdc.nic.in; Apr 15–July 15 and Sept 15–Jan 1 daily 9am–8pm, rest of year daily 9am–6pm) is along The Mall, near Scandal Point. The Mall has an abundance of travel agencies; use them to arrange transport, tours, and trekking around the state.

FAST FACTS: **Shimla**

Ambulance Dial ✆ **0177/280-4648** or 0177/265-2102.

ATMs, Banks & Currency Exchange The Mall has outlets of HDFC, City Banks, ICICI Bank, and UTI Bank. You can change cash and traveler's checks, and organize cash advances on certain credit cards Monday to Saturday 8am to 8pm. In an emergency, guests at the Cecil and Wildflower Hall can also draw money against their credit cards for a small percentage.

Hospital For around-the-clock service, call **Tara Hospital** (✆ **0177/280-3275**).

Police There's a police office (✆ **0177/281-2344**) adjacent to the Town Hall, on The Mall. It's closed on Sunday.

Post Office The **General Post Office** (Mon–Sat 10am–6pm) is located just above Scandal Corner.

WHAT TO SEE & DO

Shimla's main promenade is **The Mall,** a pedestrian avenue stretching across the length of the city from Gopal Mandir in the west to the suburb of Chhota Shimla, roughly south of the town center. Along this stretch, crumbling remnants of the British Raj abound. Above The Mall is **The Ridge,** a wide-open esplanade watched over by a statue of Gandhi to the east, where the nearby Gothic **Christchurch** is one of Shimla's most imposing structures, situated adjacent the faux-Tudor half-timbered **library.** Note the fresco around the chancel window, designed by Lockwood Kipling, Rudyard's father.

Also on The Mall are the **Telegraph Office,** an interesting example of stone ashlar work completed in 1922 and, to its right, the old **Railway Booking Office,** a sadly decaying building frequently overrun by obnoxious monkeys. Marking the area where The Ridge joins up with The Mall, **Scandal Point** continues to be a popular social hangout, supposedly taking its name from an unconfirmed scandal involving the elopement of a handsome Patiala prince with the daughter of a British commander-in-chief. Beyond the fire station, after the dressed stone building housing the Municipal Offices, is the **Gaiety Theatre,** originally the Town Hall. Renowned for its excellent acoustics, the Gaiety continues to showcase local dramas on a stage where notable personalities, including Lord Robert Baden-Powell and novelist M. M. Kaye, once graced the planks—not all with great success; a fashionable piece of gossip tells how Rudyard Kipling was booed off the stage.

A short walk east of The Ridge will take you to the start of a rather strenuous but worthwhile hike to the summit of **Jakhu Hill** ⋐ which, at an altitude of 2,445m (8,020 ft.), is Shimla's highest point and affords excellent views of the city and surrounding valleys. You need to trudge up a steep 1.5km (1-mile) path, commencing at The Ridge and culminating at Shimla's highest point, to get to the Hanuman Temple on Jakhu's summit. Try to make it to the top in time for sunrise or sunset, either of which is glorious. The little temple is dedicated to Hinduism's popular monkey god (who is said to have rested on Jakhu Hill on his return from a mission in the Himalayas). Today his brazen descendants continue to patrol the path, so beware of carrying food or doing *anything* likely to provoke them. After you sound the bell at the temple entrance, enter to discover a curious concoction of serious Hindu faith and jovial Christmas pomp suggested by the tinsel and streamer decorations; the priest will happily give you a blessing.

To the west of the city, beyond The Cecil Hotel, is the vast six-story Scottish baronial mansion formerly known as **Viceregal Lodge** (Observatory Hill; Tues–Sun 9am–1pm and 2–5pm). The admission fee of Rs 100 ($2.45/£1.25) includes a guide. Built in 1888 at the behest of the British viceroy in an approximation of the Elizabethan style, the lodge is Shimla's single greatest architectural testament to the influence of the British Raj, and its luxuriant woodwork and lovely views attract numerous visitors. Even in 1888 it had electric light and an indoor tennis court, both rare for the times. The building was the summer residence of all viceroys until 1947, when India was granted independence and the building renamed Rashtrapati Niwas, a retreat for the president of India. The first president of India thought it should be put to better use, however, and in 1964 it was inhabited by the Indian Institute of Advanced Study, an academic foundation still housed here. It has a museum of photographs and other artifacts that highlight the important events that took place in Shimla during the pre-independence days.

SHIMLA EXCURSIONS

A mere 12km (7½ miles) from Shimla, the forested village of **Mashobra** is great for scenic walks but is best visited as an excuse to step into one of India's loveliest hotels, **Wildflower Hall** (see "Where to Stay & Dine," below), for high tea or lunch. From the village, you can attempt a trek to the area's highest peak—Shali—which reaches 3,200m (10,496 ft.), or take the 2km (1¼-mile) pedestrian track to the "sacred grove" of Sipur, which is where you'll find the charming, indigenous-style temple dedicated to the local deity, Seep. Because they are considered the personal property of Seep, no trees may be cut here; so superstitious are the locals that they pat themselves down before leaving to ensure no fallen cedar needles have accidentally dropped on them. Beyond Mashobra is the popular picnicking resort of **Naldehra** (23km/14 miles from Shimla), which has an extraordinary 9-hole golf course designed by Lord Curzon (British viceroy of India, 1899–1905). Golfing on the world's highest course is best arranged through your hotel in Shimla, or you can opt to stay at one of the local "resorts"—**The Châlets Naldehra** (⟨⟨ **0177/274-7715** or 98-1606-2007; www.chaletsnaldehra.com; Rs 5,000–Rs 10,500/$122–$256/£62–£130) has a pleasing alpine feel, with clean, comfortable, Scandinavian prefab wood cabins. Staff will arrange golf, river rafting, horseback-riding, fishing, and a range of hikes. The hot sulfur springs of **Tattapani** lie 28km (17 miles) farther away.

WHERE TO STAY & DINE

A destination in its own right, the Oberoi's **Wildflower Hall** (reviewed below) is by far your best option, but if the rates exceed your budget, nothing can beat the homey Raj-era experience of **Chapslee,** run by the aristocratic Kapurthalas (see below). If this is not available, you could try **Clarke's** (✆ **0177/265-1010;** clarkesreservations@ sancharnet.in), a small, modest, Oberoi-owned hotel, interesting in some respects because it was the hotel on which the Oberoi empire was built, with dull but perfectly comfortable accommodations (doubles from Rs 7,500/$183/£93). A member of the Welcomheritage group, **Woodville Palace** is runner-up to Chapslee in "the most charming heritage property" category, but lacks the latter's atmosphere and is looking terribly run-down (Raj Bhavan Rd.; ✆ **0177/262-3919;** doubles Rs 2,600/$63/£32 and up; ask for a room in the new block). Its location in the posh Raj Bhavan area is superb, however, surrounded as it is by large gardens—a luxury in Shimla. It also has some fantastic furniture and antiques, unfortunately languishing dispiritedly in corners, along with great photographic displays that provide an interesting insight into the lives of Indian royalty.

Shimla has no dearth of dining options; **Café Coffee Day** and **Barista** are both on the Mall, and **Balijee's** (The Mall; ✆ **0177/265-8926**) is excellent for Indian fast food. If you want to have a taste of a local specialty, then don't miss the *aloo sabzi and poori* (potato curry with deep-fried pancakelike bread) at **Mehar Chand** (lower Bazaar; ✆ **0177/329-475**). **The Restaurant** at Cecil keeps the Oberoi flag high—the *Baluchi Raan* (tandoor roasted lamb leg flavored with mace, cardamom, and saffron) in particular is excellent.

Finally, **high tea** at Wildflower Hall is legendary—sample the local infusions along with traditional Irish tea brack bread—a baked reminder of the Raj, speckled with raisins and sultanas, steeped in Darjeeling tea, and served with unsalted butter and lemon curd. The restaurant at Wildflower is also by far the best in and around Shimla, where you can sample everything from traditional *Chaa gosht* (a Himachali preparation of baby lamb in yogurt) to delicious ravioli and risotto.

Camp Potter's Hill 🌟 (Value)   If hotels are not your thing, and roads and shops teeming with tourists are a big turn-off, don't think twice: Head for Camp Potter's Hill, a delightfully simple and comfortable refuge in the middle of a 100-hectare (250-acre) pine, cedar, and oak forest. As part of an eco-tourism drive, the designers have ensured that nothing clashes with the beauty of the natural surroundings. Cottages and tents, machans (raised platforms, often in trees) and hidden trails, and being completely oblivious to the outside world—that is what Potter's Hill is all about.

Van Vihar, Summer Hill, Shimla 171 005. ✆ **0177/55-36501** or 94-1806-5001. Fax 0177/265-4774. www.pottershill. com. 11 luxury cottages, 7 deluxe tents. Rs 3,300 ($81/£41) cottages; Rs 2,200 ($54/£27) tents. Includes meals and taxes. 2-day/3-night packages available as well. MC, V. **Amenities:** Restaurant with bar; rock climbing; rappelling; day and night treks; bird-watching; mountain biking; river rafting; sightseeing and temple tours; nature walks; indoor games. *In room:* 24-hr. water and electricity, gas geysers.

The Cecil 🌟🌟🌟   Originally built as a private residence back in 1884, the Cecil has hosted the likes of Mahatma Gandhi and continues to draw political figures and noted celebrities. It was rebuilt in the Gothic style of Shimla's most elegant Raj monuments, and the interiors are luxurious with plenty of wood paneling, leather, and opulent furniture. Guest rooms are tasteful, with wooden flooring, rich fabrics, and considerable attention to detail; each has a dressing room and a large bathroom with separate tub and shower. Opt for one of the south-facing rooms (nos. 411–415 are best) with spectacular views of the Shimla Valley foothills or ask for the premier rooms or luxury suites, which come with balconies. Avoid the rooms in the older "Tudor Block," which feel a little claustrophobic and removed from the atmosphere of the main hotel. Facilities include a wonderful spa with a heated pool and a complete range of treatments to add a bit of decadence to your Himalayan sojourn. This is a less intimate, personal experience than Chapslee, but it will suit those who prefer the anonymity of luxury hotels and don't want to shell out for Wildflower Hall.

Chaura Maidan, Shimla 171 004. ☎ 0177/280-4848. Toll-free reservations in India: ☎ 1600/11-2030. Fax 0177/281-1024. www.oberoihotels.com. reservations@oberoi-cecil.com. 79 units. $260 (£132) deluxe; $310 (£157) premier; $485 (£245) deluxe suite; $575 (£291) luxury suite. Taxes extra. AE, DC, MC, V. **Amenities:** Restaurant; lounge bar; garden lounge; indoor pool; health center; spa w/Thai, Ayurvedic, and Balinese massage and aromatherapy; activity center w/billiards; children's activity center; 24-hr. room service; babysitting; laundry; Wi-Fi enabled; library. *In room:* A/C, TV, minibar, tea- and coffee-making facilities, hair dryer, safe (except superior rooms), DVD player.

Chapslee ✿✿ On the northeastern spur of the Shimla range, this charming home is the most authentically old-world lodging in town. Owned and lovingly managed by Ratanjit "Reggie" Singh, the regal grandson of Raja Charanjit Singh of Kapurthala, who bought the estate in 1938, Chapslee remains the quintessential creaky-floorboards Shimla homestead, its Raj-era aura hardly dented by modern conveniences or the slightly fraying Art Deco wallpaper. Originally built in 1835 as the summer residence of a British family, the house received an Edwardian face-lift in 1896 with teak paneling (part of the same consignment used for the Viceregal Lodge), wood parquet floors, and a dramatic staircase. Its current incarnation was undertaken when it became the summer residence of the Kapurthala royals. Be sure to request either of the two upstairs suites; the original master bedroom in each affords lovely valley views, a massive brass four-poster bed, and delicate ornamentation, as well as a vast bathroom with a raised tub, an enormous shower, a bidet, and its own fireplace. Chapslee's obvious aesthetic pleasures are a good match for the fairy-tale view of Shimla at twilight; with whiskey in hand, you can watch the city's lights come on from the garden terrace. Chapslee's excellent kitchen prepares British-influenced dishes, as well as delectable tandoori chicken and mouthwatering *shami* kebabs.

Chapslee, Shimla 171 001. ☎ 0177/280-2542. Fax 0177/265-8663. www.chapslee.com. chapslee@vsnl.com. 6 units. Rs 9,500–Rs 12,500 ($232–$305/£117–£154) double. Rates inclusive of all meals, taxes, and service charges in lieu of tips; Rs 750–Rs 1,000 ($18–$24/£9.25–£12) winter surcharge Oct 15–Mar 31 includes heaters, fire. Foreigners may need to pay by international credit card; MC, V. **Amenities:** Dining room; tennis court; bed tea and packed lunches; croquet lawn; card room; library.

Wildflower Hall ✿✿✿ Smack-dab in the middle of magnificent deodar cedar forests, atop its own hill a thousand feet above Shimla, surrounded by swirling mist and snowy peaks, this inspired remake of the fire-gutted mountain retreat of Lord Kitchener is the ideal setting for a beautifully eerie alpine fantasy. Affording showstopping views of some of the most spectacularly scenic mountains and valleys in India, this opulent yet surprisingly unpretentious Himalayan resort has all the seductive charms of a luxury hotel in a heritage property, with top-notch facilities and fine service. It's also dressed to perfection: Stately architecture is matched with tasteful reproduction furniture and carefully selected artworks and objets d'art. Guest rooms are well-appointed and spacious, with wood paneling, walk-in closets, and exquisite bathrooms. Burmese teak wood and Italian marble have been used lavishly. Valley-view premium rooms are excellent (nos. 101, 201, 301, and 327 are most prized). Deluxe rooms have the added benefit of private balconies. The billiards room is almost in the exact spot as Lord Kitchener's was, with classic lifted benches, high stools and chairs, and lights from England dating back to 1911. Besides the outstanding restaurant (don't miss the traditional Himachali thali), a spa menu serves healthy meals; each dish comes with a card indicating the calories and food value. But the hotel's *pièce de résistance* is the spa itself, which offers an impressive range of services and massage treatments (including private spa suites for couples). If you're fortunate to be at Wildflower during a full moon, spend an evening in the outdoor Jacuzzi surrounded by nothing but snowcapped mountain peaks.

Chharabra, Shimla 171 012. ⓒ 0177/264-8585. Toll-free reservations in India: ⓒ 1800/11-2030. Fax 0177/264-8686. www.oberoihotels.com. reservations@eih-india.com. 85 units. $360 (£182) premier single; $390 (£197) premier double; $625 (£316) deluxe suite; $925 (£468) Lord Kitchener Suite. Taxes extra. AE, DC, MC, V. **Amenities:** Restaurant; spa restaurant; bar; tennis court; heated indoor pool; spa w/gym, sauna, steam, Jacuzzi, and massage facilities, separate spa pavilion, and 2 private spa suites; outdoor Jacuzzi; travel arrangements; car hire; currency exchange; Wi-Fi enabled; horses and horse trail; hiking and picnicking; trekking; bird-watching; archery; mountain biking; ice skating (winter); river-rafting; card room; billiards; library. *In room:* A/C, TV, dataport, minibar, tea- and coffee-making facilities, electronic safe, DVD player, butler.

SHOPPING

The cool nip in the evening air may well have you stocking up on colorful Kinnauri shawls, mufflers, and caps; Pangwali blankets from Chamba; and multicolored hand-knitted woolen socks from Lahaul. The best place to shop for these items and more is **Himachal Emporium** (3 The Mall; ⓒ 0177/201-234). But before you purchase, the **Tibetan Handloom Shop** (5 Willow Bank, The Mall; ⓒ 0177/280-8163) is also worth visiting, good for Tibetan handicrafts and unique knits. You can also try the very old and renowned **Dewanchand Atmaram** (47 The Mall; ⓒ 0177/203-000; closed Sun) for woolen items, while **Shezadi** (ⓒ 0177/213-333) is a favorite for those interested in bringing home some traditional Indian clothes jazzed up by innovative design. A side trail from The Mall takes you to the **Lakkar Bazaar** (timber market), famous for wooden souvenirs (closed Sun), while another detour into the **Lower Bazaar** leads to an assortment of interesting shops, some barely big enough for two people—drop in at **Thakur Bhrata,** where you will find a fascinating display of homemade pickles and preserves. If you are an avid collector of first editions, **Maria Brothers** (78 The Mall; ⓒ 0177/255-388; closed Sun) is an absolute gem, known for rare books, antique maps, old prints, and photographs. For a more contemporary selection, try **Asia Book House** (40 The Mall; ⓒ 0177/212-217) or **Minerva** (46 The Mall; ⓒ 0177/203-078; closed Sun).

4 Exploring Kinnaur & Spiti ⭑⭑⭑

The arid, dust-covered, snowcapped slopes in the Indo-Tibetan regions of Kinnaur, Spiti, and Lahaul are the stuff adventurers' dreams are made of, offering sublime mountainscapes, twisting roads, and fascinating Tibetan Buddhist communities with atmospheric *gompas* (monasteries). Negotiating the rough, drop-off ledges of the **Hindustan-Tibet Road** (bizarrely enough, known as "National Highway" 22) is an action-packed art in itself, and the impossible road is made all the more unnerving when buses, trucks, and jeeps headed in the opposite direction seem to appear out of nowhere. Although the spectacular scenery is undoubtedly the highlight of any trip through Kinnaur and Spiti, there are also marvelous monuments, including some of the world's most intriguing Buddhist complexes (such as the World Heritage Site of **Tabo Monastery** in Spiti), as well as high-altitude villages that seem to cling to the sides of mountains or balance on the edges of sharp cliffs.

ESSENTIALS

VISITOR INFORMATION   Pick up information from the **tourism office in Shimla** (or Manali if you're doing the trip in reverse), and make detailed inquiries regarding accessibility and weather developments. Ajay Sud, an ex-army captain and adventurer who together with Rajesh Ojha founded **Banjara Camps,** is one of the best sources of information, tips, and assistance in the Kinnaur region. He's also a very experienced trekker and can give great advice and suggestions for treks throughout the Himalayas. He and the equally helpful Rajesh take turns manning the Sangla camp; best to reach either through the **head office** (1A Hauz Khas Village, New Delhi 110 016; © **011/2686-1397;** fax 011/2685-5152; www.banjaracamps.com).

If you'd like to have a more interactive holiday, staying with (and getting to know) local folk, contact **Ecosphere** (Ishita Khanna; © **98-99492417** or 01906/22-2724; www.spitiecosphere.com). Ecosphere has pioneered homestays and grassroots community participation in the Spiti region and can help put together a really memorable trip. If you're a hiker, **Aquaterra Adventures** (www.aquaterra.in), one of India's leading adventure travel specialists, runs "homestay trails"—fantastic hiking holidays through the rugged terrain with accommodations arranged in local village homes rather than tented camps—thereby providing a glimpse into the lifestyle and culture of this region. Aquaterra also organizes a yearly descent of the Spiti-Pin rivers from Kiato to Sumdo.

GETTING AROUND   Ultra-budget-conscious travelers undertake the journey in state buses that rely on luck as much as faith to reach their destination, while born-to-be-wild adventurers do it on the back of a motorbike—sign up with Capt. Raaj Kumar of **Shepherds Realms** (see "Jeep & Motorcycle Safari Specialists" above). For the rest, we highly recommend renting a jeep and driver—the heftier the jeep (a Toyota Qualis or a Mahindra Scorpio), the better your chances of actually enjoying the adventure. Most of the villages can be explored on foot, and the region lends itself to trekking (see "Staying Active," earlier in this chapter). For one-stop shopping, we recommend you utilize the services of Banjara Camps (see "Visitor Information," above), which offers most of the best lodging options in the area and can arrange your entire jeep safari.

INNER LINE PERMITS   Foreigners may not travel through the zone closest to the Tibetan border without first obtaining an **Inner Line Permit** from one of several government offices in Himachal. It's a fairly easy, if laborious and frustrating, process (taking anywhere from 3 hr. to a whole day); you will need your passport, three passport-size photographs, and two copies of both the main page of your passport and your visa, before heading for the SDM (Sub-Divisional Magistrate) office where you complete an application form. It's best to have this prearranged from Shimla; alternatively, the place to apply is Recong Peo—the SDM's office is located in the Deputy Commissioner's Building near the town's bus stand, next door to the Hotel Snowview. One way of dealing with the slow pace is to apply and then collect your papers the following day after overnighting in beautiful Kalpa nearby. It's a good idea to phone ahead to ensure that the **SDM office** (© **01786/222-253;** Mon–Sat 10am–5pm) is definitely open on the day you plan to apply.

THE JOURNEY

Heading east out of Shimla, National Highway 22 takes you to **Narkanda** (2,708m/8,882 ft.), a ski resort (Jan–Mar) where you can take in excellent views from Hatu Peak. From Narkanda, a 16km (10-mile) detour off the main highway brings you to the vast apple orchards of Thanedar, heavy with fruit in summer. (Samuel Stokes, an

American who settled here in the early 1900s, is credited with bringing over and planting the region's first apple trees.) Set in the midst of this sea of apple trees is the whitewashed **Banjara Camps' Orchard Retreat** ⭐, its pleasant rooms decked with thick, colorful throws and attached bathrooms. It's a very comfortable place to kick back and relax and enjoy astonishingly beautiful sunsets. Prakash Thakur, host and owner of this lovely Himalayan getaway, is also the resident expert on local history and culture, and you can request a guide to take you for a fabulous 3-hour trek through the shady forest. Evenings are spent around a bonfire, where Prakash serves up anecdotes, *paneer*-on-a-toothpick, and spicy chicken snacks before an Indian buffet is laid out. Do taste the homemade apple juice, chutneys, and other concoctions Prakash makes from the orchard fruit (Rs 3,600/$88/£44 double; see "Visitor Information," above).

From Thanedar you can either backtrack to Narkanda or continue farther on the Narkanda-Thanedar road which meets the highway at Bithal, 21km (13 miles) from the retreat. Then continue north past the commercial town of **Rampur,** a former princely capital. The road descends towards the raging Sutlej River, following its contours until you come upon the dusty village of **Jeori.** From here, a twisting, hairpin-heavy climb leads to the charming village of **Sarahan** (2,165m/7,101 ft., 6 hr. from Shimla), which enjoys spectacular views of the snowcapped peaks across the river. Trapped in time, Sarahan is the site of the famous pagoda-style **Bhimakali Temple** ⭐⭐⭐. You can overnight in Sarahan at the recently renovated government-run **Hotel Shrikhand** (© 01782/27-4234; www.hptdc.nic.in); the setting is out-of-this-world, rates are low (from Rs 400/$9.75/£5), and you'll enjoy incredible views from your room. For the best room deal, book "half the cottage" (Rs 1,200/$29/£15), which gets you a spacious, high-ceilinged room in a separate block with a fireplace, television, and enclosed porch/sitting room. The hotel has a small bar and a restaurant. Alternatively, try **Wildside: Off Beat Nature Retreat** (© 94-1800-0056 or 98-1535-7866; www.wildside.in)—these nine rooms (Rs 2,800/$68/£35), located in an interesting teakwood building, are probably your best option in Sarahan.

The next morning, follow the same road back down to Jeori. About 3km (2 miles) ahead of Karchham (Baspa–Sutlej Junction), take a U-turn to come back to Karcham and then follow the steep dirt tracks (the road from Karcham to Sangla is fairly wide now, and two small cars/jeeps can comfortably pass by each other) of the **Sangla Valley** ⭐⭐⭐, through which the raging Baspa River flows. You won't find any flashy accommodations, but comfortable **Banjara Camp,** 8km (5 miles) beyond, is an excellent place to spend a night or two, and serves as the perfect base from which to explore the remote hamlet of **Chitkul** ⭐⭐ (3,450m/11,316 ft.). This Banjara Camp (see "Visitor Information" above; Rs 3,800/$93/£47 double, includes all meals and taxes; open Apr–Oct) comprises 17 comfortable tents with attached toilets and running water, in a gorgeous open meadow (wildflowers in full bloom July–Oct) alongside the Baspa River, beneath towering Khargala Peak. Make use of the opportunity to pick the brains of Banjara founders Ajay or Rajesh (one of whom is generally in camp) for details of the best treks in the area. Both are wonderful hosts, with plenty of ideas for what you can do (besides lying in one of the inviting hammocks overlooking the river). A selection of tasty Indian and Tibetan-inspired dishes is prepared at mealtimes and served in Makuti, the thatched dining area; but there's nothing stopping you from picking up fresh fish from a local farm (the area is known for trout fishing) and having the kitchen team cook it for you.

From Sangla, you will have to double back to "National Highway" 22 to continue east towards Kinnaur's main town of **Recong Peo** (2,670m/8,758 ft.), where you must complete the paperwork for your Inner Line Permit, which will permit you to enter the zone closest to the Tibetan border. While waiting for the bureaucratic wheels to turn, spend the night in the village of **Kalpa** ✵✵ (2,960m/9,709 ft.), well worth a visit for its crisp, clear air and view across the valley of the majestic Kinner-Kailash massif; it's a 30-minute drive into the mountain above Recong Peo. **Hotel Kinner Villa** (✆ **01786/22-6006;** from Rs 1,300/$32/£16 double) is the best place to stay (well at least service is a notch better given that it is privately run), with simple, clean, and comfortable accommodations. Room no. 201 has the most exquisite view; nos. 101, 104, 202, and 207 aren't bad, either. When the hotel is quiet, you'll have to book meals in advance. Note, too, that Kalpa suffers from interminable power failures, so make sure the manager supplies you with candles. Also affording good views are rooms at the **Tourist Complex** of Kinner Kailash, an HPTDC (state-run) hotel (✆ **01786/22-6159**). Double rooms (without meals) start from Rs 900 ($22/£11).

Set out early the following day; once you pass the first Inner Line checkpoint at Jangi, you will notice dramatic changes in the landscape, as fir trees give way to rock and stone sloping up toward distant summits and down into the raging River Sutlej. The journey through Inner Line territory takes you past the off-limits turnoff for 5,500m-high (18,040-ft.) Shipki-La Pass, which heads into China. **Nako Lake** ✵ and its village lie farther along; beyond the turnoff for Nako, the road attains its most sinister aspect as you enter the notorious section known as the Malling Slide, heavily punctuated with precipitous drops—an ideal place to strengthen your faith in the divine. The bypass to Malling via Nako was operational throughout 2006—though not "fault" free, there is every chance that you will get through; this road meets the highway again at Chango. Upon reaching the final Inner Line check-post at Sumdo—some 115km (71 miles) from Recong Peo and 363km (225 miles) from Shimla—the road heads northwest into the alien landscapes of Spiti.

The Buddhist town of **Tabo** ✵✵✵ (some 6 hr. from Recong Peo) is the most frequented stop in Spiti, and for good reason (see "Top Attractions," below). We recommend you stay at **Banjara Camps' Tabo Retreat** (see "Visitor Information" above; doubles from Rs 3,600/$88/£44; Apr–Oct). Architecturally, the building echoes Ladakhi style: simple, clean, comfortable, en-suite guest rooms have small, private balconies. Ask for an upper-level room facing the monastery. Om Parkash Thakur is not only an efficient manager, but something of a culinary wizard, so there's plenty of carefully prepared food available. Many visitors traveling on a tight budget stay at the **rest house** in the monastery run by monks (✆ **01906/23-3313** or -3315; www.aarogya. com/tabo/location.html; Rs 300–Rs 550/$7.30–$13/£3.70–£6.80). It has simple guest rooms with attached bathrooms, all arranged around a peaceful central courtyard. You will most likely have to arrive here to arrange a room—phones in the area are notoriously unreliable. If you run into problems, another solid option is the **Torzan Guest House,** located on the main road. Doubles run about Rs 1,000 ($24/£12), but rates are flexible.

Not far from Tabo is the village of **Dhankar** ✵✵✵, which hugs the side of a hill and offers breathtaking glimpses of the surrounding mountains and valley below—a visit to the precariously perched monastery makes for an excellent diversion. Legend has it that Ladhaki invaders posing a threat to the monastery were invited for a feast. As was customary, a strong local brew was served, and once inebriated, the guests were rolled down the steep precipice by the hosts—no need, however, to regard the butter tea offered by the warm monks with suspicion! Visit Dhankar on your way from Tabo, and then continue on to the town of **Kaza.** As the administrative headquarters of

Spiti, Kaza offers little excitement, but unless you really want to spend an entire day on the road, it's a useful base from which to visit the beautiful, fortresslike *gompa* of **Ki** 🦚🦚🦚 and the high-altitude village of **Kibber** 🦚🦚. Plan on spending the night here at **Kaza Retreat,** another inn operated by the Banjara group (see "Visitor Information," above; doubles from Rs 2,800/$68/£35). Guest rooms are simple but have attached Western bathrooms. If you're on a tighter budget, get a room at **Sakya's Abode** (© **01906/22-2256** or -2254). If you're traveling from Manali, make reservations through Ritesh Sood at the Himalayan Saga travel agency, near Club House, Manali (© **01902/25-1848** or 98-1614-6191). Doubles start at Rs 800 ($20/£10).

From Kaza, either head for Manali to catch your breath, or travel directly to Leh. North of Spiti is **Lahaul** 🦚🦚🦚. Linked to the rest of Himachal by the Rohtang Pass, dotted with villages of flat-roofed houses, fluttering prayer flags, and whitewashed *chortens,* Lahaul is cut off from the world by heavy snow for 8 months of the year. This mountainous region attracts adventurers to its Buddhist monasteries, mountain passes, spectacular glaciers, and high-altitude lakes. Visitors traveling by road to Leh in Ladakh, farther north, pass through Lahaul.

TOP ATTRACTIONS

Bhimakali Temple 🦚🦚   Chanting and music blast from the temple loudspeakers very early each morning and again in the evenings, transforming Sarahan village into a place that literally resonates with spirituality. Combining Hindu and Buddhist architectural elements, the main section of the temple comprises two pagoda-style pitched slate-roof towers. Built from layers of interlaced stone and timber, the towers rise from a courtyard around which are living quarters and a small museum with a collection of weapons and other unusual ritual objects and relics. Had you visited the temple 200 years ago, you might have witnessed one of the annual human sacrifices that kept the gods satisfied; today, animals suffice. The tower on the right was damaged in an earthquake a century ago, and the presiding deity was relocated to the tower on the left. Climb the stairs to get to the main shrine with its family of idols. Bhimakali is the main deity, while Durga, Ganesha, and even Buddha are all in attendance. The priests don't speak English, but it's worth taking part in the small *puja* (prayer) ceremony, so bring your rupees. Morning and evening prayers are scheduled but don't always take place.
Sarahan village center. No shoes, cameras, leather, or weapons. Daily 7am–8pm.

Dhankar Monastery 🦚🦚🦚   *Dhankar* means "fort," and a glimpse of this monastery precariously perched on a hill jutting against a sharp mountainside certainly suggests its usefulness as a protective stronghold. Once the castle of the Nono, the ruler of Spiti, the building typifies the traditional architecture of the town. As if wedged between massive craggy outcrops, the rather dirty whitewashed flat-topped structures create a dramatic effect against stark fingers of hard rock. Entry to the temple is nerve-wracking; access steps and uppermost rooftops drop away to perilously steep rocky slopes. Today, Dhankar is a repository of Bhoti-scripted Buddhist scriptures. You can visit this hilltop monastery as an excursion from Tabo, or en route to your next destination. It makes a sublime detour because it attracts considerably fewer visitors than relatively busy Tabo, and although the monastery interiors are rather small, the astonishing location and wonderful views more than make up for this.
Dhankar Tashi Choling Monastery, Spiti. Small entrance fee.

Kibber & Ki Gompa 🦚🦚🦚   Just north of Kaza, a road veers off the main highway and zigzags its way up a steep mountainside. At the end of this stretch is Kibber, perched on a rocky spur at an altitude of 4,205m (13,792 ft.). Kibber enjoys a reputation as the highest permanent settlement with electricity and accessibility by motor road. Surrounded by limestone rocks and cliffs, the remote and isolated village offers stunning views of the barren valley below. There's even a handful of guesthouses should you require accommodations. Between Kibber and Kaza is Spiti's largest monastery, Ki Gompa, which is about 700 years old. Home to a large community of lamas (of the Gelugpa sect), Ki Gompa is well accustomed to receiving visitors; the monk on duty will brew you a welcoming cup of tea and show you around the different prayer rooms and assembly halls filled with holy relics. The most exciting time to visit is late June or early July, when a festival involving *chaam* dancing and the ceremonial burning of butter sculptures draws large numbers of pilgrims.

Ki Gompa is 12km (7½ miles) northwest of Kaza. Kibber is 4km (2½ miles) farther.

Tabo ⟨★★★⟩   With a population of some 900, this Buddhist settlement, situated at 3,050m (10,004 ft.) in lower Spiti, is centered around its celebrated 1,000-year-old monastic complex, said to be the place where the present Dalai Lama will "retire." A serene village of flat-roofed houses topped by thatch packed with branches, mud, and grass, Tabo has as its focus its monastery—or "doctrinal enclave"—consisting of nine temple buildings, chambers for monks and nuns, 23 snow-white *chortens,* and piles of stones, each inscribed with scripture. The sanctity of this World Heritage Site is topped only by Tholing monastery in Tibet. Don't arrive expecting some cathedral-like masterpiece; Tabo Gompa is a rustic center that is more spiritually than architecturally engaging. A high mud wall surrounds the compound, and the pale mud-covered low-rise monastery buildings suggest nothing of the exquisite wall paintings and stucco statues within. You'll need a flashlight to properly appreciate many of the frescoes and other artworks that adorn the various dark, ancient spaces; only narrow shafts of natural light from small skylights illuminate the frescoed walls, saturated with rich colors and an incongruous variety of scenes. There's a distinctly surreal, often nightmarish quality to the work—gruesome torture scenes compete with images of meditative contemplation and spiritual discovery.

At the core of the complex is the **Temple of Enlightened Gods (Tsug Lha-khang),** which includes the **Assembly Hall** (or *du-khang*) housing a 2m-high (6½-ft.) white stucco image of Vairocana, one of the five spiritual sons of the primordial, self-creative Buddha, or Adibuddha. Below this are two images of the great translator and teacher Rin-Chan-Sang-Po, who is believed to have founded Tabo in A.D. 996. Thirty-three other life-size stucco deities surrounded by stylized flaming circles are bracketed along the walls. Directly behind the assembly hall is the **sanctum,** with five bodhisattvas of the Good Age and beautifully rendered Indian-style frescoes depicting the life of the Buddha. Monks are initiated in the smaller **Mystic Mandala Temple (dKyil-hKhor-khang),** situated behind the main temples. At the northern edge of the complex is the **Temple of Dromton (Brom-ston Lha-khang),** entered via a small portico and long passage. Only enter the **Mahakala Vajra-Bhairava Temple (Gon-Khang)** once you've performed a protective meditation—it's filled with fierce deities that inspire its nickname, "the temple of horrors." Just outside the complex are several contemporary monastic buildings, including an atmospheric guesthouse run by the monks. Above Tabo, across the highway, a group of caves on a sheer cliff-face was once used as monastic dwellings. (*Note:* No photography allowed inside the monastery.)

365km (226 miles) from Shimla, 295km (183 miles) from Kullu, 47km (29 miles) from Kaza. www.aarogya.com/tabo/index.html.

5 The Valley of the Gods: Central Himachal

Central Himachal's fertile valleys—centered around the towns of Mandi, Kullu, and Manali—are watered by the Beas River, and are famous for a variety of fruits, excellent treks, and what is considered—by the stoned hippies of Manali, at least—the finest marijuana in the world.

The drive from Shimla to Manali—starting point for the spectacular road journey to Leh and a number of adventure activities—is around 280km (174 miles) and can be done in a day. The route is scenic, especially in July and August, when the heavy monsoon rains cause the river to swell and waterfalls to cascade spectacularly. Time allowing, it's a good idea to spend the night en route in the scruffy town of Mandi, where you can use the atmospheric Raj Mahal palace hotel as a base for a visit to the nearby hill hamlet of **Rewalsar** ☀. The fascinating confluence of Buddhist, Sikh, and Hindu spirituality, centered around a small black lake teeming with fish (supposedly holy), beautifully reflects the soaring mountain ranges above. Sacred to all three religions, the lake's banks sport lively Buddhist *gompas,* an important Sikh *gurudwara* (place of worship), and a Hindu temple.

Farther north (about 70km/43 miles), in the heart of the Valley of the Gods, is the unattractive town of **Kullu,** famous for its sheer volume of Hindu temples and the Dussehra Festival (usually in Oct), which attracts substantial crowds and hundreds of valley gods to take part in the annual festivities: 7 days of jubilant processions, music, dancing, and markets. Unless you stop specifically to catch any festival action or want to visit the "first and biggest angora farm in Asia," there's no real reason to linger in Kullu.

Bhuntar, not too far south of Kullu, is the turnoff point for drives to Jari, Kasol, and the therapeutic hot springs of **Manikaran,** which is the main jumping-off point for a variety of treks to less-visited villages. **Khirganga,** farther east, is the site of even more thermal water springs, while isolated **Malana,** to the north, is an anthropologist's dream and home of the world's top-rated *ganja,* the famous Malana Gold, according to a recent competition held in Amsterdam. Adventures to any of these remote areas should not be undertaken without the help of a recognized guide—not only is getting lost a strong possibility, but there have been reports of what are believed to be drug-related crimes, including the assault and "disappearance'" of travelers.

ESSENTIALS

GETTING THERE & AROUND It's possible to avoid Shimla entirely by flying directly to **Bhuntar Airport** 10km (6¼ miles) south of Kullu. In Manali, taxis and auto-rickshaws charge ridiculously inflated rates that fluctuate seasonally and according to the whim of the near-militant local taxi union. Hire a car for the duration of your stay; if you've used a car and driver to get to Manali, you might consider planning ahead to retain the service for any further travel, bearing in mind that a sturdy vehicle with off-road capabilities and a driver who knows the terrain will be essential if you plan on getting to Ladakh or the regions east of the Beas River.

VISITOR INFORMATION & TRAVEL AGENTS For information about the Kullu and Parvati valleys, visit **Himachal Pradesh Tourism** (✆ 01902/22-2349; www.himachaltourism.nic.in) in Kullu, near the maidan. In Manali, the **Tourist Information Centre** (The Mall, Manali; ✆ 01902/25-2175; Mon–Sat 10am–1pm and 1:30–5pm) can give you a pile of booklets on destinations throughout the state (most of these are available from the far friendlier office in Shimla). Alternatively, try the **HPTDC** office ✆ 01902/25-2360. An ad-saturated tourist map of Manali is available for Rs 15

Tips **Avoid the Rush**

The low-level but ongoing threat of war in Kashmir has meant that Manali's popularity has soared over the last decade. Visitors who once would have gone to Kashmir for the snow and possibility of skiing now swamp Manali during the Indian high season, which stretches from April until the rains hit in early July, and then again from September to November. Manali's charms have been all but eroded by this tourist explosion, which sets off a soulless cash-rally that seems to involve every proprietor, merchant, and taxi-tour operator in town; hotel tariffs also soar during this period. *Bottom line:* Try to avoid this usually peaceful town during these months.

(35¢/20p), and more detailed books and booklets are available for purchase. **Matkon Travels** (*C* **01902/25-3738** or 98-1600-3738) can also help you with domestic flights and deluxe-bus bookings. Matkon works in conjunction with the **Himalayan Institute of Adventure Sports** (Roshan Thakur; *C* **981601-6554**) and offers sightseeing, trekking, rafting, paragliding, and skiing opportunities with reliable guides.

MANALI

Yes, it's set amid dense pine forests and shadowed by snowy peaks, but Manali's reputation as a spectacular Himalayan resort is much exaggerated. The primary reason to be here is to set off for Leh in Ladakh, a 2-day drive away, or to participate in the many treks or adventure sports, including heli-skiing.

Manali comprises several neighborhoods, each with a distinct personality. North of the Manalsu Nala River is **Old Manali,** with its historic stone buildings; to the west is the pleasant village of **Dhungri;** while messy **Model Town** is a motley collection of concrete buildings tucked behind the main bazaar area, concentrated around The Mall. East of the Beas River, a few kilometers north of Manali is **Vashisht,** a village known for its hot springs and laid-back atmosphere. Unfortunately, Vashisht has lost much of its charm thanks to an influx of long-stay budget tourists; a dunk in the communal hot-water bath of the local temple is hardly reason enough to visit.

The most peaceful area is **Dhungri Village** (around 2km/1¼ miles from the bazaar), where you can stroll through deodar forests or visit a 450-year-old temple where animal sacrifice is still practiced. On the outskirts of the neighborhood, the multi-tiered wooden pagoda-style **Hadimba Devi Temple** *✪*, built in 1553, is Manali's oldest and most interesting shrine, dedicated to the demon goddess Hadimba (an incarnation of Kali). Look around for the sheltered sacrificial stone used for blood rituals during important ceremonies; the central hollow is where the blood from a slain buffalo or goat drains into Hadimba's mouth.

Another good walk takes you through Old Manali (center of cheap backpackers' accommodations), the temple dedicated to Manu, and beyond to silent hillside paths where you'll encounter village women passing the day over idle gossip while their men unhurriedly herd goats and cows toward greener pastures at higher altitudes. Most visitors pay a visit to Manali's two rather modern Buddhist *gompas* in the town's Tibetan quarter south of the bazaar. **Gadhan Thekchhokling gompa** was built in 1969, and is recognizable by its yellow, pagoda-style roof; memorial notices outside draw attention to the extermination of Tibetans in China.

Just 24km (15 miles) short of Manali is **Naggar,** which like Manali is slowly being wrecked by unchecked construction and tourism. Visit the **Nicholas Roerich Museum** (© **01902/24-8290** or -8590; Tues–Sun 10am–1pm and 1:30–6pm), where the famous Russian artist lived from 1923 until he died in 1947. In this small but well-maintained museum, paintings and books by the prolific artist and philosopher are on display. In this stunning location, it's easy to see why Roerich and his wife, Helena, were so inspired by their surroundings (though not everyone feels the same about his artworks). Also part of the estate is the **Urusvati Himalayan Folk Art Museum** (Tues–Sun 10am–6pm), created for the preservation of folk art and craft.

WHERE TO STAY
MANDI & KULLU
If you're traveling by road from Shimla direct to either Manali or Dharamsala, it's a good idea to take a break en route. In Mandi, 70km (43 miles) south of Kullu, **Raj Mahal** (© **01905/22-2401,** -3434 or 98-1602-1126), a creaky-floorboards "palace," is recommended for its serious time-warp character. Book one of the four enormous Royal Suites (Rs 4,400/$107/£54 double), which showcase an assortment of kitsch furnishings and objets d'art (in one room a stuffed leopard grimaces on a table with rifles for legs!). Generally, the service at Raj Mahal is quite awful, and the ancient plumbing acts up at times, but as a place to lay your head for a night and as a base for visiting nearby Rewalsar, it's adequate. If you're after a more typical hotel experience, head on to **Apple Valley Resort** (© **01902/26-0001** or -0006), just short of Kullu town. Set on the banks of the Beas River, the luridly decorated country-style cabins with ivy-covered walls and stone chimneys are Rs 2,700 ($66/£33) double, with meals; ask for a cabin with a good view.

MANALI
For the most atmospheric room in town, you're best off in an original lodge apartment at **Jimmy Johnson's Lodge** (not to be confused with the adjacent Johnson's Lodge) or the privacy of **Leela Huts;** alternatively, stay at **Negi's Hotel Mayflower** or **Span Resorts** for their riverside location (see below for reviews of all). For those keen on outdoor pursuits like paragliding in summer and skiing in winter, **Solang Valley Resort** (© **01902/25-6132;** www.solangvalleyresorts.com; doubles from Rs 4,500/$110/£56) is probably the best option as it is situated only half a kilometer from the beautiful Solang Valley (about 45 min. from Manali town). If none of the following recommendations are available, Manali's **Private Hoteliers' Information Centre** (The Mall, near the taxi stand) is well established and can assist you in finding suitably priced accommodations if you haven't prebooked. Note that during the busy season (mid-Apr to early July) you will have difficulty finding any upmarket guest room in Manali at all.

Jimmy Johnson's Lodge ⚡ Set among lovely lawns, this "lodge" was the first inhabited property in New Manali, and it offers a choice of vintage or modern accommodations not too far from the thick of things. Now run by Piya, the cosmopolitan granddaughter of the man who built the original stone lodge apartments, Johnson's may be relatively close to the bazaar, but it remains a tranquil spot with lovely views. If you opt for one of the slate, stone, and wood guest rooms in the upper complex, ask for a corner unit—these are larger and have extra windows from which to enjoy the mountain scenes. If you'd prefer an old-fashioned experience, the three huge ivy-covered stone-walled balconied suites in the original building are atmospheric curiosities, with aging furnishings, original fittings, and loads of space. Wood-beam ceilings, screened windows, and small, homey kitchens add to the ambience. Ask for cottage no. 2, which is the neatest and quietest. A pleasant, cafe-style restaurant offers all-day dining.

Circuit House Rd., Manali 175 131. ℂ **01902/25-3023** or 01902/25-3764. Fax 01902/24-5123. johnsonshotel@ gmail.com. 18 units. New Wing: May 11–July 15 Rs 1,800 ($44/£22) standard double, Rs 2,000 ($49/£25) deluxe double, taxes extra; rest of the year flat rate of Rs 1,500 ($37/£19) on all rooms. Original suites, for 4: Rs 4,500 ($110/£56) May 15–July 15; Rs 1,000 ($24/£12) less rest of the year. No credit cards. **Amenities:** Restaurant; laundry on request; doctor-on-call. *In room:* TV, heaters.

Leela Huts ℱ *(Kids)*   Popular with diplomats in need of a real break, this collection of five stone cottages is ideal if you're traveling with children or a group of friends. Set in a large garden of potted plants, fruit trees, and neatly hedged pathways, these rustic, comfortable, and rather large holiday cabins offer a pleasant respite from Manali's bustle, even during the height of the domestic tourist season. It's owned and run by the affable Mrs. Thakur and her family, and you are assured of friendly, helpful assistance throughout your stay. When the power goes down, as it tends to throughout Himachal, someone soon arrives to tend to your gas lanterns. Although the cottages are self-catering, you have the option of investing in a "cook-on-request" to tend to your culinary desires.

Sunshine Orchards, Club House Rd., Manali 175 131. ℂ **01902/25-2464.** Fax 01902/25-4035. www.leelahuts.com. leelahuts@rediffmail.com. 5 units. Apr 15–June 30 and Sept 15–Jan 15 Rs 4,500 ($110/£56) 3-bedroom cottage, Rs 3,500 ($85/£43) 2-bedroom cottage; July 1–Sept 15 Rs 3,500 ($85/£43) 3-bedroom cottage, Rs 2,500 ($61/£31) 2-bedroom cottage. No credit cards. **Amenities:** Cook on request; tour and taxi arrangements; laundry; in-house doctor; badminton; basketball court; children's play area. *In room:* TV, kitchenette, fridge, gas cooker, fireplace, heater in winter.

Negi's Hotel Mayflower ℱ *(Finds)*   In a town overflowing with characterless hotels, this handsome, unpretentious, and comfortable option is a relief to find. Rooms are massive, with wooden floors and paneling, rocking chairs by the fireplace, tasteful lamps with rice-paper shades, desks in cozy corners, warm sitting areas, and spotless bathrooms (with bathtubs) overlooking the pine forests—what more could you possibly want? Best of all is the veranda that runs the length of the facade, furnished with wicker chairs to lounge around in while sipping cups of lemon tea. The extremely reserved proprietor keeps a low profile, but thankfully not in the kitchen—his Irish stew, roast lamb, caramel custard with stewed apricots, and bread and butter pudding are legendary. Manager Dharamendra looks after each of his guests with real care and can help with planning a detailed itinerary.

Club House Rd., Manali 175 131. ℂ **01902/25-2104** or -0256. Fax 01902/25-3923. www.negismayflower.com. negismayflower@sancharnet.in. 21 units. Rs 2,000 ($49/£25) double (excluding taxes and meals). AE, MC, V. **Amenities:** Restaurant; bar; taxis; tours; adventure activities; room service; laundry; doctor-on-call; Internet. *In room:* TV, heater, fireplace.

Span Resorts ℱ   A riverside location, 15km (9⅓ miles) from the center of Manali, makes this resort a peaceful respite from the crowds, enhanced by the generous range of amenities and outdoor activities on offer. Accommodations are in stone-and-wood cottages shaped like stars and spread around well-maintained grounds; they're comfortable and offer a fair degree of privacy. Riverside units, with wooden floors, are the best. There isn't a heck of a lot of space, but each cottage has a fireplace and a covered porch from which to appreciate the relaxed setting and mountain views. There is plenty to keep you occupied during the snowy season, including what may be the best-stocked bar in the state.

Kullu–Manali Hwy., P.O. Katrain 175 129. © **01902/24-0138** or -0538. Fax 01902/24-0140. www.spanresorts.com. spanres@del3.vsnl.net.in. Reservations: Vijaya (1st Floor), 17 Barakhamba Rd., New Delhi 110 001. © **011/2331-1434.** Fax 011/2335-3148. 24 units. Rs 5,000 ($122/£62) double; Rs 1,500 ($37/£19) more for riverside double. Rs 375 ($9.15/£4.60) children ages 5–12, Rs 750 ($18/£9.25) children above 12. Rates include breakfast. AE, DC, MC, V. **Amenities:** Restaurant; bar; pool; minigolf; tennis; travel assistance, taxis, tours, sightseeing; 24-hr. room service; laundry; doctor-on-call; basketball; gym; darts; croquet; card room; library; table tennis; children's park; billiards; badminton; fishing, river rafting, skiing, horseback riding, trekking, and paragliding by arrangement. *In room:* A/C, TV, minibar.

WHERE TO DINE

With Manali's tourism boom has come a flood of eating establishments, many of which indulge in unchecked fly-by-night copycat techniques; be sure to check details beyond the name of whichever establishment you choose. Bear in mind that none take credit cards, and most stay open from 9am to 11pm.

The best Indian restaurant is **Mayur** (© **01902/25-2316;** average meal Rs 150/ $3.65/£1.85). Kangra Valley–born Rajesh Sud has been in the restaurant business since 1970 and opened this Manali institution back in 1978. Try the *murgh tikka masala* (barbecued chicken with spices) or the fresh, locally caught wild trout, prepared in the tandoor oven with a subtle blend of yogurt and aromatic spice. For the best Tibetan cuisine, head for **Phunsok,** run by a Tibetan family. Food is freshly cooked and thus takes a bit longer than usual; seating is outdoors, on the riverbank (2.5km/1½ miles from Manali toward Solang, on the left-hand side just ahead of the turn to Vashisht). For Italian (including reasonably good coffee), **Il Forno,** housed in a century-old house in Dunghri en route to the Hadimba Temple, is your most authentic option, also with good views. Roberta Angelone, who is from Naples, creates outstanding fresh-made pastas (ask if the ravioli is available) and authentic pizzas (no phone; average meal Rs 300/$7.30/£3.70). **Johnson's Café** (Johnson's Lodge, The Mall; © **01902/24-3764;** Rs 90–Rs 350/$2.20–$8.55/£1–£4.30) is a cozy, informal venue that enjoys a lively atmosphere and has garden seating. It also has Italian cuisine and the ubiquitous fresh trout—locally caught—on the menu, and it's a fine place to have coffee and breakfast while you plan the day's trek.

6 Exploring Dharamsala & the Kangra Valley

Tenzin Gyatso, the 14th Dalai Lama, chose Dharamsala as the capital-in-exile of the Tibetan people after fleeing Chinese oppression in 1959, and whether it's the endless spinning of Buddhist prayer wheels or simply the divine presence of the Dalai Lama, the Tibetan enclave at Dharamsala draws seekers of spiritual enlightenment from all over the world.

Admittedly, a visit to Everyman's spiritual center of the universe seems like the ultimate New Age cliché, but the town and its environs have much more to recommend than the fervent chanting of *Om mani padme hum* ("Hail to the jewel in the lotus"). The natural beauty of the surrounding mountains and mist-soaked valleys compares favorably with that of any of Himachal's best-loved resort towns, and for those not single-mindedly wrapped up in a quest for spiritual fine-tuning with Buddhist lectures and meditation courses, this is an ideal base for walks and treks into the Dhauladhar range. It's also a good place to simply experience a toned-down India at a more leisurely pace.

The hillside town stretches along a spur of the Dhauladhar mountain range and is divided into two very distinct parts—**Lower Dharamsala** and **McLeod Ganj** (often called Little Lhasa). Only the latter is worth considering as a place to stay and explore;

here you will encounter brightly robed Buddhist monks with umbrellas and Doc Marten boots, traditionally attired Tibetan women reciting holy mantras, and spiritual tourists in search of enlightenment. A former British hill station rocked by an earthquake in the early 1900s, McLeod Ganj today harbors several institutes and organizations dedicated to raising funds for the Tibetan people and promoting and preserving Buddhist culture. Among these is the Government-in-Exile's administration complex, or *Gangchen Kyishong,* where you'll find the fascinating **Library of Tibetan Works and Archives.** North of Dharamsala are spectacular mountain-hugging drives to the remote towns of Dalhousie and Chamba, while farther south you can visit the charming heritage village of **Pragpur** *ƒƒ* and explore the tea-covered valleys around historical **Taragarh Palace Hotel** *ƒ*, not far from the town of Palampur.

ESSENTIALS

VISITOR INFORMATION   There's a **Tourist Information Office** (*✆* 01892/22-1205 or -1232; Mon–Sat 10am–1:30pm and 2–5pm) in McLeod Ganj, but you'll be hard-pressed to squeeze anything worthwhile out of the lackluster staff; you'd do better to make inquiries at your hotel. *CONTACT* is a free monthly newsletter distributed in and around McLeod Ganj. Although its primary aim is to promote Buddhist issues, it also carries up-to-date information and advertisements regarding cultural events and activities likely to be of interest to foreign visitors. If you are here for massage, meditation, alternative healing, yoga, or Tibetan cooking classes, this publication will point you in the right direction. Also visit **www.dharamsalanet.com**.

GETTING THERE & AROUND   It's possible to drive from Shimla or Chandigarh to Dharamsala, and there are two great overnight options along the way—choose between **Taragarh Palace,** outside Palampur, or **The Judge's Court,** in Pragpur (see later in this chapter). The most pleasant way to get to the Kangra Valley directly from Delhi is by train (driving by car takes almost 12 hr.). The overnight Jammu Mail from Delhi allows you to rest up before hiring a car for the scenic 3-hour road trip from Pathankot to Dharamsala (80km/50 miles). Another option is to fly—Air Deccan operates daily to Kangra's Gaggal Airport, 15km (9⅓ miles) from Dharamsala. In Dharamsala, you will find it easy to get either a taxi or auto-rickshaw. (Auto-rickshaws are incredibly impractical, however, because of the engine-killing gradient of the town.) **Ways Tours & Travels** (Temple Rd., McLeod Ganj; *✆* **01892/22-1910,** -1355, or -1988; waystour@gmail.com) hires out cars with drivers for local sightseeing, and can help with all your travel arrangements as well as organize individually packaged tours throughout the region. You can also contact them in New Delhi, at House no. 45, New Tibetan Camp, Majnu-Ka-Tilla; call *✆* **011/2381-3254** or 98-1128-9552.

THE TOP ATTRACTIONS

Church of St. John in the Wilderness *ƒ*   Ten minutes of downhill walking from McLeod Ganj brings you to the Church of St. John in the Wilderness, surrounded by deodar cedars. It's a neo-Gothic stone construction, with its original Belgian stained glass intact in spite of a severe earthquake in 1905 that leveled the rest of town. Buried in the grassy adjoining graveyard is British Viceroy Lord Elgin (whose somewhat infamous father was responsible for the controversial Elgin Marbles).

Daily 10am–5pm.

Norbulingka Institute *ƒƒƒ*   If you're interested in getting a firsthand understanding of the techniques (and unbelievable patience) required to produce authentic

Tibetan arts and crafts, the institute is a good starting point. Set in well-tended grounds some 40 minutes from Dharamsala, it comprises workshops, training centers, a temple, a guesthouse, a cafe, and a doll museum. You can contact the management in advance to organize a tour through the facilities, where you can witness the creation of colorful tantric *thangkas* (embroidered wall hangings), paintings, metalware, furniture, and traditional garments. Tibetan language lessons are available for interested foreigners. The beautiful **Seat of Happiness Temple** 𝒢★★ features astounding murals, including impressions of all 14 Dalai Lamas and 1,173 images of the Buddha, which decorate the 13m-high (43-ft.) temple hall. The gilded copper Buddha Sakyamuni was crafted by Norbulingka's master statue-maker, Pemba Dorje, and is one of the largest of its kind outside Tibet; the arch behind the statue is decorated with sculpted clay images. Head for the richly ornamented temple rooftop for magnificent views of the surrounding landscape. The Institute's **Losel Doll Museum** 𝒢★★ features diorama-style displays of miniature figures (Tibetan dolls) in traditional costumes and historical regalia.

P.O. Sidhpur. ☏ **01892/24-6402** or 01892/24-6405. www.norbulingka.org. Free admission (except for doll museum Rs 20/50¢/25p). Daily 9am–5:30pm.

Thekchen Chöling Temple Complex 𝒢★★   Life in McLeod Ganj revolves around this Buddhist temple complex, linked to the off-limits private residence of the Dalai Lama. A good example of Buddhism's spiritual and artistic traditions, the complex comprises **Namgyal Monastery** and **Tsuglakhang Temple,** both worth a visit if you're keen to get a sense of active lamaistic practice. You'll often encounter monks debating in the courtyard or meditatively preparing colorful sand *mandalas,* diagrams that symbolize the universe and are used in the ritual of spiritual empowerment known as the *kalachakra* ceremony, after which the meticulous designs are destroyed. The *gompa* houses various cultural relics brought from Lhasa during the Cultural Revolution, including a 1,500-year-old idol of Guru Padmasambhav, and a life-size image of Avalokiteshvara, of whom the Dalai Lama is believed to be an incarnation. Public appearances by the Dalai Lama occur from time to time; consult the local authorities for information. The complex courtyard is the venue for an all-day festival of traditional dance held in honor of His Holiness's birthday on July 6, although the Dalai Lama is not always in attendance on this auspicious day. It's worthwhile to take a break from the prayer wheels and settle in at the tiny, laid-back cafe in the temple complex (which serves primarily as a vocational training opportunity for young Tibetans) to try out the international vegetarian dishes ranging from Indonesian *gado-gado* to Cuban *arro a la cubana.* This is a great place for a cup of pure South Indian coffee or Tibetan herbal tea. Snag the window-side table for beautiful views over the valley below.

Temple Rd. To obtain clearance for a public audience with the Dalai Lama, it's necessary to apply, with your passport, at the Security Office on Bhagsu Rd.

Tibetan Institute for Performing Arts (TIPA)   One hour from McLeod Ganj is TIPA, one of the first institutes set up by the Dalai Lama when he settled in McLeod Ganj, for the study and preservation of traditional Tibetan opera, dance, and music. Tibetan opera *(Lhamo)* performances can be long (some last 6 hr.) and are best experienced during the annual 9-day-long Shoton Opera Festival held in February and March (usually in Dharamsala, but in 2005 at the Tibetan settlement of Bylakuppe, Karnataka). Many other performances are held throughout the year as well, and interested visitors are welcome to watch classes. Ask at your hotel, check bulletin boards in local cafes for announcements, or go to the website for details.

P.O. McLeod Ganj. ℂ **01892/22-0657.** www.tibetanarts.org.

The Tibet Museum If you'd like to learn more about the plight of the Tibetan people, then step into this sophisticated but rather depressing installation that provides a historical overview of the situation in Tibet. *A Long Look Homeward,* the main exhibition, consists of two parts. The downstairs display highlights the atrocities that have been carried out against millions of Tibetans during the Chinese occupation. Although events are detailed primarily through textual displays, the collection of data is emotionally challenging. Upstairs, the exhibition focuses more on Tibetan history. Particularly moving is the "testimony corner," where visitors can record the names of loved ones whose deaths are a result of the occupation. Lectures, presentations, and video screenings are presented in the small lecture hall; visit **www.thetibetmuseum. org** if you're interested in upcoming events.

Near the main temple and Namgyal Monastery Gate. Admission Rs 5 (10¢/5p). Tues–Sun 10am–6pm.

WHERE TO STAY & DINE

The best place to stay is the Norbulingka Institute–run **Chonor House,** not least for its dining. If you have a yearning to live in a forest surrounded by nature's bounty, the other top option is **Glenmoor Cottages.** (Both options are reviewed below.)

For a real budget option, consider peaceful **Cheryton Cottage** (Jogibara Rd.; ℂ **01892/22-1993;** tcheryl_89@yahoo.com), where Alan and Cheryl Templeton rent out four rooms with attached bathrooms and hot showers (Rs 450/$11/£5.60 single; Rs 550/$13/£6.80 double). The rooms are spartan 1970s throwbacks dressed in outrageous colors (of the four units, the aptly named "Blue" and "Pink" have views). Above the guesthouse is an entire apartment (one double bedroom with attached bathroom, living room with television, equipped kitchenette including gas range, and balcony). The rate for the apartment is Rs 1,500 ($37/£19) per night; or Rs 15,000 ($366/£185) single and Rs 21,000 ($512/£259) double for the month. Electricity and gas are additional, based on usage. The owners have also started the first winery in the Kangra district, called **Wine Oaks,** where you can sample their grandfather's Italian recipes for wines made from grapes, ginger, and black currants.

Away from the noise of the central square and yet only a stone's throw from it, the very likable **Pema Thang** guesthouse has spotless rooms with wood floors, an excellent restaurant, and a friendly, helpful manager, Mr. Tseten Dorjee. Ask for a room on one of the higher floors, though all overlook the valley (ℂ **01892/22-1871;** doubles Rs 660–Rs 990/$16–$24/£8.15–£12).

For those who prefer a more secluded stay, head out to **Dharamkot,** a small borough just outside McLeod Ganj with stupendous views of the Dhauladhar mountains and Kangra Valley. **Dev Cottages** (ℂ **01892/22-1558**) has pleasant rooms with large windows, balconies, and lovely views, for Rs 1,500 ($37/£19). Another option far from town but worth considering is **Norling Guesthouse** (at the Norbulingka Institute), which has six charming rooms from Rs 1,150 ($28/£14). All the recommendations are for places in McLeod Ganj; if McLeod Ganj is full, the two best options in Dharamsala are White Haven Estate (reviewed below) and **Grace Hotel,** a 200-year-old haveli converted into a heritage hotel. Although its approach isn't too inspiring (through the congested clutter of the main street into a narrow over-concretized lane),

The Dalai Lama Speaks Here & Richard Gere Slept There

Tenzin, from Nick's Italian Kitchen (above), is one of the best people to speak to if you're eager to organize an audience with His Holiness. A proud and committed follower of the Dalai Lama, he also organizes occasional talks on Tibet and Buddhism at the restaurant, and is overflowing with personal theories about the local community and the diplomatic situation with the Chinese government. Staunch Richard Gere fans traveling on a limited budget can try to get the Gere Suite of the **Kunga Guesthouse** upstairs from the restaurant; Richard was the first guest when it opened on January 24, 1996.

the views of the valley from the other side are splendid. The house is built in the traditional hill style, with narrow galleries, 200-year-old deodar tree pillars, alcoves, balconies and terraces, wooden latticed screens and doors, antique brass locks, and some beautiful pieces of furniture—it may not be very polished or sophisticated but it certainly is atmospheric (558 Old Chari Rd., Kotwali Bazaar, Dharamsala; © **01892/22-3265;** www.welcomheritagegracehotel.com; Rs 2,800/$68/£35 double).

As with many of the towns popular with tourists, McLeod Ganj is disproportionately restaurant-heavy. The best by far is Chonor House, which specializes in Tibetan cuisine (see below). Other Tibetan food restaurants worth highlighting are **Green Restaurant** (Bhagsunag Rd.; © **01892/22-1200**), which uses only organic produce; and **Namgyal Café** ★★ (at the Tsuglakhang or Main temple; © **01892/24-6402**), which serves what might be called Tibetan fusion. Try the tofu stroganoff or *tsampa* (roasted flour) crepes; if you're not feeling too experimental, stick to noodles, *momos,* or the brilliant thin-crust pizzas.

While Tibetan fare would appear to be the way to go, you'll pretty much find something for everyone—from falafels to focaccia, *momos* (dumplings) to tempura. At least four German bakeries and as many pizzerias also cater to the large number of foreigners who come to McLeod Ganj. There's even a nifty grub-'n'-pub style restaurant called **Mc'Llo** (at the top of Temple Rd.; © **01892/22-1280**), an extremely popular hangout for travelers that prides itself on having once entertained Pierce Brosnan (celebrity culture having few geographical boundaries). Another informal and extremely popular hangout is **Om** restaurant, located just off Nowrojee Road, which serves a safe and Indianized version of world cuisine. If you have a yen for Japanese, **Lung Ta,** an intimate diner with meat-free dishes from the land of the rising sun, includes a small floor-seating area with traditional low tables (Jogibara Rd.; © **01892/22-0689**). Daily set meals feature a curious mix of Japanese vegetarian dishes; on a typical day, you may be offered glass noodle (or other) salad, miso soup, and rice (on Tues and Fri rice is replaced with a healthy number of assorted sushi rolls), all meals a real steal at under Rs 100 ($2.45/£1.25).

For Italian, head for **Nick's Italian Kitchen** (in the Kunga Guesthouse, Bhagsu Rd., McLeod Ganj; © **01892/22-1180**), which is something of a local institution. Tenzin, whose father worked as security officer for the Dalai Lama from the age of 18, is—like His Holiness—a proponent of vegetarianism, and his kitchen is therefore strictly non-meat. Gnocchi, cannelloni, and ravioli are prepared fresh every morning. The eggplant, spinach, and cheese lasagnas are star attractions, as is the aptly named "Pizza Everything." Nick's has the edge, but if you're passing **The Pizzeria** (past Tushita into

Dharamkot village—ask anyone), you'll find simple, tasty pizzas prepared by a local *gaddi* family, apparently taught how to make wood-fire pizzas by a visiting Italian.

At the immaculate Norbulingka Institute, **Norling Café** ✿✿ (✆ **01892/24-6402** or -6405; www.norbulingka.org) is great for healthy, wholesome dishes that can be taken on the patio, where you're likely to spot paradise flycatchers darting among the lush vegetation. You can also pre-order meals through the guesthouse. If it's cold outside, sit in the cozy dining room, adorned with paintings by the institute's artists.

Chonor House ✿✿✿ (Value   One of the best reasons to spend any amount of time in Dharamsala is to sample each of the exquisitely decorated rooms that make up this charming Tibetan guesthouse at the toe-end of McLeod Ganj, a stone's throw away from the main *gompa*. Each room is uniquely themed according to aspects of Tibetan culture; the museum-standard murals created by different experts in conjunction with artists from the Norbulingka Institute (see above) neatly balance the beautifully crafted teak-and-rosewood furniture and hand-knotted carpets rendered by other Norbulingka teams. There are three categories of rooms, each offering different amenities: Some have balconies, some have tubs, and some (like the magnificent "Voyage at Sea" rooms) are simply enormous. "Nomad" features strikingly painted yaks, goats, and traveling tribes-people and also has a lovely balcony from which you have a direct view of the main *gompa.* The terrifically colorful Songsten Suite not only has a separate lounge and private balcony, but its own shrinelike cabinet showcasing statues of the three great kings of Tibet. There's a public homey sitting room furnished with plush sofas and a combination of parquet wood flooring and thick rugs. Indeed, you need hardly step outside the front door to get a good feel for Tibetan art and culture—this is a treasure chest of style and meticulous attention to details most Westerners probably don't think about. Dharamsala's best guesthouse also offers its most impressive dining opportunity. The menu is a veritable encyclopedia of Tibetan dishes—which have a way of becoming quite addictive. Share a plate of *momos* to start—these butter dumplings are steamed to perfection and filled with tasty fresh white cheese. Or experiment with the excellent *bobi,* which allows you to build your own Tibetan spring rolls, a fun alternative to the greasy version popular in Chinese takeout joints. You can build all night, using thinly grilled bread wraps, seasoned glass noodles, mixed vegetables, tofu, and Basmati rice. Or have the *bobi* as a starter, after which you can try the delicious fried *pishi* (wontons), deliciously seasoned *shabri* (meat or vegetable balls in garlic sauce), or steaming mutton-filled *shabalay* (bread pie). There's even a selection of scrumptious salads (try the cheese, carrot, apple, walnut, and spinach concoction). *Note:* Tibetan hospitality at its very best can, of course, do nothing to stop the chorus of barking hounds that seems to be the typical prelude—or interruption—to a good night's sleep.

Thekchen Choling Rd. (road ends at Pema Thang, walk the last 50m/164 ft.), P.O. McLeod Ganj, Dharamsala 176 219. ✆ **01892/22-1468** or -1006. Fax 01892/22-0815. www.norbulingka.org/visitors/chonor.htm. chonorhs@norbulingka. org. 11 units. Rs 2,100–Rs 2,700 ($51–$66/£26–£33) double; Rs 3,100 ($76/£38) suite. Rs 600 ($15/£7.40) extra bed. Taxes extra. MC, V. **Amenities:** Restaurant; boutique; room service 6:30am–10:30pm; laundry; TV room; cybercafe; library; can arrange transfers. *In room:* Heater, tea-making facility.

Glenmoor Cottages ✿✿   Located on a magnificent property in the midst of a hillside forest, 1km (½ mile) beyond McLeod Ganj, Glenmoor comprises five private cottages situated around an original colonial manor house, Om Bhawan, built by a Scotsman in the early–20th century. Dharamsala's most remote and peaceful lodging (you feel as if you're a thousand miles from anything), Glenmoor is owned and run by Ajai Singh, whose family bought the lovely, tree-covered property 6 decades back. The

A Taste of Tibet

Confused by what's on offer in the Tibetan restaurants of the Indian Himalayan region? Here's a guide: *Gyathuk* is a traditional egg noodle soup, typically prepared with tofu and black-and-white mushrooms. *Thenthuk* is a broth made with handmade noodles. *Pishi* is another name for wontons, often served in a vegetable broth with Tibetan tofu. You'll find Tibetan tofu and dumplings swimming in your *mothuk,* another traditional Tibetan broth. *Shabaklab* or *shabalay* is the Tibetan version of a pie, typically accompanied by broth. *Momos* are Tibetan dumplings, filled with cheese, vegetables, or meat. *Shabri* are seasoned meat or vegetable balls. *Bobi* are Tibetan spring rolls, filled with glass noodles, tofu, and mixed vegetables. Most Tibetan dishes can be served with vegetables, chicken, mutton, or even pork. *Bod-jha* is the staple Tibetan tea, copious quantities of which are consumed by Tibetans everywhere, and by almost no one else. It tastes nothing like any tea you've ever had—besides tea and milk, it contains salt and butter.

cottages are simple stone structures with pleasant pine interiors and private verandas from which to appreciate the infinite peace and quiet (save for the ceaseless chorus of cicadas) or to watch for exotic birds. The upper cottages are roomier and include both a dressing area and a larger split-level living room; there are only two of these, so book ahead. Guests can enjoy wholesome home-cooked Indian meals and simple continental breakfasts in the small restaurant at the manor house.

Mall Rd., Upper Dharamsala 176 219. © 01892/22-1010. Fax 01892/22-1021. www.glenmoorcottages.com. info@glenmoorcottages.com. 5 units. Rs 3,450 ($84/£43) upper cottages; Rs 2,350 ($57/£29) lower cottages. There are also 2 rooms with double beds and common bathroom at Rs 750 ($18/£9.25). Rates exclude meals and taxes. **Amenities:** Restaurant; room service 7am–9pm; can arrange laundry and make travel arrangements; doctor-on-call; Wi-Fi enabled. *In room:* Satellite TV, fridge, heater.

White Haven Estate ★ *(Finds*   Built of grey stone with a green tin roof, cream chimney, and white window frames, surrounded by the Dhauladhar range and huge open spaces with little else in the vicinity, the White Haven is perhaps the best-kept secret in Dharamsala, and your best option if you have to stay this side of town. Rooms are huge, with plush sofas, wood paneling, fireplaces, beautiful cupboards, dressing rooms, and impeccably clean, large bathrooms—pick room no. 1 or 2. There are plenty of windows in the house to drench it with light, a lovely and spacious dining hall with dark wooden flooring, simple but tasteful furniture, warm lounges with fireplaces or *bukharis,* Kashmiri carpets, and photographs galore. Outside, you can sit in the lovely garden overflowing with roses or have breakfast on the terrace.

P.O. Box 26, Chilgarhi, Dharamsala 176 215. © 01892/22-6162. Fax 01892/22-6768. Chandigarh office: © 0172/ 265-9699. Fax 0172/263-9387. www.hotelwhitehaven.com. marketing@hotelwhitehaven.com. 8 units. Rs 3,850 ($94/£48) standard double; Rs 4,650 ($113/£57) deluxe double. Rates exclude meals and taxes. **Amenities:** Kitchen; laundry; library. *In room:* Heater, hot water.

SHOPPING

McLeod Ganj is full of shops selling curios, books, or trekking gear and unlikely combinations like "laundry and bakery." You can buy reasonably priced Tibetan rugs and handicrafts from the **Tibetan Handicraft Centre** (near Post Office, Jogibara Rd.; © 01892/22-1415) and the **Tibetan Children's Village Handicraft Centre** (© 01892/

22-1592). **Stitches of Tibet** (Temple Rd.; © **01892/22-1198** or -1527) is an enterprise that trains local women in handicraft production. Their shop stocks the completed handicrafts as well as Tibetan clothing. If you want to buy a traditional Tibetan *thangka* (painted or embroidered banner or wall decoration), the **Norbulingka Institute** is where this art is preserved and taught; they also take orders. Shop at the institute or at Chonor House, knowing that your purchase will actually contribute to the development of Tibetan craftsmanship. For books, visit **Namgyal Bookstore** in the temple complex; its excellent collection focuses primarily on Tibetan culture and Buddhism, but it has a good number of beautiful publications on Himachal Pradesh and other Himalayan regions as well. Also filled with an interesting assortment of books on the history, culture, and art of the region is **Youtse Book Shop** (Mount View Complex, Temple Rd.). Finally, don't miss stopping at **Nowrojee Store** ✿ (near the Bus Stand), run for six generations by a Parsi family, one of whom is said to have been the person who encouraged the Dalai Lama to settle here in 1959. This quaint place is worth a visit for its history alone, if not to pick up some interesting knickknacks.

Tip: If you're looking for cash, an SBI (State Bank of India) ATM is located on the main street of McLeod Ganj, while ICICI and HDFC banks operate in lower Dharamsala. For changing or transferring foreign exchange, you can use Thomas Cook (next to SBI) or any of the Western Union outlets.

NEAR DHARAMSALA

If you have the time and want to veer slightly off the beaten track, definitely head southeast of Dharamsala toward the gently undulating tea-covered hills of Kangra Valley. Although it lacks any particular charms of its own, **Palampur** is a popular starting point for Kangra Valley. Nearby is **Tashijong Monastery,** a colorful *gompa* established in the years after the Dalai Lama made his home in Dharamsala. The neighboring town of Baijnath is the site of the beautiful **Saivite Vaidyanath Temple complex** ✿✿ (Baijnath Main Rd.; daily 5am–9pm in summer and 6am–8pm in winter), one of the more interesting and best-preserved Hindu shrines in Himachal Pradesh, dating back to the early–13th century. Surrounded by a wall decorated by fine carvings, the main temple enshrines a squat Shiva lingam protected by a five-headed metallic cobra; devotees usually cover the lingam with flowers and other offerings. A half-hour drive in the other direction will take you to **Andretta Pottery and Craft Society** (© **01894/25-4243;** www.andrettapottery.com), where the extremely passionate Jugal Kishore will be happy to explain the objectives behind this training school—modest accommodation is available for those who feel like attending short-term classes.

Pragpur ✿✿✿ (6 hr. from Shimla; 7 hr. from Manali; 4 hr. from Taragarh) is a time-trapped village with mud-plastered, slate-roofed houses, elegant *havelis* (mansions), Italianate buildings, and narrow cobblestone roads. Designated India's first official "Heritage Village," this tiny hamlet was founded as a memorial to a brave warrior princess who led a resistance against invaders in the 17th century. Pragpur is wonderful to explore, a veritable warren of tiny lanes and old, atmospheric buildings. The surrounding landscape offers opportunities for nature walks, cycling, bird-watching, and fishing. Upper Pragpur is known for its home-weaving industry, so this is the place to look for good deals on local crafts. Spend the night in Pragpur's beautiful **Judge's Court,** one of Himachal's most enchanting hotels (reviewed below). Near Pragpur is the strangely named **Pong Lake,** officially known as Maharana Pratap Sagar—a reservoir that attracts local and migratory birds, mostly from Siberia (best time to visit: Oct/Nov–Mar/Apr). Some 1,300 hundred species of birds are found in the Indian subcontinent, of which more than 500 species are present in Kangra—if you're interested it's worth picking up a copy of the *Birds of Kangra* by Jan Willem den Besten, a very comprehensive book on the extensive birdlife of this region.

WHERE TO STAY

Besides the romantic **Taragarh Palace** (reviewed below), the heritage hotel near Palampur (14km/8⅔ miles away), the delightful **Country Cottage** (Chandpur Tea Estate; ✆ **01894/23-0647;** www.countrycottageindia.com; cottages Rs 1,500–2,500/ $37–$61/£19–£31) has only five stone cottages, set in the cantonment area of Palam-pur amid a small tea plantation. It's a simple and unpretentious family-run enterprise, at press time still smelling faintly of fresh paint and experiencing a few teething prob-lems but none too exasperating to handle, and very good value.

The Judge's Court ✿✿   This atmospheric Indo-European haveli, architecturally detailed with domes, galleries, terraces, and porticoes, is filled with the sort of tranquil charm that whisks guests straight back into a bygone age. Set on a magnificent property with orchards of mango, litchi, plum, persimmon, and citrus-fruit trees, the main manor house was built in 1918 by a descendant of Pragpur's founders as a gift for his son, a well-known judge of the Punjab High Court. Laboriously restored, the hotel offers a variety of accommodations. The very best guest room is the spookily romantic Judge's Suite, which has its own sitting room and two plush armchairs strategically placed in front of the fireplace. The Kangra room is spacious as well, although the Kipling suite has a more antique feel. Bathroom sizes vary considerably; ask for a big one if this is important to you. Staff can assist you with exploring the village or finding adventure in Kangra Valley. Ask the cook to prepare the unique cauliflower with sesame seeds dish, and don't miss sampling the delicious mushroom pickle prepared by the owner.

Note: If you want to stay in the heart of the medieval village, look into the avail-ability of one of the two Judge's Court annexes: semi-detached 17th-century houses in Pragpur's highly atmospheric Kuthiala Courtyard. Visitors can rent these to experience life along the narrow lanes and cobbled walkways of the village—perfect for families, and ideal for romance. Marble floors are offset by mud-themed walls, an ancient gas-powered kitchen, and big bedrooms with tiny shuttered windows. We recommend the Kuthiala suite in this part of the property.

Heritage Village Pragpur, Tehsil Dehra, District Kangra 177 107. ✆ **01970/24-5035** or 01970/24-5335. Reservations: 3/44, Shanti Niketan, New Delhi 110 021. ✆ **011/2411-4135.** Fax 011/2411-5970. www.judgescourt.com. 10 units. Rs 2,900 ($71/£36) double at Orchard Complex; Rs 3,300 ($81/£41) double at Museum Mews; Rs 3,500 ($85/£43) Suite. Rs 800 ($20/£10) extra bed. Taxes extra. AE, MC, V. **Amenities:** Restaurant; local sightseeing, taxi, and travel arrange-ments; laundry; cultural performances. *In room:* A/C in some rooms, tea- and coffee-making facilities, heater, flashlight.

Taragarh Palace Hotel ✿   A pleasant change from more commercial hill-station retreats such as Shimla and Mussourie, Kangra Valley attracts travelers seeking peace and tranquillity. At this 6-hectare (15-acre) forested estate, a touch of pre-independence class is thrown in for good measure. Once known as Al Hilal (The Land of the Crescent Moon), this Art Deco mansion (now described as the Heritage Wing) was built in the 1930s as the summer resort of the Nawab of Bahawalpur until he fled to Pakistan after Partition. One of the least-visited destinations in the heart of the scenic and serene Kan-gra Valley, Taragarh is enveloped in thick vegetation, moss-covered walls, and gorgeous grounds, making it particularly popular with meditation groups who come here for the clean air and idyllic environment. Reminiscent of the setting for a brooding Agatha Christie whodunit, the mansion is all high ceilings, broad staircases, chandeliers, and long passages. Book the characterful Maharajah, Maharani, or Princess suites—smart, spacious, and elegantly decorated with charming touches entirely absent from the rather dull double rooms, which are more reminiscent of English country-hotel rooms with musty carpets than royal retiring quarters (and which are also a tad on the small side). If the suites are above your budget, then opt for the newer Palace Wing, with 14 units (all rooms except 306 and 406 have lovely views of the Dhauladar range), as well as a business and fitness center. Traditional Indian, Kashmiri, and local dishes are served in the charming wood-paneled dining room with a gorgeous old copper *bukhari* almost hidden in the fireplace.

Taragarh Palace, P.O. Taragarh, District Kangra 176 081. ©/fax **01894/242-034** or 01894/243-077. www.taragarh. com. reservations@taragarh.com. Reservations: 15 Institutional Area, Lodhi Rd., New Delhi 110 003. © **011/2464-3046.** Fax 011/2469-2317. 26 units. Rs 3,500 ($85/£43) heritage; Rs 4,500 ($110/£56) superior deluxe; Rs 5,000 ($122/£62) suite. Extra bed 25% of room rent. AE, MC, V. **Amenities:** Restaurant; bar; pool; tennis court; fitness center w/steam room; sightseeing, taxi, and travel arrangements; business center; room service (snacks and tea) 7am–10pm; cybercafe; badminton court; children's park. *In room:* TV, heater; A/C, minibar, and tea- and coffee-making facilities in suites.

7 Leh & Environs ✶✶✶

Leh is 475km (295 miles) from Manali

The region of Ladakh, in the state of Jammu and Kashmir, has often been described as a moonscape, a desolate high-altitude desert kingdom of mysticism and mystery. It is all of these, and more, a thoroughly awe-inspiring world of harsh reality, with few luxuries. Local lives are centered around Buddhism, yaks, and survival, and more recently on the small tourism industry that sprouts in the relatively warmer months of the year (July–Sept).

Leh, Ladakh's capital city, is little touched by rain, but the extreme cold during the long winter season means that this remote region remains isolated for much of the year. Come June, however, when the tourists begin to trickle into Leh, the sober, somber slumber of this remote high-altitude town lifts along with the temperatures. Situated in a fertile valley at the foot of Namgyal Tsemo peak, 8km (5 miles) northeast of the Indus River, Leh is deeply reliant on this short, intense tourist season. From June to September the surrounding barren mountains and distant snowcapped peaks are the perfect natural backdrop for the verdant fields and avenues of trees that cluster around the whitewashed, flat-roofed buildings.

Developed as a market for traders from across the North India belt, Leh was an important stop for travelers traversing the challenging caravan routes to Yarkand and Kashgar. The Silk Road brought Buddhist travelers, and today the population remains predominantly Buddhist. You can spend up to a week exploring the town and the numerous Buddhist monuments within a 2- or 3-hour drive of Leh. Adventure-seekers can get caught up in river-rafting on the Zanskar and Indus, high-level mountain-climbing, or treks into remote, barren wilderness regions, which can easily extend your stay by an additional week. The more laid-back traveler will be rewarded by awe-inspiring excursions to high-altitude lakes such as Pangong Tso and Tso Moriri.

ESSENTIALS
GETTING THERE   By Air   If you'd rather save time and get to Leh without the arduous cliff-hanging road journey, the ever-professional **Jet Airways** (Dreamland Complex, Main Bazaar; © **01982/25-0444;** Mon–Sat 10am–5pm, Sun 10am–3pm)

Negotiating the Manali–Leh Highway

Nearly 475km (295 miles) of tricky roads, mountain passes, and exceptional roller-coaster scenery separates Leh from Manali. For most of the year, this spectacular stretch of road is closed to traffic, covered by thick snow. Even when the road is officially open in late June and early July, the danger of unexpected snowfall looms, bringing with it various risks associated with getting stuck in the middle of vast unpopulated areas with only freezing cold nights for company. Once summer has set in, a variety of makeshift *dhabas* and *chai* stalls are gathered in minicolonies along the way. You'll need your passport for a string of checkpoints, the first of which is just beyond the Rohtang Pass at the head of the Kullu Valley. Beyond this, you enter **Lahaul,** a vast Trans-Himalayan landscape dotted with flat-roofed, whitewashed houses built from sun-dried bricks. **Sarchu,** a motley collection of tented camps, is where you'll probably bed down for the night; you'll be too cold to complain about the limited facilities. You reach the world's second-highest motorable road at the summit of the Tanglang-La Pass (5,241m/17,190 ft.); here you will find a small multifaith shrine adorned by images of gurus, deities, and religious icons. Beyond the pass, exquisite mountains in a host of unbelievable colors compete with charming villages for your attention.

Your cheapest viable option is an ostensibly "luxury" bus operated by **HPTDC** (© **0177/265-2651;** www.hptdc.nic.in). For Rs 1,500 ($37/£19) you get an ass-numbing 2-day trip with spartan tented accommodations and dinner en route near Sarchu. Occasional stops for *chai* and photographs are obligatory, but bring plenty of camera film and refreshments. Bottled water is particularly important because dehydration is one of the symptoms of altitude sickness. Garlic in any form also apparently helps. Jeeps and minivan taxis are pricier but represent relative luxury and the opportunity to explore villages and off-road sites along the way. Hiring your own vehicle and driver is an even better way to go—it costs Rs 12,000 ($293/£148) for the whole vehicle divided by the number of passengers. Bernard Lazarevitch is an adventurous European who offers "motorbike safaris" to fascinating destinations throughout northern India. When the Manali–Leh highway opens in late June, you can experience this legendary route by hopping onto the back of Bernard's bike or by joining one of his expeditions. For details, contact **AventureMoto** (www.AventureMoto.com; aventuremoto@yahoo.com). Another experienced Indian operator is Capt. Raaj Kumar of **Shepherds Realms, Camps & Adventures,** who offers 14- to 21-day tailor-made safaris (© **98-1871-2970;** www.asiasafari.com; shepherdsrealms@gmail.com).

offers daily flights between New Delhi and Leh in the summer. The disadvantage of flying in is that you may need to spend up to 48 hours acclimatizing anyway, whereas the road journey gently puts you through your paces. Flying out of Leh is definitely a good idea; reserve a window seat. Indian Airlines also flies to Leh, but these flights are often booked up by military personnel.

By Road   Two rather tiring days are required to get from Manali to Leh. But for those seeking an adventurous road trip coupled with exquisite, endlessly changing scenery, the journey—by off-road vehicle or bus—is highly recommended. See "Negotiating the Manali–Leh Highway," below.

VISITOR INFORMATION   Leh has a Tourist Information Center, but you are advised not to waste your time there. Speak to your hotel manager or any of the many tour operators who offer various services throughout Ladakh.

GETTING AROUND   By Car   Thanks to a strong military presence in the region, Ladakh's roads are excellent and the network of accessible destinations extensive.

By Taxi   Although Leh has but one auto-rickshaw, it has as many as 1,500 taxis, but the fixed rates to practically any place in the state are high. *Note:* You cannot rent a vehicle outside Leh if you want to tour within Ladhak. Your best bet is to share a jeep (booked only through a travel agency) with fellow travelers interested in visiting similar destinations. For taxi rates and bookings, call the **Leh Taxi Stand** (② 01982/ 25-2723). Note that if you travel from Leh to Zanskar or Kargil by taxi, you will have to hire a separate local taxi for internal travel in these districts. Inconvenient as it may be, it's a taxi union rule that is meant to protect the livelihood of the drivers in these less-visited districts.

GUIDED TOURS AND ADVENTURE & TREKKING COMPANIES   It's easy to plan your own outings and give the instructions to your jeep or taxi driver. If you want to deal with an outfitter, refer to the "Staying Active" section earlier in this chapter. If you are very keen on receiving expert information as you explore monasteries and other sights, then a licensed operator may be useful. Speak to Ghulam Mohiuddin at **Adventure North** (Hotel Dragon; ② 01982/25-1227; fax 01982/25-5885; advnorth@sancharnet.in) about organizing treks and adventures throughout Ladakh. **Banjara Camps,** also highly recommended, is the only outfit to use the services of a qualified geologist (Delhi office: ② 011/2686-1397 or 011/2685-5153; www.banjara camps.com).

San Francisco–based **Geographic Expeditions** 𝕽𝕽𝕽 (② 800/777-8183 in the U.S.; www.geoex.com) offers a 21-day Trans-Himalayan trek that passes through the old kingdom of Zanskar through Ladakh, hitting an altitude of 5,064m (16,610 ft.); though not for the fainthearted, it's an exhilarating way to experience one of India's most untouched regions. For more leisure-oriented travelers, the same company conducts jeep safaris of Ladakh. In Leh itself, **Rimo Expeditions** (Hotel Kanglhachen Complex, opposite the Police Station; ② 01982/25-3257; Gurgaon contact: 0124/ 2680-6027 through -6029; www.rimoexpeditions.com; info@rimoexpeditions.com)

⸂Tips **Altitude Sickness**

Arriving by air into Leh makes most people feel slightly knocked out, with headaches, loss of appetite, drowsiness, and disturbed sleep—all early signs of altitude sickness. It's necessary to stay put and drink lots of fluids for 48 hours to acclimatize before venturing higher into the mountains. Monitor your body and health, and don't ignore worsening symptoms, which could lead to a pulmonary or cerebral edema. In Leh you can get 24-hour medical help for altitude sickness at **Sonam Norbu Memorial (SNM) Hospital** (② 01982/252-012).

is a very reliable outfit that undertakes various expeditions. The company also arranges less-hectic trekking expeditions, as well as jeep and yak safaris, and skiing, mountain biking, and challenging mountaineering packages for serious climbers. English-speaking mountain guides are provided, as well as all equipment, porters, cooks, and other staff. Another highly recommended operator is **Project Himalaya** ✮✮✮ (✆ 977/ 1436-0005 in Kathmandu; www.project-himalaya.com; info@project-himalaya. com), a Kathmandu-based company run by the professional, dynamic trio of Jamie McGuiness, Joel Schone, and Kim Bannister. Joel and Kim lead the Ladakh treks, which run 20 to 24 days; the adventurous should definitely consider taking their exploratory trek to uncommon regions that you won't find on a map. One of the best treks offered is the arduous 16-day **Chadar Trek** ✮✮✮ in winter along the semi-frozen Zanskar River. At night, outside temperatures plummet to a bone-chilling –22°F (–30°C), while all day long you defy the slippery ice, which is thick enough to support your weight only 2 months a year, and perhaps meet local Zanskaris as they traverse this ancient route. Peruse their friendly, regularly updated website for more information. This is an outfit that does things differently, with small groups, highly personalized service, and a real concern for local support staff. Also operating along the Chadar route is **Himalayan River Runners** (www.hrrindia.com) and **Aquaterra Adventures** ✮✮✮ (✆ 011/2921-2641 or -2760; www.treknraft.com), the latter one of the best Indian adventure operators, which runs a wide range of tours and treks customized to suit your personal interests and abilities. Working with highly experienced and knowledgeable guides, Aquaterra is possibly the best choice for discerning travelers looking to raft the Indus or Zanskar rivers in Ladakh. You can also combine trekking and rafting trips or opt for a unique bicycle camping expedition.

WHAT TO SEE & DO

Leh's wide street **bazaar** runs east-west. Together with the labyrinth of adjoining side streets and alleys, the bazaar is the center of business and shopping—particularly for visitors who find the plethora of antiques shops irresistible. Locals tend to visit the alternative market nearer the Leh **polo ground,** east of the center. For a truly exotic and atmospheric experience, visit the **Old Village** ✮, a disorganized cluster of cobble-stone lanes, ancient homes, and low-vaulted tunnels. It's well worth an exploratory jaunt, during which you should sample the freshly baked breads sold by local bakers. Walking northwest of the city (beyond the **Women's Alliance of Ladakh** headquarters, where you can shop for traditional Ladakhi handicrafts), you will quickly discover a **rural farmlike community.** Gone are the shops and eager sellers—here you'll find only fields of green sprinkled with bright yellow blossoms, gentle streams trickling past squat stone walls, and small Ladakhi houses with little vegetable gardens. To the west are the cobbled streets of the popular **Changspa** neighborhood, characterized by the number of guesthouses, restaurants, and laid-back marijuana-smoking travelers who come here for the pastoral atmosphere. To the west of Changspa lies **Shanti Stupa,** a Buddhist monument most easily reached by motorable road. Inaugurated by the Dalai Lama in the 1980s, the large white *stupa* (commemorative cairn) was conceived as part of a Japanese-inspired peace movement to spread Buddhism throughout the world. From the vast courtyard at the base of the stupa you can enjoy matchless **panoramic views** ✮✮✮ of Leh and the rugged beauty of the surrounding mountains, which seem to stretch on forever. Northeast of the main bazaar area is **Leh Palace,** which unfortunately is in a sorry state of disrepair. At press time reconstruction and repairs were ongoing, but until they are completed, the palace is best enjoyed from a distance.

WHERE TO STAY

With tourism the single most important industry in town, Leh is inundated with accommodations, but don't expect luxury, particularly when it comes to bathrooms, which can only be described as functional (though the new Grand Dragon hotel may inject a little much needed modernity). Hotels are priced according to unfathomable government regulations and categorized as "A," "B," "C," and "guesthouse," so despite mediocre facilities, you may be paying unreasonable rates based on the fact that, theoretically at least, you have hot running water. **Shambha-La Hotel** is a little out of the center of things, but this is, together with **Hotel Kanglachen** ("A," opposite the police station; © **01982/25-2144;** klcleh@sancharnet.in; doubles from Rs 2,970/ $72/£37), one of the better accommodations in town. The terrace dining offers good views of the Leh Palace especially at night when it's all lit up. Farther out, near Shey (8km/5 miles away; 10 min. from Leh), is **Whispering Willows,** a 14-room hotel run by the affable Dr. C. P. Dorjay, who is a huge source of information on the geology of Ladakh (Rs 3,200–Rs 4,500/$78–$110/£40–£56 double/suite; bookings can be done through the Banjara office at www.banjaracamps.com).

Hotel Dragon   Owned by Ghulam Mustafa and his brother Mohiuddin since 1974, this remains one of the best places to stay in Leh. Each floor of the squat, traditionally styled building has its own terrace, and you can catch fantastic 360-degree views of Leh from the rooftop. The suites are well worth the extra dollars—they're considerably better than the doubles. Upstairs, room nos. 131 through 133 are more spacious than the other, typically small doubles. At night, when a campfire is lit, the small garden courtyard becomes an ideal spot in which to wind down the day. Good Ladakhi and Tibetan meals are served in the dining room, which is decorated with gorgeous paintings by Ghulam Mustafa. (*Note:* At press time, **Grand Dragon,** an affiliate of the Hotel Dragon, was scheduled to open—this will perhaps be the largest and most modern hotel in Leh; we're talking elevators, card keys, and a coffee shop; all fittings will be spanking new, making this the best option in town.)

Leh 194 101. © **01982/25-2139** or -2720. Fax 01982/25-2720. www.travelladakh.com. 33 units. Rs 2,990 ($73/ £37) standard double; Rs 3,300 ($81/£41) deluxe double; Rs 4,400 ($107/£54) suite. Rates include all meals. MC, V. **Amenities:** Dining hall; tours and sightseeing; shop; limited room service 24-hr.; laundry; doctor-on-call; currency exchange; conferencing.

Omasila   Built in the early 1980s, this intimate hotel occupying a pleasant Ladakhi-style building and offering an array of accommodations is favored by film crews. But Omasila enjoys a peaceful setting despite the occasional presence of an overbearing Bollywood director and its proximity to the backpackers' haven of Changspa. Fresh vegetables, apricots, and apples are grown in an adjoining garden, and the stream alongside is a natural aural tonic during laid-back afternoons on cane chairs on the terrace. In summer the mountains surrounding Leh provide the perfect backdrop for magnificent sweeps of colorful flora perfectly visible from each room in the hotel. The suites offer the most comfortable stay and a faint Tibetan-design aesthetic. For views to match the price, ask for suite no. 21, 23, or 26. Buffet meals are served in the relatively stylish "Ladakhi-Tibetan" restaurant, which features colorful murals. (Note that Omasila is one of the very few hotels to remain open throughout the year. It features a gas-regulated heating system, which makes it popular with the Chadar trekkers and ice hockey players who come during the winter months.)

Karzoo-Changspa, Leh 194 101. Ⓒ 01982/25-2119, -1178, or -0207. www.omasila.com. 40 units. Rs 2,970 ($72/£37) standard double; Rs 3,100 ($76/£38) deluxe double; Rs 4,400 ($107/£54) suite. Rates include all meals. No credit cards. **Amenities:** Restaurant; tour and travel arrangements; room service; laundry; doctor-on-call; cybercafe; oxygen facilities. *In room:* TV, central heating.

Shambha-La Hotel Ⓕ This hotel was once a part of the excellent Oberoi chain, and while it no longer has this pedigree, Shambha-La offers straightforward but dignified accommodations in a flat-roofed Ladakhi-style lodge with fluttering prayer flags and comfortable hammocks in the neat garden. Public areas—including a colorful Tibetan lounge area—are attractive, and the views from the upstairs terrace are mesmerizing. As with all of Leh's hotels, the bathroom facilities are merely adequate. Guest rooms are far from lavish, but you get a warm bed and you can book a stove-heated unit in the colder months. Power outages can be a serious problem this far from the town center, so have your hot shower early, just in case. A hotel jeep is on hand to drop you in town whenever you require a lift, and the helpful manager is a mine of useful information. The hotel also organizes tours to any destination in Ladakh; ask about their campsites in the Nubra Valley.

South of the bazaar, Leh 194 101. Ⓒ 01982/25-1100, -2607, or -3500. Fax 01982/25-1100. 26 units. Rs 2,800 ($68/£35) double. Rs 800 ($20/£10) extra bed. Rates exclude taxes. AE, MC, V. **Amenities:** Restaurant; travel assistance, tours, treks, sightseeing, and taxi arrangements; laundry; doctor-on-call; TV lounge; billiards; small library. *In room:* TV.

WHERE TO DINE

For the best Tibetan dishes in Leh, dinner at **The Tibetan Kitchen** (reviewed below) is recommended. In the Main Street Bazaar, you might be forgiven for not even noticing the reliable **Himalaya Café** (Ⓒ 01982/25-0144; Rs 45–Rs 150/$1–$3.65/50p–£2; no credit cards), where marvelous Tibetan and Chinese dishes are served in the Ladakhi version of a dimly lit bistro—one of the few eating establishments in Leh where you'll experience some sort of atmosphere. At first glance it would appear that the only real attraction at **Ibex Bar & Restaurant** (Fort Rd.; Ⓒ 01982/25-2281; everything under $12/£6) is the fact that you can order beer with your meal, but the extensive Indian menu is well worth perusing; the *seekh* kebabs are served with a delicious mint sauce *(pudina chutney),* and mutton and chicken curries are exceptional—perfect with steaming-hot *naan* bread.

For a Continental fix of filter coffee and croissants, a disproportionate number of German bakeries are scattered around the town. Main Street's upstairs eatery, **La Terrasse,** is a welcoming wannabe-Italian joint where you can order pizzas while enjoying views of Leh Palace from the alfresco terrace; alternatively, you could try the wood-oven pizza at **World Garden Café** (near the Leh Police Station). In the Main Street Bazaar, **Cafe Amdo** has brilliant *thupka*—the local staple, a soup noodle mixed with veggies, succulent meat, and a round of hot, yummy sauces that'll clear your sinuses. If you're walking up to Shanti Stupa, pop in at **Café Wonderland** en route (on Changspa) for scrumptious *momos* (dumplings) and *kothey* (a slightly fried version of the momo). For a spacious, outdoorsy cafe experience, head to **Penguin Garden Restaurant & Bar & German Bakery** (Shamshu Complex, Fort Rd.; average meal Rs 200/$4.85/£2.45), a laid-back hangout set in a large leafy courtyard with seating under a couple of apple trees decorated with speakers from which cool lounge tunes resonate. This is a lovely place to chill out with the locals, who gather here to play cards and catch up on the latest Leh gossip; there's the added advantage of being able to order liquor with your meal. If you're looking for a great Indian lunch or dinner, be prepared to wait 30 minutes for the highly recommended *reshmi kebab,* a melt-in-the-mouth blend of minced chicken, mixed spices, and fresh herbs. While you wait, try a piece of delicious *kulcha,* which is similar to *naan* bread but comes filled with onions or a blend of spices. Penguin is also great for health food and salads and is the ideal spot to kick off your day with a filling breakfast. **Note:** On request, the Penguin staff will happily prepare special meals for road journeys or trekking trips. Their long-lasting trekking bread made from specially prepared sour dough lasts up to a week.

The Tibetan Kitchen ₢₢ *(Value* TIBETAN   Tibetan fare is de rigueur in Leh, and after more than a decade, the town's best restaurant does not disappoint. Pre-order (1 day ahead) the traditional Tibetan hot pot, or *gyako,* suitable for four fairly hungry diners: A brass pot with a communal broth is heated at the table, while salads, *papads,* fine noodles, rice, and mutton are served in abundance for you to cook at will. Note that the restaurant has only one pot, so be sure to book well ahead. If you'd prefer to have your food cooked for you by skilled Tibetan and Nepalese chefs, there's plenty to choose from. Try wonton *pishi* soup, Tibetan salad (avocado, tomato, and mint), or delicious *shabalay* (a freshly baked meat- or vegetable-filled bun). The steamed mutton *momos,* prepared with garlic and onion and served with a salad, are probably the best you'll find this side of the Indo-Tibetan border.

Opposite Hotel Tso-Kar, Fort Rd. 🕐 **01982/25-3071.** Main courses Rs 80–Rs 230 ($1.95–$5.60/£1–£2.85); Tibetan hot pot for 4 Rs 1,600 ($39/£20). No credit cards. Daily 8am–10pm.

DISCOVERING LADAKHI GOMPAS & OTHER DIVERSIONS
NORTH OF LEH
There are enough Buddhist *gompas* within easy reach of Leh to keep enthusiasts busy for several days. North along the road to Srinagar are **Phyang Gompa** ₢₢ (16km/10 miles from Leh), and 15th-century **Spituk Gompa** ₢₢ (8km/5 miles from Leh), which sits atop a lone rocky hill. If you're prepared to spend some time on the road (a scintillating journey), **Alchi** ₢₢₢ (along the left bank of the Indus around 70km/43 miles northwest of Leh, a short way off the Srinigar–Leh Rd.) is highly recommended. One of the oldest monasteries in the region, it dates back to the 11th century, and is unique for the influence of Kashmiri art versus the pure Buddhist styles prevalent in most other monasteries. Situated in a quiet hamlet with a handful of souvenir and snack stalls and some very modest budget accommodations, Alchi is centered around its inactive five-temple *gompa* complex, administered by the Yellow-Hat Gelugpa monks of Likir Monastery 30km (19 miles) across the river. You'll need a flashlight to explore the temple interiors, which are covered with vibrant, colorful, detailed murals and wooden figures (note the painted wooden ceiling of the gate. A courtyard leads to the *dukhang,* or assembly hall, where the statue of Avalokiteshvara is believed to be of pure gold.

On the way to Alchi, stop at **Basgo** ₢₢, where a hillside citadel consists of several Buddhist temples attached to a ruined castle. A two-story-high golden statue of the future Buddha is housed in the Maitreya Temple, which has fantastic murals of fierce divinities that were the guardian deities of the royal family once resident here. If you decide to venture all the way into Zanskar, you will come across another fantastic monastery about 4 hours from Leh, en route to Kargil—**Lamayuru** ₢ is not only interesting as a monastery but offers a unique moonscape landscape as well, with a stunning cliffside positioning.

SOUTH & EAST OF LEH

Venturing south of Leh along the same road that goes all the way to Manali, you can take in a number of monasteries, and one or two Ladakhi palaces. Located across from Choglamsar on the opposite side of the Indus, **Stok Palace** ✶✶ (Rs 25/60¢/30p; May–Oct daily 8am–7pm) is the only inhabited palace in Ladakh, home to the 74th generation of the Namgyal dynasty. The land-holding rights of Stok were granted to the royal family by Gen. Zorawar Singh in 1834 when he deposed Tshe-spal-Nam-gyal, the *Gyalpo* (king) of Ladakh. It's an imposing complex, with around 80 rooms, only a few of which are still used by the current widowed *Gyalmo* (queen), who is sometimes in residence with her immediate family. Several rooms are taken up by the modest museum housed in one section. Museum highlights include a vast *thangka* collection, weapons, jewels, and, of special note, the queen's *perak*, a turquoise-studded headdress. The ghostly Buddhist shrine is an experience not to be missed.

Fifteen kilometers (9 miles) from Leh, **Shey Palace and Monastery** ✶✶ (Rs 20/50¢/25p; May–Oct daily 8am–7pm) is worthwhile for the *gompa*, but the palace is little more than crumbling ruins. **Thikse Gompa** ✶✶✶ (daily 6am–6pm) located 25km (16 miles) south of Leh, is a striking 12-story edifice with tapering walls that sits atop a craggy peak. From here you get magnificent views of the valley, strewn with whitewashed stupas. Note that 6am morning prayers at Thikse are worth rising early to witness (but it's quite popular with tourists so don't expect to see it alone).

Hidden from the world on a remote verdant hillock, **Hemis Gompa** ✶✶✶ (45km/ 28 miles from Leh) is considered the wealthiest Ladakhi monastery, its atmospheric prayer and assembly halls rich with ancient relics and ritual symbols. During the summer season in June and July, the monastery comes alive for the annual **Hemis Tsechu** ✶✶✶, a festival commemorating Guru Padmasambhava's birth. Masked dancing by the lamas and ritual dramas are played out in the courtyard, and the locals sell Ladakhi handicrafts and jewelry. Every 12 years, a magnificent embroidered silk *thangka* (tantric wall hanging) is displayed to the public; the next such unveiling takes place in June 2016, when the Year of the Monkey comes around again. On your daylong trip into **Hemis National Park,** you may—with luck—come across brown bear, ibex, or (if the stars are truly aligned in your favor) the extremely elusive snow leopard. The popular Markha Valley trek also traverses this park.

East of Leh are two stunning high-altitude lakes that can be visited on a 2- to 3-day jeep safari. The only way to visit these lakes, close to the sensitive border with Tibet, is to book though an agent who can organize everything, including travel, guides, basic accommodations in tents or a village, and special permits. **Pangong Tso** ✶✶ is a huge lake, a large chunk of which lies across the border in China (**Note:** There are practically no accommodations at the lake itself, so many prefer to return the same day—start, say by 5am for the 5- to 6-hr. one-way drive and return after a 3- to 4-hr. stay; back by late evening); farther south is **Tso Moriri** ✶✶✶, where the colors of the water are as lovely as the birds you'll spot. Korzok village, on the northern tip of Tso Moriri, is the only place that has basic accommodation, in tents and guesthouses.

NUBRA VALLEY

A 5-hour jeep drive over the world's highest motorable pass, **Khardung-La** (5,578m/18,296 ft.), now a veritable vehicle scrap dump, leads to northern Ladakh's

Rafting on the Indus & Zanskar 🏕🏕

Without doubt, Zanskar offers one of the most exhilarating and challenging white-water rafting journeys in India. Beginning on the Stod River in Zanskar, the multiday river adventure descends through rapids of grade IV and V, passes incredibly desolate, scenic gorges and stupendous cliffs down the Zanskar River, and ends at the Indus, near Alchi Monastery. The trips take a minimum of 12 days round-trip from Leh and are best attempted as part of an organized expedition. **Aquaterra Adventures** (www.aquaterra.in) runs a yearly departure every August. If you're looking for something less hairy, there are tamer options close to Leh: a half-day rafting trip from Nimoo to Alchi that's got some adrenaline packed in, a 3-hour gentle rafting trip from Hemis to Choglamsar where your guide does most of the paddling work with well-practiced efficiency, or a 4-hour trip from Phey to Nimoo that packs in a bit of both. Trips cost about Rs 1,000 to Rs 1,500 ($24–$37/£12–£19) per head for the day. Daily trips are run by **Rimo Expeditions** (www.rimoexpeditions.com) and **Indus Himalayan Explorers** (⟨ 01982/253-454 or 01982/252-788).

lush **Nubra Valley** 🏕🏕🏕, a fertile region with *gompas,* hot sulfur springs (at Panamik), and double-humped camels. Deep within the breathtaking Karakoram mountain range, the valley combines terrific desertscapes and fertile fields watered by the Siachen and Shayok rivers.

For centuries, the route into Nubra was part of the legendary Silk Route used by caravans of traders operating between the Punjab and various regions within central Asia. The valley is dotted with peaceful, pleasant, sparsely populated villages, but its little-explored landscape is the ultimate getaway for the traveler in search of escape; rent a bike and take time to explore. You need to arrange an Inner Line Permit in Leh (which can be done through any travel agent or through your hotel), and technically you must be traveling in a group of at least two people. Hire a jeep with driver (count on spending Rs 7,000/$171/£86 for 3 days), and set off early in the day. **Shambha-La Hotel** (reviewed above) offers all-inclusive tours to the Nubra Valley, with accommodations at their own camping site. For a comfortable night's stay, try the village of Tegar, along the Nubra River, where **Hotel Yarab Tso** (reservations in Leh: ⟨ 01982/25-2480, -2016, or 01982/22-3544; Rs 1,850/$45/£23 double, including all meals) has clean accommodations with attached Western bathrooms. **Hotel Rimo,** a new option in Tegar village, was due to be operational at press time; bookings can be made through Rimo Expeditions (details above).

12

Uttaranchal: Sacred Source of the Ganges

For devout Hindus, a trip into the Himalayan ranges of Uttarakhand—source of the sacred **Ganges**—is no mere journey, but a *yatra,* or spiritual pilgrimage. For the city-smothered traveler, it's balm for the soul, particularly Kumaon. This relatively untouched area sees far less tourist traffic than the more hyped neighboring Himachal Pradesh, yet is in many ways more accessible, with plenty of wonderful places to stay.

Comprising the territories of Garhwal (west) and Kumaon (east), tiny Uttarakhand is one of India's newest states, carved from Uttar Pradesh in 2000, when it was named Uttaranchal. In 2007 it adopted the name bestowed upon it in the ancient Hindu scriptures, the Puranas: Uttarakhand. Besides Hindu pilgrims and adventurous trekkers and river rafters, Garhwal attracts New Age Westerners who flock to the ashrams of **Rishikesh** on the banks of the holy river Ganges, and to nearby **Ananda-in-the-Himalayas,** one of the top spa destinations in the world. For visitors looking for a gentle road trip, the picturesque lower-altitude **hill stations of the Kumaon** offer glorious views of snowcapped mountains and a chance to spot tigers in one of the country's best-known wildlife sanctuaries, **Corbett National Park,** which vies with Rajasthan's Ranthambore National Park in terms of accessibility (264km/164 miles from Delhi; 6–7 hr. by road or rail).

1 Garhwal

Sacred source of the Ganges, the western part of Uttarakhand is where Hindu devotees come on mountain *yatras* (pilgrimages) to Badrinath, Kedarnath, Gangotri, and Yamunotri. Westerners tend to head for **Rishikesh,** said to be the "birthplace" of yoga. Today scores of garish concrete ashrams and temples line the banks of the Ganges, and draw visitors who seek out yogis and tantric enlightenment, as well as hippies and backpackers keen to contemplate life, the universe, and everything through an edifying cloud of hash smoke. Up in the hills, with staggering views of the vast Doon Valley and western Garhwal's Himalayan peaks, **Mussoorie** is the quintessential Raj-era hill station, but it gets crowded and detestable in summer (and on weekends), packed with honeymooning and vacationing domestic tourists who send the decibel level skyrocketing. In winter, however, much of its near-haunted charm returns.

ESSENTIALS

GETTING THERE & AWAY   **By Air**   Dehra Dun's **Jolly Grant Airport** is a 50-minute flight from Delhi. From there, catch a taxi to either Mussoorie or Rishikesh, or have your hotel pick you up.

Uttarakhand

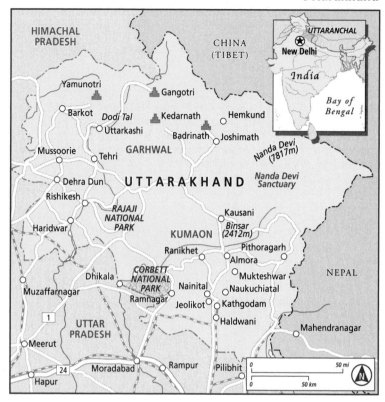

By Train   Dehra Dun is the terminus of the Northern Railway, and is the jumping-off point for Mussoorie. For Rishikesh, Haridwar is the more convenient terminal, 30 minutes away by taxi. There are several good connections between the capital and both Dehra Dun and Haridwar, including the **Dehra Dun Shatabdi** and the **Dehra Dun Janshatabdi** (Mon–Sat), which both stop at Haridwar. An overnight alternative is the **Mussoorie Express.**

By Road   The drive from Delhi to Rishikesh (250km/155 miles) takes between 5 and 6 hours. If you're at Corbett, the drive to Rishikesh takes around 4 hours. There are regular buses from Delhi to Haridwar and Rishikesh. Mussoorie is 280km (173 miles) from Delhi, including a final 33km (20 miles) from Dehra Dun, along a steeply ascending series of troublesome hairpin bends.

VISITOR INFORMATION   In Mussoorie, the **Tourist Bureau** (☎ **0135/263-2863;** Mon–Sat 10am–5pm, closed 2nd Sat of the month) is located near the rope-way, on the Mall. In Rishikesh, visit the **Garhwal Mandal Vikas Nigam (GMVN) Tourist Office** (Shail Vihar, Haridwar By Pass Rd.; ☎ **0135/243-1793,** or -1783, or -2648; www.gmvnl.com; same hours as above); you can contact the same office for rafting (Nov–May) and other adventure inquiries. Dehra Dun's GMVN office is at 74/1 Rajpur Rd. (☎ **0135/274-7898,** -6817, or -9308).

GETTING AROUND   Hire a car and driver for the duration of your visit, unless you plan on trekking. Note that in Mussoorie, the taxi union frowns upon outside taxis.

MUSSOORIE

278km (172 miles) NE of Delhi; 35km (22 miles) N of Dehra Dun; 67km (42 miles) NW of Rishikesh

Smaller than Shimla and some 450m (1,500 ft.) lower, this hill station enjoys a more spectacular setting but has rather gone to seed, its regal colonial mansions all peeling plaster and overgrown hedges. It was once a favorite summer refuge of the Raj, but these days the strutting sahibs and memsahibs have been replaced by hordes of visitors escaping Delhi's blistering summer heat (which is when Mussoorie is best avoided). Until recently, Mussoorie's historical ambience was also overwhelmed by unchecked urban development; the government has now intervened (a little late, it must be said).

Unlike Shimla, Mussoorie in its glory days was pleasantly free of administrators, with plenty of nocturnal cavorting between young men and the wives of the hard-working bureaucrats who had remained back in the plains—it is said that a bell was rung just before dawn at the famous **Savoy Hotel** to encourage impious lovers to get back to their own beds. The quintessential crumbling relic, the Savoy has been visited by Indira Gandhi, the Dalai Lama, Jawaharlal Nehru, Haile Selassie, the king of Nepal, and Queen Mary, but it now tries to push barren, moldy rooms on unsuspecting travelers seeking Raj-era glory. Still, do ask the manager, Mr. Bhandari, to take you on a tour of the "best" rooms and of the melancholic **Writers' Bar,** which has hosted Rudyard Kipling, Pearl S. Buck, and Arthur Conan Doyle—but you'd better rush to pay your respects before the whole thing collapses.

The town's lifeline is the **Mall,** a stretch of pedestrian road that links its two centers, **Library Bazaar** and **Kulri Bazaar.** You can walk the entire length of the ridge, from the bandstand at the western end of the Mall to the old churches and cemeteries at the quieter end of Kulri. Above the town is **Gun Hill,** from where the British punctually fired their noonday guns. Today, visitors reach the summit by means of a ropeway, or rent horses for a 15-minute ride from the central police station. Along Mussoorie's upper ridge, **Camel's Back Road** is another fine place for a stroll. Farther east of Kulri Bazaar is **Landour,** which is quieter and better-preserved than touristy Mussoorie. Continue on foot for an hour beyond Kulri Bazaar and you'll reach **Lal Tibba,** where the lookout point provides sensational views of the Himalayas. Farther still is **Sisters' Bazaar,** a wooded area named for the nurses who attended to convalescing soldiers, and where you can explore an empty colonial mansion, said to be haunted.

WHERE TO STAY & DINE

In the heart of town, **Kasmanda Palace Hotel** (© **0135/263-0007** or -3949; www.welcomheritagehotels.com) is a stately, airy mansion where you can negotiate a 20% discount on a double room in low season. The well-preserved former holiday palace of the Maharajah of Kasmanda is packed with antiques, animal skins, and hunting trophies, including an elephant's-foot piano stool. Book a suite for exceptional views of the Doon Valley, but be warned that you'll have to put up with stuffed animal heads mounted on the walls and a liberal use of gaudy floral fabrics; doubles run from Rs 3,500 ($85/£43). Set on the outskirts of town, **Claridges Nabha Retreat** ⭐ (© **0135/263-1426,** -1427, or 011/2301-0211; fax 011/263-1425; www.claridges-hotels.com; doubles from $250/£125, breakfast and dinner included; ask about off-season discounts) is a serene and lovely estate (ca. 1845), once used by the Maharajah of Nabha for his summer escapades. In the surrounding cedar forest, langur monkeys perform acrobatic feats watched by visitors lounging on the terrace. Accommodations are relatively smart and a good deal more stylish than at Kasmanda; the best are room nos. 110 through 115, which enjoy attractive forest views (no. 114 is the biggest). The hotel conducts courtesy pick-ups from the Mall throughout the day.

RISHIKESH
238km (148 miles) NE of Delhi

It was The Beatles, who came here during the 1960s to visit the maharishi (a visit that inspired much of *Sgt. Pepper*), who put Rishikesh on the map, and today the town is full of ashrams and yoga schools catering to Westerners keen to fine-tune their spiritual tool kits. *Sadhus* (holy men) in ginger robes, hippies in tie-dyed cheesecloth, and backpackers with plenty of time (and plenty of First World credit) gather on the banks of the Ganga to talk about the evils of the West and the failure of communism. By day, it's a spiritual Disneyland, where the commercial excesses of packaged meditation hang heavily about the concrete ashrams, bedecked with gaudy statues of Vishnu and Shiva. The place to concentrate your time is around the Lakhsman Jhula area, where there are plenty of simple eateries and stores selling all kinds of devotional paraphernalia; books and CDs in particular are worth browsing for. To get to the far side of the Ganga, where the most interesting *ghats,* ashrams, and people are concentrated, you'll need to cross the suspension bridge on foot. Here you can undertake any and every sort of self-improvement course, from yoga and reiki to cooking and music. A visit here in time for the sunset **Ganga Aarti** on the *ghat* of the Parmarth Niketan Ashram is highly recommended—to the accompaniment of hypnotic prayers and harmonious singing, Rishikesh undergoes a magical transformation, reminding all that this really is a spiritual retreat.

WHERE TO STAY & DINE

In a town full of ashrams and *sadhus,* you might very well expect Rishikesh luxury to involve a bed of sharpened nails. Fortunately, you can indulge in the unadulterated luxury of one of the country's finest spa resorts: **Ananda-in-the-Himalayas** (reviewed below). Of course, you won't be in Rishikesh itself (potentially a very good thing). But for a truly unusual and lovely place to stay, don't miss **The Glasshouse on the Ganges** (reviewed below), which enjoys a remarkable location slap-bang on the edge of the great Ganga; if you book the right room, you can hear the waters roaring by from the comfort of your four-poster bed; in terms of value and location it gets our top recommendation. Also well-situated, and about 19km (12 miles) from Rishikesh is **Himalayan Hideaway** ☆ (© **011/2685-2602**), a lodge owned by the couple who run the Himalayan River Runners outfit (their riverside camp is 2km/1¼ miles away). Accommodations are in stone cottages set in a forest near the Ganges (an 8-min. walk); all have air-conditioning and decent bathrooms (shower only) done out in stone and tile. Select a river-view room (Rs 3,500–Rs 4,700/$85–$114/£43–£58, double with breakfast and tea), gorge on delicious meals, go rafting, or while away the hours watching the river; trips to Rishikesh for sightseeing and the evening Ganga Aarti are easily arranged. If you really want to be near the action (and the noise), the most acceptable choice is **Hotel The Great Ganga** (Muni-ki-Reti, Rishikesh 249 201; © **0135/244-2243;** www.thegreatganga.com; doubles from Rs 1,650/$40/£20), which is fine if you just need a place to sleep and don't plan on hanging around during the day. Some of the rooms have little terraces that overlook the Ganges, but be aware that you'll be picking up a lot of traffic noise. Accommodations have marble floors, kitschy fabrics, and very firm mattresses, and the small tiled bathrooms have aging tubs. Do not even consider the suites, which are in a grotty apartment block next door.

Ananda-in-the-Himalayas ⊛⊛⊛   At this destination spa, high-class pampering is the order of the day. The resort's immaculate, palatial reception rooms are in the restored Viceregal Palace, added to the palace of the Maharaja of Tehri Garhwal in 1910 to accommodate the likes of Lord Mountbatten. Now the grounds have been fabulously landscaped, enhanced with flower beds and water features, and primped to satisfy Western tastes. Some distance from the palace, in a somewhat characterless five-story block overlooking Rishikesh far below, guest accommodations are elegant, with chic-modern decor, teak parquet wood flooring, coir mats, ultra-comfortable beds, and balconies (the more expensive "valley view" is the category to go for). In 2007, three free-standing villas, each with a private pool, were added. Yoga mats are placed in each room for personal use when attending the yoga and meditation classes. The comfortable, light-fitting *kurta* pajamas provided for you to wear throughout your stay are ideal if you're going to spend lots of time receiving treatments in the 1,951-sq.-m (21,000-sq.-ft.) Wellness Center. Guests generally start their spa experience with a brief session with the resident Ayurvedic doctor, who makes an assessment of your body type and issues an ideal dietary plan. But the real pleasures lie in the overwhelming choice of relaxing, soothing, and restorative treatments provided by a lineup of excellent therapists from all over the world. Choose among Thai, Ayurvedic, or Swedish massage, or lie back for an Ananda royal facial, seaweed body wrap, or Indian body mask. From the moment you wake (to a steaming cup of honey, lemon, and ginger tea) until you retire to a bath (for which a candle is lit to heat fragrant essential oils) and bed (warmed by a hot-water bottle), you'll feel extremely nurtured. There are also talks on spirituality, treks, yoga sessions, and escorted excursions to Rishikesh for the highly recommended evening Ganga Aarti.

The Palace Estate, Narendra Nagar, Tehri Garhwal 249 175. ℭ **01378/22-7500.** Fax 01378/22-7550 or 01378/22-7555. www.anandaspa.com. 78 units. $500 (£250) deluxe palace-view double; $575 (£288) deluxe valley-view double; $800–$1,250 (£400–£625) suite; $1,250–$1,750 (£625–£875) villa with private pool. AE, MC, V. **Amenities:** Restaurant; pool; 6-hole golf course; spa; limousine service; room service; laundry service; dry-cleaning; in-house doctor; squash court; jogging track; daily health and relaxation program; safaris; trekking; white-water rafting; ashram; library. *In room:* A/C, TV, dataport, minibar, tea- and coffee-making facilities, hair dryer, electronic safe, scale, DVD player; villas have private pool.

The Glasshouse on the Ganges ⊛⊛ *Value*   Spectacularly situated on the banks of the Ganges, 23km (14 miles) north of Rishikesh, this former garden retreat of the Maharajahs of Tehri Garhwal is thrillingly close to the Ganges, which is why it gets two stars: There's even a little "beach" where you can swim in the clean, refreshing waters of one of the world's most famous rivers. Location is certainly the key ingredient here, supported by the marriage of heritage, simple and lovely design elements, and—again—the sound of the Ganges waters rushing by. Accommodations are individual and unique. You have two general choices: Either stay in the main block, fronted by a pillared veranda with relaxing planter's chairs, or in cottages in the lush gardens of hammock-strung mango, litchi, and citrus trees and tropical plants. The best of the lot (book well in advance!) is Gangeshwari (on the top floor of one of the cottages)—immaculately laid out and spacious, with fantastic views from the terrace, and a most unusual bathroom with a sunken tub built right into the rock; there's also a working fireplace. If it's not available, ask about the Jamuna Room, where simple antique furnishings (four-poster bed), a working fireplace, and soft white linen provide superb comfort. Of the cheaper rooms, which are much smaller, ask for the Gomti Room or the unit above it, and you'll enjoy views through large windows in a spacious environment. While we greatly admire the beautiful location of this very special "non-hotel," the grounds have grown slightly shabby over the years—some maintenance work is sorely needed—and the service standards are not the greatest. Also bear in mind that alcohol is not available, due to the retreat's proximity to the holy river.

23rd Milestone, Rishikesh-Badrinath Rd., Village and P.O. Gular-Dogi, Tehri-Garhwal District 249 303. ℭ **01378/ 26-9218.** Fax 01378/26-9224. Reservations: 13 Main Market, New Delhi 110 013. ℭ **011/2435-6145** or 011/4182-5001. Fax 011/2435-1112. www.neemranahotels.com. 15 units. Rs 3,000–Rs 6,000 ($73–$146/£37–£74) standard and "grand" doubles and triples; Rs 4,200 ($102/£52) triple suite; Rs 6,600 ($161/£81) luxury triple suite; Rs 9,000 ($220/£111) Gangeshwari suite. Rs 300 ($6.85) extra bed. AE, MC, V. **Amenities:** Restaurant; dining terrace; Ayurvedic spa; travel assistance; health and beauty shop; laundry; doctor-on-call, TV lounge; yoga. *In room:* A/C, tea-and coffee-making facilities, TV in some, no phone in some.

2 Kumaon

It's not hard to fathom why the British Raj claimed this eastern pocket of Himalayan India from Nepal in 1815. Free of the hustle and bustle of urban India and blessed with a gentle, laid-back quality, the Kumaon, studded with gorgeous lakes, not all of which are overcrowded with construction, is great for viewing breathtaking scenery, breathing in restorative oxygen-rich air, taking wonderful walks, and seeing decaying reminders of the British preoccupation with transforming remote villages into proper English towns. Prominent among these are **Nainital** and **Ranikhet.** Both are surrounded by pine forests and are good spots for taking a break; the latter is prettier and arguably the most evocative former British hill station in India. A good route is to set off from Nainital, overnight at Mukteshwar, then set off for Binsar or Almora surrounds—this is untouched Kumaon, and we have listed two great accommodations. Next, either head east to Ranikhet or return back south to Naukuchiatal (or Jilling) for your next stop, ending your journey at Corbett National Park. Wherever you overnight, the road journeys between these destinations are the real joy of the Kumaon; when you're this close to gorgeous Himalayan mountain ranges, you simply cannot escape breathtaking views.

ESSENTIALS

GETTING THERE & AROUND   There are many trains heading out of both Delhi and Lucknow towards Kathgodam, 35km (22 miles) from Nainital. The overnight Ranikhet Express leaves Old Delhi at 10:45pm and arrives at 6:05am. There are always taxis (from Rs 350/$8.50/£4.30) and share-taxis available (from Rs 50/$1.25/60p a seat), or you can have your hotel pick you up from the station. There are also overnight private deluxe buses (pick the Volvo) from Delhi to Nainital (Rs 300/$7.30/£3.70). Ranikhet is an additional 60km (37 miles) from Nainital, or a 3½-hour journey from the Kathgodam railway station. Once you've found your bearings, hire a car (preferably a four-wheel-drive) and driver for the duration of your stay in Uttarakhand. You can expect to pay around Rs 8 (20¢/10p) per kilometer, plus an additional fee per day and a reasonable contribution (Rs 250/$6.10/£3.10) towards the driver's overnight expenses.

VISITOR INFORMATION   While in Delhi, you can visit the **KMVN Tourist Information Office** (103 Indraprakash Building, 21 Barakhamba Rd.; ℭ **011/5151-9366;** fax 011/2331-9835; www.kmvn.org). In Nainital, the KMVN is at Oak Park House (ℭ **05942/23-6356**).

A ROAD TRIP THROUGH KUMAON

Your first stop, Nainital, is set around the ebony-emerald **Naini Tal (Lake)**—according to Hindu mythology, one of the eyes of Shiva's wife, Sati. **Naina Devi Temple** is said to be the precise spot where Sati's eye fell when her body parts were scattered throughout the country in a bid to stop Shiva's "dance of cosmic destruction," which began when he discovered that Sati had immolated herself, an act provoked by her father's incessant insults of Shiva. High above the town, at 2,235m (7,450 ft.), is the aptly named **Snow View,** a hilltop area from where you can see Nanda Devi, India's second-highest peak. Make use of the Aerial Express ropeway; round-trips (daily 10am–5pm) cost Rs 70 ($1.70/90p). You can overnight here, but Nainital is as ghastly as most of Himachal's towns, so we recommend you head just 26km (16 miles) east of Nainital to picturesque **Naukuchiatal (Nine-Cornered Lake).** According to local folklore, when you get to a point where you can see all nine corners of the lake, make a wish and it will come true. This is certainly the case if you're looking for picture-perfect serenity, solitude, and enchanting trails, filled with wildflowers. Even if you don't opt to overnight here, make time for a day trip and take a leisurely ride or a swim in the lake. Alternatively, head north from Nainital to remote and lovely **Mukteshwar** some 50km (30 miles) away.

On a ridge some 2,254m (7,513 ft.) above sea level, where you are surrounded by little more than dramatic views of the Himalayas, conifer forests, fruit orchards, and fresh, clean air, Mukteshwar enjoys one of the most charming settings in the Kumaon. At the edge of town, atop a cliff, is century-old **Mukteshwar Temple,** dedicated to Lord Shiva. On the same hill is an ashram administered by a hermit whose disciples come from around the world. Behind the temple, a rocky cliff juts out of the hillside at Chauthi Jaali; take an early-morning walk here for stunning views.

Then set off for Binsar for the best view in motorable Kumaon. Here, in another of the region's most untouched areas, you can watch the sunrise over Nepal and the sunset on Garhwal. Time allowing, visit the **Jageshwar Temple** complex, and explore **Binsar Sanctuary** (Rs 100/$2.45/£1.25 per head, Rs 50/$1.25/60p per car) to view Himalayan wildlife. Overnight at **Kalmatia Sangam,** near Almora (66km/41 miles from Nainital). If you haven't done so yet, head back to spend some time at Naukuchiatal, or set off east for Ranikhet.

Even more than Nainital, Ranikhet—surrounded by slopes draped with forests of thick pine and deodar and impeccable views of Nanda Devi—exudes the ambience of a haunted English Gothic township, forever waiting for a cloak of thick mist and the echoes of a long-lost era to descend.

Whether you arrive from Nainital (60km/37 miles away) or Binsar, you'll first encounter the typically Indian **Sadar Bazaar,** an unappealing town center that is entirely avoidable. Take the turnoff for the **Mall,** and head into the peaceful Cantonment area. Ranikhet is occupied by the army's Kumaon Regiment, which maintains a strict code that seems to have had a positive impact on the Sleepy Hollow serenity evident here. You'll encounter an abundance of flagstone colonial buildings topped by tin roofs, many used by the military and in fairly attractive condition, surrounded by hedges and greenery. **Lower Mall Road,** as you head farther south, is good for walks, with only ancient trees for company. Continue on, past 14th-century **Jhula Devi Temple,** and 10km (6¼ miles) south you'll come upon the state-run **Chaubatia Orchards,** a great place (though best avoided May–June) for a picnic (ask your hotel to pack one).

From here it's an easy drive to Corbett.

WHERE TO STAY & DINE

The Kumaon Hills are dotted with laid-back, atmospheric accommodations that offer guests the more intimate experience of a homestay and the opportunity to mingle with Indian families who live in the hills—a wonderful reprieve from overcrowded tourist hubs. Note, though, that because these are not hotels, hot water in the bathrooms often comes via a geyser, which must be switched on when required (or in buckets carried into your bathroom). Room service is limited, and food cannot be rustled up in minutes, on demand. If you'd prefer more conventional hotel-style accommodations, several of these are listed as well.

NAINITAL TO MUKTESHWAR

Besides Emily Lodge, reviewed below, a good place to stay in Nainital is the **Palace Belvedere** ⚐ (© **05942/23-7434;** www.welcomheritagehotels.com). Built in 1897, this former summer palace offers a casual historic ambience with personal, attentive service. Book a lake-facing room (from Rs 4,700/$115/£58 double), which has an enclosed porch-cum-study (no. 19 is particularly large) from where the view of the sun rising over Nainital Lake is simply exquisite; even the bathrooms have views of the lake. Other than this, consider **The Claridges Naini Retreat** (© **05942/23-5105** or -5108; www.nivalink.com/nainiretreat). The gabled bluestone summer retreat of the Maharajah of Pilibhit, situated above Naini Lake, underwent a major overhaul early in 2003 but retains much of its charm. Standard ("deluxe") rooms are neat but a tad cramped (book nos. 304–311; doubles from Rs 7,555/$184/£93, including breakfast and dinner, in low season), so it's best to reserve one of three "garden" units, which share a common balcony, or opt for a lake-facing room (from Rs 9,555/$233/£118 double in low season). Another option worth considering is **Balrampur House** (© **05942/23-6236** or -9902; www.balrampurhotels.com; doubles from Rs 4,000/$98/ £49), once the summer home of the Maharaja of Balrampur and now a heritage hotel run by his descendant Jayendra Pratap Singh. Deluxe rooms are huge with big bathrooms but have shoebox cupboards and slightly worn carpets. Ask for one of the super deluxe rooms (nos. 001, 004, 007), which are better furnished.

Nainital offers many accommodations, but a visit during peak season is likely to be accompanied by crowds, noise, and irritation. Duck the crowds by opting for one of the following fully reviewed options or for one of two recommendations at Naukuchiatal. **Déjà-vu** (reservations through Corbett Trails, New Delhi; © **011/4172-1601;** www.naukuchiatal.com; Rs 4,500/$110/£56 four-person cottage) is a small, cozy, two-bedroom stand-alone overlooking the lake. It comes with cable TV, DVD, and a music system, as well as housekeeping attendants and a cook who will prepare meals on demand; you just need to pay for ingredients. Be prepared for frequent power outages; there is a back-up generator but you may be expected to arrange and pay for fuel to run it. For more hotel-style amenities (albeit in a concrete and stone block with plenty of face-brick and mortar), **The Lake Resort** (© **05942/24-7183** or -7184; www.lakeresort.in; from Rs 2,400/$59/£30 double) is a newer hotel whose sprawling grounds hug Naukuchiatal Lake. Every room has a view of the lake; ask for the pricier log hut with wooden floors and a bathtub for two. Room nos. 1, 5, and 12 have lounge areas and fine views, but bathrooms are small with no tubs.

The Cottage ⭒*Value*   This 100-year-old house set in a 3-hectare (8-acre) orchard has herringbone-patterned wood floors, ivy-covered stone walls, and a sloping red tiled roof—all of which give it a distinctly English appearance and old-world charm, offset by the carved Kumaoni door and window frames. Owner Bhuvan Kumari loves to tell how she painstakingly created this dream house, a lovely, value-for-money homestay. Each room has a private patio with wonderful views of lush green mountains. The Middle Room (where floral drapes decorating the ceiling are a tad kitschy) is the best in the house; the Blue Room is great for more privacy and better views, but a little too blue for our liking. The bed heights in the various guest rooms have been thoughtfully adjusted to give guests the best possible views. Simple, tasty meals are served in the homey living room–cum–dining area.

Jeolikot, District Nainital. (C) 05942/22-4013. Fax 05942/22-4182 www.jeolikot.com. 5 units. Rs 3,500 ($85/£43) double. Rates include breakfast, dinner, tea, and coffee. No credit cards. **Amenities:** Dining room; transfers; room service for snacks (7am–10 pm); laundry; doctor-on-call; badminton; board games; trekking; driver lodging facility. *In room:* Air cooler.

Emily Lodge 🏵🏵   This colonial-era bungalow is the nicest homestay in Nainital. Gracious hosts Siddharth Singh and his family have a homey cottage well away from the main mall, done up in subdued floral drapes and country-home decor. Figures of elephants and birds stenciled on the walls give the place a lively ambience in spite of the hunting-lodge atmosphere created by the old teak wood furniture, deer horns, swords, and rifles adorning the walls. Warm and comfortable, the living room has an old fireplace that's lighted at mealtimes in cold weather; it's also where wholesome home-cooked meals are served. Rooms (of which there are only four) are clean and bathrooms spacious. Jim Corbett's house (Gurney House) is just a stone's throw away, and if you are lucky the caretaker might let you in.

Ayarpata Hill, near Sherwood College, Nainital. (C) 05942/23-5857 or 98-3737-3444. 4 units. Rs 3,000–Rs 3,500 ($73–$85/£37–£43) double. Rates include breakfast, dinner, tea, and coffee. No credit cards. **Amenities:** Dining hall; transfers; laundry facilities; doctor-on-call; board games; driver lodging facility.

Jilling Estate 🏵   For a real outback experience in a magnificent setting, just 17km (11 miles) from Nainital, Jilling Estate is your best choice—though not for the faint-hearted or unfit. Access to this huge estate, where arch-conservationist Steve Lall, his wife, Parvati, and daughter Nandini live a couple of kilometers from the nearest drivable road, is only by foot or horseback; and you'll have to lug yourself up this distance just to get through the front door. All four cottages are completely private—you won't run into your neighbors even by chance. Facilities are rustic but extremely quaint; each room has an eclectic collection of books, and hot water for your bucket bath is heated on wooden fires by an attendant assigned to your room. Evenings are spent around a bonfire with the Lalls and their three friendly mutts. Steve may even encourage you to go for a completely private hike in the woods of his estate, in the buff. Or let Parvati teach you how to milk cows. The land phone here rarely works, but there is a mobile phone for emergencies.

P.O. Padampuri, District Nainital 263 136. (C) 05942/23-5493. Reservations: Neelam Rai Singh, Beckon Tours Pvt. Ltd., G22 1st floor, Lajpat Nagar Part 1, New Delhi 110 024. (C) 011/2981-3546 or -0225. Fax 011/2981-4259. www.jilling.net. 4 units. Rs 2,800 ($68/£35) double. Rate includes all meals; taxes extra. No credit cards. **Amenities:** Room service; laundry; campfire; picnic baskets; trekking; camping; table tennis.

Mountain Quail Camp & Tented Lodge 🏵   The drive from Nainital to this out-of-the-way mountainside resort provides jaw-dropping views back down over the town and lake, as well as intoxicating vistas of the Himalayan range—particularly gorgeous just after sunrise, when a striking color palette whips over mountain peaks. The hill-hugging half-hour journey brings you to a remote, exquisitely peaceful site with deluxe tents and a lodge in a clearing between forested hills and terraced farmland.

Opt for the tented accommodations, half of which have attached bathrooms with basin, shower (with hot water), and Western toilet. The bedroom interiors have patterned "walls," pitched roofs, carpets, and thick but uneven mattresses. The resort is ideal for scenic walks, bird-watching (aided by the resident birder), and easy treks, and even more perfect for doing nothing; there are also all kinds of adventure activities if you're feeling limber. Be warned that this is a popular place for groups (notably youngsters) engaged in outdoor team-building events; you might want to check that you're not sharing the place with noisy, city-slicking teenagers.

Pangot 263 001. (𝐶) **05942/24-2126.** Fax 05942/23-5493. Reservations: Blaze a Trail Adventures. (𝐶) **98-3707-7537.** www.blazeatrailadventures.com. 10 tents, 3 lodge units. $90 (£45) tent double; $120 (£60) lodge double. Rates include all meals. No credit cards. **Amenities:** Restaurant; doctor-on-call; trekking; horse safaris; mountain biking; rock climbing; fishing; jeep safaris; white-water rafting; games.

Mountain Trail   This is the best place to overnight if you want to stay in Mukteshwar itself. Mountain Trail is well-maintained and is on a terraced slope with a lovely rose garden and direct views of the Himalayas. Accommodations are large, neat, and simple. Ask for a deluxe double room; each has high-pitched ceilings, enclosed porch with exquisite views, large tiled shower, and fridge. All rooms are comfortable and spotless, and the pleasant restaurant has a working fireplace. There's no bar or room service, but most other facilities are available, and there's a game room with table tennis and a small library. The resort also runs a *chocolaterie,* where delicious center-filled chocolates are made with ingredients imported from Belgium.

P.O. Sargakhet, Mukteshwar 263 132. (𝐶) **05942/28-6040** or -6240. www.mountaintrail.com. Reservations: Mountain Trail Holidays, 224 Vardhaman Plaza, 9 Local Shopping Centre, I.P. Extension, Delhi 110 092. (𝐶) **011/2272-0675** or -0677. 12 units. Rs 2,500 ($61/£31) double; Rs 3,500 ($85/£43) 4-bed family room. During high season (May–June) full-board packages only, from Rs 4,000 ($98/£49) double. AE, MC, V. **Amenities:** Restaurant; game room; room service; laundry; doctor-on-call; river rafting; adventure activities; TV lounge; library; yoga and meditation in summer.

The Ramgarh Bungalows 𝒌𝒌   For a restful, soul-calming sojourn in atmospheric colonial accommodations that aren't quite hotels and are definitely not homestays, Neemrana's Ramgarh Bungalows is hard to match. A great base from which to explore the Kumaon Hills, these 19th-century British bungalows feature deep verandas, bay windows, fireplaces, and dainty gardens bordered by chestnut trees. The Writers' Bungalow was built in 1860, while the Old Bungalow dates back to 1830; both have been given a bright, homey atmosphere with floral fabrics. Two additional bungalows, the Vista Bungalow and the Rose Cottage, were added more recently, all dressed in the same 19th-century English ambience; the Rose Cottage is perfect if you desire exclusivity and privacy: It comprises one luxury suite with a sleeping room for one couple and three children, and has a great private terrace. Many of the various and varied rooms and suites sleep three or four, making them ideal for families. Ramgarh is 24km (15 miles) from Mukteshwar; because of the remote location you must make travel arrangements and reservations in advance. There's no room service, but morning tea is brought to your room. Lawn tables, views, and the possibility of walks are all so alluring that even the laziest will be drawn outdoors. Rates quoted below are for a double room or a suite that also has additional single beds.

Ramgarh (Malla), Kumaon Hills, Nainital District 263 137. (𝐶) **05942/28-1156** or -1137. Reservations: Neemrana Hotels Pvt. Ltd., A-58 Nizamuddin E., New Delhi 110 013. (𝐶) **011/2461-6145,** -8962, or -5214. Fax 011/2462-1112. www.neemranahotels.com. 11 units. Rs 1,200–Rs 4,800 ($29–$117/£15–£59) Old Bungalow; Rs 3,000–Rs 6,000 ($73–$146/£37–£74) Writers' Bungalow; Rs 1,500–Rs 3,600 ($37–$88/£19–£44) Vista Bungalow; Rs 3,600–Rs 7,200 ($88–$176/£44–£89) Rose Cottage. Rates vary according to season. Taxes extra. AE, MC, V accepted at main office. **Amenities:** Restaurant; laundry; doctor-on-call; trekking; river rafting; yoga.

Sitla Estate ★ *Kids*   This is a wonderful place to unwind, spot rare birds, and explore the Kumaon forests. Facilities are a bit rustic (hot water is available for only 2 hr. in the morning), but the stunning views of Himalayan peaks from your window more than make up for it. Deluxe rooms are lovely, with bay windows that allow you to sip tea and enjoy the sunrise from your bed. Vikram Maira, the genial owner-host, can suggest the best trails to take through dense forests, but just walking around the 16 hectares (39 acres) of orchards and organic gardens is a cleansing experience. Since Vikram is the head chef, spontaneous local counselor, and organizer of treks, river rafting, and jeep safaris, make sure you plan your next day with him the night before. And yes, he does cook up lip-smacking meals—his mulberry crumble is legendary. With farm animals and ponies around, there's plenty to keep kids occupied.

P.O. Mukteshwar, District Nainital 263 138. ℂ **05942/28-6330** or -6030. www.sitlaestate.net. 7 units. Rs 3,500 ($85/£43) regular double; Rs 4,000 ($98/£49) deluxe double; Rs 4,500 ($110/£56) suite. Rates include all meals, tea, and coffee. Taxes extra. No credit cards. **Amenities:** Dining hall; transfers; laundry; doctor-on-call; board games; river rafting; adventure activities; picnic lunch. *In room:* Tea- and coffee-making facilities, sawdust heater.

BINSAR & ALMORA SURROUNDS

High on the hill within Binsar Wildlife Sanctuary, the **Forest Resthouse** is characterized by long, musty rooms, high ceilings, old-fashioned furnishings, a lack of electricity, and ridiculously low room rates. The resthouse is looked after by a *chowkidar* (caretaker), who may even prepare meals for you if you bring your own supplies. Book a room through the **Almora Forest Office** (ℂ **05962/23-1089;** http://almora.nic.in). Avoid the 500-year-old Almora town (34km/21 miles southwest of Binsar) entirely, but consider staying at wonderful Kalmatia Sangam (reviewed below) on the road to Kasardevi Temple. Also near Almora, within a forest, the **Deodars** (Papparsalle; ℂ **05962/23-3025;** rwheeler@rediffmail.com) is a family-run lodging with three guest rooms in an old stone cottage; solitude is guaranteed for just Rs 4,000 ($98/£49) double, including all meals. Guest rooms have fireplaces, and one unit has a bathtub. If you're less adventurous, you might settle on **Club Mahindra Valley Resort Binsar** (Bhainsori P.O., Binsar, Almora 263 684; ℂ **05962/25-3028,** -3062, or -3174; fax 05962/25-3035; www.clubmahindra.com), a resort-style option for those wanting typical hotel luxuries and amenities. The setting is pleasant enough, with stone pathways and slate stairways running between the studios and one-bedroom apartments spread across a terraced hillside. Each apartment (club suite) is huge, with kitchenette, separate dining and sitting areas, Zen-style bedroom with rugs, and private balcony. Decor is upbeat and modern, and bathrooms are large with curtained drench showers. Management organizes a range of activities and excursions, primarily aimed at keeping well-heeled Indian guests busy, but be warned that this is part of a timeshare scheme, so you'll undoubtedly be hard-pressed to find any sort of tranquillity during the popular summer months. The low season is from January through March and mid-July through September; peak season rates start at Rs 5,760 ($140/£71) double.

Kalmatia Sangam ★★   Owners Geeta and Dieter Reeb believe in eco-conscious tourism, and the focus here is on nature and wellness. You won't find fancy amenities in any of the resort's nine cottage rooms, but each has a little balcony overlooking the valley and oozes charm. Eagle's Nest is the largest of the rooms, with the best views. Food is good and wholesome; alcohol is not available but you're free to bring your own. Though you can wander around endlessly on your own, the Reebs also conduct fascinating guided walks—including a village walk, which allows guests to observe the local architecture, walk through fields, and interact with locals. Everything about Kalmatia is geared toward de-stressing, so you can forget about walking if you don't want to, and instead get yourself a glass of rhododendron squash and retire to the library, or book a treatment or aromatherapy session with the resident reflexologist. For the higher price (compared with other Kumaon properties), you are assured utmost privacy, personalized attention, and serenity. The resort makes a point of employing people who live nearby, and also supports the local economy through a boutique (Kasa) that carries locally made linens, shawls, bamboo, and copper products.

Kalimat Estate, Post Bag 002, Almora 263 601. ℂ 05962/23-3625. Fax 05962/23-1572. www.kalmatia-sangam.com. Reservations: Kalmatia Sangam Travels Pvt. Ltd., c/o Triage Overseas, Mr. Basu or Mr. Khanduri, B-11, Gulmohar Park, New Delhi 110 049. 9 units. 85€–127€ ($114–$170/£58–£86) double; 160€ ($214/£109) Eagles Nest double; 39€ ($52/£27) extra bed. These rates include breakfast; all-meal inclusive packages available. MC, V. Full advance payment required for reservation confirmation. **Amenities:** Restaurant; transfers; room service only for snacks (6am–10:30pm); laundry; doctor-on-call; reflexology; aromatherapy; yoga; Ayurvedic diet advice; music library; book library; guided walks; picnic lunches; bonfire; generator. *In room:* Wood-burning stove, fan.

RANIKHET

An attractive alternative to the hotel reviewed below is **Chevron Rosemount** (ℂ **05966/ 22-1391** or -0989; www.chevronhotels.com), a century-old, two-story colonial bungalow in a forest clearing that's showing its age in a charmingly dilapidated way. Reserve room no. 202, the Nirvana Suite (Rs 4,200/$102/£52). Unwind on the armchairs, chaise longue, or large comfortable bed; the large bathroom has plenty of natural light. Another option worth considering is **Holm Farm** ⋆, the first bungalow in Ranikhet, with suites from Rs 2,500 ($61/£31), and even cheaper Swiss huts. This is ideal for those looking for relaxed, old-world atmosphere—though when the place is full, you'll find tents pitched outside for guests (ℂ **05966/22-0891** or 94-1152-0445; www.holmfarmranikhet.com); there are also indoor and outdoor activities for children.

West View Hotel ⋆   This stone brick colonial mansion—an atmospheric relic of the Raj set in a lovely garden—offers spacious accommodations with carpeted bedrooms, old dark wooden furniture, upholstered armchairs, hard mattresses on big beds, and massive bathrooms with drench showers and natural light. Deluxe guest rooms have working stone fireplaces, half-canopied two-poster beds, and floral blinds and bed frills. Ask for the best room in the house, no. 21, which also has a view. Suites feature four-poster beds and separate lounges. Some of the rooms are only accessible via creaking wooden stairways. The public lounge is quaint and old-fashioned; the homey dining room with log fire has wallpapered walls decorated with blue-patterned porcelain plates. Note that hot water is only available mornings and evenings. The outdoor cafe is a pleasant spot at which to relax with a cappuccino and cake after traipsing around the hills nearby.

Mahatma Gandhi Rd., Ranikhet 263 645. ℂ **05966/22-0261** or -1075. Fax 05966/22-0396. www.westviewhotel. com. westview@ajitjain.com. Reservations: 115, Pushpanjali, New Delhi 110 092. ℂ **011/2237-3389.** Fax 011/2237-2996. 18 units. Rs 3,500 ($85/£43) deluxe double; Rs 4,500 ($110/£56) luxury suite; Rs 5,500 ($134/£68) family suite. Children 5–12 pay 25%. Rates include breakfast and dinner. Taxes extra. Check for off-season discounts. No credit cards. **Amenities:** Restaurant; coffee shop; limited transport assistance; room service 7am–10pm; laundry; doctor-on-call; badminton; table tennis; rock climbing; indoor games. *In room:* TV.

3 Corbett National Park ★★★

264km (164 miles) NE of Delhi; 436km (270 miles) NW of Lucknow

Covering 1,319 sq. km (509 sq. miles), Corbett became India's first national park on August 8, 1936. When renowned conservationist Jim Corbett passed away in Kenya in 1955, it was renamed to honor the role he played in establishing the park.

The biggest draw of the park, of course, is the possibility of spotting a tiger in the wild. Project Tiger, a government undertaking aimed at saving India's dwindling tiger population, was launched here in 1973. Despite the fact that 140 or so tigers reside here, sightings are not to be taken for granted, and your chances of an encounter are far better at Ranthambore (Rajasthan) and Bandavgarh (Madhya Pradesh). The advantage of Corbett, however, is that you can overnight in the park. The landscape consists of *Sal* forests and bamboo trees, with an abundance of other wildlife, including leopards, wild elephants, boars, black bears, sambar, four-horned antelope *(chausingha),* monkeys, and, among the reptile population, pythons and the endangered gharial crocodile. Corbett's many water bodies are a birder's delight, with more than 400 species recorded. Inside the park, you can hole up in a watchtower near a waterhole for hours. Areas outside the park, especially along the Kosi River, are almost as good.

VISITING THE PARK

Corbett is open from November 15 through June 15, much of it closed when the monsoon causes rivers to flood their banks. Sightings are best between March and June. Access to the park is via the town of Ramnagar, where the **Park Office** (opposite the Ramnagar bus stand; ✆ **05947/25-1489;** www.jimcorbettnationalpark.com; Dec–May daily 8:15am–noon and 1–4pm, June–Nov daily 10am–noon and 1–5pm) processes and issues the required permits, and handles all park-managed accommodations as well as jeep safaris. There are direct trains from Delhi to Ramnagar; driving takes 6 to 8 hours (about 300km/186 miles). Corbett is divided into five mutually exclusive tourist zones, and you can visit only one zone at a time. If you do not have your own vehicle, hire one in Ramnagar or at Dhangari Gate for around Rs 700 ($17/£9). It's best to undertake jeep safaris early in the morning; you'll spend a total of around Rs 350 ($9/£4) on entry and vehicle fees, depending on which zone you visit, and you'll need to be accompanied by a licensed guide (Rs 150/$3.65/£1.85); an English-speaking naturalist (best organized through your lodge) usually charges Rs 850 ($21/£11) per trip. The park is open daily 7am to 5pm in winter, and 6am to 6pm when the days are longer. You are not permitted to enter the park less than 30 minutes before the sun descends, and nighttime driving within Corbett is not allowed. Don't make the mistake of arriving in Ramnagar too late in the day; you will have to fill out forms, pay for permits and accommodations, and still get to the gate 30 minutes before sunset. Corbett is extremely popular and likely to be fully booked, so don't arrive unprepared.

Perhaps the most visually attractive area of the park is **Jhirna,** which is the only section that does not close during the monsoon season (June 15–Nov 15); entry to this zone is Rs 100 ($2.45/£1.25) plus Rs 75 ($1.85/95p) for vehicle entry. Try to visit **Ramganga Reservoir,** where endangered gharial crocodiles bask on the banks and a sign warning against swimming proclaims that SURVIVORS WILL BE PROSECUTED. Surrounded by vast elephant grassland savannahs, **Dhikala** has the greatest selection of accommodations, and substitutes solitude for access to facilities like restaurants and film screenings. Dhikala is reached via **Dhangarhi Gate** (16km/10 miles north of Ramnagar), and is only accessible to visitors with accommodations reserved inside this zone; entry to Dhikala costs Rs 450 ($11/£6) per person for 2 nights, plus Rs 150 ($3.65/£1.85) for a car or Jeep. **Elephant rides,** available from Dhikala and Bijrani, are the most promising and nature-friendly way of tracking tigers through the *chaur.* Departing at sunrise and sunset, the ride through the forests and across the plains costs just Rs 300 ($7.30/£3.70) for 2 hours. You need to reserve well in advance (a full day is recommended), and reward your *mahout* (elephant handler) with a tip if you do, indeed, spot a tiger.

Tip: If you plan to go exploring by yourself for flexibility, you'll need your own vehicle from Delhi or you can hire a vehicle (preferably a jeep) with driver once you arrive; otherwise all accommodations will arrange pickups from Ramnagar Station. If you don't plan on staying in the park, it's far easier (particularly if you're staying at one of the resorts below) to have your hotel management make all your safari arrangements; the bureaucracy and form-filling that go along with acquiring the necessary permits can be exasperating.

WHERE TO STAY & DINE
INSIDE THE PARK

Finally the park has relatively upmarket, privately managed accommodations—something of a milestone in Indian nature reserves. **The Hideaway River Lodge** 𝒢𝒢 (𝒞 **05947/28-4132** or -4134; www.corbetthideaway.com.) is owned by the same group responsible for Corbett Hideaway (reviewed below). Besides offering pleasing digs and the best meals you'll find anywhere inside the park (not to mention the *only* alcohol!), the lodge is located right on the Ramganga River and spread out over 1.2 hectares (3 acres) deep within the reserve. Accommodations are in luxury en-suite tents; each tent has a private veranda with a rocking chair and a lovely view. Hot water is only available in the mornings and evenings, but this should not be a major drawback. Besides the regular safari activities (in a jeep or on an elephant), the lodge also offers fishing, and the location is ideal for birders; there's also a natural pool where you can laze away the hotter parts of the day. Tents (specify if you want a double bed) go for $300 (£150) for a deluxe double, and $325 (£163) for a superior double; this includes all meals, transfers from Corbett Hideaway, all entrance fees, tea and coffee, safaris, the services of a naturalist, angling, and all taxes. It makes for a highly convenient and comfortable getaway.

Although overnighting at one of the official park lodges has many advantages (particularly for your budget), comfort and service are not among them. The popular and often crowded **Dikhala** camp is one of the few places (others are Gairal and Bijrani) where you can get food in the park; it has two vegetarian restaurants (non-vegetarian food and alcohol are forbidden in the park and at park lodges). Dikhala's accommodations include cabins and three-bed "hutments" with attached bathrooms, and dorms that sleep 12 and are serviced by a separate washroom. **Forest bungalows (resthouses)** are scattered throughout the reserve and are best booked at least 1 month in advance; they offer seclusion and complete privacy, but—as with all of the resthouses outside Dikhala—you'll have to bring your own supplies. (Don't leave food lying around—there are reports of elephants ripping out the screen windows of forest resthouses to get to the provisions inside.) One of the best bungalows is at **Gairal,** near the Ramganga River and close to a hide bank. **Kandha Resthouse** is set on the highest point within the park. If you're up for a little more style, ask about **lodges** once used by British hunters; these have such unexpected luxuries as attached bathrooms, fireplaces, and carpets. For reservations at any of these camps, contact the Director,

Corbett Reserve Reception Centre, Ramnagar 244 715 (© **05947/25-1489; fax** 05947/ 25-1376; www.corbettnationalpark.in). At Dhikala, rates range from Rs 200 ($5/£2.50) per person for a log-hut dorm to Rs 1,400 ($34/£17) for a room in a cabin, and up to Rs 2,000 or Rs 2,800 ($49–$68/£25–£35) for a room in a more private forest bungalow. Rooms in various other resthouses throughout the park cost between Rs 800 and Rs 2,800 ($20–$68/£10–£35). Credit cards are not accepted.

OUTSIDE THE PARK

There are dozens of accommodations from Ramnagar to Corbett and beyond. Nature lovers who don't necessarily require top-notch hotel amenities will love the rustic but terrific **Camp Forktail Creek** ⚜ (© **05947/28-7804;** www.campforktailcreek.com). The place is run by a young, enthusiastic couple, Ritish Suri and Minakshi Pandey. Accommodations are in safari tents, with elevated wooden floors and attached toilets, or in mud huts with thatched roofs and verandas. Customized walks, safaris, and birding and angling trips include the services of a resident naturalist or tracker. A double at Rs 4,400 ($107/£54) includes all meals, cold drinks, and escorted walks; no credit cards. Half- or full-day game drives are offered, and you can also opt for a camping trip into the forest reserve or multi-day elephant safaris. Delicious buffet-style meals are served in "The Thatch"; lit by lanterns at night (there is no electricity), it houses a collection of some 700 books for guests to peruse. For more conventional lodgings, book one of the following.

Corbett Hideaway ⚜⚜   Pebbled pathways interweave with pretty gardens and cozy mustard-colored cottages in a mango orchard. The older, "jungle-themed" cottages have thatched pitched ceilings, stone-tile flooring, comfortable beds, and separate sitting areas with fireplaces. A lovely place to relax is the thatched-roof bar, with its distinguished air. There's a well-stocked library with a selection of Jim Corbett's books to get you in the mood for tiger-spotting safaris. If you don't feel like lazing, and you're not on the back of a pachyderm, you may wish to go river rafting on the Kosi River. Or check out the resort's herd of water buffalo. The evening's entertainment features Kumaoni folk dancing, a wildlife movie, or a slide show.

Zero Garjia, Dhikuli 224 715. © **05947/28-4132** or -4134. Fax 05947/28-4133. www.corbetthideaway.com. 52 cottages. $325 (£163) deluxe double; $360 (£180) superior double. Rates include all meals, jeep and elephant safaris, and nature walk. Taxes extra. AE, MC, V. **Amenities:** 2 restaurants; bar; pool; kids' pool; nature shop; Ayurvedic massage; laundry; doctor-on-call; jeep, elephant, and coach safaris; river rafting; nature walks; fishing; archery; table tennis; badminton; bird-watching; indoor games; billiards; cultural performances. *In room:* A/C, tea- and coffee-making facilities.

Corbett Ramganga Resort ⚜   Tiger-spotting is not the only reason to venture into the lower Kumaon Mountains. Die-hard anglers head here in hope of bagging India's ultimate big-game fishing trophy: the mighty *mahseer*. This decade-old resort, on the banks of the Ramganga River, is not as attractive as its riverfront neighbor Solluna, but it draws an interesting mix of people, many here only to fish—the world record *mahseer* was bagged just 500m (1,600 ft.) from the Corbett Resort. Guest rooms are large and simple, in semicircular brick cabins with stone tile floors. We prefer the tented accommodations—each large, air-cooled, army-style structure is encased in a thatch shell, with a tiny dressing room and a small shower room attached; mattresses here are also more comfortable. At night, guests—mostly moneyed Indians and diplomats—gather around a bonfire and share rum-induced fishing tales; in

Sightings from the Saddle

Saddle up for a 3-day (or 6-day) horse safari in the reserve forest bordering Corbett National Park. **Corbett Horse Safari** takes you out on thoroughbred horses retired from Mumbai's racetracks across the Kosi River, up and down ridges and mountains, through thick forests of *sal* and elephant and tiger country to Kaladungi, where Jim Corbett lived. Trips are professionally led, and horses have accompanying *syces* (stable-hands). Riders overnight in spartan 19th-century forest resthouses (or tents) along the way. The whole experience is a step back in time. Call ✆ **05947/28-4125**, 011/2955-1191, or 98-1110-9596; or go to www.corbettriverside.com. Customized trips with accommodation and all meals cost approximately Rs 6,000 ($146/£74) per person, per day. Or saddle up for 3 hours for Rs 500 ($12/£6).

the background, the gurgling Ramganga reminds you that you're miles away from the pollution, congestion, and ceaseless traffic of the cities. You might like to ask manager Surender Pal about a rainy night when he witnessed a standoff between a tiger and a boar outside his office; although this was quite a number of years back, he still recalls the event vividly. The resort organizes night safaris (from Rs 1,000/$24/£12 per jeep) through the surrounding valleys, providing an opportunity for nocturnal tiger and leopard sightings. Buffet meals, served in a high-ceilinged, circular restaurant, are wonderful.

Village Jhamaria, P.O. Sankar, Marchula. ✆ 05966/28-1592 or -1692. Reservations: Surbhi Adventures, No. 5, C-1 Lane, Sainik Farms, Khanpur Gate, New Delhi 110 062. ✆ 011/3298-9876. Fax 011/2955-1428. www.ramganga. com. 30 units. Rs 5,500 ($134/£68) safari tent double; Rs 6,500 ($159/£80) deluxe double; Rs 7,050 ($172/£87) super deluxe double; Rs 8,300 ($202/£102) suite. Rs 1,850 ($45/£23) extra bed. Rates include all meals, bed tea, and taxes. AE, DC, MC, V. **Amenities:** Restaurant; bar service; pool; children's pool; tennis court; snacks-only room service; laundry; doctor-on-call; fishing; night safaris; river-rafting; rappelling and other adventure activities for groups only; badminton; cycling; indoor and outdoor games; day excursions. *In room:* A/C (tents are air-cooled only), heater. Suites have kitchenettes and tea- and coffee-making facilities.

Infinity Resorts 🏕   Activities at this pleasant riverside hotel center around a huge enclosed octagonal building with a terrace and indoor bonfire; this is where meals are served, wildlife movies are shown, and cultural performances are held. The deluxe guest rooms are worth paying a little more for; they lead off open corridors on the floor above the standard units. They're spacious (though not particularly tasteful), and each one has a large terrace with a river view. From your room, you can hear the river and enjoy great bird-watching. The setting is peaceful, perhaps more so than at Claridges Corbett Hideaway. There's a relaxing swimming pool, and a terraced rock embankment leads down to a riverside pond filled with *mahseer* and a nearby shrine to Ganesha. Hammocks are strung up between the mango trees and rhododendrons. The idyllic setting is wonderful for stretching out with a copy of Jim Corbett's memoirs.

P.O. Dhikuli, Ramnagar 244 715. ✆ 05947/25-1279 or -1280. Fax 05947/25-1280. www.infinityresorts.com. Reservations: 405, International Trade Tower, Nehru Place, New Delhi 110 017. ✆ 011/4160-8508 or 011/4100-8510. Fax 011/4160-8509. 24 units. Oct 1–June 30/July 1–Sept 30: $240/$200 (£120/£100) standard double; $250/$210 (£125/£110) luxury double. Rates include all meals and 1 safari per day. AE, DC, MC, V. **Amenities:** Restaurant; bar; pool; health club; souvenir shop; room service; laundry; medical center; cultural events; billiards and pool table; fishing; park jeep safaris; elephant safaris; nature walks; wildlife film shows; conference hall. *In room:* A/C, heater.

The Solluna Resort ✿   Not as well-known as its older neighbor, Corbett Ramganga, this 10-hectare (25-acre) resort—named for the sun and the moon, and situated on the riverbank—has better rooms (gorgeous cottages, each with comfortable mattress, bay window seats, a skylight that allows you to watch the stars from your bed, a good tiled shower room, cupboard space, working surfaces, and two small private verandas with wicker chairs and a cane swing). However, it's not as popular as Corbett Ramganga, and not as convivial. Above the reception area (where there's a small dining area), a lovely viewing terrace with comfortable wicker chairs is great for lazing and drinking in the natural spectacle all around you. Expansive lawns surround the cottages, scattered with bougainvillea and mango and cherry trees. At night, pathways glow from the light of storm lanterns, and a bonfire is lit for a communal chinwag. Alcohol isn't available, but you're welcome to bring your own.

Marchula 244 715. Reservations: ✆ **011/2354-0456** or 011/2331-0227. Fax 011/2362-7738. www.sollunaresort.com. 23 units. Rs 4,500 ($110/£56) double; Rs 1,800 ($44/£22) extra person. 2 children under 7 stay free in parent's room. Rates include all meals. Discounts of up to 50% mid-June to mid-Nov. Taxes extra. No credit cards. **Amenities:** Restaurant; 24-hr. coffee shop; pool; limited room service; laundry; doctor-on-call; minitheater; safaris; fishing; birdwatching; sightseeing. *In room:* A/C, fridge, tea- and coffee-making facilities, heater.

13

Kolkata (Calcutta) & East India

The image most people have of Calcutta is one of abject poverty and misery—the residual effect of the many years the media focused on Mother Teresa's good works. Despite this unfortunate perception, Kolkata (as the Communist-ruled West Bengal Capital became known in 2001) attracts its fair share of visitors, many of whom are pleasantly surprised by the seductive charms of this intoxicating city.

Believed to be the ethereal abode of the goddess Kali, who embodies *shakit*—fortitude and strength—it is home to a joyous, cerebral, and sophisticated community; some of the best Raj-era architecture in India; many of the country's best artists; a thriving film industry; and a host of superb restaurants.

Kolkata is also the natural starting point for a trip to the Himalayan mountains of the North, where you can drink in the crystal-clear air of **Darjeeling,** India's most famous hill station, imbibing the "champagne of teas" before picking up a permit to hike the tiny state of **Sikkim.** One of the least-explored regions of India, Sikkim is a world apart, surrounded by jagged peaks and home to snow-fed lakes, remote Buddhist monasteries, yak-herding Tibetans, high-altitude forests, and some 4,000 varieties of wildflowers (including 600 varieties of orchid).

South of West Bengal, in the coastal state of Orissa—often called the "soul of India"—you can join the pilgrims who gather by the thousands to pay homage to the Lord of the Universe, who resides at the seaside town of Puri. Within easy striking distance from here is Konark's **Sun Temple,** a World Heritage Site, a testament to the technical and artistic brilliance of Orissa in the 13th century, and unreservedly one of India's top attractions.

To cover all three eastern states, you will need a minimum of 9 days, ideally flying directly to Bhubaneswar, capital of Orissa, to visit Puri and Konark, then heading northward to West Bengal to visit the capital, Kolkata, and the state's idyllic hill station, Darjeeling. End your tour in laid-back Sikkim before flying back to Delhi from nearby Bagdogra Airport. Set aside extra time for trekking in Sikkim or a tribal tour in Orissa.

1 Kolkata

1,310km (812 miles) SE of Delhi

Once the proud capital of the British Raj, Kolkata is deeply evocative of an era and sensibility lost in time. Established as the trading post for the East India Company on the banks of the Hooghly River by Job Charnock in 1690, it grew to be the biggest colonial trade center in Asia, earning it the name "Jewel of the East." With its splendid Victorian buildings, ornamental pools, stone-paved footpaths, figured lampposts, and sweeping esplanade, it was entirely European in its architecture and sensibility, and the burgeoning city became the stomping ground of a new breed of sahibs and

The Dance of Destruction

For Hindus, India is a Holy Land, with thousands of *tirthas*—celestial "cross-over" points where mortals can access the world of the gods. Legend has it that these were created after Lord Shiva's wife, Sati, jumped into a fire in an act of shame because her father, Raja Daksha, had neglected to invite Shiva to an important ritual. Unable to bear the loss, the grief-struck Shiva—carrying Sati's body—began to pace India in a *tandava nritya,* or "dance of destruction." Terrified that his fury and pain would destroy the universe, Brahma, Vishnu, and Shani dispersed her body across the vast plains and peaks of India, and wherever a body part fell, this became a *tirtha.* Many of these are important pilgrimage sites Hindu believers must visit at least once in their lifetime, such as those at Varanasi (see chapter 9). One of Sati's toes also fell in a dense forest in southwest Bengal. Today, this site—now **Kalighat Temple**—is one of India's most important pilgrimage centers, where the goddess is worshipped as Kali. The toe is supposedly housed in a chamber of the temple. Every year in June, as part of a secretive ritual, the toe is bathed.

memsahibs who wore their white skins and British manners as though they were royal insignias. But Kolkata was effectively built on a disease-breeding swamp—the marshy delta of the Ganges and Brahmaputra rivers—and this, combined with the heat, humidity, and the Bengalis' prominence in the struggle for independence, finally persuaded the British to transfer the capital. In 1911 they left for Delhi, leaving Calcutta to rot.

Today, much of the city's architectural heritage stands crumbling and in ruins, its monumental colonial structures not nearly as well maintained as those of Mumbai. Moss and grime cover tattered buildings that should be celebrated as the city's finest—the collapsing masonry, peeling paint, and sun-scorched woodwork testaments to the indifference of time. Unable to stem the long-term industrial and commercial decline of the city, or the flood of refugees that have continually arrived from Bangladesh since the first days of Partition, the Communist ruling parties (CPI and CPIM) struggle to adequately provide for the city's 14 million inhabitants. The second-largest city on the subcontinent (after Mumbai), it is packed to capacity, politically beleaguered, and an entrepôt of India's social woes.

Yet its proud citizens, who speak rapturously of its benefits over the other big Indian metropolises, fiercely tout the charms of Kolkata. In fact, meeting Bengalis is one of the best aspects of traveling here—Kolkata is the self-proclaimed capital of India's intellectuals, home to three Nobel Prize laureates (including the revered Rabindranath Tagore, who became Asia's first Nobel laureate in 1913) and an Oscar-winning film director (Satyajit Ray). Warm, helpful, and imbued with a great sense of humor (not to mention a famously keen appreciation for dining), the Bengalis live by the maxim that "what Bengal does today, India will do tomorrow," and engaging in lively discussion on the benefits or drawbacks of Communism, or on the original recipe for *sandesh* (milk-based sweets, a Bengali specialty), is likely to be one of your more memorable experiences in India.

In some ways, the city is as frightening as you might fear, a degraded mess where squalor, filth, and the ubiquitous *bustees* (slums) can overwhelm the senses. If you're in India to enjoy the country's softer side, don't tarry here. Head for the Himalayan

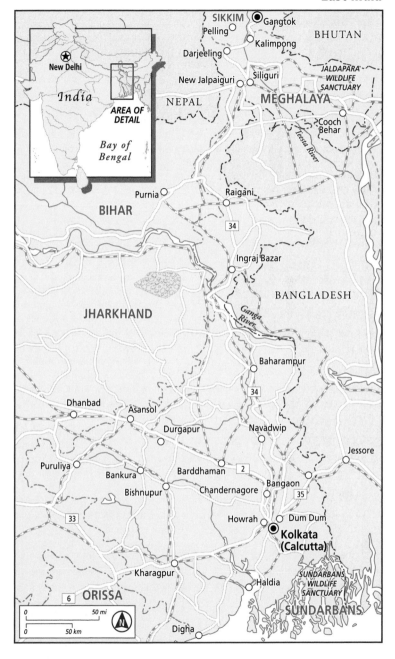

East India

SIKKIM

Gangtok

Pelling

Kalimpong

BHUTAN

Darjeeling

JALDAPARA
WILDLIFE
SANCTUARY

New Jalpaiguri

Siliguri

MEGHALAYA

NEPAL

Teesta River

Cooch
Behar

Purnia

Raigani

BIHAR

34

Ingraj Bazar

BANGLADESH

JHARKHAND

Ganga River

Baharampur

34

Dhanbad

Asansol

Durgapur

Navadwip

Jessore

Puruliya

Bankura

Barddhaman

2

Chandernagore

Bangaon

Bishnupur

35

33

Howrah

Dum Dum

**Kolkata
(Calcutta)**

Kharagpur

6

ORISSA

Haldia

SUNDARBANS
WILDLIFE
SANCTUARY

SUNDARBANS

0   50 mi

0   50 km

N

Digha

Locator inset

New Delhi

India

AREA OF
DETAIL

*Bay of
Bengal*

Kolkata (Calcutta)

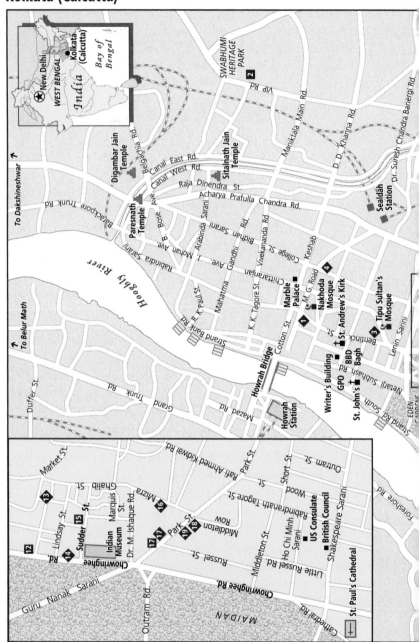

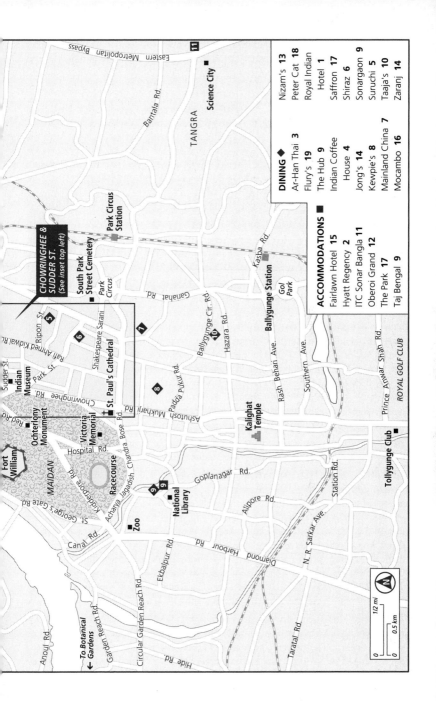

CHOWRINGHEE & SUDDER ST.
(See inset top left)

DINING ◆

Ar-Han Thai **3**
Flury's **19**
The Hub **9**
Indian Coffee
   House **4**
Jong's **14**
Kewpie's **8**
Mainland China **7**
Mocambo **16**
Nizam's **13**
Peter Cat **18**
Royal Indian
   Hotel **1**
Saffron **17**
Shiraz **6**
Sonargaon **9**
Suruchi **5**
Taaja's **10**
Zaranj **14**

ACCOMMODATIONS ■

Fairlawn Hotel **15**
Hyatt Regency **2**
ITC Sonar Bangla **11**
Oberoi Grand **12**
The Park **17**
Taj Bengal **9**

mountainscapes of Sikkim or Darjeeling, or the temples and beaches of Orissa, farther south. But if you delight in eclectic city culture, spend at least 2 or 3 nights in this thrilling city.

ESSENTIALS

VISITOR INFORMATION   The **West Bengal Tourism Centre** (3/2 B.B.D. Bagh E.; ✆ **033/2248-8271** or -8272; www.wbtourism.com; Mon–Sat 10am–6pm) is good for up-to-date information and you can also arrange city tours here. Visit the **India Tourism Kolkata** (MSE Building, 4 Shakespeare Sarani; ✆ **033/2282-5813,** -1475, or -7731) for (limited) information on the entire subcontinent. *Cal Calling* is a monthly catalog of events and general information (✆ **98-3121-4445**).

GETTING THERE & AWAY   **By Air**   Kolkata is served by domestic flights from most major destinations in India. Netaji Subhash Chandra Bose International Airport, formerly Dum Dum Airport (✆ **033/2511-8787** or -9721; www.calcuttaairport.com) is 15km (9⅓ miles) northeast. You can exchange currency and get tourist information from two separate booths here. Use the prepaid taxi stand (✆ **033/2511-1201**); the 40-minute trip into town should cost Rs 300 ($7.30/£3.70).

By Train   Kolkata's **Howrah Junction** (✆ **033/2638-2217**), just south of Howrah Bridge, connects the city with most other parts of the country. It's made up of the adjoining Old and New Howrah stations. You should purchase tickets through your hotel or a travel agent, but there is a section specifically for foreigners in the main **reservations office** (daily 10am–5pm). For general inquiries, call ✆ **1310;** for prere-corded information, call ✆ **1331.** Trains to destinations farther east and to the north-ern areas of West Bengal often depart from **Sealdah Station** (Bepin Behari Ganguly St.; ✆ **033/2350-3535** or -3537); check your ticket to confirm which station you need to be at. Also arrive with time to spare so that you can navigate through the crowds and find out about any changes to the schedule. You can also log on to **www.indianrail.gov.in** for information (see chapter 2).

By Road   Don't consider getting to or from Kolkata by motor vehicle (either driving yourself or by bus); otherwise you'll waste a great deal of your vacation time.

GETTING AROUND   **By Taxi & Auto-Rickshaw**   The full-to-capacity streets of Kolkata can be the very devil to get around, but a jaunt in a hired Ambassador is a good way to experience the city. Taxi drivers here are notoriously keen on ripping you off, even after you've negotiated a fare. Ask your hotel concierge for an approximate idea of the fare for your route, check that the meter is reset, and make sure that the driver knows where you're going (use a street map to ensure you aren't taken on a detour). You can hire a good car and driver through **Avis** (Oberoi Grand; ✆ **033/ 2249-2323,** ext. 6325 or 6335) or through **Car-Cab** (2 Manook Lane, off Ezra St.; ✆ **033/2235 -3535** or 98-3104-1614). See "Car Rentals" under "Fast Facts: Kolkata," below. Note that rickshaws are outlawed from entering many of the city's major streets.

The Metro   India's first underground railway was started in Calcutta in 1984; it cur-rently connects Tollygunge in the south with Dum Dum Station in the north. It's a reliable, clean, and surprisingly uncrowded transport option, and tickets are cheap (Rs 4–Rs 8/10¢–20¢/5p–10p). The Metro operates Monday through Saturday from 7am to 9:45pm, and on Sunday from 3 to 9:45pm. For information, contact the **Metro Rail Bhavan** (33/1 Jawaharlal Nehru Rd.; ✆ **033/2226-7280** or -1054).

By Bus or Tram   To experience India at its most confusing, claustrophobic, and unpredictable, by all means hop aboard one of Kolkata's battered buses or road-clogging trams. If you're looking for a joyride, take a tram around Victoria Memorial.

On Foot   If you don't mind breaking a sweat and rubbing shoulders with the *aam janta* (common man), Kolkata is quite a walkable city, at least in parts, with its pavements lined end to end with makeshift shacks selling practically anything that is sellable! Early morning is the best time to get out and stroll through the streets; it's still relatively quiet, and the air is cooler and less choked by pollution. Pick up a cup of tea from the *chai-wallas* who serve their sweet brew in tiny unfired clay cups—India's answer to the polystyrene cup, these are simply discarded after use. A great way to get acquainted with Kolkata is to pick up a copy of *Ten Walks in Calcutta* by Prosenjit Das Gupta (Hermes Inc.) from a bookstore (see "Shopping," below).

GUIDED TOURS   The guide services of the following two men are worth booking before you arrive. **Shanti Bhattacharjee** is a retired history teacher with a profound knowledge of his city, who provides in-depth tours of Kolkata (✆ **033/2350-1576** or 98-3024-2803). He charges Rs 800 ($20/£10) per day for a group of four people (all entrance and transport costs to be paid by tourists). Architect **Manish Chakrabovti** conducts excellent **heritage walks** 😺😺 (usually on Sun) of northern Kolkata on behalf of Action Research in Conservation of Heritage (✆ **033/2337-5757** or 033/2359-6303; archeritage@yahoo.co.uk). There is also a shopping tour (see "Shop 'till You Drop: A Unique Tour of Kolkata," later in this chapter). **The Tourism Centre** (3/2 B.B.D. Bagh E.; ✆ **033/2248-8271** or -8272) conducts two different daily sightseeing tours of the city; these inevitably involve a great deal of bus travel and little sightseeing. In the same center, the **West Bengal Tourist Development Corporation** (✆ **033/2243-7260**) organizes short and long-distance tours of the state and selected destinations around the country.

FAST FACTS: Kolkata

Airlines   Jet Airways: ✆ 033/2229-2227, or -2084. **Kingfisher Airlines:** ✆ 1800-1800-101. **Air Sahara:** ✆ 033/2282-6118 or 033/2511-9545. **Indian Airlines:** ✆ 033/2511-9720.

Ambulance   **Bellevue Clinic,** 9 Loudon St. (✆ 033/2247-2321 or -6925) has a 24-hour ambulance service.

American Express   The office is located at 21 Old Court House St., near Raj Bhavan (✆ 033/2222-3001 or -3026). Open Monday to Friday 10am to 2pm and Saturday 10am to noon.

Area Code   The area code for **Kolkata** is **033.**

ATMs   There are plenty of 24-hour ATMs: **Citibank** (Kanak Building, 41 J.L. Nehru [Chowringhee] Rd.; ✆ 033/2283-2484), **UTI Bank** (7 Shakespeare Sarani; ✆ 033/2282-2933), **HDFC Bank** (Stephen House, 4 B.B.D. Bagh E.; ✆ 033/2281-3838), **Standard Chartered Grindlays Bank** (41 J.L. Nehru [Chowringhee] Rd.; ✆ 033/2242-8888), and **HSBC Bank** (8 Netaji Subhash Rd., 31 B.B.D. Bagh; ✆ 033/2243-8585).

Banks Most banks are open Monday to Friday 10am to 2 or 3pm, and Saturday 10am to noon.

Car Rentals Contact **Car-Cab** (2 Manook Lane, off Ezra St., Kolkata 1; ✆ **033/2235-3535;** vayuseva@cal.vsnl.net.in), Rs 1,500 ($37/£19) for 5 hours and maximum 50km (31 miles), Rs 19 (45¢/25p) per extra kilometer; rates include driver. **Avis Rent-A-Car** is at the Oberoi Grand (15 Jawaharlal Nehru Rd.; ✆ **033/2249-2323,** ext. 6325 or 6335).

Consulates **United States:** 5/1 Ho Chi Minh Sarani; ✆ **033/2282-3611;** Monday to Friday 8am to 1pm and 2 to 5pm. **United Kingdom:** 1A Ho Chi Minh Sarani; ✆ **033/2288-5172;** Monday to Friday 8:30am–1pm and 1:30–4pm. **Canada:** Duncan House, 31 N.S. Rd.; ✆ **033/2230-8515;** Monday to Friday 9:30am–1pm.

Currency Exchange **Thomas Cook** is at 19B Shakespeare Sarani, first floor (✆ **033/2283-0473** or -0475); hours are Monday to Saturday 9:30am to 6pm.

Drugstores Twenty-four-hour chemists include **AMRI Apollo Hospital Pharmacy** (P4 Gariahat Rd., Block A-29; ✆ **033/2461-2626,** ext. 606), **Dhanwantary** (48A/1 Diamond Harbour Rd.; ✆ **033/2449-3204**), **Jeevan Deep** (1-14B Hazra Rd.; ✆ **033/2455-0926**), and **Life Care** (1/2A Hazra Rd.; ✆ **033/2475-4628**).

Emergencies For fire brigade, dial ✆ **101** or 033/2244-0101.

Hospitals **Belle Vue Clinic** (9 U.N. Brahmachari St.; ✆ **033/2247-2321,** -6921, -6925, or -7473) also has a blood bank. There are English-speaking doctors at the 24-hour **B.M. Birla Heart Research Center** (1/1A National Library Ave.; ✆ **033/2456-7001** to -7009).

Newspapers & Magazines Peruse the pages of *The Statesman,* one of India's oldest English dailies, for information about special events. Kolkata's other very popular paper is *The Telegraph,* which has a metro section that lists local events.

Police Dial ✆ **100** or **033/2250-5000** through -5004. Police headquarters are in Lal Bazaar (✆ **033/2214-3230** or -3024).

Post Office B.B.D. Bagh; Monday to Saturday 8am to 8:30pm and Sunday 8am to 3:30pm.

ORIENTATION

Kolkata is a huge, sprawling city, divided into **north** and **south,** both spread along the eastern bank of the Hooghly River, which divides it from the vast suburb of **Howrah,** located on the western bank. Howrah is where you'll be deposited if you arrive by train; the main station is close to the Howrah Bridge, which connects with the city proper. Just east and south of Howrah Bridge are Kolkata's commercial and tourist hubs, centered around **B.B.D. Bagh,** still known by its colonial name, Dalhousie Square, and the long stretch of road once known as **Chowringhee** (now Jawaharlal Nehru Rd.) that runs southward, alongside the Maidan, Kolkata's vast urban park. Many visitors base themselves around Chowringhee; nearby Sudder Street teems with budget accommodations, while Park Street has plenty of boutiques and fine restaurants.

To the northeast is the rapidly expanding business district of **Salt Lake City,** which has few historical sites but is steadily developing a reputation for its upscale business hotels and high-tech entertainment facilities. It's the closest district to the airport.

Tips **Sorry, Wrong Number . . .**

Dial ℂ **1952** for a recorded message (in English) if the number you're dialing has been changed.

WHAT TO SEE & DO

You need at least 2 full days to cover Kolkata. Spend the first day exploring central and south Kolkata, and the second visiting sites in the north, for which you should hire a car and driver.

DAY 1 (CENTRAL & SOUTH KOLKATA)

Start by catching a taxi south to the city's most famous temple, **Kalighat Kali** (p. 556). After this, visit Mother Teresa's **Nirmal Hriday** home for the destitute and dying, right next door (see "The Miracle of Mother Teresa & the 'Pure Hearts,'" on p. 558). Or, if you're a bookworm, check out the **National Library** in the 300-year-old former summer residence of Prince Azim-us-Shan, the grandson of Emperor Aurangzeb. The library has a catalog of over 2 million books. Our recommendation is to enjoy the relaxing, tranquil atmosphere of **South Park Street Cemetery** (p. 557) before you head into the chaos of central Kolkata. If you're hungry, nearby **Suruchi** (89 Elliot Rd., near Mallik Bazaar; ℂ **033/2229-1763;** no credit cards; open Mon–Sat 10am–5:45pm, Sun 10am–2:45pm) is an authentic Bengali restaurant, with a no-frills, homegrown atmosphere.

You can save time by using a vehicle to move on to central Kolkata, or enjoy the walk along Park Street to **Chowringhee Road,** taking in the upmarket shops and boutiques and perhaps stopping at **Flury's** (ℂ **033/2229-7664;** credit cards accepted; daily 7:30am–10pm) for tea and a sandwich. Now officially known as "Jawaharlal Nehru Road," Chowringhee is Kolkata's main drag, with less human excrement along its sidewalks than almost anywhere else in the city. It is lined with colonial Victoriana—including the monumental **Indian Museum** (see below) and that pinnacle of Calcutta's society life, the **Oberoi Grand.** Continue north along Chowringhee into the heart of the city, where you can explore the roads around **B.B.D. Bagh** (see below).

When you've had your fill of life on the sidewalks, make your way south again, along Government Place East. You'll soon find yourself in the green expanse that is the **Maidan**—one of the largest city-center parks in the world—where the Ochterlony Monument, or **Shahid Minar (Martyr's Tower),** is worth noting. Walking west through the Maidan will bring you to **Eden Gardens,** India's most famous cricket stadium, while much farther south is the imperious **Victoria Memorial** (see below). Buy a ticket and venture in if you are keen to broaden your knowledge of the city's history. But don't feel guilty if you just want to lie on the lawn and watch Bengalis socializing. Otherwise, brave the traffic and catch a cab to Howrah to explore the 18th-century **Indian Botanical Gardens** (Shibpur; ℂ **033/2668-0554;** Rs 5/10¢/5p; closes 1 hr. before sunset), said to house the largest banyan tree on earth. Scientists, when they are available (usually after 11:30am), will act as guides at no charge.

TOP ATTRACTIONS

B.B.D. Bagh ✸✸✸   For those interested in colonial architecture, this part of central Kolkata makes for very worthwhile exploration on foot. Once called Dalhousie Square, B.B.D. refers to the names of three Indian freedom fighters (Benoy, Badal, and Dinesh) who shot a British police inspector-general in 1930. At the center of the square *(bagh)* is Lal Dighi Tank, where locals wade and bathe in the dodgy-looking, spring-fed water. Most impressive of the surrounding monuments is the **Writers' Building,** the office of the West Bengal government, which stretches along B.B.D. Bagh North Road; it was built to house the British bachelors imported to serve the East India Company. Across the road is the early-19th-century **St. Andrew's Kirk,** recognizable by its tall white steeple. At the other end of B.B.D. Bagh North is the **General Post Office,** with a monumental rotunda; it's thought to be the site of the notorious Black Hole of Calcutta incident (see the appendix). Southwest of the tank is the St. Martin-in-the-Fields–inspired **St. John's Church** (© **033/2243-6098;** Rs 10/25¢/15p; daily 9am–6pm) and, within the grounds, the tomb of Calcutta's founding father, Job Charnock. East of B.B.D. Bagh, to the south of Lal Bazaar, you'll find numerous tea merchants, where teas from Darjeeling, the Dooars, and Assam are packed and exported. **Nilhat House,** located behind the Old Mission Church, is the oldest tea auction house in India—join the action on Monday and Tuesday mornings.

Central Kolkata, south of Howrah Bridge, and north of Jawaharlal Nehru Rd.

Indian Museum 🌸🌸🌸 Containing things beautiful, unusual, and ancient, the museum is known to locals as *Jadu Ghar,* the House of Magic. The oldest institution of its kind in the Asia–Pacific region, it holds the country's largest repository of artifacts (over 100,000 exhibits). Among the dinosaur and mammoth skeletons and the 4,000-year-old Egyptian mummy are extraordinary Indian cultural items, including Shah Jahan's emerald goblet, and an urn said to contain the Buddha's ashes. Don't miss the cultural anthropology section—accompanied by good explanations—if you are interested in India's many tribal groups. The textiles-and-decorative-arts gallery is most impressive. It can be difficult to find, however—ask for assistance.

27 Jawaharlal Nehru Rd., at the corner of Sudder St. © 033/2286-1699. Rs 150 ($3.65/£1.85). Tues–Sun 10am–4pm.

Kalighat Kali Temple 🌸🌸 Violent, vengeful Kali is the patron goddess of Kolkata, and this temple complex—believed to be the site where the toe of Shiva's wife fell when her body was scattered across the earth by the gods anxious to stop Lord Shiva's dance of destruction (see "The Dance of Destruction," p. 548)—is a major pilgrimage center, drawing some 20,000 visitors each day. If you're a non-Hindu, you cannot enter the inner sanctum, sticky with the rotted remains of fresh flowers offered by devotees every day, but it's worth your while to explore the courtyards and the various stalls selling flowers, fruit, and religious paraphernalia. If you're uneasy about the idea of animal sacrifice, avoid the enclosure to the south of the temple where at least one goat is offered to Kali every day (a ritual that allegedly replaced the ancient practice of human sacrifice). Be equally wary of the so-called priests—temple "guides" who usher you into

---

The Tollywood Oscar Achiever

Kolkata has its own film industry, known throughout the Bengali world as Tollywood. In fact, it was this city that gave birth to India's finest filmmaker, **Satyajit Ray,** who died in 1992—the same year he received a Lifetime Achievement Oscar. While Bollywood was churning out dazzling choreographic daydreams, Ray made classic films that filled art-house cinemas around the world. For more on Ray, go to the appendix.

Tigers in the Sundarbans: India's Best-Kept Secret

One of the most enigmatic national parks in India, the **Sundarbans** is the largest delta in the world, with saline mud flats and thick mangrove forests teeming with wildlife, of which the Royal Bengal tiger is the most exotic inhabitant. Spanning around 4,264 sq. km (1,663 sq. miles) in India and an even larger area in neighboring Bangladesh, and surrounded by the Ganga, Brahmaputra, and Meghna rivers, it was declared a World Heritage Site by UNESCO in 1987 but remains one of the least developed parks in Asia, as access is only via water. Although there are affordable government ferries (West Bengal Tourism Development Corporation; © 033/2248-7302) offering overnight trips, it is a bit of a slog just to get to the ferry itself, as it involves several switches between cabs and smaller boats, and accommodation is below par. But the elusive nature of the Sundarbans is set to change with **Vivada Inland Waterways** (© 98-3002-9359, or 99-0300-0268; www.vivada.com; sunderbancruises@ vivada.com), which now offers comfortable accommodation in boats, as well as relatively easy access; packages vary, but be prepared to shell out in the region of $245 to $295 (£124–£149) for a 4-day luxury cruise. If you're lucky, you'll spot a tiger lapping at the water's edge, but even if his or her royal highness deign not to make an appearance during your stay, the mangrove forests are alive with fabulous birdlife, and you will get to visit a few far-flung villages where life continues as it has for centuries.

the complex and conduct a whirlwind tour of the facilities, only to present you with a donation book that records the radically generous donations of other foreigners.

Kalighat Rd., Kalighat. Free admission. Daily 5am–1:30pm and 3–10pm (Tues, Sat, Sun, and festival days are terribly crowded with mile-long lines of devotees; Wed and Thurs are least congested).

South Park Street Cemetery ⊕⊕   This is Kolkata's most famous cemetery, where monumental gravestones and lichen- and moss-covered tombstones to large numbers of ill-fated Brits buried on Indian soil provide a tranquil retreat. A really atmospheric place to wander around, the cemetery contains headstones that bear unlikely epitaphs like MAJ. GEN. C. GREEN DIED 51TH OF JULY.

Park St. and southeast end of Cemetery Rd. Free admission. Daily 7:30am–4:30pm.

Victoria Memorial ⊕   Conceived of by Lord Curzon as a monument to his queen 4 years after her death, this domed structure is Kolkata's most recognizable landmark. It's billed as one of the city's top attractions, but with portraits of fairly boring-looking individuals filling many of the walls, it's more likely to excite Rajophiles. There are 25 galleries in the central hall, and about 3,500 articles relating to the Raj on display, including the queen's rosewood piano. Exhibits are not restricted to Raj-artifacts; the black marble throne that belonged to Siraj-ud-Daulah is impressive, as is a gigantic painting of a Jaipur royal procession, said to be one of the largest paintings in Asia.

Queen's Way. © 033/2223-1889, -1890, or -1891. www.victoriamemorial-cal.org. Rs 150 ($3.75/£1.90). Tues–Sun 10am–4:30pm. Sound-and-light show: Winter Tues–Sun 7:15pm (in English); Summer 7:45pm (in English); Rs 20 (50¢/25p).

DAY 2 (NORTH KOLKATA)

Early in the morning, head toward **Howrah Bridge,** where you can witness people bathing at the *ghats* (steps leading down to the Hooghly River) or the pandemonium

The Miracle of Mother Teresa & the "Pure Hearts"

Mother Teresa's **Missionaries of Charity (MOC)** is now headed by Sister Nirmala, a converted Brahmin. There are some 3,500 MOC sisters around the world, working in 569 centers in 120 countries, but their selfless efforts are not without controversy. Even during Mother Teresa's time, tales of pecuniary troubles and controversies over the way in which the poor and dying were being treated (and converted) beleaguered the MOC. There have always been plenty of cynics, despite the Vatican's confirmation of Mother Teresa's "miraculous" healing of a young woman's malignant tumor (the woman claims to have been cured after seeing Mother Teresa in her dreams), a move that has irritated rationalists and the medical profession. Still, in Kolkata alone, more than 50,000 destitute sick and dying are looked after by the blue-and-white-sari-wearing nuns of the MOC, a demonstration of selflessness that you might deem miraculous in itself. Adjacent to the Kali Temple is "Pure Heart," or **Nirmal Hriday** (251 Kalighat Rd.; ✆ 033/2464-4223; Fri–Wed 8–11:30am and 3–5:30pm), the very first MOC center. **Mother House** (54 A.J.C. Bose Rd.; ✆ 033/2249-7115; same hours as Nirmal Hriday) is the MOC headquarters, where Mother Teresa is buried. Nearby is **Nirmal Shishu Bhawan** (78 A.J.C. Bose Rd.; same hours as Nirmal Hriday), where some 250 orphans are cared for.

at the colorful **flower market** (you need to arrive before 7am). There you can sip *chai* and watch the stall holders deftly thread marigold garlands for the gods and bridal headgear from tuberoses and dahlias. Crossing over Howrah Bridge, head toward the **Belur Math Shrine** (see below). From here you can either incorporate a short stop at popular **Dakshineshwar Temple** (across Vivekananda Bridge; ✆ 033/2564-5222; daily 6:45am–12:30pm and 3:30–8:30pm), or take a look at the potters' village at **Kumartuli** (N. Chitpur Rd.), a warren of alleys where clay deities and images of Mother Teresa are produced by the thousands. If you prefer to slow the pace, however, skip these and head south to beautiful **Paresnath Temple** (see below)—not as famous as the Kali temple, but certainly Kolkata's prettiest, and north Kolkata's star attraction. From here, you can head east to shop and eat at **Swabhumi Heritage Plaza,** a mall with 2.4 hectares (6 acres) of shopping, dining, and entertainment diversions; or head south to **Rabindra Bharati University Museum** (✆ 033/2269-5241; Rs 50/$1.20/60p; Tues–Sun 10:30am–4:30pm; no photography) to visit the **Rabindranath Tagore House Museum.** Born to a wealthy entrepreneurial family in 1861, Tagore remains Bengal's best-loved artist and intellectual, and his home is filled with artworks and collectibles (closed Sun, and open only until 1:30pm on Sat). Move on to the nearby **Marble Palace** (see below).

By now, you may be in serious need of sustenance, which you'll find in the vicinity of the enormous **Nakhoda,** Calcutta's largest mosque (Rabindra Sarani and M.G. Rd.). The mosque is closed to non-Muslims during prayers, but is set within a busy bazaar area where Muslim tradespeople sell all sorts of goods, as well as a range of breads, sweetmeats, and snacks. Alternatively, enjoy a cheap, substantial Kolkata-Mughlai meal at the century-old **Royal Indian Hotel** (147 Rabindra Sarani; ℂ **033/2268-1073;** daily 9am–11:30pm). Browse through the thousands of bookstalls along **College Street,** and finish with coffee at the **Indian Coffee House** (see below).

TOP ATTRACTIONS

Belur Math Shrine ⭐⭐ The headquarters of the international Ramakrishna Order, Belur Math combines the architectural elements of a church, a mosque, and a temple, symbolically embodying the teachings of the monk and seer Sri Ramakrishna Paramahansa. It was established in 1897, and the ashes of Sri Ramakrishna were placed here by his most prominent disciple, Swami Vivekananda, who also set up the Order. The location is lovely: Smaller shrines line the riverbank, and devotees and seekers of spiritual peace roam the grounds. Within the immaculate main shrine, activity is enlivened by evening *aarti* (musical prayers).

Belur Rd., Howrah. ℂ **033/2654-5700.** Daily 6:30–11:30am and 3:30–6pm; prayer *(aarti)* time: 5:30pm.

College Street ⭐⭐ This stretch of road, deep in the heart of the university quarter, is famous for its 5,000 or so secondhand bookstalls, and for the renowned Presidency College, where India's greatest filmmaker, Satyajit Ray, studied. Many of the booksellers here are semi-literate, but remarkably, each is able to recall the titles and prices of thousands of academic and technical books, the volumes typically piled meters high. Look for the bust commemorating the father of Bengali prose literature, the reformer and philanthropist Pandit Iswar Chandra Vidyasagar, who also introduced a ban on forced marriages.

Bidhan Sarani, N. Kolkata.

Marble Palace ⭐⭐ Up a back street, in what was once known as Black Town, stands a vast mansion—a wonder to behold—sporting a plush Romanesque veneer that incorporates at least 90 different varieties of marble. Built in 1835 by the wealthy *zamindar* (landowner) Raja Rajendra Mullick Bahadur, this palatial family home has

---

Moments Meeting Bengalis

The **Indian Coffee House** (15 Bankin Chatterjee St., first floor; ℂ **033/2241-4869;** Mon–Sat 9am–9pm, Sun 9am–12:30pm and 5–9pm), where the Young Bengal Movement started, is the quintessential College Street haunt. This is where M. N. Roy, founder of the Communist Party of India (as well as the Mexican Communist Party), Satyajit Ray, Nobel Laureate Dr. Amartya Sen, and a host of other famous personalities discussed the future of India over platefuls of fish fingers and coffee. A lone photograph of Rabindranath Tagore looks across a vast former 1930s dance hall with sagging ceiling fans and scattered tables around which men, young and old, demonstratively argue the issues of the day. Surly waiters plod around rather aimlessly, so be patient while waiting for your greasy *pakora* and a strong Coorg. Meals are not the reason to come, but it's a good place to strike up a conversation over a cup of coffee. For an even more animated and authentic interaction with locals, head for the **Calcutta races** (www.rctconline.com); ask any waiter or at your hotel about the next event. All walks of life are to be seen here, many in their finest glad rags. As everyone celebrates the chance to escape their dharma, the atmosphere is electric.

Moments **Durga Puja—Not Just Another Festival**

Indians celebrate all year long throughout the country, but the grande dame of festivals is the **Durga Puja** ★★ (signifying the return of the goddess to her parents' home), the most sacred festival for the Bengalis. Though it is celebrated with much pomp all over northeastern India, Kolkata does it best, and if you're traveling here in September or October you simply have to include Kolkata in your itinerary. Literally every family is involved, not just in their own celebrations, but also as participants of the collective neighborhood presentation of Goddess Durga. *Pandals,* a kind of marquee used to shelter the idol, abound in the city, and have over the last decade become a commercial enterprise, with lucrative cash prizes for the most impressive—this has led to some highly innovative designs, where the raw materials include everything from bamboo and cloth to futuristic hi-tech gizmos. The mode of transport for Durga is declared by the pundits just before the festival commences, and for many orthodox Bengalis, it is a sign of what awaits them in the coming year—for instance, an elephant could mean prosperity, while a boat may signify natural disasters. The festivities last for 4 days, with dances and frenzied drumming, lots of food, and endless bouts of shopping—it is mayhem on a grand scale and well worth experiencing. On the last day, idols (ranging from 1 inch to grandiose figures of over 9m/30 ft.) are immersed in the Hoogly, which carries many a prayer into deeper realms.

seen better days, and is now the center of a bitter feud between relatives, some of whom have been accused of sneaking off with the more valuable displays. But several works attributed to Titian and Renoir remain, while Venetian chandeliers; Ming vases; Egyptian statuary; and paintings, sculptures, furniture, and antique vases accumulated from 90 countries crowd the enormous, dimly lit rooms that open off deep verandas around an inner courtyard. Get there soon, since the feuding of the Mullicks makes it uncertain which prized item might next disappear. Admission is free, but you need a pass from the India Tourism Kolkata Office; if you arrive without one, the guard will let you in for a small fee (although this simply adds to the culture of corruption in India). A guide (at times, a young boy trying to make pocket money) is sent with you but it's pretty much a sham—insist on someone knowledgeable. In the same compound, you'll find a small garden and an animal enclosure.

46 Muktaram Basu St., off Chittaranjan Ave. © 033/2269-3310. Free admission but you need a pass from the India Tourism Kolkata Office. Tues–Wed and Fri–Sun 10am–4pm.

Paresnath Temple ★★★   Jain temples are generally the most beautifully adorned in India, and Paresnath, dedicated to Sithalnath—one of the 24 perfect souls *(tirthankaras)* of the Jain religion—is no exception. Built in 1867 by a jeweler whose love of intricate designs, mirrors, and colored glass is evident everywhere, it boasts lavishly adorned patterned marble, beautiful European chandeliers, and stained-glass windows. A quiet garden is dotted with silver statues, and the temple houses an eternal flame that's apparently never gone out.

Badridas Temple St. Free admission. Daily 6am–noon and 3–7pm.

WHERE TO STAY

Decent budget rooms are all but nonexistent in Kolkata, and quality mid-range accommodations are also hard to find. For rooms under $70 (£35) you have two good options, both downtown in the busy Chowringhee area. **Fairlawn Hotel** is a famous option (see below) but **Middleton Inn,** a neat 21-room business hotel at 10 Middleton St. (✆ **033/2216-0449** through -0452) may suit you more. The Inn's dull entrance belies the scrupulously clean deluxe air-conditioned doubles that go for just Rs 2,500 ($61/£31), including breakfast. Service in general is crisp and courteous, and though there's no restaurant, they have 24-hour room service. If neither of these options is available, we highly recommend that you revise your budget to stay at one of the higher-end properties below.

Fairlawn Hotel ⟨ⁱ⟩ ⟨Value⟩ Hollywood's production of *City of Joy* made use of this small, popular heritage hotel and its neoclassical facade for several days of shooting, and in its heyday it played host to British playwright Tom Stoppard, actress Felicity Kendal, and the musician Sting. Established by Armenian refugees who escaped Eastern Europe in 1917, the hotel is a little run-down, but it's still the most characterful place to stay: a real family enterprise run by the enthusiastic 84-year-old Mrs. Violet Smith. News clippings, hotel awards, and copious family and celebrity photographs cover the walls, while old wicker chairs, vases, decorative plates, and even Buddhas and Ganeshas are used to create a homey atmosphere. Guest rooms (book nos. 16–21) are cozy, if simply furnished. In the kitchen, a wood- and coal-fire stove is used to prepare wholesome home-style meals from a menu that changes daily, but meal times are strict. The pleasant garden terrace has abundant greenery and is host to Rajophiles and beer-swilling travelers. Service standards have lagged significantly of late, and the heritage property is also starting to show wear and tear, so don't overnight here if you prefer bland but pristine accommodations (such as the Middleton Inn; see above), but do pop in for a drink.

13/A Sudder S., Kolkata 700 016. ✆ **033/2252-1510** or -8767. Fax 033/2252-1835. www.fairlawnhotel.com. 18 units. $65 (£33) double with all meals; $60 (£30) double with breakfast. 20% discount Apr–Sept. AE, MC, V. **Amenities:** Restaurant; bar; travel assistance; limited room service; laundry; small library. *In room:* A/C, TV, tea-making facility. 1st-floor rooms have fridges.

Hyatt Regency ⟨ⁱ⟩⟨ⁱ⟩ ⟨Value⟩ If it's a design-conscious luxury hotel near the airport you're after, book yourself into the Hyatt, right next door to Swabhumi Heritage Park in the rapidly expanding business district of Salt Lake City, a good 45 minutes away from the tourist hub. Stylish rooms (32 of which are nonsmoking) have warm teakwood floors, sunken baths, panoramic floor-to-ceiling windows, and walk-in closets. The large pool is backed by tall trees, while inside, a trendy cigar lounge appears suspended in mid-air. It's a schlep getting into the city from here, but if you're more or less in transit, with just a day to spare in Kolkata, this is a very good option, particularly if the rate drops to $150 (£76) double, which it does at certain times—check the website for the latest "Rate of the Day" tariff.

JA-1, Sector III, Salt Lake City, Kolkata 700 098. ✆ **033/2335-1234.** Fax 033/2335-1235. www.kolkata.regency. hyatt.com. Toll-free reservations from within India: ✆ 1-800/228-001. 235 units. There is no fixed tariff with the Hyatt working on a "Rate of the Day" system fluctuating between $150–$400 (£76–£202) double, depending on the month; check the website or call reservations. AE, DC, MC, V. **Amenities:** 3 restaurants; bar; pool bar; pool; tennis; fitness center and spa; concierge; business center; salon; 24-hr. room service; babysitting; laundry and valet service; doctor-on-call; Wi-Fi; squash; bakery; flower shop. *In room:* A/C, TV, dataport, tea- and coffee-making facilities, hair dryer, voice mail.

ITC Sonar Bangla Sheraton Hotel and Towers &&&   If you want to stay far from the congested heart of Kolkata, like large open spaces, and want the pampering of a good spa, the Sonar Bangla offers just that, and the Executive Club rooms offer good value. (If, however, you want the added benefits of having the sights on your doorstep and prefer not to deal with endless taxi rip-offs, Oberoi Grand and The Park are better options.) Priding itself as a "business resort hotel," the ITC looks from the outside like the quintessential grotesque concrete structure rising from open marshland; once inside, you'll find a soporific escape from the intense reality of Kolkata. Courtyards and lily ponds separate accommodations blocks, each with its own lounge area and exclusive facilities. While some rooms in the Sheraton Tower overlook the pretty lily ponds, the rooms to ask for are the ITC One rooms that overlook the Sundarbans (littoral forests in the Ganges delta). Every room in the latter category (and above) also has a plush black leather massage lounger. The hotel's huge pool and spa are welcome respites after a day trudging Kolkata's streets. Schedule a meal at **Dum Pukht** or **Peshawari** to get a taste of Lucknowi or North West Frontier cuisine, respectively.

1 JBS Halden Ave., opposite Science City (Eastern Metropolitan Bypass), Kolkata 700 046. ℭ **033/2345-4545.** Fax 033/2345-4555. www.starwoodhotels.com. 239 units. $275 (£139) Executive Club double; $350 (£177) Sheraton Towers double; $400 (£203) ITC One double; $500 (£253) junior suite; $800 (£405) queen suite; $1,000 (£506) presidential suite. Rates include breakfast. Some rates include airport transfers and other privileges. Taxes extra. Check online for specials for stays of 2 nights or more. AE, DC, MC, V. **Amenities:** 5 restaurants; bar; lounges; nightclub; pool; chip and putt golf course; tennis courts; health club; spa; travel desk; business services; salon; 24-hr. room service; babysitting; laundry; dry cleaning; Wi-Fi enabled; pastry shop; jogging track. *In room:* TV, dataport, minibar, tea-and coffee-making facilities, safe, weighing scale.

Oberoi Grand &&&   This quintessential Kolkata monument is the city's top accommodations and one of the best hotels in India. Elegant, with regal old-world charm, its guest rooms draw ambassadors, diplomats, heads of state, and royalty (although the Hollywood party crowd heads for The Park). Deluxe suites, elegant and never too opulent, come with balconies, wooden floors, and Victorian furniture. Premier guest rooms (city or garden view) are marvelous; if you want a private balcony, book a room on the third floor. In the central courtyard, amid palms and gnarled frangipani trees, you can sip gin and tonics around the best pool in town. Or opt for the smoky ambience of the **Chowringhee bar** with its pool table and ancient models of binoculars and cameras hanging on the walls. Despite being cheek-by-jowl with one of the most chaotic streets, not a honk can be heard, courtesy of the old thick stone walls. The **Spa,** operating under the banner of famous Banyan Tree, is exclusively for guests and reason enough to stay here. And for inspiration about what to do when you run out of sights and restaurants, speak to the head concierge, Amitava Sarkar, whose knowledge and enthusiasm will deepen your appreciation of the city.

15 Jawaharlal Nehru Rd., Kolkata 700 013. ℭ **033/2249-2323.** Fax 033/2249-1217. www.oberoihotels.com. 213 units. Doubles: $400 (£203) classic rooms; $450 (£228) deluxe rooms; $550 (£278) premier rooms; $750–$1,500 (£354–£759) suites; rates exclusive of meals and taxes. Premier room and suite rates include breakfast and airport transfers. Check website for online discounts. AE, DC, MC, V. **Amenities:** 2 restaurants; bar; pool; health club and spa; shopping arcade; 24-hr. room service; babysitting; laundry; dry cleaning; doctor-on-call. *In room:* A/C, TV, minibar, tea-and coffee-making facilities, hair dryer, Wi-Fi enabled, DVD player. Fax machines in deluxe rooms.

The Park &&&   Space is something of a premium in Calcutta, and a stylish overhaul has transformed this tiny sliver of Park Street into a model of urban chic, the abode of choice for the likes of Penelope Cruz and Melanie Griffith. A five-star property, this boutique hotel is in the best downtown location, with proximity to both the business and entertainment hubs of the city. But the real reason many choose to stay here is the on-tap party: Like so many Park properties, this hotel has four top "after dark" destinations under one roof—a pub, a nightclub, a cocktail bar, and a poolside alfresco bar lounge (see "Kolkata After Dark," below), providing easy access to the city's hippest, most happening nightlife. Guest rooms are small, but they're neat, functional, and bright, with bold color combinations. If you're in town for a while, book a Residence Room and you get a private lounge, a slightly larger bedroom with walk-in dressing room, stylish furniture, a thick mattress on a queen-size bed, a floor butler, and a Jacuzzi in the bathroom.

17 Park St., Kolkata 700 016. ☏ 033/2249-3121, or -9000. Fax 033/2249-7343 or -4000. www.theparkhotels.com. 174 units. $350 (£177) deluxe double; $400 (£203) luxury double; $450 (£228) The Residence suite double; $500 (£253) Presidential suite. $25 (£13) extra bed. AE, DC, MC, V. **Amenities:** 4 restaurants; pub; disco; pool; golf on request; health club/fitness center; travel desk; 24-hr. butler service; doctor-on-call; 24-hr. currency exchange; Wi-Fi enabled. *In room:* A/C, TV, dataport, minibar, hair dryer, DVD, Jacuzzi.

Taj Bengal ⭐⭐ This smart hotel, popular with businesspeople and politicos like Hillary Clinton, is a good choice if you want to stay south of the city, enjoy views of the Maidan, and dine in-house—Taj Bengal boasts some of Kolkata's most impressive restaurants, under the aegis of the highly experienced chef Sujan Mukherjee. Besides **Sonargaon** and **The Hub,** it houses one of India's best Chinese restaurants, **Chinoiserie** (all reviewed below). Quieter rooms face the pool, or you can ask for a room with a view of the Victoria Memorial. All rooms have tasteful decor, and color schemes change from room to room; guest rooms on the third and fourth floors feature dark teakwood parquet floors, rugs, shimmering olive curtains, and paintings depicting Calcuttan city scenes; bar a few exceptions the bathrooms are a bit on the small side. Club Rooms (top floor) have added space (thanks to a window alcove), personal butler service, and access to posh lounges and exclusive restaurants (with strict dress codes) where the city's elite plot and play. The "gentlemen's club" ambience in the residents' lounge goes down well with a game of pool, a book from the small library, or time at the Internet bar. In the evenings, you can sit in the atrium at **By The Way** amidst palms and enjoy live instrumental music with a vast assortment of teas and coffees from across the world.

34B Belvedere Rd., Alipore, Kolkata 700 027. ☏ 033/2223-3939. Fax 033/2223-1766 or -8805. www.tajhotels.com. calcutta@tajhotels.com. 229 units. $300 (£152) superior double; $320 (£162) deluxe double; $350 (£177) luxury double; $395 (£200) Taj Club; $500 (£253) executive suite; $600 (£304) luxury suite; $1,200 (£607) presidential suite; $25 (£13) extra bed. Rates include breakfast. Rates up to 50% lower Apr–Sept. AE, DC, MC, V. **Amenities:** 3 restaurants; bar; tea lounge; patisserie; pool; health club; concierge; travel desk and car hire; salon; 24-hr. room service; laundry; currency exchange; in-house doctor; high-speed Internet access. *In room:* A/C, TV, minibar, tea- and coffee-making facilities, hair dryer, electronic safe, Wi-Fi enabled.

WHERE TO DINE

Bengalis are known for their fine palates and love of dining out, and a wide range of cuisines are theirs to choose from. Make sure to sample **Kolkata-Mughlai food**—blending the best of the Bengali *Nawabs'* cuisine with influences from the Deccan, Awadh, and North India—at least once. **Nizam's,** which has been given a makeover recently (1 Corporation Place, just behind the Oberoi Grand), claims to be the place where the *kathi* kebab roll (kebabs wrapped in a *paratha*—fried bread) was invented. The food is legendary, and the prices unbeatable. Another popular Bengali-Muslim joint is **Shiraz** (56 Park St., at the intersection of Park St. and A.J.C. Bose Rd.; ☏ **033/2287-7702** or 033/2280-5006). Go to the first floor for air-conditioned comfort, or up to the rooftop. The extensive menu includes numerous exotic-sounding Kolkata-Mughlai items, as well as a range of kebabs.

If you're in the vicinity of Nakhoda Mosque, try the **Royal Indian Hotel** (147 Rabindra Sarani; ℂ **033/2268-1073**), which opened in 1905 and is the oldest restaurant of its kind. On Thursday or Sunday, you can order *murgh mussalam* (chicken); mutton *chanps tikiya* (chops) is another specialty (available on all days except Thurs).

Chinese cuisine is popular with Kolkatans—**Mainland China** 𝕳 (Uniworth House, 3A Gurusadary Rd.; ℂ **033/2283-7964** through -7969) is one of the most popular, but serves typical Indian-Chinese: a tomato base, and heavy emphasis on chilies. Good choices include Peking-style lamb cooked in black pepper sauce, Hunan-style prawns, and Szechuan chili crab.

Park Street, one of the city's busiest hubs, is lined cheek-by-jowl with restaurants and stalls serving all kinds of interesting food. **Peter Cat** (18A Park St.; ℂ **033/2229-8841** or 033/2217-2942), set in a pleasant colonial bungalow, serves an outstanding *chelo kebab* platter (Rs 142/$3.45/£1.75), skewered meat kebabs on a bed of flavored rice. This is a popular after-work watering hole, though service is often shoddy. Avoid it at lunchtime on weekdays when it's packed with local office-goers. Also on Park Street is **Mocambo** (25B Park St.; ℂ **033/2246-4300,** 033/2229-0095, or 033/2217-5372), which serves decent Western fare (try the tasty deviled crabs—Rs 138/$3.35/£1.70) and sizzlers (steak or kebab and vegetable platters). Close by is the **Blue Potato** (reviewed below), which is fast gaining popularity as one of the few stand-alone fine-dining venues in Kolkata.

For Bengali cuisine, try **O Calcutta** (10/3 Elgin Rd., fourth floor, Forum Mall; ℂ **033/2283-7162**) and ask for specials like *dab chingri* (prawns in coconut gravy) or *kanka chingri bapa* (crabmeat and minced prawn cooked with mustard sauce, wrapped in banana leaf, and steamed). But if you don't mind sitting in cramped surroundings, **Bhojohari Manna** (ℂ **033/2440-1933**) is where you get the most authentic Bengali fare at dirt-cheap prices. There are four branches; best to give a call and ask which one is closest to you.

Anyone with a sweet tooth is headed for heaven: *Mishti doi* (yogurt with caramelized sugar) is a must-try, as are Bengali staples like *sandesh* (cottage cheese with jaggery), *chanar payesh* (cottage cheese or milk with nuts and raisins), *ledikeni* (said to be named after Lady Canning who was a great admirer of this sweet!), *rossogolla* (spongy balls of cottage cheese dipped in sugar syrup), and *khir kadom,* more delicately sweetened than the *gulab jamuns* (sweet milk-and-dough balls) and *halwas* (semolina desserts) of the north, and available all over the city. Shop where sweet gourmands do, at the most popular **K.C. Das** (11A Planet East, Dharamtala; ℂ **033/2248-5920**). You could also try **Ganguram** (11 C.R. Ave.; ℂ **033/2236-5502**), **Gokul** (1 A.J.C. Bose Rd.), **Mithai** (48B Syed Amir Ali Ave.), and **Bhim Nag** (Bidhan Sarani).

Baan Thai 𝕳𝕳𝕳 THAI   South Asian and Thai cuisine have become increasingly popular in India over the last few years, but there are still too few restaurants that manage to stay true to the tastes and flavors of Thailand without "Indianizing" it. Oberoi's Baan Thai is one of those rare places where you are assured of real authenticity, with chefs Thida and Prayong earning the *Times Food Guide* award for Best Thai Restaurant for 3 consecutive years. We recommend you start with *kai rue koong hor bai toey* (marinated chicken or prawn morsels wrapped in pandana leaf, deep fried, and served with soy sesame dip) or the *som tam esan* (tangy salad of young papaya, peanut, and tomato dressed with lemon juice and palm). Follow this with the spicy

Moments Fast Food, Kolkata Style

At almost any time of the day you'll see expectant customers standing outside the various *kathi* roll booths all over the city. They're waiting for one of Kolkata's favorite lunchtime snacks, a *paratha* (thick *chapati*, or fried bread) filled with spiced chicken, mutton, egg, potato, or *paneer* (Indian cheese) topped off with *chaat* masala, onion, and lemon juice—simply delicious. The hygiene at many of these places is often suspect, so look for a stall with lots of customers. (Try **Kusum** at 21 Park St., the one outside Oxford Book Store; or another stall next to Peter Cat.) Order the double-side egg mutton roll and avoid the accompanying green chutney. *Puchkas* (deep-fried hollow balls made of wheat, filled with mashed and spiced potato along with tangy mint), omelet bread (where the bread is cooked inside the egg!), and *jhalmuri* (a mix of a dozen snack items, served dry or with onions, tomatoes, and spicy chutneys), are also favorites with the local people and a must-have if you really want a taste of Kolkatan life.

---

tom yam soup flavored with lemon grass and kafir lime leaf. For the main course try *phad thai* (traditional flat rice noodles with tamarind and crushed peanut) accompanied by *kaeng kiew wan* (spicy green curry), *pla kapong/phet samros* (deep-fried *bekti* (fish)/duck in spicy sweet and sour sauce), *patani* (stir-fried lamb with ginger), or *kai takrai* (traditional stir-fried chicken). Don't forget to order a most refreshing Chendol Ice, a mix of pineapple juice and coconut milk. The ambience is nicer in the evening, but if it's purely the cuisine you're after, any time is a good time.

The Oberoi Grand, 15 Jawaharlal Nehru Rd., Kolkata. © **033/2249-2323**. Fax 033/2249-1217. www.oberoihotels.com. Average meal for 2 Rs 2,000 ($49/£25). AE, DC, MC, V. Daily 12:30–2:30pm and 7:30–11:30pm.

Blue Potato ✿✿ MULTI-CUISINE/WESTERN   In a city where fine dining is dominated by five-star hotel restaurants, the stand-alone chef-owned Blue Potato is a welcome relief, particularly for those stomachs not yet sensitized to spicy Indian cooking. Chef Shaun Kenworthy, who originally hails from the U.K., has been in India for the last 7 years, working in various parts of the country. In the short time since he opened this place in December 2006 near the popular Park Street area, it has become increasingly popular (and it can't hurt having a catchy name like the Blue Potato). Sensibly, he stuck with what he knows best, producing a menu that is predominantly Western. You could start with the bacon-wrapped chicken, then follow it with pan-fried sea bass or the New Zealand lamb chops, and end off with an old-fashioned trifle (though we'd opt for the mascarpone tart with port-soaked figs). The real challenge for Shaun lies in creating a stand-alone restaurant in a city that associates this kind of cuisine with in-house hotel restaurants—and for a single owner to deal with such constraints as high excise duties. But looking at the waves Shaun has made since he opened, this may be the start of a slow revolution.

27 Shakespeare Sarani; Circus Ave., Kolkata. © **033/3259-7833**. Main courses Rs 380–Rs 575 ($9.25–$12/£4.70–£6.05). AE, MC, V. Tues–Sun 11:30am–3pm and 7:30–11pm.

Chinoiserie ✿✿✿ CHINESE   The finest Chinese restaurant in Kolkata dishes out delicious Szechuan and Cantonese cuisine. Centered around a beautiful raindrop chandelier, with private corners for business lunches and romantic dinners, cloth paintings done by an artist from Shantiniketan, photographs of ancient Chinese arti-facts, and, bizarrely, a blues and soul soundtrack—Chinoiserie breaks all stereotypes. If the menu proves bewildering, turn to chef Lian for guidance, but be warned: He is passionate about almost everything! Our recommendation would be to start with crispy duck with pancakes and sweet bean sauce or the delicious banana fish roll. Amazingly light golden-fried prawns are accompanied by Lian's special green sauce. For the main course try stir-fried chicken with pickled chilies, braised Chinese cab-bage with ginger, and fish with oyster sauce. End with white fungus (which, contrary to its name, is delicious) or tofu with coconut—and wash the whole meal down with cups of Chinese tea. Unlike in most other Chinese restaurants, the emphasis here is on flavor, which comes across in everything you eat.

Taj Bengal, 34B Belvedere Rd., Alipore. (𝒞 **033/2223-3939**. Average meal for 2 Rs 2,000 ($49/£25). AE, DC, MC, V. Daily 12:30–2:45pm and 7:30pm–11:45pm.

Fire and Ice 𝒜 ITALIAN   When Annamaria started out selling tomato sauce to hotels it probably never crossed her mind that a decade later she would be serving her brand of simple, authentic Italian in two restaurants (in India and Nepal). Fire and Ice is excellent value for money and the spacious restaurant an unpretentious haven, with exposed brick walls, photographs of Hollywood and Bollywood classics, and an open kitchen where you can see Annamaria puttering around, making sure the pizzas are just right. If she's too busy, ask her son Stephen to suggest what to dive into. The *antipasta misto* and penne pesto are highly recommended, as is the Fire of Bengal pizza. Make sure you save space for the delicious homemade apple pie served with imported vanilla ice cream. The evenings are great here, but it's also a lovely place to hang out during the day over a cup of excellent coffee or iced tea.

Kanak Building, 41, J.L. Nehru Rd., opposite Jeevan Deep Building. (𝒞 **033/2288-4073**. www.fireandicepizzeria.com. Meal for 2 Rs 500 ($12/£6.15). AE, DC, MC, V. Daily 11am–midnight.

The Hub 𝒜𝒜 ECLECTIC   Alex Bignotti, the Italian chef at this bright restaurant overlooking the Taj pool, likes to experiment. Not only was he the first international chef to come to the city, but this is also Kolkata's first interactive kitchen: A highlight is the "food theater" experience, during which guests can watch a five-course meal being prepared, and then dig into the results. Start with the intriguing souplike con-coction called *porcini cappucino* (porcini mushrooms, white wine, pepper, cream, and butter), followed by the pan-fried *bhetki* (fish) with grilled vegetables, white wine, and garlic bisque sauce; leave enough space to end with the scrumptious mud pie with banana caramel ice cream.

Taj Bengal, 34B Belvedere Rd., Alipore. (𝒞 **033/2223-3939**. Main courses Rs 450–Rs 1,500 ($11–$37/£5.55–£19); buffet Rs 800 ($20/£10). Food theater Rs 425–Rs 850 ($10–$21/£5.25–£11). AE, DC, MC, V. Open 24 hr.

Kewpie's BENGALI   Popular with local celebrities and bigwig visitors to the city, this tiny family kitchen has been well marketed but is not necessarily the most authen-tic (for that you're better off visiting **Suruchi,** ideally combined with a visit to South Park Cemetery). The menu changes daily, but the highlight is Kewpie's thali (multi-course platter)—various fish, vegetable, and meat items (or strictly vegetarian items), served with different breads.

2 Elgin Lane, off Heysham Rd., behind Netaji Bhavan. (𝒞 **033/2475-9880** or 033/2476-9929. Minimum charge (thali) Rs 200 ($5/£2.45) per person. MC, V. Tues–Sun 12:30–3pm and 7:30–11pm.

Saffron ⟨★★★ CONTEMPORARY INDIAN/FUSION   Saffron's executive chef Rajiv Khullar has transformed the menu to showcase local Bengali cuisine as well as a host of pan-Indian specialties, all cooked strictly using Indian methods, but often with ingredients from around the world. The *daab chingri,* prawns simmered in coconut milk gravy, is a real treat, as is the *kadai masala duck* (Punjabi style). *Bhatti ka champ,* a succulent piece of mutton marinated in balsamic vinegar and cooked in a tandoor, is one of the restaurant's signature dishes. Or try the more traditional saffron-infused *kacchi gosht biryani* or chicken Chettinad. Vegetarians are also well catered to. Leave space for *gulab jamun,* a dessert based on an old family recipe (topped with honey and stuffed with saffron and nuts). Note that The Park has a second restaurant, **Zen House** ⟨★, where Bangkok-born master chef Nut Kunlert serves Asian specialties like prawns, barbecued whole with a chili sauce; sweet-and-sour chicken prepared with a hint of ginger and jalapeño; or lemon-grass soufflé. Prices are similar to those at Saffron. (At press time it was undergoing renovation but promised to be back in a new avatar by the end of 2008.)

The Park hotel, 17 Park St. ⓒ **033/2249-3121.** Main courses Rs 335–Rs 725 ($8.15–$18/£4.15–£9). AE, DC, MC, V. Daily 12:45–2:45pm and 7:30–11:45pm (last orders).

Sonargaon ⟨★★★ BENGALI/NORTH INDIAN   Exposed stone masonry, a well, whitewashed walls, wooden tables, tribal wall hangings, a separate fish-market kitchen (where guests can watch their fish being cooked), and enormous storm lanterns set the atmosphere for this upmarket take on village-style North Indian and Bengali dining. Order a large glass of the most delicious *ganne ka ras* (fresh sugar cane juice) to go along with a traditional Bengali thali (multicourse meal; it's not on the menu, but you can order it in advance), served on a silver platter, and give yourself plenty of time to recover; diners tend to leave with full stomachs. For an excellent starter, get the melt-in-your-mouth *kakori kebab* (tender minced mutton kebab blended with rose petals, cardamom, saffron, and secret spices), introduced by Sonargaon to Kolkata 15 years ago. You could also try the kebab *sonargaon* (star-anise-flavored marinated chicken legs cooked in charcoal-fired clay oven). If you're in the mood for North Indian cuisine, try the *dal Sonargaon* (a house speciality—black lentils simmered overnight with butter and cream) and *Rogani Nalli Amritsari* (lamb shanks in a northwest frontier curry). Leave space for *rossogolla payesh,* a Bengali dessert made from *paneer* (cheese) and thickened sweet milk or the innovative *Baileys kulfi* (frozen thick ice-cream-like milk dessert flavored with Baileys Irish Cream).

Taj Bengal, 34B Belvedere Rd., Alipore. ⓒ **033/2223-3939.** Main courses Rs 395–Rs 800 ($9.65–$20/£5–£10). AE, DC, MC, V. Daily 12:30–2:45pm and 7:30–11:45pm.

Zaranj ⟨★ NORTHWEST FRONTIER   Named for a hamlet in Afghanistan, this upmarket restaurant is one of the city's most opulent dining options, where miniature waterfalls and plush seating provide a warm, luxurious atmosphere. The **Raphael Lounge** is an ideal spot to kick off the evening in style, with its fine selection of imported wines and champagnes. Affable manager Protik Dey will help you pick fare to suit your taste buds, but if you like lamb, his hands-down recommendation is the Zaranj *raan.* Other popular dishes include *macchli masala* kebabs (*bhetki* fish mixed with the chef's secret spices), tandoori prawns (*jhinga),* and *dahi ka* kebab, prepared in the display kitchen behind a wall of glass. For dinner, be sure to reserve in advance, or you'll be watching the city's movers and groovers feasting while you wait. Sharing the entrance with Zaranj is **Jongs,** which serves decent Asian fare.

Tips **Shop 'till You Drop: A Unique Tour of Kolkata**

Given that there is so much to see and do, one practical and rather enjoyable alternative way to see the city is to opt for a personalized **shopping tour,** which enables you to visit antique furniture bazaars, textile shops, art galleries, and food and flower markets. A typical day with **Devika Duncan** (✆ 033/2288-5630; info@glenburnteaestate.com) also includes sampling local Bengali cuisine and paying a visit to the famous Bengal Club, not normally accessible to regular tourists.

---

26 Jawaharlal Nehru Rd. ✆ 033/2249-5572, -9744, -0369, or -0370. Reservations essential. Main courses Rs 200–Rs 525 ($5–$13/£2.45–£6.50). AE, DC, MC, V. Daily 12:30–3pm and 7:30–11pm; closed at lunchtime on Tues.

SHOPPING

Kolkata is also renowned for its fashion designers. Look for garments by the promising local **Sabyasachi Mukherjee,** who is taking Kolkata's fashion industry to new heights (there's an outlet at 37/1C Hazra Rd.; ✆ 033/2454-3005). Another name to reckon with is Anamika Khanna, recognized for her flamboyant fashions for both men and women. If time is short, drop in at **85 Landsdowne Road** (✆ 033/2486-2136), a one-stop shop stocking all the major Indian labels. However, if you're looking for something very ethnic and traditional, **Shamlu Dudeja's** workshop is where you should head (4/1 Alipore Park Rd.; ✆ 98-3002-6288; call for appointment). With a team of rural women, Shamlu has successfully revived the art of Kantha embroidery, making it into a much sought-after craft both locally and abroad. Smaller but also worth visiting are **Women's Friendly Society** (29 Park Lane; ✆ 033/2229-5285) and **Good Companions** (13 C, Russell St.; ✆ 033/3292-9612) for hand-embroidered linen from the villages of West Bengal. For Bengali handicrafts, visit **Bengal Home Industries** (11 Camac St.; ✆ 033/2282-1562) or **Sasha** (27 Mirza Ghalib St.; ✆ 033/ 2252-1586). You can pick up a wide range of Indian curios, along with everything from saris to silk carpets, from the government-operated **Central Cottage Industries Emporium** in Chowringhee (7 Jawaharlal Nehru Rd.; ✆ 033/2228-4139 or -3205). **Hugli** (Hastings Court, 96 Garden Reach Rd.; ✆ 033/2489-2104) and **Khazana** at the Taj Bengal hotel are two good options for handicrafts as well; although the prices are high, quality is excellent. If you feel you can lug some heavier stuff back home, drop in at **Minnoli** (Karnani Estate, Unit G-I 209, AJC Bose Rd.; ✆ 033/2289-1307), where owner Sharad Narula shows his obvious passion for antique furniture. Proud of a collection that includes everything from silver spoons dating back to the first World War to 60-year-old glass lamps, Minnoli encapsulates the very spirit of Kolkata.

Inevitably, Kolkata is also home to one of India's best bookstores, **Oxford Bookstore** (17 Park St., Kolkata; ✆ 033/2229-7662 or 033/2217-5266; oxfordmail@ apeejaygroup.com), which carries a good range of local and imported periodicals, books on India and Kolkata, and fiction. Another shop worth investigating is **Family Book Shop** (1A Park St.; ✆ 033/2229-3486 or 033/3290-6003); it's tiny but has an interesting upstairs section. You can also try **Crossword** on Elgin Road or **Starmark** on Lord Sinha Road.

KOLKATA AFTER DARK
DRINKING & PARTYING

Kolkata is officially dry on Thursday, but this doesn't affect the upscale hotels. Local laws supposedly prohibit the sale of alcohol after 10:30pm, so if you're keen for an all-nighter, be sure to ask the exact time for last rounds at any bar you visit. In the budget-oriented Sudder Street precinct, the open-air bar at the **Fairlawn Hotel** (13/A Sudder St.; ✆ **033/2252-1510**) is an atmospheric place for sundowners and early-evening drinks. **The Park** (✆ **033/2249-3121** or -7336) is *the* place to hang out after hours—despite a postage stamp–size dance floor, **Someplace Else** 👯👯 rocks all night long with live bands belting out retro rock and blues every night of the week. Together with vibrantly hued **Tantra** 👯 (also at The Park; Rs 500/$12/£6.15 on weekdays per couple), which has the largest dance floor in the city, it attracts the city's hippest crowd. The '60s-styled and -themed cocktail bar **Roxie's** (The Park; entry is free if staying at the hotel or on recommendation by an existing guest) is worth trying to get an invite to, if not for the decor, then definitely for the music that darts between the '50s, '60s, and '70s, enjoyed best with what the bar prides itself on—"mood cocktails." If this wasn't already enough, The Park now has **Aqua,** a poolside alfresco lounge. Wooden loungers and deck beds, suspended timber deck, hot tub, and cool pool—Aqua has it all. **Cinnamon Restaurant and Lounge** (24 Park St.; ✆ **033/2227-4974**) and **Virgose,** at the Hotel Hindustan International (235/1ACJ Bose Rd.; ✆ **033/2283-0505**), are also popular, especially with those who want to stray far from the bustling crowds that throng in and around The Park.

LIVE PERFORMANCE

Theater, music, dance, and poetry recitals all thrive here. Check out the listings in the "Bulletin Board" section of *The Times of India.* Upscale hotels also carry the useful monthly booklet *Cal Calling.* **Rabindra Sadan** concert hall (A.J.C. Bose Rd. and Cathedral Rd.; ✆ **033/2223-9936** or -9917) hosts regular theater and musical events, as well as dance-drama performances and local-flavored Bengali poetry evenings. Cultural events also take place at the **Academy of Fine Arts** (2 Cathedral Rd.; ✆ **033/2223-4302**). The **British Council** (5 Shakespeare Sarani; ✆ **033/2242-5478**) often offers plays and performances in English. Bengali and English dramas are performed at **Kala Mandir** (48 Shakespeare Sarani; ✆ **033/2287-9086**). For musical programs, contact **Sisir Mancha** (1/1 A.J.C. Bose Rd.; ✆ **033/2223-5317**). Indo-German productions are occasionally held at **Max Mueller Bhavan** (8 Pramathesh Barua Sarani; ✆ **033/2486-6398**).

CINEMA, GALLERIES & EXHIBITIONS

Considered the art capital of India, Kolkata hosts a huge number of art exhibitions. Scan the newspapers for information about what's on while you're in town. Or check out the **Birla Academy of Art and Culture** (108–109 Southern Ave.; ✆ **033/2466-2843**) or the **Centre for International Modern Art** (Sunny Towers, 43 Ashutosh Chowdhari Ave.; ✆ **033/2485-8717**; Tues–Sat 11am–7pm, Mon 3–7pm, closed Sun). The **Academy of Fine Arts** (2 Cathedral Rd.; ✆ **033/2223-4302**) has art galleries (daily 3–8pm) and a museum (Tues–Sun noon–6:30pm; admission Rs 5/10¢/5p), where you can see works by Rabindranath Tagore.

The best cinema complex in the city is **Nandan** (1/1 A.J.C. Bose Rd.; ✆ **033/2223-1210** or -0970), with excellent screens and a fantastic sound system. Nandan also regularly hosts art-film screenings and retrospectives. There are a number of cinemas in Chowringhee where you can watch movies in the company of feverishly excitable Indian audiences.

2 Orissa's Golden Temple Triangle

The tropical state that flourished during the 13th century on India's central eastern seaboard, Orissa is famous for its temples, which draw thousands of pilgrims here throughout the year, predominantly to **Jagannath Temple** in the coastal town of **Puri,** to worship Vishnu in his avatar as the Lord of the Universe. Architecturally, the **Sun Temple** at **Konark** is of even greater significance, with its massive stone-carved chariot adorned with sculptures, rising to carry Surya, the sun god, to the heavens. Even Orissa's capital, **Bhubaneswar** (the third point of Orissa's Golden Triangle), is more important for its enormous collection of Hindu temples—at one time 7,000—than it is as an administrative or industrial center.

Orissa remains largely tribal, with many villages still off-limits to outsiders, but the state is also well-known for its "Tribal Tourism." For the anthropologically inclined, this offers you a chance to get way off the beaten track and meet people who live on the fringes of civilization. The state is also a good place to pick up crafts, particularly textiles and paintings—even when tending to the rice paddies, the women of Orissa are dressed in glamorous saris. Cottage textile industries are the mainstays for entire villages, which produce beautiful *ikat* (patterned) textiles, palm-leaf paintings, and bright *patachitra* (cloth) paintings (the best-known of Orissa's handicrafts). *Note:* Although Orissa has long, golden beaches that curve around the Bay of Bengal, the infrastructure here is limited and the sea can be treacherous; beach lovers are best off heading for Kerala or Goa.

BHUBANESWAR

485km (300 miles) SW of Kolkata

Orissa's capital emerged in the 7th century as a center of prolific and accomplished temple building, and by the 11th century the city of Bhubaneswar (derived from Shiva's incarnation as Tribhubaneswar, Lord of the Three Worlds) had become a significant religious hub, with an estimated 7,000 temples. Of these, only several hundred remain, but those that survive reveal the evolution of the Nagara style into an architectural form unique to Orissa. You won't need to stay here more than a day— Konark's Sun Temple, one of India's top attractions, is just under an hour's drive away.

ESSENTIALS

VISITOR INFORMATION   You can try the **Government of Orissa Tourist Office** (5 Jaydev Nagar; © 0674/243-1299; Mon–Sat 10am–5pm, closed on the second Sat of each month) for information about the region.

GETTING THERE   By Air   Air Sahara (www.airsahara.net) and **Indian Airlines** (© **0674/253-0533** or –0544; http://indian-airlines.nic.in) have 55-minute daily flights from Kolkata. Indian Airlines also operates regular flights to and from Delhi (2 hr.), and Mumbai (3 hr.), and to and from several destinations in South India, including Chennai and Hyderabad. **Bhubaneswar's Biju Patnaik Airport** is about 4km (2½ miles) from the center, in the southwest. The airport has a tourist information counter, as well as a taxi service; though this is not a prepaid service, transfers into the city should cost no more than Rs 150 ($3.75/£1.85).

By Train   The best train from Delhi is the **Rajdhani Express,** but the trip is lengthy—25 hours—and departures are only 2 days per week; other trains may take 30 to 42 hours. From Kolkata, the **Howrah-Puri Express** is the most convenient (it's overnight); however, the quickest is the **Faluknama Express** (under 7 hr.). Puri is 1½ hours from Bhubaneswar, and there is regular train service between the two cities. For inquiries and reservations, your best bet is to see a travel agent or to visit the train reservation office personally (see chapter 2).

By Road   If you want to drive or bus it here from Kolkata (500km/310 miles away), count on spending 13 hours propped up in your seat.

GETTING AROUND   By Taxi & Auto-Rickshaw   Auto-rickshaws in Bhubaneswar are unusually comfortable and well maintained. Drivers are genuinely helpful, if sometimes unable to understand you. Taxis from Bhubaneswar to Puri or Konark are readily available; for taxi excursions, be clear about the duration of your journey, and the sights you wish to cover. Hiring a car and driver is a good way to save time. Try **Mercury Travels** at the Trident Hilton (Nayapalli; ✆ **0674/230-1010,** ext. 49), or **Swosti Travels** (103 Janpath; ✆ **0674/253-5773** or -5771)—each of which handles flights, car rentals, and tours of the state. Inexpensive full-day coach tours of the city and the entire Golden Triangle region are administered by the **O.T.D.C. Head Office** (✆ **0674/243-2382;** www.orissa-tourism.com), but these are targeted at domestic visitors.

Tip: **Heritage Tours** (www.heritagetoursorissa.com) is a reputable outfit with years of experience. Located at the entrance of the Mayfair Beach Resort in Puri, it specializes in "Lifestyle Tours" (including learning trips on such subjects as yoga, Odissi dance, Ayurveda, stone carving, and sand sculpting) as well as rural and tribal excursions. Besides organizing every aspect of trips lasting anything from 1 to 20 days, Heritage Tours also deals with ticketing and transportation matters.

BHUBANESWAR'S TOP ATTRACTIONS

In the heart of Bhubaneswar's Old Town, the most important temples—almost all Shaivite—are clustered around **Bindusagar Lake,** a holy reservoir believed to hold water from each and every holy river and lake in India. Of the 7,000 temples that are said to have once surrounded the tank, only around 500 remain. Traditionally, pilgrims perform their ablutions in the lake before heading into the temples to perform *puja* (a ritual of respect, such as prayer). The best are easily visited in a morning (more than three or four is overkill), leaving you time to explore some of the outlying sights during the afternoon.

The best of the city's Nagara-style temples (7th c. and 12th c. A.D.) are testament to both a radical resurgence of Hinduism and Buddhist defeat—frequently represented in temple sculptures by the image of a lion lunging for an elephant. With the exception of wonderful **Rajarani Temple** (see below), all of those worth visiting are living temples. The best are magnificently carved **Mukteshwar Temple**—the 10th-century "Gem of Orissan Architecture," where a squat, cobra-protected lingam stands in the sanctum sanctorum—and **Lingaraj Temple;** although the complex is off-limits to non-Hindus, you can admire it from a well-known vantage point, a raised platform built by the British, where you'll be harassed by a hood with a phony register of donations from other foreigners (ignore his advances and mention the police). If you have time, make a stop at the well-preserved 7th-century **Parasurameswar Temple (Brahmeswar),** for its lavish carvings, including a number of amorous couples. For something more "exotic," visit **Vaital Temple** 🏵 and view its creepy tantric carvings;

you'll need a flashlight to see the images of humans being put to death while the goddess Chamunda looks on.

Chilka Lake ✸✸ A unique ecosystem of marine, brackish, and fresh water, this Wetlands of International Importance is a haven for migratory birds: Come in October and the 1,100 sq. km (429 sq. miles) of Asia's largest brackish water lake resound with the delightful cacophony of thousands of birds. Besides birdlife, the lake has pods of dolphins and a central island with an important Hindu temple dedicated to Goddess Kalijai. There isn't much infrastructure around, so best to keep it as a day trip, preferably from Puri. Contact the Orissa tourism office (✆ **0674/243-2382;** www.orissa-tourism.com) for help in planning your trip.

Best time to visit: Oct–Mar.

Dhauli ✸ The glistening, white-domed **Shanti Stupa (Peace Pagoda)** at the top of Dhauli Hill is visible from the main road as you head toward this site, where historic Ashokan rock edicts are carved. Guarded by pale yellow Ashokan lions, the Kalinga World Peace Pagoda is a celebration of Ashoka's decision, 2,300 years ago, to renounce violence and war and embrace Buddhism—a decision made in the wake of his massacre against the Kalinga people, then rulers of Orissa. A plaque here notes that Ashoka built 84,000 *stupas* (commemorative cairns), some as far away as Greece.

Free admission. Daily 5am–8pm.

Museum of Tribal Art and Artifacts ✸ Anything and everything connected with the life of Orissa's tribal people is on display in the exhibition rooms at this newly built museum decorated with primitive murals. Traditional costumes, jewelry, household appliances, and hunting equipment such as bows and arrows, axes, and traps for birds and fish indicate the ways of life of the tribal peoples of Orissa.

Near C.R.P. Sq., NH 5. ✆ **0674/256-1635** or -3649. Free admission. Tues–Sun 10am–5pm; closed 2nd Sat of each month.

Orissa State Museum ✸ This collection convincingly explains the religious context of Hindu sculptures, but you may be more fascinated by the erotic friezes that date back as far as the 7th century A.D. Upstairs, the **Manuscript Gallery** includes early examples of the type of work you'll encounter in some Orissan crafts villages. Along with a collection of musical instruments, a number of dioramas depict different Orissan tribes. Next door is a collection of *patachitra* (cloth) paintings dealing primarily with the Jagannath cult and tales from the *Ramayana*.

Lewis Rd., near Kalpana Sq. ✆ **0674/243-1597.** Rs 50 ($1.20/£60). Tues–Sun 10am–5pm.

Rajarani Temple ✸✸ Surrounded by open space and paddy fields, this 11th-century temple—maintained by the Archaeological Survey of India—glimmers in the light of day, built as it was using a superior-quality burgundy-gold sandstone. Unusual for Orissan temples, the tower *(shikhara)* features miniature versions of itself. Sculptural representations of lotus flowers with the guardians of the eight cardinal directions are a standout feature of the temple walls, which also feature delightful female figures engaged in mundane (but beautiful) daily activities.

Tankapani Rd. Rs 220 ($5.40/£2.70). Daily 6am–6pm.

Udaygiri and Khandagiri caves ✸ Barely 7km (4⅓ miles) from the chaos of Bhubaneswar, the twin caves of Udaygiri and Khandagiri were once home to aspiring Jain monks. They were built in the 1st century B.C. by King Kharevala, and each complex numbers roughly 15 to 18 caves. Of the two, Udaygiri is more interesting, with caves filled with ornate carvings—look for caves 1, 3, 5, 9, 10, and 14; Khandagiri's cave no. 3 is also rich in carvings. If you go in the evening, the atmosphere gets a little more interesting, with monkeys gamboling from one cave to another and the odd lone *sadhu* playing his flute. The caves bathed in golden light around sunset look very beautiful and serene despite the tourist influx. (For those interested in other cave sites, the **Lalitgiri, Udaigiri,** and **Ratnagiri** trio are located 100km (62 miles) from Bhubanswar and contain Buddhist sculptures and stupas.)

Small entry fee. Daily 8am–6pm.

WHERE TO STAY

Mayfair Lagoon 🐾   It's not as luxe as the Trident, but the Mayfair is a better bet for those who want to stay within the city, a location that gives you the opportunity to sightsee and shop at the drop of a hat. Cottages and villas with plush interiors and views of the lake are set amid gardens, and facilities like the in-house spa are good. Finally, you can dine in the open-air **Nakli Dhaba:** an imitation of a typical roadside eatery in India that serves the night highway traffic, there's even a faux petrol pump and truck.

8-B Jaydev Vihar, Bhubaneswar 751 013. ℃ 0674/236-0101. Fax 0674/236-0236. www.mayfairhotels.com. 70 units. Rs 6,500 ($159/£80) executive cottage/club room; Rs 12,000 ($293/£148) deluxe cottage/club suite; Rs 25,000 ($610/£309) villa; Rs 1,500 ($37/£19) extra bed. Check website for online specials. AE, DC, MC, V. **Amenities:** Restaurant; bar; pool; spa; butler service; concierge; travel desk; business center; salon; 24-hr. room service; babysitting; laundry, doctor-on-call; currency exchange. *In room:* A/C, TV, minibar, tea- and coffee-making facilities, hair dryer, safe, Wi-Fi enabled, DVD player; villas come with a Jacuzzi and a lake-view deck.

Trident Hilton 🐾🐾   Situated some distance out of the city center, this classy low-rise hotel is surrounded by 5.6 hectares (14 acres) of exquisite lawns, mango groves, and rock gardens. Drawing businesspeople, travelers, and even the English cricket team, this is Bhubaneswar's most fabulous, and expensive, hotel. Stepping inside the lobby is like entering a temple, sans the usual chaos brought by thronging worshipers. The space has been carefully designed with stone columns, beautiful brickwork, and trellised railings enhanced by concealed lighting and spectacular brass-bell lighting features. Mythical lions perch above, looking down on guests as they arrive, and in the evenings, live Indian music is featured. Guest rooms are smart, stylish, and well laid out. Bird-watchers should ask for a room facing the rose garden. The kitchen will prepare a picnic hamper for you should you be heading out on a long day of temple-exploring.

C.B.-1, Nayapalli, Bhubaneswar 751 013. ℃ 0674/230-1010. Fax 0674/230-1302. www.hilton.com. 62 units. Rs 7,000 ($171/£86) standard double; Rs 8,000 ($195/£99) superior double and junior suite; Rs 11,000 ($268/£136) executive suite; Rs 16,000 ($390/£198) deluxe suite. Check website for online specials. AE, DC, MC, V. **Amenities:** Restaurant; bar; pool; 2 floodlit tennis courts; travel agency; business center; secretarial services; 24-hr. room service; babysitting; laundry; dry-cleaning; doctor-on-call; badminton court; jogging track. *In room:* A/C, TV, minibar, tea- and coffee-making facilities, hair dryer, safe, Wi-Fi enabled, DVD player in suites.

WHERE TO DINE

Ignore the seedy neighborhood and dour look of the lodge where this upstairs eatery, **Venus Inn** (217 Bapuji Nagar; ℃ 0674/253-1908), is and you'll find a good location for a quick South Indian *dosa.* Soft Hindi music fills the neat, clean interior as you dine on butter paper *masala dosa* (crepe-thin filled pancake), the onion *rawa masala dosa,* a *dosa* stuffed full of *potato,* or an *uttapam* (thicker pancake) with coconut. For the best chicken in town, **Cook's Kitchen** (260 Bapuji Nagar; ℃ 0674/253-0025) is the place to be—chicken *tikka* butter masala is for those who can handle their spices.

Order an Orissan thali at Swosti Plaza's **Chandan** 🛪 (© 0674/230-1936 through -1939), where waiters can talk you through the evening's selection while old Hindi film music provides prerecorded entertainment. The menu changes daily, but a typical selection might include fragrant dry Oriya mutton *(mangsha kasha);* Rohu fish (beware of the fine bones) cooked in a mustard sauce *(sorisa machha);* traditionally prepared mixed vegetables *(santula);* and soft *paneer* (Indian cheese) cooked under charcoal and then caramelized *(chhena poda)*—all served with breads and condiments on a brass platter.

Hare Krishna 🛪 PURE VEGETARIAN   You won't find garlic or onion (Hare Krishna culinary no-nos) in the vegetarian dishes served at this surreally decorated restaurant reached via a series of Art Deco linoleum steps. The food is rich and flavorful, so don't over-order. Lord Krishna's favorite is apparently Govinda's Pasanda, a *paneer* (Indian cheese) based dish that's heavy on the spices and includes cashew nuts, tomato, and fresh vegetables. Also spicy, but with an added hint of sour, is Chaitanya's Pasanda, made with *paneer* as well. We can heartily recommend Nanda Moharaja's *palak paneer,* which makes good use of mineral-rich spinach and is accompanied by thick, warm, fresh *naan.* The steaming-hot vegetable *biryani* is known as Bhaktivinod's Delight, and it's good.

1st floor, Lalchand Market, Jan Path. © 0674/253-4188. Main courses Rs 50–Rs 85 ($1.20–$2). No credit cards. Daily 11am–3pm and 6:30–10:30pm.

SHOPPING

Sixteen kilometers (10 miles) north of Puri, **Raghurajpur Crafts Village,** a quaint rural village of thatched-roof houses, offers a variety of traditional Oriya crafts. Craftspeople will meet you as you emerge from your taxi or auto-rickshaw and lead you to their homes, which double as production centers for specific art forms. Along with a cup of *chai,* you'll be given a thorough account of the creative process. *Patachitra* paintings, the best-known of Orissa's handicrafts, fetch up to Rs 15,000 ($367/£185) and are created on a cloth canvas, using a brush made from mouse hair. Vibrant colors are used to create extraordinarily detailed depictions of mythological events—most of these revolve around the life of Krishna. Also impressive are traditional palm-leaf drawings made with an iron pen. These are typically presented as a concertina-style fold-up poster made from palm fronds and featuring concealed erotic images and Sanskrit inscriptions. Those who want to watch artisans at work can spend time at the **Chitrakara** workshop (© 0675/227-4359; daily 9am–7pm). *Note:* Although prices are reasonable, they are slightly inflated, and you shouldn't feel pressured to buy something you don't want. You can also try and get these at any of the **Utkalika** showrooms present in all the cities within the state.

If you are traveling to Konark by road, you will come across a sudden splash of color spilling on to the blue tar—welcome to **Pipli,** a tiny village where almost everyone is involved in appliqué work. The street is lined with shops on both sides selling massive umbrellas, cushion covers, bedspreads, wall hangings, and lampshades, all in bright colors and bold patterns. Every shop has a couple of tailors (often the owners themselves are on the machines), and it's fascinating to watch them at work. Orissa is also well known for its textiles, especially **ikat,** a kind of tie-and-dye, which comes in exquisite colors and weaves. Available in scores of shops, you can choose from several varieties, each of which hails from a different corner of the state.

EXPLORING PURI & THE SUN TEMPLE AT KONARK

Puri is 65km (40 miles) S of Bhubaneswar; Konark is 35km (22 miles) NE of Puri

Puri is considered one of the four holiest places in India, home to magnificent 15th-century **Sri Jagannath Temple,** where pilgrims throng to be absolved of past sins by the Lord of the Universe. But given that this is off-limits to non-Hindus, the real highlight lies farther up the coast, in the mellow town of Konark, site of the legendary 13th-century **Sun Temple.**

Sri Jagannath Temple ⚑   Topped by Vishnu's wheel and flag, the 64m (210-ft.) *shikhara* (spire) of Jagannath Temple dominates Puri's skyline, and it's possible to circumambulate the entire complex by wandering through the market streets around the periphery walls. However, for non-Hindus, the best view of this mighty Kalinga temple is from the balcony of **Raghunandan Library,** across the street. From here, you not only get a glimpse of the tremendously active temple life, but you'll be privy to the colorful activity around the souvenir stalls that spread around the temple in every direction. From this viewing point, both the size of the temple and the sheer numbers of swarming people are impressive; the temple buildings themselves are filthy with mildew. Incidentally, you will find images of Lord Jagannath and his siblings everywhere in this part of India. Pitch-black with squat physiques and exaggerated features, they could well have been inspiration for the animation technique used by the creators of *South Park:* The crude, flat-featured, raccoon-eyed faces have thin red curling grins. You will be asked to sign a register on your way out with a column for donations with suspiciously high figures (for instance, two zeros added after Rs 20/50¢/25p); in all fairness, make a donation, but don't get conned.

Raghunandan Library is open daily 7am–noon and 4–8pm. All rickshaw drivers can show you the way.

Sun Temple ⚑⚑⚑   Visualized as the gigantic chariot of Surya, the sun god, emerging from the ocean, the Sun Temple at Konark was built (though not completed) at the zenith of Orissan architectural development, at the edge of a 483km (300-mile) beach. Guarded by stone elephants and mythical lions, the immense structure was carved from rock so as to look like an enormous war chariot (originally drawn by seven galloping horses), with detailed sculpted scenes of everyday facets of life. Even the spokes of the 24 giant wheels that adorn the base of the temple are intricately carved. The temple was at some point submerged by sand; when the ocean retreated just over a century ago, the temple that had been lost to the world was uncovered and excavated by the British. The entire complex is surrounded by a periphery wall. To first get an idea of the enormity of the project, circumnavigate the temple by slowly skirting this outer wall. The sanctum has collapsed inward, so it is no longer possible to enter the temple building, but you can clamber over most of the exterior for close-up views of the various scenes of love and war, trade and commerce, sports and mythical figures, and of course the four depictions of Surya in each of the directions. Among the friezes are those depicting amorous dalliances between entwined couples—these provide stiff competition for the world-renowned sculpted erotica at Khajuraho—including spokes with miniature examples of the erotic carvings found all over the rest of the temple.

The earlier you arrive, the better your chances of enjoying this World Heritage Site in peace. Definitely avoid visiting the temple on the weekend, when day-tripping local visitors swarm to Konark as part of a high-paced pilgrimage around Orissa's golden circuit.

If you're here during the first week of December, you may be able to catch the 5-day **Konark Dance Festival** ✦✦✦, which offers performances by some of the country's most sought-after dancers. The monument forms a remarkable backdrop to traditional dance styles accompanied by music played on classical Indian instruments.

Konark, 64km (40 miles) southeast of Bhubaneswar; 35km (21 miles) northeast of Puri. Rs 205 ($5/£2.55). Sunrise–sunset. For information on the Konark Dance Festival, contact O.T.D.C. in Bhubaneswar (✆ **0674/243-2382**).

WHERE TO STAY

Small, intimate, peaceful, and close to the beach, **Z Hotel**—the former seaside residence of the Raja of Serampore—is the best budget lodging in the state, offering huge, simply furnished guest rooms with sea views. Reserve room no. 25, 26, or 27 (✆ **06752/22-2554;** www.zhotelindia.com; Rs 600/$15/£7.40; no credit cards) well in advance to secure an upstairs unit with attached bathroom (drench shower only). Don't miss the beach view from the rooftop which, unfortunately, also reveals Puri's unchecked development. Alternatively, try **Toshali Sands,** en route to Konark (✆ **06752/25-0571** through -0574; www.toshalisands.com; doubles from Rs 3,200/ $78/£40). Though it's never going to win any design awards, this is the closest acceptable accommodations to the Sun Temple. A beach lies nearby, and the restaurant's not bad. "Villa" units are the best choices; they feature small sitting rooms, porches, shared kitchenettes, and big bathrooms with tubs.

Mayfair Beach Resort   This is the best place to stay in the vicinity of the Sun Temple by a long shot, popular with middle-class Indian families who come to strut their stuff on the wide expanse of beach, a short walk from the resort. However, service can be pretty surly. Disinterested staff members wear bright Hawaiian shirts, and the entrance and lobby areas are equally colorful, playing off the Jagannath Temple theme. The rough-hewn red-brick resort makes the most of its limited space, its gardens profuse with lovely trees, potted plants, and stone statues of various deities. Unless you can afford the presidential suite, book a garden cottage; it has a small sitting area, a semi-private veranda, and a small shower room. Beyond the crow-infested pool, which is neatly lined with white wood loungers, a nicely maintained stretch of beach is constantly watched by the resort's lifeguards, although hawkers still ply their trades. The major drawback here is an inconvenient 8am checkout, but if this doesn't suit you, say so, and the management may be able to accommodate you with a later checkout.

Chakratirtha Rd., Puri 752 002. ✆ **06752/22-7800** through -7809. Fax 06752/22-4242. www.mayfairhotels.com. 34 units. Rs 5,000 ($122/£62) deluxe room/cottage; Rs 7,500 ($183/£93) premier suite. Rs 900 ($22/£11) extra person. Ask about discounts. AE, MC, V. **Amenities:** 2 restaurants; 2 bars; pool; health club; steam; Jacuzzi; indoor games; travel desk; boutique; 24-hr. room service; doctor-on-call; currency exchange; table tennis; pool table. *In room:* A/C, TV, minibar.

WHERE TO DINE

Besides **Mayfair's Aquarium & Veranda** (✆ **06752/22-7800**), where you can sample Orissan seafood specialties (*chingudi tarkari,* prawns prepared in a traditional Orissan gravy, is delicious), you can dine at **Wild Grass** (V.I.P. Rd.; ✆ **06752/22-9293;** daily 11am–11pm; reasonably priced Ayurvedic spa), a self-consciously eco-friendly open-air restaurant set in a lush garden with stone and slate pathways and tables arranged in various nooks at different levels. Come for the delightful ambience, but don't expect the most spectacular food or service. One of the highlights here is an Orissan thali, but it must be ordered at least 6 hours in advance (well worth it). Grilled *brinjal* (eggplant, known as *baigan poda*) is another favorite; or try tandoori prawns, *nargisi* fish kebab, or prawn *malai* curry. For dessert, try the local cheesecake, *chhena poda*. **Restaurant Peace** is an utterly laid-back cafe-style eatery with plastic chairs under thatched roofing. Owner-manager Velu serves fresh locally caught fish and shellfish at ridiculously low prices: 10 grilled prawns cost around $2 (£1). Restaurant Peace opens early and serves the best bowl of muesli in India. A genuinely huge portion of fresh fruit, mixed nuts, curd, and honey is a perfect way to start the day (C.T. Rd.; ✆ **06752/22-6642;** no credit cards; daily 7am–11pm).

TRIBAL TOURS IN ORISSA

Venturing into Orissa's tribal heartland is a true off-the-beaten-track adventure, allowing you to meet people with social, cultural, and agricultural practices that have remained unchanged for centuries. Many of Orissa's tribal people are still hunter-gatherers, and are physically distinct from any other ethnic group on the subcontinent. Opportunities for travelers to interact with members of these unique societies are generally limited to weekly markets held at various tribal centers. Visitors with an especially strong interest in anthropology can arrange to spend a night or two in a traditional village, but expect plenty of walking—and forget any modern conveniences. You may, however, want to consider the fact that you will be visiting one of India's poorest regions. Also check whether any of the spoils of your tourist venture are actually reaching these village folk. Visitors have reported that some tribal tours are exploitative, making a freak-show/spectacle of the poor. In Puri, your best option for a responsibly organized tribal tour is **Heritage Tours** (p. 571); to ensure that a suitable trip is planned around your specific interests, e-mail the highly knowledgeable Bubu in advance (✆ **06752/22-3656** or 94-3702-3656; www.heritagetoursorissa. com). A typical tribal tour for two persons will cost in the vicinity of $60 to $80 (£30–£41) per person per day, for a minimum of 6 or 7 days. The fee factors in the services of a guide, an Ambassador car and driver, food, and (ultra-basic) accommodations.

3 Darjeeling

500km (310 miles) N of Kolkata

Darjeeling, "Land of the Celestial Thunderbolt," was given to the British as a "gift" from the once-independent kingdom of Sikkim. Lying in the Himalayan foothills and entirely surrounded by snowcapped vistas, Darjeeling soon became the favorite summer resort of the British Raj during the heyday of Calcutta—when Mark Twain visited, he exclaimed it was "the one land that all men desire to see, and having seen once by even a glimpse would not give that glimpse for the shows of the rest of the world combined." Today, the incredible view of the world's third-highest mountain, Mount Kanchenjunga (8,220m/27,400 ft.), is undoubtedly Darjeeling's best-loved attraction, though the town has also acquired a global reputation for producing the "champagne of teas," and retains some of its haunting Gothic Victorian ambience. Most visitors are here to pick up a permit and get acclimatized for hikes through the mountainous state of Sikkim. It's worth noting that if you want a sleepy colonial hill-station environment, with splendid flower-filled walks, this is not it. Head instead for nearby **Kalimpong,** which offers a number of charming old-world accommodations.

Two nights in Darjeeling should be more than enough, particularly if you're moving on to other Himalayan foothill towns. As with most hill stations, Darjeeling involves a considerable amount of climbing, and you'll do well to avoid the ugly mess of lower Darjeeling, which is typically congested, with suspicious odors, confusing back alleys, and a jumble of paths and stairways. Stick to The Mall and Chowrasta (crossroads) in upper Darjeeling, where life proceeds at a polite pace, and you can enjoy leisurely walks, stopping for a cup of tea or to browse shops stuffed full of trinkets and artifacts.

ESSENTIALS

VISITOR INFORMATION   Darjeeling's **Tourist Information Centre** (The Mall; ✆ **0354/225-5351** or -4214; www.wbtourism.com/darjeeling; June to mid-Mar Mon–Sat 10am–4:30pm, mid-Mar to May daily 9am–7pm) is helpful and will give you a free map of the area.

ACQUIRING YOUR SIKKIM PERMIT IN DARJEELING   *Be warned:* Getting your Sikkim permit is a laborious process that will last at least an hour. Take your passport to the **District Magistrate's Office** (off Hill Cart Rd.; Mon–Fri 10am–1pm and 2:30–4:30pm). Fill in a permit application form (remember to have it stamped), then go to the **Foreigners' Registration Office** (Laden La Rd.; ✆ **0354/225-4203;** daily 10am–7pm), where a policeman will endorse your form. Finally, head back to the District Magistrate's Office, making sure you arrive before closing time, and your passport will be stamped and the permit issued free of charge. Valid for 15 days, it states clearly which areas you may enter. (Permits are also available from the Ministry of Home Affairs in New Delhi or from Indian consulates abroad.)

GETTING THERE   By Road   Darjeeling is 80km (50 miles) from Siliguri, which is the nearest main transit point. Buses from Darjeeling usually leave from the Bazaar bus stand on Hill Cart Road. Darjeeling is connected by road with Siliguri, Bagdogra, Gangtok, and Kathmandu across the Nepali border. Kalimpong is 2½ hours from Bagdogra as well as Darjeeling.

By Air   The nearest airport is at Bagdogra (near Siliguri), 90km (56 miles) away. **Jet Airways, Air Deccan,** and **Indian Airlines** (see chapter 2 for contact details) have flights to Bagdogra from Kolkata (55 min.) and Delhi (via Guwahati). A taxi ride from Bagdogra to Darjeeling should take 3½ hours and cost about Rs 2,000 to Rs 2,500 ($49–$61/£25–£31). From Siliguri, catch the **toy train** (8 hr.; see below) or a **taxi** (2–3 hr.; Rs 1,000/$24/£12) to get to Darjeeling.

By Train   From Kolkata (Sealdah Station), the best option is the overnight Darjeeling Mail, which is supposed to arrive at the New Jalpaiguri railway station (scheduled arrival 8:40am) in time to connect with the Darjeeling Himalayan Railway's famous **toy train.** The toy train departs at 9am for the scenic 8-hour journey (see "The Most Spectacular Train Journey," below). Or you can hire a taxi or share a jeep (readily available), directly from the station, for the 3-hour, 88km (54-mile) journey to Darjeeling. Although the toy train runs daily, bad weather may disrupt services. If you intend to catch the toy train out of Darjeeling at the end of your stay, and wish to travel in first class (Rs 247/$6/£3), you must book your ticket in advance at the counter at New Jalpaiguri Station. You can reserve other tickets for major trains out of New Jalpaiguri at the Darjeeling railway station daily between 8am and 2pm.

GETTING AROUND   It's best to explore Darjeeling on foot, and if you need to haul luggage, ask for a porter and pay him well. Taxis are overpriced and unnecessary (with the exception of excursions to places some distance from the town). For local sightseeing tours or even jeep trips to Gangtok and other mid-distance destinations, contact the helpful **Darjeeling Transport Corporation** (30 Laden La Rd., opposite

⟮Moments⟯ The Most Spectacular Train Journey

A polite voice at New Jalpaiguri railway station frequently announces that "... the train is running 30 minutes late, the inconvenience caused is deeply regretted ..." It's a small price to pay for what must be one of the slowest, most spectacular train journeys in the world. Since July 4, 1881, Darjeeling's aptly named **toy trains**—including the world's oldest functioning steam locomotive—have puffed and wheezed their ways between the hill station and the plains. In December 1999, the railway became India's 22nd World Heritage Site, only the second railway in the world to be so recognized on the list. The trip between New Jalpaiguri and Darjeeling covers a mere 87km (54 miles) but takes almost an entire day to transport passengers up 2,055m (6,850 ft.). En route, with rhododendron slopes, rolling hills, and Kanchenjunga in almost constant view, you pass through villages with names like Margaret's Hope, and puff right past the front doors of homes that range from shacks to quaint red-tiled cottages surrounded by potted flowers. You also traverse a total of **498 bridges** and **153 unmanned level crossings.** The final stop before Darjeeling is **Ghum (Ghoom),** the second-highest railway station in the world. For details, see "Getting There: By Train," above, or **www.dhr.in**.

Apsara Hotel). It's open from 8am until 8pm and can advise you on alternatives if they're unable to accommodate you.

TREKKING & ADVENTURE ACTIVITIES   Darjeeling is a good base for various "acclimatization treks" at lower altitudes than those you're going to come up against if you intend to trek in Sikkim. For sightseeing as well as trekking tours around Darjeeling and western Sikkim **Travel Slique** (J.P. Sharma Rd.; ✆ **94-3404-4218**) comes highly recommended. For white-water rafting, contact **D.G.H.C. Tourism** (Silver Fir Building, The Mall; ✆ **0354/225-5351**). A well-established tour and travel agency in Sikkim, with a branch in Darjeeling, is **Himali Travel Specialists** (30 D.B Giri Rd., Darjeeling; ✆ **0354/225-2741** or 98-3204-5091; himalits@satyam.net.in).

Darjeeling is the type of place where you might easily find yourself wanting to do very little other than drink in the restorative climate and tea. There are over 70 different tea plantations in the area, and a typical tour demonstrates everything from harvesting to how different varieties of tea are sorted and prepared for export around the globe. For the finest selection of organic and non-organic teas—20 to 30 plantations are represented—pay a visit to **Nathmulls** (✆ **0354/225-6437;** www.nathmulltea.com; Mon–Sat 9am–7pm), a family business that's been selling tea since 1931. Better still, stay at the Glenburn Tea Estate (reviewed below). For a good vantage point, climb **Observatory Hill,** held sacred by Hindus and Buddhists. A Kali shrine is guarded by foul-tempered monkeys that play on the colorful Buddhist prayer flags strung between the pine trees.

Darjeeling has a sizable Tibetan presence and a number of Buddhist monasteries you can visit. Set against the backdrop of Kanchenjunga, colorful **Bhutia Busty Gompa,** near Chowrasta, is famous for the contents of its upstairs Buddhist library—one of the texts kept there is the original *Tibetan Book of the Dead.* On Tenzing Norgay Road, you may be able to buy Tibetan and Sikkimese handicrafts at **Aloobari Monastery.**

An hour's walk from town is **Padmaja Naidu Zoological Park,** where you can give the animals a miss and head straight for the secluded **Snow Leopard and Red Panda Breeding Programme,** the only successful breeding program of these endangered species in the world. Sit patiently and watch snow leopards in their cages or a red panda in the trees, or chat with Kiran Motane, the program's dedicated zoologist.

A GLORIOUS SUNRISE

Watching the sun rise from **Tiger Hill,** near the sleepy town of Ghoom, is one of the best things to do in the area (11km/7 miles from Darjeeling; private taxi costs Rs 450/$11/£5.55 round-trip): The sight of the first rays of dawn carving a dramatic, golden silhouette around the not-too-distant eastern Himalayan peaks is brilliant. Occasionally, Mount Everest is also visible, just 225km (140 miles) away. Come armed with spare film and warm clothing—at an altitude of 2,550m (8,160 ft.), predawn Tiger Hill is bone-jarringly cold, and if you want to join the crowds who flock here each morning, you have to be up before dawn. The entry fee is Rs 5 (10¢/5p), but you can pay a little extra for VIP treatment inside a special observation tower (Rs 40/$1/50p), where heating is accompanied by soothing Darjeeling tea. On the way back, visit **Ghoom (Liga Choling) Gompa;** possibly the best-known Buddhist monastery around Darjeeling, it was founded in the late 1800s and enshrines a 5m-high (16-ft.) clay statue of the Maitreya Buddha. In the early morning light, the colorfully painted figures over the facade and rooftops—intended to scare away evil spirits—are radiant. Along the exterior walls are prayer wheels that are spun in order to send countless prayers to the heavens, while inside, butter lamps are lit in offering to the deity.

WHERE TO STAY

Darjeeling is a great place to experience real colonial coziness, with several charming heritage hotels. In this category our preference is for **Mayfair Hill,** but **Windamere Hotel** (© 0354/225-4041 or -4042; www.windamerehotel.com; doubles from $160/£81), originally a Victorian boardinghouse for English tea-planters on Observatory Hill, has atmospheric public spaces (though the list of do's and don'ts put a slight damper on the holiday). Its huge heritage rooms come with immense charm, but the hotel is showing signs of wear and tear (as you'd expect from a place built in 1889), as does the service. Another heritage property (and better bet) is the **New Elgin Hotel** (© 0354/225-7226 or -7227; www.elginhotels.com; doubles from Rs 4,400/$107/£54). With the air of a country manor, the hotel is frequented by an upmarket foreign crowd looking to relive the splendor of the British Raj. Like that of Windamere, its public spaces are filled with old-world charm—old-fashioned sofas, deep armchairs, fireplaces, and beautiful rugs—but some of the rooms aren't quite as grand (some odd color combinations, too), and the bathrooms are small. The best views are from room nos. 21 to 23, 31 to 33, and 51 to 53. More in the standard category of hotels is the **Cedar Inn** (Jalapahar Rd.; © 0354/225-4446; www.cedarinndarjeeling.com; doubles with half-board from Rs 4,500/$110/£56)—it has rooms with fireplaces (ask for the observatory suite or the attic rooms) and a lovely garden with good views; the only drawback are frayed towels in the small bathrooms.

Finally, if you want to be assured of absolute peace and quiet, head for the nearby hill station of Kalimpong (see "Looking for Orchids in Kalimpong," below).

Dekeling Hotel 🎯 *Value*   Some of the cedar-paneled guest rooms at this charming hotel (the best choice if you're on a tight budget) have the best views in town. Spotlessly clean and simple, this is the place to go for Tibetan hospitality (run by the wonderfully warm Norbu and Sangay Dekeva) rather than Raj-style sophistication. An old iron chimney heater keeps the lounge/library (stone tile floors, Tibetan sofas, *thangkas*, Tibetan paintings) cozy and warm; it's a wonderful place to kick back with a book, watched by the family dog, Doma. Guest rooms are basic, and although the bathrooms are a little small (with shower only), they're immaculately clean. On cold nights, a hot-water bottle is usually tucked into your bed. On the attic floor, room no. 3 has a 180-degree view that takes in Darjeeling town and Mount Kachenchunga in all its snowcapped magnificence. For security reasons, the hotel, located high above Dekevas Restaurant, is locked up at 11pm; inform the management by 9pm if you expect to be late, and a watchman will wait up for you.

51 Gandhi Rd., Darjeeling 734 101. ⓒ 0354/225-3298 or -4159. Fax 0354/225-3298. www.dekeling.com. 22 units. Rs 900 ($22/£11) back-facing double; Rs 1,100 ($27/£14) standard and attic double; Rs 1,350 ($33/£17) deluxe double. Rs 250 ($6/£3) extra bed. Discounts of up to 50% off season (July 1–Sept 14 and Jan 15–Mar 14). AE, MC, V. **Amenities:** Restaurant; travel, sightseeing, and car rental assistance; limited room service; laundry; library. *In room:* TV, electric heater on request.

Dekeling Resort 𝒦 *Value*   This guesthouse (resort is an ill-chosen descriptor) is the best value-for-money deal in town. A stiff, athletic climb leads you to "Hawke's Nest," the colonial bungalow with a commanding location high above the town, now re-dubbed Dekeling Resort. Prayer flags flutter around this 120-year-old green-roofed, bay-windowed, two-leveled, all-suite cottage offering simple comfort, effortless charm, and complete privacy. There's a small, one-table dining room where breakfasts and home-cooked meals are served; or you can be served in bed, which the obliging staff of two will arrange. Ask for a double bed in an upstairs room; accommodations there are huge and charming, with wood floors, carved antique dressers, Tibetan rugs, pale floral fabrics, and lovely fireplaces. Bathrooms have large drench showers and plenty of natural light. This is a true haven if you don't mind the 20-minute walk to The Mall.

2 A.J.C. Bose Rd., Darjeeling 734 101. ⓒ 0354/225-3092 or -3347. Fax 0354/225-3298. www.dekeling.com. 4 units. Rs 2,500 ($61/£31) double without meals; Rs 3,800 ($93/£47) double with meals. Up to 40% discount off season. AE, MC, V. **Amenities:** Dining room; lounge; assistance w/travel; sightseeing; car rental; room service; laundry. *In room:* TV, fireplace.

The Glenburn Tea Estate 𝒦𝒦𝒦   Homestays are aplenty in India, as are tea gardens and luxurious resorts, but a combination of all three is very rare. The creative offspring of the dynamic Husna-Tara Prakash, Glenburn centers around the 100-year-old Burra Bungalow, which offers just four magnificent rooms, a cozy sitting room, and a traditional dining room where one can eat a multicourse meal in the true planter's style. Each of the rooms is unique and makes delightful use of space, light, and color. Birds and butterflies embroidered on linens, splashes of blues and pinks, beds made of Spanish mahogany and Victorian teak, antique bathtubs, and floral tiles are just some of the features. Add to that the gorgeous views of the Kanchenjunga that can be had from the sit-outs and verandas, while sipping endless cups of Glenburn tea accompanied by the most delicious homemade brownies, and you can see why we think Glenburn is a little chunk of heaven. Trails wind through pockets of forest or slopes of tea all the way from 1,110m (3,700 ft.) to the banks of the rivers Rungeet and Rung Dung, across which lies the neighboring state of Sikkim. Guests have an option to enjoy the day or even stay overnight at the Glenburn Lodge by the river, without giving up their room at the Bungalow—the two rooms here are charming, especially at night when bathed in the orange glow of hurricane lamps (no electricity)

Tips Looking for Orchids in Kalimpong

For even more peace and quiet, head for this nearby hill station. At an altitude of 1,250m (4,000 ft.), Kalimpong is a restorative destination, with magnificent views, relaxing walks, a number of monasteries (Thara Choeling, Tongsa Gompa, Durpin) and an abundance of wild orchids. Also check out the interesting **Pine View Nursery** with its amazing assortment of cacti (Attisha Rd.; ✆ **03552/25-5843**). Kalimpong is known for its cheese and deadly red-chili pickle, both of which you can buy from **Larks Provision Store** (Rishi Rd.; ✆ **03552/25-9774**). You'll find a variety of places to stay, including several charming hotels that will delight Rajophiles. **Silver Oaks** (Rinkingpong Rd.; ✆ **03552/25-5296**, -5766, or -5767; www.elginhotels.com) has lovely exteriors with flowers spilling from every crevice and terrific old-world ambience; the luxurious doubles go for Rs 4,100 ($100/£51) including all meals (request Tibetan cuisine). However, the views aren't great and sound carries through the walls quite easily. On the flip side, the staff is extra chirpy in the mornings and you can enjoy their singing as they clean the rooms down the hall! Barely a 5-minute walk from here, representing real heritage, the **Himalayan Hotel** (Upper Cart Rd.; ✆ **03552/25-5248**; himhot@satyam.net.in) feels like the setting for a Sherlock Holmes mystery. Crammed full of history, it has a wonderful hilltop location (full-board doubles from Rs 4,100/$100/£51). Originally owned by David Macdonald, who also assisted in the escape of the 13th Dalai Lama in 1910, it has played host to the likes of Hillary and Tenzing, Mme. Alexandra David-Neel, and Shirley MacLaine. The old heritage cottage has eight rooms, with oak ceilings, teak pillars, a porch with an assortment of lovely wicker and wooden chairs, and stunning views—ask for no. 5 or 6. Another option is a homestay called **Orchid Retreat** (Ganesh Villa; ✆ **03552/27-4489**; www.theorchidretreat. com), situated 4km (2½ miles) from the main town, away from the noise and set amid a terraced nursery (full-board doubles 2,000/$49/£25). Run by the Pradhan family, it offers good cuisine and simple but lovely cottages surrounded by native and exotic species of plants. Rooms are spacious, but bathrooms (showers only) are a little tacky. The extremely interesting Ganesh Mani Pradhan, expert in the flora and fauna of the area, will be more than happy to show you around. Ask him to take you to Pedong, half an hour away along a lovely road lined with old trees—it's a small village with some great views and an ancient Bhutanese monastery, with rare and unusual paintings of the Buddha.

with only the burbling of the river for music. Picnics can be arranged anywhere on the estate and will be served by liveried bearers on portable tables complete with a tablecloth, delicate crockery, and a vase of fresh flowers—all that is lacking is a chandelier. City Office: Kanak Building, 41, Chowringhee Rd., Kolkata 700 071. Darlene Khan ✆ **033/2288-5630** or -1805; Husna-Tara Prakash ✆ **98-3007-0213**. Fax 033/2288-3581. www.glenburnteaestate.com. U.K. ✆ **+44 (0)1295/758-150**. www.mahoutuk.com. Burra Bungalow 4 units (at press time, there were plans to build an annex with an additional 2 rooms). The Planters' Suite, the Rose Suite, the Kanchenjunga Suite: $400 (£203) double; $70 (£36) extra person. Simbong Butterfly Room (smaller than the rest): $375 (£190) double; $250 (£127) single. Children under 3 stay free in parent's room. Entire estate rental: $2,150 (£1,088) per night. 10% discount for stays of 4 nights or more. Off-season discounts May–Sept. Rates include taxes; transfers from Bagdogra Airport, NJP, Darjeeling, Sikkim; all meals; laundry; complimentary tea, coffee, mineral water, fresh juice, and soft drinks; day trips to Darjeeling town/Kalimpong; fishing (seasonal); and activities within the estate. **Amenities:** Dining; library; board games; vehicle at disposal; guide/naturalist; shop. *In room:* Hot water bottles/electric blankets, fresh fruit and flowers, heater, fireplace (except Rose and Kanchenjunga suites).

Mayfair Hill Resort ★★   Once the summer palace of the Maharajah of Nazargunj, this class act has warmer staff and better ambience than popular New Elgin, and the views are far superior. Two copper elephants guard the entrance of the main building, and a signboard informs guests of daily weather conditions. It's set in a lovely garden with potted plants, sculpted deities, and its own temple. The partially wood-paneled guest rooms—in ivy-covered buildings, which feel more like cozy cottages—are a tad feminine (floral fabrics, predominantly pink) but lovely, featuring Tibetan rugs, fireplaces, fine wooden furnishings, bay windows with seats, and entrance/dressing rooms. They receive plenty of natural light and enjoy superb views of the town, the mountains, and the valley below. The tiled, well-spaced bathrooms have good shelving and vintage-style free-standing wooden towel racks. Guests are allowed use of sports facilities at the Darjeeling Gymkhana Club.

Opposite Governor's House, The Mall, Darjeeling 734 101. ☏ 0354/225-6376 or -6476. Fax 0354/225-2674. www. mayfairhotels.com. darjeeling@mayfairhotels.com. 41 units. Rs 6,000 ($146/£74) Premium cottage double; Rs 8,000 ($195/£99) heritage cottage double. Rs 2,000 ($49/£25) extra bed. Rates include all meals. MC, V. **Amenities:** Restaurant; bar; health club and tennis privileges; travel assistance; car rental; babysitting; laundry; doctor-on-call; currency exchange; library; tea-leaf shop; pool table; billiards; squash; ice-skating. *In room:* TV, tea- and coffee-making facilities, hair dryer, DVD player, fireplace, heater.

WHERE TO DINE

The following recommendations are all within walking distance of each other; ask for directions before you set out. For Tibetan food, **Dekevas Restaurant** (☏ 0354/225-4159; no credit cards) has some delicious favorites, including *momos* (dumplings) and wonton soup, with a choice of chicken, pork, or vegetable as a base. Try a delicious *shabalay,* Tibetan pie filled with mince, onion, and spring onion; spice it up with a hint of chili sauce. Also sample the awesome *tsampa*—roasted barley served with cheese, butter, and a glass of milk. For those extra-cold days, it has a selection of soups. Also available are Chinese dishes, pizzas, and burgers. Adjacent is the no-frills matchbox-size **Kunga,** where the beef or pork *thenthuk* (flat noodles) soup is excellent. At **Lemon Grass** (also known as The Park), you can order from the Thai or Indian menu—the Indian tandoori chicken is a standout (☏ 0354/225-5270; no credit cards). Part of a three-floor food center, with a delicatessen and Internet cafe one floor below and an American diner at the basement level, **Glenary's** has been serving guests since 1935. Although staff may boast about the Continental cuisine, the best options are Indian—try *mahi tikka* (spicy fish tandoori) or *bhuna gosht,* a mutton curry cooked with ginger, garlic, and masala in its own juices (☏ 0354/225-7554). A new addition in the basement, the **Buzz** acts as a pub, dishing out great music and hosting live bands in the evenings from Thursday to Sunday. **Joey's Pub** (☏ 0354/225-8216; no credit cards) is your quintessential bar, and that just about sums up Darj's nightlife. Spectacular views of Mount Kachenjunga make **Keventer's Snack Bar** (1 Nehru Rd.; ☏ 0354/225-6542 or -4026) something of a Darjeeling institution, even if the food is nothing to write home about. Sit upstairs on the terrace for breakfast served by disaffected waiters. Darjeeling also boasts an **Inox multiplex** and **Rink Mall** where you can have a good cuppa at the tea lounge or Café Coffee Day. Finally, for Nepali cuisine (a must if you're in the region), there's no better place than **Penangs** (just opposite the Rink Mall on the first floor of a shabby building), where you should order the traditional Nepali thali (multicourse platter) and *momos* (dumplings).

4 Sikkim

Sikkim's original inhabitants are the Lepchas, also called Rongtub (literally "the dearest people of Mother Earth"), who call their land *Ney Mayal Lyang,* or "heaven." And how! Crammed in between Tibet, Nepal, Bhutan, and West Bengal, this tiny, mountainous state is as pristine a pocket of India as you are likely to encounter, with some 4,000 varieties of wildflowers (including 600 varieties of orchids), snow-fed lakes, high-altitude mountain forests, and hidden Buddhist monasteries. Some travelers come simply to enjoy the refreshing views and clean air, but most are here to tackle the fantastic treks through western Sikkim, exploring remote valleys and villages of yak-herding Tibetans. Ideally, you should spend a day or two in the state capital, **Gangtok,** to organize permits and transport/trekking arrangements, then head to **Pelling** before undertaking a demanding high-altitude trek for several days. Or you can skip Gangtok and either hire a jeep that goes directly from Siliguri (near the railway station at New Jalpaiguri) to Pelling, or travel from Bagdogra, the nearest airport; both are about 6 hours away by road. If you want to avoid serious trekking and enjoy easier hikes, you can opt for **Tendong Hill** or **Menam Hill,** which can be accessed via Namchi and Rawangla in South Sikkim. There is relatively very little to offer in terms of accommodation in these areas, but the scenery of endless terraced paddy fields with dense forests higher up is worth the visit—this is also home to the famous Temi Tea Garden. Remoter still and even more gorgeous is **North Sikkim,** with some spectacular drives—the Chungthang-to-Lachung stretch is riddled with waterfalls, while Lachung to Yumthang ascends 1,000m (3,280 ft.) in just 25km (16 miles), cruising through the Singba Rhododendron Reserve, which in spring is a riot of colors. If you've come this far, make sure you dip your weary bones in the hot sulfur springs at Yumthang. (*Note:* North Sikkim is accessible only via a tour agency—the government does not want to overburden the natural resources with an uncontrolled tourist influx.)

ESSENTIALS

PERMITS   In addition to the standard visa, foreign visitors must be in possession of an **Inner Line Permit** (see "Acquiring your Sikkim Permit in Darjeeling," earlier in this chapter). This, together with your passport, must be carried at all times. If you wish to travel north of Gangtok or Pelling, you will require an additional endorsement or **Protected Area Permit** from Sikkim Tourism in Gangtok.

VISITOR INFORMATION   Sikkim Tourism (Mahatma Gandhi Marg; ✆ 03592/20-2634 or -2352; www.sikkimindia.com) is open Monday to Saturday, May through August, 10am to 4pm; March through April and September through October daily 9am to 7pm. The center has a computerized touch-screen kiosk that will provide more-or-less up-to-date tourist information (when it's working). This is where you can book highly recommended scenic helicopter rides. The office downstairs is where you must have your Sikkim permit endorsed if you intend to visit certain restricted areas in the state. There's also an **Information Counter** (✆ 0353/255-1036; daily 10am–2:30pm) at Bagdogra Airport.

GETTING THERE   **Bagdogra** in neighboring West Bengal is the closest airport, and is served by flights from major cities like Kolkata and Delhi. From Bagdogra, Sikkim Helicopter Service runs daily 30-minute flights to Gangtok for around Rs 1,700 ($41/£21), well worth it just for the views. Alternatively, taxis (4 hr.) and buses are available. Shared jeep services are also available from Darjeeling, Siliguri, and Kalimpong, all in West Bengal. These are highly affordable; book more than one seat for yourself, preferably the two front seats for the best views. If you're coming from Kathmandu, fly to **Bhadrapur** in east Nepal, and head to Gangtok via Kakarbhitta (on the Nepalese-Indian border) and Siliguri in West Bengal.

GETTING AROUND SIKKIM   Unless you pick up a helicopter from Bagdogra Airport, you will travel in Sikkim by road. Use either a private or shared jeep. Although roads are open throughout the year, bear in mind that all of Sikkim is mountainous and routes inevitably take far longer than they appear on maps. The shared taxi and jeep services from Gangtok to Pelling (Rs 150/$3.65/£1.85) that depart twice a day at 7am and 12:30pm are served by **Nam Nam taxi stand;** book your seat in advance. Again, book both front seats, for the views, and also because drivers tend to pack way more people into the car than you'd have imagined possible. Sikkim's roads invariably traverse steep mountains and deep valleys, so travel can be exhausting (the journey to Pelling, via Ravangla, takes 5 hr.), but the scenery is spectacular. Alternatively, you could break journey at the delightful Yangsum Farm (reviewed below) at Rinchenpong (1½ hr. from Pelling). Within **Gangtok,** you're best off doing most of your wandering on foot; because of one-way roads, taxis are frequently required to skirt much of the city. To get to the Tibetology Institute and to Rumtek Monastery, you'll have to use a taxi.

GUIDED TOURS & TRAVEL AGENTS   For all kinds of adventure tourist activities as well as tour arrangements, contact Saom Tshering Namchu of **Himali Travel Specialists** (Karma Bhutia Building, Gairi Gaon, Tadong, Gangtok; ✆ 94-3420-9819 or 0354/23-2421). **Blue Sky Tours & Travel** (Tourism Building, Mahatma Gandhi Marg; ✆ 03592/20-5113) specializes in jeep tours of northern Sikkim. They can also help you with local sightseeing, and offer a 2-day Monastery Tour that takes in several Buddhist monasteries in the state. Like all tour operators in Gangtok, their rates depend on the number of riders.

For trekking arrangements, try **Sikkim Tours & Travels** (Church Rd.; ✆ 03592/20-2188; www.sikkimtours.com). **Tashila Tours & Travels** (✆ 03592/20-2978; www.tashila.com) undertakes a range of services, including trekking, rafting, and specialist tours. **Siniolchu Tours and Travels** (✆ 03592/20-5569 or 94-3402-4572; slg_sinolchu@sancharnet.in; Mon–Sat 9am–1pm and 2–8pm) is reliable. Headquartered in Gangtok, it undertakes a wide range of spectacular treks and tours in various regions of Sikkim and beyond. Most treks cost in the vicinity of $60 (£30) per person per day, and include tents, food, porters, yaks, and guides.

GANGTOK & ENVIRONS

Sikkim's capital sits at an altitude of 1,780m (5,800 ft.), straddling a high ridge where houses and concrete blocks spill down the hillside; below is the Ranipul River. With only 29,000 inhabitants, it's relatively laid-back and generally free from the malaise that stalks India's many overpopulated towns and cities. For visitors, the most noble of Gangtok's charms is its proximity to marvelous mountain vistas; the town itself is threatened by unchecked construction. A base for visitors who come to organize treks or wind down after a high-altitude experience, it's pleasant to roam around but certainly not packed with attractions. The town's most significant drawing card is the **Namgyal Institute of Tibetology** ⍟ (admission Rs 10/25¢/15p; Mon–Sat 10am–4pm), which houses a collection of Tibetan, Sanskrit, and Lepcha manuscripts, as well as statues, Buddhist icons, masks, scrolls, musical instruments, jewelry, incense burners, and beautiful *thangkas* (painted or embroidered tapestry wall hangings).

Nearby, **Do-Drul Chorten** is a fine example of a whitewashed Buddhist stupa, encircled by prayer wheels. **Enchey Monastery** is a Tibetan Buddhist lamasery worth visiting, and the **Flower Exhibition Centre** (Rs 5/10¢/5p adults, Rs 5/10¢/5p camera), near White Hall, attracts orchid buffs. In the manner of traditional hill kingdom forts and castles, Sikkim's royalty once resided within the yellow tin-roofed palace in the uppermost reaches of the town. From here, the Chogyal and his family enjoyed the best views in Gangtok. Sadly, the Chogyal palace is off-limits to visitors. When the British turned up, they installed their own very own "White Hall" alongside the palace and, despite initial bickering, soon got round to several decades of contented socializing. A good morning excursion (8am–noon) is to the stunning high-altitude **Changu Lake.** This is barely 18km (11 miles) from the Indo-Chinese border post **Nathu-La,** which has only recently been opened up for trade. It is extremely cold here, even in the summer, so come prepared. Permits are a must for all travelers, and the 90-minute return journey by taxi will cost Rs 1,200 to Rs 1,800 ($29–$44/£15–£22).

Rumtek Monastery ⍟⍟   The region's top attraction lies 24km (15 miles) from Gangtok. Rigpe Dorjee, the "supreme head" of one of Tibetan Buddhism's four major sects—the Kagyu, or "Black Hat" order—revived it in 1959 after the Chinese invaded Tibet. Regarded as the richest Buddhist monastic center in India, Rumtek houses some of the world's rarest and most unique religious artifacts; its design is said to replicate that of the original Kagyu headquarters in Tibet. Try to get here during prayer times, when the red-carpeted benches are occupied by the Vajra chant and disciplinary master, who leads the chanting of prayers. The venerated part of the complex is the **Golden Stupa,** a 4m-high (13-ft.) *chorten* in which the mortal remains of the 16th Gyalwa Karmapa (founder of the Black Hat order; see box below) are enshrined. Gold-plated and embedded with jewels, turquoise, and coral, the stupa is kept in a locked shrine room, which must be specially unlocked for visitors. Ask a monk to help you track down the keeper of the key. (*Note:* If you come in Feb, you will be able to

---

⍟ Fun Fact   **Who Will Rule the Black Hat Order?**

In September 1992, an 8-year-old Tibetan boy named Ugyen Thinley Dorje was officially sanctified as the 17th Gyalwa Karmapa and new head of the "Black Hat" order, and recognized by the Dalai Lama as the true reincarnation of the 16th Karmapa. But controversy has surrounded Dorje ever since his coronation at Tibet's Tshurpu monastery. Chinese authorities, welcoming him as a state guest, have been intent on using him as a political puppet, while a group of rival lamas have identified another candidate as the true reincarnation. In January 2000, Dorje undertook a grueling 1,400km (868-mile) trek and escaped from Chinese-controlled Tibet to join the Dalai Lama in Dharamsala. There he awaits permission from the Indian government to take his place at Rumtek Monastery, which has been without a head since 1981.

witness the fascinating annual mask dance and other ceremonies that take place in all the monasteries in the region, all celebrating the Tibetan New Year.) For more information, go to www.rumtek.org.

WHERE TO STAY & DINE

If you're traveling on a budget, **Mintokling Guest House** (© **03592/20-4226;** mintokling@hotmail.com; doubles Rs 650–Rs 1,500 ($16–$37/£8–£19); all credit cards except AE) is a Sikkimese home with fairly spacious, clean guest rooms; our favorite is no. 304. The owner is a fantastic source of information on Sikkimese history, especially if you're interested in the political lowdown; his mother was the niece of the last king of Sikkim.

Sikkim's smartest hotel, **Nor-Khill** (see below), also hosts one of the better restaurants, **Shangri-La** (© **03592/20-5637**). Splurge on an all-inclusive full-course Sikkimese meal, which you will have to order beforehand. Find out if the stir-fried fiddlehead ferns or the popular *sisnu* (a dish made from stinging nettle) are available, and do try their juicy chicken/pork *momos* (Tibetan dumplings). Book a table at the window. Nor-Khill also has the best pub in town, the cozy **Dragon Bar. Snowlion** (© **03592/20-2523** or -4962; all credit cards accepted) is equally good for Tibetan fare, including chicken *sha-dre* (rice noodles with a curry sauce) and *sumei,* or open *momos.* Adventurous diners can sample traditional *dre-thuk,* a thick, porridgelike rice soup topped with a mountain of finely grated cheese. It serves delicious, body-warming beverages—try the hot toddy with brandy, rum, and cloves, or the hot whiskey lemonade. **Little Italy** (SNOD Complex, Deorali; © **03592/28-1980**) rustles up good pizzas and pastas and plays great music, with a live band on the weekends (bar attached). **Bakers Café** (M.G. Marg; © **03592/22-0195**) is also a good place to hang out over coffee and freshly baked cakes and croissants.

The Hidden Forest Retreat 𝒜𝒜   Offering an authentic homestay experience, this is a fabulous alternative to the hotels in Gangtok. It's owned by a family that admits it's a little crazy because their plants come first before all else. Spending a few days here, surrounded by the 30-year-old nursery, taking in lots of fresh air and mountain views and being overfed by the lovely Kesang, is a rare pleasure. A great cook, Kesang will feed you a range of delectable snacklike meals—the only drawback is that at some point you have to stop eating! With one cottage and six double rooms, it's a small, personal affair—interiors are similar with colorful Sikkimese *tenthis* (low stools) and *choktsis* (low tables), pinewood floors and ceilings, and dimly lit but clean bathrooms. Spend the evening on the patio with wind chimes for company, and warm up with *chang* (a local alcoholic beverage made with millet) served in a beautiful container fashioned out of old wood and silver.

The Hidden Forest Retreat, Sinchey Busty, Gangtok 737 101. ©/fax **03592/20-5197.** www.hiddenforestretreat.com. 7 units. Rs 1,800 ($44/£22) single; Rs 2,500 ($61/£31) double. Rs 500 ($12/£6.15) extra bed. Rates include all meals. At press time could not process credit cards but plans to do so; please check. **Amenities:** Dining; travel assistance; laundry; doctor-on-call; television; heater; complimentary tea/coffee; Internet after 9pm.

Netuk House 𝒜𝒜 (𝓥𝒶𝓁𝓊𝑒   Buddhist prayer flags flutter above this gorgeously situated and well-run family guesthouse with real Sikkimese flavor. The warmly aristocratic Denzong family, who are always pleased to introduce guests to local culture, owns it. All accommodations are unique; four guest rooms are in the main house and six are in the colorful annex, with its traditional rainbow-hued Sikkimese-style facade. Guest rooms are simple but lovely, and have good, comfortable mattresses covered in crisp white linen. Carefully prepared traditional four-course Sikkimese meals are served in the dining room; just below is a charming Sikkimese-style living room with an old-fashioned wood-burning heater. There's also a lovely bar.

Tibet Rd., Gangtok 737 101. © 03592/20-2374 or 3592/22-6778. slg_netuk@sancharnet.in. 12 units. Rs 4,180 ($102/£52) double. Rs 1,300 ($32/£16) extra person; Rs 750 ($18/£9.25) children 8–12; Rs 375 ($9.15/£4.60) children 4–7; free for children under 4. Rates include all meals. No credit cards. **Amenities:** Restaurant; bar; travel assistance; car hire; laundry; doctor-on-call; TV lounge; sightseeing.

Nor-Khill 🏵🏵🏵 This stylish hotel, once the royal guest house of the former king, offers the priciest and most luxurious accommodations in the state of Sikkim, fronted by a lovely lawn (sadly, overlooking Gangtok's sports stadium). The renovated deluxe units resemble suites, with a large bedroom area extending off a comfortable and beautiful living area; views are excellent. Huge floral or dragon-motif rugs cover the wood tile floors, and the furnishings and fittings are carved and painted Sikkimese-style. Beds are a little narrow and slightly soft, but have lovely fabrics and scatter cushions. Bathrooms are spacious, with tubs and natural light. Standard doubles are spacious and equally beautiful; reserve room no. 43 or 44, which are large and well-positioned. The room rate includes all meals, served as a set-menu in the formal **Shangri-La Restaurant.**

Paljor Stadium Rd., Gangtok 737 101. © **03592/20-5637** or 0359/22-0064. Fax 03592/20-5639. Reservations: 5 Park Row, 47 Park St., Kolkata 700 016. © 033/2226-9878. Fax 033/2246-6388. www.elginhotels.com. 25 units. Rs 4,800 ($117/£59) single; Rs 5,100 ($124/£63) standard double. Rs 2,150 ($52/£27) extra bed. Rates include all meals. AE, MC, V. **Amenities:** Restaurant; bar; travel assistance; gift shop; 24-hr. room service; babysitting; laundry; doctor-on-call; currency exchange. *In room:* TV, heater.

Near Rumtek

There are plenty of small guesthouses in the area, but the biggest and best would be **Martam Village Resort** (reviewed below) and the **Bamboo Resort** (© **03592/25-2516;** www.sikkim.ch/bamboo-resort.html; Rs 3,800/$93/£47 double) set amid paddy fields. The rooms are small but clean; some come with balconies. Each has its own color scheme according to Feng Shui principles—frankly, the red and blue is a trifle overpowering. Sadly, the **Shambhala Mountain Resort,** located right next to the monastery, has become quite seedy and is to be avoided.

Martam Village Resort 🏵 🏵alue Although it's small, covering barely an acre of land, this lovely resort (a bit of a misnomer) is an excellent place to stay for several reasons. Just half an hour from Rumtek, it is one of the few places where you get fantastic views, not of Kanchenjunga for once, but of the lower hills, their terraced fields of mustard, corn, and paddy creating a ripple effect: brown in winters and green and golden in the summers. Awakened by boisterous roosters, guests are taken for short or long walks through villages and forests full of giant bamboo and wild orchids by the

---

Himalayan Brew

Chang, made from fermented millet, is the brew of choice in Sikkim. It's usually served in a wooden tumbler (a *tomba*) with a bamboo straw and should look like a small mountain of chestnut-colored caviar sprinkled with a few grains of rice. Believed to aid sleep, it supposedly never causes hangovers. Many Western travelers would disagree. The locals advise you to not gulp it but let it sit as long as possible in the *tomba,* thereby allowing it to get stronger.

Husbands, Inc.

Part of Sikkim's unique high-altitude culture is the continued existence—typically in remote regions—of polyandrous communities, where one woman is married to a number of men. In some cases, a woman marries all the brothers from a single family. With the increasing modernization, however, such practices have now become rare.

enthusiastic Pema, who will point out the many varieties of natural herbs used for everything from toothaches and antiseptics to writing ink and paper. Facilities in the 14 thatched cottages are basic—rooms spartan, doddering heaters, bathrooms just okay, cuisine unimaginative—but the atmosphere all around more than makes up for these small inconveniences.

Gangkha, Martam, East Sikkim. ✆ 03592/23-6843. martam31@hotmail.com. 14 units. Rs 3,000 ($73/£37) full-board double; Rs 2,300 ($56/£28) single. Extra bed Rs 1,200 ($29/£15). No credit cards. **Amenities:** Bar; travel arrangements; laundry; currency exchange. *In room:* Hot water, room heater, no phone.

PELLING & ENVIRONS

Traditionally a stopover for trekkers headed for Yoksum, Dzongri, and similar high-altitude spots in western Sikkim, Pelling has begun to establish itself as a tourist destination in its own right, and as a result, concrete lodges have sprung up indiscriminately to cash in on the passing trade. Nevertheless, the surrounding scenery is spectacular, and the sunrise behind snow-clad Khangchendzonga will leave you breathless. Besides hiking or rafting, the top attractions are the nearby monasteries. From Pelling, a pleasant 30-minute walk along the main road toward Geyzing will lead you to one of Sikkim's oldest and most revered monasteries, **Pemayangtse** ✿ (entry Rs 5/10¢/5p; daily 7am–4pm), situated at 2,085m (6,672 ft.) in a cliff-top forest clearing. Set up as a monastery for *Ta-Sang,* or "pure monks" of the Nyingmapa order, Pemayangtse was established in 1705 by Lhatsun Chempo, one of the lamas who performed the consecration ritual of Sikkim's first king. Its prized treasure is a 7m-tall (22-ft.) wooden depiction of Guru Rinpoche's *Sang-tok-palri,* or "heavenly palace," encased in glass in the monastery's upper room. Note that it's worth trying to contact Yapo S. Yongda, who resides here—he's a fascinating source of information on Sikkimese history.

Southeast of Pemayangtse (30-min. walk), on a lower hillock, are the ruins of the late-17th-century **Rabdentse Palace,** from where you can see **Tashiding Monastery** ✿✿, one of the most idyllic, peaceful, and sublime monasteries in India. Hire a jeep from Pelling to get here (Rs 1,400/$34/£17 round-trip). A mere glance at Tashiding's **Thongwa Rangdol,** Sikkim's most venerated *chorten,* will (if Buddhist legends are to be believed) absolve you of all your sins. Also of special significance is the *bhumpa,* a copper vase that contains the holy water used each year during the *Bhumchu* festival, when a sacred ritual reveals Sikkim's fate for the upcoming year. It's a somewhat stiff 50-minute hike in the opposite direction to hilltop **Sanga Choling Monastery** ✿—but it's worth it, for the most panoramic views around. Constructed in 1697, this is believed to be the second-oldest Buddhist monastery in Sikkim. Go when morning or evening prayers are held. For more information on the region, call the **Tourism Information Office** at ✆ 03595/25-0756. There is, however, one more optional stopover for those with more time to explore—2 hours south of Pelling is the small town of Rinchenpong—worth including just so you can overnight at **Yangsum Farm** (reviewed below).

WHERE TO STAY & DINE

With basics like electricity and water in short supply, don't expect luxury in Pelling. The town is spilling over with tour and travel agents, many of whom are quite suspect in their dealings—single women travelers would do well to be cautious and use only accredited travel agents, based preferably in Gangtok. Aside from Norbu, the best place to stay is newly opened **The Mount Pandim** $\mathcal{R}$, set atop a hill, with the most terrific views of the mighty Kanchenjunga, and a 10-minute amble distance from the Pemayangtse Monastery (and 30 min. from the Rabdentse Ruins). The hotel had only just opened at press time, but guest rooms and facilities are in keeping with the Elgin chain of hotels: comfortable and positively luxurious when compared with your other options. Try to reserve deluxe room no. 203 (© **03595/25-0756** or -0573; www.elgin hotels.com; doubles Rs 3,800/$93/£47). If you're keen on the homestay experience, your best bet is the delightful Yangsum, a working farm reviewed below, near the village of Rinchenpong. If you want to be based in Pelling itself (and you're watching your rupees), a good budget option is **Hotel Phamrong** (Upper Pelling; © **03595/ 25-8218** or -0660; mailphamrong@yahoo.com; doubles from Rs 950–Rs 1,800/ $23–$44/£12–£22), which have large en-suite rooms that generally come with fantastic views. Don't expect luxury, but the sunrises are brilliant. Pelling's best dining is at the Norbu Ghang Resort (see below), but the restaurant at tiny **Garuda** guest lodge (next door to Hotel Phamrong) serves a solid selection, including Tibetan and Sikkimese specialties.

Norbu Ghang Resort $\mathcal{R}$ Norbu Ghang (which means "Jewel on the Hilltop") has the most tasteful accommodations in western Sikkim (the Mount Pandim has the edge with its glorious views, but it's located outside of town, which may not suit you if you're just here to arrange trekking). The resort is built on four levels over a 2-hectare (5-acre) stretch of flower-speckled terraced hillside. The corrugated-roof cottages are fairly decent in size. All the best rooms and cottages have views of mighty Khangchendzonga (book cottage no. 601, 801, or 804). You can also opt for the cozy Denzong suite, with its atticlike feel, where even the tiny windows are excusable. The resort also has Pelling's best restaurant, serving traditional Sikkimese cuisine.

Pelling 737 113. © **03595/25-8245**, -8272, or -0566. Fax 03595/25-8271. www.sikkiminfo.net/norbughang. 30 units. Rs 2,200 ($54/£27) deluxe double; Rs 2,700 ($66/£33) super deluxe double; Rs 3,300 ($81/£41) Denzong Suite. Rs 600 ($15/£7.40) extra bed. MC, V. **Amenities:** Restaurant; bar; travel assistance; gift shop; room service; doctor-on-call; currency exchange; Internet. *In room:* TV, heater.

Yangsum Farm $\mathcal{R}$ *(Finds*   With an idyllic location, surrounded by fields and edge-to-edge mountain ranges, Yangsum Farm is a real find. Owner-run by Thendup Tashi and Pema, this is a working farm: The resident rooster and watchdog geese ensure that everyone is up at the crack of dawn to welcome the early morning rays and contemplate another relaxing day. You'll spend your time soaking in views, or getting fat on Sikkimese cuisine. (Growing everything from mandarin, plums, pears, and peaches to spinach, radish, cauliflower, and cardamom, this is one place you won't be going hungry.) Burn it all off with long, lovely walks around the countryside, coming across monasteries, ancient *lepcha* houses, and fog-filled forests (not to mention a leech or two). Of the four rooms, the heritage and the mud cottage are the best—spacious with curtains fashioned out of silks, *thangkas* on walls, and tiny balconies overlooking the fields with the range in the backdrop.

Moments Wildlife Safari by Boat

The Brahmaputra flows for some 644km (400 miles) through Assam, and a river cruise is the best way to visit this little-known region in comfort. There is hardly any traffic on the river, just the occasional country boat taking fishermen to their traps. Otherwise you'll find total solitude, rare indeed in India. The two 12-double-cabin riverboats of **Assam Bengal Navigation** (www.assambengal navigation.com; assambengal@aol.com) are comfortable without being pretentious. Rooms are all air-conditioned, the en-suite bathrooms are workmanlike, and the furnishings, which make use of local weaving, rattan, and bamboo, are simple and unfussy. Each boat has a saloon and bar with glass doors looking out on a small foredeck and the river ahead, while upper sun decks are furnished with sun loungers and generous seating. ABN's cruises range in length from 4 to 14 nights and cost from $275 (£140) per person per night. Most days the boat stops for a visit on land, whether to a wildlife park, tea garden, temple, or tribal village. A fleet of jeeps is used to take guests on longer excursions, but be warned, Assam's road surfaces leave a lot to be desired. Transfers are included in the tariff. Pickups can be done at either of the two airports in Dibrugarh or Guwahati, both of which are connected to Delhi and Kolkata.

Yangsum Farm, P.O. Rinchenpong, West Sikkim 737 111. © 97-3308-5196. www.yangsumfarm.com. 4 units. $81 (£41) doubles with full board; $60 (£30) singles. No credit cards. **Amenities:** Travel assistance; doctor-on-call; running hot water; room heaters; village walks and local sightseeing. *In room:* No phone.

TREKS THROUGH WESTERN SIKKIM ★★★

Treks around western Sikkim are justifiably popular because of the spectacular views afforded throughout. If you want something relatively short and undemanding, the 4-day trek from Pelling to Tashiding and back is ideal, covering both cultural sights and majestic scenery. Far more challenging, and requiring more time and extra stamina, are the high-altitude treks to **Dzongri** (3,861m/12,870 ft.; 6 days) and **Goeche La** (4,740m/15,800 ft.; 9–10 days). There are also other treks to Singalila and Versay in the west, Greenlake in the north, and Kedi and Teenjure in the east. Trekking here is only allowed with a recognized trekking operator in Gangtok; a daily fee of $45 to $60 (£23–£30) will include guides, porters, yaks, tents, and food. March through May, the fabulous—and less strenuous—5-day **Rhododendron Trek** through the exotic forests of the Singalila Range, near the border with Nepal, become possible. For trek operators, see "Essentials: Guided Tours & Travel Agents," above.

EXPLORING THE WILDS OF ASSAM ★★★

To most, Assam means tea, and indeed some 20% of the world's tea is grown here. But Assam's remote location (best reached by plane from Kolkata or Bagdogra, flying into Guwahati, after which you need to travel by road, with the closest park approximately 4 hr. away) has meant that it remains one of India's best-kept secrets, despite boasting two out of India's five World Heritage environmental sites—Manas and Kaziranga. In **Manas,** apart from a small and extremely basic but superbly located **Forest Rest House** at Mothanguri (contact the Field Director, Manas Tiger Reserve; © 03666/233-413), deep in the park, the only place to stay is the **Bansbari Lodge** (www.assambengalnavigation.com; assambengal@aol.com), right beside the park entrance. The 16 fan-cooled rooms are spacious and have small balconies. The lodge arranges performances of Bodo tribal dancing. Be warned—the access road to the park from the National Highway is in dire need of attention. The more popular **Kaziranga** is among the top five places to see wildlife in India. This marshy plain beside the Brahmaputra was turned into a wildlife sanctuary by Lord Curzon, Viceroy of India, in 1908. At that time there were only a handful of rhinos left; now around 1,800 graze the park; they constitute the vast majority of the world population of the Asian one-horned rhinoceros. Also present here are wild elephant, buffalo, swamp deer, hog deer, sambar, wild boar, as well as the densest tiger population in India. But don't get your hopes up—tiger in Kaziranga are harder to spot than almost anywhere else, thanks to the lush vegetation. The best way to get close to the rhinos is atop an elephant: Every morning cavalcades of 20 or so elephants head out rhino tracking—and visitors are seldom disappointed. If you aren't staying on board one of Assam Bengal Navigation's river cruise ships (see box below), the only possible alternative is **Wild Grass** (© **03776/226-2011**), which offers a good standard of comfort and is close to the entrance to Kaziranga's Central Range. At press time, **Diphlu River Lodge** was being constructed by Assam Bengal Navigation (see details below); once completed, this will in all likelihood be the best place to stay on terra firma.

Appendix: India in Depth

A great triangle of land thrusting out of Asia, past the Bay of Bengal and the Arabian Sea, and deep into the Indian Ocean, India is a vast country (similar in size to Europe) and home to an ancient culture with a host of historic and architectural treasures unparalleled in the world. But more than anything else, it is India's enigmatic "otherness" that so fascinates the first-time visitor, for perhaps no other country on earth can offer so much contrast—traveling within the subcontinent feels at times like traveling through time. From the snowy peaks of the Himalayas, where prayer flags flutter against an impossibly blue sky, to the golden deserts of Rajasthan and Gujarat, where women wear saris saturated with fuchsia and saffron; from the vast plains of Madhya Pradesh, dotted with ruins and tiger parks, to the lush tropical mountains and paradisiacal beaches off the Malabar Coast, the spectrum of images and experiences is stupendous. Perhaps one of the most heterogeneous cultures in the world, with a mosaic of languages, dialects, religions, races, customs, and cuisines, India and its people cannot be defined, labeled, or pigeonholed—only experienced. Whether you're planning your trip to do a spiritual pilgrimage, view (or shop for) its myriad treasures, live like royalty in medieval palaces, unwind on unspoiled beaches, or simply indulge in the most holistic spa therapies known to man, India will leave an indelible impression on you. The following essays are merely a backdrop; to come to grips with the strange and fascinating world that is India, you will need to immerse yourself in some of the reading suggested at the end of this chapter. And travel to India again. And again. And again.

1 India Today

by Frommer's authors & Anita Pratap

Pratap is a former CNN bureau chief for South Asia, freelance journalist, and columnist for *Outlook,* India's weekly newsmagazine

Whatever your understanding of India today, the exact opposite is probably equally true. Life has changed dramatically since India began to liberalize its economy in the 1990s, and yet it remains a land where several centuries exist simultaneously. If you visit one of its scientific centers, you could well believe you are at NASA, but walk to a village that still has no connection to a drivable road (and there are thousands of them), and you will find people living exactly as they did 2,000 years ago. More than 25% of the world's software engineers are Indian, but another 25% of the Indian population goes to bed hungry every night. Women like Pratibha Patil, the female president of India elected in July 2007, have risen to top positions of power and authority in both the political and corporate world, yet millions struggle without the most basic human rights. India has the world's highest number of malnourished children, yet obesity in urban children is a new and menacing problem. The country has armed itself with nuclear weapons, but has difficulty providing drinking water to millions of its citizens. It ranks low in the United Nations' Human Development Index, which measures quality of life, but in terms of purchasing parity, India is the third-biggest economy in the world after the United States and China. As more and more countries outsource their call centers to Indian companies, the BPO boom has created a large new class of young urbanites keen to flash their disposable incomes, and as a result the luxury market in India has exploded, with every international brand from Louis Vuitton to Greubel Forsey vying for their slice of this burgeoning market. Meanwhile, a real agrarian crisis continues to brew in rural India, with newspapers and 24/7 news channels (of which there are now dozens) reporting debt-related farmer suicides on an almost daily basis. In Maharashtra alone 1,448 cotton farmers committed suicide in 2006, because basic issues of debt, water shortage, food security, and social inequities remain unaddressed. No wonder India is confusing, confounding, incomprehensible. How can you make sense of this land? It's like emptying an ocean with a spoon.

All through the 1970s and even 1980s, Western diplomats and journalists predicted the "Balkanization" of India. It didn't happen, but in 1991 India's foreign exchange reserves plunged to a catastrophic $1 billion, barely sufficient to service 2 weeks of imports. India was forced to embark on its radical liberalization program. Since then, India's economy has grown at a rate rivaled only by neighbor China: 2006–07 saw India's $1,103-billion economy grow by a whopping 9.4%, the fastest in 18 years. India's reserves have reached a staggering $212.4 billion and the stock market has soared to unheard-of numbers, while the dollar exchange rate continues to dip. But this growth has also spurred inflation (said to be at 5.06%) and a rise in interest rates. Statistics show that the overall standard of living has improved drastically, but the truth is that the benefits of a booming economy have not reached a vast percentage of the population, and India still has the world's largest concentration of poor. Nearly 300 million people live without the basic necessities of life: water, food, roads, education, medical care, and jobs. These are the Indians living on the outer edges of the nation's consciousness, far away in remote tribal areas, barren wastelands, and dirty slums, totally outside the market economy.

With a billion voters, every national election here is the biggest spectacle of fair and peaceful democracy that humankind has ever witnessed. And yet increasingly democracy is often a masquerade for a modern version of feudalism. Clan loyalties propel electoral victories. The victor rules his or her province like a medieval tribal chieftain, often showing scant respect for merit or rule of law. Cronies are hand-picked for jobs, rivals are attacked or harassed, public funds are misused to promote personal agendas. Modern-day versions of Marie Antoinette abound in Indian democracy—while the poor were dying of cold in January 2003 in Uttar Pradesh, India's most populous state, its chief minister, Mayawati, was strutting around in diamonds and celebrating her birthday with a cake the size of a minibus. Later that year, having been indicted by the Supreme Court in a case of alleged corruption, Mayawati resigned only to return to power with a resounding victory. Proof that real choices are limited? Perhaps, but many low-caste people, whose cause Mayawati (herself of low-caste origin) supposedly champions, support her fiery attitude and are inspired that she too can celebrate like India's rich.

In fact, according to a seminal paper presented by Dheeraj Sinha in 2007, the mindset of India as a nation is changing—gone (or fading) are the priestly Brahminical values of knowledge, adjustment, simplicity, and restraint, and "in"

Impressions

Who is an authentic Indian and who isn't? Is India Indian? Does it matter? Let's just say we're an ancient people learning to live in a recent nation . . .
—Arundhati Roy, *The Algebra of Injustice*

are the warrior-like Kshatriya values of success, winning, glory, and heroism. Whereas Indians traditionally took refuge in the idea of karma and fate (see "Hinduism," below), the emerging mindset believes that karma is shaped by one's actions—that it is possible to achieve a life that one desires rather than one that's destined.

This represents a huge shift, and is both the result and driver of the economic engine that is powering India. But there is one growth industry guaranteed to stymie, if not wreck, genuine progress: the feud between Muslim and Hindu fundamentalists. At the heart of the latter ideology—most acutely represented by the RSS and Bajrang Dal—is the belief that today's Muslims should be punished for historical wrongs perpetrated by medieval Muslim conquerors. It's a belief that is fired by modern-day resentments (such as the concern that Muslims have, proportionally, the highest birth rate in India) and fears that *madrasas* are creating hotbeds of Muslim fundamentalism. The worst Hindu-Muslim rioting and looting happened in the western state of Gujarat in 2002, but bomb blasts still occur almost annually (most recently in Hyderabad) and are proof that sectarian trouble is simply on slow-brew.

Nationalism also takes its toll in the Kashmir dispute that bedevils relations between the nuclear-capable neighbors India and Pakistan. The two countries have fought two of their three wars over Kashmir, engaged in another low-level conflict in 1998, and came to the brink of another in 2002. Driven by popular enthusiasm and political initiatives on either side, there has been a thawing in India-Pakistan relations since then, and the peace process has enjoyed a visible momentum with issues such as visa issuance significantly improved. That said, there is still a lack of progress in resolving many bilateral problems, and any further improvements are unlikely given the recent spike in terrorist incidences and with Pakistan now battling its own internal crises.

The problems of nationalism are exacerbated by politicians who try to pit Hindus, who constitute 80% of the population, against the 150-million Muslim minority before elections in order to garner votes—this happened again in 2006 and 2007 in the UP elections, when the BJP released a highly inflammatory CD featuring Muslims slaughtering cows and kidnapping Hindu women.

Yet the last general election, held in 2004, proved that the masses cannot be won over for long through this diabolical strategy of dividing communities, and in some subconscious way there seems to be a recognition that if divisive politics win, India will lose. Deviating from the script, the Indian masses proved the media barons, opinion-makers, psephologists (political scientists who study and even predict elections), exit-pollsters, and astrologers all wrong and voted the Congress party back into power. The 2004 electoral upset for the BJP-led government was also in many ways a vote against the highly personalized campaign against Sonia Gandhi's foreign origins. Ms. Gandhi responded by declining the post of Prime Minister, citing the potential divide it would cause, and asking former Finance Minister Manmohan Singh—highly respected for the role he played in the liberalization of India's economy in the '90s—to take the helm. It was a smart move, although many feel that Singh is in fact just a puppet (and Ms. Gandhi still pulls the strings) and look forward to registering their protest in the next general election, in 2009.

Bill Clinton once said: "India remains a battleground for every single conflict the world has to win." Certainly India copes with huge problems—massive corruption, joblessness, judicial bottlenecks with few convictions and delays of up to 20 years for delivering justice, AIDS, acute water shortages, poverty, disease, environmental degradation, unbearable overcrowding in metropolitan cities, crises of governance, sectarian violence, and terrorism. India adds one Australia to itself every year—*18 million people.* The rural poor (who form the majority) see children as an economic resource, the only security net for old age, and high child-mortality rates necessitate the need for more than one, or two. Apart from India's huge natural growth rate, an estimated two million poor Bangladeshis slip into India every year in search of work.

But this is a country of remarkable stamina. As Manmohan Singh recently put it, "Our real strength has always been our willingness to live and let live." Home to scores of languages, cuisines, landscapes, and cultures, India is a giant. But she will move at her own pace. She is not an Asian tiger. She is more like a stately Indian elephant. No one can whip or crack her into a run. If you try, the stubborn elephant will dig in her heels and refuse to budge. No power on earth can then force her to move. But equally so, she cannot be stopped once she's on the move. And with the slow but fundamental shift from silent acceptance of karma to the belief that one can—and should—give shape to destiny, she is most certainly on the move. There is no point arguing whether this is good or bad. It is good and bad. And it is many things in between.

After all, this is India.

2 India Past to Present

by Nigel Worden

A professor of history specializing in Indian Ocean history

No visitor to India can fail to be overwhelmed by the combination of a bustling, modernizing nation and an ancient but omnipresent past. India's history is everywhere, in its temples and mosques, forts and palaces, tombs and monuments, but it has only recently become a single country, which makes its history a complex one. Successions of kingdoms and empires have controlled parts of the subcontinent, but none unified the whole—even the British Raj's "Jewel in the Crown of the Empire" excluded large swaths of territory ruled by independent princes. Thus the accounts of history vary, and competing versions have often been the cause of bitter conflict. Given the tensions between Hindus and Muslims in South Asia, it is hardly surprising that the Islamic era in particular is highly controversial. Were the Muslims invaders and pillagers of an ancient Indian tradition, as Hindu nationalist historians claim? Or were they Indians who created a distinctive culture of architecture, painting, and literature by blending indigenous forms with Islamic influences? Is the Taj Mahal a uniquely Indian masterpiece, or a symbol of the Islamic oppressor? As is usually the case with history, it all depends on where you are, and to whom you're talking.

ANCIENT INDIA Historical accounts of India usually begin with the **Harappan civilization** of the Indus Valley, a sophisticated agricultural and urban society that flourished from 3000 to 1700 B.C. (about the same time as the earliest Egyptian civilization); although many of its sites are now located in latter-day Pakistan, you can view Harappan artifacts in places like the National Museum in New Delhi. Not much is known about the people, not least because their writing system has yet to be deciphered, but their active trade with the civilizations of the Euphrates (contemporary Iran and Iraq) show that northern India had links from very early on with the rest of Asia.

A more recognizably and distinctive "Indian" culture developed from around 1500 B.C. in the northern part of the subcontinent, spreading steadily eastward in the 1st millennium B.C., although never penetrating to the far south. This is usually referred to as the **Vedic period**. The ancient written *Vedas* provide a rich record of this era, led by a Sanskrit-speaking elite, which embedded into India Hinduism the caste system (led by a Brahmin priesthood), and the dichotomy between a rural farming majority and an urbanized merchant class, all ruled by local kings and princes. A series of Vedic kingdoms r ose and fell, each centered on a city, of which Varanasi is today the oldest-living and best-known example. Much controversy surrounds the interpretation of the "Aryans," as the Vedic culture is known— some claim that they originated as invaders from the north who conquered and subjugated the local population, while Hindu nationalists today see them as the archetypal indigenous Indian—a controversy that makes Indian archaeology a tempestuous field of study. Whichever interpretation you buy into, the influence of the Vedic era is all-pervasive in modern Indian life, and the historical focus of a modern Hindu identity.

From the 6th century B.C., the Aryan states were themselves subject to invasions from the north, in a cycle of incursion and subsequent local adaptation that was to dominate much of India's history. Even Alexander the Great, hearing of the wealth and fertility of the area, tried to invade, but his army apparently refused to cross the Indus River and instead made their way back to Macedonia. Other invaders (or settlers, depending on your preference) of Greek, Persian, and central Asian origin moved in, challenging some of the indigenous states, such as Shakas of western India and the Magadha state of the northeast. In time, all of these newcomers were absorbed into the local population. It was during this period that Siddhartha Gautama (Buddha) was born in latter-day Nepal; he later moved to India, where he sought—and found—enlightenment at

Dateline

- **Circa 3000–1700 B.C.** Harappan civilization of the Indus Valley marks earliest farming communities in the region.
- **1500–600 B.C.** Vedic states in the north establish the basis of Hinduism and the caste system.
- **326 B.C.** Alexander the Great's army halts at the Indus.
- **322–185 B.C.** Mauryan state in North India; conversions to Buddhism under Asoka (reigned 272–232 B.C.).
- **A.D. 319–540** Gupta empire reunites northern India.
- **300–900** Pallava empire in Dravidian southern India.
- **900–1300** Chola empire in southern India.
- **1206–1400s** Islamic Delhi sultanates established in north.
- **1510** Portuguese establish first European coastal settlement in India.
- **1526** Mughal conquest of Delhi (returned permanently in 1555).
- **1556–1605** Akbar extends Mughal power.
- **1600** Founding of British East India Company.
- **1658–1707** Aurangzeb conquers south for Mughal empire.

(continues)

Bodghaya, and starting teaching at Sarnath, just outside Varanasi.

The first large state to emerge in this region was under the **Mauryan rulers** (322–185 B.C.), who incorporated much of northern India, including the region west of the Indus; at its largest, it even reached south to Karnataka. The most famous of these rulers was **Asoka,** who converted to Buddhism after a particularly murderous episode of conquest pricked his conscience; he spread the Buddha's teachings throughout northern India, particularly at Sarnath and Sanchi, where you can still view the *stupas* (commemorative cairns) he built. Asoka's decrees, which were inscribed onto rock (literally), carved his reputation throughout the region, while his emblem of four back-to-back lion heads (which you can also view at Sarnath) has been adopted as the modern symbol of India.

Asoka's empire barely survived his death in 232 B.C., however, and in the subsequent centuries local states rose and fell in the north with alacrity. The **Gupta empire** emerged from A.D. 319 to 540 under Sumadra Gupta, who conquered the small kingdoms of much of northern India and Bengal, while his son extended its range to the west. This loose confederacy was marked by a reinvigoration of Hinduism and the power of the Brahmins, which

reduced the influence of Buddhism in the subcontinent (though it had taken strong root in Sri Lanka and Southeast Asia). But Hun invasions from the north in turn destroyed Gupta power, and northern India was again split into numerous small kingdoms.

It should be noted that the southern part of India remained unaffected by these developments. With the exception of Asoka's Mauryan empire, none of the northern states extended their influence beyond the central plains, and South India developed its own economic systems, trading with Southeast Asia and across the western Indian Ocean as far afield as the Roman Empire. Dravidian kingdoms emerged, some of which established sizable empires such as the **Pallava** (A.D. 300–900) and **Chola** (A.D. 900–1300). Hinduism flourished, evident in the rich legacy of Dravidian temple architecture (notably at Thanjavur).

THE ISLAMIC ERA Even Indian historians refer to the period from the 10th to the 16th centuries as "medieval," but a more accurate characterization of it relates to the impact of Islam. Muslim influence from the northwest was evident in northern India from at least A.D. 1000, but it was only with the arrival of Islamic forces from the 13th century onward that its presence became dominant. A succession

- **1739** Persian sacking of Delhi and removal of the Peacock Throne accelerates Mughal decline.
- **1757** Clive defeats *Nawab* of Bengal at Battle of Plassey, establishing British rule in Bengal.
- **1790s–1820s** British extend power in southern, western, and central India.
- **1856–57** Indian "Mutiny": uprising against British.

British sacking of Delhi and expulsion of Mughals.
- **1858** Dissolution of East India Company; India to be ruled directly from London.
- **1877** Queen Victoria declared Queen-Empress of India.
- **1885** Foundation of the Indian National Congress.
- **1890s** Bengal famine and plague epidemics.
- **1903** British capital moved from Calcutta to Delhi.

- **1905** Division of Bengal provokes boycott campaigns against British.
- **1906** Muslim League founded.
- **1915** Gandhi returns to India.
- **1919** Amritsar massacre galvanizes Indian nationalist opposition to British.
- **1930** Gandhi leads salt march to protest British taxation policies.

of fragmented and unstable Moslem states emerged around new centers such as Lahore (Pakistan), Delhi, and Agra, collectively known as the Delhi Sultanates. Conversions to Islam were made among the local population, mainly from the lower castes or where Hinduism was weaker, like in Bengal, but the majority of the population remained Hindu. In most areas the Muslim rulers and their administrators were but a thin layer, ruling societies that followed earlier traditions and practices.

In the south, Muslims made much less impact. Muslim raids in the 14th century instead led to unified Hindu resistance by the Vijayanagar empire centered in Hampi, which flourished in the south as one of the strongest Hindu states in Indian history, surviving until the 16th century.

By this stage a more vigorous wave of Islamization had emerged in the form of the **Mughals**, a dynasty that originated in the Persian borderlands (and was possibly driven south by the opposing might of Genghis Khan in central Asia). The Mughals established themselves initially in Kabul, then the Punjab, and in 1555 they finally conquered Delhi, became their capital. Under **Akbar** (1556–1605) and **Aurangzeb** (1658–1707), the Mughals extended their empire south into the Deccan and, after defeating the Vijayanagar state, deep into the south, although their ambitions to conquer the entire subcontinent were stymied by the opposition of the Hindu Maratha states in the southwest.

Rulers such as Aurangzeb were not slow to show merciless terror against those who opposed them, but previous images of the Mughal empire's ruthless despotism have now been challenged by many historians, who point out that, other than Aurangzeb, the Mughal emperors were happy to allow local rulers to continue in power, provided they regularly sent tribute to Delhi and provided troops and cavalry when needed. Close to Delhi, the fiercely independent Hindu princes of Rajasthan retained their authority so long as they did not openly flout Mughal rule. Taxes were levied on landowners, but the levels were in general no higher than before. Trade and local textile production flourished in many regions, notably in Bengal and Gujarat. Muslim law, Persian language, and administrative structures were introduced, although in many outlying parts of the empire, local customs continued.

But by the 18th century, the Mughal empire was in decline. Some of this was the result of direct opposition, especially from the Marathas, who were consolidating their power in the southwest, but in other respects, decline might have been a

(continues)

product of the Mughal empire's own prosperity. Local regions such as Bengal, Oudh, and the Punjab began to benefit from economic growth and to assert their independence. When Delhi was attacked by yet more incursions from the north, culminating in the sacking of the city by Persians in 1739 and the hauling off of the fabulously valuable Peacock Throne, symbol of Mughal power, local regions went their own way. In Bengal, the local ruler made an agreement with foreign merchants who had appeared along the coast in the 17th century, allowing them to built a small settlement at the mouth of the Hooghly River (later to become Calcutta) and to trade in cotton and cloth in return for tribute. These foreign merchants were members of the British East India Company, formed in 1600, which had failed to establish a niche in the more lucrative spice trade of Southeast Asia, and was thus forced to settle for less-plum pickings along the Indian coastline: They obtained permission from locals to set up stations at Surat and what were to become the cities of Madras and Bombay. They were not the only Europeans to settle in India; the Portuguese had first established a base in Goa in 1510, and in the 17th century the Dutch made similar agreements with local rulers in Bengal, Nagapatnam, and the Malabar coast, while the French set up shop in Pondicherry. Even the Belgians, Danes, and Swedes formed trading companies, but unlike the others, they had little impact on the indigenous culture.

As was the case elsewhere, it was the British who moved from trade to empire in India. In part this was the outcome of inter-European rivalries: The English grabbed French ships and produce in India (along with French Canada) in the **Seven Years' War** (1756–63), then moved on Dutch posts in India and Sri Lanka after the Napoleonic wars. But the main impetus came from their dealings with Indian rulers. In Bengal, English traders were making a killing, often marrying local women and living the high life. Frustrated by their continued and unwelcome presence, the local *Nawab* attacked the English settlement at Calcutta in 1756, imprisoning a number of people in a cramped cell, where some suffocated. The "Black Hole of Calcutta" martyrs became a rallying cry to justify further incursions by the British: Troops were shipped to Calcutta, which defeated the *Nawab* at Plassey the following year and again in 1764. The British East India Company filled the local power vacuum—and although nominal vassals of the Mughals still lived in the Red Fort in Delhi, the East India Company was effectively the local government.

In the course of the late 18th and early 19th centuries, the Company's area of influence grew apace. Presenting itself as the "defenders of Bengal," it forged alliances and provided military support for local rulers in areas such as Bihar and the northwestern regions, then moved in when they defaulted on repayments. By the mid–19th century, English armies (manned overwhelmingly by Indian troops) overran Oudh and the Punjab. In the south the Company moved inland from Madras to the Carnatic and across to Malabar. It inherited the Mughals' rivalry with the Marathas (the region around latter-day Mumbai), which erupted into open warfare in 1810 and led to the Company's conquest of the western coast and its hinterland.

While extending their power base, the Company still claimed allegiance to the Mughals, whose emperor retained nominal control in Delhi. But this, too, was to end. In 1856 and 1857, following decades of resentment against British policies and their impact, an army mutiny (caused by the use of animal fat on bullet cartridges, which affronted the Hindus) triggered uprisings against the British across northern and central India. Despite claims by later nationalist historians that this was a united revolt against the foreign oppressor, most of the violence in the "Indian Mutiny" of 1856 to 1857 was by Indians against other Indians, in which old scores of class, religious, or regional rivalries were festering. Nonetheless, epic stories abounded of Indian valor or British heroism and martyrdom (depending, again, on which side told them). The British, taken by surprise, only regained control by the skin of their teeth—and by ruthless retaliation. Some of the resisters had appealed to the Mughal emperor to reassert control over India, which in an unwise moment he had agreed to do. The British army sacked Delhi, forced the emperor into exile, and declared the end of the Mughal empire. But London was unimpressed by the chaos that the East India Company rule and policies had brought, and moved to abolish the Company's charter, effectively establishing direct rule from London. The pretence was over. India was now to be ruled by a new foreign power.

THE RAJ The East India Company was replaced by a new system of government. The British Crown was represented in India by a viceroy sent out from London who presided over a professional class of British-born and (mainly) Oxbridge-educated administrators appointed through the Indian Civil Service. Most Indians never saw this relatively small body of men (never exceeding 5,000 at any one time), and they in turn were dependent on the military (still primarily composed of Indian troops, or *sepoys,* lorded over by a British officer class) and on another army of Indian lesser-ranking administrators, lawyers, and civil servants, who were prevented by race from rising to the upper ranks. For India, unlike British Africa and Australasia, was not to be a settler colony. The British initially played on the fiction that they were the legitimate successors to the Mughals, mounting spectacular *durbars* (receptions) to demonstrate their power and the loyalty of India's princes—in 1877 the occasion was used to declare an absent Victoria "Queen-Empress of India"; it was only in 1911 that the reigning British monarch finally attended a *durbar.* The British built a set of administrative buildings in "New Delhi," declared the capital in 1903, that today are considered the finest architectural achievements of the empire.

In many ways, British rule was a new experience for India. For one thing, the entire subcontinent was viewed as a single whole, despite the continuation of nominally independent princely states in many of its central regions. With a mania characteristic of the Victorian, the British mapped the landscape; surveyed the diverse systems of landholding; separated inhabitants by race, language, and caste (for census purposes); and built the huge railway network that connects the country today. Much of this had the practical purpose of raising revenues from trade and taxation, since the British were determined that the Raj should be self-financing. But it also created a body of knowledge that was to shape many of their political and social policies, and to solidify categories of race and caste that had earlier been somewhat more permeable.

The Indian economy in the era of the Raj became closely dependent on British and other imperial markets, with promotion of the export of raw materials rather than internal industrialization, although by the early–20th century, parts of Bengal and the region around Bombay were starting to manufacture for local purchasers. It was from the "new" Indian administrative and mercantile classes that the first stirrings of opposition to British rule came. The local modernizers demanded equal access to economic and political opportunities, rather than a return to India's precolonial past. Thus the first **Indian National Congress (INC)** was formed in 1885, with members primarily from Bengal, Bombay Presidency, and Madras. The INC carried out its proceedings in English, and called for access to the higher ranks of the civil service (with examinations for entry held in India, not in Britain) and for relief of the heavy levies on Indian-produced local textiles. By the turn of the 20th century, after the disastrous famine and plague epidemic that broke out in Bengal in the 1890s, more extremist members of the INC were demanding *swaraj,* or "self-rule," although what they had in mind was a degree of self-government akin to the British dominions in Canada, Australia, or South Africa, rather than total independence. An unpopular administrative division of Bengal in 1905 led to a boycott of British imports, and some Bengali intellectuals began to evoke Hindu notions of a free Indian nation. The British conceded limited electoral reform, granting a local franchise to a tiny percentage of the propertied, but they ominously listed voters in separate voter rolls according to whether they were Muslim or Hindu; a separate **Muslim League (ML)** was formed in 1906.

World War I, in which large numbers of Indian troops served the British cause, dampened anti-British protests and saw a pact between the ML and the INC, not least because of vague British promises of meaningful change once the war was won. But in 1919, British General Dwyer opened fire on a demonstration held in the enclosed space of the Jallianwala Bagh in Amritsar, killing and wounding over 2,000. This gave Indian nationalism its first clear martyrs, and the callousness with which Dwyer's actions were applauded by the British general public inflamed matters further.

The period between the two world wars saw a seismic transformation of Indian nationalism, growing from the protests of a small elite to a mass-based movement that overwhelmed the British. The figure with whom Indian nationalism is most associated is **Mohandas Karamchand Gandhi,** the "Mahatma." After an early career in law, he developed his concepts of *satyagraha* (nonviolent protest) and passive resistance in defending Indian interests in colonial South Africa before he returned to his native India in 1915. Gandhi persuaded the INC to embrace a concept of a united India that belonged to all Indians, irrespective of religion or caste. Mass support for Congress campaigns of non-cooperation with the colonial state was ensured by well-publicized and symbolic campaigns such as the 1930 march from Ahmedabad to the Gujarat coast to defy a salt tax by making salt from sea water. Membership of the INC soared to over two million. But not all of Gandhi's ideas were triumphs—he was much criticized by some for his failure to support the socialist leanings of Bombay factory workers, while others took little interest in his appeal for religious tolerance or equal acceptance of the outcast *dalits*. The British granted a degree of self-government to India in 1935, although only at the provincial level. Another group that did not accept INC's call for unity was the Muslim League. Fearing Hindu domination in a united India (revealed by the 1935 elections), they began, under their leader Mohammed Ali Jinnah, to call for a separatist Islamic state named "Pakistan" (after the initials of areas they claimed: Punjab, the Afghan states, Kashmir, and Sind). At first, few took this seriously, although Gandhi was alarmed at the divisive trends.

World War II was to change everything. Gandhi and INC leaders called in 1942 for the British to "quit India" and were imprisoned. Although many Indian regiments in the British army supported the Allies, a number of other Indians joined the Japanese-trained Indian National Army under the INC leader Subhas Chandra Bose. After 1945, Muslim and Hindu violence broke out, with each side claiming power. The new Labor government in Britain was now anxious to divest itself of its troublesome Raj and sent Lord Mountbatten as a new viceroy to oversee the process. Mountbatten's decision that the British should cut their losses as quickly as possible by leaving in August 1947 took everyone by surprise. More seriously, he agreed to partition the country to appease Jinnah and the Muslim League rather than risk continuing civil war in the new state. In a frenzy of activity, "Partition" became official, and the boundaries of the new Pakistan were summarily drawn across the map, splitting the Punjab into two and dividing communities. Millions of refugees spent Independence Day desperately trying to get to the "right" side of the border, amid murderous attacks in which well over a million lost their lives. The trauma of these months still casts a deep shadow over the subcontinent. While the British Raj in India lasted less than a hundred years, the processes that led the British to divide the country into two states, India and Pakistan, have fundamentally shaped the modern nation state.

INDEPENDENT INDIA   For almost 4 decades, independent India was to be governed by the INC, initially under its leader Jawaharlal Nehru, who had led Congress in the negotiations of 1946 and 1947. Gandhi was bitterly disillusioned by Partition, even proposing at one stage that Jinnah be made prime minister of India to restore unity. This was enough to alienate him from some Hindu nationalists, one of whom assassinated the Mahatma in 1948. Such rival visions of the Indian nation were to plague the new country.

The most pressing political issues centered around India's relations with Pakistan. The Indian government was (rightly) accused of fomenting dissent in East Pakistan in the late 1960s, leading to war in 1971. Continued conflict has centered around Kashmir, an independent princely state with a predominantly Muslim population but whose Hindu ruler, under threat from Muslim forces from Pakistan, placed it under Indian rule in 1948. Pakistani and Indian troops have tensely faced each other in the territory ever since. With the development of nuclear weapons by both states, and a militant Kashmiri independence movement, the area is a potential powder keg of international concern.

Under Nehru, internal stability was obtained, remarkable considering the circumstances of India's independence, and until his death in 1964, he established India as the world's leading postcolonial democracy, a key player (along with Sukarno's Indonesia) in the non-alignment movement that avoided Cold War conflicts. Communal rivalries were downplayed by a focus on India's secular status. Regional separatism continued to threaten unity, especially Tamil opposition to Hindi linguistic domination from Delhi, but this was resolved by a reorganization of local states along linguistic lines.

Nonetheless, Congress never obtained more than 45% of the national vote and only held power because of the division of its political opponents. After Nehru's death, its attraction weakened. In an attempt to restore its popularity, his daughter, Indira Gandhi (no relation to the Mahatma), became prime minister in 1966. From 1969, she implemented a more populist program of social change, including land reform and a planned economy—a program that was to alienate some of the richer landowners and regional party leaders. Economic restructuring led to strikes and civil opposition in the cities, and in 1975, a State of Emergency was declared that lasted 2 years. Believing that she had reasserted control, Indira Gandhi held elections in 1977. The result was the first defeat for Congress, although no party was able to form a united government to replace it, and by 1980 Gandhi was back in power.

The INC never regained its previous level of control, however. Resentment by Sikhs at their failure to secure autonomy in the Punjab culminated in 1984 with the Indian army's siege and capture of the main Sikh temple at Amritsar with thousands of casualties, and Indira Gandhi was assassinated by her Sikh bodyguards. Her son, Rajiv Gandhi, succeeded her, and instituted new programs of economic liberalization, but he also embroiled India unsuccessfully in the ongoing civil war in Sri Lanka, leading to his assassination in 1991 by a Tamil activist. Although his widow, the Italian-born Sonia Gandhi, inherited leadership of Congress, the era of the Nehru family's domination of Indian politics (which has been compared to the Kennedy family's political impact in the U.S.) was thought by many to be over.

In 1989, Congress was again defeated at the polls, this time led by the Hindu nationalist **Bharatiya Janata Party (BJP).** Although the BJP initially failed to hold together a coalition government, its strength grew. It accused Congress of allowing India to be dominated by outside interests, including globalized economic forces, but more specifically by Indian Muslims who it considered to be unduly tolerated under Congress's secular state policies. In 1992, a BJP-led campaign led to the destruction of the mosque at Ayodhya, believed to be the birthplace of the Hindu god Ram.

In the 1996 elections the BJP defeated a Congress government plagued by accusations of corruption and emerged as the leading group in the coalition governments that have ruled India since. Under the BJP Prime Minister Atal Behari Vajpayee, tensions with Muslim Pakistan increased, with both sides testing and threatening the use of nuclear weapons, especially in conflicts over Kashmir. Fortunately, 2003 saw a welcome cooling. In 2004 the confident BJP government called for early elections, hoping to cash in on a booming economy and developments in the India-Pakistan peace process. Contrary to all expectations, however, the BJP did not win. Instead the Congress, which had been the opposition party for 8 years, took much of the vote, as did the Left (which unexpectedly won more than 60 seats in the 543-member house). Together with other parties, they formed a ruling coalition, the UPA (United Progressive Alliance). The next surprise came soon after, when the victorious Sonia

Gandhi, leader of the Congress, declined to take on the job of prime minister, appointing instead Manmohan Singh, a former Indian finance minister, to the chair.

By mid-2005, the Congress had been in power for just one year; the opposition BJP was in disarray, its political plans to disrupt the functioning of the Congress-led government a mess, and its own dirty linen being washed in public view almost daily. Simultaneously, the normally tenuous relations between India and Pakistan had reached a new high—despite obstacles like unresolved disputes and cross-border terrorism—a strategic factor in the development of the region as a whole.

3 The Religions of India

The diversity of religious belief and practice in India is both unique and somewhat confounding. What follows is a very brief introduction to the religions that took root in India; this will hopefully provide some insight into the patterns and diversity that exist. Tribal religions, ostensibly pagan, often mixed with elements and practices of mainstream religions, still exist in isolated pockets, but are declining rapidly and are not covered here.

HINDUISM To begin the unending journey of studying India, you need to take the first step toward understanding Hinduism, the religion of some 80% of India's population. It can only be a "first step" for, like India itself, Hinduism defies attempts to clearly define or categorize, and what may be described as universal Hindu religious practice in one place may very well be contradicted by others elsewhere.

Hinduism has no ecclesiastical order, nor is there a central religious book. (While many religious texts like the ancient *Upanishads* and *Bhagavad-Gita* exist, they are not the "word of god" like the Bible or the Koran.) It is not possible to convert to Hinduism; you are born Hindu, usually into one of the four main hierarchical castes (Brahmin, or "priest"; Kshatriya, or "warrior"; Vaisya, or "merchant"; Sudra, or "peasant") or—at the very bottom of the social order—you are born Dalit, better known as the "untouchables." Unlike organized religions such as Christianity or Islam where truth is specified, categorical, linear, and uni-dimensional, truth in Hinduism is in fact extremely multidimensional—contradictions are not bad, but inevitable. Unlike Christianity and Islam, which say there is one true path that leads to one God, Hinduism says there are many paths that lead to many gods (some say—probably hyperbolically—330 million gods, who epitomize a host of human qualities, from gluttony to vengefulness). This intrinsic Hindu acceptance of diversity and multiplicity has defined India's history, allowing it to successfully adapt by absorbing the beliefs of successive invaders. Even today it is not difficult for Hindus to look upon Allah or Jesus as deities worthy of veneration—more than half the devotees who flock to pray at the famous Muslim shrine in Ajmer in North India or at the fabled Velankanni Church in South India are Hindus.

Rather than a formal religion, Hinduism is considered a way of life, or *Sanatan Dharma* (an eternal path), in which the universe is part of an endless cycle of creation, preservation, and dissolution. The human soul is also part of this cycle, endlessly reincarnated, and seeking freedom. According to Hindu philosophy, we determine our destiny by our actions. *Karma* is the law of cause and effect through which individuals create their own destiny by virtuous thoughts, words, and deeds. Each of us can control the nature and experiences of the next life *(karma)* by "living right" or *dharma*—through *dharma* (a righteous pattern of conduct), individuals determine their *karma*. By resolving all *karmas,* the soul can finally attain *moksha,* an escape from the cycle of life.

There are many sects and denominations within Hinduism, and priests, *sadhus* (holy men), and other spiritually enlightened individuals are important parts of the religious process: *Bhakti* is devotion to and communication with the gods, which devotees express in the performance of *puja* (religious ritual-like prayer), *bhajan* (devotional singing), and meditation. *Puja* may be performed at home or in a temple in front of an idol(s) of god(s). It involves some kind of offering to the gods (flowers being the most common) and is an essential part of the practice of Hindu faith. For Hindus the physical symbol or idol of god is the material form through which god appears in this world. Hindu devotees may worship Shiva, Kali, Ganesha, or any one of thousands of gods and manifestations of gods in the Hindu pantheon, and may believe in a Supreme Being who is either their chosen deity or some unnamed force even higher than the gods. Hinduism believes in the existence of three worlds: The material universe we live in, the astral plane where angels and spirits live and, finally, the spiritual world of the gods.

BUDDHISM   Though Buddhism originated in India around 500 B.C., when the Indian prince Siddhartha Gautama attained enlightenment and became the Buddha (Enlightened One) at Bodhgaya, only some eight million still practice the belief in India, the majority of them from Tibet or Nepal or converted during the mass conversion of lower castes by the anti-caste leader Dr. Ambedkar in 1956. (The Buddhist following is, of course, far higher outside India, particularly in the rest of Asia; even in the West, Buddhism appears to be on the rise.)

Unlike any other religion, Buddhism does not advocate belief in a godhead; it instead expects the individual to seek truth within his own experience and control his dharma and karma without relying on divine intervention. Buddhist philosophy is based on the idea that life is riddled with conflict and pain caused by desire (or craving) and ignorance, and to escape from this suffering you need to follow the Eight-Fold Path to gain Enlightenment, or *nirvana.* The Eight-Fold Path advocates Right Understanding, Right Thought, Right Speech, Right Action, Right Mode of Living, Right Endeavor, Right Mindfulness, and Right Concentration. As is the case in Hinduism, each of us carries our karma through a cycle of rebirths until the attainment of nirvana. Meditation, chanting, counting beads, and lighting lamps are some of the ways in which Buddhists pursue their spiritual goal of enlightenment.

JAINISM   This began as a reform movement and became a religion under the 24th Jain *trithankara* (prophet) Vardhaman, later called Mahavira (incidentally, a contemporary of Buddha), in the 6th century B.C. Though it never spread beyond India, today some four million Jains live here, predominantly in Maharashtra and Gujarat. The principles of Jainism include strict vegetarianism and extreme reverence for all forms of life—even insects and plants are believed to have *jives,* or souls. Jains believe in reincarnation and salvation (or *moksha*), which can be achieved through respect for and consideration of all forms of life, and living a life of asceticism, meditation, fasting, and pilgrimage to holy places. According to Jain philosophy, the soul journeys through 14 stages before the final burning up of all karma and freedom from bondage.

There are two sects of Jains—Svetambara and Digambara. Svetambara followers vow to avoid intentional injury to others and to lead a life of honesty and detachment from worldly passions. The Digambaras are even more strict in their beliefs and practices—as a symbol of their complete detachment from material possessions, the highest monks of this sect wear no clothes. In addition, unlike Svetamabaras, Digambaras believe women cannot achieve *moksha.* Their temples are among the finest in India: Karnataka's famous Sravanbelagola Temple is a Digambara temple, while the celebrated Dilwara (Mount Abu, Rajasthan) and Shatrunjaya (Palitana, Gujarat) temples are important Svetambara places of pilgrimage.

SIKHISM This religion emerged in the 15th century out of a rejection of caste distinctions and idolatry under the founder, Guru Nanak, who wanted to bring together the best of Hinduism and Islam. Nine gurus, all of whom are equally revered by Sikhs, followed him, and today there are over 19 million Sikhs in India, mostly in Punjab. Like Hinduism, Sikhism accepts the doctrine of reincarnation, but worship is based on meditation and not ritual or asceticism. Like Muslims, Sikhs believe in one omnipresent universal God; worship takes place in *gurdwaras,* and the holy book is the *Granth Sahib.* The 16th-century Golden Temple at Amritsar is the holiest Sikh place of worship (and has a truly sacred atmosphere).

Charity is an important aspect of the religion, and the *gurdwaras* always run community kitchens where anyone can eat free. Sikhs are expected to never cut their hair—which makes Sikh men, who wind their long hair under large turbans and sport large beards, one of the most easily recognized male communities in India.

OTHER RELIGIONS Zoroastrianism, Judaism, Islam, and Christianity did not originate in India, but are all represented, with Islam and Christianity (which, incidentally, originated within 600 years of each other) the second- and third-largest religious groups, respectively, in India. Muslims comprise about 13% of the population, while Christians form just 2%. Every major Christian and Muslim sect and denomination is represented, and the beliefs and practices of each group vary accordingly, some with indigenous nuances. But overall they tend to follow the main tenets of these religions as practiced worldwide. It is estimated that only some 5,000 Jews still live in India, mostly in Mumbai, and these numbers continue to dwindle. Zoroastrianism, one of the world's oldest religions, dating back to the 7th or 6th century B.C., arrived in India in the 10th century A.D. with refugees fleeing religious persecution in Persia (latter-day Iran). Though numerically they are a tiny religious minority (70,000), the descendants of these refugees (called **Parsis**) have made a distinctive mark as a social and economic group in India. Followers believe in a single God, Ahura Mazda, whose prophet Zarathustra is their guide, and fire is considered sacred and symbolic of God. Parsis therefore worship in a Fire Temple (closed to non-Parsis), and Zoroastrian philosophy regards life as an eternal battle between the forces of good and evil. Again, the path to overcome evil is through good thoughts, words, and deeds. Where possible, their dead are placed in dry wells at a Tower of Silence to be consumed by vultures. This practice is based on the belief that since dead matter pollutes, cremation and burial would pollute the respective elements. Today's Parsis regard this unique method of disposing of the dead as being useful to the cycle of life even after death.

by Niloufer Venkatraman
Anthropologist, writer, and dedicated foodie

Indian cooking is one of the great cuisines of the world. Like the country itself, however, it varies greatly from region to region, and you'll discover a great deal more to savor than the ubiquitous *kormas* and *tikka* masalas (known to the naive simply as "curry") with which most Westerners are familiar. Not only does each Indian community and ethnic and regional group have a distinct cuisine, but there is a great deal of fusion within the country—subtle variations and combinations you're only likely to pick up once you are familiar with the basics. A good way to sample a variety of dishes in a particular region is to order a thali (multicourse meal), in which an assortment of items is served. Basic staples that tend to be served with every meal throughout the subcontinent are rice, *dal* (lentils), and/or some form of *roti* (bread). The following is a brief summary of regional variations and general dining tips.

SOUTHERN STATES   Food from the coastal areas of India almost always contains a generous quantity of coconut—besides using it in cooking, most Maharashtrian homes offer grated coconut as a garnish to every dish. Rice also dominates the food of southern India, as do their "breads," which are more like pancakes and made of a rice (and/or *dal*) batter—these *appams, idiapams,* and *dosas* are found throughout the south. *Dosas* are in fact a South Indian "breakfast" favorite (consumed anytime), as are *idlis* and *vadas,* all of which have become part of mainstream cooking in many parts of India. *Idli* is a steamed rice and lentil dumpling, *dosa* a pancake (similar batter), and *vada* a deep-fried doughnut-shaped snack. All should be eaten fresh and hot with a coconut chutney and

sambar, which is a specially seasoned *dal* (lentils), also eaten with steamed rice. In Tamil Nadu a large number of people are vegetarian, but in Kerala, Goa, and Mumbai, you must sample the fresh fish! Delicious kebabs and slow-cooked meals are what you'll find in Hyderabadi cuisine; inspired by the courts of the *Nawabs* (nobles), it's similar to Mughlai cooking, but stronger in flavor.

NORTHERN STATES   India's great meat-eating tradition comes from the Mughals and Kashmiris, whose *rogan josh* and creamy *korma* dishes, along with kebabs and *biryanis,* have become the backbone of Indian restaurants overseas. The most popular tradition—tandoor (clay oven) cooking—is part of India's Mughal gastronomic heritage. Tandoor dishes are effectively "barbecued" vegetables, *paneer* (Indian cheese), or meat that has been marinated and tenderized in spiced yogurt, cooked over coals, and then either served "dry" as a kebab or in a rich spiced gravy like the *korma.* Recently revived is the tradition of *dum pukht,* enjoyed by the erstwhile *Nawabs* of Awadh in Lucknow and the surrounding area. All the ingredients are sealed and slow-cooked in a pot, around which coals are placed. Nothing escapes the sealed pot, preserving the flavors.

NORTHWEST (PUNJAB) SPECIALS   Besides trying the various tandoor dishes, you should order *parathas:* A Punjabi specialty, this thick version of the traditional chapati is stuffed with potatoes, cabbage, radish, or a variety of other fillings. Be aware that many North Indians love their ghee (clarified butter); sensitive stomachs (or those watching their weight) should simply specify that they would prefer their *paratha* without ghee. A general note of caution when dining in North India: If the menu specifies a choice between oil and ghee as a cooking method, you should probably specify the former. And keep in mind that if you exclusively eat oily, highly pungent, so-called Punjabi fare, you are bound to feel ill, so make sure you vary your meals by dining at South Indian restaurants, which combine a healthy balance of carbohydrate and protein (rice and *dal*); in northern states you will find *rotis* (breads) combined with *rajma* (kidney beans), *puris* (bread) with *chole* (chickpeas), and so on.

EASTERN STATES Freshwater fish (such as *hilsa, bekti,* and *rohu*) take pride of place at the Bengali table, which incidentally considers itself to be the apotheosis of Indian cooking. In Bengal, mustard oil (which has its own powerful flavor) is the preferred cooking oil. Sweets are another Bengali gift to the world; these are made from milk that has been converted to *paneer* (Indian cheese) and that has names like *rosogolla* (or *rasgulla*) and *sandesh.*

SPICES Literally hundreds of spices (masalas) and spice combinations form the culinary backdrop to India, but a few are used so often that they are considered indispensable. Turmeric *(haldi)*—in its common form a yellow powder with a slightly bitter flavor—is the foremost, not least for its antiseptic properties. Mustard seeds are also very important, particularly in the South. Cumin seeds and coriander seeds and their powders are widely used in different forms—whether you powder, roast, or fry a spice, and how you do so, makes a big difference in determining the flavors of a dish. Chili powder is another common ingredient, available in umpteen different varieties and potencies. Then there are the vital "sweet" spices—cardamom *(elaichi),* clove *(lavang),* cinnamon *(dalchini)*—which, along with black pepper *(kali miri),* make up the key ingredients of the spice combination known as

garam masala. Though tolerance to spicy food is extremely subjective, let your preference be known by asking whether the item is spicy-hot *(tikha hai?)* and indicating no-chili, medium-spicy, and so on. "Curry powder" as it is merchandised in the West is rarely found or used in India. "Curry" more or less defines the complex and very diverse combination of spices freshly ground together, often to create a spicy saucelike liquid that comes in varying degrees of pungency and varies in texture and consistency, from thin and smooth to thick and grainy, ideally accompanied by rice or breads.

STAPLES & ACCOMPANIMENTS All over the country, Indian food is served with either the staple of rice or bread, or both—the most popular being unleavened (pan-roasted) breads (called *rotis*); tandoor-baked breads; deep-fried breads (*puris* and *bhaturas*) or pancake-style ones. Chapatis, thin whole-wheat breads roasted in a flat iron pan *(tava),* are the most common bread eaten in Indian homes, though these are not as widely available as restaurant breads. The thicker version of chapatis are called *parathas,* which can be stuffed with an assortment of vegetables or even ground meat. Tandoor-roasted breads are made with a more refined flour and include *naans,* tandoori *rotis,* and the super-thin *roomali* (handkerchief) *rotis.* Tandoor breads turn a little leathery when cold and are best eaten fresh.

Dal, made of lentils (any of a huge variety) and seasoned with mustard, cumin, chilies, and/or other spices, is another Indian staple eaten throughout the country. *Khichdi,* a mixture of rice, lentils, and spices, is a great meal by itself and considered comfort food. In some parts it's served with *kadhi*—a savory sour yogurt–based stew to which chickpea flour dumplings may be added. You'll usually be served accompaniments in the form of onion and lime, chutneys, pickles, relishes, and a variety of yogurt-based salads called *raita*. *Papads* (roasted or fried lentil flour discs) are another favorite food accompaniment that arrives with your meal in a variety of shapes, sizes, and flavors.

MEAT A large number of Indians are vegetarian for religious reasons, with entire towns serving only vegetarian meals, but these are so delicious that meat lovers are unlikely to feel put out. Elsewhere, meat lovers should probably (unless you're dining in a top-end big-city restaurant) opt for the chicken and fish dishes—not only are these usually very tender and succulent, but the "mutton" or "lamb" promised on the menu is more often than not goat, while "beef" (seldom on the menu—beef is taboo for most Hindus, and the ban on cow slaughter continues to be a raging national debate) is usually water buffalo. Again, there are regional differences, like in "Portuguese" Goa, where pork is common.

SWEETS Indians love sweets (called *mithais, mishtaan,* or "sweet meats'"), and they love them very sweet. In fact, Western palates often find Indian sweets *too* sweet; if this is the case, sample the dry-fruit-based sweets. Any occasion for celebration necessitates a round of sweets as a symbol of spreading sweetness (happiness). Every region of the country has a variety of specialty sweets made from an array of ingredients, but they are largely milk-based. This includes *pedas* and *laddus* (soft, circular), *barfis* (brownielike), *halwas* (sticky or wet), *kheer* (rice pudding–like), and so on. Whatever you do, don't miss the Indian *kulfi,* a creamy, rich ice cream flavored with saffron, nuts, or seasonal fruit.

FRUITS If the spiciness of the meals unsettles your stomach, try living on fruit for a day. You'll get a whole range of delicious tropical varieties (with any luck, in a basket in your hotel room) ranging from guavas and jackfruit to lychees and the most coveted fruit of them all, the mango. More than 200 varieties of mangoes are grown in India, but the most popular ones (Alphonso or *aphoos*) come from Maharashtra (Mar–June); try to taste one when you're in Mumbai.

BEVERAGES *Chai* (tea) is India's national drink. Normally served in small quantities, it is hot, made with milk usually flavored with ginger and/or cardamom, and rather sweet unless you request otherwise. Instant coffee is widely available (and may be mixed in your five-star hotel's "filter coffee" pot), but in South India you'll get excellent fresh brews. Another drink worth trying is *lassi,* liquefied sweetened yogurt. *Note:* The yogurt is sometimes thinned with water, so you're only safe consuming lassis in places where they can assure you no water was added at all, or where they will make it with bottled water (that you purchase separately). Lassi's close companion is *chaas,* a savory version that is very thin and served with Gujarati/Rajasthani meals. With southern food, it is served with a flavorful assortment of herbs and spices. In general, you should avoid ice in any beverage unless you are satisfied that it is made from boiled water.

EATING ETIQUETTE Eating with your hands: Indians generally eat with their hands, and although many don't do so in five-star Westernized restaurants, the majority will in most other places. Even the simplest restaurant will be able to provide a spoon as cutlery, but if you really want to experience your meal in an authentic manner, follow suit. Note that you should ideally only use your right hand (though in places where tourists go, people are unlikely to be offended if you use your left). In the North, where the food is "drier," you are traditionally not supposed to dirty more than the first two digits of your fingers. In the South, where the food is much "wetter," you may use the whole hand to eat.

Sharing your food: It is typically Indian to share food or drinks, even if you don't really want to. On long train journeys, you're likely to meet Indian families carrying a lot of food, which they will invite you to share—do sample some, if only to get a taste of home cooking. In return, you can buy them a round of tea or cold drinks when the vendors come by.

Sharing food at a restaurant is another Indian norm; menus are set up to cater to this style of dining. So, for example, if two or more of you go to a Mughlai restaurant, you would order perhaps two kinds of kebabs, two kinds of meat/vegetable entrees, one rice, and several breads *(rotis)*. It's a good way to try a range of items.

The hygiene of *jootha*: While sharing is good manners, *jootha* is considered offensive in many parts. This refers to drinking from the same glass, eating with the same spoon, taking a bite out of someone's sandwich, or "double dipping." To share a bread or snack, break off a piece; when sharing a bottle of water, don't put your mouth to it but tilt your head back and pour. Although there are no definite rules about what is permissible or not, just make sure that you use common courtesy when sharing a meal with others.

SALADS The practice of eating Western-style salads (except raw onion) is not very common, but most restaurants do have them on the menu. Beware that it is only advisable to eat these in top-end restaurants, and make sure that the vegetables have been freshly cut and washed in boiled water.

STREET FOOD Even in smaller cities like Indore and Jaipur, street food has a fantastic tradition and following. *Samosas, vadas, bhelpuri, sev, bhajias,* and a host of deep-fried foods are all delicious, and you should try them on your trip. It's not easy for the first-time visitor to figure out which street foods are safe to eat, however—best to look for an outlet where loads of people are lined up; this means that neither the food nor the oil have been around long. Alternatively, ask your hotel for suggestions.

5 Reading India

by Jerry Pinto
Author, journalist, and poet

More than almost any other destination, India demands that you immerse yourself in the local culture to make sense of all you see and experience. And wherever you're headed in India, there's probably a novel you can read to explore the ways people are shaped by the landscape and history around them.

LITERATURE The late R. K. Narayan, one of the grand old men of Indian letters, offers a panoramic view of village life in India. He focuses on a gentle prelapsarian village in *Malgudi Days* (Penguin), a good introduction to his work. For a more politicized investigation of the caste system, you might want to read U. R. Ananthamurthy's **Samskara** (Oxford University Press, translated from Kannada), which deals with a dilemma that convulses a village after the death of an unclean Brahmin; or Raja Rao's **Kanthapura** (New Directions), set in a village in South India that has to face the storms of Mahatma Gandhi's civil disobedience movement.

Small-town India is well represented in Arundhati Roy's Booker Prize–winning novel, **The God of Small Things** (HarperCollins), which will make you want to travel the waterways of Kerala to see the village life she describes so vividly. And then there's Bhalchandra Nemade's **Cocoon** (National Book Trust), often referred to as India's *Catcher in the Rye.*

Each of the big cities has at least one big novel. Mumbai's industrial past is presented in a charming story of two boys who grow up in a tenement in Kiran Nagarkar's **Raavan and Eddie** (Penguin India), but if you're looking for a page-turner one of the most unputdownable books you're likely to read this year is the thrilling and enlightening **Shantaram** (Abacus; St. Martin's Griffin), written by Australian Gregory David Roberts and set in a Mumbai that really comes alive. Roberts potently describes the pulsating rhythm of one of the world's headiest cities, penetrating its nefarious underground crime syndicates and getting deep inside the soul of the city's shantytowns. The book has not only taken the world by storm, but is phenomenally popular in Mumbai itself, particularly as the city prepares to become the central location for a big-budget movie based on the book with Johnny Depp in the titular role. Equally captivating, and also an international bestseller, is Vikram Chandra's **Sacred Games** (HarperCollins), a beautifully narrated and utterly gripping account of Mumbai's criminal underworld, seen through the eyes of its most wanted gangster and down-to-earth detective.

Mumbai is also where Salman Rushdie grew up, and the city is one of the backdrops of his Booker of Bookers, **Midnight's Children** (Vintage), which tells of two babies swapped at birth, one Hindu and one Muslim, one rich and one poor, both born on the stroke of midnight at India's independence. Mumbai is also the backdrop for his more notorious **The Satanic Verses** (Viking). Rushdie's style of magic realism laced with Mumbai's street lingo was anticipated in G. V. Dessani's single brilliant novel, **All About H Hatterr** (Penguin India).

Kolkata has inspired a plethora of books, including Amit Chaudhuri's plangent tale of growing up in **A Strange and Sublime Address** (Vintage) and Amitav Ghosh's **The Hungry Tide** (Houghton Mifflin), which takes off from the 300-year-old city and stirs up sediment of language and memory in the distributaries of the Ganga, in the Sundarbans. Delhi has an eponymous novel, **Delhi** (Viking India), by one of India's most widely read writers, Khushwant Singh; the book deftly mixes history with contemporary life. (Singh's **Train to Pakistan** [Penguin India] should be read alongside Bhisham Sahni's **Tamas** [Penguin India] to understand the complicated ambivalence of India's relationship with its Islamic neighbor, Pakistan.) But if you're looking for a light, highly readable introduction to India's myriad religious and spiritual paths, pick up a copy of the wholly delightful **Holy Cow** (Bantam Books), written by another Australian, Sarah Macdonald. It's a witty autobiographical account of the author's life as an expat living in Delhi and traveling around the subcontinent in various hysterical attempts to get to grips with a very different culture. Chennai has been well-captured in C. S. Lakshmi's collection of short stories, **A Purple Sea** (University of Nebraska Press).

Another novel to sample is Vikram Seth's compendious look at arranged marriage, **A Suitable Boy** (HarperCollins). This enjoyable novel is set in several cities. If you drive from Varanasi to Agra, you will pass by the scene, described by Seth, of a disaster that befell pilgrims there in the 1980s. (You may also find yourself incorporating the phrase "a tight slap" into your speech; don't ask—just read.) Other novels of repute include Rohinton Mistry's charming stories of the minuscule Parsi community in **Such A Long Journey** (Random House) and **A Fine Balance** (Faber & Faber), with its unforgettable characters, set during 1975's State of Emergency; I. Allan Sealey's fictionalization of the life of the adventurer Claude Martin in *The Trotternama;* and Anita Desai's *Baumgartner's Bombay,* which takes a compassionate but clear-eyed look at German Jews, refugees from the Holocaust, who stayed on after the British left.

NONFICTION A good way to start a hot debate (as if an excuse were needed) is to be seen reading V. S. Naipaul's *India: A Million Mutinies Now* (Vintage). Many Western readers respond to the mixture of fear and fascination with which Naipaul considers the subcontinent. A far more contemporary and intriguing account of the nation-state that has remained a democracy for most of its 50-year history is offered by Sunil Khilnani's *The Idea of India* (Farrar, Straus & Giroux).

Don't pass up William Dalrymple's wonderful journalistic prose in either *The Age of Kali* or *City of Djinns.* The former looks at some of the pressingly negative issues that affect the people of India. The latter gives a refreshing account of life in modern Delhi while touching on poignant moments in the city's fascinating history.

Journalist P. Sainath's *Everybody Loves A Good Drought* (Penguin India) has won 13 international awards at last count for his account of the country's poorest districts and the ways in which development schemes almost never help the ostensible beneficiaries. Suketu Mehta's *Maximum City* (Viking) captures the frenetic mood of living in Mumbai when the author moves back here, and offers a fascinating scrutiny of the city's underbelly. Read it in association with *Bombay, Meri Jaan* (Penguin India; edited by Jerry Pinto and Naresh Fernandes), an anthology of writings about the city that includes names as varied as Andre Gidé and Duke Ellington. Gita Mehta's *Karma Cola* (Vintage) is an acerbic and witty investigation into the way in which unscrupulous gurus marketed Indian spirituality to credulous Westerners in search of "enlightenment."

Those interested in Indian spirituality will uncover a wealth of material. Besides picking up the light-hearted *Holy Cow* (above), you should find a copy of Kamala Subramaniam's *The Mahabharata* (Bharatiya Vidya Bhavan), the great epic tale of the war between two clans related by the ties of kinship. *The Mahabharata* also contains the *Bhagavad–Gita* or "The Celestial Song," which is often seen as the core of Hindu beliefs. *The Ramayana* (Penguin) by R. K. Narayan offers a good introduction to the epic of Rama, who is exiled and whose wife, Sita, is abducted by the demon king Ravana. Penguin India also does a compact series that includes *The Book of Krishna* by Pavan K. Varma, *The Book of the Buddha* by Arundhathi Subramaniam, and *The Book of the Devi* by Bulbul Sharma.

For a more academic approach to Indian history, try the somewhat pedantic *Modern South Asia: History, Culture, Political Economy,* by Sugata Bose and Ayesha Jalal (Routledge); *A History of India,* by Peter Robb (Palgrave); or *A Concise History of India* by Barbara Metcalf and Thomas Metcalf (Cambridge University Press).

This is just a start. But be warned—the writing on India is as seductive as the place it describes. Once hooked, you'll want more.

by Jerry Pinto & Keith Bain

Mumbai's Hindi film industry, popularly known as Bollywood, is the biggest producer of films in the world, churning out hundreds of movies annually, all of which feature super-kitschy images of buxom, bee-stung-lipped heroines gyrating to high-pitched melodies while strapping studs thrust their groins in time to lip-synched banal-and-breezy lyrics. These are wonderful, predictable melodramas in which the hero is always valiant and virile, the woman always voluptuous and virtuous. The battle between good and evil (a bankable hero and a recognizably nasty villain) must be intense, long-winded, and ultimately unsurprising— audiences do not pay good money to be challenged, but to be entertained.

Before you choose to spend a hot subtropical afternoon watching a Hindi film, know that these films are long, averaging about 3 hours. This is because they are constructed more like Elizabethan plays or old operas. Their audiences do not come for tragedies or for comedies but for full-scale performances that give them everything: the chance to laugh and cry, to bemoan the violence done unto the hero, and the opportunity to cheer as justice is done. These films are also made in defiance of the Aristotelian requirements of unity in time and space, and require from you a willing suspension of disbelief. And though the genre film has just begun—a few historicals such as *Devdas* and *Parineeta* (The Espoused) (2005); some horror films like *Kaal* (Time) (2005) and *Darna Mana Hai* (Fear is Forbidden) (2003); and some war films, including *Lakshya* (Goal) (2004) and *Mission Kashmir* (2000)—most Hindi films still work on this principle.

The top-bracket Bollywood stars, including Amitabh Bachchan (who is nearing 70), the 40-something Shah Rukh Khan, and heartthrob Aamir Khan, are paid incredible sums by Indian standards, earning close to a million dollars for a film simply because they are the names that will bring in the audiences and the "repeat audiences." As it is all over the world, women get paid much less, often half of what the male stars are paid, but stars like Rani Mukherjee and Preity Zinta have their devoted followings.

Increasingly, the influence of Hollywood production values and obsession with consumer culture is becoming evident in major Bollywood releases; in an effort to keep the MTV generation (and yes, India has its very own MTV) interested, you can expect to see younger stars with an ever more visible sex appeal engaged in plots that echo some of the preoccupations of the Western silver screen. Bigger bangs, more powerful explosions, and longer chase scenes combine with racier moments, tighter outfits, and about enough attitude to put even the most self-indulgent posers to shame. But it's not all bad. In fact, some wonderful experiments in storytelling have produced screenplays that pack a punch and wow with the twists and turns invented to keep more world-wise audiences on their toes. Also, collaborative efforts between Bollywood studios and the West are making for enterprising transnational storylines; perhaps the most interesting of these is the intricately crafted *Salaam-E-Ishq,* which travels between continents and across genres and generations to provide a fantasy romance that innovatively blends narrative techniques borrowed from a broad pedigree. It's the type of cinema that cannot fail to steal your heart.

To view Bollywood movies as the be-all and end-all of India's film industry would be akin to thinking that big-budget blockbusters are the only movies made by the U.S. film industry; in fact, Bollywood is only responsible for a small part of the huge number of films produced by India in several languages. The first Indian director to make international art audiences sit up and take notice was Kolkata-based Satyajit Ray. Although he made his films in the 1950s, he received a Lifetime Achievement Oscar for his prolific body of work in 1992. Operating out of West Bengal's "Tollywood," Ray made movies that were the antithesis of Bollywood's; he was the director who stated that "the man in the street is a more challenging subject for exploration than people in the heroic mold" and that he found "muted emotions more interesting and challenging." Ray directed some 40 feature films, documentaries, and short subjects, of which *Pather Panchali* (Song of the Little Road) in 1955, *Aparajito* (The Unvanquished) in 1956, *Apur Sansar* (The World of Apu) in 1959, and *Goopy Gyne Bagha Byne* (The Adventures of Goopy and Bagha) in 1968 were the most internationally acclaimed. There are, of course, other exceptions, like Guru Dutt, one of Bollywood's most successful directors of the 1950s, whose film *Pyaasa* (1957) has been nominated one of the world's 100 best films by *Time* magazine.

Because India produces more than 700 films a year, it is in fact impossible to be monolithic about all products and speak of only a certain kind of film. Until recently, the government financed arthouse cinema, and there are signs of a growing "indie" movement in which young directors scrape together the finances and make the kind of films they want as opposed to the formulaic catch-all colorful song-and-dance extravaganzas that financiers are comfortable backing.

These are probably more likely to be the types of films that provide insight into what India looks and feels like. If you want a deep, hard look at the social consciousness of the country, look to the wonderful works of Mira Nair, who has crafted fantastic entertainments that tug at the heartstrings and probe many issues without stooping to cheap preachy politicking (the notable exception being her recent work, *The Namesake*). You would be amiss not to see her *Salaam Bombay!*, about the life of a group of Mumbai street urchins, and *Monsoon Wedding*, a beautiful and poignant romantic comedy about a well-to-do Delhiite family dealing with generational conflicts that complicate traditional marriage arrangements. In 2008 look for the much-vaunted *Shantaram*, which Nair is directing; based on the riveting best-selling novel (see above), the Johnny Depp–headliner is destined to take the world by storm.

Another top-rated woman director to look for is Deepa Mehta, whose trilogy *Fire* (1996), *Earth* (1998), and *Water* (2005) are superbly moving works of high-grade cinema—and certainly preferable to her slightly irritating and kitschy *Bollywood/Hollywood* (2002), set in Canada.

Art listings aside, playing in a theater near you in any city in India will be a film in which the rich hero meets the poor heroine and falls almost instantly in love. He will declare this in song, and the scene will change to New Zealand, Switzerland, or Southeast Asia, depending on which country is most eager to attract the new beneficiaries of India's globalization. The couple will find obstacles put in their path, some by their parents and others by the villain, who will at some point have cast his lecherous eyes on the heroine. Fairly standardized violence will follow—after this comes a misunderstanding that paves the way for another song expressing the grief of betrayal or the pain of parting or that sets up what the industry calls an "item number" (which may have derived from Mumbai slang for a pretty young thing, or an "item") in which a young dancer performs the equivalent of a pole dance for the audience. When the air is cleared, justice and peace have returned to the world, the good have been rewarded, and the villains are dead or rounded up. At the film's end, you will either be floored by the extravagant color, ravished by floods of emotion, and converted to another way of telling stories; or you will be repulsed by excess and sickened by melodrama and the way in which Caucasian extras are used to represent the decadent sexualized Other. But you will not be unmoved.

Index

I don't speak sign language.

A hotel can close for all kinds of reasons.

Our Guarantee ensures that if your hotel's undergoing construction, we'll let you know in advance. In fact, we cover your entire travel experience. See www.travelocity.com/guarantee for details.

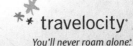

You'll never roam alone.

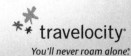